The Oxford French Dictionary and Grammar

Second Edition

DICTIONARY
FRENCH–ENGLISH
ENGLISH–FRENCH

GRAMMAR
WILLIAM ROWLINSON

OXFORD
UNIVERSITY PRESS

OXFORD
UNIVERSITY PRESS

Great Clarendon Street, Oxford OX2 6DP

Oxford University Press is a department of the University of Oxford.
It furthers the University's objective of excellence in research, scholarship,
and education by publishing worldwide in

Oxford New York

Athens Auckland Bangkok Bogotá Buenos Aires
Cape Town Chennai Dar es Salaam Delhi Florence Hong Kong Istanbul
Karachi Kolkata Kuala Lumpur Madrid Melbourne Mexico City Mumbai Nairobi
Paris São Paulo Shanghai Singapore Taipei Tokyo Toronto Warsaw

with associated companies in Berlin Ibadan

British Library Cataloguing in Publication Data
Data available

Library of Congress Cataloging in Publication Data
Data available
ISBN 0–19–860387–8

10 9 8 7 6 5 4 3

Typeset by Tradespools
Printed in Great Britain by
Mackays of Chatham plc, Chatham, Kent

Contents

List of contributors

First Edition

Editors:

Michael Janes
Dora Latiri-Carpenter
Edwin Carpenter

Second Edition

Editors:

Marianne Chalmers
Rosalind Combley
Catherine Roux
Laura Wedgeworth

Proof-reading:
Andrew Hodgson

Grammar:
William Rowlinson

Preface

Part of the Oxford Dictionary and Grammar series, the present work combines up-to-date and compact dictionary, offering comprehensive coverage of modern French and English, with a practical and user-friendly guide to French grammar. This unique feature makes it the perfect all-in-one reference tool for students, tourists, and business people alike.

Introduction to the dictionary

Enhanced coverage

The wordlist has been comprehensively revised to reflect recent additions to both languages and to cover such topics as **computing** and the **Internet**.

A further new feature of the dictionary is the special status given to more complex grammatical words which provide the basic structure of both languages. These *function words* are given a special layout to make them instantly accessible and offer clearly presented translation options and examples, with **short usage notes** to warn of possible pitfalls.

Coverage of verbs has been significantly extended so that all **French verbs** in the text are cross-referenced to the appropriate section of the expanded verb tables. Examples of the three main French verb groups, as well as *avoir* and *être*, are conjugated in the most commonly used tenses. A quick **reference guide** giving the English translation of an example verb in the principal tenses has been included, as well as exemplified guidance on **how to conjugate a reflexive verb**.

Easy reference

The dictionary layout has been designed to be **clear**, streamlined, and easy to consult. The wordlist has been fully **alphabetized**, with all English compounds and French hyphenated compounds in their correct alphabetical positions. **Bullet points** separate each new part of speech within an entry, making it easy to scan. Nuances of sense or usage are pinpointed by semantic indicators (in condensed type in round brackets) or by typical collocates (*in italics in round brackets*) with which the word frequently occurs, quickly guiding the user to the appropriate translation. Extra help is given in the form of **symbols** to mark the register of language unambiguously. An exclamation mark 🄵 indicates colloquial language and a cross 🄴 indicates slang.

Proprietary terms

This dictionary includes some words which are, or are asserted to be, proprietary terms or trademarks. The presence or absence of such assertions should not be regarded as affecting the legal status of any proprietary name or trademark.

The pronunciation of French

Vowels

a	*as in*	patte	/pat/		ɑ	*as in*	pâte	/pɑt/
ã		clan	/klã/		e		dé	/de/
ɛ		belle	/bɛl/		ɛ̃		lin	/lɛ̃/
ə		demain	/dəmɛ̃/		i		gris	/gʀi/
o		gros	/gʀo/		ɔ		corps	/kɔʀ/
ɔ̃		long	/lɔ̃/		œ		leur	/lœʀ/
œ̃		brun	/bʀœ̃/		ø		deux	/dø/
u		fou	/fu/		y		pur	/pyʀ/

Semi-Vowels

j	*as in*	fille	/fij/
ɥ		huit	/ɥit/
w		oui	/wi/

Consonants

Aspiration of 'h'

Where it is impossible to make a liason this is indicated by /'/ immediately after the slash e.g. *haine* /'ɛn/.

b	*as in*	bal	/bal/		ŋ	*as in*	camping	/kãpiŋ/
d		dent	/dã/		p		porte	/pɔʀt/
f		foire	/fwaʀ/		ʀ		rire	/ʀiʀ/
g		gomme	/gɔm/		s		sang	/sã/
k		clé	/kle/		ʃ		chien	/ʃjɛ̃/
l		lien	/ljɛ̃/		t		train	/tʀɛ̃/
m		mer	/mɛʀ/		v		voile	/vwal/
n		nage	/naʒ/		z		zèbre	/zɛbʀ/
ɲ		gnon	/ɲɔ̃/		ʒ		jeune	/ʒœn/

Abbreviations

adjective	*adj*	adjectif
abbreviation	*abbr, abrév*	abréviation
adverb	*adv*	adverbe
anatomy	*Anat*	anatomie
archeology	*Archeol, Archéol*	archéologie
architecture	*Archit*	architecture
motoring	*Auto*	automobile
auxiliary	*aux*	auxiliaire
aviation	*Aviat*	aviation
botany	*Bot*	botanique
commerce	*Comm*	commerce
computing	*Comput*	informatique
conjunction	*conj*	conjonction
cookery	*Culin*	culinaire
determiner	*det, dét*	déterminant
electricity	*Electr, Électr*	électricité
figurative	*fig*	sens figuré
geography	*Geog, Géog*	géographie
geology	*Geol, Géol*	géologie
grammar	*Gram*	grammaire
humorous	*hum*	humoristique
interjection	*interj*	interjection
invariable	*inv*	invariable
law	*Jur*	droit
linguistics	*Ling*	linguistique
literal	*lit*	littéral
phrase	*loc*	locution
medicine	*Med, Méd*	médecine
military	*Mil*	armée
music	*Mus*	musique
noun	*n*	nom
nautical	*Naut*	nautisme
feminine noun	*nf*	nom féminin
masculine noun	*nm*	nom masculin
masculine and feminine noun	*nm,f* or *nmf* or *nm/f*	nom masculin et féminin
computing	*Ordinat*	informatique

pejorative	*pej, péj*	péjoratif
philosophy	*Phil*	philosophie
photography	*Photo*	photographie
plural	*pl*	pluriel
politics	*Pol*	politique
possessive	*poss*	possessif
past participle	*pp*	participe passé
prefix	*pref, préf*	préfixe
preposition	*prep, prép*	préposition
present participle	*pres p*	participe présent
pronoun	*pron*	pronom
psychology	*Psych*	psychologie
past	*pt*	prétérit
something	*qch*	quelque chose
somebody	*qn*	quelqu'un
railway	*Rail*	chemin de fer
relative pronoun	*rel pron, pron rel*	pronom relatif
religion	*Relig*	religion
somebody	*sb*	quelqu'un
school	*School, Scol*	scolaire
sport	*Sport*	sport
something	*sth*	quelque chose
technology	*Tech*	technologie
theatre	*Theat, Théât*	théâtre
television	*TV*	télévision
university	*Univ*	université
American English	*US*	anglais américain
auxiliary verb	*v aux*	verbe auxiliaire
intransitive verb	*vi*	verbe intransitif
reflexive verb	*vpr*	verbe pronominal
transitive verb	*vt*	verbe transitif
transitive and intransitive verb	*vt/i*	verbe transitif et intransitif
translation equivalent	≈	équivalent approximatif
trademark	®	marque déposée
colloquial	▯	familier
slang	▣	argot

Aa

a /a/ ⇒AVOIR [5].

à /a/ *préposition*

   à+le = au
   à+les = aux

••••➤ (avec verbe de mouvement) to.

••••➤ (pour indiquer où l'on se trouve) ∼ **la maison** at home; ∼ **Nice** in Nice.

••••➤ (âge, date, heure) ∼ **l'âge de...** at the age of...; **au XIXe siècle** in the 19th century; ∼ **deux heures** at two o'clock.

••••➤ (description) with; **aux yeux verts** with green eyes.

••••➤ (appartenance) ∼ **qui est ce stylo?** whose pen is this?; **c'est** ∼ **vous?** is this yours?

••••➤ (avec nombre) ∼ **90 km/h** at 90 km per hour; ∼ **10 minutes d'ici** 10 minutes from here; **des tomates** ∼ **3 francs le kilo** tomatoes at 3 francs a kilo; **un timbre** ∼ **3 francs** a 3-franc stamp; **nous avons fait le travail** ∼ **deux** two of us did the work; **mener 5** ∼ **4** to lead 5 (to) 4.

••••➤ (avec être) **c'est** ∼ **moi** it's my turn; **je suis** ∼ **vous tout de suite** I'll be with you in a minute; **c'est** ∼ **toi de décider** it's up to you to decide.

••••➤ (hypothèse) ∼ **ce qu'il paraît** apparently; ∼ **t'entendre** to hear you talk.

••••➤ (exclamatif) ∼ **ta santé!** cheers!; ∼ **demain/bientôt!** see you tomorrow/ soon!

••••➤ (moyen) ∼ **la main** by hand; ∼ **vélo** by bike; ∼ **pied** on foot; **chauffage au gaz** gas heating.

abaissement /abɛsmã/ *nm* (de taux, de prix) cut; (de seuil) lowering.

abaisser /abese/ [1] *vt* lower; (*levier*) pull ou push down; (fig) humiliate. □ **s'**∼ *vpr* go down, drop; (fig) demean oneself; **s'**∼ **à** stoop to.

abandon /abãdɔ̃/ *nm* abandonment; (de personne) desertion; (de course) withdrawal; (naturel) abandon; **à l'**∼ in a state of neglect.

abandonner /abãdɔne/ [1] *vt* abandon; (*épouse, cause*) desert; (renoncer à) give up, abandon; (céder) give (à to); (*course*) withdraw from; (Ordinat) abort. □ **s'**∼ **à** *vpr* give oneself up to.

abasourdir /abazuʀdiʀ/ [2] *vt* stun.

abat-jour /abaʒuʀ/ *nm inv* lampshade.

abats /aba/ *nmpl* offal.

abattement /abatmã/ *nm* dejection; (faiblesse) exhaustion; (Comm) reduction; ∼ **fiscal** tax allowance.

abattre /abatʀ/ [11] *vt* knock down; (*arbre*) cut down; (*animal*) slaughter; (*avion*) shoot down; (affaiblir) weaken; (démoraliser) demoralize; **ne pas se laisser** ∼ not let things get one down. □ **s'**∼ *vpr* come down, fall (down).

abbaye /abei/ *nf* abbey.

abbé /abe/ *nm* priest; (supérieur d'une abbaye) abbot.

abcès /apsɛ/ *nm* abscess.

abdiquer /abdike/ [1] *vt/i* abdicate.

abdomen /abdɔmɛn/ *nm* abdomen.

abdominal (*pl* **-aux**) /abdɔminal/ *adj* abdominal. **abdominaux** *nmpl* (Sport) stomach exercises.

abeille /abɛj/ *nf* bee.

aberrant, ∼**e** /abɛʀã, -t/ *adj* absurd.

abêtir /abetiʀ/ [2] *vt* turn into a moron.

abîme /abim/ *nm* abyss.

abîmer /abime/ [1] *vt* damage, spoil. □ **s'**∼ *vpr* get damaged ou spoilt.

ablation /ablasjɔ̃/ *nf* removal.

aboiement /abwamã/ *nm* bark, barking; ∼**s** barking.

abolir /abɔliʀ/ [2] *vt* abolish.

abondance /abɔ̃dãs/ *nf* abundance; (prospérité) affluence. **abondant**, ∼**e** *adj* abundant, plentiful.

abonder /abɔ̃de/ [1] *vi* abound (**en** in); ~ **dans le sens de qn** agree wholeheartedly with sb.

abonné, ~**e** /abɔne/ *nm,f* (lecteur) subscriber; (voyageur, spectateur) season-ticket holder.

abonnement /abɔnmã/ *nm* (à un journal) subscription; (de bus, Théât) season-ticket; (au gaz) standing charge.

abonner (**s'**) /(s)abɔne/ [1] *vpr* subscribe (**à** to).

abord /abɔʀ/ *nm* access; ~**s** surroundings; **d'**~ first.

abordable /abɔʀdabl/ *adj* (*prix*) affordable; (*personne*) approachable; (*texte*) accessible.

aborder /abɔʀde/ [1] *vt* approach; (*lieu*) reach; (*problème*) tackle. ● *vi* reach land.

aborigène /abɔʀiʒɛn/ *nm* aborigine.

aboutir /abutiʀ/ [2] *vi* succeed, achieve a result; ~ **à** end (up) in, lead to; **n'**~ **à rien** come to nothing.

aboutissement /abutismã/ *nm* outcome; (de carrière, d'évolution) culmination.

aboyer /abwaje/ [31] *vi* bark.

abrégé /abʀeʒe/ *nm* summary.

abréger /abʀeʒe/ [14] [40] *vt* (*texte*) shorten, abridge; (*mot*) abbreviate, shorten; (*visite*) cut short.

abreuver /abʀœve/ [1] *vt* water; (fig) overwhelm (**de** with). □ **s'**~ *vpr* drink.

abréviation /abʀevjasjɔ̃/ *nf* abbreviation.

abri /abʀi/ *nm* shelter; **à l'**~ under cover; (en lieu sûr) safe; **à l'**~ **de** sheltered from; **se mettre à l'**~ take shelter.

abricot /abʀiko/ *nm* apricot.

abriter /abʀite/ [1] *vt* shelter; (recevoir) house. □ **s'**~ *vpr* (take) shelter.

abrupt, ~**e** /abʀypt/ *adj* steep, sheer; (fig) abrupt.

abruti, ~**e** /abʀyti/ *nm,f* 🖾 idiot.

absence /apsɑ̃s/ *nf* absence; **il a des** ~**s** sometimes his mind goes blank.

absent, ~**e** /apsɑ̃, -t/ *adj* (personne) absent, away; (chose) missing; **il est**

toujours ~ he's still away; **d'un air** ~ absently. ● *nm,f* absentee.

absenter (**s'**) /(s)apsɑ̃te/ [1] *vpr* go *ou* be away; (sortir) go out, leave.

absolu, ~**e** /apsɔly/ *adj* absolute.

absorbant, ~**e** /apsɔʀbɑ̃, -t/ *adj* (*travail*) absorbing; (*matière*) absorbent.

absorber /apsɔʀbe/ [1] *vt* absorb; **être absorbé par qch** be engrossed in sth.

abstenir (**s'**) /(s)apstəniʀ/ [58] *vpr* abstain; **s'**~ **de** refrain from.

abstrait, ~**e** /apstʀɛ, -t/ *a & nm* abstract.

absurde /apsyʀd/ *adj* absurd.

abus /aby/ *nm* abuse, misuse; (injustice) abuse; ~ **de confiance** breach of trust.

abuser /abyze/ [1] *vt* deceive. ● *vi* go too far; ~ **de** abuse, misuse; (profiter de) take advantage of; (*alcool*) overindulge in. □ **s'**~ *vpr* be mistaken.

abusif, -ive /abyzif, -v/ *adj* excessive; (impropre) wrong; (injuste) unfair.

académie /akademi/ *nf* academy; (circonscription) local education authority.

acajou /akaʒu/ *nm* mahogany.

accablant, ~**e** /akablɑ̃, -t/ *adj* (*chaleur*) oppressive; (*fait, témoignage*) damning.

accabler /akɑble/ [1] *vt* overwhelm; ~ **d'impôts** burden with taxes; ~ **d'injures** heap insults upon.

accéder /aksede/ [14] *vi* ~ **à** (*lieu*) reach; (*pouvoir, trône*) accede to; (*requête*) grant; (Ordinat) access; ~ **à la propriété** become a homeowner.

accélérateur /akseleʀatœʀ/ *nm* accelerator.

accélérer /akseleʀe/ [14] *vt/i* accelerate. □ **s'**~ *vpr* speed up.

accent /aksɑ̃/ *nm* accent; (sur une syllabe) stress, accent; **mettre l'**~ **sur** stress; ~ **aigu/grave/circonflexe** acute/grave/circumflex accent.

accentuer /aksɑ̃tɥe/ [1] *vt* (*lettre, syllabe*) accent; (fig) emphasize, accentuate. □ **s'**~ *vpr* become more pronounced, increase.

accepter /aksɛpte/ [1] *vt* accept; ~ de faire agree to do.

accès /aksɛ/ *nm* access; (porte) entrance; (de fièvre) bout; (de colère) fit; (d'enthousiasme) burst; (Ordinat) access; **les ~ de** (voies) the approaches to; **facile d'~** easy to get to.

accessoire /aksɛswaʀ/ *adj* secondary, incidental. ● *nm* accessory; (Théât) prop.

accident /aksidɑ̃/ *nm* accident; ~ **de train/d'avion** train/plane crash; **par ~** by accident. **accidenté**, **~e** *adj* (*personne*) injured (in an accident); (*voiture*) damaged; (*terrain*) uneven, hilly. **accidentel**, **~le** *adj* accidental.

acclamer /aklame/ [1] *vt* cheer, acclaim.

accommoder /akɔmɔde/ [1] *vt* adapt (à to); (cuisiner) prepare; (assaisonner) flavour. □ **s'~ de** *vpr* make the best of.

accompagnateur, -trice /akɔ̃paɲatœʀ, -tʀis/ *nm,f* (Mus) accompanist; (guide) guide; ~ **d'enfants** accompanying adult.

accompagner /akɔ̃paɲe/ [1] *vt* accompany. □ **s'~ de** *vpr* be accompanied by.

accomplir /akɔ̃pliʀ/ [2] *vt* carry out, fulfil. □ **s'~** *vpr* take place, happen; (*vœu*) be fulfilled.

accord /akɔʀ/ *nm* agreement; (harmonie) harmony; (Mus) chord; **être d'~** agree (**pour** to); **se mettre d'~** come to an agreement, agree; **d'~!** all right!, OK!

accorder /akɔʀde/ [1] *vt* grant; (*couleurs*) match; (Mus) tune; (attribuer) (*valeur, importance*) assign. □ **s'~** *vpr* (se mettre d'accord) agree; (s'octroyer) allow oneself; **s'~ avec** (s'entendre avec) get on with.

accotement /akɔtmɑ̃/ *nm* verge; ~ **non stabilisé** soft verge.

accouchement /akuʃmɑ̃/ *nm* childbirth; (travail) labour.

accoucher /akuʃe/ [1] *vi* give birth (de to); (être en travail) be in labour. ● *vt* deliver. **accoucheur** *nm* **médecin ~** obstetrician.

accoudoir /akudwaʀ/ *nm* arm-rest.

accoupler /akuple/ [1] *vt* (Tech) couple. □ **s'~** *vpr* mate.

accourir /akuʀiʀ/ [20] *vi* run up.

accoutumance /akutymɑ̃s/ *nf* familiarization; (Méd) addiction.

accoutumer /akutyme/ [1] *vt* accustom. □ **s'~** *vpr* get accustomed.

accro /akʀo/ *nmf* Ⓘ (drogué) addict; (amateur) fan.

accroc /akʀo/ *nm* tear, rip; (fig) hitch.

accrochage /akʀɔʃaʒ/ *nm* hanging; hooking; (Auto) collision; (dispute) clash; (Mil) encounter.

accrocher /akʀɔʃe/ [1] *vt* (suspendre) hang up; (attacher) hook, hitch; (déchirer) catch; (heurter) hit; (attirer) attract. □ **s'~** *vpr* cling, hang on (à to); (se disputer) clash.

accroissement /akʀwasmɑ̃/ *nm* increase (de in).

accroître /akʀwɑtʀ/ [24] *vt* increase. □ **s'~** *vpr* increase.

accroupir (s') /(s)akʀupiʀ/ [2] *vpr* squat.

accru, ~e /akʀy/ *adj* increased, greater.

accueil /akœj/ *nm* reception, welcome.

accueillant, ~e /akœjɑ̃, -t/ *adj* friendly, welcoming.

accueillir /akœjiʀ/ [25] *vt* receive, welcome; (*film, livre*) receive; (prendre en charge) (*réfugiés, patients*) take care of, cater for.

accumuler /akymyle/ [1] *vt* (*énergie*) store up; (*capital*) accumulate. □ **s'~** *vpr* (*neige, ordures*) pile up; (*dettes*) accrue.

accusation /akyzasjɔ̃/ *nf* accusation; (Jur) charge; **l'~** (magistrat) the prosecution.

accusé, ~e /akyze/ *adj* marked. ● *nm,f* defendant, accused.

accuser /akyze/ [1] *vt* accuse (**de** of); (blâmer) blame (**de** for); (Jur) charge (**de** with); (fig) emphasize; ~ **réception de** acknowledge receipt of.

acharné, ~e /aʃaʀne/ *adj* relentless, ferocious. **acharnement** *nm* (énergie) furious energy; (ténacité) determination.

acharner (s') /(s)aʃaʀne/ [1] *vpr* persevere; **s'~ sur** set upon;

(poursuivre) hound; **s'~ à faire** (s'évertuer) try desperately; (s'obstiner) keep on doing.

achat /aʃa/ *nm* purchase; **~s** shopping; **faire l'~ de** buy; **faire des ~s** do some shopping.

acheminer /aʃ(ə)mine/ [1] *vt* dispatch, convey; (*courrier*) handle. □ **s'~ vers** *vpr* head for.

acheter /aʃ(ə)te/ [6] *vt* buy; **~ qch à qn** (pour lui) buy sth for sb; (chez lui) buy sth from sb. **acheteur, -euse** *nm,f* buyer; (client de magasin) shopper.

achèvement /aʃɛvmɑ̃/ *nm* completion.

achever /aʃ(ə)ve/ [6] *vt* finish (off). □ **s'~** *vpr* end.

acide /asid/ *adj* acid, sharp. ● *nm* acid.

acier /asje/ *nm* steel.

acné /akne/ *nf* acne.

acompte /akɔ̃t/ *nm* deposit, part-payment.

à-côté (*pl* ~s) /akote/ *nm* side issue; ~s (argent) extras.

acoustique /akustik/ *nf* acoustics (+ *sg*). ● *adj* acoustic.

acquéreur /akerœr/ *nm* purchaser, buyer.

acquérir /akerir/ [7] *vt* acquire, gain; (*biens*) purchase, acquire.

acquis, ~e /aki, -z/ *adj* acquired; (*fait*) established; **tenir qch pour ~** take sth for granted. ● *nm* experience. **acquisition** *nf* acquisition; purchase.

acquitter /akite/ [1] *vt* acquit; (*dette*) settle. □ **s'~ de** *vpr* (*promesse*) fulfil; (*devoir*) discharge.

âcre /ɑkr/ *adj* acrid.

acrobatie /akrɔbasi/ *nf* acrobatics (+ *pl*); ~ **aérienne** aerobatics (+ *pl*).

acte /akt/ *nm* act, action, deed; (Théât) act; (Jur) deed; ~ **de naissance/mariage** birth/marriage certificate; ~s (compte rendu) proceedings; **prendre ~ de** note.

acteur /aktœr/ *nm* actor.

actif, -ive /aktif, -v/ *adj* active; (*population*) working. ● *nm* (Comm) assets; **avoir à son ~** have to one's credit *ou* name.

action /aksjɔ̃/ *nf* action; (Comm) share; (Jur) action; (effet) effect; (initiative) initiative. **actionnaire** *nmf* shareholder.

activer /aktive/ [1] *vt* speed up; (*feu*) boost. □ **s'~** *vpr* hurry up; (s'affairer) be very busy.

activité /aktivite/ *nf* activity; **en ~** (*volcan*) active; (*fonctionnaire*) working; (*usine*) in operation.

actrice /aktris/ *nf* actress.

actualité /aktɥalite/ *nf* topicality; **l'~** current affairs; **les ~s** news; **d'~** topical.

actuel, ~le /aktɥɛl/ *adj* current, present; (d'actualité) topical. **actuellement** *adv* currently, at the present time.

acupuncture /akypɔ̃ktyr/ *nf* acupuncture.

adaptateur /adaptatœr/ *nm* (Électr) adapter.

adapter /adapte/ [1] *vt* adapt; (fixer) fit. □ **s'~** *vpr* adapt (oneself); (Tech) fit.

additif /aditif/ *nm* (note) rider; (substance) additive.

addition /adisjɔ̃/ *nf* addition; (au café) bill; (US) check. **additionner** [1] *vt* add; (totaliser) add (up).

adepte /adɛpt/ *nmf* follower; (d'activité) enthusiast.

adéquat, ~e /adekwa, -t/ *adj* suitable; (suffisant) adequate.

adhérent, ~e /aderɑ̃, -t/ *nm,f* member.

adhérer /adere/ [14] *vi* adhere, stick (à to); ~ **à** (*club*) be a member of; (s'inscrire à) join.

adhésif, -ive /adezif, -v/ *adj* adhesive; **ruban ~** sticky tape.

adhésion /adezjɔ̃/ *nf* membership; (soutien) support.

adieu (*pl* ~x) /adjø/ *interj & nm* goodbye, farewell.

adjectif /adʒɛktif/ *nm* adjective.

adjoint, ~e /adʒwɛ̃, -t/ *nm,f* assistant; ~ **au maire** deputy mayor. ● *adj* assistant.

adjuger /adʒyʒe/ [40] *vt* award; (aux enchères) auction. □ **s'~** *vpr* take (for oneself).

agresser /agʀese/ [1] *vt* attack; (pour voler) mug.

agressif, **-ive** /agʀesif, -v/ *adj* aggressive. **agression** *nf* attack; (pour voler) mugging; (Mil) aggression.

agricole /agʀikɔl/ *adj* agricultural; (*ouvrier*, *produit*) farm. **agriculteur** *nm* farmer. **agriculture** *nf* agriculture, farming.

agripper /agʀipe/ [1] *vt* grab. □ **s'∼** *vpr* cling (à to).

agroalimentaire /agʀɔalimɑ̃tɛʀ/ *nm* food industry.

agrumes /agʀym/ *nmpl* citrus fruit (s).

ai /e/ ⇒AVOIR [5].

aide /ɛd/ *nf* help, assistance; (en argent) aid; **à l'∼ de** with the help of; **venir en ∼ à** help; **∼ à domicile** home help; **∼ familiale** mother's help; **∼ sociale** social security; (US) welfare. ● *nmf* assistant. **aide-mémoire** *nm inv* handbook of key facts.

aider /ede/ [1] *vt/i* help, assist; (subventionner) aid, give aid to; **∼ à faire** help to do. □ **s' ∼ de** *vpr* use.

aïeul, **∼e** /ajœl/ *nm,f* grandparent.

aigle /ɛgl/ *nm* eagle.

aigre /ɛgʀ/ *adj* sour, sharp; (fig) sharp.

aigrir /egʀiʀ/ [2] *vt* embitter. □ **s'∼** *vpr* turn sour; (*personne*) become embittered.

aigu, **∼ë** /egy/ *adj* (*douleur*, *problème*) acute; (*objet*) sharp; (*voix*) shrill; (Mus) high(-pitched); (*accent*) acute.

aiguille /egɥij/ *nf* needle; (de montre) hand; (de balance) pointer; **∼ à tricoter** knitting needle.

aiguilleur /egɥijœʀ/ *nm* pointsman; **∼ du ciel** air traffic controller.

aiguiser /eg(ɥ)ize/ [1] *vt* sharpen; (fig) stimulate.

ail (*pl* **∼s** *ou* **aulx**) /aj, o/ *nm* garlic.

aile /ɛl/ *nf* wing.

ailier /elje/ *nm* winger; (US) end.

aille /aj/ ⇒ALLER [8].

ailleurs /ajœʀ/ *adv* elsewhere, somewhere else; **d'∼** besides, moreover; **nulle part ∼** nowhere else;

par ∼ moreover, furthermore; **partout ∼** everywhere else.

aimable /ɛmabl/ *adj* kind.

aimant /ɛmɑ̃/ *nm* magnet.

aimer /eme/ [1] *vt* like; (d'amour) love; **j'aimerais faire** I'd like to do; **∼ bien** quite like; **∼ mieux** *ou* **autant** prefer.

aîné, **∼e** /ene/ *adj* eldest; (de deux) elder. ● *nm,f* eldest (child); (premier de deux) elder (child); **∼s** elders; **il est mon ∼** he is older than me *ou* my senior.

ainsi /ɛ̃si/ *adv* like this, thus; (donc) so; **et ∼ de suite** and so on; **pour ∼ dire** so to speak, as it were; **∼ que** as well as; (comme) as.

air /ɛʀ/ *nm* air; (mine) look, air; (mélodie) tune; **∼ conditionné** air-conditioning; **avoir l'∼** look, appear; **avoir l'∼ de** look like; **avoir l'∼ de faire** appear to be doing; **en l'∼** (up) in the air; (*promesses*) empty; **prendre l'∼** get some fresh air.

aire /ɛʀ/ *nf* area; **∼ d'atterrissage** landing-strip; **∼ de pique-nique** picnic area; **∼ de repas** rest area; **∼ de services** (motorway) services.

aisance /ɛzɑ̃s/ *nf* ease; (richesse) affluence.

aise /ɛz/ *nf* joy; **à l'∼** (sur un siège) comfortable; (pas gêné) at ease; (fortuné) comfortably off; **mal à l'∼** uncomfortable; ill at ease; **aimer ses ∼s** like one's creature comforts; **mettre qn à l'∼** put sb at ease; **se mettre à l'∼** make oneself comfortable.

aisé, **∼e** /eze/ *adj* easy; (fortuné) well-off.

aisselle /ɛsɛl/ *nf* armpit.

ait /ɛ/ ⇒AVOIR [5].

ajourner /aʒuʀne/ [1] *vt* postpone; (*débat*, *procès*) adjourn.

ajout /aʒu/ *nm* addition.

ajouter /aʒute/ [1] *vt* add (à to); **∼ foi à** lend credence to. □ **s'∼** *vpr* be added.

ajuster /aʒyste/ [1] *vt* adjust; (*cible*) aim at; (adapter) fit; **∼ son coup** adjust one's aim.

alarme /alaʀm/ *nf* alarm; **donner l'∼** raise the alarm.

alarmer /alaʀme/ [1] *vt* alarm. □ **s'∼** *vpr* become alarmed (de at).

Albanie /albani/ *nf* Albania.

alcool /alkɔl/ *nm* alcohol; (eau de vie) brandy; ~ **à brûler** methylated spirit. **alcoolique** *a* & *nmf* alcoholic. **alcoolisé**, ~**e** *adj* (*boisson*) alcoholic. **alcoolisme** *nm* alcoholism.

alcootest /alkɔtɛst/ *nm* breath test; (appareil) Breathalyser®.

aléa /alea/ *nm* hazard. **aléatoire** *adj* unpredictable, uncertain; (Ordinat) random.

alentours /alɑ̃tuʀ/ *nmpl* surroundings; **aux ~ de** (de lieu) around; (de chiffre, date) about, around.

alerte /alɛʀt/ *adj* (*personne*) alert; (vif) lively. ● *nf* alert; ~ **à la bombe** bomb scare. **alerter** [1] *vt* alert.

algèbre /alʒɛbʀ/ *nf* algebra.

Algérie /alʒeʀi/ *nf* Algeria.

algue /alg/ *nf* seaweed; **les ~s** (Bot) algae.

aliéné, ~**e** /aljene/ *nm,f* insane person.

aliéner /aljene/ [14] *vt* alienate; (céder) give up. □ **s'~** *vpr* alienate.

aligner /aliɲe/ [1] *vt* (*objets*) line up, make lines of; (*chiffres*) string together; ~ **sur** bring into line with. □ **s'~** *vpr* line up; **s'~ sur** align oneself on.

aliment /alimɑ̃/ *nm* food.

alimentaire /alimɑ̃tɛʀ/ *adj* (*industrie*) food; (*habitudes*) dietary; **produits ~s** foodstuffs.

alimentation /alimɑ̃tasjɔ̃/ *nf* feeding, supply(ing); (régime) diet; (aliments) food; **magasin d'~** grocery shop *ou* store.

alimenter /alimɑ̃te/ [1] *vt* feed; (fournir) supply; (fig) sustain. □ **s'~** *vpr* eat.

allaiter /alete/ [1] *vt* (*bébé*) breast-feed; (US) nurse; (*animal*) suckle.

allée /ale/ *nf* path, lane; (menant à une maison) drive(way); (dans un cinéma, magasin) aisle; (rue) road; **~s et venues** comings and goings.

allégé, ~**e** /aleʒe/ *adj* diet; (*beurre, yaourt*) low-fat.

alléger /aleʒe/ [14] [40] *vt* make lighter; (*fardeau, chargement*) lighten; (fig) (*souffrance*) alleviate.

allégresse /alegʀɛs/ *nf* gaiety, joy.

alléguer /alege/ [14] *vt* (*exemple*) invoke; (prétexter) allege.

Allemagne /almaɲ/ *nf* Germany.

allemand, ~**e** /almɑ̃, -d/ *adj* German. ● *nm* (Ling) German. **A~**, ~**e** *nm,f* German.

aller /ale/ [8]

● *verbe auxiliaire*

····➤ **je vais l'appeler** I'm going to call him; **j'allais partir** I was about to leave; **va savoir!** who knows?; ~ **en s'améliorant** be improving.

● *verbe intransitif*

····➤ (se déplacer) go; **allons-y!** let's go!; **allez!** come on!

····➤ (se porter) **comment allez-vous?**, **comment ça va?** how are you?; **ça va (bien)** I'm fine; **qu'est-ce qui ne va pas?** what's the matter?; **ça ne va pas la tête?** 🖪 are you mad? 🖪.

····➤ (mettre en valeur) ~ **à qn** suit sb; **ça te va bien** it really suits you.

····➤ (convenir) **ça va ma coiffure?** is my hair OK?; **ça ne va pas du tout** that's no good at all.

□ **s'en aller** *verbe pronominal*

····➤ go; **va-t'en!** go away!; **ça ne s'en va pas** (*tache*) it won't come out.

● *nom masculin*

····➤ outward journey; ~ **(simple)** single (ticket); (US) one-way (ticket); ~ **retour** return (ticket); (US) round trip (ticket); **à l'~** on the way out.

allergie /alɛʀʒi/ *nf* allergy. **allergique** *adj* allergic (à to).

alliance /aljɑ̃s/ *nf* alliance; (bague) wedding-ring; (mariage) marriage.

allier /alje/ [45] *vt* combine; (Pol) ally. □ **s'~** *vpr* combine; (Pol) form an alliance; (*famille*) become related (à to).

allô /alo/ *interj* hallo, hello.

allocation /alɔkasjɔ̃/ *nf* allowance; ~ **chômage** unemployment benefit; **~s familiales** family allowance.

allonger /alɔ̃ʒe/ [40] *vt* lengthen; (*bras, jambe*) stretch (out); (coucher) lay down. □ **s'~** *vpr* get longer;

(s'étendre) lie down; (s'étirer) stretch (oneself) out.

allouer /alwe/ [1] *vt* allocate; (*prêt*) grant.

allumer /alyme/ [1] *vt* (*bougie, gaz*) light; (*lampe, appareil*) turn on; (*pièce*) switch the light(s) on in; (fig) arouse. □ **s'**~ *vpr* (*lumière, appareil*) come on.

allumette /alymɛt/ *nf* match.

allure /alyʀ/ *nf* speed, pace; (*démarche*) walk; (*apparence*) appearance; **à toute** ~ at full speed; **avoir de l'**~ have style; **avoir des** ~s **de** look like; **avoir une drôle d'**~ be funny-looking.

allusion /alyzjɔ̃/ *nf* allusion (à to); (*implicite*) hint (à at); **faire** ~ à allude to; hint at.

alors /alɔʀ/ *adv* (à ce moment-là) then; (de ce fait) so; (dans ce cas-là) then; **ça** ~! well!; **et** ~? so what? ● *conj* ~ **que** (pendant que) while; (tandis que) when, whereas.

alouette /alwɛt/ *nf* lark.

alourdir /aluʀdiʀ/ [2] *vt* weigh down; (rendre plus important) increase.

aloyau (*pl* ~**x**) /alwajo/ *nm* sirloin.

Alpes /alp/ *nfpl* **les** ~ the Alps.

alphabet /alfabɛ/ *nm* alphabet. **alphabétique** *adj* alphabetical.

alphabétiser /alfabetize/ [1] *vt* teach to read and write.

alpinist /alpinist/ *nmf* mountaineer.

altérer /alteʀe/ [14] *vt* (*fait, texte*) distort; (*abîmer*) spoil; (*donner soif à*) make thirsty. □ **s'**~ *vpr* deteriorate.

alternance /altɛʀnɑ̃s/ *nf* alternation; **en** ~ alternately.

altitude /altityd/ *nf* altitude, height.

amabilité /amabilite/ *nf* kindness.

amaigrir /amegʀiʀ/ [2] *vt* make thin(ner).

amande /amɑ̃d/ *nf* almond; (d'un fruit à noyau) kernel.

amant /amɑ̃/ *nm* lover.

amarre /amaʀ/ *nf* (mooring) rope; ~**s** moorings.

amas /amɑ/ *nm* heap, pile.

amasser /amase/ [1] *vt* amass, gather; (empiler) pile up. □ **s'**~ *vpr* pile up; (*gens*) gather.

amateur /amatœʀ/ *nm* amateur; ~ **de** lover of; **d'**~ amateur; (péj) amateurish.

ambassade /ɑ̃basad/ *nf* embassy. **ambassadeur, -drice** *nm, f* ambassador.

ambiance /ɑ̃bjɑ̃s/ *nf* atmosphere. **ambiant,** ~**e** *adj* surrounding.

ambigu, ~**ë** /ɑ̃bigy/ *adj* ambiguous.

ambitieux, -ieuse /ɑ̃bisjø, -z/ *adj* ambitious. **ambition** *nf* ambition.

ambulance /ɑ̃bylɑ̃s/ *nf* ambulance.

ambulant, ~**e** /ɑ̃bylɑ̃, -t/ *adj* itinerant, travelling.

âme /am/ *nf* soul; ~ **sœur** soul mate.

amélioration /ameljɔʀasjɔ̃/ *nf* improvement.

améliorer /ameljɔʀe/ [1] *vt* improve. □ **s'**~ *vpr* improve.

aménagement /amenaʒmɑ̃/ *nm* (de magasin) fitting out; (de grenier) conversion; (de territoire) development; (de cuisine) equipping.

aménager /amenaʒe/ [40] *vt* (*magasin*) fit out; (*transformer*) convert; (*territoire*) develop; (*cuisine*) equip.

amende /amɑ̃d/ *nf* fine; **faire** ~ **honorable** make amends.

amener /am(ə)ne/ [6] *vt* bring; (causer) bring about; ~ **qn à faire** cause sb to do. □ **s'**~ *vpr* [] turn up.

amer, -ère /amɛʀ/ *adj* bitter.

américain, ~**e** /ameʀikɛ̃, -ɛn/ *adj* American. **A**~, ~**e** *nm, f* American.

Amérique /ameʀik/ *nf* America; ~ **centrale/latine** Central/Latin America; ~ **du Nord/Sud** North/ South America.

amertume /amɛʀtym/ *nf* bitterness.

ami, ~**e** /ami/ *nm, f* friend; (amateur) lover; **un** ~ **des bêtes** an animal lover. ● *adj* friendly.

amiable /amjabl/ *adj* amicable; **à l'**~ (*divorcer*) by mutual consent; (se séparer) on friendly terms; (*séparation*) amicable.

amical, ~**e** (*mpl* **-aux**) /amikal, -o/ *adj* friendly.

amiral (*pl* **-aux**) /amiʀal, -o/ *nm* admiral.

amitié /amitje/ *nf* friendship; **~s** (en fin de lettre) kind regards; **prendre qn en ~** take a liking to sb.

amnistie /amnisti/ *nf* amnesty.

amoindrir /amwɛ̃dʀiʀ/ [2] *vt* reduce.

amont: en ~ /ãnamɔ̃/ *loc* upstream.

amorcer /amɔʀse/ [10] *vt* start; (*hameçon*) bait; (*pompe*) prime; (*arme à feu*) arm.

amortir /amɔʀtiʀ/ [2] *vt* (*choc*) cushion; (*bruit*) deaden; (*dette*) pay off; **~ un achat** make a purchase pay for itself.

amortisseur /amɔʀtisœʀ/ *nm* shock absorber.

amour /amuʀ/ *nm* love; **pour l'~ de** for the sake of.

amoureux, -euse /amuʀø, -z/ *adj* (*personne*) in love; (*relation, regard*) loving; (*vie*) love; **~ de qn** in love with sb. ● *nm, f* lover.

amour-propre /amuʀpʀɔpʀ/ *nm* self-esteem.

amphithéâtre /ãfiteatʀ/ *nm* amphitheatre; (d'université) lecture hall.

ampleur /ãplœʀ/ *nf* extent, size; (de vêtement) fullness; **prendre de l'~** spread, grow.

amplifier /ãplifje/ [45] *vt* amplify; (fig) expand, develop. □ **s'~** *vpr* (*son*) grow; (*scandale*) intensify.

ampoule /ãpul/ *nf* (électrique) bulb; (sur la peau) blister; (Méd) phial, ampoule.

amusant, ~e /amyzã, -t/ *adj* (*blague*) funny; (*soirée*) enjoyable, entertaining.

amuse-gueule /amyzgœl/ *nm inv* cocktail snack.

amusement /amyzmã/ *nm* amusement; (passe-temps) entertainment.

amuser /amyze/ [1] *vt* amuse; (détourner l'attention de) distract. □ **s'~** *vpr* enjoy oneself; (jouer) play.

amygdale /amidal/ *nf* tonsil.

an /ã/ *nm* year; **avoir dix ~s** be ten years old; **un garçon de deux ~s** a two-year-old boy; **à soixante ~s** at the age of sixty; **les moins de dix-huit ~s** under eighteens.

analogie /analɔʒi/ *nf* analogy.

analogue /analɔg/ *adj* similar, analogous (à to).

analphabète /analfabɛt/ *a & nmf* illiterate.

analyse /analiz/ *nf* analysis; (Méd) test. **analyser** [1] *vt* analyse; (Méd) test.

ananas /anana(s)/ *nm* pineapple.

anarchie /anaʀʃi/ *nf* anarchy.

anatomie /anatɔmi/ *nf* anatomy.

ancêtre /ãsɛtʀ/ *nm* ancestor.

anchois /ãʃwa/ *nm* anchovy.

ancien, ~ne /ãsjɛ̃, -jɛn/ *adj* old; (de jadis) ancient; (*meuble*) antique; (*précédent*) former, ex-, old; (dans une fonction) senior; **~ combattant** veteran. ● *nm, f* senior; (par l'âge) elder. **anciennement** *adv* formerly. **ancienneté** *nf* age, seniority.

ancre /ãkʀ/ *nf* anchor; **jeter/lever l'~** cast/weigh anchor.

andouille /ãduj/ *nf* sausage (*filled with chitterlings*); (idiot 🔢) fool; **faire l'~** fool around.

âne /an/ *nm* donkey, ass; (imbécile 🔢) dimwit 🔢.

anéantir /aneãtiʀ/ [2] *vt* destroy; (exterminer) annihilate; (accabler) overwhelm.

anémie /anemi/ *nf* anaemia.

ânerie /anʀi/ *nf* stupid remark.

anesthésie /anɛstezi/ *nf* (opération) anaesthetic.

ange /ãʒ/ *nm* angel; **aux ~s** in seventh heaven.

angine /ãʒin/ *nf* throat infection.

anglais, ~e /ãglɛ, -z/ *adj* English. ● *nm* (Ling) English. **A~, ~e** *nm, f* Englishman, Englishwoman.

angle /ãgl/ *nm* angle; (coin) corner.

Angleterre /ãglətɛʀ/ *nf* England.

anglophone /ãglɔfɔn/ *adj* English-speaking. ● *nmf* English speaker.

angoissant, ~e /ãgwasã, -t/ *adj* alarming; (effrayant) harrowing.

angoisse /ãgwas/ *nf* anxiety. **angoissé, ~e** *adj* anxious. **angoisser** [1] *vi* worry.

animal (*pl* **-aux**) /animal, -o/ *nm* animal; **~ familier**, **~ de compagnie** pet. ● *adj* (*mpl* **-aux**) animal.

animateur, **-trice** /animatœʀ, -tʀis/ *nm, f* organizer, leader; (TV) host, hostess.

animation /animasjɔ̃/ *nf* liveliness; (*affairement*) activity; (au cinéma) animation; (*activité dirigée*) organized activity.

animé, **~e** /anime/ *adj* lively; (*affairé*) busy; (*être*) animate.

animer /anime/ [1] *vt* liven up; (*débat, atelier*) lead; (*spectacle*) host; (*pousser*) drive; (*encourager*) spur on. □ **s'~** *vpr* liven up.

anis /ani(s)/ *nm* (Culin) aniseed; (Bot) anise.

anneau (*pl* **~x**) /ano/ *nm* ring; (de chaîne) link.

année /ane/ *nf* year; **~ bissextile** leap year; **~ civile** calendar year.

annexe /anɛks/ *adj* (*document*) attached; (*question*) related; (*bâtiment*) adjoining. ● *nf* (bâtiment) annexe; (US) annex; (*document*) appendix; (électronique) attachment. **annexer** [1] *vt* annex; (*document*) attach.

anniversaire /anivɛʀsɛʀ/ *nm* birthday; (d'un événement) anniversary. ● *adj* anniversary.

annonce /anɔ̃s/ *nf* announcement; (*publicitaire*) advertisement; (*indice*) sign.

annoncer /anɔ̃se/ [10] *vt* announce; (*prédire*) forecast; (être l'indice de) herald. □ **s'~** *vpr* (*crise, tempête*) be brewing; **s'~ bien/mal** look good/ bad. **annonceur** *nm* advertiser.

annuaire /anɥɛʀ/ *nm* year-book; **~ (téléphonique)** (telephone) directory.

annuel, **~le** /anɥɛl/ *adj* annual, yearly.

annulation /anylasjɔ̃/ *nf* cancellation; (de sanction, loi) repeal; (de mesure) abolition.

annuler /anyle/ [1] *vt* cancel; (*contrat*) nullify; (*jugement*) quash; (*loi*) repeal. □ **s'~** *vpr* cancel each other out.

anodin, **~e** /anɔdɛ̃, -in/ *adj* insignificant; (sans risques) harmless, safe.

anonymat /anɔnima/ *nm* anonymity; **garder l'~** remain anonymous. **anonyme** *adj* anonymous.

anorexie /anɔʀɛksi/ *nf* anorexia.

anormal, **~e** (*mpl* **-aux**) /anɔʀmal, -o/ *adj* abnormal.

anse /ɑ̃s/ *nf* handle; (baie) cove.

Antarctique /ɑ̃taʀktik/ *nm* Antarctic.

antenne /ɑ̃tɛn/ *nf* aerial; (US) antenna; (d'insecte) antenna; (*succursale*) agency; (Mil) outpost; **à l'~** on the air; **~ chirurgicale** mobile emergency unit; **~ parabolique** satellite dish.

antérieur, **~e** /ɑ̃teʀjœʀ/ *adj* previous, earlier; (*placé devant*) front; **~ à** prior to.

antiaérien, **~ne** /ɑ̃tiaeʀjɛ̃, -ɛn/ *adj* anti-aircraft; **abri ~** air-raid shelter.

antiatomique /ɑ̃tiatɔmik/ *adj* **abri ~** nuclear fall-out shelter.

antibiotique /ɑ̃tibjɔtik/ *nm* antibiotic.

anticipation /ɑ̃tisipasjɔ̃/ *nf* **d'~** (*livre, film*) science fiction; **par ~** in advance.

anticiper /ɑ̃tisipe/ [1] *vt* **~ (sur)** anticipate; (effectuer à l'avance) bring forward.

anticorps /ɑ̃tikɔʀ/ *nm* antibody.

antidater /ɑ̃tidate/ [1] *vt* backdate, antedate.

antigel /ɑ̃tiʒɛl/ *nm* antifreeze.

Antilles /ɑ̃tij/ *nfpl* **les ~** the West Indies.

antipathique /ɑ̃tipatik/ *adj* unpleasant.

antiquaire /ɑ̃tikɛʀ/ *nmf* antique dealer.

antiquité /ɑ̃tikite/ *nf* (objet) antique; **l'A~** antiquity.

antisémite /ɑ̃tisemit/ *adj* anti-Semitic.

antiseptique /ɑ̃tisɛptik/ *a & nm* antiseptic.

antivol /ɑ̃tivɔl/ *nm* anti-theft device; (Auto) steering lock.

anxiété /ɑ̃ksjete/ *nf* anxiety.

anxieux, **-ieuse** /ɑ̃ksjø, -z/ *adj* anxious. ● *nm, f* worrier.

août /u(t)/ *nm* August.

apaiser /apeze/ [1] *vt* calm down; (*colère, militant*) appease; (*douleur*) soothe; (*faim*) satisfy. □ **s'~** *vpr* (*tempête*) die down.

apathie /apati/ *nf* apathy.
apathique *adj* apathetic.

apercevoir /apɛRsəvwaR/ [52] *vt* see. □ **s'~ de** *vpr* notice; **s'~ que** notice *ou* realize that.

aperçu /apɛRsy/ *nm* (échantillon) glimpse, taste; (intuition) insight.

apéritif /apeRitif/ *nm* aperitif, drink.

aphte /aft/ *nm* mouth ulcer.

apitoyer /apitwaje/ [31] *vt* move (to pity). □ **s'~** *vpr* **s'~ sur** (le sort de) **qn** feel sorry for sb.

aplanir /aplaniR/ [2] *vt* level; (fig) iron out.

aplatir /aplatiR/ [2] *vt* flatten (out). □ **s'~** *vpr* (s'immobiliser) flatten oneself.

aplomb /aplɔ̃/ *nm* balance; (fig) self-confidence; **d'~** (en équilibre) steady; **je ne suis pas bien d'~** Ⓘ I don't feel very well.

apogée /apɔʒe/ *nm* peak.

apologie /apɔlɔʒi/ *nf* panegyric.

apostrophe /apɔstRɔf/ *nf* apostrophe; (remarque) remark.

apothéose /apoteoz/ *nf* high point; (d'événement) grand finale.

apparaître /apaRɛtR/ [18] *vi* appear; **il apparaît que** it appears that.

appareil /apaRɛj/ *nm* device; (électrique) appliance; (Anat) system; (téléphone) phone; (avion) plane; (Culin) mixture; (système administratif) apparatus; **~ (dentaire)** brace; (dentier) dentures; **~ (photo)** camera; **c'est Gabriel à l'~** it's Gabriel on the phone; **~ auditif** hearing aid; **~ électroménager** household electrical appliance.

appareiller /apaReje/ [1] *vi* (navire) cast off, put to sea.

apparemment /apaRamɑ̃/ *adv* apparently.

apparence /apaRɑ̃s/ *nf* appearance; **en ~** outwardly; (apparemment) apparently.

apparent, **~e** /apaRɑ̃, -t/ *adj* apparent; (visible) conspicuous.

apparenté, **~e** /apaRɑ̃te/ *adj* related; (semblable) similar.

apparition /apaRisjɔ̃/ *nf* appearance; (spectre) apparition.

appartement /apaRtəmɑ̃/ *nm* flat; (US) apartment.

appartenir /apaRtəniR/ [58] *vi* belong (à to); **il lui appartient de** it is up to him to.

appât /apɑ/ *nm* bait; (fig) lure.

appauvrir /apovRiR/ [2] *vt* impoverish. □ **s'~** *vpr* become impoverished.

appel /apɛl/ *nm* call; (Jur) appeal; (supplique) appeal, plea; (Mil) call-up; (US) draft; **faire ~** appeal; **faire ~ à** (recourir à) call on; (invoquer) appeal to; (évoquer) call up; (exiger) call for; **faire l'~** (Scol) call the register; (Mil) take a roll-call; **~ d'offres** (Comm) invitation to tender; **faire un ~ de phares** flash one's headlights.

appeler /aple/ [38] *vt* call; (téléphoner) phone, call; (nécessiter) call for; **en ~ à** appeal to; **appelé à** (destiné) destined for. □ **s'~** *vpr* be called; **il s'appelle Tim** his name is Tim *ou* he is called Tim.

appellation /apelasjɔ̃/ *nf* name, designation.

appendice /apɛ̃dis/ *nm* appendix.
appendicite *nf* appendicitis.

appesantir /apəzɑ̃tiR/ [2] *vt* weigh down. □ **s'~** *vpr* grow heavier; **s'~ sur** dwell upon.

appétissant, **~e** /apetisɑ̃, -t/ *adj* appetizing.

appétit /apeti/ *nm* appetite; **bon ~!** enjoy your meal!

applaudir /aplodiR/ [2] *vt/i* applaud.
applaudissements *nmpl* applause.

application /aplikasjɔ̃/ *nf* (soin) care; (de loi) (respect) application; (mise en œuvre) implementation; (Ordinat) application program.

appliqué, **~e** /aplike/ *adj* (travail) painstaking; (sciences) applied; (élève) hard-working.

appliquer /aplike/ [1] *vt* apply; (loi) enforce. □ **s'~** *vpr* apply oneself (à to), take great care (à faire to do); **s'~ à** (concerner) apply to.

appoint /apwɛ̃/ *nm* support; **d'~** extra; **faire l'~** give the correct money.

apport /apɔʀ/ *nm* contribution.

apporter /apɔʀte/ [1] *vt* bring; *(aide, précision)* give; *(causer)* bring about.

appréciation /apʀesjasjɔ̃/ *nf* estimate, evaluation; *(de monnaie)* appreciation; *(jugement)* assessment.

apprécier /apʀesje/ [45] *vt* appreciate; *(évaluer)* assess; *(objet)* value, appraise.

appréhender /apʀeɑ̃de/ [1] *vt* dread, fear; *(arrêter)* apprehend.

apprendre /apʀɑ̃dʀ/ [50] *vt* learn; *(être informé de)* hear, learn; *(de façon indirecte)* hear of; ~ **qch à qn** teach sb sth; *(informer)* tell sb sth; ~ **à faire** learn to do; ~ **à qn à faire** teach sb to do; ~ **que** learn that; *(être informé)* hear that.

apprenti, ~**e** /apʀɑ̃ti/ *nm,f* apprentice. **apprentissage** *nm* apprenticeship; *(d'un sujet)* learning.

apprêter /apʀete/ [1] *vt* prepare; *(bois)* prime; *(mur)* size. □ **s'**~ **à** *vpr* prepare to.

apprivoiser /apʀivwaze/ [1] *vt* tame.

approbation /apʀɔbasjɔ̃/ *nf* approval.

approchant, ~**e** /apʀɔʃɑ̃, -t/ *adj* close, similar.

approcher /apʀɔʃe/ [1] *vt* *(objet)* move near(er) *(de* to); *(personne)* approach; ~ **de** get nearer *ou* closer to. ● *vi* approach. □ **s'**~ **de** *vpr* approach, move near(er) to.

approfondir /apʀɔfɔ̃diʀ/ [2] *vt* deepen; *(fig)* *(sujet)* go into sth in depth; *(connaissances)* improve.

approprié, ~**e** /apʀɔpʀije/ *adj* appropriate.

approprier (s') /(s)apʀɔpʀije/ [45] *vpr* appropriate.

approuver /apʀuve/ [1] *vt* approve; *(trouver louable)* approve of; *(soutenir)* agree with.

approvisionner /apʀɔvizjɔne/ [1] *vt* supply *(en* with); *(compte en banque)* pay money into. □ **s'**~ *vpr* stock up.

approximatif, -**ive** /apʀɔksimatif, -v/ *adj* approximate.

appui /apɥi/ *nm* support; *(de fenêtre)* sill; *(pour objet)* rest; **à l'**~ **de** in support of; **prendre** ~ **sur** lean on.

appui-tête *(pl* **appuis-tête)** /apɥitɛt/ *nm* headrest.

appuyer /apɥije/ [31] *vt* lean, rest; *(presser)* press; *(soutenir)* support, back. ● *vi* ~ **sur** press (on); *(fig)* stress. □ **s'**~ **sur** *vpr* lean on; *(compter sur)* rely on.

après /apʀɛ/ *prép* after; *(au-delà de)* after, beyond; ~ **avoir fait** after doing; ~ **tout** after all; ~ **coup** after the event; **d'**~ *(selon)* according to; *(en imitant)* from; *(adapté de)* based on. ● *adv* after(wards); *(plus tard)* later; **le bus d'**~ the next bus. ● *conj* ~ **qu'il est parti** after he left. **après-demain** *adv* the day after tomorrow. **après-guerre** *(pl* ~**s)** *nm ou f* postwar period. **après-midi** *nm ou f inv* afternoon. **après-rasage** *(pl* ~**s)** *nm* aftershave. **après-ski** *nm inv* moonboot. **après-vente** *a inv* after-sales.

a priori /apʀijɔʀi/ *adv* *(à première vue)* offhand, on the face of it; *(sans réfléchir)* out of hand. ● *nm* preconception.

à-propos /apʀɔpo/ *nm* timing, timeliness; *(fig)* presence of mind.

apte /apt/ *adj* capable *(à* of); *(ayant les qualités requises)* suitable *(à* for); *(en état)* fit *(à* for).

aptitude /aptityd/ *nf* aptitude, ability.

aquarelle /akwaʀɛl/ *nf* watercolour.

aquatique /akwatik/ *adj* aquatic; *(Sport)* water.

arabe /aʀab/ *adj* Arab; *(Ling)* Arabic; *(désert)* Arabian. ● *nm* *(Ling)* Arabic. **A**~ *nmf* Arab.

Arabie /aʀabi/ *nf* ~ **Saoudite** Saudi Arabia.

arachide /aʀaʃid/ *nf* groundnut; **huile d'**~ groundnut oil.

araignée /aʀeɲe/ *nf* spider.

arbitraire /aʀbitʀɛʀ/ *adj* arbitrary.

arbitre /aʀbitʀ/ *nm* referee; *(au cricket, tennis)* umpire; *(expert)* arbiter; *(Jur)* arbitrator. **arbitrer** [1] *vt* *(match)* referee, umpire; *(Jur)* arbitrate in.

arbre /aʀbʀ/ *nm* tree; *(Tech)* shaft.

arbuste /aʀbyst/ *nm* shrub.

arc /aʀk/ nm (arme) bow; (courbe) curve; (voûte) arch; ~ **de cercle** arc of a circle.

arc-en-ciel (pl **arcs-en-ciel**) /aʀkɑ̃sjɛl/ nm rainbow.

arche /aʀʃ/ nf arch; ~ **de Noé** Noah's ark.

archéologie /aʀkeɔlɔʒi/ nf archaeology.

archevêque /aʀʃəvɛk/ nm archbishop.

architecte /aʀʃitɛkt/ nmf architect. **architecture** nf architecture.

Arctique /aʀktik/ nm Arctic.

ardent, ~**e** /aʀdɑ̃, -t/ adj burning; (passionné) ardent; (foi) fervent. **ardeur** nf ardour; (chaleur) heat.

ardoise /aʀdwaz/ nf slate; ~ **électronique** notepad computer.

arène /aʀɛn/ nf arena; ~**s** amphitheatre; (pour corridas) bullring.

arête /aʀɛt/ nf (de poisson) bone; (bord) ridge.

argent /aʀʒɑ̃/ nm money; (métal) silver; ~ **comptant** cash; **prendre pour** ~ **comptant** take at face value; ~ **de poche** pocket money.

argenté, ~**e** /aʀʒɑ̃te/ adj silver(y); (métal) (silver-)plated.

argenterie /aʀʒɑ̃tʀi/ nf silverware.

Argentine /aʀʒɑ̃tin/ nf Argentina.

argile /aʀʒil/ nf clay.

argot /aʀɡo/ nm slang.

argument /aʀɡymɑ̃/ nm argument; ~ **de vente** selling point. **argumenter** [1] vi argue.

aristocratie /aʀistɔkʀasi/ nf aristocracy.

arithmétique /aʀitmetik/ nf arithmetic. ● adj arithmetical.

armature /aʀmatyʀ/ nf framework; (de tente) frame.

arme /aʀm/ nf arm, weapon; ~ **à feu** firearm; ~**s** (blason) coat of arms.

armée /aʀme/ nf army; ~ **de l'air** Air Force; ~ **de terre** Army.

armer /aʀme/ [1] vt arm; (fusil) cock; (navire) equip; (renforcer) reinforce; (Photo) wind on; ~ **de** (garnir de) fit with. □ **s'**~ **de** vpr arm oneself with.

armoire /aʀmwaʀ/ nf cupboard; (penderie) wardrobe; (US) closet; ~ **à pharmacie** medicine cabinet.

armure /aʀmyʀ/ nf armour.

arnaque /aʀnak/ nf 🔲 swindling; **c'est de l'**~ it's a swindle ou con 🔲.

aromate /aʀɔmat/ nm herb, spice.

aromatisé, ~**e** /aʀɔmatize/ adj flavoured.

arôme /aʀom/ nm aroma; (additif) flavouring.

arpenter /aʀpɑ̃te/ [1] vt pace up and down; (terrain) survey.

arqué, ~**e** /aʀke/ adj arched; (jambes) bandy.

arrache-pied: d'~ /daʀaʃpje/ loc relentlessly.

arracher /aʀaʃe/ [1] vt pull out ou off; (plante) pull ou dig up; (cheveux, page) tear ou pull out; (par une explosion) blow off; ~ **à** (enlever à) snatch from; (fig) force ou wrest from. □ **s'**~ **qch** vpr fight over sth.

arranger /aʀɑ̃ʒe/ [40] vt arrange, fix up; (réparer) put right; (régler) sort out; (convenir à) suit. □ **s'**~ vpr (se mettre d'accord) come to an arrangement; (se débrouiller) manage (**pour** to).

arrestation /aʀɛstasjɔ̃/ nf arrest.

arrêt /aʀɛ/ nm stopping; (de combats) cessation; (de production) halt; (lieu) stop; (pause) pause; (Jur) ruling; **aux** ~**s** (Mil) under arrest; **à l'**~ (véhicule) stationary; (machine) idle; **faire un** ~ (make a) stop; **sans** ~ (sans escale) nonstop; (sans interruption) constantly; ~ **maladie** sick leave; ~ **de travail** (grève) stoppage; (Méd) sick leave.

arrêté /aʀete/ nm order; ~ **municipal** bylaw.

arrêter /aʀete/ [1] vt stop; (date) fix; (appareil) turn off; (renoncer à) give up; (appréhender) arrest. ● vi stop. □ **s'**~ vpr stop; **s'**~ **de faire** stop doing.

arrhes /aʀ/ nfpl deposit; **verser des** ~ pay a deposit.

arrière /aʀjɛʀ/ a inv back, rear. ● nm back, rear; (football) back; **à l'**~ in ou at the back; **en** ~ behind; (marcher, tomber) backwards; **en** ~ **de** behind. **arrière-boutique** (pl ~**s**) nf back room (of the shop). **arrière-garde** (pl ~**s**) nf

rearguard. **arrière-goût** (*pl* ~s)
nm after-taste. **arrière-grand-
mère** (*pl* **arrière-grands-mères**)
nf great-grandmother. **arrière-
grand-père** (*pl* **arrière-grands-
pères**) *nm* great-grandfather.
arrière-pays *nm inv* backcountry.
arrière-pensée (*pl* ~s) *nf* ulterior
motive. **arrière-plan** *nm* (*pl* ~s)
background.

arrimer /aRime/ [1] *vt* secure;
(*cargaison*) stow.

arrivage /aRivaʒ/ *nm* consignment.

arrivée /aRive/ *nf* arrival; (Sport)
finish.

arriver /aRive/ [1] *vi* (*aux être*)
arrive, come; (*réussir*) succeed; (*se
produire*) happen; ~ à (*atteindre*) reach;
~ à faire manage to do; **je n'arrive
pas à faire** I can't do; **en ~ à faire** get
to the stage of doing; **il arrive que** it
happens that; **il lui arrive de faire** he
(sometimes) does.

arriviste /aRivist/ *nmf* go-getter,
self-seeker.

arrondir /aRɔ̃diR/ [2] *vt* (make)
round; (*somme*) round off. □ **s'~** *vpr*
become round(ed).

arrondissement /aRɔ̃dismɑ̃/ *nm*
district.

arroser /aRoze/ [1] *vt* water; (*repas*)
wash down (with a drink); (*rôti*)
baste; (*victoire*) drink to. **arrosoir**
nm watering-can.

art /aR/ *nm* art; (*don*) knack (**de faire**
of doing); ~s **et métiers** arts and
crafts; ~s **ménagers** home
economics (+ *sg*).

artère /aRtɛR/ *nf* artery; (**grande**) ~
main road.

arthrite /aRtRit/ *nf* arthritis.

arthrose /aRtRoz/ *nf* osteoarthritis.

artichaut /aRtiʃo/ *nm* artichoke.

article /aRtikl/ *nm* article; (Comm)
item, article; **à l'~ de la mort** at
death's door; ~ **de fond** feature
(article); ~s **de voyage** travel goods.

articulation /aRtikylasjɔ̃/ *nf*
articulation; (Anat) joint.

articuler /aRtikyle/ [1] *vt* articulate;
(*structurer*) structure; (*assembler*)
connect (**sur** to).

artificiel, ~**le** /aRtifisjɛl/ *adj*
artificial.

artisan /aRtizɑ̃/ *nm* artisan,
craftsman; **l'~ de** (fig) the architect
of.

artisanal, ~**e** (*mpl* ~**aux**)
/aRtizanal/ *adj* craft; (*méthode*)
traditional; (*amateur*) home-made; **de
fabrication** ~**e** hand-made, hand-
crafted.

artiste /aRtist/ *nmf* artist.
artistique *adj* artistic.

as[1] /a/ ⇒AVOIR [5].

as[2] /ɑs/ *nm* ace.

ascenseur /asɑ̃sœR/ *nm* lift; (US)
elevator.

ascension /asɑ̃sjɔ̃/ *nf* ascent; **l'A~**
Ascension.

aseptiser /asɛptize/ [1] *vt* disinfect;
(*stériliser*) sterilize; **aseptisé** (péj)
sanitized.

asiatique /azjatik/ *adj* Asian. **A~**
nmf Asian.

Asie /azi/ *nf* Asia.

asile /azil/ *nm* refuge; (Pol) asylum;
(**pour malades, vieillards**) home; ~ **de
nuit** night shelter.

aspect /aspɛ/ *nm* appearance;
(*facettes*) aspect; (*perspective*) side; **à
l'~ de** at the sight of.

asperge /aspɛRʒ/ *nf* asparagus.

asperger /aspɛRʒe/ [40] *vt* spray.

asphyxier /asfiksje/ [45] *vt*
(*personne*) asphyxiate; (*entreprise,
réseau*) paralyse. □ **s'~** *vpr*
suffocate; gas oneself; (*entreprise,
réseau*) become paralysed.

aspirateur /aspiRatœR/ *nm*
vacuum cleaner.

aspirer /aspiRe/ [1] *vt* inhale;
(*liquide*) suck up. ● *vi* ~ **à** aspire to.

aspirine® /aspiRin/ *nf* aspirin.

assainir /aseniR/ [2] *vt* clean up.

assaisonnement /asɛzɔnmɑ̃/ *nm*
seasoning.

assassin /asasɛ̃/ *nm* murderer; (Pol)
assassin. **assassiner** [1] *vt* murder;
(Pol) assassinate.

assaut /aso/ *nm* assault, onslaught;
donner l'~ à, prendre d'~ storm.

assemblage /asɑ̃blaʒ/ *nm*
assembly; (*combinaison*) collection;
(Tech) joint.

assemblée /asɑ̃ble/ *nf* meeting;
(**gens réunis**) gathering; (Pol) assembly.

assembler /asɑ̃ble/ [1] *vt* assemble, put together; (réunir) gather. □ **s'~** *vpr* gather, assemble.

asseoir /aswaʀ/ [9] *vt* sit (down), seat; (*bébé, malade*) sit up; (affermir) establish; (baser) base. □ **s'~** *vpr* sit (down).

assermenté, **~e** /asɛʀmɑ̃te/ *adj* sworn.

assez /ase/ *adv* (suffisamment) enough; (plutôt) quite, fairly; **~ grand/rapide** big/fast enough (**pour** to); **~ de** enough; **j'en ai ~ (de)** I've had enough (of).

assidu, **~e** /asidy/ *adj* (zélé) assiduous; (régulier) regular; **~ auprès de** attentive to. **assiduité** *nf* assiduousness, regularity.

assiéger /asjeʒe/ [14] [40] *vt* besiege.

assiette /asjɛt/ *nf* plate; (équilibre) seat; **~ anglaise** assorted cold meats; **~ creuse/plate** soup-/dinner-plate; **ne pas être dans son ~** feel out of sorts.

assigner /asiɲe/ [1] *vt* assign; (*limite*) fix.

assimilation /asimilasjɔ̃/ *nf* assimilation; (comparaison) likening, comparison.

assimiler /asimile/ [1] *vt* **~ à** liken to; (classer) class as. □ **s'~** *vpr* assimilate; (être comparable) be comparable (**à** to).

assis, **~e** /asi, -z/ *adj* sitting (down), seated. ● ⇒ASSEOIR [9].

assise /asiz/ *nf* (base) foundation; **~s** (tribunal) assizes; (congrès) conference, congress.

assistance /asistɑ̃s/ *nf* audience; (aide) assistance; **l'A~ (publique)** welfare services.

assistant, **~e** /asistɑ̃, -t/ *nm,f* assistant; (Scol) foreign language assistant; **~s** (spectateurs) members of the audience; **~e sociale** social worker.

assister /asiste/ [1] *vt* assist; **~ à** attend, be (present) at; (*accident*) witness; **assisté par ordinateur** computer-assisted.

association /asɔsjasjɔ̃/ *nf* association.

associé, **~e** /asɔsje/ *nm,f* partner, associate. ● *adj* associate.

associer /asɔsje/ [45] *vt* associate; (mêler) combine (**à** with); **~ qn à** (*projet*) involve sb in; (*bénéfices*) give sb a share of. □ **s'~** *vpr* (*sociétés, personnes*) become associated, join forces (**à** with); (s'harmoniser) combine (**à** with); **s'~ à** (*joie, opinion de qn*) share; (*projet*) take part in.

assommer /asɔme/ [1] *vt* knock out; (*animal*) stun; (fig) overwhelm; (ennuyer Ⅱ) bore.

Assomption /asɔ̃psjɔ̃/ *nf* Assumption.

assortiment /asɔʀtimɑ̃/ *nm* assortment.

assortir /asɔʀtiʀ/ [2] *vt* match (**à** with, to); **~ de** accompany with. □ **s'~** *vpr* match; **s'~ à qch** match sth.

assoupir (s') /(s)asupiʀ/ [2] *vpr* doze off; (s'apaiser) subside.

assouplir /asupliʀ/ [2] *vt* make supple; (fig) make flexible.

assourdir /asuʀdiʀ/ [2] *vt* (*personne*) deafen; (*bruit*) muffle.

assouvir /asuviʀ/ [2] *vt* satisfy.

assujettir /asyʒetiʀ/ [2] *vt* subjugate, subdue; **~ à** subject to.

assumer /asyme/ [1] *vt* assume; (*coût*) meet; (accepter) come to terms with, accept.

assurance /asyʀɑ̃s/ *nf* (self-) assurance; (garantie) assurance; (contrat) insurance; **~s sociales** social insurance; **~ automobile/maladie** car/health insurance.

assuré, **~e** /asyʀe/ *adj* certain, assured; (sûr de soi) confident, assured. ● *nm,f* insured party.

assurer /asyʀe/ [1] *vt* ensure; (fournir) provide; (exécuter) carry out; (Comm) insure; (stabiliser) steady; (*frontières*) make secure; **~ à qn que** assure sb that; **~ qn de** assure sb of; **~ la gestion/défense de** manage/defend. □ **s'~** *vpr* take out insurance; **s'~ de/que** make sure of/ that; **s'~ qch** (se procurer) secure sth.

assureur *nm* insurer.

astérisque /asteʀisk/ *nm* asterisk.

asthmatique /asmatik/ *a & nmf* asthmatic.

asthme /asm/ *nm* asthma.

asticot /astiko/ *nm* maggot.

astreindre /astʀɛ̃dʀ/ [22] *vt* ~ qn à qch force sth on sb; ~ qn à faire force sb to do.

astrologie /astʀɔlɔʒi/ *nf* astrology. **astrologue** *nmf* astrologer.

astronaute /astʀonot/ *nmf* astronaut.

astronomie /astʀɔnɔmi/ *nf* astronomy.

astuce /astys/ *nf* smartness; (truc) trick; (plaisanterie) wisecrack.

astucieux, -ieuse /astysjø, -z/ *adj* smart, clever.

atelier /atəlje/ *nm* (local) workshop; (de peintre) studio; (séance de travail) workshop.

athée /ate/ *nmf* atheist. ● *adj* atheistic.

athlète /atlɛt/ *nmf* athlete. **athlétisme** *nm* athletics.

Atlantique /atlɑ̃tik/ *nm* Atlantic (Ocean).

atmosphère /atmɔsfɛʀ/ *nf* atmosphere.

atomique /atɔmik/ *adj* atomic; (énergie, centrale) nuclear.

atomiseur /atɔmizœʀ/ *nm* spray.

atout /atu/ *nm* trump (card); (avantage) asset.

atroce /atʀɔs/ *adj* atrocious.

attabler (s') /(s)atable/ [1] *vpr* sit down at table.

attachant, ~e /ataʃɑ̃, -t/ *adj* charming.

attache /ataʃ/ *nf* (agrafe) fastener; (lien) tie.

attaché, ~e /ataʃe/ *adj* être ~ à (aimer) be attached to. ● *nm,f* (Pol) attaché.

attacher /ataʃe/ [1] *vt* tie (up); (ceinture, robe) fasten; (bicyclette) lock; ~ à (attribuer à) attach to. ● *vi* (Culin) stick. □ **s'~** *vpr* fasten, do up; **s'~ à** (se lier à) become attached to; (se consacrer à) apply oneself to.

attaquant, ~e /atakɑ̃, -t/ *nm,f* attacker; (au football) striker; (au football américain) forward.

attaque /atak/ *nf* attack; ~ (cérébrale) stroke; il va en faire une ~ he'll have a fit; ~ à main armée armed attack.

attaquer /atake/ [1] *vt* attack; (banque) raid. ● *vi* attack. □ **s'~ à** *vpr* attack; (problème, sujet) tackle.

attardé, ~e /ataʀde/ *adj* backward; (idées) outdated; (en retard) late.

attarder (s') /(s)ataʀde/ [1] *vpr* linger.

atteindre /atɛ̃dʀ/ [22] *vt* reach; (blesser) hit; (affecter) affect.

atteint, ~e /atɛ̃, -t/ *adj* ~ de suffering from.

atteinte /atɛ̃t/ *nf* attack (à on); porter ~ à attack; (droit) infringe.

atteler /atle/ [38] *vt* (cheval) harness; (remorque) couple. □ **s'~ à** *vpr* get down to.

attelle /atɛl/ *nf* splint.

attenant, ~e /atnɑ̃, -t/ *adj* ~ (à) adjoining.

attendant: en ~ /ɑ̃natɑ̃dɑ̃/ *loc* meanwhile.

attendre /atɑ̃dʀ/ [3] *vt* wait for; (bébé) expect; (être le sort de) await; (escompter) expect; ~ que qn fasse wait for sb to do. ● *vi* wait; (au téléphone) hold. □ **s'~ à** *vpr* expect.

attendrir /atɑ̃dʀiʀ/ [2] *vt* move (to pity). □ **s'~** *vpr* be moved to pity.

attendu¹ /atɑ̃dy/ *prép* given, considering; ~ que considering that.

attendu², ~e /atɑ̃dy/ *adj* (escompté) expected; (espéré) long-awaited.

attentat /atɑ̃ta/ *nm* assassination attempt; ~ (à la bombe) (bomb) attack.

attente /atɑ̃t/ *nf* wait(ing); (espoir) expectations (+ *pl*).

attenter /atɑ̃te/ [1] *vi* ~ à make an attempt on; (fig) violate.

attentif, -ive /atɑ̃tif, -v/ *adj* attentive; (scrupuleux) careful; ~ à mindful of; (soucieux) careful of.

attention /atɑ̃sjɔ̃/ *nf* attention; (soin) care; ~ (à)! watch out (for)!; faire ~ à (écouter) pay attention to; (prendre garde à) watch out for; (prendre soin de) take care of; faire ~ à faire be careful to do. **attentionné, ~e** *adj* considerate.

attentisme /atɑ̃tism/ *nm* wait-and-see policy.

atténuer /atenɥe/ [1] vt (*violence*) reduce; (*critique*) tone down; (*douleur*) ease; (*faute*) mitigate. □ s'~ vpr subside.

atterrir /ateʀiʀ/ [2] vi land. **atterrissage** nm landing.

attestation /atɛstasjɔ̃/ nf certificate.

attester /atɛste/ [1] vt testify to; ~ que testify that.

attirant, ~e /atiʀɑ̃, -t/ adj attractive.

attirer /atire/ [1] vt draw, attract; (*causer*) bring. □ s'~ vpr bring upon oneself; (*amis*) win.

attiser /atize/ [1] vt (*feu*) poke; (*sentiment*) stir up.

attitré, ~e /atitre/ adj accredited; (*habituel*) usual, regular.

attitude /atityd/ nf attitude; (*maintien*) bearing.

attraction /atʀaksjɔ̃/ nf attraction.

attrait /atʀɛ/ nm attraction.

attraper /atʀape/ [1] vt catch; (*corde, main*) catch hold of; (*habitude, accent*) pick up; (*maladie*) catch; se faire ~ 🆒 get told off.

attrayant, ~e /atʀɛjɑ̃, -t/ adj attractive.

attribuer /atʀibɥe/ [1] vt allocate; (*prix*) award; (imputer) attribute. □ s'~ vpr claim (for oneself).

attribution nf awarding, allocation.

attrouper (s') /(s)atʀupe/ [1] vpr gather.

au /o/ ⇨À.

aubaine /obɛn/ nf godsend, opportunity.

aube /ob/ nf dawn, daybreak.

auberge /obɛʀʒ/ nf inn; ~ de jeunesse youth hostel.

aubergine /obɛʀʒin/ nf aubergine; (US) eggplant.

aucun, ~e /okœ̃, okyn/ adj (dans une phrase négative) no, not any; (positif) any. ● pron (dans une phrase négative) none, not any; (positif) any; ~ des deux neither of the two; d'~s some.

aucunement adv not at all, in no way.

audace /odas/ nf daring; (impudence) audacity.

audacieux, **-ieuse** /odasjø, -z/ adj daring.

au-delà /od(ə)la/ adv beyond. ● prép ~ de beyond.

au-dessous /od(ə)su/ adv below. ● prép ~ de below; (couvert par) under.

au-dessus /od(ə)sy/ adv above. ● prép ~ de above.

au-devant /od(ə)vɑ̃/ prép aller ~ de qn go to meet sb; aller ~ des désirs de qn anticipate sb's wishes.

audience /odjɑ̃s/ nf audience; (d'un tribunal) hearing; (succès, attention) success.

audimat® /odimat/ nm l'~ the TV ratings.

audiovisuel, ~le /odjovizɥɛl/ adj audio-visual.

auditeur, **-trice** /oditœʀ, -tʀis/ nm,f listener.

audition /odisjɔ̃/ nf hearing; (Théât, Mus) audition.

auditoire /oditwaʀ/ nm audience.

augmentation /ogmɑ̃tasjɔ̃/ nf increase; ~ (de salaire) (pay) rise; (US) raise.

augmenter /ogmɑ̃te/ [1] vt/i increase; (*employé*) give a pay rise ou raise to.

augure /ogyʀ/ nm (devin) oracle; être de bon/mauvais ~ be a good/bad sign.

aujourd'hui /oʒuʀdɥi/ adv today.

auparavant /opaʀavɑ̃/ adv (avant) before; (précédemment) previously; (en premier lieu) beforehand.

auprès /opʀɛ/ prép ~ de (à côté de) beside, next to; (comparé à) compared with; s'excuser/se plaindre ~ de apologize/complain to.

auquel /okɛl/ ⇨LEQUEL.

aura, **aurait** /oʀa, oʀɛ/ ⇨AVOIR [5].

aurore /oʀoʀ/ nf dawn.

aussi /osi/ adv (également) too, also, as well; (dans une comparaison) as; (si, tellement) so; ~ bien que as well as. ● conj (donc) so, consequently.

aussitôt /osito/ adv immediately; ~ que as soon as, the moment; ~ arrivé as soon as he arrived.

austère /ostɛʀ/ adj austere.

Australie /ɔstʀali/ nf Australia.

australien, **~ne** /ɔstraljɛ̃, -ɛn/ *adj* Australian. **A~**, **~ne** *nm,f* Australian.

autant /otɑ̃/ *adv* (*travailler, manger*) as much (**que** as); **~** (**de**) (quantité) as much (**que** as); (nombre) as many (**que** as); (tant) so much, so many; **~ faire** one had better do; **d'~ plus que** all the more than; **en faire ~** do the same; **pour ~** for all that.

autel /otɛl/ *nm* altar.

auteur /otœR/ *nm* author; **l'~ du crime** the perpetrator of the crime.

authentifier /otɑ̃tifje/ [45] *vt* authenticate.

authentique /otɑ̃tik/ *adj* authentic.

auto /oto/ *nf* car; **~ tamponneuse** dodgem, bumper car.

autobus /otobys/ *nm* bus.

autocar /otokaR/ *nm* coach.

autochtone /otɔktɔn/ *nmf* native.

autocollant, **~e** /otɔkɔlɑ̃, -t/ *adj* self-adhesive. ● *nm* sticker.

autodidacte /otɔdidakt/ *nmf* self-taught person.

auto-école (*pl* **~s**) /otoekɔl/ *nf* driving school.

automate /otɔmat/ *nm* automaton, robot.

automatique /otɔmatik/ *adj* automatic.

automatisation /otɔmatizasjɔ̃/ *nf* automation.

automne /otɔn/ *nm* autumn; (US) fall.

automobile /otɔmɔbil/ *adj* motor, car; (US) automobile. ● *nf* (motor) car; **l'~** the motor industry; (Sport) motoring. **automobiliste** *nmf* motorist.

autonome /otɔnɔm/ *adj* autonomous; (Ordinat) stand-alone.

autoradio /otɔRadjo/ *nm* car radio.

autorisation /otɔRizasjɔ̃/ *nf* permission, authorization; (permis) permit.

autorisé, **~e** /otɔRize/ *adj* (*opinions*) authoritative; (approuvé) authorized.

autoriser /otɔRize/ [1] *vt* authorize, permit; (rendre possible) allow (of);

(donner un droit) **~ qn à faire** entitle sb to do.

autoritaire /otɔRitɛR/ *adj* authoritarian.

autorité /otɔRite/ *nf* authority; **faire ~** be authoritative.

autoroute /otɔRut/ *nf* motorway; (US) highway; **~ de l'information** (Ordinat) information superhighway.

auto-stop /otɔstɔp/ *nm* hitch-hiking; **faire de l'~** hitch-hike; **prendre qn en ~** give a lift to sb.

autour /otuR/ *adv* around; **tout ~** all around. ● *prép* **~ de** around.

autre /otR/ *adj* other; **un ~ jour/livre** another day/book; **~ chose/part** something/somewhere else; **quelqu'un/rien d'~** somebody/ nothing else; **quoi d'~?** what else?; **d'~ part** on the other hand; (de plus) moreover, besides; **vous ~s Anglais** you English. ● *pron* **un ~**, **une ~** another (one); **l'~** the other (one); **les ~s** the others; (autrui) others; **d'~s** (some) others; **l'un l'~** each other; **l'un et l'~** both of them; **d'un jour à l'~** (bientôt) any day now; **entre ~s** among other things.

autrefois /otRəfwa/ *adv* in the past; (précédemment) formerly.

autrement /otRəmɑ̃/ *adv* differently; (sinon) otherwise; (plus 🄸) far more; **~ dit** in other words.

Autriche /otRiʃ/ *nf* Austria.

autrichien, **~ne** /otRiʃjɛ̃, -jɛn/ *adj* Austrian. **A~**, **~ne** *nm,f* Austrian.

autruche /otRyʃ/ *nf* ostrich.

autrui /otRɥi/ *pron* others, other people.

aux /o/ ⇒À.

auxiliaire /oksiljɛR/ *adj* auxiliary. ● *nmf* (assistant) auxiliary. ● *nm* (Gram) auxiliary.

auxquels, **-quelles** /okɛl/ ⇒LEQUEL.

aval: **en ~** /ɑ̃naval/ *loc* downstream.

avaler /avale/ [1] *vt* swallow.

avance /avɑ̃s/ *nf* advance; (sur un concurrent) lead; **~** (**de fonds**) advance; **à l'~** in advance; **d'~** already; **en ~** early; (*montre*) fast; **en ~** (**sur**) (*menant*) ahead (of).

avancement /avɑ̃smɑ̃/ *nm* promotion.

avancé, **~e** /avɑ̃se/ adj advanced.

avancer /avɑ̃se/ [10] vi move forward, advance; (travail) make progress; (montre) be fast; (faire saillie) jut out. ● vt move forward; (dans le temps) bring forward; (argent) advance; (montre) put forward. □ **s'~** vpr move forward, advance; (se hasarder) commit oneself.

avant /avɑ̃/ nm front; (Sport) forward. ● a inv front. ● prép before; **~ de faire** before doing; **en ~ de** in front of; **~ peu** shortly; **~ tout** above all. ● adv (dans le temps) before, beforehand; (d'abord) first; **en ~** (dans l'espace) forward(s); (dans le temps) ahead; **le bus d'~** the previous bus. ● conj **~ que** before; **~ qu'il (ne) fasse** before he does.

avantage /avɑ̃taʒ/ nm advantage; (Comm) benefit.

avantager /avɑ̃taʒe/ [40] vt favour; (embellir) show off to advantage.

avantageux, **-euse** /avɑ̃taʒø, -z/ adj advantageous, favourable; (prix) attractive.

avant-bras /avɑ̃bʀa/ nm inv forearm.

avant-centre (pl **avants-centres**) /avɑ̃sɑ̃tʀ/ nm centre forward.

avant-coureur (pl **~s**) /avɑ̃kuʀœʀ/ adj precursory, foreshadowing.

avant-dernier, **-ière** (pl **~s**) /avɑ̃dɛʀnje, -jɛʀ/ a & nm,f last but one.

avant-goût (pl **~s**) /avɑ̃gu/ nm foretaste.

avant-hier /avɑ̃tjɛʀ/ adv the day before yesterday.

avant-poste (pl **~s**) /avɑ̃pɔst/ nm outpost.

avant-première (pl **~s**) /avɑ̃pʀəmjɛʀ/ nf preview.

avant-propos /avɑ̃pʀɔpo/ nm inv foreword.

avare /avaʀ/ adj miserly; **~ de** sparing with. ● nmf miser.

avarié, **~e** /avaʀje/ adj (aliment) spoiled.

avatar /avataʀ/ nm misfortune.

avec /avɛk/ prép with. ● adv 🆃 with it ou them.

avènement /avɛnmɑ̃/ nm advent; (d'un roi) accession.

avenir /avniʀ/ nm future; **à l'~** in future; **d'~** with (future) prospects.

aventure /avɑ̃tyʀ/ nf adventure; (sentimentale) affair. **aventureux**, **-euse** adj adventurous; (hasardeux) risky.

avérer (s') /(s)aveʀe/ [14] vpr prove (to be).

averse /avɛʀs/ nf shower.

avertir /avɛʀtiʀ/ [2] vt inform; (mettre en garde, menacer) warn. **avertissement** nm warning.

avertisseur /avɛʀtisœʀ/ nm alarm; (Auto) horn; **~ d'incendie** fire-alarm; **~ lumineux** warning light.

aveu (pl **~x**) /avø/ nm confession; **de l'~ de** by the admission of.

aveugle /avœgl/ adj blind. ● nmf blind man, blind woman.

aviateur, **-trice** /avjatœʀ, -tʀis/ nm,f aviator.

aviation /avjasjɔ̃/ nf flying; (industrie) aviation; (Mil) air force.

avide /avid/ adj greedy (de for); (anxieux) eager (de for); **~ de faire** eager to do.

avion /avjɔ̃/ nm plane, aeroplane, aircraft; (US) airplane; **~ à réaction** jet.

aviron /aviʀɔ̃/ nm oar; **l'~** (Sport) rowing.

avis /avi/ nm opinion; (conseil) advice; (renseignement) notification; (Comm) advice; **à mon ~** in my opinion; **changer d'~** change one's mind; **être d'~ que** be of the opinion that; **~ au lecteur** foreword.

avisé, **~e** /avize/ adj sensible; **être bien/mal ~ de** be well-/ill-advised to.

aviser /avize/ [1] vt advise, notify. ● vi decide what to do. □ **s'~ de** vpr suddenly realize; **s'~ de faire** take it into one's head to do.

avocat, **~e** /avɔka, -t/ nm,f barrister; (US) attorney; (fig) advocate; **~ de la défense** counsel for the defence. ● nm (fruit) avocado (pear).

avoine /avwan/ nf oats (+ pl).

avoir /avwaʀ/ [5]

● *verbe auxiliaire*

····▸ have; **il nous a appelés hier** he called us yesterday.

● *verbe transitif*

····▸ (possession) have (got).

····▸ (obtenir) get; (au téléphone) get through to.

····▸ (duper) 🅵 have; **on m'a eu!** I've been had!

····▸ ~ **chaud/faim** be hot/hungry.

····▸ ~ **dix ans** be ten years old.

● **avoir à** *verbe + préposition*

····▸ to have to; **j'ai beaucoup à faire** I have a lot to do; **tu n'as qu'à leur écrire** all you have to do is write to them.

● **en avoir pour** *verbe + préposition*

····▸ **j'en ai pour une minute** I will only be a minute; **j'en ai eu pour 100 francs** it cost me 100 francs.

● **il y a** *verbe impersonnel*

····▸ there is; (pluriel) there are; **qu'est-ce qu'il y a?** what's the matter?; **il est venu il y a cinq ans** he came here five years ago; **il y a au moins 5 km jusqu'à la gare** it's at least 5 km to the station.

● *nom masculin*

····▸ (dans un magasin) credit note.

····▸ (biens) asset (+ *pl*).

avortement /avɔʀtəmɑ̃/ *nm* (Méd) abortion.

avorter /avɔʀte/ [1] *vi* (*projet*) abort; **(se faire)** ~ have an abortion.

avoué, **-e** /avwe/ *adj* avowed. ● *nm* solicitor; (US) attorney.

avouer /avwe/ [1] *vt* (*amour*, *ignorance*) confess; (*crime*) confess to, admit. ● *vi* confess.

avril /avʀil/ *nm* April.

axe /aks/ *nm* axis; (essieu) axle; (d'une politique) main line(s), basis; ~ **(routier)** main road.

ayant /ɛjɑ̃/ ⇒AVOIR [5].

azote /azɔt/ *nm* nitrogen.

azur /azyʀ/ *nm* sky-blue.

Bb

baba /baba/ *nm* ~ **(au rhum)** (rum) baba; **en rester** ~ 🅵 be flabbergasted.

babillard /babijaʀ/ *nm* ~ **électronique** (Internet) bulletin board system, BBS.

babines /babin/ *nfpl* **se lécher les** ~ lick one's chops.

babiole /babjɔl/ *nf* trinket.

bâbord /bɑbɔʀ/ *nm* port (side).

baby-foot /babifut/ *nm inv* table football.

bac /bak/ *nm* (Scol) ⇒BACCALAURÉAT; (bateau) ferry; (récipient) tub; (plus petit) tray.

baccalauréat /bakalɔʀea/ *nm* school leaving certificate.

bâche /bɑʃ/ *nf* tarpaulin.

bachelier, **-ière** /baʃəlje, -jɛʀ/ *nm, f* holder of the *baccalauréat*.

bachoter /baʃote/ [1] *vi* cram (for an exam).

bâcler /bɑkle/ [1] *vt* botch (up).

bactérie /bakteʀi/ *nf* bacterium; ~**s** bacteria.

badaud, ~**e** /bado, -d/ *nm, f* onlooker.

badigeonner /badiʒɔne/ [1] *vt* whitewash; (barbouiller) daub.

badiner /badine/ [1] *vi* banter.

baffe /baf/ *nf* 🅵 slap.

baffle /bafl/ *nm* speaker.

bafouiller /bafuje/ [1] *vt/i* stammer.

bagage /bagaʒ/ *nm* bag; (connaissances) knowledge; ~**s** luggage; ~ **à main** hand luggage.

bagarre /bagaʀ/ *nf* fight.

bagatelle /bagatɛl/ *nf* trifle; (somme) trifling amount.

bagnard /baɲaʀ/ *nm* convict.

bagnole /baɲɔl/ *nf* 🅵 car.

bague /bag/ *nf* (bijou) ring.

baguette /baɡɛt/ *nf* stick; (de chef d'orchestre) baton; (chinoise) chopstick; (pain) baguette; ~ **magique** magic wand; ~ **de tambour** drumstick.

baie /bɛ/ *nf* (Géog) bay; (fruit) berry; ~ (**vitrée**) picture window; (Ordinat) bay.

baignade /bɛɲad/ *nf* swimming.

baigner /beɲe/ [1] *vt* bathe; (*enfant*) bath. ● *vi* ~ **dans l'huile** swim in grease. □ **se** ~ *vpr* have a swim. **baigneur, -euse** *nm, f* swimmer.

baignoire /bɛɲwaʀ/ *nf* bath(tub).

bail (*pl* **baux**) /baj, bo/ *nm* lease.

bâiller /baje/ [1] *vi* yawn; (être ouvert) gape.

bailleur /bajœʀ/ *nm* ~ **de fonds** (Comm) sleeping partner.

bain /bɛ̃/ *nm* bath; (baignade) swim; **prendre un** ~ **de soleil** sunbathe; ~ **de bouche** mouthwash; **être dans le** ~ (fig) be in the swing of things; **se remettre dans le** ~ get back into the swing of things; **prendre un** ~ **de foule** mingle with the crowd.

bain-marie (*pl* **bains-marie**) /bɛ̃maʀi/ *nm* double boiler.

baiser /beze/ [1] *vt* (*main*) kiss; ☒ screw ☒. ● *nm* kiss.

baisse /bɛs/ *nf* fall, drop; **être en** ~ be going down.

baisser /bese/ [1] *vt* lower; (*radio, lampe*) turn down. ● *vi* (*niveau*) go down, fall; (*santé, forces*) fail. □ **se** ~ *vpr* bend down.

bal (*pl* ~**s**) /bal/ *nm* dance; (habillé) ball; (lieu) dance-hall; ~ **costumé** fancy-dress ball.

balade /balad/ *nf* stroll; (en auto) drive.

balader /balade/ [1] *vt* take for a stroll. □ **se** ~ *vpr* (à pied) (go for a) stroll; (en voiture) go for a drive; (voyager) travel.

baladeur /baladœʀ/ *nm* personal stereo.

balafre /balafʀ/ *nf* gash; (cicatrice) scar.

balai /balɛ/ *nm* broom.

balance /balɑ̃s/ *nf* scales (+ *pl*); **la B**~ Libra.

balancer /balɑ̃se/ [10] *vt* swing; (doucement) sway; (lancer ☒) chuck ☒; (se débarrasser de ☒) chuck out ☒.

● *vi* sway. □ **se** ~ *vpr* swing; sway; **s'en** ~ ☒ not to give a damn ☒.

balancier /balɑ̃sje/ *nm* (d'horloge) pendulum; (d'équilibriste) pole.

balançoire /balɑ̃swaʀ/ *nf* swing.

balayage /balɛjaʒ/ *nm* sweeping; (cheveux) highlights.

balayer /balɛje/ [31] *vt* sweep (up); (*vent*) sweep away; (se débarrasser de) sweep aside.

balbutiement /balbysimɑ̃/ *nm* stammering; **les** ~**s** (fig) the first steps.

balcon /balkɔ̃/ *nm* balcony; (Théât) dress circle.

baleine /balɛn/ *nf* whale.

balise /baliz/ *nf* beacon; (bouée) buoy; (Auto) (road) sign. **baliser** [1] *vt* mark out (with beacons); (*route*) signpost; (*sentier*) mark out.

balivernes /balivɛʀn/ *nfpl* nonsense.

ballant, ~**e** /balɑ̃, -t/ *adj* dangling.

balle /bal/ *nf* (projectile) bullet; (Sport) ball; (paquet) bale.

ballerine /balʀin/ *nf* (danseuse) ballerina; (chaussure) ballet pump.

ballet /balɛ/ *nm* ballet.

ballon /balɔ̃/ *nm* (Sport) ball; ~ (**de baudruche**) balloon; ~ **de football** football.

ballonné, ~**e** /balɔne/ *adj* bloated.

balnéaire /balneɛʀ/ *adj* seaside.

balourd, ~**e** /baluʀ, -d/ *nm, f* oaf. ● *adj* uncouth.

balustrade /balystʀad/ *nf* railing.

ban /bɑ̃/ *nm* round of applause; ~**s** (de mariage) banns; **mettre au** ~ **de** cast out from.

banal, ~**e** (*mpl* ~**s**) /banal/ *adj* commonplace, banal.

banane /banan/ *nf* banana.

banc /bɑ̃/ *nm* bench; (de poissons) shoal; ~ **des accusés** dock; ~ **d'essai** (test) testing ground.

bancaire /bɑ̃kɛʀ/ *adj* (*secteur*) banking; (*chèque*) bank.

bancal, ~**e** (*mpl* ~**s**) /bɑ̃kal/ *adj* wobbly; (*solution*) shaky.

bande /bɑ̃d/ *nf* (groupe) gang; (de papier) strip; (rayure) stripe; (de film) reel; (pansement) bandage; ~ **dessinée**

comic strip; ~ **(magnétique)** tape; ~ **sonore** sound-track.

bande-annonce (*pl* **bandes-annonces**) /bãdanɔ̃s/ *nf* trailer.

bandeau (*pl* ~**x**) /bãdo/ *nm* headband; (sur les yeux) blindfold.

bander /bãde/ [1] *vt* bandage; (*arc*) bend; (*muscle*) tense; ~ **les yeux à** blindfold.

banderole /bãdʀɔl/ *nf* banner.

bandit /bãdi/ *nm* bandit. **banditisme** *nm* crime.

bandoulière: en ~ /ãbãduljɛʀ/ *loc* across one's shoulder.

banlieue /bãljø/ *nf* suburbs; **de ~** suburban. **banlieusard**, ~**e** *nm,f* (suburban) commuter.

bannir /baniʀ/ [2] *vt* banish.

banque /bãk/ *nf* bank; (activité) banking; ~ **de données** databank.

banqueroute /bãkʀut/ *nf* bankruptcy.

banquet /bãkɛ/ *nm* banquet.

banquette /bãkɛt/ *nf* seat.

banquier, -ière /bãkje, -jɛʀ/ *nm,f* banker.

baptême /batɛm/ *nm* baptism, christening. **baptiser** [1] *vt* baptize, christen; (nommer) call.

bar /baʀ/ *nm* (lieu) bar.

baragouiner /baʀagwine/ [1] *vt/i* gabble; (*langue*) speak a few words of.

baraque /baʀak/ *nf* hut, shed; (maison 🔲) house.

baratin /baʀatɛ̃/ *nm* 🔲 sweet *ou* smooth talk.

barbare /baʀbaʀ/ *adj* barbaric. ● *nmf* barbarian.

barbe /baʀb/ *nf* beard; ~ **à papa** candy-floss; (US) cotton candy; **quelle ~!** 🔲 what a drag!. 🔲.

barbelé /baʀbəle/ *adj* **fil ~** barbed wire.

barber /baʀbe/ [1] *vt* 🔲 bore.

barboter /baʀbɔte/ [1] *vi* (dans l'eau) paddle, splash. ● *vt* (voler 🔲) pinch.

barbouiller /baʀbuje/ [1] *vt* (souiller) smear (de with); **tu es tout barbouillé** your face is all dirty; **être barbouillé** feel queazy.

barbu, ~**e** /baʀby/ *adj* bearded.

barème /baʀɛm/ *nm* list, table; (échelle) scale.

baril /baʀil/ *nm* barrel; (de poudre) keg.

bariolé, ~**e** /baʀjɔle/ *adj* multicoloured.

baromètre /baʀɔmɛtʀ/ *nm* barometer.

baron, ~**ne** /baʀɔ̃, -ɔn/ *nm,f* baron, baroness.

barque /baʀk/ *nf* (small) boat.

barrage /baʀaʒ/ *nm* dam; (sur route) roadblock.

barre /baʀ/ *nf* bar; (trait) line, stroke; (Naut) helm; ~ **de boutons** (Ordinat) toolbar.

barreau (*pl* ~**x**) /baʀo/ *nm* bar; (d'échelle) rung; **le ~** (Jur) the bar.

barrer /baʀe/ [1] *vt* block; (*porte*) bar; (rayer) cross out; (Naut) steer. □ **se ~** *vpr* 🔲 leave.

barrette /baʀɛt/ *nf* (hair) slide.

barrière /baʀjɛʀ/ *nf* (porte) gate; (clôture) fence; (obstacle) barrier.

bar-tabac (*pl* **bars-tabac**) /baʀtaba/ *nm* café (*selling stamps and cigarettes*).

bas, basse /ba, bas/ *adj* (niveau, table) low; (action) base; **au ~ mot** at the lowest estimate; **en ~ âge** young; ~ **morceaux** (viande) cheap cuts. ● *nm* bottom; (chaussette) stocking; ~ **de laine** (fig) nest-egg. ● *adv* low; **en ~** down below; (dans une maison) downstairs; **en ~ de la page** at the bottom of the page; **plus ~** further *ou* lower down; **mettre ~** give birth (to). **bas de casse** *nm inv* lower case. **bas-côté** (*pl* ~**s**) *nm* (de route) verge; (US) shoulder.

bascule /baskyl/ *nf* (balance) scales (+ *pl*); **cheval/fauteuil à ~** rocking-horse/-chair.

basculer /baskyle/ [1] *vi* topple over; (benne) tip up.

base /baz/ *nf* base; (fondement) basis; (Pol) rank and file; **de ~** basic. **base de données** *nf* data-base.

baser /baze/ [1] *vt* base. □ **se ~ sur** *vpr* go by.

bas-fonds /baf ɔ̃/ *nmpl* (eau) shallows; (fig) dregs.

basilic /bazilik/ *nm* basil.

basilique /bazilik/ *nf* basilica.

basque /bask/ *adj* Basque. **B~** *nmf* Basque.

basse /bɑs/ ⇨BAS.

basse-cour (*pl* **basses-cours**) /baskuʀ/ *nf* farmyard.

bassesse /bɑsɛs/ *nf* baseness; (action) base act.

bassin /basɛ̃/ *nm* (pièce d'eau) pond; (de piscine) pool; (Géog) basin; (Anat) pelvis; (plat) bowl; **~ houiller** coalfield.

bassine /basin/ *nf* bowl.

basson /basɔ̃/ *nm* bassoon.

bas-ventre (*pl* **~s**) /bavɑ̃tʀ/ *nm* lower abdomen.

bat /ba/ ⇨BATTRE [11].

bataille /batɑj/ *nf* battle; (fig) fight.

bâtard, ~e /bɑtaʀ, -d/ *adj* (solution) hybrid. ● *nm,f* bastard.

bateau (*pl* **~x**) /bato/ *nm* boat; **~ pneumatique** rubber dinghy. **bateau-mouche** (*pl* **bateaux-mouches**) *nm* sightseeing boat.

bâti, ~e /bɑti/ *adj* **bien ~** well-built.

bâtiment /bɑtimɑ̃/ *nm* building; (industrie) building trade; (navire) vessel.

bâtir /bɑtiʀ/ [2] *vt* build.

bâton /bɑtɔ̃/ *nm* stick; **conversation à ~s rompus** rambling conversation; **~ de rouge** lipstick.

battant /batɑ̃/ *nm* (vantail) flap; **porte à deux ~s** double door.

battement /batmɑ̃/ *nm* (de cœur) beat(ing); (temps) interval; (Mus) beat.

batterie /batʀi/ *nf* (Mil, Électr) battery; (Mus) drums; **~ de cuisine** pots and pans.

batteur /batœʀ/ *nm* (Mus) drummer; (Culin) whisk.

battre /batʀ/ [11] *vt/i* beat; (cartes) shuffle; (Culin) whisk; (l'emporter sur) beat; **~ des ailes** flap its wings; **~ des mains** clap; **~ des paupières** blink; **~ en retraite** beat a retreat; **~ la semelle** stamp one's feet; **~ son plein** be in full swing. □ **se ~** *vpr* fight.

baume /bom/ *nm* balm.

bavard, ~e /bavaʀ, -d/ *adj* talkative. ● *nm,f* chatterbox.

bavardage /bavaʀdaʒ/ *nm* chatter, gossip. **bavarder** [1] *vi* chat; (jacasser) chatter, gossip.

bave /bav/ *nf* dribble, slobber; (de limace) slime. **baver** [1] *vi* dribble, slobber. **baveux, -euse** *adj* dribbling; (omelette) runny.

bavoir /bavwaʀ/ *nm* bib.

bavure /bavyʀ/ *nf* smudge; (erreur) blunder; **~ policière** police blunder.

bazar /bazaʀ/ *nm* bazaar; (objets 🇫) clutter.

BCBG *abrév mf* (**bon chic bon genre**) posh.

BD *abrév f* (**bande dessinée**) comic strip.

béant, ~e /beɑ̃, -t/ *adj* gaping.

béat, ~e /bea, -t/ *adj* (hum) blissful; **~ d'admiration** wide-eyed with admiration.

beau (**bel** *before vowel or mute h*), **belle** (*mpl* **~x**) /bo, bɛl/ *adj* beautiful; (femme) beautiful; (homme) handsome; (temps) fine, nice. ● *nm* beauty. ● *adv* **il fait ~** the weather is nice; **au ~ milieu** right in the middle; **bel et bien** well and truly; **de plus belle** more than ever; **faire le ~** sit up and beg; **on a ~ essayer/insister** however much one tries/insists.

beaucoup /boku/ *adv* a lot, very much; **~ de** (nombre) many; (quantité) a lot of; **pas ~ de** not many; (quantité) not much; **~ plus/mieux** much more/better; **~ trop** far too much; **de ~** by far.

beau-fils (*pl* **beaux-fils**) /bofis/ *nm* (remariage) stepson.

beau-frère (*pl* **beaux-frères**) /bofʀɛʀ/ *nm* brother-in-law.

beau-père (*pl* **beaux-pères**) /bopɛʀ/ *nm* father-in-law; (remariage) stepfather.

beauté /bote/ *nf* beauty; **finir en ~** end magnificently.

beaux-arts /bozaʀ/ *nmpl* fine arts.

beaux-parents /bopaʀɑ̃/ *nmpl* parents-in-law.

bébé /bebe/ *nm* baby. **bébé-éprouvette** (*pl* **bébés-éprouvette**) *nm* test-tube baby.

bec /bɛk/ nm beak; (de théière) spout; (de casserole) lip; (bouche 🆃) mouth; ~ de gaz gas street-lamp.

bécane /bekan/ nf 🆃 bike.

bêche /bɛʃ/ nf spade.

bégayer /begeje/ [31] vt/i stammer.

bègue /bɛg/ nmf stammerer. ● adj être ~ stammer.

bégueule /begœl/ adj prudish.

beige /bɛʒ/ a & nm beige.

beignet /bɛɲɛ/ nm fritter.

bel /bɛl/ ⇒BEAU.

bêler /bele/ [1] vi bleat.

belette /bəlɛt/ nf weasel.

belge /bɛlʒ/ adj Belgian. **B~** nmf Belgian.

Belgique /bɛlʒik/ nf Belgium.

bélier /belje/ nm ram; le B~ Aries.

belle /bɛl/ ⇒BEAU.

belle-fille (pl **belles-filles**) /bɛlfij/ nf daughter-in-law; (remariage) stepdaughter.

belle-mère (pl **belles-mères**) /bɛlmɛʀ/ nf mother-in-law; (remariage) stepmother.

belle-sœur (pl **belles-sœurs**) /bɛlsœʀ/ nf sister-in-law.

belliqueux, -euse /belikø, -z/ adj warlike.

bémol /bemɔl/ nm (Mus) flat.

bénédiction /benediksjɔ̃/ nf blessing.

bénéfice /benefis/ nm (gain) profit; (avantage) benefit.

bénéficiaire /benefisjɛʀ/ nmf beneficiary.

bénéficier /benefisje/ [45] vi ~ de benefit from; (jouir de) enjoy, have.

bénéfique /benefik/ adj beneficial.

Bénélux /benelyks/ nm Benelux.

bénévole /benevɔl/ adj voluntary.

bénin, -igne /benɛ̃, -iɲ/ adj minor; (tumeur) benign.

bénir /beniʀ/ [2] vt bless. **bénit, ~e** adj (eau) holy; (pain) consecrated.

benjamin, ~e /bɛ̃ʒamɛ̃, -in/ nm, f youngest child.

benne /bɛn/ nf (de grue) scoop; ~ à ordures (camion) waste disposal truck; (conteneur) skip; ~ (basculante) dump truck.

béquille /bekij/ nf crutch; (de moto) stand.

berceau (pl ~x) /bɛʀso/ nm (de bébé, civilisation) cradle.

bercer /bɛʀse/ [10] vt (balancer) rock; (apaiser) lull; (leurrer) delude.

béret /beʀɛ/ nm beret.

berge /bɛʀʒ/ nf (bord) bank.

berger, -ère /bɛʀʒe, -ɛʀ/ nm, f shepherd, shepherdess.

berne: en ~ /ɑ̃bɛʀn/ loc at half-mast.

berner /bɛʀne/ [1] vt fool.

besogne /bəzɔɲ/ nf task, job.

besoin /bəzwɛ̃/ nm need; avoir ~ de need; au ~ if need be; dans le ~ in need.

bestiole /bɛstjɔl/ nf 🆃 bug.

bétail /betaj/ nm livestock.

bête /bɛt/ adj stupid. ● nf animal; ~ noire pet hate; ~ sauvage wild beast; chercher la petite ~ be overfussy.

bêtise /betiz/ nf stupidity; (action) stupid thing.

béton /betɔ̃/ nm concrete; ~ armé reinforced concrete; en ~ (mur) concrete; (argument 🆃) watertight. **bétonnière** nf concrete mixer.

betterave /bɛtʀav/ nf beet; ~ rouge beetroot.

beugler /bøgle/ [1] vi bellow; (radio) blare out.

beur /bœʀ/ nmf & a 🆃 second-generation North African living in France.

beurre /bœʀ/ nm butter. **beurré, ~e** adj buttered; 🆃 drunk. **beurrier** nm butter-dish.

bévue /bevy/ nf blunder.

biais /bjɛ/ nm (moyen) way; par le ~ de by means of; de ~, en ~ at an angle; regarder qn de ~ look sideways at sb.

bibelot /biblo/ nm ornament.

biberon /bibʀɔ̃/ nm (feeding) bottle; nourrir au ~ bottle-feed.

bible /bibl/ nf bible; la B~ the Bible. **bibliographie** /biblijɔgʀafi/ nf bibliography.

bibliothécaire /biblijotekɛʀ/ nmf librarian.

bibliothèque /biblijotɛk/ nf library; (meuble) bookcase.

bic® /bik/ nm biro®.

bicarbonate /bikaʀbɔnat/ *nm* ~ (de soude) bicarbonate (of soda).

biceps /bisɛps/ *nm* biceps.

biche /biʃ/ *nf* doe; **ma** ~ darling.

bichonner /biʃɔne/ [1] *vt* pamper.

bicyclette /bisiklɛt/ *nf* bicycle.

bide /bid/ *nm* (ventre 🎦) paunch; (échec 🎦) flop.

bidet /bidɛ/ *nm* bidet.

bidon /bidɔ̃/ *nm* can; (plus grand) drum; (ventre 🎦) belly; **c'est du** ~ 🎦 it's a load of hogwash 🎦. ● *a inv* 🎦 phoney.

bidonville /bidɔ̃vil/ *nf* shanty town.

bidule /bidyl/ *nm* 🎦 thing.

Biélorussie /bjelɔʀysi/ *nf* Byelorussia.

bien /bjɛ̃/ *adv* well; (très) quite, very; ~ **des** (nombre) many; **tu as** ~ **de la chance** you are very lucky; **j'aimerais** ~ I would like to; **ce n'est pas** ~ **de** it is not nice to; ~ **sûr** of course. ● *nm* good; (patrimoine) possession; ~**s de consommation** consumer goods. ● *a inv* good; (passable) all right; (en forme) well; (à l'aise) comfortable; (beau) attractive; (respectable) nice, respectable. ● *conj* ~ **que** (al-) though; ~ **que ce soit** although it is. **bien-aimé**, ~**e** *a & nm,f* beloved. **bien-être** *nm* well-being.

bienfaisance /bjɛ̃fəzɑ̃s/ *nf* charity; **fête de** ~ charity event. **bienfaisant**, ~**e** *adj* beneficial.

bienfait /bjɛ̃fɛ/ *nm* (kind) favour; (avantage) beneficial effect. **bienfaiteur**, **-trice** *nm,f* benefactor.

bien-pensant, ~**e** /bjɛ̃pɑ̃sɑ̃, -t/ *adj* right-thinking.

bienséance /bjɛ̃seɑ̃s/ *nf* propriety.

bientôt /bjɛ̃to/ *adv* soon; **à** ~ see you soon.

bienveillance /bjɛ̃vɛjɑ̃s/ *nf* kind(li)ness.

bienvenu, ~**e** /bjɛ̃vny/ *adj* welcome. ● *nm,f* **être le** ~, **être la** ~**e** be welcome.

bienvenue /bjɛ̃vny/ *nf* welcome; **souhaiter la** ~ **à** welcome.

bière /bjɛʀ/ *nf* beer; (cercueil) coffin; ~ **blonde** lager; ~ **brune** ≈ stout; ~ **pression** draught beer.

bifteck /biftɛk/ *nm* steak.

bifurquer /bifyʀke/ [1] *vi* branch off, fork.

bigarré, ~**e** /bigaʀe/ *adj* motley.

bigoudi /bigudi/ *nm* curler.

bijou (*pl* ~**x**) /biʒu/ *nm* jewel; ~**x en or** gold jewellery. **bijouterie** *nf* (boutique) jewellery shop; (Comm) jewellery. **bijoutier**, **-ière** *nm,f* jeweller.

bilan /bilɑ̃/ *nm* outcome; (d'une catastrophe) (casualty) toll; (Comm) balance sheet; **faire le** ~ **de** assess; ~ **de santé** check-up.

bile /bil/ *nf* bile; **se faire de la** ~ 🎦 worry.

bilingue /bilɛ̃g/ *adj* bilingual.

billard /bijaʀ/ *nm* billiards (+ *pl*); (table) billiard-table.

bille /bij/ *nf* (d'enfant) marble; (de billard) billiard-ball.

billet /bijɛ/ *nm* ticket; (lettre) note; (article) column; ~ (de banque) (bank) note; ~ **de 50 francs** 50-franc note.

billetterie /bijɛtʀi/ *nf* cash dispenser.

billion /biljɔ̃/ *nm* billion; (US) trillion.

bimensuel, ~**e** /bimɑ̃sɥɛl/ *adj* fortnightly, bimonthly. ● *nm* fortnightly magazine.

binette /binɛt/ *nf* hoe; (visage) face; (Internet) smiley.

biochimie /bjoʃimi/ *nf* biochemistry.

biodégradable /bjodegʀadabl/ *adj* biodegradable.

biographie /bjogʀafi/ *nf* biography.

biologie /bjolɔʒi/ *nf* biology. **biologique** *adj* biological; (produit) organic.

bis /bis/ *nm & interj* encore.

biscornu, ~**e** /biskɔʀny/ *adj* crooked; (bizarre) cranky 🎦.

biscotte /biskɔt/ *nf* continental toast.

biscuit /biskɥi/ *nm* biscuit; (US) cookie; ~ **salé** cracker; ~ **de Savoie** sponge-cake.

bise /biz/ *nf* 🎦 kiss; (vent) north wind.

bison /bizɔ̃/ *nm* buffalo.

bisou /bizu/ *nm* 🎦 kiss.

bistro(t) /bistʀo/ nm 🔲 café, bar.

bit /bit/ nm (Ordinat) bit.

bitume /bitym/ nm asphalt.

bizarre /bizaʀ/ adj odd, strange. **bizzarerie** nf peculiarity.

blafard, **~e** /blafaʀ, -d/ adj pale.

blague /blag/ nf 🔲 joke; **sans ~!** no kidding! 🔲.

blaguer /blage/ [1] 🔲 vi joke.

blaireau (pl **~x**) /blɛʀo/ nm shaving-brush; (animal) badger.

blâmer /blame/ [1] vt criticize.

blanc, **blanche** /blɑ̃, blɑ̃ʃ/ adj white; (papier, page) blank. ● nm white; (espace) blank; **~ d'œuf** egg white; **~ de poireau** white part of the leek; **~ (de poulet)** chicken breast; **le ~** (linge) whites; **laisser en ~** leave blank. **B~**, **Blanche** nm,f white man, white woman. **blanche** nf (Mus) minim.

blanchiment /blɑ̃ʃimɑ̃/ nm (d'argent) laundering.

blanchir /blɑ̃ʃiʀ/ [2] vt whiten; (personne: fig) clear; (argent) launder; (Culin) blanch; **~ (à la chaux)** whitewash. ● vi turn white.

blanchisserie /blɑ̃ʃisʀi/ nf laundry.

blason /blazɔ̃/ nm coat of arms.

blasphème /blasfɛm/ nm blasphemy.

blé /ble/ nm wheat.

blême /blɛm/ adj pallid.

blessant, **~e** /blesɑ̃, -t/ adj hurtful.

blessé, **~e** /blese/ nm,f casualty, injured person.

blesser /blese/ [1] vt injure, hurt; (par balle) wound; (offenser) hurt. □ **se ~** vpr injure ou hurt oneself. **blessure** nf wound.

bleu, **~e** /blø/ adj blue; (Culin) very rare; **~ marine/turquoise** navy blue/ turquoise; **avoir une peur ~e** be scared stiff. ● nm blue; (contusion) bruise; **~ (de travail)** overalls (+ pl).

bleuet /bløɛ/ nm cornflower.

blindé, **~e** /blɛ̃de/ adj armoured; (fig) immune (**contre** to); **porte ~e** security car. ● nm armoured car, tank.

blinder /blɛ̃de/ [1] vt armour; (fig) harden.

bloc /blɔk/ nm block; (de papier) pad; **serrer à ~** tighten hard; **en ~** (matériau) in a block; (nier) outright.

blocage /blɔkaʒ/ nm (des prix) freeze, freezing; (des roues) locking; (Psych) block.

bloc-notes (pl **blocs-notes**) /blɔknɔt/ nm note-pad.

blocus /blɔkys/ nm blockade.

blond, **~e** /blɔ̃, -d/ adj fair, blond. ● nm,f fair-haired man, fair-haired woman.

bloquer /blɔke/ [1] vt block; (porte, machine) jam; (roues) lock; (prix, crédits) freeze. □ **se ~** vpr jam; (roues) lock; (freins) jam; (ordinateur) crash; **bloqué par la neige** snowbound.

blottir (se) /(sə)blɔtiʀ/ [2] vpr snuggle, huddle (**contre** against).

blouse /bluz/ nf overall. **blouse blanche** nf white coat.

blouson /bluzɔ̃/ nm jacket, blouson.

bluffer /blœfe/ [1] vt/i bluff.

bobine /bɔbin/ nf (de fil, film) reel; (Électr) coil.

bobo /bɔbo/ nm 🔲 sore, cut; **avoir ~** have a pain.

bocal (pl **-aux**) /bɔkal, -o/ nm jar.

bœuf (pl **~s**) /bœf, bø/ nm bullock; (US) steer; (viande) beef; **~s** oxen.

bogue /bɔg/ nm (Ordinat) bug.

bohème /bɔɛm/ a & nmf bohemian.

boire /bwaʀ/ [12] vt/i (personne, plante) drink; (argile) soak up; **~ un coup** 🔲 have a drink.

bois /bwa/ ⇒BOIRE [12]. ● nm (matériau, forêt) wood; **de ~**, **en ~** wooden. ● nmpl (de cerf) antlers.

boiseries /bwazʀi/ nfpl panelling.

boisson /bwasɔ̃/ nf drink.

boit /bwa/ ⇒BOIRE [12].

boîte /bwat/ nf box; (de conserves) tin, can; (entreprise 🔲) firm; **en ~** tinned, canned; **~ à gants** glove compartment; **~ aux lettres** letter-box; **~ aux lettres électronique, blé** mailbox; **~ de nuit** night-club; **~ postale** post-office box; **~ de vitesses** gear box.

boiter /bwate/ [1] vi limp. **boiteux**, **-euse** adj lame; (raisonnement) shaky.

boîtier /bwatje/ *nm* case.

bol /bɔl/ *nm* bowl; ~ **d'air** a breath of fresh air; **avoir du ~** 🆒 be lucky.

bolide /bɔlid/ *nm* racing car.

Bolivie /bɔlivi/ *nf* Bolivia.

bombardement /bɔ̃baʀdəmɑ̃/ *nm* bombing; shelling.

bombarder /bɔ̃baʀde/ [1] *vt* bomb; (par obus) shell; ~ **qn de** (fig) bombard sb with. **bombardier** *nm* (Aviat) bomber.

bombe /bɔ̃b/ *nf* bomb; (atomiseur) spray, aerosol.

bombé, ~**e** /bɔ̃be/ *adj* rounded; (route) cambered.

bon, bonne /bɔ̃, bɔn/ *adj* good; (qui convient) right; ~ **à/pour** (approprié) fit to/for; **bonne année** happy New Year; ~ **anniversaire** happy birthday; ~ **appétit/voyage** enjoy your meal/trip; **bonne chance/nuit** good luck/night; ~ **sens** common sense; **bonne femme** (péj) woman; **de bonne heure** early; **à quoi ~?** what's the point? ● *adv* **sentir** ~ smell nice; **tenir** ~ stand firm; **il fait** ~ the weather is mild. ● *interj* right, well. ● *nm* (billet) voucher, coupon; ~ **de commande** order form; **pour de** ~ for good. **bonne** *nf* (domestique) maid.

bonbon /bɔ̃bɔ̃/ *nm* sweet; (US) candy.

bonbonne /bɔ̃bɔn/ *nf* demijohn; (de gaz) cylinder.

bond /bɔ̃/ *nm* leap; **faire un** ~ (de surprise) jump.

bonde /bɔ̃d/ *nf* plug; (trou) plughole.

bondé, ~**e** /bɔ̃de/ *adj* packed.

bondir /bɔ̃diʀ/ [2] *vi* leap; (de surprise) jump.

bonheur /bɔnœʀ/ *nm* happiness; (chance) (good) luck; **au petit** ~ haphazardly; **par** ~ luckily.

bonhomme (*pl* **bonshommes**) /bɔnɔm, bɔ̃zɔm/ *nm* fellow; ~ **de neige** snowman. ● *a inv* good-hearted.

bonifier (se) /(sə)bɔnifje/ [45] *vpr* improve.

bonjour /bɔ̃ʒuʀ/ *nm & interj* hallo, hello, good morning *ou* afternoon.

bon marché /bɔ̃maʀʃe/ *a inv* cheap. ● *adv* cheap(ly).

bonne /bɔn/ ⇒BON.

bonne-maman (*pl* **bonnes-mamans**) /bɔnmamɑ̃/ *nf* 🆒 granny.

bonnement /bɔnmɑ̃/ *adv* **tout** ~ quite simply.

bonnet /bɔnɛ/ *nm* hat; (de soutien-gorge) cup; ~ **de bain** swimming cap.

bonneterie *nf* hosiery.

bonsoir /bɔ̃swaʀ/ *nm* good evening; (en se couchant) good night.

bonté /bɔ̃te/ *nf* kindness.

bonus /bɔnys/ *nm* (Auto) no-claims bonus.

boots /buts/ *nmpl* ankle boots.

bord /bɔʀ/ *nm* edge; (rive) bank; **à** ~ **(de)** on board; **au** ~ **de la mer** at the seaside; **au** ~ **des larmes** on the verge of tears; ~ **de la route** roadside.

bordeaux /bɔʀdo/ *a inv* maroon. ● *nm inv* Bordeaux.

bordel /bɔʀdɛl/ *nm* brothel; (désordre 🆒) shambles.

border /bɔʀde/ [1] *vt* line, border; (tissu) edge; (personne, lit) tuck in.

bordereau (*pl* ~**x**) /bɔʀdəʀo/ *nm* (document) slip.

bordure /bɔʀdyʀ/ *nf* border; **en** ~ **de** on the edge of.

borgne /bɔʀɲ/ *adj* one-eyed.

borne /bɔʀn/ *nf* boundary marker; (pour barrer le passage) bollard; ~ **(kilométrique)** ≈ milestone; ~**s** limits.

borné, ~**e** /bɔʀne/ *adj* (esprit) narrow; (personne) narrow-minded.

borner (se) /(sə)bɔʀne/ [1] *vpr* confine oneself (**à** to).

bosniaque /bɔsnjak/ *adj* Bosnian. **B**~ *nmf* Bosnian.

Bosnie /bɔsni/ *nf* Bosnia.

bosse /bɔs/ *nf* bump; (de chameau) hump; **avoir la** ~ **de** 🆒 have a gift for; **avoir roulé sa** ~ have been around. **bosselé**, ~**e** *adj* dented; (terrain) bumpy.

bosser /bɔse/ [1] *vi* 🆒 work (hard).

bossu, ~**e** /bɔsy/ *adj* hunchbacked. ● *nm, f* hunchback.

botanique /bɔtanik/ *nf* botany. ● *adj* botanical.

botte /bɔt/ *nf* boot; (de fleurs, légumes) bunch; (de paille) bundle, bale; ~**s de caoutchouc** wellingtons.

botter /bɔte/ [1] *vt* 🅻 ça me botte I like the idea.

bottin® /bɔtɛ̃/ *nm* phone book.

bouc /buk/ *nm* (billy-)goat; (barbe) goatee; ~ émissaire scapegoat.

boucan /bukɑ̃/ *nm* 🅻 din.

bouche /buʃ/ *nf* mouth; (lèvres) lips; ~ bée open-mouthed; ~ d'égout manhole; ~ d'incendie (fire) hydrant; ~ de métro entrance to the underground *ou* subway (US). **bouche-à-bouche** *nm inv* mouth-to-mouth resuscitation. **bouche-à-oreille** *nm inv* word of mouth.

bouché, ~e /buʃe/ *adj* (*profession, avenir*) oversubscribed; (stupide: péj) stupid.

bouchée /buʃe/ *nf* mouthful.

boucher¹ /buʃe/ [1] *vt* block; (*bouteille*) cork. □ **se** ~ *vpr* get blocked; **se** ~ **le nez** hold one's nose.

boucher², -ère /buʃe, -ɛʀ/ *nm,f* butcher. **boucherie** *nf* butcher's (shop); (carnage) butchery.

bouchon /buʃɔ̃/ *nm* stopper; (en liège) cork; (de stylo, tube) cap; (de pêcheur) float; (embouteillage) traffic jam; ~ de cérumen plug of earwax.

boucle /bukl/ *nf* (de ceinture) buckle; (de cheveux) curl; (forme) loop; ~ d'oreille earring. **bouclé**, ~e *adj* (*cheveux*) curly.

boucler /bukle/ [1] *vt* fasten; (enfermer 🅻) shut up; (encercler) seal off; (*budget*) balance; (terminer) finish off. ● *vi* curl.

bouclier /buklije/ *nm* shield.

bouddhiste /budist/ *a & nmf* Buddhist.

bouder /bude/ [1] *vi* sulk. ● *vt* stay away from.

boudin /budɛ̃/ *nm* black pudding.

boue /bu/ *nf* mud.

bouée /bwe/ *nf* buoy; ~ de sauvetage lifebuoy.

boueux, -euse /buø, -z/ *adj* muddy.

bouffe /buf/ *nf* 🅻 food, grub.

bouffée /bufe/ *nf* puff, whiff; (d'orgueil) fit; ~ de chaleur (Méd) hot flush.

bouffi, ~e /bufi/ *adj* bloated.

bouffon, ~ne /bufɔ̃, -ɔn/ *adj* farcical. ● *nm* buffoon.

bougeoir /buʒwaʀ/ *nm* candlestick.

bougeotte /buʒɔt/ *nf* avoir la ~ 🅻 have the fidgets.

bouger /buʒe/ [40] *vt/i* move. □ **se** ~ *vpr* 🅻 move.

bougie /buʒi/ *nf* candle; (Auto) spark(ing)-plug.

bouillant, ~e /bujɑ̃, -t/ *adj* boiling; (très chaud) boiling hot.

bouillie /buji/ *nf* (pour bébé) baby cereal; (péj) mush; en ~ crushed, mushy.

bouillir /bujiʀ/ [13] *vi* boil; (fig) seethe; faire ~ boil.

bouilloire /bujwaʀ/ *nf* kettle.

bouillon /bujɔ̃/ *nm* (de cuisson) stock; (potage) broth.

bouillonner /bujɔne/ [1] *vi* bubble.

bouillotte /bujɔt/ *nf* hot-water bottle.

boulanger, -ère /bulɑ̃ʒe, -ɛʀ/ *nm,f* baker. **boulangerie** *nf* bakery. **boulangerie-pâtisserie** *nf* bakery (*selling cakes and pastries*).

boule /bul/ *nf* ball; ~s (jeu) boules; jouer aux ~s play boules; une ~ dans la gorge a lump in one's throat; ~ de neige snowball.

bouleau (*pl* ~x) /bulo/ *nm* (silver) birch.

boulet /bulɛ/ *nm* (de forçat) ball and chain; ~ (de canon) cannonball; ~ de charbon coal nut.

boulette /bulɛt/ *nf* (de pain, papier) pellet; (bévue) blunder; ~ de viande meat ball.

boulevard /bulvaʀ/ *nm* boulevard.

bouleversant, ~e /bulvɛʀsɑ̃, -t/ *adj* deeply moving. **bouleversement** *nm* upheaval. **bouleverser** [1] *vt* turn upside down; (*pays, plans*) disrupt; (émouvoir) upset.

boulimie /bulimi/ *nf* bulimia.

boulon /bulɔ̃/ *nm* bolt.

boulot, ~te /bulo, -ɔt/ *adj* (rond 🅻) dumpy. ● *nm* (travail 🅻) work.

boum /bum/ *nm & interj* bang. ● *nf* (fête 🅻) party.

bouquet /bukɛ/ *nm* (de fleurs) bunch, bouquet; (d'arbres) clump; c'est le ~! 🅻 that's the last straw!

bouquin /bukɛ̃/ nm 🔲 book.
bouquiner [1] vt/i 🔲 read.
bouquiniste nmf second-hand
bookseller.

bourbier /buʀbje/ nm mire; (fig)
tangle.

bourde /buʀd/ nf blunder.

bourdon /buʀdɔ̃/ nm bumble-bee.
bourdonnement nm buzzing.

bourg /buʀ/ nm (market) town
(centre), village centre.

bourgeois, **∼e** /buʀʒwa, -z/ a &
nm,f middle-class (person); (péj)
bourgeois. **bourgeoisie** nf middle
class(es).

bourgeon /buʀʒɔ̃/ nm bud.

bourgogne /buʀgɔɲ/ nm
Burgundy.

bourlinguer /buʀlɛ̃ge/ [1] vi 🔲
travel about.

bourrage /buʀaʒ/ nm ∼ de crâne
brainwashing.

bourratif, **-ive** /buʀatif, -v/ adj
stodgy.

bourreau (pl ∼x) /buʀo/ nm
executioner; ∼ de travail (fig)
workaholic.

bourrelet /buʀlɛ/ nm weather-strip,
draught excluder; (de chair) roll of fat.

bourrer /buʀe/ [1] vt cram (de with);
(pipe) fill; ∼ de (nourriture) stuff
with; ∼ de coups thrash; ∼ le crâne
à qn brainwash sb.

bourrique /buʀik/ nf donkey; 🔲
pig-headed person.

bourru, **∼e** /buʀy/ adj gruff.

bourse /buʀs/ nf purse; (subvention)
grant; la B∼ the Stock Exchange.

boursier, **-ière** /buʀsje, -jɛʀ/ adj
(valeurs) Stock Exchange. ● nm,f
grant holder.

boursoufler /buʀsufle/ [1] vt (visage) cause to swell; (peinture) blister.

bousculade /buskylad/ nf crush;
(précipitation) rush. **bousculer** [1] vt
(pousser) jostle; (presser) rush;
(renverser) knock over.

bousiller /buzije/ [1] vt 🔲 wreck.

boussole /busɔl/ nf compass.

bout /bu/ nm end; (de langue, bâton)
piece; (morceau) bit; à ∼ exhausted; à
∼ de souffle out of breath; à ∼
portant point-blank; au ∼ de (après)

after; venir à ∼ de (finir) manage to
finish; d'un ∼ à l'autre throughout;
au ∼ du compte in the end; ∼ filtre
filter-tip.

bouteille /butɛj/ nf bottle; ∼
d'oxygène oxygen cylinder.

boutique /butik/ nf shop; (de mode)
boutique.

bouton /butɔ̃/ nm button; (sur la
peau) spot, pimple; (pousse) bud; (de
porte, radio) knob; ∼ de manchette
cuff-link. **boutonner** [1] vt button
(up). **boutonnière** nf buttonhole.
bouton-pression (pl boutons-
pression) nm press-stud; (US) snap.

bouture /butyʀ/ nf cutting.

bovin, **∼e** /bɔvɛ̃, -in/ adj bovine.
bovins nmpl cattle (pl).

box (pl ∼ ou boxes) /bɔks/ nm
lock-up garage; (de dortoir) cubicle;
(d'écurie) (loose) box; (Jur) dock.

boxe /bɔks/ nf boxing.

boyau (pl ∼x) /bwajo/ nm gut;
(corde) catgut; (galerie) gallery; (de
bicyclette) tyre; (US) tire.

boycotter /bɔjkɔte/ [1] vt boycott.

BP abrév f (boîte postale) PO Box.

bracelet /bʀaslɛ/ nm bracelet; (de
montre) watchstrap.

braconnier /bʀakɔnje/ nm
poacher.

brader /bʀade/ [1] vt sell off.
braderie nf clearance sale.

braguette /bʀagɛt/ nf fly.

braille /bʀaj/ nm & a Braille.

brailler /bʀaje/ [1] vt/i bawl.

braise /bʀɛz/ nf embers (+ pl).

braiser /bʀeze/ [1] vt (Culin) braise.

brancard /bʀɑ̃kaʀ/ nm stretcher;
(de charrette) shaft.

branche /bʀɑ̃ʃ/ nf branch.

branché, **∼e** /bʀɑ̃ʃe/ adj 🔲 trendy.

branchement /bʀɑ̃ʃmɑ̃/ nm
connection. **brancher** [1] vt (prise)
plug in; (à un réseau) connect.

brandir /bʀɑ̃diʀ/ [2] vt brandish.

branler /bʀɑ̃le/ [1] vi be shaky.

braquer /bʀake/ [1] vt (arme) aim;
(regard) fix; (roue) turn; (banque: 🔲)
hold up; ∼ qn contre turn sb
against. ● vi (Auto) turn (the wheel).
□ se ∼ vpr dig one's heels in.

bras /bʀa/ nm arm; (de rivière) branch; (Tech) arm; ~ dessus ~ dessous arm in arm; ~ droit (fig) right hand man; ~ de mer sound; en ~ de chemise in one's shirtsleeves. ● nmpl (fig) labour, hands.

brasier /bʀazje/ nm blaze.

brassard /bʀasaʀ/ nm armband.

brasse /bʀas/ nf breast-stroke; ~ papillon butterfly (stroke).

brasser /bʀase/ [1] vt mix; (bière) brew; (affaires) handle a lot of. **brasserie** nf brewery; (café) brasserie.

brave /bʀav/ adj (bon) good; (valeureux) brave. **braver** [1] vt defy.

bravo /bʀavo/ interj bravo. ● nm cheer.

bravoure /bʀavuʀ/ nf bravery.

break /bʀɛk/ nm estate car; (US) station-wagon.

brebis /bʀəbi/ nf ewe.

brèche /bʀɛʃ/ nf gap, breach; être sur la ~ be on the go.

bredouille /bʀəduj/ adj empty-handed.

bredouiller /bʀəduje/ [1] vt/i mumble.

bref, brève /bʀɛf, -v/ adj short, brief. ● adv in short; en ~ in short.

Brésil /bʀezil/ nm Brazil.

Bretagne /bʀətaɲ/ nf Brittany.

bretelle /bʀətɛl/ nf (de sac, maillot) strap; (d'autoroute) access road; ~s (pour pantalon) braces; (US) suspenders.

breton, ~ne /bʀətɔ̃, -ɔn/ a & nm (Ling) Breton. **B~, ~ne** nm,f Breton.

breuvage /bʀœvaʒ/ nm beverage.

brève /bʀɛv/ ⇒BREF.

brevet /bʀəvɛ/ nm ~ (d'invention) patent; (diplôme) diploma.

breveté, ~e /bʀəvte/ adj patented.

bribes /bʀib/ nfpl scraps.

bricolage /bʀikɔlaʒ/ nm do-it-yourself (jobs).

bricole /bʀikɔl/ nf trifle.

bricoler /bʀikɔle/ [1] vi do DIY; (US) fix things, tinker with.

bricoleur, -euse /bʀikɔlœʀ, -øz/ nm,f handyman, handywoman.

bride /bʀid/ nf bridle.

bridé, ~e /bʀide/ adj yeux ~s slanting eyes.

brider /bʀide/ [1] vt (cheval) bridle; (fig) keep in check.

brièvement /bʀijɛvmɑ̃/ adv briefly.

brigade /bʀigad/ nf (de police) squad; (Mil) brigade; (fig) team. **brigadier** nm (de gendarmerie) sergeant.

brigand /bʀigɑ̃/ nm robber.

brillant, ~e /bʀijɑ̃, -t/ adj (couleur) bright; (luisant) shiny; (remarquable) brilliant. ● nm (éclat) shine; (diamant) diamond.

briller /bʀije/ [1] vi shine.

brimade /bʀimad/ nf vexation. **brimer** [1] vt bully, harass; se sentir brimé feel put down.

brin /bʀɛ̃/ nm (de muguet) sprig; (d'herbe) blade; (de paille) wisp; un ~ de (un peu) a bit of.

brindille /bʀɛ̃dij/ nf twig.

brioche /bʀijɔʃ/ nf brioche, sweet bun; (ventre 🗊) paunch.

brique /bʀik/ nf brick.

briquet /bʀikɛ/ nm (cigarette-) lighter.

brise /bʀiz/ nf breeze.

briser /bʀize/ [1] vt break. □ se ~ vpr break.

britannique /bʀitanik/ adj British. **B~** nmf Briton; les **B~s** the British.

brocante /bʀɔkɑ̃t/ nf bric-à-brac trade; (marché) flea market.

broche /bʀɔʃ/ nf brooch; (Culin) spit; à la ~ spit-roasted.

broché, ~e /bʀɔʃe/ adj paperback.

brochet /bʀɔʃɛ/ nm pike.

brochette /bʀɔʃɛt/ nf skewer.

brochure /bʀɔʃyʀ/ nf brochure, booklet.

broder /bʀɔde/ [1] vt/i embroider. **broderie** nf embroidery.

broncher /bʀɔ̃ʃe/ [1] vi sans ~ without turning a hair.

bronchite /bʀɔ̃ʃit/ nf bronchitis.

bronze /bʀɔ̃z/ nm bronze.

bronzé, ~e /bʀɔ̃ze/ adj (sun-) tanned.

bronzer /bʀɔ̃ze/ [1] vi (personne) get a (sun-)tan.

brosse /brɔs/ *nf* brush; ~ à dents toothbrush; ~ à habits clothes brush; **en** ~ (*coiffure*) in a crew cut.

brosser /brɔse/ [1] *vt* brush; (fig) paint. □ **se** ~ *vpr* se ~ les dents/les cheveux brush one's teeth/hair.

brouette /bruɛt/ *nf* wheelbarrow.

brouhaha /bruaa/ *nm* hubbub.

brouillard /brujaʀ/ *nm* fog.

brouille /bruj/ *nf* quarrel.

brouiller /bruje/ [1] *vt* (*vue*) blur; (*œufs*) scramble; (*amis*) set at odds; ~ les pistes cloud the issue. □ **se** ~ *vpr* (*ciel*) cloud over; (*amis*) fall out.

brouillon, ~**ne** /brujɔ̃, -ɔn/ *adj* untidy. ● *nm* (rough) draft.

brousse /brus/ *nf* la ~ the bush.

brouter /brute/ [1] *vt/i* graze.

broyer /brwaje/ [31] *vt* crush; (*moudre*) grind.

bru /bry/ *nf* daughter-in-law.

bruine /bruin/ *nf* drizzle.

bruissement /bruismã/ *nm* rustling.

bruit /brui/ *nm* noise; ~ de couloir (fig) rumour.

bruitage /bruitaʒ/ *nm* sound effects.

brûlant, ~**e** /brylã, -t/ *adj* burning (hot); (*sujet*) red-hot; (*passion*) fiery.

brûlé /bryle/ *nm* burning; ça sent le ~ I can smell something burning. ● ⇒BRÛLER [1].

brûler /bryle/ [1] *vt/i* burn; (*essence*) use (up); (*cierge*) light (à to); ~ un feu (rouge) jump the lights; ~ d'envie de faire be longing to do. □ **se** ~ *vpr* burn oneself.

brûlure /brylyr/ *nf* burn; ~s d'estomac heartburn.

brume /brym/ *nf* mist. **brumeux**, -**euse** *adj* misty; (*esprit*) hazy.

brun, ~**e** /brœ̃, -yn/ *adj* brown, dark. ● *nm* brown. ● *nm,f* dark-haired person. **brunir** [2] *vi* turn brown; (*bronzer*) get a tan.

brushing /brœʃiŋ/ *nm* blow-dry.

brusque /brysk/ *adj* (*personne*) abrupt; (*geste*) violent; (*soudain*) sudden.

brusquer /bryske/ [1] *vt* be abrupt with; (*précipiter*) rush.

brut, ~**e** /bryt/ *adj* (*diamant*) rough; (*champagne*) dry; (*pétrole*) crude; (Comm) gross.

brutal, ~**e** (*mpl* -**aux**) /brytal, -o/ *adj* brutal. **brutalité** *nf* brutality.

brute /bryt/ *nf* brute.

Bruxelles /brysɛl/ *npr* Brussels.

bruyant, ~**e** /bruijã, -t/ *adj* noisy.

bruyère /bryjɛr/ *nf* heather.

bu /by/ ⇒BOIRE [12].

bûche /byʃ/ *nf* log; ~ de Noël Christmas log; **ramasser une** ~ 🄸 fall.

bûcher /byʃe/ [1] *vt/i* 🄸 slog away (at) 🄸. ● *nm* (*supplice*) stake.

bûcheron /byʃrɔ̃/ *nm* lumberjack.

budget /bydʒɛ/ *nm* budget. **budgétaire** *adj* budgetary.

buée /bɥe/ *nf* condensation.

buffet /byfɛ/ *nm* sideboard; (*table garnie*) buffet.

buffle /byfl/ *nm* buffalo.

buisson /bɥisɔ̃/ *nm* bush.

buissonnière /bɥisɔnjɛr/ *af* faire l'école ~ play truant.

bulbe /bylb/ *nm* bulb.

bulgare /bylgaʀ/ *a & nm* Bulgarian. **B**~ *nmf* Bulgarian.

Bulgarie /bylgaʀi/ *nf* Bulgaria.

bulldozer /byldozɛʀ/ *nm* bulldozer.

bulle /byl/ *nf* bubble.

bulletin /byltɛ̃/ *nm* bulletin, report; (Scol) report; ~ d'information news bulletin; ~ météorologique weather report; ~ (de vote) ballot-paper; ~ de salaire pay-slip.

buraliste /byʀalist/ *nmf* tobacconist.

bureau (*pl* ~**x**) /byʀo/ *nm* office; (*meuble*) desk; (*comité*) board; ~ d'études design office; ~ de poste post office; ~ de tabac tobacconist's (shop); ~ de vote polling station.

bureaucrate /byʀokʀat/ *nmf* bureaucrat. **bureaucratie** *nf* bureaucracy. **bureaucratique** *adj* bureaucratic.

bureautique /byʀotik/ *nf* office automation.

burlesque /byʀlɛsk/ *a* (*histoire*) ludicrous; (*film*) farcical.

bus /bys/ *nm* bus.

buste /byst/ *nm* bust.

but /by(t)/ nm target; (dessein) aim, goal; (football) goal; **avoir pour ~ de** aim to; **de ~ en blanc** point-blank; **dans le ~ de** with the intention of; **aller droit au ~** go straight to the point.

butane /bytan/ nm butane, Calor gas®.

buté, **~e** /byte/ adj obstinate.

buter /byte/ [1] vi **~ contre** knock against; (problème) come up against. ● vt antagonize. □ **se ~** vpr (s'entêter) become obstinate.

buteur /bytœʀ/ nm (au football) striker.

butin /bytɛ̃/ nm booty, loot.

butte /byt/ nf mound; **en ~ à** exposed to.

buvard /byvaʀ/ nm blotting-paper.

buvette /byvɛt/ nf (refreshment) bar.

buveur, **-euse** /byvœʀ, -øz/ nm,f drinker.

Cc

c' /s/ ⇒CE.

ça /sa/
● pronom démonstratif
····▸ (sujet) it; that; **~ flotte** it floats; **~ suffit!** that's enough!; **~ y est!** that's it!; **~ sent le brûlé** there's a smell of burning; **~ va?** how are things?
····▸ (objet) (proche) this; (plus éloigné) that; **c'est ~** that's right.
····▸ (dans expressions) **où ~?** where?; **quand ~?** when?; **et avec ~?** anything else?

çà /sa/ adv **~ et là** here and there.

cabane /kaban/ nf hut; (à outils) shed.

cabaret /kabaʀɛ/ nm cabaret.

cabillaud /kabijo/ nm cod.

cabine /kabin/ nf (à la piscine) cubicle; (de bateau) cabin; (de camion) cab; (d'ascenseur) cage; **~ d'essayage** fitting room; **~ de pilotage** cockpit; **~ de plage** beach hut; **~ (téléphonique)** phone booth, phone box.

cabinet /kabinɛ/ nm (de médecin) surgery; (US) office; (d'avocat) office; (clientèle) practice; (cabinet collectif) firm; (Pol) Cabinet; (pièce) room; **~s** (toilettes) toilet; (US) bathroom; **~ de toilette** bathroom.

câble /kɑbl/ nm cable; (corde) rope; (TV) cable TV. **câbler** vt [1] cable; (TV) install cable television in.

cabosser /kabose/ [1] vt dent.

cabotage /kabotaʒ/ nm coastal navigation.

cabrer (se) /(sə)kabʀe/ [1] vpr (cheval) rear; **se ~ contre** rebel against.

cabriole /kabʀijɔl/ nf **faire des ~s** caper about.

cacahuète /kakawɛt/ nf peanut.

cacao /kakao/ nm cocoa.

cachalot /kaʃalo/ nm sperm whale.

cache /kaʃ/ nm mask. ● nf hiding place; **~ d'armes** arms cache.

cache-cache /kaʃkaʃ/ nm inv hide-and-seek.

cache-nez /kaʃne/ nm inv scarf.

cacher /kaʃe/ [1] vt hide, conceal (à from). □ **se ~** vpr hide; (se trouver caché) be hidden.

cachet /kaʃɛ/ nm (de cire) seal; (à l'encre) stamp; (de la poste) postmark; (comprimé) tablet; (d'artiste) fee; (chic) style, cachet.

cachette /kaʃɛt/ nf hiding-place; **en ~** in secret.

cachot /kaʃo/ nm dungeon.

cachottier, **-ière** /kaʃotje, -jɛʀ/ adj secretive.

cacophonie /kakɔfɔni/ nf cacophony.

cactus /kaktys/ nm cactus.

cadavérique /kadaveʀik/ adj (teint) deathly pale.

cadavre /kadavʀ/ nm corpse; (de victime) body.

caddie /kadi/ nm (de supermarché)® trolley; (au golf) caddie.

cadeau (*pl* ~**x**) /kado/ *nm* present, gift; **faire un ~ à qn** give sb a present.

cadenas /kadna/ *nm* padlock.

cadence /kadɑ̃s/ *nf* rhythm, cadence; (de travail) rate; **en ~** in time; (*marcher*) in step.

cadet, ~**te** /kadɛ, -t/ *adj* youngest; (entre deux) younger. ● *nm, f* youngest (child); younger (child).

cadran /kadʁɑ̃/ *nm* dial; ~ **solaire** sundial.

cadre /kɑdʁ/ *nm* frame; (lieu) setting; (milieu) surroundings; (limites) scope; (contexte) framework; **dans le ~ de** (à l'occasion de) on the occasion of; (dans le contexte de) in the framework of. ● *nm* (personne) executive; **les ~s** the managerial staff.

cadrer /kadʁe/ [1] *vi* ~ **avec** tally with. ● *vt* (*photo*) centre.

cafard /kafaʁ/ *nm* (insecte) cockroach; **avoir le ~** 🗉 be down in the dumps.

café /kafe/ *nm* coffee; (bar) café; ~ **crème** espresso with milk; ~ **en grains** coffee beans; ~ **au lait** white coffee.

cafetière /kaftjɛʁ/ *nf* coffee-pot; ~ **électrique** coffee machine.

cage /kaʒ/ *nf* cage; ~ **d'ascenseur** lift shaft; ~ **d'escalier** stairwell; ~ **thoracique** rib cage.

cageot /kaʒo/ *nm* crate.

cagibi /kaʒibi/ *nm* storage room.

cagneux, -**euse** /kaɲø, -z/ *adj* **avoir les genoux ~** be knock-kneed.

cagnotte /kaɲɔt/ *nf* kitty.

cagoule /kagul/ *nf* hood; (passe-montagne) balaclava.

cahier /kaje/ *nm* notebook; (Scol) exercise book; ~ **de textes** homework notebook; ~ **des charges** (Tech) specifications (+ *pl*).

cahot /kao/ *nm* bump, jolt. **cahoteux**, -**euse** *adj* bumpy.

caïd /kaid/ *nm* 🗉 big shot.

caille /kɑj/ *nf* quail.

cailler /kɑje/ [1] *vi* curdle; **ça caille** 🗉 it's freezing. ☐ **se ~** *vpr* (*sang*) clot; (*lait*) curdle. **caillot** *nm* (blood) clot.

caillou (*pl* ~**x**) /kaju/ *nm* stone; (galet) pebble.

caisse /kɛs/ *nf* crate, case; (tiroir, machine) till; (guichet) cash desk; (au supermarché) check-out; (bureau) office; (Mus) drum; ~ **enregistreuse** cash register; ~ **d'épargne** savings bank; ~ **de retraite** pension fund. **caissier**, -**ière** *nm, f* cashier.

cajoler /kaʒɔle/ [1] *vt* coax.

calcaire /kalkɛʁ/ *adj* (sol) chalky; (*eau*) hard.

calciné, ~**e** /kalsine/ *adj* charred.

calcul /kalkyl/ *nm* calculation; (Scol) arithmetic; (différentiel) calculus; ~ **biliaire** gallstone.

calculatrice /kalkylatʁis/ *nf* calculator. **calculer** [1] *vt* calculate. **calculette** *nf* (pocket) calculator.

cale /kal/ *nf* wedge; (pour roue) chock; (de navire) hold; ~ **sèche** dry dock.

calé, ~**e** /kale/ *adj* 🗉 clever.

caleçon /kalsɔ̃/ *nm* boxer shorts (+ *pl*); underpants (+ *pl*); (de femme) leggings.

calembour /kalɑ̃buʁ/ *nm* pun.

calendrier /kalɑ̃dʁije/ *nm* calendar; (fig) schedule, timetable.

calepin /kalpɛ̃/ *nm* notebook.

caler /kale/ [1] *vt* wedge. ● *vi* stall; (abandonner 🗉) give up.

calfeutrer /kalføtʁe/ [1] *vt* (*fissure*) stop up; (*porte*) draught proof.

calibre /kalibʁ/ *nm* calibre; (d'un œuf, fruit) grade.

calice /kalis/ *nm* (Relig) chalice; (Bot) calyx.

califourchon: **à ~** /akalifuʁʃɔ̃/ *loc* astride.

câlin, ~**e** /kɑlɛ̃, -in/ *adj* (regard, ton) affectionate; (*personne*) cuddly.

calmant /kalmɑ̃/ *nm* sedative.

calme /kalm/ *adj* calm. ● *nm* peace; calm; (maîtrise de soi) composure; **du ~!** calm down!

calmer /kalme/ [1] *vt* (*personne*) calm down; (*situation*) defuse; (*douleur*) ease; (*soif*) quench. ☐ **se ~** *vpr* (*personne, situation*) calm down; (*agitation, tempête*) die down; (*douleur*) ease.

calomnie /kalɔmni/ *nf* (orale) slander; (écrite) libel. **calomnier** [45]

vt slander; libel. **calomnieux,
-ieuse** *adj* slanderous; libellous.

calorie /kalɔʀi/ *nf* calorie.

calque /kalk/ *nm* tracing; (**papier**) ~
tracing paper; (fig) exact copy.

calquer /kalke/ [1] *vt* trace; (fig)
copy; ~ **qch sur** model sth on.

calvaire /kalvɛʀ/ *nm* (croix) Calvary;
(fig) suffering.

calvitie /kalvisi/ *nf* baldness.

camarade /kamaʀad/ *nmf* friend;
(Pol) comrade; ~ **de jeu** playmate.
camaraderie *nf* friendship.

cambouis /kãbwi/ *nm* dirty oil.

cambrer /kãbʀe/ [1] *vt* arch. □ **se**
~ *vpr* arch one's back.

cambriolage /kãbʀijɔlaʒ/ *nm*
burglary. **cambrioler** [1] *vt* burgle.
cambrioleur, -euse *nm,f* burglar.

camelot /kamlo/ *nm* Ⓕ street
vendor.

camelote /kamlɔt/ *nf* Ⓕ junk.

caméra /kameʀa/ *nf* (cinéma,
télévision) camera.

caméscope® /kameskɔp/ *nm*
camcorder.

camion /kamjõ/ *nm* lorry, truck.
camion-citerne (*pl* **camions-
citernes**) *nm* tanker.
camionnage *nm* haulage.
camionnette *nf* van.
camionneur *nm* lorry *ou* truck
driver; (entrepreneur) haulage
contractor.

camisole /kamizɔl/ *nf* ~ (**de force**)
straitjacket.

camoufler /kamufle/ [1] *vt*
camouflage.

camp /kã/ *nm* camp; (Sport, Pol) side.

campagnard, ~e /kãpaɲaʀ, -d/
adj country. ● *nm,f* countryman,
countrywoman.

campagne /kãpaɲ/ *nf* country;
countryside; (Mil, Pol) campaign.

campement /kãpmã/ *nm* camp,
encampment.

camper /kãpe/ [1] *vi* camp. ● *vt*
(esquisser) sketch. □ **se** ~ *vpr* plant
oneself. **campeur, -euse** *nm,f*
camper.

camping /kãpiŋ/ *nm* camping; **faire
du** ~ go camping; (**terrain de**) ~
campsite. **camping-car** (*pl* ~**s**) *nm*

camper-van; (US) motorhome.
camping-gaz® *nm inv* (réchaud)
camping stove.

Canada /kanada/ *nm* Canada.

canadien, ~ne /kanadjɛ̃, -ɛn/ *adj*
Canadian. **C~, ~ne** *nm,f* Canadian.
canadienne *nf* (veste) fur-lined
jacket; (tente) ridge tent.

canaille /kanaj/ *nf* rogue.

canal (*pl* **-aux**) /kanal, -o/ *nm*
(artificiel) canal; (bras de mer) channel;
(Tech, TV) channel; (moyen) channel;
par le ~ **de** through. **canalisation**
nf (tuyaux) mains (+ *pl*). **canaliser**
[1] *vt* (eau) canalize; (fig) channel.

canapé /kanape/ *nm* sofa.

canard /kanaʀ/ *nm* duck; (journal Ⓕ)
rag.

canari /kanaʀi/ *nm* canary.

cancans /kãkã/ *nmpl* Ⓕ gossip.

cancer /kãsɛʀ/ *nm* cancer; **le C~**
Cancer. **cancéreux, -euse** *adj*
cancerous. **cancérigène** *adj*
carcinogenic.

cancre /kãkʀ/ *nm* dunce.

candeur /kãdœʀ/ *nf* ingenuousness.

candidat, ~e /kãdida, -t/ *nm,f* (à
un examen, Pol) candidate; (à un poste)
applicant; candidate (**à** for).

candidature /kãdidatyʀ/ *nf*
application; (Pol) candidacy; **poser sa**
~ **à un poste** apply for a job.

candide /kãdid/ *adj* ingenuous.

cane /kan/ *nf* (female) duck.
caneton *nm* duckling.

canette /kanɛt/ *nf* (bouteille) bottle;
(boîte) can.

canevas /kanva/ *nm* canvas;
(ouvrage) tapestry; (plan) framework,
outline.

caniche /kaniʃ/ *nm* poodle.

canicule /kanikyl/ *nf* scorching
heat; (vague de chaleur) heatwave.

canif /kanif/ *nm* penknife.

canine /kanin/ *nf* canine (tooth).

caniveau (*pl* ~**x**) /kanivo/ *nm*
gutter.

cannabis /kanabis/ *nm* cannabis.

canne /kan/ *nf* (walking) stick; ~ **à
pêche** fishing rod; ~ **à sucre** sugar
cane.

cannelle /kanɛl/ *nf* cinnamon.

cannibale /kanibal/ *a & nmf* cannibal.

canoë /kanɔe/ *nm* canoe; (Sport) canoeing.

canon /kanɔ̃/ *nm* (big) gun; (ancien) cannon; (d'une arme) barrel; (principe, règle) canon.

canot /kano/ *nm* dinghy, (small) boat; ~ **de sauvetage** lifeboat; ~ **pneumatique** rubber dinghy. **canotier** *nm* boater.

cantatrice /kɑ̃tatʀis/ *nf* opera singer.

cantine /kɑ̃tin/ *nf* canteen.

cantique /kɑ̃tik/ *nm* hymn.

cantonner /kɑ̃tɔne/ [1] *vt* (Mil) billet. □ **se** ~ **dans** *vpr* confine oneself to.

cantonnier /kɑ̃tɔnje/ *nm* road mender.

canular /kanylaʀ/ *nm* hoax.

caoutchouc /kautʃu/ *nm* rubber; (élastique) rubber band; ~ **mousse** foam rubber.

cap /kap/ *nm* cape, headland; (direction) course; (obstacle) hurdle; **franchir le** ~ **de la cinquantaine** pass the fifty mark; **mettre le** ~ **sur** steer a course for.

capable /kapabl/ *adj* capable (**de** of); ~ **de faire** able to do, capable of doing.

capacité /kapasite/ *nf* ability; (contenance, potentiel) capacity.

cape /kap/ *nf* cape; **rire sous** ~ laugh up one's sleeve.

capillaire /kapilɛʀ/ *adj* (lotion, soins) hair; (vaisseau) ~ capillary.

capitaine /kapitɛn/ *nm* captain.

capital, ~**e** (*mpl* **-aux**) /kapital, -o/ *adj* key, crucial, fundamental; (peine, lettre) capital. ● *nm* (*pl* **-aux**) (Comm) capital; (fig) stock; **capitaux** (Comm) capital. **capitale** *nf* (ville, lettre) capital.

capitalisme /kapitalism/ *nm* capitalism.

capitonné, ~**e** /kapitɔne/ *adj* padded.

capituler /kapityle/ [1] *vi* capitulate.

caporal (*pl* **-aux**) /kapɔʀal, -o/ *nm* corporal.

capot /kapo/ *nm* (Auto) bonnet; (US) hood.

capote /kapɔt/ *nf* (Auto) hood; (US) top; (préservatif 🔲) condom.

capoter /kapɔte/ [1] *vi* overturn; (fig) collapse.

câpre /kɑpʀ/ *nf* (Culin) caper.

caprice /kapʀis/ *nm* whim; (colère) tantrum; **faire un** ~ throw a tantrum. **capricieux**, **-ieuse** *adj* capricious; (appareil) temperamental.

Capricorne /kapʀikɔʀn/ *nm* **le** ~ Capricorn.

capsule /kapsyl/ *nf* capsule; (de bouteille) cap.

capter /kapte/ [1] *vt* (eau) collect; (émission) get; (signal) pick up; (fig) win, capture.

captif, **-ive** /kaptif, -v/ *a & nmf* captive.

captiver /kaptive/ [1] *vt* captivate.

capturer /kaptyʀe/ [1] *vt* capture.

capuche /kapyʃ/ *nf* hood. **capuchon** *nm* hood; (de stylo) cap.

car /kaʀ/ *conj* because, for. ● *nm* coach; (US) bus.

carabine /kaʀabin/ *nf* rifle.

caractère /kaʀaktɛʀ/ *nm* (lettre) character; (nature) nature; ~**s** **d'imprimerie** block letters; **avoir bon/ mauvais** ~ be good-natured/ bad-tempered; **avoir du** ~ have character.

caractériel, ~**le** /kaʀakteʀjɛl/ *adj* (trait) character; (enfant) disturbed.

caractériser /kaʀakteʀize/ [1] *vt* characterize. □ **se** ~ **par** *vpr* be characterized by. **caractéristique** *a & nf* characteristic.

carafe /kaʀaf/ *nf* carafe.

Caraïbes /kaʀaib/ *nfpl* **les** ~ the Caribbean.

carambolage /kaʀɑ̃bɔlaʒ/ *nm* pile-up.

caramel /kaʀamɛl/ *nm* caramel; (bonbon) toffee.

carapace /kaʀapas/ *nf* shell.

caravane /kaʀavan/ *nf* (Auto) caravan; (US) trailer; (convoi) caravan.

carbone /kaʀbɔn/ nm carbon;
(papier) ~ carbon (paper).
  carboniser [1] vt burn (to ashes).
carburant /kaʀbyʀɑ̃/ nm (motor)
fuel.
carburateur /kaʀbyʀatœʀ/ nm
carburettor; (US) carburetor.
carcan /kaʀkɑ̃/ nm constraints (+
pl).
carcasse /kaʀkas/ nf (squelette)
carcass; (armature) frame; (de voiture)
shell.
cardiaque /kaʀdjak/ adj heart.
  ● nmf heart patient.
cardinal, ~e (mpl -aux) /kaʀdinal,
-o/ a & nm cardinal.
Carême /kaʀɛm/ nm le ~ Lent.
carence /kaʀɑ̃s/ nf shortcomings (+
pl); inadequacy; (Méd) deficiency;
(absence) lack.
caresse /kaʀɛs/ nf caress; (à un
animal) stroke. **caresser** [1] vt
caress, stroke; (espoir) cherish.
cargaison /kaʀɡɛzɔ̃/ nf cargo.
cargo /kaʀɡo/ nm cargo boat.
caricature /kaʀikatyʀ/ nf
caricature.
carie /kaʀi/ nf (trou) cavity; la ~
(dentaire) tooth decay.
carillon /kaʀijɔ̃/ nm chimes (+ pl);
(horloge) chiming clock.
caritatif, **-ive** /kaʀitatif, -v/ adj
association caritative charity.
carnage /kaʀnaʒ/ nm carnage.
carnassier, **-ière** /kaʀnasje, -jɛʀ/
adj carnivorous.
carnaval (pl ~s) /kaʀnaval/ nm
carnival.
carnet /kaʀnɛ/ nm notebook; (de
tickets, timbres) book; ~ d'adresses
address book; ~ de chèques
chequebook.
carotte /kaʀɔt/ nf carrot.
carpe /kaʀp/ nf carp.
carré, ~e /kaʀe/ adj (forme, mesure)
square; (fig) straightforward; un
mètre ~ one square metre. ● nm
square; (de terrain) patch.
carreau (pl ~x) /kaʀo/ nm
(window) pane; (par terre, au mur) tile;
(dessin) check; (aux cartes) diamonds
(+ pl); à ~x (tissu) check(ed);
(papier) squared.

carrefour /kaʀfuʀ/ nm crossroads
(+ sg).
carrelage /kaʀlaʒ/ nm tiling; (sol)
tiles.
carrément /kaʀemɑ̃/ adv
(complètement) completely; (stupide,
dangereux) downright; (dire) straight
out; elle a ~ démissionné she went
straight ahead and resigned.
carrière /kaʀjɛʀ/ nf career; (terrain)
quarry.
carrossable /kaʀɔsabl/ adj
suitable for vehicles.
carrosse /kaʀɔs/ nm (horse-drawn)
coach.
carrosserie /kaʀɔsʀi/ nf (Auto)
body(work).
carrure /kaʀyʀ/ nf shoulders; (fig)
necessary qualities, calibre.
cartable /kaʀtabl/ nm satchel.
carte /kaʀt/ nf card; (Géog) map;
(Naut) chart; (au restaurant) menu; ~s
(jeu) cards; à la ~ (manger) à la
carte; (horaire) personalized; donner
~ blanche à give a free hand to; ~
de crédit credit card; ~ grise (car)
registration document; ~ d'identité
identity card; ~ magnétique swipe
card; ~ de paiement debit card; ~
postale postcard; ~ à puce smart
card; ~ de séjour resident's permit;
~ des vins wine list; ~ de visite
(business) card.
cartilage /kaʀtilaʒ/ nm cartilage.
carton /kaʀtɔ̃/ nm cardboard; (boîte)
(cardboard) box; ~ à dessin
portfolio; faire un ~ 🄳 do well.
cartonné, ~e /kaʀtɔne/ adj livre ~
hardback.
cartouche /kaʀtuʃ/ nf cartridge;
(de cigarettes) carton. **cartouchière**
nf cartridge-belt.
cas /kɑ/ nm case; au ~ où in case; ~
urgent emergency; en aucun ~ on no
account; en tout ~ in any case; (du
moins) at least; faire ~ de set great
store by; ~ de conscience moral
dilemma.
casanier, **-ière** /kazanje, -jɛʀ/ adj
home-loving.
cascade /kaskad/ nf waterfall; (au
cinéma) stunt; (fig) spate, series (+ sg).

cascadeur, -euse /kaskadœʀ, -øz/ *nm, f* stuntman, stuntwoman.

case /kaz/ *nf* hut; (de damier) square; (compartiment) pigeon-hole; (sur un formulaire) box.

caser /kaze/ [1] *vt* ⊞ (mettre) put; (loger) put up; (dans un travail) find a job for; (marier: péj) marry off.

caserne /kazɛʀn/ *nf* barracks; ~ de sapeurs-pompiers fire station.

casier /kazje/ *nm* pigeon-hole, compartment; (à bouteilles, chaussures) rack; ~ judiciaire criminal record.

casque /kask/ *nm* (de motard) crash helmet; (de cycliste) cycle helmet; (chez le coiffeur) (hair-)drier; ~ (à écouteurs) headphones; ~ anti-bruit ear defenders; ~ de protection safety helmet.

casquette /kaskɛt/ *nf* cap.

cassant, ~e /kasɑ̃, -t/ *adj* brittle; (brusque) curt.

cassation /kasasjɔ̃/ *nf* cour de ~ appeal court.

casse /kas/ *nf* (objets) breakages; (lieu) breaker's yard; mettre à la ~ scrap.

casse-cou /kasku/ *nmf inv* daredevil.

casse-croûte /kaskʀut/ *nm inv* snack.

casse-noix /kasnwa/ *nm inv* nutcrackers (+ *pl*).

casse-pieds /kaspje/ *nmf inv* ⊞ pain (in the neck) ⊞.

casser /kase/ [1] *vt* break; (annuler) annul; ~ les pieds à qn ⊞ annoy sb. ● *vi* break. □ se ~ *vpr* break; (partir ⊞) be off ⊞.

casserole /kasʀɔl/ *nf* saucepan.

casse-tête /kastɛt/ *nm inv* (problème) headache; (jeu) brain teaser.

cassette /kasɛt/ *nf* casket; (de magnétophone) cassette, tape; (de vidéo) video tape; ~ audionumérique digital audio tape.

cassis /kasi(s)/ *nm inv* blackcurrant.

cassure /kasyʀ/ *nf* break.

castor /kastɔʀ/ *nm* beaver.

castration /kastʀasjɔ̃/ *nf* castration.

catalogue /katalɔg/ *nm* catalogue.

catalyseur /katalizœʀ/ *nm* catalyst; (Auto) catalytic convertor.

catastrophe /katastʀɔf/ *nf* disaster, catastrophe.

catastrophique *adj* catastrophic.

catch /katʃ/ *nm* (all-in) wrestling.

catéchisme /kateʃism/ *nm* catechism.

catégorie /kategɔʀi/ *nf* category.

catégorique *adj* categorical.

cathédrale /katedʀal/ *nf* cathedral.

catholique /katɔlik/ *adj* Catholic; pas très ~ a bit fishy.

catimini: en ~ /ãkatimini/ *loc* on the sly.

cauchemar /koʃmaʀ/ *nm* nightmare.

cause /koz/ *nf* cause; (raison) reason; (Jur) case; à ~ de because of; en ~ (en jeu, concerné) involved; pour ~ de on account of; mettre en ~ implicate; remettre en ~ call into question.

causer /koze/ [1] *vt* cause; (discuter de ⊞) ~ travail talk shop; ~ de talk about. ● *vi* chat. **causerie** *nf* talk.

causette /kozɛt/ *nf* faire la ~ have a chat.

caution /kosjɔ̃/ *nf* surety; (Jur) bail; (appui) backing; (garantie) deposit; libéré sous ~ released on bail.

cautionner [1] *vt* guarantee; (soutenir) back.

cavalcade /kavalkad/ *nf* stampede, rush.

cavalier, -ière /kavalje, -jɛʀ/ *adj* offhand; allée cavalière bridle path. ● *nm, f* rider; (pour danser) partner. ● *nm* (aux échecs) knight.

cave /kav/ *nf* cellar. ● *adj* sunken.

caveau (*pl* ~x) /kavo/ *nm* vault.

caverne /kavɛʀn/ *nf* cave.

CCP *abrév m* (**compte chèque postal**) post office account.

CD *abrév m* (**compact disc**) CD.

CD-ROM *abrév m inv* (**compact disc read only memory**) CD-ROM.

ce, c', cet, cette (*pl* **ces**) /sə,s, sɛt, se/

c' before e. cet before vowel or mute h.

●**ce**, **cet**, **cette** (*pl* **ces**) *adjectif démonstratif*

····▸ this; (plus éloigné) that; **ces** these; (plus éloigné) those; **cette nuit** (passée) last night; (à venir) tonight.

●**ce**, **c'** *pronom démonstratif*

····▸ **c'est** it's *ou* it is; **c'est un policier** he's a policeman; ~ **sont eux qui l'ont fait** THEY did it; **qui est-~?** who is it?

····▸ **ce que/qui** what; ~ **que je ne comprends pas** what I don't understand; **elle est venue, ~ qui est étonnant** she came, which is surprising; ~ **que tu as de la chance!** how lucky you are!; **tout ~ que je sais** all I know; **tout ~ qu'elle trouve/peut** everything she finds/can.

CE *abrév f* (**Communauté européenne**) EC.

ceci /səsi/ *pron* this.

cécité /sesite/ *nf* blindness.

céder /sede/ [14] *vt* give up; ~ **le passage** give way; (vendre) sell. ● *vi* (se rompre) give way; (se soumettre) give in.

cédérom /sederɔm/ *nm* CD-ROM.

cédille /sedij/ *nf* cedilla.

cèdre /sɛdʀ/ *nm* cedar.

CEI *abrév f* (**Communauté des États indépendants**) CIS.

ceinture /sɛ̃tyʀ/ *nf* belt; (taille) waist; ~ **de sauvetage** lifebelt; ~ **de sécurité** seatbelt.

cela /səla/ *pron* it, that; (pour désigner) that; ~ **va de soi** it is obvious; ~ **dit/fait** having said/done that.

célèbre /selɛbʀ/ *adj* famous. **célébrer** [14] *vt* celebrate. **célébrité** *nf* fame; (personne) celebrity.

céleri /sɛlʀi/ *nm* (en branches) celery. **céleri-rave** (*pl* **céleris-raves**) *nm* celeriac.

célibat /seliba/ *nm* celibacy; (état) single status.

célibataire /selibatɛʀ/ *adj* single. ● *nm* bachelor. ● *nf* single woman.

celle, **celles** /sɛl/ ⇒CELUI.

cellier /selje/ *nm* wine cellar.

cellulaire /selylɛʀ/ *adj* cell; **emprisonnement** ~ solitary confinement; **fourgon** *ou* **voiture** ~ prison van; **téléphone** ~ cellular phone.

cellule /selyl/ *nf* cell.

celui, **celle** (*pl* **ceux**, **celles**) /səlɥi, sɛl, sø/ *pron* the one; ~ **de mon ami** my friend's; ~-**ci** this (one); ~-**là** that (one); **ceux-ci** these (ones); **ceux-là** those (ones).

cendre /sɑ̃dʀ/ *nf* ash.

cendrier /sɑ̃dʀije/ *nm* ashtray.

censé, ~**e** /sɑ̃se/ *adj* **être** ~ **faire** be supposed to do.

censeur /sɑ̃sœʀ/ *nm* censor; (Scol) administrator in charge of discipline.

censure /sɑ̃syʀ/ *nf* censorship. **censurer** [1] *vt* censor; (critiquer) censure.

cent /sɑ̃/ *a* & *nm* (a) hundred; ~ **un** a hundred and one; **20 pour** ~ 20 per cent.

centaine /sɑ̃tɛn/ *nf* hundred; **une** ~ (**de**) (about) a hundred.

centenaire /sɑ̃tnɛʀ/ *nm* (anniversaire) centenary.

centième /sɑ̃tjɛm/ *a* & *nmf* hundredth.

centimètre /sɑ̃timɛtʀ/ *nm* centimetre; (ruban) tape-measure.

central, ~**e** (*mpl* -**aux**) /sɑ̃tʀal, -o/ *adj* central. ● *nm* (*pl* -**aux**) ~ (**téléphonique**) (telephone) exchange. **centrale** *nf* power-station.

centre /sɑ̃tʀ/ *nm* centre; ~ **commercial** shopping centre; (US) mall; ~ **de formation** training centre; ~ **hospitalier** hospital. **centrer** [1] *vt* centre. **centre-ville** (*pl* **centres-villes**) *nm* town centre.

centuple /sɑ̃typl/ *nm* **le** ~ **de** a hundred times; **au** ~ a hundredfold.

cep /sɛp/ *nm* vine stock.

cépage /sepaʒ/ *nm* grape variety.

cèpe /sɛp/ *nm* cep.

cependant /səpɑ̃dɑ̃/ *adv* however.

céramique /seʀamik/ *nf* ceramic; (art) ceramics (+ *sg*).

cercle /sɛʀkl/ *nm* circle; (cerceau) hoop; (association) society, club; ~ **vicieux** vicious circle.

cercueil /sɛʀkœj/ *nm* coffin.

céréale /seʀeal/ *nf* cereal; ~**s** (Culin) (breakfast) cereal.

cérébral, ~**e** (*mpl* -**aux**) /seʀebʀal, -o/ *adj* cerebral; (*travail*) intellectual.

cérémonie /seʀemɔni/ *nf* ceremony; **sans** ~**s** (*repas*) informal; (*recevoir*) informally.

cerf /sɛʀ/ *nm* stag.

cerfeuil /sɛʀfœj/ *nm* chervil.

cerf-volant (*pl* **cerfs-volants**) /sɛʀvɔlɑ̃/ *nm* kite.

cerise /s(ə)ʀiz/ *nf* cherry. **cerisier** *nm* cherry tree.

cerne /sɛʀn/ *nm* ring.

cerner /sɛʀne/ [1] *vt* surround; (*question*) define; **avoir les yeux cernés** have rings under one's eyes.

certain, ~**e** /sɛʀtɛ̃, -ɛn/ *adj* certain; (*sûr*) certain, sure (**de** of; **que** that); **d'un** ~ **âge** no longer young; **un** ~ **temps** some time. **certainement** *adv* (*probablement*) most probably; (*avec certitude*) certainly. **certains**, -**es** *pron* some people.

certes /sɛʀt/ *adv* (*sans doute*) admittedly; (*bien sûr*) of course.

certificat /sɛʀtifika/ *nm* certificate.

certifier /sɛʀtifje/ [45] *vt* certify; ~ **qch à qn** assure sb of sth; **copie certifiée conforme** certified true copy.

certitude /sɛʀtityd/ *nf* certainty.

cerveau (*pl* ~**x**) /sɛʀvo/ *nm* brain.

cervelle /sɛʀvɛl/ *nf* (Anat) brain; (Culin) brains.

ces /se/ ⇒CE.

césarienne /sezaʀjɛn/ *nf* Caesarean (section).

cesse /sɛs/ *nf* **n'avoir de** ~ **que** have no rest until; **sans** ~ constantly, incessantly.

cesser /sese/ [1] *vt* stop; ~ **de faire** stop doing. ● *vi* cease; **faire** ~ put an end to.

cessez-le-feu /seselfø/ *nm inv* ceasefire.

cession /sesjɔ̃/ *nf* transfer.

c'est-à-dire /sɛtadiʀ/ *conj* that is (to say).

cet, **cette** /sɛt/ ⇒CE.

ceux /sø/ ⇒CELUI.

chacun, ~**e** /ʃakœ̃, -yn/ *pron* each (one), every one; (tout le monde) everyone; ~ **d'entre nous** each (one) of us.

chagrin /ʃagʀɛ̃/ *nm* sorrow; **avoir du** ~ be sad.

chahut /ʃay/ *nm* row, din.

chahuter /ʃayte/ [1] *vi* make a row. ● *vt* (*enseignant*) be rowdy with; (*orateur*) heckle.

chaîne /ʃɛn/ *nf* chain; (de télévision) channel; ~ (**d'assemblage**) assembly line; ~**s** (Auto) snow chains; ~ **de montagnes** mountain range; ~ **de montage/fabrication** assembly/ production line; ~ **hi-fi** hi-fi system; ~ **laser** CD player; **en** ~ (*accidents*) multiple; (*réaction*) chain. **chaînette** *nf* (small) chain. **chaînon** *nm* link.

chair /ʃɛʀ/ *nf* flesh; **bien en** ~ plump; **en** ~ **et en os** in the flesh; ~ **à saucisses** sausage meat; **la** ~ **de poule** goose pimples. ● *a inv* (couleur) ~ flesh-coloured.

chaire /ʃɛʀ/ *nf* (d'église) pulpit; (Univ) chair.

chaise /ʃɛz/ *nf* chair; ~ **longue** deckchair.

châle /ʃɑl/ *nm* shawl.

chaleur /ʃalœʀ/ *nf* heat; (moins intense) warmth; (d'un accueil, d'une couleur) warmth. **chaleureux**, -**euse** *adj* warm.

chalumeau (*pl* ~**x**) /ʃalymo/ *nm* blowtorch.

chalutier /ʃalytje/ *nm* trawler.

chamailler (**se**) /(sə)ʃamaje/ [1] *vpr* squabble.

chambre /ʃɑ̃bʀ/ *nf* (bed)room; (Pol, Jur) chamber; **faire** ~ **à part** sleep in separate rooms; ~ **à air** inner tube; ~ **d'amis** spare *ou* guest room; ~ **de commerce** (**et d'industrie**) Chamber of Commerce; ~ **à coucher** bedroom; ~ **à un lit/deux lits** single/twin room; ~ **pour deux personnes** double room; ~ **forte** strong-room; ~ **d'hôte** bed and breakfast, B and B.

chambrer [1] *vt* (*vin*) bring to room temperature.

chameau (*pl* ~**x**) /ʃamo/ *nm* camel.

chamois /ʃamwa/ *nm* chamois.

champ /ʃɑ̃/ *nm* field; ~ **de bataille** battlefield; ~ **de courses** racecourse; ~ **de tir** firing range.

champêtre /ʃɑ̃pɛtʀ/ *adj* rural.

champignon /ʃɑ̃piɲɔ̃/ *nm* mushroom; (moisissure) fungus; ~ **de Paris** button mushroom.

champion, ~**ne** /ʃɑ̃pjɔ̃, -ɔn/ *nm,f* champion. **championnat** *nm* championship.

chance /ʃɑ̃s/ *nf* (good) luck; (possibilité) chance; **avoir de la** ~ be lucky; **quelle** ~**!** what luck!

chanceler /ʃɑ̃sle/ [38] *vi* stagger; (fig) falter, waver.

chancelier /ʃɑ̃səlje/ *nm* chancellor.

chanceux, -euse /ʃɑ̃sø, -z/ *adj* lucky.

chandail /ʃɑ̃daj/ *nm* sweater.

chandelier /ʃɑ̃dəlje/ *nm* candlestick.

chandelle /ʃɑ̃dɛl/ *nf* candle; **dîner aux** ~**s** candlelight dinner.

change /ʃɑ̃ʒ/ *nm* (foreign) exchange; (taux) exchange rate.

changement /ʃɑ̃ʒmɑ̃/ *nm* change; ~ **de vitesse** (dispositif) gears.

changer /ʃɑ̃ʒe/ [40] *vt* change; ~ **qch de place** move sth; (échanger) change (**pour, contre** for); ~ **de nom/ voiture** change one's name/car; ~ **de place/train** change places/trains; ~ **de direction** change direction; ~ **d'avis** *ou* **d'idée** change one's mind; ~ **de vitesse** change gear. □ **se** ~ *vpr* change, get changed.

chanson /ʃɑ̃sɔ̃/ *nf* song.

chant /ʃɑ̃/ *nm* singing; (chanson) song; (Relig) hymn.

chantage /ʃɑ̃taʒ/ *nm* blackmail.

chanter /ʃɑ̃te/ [1] *vt* sing; **si cela vous chante** 🆃 if you feel like it. ● *vi* sing; **faire** ~ (délit) blackmail. **chanteur, -euse** *nm,f* singer.

chantier /ʃɑ̃tje/ *nm* building site; ~ **naval** shipyard; **mettre en** ~ get under way, start.

chaos /kao/ *nm* chaos.

chaparder /ʃapaʀde/ [1] *vt* 🆃 pinch 🆃, filch.

chapeau (*pl* ~**x**) /ʃapo/ *nm* hat; ~**!** well done!

chapelet /ʃaplɛ/ *nm* rosary; (fig) string.

chapelle /ʃapɛl/ *nf* chapel.

chapelure /ʃaplyʀ/ *nf* (Culin) breadcrumbs.

chaperonner /ʃapʀɔne/ [1] *vt* chaperone.

chapiteau (*pl* ~**x**) /ʃapito/ *nm* marquee; (de cirque) big top; (de colonne) capital.

chapitre /ʃapitʀ/ *nm* chapter; (fig) subject.

chaque /ʃak/ *adj* every, each.

char /ʃaʀ/ *nm* (Mil) tank; (de carnaval) float; (charrette) cart; (dans l'antiquité) chariot.

charabia /ʃaʀabja/ *nm* 🆃 gibberish.

charade /ʃaʀad/ *nf* riddle.

charbon /ʃaʀbɔ̃/ *nm* coal; ~ **de bois** charcoal.

charcuterie /ʃaʀkytʀi/ *nf* pork butcher's shop; (aliments) (cooked) pork meats. **charcutier, -ière** *nm,f* pork butcher.

chardon /ʃaʀdɔ̃/ *nm* thistle.

charge /ʃaʀʒ/ *nf* load, burden; (Mil, Électr, Jur) charge; (responsabilité) responsibility; **avoir qn à** ~ be responsible for; ~**s** expenses; (de locataire) service charges; **être à la** ~ **de** (*personne*) be the responsibility of; (*frais*) be payable by; ~**s sociales** social security contributions; **prendre en** ~ take charge of.

chargé, ~**e** /ʃaʀʒe/ *adj* (véhicule) loaded; (journée, emploi du temps) busy; (langue) coated. ● *nm,f* ~ **de mission** head of mission; ~ **d'affaires** chargé d'affaires, ~ **de cours** lecturer.

chargement /ʃaʀʒəmɑ̃/ *nm* loading; (objets) load.

charger /ʃaʀʒe/ [40] *vt* load; (Ordinat, Photo) load; (attaquer) charge; (*batterie*) charge; ~ **qn de** (*fardeau*) weigh sb down with; (*tâche*) entrust sb with; ~ **qn de faire** make sb responsible for doing. ● *vi* (attaquer) charge. □ **se ~ de** *vpr* take charge *ou* care of.

chariot /ʃaʀjo/ *nm* (à roulettes) trolley; (US) cart; (charrette) cart.

charitable /ʃaʀitabl/ *adj* charitable.

charité /ʃaʀite/ *nf* charity; **faire la ~ à** give (money) to.

charlatan /ʃaʀlatɑ̃/ *nm* charlatan.

charmant, ~e /ʃaʀmɑ̃, -t/ *adj* charming.

charme /ʃaʀm/ *nm* charm; (qui envoûte) spell. **charmer** [1] *vt* charm. **charmeur, -euse** *nm, f* charmer.

charnel, ~le /ʃaʀnɛl/ *adj* carnal.

charnière /ʃaʀnjɛʀ/ *nf* hinge; **à la ~ de** at the meeting point between.

charnu, ~e /ʃaʀny/ *adj* plump, fleshy.

charpente /ʃaʀpɑ̃t/ *nf* framework; (carrure) build.

charpentier /ʃaʀpɑ̃tje/ *nm* carpenter.

charpie /ʃaʀpi/ *nf* **en ~** in shreds.

charrette /ʃaʀɛt/ *nf* cart.

charrue /ʃaʀy/ *nf* plough.

chasse /ʃas/ *nf* hunting; (au fusil) shooting; (poursuite) chase; (recherche) hunt(ing); **~ (d'eau)** (toilet) flush; **~ sous-marine** harpoon fishing.

chasse-neige /ʃasnɛʒ/ *nm inv* snowplough.

chasser /ʃase/ [1] *vt* hunt; (au fusil) shoot; (faire partir) chase away; (odeur, employé) get rid of. ● *vi* go hunting; (au fusil) go shooting.

chasseur, -euse /ʃasœʀ, -øz/ *nm, f* hunter. ● *nm* bellboy; (US) bellhop; (avion) fighter plane.

châssis /ʃasi/ *nm* frame; (Auto) chassis.

chasteté /ʃastəte/ *nf* chastity.

chat /ʃa/ *nm* cat; (mâle) tomcat.

châtaigne /ʃatɛɲ/ *nf* chestnut. **châtaignier** *nm* chestnut tree. **châtain** *a inv* chestnut (brown).

château (*pl* ~**x**) /ʃato/ *nm* castle; (manoir) manor; **~ d'eau** water tower; **~ fort** fortified castle.

châtiment /ʃatimɑ̃/ *nm* punishment.

chaton /ʃatɔ̃/ *nm* (chat) kitten.

chatouillement /ʃatujmɑ̃/ *nm* tickling. **chatouiller** [1] *vt* tickle. **chatouilleux, -euse** *adj* ticklish; (susceptible) touchy.

châtrer /ʃatʀe/ [1] *vt* castrate; (chat) neuter.

chatte /ʃat/ *nf* female cat.

chaud, ~e /ʃo, -d/ *adj* warm; (brûlant) hot; (vif; fig) warm. ● *nm* heat; **au ~** in the warm(th); **avoir ~** be warm; be hot; **il fait ~** it is warm; it is hot; **pour te tenir ~** to keep you warm. **chaudement** *adv* warmly; (disputé) hotly.

chaudière /ʃodjɛʀ/ *nf* boiler.

chaudron /ʃodʀɔ̃/ *nm* cauldron.

chauffage /ʃofaʒ/ *nm* heating; **~ central** central heating.

chauffard /ʃofaʀ/ *nm* (péj) reckless driver.

chauffer /ʃofe/ [1] *vt/i* heat (up); (moteur, appareil) overheat. □ **se ~** *vpr* warm oneself (up).

chauffeur /ʃofœʀ/ *nm* driver; (aux gages de qn) chauffeur.

chaume /ʃom/ *nm* (de toit) thatch.

chaussée /ʃose/ *nf* road(way).

chausse-pied (*pl* ~**s**) /ʃospje/ *nm* shoehorn.

chausser /ʃose/ [1] *vt* (chaussures) put on; (enfant) put shoes on (to). ● *vi* **~ bien** (aller) fit well; **~ du 35** take a size 35 shoe. □ **se ~** *vpr* put one's shoes on.

chaussette /ʃosɛt/ *nf* sock.

chausson /ʃosɔ̃/ *nm* slipper; (de bébé) bootee; **~ de danse** ballet shoe; **~ aux pommes** apple turnover.

chaussure /ʃosyʀ/ *nf* shoe; **~ de ski** ski boot; **~ de marche** hiking boot.

chauve /ʃov/ *adj* bald.

chauve-souris (*pl* **chauves-souris**) /ʃovsuʀi/ *nf* bat.

chauvin, ~e /ʃovɛ̃, -in/ *adj* chauvinistic. ● *nm, f* chauvinist.

chavirer /ʃaviʀe/ [1] *vt* (bateau) capsize; (objets) tip over.

chef /ʃɛf/ *nm* leader, head; (supérieur) boss, superior; (Culin) chef; (de tribu) chief; **architecte en ~** chief *ou* head architect; **~ d'accusation** (Jur) charge; **~ d'équipe** foreman; (Sport) captain; ~ **d'État** head of State; ~ **de famille** head of the family; ~ **de file** (Pol) leader; ~ **de gare** stationmaster; ~ **d'orchestre** conductor; ~ **de service** department head; ~ **de train** guard; (US) conductor.

chef-d'œuvre (*pl* **chefs-d'œuvre**) /ʃɛdœvR/ *nm* masterpiece.

chef-lieu (*pl* **chefs-lieux**) /ʃɛfljø/ *nm* county town, administrative centre.

chemin /ʃəmɛ̃/ *nm* road; (étroit) lane; (de terre) track; (pour piétons) path; (passage) way; (direction, trajet) way; **avoir du ~ à faire** have a long way to go; ~ **de fer** railway; **par ~ de fer** by rail; ~ **de halage** towpath; ~ **vicinal** country lane.

cheminée /ʃəmine/ *nf* chimney; (intérieure) fireplace; (encadrement) mantelpiece; (de bateau) funnel.

cheminot /ʃəmino/ *nm* railwayman; (US) railroad man.

chemise /ʃəmiz/ *nf* shirt; (dossier) folder; (de livre) jacket; ~ **de nuit** nightdress. **chemisette** *nf* short-sleeved shirt. **chemisier** *nm* blouse.

chêne /ʃɛn/ *nm* oak.

chenil /ʃəni(l)/ *nm* (pension) kennels (+ *sg*).

chenille /ʃənij/ *nf* caterpillar; **véhicule à ~s** tracked vehicle.

cheptel /ʃɛptɛl/ *nm* livestock.

chèque /ʃɛk/ *nm* cheque; ~ **sans provision** bad cheque; ~ **de voyage** traveller's cheque. **chéquier** *nm* chequebook.

cher, chère /ʃɛR/ *adj* (coûteux) dear, expensive; (aimé) dear; (dans la correspondance) dear. ● *adv* (coûter, payer) a lot (of money); (en importance) dearly. ● *nm, f* **mon ~, ma chère** my dear.

chercher /ʃɛRʃe/ [1] *vt* look for; (aide, paix, gloire) seek; **aller ~** go and get *ou* fetch, go for; ~ **à faire** attempt to do; ~ **la petite bête** be finicky.

chercheur, -euse /ʃɛRʃœR, -øz/ *nm, f* research worker.

chèrement /ʃɛRmã/ *adv* dearly.

chéri, ~e /ʃeRi/ *adj* beloved. ● *nm, f* darling.

chérir /ʃeRiR/ [2] *vt* cherish.

chétif, -ive /ʃetif, -v/ *adj* puny.

cheval (*pl* **-aux**) /ʃəval, -o/ *nm* horse; **à ~** on horseback; **à ~ sur** astride, straddling; **faire du ~** ride, go horse-riding.

chevalerie /ʃəvalRi/ *nf* chivalry.

chevalet /ʃəvalɛ/ *nm* easel; (de menuisier) trestle.

chevalier /ʃəvalje/ *nm* knight.

chevalière /ʃəvaljɛR/ *nf* signet ring.

cheval-vapeur (*pl* **chevaux-vapeur**) /ʃəvalvapœR/ *nm* horsepower.

chevaucher /ʃəvoʃe/ [1] *vt* sit astride. □ **se ~** *vpr* overlap.

chevelu, ~e /ʃəvly/ *adj* (péj) long-haired; (Bot) hairy.

chevelure /ʃəvlyR/ *nf* hair.

chevet /ʃəvɛ/ *nm* **au ~ de** at the bedside of; **livre de ~** bedside book.

cheveu (*pl* **~x**) /ʃəvø/ *nm* (poil) hair; **~x** (chevelure) hair; **avoir les ~x longs** have long hair.

cheville /ʃəvij/ *nf* ankle; (fiche) peg, pin; (pour mur) (wall) plug.

chèvre /ʃɛvR/ *nf* goat.

chevreuil /ʃəvRœj/ *nm* roe (deer); (Culin) venison.

chevron /ʃəvRɔ̃/ *nm* (poutre) rafter; **à ~s** herringbone.

chez /ʃe/ *prép* (au domicile de) at the house of; (parmi) among; (dans le caractère ou l'œuvre de) in; **aller ~ qn** go to sb's house; ~ **le boucher** at *ou* to the butcher's; ~ **soi** at home; **rentrer ~ soi** go home. **chez-soi** *nm inv* home.

chic /ʃik/ *a inv* smart; (gentil) kind. ● *nm* style; **avoir le ~ pour** have a knack for; ~ **(alors)!** great!

chicane /ʃikan/ *nf* double bend; **chercher ~ à qn** pick a quarrel with sb.

chiche /ʃiʃ/ *adj* mean (de with); ~ **que je le fais!** 🛠 I bet you I can do it.

chichis /ʃiʃi/ *nmpl* 🛠 fuss.

chicorée /ʃikɔRe/ *nf* (frisée) endive; (à café) chicory.

chien /ʃjɛ̃/ *nm* dog; ~ **d'aveugle** guide dog; ~ **de garde** watch-dog. **chienne** *nf* dog, bitch.

chiffon /ʃifɔ̃/ nm rag; (pour nettoyer) duster; ∼ **humide** damp cloth. **chiffonner** [1] vt crumple; (préoccuper Ⅰ) bother.

chiffre /ʃifʀ/ nm figure; (numéro) number; (code) code; ∼**s arabes/romains** Arabic/Roman numerals; ∼**s (statistiques)** statistics; ∼ **d'affaires** turnover.

chiffrer /ʃifʀe/ [1] vt put a figure on, assess; (texte) encode. □ **se** ∼ **à** vpr come to.

chignon /ʃiɲɔ̃/ nm bun, chignon.

Chili /ʃili/ nm Chile.

chimère /ʃimɛʀ/ nf fantasy.

chimie /ʃimi/ nf chemistry. **chimique** adj chemical. **chimiste** nmf chemist.

chimpanzé /ʃɛ̃pɑ̃ze/ nm chimpanzee.

Chine /ʃin/ nf China.

chinois, ∼**e** /ʃinwa, -z/ adj Chinese. ● nm (Ling) Chinese. **C**∼, ∼**e** nm,f Chinese.

chiot /ʃjo/ nm pup(py).

chipoter /ʃipɔte/ [1] vi (manger) pick at one's food; (discuter) quibble.

chips /ʃips/ nf inv crisp; (US) chip.

chirurgie /ʃiʀyʀʒi/ nf surgery; ∼ **esthétique** plastic surgery. **chirurgien** nm surgeon.

chlore /klɔʀ/ nm chlorine.

choc /ʃɔk/ nm (heurt) impact, shock; (émotion) shock; (collision) crash; (affrontement) clash; (Méd) shock; **sous le** ∼ in shock.

chocolat /ʃɔkɔla/ nm chocolate; (à boire) drinking chocolate; ∼ **au lait** milk chocolate; ∼ **chaud** hot chocolate; ∼ **noir** plain ou dark chocolate.

chœur /kœʀ/ nm (antique) chorus; (chanteurs, nef) choir; **en** ∼ in chorus.

choisir /ʃwaziʀ/ [2] vt choose, select.

choix /ʃwa/ nm choice, selection; **fromage ou dessert au** ∼ a choice of cheese ou dessert; **de** ∼ choice; **de premier** ∼ top quality.

chômage /ʃomaʒ/ nm unemployment; **au** ∼, **en** ∼ unemployed; **mettre en** ∼ **technique** lay off.

chômeur, **-euse** /ʃomœʀ, -øz/ nm,f unemployed person; **les** ∼**s** the unemployed.

choquer /ʃɔke/ [1] vt shock; (commotionner) shake.

choral, ∼**e** (mpl ∼**s**) /kɔʀal/ adj choral. **chorale** nf choir, choral society.

chorégraphie /kɔʀegʀafi/ nf choreography.

choriste /kɔʀist/ nmf (à l'église) chorister; (à l'opéra) member of the chorus ou choir.

chose /ʃoz/ nf thing; (très) **peu de** ∼ nothing much; **pas grand** ∼ not much.

chou (pl ∼**x**) /ʃu/ nm cabbage; ∼ (à **la crème**) cream puff; ∼ **de Bruxelles** Brussels sprout; **mon petit** ∼ Ⅰ my dear.

chouchou, ∼**te** /ʃuʃu, -t/ nm,f (de professeur) pet; (du public) darling.

choucroute /ʃukʀut/ nf sauerkraut.

chouette /ʃwɛt/ nf owl. ● adj Ⅰ super.

chou-fleur (pl **choux-fleurs**) /ʃuflœʀ/ nm cauliflower.

choyer /ʃwaje/ [31] vt pamper.

chrétien, ∼**ne** /kʀetjɛ̃, -jɛn/ a & nm,f Christian.

Christ /kʀist/ nm **le** ∼ Christ.

chrome /kʀom/ nm chromium, chrome.

chromosome /kʀɔmozom/ nm chromosome.

chronique /kʀɔnik/ adj chronic. ● nf (rubrique) column; (nouvelles) news; (annales) chronicle.

chronologique /kʀɔnɔlɔʒik/ adj chronological.

chronomètre /kʀɔnɔmɛtʀ/ nm stopwatch. **chronométrer** [14] vt time.

chrysanthème /kʀizɑ̃tɛm/ nm chrysanthemum.

chuchoter /ʃyʃɔte/ [1] vt/i whisper.

chut /ʃyt/ interj shh, hush.

chute /ʃyt/ nf fall; (déchet) offcut; ∼ (**d'eau**) waterfall; ∼ **de pluie** rainfall; ∼ **des cheveux** hair loss; ∼ **des ventes** drop in sales; ∼ **de 5%** 5% drop. **chuter** [1] vi fall.

Chypre /ʃipʀ/ *nf* Cyprus.

ci /si/ *adv* here; **~-gît** here lies; **cet homme-~** this man; **ces maisons-~** these houses.

ci-après /siapʀɛ/ *adv* below.

cible /sibl/ *nf* target.

ciboulette /sibulɛt/ *nf* (Culin) chives (+ *pl*).

cicatrice /sikatʀis/ *nf* scar.

cicatriser /sikatʀize/ [1] *vt* heal. □ **se ~** *vpr* heal.

ci-dessous /sidəsu/ *adv* below.

ci-dessus /sidəsy/ *adv* above.

cidre /sidʀ/ *nm* cider.

ciel (*pl* **cieux, ciels**) /sjɛl, sjø/ *nm* sky; (Relig) heaven; **cieux** (Relig) heaven.

cierge /sjɛʀʒ/ *nm* (church) candle.

cigale /sigal/ *nf* cicada.

cigare /sigaʀ/ *nm* cigar.

cigarette /sigaʀɛt/ *nf* cigarette.

cigogne /sigɔɲ/ *nf* stork.

ci-joint /siʒwɛ̃/ *adv* enclosed.

cil /sil/ *nm* eyelash.

cime /sim/ *nf* peak, tip.

ciment /simɑ̃/ *nm* cement.

cimetière /simtjɛʀ/ *nm* cemetery, graveyard; **~ de voitures** breaker's yard.

cinéaste /sineast/ *nmf* film-maker.

cinéma /sinema/ *nm* cinema; (US) movie theater. **cinémathèque** *nf* film archive; (salle) film theatre. **cinématographique** *adj* cinema.

cinéphile /sinefil/ *nmf* film lover.

cinglant, ~e /sɛ̃glɑ̃, -t/ *adj* (*vent*) biting; (*remarque*) scathing.

cinglé, ~e /sɛ̃gle/ *adj* Ⅱ crazy.

cinq /sɛ̃k/ *a & nm* five.

cinquante /sɛ̃kɑ̃t/ *a & nm* fifty.

cinquième /sɛ̃kjɛm/ *a & nmf* fifth.

cintre /sɛ̃tʀ/ *nm* coat-hanger; (Archit) curve.

cirage /siʀaʒ/ *nm* polish.

circoncision /siʀkɔ̃sizjɔ̃/ *nf* circumcision.

circonflexe /siʀkɔ̃flɛks/ *adj* circumflex.

circonscription /siʀkɔ̃skʀipsjɔ̃/ *nf* district; **~ électorale** constituency; (US) district; (de conseiller, maire) ward.

circonscrire /siʀkɔ̃skʀiʀ/ [30] *vt* (*incendie, épidémie*) contain; (*sujet*) define.

circonspect, ~e /siʀkɔ̃spɛkt/ *adj* circumspect.

circonstance /siʀkɔ̃stɑ̃s/ *nf* circumstance; (situation) situation; (occasion) occasion; **~s atténuantes** mitigating circumstances.

circuit /siʀkɥi/ *nm* circuit; (trajet) tour, trip.

circulaire /siʀkylɛʀ/ *a & nf* circular.

circulation /siʀkylasjɔ̃/ *nf* circulation; (de véhicules) traffic.

circuler /siʀkyle/ [1] *vi* (se répandre, être distribué) circulate; (aller d'un lieu à un autre) get around; (en voiture) travel; (*piéton*) walk; (être en service) (*bus, train*) run; **faire ~** (*badauds*) move on; (*rumeur*) spread.

cire /siʀ/ *nf* wax.

ciré /siʀe/ *nm* oilskin.

cirer /siʀe/ [1] *vt* polish.

cirque /siʀk/ *nm* circus; (arène) amphitheatre; (désordre: fig) chaos; **faire le ~** Ⅰ make a racket Ⅰ.

ciseau (*pl* **~x**) /sizo/ *nm* chisel; **~x** scissors.

ciseler /sizle/ [6] *vt* chisel.

citadelle /sitadɛl/ *nf* citadel.

citadin, ~e /sitadɛ̃, -in/ *nm,f* city-dweller. ● *adj* city.

citation /sitasjɔ̃/ *nf* quotation; (Jur) summons.

cité /site/ *nf* city; (logements) housing estate; **~ universitaire** (university) halls of residence.

citer /site/ [1] *vt* quote, cite; (Jur) summon.

citerne /sitɛʀn/ *nf* tank.

citoyen, ~ne /sitwajɛ̃, -ɛn/ *nm,f* citizen.

citron /sitʀɔ̃/ *nm* lemon; **~ vert** lime. **citronnade** *nf* lemon squash, (still) lemonade.

citrouille /sitʀuj/ *nf* pumpkin.

civet /sivɛ/ *nm* stew; **~ de lièvre** jugged hare.

civière /sivjɛʀ/ *nf* stretcher.

civil, ~e /sivil/ *adj* civil; (non militaire) civilian; (poli) civil. ● *nm* civilian;

dans le ~ in civilian life; **en** ~ in plain clothes.

civilisation /sivilizasjɔ̃/ *nf* civilization.

civiliser /sivilize/ [1] *vt* civilize. □ **se** ~ *vpr* become civilized.

civique /sivik/ *adj* civic.

clair, ~**e** /klɛʀ/ *adj* clear; (*éclairé*) light, bright; (*couleur*) light; **le plus** ~ **de** most of. ● *adv* clearly; **il faisait** ~ it was already light. ● *nm* ~ **de lune** moonlight; **tirer une histoire au** ~ get to the bottom of things.

clairement *adv* clearly.

clairière /klɛʀjɛʀ/ *nf* clearing.

clairsemé, ~**e** /klɛʀsəme/ *adj* sparse.

clamer /klame/ [1] *vt* proclaim.

clameur /klamœʀ/ *nf* clamour.

clan /klɑ̃/ *nm* clan.

clandestin, ~**e** /klɑ̃dɛstɛ̃, -in/ *adj* secret; (*journal*) underground; (*immigration, travail*) illegal; **passager** ~ stowaway.

clapier /klapje/ *nm* (rabbit) hutch.

clapoter /klapɔte/ [1] *vi* lap.

claquage /klakaʒ/ *nm* strained muscle; **se faire un** ~ pull a muscle.

claque /klak/ *nf* slap; **en avoir sa** ~ (**de**) ⊞ be fed up (with) ⊞.

claquer /klake/ [1] *vi* bang; (*porte*) slam, bang; (*fouet*) crack; (*se casser* ⊞) conk out; (*mourir* ⊞) snuff it ⊞; ~ **des doigts** snap one's fingers; ~ **des mains** clap one's hands; **il claque des dents** his teeth are chattering. ● *vt* (*porte*) slam, bang; (*dépenser* ⊞) blow; (*fatiguer* ⊞) tire out.

claquettes /klakɛt/ *nfpl* tap dancing.

clarifier /klaʀifje/ [45] *vt* clarify.

clarinette /klaʀinɛt/ *nf* clarinet.

clarté /klaʀte/ *nf* light, brightness; (*netteté*) clarity.

classe /klas/ *nf* class; (*salle*: Scol) classroom; (*cours*) class, lesson; **aller en** ~ go to school; **faire la** ~ teach; ~ **ouvrière/moyenne** working/middle class.

classement /klasmɑ̃/ *nm* classification; (*d'élèves*) grading; (*de documents*) filing; (*rang*) place, grade; (*de coureur*) placing.

classer /klase/ [1] *vt* classify; (*par mérite*) grade; (*papiers*) file; (Jur) (*affaire*) close. □ **se** ~ *vpr* rank.

classeur /klasœʀ/ *nm* (*meuble*) filing cabinet; (*chemise*) file; (*à anneaux*) ring binder.

classification /klasifikasjɔ̃/ *nf* classification.

classique /klasik/ *adj* classical; (*de qualité*) classic; (*habituel*) classic, standard. ● *nm* classic; (*auteur*) classical author.

clavecin /klavsɛ̃/ *nm* harpsichord.

clavicule /klavikyl/ *nf* collarbone.

clavier /klavje/ *nm* keyboard; ~ **numérique** keypad.

clé, clef /kle/ *nf* key; (*outil*) spanner; (Mus) clef; ~ **anglaise** (monkey-) wrench; ~ **de contact** ignition key; ~ **à molette** adjustable spanner; ~ **de voûte** keystone; **prix** ~**s en main** (*de voiture*) on-the-road price. ● *a inv* key.

clémence /klemɑ̃s/ *nf* (*de climat*) mildness; (*indulgence*) leniency.

clergé /klɛʀʒe/ *nm* clergy.

clérical, ~**e** (*mpl* -**aux**) /klerikal, -o/ *adj* clerical.

cliché /kliʃe/ *nm* cliché; (Photo) negative.

client, ~**e** /klijɑ̃, -t/ *nm, f* customer; (*d'un avocat*) client; (*d'un médecin*) patient; (*d'hôtel*) guest; (*de taxi*) passenger.

clientèle /klijɑ̃tɛl/ *nf* customers, clientele; (*d'un avocat*) clients, practice; (*d'un médecin*) patients, practice; (*soutien*) custom.

cligner /kliɲe/ [1] *vi* ~ **des yeux** blink; ~ **de l'œil** wink.

clignotant /kliɲɔtɑ̃/ *nm* (Auto) indicator, turn.

clignoter /kliɲɔte/ [1] *vi* blink; (*lumière*) flicker; (*comme signal*) flash.

climat /klima/ *nm* climate.

climatisation /klimatizasjɔ̃/ *nf* air-conditioning.

clin d'œil /klɛ̃dœj/ *nm* wink; **en un** ~ in a flash.

clinique /klinik/ *adj* clinical. ● *nf* (*private*) clinic.

clinquant, ~**e** /klɛ̃kɑ̃, -t/ *adj* showy.

clip /klip/ nm video.

cliquer /klike/ [1] vi (Ordinat) click (sur on).

cliqueter /klikte/ [38] vi (couverts) clink; (clés, monnaie) jingle; (ferraille) rattle. **cliquetis** nm clink(ing), jingle, rattle.

clivage /klivaʒ/ nm divide.

clochard, **~e** /klɔʃaR, -d/ nm, f tramp.

cloche /klɔʃ/ nf bell; (imbécile 🄵) idiot; **~ à fromage** cheese-cover.

cloche-pied: **à ~** /aklɔʃpje/ loc **sauter à ~** hop on one leg.

clocher /klɔʃe/ nm bell-tower; (pointu) steeple; **de ~** parochial.

cloison /klwazɔ̃/ nf partition; (fig) barrier.

cloître /klwatR/ nm cloister. **cloîtrer (se)** [1] vpr shut oneself away.

cloque /klɔk/ nf blister.

clos, **~e** /klo, -z/ adj closed.

clôture /klotyR/ nf fence; (fermeture) closure; (de magasin, bureau) closing; (de débat, liste) close; (en Bourse) close of trading. **clôturer** [1] vt enclose, fence in; (festival, séance) close.

clou /klu/ nm nail; (furoncle) boil; (de spectacle) star attraction; **les ~s** (passage) pedestrian crossing; (US) crosswalk.

clouer /klue/ [1] vt nail down; (fig) pin down; **être cloué au lit** be confined to one's bed; **~ le bec à qn** shut sb up.

clouté, **~e** /klute/ adj studded; **passage ~** pedestrian crossing; (US) crosswalk.

coaliser (se) /(sə)kɔalize/ [1] vpr join forces.

coalition /kɔalisjɔ̃/ nf coalition.

cobaye /kɔbaj/ nm guinea-pig.

cocaïne /kɔkain/ nf cocaine.

cocasse /kɔkas/ adj comical.

coccinelle /kɔksinɛl/ nf ladybird; (US) ladybug.

cocher /kɔʃe/ [1] vt tick (off), check. ● nm coachman.

cochon, **~ne** /kɔʃɔ̃, -ɔn/ nm, f (personne 🄵) pig. ● adj 🄵 filthy. ● nm pig. **cochonnerie** nf (saleté 🄵) filth; (marchandise 🄵) rubbish, junk.

cocon /kɔkɔ̃/ nm cocoon.

cocorico /kɔkɔriko/ nm cock-a-doodle-doo.

cocotier /kɔkɔtje/ nm coconut palm.

cocotte /kɔkɔt/ nf (marmite) casserole; **~ minute®** pressure-cooker; **ma ~** 🄵 my dear.

cocu, **~e** /kɔky/ nm, f 🄵 deceived husband, deceived wife.

code /kɔd/ nm code; **~s** dipped headlights; **se mettre en ~s** dip one's headlights; **~ (à) barres** bar code; **~ confidentiel** (d'identification) PIN number; **~ postal** post code; (US) zip code; **~ de la route** Highway Code. **coder** [1] vt code, encode.

coéquipier, **-ière** /kɔekipje, -jɛR/ nm, f team mate.

cœur /kœR/ nm heart; (aux cartes) hearts (+ pl); **~ d'artichaut** artichoke heart; **~ de palmier** palm heart; **à ~ ouvert** (opération) open-heart; (parler) freely; **avoir bon ~** be kind-hearted; **de bon ~** willingly; (rire) heartily; **par ~** by heart; **avoir mal au ~** feel sick ou nauseous; **je veux en avoir le ~ net** I want to be clear in my own mind (about it).

coffre /kɔfR/ nm chest; (pour argent) safe; (Auto) boot; (US) trunk. **coffre-fort** (pl **coffres-forts**) nm safe.

coffret /kɔfrɛ/ nm casket, box; (de livres, cassettes) boxed set.

cogner /kɔɲe/ [1] vt/i knock. □ **se ~** vpr knock oneself; **se ~ la tête** bump one's head.

cohabiter /kɔabite/ [1] vi live together.

cohérent, **~e** /kɔerɑ̃, -t/ adj coherent; (homogène) consistent.

cohue /kɔy/ nf crowd.

coi, **~te** /kwa, -t/ adj silent.

coiffe /kwaf/ nf headgear.

coiffer /kwafe/ [1] vt do the hair of; (chapeau) put on; (surmonter) cap; **~ qn d'un chapeau** put a hat on sb; **coiffé de** wearing; **être bien/mal coiffé** have tidy/untidy hair. □ **se ~** vpr do one's hair.

coiffeur, **-euse** /kwafœR, -øz/ nm, f hairdresser. **coiffeuse** nf dressing-table.

coiffure /kwafyʀ/ *nf* hairstyle; (métier) hairdressing; (chapeau) hat.

coin /kwɛ̃/ *nm* corner; (endroit) spot; (cale) wedge; **au ~ du feu** by the fireside; **dans le ~** locally; **du ~** local.

coincer /kwɛ̃se/ [10] *vt* jam; (caler) wedge; (attraper 🄸) catch. ▫ **se ~** *vpr* get jammed.

coïncidence /kɔɛ̃sidɑ̃s/ *nf* coincidence.

coing /kwɛ̃/ *nm* quince.

coït /kɔit/ *nm* intercourse.

col /kɔl/ *nm* collar; (de bouteille) neck; (de montagne) pass; **~ blanc** white-collar worker; **~ roulé** polo-neck; (US) turtle-neck; **~ de l'utérus** cervix; **se casser le ~ du fémur** break one's hip.

colère /kɔlɛʀ/ *nf* anger; (accès) fit of anger; **en ~** angry; **se mettre en ~** lose one's temper; **faire une ~** throw a tantrum.

coléreux, -euse /kɔleʀø, -z/ *adj* quick-tempered.

colin /kɔlɛ̃/ *nm* (merlu) hake; (lieu noir) coley.

colique /kɔlik/ *nf* diarrhoea; (Méd) colic.

colis /kɔli/ *nm* parcel.

collaborateur, -trice /kɔlabɔʀatœʀ, -tʀis/ *nm,f* collaborator; (journaliste) contributor; (collègue) colleague.

collaboration /kɔlabɔʀasjɔ̃/ *nf* collaboration (**à** on); (à ouvrage, projet) contribution (**à** to).

collaborer /kɔlabɔʀe/ [1] *vi* collaborate (**à** on); **~ à** (*journal*) contribute to.

collant, ~e /kɔlɑ̃, -t/ *adj* (moulant) skin-tight; (poisseux) sticky. ● *nm* (bas) tights; (US) panty hose.

colle /kɔl/ *nf* glue; (en pâte) paste; (problème 🄸) poser; (Scol 🄸) detention.

collecter /kɔlɛkte/ [1] *vt* collect.

collectif, -ive /kɔlɛktif, -v/ *adj* collective; (*billet, voyage*) group.

collection /kɔlɛksjɔ̃/ *nf* collection; (ouvrages) series (+ *sg*); (du même auteur) set. **collectionner** [1] *vt* collect. **collectionneur, -euse** *nm,f* collector.

collectivité /kɔlɛktivite/ *nf* community; **~ locale** local authority.

collège /kɔlɛʒ/ *nm* secondary school (*up to age 15*); (US) junior high school; (assemblée) college.

collégien, ~ne *nm,f* schoolboy, schoolgirl.

collègue /kɔlɛg/ *nmf* colleague.

coller /kɔle/ [1] *vt* stick; (avec colle liquide) glue; (*affiche*) stick up; (mettre 🄸) stick; (par une question 🄸) stump; (Scol 🄸) **se faire ~** get a detention; **je me suis fait ~ en maths** I failed *ou* flunked maths. ● *vi* stick (**à** to); (être collant) be sticky; **~ à** (convenir à) fit, correspond to.

collet /kɔlɛ/ *nm* (piège) snare; **~ monté** prim and proper; **mettre la main au ~ de qn** collar sb.

collier /kɔlje/ *nm* necklace; (de chien) collar.

colline /kɔlin/ *nf* hill.

collision /kɔlizjɔ̃/ *nf* (choc) collision; (lutte) clash; **entrer en ~ (avec)** collide (with).

collyre /kɔliʀ/ *nm* eye drops (+ *pl*).

colmater /kɔlmate/ [1] *vt* plug, seal.

colombe /kɔlɔ̃b/ *nf* dove.

Colombie /kɔlɔ̃bi/ *nf* Colombia.

colon /kɔlɔ̃/ *nm* settler.

colonel /kɔlɔnɛl/ *nm* colonel.

colonie /kɔlɔni/ *nf* colony; **~ de vacances** children's holiday camp.

colonne /kɔlɔn/ *nf* column; **~ vertébrale** spine; **en ~ par deux** in double file.

colorant /kɔlɔʀɑ̃/ *nm* colouring.

colorier /kɔlɔʀje/ [45] *vt* colour (in).

colosse /kɔlɔs/ *nm* giant.

colza /kɔlza/ *nm* rape(-seed).

coma /kɔma/ *nm* coma; **dans le ~** in a coma.

combat /kɔ̃ba/ *nm* fight; (Sport) match; **~s** fighting. **combatif, -ive** *adj* eager to fight; (*esprit*) fighting.

combattre /kɔ̃batʀ/ [11] *vt/i* fight.

combien /kɔ̃bjɛ̃/ *adv* **~ (de)** (quantité) how much; (nombre) how many; (temps) how long; **~ il a changé!** (comme) how he has changed!; **~ y a-t-il d'ici à ...?** how far is it to ...?; **on est le ~ aujourd'hui?** what's the date today?

combinaison /kɔ̃binɛzɔ̃/ *nf* combination; (de femme) slip; (bleu de travail) boiler suit; (US) overalls; ~ **d'aviateur** flying-suit; ~ **de plongée** wetsuit.

combine /kɔ̃bin/ *nf* trick; (fraude) fiddle; (intrigue) scheme.

combiné /kɔ̃bine/ *nm* (de téléphone) receiver, handset.

combiner /kɔ̃bine/ [1] *vt* (réunir) combine; (calculer) devise; ~ **de faire** plan to do.

comble /kɔ̃bl/ *adj* packed. ● *nm* height; ~**s** (mansarde) attic, loft; **c'est le** ~**!** that's the (absolute) limit!

combler /kɔ̃ble/ [1] *vt* fill; (perte, déficit) make good; (désir) fulfil; ~ **qn de cadeaux** lavish gifts on sb.

combustible /kɔ̃bystibl/ *nm* fuel.

comédie /kɔmedi/ *nf* comedy; (histoire 🔢) fuss; ~ **musicale** musical; **jouer la** ~ put on an act. **comédien, ~ne** *nm, f* actor, actress.

comestible /kɔmɛstibl/ *adj* edible.

comète /kɔmɛt/ *nf* comet.

comique /kɔmik/ *adj* comical, funny; (genre) comic. ● *nm* (acteur) comic; (comédie) comedy; (côté drôle) comical aspect.

commandant /kɔmɑ̃dɑ̃/ *nm* commander; (dans l'armée de terre) major; ~ **(de bord)** captain; ~ **en chef** Commander-in-Chief.

commande /kɔmɑ̃d/ *nf* (Comm) order; (Tech) control; ~**s** (d'avion) controls.

commandement /kɔmɑ̃dmɑ̃/ *nm* command; (Relig) commandment.

commander /kɔmɑ̃de/ [1] *vt* command; (acheter) order; (étude, œuvre d'art) commission; ~ **à** (maîtriser) control; ~ **à qn de** command sb to. ● *vi* be in command.

comme /kɔm/ *adv* **c'est bon!** it's so good!; ~ **il est mignon!** isn't he sweet! ● *conj* (dans une comparaison) as; (dans une équivalence, illustration) like; (en tant que) as; (puisque) as, since; (au moment où) as; **vif** ~ **l'éclair** as quick as a flash; **travailler** ~ **sage-femme** work as a midwife; ~ **ci** ~ **ça** so-so; ~ **il faut** properly; ~ **pour faire** as if to do; **jolie** ~ **tout** as pretty as

anything; **qu'est-ce qu'il y a** ~ **légumes?** what is there in the way of vegetables?

commencer /kɔmɑ̃se/ [10] *vt/i* begin, start; ~ **à faire** begin *ou* start to do.

comment /kɔmɑ̃/ *adv* how; ~**?** (répétition) pardon?; (surprise) what?; ~ **est-il?** what is he like?; **le** ~ **et le pourquoi** the whys and wherefores.

commentaire /kɔmɑ̃tɛʀ/ *nm* comment; (d'un texte, événement) commentary. **commentateur, -trice** *nm, f* commentator.

commenter /kɔmɑ̃te/ [1] *vt* comment on; (film, visite) provide a commentary for; (radio, TV) commentate.

commérages /kɔmeʀaʒ/ *nmpl* gossip.

commerçant, ~e /kɔmɛʀsɑ̃, -t/ *adj* (rue) shopping; (personne) business-minded. ● *nm, f* shopkeeper.

commerce /kɔmɛʀs/ *nm* trade, commerce; (magasin) business; **faire du** ~ be in business.

commercial, ~e (*mpl* **-iaux**) /kɔmɛʀsjal, -jo/ *adj* commercial. **commercialiser** [1] *vt* market.

commettre /kɔmɛtʀ/ [42] *vt* commit.

commis /kɔmi/ *nm* (de magasin) assistant; (de bureau) clerk.

commissaire /kɔmisɛʀ/ *nm* commissioner; (Sport) steward; ~ **(de police)** (police) superintendent. **commissaire-priseur** (*pl* **commissaires-priseurs**) *nm* auctioneer.

commissariat /kɔmisaʀja/ *nm* ~ **(de police)** police station.

commission /kɔmisjɔ̃/ *nf* commission; (course) errand; (message) message; ~**s** shopping.

commode /kɔmɔd/ *adj* handy, convenient; (facile) easy; **il n'est pas** ~ he's a difficult customer. ● *nf* chest (of drawers). **commodité** *nf* convenience.

commotion /kɔmosjɔ̃/ *nf* ~ **(cérébrale)** concussion.

commun, ~e /kɔmœ̃, -yn/ *adj* common; (effort, action) joint; (frais,

pièce) shared; **en ~** jointly; **avoir** *ou*
mettre en ~ share; **le ~ des mortels**
ordinary mortals. **communal, ~e**
(*mpl* **-aux**) *adj* of the commune,
local.

communauté /kɔmynote/ *nf*
community; **~ de biens** joint
ownership.

commune /kɔmyn/ *nf* (circonscription,
collectivité) commune.

communicatif, -ive /kɔmynikatif,
-v/ *adj* (*personne*) talkative; (*gaieté*)
infectious.

communication /kɔmynikasjɔ̃/ *nf*
communication; (téléphonique) call; **~s**
(relations) communications (+ *pl*);
voies *ou* **moyens de ~**
communications (+ *pl*).

communier /kɔmynje/ [45] *vi*
(Relig) receive communion; (fig)
commune.

communiqué /kɔmynike/ *nm*
statement; (de presse) communiqué.

communiquer /kɔmynike/ [1] *vt*
pass on, communicate; (*date,
décision*) announce. ● *vi*
communicate. □ **se ~ à** *vpr* spread
to.

communiste /kɔmynist/ *a & nmf*
communist.

commutateur /kɔmytatœʀ/ *nm*
(Électr) switch.

compagne /kɔ̃paɲ/ *nf* companion.

compagnie /kɔ̃paɲi/ *nf* company;
tenir ~ à keep company; **en ~ de**
together with; **~ aérienne** airline.

compagnon /kɔ̃paɲɔ̃/ *nm*
companion.

comparable /kɔ̃paʀabl/ *adj*
comparable (à to). **comparaison** *nf*
comparison; (littéraire) simile.

comparaître /kɔ̃paʀɛtʀ/ [18] *vi*
(Jur) appear (**devant** before).

comparatif, -ive /kɔ̃paʀatif, -v/ *a*
& nm comparative.

comparer /kɔ̃paʀe/ [1] *vt* compare
(à with). □ **se ~** *vpr* compare
oneself; (être comparable) be
comparable.

compartiment /kɔ̃paʀtimã/ *nm*
compartment.

comparution /kɔ̃paʀysjɔ̃/ *nf* (Jur)
appearance.

compas /kɔ̃pa/ *nm* (pair of)
compasses; (boussole) compass.

compassion /kɔ̃pasjɔ̃/ *nf*
compassion.

compatible /kɔ̃patibl/ *adj*
compatible.

compatir /kɔ̃patiʀ/ [2] *vi*
sympathize; **~ à** share in.

compatriote /kɔ̃patʀijɔt/ *nmf*
compatriot.

compensation /kɔ̃pɑ̃sasjɔ̃/ *nf*
compensation. **compenser** [1] *vt*
compensate for, make up for.

compère /kɔ̃pɛʀ/ *nm* accomplice.

compétence /kɔpetɑ̃s/ *nf*
competence; (fonction) domain,
sphere; **entrer dans les ~s de qn** be
in sb's domain. **compétent, ~e**
adj competent.

compétition /kɔ̃petisjɔ̃/ *nf*
competition; (sportive) event; **de ~**
competitive.

complaire (se) /(sə)kɔ̃plɛʀ/ [47]
vpr **se ~ dans** delight in.

complaisance /kɔ̃plɛzɑ̃s/ *nf*
kindness; (indulgence) indulgence.

complément /kɔ̃plemã/ *nm*
supplement; (Gram) complement; **~
(d'objet)** (Gram) object; **~
d'information** further information.
complémentaire *adj*
complementary; (*renseignements*)
supplementary.

complet, -ète /kɔ̃plɛ, -t/ *adj*
complete; (*train, hôtel*) full. ● *nm*
suit.

compléter /kɔ̃plete/ [14] *vt*
complete; (agrémenter) complement.
□ **se ~** *vpr* complement each other.

complexe /kɔ̃plɛks/ *adj* complex.
● *nm* (sentiment, bâtiments) complex.

complexé, ~e /kɔ̃plekse/ *adj* **être
~** have a lot of hang-ups.

complice /kɔ̃plis/ *nm* accomplice.

compliment /kɔ̃plimã/ *nm*
compliment; **~s** (félicitations)
compliments, congratulations.

compliquer /kɔ̃plike/ [1] *vt*
complicate. □ **se ~** *vpr* become
complicated.

complot /kɔ̃plo/ *nm* plot.

comportement /kɔ̃pɔʀtəmã/ *nm*
behaviour; (de joueur, voiture)
performance.

comporter /kɔ̃pɔʀte/ [1] vt (être composé de) comprise; (inclure) include; (risque) entail. □ se ~ vpr behave; (joueur, voiture) perform.

composant /kɔ̃pozɑ̃/ nm component.

composé, ~e /kɔ̃poze/ adj composite; (salade) mixed; (guindé) affected. ● nm compound.

composer /kɔ̃poze/ [1] vt make up, compose; (chanson, visage) compose; (numéro) dial; (page) typeset. ● vi (transiger) compromise. □ se ~ de vpr be made up ou composed of.

compositeur, -trice nm, f (Mus) composer.

composter /kɔ̃pɔste/ [1] vt (billet) punch.

compote /kɔ̃pɔt/ nf stewed fruit; ~ de pommes stewed apples.

compréhensible /kɔ̃pʀeɑ̃sibl/ adj understandable; (intelligible) comprehensible.

compréhensif, -ive /kɔ̃pʀeɑ̃sif, -v/ adj understanding.

compréhension /kɔ̃pʀeɑ̃sjɔ̃/ nf understanding, comprehension.

comprendre /kɔ̃pʀɑ̃dʀ/ [50] vt understand; (comporter) comprise, be made up of. □ se ~ vpr (personnes) understand each other; ça se comprend that is understandable.

compresse /kɔ̃pʀɛs/ nf compress.

comprimé /kɔ̃pʀime/ nm tablet.

comprimer /kɔ̃pʀime/ [1] vt compress; (réduire) reduce.

compris, ~e /kɔ̃pʀi, -z/ adj included; (d'accord) agreed; ~ entre (contained) between; service (non) ~ service (not) included; tout ~ (all) inclusive; y ~ including.

compromettre /kɔ̃pʀɔmɛtʀ/ [42] vt compromise. **compromis** nm compromise.

comptabilité /kɔ̃patibilite/ nf accountancy; (comptes) accounts; (service) accounts department.

comptable /kɔ̃tabl/ adj accounting. ● nmf accountant.

comptant /kɔ̃tɑ̃/ adv (payer) (in) cash; (acheter) for cash.

compte /kɔ̃t/ nm count; (facture, comptabilité) account; (nombre exact) right number; ~ bancaire, ~ en

banque bank account; prendre qch en ~, tenir ~ de qch take sth into account; se rendre ~ de realize; demander/rendre des ~s ask for/ give an explanation; à bon ~ cheaply; s'en tirer à bon ~ get off lightly; travailler à son ~ be self-employed; faire le ~ de count; pour le ~ de on behalf of; sur le ~ de about; au bout du ~ all things considered; à rebours countdown.

compte-gouttes /kɔ̃tgut/ nm inv (Méd) dropper; au ~ (fig) in dribs and drabs.

compter /kɔ̃te/ [1] vt count; (prévoir) allow, reckon on; (facturer) charge for; (avoir) have; (classer) consider; ~ faire intend to do. ● vi (calculer, importer) count; ~ avec reckon with; ~ parmi (figurer) be considered among; ~ sur rely on, count on.

compte(-)rendu /kɔ̃tʀɑ̃dy/ nm report; (de film, livre) review.

compteur /kɔ̃tœʀ/ nm meter; ~ de vitesse speedometer.

comptine /kɔ̃tin/ nf nursery rhyme.

comptoir /kɔ̃twaʀ/ nm counter; (de café) bar.

comte /kɔ̃t/ nm count.

comté /kɔ̃te/ nm county.

comtesse /kɔ̃tɛs/ nf countess.

con, ~ne /kɔ̃, kɔn/ adj 🔲 bloody stupid 🔲. ● nm, f 🔲 bloody fool 🔲.

concentrer /kɔ̃sɑ̃tʀe/ [1] vt concentrate. □ se ~ vpr be concentrated.

concept /kɔ̃sɛpt/ nm concept.

concerner /kɔ̃sɛʀne/ [1] vt concern; en ce qui me concerne as far as I am concerned.

concert /kɔ̃sɛʀ/ nm concert; de ~ in unison.

concerter /kɔ̃sɛʀte/ [1] vt organize, prepare. □ se ~ vpr confer.

concession /kɔ̃sesjɔ̃/ nf concession; (terrain) plot.

concevoir /kɔ̃svwaʀ/ [52] vt (imaginer, engendrer) conceive; (comprendre) understand; (élaborer) design.

concierge /kɔ̃sjɛʀʒ/ nmf caretaker.

concilier /kɔ̃silje/ [45] vt reconcile. □ se ~ vpr (s'attirer) win (over).

concis, ~e /kɔ̃si, -z/ adj concise.

conclure /kɔ̃klyʀ/ [16] *vt* conclude; ～ à conclude in favour of. ● *vi* ～ en faveur de/contre find in favour of/against. **conclusion** *nf* conclusion.

concombre /kɔ̃kɔ̃bʀ/ *nm* cucumber.

concordance /kɔ̃kɔʀdɑ̃s/ *nf* agreement.

concourir /kɔ̃kuʀiʀ/ [20] *vi* compete. ● *vt* ～ à contribute towards.

concours /kɔ̃kuʀ/ *nm* competition; (examen) competitive examination; (aide) help; (de circonstances) combination.

concret, -ète /kɔ̃kʀɛ, -t/ *adj* concrete.

concrétiser /kɔ̃kʀetize/ [1] *vt* give concrete form to. □ se ～ *vpr* materialize.

conçu, ～e /kɔ̃sy/ *adj* bien/mal ～ well/badly designed.

concubinage /kɔ̃kybinaʒ/ *nm* cohabitation; vivre en ～ live together, cohabit.

concurrence /kɔ̃kyʀɑ̃s/ *nf* competition; faire ～ à compete with; jusqu'à ～ de up to a limit of.

concurrencer /kɔ̃kyʀɑ̃se/ [10] *vt* compete with.

concurrent, ～e /kɔ̃kyʀɑ̃, -t/ *nm, f* competitor; (Scol) candidate. ● *adj* rival.

condamnation /kɔ̃danasjɔ̃/ *nf* condemnation; (peine) sentence; ～ centralisée des portières central locking. **condamné, ～e** *nm, f* condemned man, condemned woman. **condamner** [1] *vt* (censurer, obliger) condemn; (Jur) sentence; (porte) block up.

condition /kɔ̃disjɔ̃/ *nf* condition; ～s (prix) terms; à ～ de *ou* que provided (that); sans ～ unconditional(ly); sous ～ conditionally.

conditionnel, ～le /kɔ̃disjɔnɛl/ *adj* conditional. ● *nm* conditional (tense).

conditionnement /kɔ̃disjɔnmɑ̃/ *nm* conditioning; (emballage) packaging.

condoléances /kɔ̃dɔleɑ̃s/ *nfpl* condolences.

conducteur, -trice /kɔ̃dyktœʀ, -tʀis/ *nm, f* driver.

conduire /kɔ̃dɥiʀ/ [17] *vt* take (à to); (guider) lead; (Auto) drive; (affaire) conduct; ～ à (faire aboutir) lead to. ● *vi* drive. □ se ～ *vpr* behave.

conduit /kɔ̃dɥi/ *nm* duct.

conduite /kɔ̃dɥit/ *nf* conduct, behaviour; (Auto) driving; (tuyau) pipe; voiture avec ～ à droite right-hand drive car.

confection /kɔ̃fɛksjɔ̃/ *nf* making; de ～ ready-made; la ～ the clothing industry.

conférence /kɔ̃feʀɑ̃s/ *nf* conference; (exposé) lecture; ～ au sommet summit meeting. **conférencier, -ière** *nm, f* lecturer.

confesser /kɔ̃fese/ [1] *vt* confess. □ se ～ *vpr* go to confession.

confiance /kɔ̃fjɑ̃s/ *nf* trust; avoir ～ en trust.

confiant, ～e /kɔ̃fjɑ̃, -t/ *adj* (assuré) confident; (sans défiance) trusting.

confidence /kɔ̃fidɑ̃s/ *nf* confidence.

confidentiel, ～le /kɔ̃fidɑ̃sjɛl/ *adj* confidential.

confier /kɔ̃fje/ [45] *vt* ～ à qn entrust sb with; ～ un secret à qn tell sb a secret. □ se ～ à *vpr* confide in.

confiner /kɔ̃fine/ [1] *vt* confine; ～ à border on. □ se ～ *vpr* confine oneself (à, dans to).

confirmation /kɔ̃fiʀmasjɔ̃/ *nf* confirmation. **confirmer** [1] *vt* confirm.

confiserie /kɔ̃fizʀi/ *nf* sweet shop; ～s confectionery.

confisquer /kɔ̃fiske/ [1] *vt* confiscate.

confit, ～e /kɔ̃fi, -t/ *adj* candied; (fruits) crystallized. ● *nm* ～ de canard confit of duck.

confiture /kɔ̃fityʀ/ *nf* jam.

conflit /kɔ̃fli/ *nm* conflict.

confondre /kɔ̃fɔ̃dʀ/ [3] *vt* confuse, mix up; (étonner) confound. □ se ～ *vpr* merge; se ～ en excuses apologize profusely.

conforme /kɔ̃fɔʀm/ *adj* être ～ à comply with; (être en accord) be in keeping with.

conformer /kɔ̃fɔrme/ [1] *vt* adapt. □ **se ~ à** *vpr* conform to.

conformité /kɔ̃fɔrmite/ *nf* compliance, conformity; **agir en ~ avec** act in accordance with.

confort /kɔ̃fɔr/ *nm* comfort; **tout ~** *adj* with all mod cons. **confortable** *adj* comfortable.

confrère /kɔ̃frɛr/ *nm* colleague.

confronter /kɔ̃frɔ̃te/ [1] *vt* confront; (*textes*) compare. □ **se ~ à** *vpr* be confronted with.

confus, **~e** /kɔ̃fy, -z/ *adj* confused; (*gêné*) embarrassed.

congé /kɔ̃ʒe/ *nm* holiday; (*arrêt momentané*) time off, leave; (*avis de départ*) notice; **en ~** on holiday *ou* leave; **~ de maladie/maternité** sick/ maternity leave; **jour de ~** day off; **prendre ~ de** take one's leave of.

congédier /kɔ̃ʒedje/ [45] *vt* dismiss.

congélateur /kɔ̃ʒelatœr/ *nm* freezer.

congeler /kɔ̃ʒle/ [6] *vt* freeze.

congère /kɔ̃ʒɛr/ *nf* snowdrift.

congrès /kɔ̃grɛ/ *nm* conference; (Pol) congress.

conjoint, **~e** /kɔ̃ʒwɛ̃, -t/ *nm,f* spouse. ● *adj* joint.

conjonctivite /kɔ̃ʒɔ̃ktivit/ *nf* conjunctivitis.

conjoncture /kɔ̃ʒɔ̃ktyr/ *nf* situation; (*économique*) economic climate.

conjugaison /kɔ̃ʒygɛzɔ̃/ *nf* conjugation.

conjugal, **~e** (*mpl* **-aux**) /kɔ̃ʒygal, -o/ *adj* conjugal, married.

conjuguer /kɔ̃ʒyge/ [1] *vt* (Gram) conjugate; (*efforts*) combine. □ **se ~** *vpr* (Gram) be conjugated; (*facteurs*) be combined.

conjurer /kɔ̃ʒyre/ [1] *vt* (*éviter*) avert; (*implorer*) beg.

connaissance /kɔnɛsɑ̃s/ *nf* knowledge; (*personne*) acquaintance; **~s** (science) knowledge; **faire la ~ de** meet; (*apprécier une personne*) get to know; **perdre/reprendre ~** lose/ regain consciousness; **sans ~** unconscious.

connaisseur /kɔnɛsœr/ *nm* expert, connoisseur.

connaître /kɔnɛtr/ [18] *vt* know; (*difficultés, faim, succès*) experience; **faire ~** make known. □ **se ~** *vpr* (se rencontrer) meet; **s'y ~ en** know (all) about.

connecter /kɔnɛkte/ [1] *vt* connect; **être/ne pas être connecté** be on-/ off-line. □ **se ~ à** *vpr* (Ordinat) log on to.

connerie /kɔnri/ *nf* 🗵 **faire une ~** do something stupid; **dire des ~s** talk rubbish.

connu, **~e** /kɔny/ *adj* well-known.

conquérant, **~e** /kɔ̃kerɑ̃, -t/ *nm,f* conqueror.

conquête /kɔ̃kɛt/ *nf* conquest.

consacrer /kɔ̃sakre/ [1] *vt* devote; (Relig) consecrate; (sanctionner) sanction. □ **se ~ à** *vpr* devote oneself to.

conscience /kɔ̃sjɑ̃s/ *nf* conscience; (perception) awareness; (de collectivité) consciousness; **avoir/prendre ~ de** be/become aware of; **perdre/ reprendre ~** lose/regain consciousness; **avoir bonne/mauvaise ~** have a clear/guilty conscience.

conscient, **~e** /kɔ̃sjɑ̃, -t/ *adj* conscious; **~ de** aware *ou* conscious of.

conseil /kɔ̃sɛj/ *nm* (piece of) advice; (assemblée) council, committee; (séance) meeting; (personne) consultant; **~ d'administration** board of directors; **~ en gestion** management consultant; **~ des ministres** Cabinet; **~ municipal** town council.

conseiller[1] /kɔ̃seje/ [1] *vt* advise; **~ à qn de** advise sb to; **~ qch à qn** recommend sth to sb.

conseiller[2], **-ère** /kɔ̃seje, -jɛr/ *nm,f* adviser, counsellor; **~ municipal** town councillor; **~ d'orientation** careers adviser.

consentement /kɔ̃sɑ̃tmɑ̃/ *nm* consent.

conséquence /kɔ̃sekɑ̃s/ *nf* consequence; **en ~** (comme il convient) accordingly; **en ~** (de quoi) as a result of which.

conséquent, **~e** /kɔ̃sekɑ̃, -t/ *adj* consistent, logical; (important) substantial; par ~ consequently, therefore.

conservateur, -trice /kɔ̃sɛʀvatœʀ, -tʀis/ *adj* conservative. ● *nm,f* (Pol) conservative; (de musée) curator. ● *nm* preservative.

conservation /kɔ̃sɛʀvasjɔ̃/ *nf* preservation; (d'espèce, patrimoine) conservation.

conservatoire /kɔ̃sɛʀvatwaʀ/ *nm* academy.

conserve /kɔ̃sɛʀv/ *nf* tinned *ou* canned food; **en ~** tinned, canned; **boîte de ~** tin, can.

conserver /kɔ̃sɛʀve/ [1] *vt* keep; (en bon état) preserve; (Culin) preserve. □ **se ~** (Culin) keep.

considérer /kɔ̃sidere/ [14] *vt* consider; (respecter) esteem; **~ comme** consider to be.

consigne /kɔ̃siɲ/ *nf* (de gare) left-luggage office; (US) baggage checkroom; (somme) deposit; (ordres) orders; **~ automatique** left-luggage lockers; (US) baggage lockers.

consistance /kɔ̃sistɑ̃s/ *nf* consistency; (fig) substance, weight. **consistant, ~e** *adj* solid; (épais) thick.

consister /kɔ̃siste/ [1] *vi* **~ en/dans** consist of/in; **~ à faire** consist in doing.

consoler /kɔ̃sɔle/ [1] *vt* console. □ **se ~** *vpr* find consolation; **se ~ de qch** get over sth.

consolider /kɔ̃sɔlide/ [1] *vt* strengthen; (fig) consolidate.

consommateur, -trice /kɔ̃sɔmatœʀ, -tʀis/ *nm,f* (Comm) consumer; (dans un café) customer.

consommation /kɔ̃sɔmasjɔ̃/ *nf* consumption; (accomplissement) consummation; (boisson) drink; **de ~** (Comm) consumer.

consommer /kɔ̃sɔme/ [1] *vt* consume, use; (manger) eat; (boire) drink; (mariage) consummate. □ **se ~** *vpr* (être mangé) be eaten; (être utilisé) be used.

consonne /kɔ̃sɔn/ *nf* consonant.

constat /kɔ̃sta/ *nm* (official) report; **~ (à l')amiable** accident report drawn up by those involved.

constatation /kɔ̃statasjɔ̃/ *nf* observation, statement of fact.

constater [1] *vt* note, notice; (certifier) certify.

consternation /kɔ̃stɛʀnasjɔ̃/ *nf* dismay.

constipé, ~e /kɔ̃stipe/ *adj* constipated; (fig) uptight.

constituer /kɔ̃stitɥe/ [1] *vt* (composer) make up, constitute; (organiser) form; (être) constitute; **constitué de** made up of. □ **se ~ prisonnier** give oneself up.

constitution /kɔ̃stitysjɔ̃/ *nf* formation, setting up; (Pol, Méd) constitution.

constructeur /kɔ̃stʀyktœʀ/ *nm* manufacturer, builder.

construction /kɔ̃stʀyksjɔ̃/ *nf* building; (structure, secteur) construction; (fabrication) manufacture.

construire /kɔ̃stʀɥiʀ/ [17] *vt* build; (système, phrase) construct.

consulat /kɔ̃syla/ *nm* consulate.

consultation /kɔ̃syltasjɔ̃/ *nf* consultation; (réception: Méd) surgery; (US) office; **heures de ~** surgery *ou* office (US) hours.

consulter /kɔ̃sylte/ [1] *vt* consult. ● *vi* (médecin) hold surgery, see patients. □ **se ~** *vpr* consult together.

contact /kɔ̃takt/ *nm* contact; (toucher) touch; **au ~ de** on contact with; (personne) by contact with, by seeing; **mettre/couper le ~** (Auto) switch on/off the ignition; **prendre ~ avec** get in touch with. **contacter** [1] *vt* contact.

contagieux, -ieuse /kɔ̃taʒjø, -z/ *adj* contagious.

conte /kɔ̃t/ *nm* tale; **~ de fées** fairy tale.

contempler /kɔ̃tɑ̃ple/ [1] *vt* contemplate.

contemporain, ~e /kɔ̃tɑ̃pɔʀɛ̃, -ɛn/ *a & nm,f* contemporary.

contenance /kɔ̃t(ə)nɑ̃s/ *nf* (volume) capacity; (allure) bearing; **perdre ~** lose one's composure.

contenir /kɔ̃t(ə)niʀ/ [58] *vt* contain; (avoir une capacité de) hold. □ **se ~** *vpr* contain oneself.

content, **~e** /kɔ̃tã, -t/ *adj* pleased, happy (**de** with); **~ de faire** pleased *ou* happy to do.

contenter /kɔ̃tãte/ [1] *vt* satisfy. □ **se ~ de** *vpr* content oneself with.

contenu /kɔ̃t(ə)ny/ *nm* (de récipient) contents (+ *pl*); (de texte) content.

conter /kɔ̃te/ [1] *vt* tell, relate.

contestation /kɔ̃tɛstasjɔ̃/ *nf* dispute; (opposition) protest.

contester /kɔ̃tɛste/ [1] *vt* question, dispute; (s'opposer) protest against. ● *vi* protest.

conteur, -euse /kɔ̃tœr, -øz/ *nm,f* storyteller.

contigu, **~ë** /kɔ̃tigy/ *adj* adjacent (**à** to).

continent /kɔ̃tinã/ *nm* continent.

continu, **~e** /kɔ̃tiny/ *adj* continuous.

continuer /kɔ̃tinɥe/ [1] *vt* continue. ● *vi* continue, go on; **~ à** *ou* **de faire** carry on *ou* go on *ou* continue doing.

contorsionner (se) /(sə)kɔ̃tɔrsjɔne/ [1] *vpr* wriggle.

contour /kɔ̃tur/ *nm* outline, contour; **~s** (d'une route) twists and turns, bends.

contourner /kɔ̃turne/ [1] *vt* go round, by-pass; (*difficulté*) get round.

contraceptif, -ive /kɔ̃trasɛptif, -v/ *adj* contraceptive. ● *nm* contraceptive. **contraception** *nf* contraception.

contracter /kɔ̃trakte/ [1] *vt* (*maladie*) contract; (*dette*) incur; (*muscle*) tense; (*assurance*) take out. □ **se ~** *vpr* contract.

contractuel, **~le** /kɔ̃traktɥɛl/ *nm,f* (agent) traffic warden.

contradictoire /kɔ̃tradiktwar/ *adj* contradictory; (*débat*) open.

contraignant, **~e** /kɔ̃trɛɲã, -t/ *adj* restricting.

contraindre /kɔ̃trɛ̃dr/ [22] *vt* force, compel (**à faire** to do).

contrainte /kɔ̃trɛ̃t/ *nf* constraint.

contraire /kɔ̃trɛr/ *adj* opposite; **~ à** contrary to. ● *nm* opposite; **au ~** on the contrary; **au ~ de** unlike.

contrarier /kɔ̃trarje/ [45] *vt* annoy; (*projet, volonté*) frustrate; (chagriner) upset.

contraste /kɔ̃trast/ *nm* contrast.

contrat /kɔ̃tra/ *nm* contract.

contravention /kɔ̃travãsjɔ̃/ *nf* (parking) ticket; **en ~** in breach (**à** of).

contre /kɔ̃tr(ə)/ *prép* against; (en échange de) for; **par ~** on the other hand; **tout ~** close by. **contre-attaque** (*pl* **~s**) *nf* counter-attack. **contre-attaquer** [1] *vt* counter-attack. **contre-balancer** [10] *vt* counterbalance.

contrebande /kɔ̃trəbãd/ *nf* contraband; **faire la ~ de** smuggle.

contrebas: **en ~** /ãkɔ̃trəba/ *loc* below.

contrebasse /kɔ̃trəbas/ *nf* double bass.

contrecœur: **à ~** /akɔ̃trəkœr/ *loc* reluctantly.

contrecoup /kɔ̃trəku/ *nm* effects, repercussions.

contredire /kɔ̃trədir/ [37] *vt* contradict. □ **se ~** *vpr* contradict oneself.

contrée /kɔ̃tre/ *nf* region; (pays) land.

contrefaçon /kɔ̃trəfasɔ̃/ *nf* (objet imité, action) forgery.

contre-indiqué, **~e** /kɔ̃trɛ̃dike/ *adj* (Méd) contra-indicated; (déconseillé) not recommended.

contre-jour: **à ~** /akɔ̃trəʒur/ *loc* against the light.

contrepartie /kɔ̃trəparti/ *nf* compensation; **en ~** in exchange, in return.

contreplaqué /kɔ̃trəplake/ *nm* plywood.

contresens /kɔ̃trəsãs/ *nm* misinterpretation; (absurdité) nonsense; **à ~** the wrong way.

contretemps /kɔ̃trətã/ *nm* hitch; **à ~** (fig) at the wrong time.

contribuable /kɔ̃tribɥabl/ *nmf* taxpayer.

contribuer /kɔ̃tribɥe/ [1] *vt* contribute (**à** to, towards).

contrôle /kɔ̃trol/ *nm* (maîtrise) control; (vérification) check; (des prix) control; (poinçon) hallmark; (Scol) test; **~ continu** continuous assessment; **~ des changes** exchange control; **~ des naissances** birth control; **~ de**

soi-même self-control; ~ **technique** (des véhicules) MOT (test).

contrôler /kɔ̃trole/ [1] *vt* (vérifier) check; (surveiller, maîtriser) control. □ **se** ~ *vpr* control oneself.

contrôleur, -euse /kɔ̃trolœr, -øz/ *nm, f* inspector.

convaincre /kɔ̃vɛ̃kr/ [59] *vt* convince; ~ **qn de faire** persuade sb to do.

convalescence /kɔ̃valesɑ̃s/ *nf* convalescence; **être en** ~ be convalescing.

convenable /kɔ̃vnabl/ *adj* (correct) decent, proper; (approprié) suitable; (acceptable) reasonable, acceptable.

convenance /kɔ̃vnɑ̃s/ *nf* **à ma** ~ to my satisfaction; **les** ~**s** convention.

convenir /kɔ̃vnir/ [58] *vt/i* be suitable; ~ **à** suit; ~ **que** admit that; ~ **de qch** (avouer) admit sth; (s'accorder sur) agree on sth; ~ **de faire** agree to do; **il convient de** it is advisable to; (selon les bienséances) it would be right to.

convention /kɔ̃vɑ̃sjɔ̃/ *nf* agreement, convention; (clause) article, clause; ~**s** (convenances) convention; **de** ~ conventional; ~ **collective** industrial agreement.

convenu, -e /kɔ̃vny/ *adj* agreed.

conversation /kɔ̃vɛrsasjɔ̃/ *nf* conversation.

convertir /kɔ̃vɛrtir/ [2] *vt* convert (à to; en into). □ **se** ~ *vpr* be converted, convert.

conviction /kɔ̃viksjɔ̃/ *nf* conviction; **avoir la** ~ **que** be convinced that.

convivial, ~e (*mpl* **-iaux**) /kɔ̃vivjal, -jo/ *adj* convivial; (Ordinat) user-friendly.

convocation /kɔ̃vɔkasjɔ̃/ *nf* (Jur) summons; (d'une assemblée) convening; (document) notification to attend.

convoi /kɔ̃vwa/ *nm* convoy; (train) train; ~ (**funèbre**) funeral procession.

convoquer /kɔ̃vɔke/ [1] *vt* (assemblée) convene; (personne) summon; **être convoqué pour un entretien** be called for interview.

coopération /kɔɔperasjɔ̃/ *nf* cooperation; (Mil) civilian national service abroad.

coordination /kɔɔrdinasjɔ̃/ *nf* coordination. **coordonnées** *nfpl* coordinates; (adresse) address and telephone number.

copain /kɔpɛ̃/ *nm* friend; (petit ami) boyfriend.

copie /kɔpi/ *nf* copy; (Scol) paper; ~ **d'examen** exam paper *ou* script; ~ **de sauvegarde** back-up copy.

copier /kɔpje/ [45] *vt/i* copy; ~ **sur** (Scol) copy *ou* crib from.

copieux, -ieuse /kɔpjø, -z/ *adj* copious.

copine /kɔpin/ *nf* friend; (petite amie) girlfriend.

coq /kɔk/ *nm* cockerel.

coque /kɔk/ *nf* shell; (de bateau) hull.

coquelicot /kɔkliko/ *nm* poppy.

coqueluche /kɔklyʃ/ *nf* whooping cough.

coquet, ~te /kɔkɛ, -t/ *adj* flirtatious; (élégant) pretty; (somme 🔢) tidy.

coquetier /kɔktje/ *nm* eggcup.

coquillage /kɔkijaʒ/ *nm* shellfish; (coquille) shell.

coquille /kɔkij/ *nf* shell; (faute) misprint; ~ **Saint-Jacques** scallop.

coquin, ~e /kɔkɛ̃, -in/ *adj* mischievous. ● *nm, f* rascal.

cor /kɔr/ *nm* (Mus) horn; (au pied) corn.

corail (*pl* **-aux**) /kɔraj, -o/ *nm* coral.

corbeau (*pl* ~**x**) /kɔrbo/ *nm* (oiseau) crow.

corbeille /kɔrbɛj/ *nf* basket; ~ **à papier** waste-paper basket.

corbillard /kɔrbijar/ *nm* hearse.

cordage /kɔrdaʒ/ *nm* rope; ~**s** (Naut) rigging.

corde /kɔrd/ *nf* rope; (d'arc, de violon) string; ~ **à linge** washing line; ~ **à sauter** skipping-rope; ~ **raide** tightrope; ~**s vocales** vocal cords.

cordon /kɔrdɔ̃/ *nm* string, cord; ~ **de police** police cordon.

cordonnier /kɔrdɔnje/ *nm* cobbler.

Corée /kɔre/ *nf* Korea.

coriace /kɔrjas/ *adj* tough.

corne /kɔrn/ *nf* horn.

corneille /kɔʀnɛj/ nf crow.

cornemuse /kɔʀnəmyz/ nf bagpipes (+ pl).

corner /kɔʀne/ [1] vt (page) turn down the corner of; **page cornée** dog-eared page. ● vi (Auto) hoot, honk.

cornet /kɔʀnɛ/ nm (paper) cone; (crème glacée) cornet, cone.

corniche /kɔʀniʃ/ nf cornice; (route) cliff road.

cornichon /kɔʀniʃɔ̃/ nm gherkin.

corporel, ~le /kɔʀpɔʀɛl/ adj bodily; (châtiment) corporal.

corps /kɔʀ/ nm body; (Mil) corps; **combat ~ à ~** hand-to-hand combat; **~ électoral** electorate; **~ enseignant** teaching profession.

correct, ~e /kɔʀɛkt/ adj proper, correct; (exact) correct.

correcteur, -trice /kɔʀɛktœʀ, -tʀis/ nm,f (d'épreuves) proofreader; (Scol) examiner; **~ liquide** correction fluid; **~ d'orthographe** spell-checker.

correction /kɔʀɛksjɔ̃/ nf correction; (d'examen) marking, grading; (punition) beating.

correspondance /kɔʀɛspɔ̃dɑ̃s/ nf correspondence; (de train, d'autobus) connection; **vente par ~** mail order; **faire des études par ~** do a correspondence course.

correspondant, ~e /kɔʀɛspɔ̃dɑ̃, -t/ adj corresponding. ● nm,f correspondent; penfriend; (au téléphone) **votre ~** the person you are calling.

correspondre /kɔʀɛspɔ̃dʀ/ [3] vi (s'accorder, écrire) correspond; (chambres) communicate. ● v + prép **~ à** (être approprié à) match, suit; (équivaloir à) correspond to. □ **se ~** vpr correspond.

corrida /kɔʀida/ nf bullfight.

corriger /kɔʀiʒe/ [40] vt correct; (devoir) mark, grade, correct; (punir) beat; (guérir) cure.

corsage /kɔʀsaʒ/ nm bodice; (chemisier) blouse.

corsaire /kɔʀsɛʀ/ nm pirate.

Corse /kɔʀs/ nf Corsica. ● nmf Corsican. **corse** adj Corsican.

corsé, ~e /kɔʀse/ adj (vin) full-bodied; (café) strong; (scabreux) racy; (problème) tough.

cortège /kɔʀtɛʒ/ nm procession; **~ funèbre** funeral procession.

corvée /kɔʀve/ nf chore.

cosmonaute /kɔsmɔnot/ nmf cosmonaut.

cosmopolite /kɔsmɔpɔlit/ adj cosmopolitan.

cosse /kɔs/ nf (de pois) pod.

cossu, ~e /kɔsy/ adj (gens) well-to-do; (demeure) opulent.

costaud, ~e /kɔsto, -d/ 🄻 adj strong. ● nm strong man.

costume /kɔstym/ nm suit; (Théât) costume.

cote /kɔt/ nf (classification) mark; (en Bourse) quotation; (de cheval) odds (**de** on); (de candidat, acteur) rating; **~ d'alerte** danger level; **avoir la ~** be popular.

côte /kot/ nf (littoral) coast; (pente) hill; (Anat) rib; (Culin) chop; **~ à ~** side by side; **la C~ d'Azur** the (French) Riviera.

côté /kote/ nm side; (direction) way; **à ~** nearby; **voisin d'à ~** next-door neighbour; **à ~ de** next to; (comparé à) compared to; **à ~ de la cible** wide of the target; **aux ~s de** by the side of; **de ~** (regarder) sideways; (sauter) to one side; **mettre de ~** put aside; **de ce ~** this way; **de chaque ~** on each side; **de tous les ~s** on every side; (partout) everywhere; **du ~ de** (vers) towards; (dans les environs de) near.

côtelette /kotlɛt/ nf chop.

coter /kɔte/ [1] vt (Comm) quote; **coté en Bourse** listed on the Stock Exchange; **très coté** highly rated.

cotiser /kɔtize/ [1] vi pay one's contributions (**à** to); (à un club) pay one's subscription. □ **se ~** vpr club together.

coton /kɔtɔ̃/ nm cotton; **~ hydrophile** cotton wool.

cou /ku/ nm neck.

couchant /kuʃɑ̃/ nm sunset.

couche /kuʃ/ nf layer; (de peinture) coat; (de bébé) nappy; (US) diaper; **~s** (Méd) childbirth; **~s sociales** social strata.

coucher /kuʃe/ [1] *vt* put to bed; (*loger*) put up; (*étendre*) lay down; ~ (*par écrit*) set down. ● *vi* sleep. □ **se** ~ *vpr* go to bed; (*s'étendre*) lie down; (*soleil*) set. ● *nm* ~ (**de soleil**) sunset; **au** ~ **du soleil** at sunset.

couchette /kuʃɛt/ *nf* (*de train*) couchette; (Naut) berth.

coude /kud/ *nm* elbow; (de rivière, chemin) bend; ~ **à** ~ side by side.

cou-de-pied (*pl* **cous-de-pied**) /kudpje/ *nm* instep.

coudre /kudʀ/ [19] *vt/i* sew.

couette /kwɛt/ *nf* duvet, continental quilt.

couler /kule/ [1] *vi* flow, run; (*fromage, nez*) run; (*fuir*) leak; (*bateau*) sink; (*entreprise*) go under; **faire** ~ **un bain** run a bath. ● *vt* (*bateau*) sink; (*sculpture, métal*) cast. □ **se** ~ *vpr* slip (**dans** into).

couleur /kulœʀ/ *nf* colour; (peinture) paint; (aux cartes) suit; ~**s** (teint) colour; **de** ~ (*homme, femme*) coloured; **en** ~**s** (*télévision, film*) colour.

couleuvre /kulœvʀ/ *nf* grass snake.

coulisse /kulis/ *nf* (de tiroir) runner; **à** ~ (*porte, fenêtre*) sliding; ~**s** (Théât) wings; **dans les** ~**s** (fig) behind the scenes.

couloir /kulwaʀ/ *nm* corridor; (Sport) lane; ~ **de bus** bus lane.

coup /ku/ *nm* blow; (choc) knock; (Sport) stroke; (de crayon, chance, cloche) stroke; (de fusil, pistolet) shot; (fois) time; (aux échecs) move; **donner un** ~ **de pied/poing à** kick/punch; **à** ~ **sûr** definitely; **après** ~ after the event; **boire un** ~ 🔟 have a drink; ~ **sur** ~ in rapid succession; **du** ~ as a result; **d'un seul** ~ in one go; **du premier** ~ first go; **sale** ~ dirty trick; **sous le** ~ **de la fatigue/colère** out of tiredness/anger; **sur le** ~ instantly; **tenir le** ~ hold out; **manquer son** ~ 🔟 blow it 🔟; ~ **de chiffon** wipe (with a rag); ~ **de coude** nudge; ~ **de couteau** stab; ~ **d'envoi** kick-off; ~ **d'État** (Pol) coup; ~ **de feu** shot; ~ **de fil** 🔟 phone call; ~ **de filet** haul, (fig) police raid; ~ **de foudre** love at first sight; ~ **franc** free kick; ~ **de frein** sudden braking;

~ **de grâce** coup de grâce; ~ **de main** helping hand; ~ **d'œil** glance; ~ **de pied** kick; ~ **de poing** punch; ~ **de soleil** sunburn; ~ **de sonnette** ring (on a bell); ~ **de téléphone** (tele-)phone call; ~ **de tête** wild impulse; ~ **de théâtre** dramatic event; ~ **de tonnerre** thunderclap; ~ **de vent** gust of wind.

coupable /kupabl/ *adj* guilty. ● *nmf* culprit.

coupe /kup/ *nf* cup; (de champagne) goblet; (à fruits) dish; (de vêtement) cut; (dessin) section; ~ **de cheveux** haircut.

couper /kupe/ [1] *vt* cut; (*arbre*) cut down; (*arrêter*) cut off; (*voyage*) break up; (*appétit*) take away; (*vin*) water down; ~ **par** take a short cut via; ~ **la parole à qn** cut sb short. ● *vi* cut. □ **se** ~ *vpr* cut oneself; **se** ~ **le doigt** cut one's finger; (*routes*) intersect; **se** ~ **de** cut oneself off from.

couple /kupl/ *nm* couple; (d'animaux) pair.

coupure /kupyʀ/ *nf* cut; (billet de banque) note; (de presse) cutting; (pause, rupture) break; ~ (**de courant**) power cut.

cour /kuʀ/ *nf* (court)yard; (du roi) court; (tribunal) court; ~ (**de récréation**) playground; ~ **martiale** court-martial; **faire la** ~ **à** court.

courageux, -euse /kuʀaʒø, -z/ *adj* courageous.

couramment /kuʀamɑ̃/ *adv* frequently; (*parler*) fluently.

courant, ~e /kuʀɑ̃, -t/ *adj* standard, ordinary; (en cours) current. ● *nm* current; (de mode, d'idées) trend; ~ **d'air** draught; **dans le** ~ **de** in the course of; **être/mettre au** ~ **de** know/tell about; (à jour) be/ bring up to date on.

courbature /kuʀbatyʀ/ *nf* ache; **avoir des** ~**s** be stiff, ache.

courber /kuʀbe/ [1] *vt* bend.

coureur, -euse /kuʀœʀ, -øz/ *nm,f* (Sport) runner; ~ **automobile** racing driver; ~ **cycliste** racing cyclist. ● *nm* womanizer.

courgette /kuʀʒɛt/ *nf* courgette; (US) zucchini.

courir /kuRiR/ [20] *vi* run; (se hâter) rush; (*nouvelles*) go round; ~ après qn/qch chase after sb/sth. ● *vt* (*risque*) run; (*danger*) face; (*épreuve sportive*) run *ou* compete in; (*fréquenter*) do the rounds of; (*filles*) chase (after).

couronne /kuRɔn/ *nf* crown; (de fleurs) wreath.

couronnement /kuRɔnmã/ *nm* coronation, crowning; (fig) crowning achievement.

courrier /kuRje/ *nm* post, mail; (à écrire) letters; ~ du cœur problem page; ~ électronique e-mail.

cours /kuR/ *nm* (leçon) class; (série de leçons) course; (prix) price; (cote) (de valeur, denrée) price; (de devises) exchange rate; (déroulement, d'une rivière) course; (allée) avenue; au ~ de in the course of; avoir ~ (*monnaie*) be legal tender; (fig) be current; (Scol) have a lesson; ~ d'eau river, stream; ~ du soir evening class; ~ particulier private lesson; ~ magistral (Univ) lecture; en ~ current; (*travail*) in progress; en ~ de route along the way.

course /kuRs/ *nf* running; (épreuve de vitesse) race; (activité) racing; (entre rivaux: fig) race; (de projectile) flight; (voyage) journey; (commission) errand; ~s (achats) shopping; (de chevaux) races; faire la ~ avec qn race sb.

coursier, -ière /kuRsje, -jɛR/ *nm,f* messenger.

court, ~e /kuR, -t/ *adj* short. ● *adv* short; à ~ de short of; pris de ~ caught unawares. ● *nm* ~ (de tennis) (tennis) court.

courtier, -ière /kuRtje, -jɛR/ *nm,f* broker.

courtiser /kuRtize/ [1] *vt* woo, court.

courtois, ~e /kuRtwa, -z/ *adj* courteous. **courtoisie** *nf* courtesy.

cousin, ~e /kuzɛ̃, -in/ *nm,f* cousin; ~ germain first cousin.

coussin /kusɛ̃/ *nm* cushion.

coût /ku/ *nm* cost; le ~ de la vie the cost of living.

couteau (*pl* ~x) /kuto/ *nm* knife; ~ à cran d'arrêt flick knife.

coûter /kute/ [1] *vt/i* cost; **coûte que coûte** at all costs; **au prix coûtant** at cost (price).

coutume /kutym/ *nf* custom.

couture /kutyR/ *nf* sewing; (métier) dressmaking; (points) seam. **couturier** *nm* fashion designer. **couturière** *nf* dressmaker.

couvée /kuve/ *nf* brood.

couvent /kuvã/ *nm* convent.

couver /kuve/ [1] *vt* (*œufs*) hatch; (*personne*) overprotect, pamper; (*maladie*) be coming down with, be sickening for. ● *vi* (*feu*) smoulder; (*mal*) be brewing.

couvercle /kuvɛRkl/ *nm* (de marmite, boîte) lid; (qui se visse) screwtop.

couvert, ~e /kuvɛR, -t/ *adj* covered (de with); (habillé) covered up; (ciel) overcast. ● *nm* (à table) place setting; (prix) cover charge; ~s (couteaux etc.) cutlery; **mettre le ~** lay the table; (abri) cover; à ~ (Mil) under cover; à ~ de (fig) safe from.

couverture /kuvɛRtyR/ *nf* cover; (de lit) blanket; (toit) roofing; (dans la presse) coverage; ~ chauffante electric blanket.

couvre-feu (*pl* ~x) /kuvRəfø/ *nm* curfew.

couvre-lit (*pl* ~s) /kuvRəli/ *nm* bedspread.

couvrir /kuvRiR/ [21] *vt* cover. □ se ~ *vpr* (s'habiller) wrap up; (se coiffer) put one's hat on; (ciel) become overcast.

covoiturage /kɔvwatyRaʒ/ *nm* car sharing.

cracher /kRaʃe/ [1] *vi* spit; (radio) crackle. ● *vt* spit (out); (fumée) belch out.

crachin /kRaʃɛ̃/ *nm* drizzle.

craie /kRɛ/ *nf* chalk.

craindre /kRɛ̃dR/ [22] *vt* be afraid of, fear; (être sensible à) be easily damaged by.

crainte /kRɛ̃t/ *nf* fear (pour for); de ~ de/que for fear of/that. **craintif, -ive** *adj* timid.

crampon /kRãpɔ̃/ *nm* (de chaussure) stud.

cramponner (se) /(sə)kRãpɔne/ [1] *vpr* se ~ à cling to.

cran /kRɑ̃/ nm (entaille) notch; (trou) hole; (courage 🆎) guts 🆎, courage; ~ **de sûreté** safety catch.

crâne /kRɑn/ nm skull.

crapaud /kRapo/ nm toad.

craquer /kRake/ [1] vi crack, snap; (plancher) creak; (couture) split; (fig) (personne) break down; (céder) give in. ● vt (allumette) strike; (vêtement) split.

crasse /kRas/ nf grime.

cravache /kRavaʃ/ nf (horse)whip.

cravate /kRavat/ nf tie.

crayon /kRɛjɔ̃/ nm pencil; ~ **de couleur** coloured pencil; ~ **à bille** ballpoint pen; ~ **optique** light pen.

créateur, -trice /kReatœR, -tRis/ adj creative. ● nm, f creator, designer.

crèche /kRɛʃ/ nf day nursery, crèche; (Relig) crib.

crédit /kRedi/ nm credit; (somme allouée) funds; **à** ~ on credit; **faire**~ give credit (**à** to).

créer /kRee/ [15] vt create; (produit) design; (société) set up.

crémaillère /kRemajɛR/ nf **pendre la** ~ have a house-warming party.

crème /kRɛm/ a inv cream. ● nm (café) ~ espresso with milk. ● nf cream; (dessert) cream dessert; ~ **anglaise** egg custard; ~ **fouettée** whipped cream; ~ **pâtissière** confectioner's custard. **crémerie** nf dairy. **crémeux, -euse** adj creamy. **crémier, -ière** nm, f dairyman, dairywoman.

créneau (pl ~x) /kReno/ nm (trou, moment) slot, window; (dans le marché) gap; **faire un** ~ parallel-park.

crêpe /kRɛp/ nf (galette) pancake. ● nm (tissu) crêpe; (matière) crêpe (rubber).

crépitement /kRepitmɑ̃/ nm crackling; (d'huile) sizzling.

crépuscule /kRepyskyl/ nm twilight, dusk.

cresson /kRəsɔ̃/ nm (water)cress.

crête /kRɛt/ nf crest; (de coq) comb.

crétin, ~e /kRetɛ̃, -in/ nm, f 🆎 moron 🆎.

creuser /kRøze/ [1] vt dig; (évider) hollow out; (fig) go into in depth.

□ **se** ~ vpr (écart) widen; **se** ~ **(la cervelle)** 🆎 rack one's brains.

creux, -euse /kRø, -z/ adj hollow; (heures) off-peak. ● nm hollow; (de l'estomac) pit; **dans le** ~ **de la main** in the palm of the hand.

crevaison /kRəvɛzɔ̃/ nf puncture.

crevasse /kRəvas/ nf crack; (de glacier) crevasse; (de la peau) chap.

crevé, ~e /kRəve/ adj 🆎 worn out.

crever /kRəve/ [1] vt burst; (pneu) puncture, burst; (exténuer 🆎) exhaust; (œil) put out. ● vi (pneu, sac) burst; (mourir 🆎) die.

crevette /kRəvɛt/ nf ~ **grise** shrimp; ~ **rose** prawn.

cri /kRi/ nm cry; (de douleur) scream, cry; **pousser un** ~ cry out, scream.

criard, ~e /kRijaR, -d/ adj (couleur) garish; (voix) shrill.

crier /kRije/ [45] vi (fort) shout, cry (out); (de douleur) scream; (grincer) creak. ● vt (ordre) shout (out).

crime /kRim/ nm crime; (meurtre) murder.

criminel, ~le /kRiminɛl/ adj criminal. ● nm, f criminal; (assassin) murderer.

crinière /kRinjɛR/ nf mane.

crise /kRiz/ nf crisis; (Méd) attack; (de colère) fit; ~ **cardiaque** heart attack; ~ **de foie** bilious attack; ~ **de nerfs** hysterics (+ pl).

crisper /kRispe/ [1] vt tense; (énerver 🆎) irritate. □ **se** ~ vpr tense; (mains) clench.

critère /kRitɛR/ nm criterion.

critique /kRitik/ adj critical. ● nf criticism; (article) review; (commentateur) critic; **la** ~ (personnes) the critics. **critiquer** [1] vt criticize.

Croate /kRɔat/ adj Croatian. **C**~ nmf Croatian.

Croatie /kRɔasi/ nf Croatia.

croche /kRɔʃ/ nf quaver.

croche-pied (pl ~s) /kRɔʃpje/ nm 🆎 **faire un** ~ **à** trip up.

crochet /kRɔʃɛ/ nm hook; (détour) detour; (signe) (square) bracket; (tricot) crochet; **faire au** ~ crochet.

crochu, ~e /kRɔʃy/ adj hooked.

crocodile /kRɔkɔdil/ nm crocodile.

croire /kʀwaʀ/ [23] *vt* believe (**à, en** in); (*estimer*) think, believe (**que** that). ● *vi* believe.

croisade /kʀwazad/ *nf* crusade.

croisement /kʀwazmɑ̃/ *nm* crossing; (fait de passer à côté de) passing; (carrefour) crossroads.

croiser /kʀwaze/ [1] *vi* (*bateau*) cruise. ● *vt* cross; (*passant, véhicule*) pass; **~ les bras** fold one's arms; **~ les jambes** cross one's legs; (*animaux*) crossbreed. □ **se ~** *vpr* (*véhicules, piétons*) pass each other; (*lignes*) cross. **croisière** *nf* cruise.

croissance /kʀwasɑ̃s/ *nf* growth.

croissant, ~e /kʀwasɑ̃, -t/ *adj* growing. ● *nm* crescent; (pâtisserie) croissant.

croix /kʀwa/ *nf* cross; **~ gammée** swastika; **C~-Rouge** Red Cross.

croquant, ~e /kʀɔkɑ̃, -t/ *adj* crunchy.

croque-monsieur /kʀɔkməsjø/ *nm inv* toasted ham and cheese sandwich.

croque-mort (*pl* **~s**) /kʀɔkmɔʀ/ *nm* 🔟 undertaker.

croquer /kʀɔke/ [1] *vt* crunch; (dessiner) sketch; **chocolat à ~** plain chocolate. ● *vi* be crunchy.

croquis /kʀɔki/ *nm* sketch.

crotte /kʀɔt/ *nf* dropping.

crotté, ~e /kʀɔte/ *adj* muddy.

crottin /kʀɔtɛ̃/ *nm* (horse) dropping.

croupir /kʀupiʀ/ [2] *vi* stagnate.

croustillant, ~e /kʀustijɑ̃, -t/ *adj* crispy; (*pain*) crusty; (fig) spicy.

croûte /kʀut/ *nf* crust; (de fromage) rind; (de plaie) scab; **en ~** (Culin) in pastry.

croûton /kʀutɔ̃/ *nm* (bout de pain) crust; (avec potage) croûton.

CRS *abrév m* (**Compagnie républicaine de sécurité**) French riot police; **un ~** *a member of the French riot police.*

cru¹ /kʀy/ ⇒CROIRE [23].

cru², ~e /kʀy/ *adj* raw; (*lumière*) harsh; (*propos*) crude. ● *nm* vineyard; (vin) vintage wine.

crû /kʀy/ ⇒CROÎTRE [24].

cruauté /kʀyote/ *nf* cruelty.

cruche /kʀyʃ/ *nf* jug, pitcher.

crucial, ~e (*mpl* **-iaux**) /kʀysjal, -jo/ *adj* crucial.

crudité /kʀydite/ *nf* (de langage) crudeness; **~s** (Culin) raw vegetables.

crue /kʀy/ *nf* rise in water level; **en ~** in spate.

crustacé /kʀystase/ *nm* shellfish.

cube /kyb/ *nm* cube. ● *adj* (*mètre*) cubic.

cueillir /kœjiʀ/ [25] *vt* pick, gather; (*personne* 🔟) pick up.

cuiller, cuillère /kɥijɛʀ/ *nf* spoon; **~ à soupe** soup spoon; (mesure) tablespoonful.

cuir /kɥiʀ/ *nm* leather; **~ chevelu** scalp.

cuire /kɥiʀ/ [17] *vt* cook; **~ (au four)** bake. ● *vi* cook; **faire ~** cook.

cuisine /kɥizin/ *nf* kitchen; (art) cookery, cooking; (aliments) food; **faire la ~** cook.

cuisiner /kɥizine/ [1] *vt* cook; (interroger 🔟) grill. ● *vi* cook.

cuisinier, -ière /kɥizinje, -jɛʀ/ *nm,f* cook. **cuisinière** *nf* (appareil) cooker, stove.

cuisse /kɥis/ *nf* thigh; (de poulet) thigh; (de grenouille) leg.

cuisson /kɥisɔ̃/ *nf* cooking.

cuit, ~e /kɥi, -t/ *adj* cooked; **bien ~** well done *ou* cooked; **trop ~** overdone.

cuivre /kɥivʀ/ *nm* copper; **~ (jaune)** brass; **~s** (Mus) brass.

cul /ky/ *nm* (derrière 🆇) backside, bottom, arse 🆇.

culbuter /kylbyte/ [1] *vi* (*personne*) tumble; (*objet*) topple (over). ● *vt* knock over.

culminer /kylmine/ [1] *vi* reach its highest point *ou* peak.

culot /kylo/ *nm* (audace 🔟) nerve, cheek; (Tech) base.

culotte /kylɔt/ *nf* (de femme) pants (+ *pl*), knickers (+ *pl*); (US) panties (+ *pl*); **~ de cheval** riding breeches; **en ~ courte** in short trousers.

culpabilité /kylpabilite/ *nf* guilt.

culte /kylt/ *nm* cult, worship; (religion) religion; (office protestant) service.

cultivateur, -trice /kyltivatœʀ, -tʀis/ *nm,f* farmer.

cultiver /kyltive/ [1] *vt* cultivate; (*plantes*) grow.

culture /kyltyʀ/ *nf* cultivation; (de plantes) growing; (agriculture) farming; (éducation) culture; (connaissances) knowledge; ∼s (terrains) lands under cultivation; ∼ **physique** physical training.

culturel, ∼**le** /kyltyʀɛl/ *adj* cultural.

cumuler /kymyle/ [1] *vt* accumulate; (*fonctions*) hold concurrently.

cure /kyʀ/ *nf* (course of) treatment.

curé /kyʀe/ *nm* (parish) priest.

cure-dent (*pl* ∼**s**) /kyʀdɑ̃/ *nm* toothpick.

curer /kyʀe/ [1] *vt* clean. □ **se** ∼ *vpr* se ∼ les dents/ongles clean one's teeth/nails.

curieux, **-ieuse** /kyʀjø, -z/ *adj* curious. ● *nm, f* (badaud) onlooker.

curiosité /kyʀjozite/ *nf* curiosity; (objet) curio; (spectacle) unusual sight.

curriculum vitae /kyʀikylɔm vite/ *nm inv* curriculum vitae; (US) résumé.

curseur /kyʀsœʀ/ *nm* cursor.

cutané, ∼**e** /kytane/ *adj* skin.

cuve /kyv/ *nf* vat; (à mazout, eau) tank.

cuvée /kyve/ *nf* (de vin) vintage.

cuvette /kyvɛt/ *nf* bowl; (de lavabo) (wash)basin; (des cabinets) pan, bowl.

CV *abrév m* (**curriculum vitae**) CV.

cyberbranché, ∼**e** /sibɛʀbʀɑ̃ʃe/ *adj* cyberwired.

cybercafé /sibɛʀkafe/ *nm* cybercafe.

cyberespace /sibɛʀsɛpas/ *nm* cyberspace.

cybernaute /sibɛʀnot/ *nmf* Netsurfer.

cybernétique /sibɛʀnetik/ *nf* cybernetics (+ *pl*).

cyclisme /siklism/ *nm* cycling.

cycliste /siklist/ *nmf* cyclist. ● *nm* cycling shorts. ● *adj* cycle.

cyclone /siklon/ *nm* cyclone.

cygne /siɲ/ *nm* swan.

cynique /sinik/ *adj* cynical. ● *nm* cynic.

Dd

d' /d/ ⇒DE.

d'abord /dabɔʀ/ *adv* first; (au début) at first.

dactylo /daktilo/ *nf* typist. **dactylographier** [45] *vt* type.

dada /dada/ *nm* hobby-horse.

daim /dɛ̃/ *nm* (fallow) deer; (cuir) suede.

dallage /dalaʒ/ *nm* paving. **dalle** *nf* slab.

daltonien, ∼**ne** /daltɔnjɛ̃, -ɛn/ *adj* colour-blind.

dame /dam/ *nf* lady; (cartes, échecs) queen; ∼**s** (jeu) draughts; (US) checkers.

damier /damje/ *nm* draught-board; (US) checker-board; **à** ∼ chequered.

damner /dane/ [1] *vt* damn.

dandiner (**se**) /(sə)dɑ̃dine/ [1] *vpr* waddle.

Danemark /danmaʀk/ *nm* Denmark.

danger /dɑ̃ʒe/ *nm* danger; **en** ∼ in danger; **mettre en** ∼ endanger.

dangereux, **-euse** /dɑ̃ʒ(ə)ʀø, -z/ *adj* dangerous.

danois, ∼**e** /danwa, -z/ *adj* Danish. ● *nm* (Ling) Danish. **D**∼, ∼**e** *nm, f* Dane.

dans /dɑ̃/ *prép* in; (mouvement) into; (à l'intérieur de) inside, in; **être** ∼ **un avion** be on a plane; ∼ **dix jours** in ten days' time; **boire** ∼ **un verre** drink out of a glass; ∼ **les 10 francs** about 10 francs.

danse /dɑ̃s/ *nf* dance; (art) dancing.

danser /dɑ̃se/ [1] *vt/i* dance. **danseur**, **-euse** *nm, f* dancer.

darne /daʀn/ *nf* steak (of fish).

date /dat/ *nf* date; ∼ **limite** deadline; ∼ **limite de vente** sell-by date; ∼ **de péremption** use-by date.

dater /date/ [1] *vt/i* date; **à ~ de** as from.

datte /dat/ *nf* (fruit) date.

daube /dob/ *nf* casserole.

dauphin /dofɛ̃/ *nm* (animal) dolphin.

davantage /davɑ̃taʒ/ *adv* more; (plus longtemps) longer; **~ de** more; **je n'en sais pas ~** that's as much as I know.

. . . .

de, d' /də, d/

d' before vowel or mute h.

● *préposition*

····▶ of; **le livre ~ mon ami** my friend's book; **un pont ~ fer** an iron bridge.

····▶ (provenance) from.

····▶ (temporel) from; **~ 8 heures à 10 heures** from 8 till 10.

····▶ (mesure, manière) **dix mètres ~ haut** ten metres high; **pleurer ~ rage** cry with rage.

····▶ (agent) by; **un livre ~ Marcel Aymé** a book by Marcel Aymé.

● **de, de l', de la, du,** (*pl* **des**) *déterminant*

····▶ some; **du pain** (some) bread; **des fleurs** (some) flowers; **je ne bois jamais ~ vin** I never drink wine.

de + le = du
de + les = des

. . . .

dé /de/ *nm* (à jouer) dice; (à coudre) thimble; **~s** (jeu) dice.

débâcle /debɑkl/ *nf* (Géog) breaking up; (Mil) rout.

déballer /debale/ [1] *vt* unpack; (révéler) spill out.

débarbouiller /debaʀbuje/ *vt* wash the face of. □ **se ~** *vpr* wash one's face.

débarcadère /debaʀkadɛʀ/ *nm* landing-stage.

débardeur /debaʀdœʀ/ *nm* (vêtement) tank top.

débarquement /debaʀkəmɑ̃/ *nm* disembarkation. **débarquer** [1] *vt/i* disembark, land; (arriver 🄸) turn up.

débarras /debaʀa/ *nm* junk room; **bon ~!** good riddance!

débarrasser /debaʀase/ [1] *vt* clear (**de** of); **~ qn de** relieve sb of; (défaut, ennemi) rid sb of. □ **se ~ de** *vpr* get rid of.

débat /deba/ *nm* debate.

débattre /debatʀ/ [11] *vt* debate. ● *vi* **~ de** discuss. □ **se ~** *vpr* struggle (to get free).

débauche /deboʃ/ *nf* debauchery; (fig) profusion.

débaucher /deboʃe/ [1] *vt* (licencier) lay off; (distraire) tempt away.

débile /debil/ *adj* weak; 🄸 stupid. ● *nmf* moron 🄸.

débit /debi/ *nm* (rate of flow); (élocution) delivery; (de compte) debit; **~ de tabac** tobacconist's shop; **~ de boissons** bar.

débiter /debite/ [1] *vt* (compte) debit; (fournir) produce; (vendre) sell; (dire: péj) spout; (couper) cut up.

débiteur, -trice /debitœʀ, -tʀis/ *nm, f* debtor. ● *adj* (compte) in debit.

déblayer /debleje/ [31] *vt* clear.

déblocage /deblɔkaʒ/ *nm* (de prix) deregulating. **débloquer** [1] *vt* (prix, salaires) unfreeze.

déboiser /debwaze/ [1] *vt* clear (of trees).

déboîter /debwate/ [1] *vi* (véhicule) pull out. ● *vt* (membre) dislocate.

débordement /debɔʀdəmɑ̃/ *nm* (de joie) excess.

déborder /debɔʀde/ [1] *vi* overflow. ● *vt* (dépasser) extend beyond; **~ de** (joie etc.) be brimming over with.

débouché /debuʃe/ *nm* opening; (carrière) prospect; (Comm) outlet; (sortie) end, exit.

déboucher /debuʃe/ [1] *vt* (bouteille) uncork; (évier) unblock. ● *vi* come out (**de** from); **~ sur** (rue) lead into.

débourser /debuʀse/ [1] *vt* pay out.

debout /dəbu/ *adv* standing; (levé, éveillé) up; **être ~, se tenir ~** be standing, stand; **se mettre ~** stand up.

déboutonner /debutɔne/ [1] *vt* unbutton. □ **se ~** *vpr* unbutton oneself; (vêtement) come undone.

débrancher /debʀɑ̃ʃe/ [1] *vt* (prise) unplug; (système) disconnect.

débrayer /debʀeje/ [31] *vi* (Auto) declutch; (faire grève) stop work.

débris /debʀi/ *nmpl* fragments; (détritus) rubbish (+ *sg*); debris.

débrouillard, **~e** /debʀujaʀ, -d/ *adj* [!] resourceful.

débrouiller /debʀuje/ [1] *vt* disentangle; (*problème*) solve. ▫ **se ~** *vpr* manage.

début /deby/ *nm* beginning; **faire ses ~s** (en public) make one's début; **à mes ~s** when I started out. **débutant**, **~e** *nm,f* beginner. **débuter** [1] *vi* begin; (dans un métier etc.) start out.

déca /deka/ *nm* [!] decaf.

deçà: **en ~** /ɑ̃dəsɑ/ *loc* this side. ● *prép* **en ~ de** this side of.

décacheter /dekaʃte/ [6] *vt* open.

décade /dekad/ *nf* ten days; (décennie) decade.

décadent, **~e** /dekadɑ̃, -t/ *adj* decadent.

décalage /dekalaʒ/ *nm* (écart) gap; **~ horaire** time difference. **décaler** [1] *vt* shift.

décalquer /dekalke/ [1] *vt* trace.

décamper /dekɑ̃pe/ [1] *vi* clear off.

décanter /dekɑ̃te/ *vt* allow to settle. ▫ **se ~** *vpr* settle.

décapant /dekapɑ̃/ *nm* chemical agent; (pour peinture) paint stripper. ● *adj* (*humour*) caustic.

décapotable /dekapɔtabl/ *adj* convertible.

décapsuleur /dekapsylœʀ/ *nm* bottle-opener.

décédé, **~e** /desede/ *adj* deceased. **décéder** [14] *vi* die.

déceler /desle/ [6] *vt* detect; (démontrer) reveal.

décembre /desɑ̃bʀ/ *nm* December.

décemment /desamɑ̃/ *adv* decently. **décence** *nf* decency. **décent**, **~e** *adj* decent.

décennie /deseni/ *nf* decade.

décentralisation /desɑ̃tʀalizasjɔ̃/ *nf* decentralization. **décentraliser** [1] *vt* decentralize.

déception /desɛpsjɔ̃/ *nf* disappointment.

décerner /desɛʀne/ [1] *vt* award.

décès /desɛ/ *nm* death.

décevant, **~e** /des(ə)vɑ̃, -t/ *adj* disappointing. **décevoir** [52] *vt* disappoint.

déchaîner /deʃene/ [1] *vt* (*enthousiasme*) rouse. ▫ **se ~** *vpr* go wild.

décharge /deʃaʀʒ/ *nf* (de fusil) discharge; **~ électrique** electric shock; **~ publique** municipal dump.

décharger /deʃaʀʒe/ [40] *vt* unload; **~ qn de** relieve sb from. ▫ **se ~** *vpr* (*batterie, pile*) go flat.

déchausser (se) /(sə)deʃose/ [1] *vpr* take off one's shoes; (*dent*) work loose.

dèche /dɛʃ/ *nf* [!] **dans la ~** broke.

déchéance /deʃeɑ̃s/ *nf* decay.

déchet /deʃɛ/ *nm* (reste) scrap; (perte) waste; **~s** (ordures) refuse.

déchiffrer /deʃifʀe/ [1] *vt* decipher.

déchiqueter /deʃikte/ [38] *vt* tear to shreds.

déchirement /deʃiʀmɑ̃/ *nm* heartbreak; (conflit) split.

déchirer /deʃiʀe/ [1] *vt* (par accident) tear; (lacérer) tear up; (arracher) tear off *ou* out; (diviser) tear apart. ▫ **se ~** *vpr* tear. **déchirure** *nf* tear.

décibel /desibɛl/ *nm* decibel.

décidément /desidemɑ̃/ *adv* really.

décider /deside/ [1] *vt* decide on; (persuader) persuade; **~ que**/**de** decide that/to; **~ de qch** decide on sth. ▫ **se ~** *vpr* make up one's mind (**à** to).

décimal, **~e** (*mpl* **~aux**) /desimal, -o/ *a & nf* decimal.

décisif, **-ive** /desizif, -v/ *adj* decisive.

décision /desizjɔ̃/ *nf* decision.

déclaration /deklaʀasjɔ̃/ *nf* declaration; (commentaire politique) statement; **~ d'impôts** tax return.

déclarer /deklaʀe/ [1] *vt* declare; (*naissance*) register; **déclaré coupable** found guilty; **~ forfait** (Sport) withdraw. ▫ **se ~** *vpr* (*feu*) break out.

déclencher /deklɑ̃ʃe/ [1] *vt* (Tech) set off; (*conflit*) spark off; (*avalanche*) start; (*rire*) provoke. ▫ **se ~** *vpr* (Tech) go off. **déclencheur** *nm* (Photo) shutter release.

déclic /deklik/ *nm* click.

déclin /deklɛ̃/ *nm* decline.

déclinaison /deklinɛzɔ̃/ *nf* (Ling) declension.

décliner /dekline/ [1] *vt* (refuser) decline; (dire) state; (Ling) decline.

décocher /dekɔʃe/ [1] *vt* (coup) fling; (regard) shoot.

décollage /dekɔlaʒ/ *nm* take-off.

décoller /dekɔle/ [1] *vt* unstick. ● *vi* (avion) take off. ◻ **se** ~ *vpr* come off.

décolleté, ~**e** /dekɔlte/ *adj* low-cut. ● *nm* low neckline.

décolorer /dekɔlɔre/ [1] *vt* fade; (cheveux) bleach. ◻ **se** ~ *vpr* fade.

décombres /dekɔ̃bʀ/ *nmpl* rubble.

décommander /dekɔmɑ̃de/ [1] *vt* cancel.

décomposer /dekɔ̃poze/ [1] *vt* break up; (substance) decompose. ◻ **se** ~ *vpr* (pourrir) decompose.

décompte /dekɔ̃t/ *nm* deduction; (détail) breakdown.

décongeler /dekɔ̃ʒle/ [6] *vt* thaw.

déconseillé, ~**e** /dekɔ̃sɛje/ *adj* not recommended, inadvisable.

déconseiller /dekɔ̃sɛje/ [1] *vt* ~ qch à qn advise sb against sth.

décontracté, ~**e** /dekɔ̃trakte/ *adj* relaxed.

déconvenue /dekɔ̃vny/ *nf* disappointment.

décor /dekɔr/ *nm* (paysage) scenery; (de cinéma, théâtre) set; (cadre) setting; (de maison) décor.

décoratif, -ive /dekɔratif, -v/ *adj* decorative.

décorateur, -trice /dekɔratœr, -tris/ *nm,f* (de cinéma) set designer. **décoration** *nf* decoration. **décorer** [1] *vt* decorate.

décortiquer /dekɔrtike/ [1] *vt* shell; (fig) dissect.

découdre (se) /(sə)dekudr/ [19] *vpr* come unstitched.

découler /dekule/ [1] *vi* ~ de follow from.

découper /dekupe/ [1] *vt* cut up; (viande) carve; (détacher) cut out.

découragement /dekuraʒmɑ̃/ *nm* discouragement.

décourager /dekuraʒe/ [40] *vt* discourage. ◻ **se** ~ *vpr* become discouraged.

décousu, ~**e** /dekuzy/ *adj* (vêtement) which has come unstitched; (idées) disjointed.

découvert, ~**e** /dekuvɛr, -t/ *adj* (tête) bare; (terrain) open. ● *nm* (de compte) overdraft; **à** ~ exposed; (fig) openly.

découverte /dekuvɛrt/ *nf* discovery; **à la** ~ **de** in search of.

découvrir /dekuvrir/ [21] *vt* discover; (voir) see; (montrer) reveal. ◻ **se** ~ *vpr* (se décoiffer) take one's hat off; (ciel) clear.

décrasser /dekrase/ [1] *vt* clean.

décrépit, ~**e** /dekrepi, -t/ *adj* decrepit. **décrépitude** *nf* decay.

décret /dekrɛ/ *nm* decree. **décréter** [14] *vt* order; (dire) declare.

décrié, ~**e** /dekrije/ *adj* criticized.

décrire /dekrir/ [30] *vt* describe.

décroché, ~**e** /dekrɔʃe/ *adj* (téléphone) off the hook.

décrocher /dekrɔʃe/ [1] *vt* unhook; (obtenir 🔲) get. ● *vi* (abandonner 🔲) give up; ~ (**le téléphone**) pick up the phone.

décroître /dekrwatr/ [24] *vi* decrease.

déçu, ~**e** /desy/ *adj* disappointed.

décupler /dekyple/ [1] *vt/i* increase tenfold.

dédaigner /dedeɲe/ [1] *vt* scorn.

dédain /dedɛ̃/ *nm* scorn.

dédale /dedal/ *nm* maze.

dedans /dədɑ̃/ *adv & nm* inside; **en** ~ on the inside.

dédicacer /dedikase/ [10] *vt* dedicate; (signer) sign.

dédier /dedje/ [45] *vt* dedicate.

dédommagement /dedɔmaʒmɑ̃/ *nm* compensation. **dédommager** [40] *vt* compensate (**de** for).

déduction /dedyksjɔ̃/ *nf* deduction; ~ **d'impôts** tax deduction.

déduire /deduir/ [17] *vt* deduct; (conclure) deduce.

déesse /dees/ *nf* goddess.

défaillance /defajɑ̃s/ *nf* (panne) failure; (évanouissement) blackout.

défaillant, ~e *adj* (*système*) faulty; (*personne*) faint.

défaire /defɛʀ/ [33] *vt* undo; (*valise*) unpack; (*démonter*) take down. □ se ~ *vpr* come undone; **se ~ de** rid oneself of.

défait, ~e /defɛ, -t/ *adj* (*cheveux*) ruffled; (*visage*) haggard; (*nœud*) undone. **défaite** *nf* defeat.

défaitiste /defetist/ *a & nmf* defeatist.

défalquer /defalke/ [1] *vt* (*somme*) deduct.

défaut /defo/ *nm* fault, defect; (d'un verre, diamant, etc.) flaw; (pénurie) shortage; **à ~ de** for lack of; **pris en ~** caught out; **faire ~** (*argent etc.*) be lacking; **par ~** (Jur) in one's absence; **~ de paiement** non-payment.

défavorable /defavɔʀabl/ *adj* unfavourable.

défavoriser /defavɔʀize/ [1] *vt* discriminate against.

défectueux, **-euse** /defɛktɥø, -z/ *adj* faulty, defective.

défendre /defɑ̃dʀ/ [3] *vt* defend; (interdire) forbid; **~ à qn de** forbid sb to. □ se ~ *vpr* defend oneself; (se protéger) protect oneself; (se débrouiller) manage; **se ~ de** (refuser) refrain from.

défense /defɑ̃s/ *nf* defence; **~ de fumer** no smoking; (d'éléphant) tusk. **défenseur** *nm* defender. **défensif, -ive** *adj* defensive.

déferler /defɛʀle/ [1] *vi* (*vagues*) break; (*violence*) erupt.

défi /defi/ *nm* challenge; (provocation) defiance; **mettre au ~** challenge.

déficience /defisjɑ̃s/ *nf* deficiency. **déficient**, ~e *adj* deficient.

déficit /defisit/ *nm* deficit. **déficitaire** *adj* in deficit.

défier /defje/ [45] *vt* challenge; (braver) defy.

défilé /defile/ *nm* procession; (Mil) parade; (fig) (continual) stream; (Géog) gorge; **~ de mode** fashion parade.

défiler /defile/ [1] *vi* march; (*visiteurs*) stream; (*images*) flash by; (*chiffres, minutes*) add up. □ se ~ *vpr* 🅸 sneak off.

défini, ~e /defini/ *adj* (Ling) definite.

définir /definiʀ/ [2] *vt* define.

définitif, **-ive** /definitif, -v/ *adj* final, definitive; **en définitive** in the end.

définition /definisjɔ̃/ *nf* definition; (de mots croisés) clue.

définitivement /definitivmɑ̃/ *adv* definitively, permanently.

déflagration /deflagʀasjɔ̃/ *nf* explosion.

déflation /deflasjɔ̃/ *nf* deflation. **déflationniste** *adj* deflationary.

défoncé, ~e /defɔ̃se/ *adj* (*terrain*) full of potholes; (*siège*) broken; (*drogué* 🅸) high.

défoncer /defɔ̃se/ [10] *vt* (*porte*) break down; (*mâchoire*) break. □ se ~ *vpr* 🅸 to give one's all.

déformation /defɔʀmasjɔ̃/ *nf* distortion. **déformer** [1] *vt* put out of shape; (*faits, pensée*) distort.

défouler (se) /(sə)defule/ [1] *vpr* let off steam.

défrayer /defʀeje/ [31] *vt* (payer) pay the expenses of; **~ la chronique** be the talk of the town.

défricher /defʀiʃe/ [1] *vt* clear.

défroisser /defʀwase/ [1] *vt* smooth out.

défunt, ~e /defœ̃, -t/ *adj* (mort) late. ● *nm, f* deceased.

dégagé, ~e /degaʒe/ *adj* (*ciel*) clear; (*front*) bare; **d'un ton ~** casually.

dégagement /degaʒmɑ̃/ *nm* clearing; (football) clearance.

dégager /degaʒe/ [40] *vt* (exhaler) give off; (désencombrer) clear; (faire ressortir) bring out; (*ballon*) clear. □ se ~ *vpr* free oneself; (*ciel, rue*) clear; (*odeur*) emanate.

dégarnir (se) /(sə)degaʀniʀ/ [2] *vpr* clear, empty; (*personne*) be going bald.

dégâts /dega/ *nmpl* damage (+ *sg*).

dégel /deʒɛl/ *nm* thaw. **dégeler** [6] *vi* thaw (out).

dégénéré, ~e /deʒeneʀe/ *a & nm,f* degenerate.

dégivrer /deʒivʀe/ [1] *vt* (Auto) de-ice; (*réfrigérateur*) defrost.

déglinguer /deglɛ̃ge/ 🅸 [1] *vt* bust. □ se ~ *vpr* break down.

dégonflé, **~e** /degɔ̃fle/ adj (pneu) flat; (lâche 🔢) yellow 🔢.

dégonfler /degɔ̃fle/ [1] vt deflate. ● vi (blessure) go down. □ **se ~** vpr 🔢 chicken out.

dégouliner /deguline/ [1] vi trickle.

dégourdi, **~e** /degurdi/ adj smart.

dégourdir /degurdir/ [2] vt (membre, liquide) warm up. □ **se ~** vpr se ~ les jambes stretch one's legs.

dégoût /degu/ nm disgust.

dégoûtant, **~e** /degutɑ̃, -t/ adj disgusting.

dégoûter /degute/ [1] vt disgust; ~ qn de qch put sb off sth.

dégradant, **~e** /degradɑ̃, -t/ adj degrading.

dégradation /degradasjɔ̃/ nf damage; **commettre des ~s** cause damage.

dégrader /degrade/ [1] vt (abîmer) damage. □ **se ~** vpr (se détériorer) deteriorate.

dégrafer /degrafe/ [1] vt unhook.

degré /dəgre/ nm degree; (d'escalier) step.

dégressif, **-ive** /degresif, -v/ adj graded; **tarif ~** tapering charge.

dégrèvement /degrɛvmɑ̃/ nm ~ **fiscal** ou **d'impôts** tax reduction.

dégringolade /degrɛ̃ɡɔlad/ nf tumble.

dégrossir /degrosir/ [2] vt (bois) trim; (projet) rough out.

déguerpir /degɛrpir/ [2] vi clear off.

dégueulasse /degœlas/ adj 🔞 disgusting, lousy.

dégueuler /degœle/ [1] vt 🔞 throw up.

déguisement /deɡizmɑ̃/ nm (de carnaval) fancy dress; (pour duper) disguise.

déguiser /deɡize/ [1] vt dress up; (pour duper) disguise. □ **se ~** vpr (au carnaval etc.) dress up; (pour duper) disguise oneself.

déguster /deɡyste/ [1] vt taste, sample; (savourer) enjoy.

dehors /dəɔr/ adv en ~ de outside; (hormis) apart from; **jeter/mettre ~** throw/put out. ● nm outside. ● nmpl (aspect de qn) exterior.

déjà /deʒa/ adv already; (avant) before, already.

déjeuner /deʒœne/ [1] vi have lunch; (le matin) have breakfast. ● nm lunch; **petit ~** breakfast.

delà /dəla/ adv & prép au ~ (de), par ~ beyond.

délai /delɛ/ nm time-limit; (attente) wait; (sursis) extension (of time); **sans ~** immediately; **dans un ~ de 2 jours** within 2 days; **finir dans les ~s** finish within the deadline; **dans les plus brefs ~s** as soon as possible.

délaisser /delese/ [1] vt (négliger) neglect.

délassement /delasmɑ̃/ nm relaxation.

délation /delasjɔ̃/ nf informing.

délavé, **~e** /delave/ adj faded.

délayer /deleje/ [31] vt mix (with liquid); (idée) drag out.

délecter (se) /(sə)delɛkte/ [1] vpr se ~ de delight in.

délégué, **~e** /delege/ nm, f delegate.

délibéré, **~e** /delibere/ adj deliberate; (résolu) determined.

délicat, **~e** /delika, -t/ adj delicate; (plein de tact) tactful. **délicatesse** nf delicacy; (tact) tact. **délicatesses** nfpl (kind) attentions.

délice /delis/ nm delight. **délicieux**, **-ieuse** adj (au goût) delicious; (charmant) delightful.

délier /delje/ [45] vt untie; (délivrer) free. □ **se ~** vpr come untied.

délimiter /delimite/ [1] vt determine, demarcate.

délinquance /delɛ̃kɑ̃s/ nf delinquency. **délinquant**, **~e** a & nm, f delinquent.

délirant, **~e** /delirɑ̃, -t/ adj delirious; (frénétique) frenzied; 🔢 wild.

délire /delir/ nm delirium; (fig) frenzy. **délirer** [1] vi be delirious (de with); 🔢 be off one's rocker 🔢.

délit /deli/ nm offence.

délivrance /delivrɑ̃s/ nf release; (soulagement) relief; (remise) issue. **délivrer** [1] vt free, release; (pays) liberate; (remettre) issue.

déloyal, ∼e (*mpl* **-aux**) /delwajal, -jo/ *adj* disloyal; (*procédé*) unfair.

deltaplane /dɛltaplan/ *nm* hang-glider.

déluge /delyʒ/ *nm* downpour; **le D∼** the Flood.

démagogie /demagɔʒi/ *nm* demagogy. **démagogue** *nmf* demagogue.

demain /dəmɛ̃/ *adv* tomorrow.

demande /dəmɑ̃d/ *nf* request; ∼ **d'emploi** job application; ∼ **en mariage** marriage proposal.

demander /dəmɑ̃de/ [1] *vt* ask for; (*chemin, heure*) ask; (nécessiter) require; ∼ **que/si** ask that/if; ∼ **qch à qn** ask sb sth; ∼ **à qn de** ask sb to; ∼ **en mariage** propose to. □ **se** ∼ *vpr* **se** ∼ **si/où** wonder if/where.

demandeur, **-euse** /dəmɑ̃dœʀ, -øz/ *nm,f* ∼ **d'emploi** job seeker; ∼ **d'asile** asylum-seeker.

démangeaison /demɑ̃ʒezɔ̃/ *nf* itch(ing).

démanteler /demɑ̃tle/ [6] *vt* break up.

démaquillant /demakijɑ̃/ *nm* make-up remover. **démaquiller (se)** [1] *vpr* remove one's make-up.

démarchage /demaʀʃaʒ/ *nm* door-to-door selling.

démarche /demaʀʃ/ *nf* walk, gait; (procédé) step.

démarcheur, **-euse** /demaʀʃœʀ, -øz/ *nm,f* (door-to-door) canvasser.

démarrage /demaʀaʒ/ *nm* start.

démarrer /demaʀe/ [1] *vi* (*moteur*) start (up); (partir) move off; (fig) get moving. ● *vt* 🄳 get moving.

démarreur /demaʀœʀ/ *nm* starter.

démêlant /demelɑ̃/ *nm* conditioner. **démêler** [1] *vt* disentangle.

déménagement /demenaʒmɑ̃/ *nm* move; (transport) removal.

déménager /demenaʒe/ [40] *vi* move (house). ● *vt* (*meubles*) remove.

déménageur /demenaʒœʀ/ *nm* removal man.

démence /demɑ̃s/ *nf* insanity.

démener (se) /(sə)demne/ [6] *vpr* move about wildly; (fig) put oneself out.

dément, ∼e /demɑ̃, -t/ *adj* insane. ● *nm,f* lunatic.

démenti /demɑ̃ti/ *nm* denial.

démentir /demɑ̃tiʀ/ [46] *vt* deny; (contredire) refute; ∼ **que** deny that.

démerder (se) /(sə)demɛʀde/ [1] *vpr* 🄳 manage.

démettre /demɛtʀ/ [42] *vt* (*poignet etc.*) dislocate; ∼ **qn de** relieve sb of. □ **se** ∼ *vpr* resign (de from).

demeure /dəmœʀ/ *nf* residence; **mettre en** ∼ **de** order to.

demeurer /dəmœʀe/ [1] *vi* live; (rester) remain.

demi, ∼e /dəmi/ *adj* half(-). ● *nm,f* half. ● *nm* (bière) (half-pint) glass of beer; (football) half-back. ● *adv* **à** ∼ half; (ouvrir, fermer) half-way; **à la** ∼**e** at half past; **une heure et** ∼**e** an hour and a half; (à l'horloge) half past one; **une** ∼**-journée/-livre** half a day/pound. **demi-cercle** (*pl* ∼**s**) *nm* semicircle. **demi-finale** (*pl* ∼**s**) *nf* semifinal. **demi-frère** (*pl* ∼**s**) *nm* half-brother, stepbrother. **demi-heure** (*pl* ∼**s**) *nf* half-hour, half an hour. **demi-litre** (*pl* ∼**s**) *nm* half a litre. **demi-mesure** (*pl* ∼**s**) *nf* half-measure. **à demi-mot** *adv* without having to express every word. **demi-pension** *nf* half-board. **demi-queue** *nm* boudoir grand piano. **demi-sel** *a inv* slightly salted. **demi-sœur** (*pl* ∼**s**) *nf* half-sister, stepsister.

démission /demisjɔ̃/ *nf* resignation.

demi-tarif (*pl* ∼**s**) /dəmitaʀif/ *nm* half-fare.

demi-tour (*pl* ∼**s**) /dəmituʀ/ *nm* about turn; (Auto) U-turn; **faire** ∼ turn back.

démocrate /demɔkʀat/ *nmf* democrat. ● *adj* democratic. **démocratie** *nf* democracy.

démodé, ∼e /demɔde/ *adj* old-fashioned.

demoiselle /dəmwazɛl/ *nf* young lady; (célibataire) single lady; ∼ **d'honneur** bridesmaid.

démolir /demɔliʀ/ [2] *vt* demolish.

démon /demɔ̃/ *nm* demon; **le D∼** the Devil. **démoniaque** *adj* fiendish.

démonstration /demɔ̃stʀasjɔ̃/ *nf* demonstration; (de force) show.

démonter /demɔ̃te/ [1] *vt* take apart, dismantle; (*installation*) take down; (fig) disconcert. □ **se ~** *vpr* come apart.

démontrer /demɔ̃tʀe/ [1] *vt* demonstrate; (indiquer) show.

démoraliser /demɔʀalize/ [1] *vt* demoralize.

démuni, **~e** /demyni/ *adj* impoverished; **~ de** without.

démunir /demyniʀ/ [2] *vt* **~ de** deprive of. □ **se ~ de** *vpr* part with.

dénaturer /denatyʀe/ [1] *vt* (*faits*) distort.

dénigrement /denigʀəmã/ *nm* denigration.

dénivellation /denivɛlasjɔ̃/ *nf* (pente) slope.

dénombrer /denɔ̃bʀe/ [1] *vt* count.

dénomination /denɔminasjɔ̃/ *nf* designation.

dénommé, **~e** /denɔme/ *nm,f* **le ~ X** the said X.

dénoncer /denɔ̃se/ [10] *vt* denounce. □ **se ~** *vpr* give oneself up. **dénonciateur**, **-trice** *nm,f* informer.

dénouement /denumã/ *nm* outcome; (Théât) dénouement.

dénouer /denwe/ [1] *vt* undo. □ **se ~** *vpr* (*nœud*) come undone.

dénoyauter /denwajote/ [1] *vt* stone.

denrée /dɑ̃ʀe/ *nf* **~ alimentaire** foodstuff.

dense /dɑ̃s/ *adj* dense. **densité** *nf* density.

dent /dɑ̃/ *nf* tooth; **faire ses ~s** teethe; **~ de lait** milk tooth; **~ de sagesse** wisdom tooth; (de roue) cog. **dentaire** *adj* dental.

denté, **~e** /dɑ̃te/ *adj* (*roue*) toothed.

dentelé, **~e** /dɑ̃te/ *adj* jagged.

dentelle /dɑ̃tɛl/ *nf* lace.

dentier /dɑ̃tje/ *nm* dentures (+ *pl*), false teeth (+ *pl*).

dentifrice /dɑ̃tifʀis/ *nm* toothpaste.

dentiste /dɑ̃tist/ *nmf* dentist.

dentition /dɑ̃tisjɔ̃/ *nf* teeth, dentition.

dénudé, **~e** /denyde/ *adj* bare.

dénué, **~e** /denɥe/ *adj* **~ de** devoid of.

dénuement /denymã/ *nm* destitution.

déodorant /deɔdɔʀã/ *nm* deodorant.

dépannage /depanaʒ/ *nm* repair; (Ordinat) troubleshooting. **dépanner** [1] *vt* repair; (fig) help out.

dépanneuse *nf* breakdown lorry.

dépareillé, **~e** /depaʀeje/ *adj* odd, not matching.

départ /depaʀ/ *nm* departure; (Sport) start; **au ~ de Nice** from Nice; **au ~** (d'abord) at first.

département /depaʀtəmã/ *nm* department.

dépassé, **~e** /depase/ *adj* outdated.

dépasser /depase/ [1] *vt* go past, pass; (*véhicule*) overtake; (excéder) exceed; (*rival*) surpass; **ça me dépasse** Ⓘ it's beyond me. ● *vi* stick out.

dépaysement /depeizmã/ *nm* change of scenery; (désagréable) disorientation.

dépêche /depɛʃ/ *nf* dispatch.

dépêcher /depeʃe/ [1] *vt* dispatch. □ **se ~** *vpr* hurry (up).

dépendance /depɑ̃dɑ̃s/ *nf* dependence; (à une drogue) dependency; (bâtiment) outbuilding.

dépendre /depɑ̃dʀ/ [3] *vt* take down. ● *vi* depend (de on); **~ de** (appartenir à) belong to.

dépens /depɑ̃/ *nmpl* **aux ~ de** at the expense of.

dépense /depɑ̃s/ *nf* expense; expenditure.

dépenser /depɑ̃se/ [1] *vt/i* spend; (*énergie etc.*) use up. □ **se ~** *vpr* get some exercise.

dépérir /depeʀiʀ/ [2] *vi* wither.

dépêtrer (se) /(sə)depetʀe/ [1] *vpr* get oneself out (de of).

dépeupler /depœple/ [1] *vt* depopulate. □ **se ~** *vpr* become depopulated.

déphasé, **~e** /defaze/ *adj* Ⓘ out of step.

dépilatoire /depilatwaʀ/ *a & nm* depilatory.

dépistage /depistaʒ/ nm screening. **dépister** [1] vt detect; (criminel) track down.

dépit /depi/ nm resentment; par ~ out of pique; en ~ de despite; en ~ du bon sens in a very illogical way. **dépité**, ~e adj vexed.

déplacé, ~e /deplase/ adj (remarque) uncalled for.

déplacement /deplasmã/ nm (voyage) trip.

déplacer /deplase/ [10] vt move. □ se ~ vpr move; (voyager) travel.

déplaire /deplɛʀ/ [47] vi ~ à (irriter) displease; ça me déplaît I don't like it.

déplaisant, ~e /deplɛzã, -t/ adj unpleasant, disagreeable.

dépliant /deplijã/ nm leaflet.

déplier /deplije/ [45] vt unfold.

déploiement /deplwamã/ nm (démonstration) display; (militaire) deployment.

déplorable /deplɔʀabl/ adj deplorable. **déplorer** [1] vt (trouver regrettable) deplore; (mort) lament.

déployer /deplwaje/ [31] vt (ailes, carte) spread; (courage) display; (armée) deploy.

déportation /depɔʀtasjõ/ nf (en 1940) internment in a concentration camp.

déposer /depoze/ [1] vt put down; (laisser) leave; (passager) drop; (argent) deposit; (plainte) lodge; (armes) lay down. ● vi (Jur) testify. □ se ~ vpr settle.

dépositaire /depozitɛʀ/ nmf (Comm) agent.

déposition /depozisjõ/ nf (Jur) statement.

dépôt /depo/ nm (entrepôt) warehouse; (d'autobus) depot; (particules) deposit; (garantie) deposit; laisser en ~ give for safe keeping; ~ légal formal deposit of a publication with an institution.

dépouille /depuj/ nf skin, hide; ~ (mortelle) mortal remains.

dépouiller /depuje/ [1] vt (courrier) open; (scrutin) count; (écorcher) skin; ~ qn de strip sb of.

dépourvu, ~e /depuʀvy/ adj ~ de devoid of; prendre au ~ catch unawares.

déprécier /depʀesje/ [45] vt depreciate. □ se ~ vpr depreciate.

déprédations /depʀedasjõ/ nfpl damage (+ sg).

dépression /depʀesjõ/ nf depression; ~ nerveuse nervous breakdown.

déprimer /depʀime/ [1] vt depress.

----

depuis /dəpɥi/

● préposition

····➤ (point de départ) since; ~ quand attendez-vous? how long have you been waiting?

····➤ (durée) for; ~ toujours always; ~ peu recently.

● adverbe

····➤ since; il a eu une attaque le mois dernier, ~ nous sommes inquiets he had a stroke last month and we've been worried ever since.

● depuis que conjonction

····➤ since, ever since; Sophie a beaucoup changé depuis que Camille est née Sophie has changed a lot since Camille was born.

----

député /depyte/ nm ≈ Member of Parliament.

déraciné, -e /deʀasine/ nm, f rootless person.

déraillement /deʀajmã/ nm derailment.

dérailler /deʀaje/ [1] vi be derailed; (fig 🔢) be talking nonsense; faire ~ derail. **dérailleur** nm (de vélo) derailleur.

déraisonnable /deʀɛzɔnabl/ adj unreasonable.

dérangement /deʀãʒmã/ nm bother; (désordre) disorder, upset; en ~ out of order; les ~s the fault reporting service.

déranger /deʀãʒe/ [40] vt (gêner) bother, disturb; (dérégler) upset, disrupt. □ se ~ vpr (aller) go; (fig) put oneself out; ça te dérangerait de...? would you mind...?

dérapage /deʀapaʒ/ *nm* skid.
déraper [1] *vi* skid; (fig) (*prix*) get
out of control.

déréglé, **~e** /deʀegle/ *adj* (*vie*)
dissolute; (*estomac*) upset; (*mécanisme, mode*) (that is) not running
properly.

dérégler /deʀegle/ [14] *vt* make go
wrong. □ **se ~** *vpr* go wrong.

dérision /deʀizjɔ̃/ *nf* mockery;
tourner en ~ ridicule.

dérive /deʀiv/ *nf* **aller à la ~** drift.

dérivé /deʀive/ *nm* by-product.

dériver /deʀive/ [1] *vi* (*bateau*) drift;
~ de stem from.

dermatologie /dɛʀmatɔlɔʒi/ *nf*
dermatology.

dernier, **-ière** /dɛʀnje, -jɛʀ/ *adj* last;
(*nouvelles, mode*) latest; (*étage*) top.
● *nm, f* last (one); **ce ~** the latter; **le
~ de mes soucis** the least of my
worries.

dernièrement /dɛʀnjɛʀmɑ̃/ *adv*
recently.

dérober /deʀɔbe/ [1] *vt* steal. □ **se
~** *vpr* slip away; **se ~ à** (*obligation*)
shy away from.

dérogation /deʀɔgasjɔ̃/ *nf* special
authorization.

déroger /deʀɔʒe/ [40] *vi* **~ à** depart
from.

déroulement /deʀulmɑ̃/ *nm* (d'une
action) development.

dérouler /deʀule/ [1] *vt* (*fil etc.*)
unwind. □ **se ~** *vpr* unwind; (avoir
lieu) take place; (*récit, paysage*)
unfold.

déroute /deʀut/ *nf* (Mil) rout.

dérouter /deʀute/ [1] *vt* disconcert.

derrière /dɛʀjɛʀ/ *prép & adv*
behind. ● *nm* back, rear; (postérieur
🄻) behind 🄸; **de ~** (*fenêtre*) back,
rear; (*pattes*) hind.

des /de/ ⇒DE.

dès /dɛ/ *prép* (right) from; **~ lors**
from then on; **~ que** as soon as.

désabusé, **~e** /dezabyze/ *adj*
disillusioned.

désaccord /dezakɔʀ/ *nm*
disagreement.

désaffecté, **~e** /dezafɛkte/ *adj*
disused.

désagréable /dezagʀeabl/ *adj*
unpleasant.

désagrément /dezagʀemɑ̃/ *nm*
annoyance, inconvenience.

désaltérer (**se**) /(sə)dezalteʀe/ [14]
vpr quench one's thirst.

désamorcer /dezamɔʀse/ [10] *vt*
(*situation, obus*) defuse.

désapprobation /dezapʀɔbasjɔ̃/
nf disapproval. **désapprouver** [1]
vt disapprove of.

désarçonner /dezaʀsɔne/ [1] *vt*
throw.

désarmement /dezaʀməmɑ̃/ *nm*
(Pol) disarmament.

désarroi /dezaʀwa/ *nm* distress.

désastre /dezastʀ/ *nm* disaster.
désastreux, **-euse** *adj* disastrous.

désavantage /dezavɑ̃taʒ/ *nm*
disadvantage. **désavantager** [40]
vt put at a disadvantage.

désaveu (*pl* **~x**) /dezavø/ *nm*
denial. **désavouer** [1] *vt* deny.

descendance /desɑ̃dɑ̃s/ *nf*
descent; (enfants) descendants (+ *pl*).
descendant, **~e** *nm, f* descendant.

descendre /desɑ̃dʀ/ [3] *vi* (*aux
être*) go down; (venir) come down;
(*passager*) get off *ou* out; (*nuit*) fall;
~ à pied walk down; **~ par
l'ascenseur** take the lift down; **~ de**
(être issu de) be descended from; **~ à
l'hôtel** go to a hotel; **~ dans la rue**
(Pol) take to the streets. ● *vt* (*aux
avoir*) (*escalier etc.*) go *ou* come
down; (*objet*) take down; (abattre 🄸)
shoot down.

descente /desɑ̃t/ *nf* descent; (à ski)
downhill; (raid) raid; **dans la ~** going
downhill; **~ de lit** bedside rug.

descriptif, **-ive** /dɛskʀiptif, -v/ *adj*
descriptive. **description** *nf*
description.

désemparé, **~e** /dezɑ̃paʀe/ *adj*
distraught.

désendettement /dezɑ̃dɛtmɑ̃/
nm reduction of the debt.

déséquilibré, **~e** /dezekilibʀe/
adj unbalanced; 🄸 crazy. ● *nm, f*
lunatic. **déséquilibrer** [1] *vt* throw
off balance.

désert, **~e** /dezɛʀ, -t/ *adj* deserted.
● *nm* desert.

déserter /dezɛRte/ [1] *vt/i* desert.
déserteur *nm* deserter.

désertique /dezɛRtik/ *adj* desert.

désespérant, **~e** /dezɛspeRɑ̃, -t/ *adj* utterly disheartening.

désespéré, **~e** /dezɛspere/ *adj* in despair; (*état, cas*) hopeless; (*effort*) desperate.

désespérer /dezɛspere/ [14] *vt* drive to despair. ● *vi* despair, lose hope; **~ de** despair of. □ **se ~** *vpr* despair.

désespoir /dezɛspwaR/ *nm* despair; **en ~ de cause** as a last resort.

déshabillé, **~e** /dezabije/ *adj* undressed. ● *nm* négligee.

déshabiller /dezabije/ [1] *vt* undress. □ **se ~** *vpr* get undressed.

désherbant /dezɛRbɑ̃/ *nm* weed-killer.

déshérité, **~e** /dezeRite/ *adj* (*région*) deprived; (*personne*) the underprivileged.

déshériter /dezeRite/ [1] *vt* disinherit.

déshonneur /dezɔnœR/ *nm* disgrace.

déshonorer /dezɔnɔRe/ [1] *vt* dishonour.

déshydrater /dezidRate/ [1] *vt* dehydrate. □ **se ~** *vpr* get dehydrated.

désigner /deziɲe/ [1] *vt* (*montrer*) point to *ou* out; (*élire*) appoint; (*signifier*) designate.

désillusion /dezilyzjɔ̃/ *nf* disillusionment.

désinence /dezinɑ̃s/ *nf* (Gram) ending.

désinfectant /dezɛ̃fɛktɑ̃/ *nm* disinfectant. **désinfecter** [1] *vt* disinfect.

désintéressé, **~e** /dezɛ̃terese/ *adj* (*personne, acte*) selfless.

désintéresser (se) /(sə)dezɛ̃te-Rese/ [1] *vpr* **se ~ de** lose interest in.

désintoxiquer /dezɛ̃tɔksike/ [1] *vt* detoxify; **se faire ~** to undergo detoxification.

désinvolte /dezɛ̃vɔlt/ *adj* casual. **désinvolture** *nf* casualness.

désir /deziR/ *nm* wish, desire; (*convoitise*) desire.

désirer /deziRe/ [1] *vt* want; (*sexuellement*) desire; **vous désirez?** what would you like?

désireux, **-euse** /deziRø, -z/ *adj* **~ de faire** anxious to do.

désistement /dezistəmɑ̃/ *nm* withdrawal.

désobéir /dezɔbeiR/ [2] *vi* **~ (à)** disobey. **désobéissant**, **~e** *adj* disobedient.

désobligeant, **~e** /dezɔbliʒɑ̃, -t/ *adj* disagreeable, unkind.

désodorisant /dezɔdɔRizɑ̃/ *nm* air freshener.

désodoriser /dezɔdɔRize/ [1] *vt* freshen up.

désœuvré, **~e** /dezœvRe/ *adj* at a loose end. **désœuvrement** *nm* lack of anything to do.

désolation /dezɔlasjɔ̃/ *nf* distress.

désolé, **~e** /dezɔle/ *adj* (*au regret*) sorry; (*région*) desolate.

désoler /dezɔle/ [1] *vt* distress. □ **se ~** *vpr* be upset (**de qch** about sth).

désopilant, **~e** /dezɔpilɑ̃, -t/ *adj* hilarious.

désordonné, **~e** /dezɔRdone/ *adj* untidy; (*mouvements*) uncoordinated.

désordre /dezɔRdR/ *nm* untidiness; (Pol) disorder; **en ~** untidy.

désorganiser /dezɔRganize/ [1] *vt* disorganize.

désorienter /dezɔRjɑ̃te/ [1] *vt* disorient.

désormais /dezɔRmɛ/ *adv* from now on.

desquels, **desquelles** /dekɛl/ ⇒LEQUEL.

dessécher /deseʃe/ [1] *vt* dry out. □ **se ~** *vpr* dry out, become dry; (*plante*) wither.

dessein /desɛ̃/ *nm* intention; **à ~** intentionally.

desserrer /desere/ [1] *vt* loosen; **il n'a pas desserré les dents** he never once opened his mouth. □ **se ~** *vpr* come loose.

dessert /desɛR/ *nm* dessert; **en ~** for dessert.

desservir /desɛRviR/ [46] *vt/i* (*débarrasser*) clear away; (*autobus*) serve.

dessin /desɛ̃/ nm drawing; (motif) design; (discipline) art; (contour) outline; **professeur de ~** art teacher; **~ animé** (cinéma) cartoon; **~ humoristique** cartoon.

dessinateur, **-trice** /desinatœr, -tris/ nm, f artist; (industriel) draughtsman.

dessiner /desine/ [1] vt/i draw; (fig) outline. □ **se ~** vpr appear, take shape.

dessoûler /desule/ [1] vt/i sober up.

dessous /dəsu/ adv underneath. ● nm underside, underneath. ● nmpl underwear; **les ~ d'une histoire** what is behind a story; **du ~** bottom; (voisins) downstairs; **en ~**, **par-~** underneath. **dessous-de-plat** nm inv (heat-resistant) table-mat. **dessous-de-table** nm inv backhander. **dessous-de-verre** nm inv coaster.

dessus /dəsy/ adv on top (of it), on it. ● nm top; **du ~** top; (voisins) upstairs; **avoir le ~** get the upper hand. **dessus-de-lit** nm inv bedspread.

destabiliser /destabilize/ [1] vt destabilize, unsettle.

destin /dɛstɛ̃/ nm (sort) fate; (avenir) destiny.

destinataire /dɛstinatɛr/ nmf addressee.

destination /dɛstinasjɔ̃/ nf destination; (fonction) purpose; **vol à ~ de** flight to.

destinée /dɛstine/ nf destiny.

destiner /dɛstine/ [1] vt **~ à** intend for; (vouer) destine for; **le commentaire m'est destiné** this comment is aimed at me; **être destiné à faire** be intended to do; (obligé) be destined to do. □ **se ~ à** vpr (carrière) intend to take up.

destituer /dɛstitɥe/ [1] vt discharge.

destructeur, **-trice** /dɛstryktœr, -tris/ adj destructive. **destruction** nf destruction.

désuet, **-ète** /dezɥɛ, -t/ adj outdated.

détachant /detaʃɑ̃/ nm stain remover.

détacher /detaʃe/ [1] vt untie; (ôter) remove, detach; (déléguer) second. □ **se ~** vpr come off, break away; (nœud etc.) come undone; (ressortir) stand out.

détail /detaj/ nm detail; (de compte) breakdown; (Comm) retail; **au ~** (vendre etc.) retail; **de ~** (prix etc.) retail; **en ~** in detail; **entrer dans les ~s** go into detail.

détaillant, **~e** /detajɑ̃, -t/ nm, f retailer.

détaillé, **~e** /detaje/ adj detailed.

détailler /detaje/ [1] vt (rapport) detail; **~ ce que qn fait** scrutinize what sb does.

détaler /detale/ [1] vi 🆄 bolt.

détartrant /detartrɑ̃/ nm descaler.

détecter /detɛkte/ [1] vt detect. **détecteur** nm detector.

détective /detɛktiv/ nm detective.

déteindre /detɛ̃dr/ [22] vi (dans l'eau) run (**sur** on to); (au soleil) fade; **~ sur** (fig) rub off on.

détendre /detɑ̃dr/ [3] vt slacken; (ressort) release; (personne) relax. □ **se ~** vpr (ressort) slacken; (personne) relax. **détendu**, **~e** adj (calme) relaxed.

détenir /det(ə)nir/ [58] vt hold; (secret, fortune) possess.

détente /detɑ̃t/ nf relaxation; (Pol) détente; (saut) spring; (gâchette) trigger; **être lent à la ~** 🆄 be slow on the uptake.

détenteur, **-trice** /detɑ̃tœr, -tris/ nm, f holder.

détention /detɑ̃sjɔ̃/ nf detention; **~ provisoire** custody.

détenu, **~e** /detny/ nm, f prisoner.

détergent /detɛrʒɑ̃/ nm detergent.

détérioration /deterjɔrasjɔ̃/ nf deterioration; (dégât) damage.

détériorer /deterjɔre/ [1] vt damage. □ **se ~** vpr deteriorate.

détermination /determinasjɔ̃/ nf determination. **déterminé**, **~e** adj (résolu) determined; (précis) definite. **déterminer** [1] vt determine.

déterrer /detere/ [1] vt dig up.

détestable /detɛstabl/ adj (caractère, temps) foul.

détester /detɛste/ [1] *vt* hate. □ **se ~** *vpr* hate each other.

détonation /detɔnasjɔ̃/ *nf* explosion, detonation.

détour /detur/ *nm* (crochet) detour; (fig) roundabout means; (virage) bend.

détournement /deturnəmã/ *nm* hijack(ing); (de fonds) embezzlement.

détourner /deturne/ [1] *vt* (attention) divert; (tête, yeux) turn away; (avion) hijack; (argent) embezzle. □ **se ~ de** *vpr* stray from.

détraquer /detrake/ [1] *vt* make go wrong; (estomac) upset. □ **se ~** *vpr* (machine) go wrong.

détresse /detrɛs/ *nf* distress; **dans la ~, en ~** in distress.

détritus /detrity(s)/ *nmpl* rubbish (+ *sg*).

détroit /detrwa/ *nm* strait.

détromper /detrɔ̃pe/ [1] *vt* set straight. □ **se ~** *vpr* **détrompe-toi!** you'd better think again!

détruire /detrɥir/ [17] *vt* destroy.

dette /dɛt/ *nf* debt.

deuil /dœj/ *nm* (période) mourning; (décès) bereavement; **porter le ~** be in mourning; **faire son ~ de qch** give sth up as lost.

deux /dø/ *a & nm* two; **~ fois** twice; **tous (les) ~** both. **deuxième** *a & nmf* second. **deux-pièces** *nm inv* (maillot de bain) two-piece; (logement) two-room flat. **deux-points** *nm inv* (Gram) colon. **deux-roues** *nm inv* two-wheeled vehicle.

dévaliser /devalize/ [1] *vt* rob, clean out.

dévalorisant, ~e /devalɔrizã, -t/ *adj* demeaning.

dévaloriser /devalɔrize/ [1] *vt* (monnaie) devalue. □ **se ~** *vpr* (personne) put oneself down.

dévaluation /devalɥasjɔ̃/ *nf* devaluation.

dévaluer /devalɥe/ [1] *vt* devalue. □ **se ~** *vpr* devalue.

devancer /dəvɑ̃se/ [10] *vt* be *ou* go ahead of; (arriver) arrive ahead of; (prévenir) anticipate.

devant /d(ə)vɑ̃/ *prép* in front of; (distance) ahead of; (avec mouvement) past; (en présence de) in front of; (face

à) in the face of; **avoir du temps ~ soi** have plenty of time. ● *adv* in front; (à distance) ahead; **de ~** front. ● *nm* front; **prendre les ~s** take the initiative.

devanture /dəvɑ̃tyr/ *nf* shop front; (vitrine) shop window.

développement /devlɔpmã/ *nm* development; (de photos) developing.

développer /devlɔpe/ [1] *vt* develop. □ **se ~** *vpr* (corps, talent) develop; (entreprise) grow, expand.

devenir /dəvnir/ [58] *vi* (aux être) become; **qu'est-il devenu?** what has become of him?

dévergondé, ~e /devɛrgɔ̃de/ *a & nm,f* shameless (person).

déverser /devɛrse/ [1] *vt* (liquide) pour; (ordures, pétrole) dump. □ **se ~** *vpr* (rivière) flow; (égout, foule) pour.

dévêtir /devetir/ [61] *vt* undress. □ **se ~** *vpr* get undressed.

déviation /devjasjɔ̃/ *nf* diversion.

dévier /devje/ [45] *vt* divert; (coup) deflect. ● *vi* (ballon, balle) veer; (personne) deviate.

devin /dəvɛ̃/ *nm* soothsayer.

deviner /dəvine/ [1] *vt* guess; (apercevoir) distinguish.

devinette /dəvinɛt/ *nf* riddle.

devis /dəvi/ *nm* estimate, quote.

dévisager /devizaʒe/ [40] *vt* stare at.

devise /dəviz/ *nf* motto; **~s** (monnaie) (foreign) currency.

dévisser /devise/ [1] *vt* unscrew.

dévitaliser /devitalize/ [1] *vt* (dent) carry out root canal treatment on.

dévoiler /devwale/ [1] *vt* reveal.

---

devoir /dəvwar/ [26]

● *verbe auxiliaire*

····▸ **~ faire** (obligation, hypothèse) must do; (nécessité) have got to do; **je dois dire que...** I have to say that...; **il a dû partir** (nécessité) he had to leave; (hypothèse) he must have left.

····▸ (prévision) **je devais lui dire** I was to tell her; **elle doit rentrer bientôt** she's due back soon.

····▸ (conseil) **tu devrais** you should.

● *verbe transitif*

····▸ *(argent, excuses)* owe; **combien je vous dois?** (en achetant) how much is it?

□ **se devoir** *verbe pronominal*

····▸ **je me dois de le faire** it's my duty to do it.

● *nom masculin*

····▸ duty; **faire son ～** do one's duty.

····▸ (Scol) ～ **(surveillé)** test; **les ～s** homework (+ *sg*); **faire ses ～s** do one's homework.

dévorer /devɔʀe/ [1] *vt* devour.
dévot, ～**e** /devo, -ɔt/ *adj* devout.
dévoué, ～**e** /devwe/ *adj* devoted.
   dévouement *nm* devotion.
dévouer (se) /(sə)devwe/ [1] *vpr* devote oneself (**à** to); (se sacrifier) sacrifice oneself.
dextérité /dɛksteʀite/ *nf* skill.
diabète /djabɛt/ *nm* diabetes.
   diabétique *a & nmf* diabetic.
diable /djabl/ *nm* devil.
diagnostic /djagnɔstik/ *nm* diagnosis. **diagnostiquer** [1] *vt* diagnose.
diagonal, ～**e** *(mpl* **-aux)** /djagɔnal, -o/ *adj* diagonal. **diagonale** *nf* diagonal; **en ～e** diagonally.
diagramme /djagʀam/ *nm* diagram; (graphique) graph.
dialecte /djalɛkt/ *nm* dialect.
dialogue /djalɔg/ *nm* dialogue.
   dialoguer [1] *vi* have talks, enter into a dialogue.
diamant /djamã/ *nm* diamond.
diamètre /djamɛtʀ/ *nm* diameter.
diapositive /djapozitiv/ *nf* slide.
diarrhée /djaʀe/ *nf* diarrhoea.
dictateur /diktatœʀ/ *nm* dictator.
dicter /dikte/ [1] *vt* dictate. **dictée** *nf* dictation.
dictionnaire /diksjɔnɛʀ/ *nm* dictionary.
dicton /diktõ/ *nm* saying.
dièse /djɛz/ *nm* (Mus) sharp.
diesel /djezɛl/ *nm & a inv* diesel.
diète /djɛt/ *nf* restricted diet.
diététicien, ～**ne** /djetetisjɛ̃, -ɛn/ *nm,f* dietician.

diététique /djetetik/ *nf* dietetics.
   ● *adj* **produit** *ou* **aliment ～** dietary product; **magasin ～** health food shop *ou* store.
dieu *(pl ～***x)** /djø/ *nm* god; **D～** God.
diffamation /difamasjõ/ *nf* slander; (par écrit) libel. **diffamer** [1] *vt* slander; (par écrit) libel.
différé: en ～ /ãdifeʀe/ *loc* (émission) pre-recorded.
différemment /difeʀamã/ *adv* differently.
différence /difeʀãs/ *nf* difference; **à la ～ de** unlike.
différencier /difeʀãsje/ [45] *vt* differentiate. □ **se ～** *vpr* differentiate oneself; **se ～ de** (différer de) differ from.
différend /difeʀã/ *nm* difference (of opinion).
différent, ～**e** /difeʀã, -t/ *adj* different (**de** from).
différer /difeʀe/ [14] *vt* postpone.
   ● *vi* differ (**de** from).
difficile /difisil/ *adj* difficult; (exigeant) fussy. **difficilement** *adv* with difficulty.
difficulté /difikylte/ *nf* difficulty; **faire des ～s** raise objections.
diffus, ～**e** /dify, -z/ *adj* diffuse.
diffuser /difyze/ [1] *vt* (émission) broadcast; (nouvelle) spread; (lumière, chaleur) diffuse; (Comm) distribute. **diffusion** *nf* broadcasting; diffusion; distribution.
digérer /diʒeʀe/ [14] *vt* digest; (endurer 🔟) stomach. **digeste** *adj* digestible.
digestif, **-ive** /diʒɛstif, -v/ *adj* digestive. ● *nm* after-dinner liqueur.
digital, ～**e** *(mpl* **-aux)** /diʒital, -o/ *adj* digital.
digne /diɲ/ *adj* (noble) dignified; (approprié) worthy; **～ de** worthy of; **～ de foi** trustworthy.
digue /dig/ *nf* dyke; (US) dike.
dilater /dilate/ [1] *vt* dilate. □ **se ～** *vpr* dilate; (estomac) distend.
dilemme /dilɛm/ *nm* dilemma.
dilettante /diletãt/ *nmf* amateur.
diluant /dilɥã/ *nm* thinner.
diluer /dilɥe/ [1] *vt* dilute.
dimanche /dimãʃ/ *nm* Sunday.

dimension /dimãsjɔ̃/ nf (taille) size; (mesure) dimension; (aspect) dimension.

diminuer /diminɥe/ [1] vt reduce, decrease; (plaisir, courage) dampen; (dénigrer) diminish. ● vi (se réduire) decrease; (faiblir) (bruit, flamme) die down; (ardeur) cool. **diminutif** nm diminutive; (surnom) pet name. **diminution** nf decrease (de in); (réduction) reduction; (affaiblissement) diminishing.

dinde /dɛ̃d/ nf turkey.

dîner /dine/ [1] vi have dinner. ● nm dinner.

dingue /dɛ̃g/ adj Ⅱ crazy.

dinosaure /dinozɔR/ nm dinosaur.

diphtongue /diftɔ̃g/ nf diphthong.

diplomate /diplɔmat/ nmf diplomat. ● adj diplomatic. **diplomatique** adj diplomatic.

diplôme /diplom/ nm certificate, diploma; (Univ) degree. **diplômé, ~e** adj qualified.

dire /diR/ [27] vt say; (secret, vérité, heure) tell; (penser) think; ~ **que** say that; ~ **à qn que** tell sb that; ~ **à qn de** tell sb to; **ça me dit de faire** I feel like doing; **on dirait que** it would seem that, it seems that; **dis/dites donc!** hey! □ **se ~** vpr (mot) be said; (penser) tell oneself; (se prétendre) claim to be. ● nm **au ~ de, selon les ~s de** according to.

direct, ~e /diRɛkt/ adj direct. ● nm (train) express train; **en ~** (émission) live.

directeur, -trice /diRɛktœR, -tRis/ nm, f director; (chef de service) manager, manageress; (de journal) editor; (d'école) headteacher; (US) principal; ~ **de banque** bank manager; ~ **commercial** sales manager; ~ **des ressources humaines** human resources manager.

direction /diRɛksjɔ̃/ nf (sens) direction; (de société) management; (Auto) steering; **en ~ de** (going) to.

dirigeant, ~e /diRiʒã, -t/ nm, f (Pol) leader; (Comm) manager. ● adj (classe) ruling.

diriger /diRiʒe/ [40] vt (service, école, parti, pays) run; (entreprise, usine)

manage; (travaux) supervise; (véhicule) steer; (orchestre) conduct; (braquer) aim; (tourner) turn. □ **se ~** vpr (s'orienter) find one's way; **se ~ vers** head for, make for.

dis /di/ ⇒DIRE [27].

discernement /disɛRnəmã/ nm discernment.

disciplinaire adj disciplinary. **discipline** nf discipline.

discontinu, ~e /diskɔ̃tiny/ adj intermittent.

discordant, ~e /diskɔRdã, -t/ adj discordant.

discothèque /diskɔtɛk/ nf record library; (boîte de nuit) disco(thèque).

discours /diskuR/ nm speech; (propos) views.

discret, -ète /diskRɛ, -t/ adj discreet.

discrétion /diskResjɔ̃/ nf discretion; **à ~** (vin) unlimited; (manger, boire) as much as one desires.

discrimination /diskRiminasjɔ̃/ nf discrimination. **discriminatoire** adj discriminatory.

disculper /diskylpe/ [1] vt exonerate. □ **se ~** vpr vindicate oneself.

discussion /diskysjɔ̃/ nf discussion; (querelle) argument.

discutable /diskytabl/ adj debatable; (critiquable) questionable.

discuter /diskyte/ [1] vt discuss; (contester) question. ● vi (parler) talk; (répliquer) argue; ~ **de** discuss.

disette /dizɛt/ nf food shortage.

disgrâce /disgRɑs/ nf disgrace.

disgracieux, -ieuse /disgRasjø, -z/ adj ugly, unsightly.

disjoindre /disʒwɛ̃dR/ [22] vt take apart. □ **se ~** vpr come apart.

disloquer /dislɔke/ [1] vt (membre) dislocate; (machine) break (apart). □ **se ~** vpr (parti, cortège) break up; (meuble) come apart.

disparaître /dispaRɛtR/ [18] vi disappear; (mourir) die; **faire ~** get rid of. **disparition** nf disappearance; (mort) death.

disparate /dispaRat/ adj ill-assorted.

disparu, ~e /dispaʁy/ adj missing.
● nm, f missing person; (mort) dead person.

dispensaire /dispɑ̃sɛʁ/ nm clinic.

dispense /dispɑ̃s/ nf exemption.

dispenser /dispɑ̃se/ [1] vt exempt (de from). □ se ~ de vpr avoid.

disperser /dispɛʁse/ [1] vt (éparpiller) scatter; (répartir) disperse. □ se ~ vpr disperse.

disponibilité /disponibilite/ nf availability. **disponible** adj available.

dispos, ~e /dispo, -z/ adj frais et ~ fresh and alert.

disposé, ~e /dispoze/ adj bien/mal ~ in a good/bad mood; ~ à prepared to; ~ envers disposed towards.

disposer /dispoze/ [1] vt arrange; ~ à (engager à) incline to. ● vi ~ de have at one's disposal. □ se ~ à vpr prepare to.

dispositif /dispozitif/ nm device; (ensemble de mesures) operation.

disposition /dispozisjɔ̃/ nf arrangement, layout; (tendance) tendency; ~s (humeur) mood; (préparatifs) arrangements; (mesures) measures; (aptitude) aptitude; **mettre à la ~ de** place ou put at the disposal of.

disproportionné, ~e /dispʁɔpɔʁsjɔne/ adj disproportionate; ~ à out of proportion with.

dispute /dispyt/ nf quarrel.

disputer /dispyte/ [1] vt (match) play; (course) run in; (prix) fight for; (gronder 🔢) tell off. □ se ~ vpr quarrel; (se battre pour) fight over; (match) be played.

disquaire /diskɛʁ/ nmf record dealer.

disque /disk/ nm (Mus) record; (Sport) discus; (cercle) disc, disk; (Ordinat) disk; ~ **compact** compact disc; ~ **dur** hard disk; ~ **optique compact** CD-ROM; ~ **souple** floppy disk.

disquette /diskɛt/ nf floppy disk, diskette; ~ **de sauvegarde** back-up disk.

disséminer /disemine/ [1] vt spread, scatter.

dissertation /disɛʁtasjɔ̃/ nf essay, paper.

disserter /disɛʁte/ [1] vi ~ **sur** speak about; (par écrit) write about.

dissident, ~e /disidɑ̃, -t/ a & nm, f dissident.

dissimulation /disimylasjɔ̃/ nf concealment; (fig) deceit.

dissimuler /disimyle/ [1] vt conceal (à from). □ se ~ vpr conceal oneself.

dissipé, ~e /disipe/ adj (élève) unruly.

dissiper /disipe/ [1] vt (fumée, crainte) dispel; (fortune) squander; (personne) distract. □ se ~ vpr disappear; (élève) grow restless.

dissolvant /disɔlvɑ̃/ nm solvent; (pour ongles) nail polish remover.

dissoudre /disudʁ/ [53] vt dissolve. □ se ~ vpr dissolve.

dissuader /disɥade/ [1] vt dissuade (de from).

dissuasion /disɥazjɔ̃/ nf dissuasion; **force de ~** deterrent force.

distance /distɑ̃s/ nf distance; (écart) gap; **à ~** at ou from a distance.

distancer /distɑ̃se/ [10] vt outdistance.

distendre /distɑ̃dʁ/ [3] vt (estomac) distend; (corde) stretch.

distinct, ~e /distɛ̃(kt), -ɛkt/ adj distinct.

distinctif, **-ive** /distɛ̃ktif, -v/ adj (trait) distinctive; (signe, caractère) distinguishing.

distinction /distɛ̃ksjɔ̃/ nf distinction; (récompense) honour.

distinguer /distɛ̃ge/ [1] vt distinguish.

distraction /distʁaksjɔ̃/ nf absent-mindedness; (passe-temps) entertainment, leisure; (détente) recreation.

distraire /distʁɛʁ/ [29] vt amuse; (rendre inattentif) distract; ~ **qn de qch** take sb's mind off sth. □ se ~ vpr amuse oneself.

distrait, ~e /distʁɛ, -t/ adj absent-minded; (élève) inattentive.

distrayant, ~e /distʁɛjɑ̃, -t/ adj entertaining.

distribuer /distribɥe/ [1] *vt* hand out, distribute; (*répartir*) distribute; (*tâches, rôles*) allocate; (*cartes*) deal; (*courrier*) deliver.

distributeur /distribytœr/ *nm* (Auto, Comm) distributor; ∼ (**automatique**) vending-machine; ∼ **de billets** (**de banque**) cash dispenser. **distribution** *nf* distribution; (du courrier) delivery; (acteurs) cast; (secteur) retailing.

district /distrikt/ *nm* district.

dit¹, dites /di, dit/ ⇒DIRE [27].

dit², ∼**e** /di, dit/ *adj* (décidé) agreed; (surnommé) known as.

diurne /djyrn/ *adj* diurnal; (*activité*) daytime.

divagations /divagasjɔ̃/ *nfpl* ravings.

divergence /divɛrʒɑ̃s/ *nf* divergence. **divergent**, ∼**e** *adj* divergent. **diverger** [40] *vi* diverge.

divers, ∼**e** /divɛr, -s/ *adj* (varié) diverse; (différent) various; (*frais*) miscellaneous; **dépenses** ∼**es** sundries. **diversifier** [45] *vt* diversify.

diversité /divɛrsite/ *nf* diversity, variety.

divertir /divɛrtir/ [2] *vt* amuse, entertain. □ **se** ∼ *vpr* amuse oneself; (passer du bon temps) enjoy oneself. **divertissement** *nm* amusement, entertainment.

dividende /dividɑ̃d/ *nm* dividend.

divin, ∼**e** /divɛ̃, -in/ *adj* divine. **divinité** *nf* divinity.

diviser /divize/ [1] *vt* divide. □ **se** ∼ *vpr* become divided; **se** ∼ **par sept** be divisible by seven. **division** *nf* division.

divorce /divɔrs/ *nm* divorce.

divorcé, ∼**e** /divɔrse/ *adj* divorced. ● *nm, f* divorcee.

divorcer /divɔrse/ [10] *vi* ∼ (**d'avec**) divorce.

dix /dis/ (/di/ *before consonant*, /diz/ *before vowel*) *a & nm* ten.

dix-huit /dizɥit/ *a & nm* eighteen.

dixième /dizjɛm/ *a & nmf* tenth.

dix-neuf /diznœf/ *a & nm* nineteen.

dix-sept /disɛt/ *a & nm* seventeen.

docile /dɔsil/ *adj* docile.

docteur /dɔktœr/ *nm* doctor.

doctorat /dɔktɔra/ *nm* doctorate, PhD.

document /dɔkymɑ̃/ *nm* document. **documentaire** *a & nm* documentary.

documentaliste /dɔkymɑ̃talist/ *nmf* information officer; (Scol) librarian.

documentation /dɔkymɑ̃tasjɔ̃/ *nf* information, literature; **centre de** ∼ resource centre.

documenté, ∼**e** /dɔkymɑ̃te/ *adj* well-documented.

documenter /dɔkymɑ̃te/ [1] *vt* provide with information. □ **se** ∼ *vpr* collect information.

dodo /dodo/ *nm* **faire** ∼ (langage enfantin) sleep.

dodu, ∼**e** /dɔdy/ *adj* plump.

dogmatique /dɔgmatik/ *adj* dogmatic. **dogme** *nm* dogma.

doigt /dwa/ *nm* finger; **un** ∼ **de** a drop of; **montrer qch du** ∼ point at sth; **à deux** ∼**s de** a hair's breadth away from; ∼ **de pied** toe. **doigté** *nm* (Mus) fingering, touch; (diplomatie) tact.

dois, doit /dwa/ ⇒DEVOIR [26].

doléances /dɔleɑ̃s/ *nfpl* grievances.

dollar /dɔlar/ *nm* dollar.

domaine /dɔmɛn/ *nm* estate, domain; (fig) domain, field.

domestique /dɔmɛstik/ *adj* domestic. ● *nmf* servant. **domestiquer** [1] *vt* domesticate.

domicile /dɔmisil/ *nm* home; **à** ∼ at home; (*livrer*) to the home.

domicilié, ∼**e** /dɔmisilje/ *adj* resident; **être** ∼ **à Paris** live *ou* be resident in Paris.

dominant, ∼**e** /dɔminɑ̃, -t/ *adj* dominant. **dominante** *nf* dominant feature.

dominer /dɔmine/ [1] *vt* dominate; (surplomber) tower over, dominate; (*sujet*) master; (*peur*) overcome. ● *vi* dominate; (*équipe*) be in the lead; (prévaloir) stand out.

domino /dɔmino/ *nm* domino.

dommage /dɔmaʒ/ *nm* (tort) harm; ∼(**s**) (dégâts) damage; **c'est** ∼ it's a pity *ou* shame; **quel** ~ what a pity *ou* shame. **dommages-intérêts** *nmpl* (Jur) damages.

dompter /dɔ̃te/ [1] *vt* tame. **dompteur, -euse** *nm, f* tamer.

DOM-TOM /dɔmtɔm/ *abrév mpl* (**départements et territoires d'outre-mer**) French overseas departments and territories.

don /dɔ̃/ *nm* (cadeau, aptitude) gift. **donateur, -trice** *nm, f* donor. **donation** *nf* donation.

donc /dɔ̃k/ *conj* so, then; (par conséquent) so, therefore; **quoi** ~? what did you say?; **tiens** ~! fancy that!

donjon /dɔ̃ʒɔ̃/ *nm* (tour) keep.

donné, ~e /dɔne/ *adj* (fixé) given; (pas cher [1]) dirt cheap; **étant** ~ **que** given that.

donnée /dɔne/ *nf* (élément d'information) fact; ~**s** data.

donner /dɔne/ [1] *vt* give; (*vieilles affaires*) give away; (distribuer) give out; (*fruits, résultats*) produce; (*film*) show; (*pièce*) put on; **ça donne soif/ faim** it makes one thirsty/hungry; ~ **qch à réparer** take sth to be repaired; ~ **lieu à** give rise to. ● *vi* ~ **sur** look out on to; ~ **dans** tend towards. □ **se** ~ **à** *vpr* devote oneself to; **se** ~ **du mal** go to a lot of trouble (**pour faire** to do).

⋯⋯⋯⋯⋯⋯⋯⋯⋯⋯

dont /dɔ̃/

● *pronom*

⋯▸ (personne) **la fille** ~ **je te parlais** the girl I was telling you about; **l'homme** ~ **la fille a dit...** the man whose daughter said...

⋯▸ (chose) which, **l'affaire** ~ **il parle** the matter which he is referring to; **la manière** ~ **elle parle** the way she speaks; **ce** ~ **il parle** what he's talking about.

⋯▸ (provenance) from which.

⋯▸ (parmi lesquels) **deux personnes** ~ **toi** two people, one of whom is you; **plusieurs thèmes** ~ **l'identité et le racisme** several topics including identity and racism.

⋯⋯⋯⋯⋯⋯⋯⋯⋯⋯

dopage /dɔpaʒ/ *nm* (de cheval) doping; (d'athlète) illegal drug-use.

doper /dɔpe/ [1] *vt* dope. □ **se** ~ *vpr* take drugs.

doré, ~e /dɔʀe/ *adj* (couleur d'or) golden; (qui rappelle l'or) gold; (avec de l'or) gilt; **la jeunesse** ~**e** gilded youth.

dorénavant /dɔʀenavɑ̃/ *adv* henceforth.

dorer /dɔʀe/ [1] *vt* gild; (Culin) brown.

dormir /dɔʀmiʀ/ [46] *vi* sleep; (être endormi) be asleep; ~ **debout** be asleep on one's feet; **une histoire à** ~ **debout** a cock-and-bull story.

dortoir /dɔʀtwaʀ/ *nm* dormitory.

dorure /dɔʀyʀ/ *nf* gilding.

dos /do/ *nm* back; (de livre) spine; **à** ~ **de** riding on; **au** ~ **de** (*chèque*) on the back of; **de** ~ from behind; ~ **crawlé** backstroke.

dosage /dozaʒ/ *nm* (mélange) mixture; (quantité) amount, proportions. **dose** *nf* dose. **doser** [1] *vt* measure out; (contrôler) use in a controlled way.

dossier /dɔsje/ *nm* (documents) file; (Jur) case; (de chaise) back; (TV, presse) special feature.

dot /dɔt/ *nf* dowry.

douane /dwan/ *nf* customs.

douanier, -ière /dwanje, -jɛʀ/ *adj* customs. ● *nm* customs officer.

double /dubl/ *a & adv* double. ● *nm* (copie) duplicate; (sosie) double; **le** ~ (**de**) twice as much *ou* as many (as); **le** ~ **messieurs** the men's doubles.

doubler /duble/ [1] *vt* double; (dépasser) overtake; (vêtement) line; (*film*) dub; (*classe*) repeat; (*cap*) round. ● *vi* double.

doublure /dublyʀ/ *nf* (étoffe) lining; (acteur) understudy.

douce /dus/ ⇒**DOUX**.

doucement /dusmɑ̃/ *adv* gently; (sans bruit) quietly; (lentement) slowly.

douceur /dusœʀ/ *nf* (mollesse) softness; (de climat) mildness; (de personne) gentleness; (friandise) sweet; (US) candy; **en** ~ smoothly.

douche /duʃ/ *nf* shower.

doucher /duʃe/ [1] *vt* give a shower to. □ **se ~** *vpr* have *ou* take a shower.

doudoune /dudun/ *nf* 🔲 down jacket.

doué, ~e /dwe/ *adj* gifted; **~ de** endowed with.

douille /duj/ *nf* (Électr) socket.

douillet, ~te /dujɛ, -t/ *adj* cosy, comfortable; (*personne*: péj) soft.

douleur /dulœr/ *nf* pain; (chagrin) sorrow, grief. **douloureux, -euse** *adj* painful.

doute /dut/ *nm* doubt; **sans ~** no doubt; **sans aucun ~** without doubt.

douter /dute/ [1] *vt* **~ de** doubt; **~ que** doubt that. ● *vi* doubt. □ **se ~ de** *vpr* suspect; **je m'en doutais** I thought so.

douteux, -euse /dutø, -z/ *adj* dubious, doubtful.

Douvres /duvr/ *npr* Dover.

doux, douce /du, dus/ *adj* (moelleux) soft; (sucré) sweet; (clément, pas fort) mild; (pas brusque, bienveillant) gentle.

douzaine /duzɛn/ *nf* about twelve; (douze) dozen; **une ~ d'œufs** a dozen eggs.

douze /duz/ *a & nm* twelve. **douzième** *a & nmf* twelfth.

doyen, ~ne /dwajɛ̃, -ɛn/ *nm, f* dean; (en âge) most senior person.

dragée /draʒe/ *nf* sugared almond.

draguer /drage/ [1] *vt* (rivière) dredge; (filles 🔲) chat up, try to pick up.

drainer /drene/ [1] *vt* drain.

dramatique /dramatik/ *adj* dramatic; (tragique) tragic. ● *nf* (television) drama.

dramatiser /dramatize/ [1] *vt* dramatize.

dramaturge /dramatyrʒ/ *nmf* dramatist.

drame /dram/ *nm* (genre) drama; (pièce) play; (événement tragique) tragedy.

drap /dra/ *nm* sheet; (tissu) (woollen) cloth.

drapeau (*pl* ~**x**) /drapo/ *nm* flag.

drap-housse (*pl* **draps-housses**) /draus/ *nm* fitted sheet.

dressage /dresaʒ/ *nm* training; (compétition équestre) dressage.

dresser /drese/ [1] *vt* put up, erect; (tête) raise; (animal) train; (liste, plan) draw up; **~ l'oreille** prick up one's ears. □ **se ~** *vpr* (bâtiment) stand; (personne) draw oneself up. **dresseur, -euse** *nm, f* trainer.

dribbler /drible/ [1] *vi* (Sport) dribble.

drive /drajv/ *nm* (Ordinat) drive.

drogue /drɔg/ *nf* drug; **la ~** drugs.

drogué, ~e /drɔge/ *nm, f* drug addict.

droguer /drɔge/ [1] *vt* (malade) drug heavily; (victime) drug. □ **se ~** *vpr* take drugs.

droguerie /drɔgri/ *nf* hardware shop. **droguiste** *nmf* owner of a hardware shop.

droit, ~e /drwa, -t/ *adj* (contraire de gauche) right; (non courbe) straight; (loyal) upright; **angle ~** right angle. ● *adv* straight. ● *nm* right; **~(s)** (taxe) duty; **le ~** (Jur) law; **avoir ~ à** be entitled to; **avoir le ~ de** be allowed to; **être dans son ~** be in the right; **~ d'auteur** copyright; **~ d'inscription** registration fee; **~s d'auteur** royalties.

droite /drwat/ *nf* (contraire de gauche) right; **à ~** on the right; (direction) to the right; **la ~** the right (side); (Pol) the right (wing); (ligne) straight line. **droitier, -ière** *adj* right-handed.

drôle /drol/ *adj* (amusant) funny; (bizarre) funny, odd. **drôlement** *adv* funnily; (très 🔲) really.

dru, ~e /dry/ *adj* thick; **tomber ~** fall thick and fast.

drugstore /drœgstɔr/ *nm* drugstore.

du /dy/ ⇒DE.

dû, due /dy/ *adj* due. ● *nm* due; (argent) dues; **~ à** due to. ● ⇒DEVOIR [26].

duc, duchesse /dyk, dyʃɛs/ *nm, f* duke, duchess.

duo /dɥo/ *nm* (Mus) duet; (fig) duo.

dupe /dyp/ *nf* dupe.

duplex /dyplɛks/ *nm* split-level apartment; (US) duplex; (émission) link-up.

duplicata /dyplikata/ *nm inv* duplicate.

duquel /dykɛl/ ⇒LEQUEL.

dur, ~e /dyʀ/ *adj* hard; (*sévère*) harsh, hard; (*viande*) tough; (*col, brosse*) stiff; **~ d'oreille** hard of hearing. ● *adv* hard. ● *nm, f* tough nut ⒤; (Pol) hardliner.

durable /dyʀabl/ *adj* lasting.

durant /dyʀɑ̃/ *prép* (au cours de) during; (avec mesure de temps) for; **~ des heures** for hours; **des heures ~** for hours and hours.

durcir /dyʀsiʀ/ [2] *vt* harden. ● *vi* (*terre*) harden; (*ciment*) set; (*pain*) go hard. ☐ **se ~** *vpr* harden.

durée /dyʀe/ *nf* length; (période) duration; **de courte ~** short-lived; **pile longue ~** long-life battery.

durer /dyʀe/ [1] *vi* last.

dureté /dyʀte/ *nf* hardness; (sévérité) harshness.

duvet /dyvɛ/ *nm* down; (sac) sleeping-bag.

dynamique /dinamik/ *adj* dynamic.

dynamite /dinamit/ *nf* dynamite.

dynamo /dinamo/ *nf* dynamo.

....

Ee

....

eau (*pl ~x*) /o/ *nf* water; **~ courante** running water; **~ de mer** seawater; **~ de source** spring water; **~ douce/salée** fresh/salt water; **~ de pluie** rainwater; **~ potable** drinking water; **~ de Javel** bleach; **~ minérale** mineral water; **~ gazeuse** sparkling water; **~ plate** still water; **~ de toilette** eau de toilette; **~x usées** dirty water; **~x et forêts** forestry commission (+ *sg*); **tomber à l'~** (fig) fall through; **prendre l'~** take in water. **eau-de-vie** (*pl* **eaux-de-vie**) *nf* brandy.

ébahi, ~e /ebai/ *adj* dumbfounded.

ébauche /eboʃ/ *nf* (dessin) sketch; (fig) attempt.

ébéniste /ebenist/ *nm* cabinet-maker.

éblouir /ebluiʀ/ [2] *vt* dazzle.

éboueur /ebwœʀ/ *nm* dustman.

ébouillanter /ebujɑ̃te/ [1] *vt* scald.

éboulement /ebulmɑ̃/ *nm* landslide.

ébouriffé, ~e /ebuʀife/ *adj* dishevelled.

ébrécher /ebʀeʃe/ [14] *vt* chip.

ébruiter /ebʀɥite/ [1] *vt* spread about. ☐ **s'~** *vpr* get out.

ébullition /ebylisjɔ̃/ *nf* boiling; **en ~** boiling.

écaille /ekaj/ *nf* (de poisson) scale; (de peinture, roc) flake; (matière) tortoiseshell.

écarlate /ekaʀlat/ *adj* scarlet.

écarquiller /ekaʀkije/ [1] *vt* **~ les yeux** open one's eyes wide.

écart /ekaʀ/ *nm* gap; (de prix) difference; (embardée) swerve; **~ de conduite** lapse in behaviour; **être à l'~** be isolated; **se tenir à l'~ de** stand apart from; (fig) keep out of the way of.

écarté, ~e /ekaʀte/ *adj* (*lieu*) remote; **les jambes ~es** (with) legs apart; **les bras ~s** with one's arms out.

écarter /ekaʀte/ [1] *vt* (séparer) move apart; (*membres*) spread; (*branches*) part; (éliminer) dismiss; **~ qch de** move sth away from; **~ qn de** keep sb away from. ☐ **s'~** *vpr* (s'éloigner) move away; (quitter son chemin) move aside; **s'~ de** stray from.

ecchymose /ekimoz/ *nf* bruise.

écervelé, ~e /esɛʀvəle/ *adj* scatterbrained. ● *nm, f* scatterbrain.

échafaudage /eʃafodaʒ/ *nm* scaffolding; (amas) heap.

échalote /eʃalɔt/ *nf* shallot.

échancré, ~e /eʃɑ̃kʀe/ *adj* low-cut.

échange /eʃɑ̃ʒ/ *nm* exchange; **en ~** (de) in exchange (for). **échanger** [40] *vt* exchange (**contre** for).

échangeur /eʃɑ̃ʒœʀ/ *nm* (Auto) interchange.

échantillon /eʃɑ̃tijɔ̃/ *nm* sample.

échappatoire /eʃapatwaʀ/ *nf* way out.

échappement /eʃapmã/ *nm* exhaust.

échapper /eʃape/ [1] *vi* ~ **à** escape; (en fuyant) escape (from); ~ **des mains de** slip out of the hands of; **ça m'a échappé** (fig) it just slipped out; **l'~ belle** have a narrow *ou* lucky escape. □ **s'~** *vpr* escape.

écharde /eʃaʀd/ *nf* splinter.

écharpe /eʃaʀp/ *nf* scarf; (de maire) sash; **en ~** (bras) in a sling.

échasse /eʃas/ *nf* stilt.

échauffement /eʃofmã/ *nm* (Sport) warm-up.

échauffer /eʃofe/ [1] *vt* heat; (fig) excite. □ **s'~** *vpr* warm up.

échéance /eʃeãs/ *nf* due date (for payment); (délai) deadline; (obligation) (financial) commitment.

échéant: **le cas ~** /ləkazeʃeã/ *loc* if need be.

échec /eʃɛk/ *nm* failure; ~**s** (jeu) chess; ~ **et mat** checkmate; **tenir en ~** hold in check.

échelle /eʃɛl/ *nf* ladder; (dimension) scale.

échelon /eʃlõ/ *nm* rung; (hiérarchique) grade; (niveau) level.

échevelé, ~**e** /eʃəvle/ *adj* dishevelled.

écho /eko/ *nm* echo; ~**s** (dans la presse) gossip.

échographie /ekɔgʀafi/ *nf* (ultrasound) scan.

échouer /eʃwe/ [1] *vi* (bateau) run aground; (ne pas réussir) fail; ~ **à un examen** fail an exam. ● *vt* (bateau) ground. □ **s'~** *vpr* run aground.

échu, ~**e** /eʃy/ *adj* (délai) expired.

éclabousser /eklabuse/ [1] *vt* splash.

éclair /eklɛʀ/ *nm* (flash of) lightning; (fig) flash; (gâteau) éclair. ● *a inv* (visite) brief.

éclairage /eklɛʀaʒ/ *nm* lighting.

éclaircie /eklɛʀsi/ *nf* sunny interval.

éclaircir /eklɛʀsiʀ/ [2] *vt* lighten; (mystère) clear up. □ **s'~** *vpr* (ciel) clear; (mystère) become clearer. **éclaircissement** *nm* clarification.

éclairer /eklɛʀe/ [1] *vt* light (up); (personne) (fig) enlighten; (situation) throw light on. ● *vi* give light. □ **s'~** *vpr* become clearer; **s'~ à la bougie** use candle-light.

éclaireur, -**euse** /eklɛʀœʀ, -øz/ *nm,f* (boy) scout, (girl) guide. ● *nm* (Mil) scout.

éclat /ekla/ *nm* fragment; (de lumière) brightness; (splendeur) brilliance; ~ **de rire** burst of laughter.

éclatant, ~**e** /eklatã, -t/ *adj* brilliant; (soleil) dazzling.

éclater /eklate/ [1] *vi* burst; (exploser) go off; (verre) shatter; (guerre) break out; (groupe) split up; ~ **de rire** burst out laughing.

éclipse /eklips/ *nf* eclipse.

éclosion /eklozjõ/ *nf* hatching, opening.

écluse /eklyz/ *nf* (de canal) lock.

écœurant, ~**e** /ekœʀã, -t/ *adj* (gâteau) sickly; (fig) disgusting. **écœurer** [1] *vt* sicken.

école /ekɔl/ *nf* school; ~ **maternelle/primaire/secondaire** nursery/primary/secondary school; ~ **normale** teachers' training college. **écolier**, -**ière** *nm,f* schoolboy, schoolgirl.

écologie /ekɔlɔʒi/ *nf* ecology. **écologique** *adj* ecological, green. **écologiste** *nmf* (chercheur) ecologist; (dans l'âme) environmentalist; (Pol) Green.

économie /ekɔnɔmi/ *nf* economy; (discipline) economics; ~**s** (argent) savings; **une ~ de** (gain) a saving of. **économique** *adj* (Pol) economic; (bon marché) economical.

économiser /ekɔnɔmize/ [1] *vt/i* save.

écorce /ekɔʀs/ *nf* bark; (de fruit) peel.

écorcher /ekɔʀʃe/ [1] *vt* (genou) graze; (animal) skin. □ **s'~** *vpr* graze oneself. **écorchure** *nf* graze.

écossais, ~**e** /ekɔsɛ, -z/ *adj* Scottish. **É~**, ~**e** *nm,f* Scot.

Écosse /ekɔs/ *nf* Scotland.

écoulement /ekulmã/ *nm* flow.

écouler /ekule/ [1] *vt* dispose of, sell. □ **s'~** *vpr* (liquide) flow; (temps) pass.

écourter /ekuʀte/ [1] *vt* shorten.

écoute /ekut/ *nf* listening; **à l'∼ (de)** listening in (to); **heures de grande ∼** prime time; **∼s téléphoniques** phone tapping.

écouter /ekute/ [1] *vt* listen to. ● *vi* listen; **∼ aux portes** eavesdrop.

écouteur *nm* earphones (+ *pl*); (de téléphone) receiver.

écran /ekrã/ *nm* screen; **∼ total** sun-block.

écraser /ekraze/ [1] *vt* crush; (*piéton*) run over; (*cigarette*) stub out. □ **s'∼** *vpr* crash (**contre** into).

écrémé, ∼e /ekreme/ *adj* skimmed; **demi-∼** semi-skimmed.

écrevisse /ekrəvis/ *nf* crayfish.

écrier (s') /(s)ekrije/ [45] *vpr* exclaim.

écrin /ekrɛ̃/ *nm* case.

écrire /ekrir/ [30] *vt/i* write; (*orthographier*) spell. □ **s'∼** *vpr* (*mot*) be spelt.

écrit /ekri/ *nm* document; (examen) written paper; **par ∼** in writing.

écriteau (*pl* **∼x**) /ekrito/ *nm* notice.

écriture /ekrityr/ *nf* writing; **∼s** (Comm) accounts.

écrivain /ekrivɛ̃/ *nm* writer.

écrou /ekru/ *nm* (Tech) nut.

écrouler (s') /(s)ekrule/ [1] *vpr* collapse.

écru, ∼e /ekry/ *adj* (*couleur*) natural; (*tissu*) raw.

écueil /ekœj/ *nm* reef; (fig) danger.

éculé, ∼e /ekyle/ *adj* (*soulier*) worn at the heel; (fig) well-worn.

écume /ekym/ *nf* foam; (Culin) scum.

écumer /ekyme/ [1] *vt* skim. ● *vi* foam.

écureuil /ekyrœj/ *nm* squirrel.

écurie /ekyri/ *nf* stable.

écuyer, -ère /ekyije, -jɛr/ *nm,f* (horse) rider.

eczéma /ɛgzema/ *nm* eczema.

EDF *abrév f* (**Électricité de France**) French electricity board.

édifice /edifis/ *nm* building.

édifier /edifje/ [45] *vt* construct; (porter à la vertu) edify.

Édimbourg /edɛ̃bur/ *npr* Edinburgh.

édit /edi/ *nm* edict.

éditer /edite/ [1] *vt* publish; (annoter) edit. **éditeur, -trice** *nm,f* publisher; (réviseur) editor.

édition /edisjõ/ *nf* (activité) publishing; (livre, disque) edition.

éditique /editik/ *nf* electronic publishing.

éditorial, ∼e (*pl* **-iaux**) /editɔrjal, -jo/ *a & nm* editorial.

édredon /edrədõ/ *nm* eiderdown.

éducateur, -trice /edykatœr, -tris/ *nm,f* youth worker.

éducatif, -ive /edykatif, -v/ *adj* educational.

éducation /edykasjõ/ *nf* (façon d'élever) upbringing; (enseignement) education; (manières) manners; **∼ physique** physical education.

éduquer /edyke/ [1] *vt* (élever) bring up; (former) educate.

effacé, ∼e /efase/ *adj* (modeste) unassuming.

effacer /efase/ [10] *vt* (gommer) rub out; (à l'écran) delete; (*souvenir*) erase. □ **s'∼** *vpr* fade; (s'écarter) step aside.

effarer /efare/ [1] *vt* alarm; **être effaré** be astounded.

effaroucher /efaruʃe/ [1] *vt* scare away.

effectif, -ive /efɛktif, -v/ *adj* effective. ● *nm* (d'école) number of pupils; **∼s** numbers. **effectivement** *adv* effectively; (en effet) indeed.

effectuer /efɛktɥe/ [1] *vt* carry out, make.

efféminé, ∼e /efemine/ *adj* effeminate.

effervescent, ∼e /efɛrvesã, -t/ *adj* **comprimé ∼** effervescent tablet.

effet /efɛ/ *nm* effect; (impression) impression; **∼s** (habits) clothes, things; **sous l'∼ d'une drogue** under the influence of drugs; **en ∼** indeed; **faire de l'∼** have an effect, be effective; **faire bon/mauvais ∼** make a good/bad impression; **ça fait un drôle d'∼** it feels strange.

efficace /efikas/ *adj* effective; (*personne*) efficient. **efficacité** *nf* effectiveness; (de personne) efficiency.

effleurer /eflœre/ [1] *vt* touch lightly; (*sujet*) touch on; **ça ne m'a**

pas effleuré it did not cross my mind.

effondrement /efɔdrəmã/ *nm* collapse. **effondrer (s')** [1] *vpr* collapse.

efforcer (s') /(s)efɔrse/ [10] *vpr* try (hard) (**de** to).

effort /efɔr/ *nm* effort.

effraction /efraksjɔ̃/ *nf* **entrer par** ~ break in.

effrayant, ~**e** /efrejã, -t/ *adj* frightening; (fig) frightful.

effrayer /efreje/ [31] *vt* frighten; (*décourager*) put off. □ **s'**~ *vpr* be frightened.

effréné, ~**e** /efrene/ *adj* wild.

effriter (s') /(s)efrite/ [1] *vpr* crumble.

effroi /efrwa/ *nm* dread.

effronté, ~**e** /efrɔ̃te/ *adj* cheeky. ● *nm,f* cheeky boy, cheeky girl.

effroyable /efrwajabl/ *adj* dreadful.

égal, ~**e** (*mpl* **-aux**) /egal, -o/ *adj* equal; (*surface, vitesse*) even. ● *nm,f* equal; **ça m'est/lui est** ~ it is all the same to me/him; **sans** ~ matchless; **d'**~ **à** ~ between equals. **également** *adv* equally; (*aussi*) as well. **égaler** [1] *vt* equal.

égaliser /egalize/ [1] *vt/i* (Sport) equalize; (*niveler*) level out; (*cheveux*) trim.

égalitaire /egaliter/ *adj* egalitarian.

égalité /egalite/ *nf* equality; (de *surface*) evenness; **être à** ~ be level.

égard /egar/ *nm* consideration; ~**s** respect (+ *sg*); **par** ~ **pour** out of consideration for; **à cet** ~ in this respect; **à l'**~ **de** with regard to; (*envers*) towards.

égarer /egare/ [1] *vt* mislay; (*tromper*) lead astray. □ **s'**~ *vpr* get lost; (se *tromper*) go astray.

égayer /egeje/ [31] *vt* (*personne*) cheer up; (*pièce*) brighten up.

église /egliz/ *nf* church.

égoïsme /egɔism/ *nm* selfishness, egoism.

égoïste /egɔist/ *adj* selfish. ● *nmf* egoist.

égorger /egɔrʒe/ [40] *vt* slit the throat of.

égout /egu/ *nm* sewer.

égoutter /egute/ [1] *vt* drain. □ **s'**~ *vpr* (*vaisselle*) drain; (*lessive*) drip dry. **égouttoir** *nm* draining-board.

égratigner /egratiɲe/ [1] *vt* scratch. **égratignure** *nf* scratch.

Égypte /eʒipt/ *nf* Egypt.

éjecter /eʒɛkte/ [1] *vt* eject.

élaboration /elabɔrasjɔ̃/ *nf* elaboration. **élaborer** [1] *vt* elaborate.

élan /elã/ *nm* (*animal*) moose; (Sport) run-up; (*vitesse*) momentum; (fig) surge.

élancé, ~**e** /elãse/ *adj* slender.

élancement /elãsmã/ *nm* twinge.

élancer (s') /(s)elãse/ [10] *vpr* leap forward, dash; (*arbre, édifice*) soar.

élargir /elarʒir/ [2] *vt* (*route*) widen; (*connaissances*) broaden. □ **s'**~ *vpr* (*famille*) expand; (*route*) widen; (*écart*) increase; (*vêtement*) stretch.

élastique /elastik/ *adj* elastic. ● *nm* elastic band; (*tissu*) elastic.

électeur, **-trice** /elɛktœr, -tris/ *nm,f* voter. **élection** *nf* election. **électoral**, ~**e** (*mpl* **-aux**) *adj* (*réunion*) election. **électorat** *nm* electorate, voters (+ *pl*).

électricien, ~**ne** /elɛktrisjɛ̃, ɛn/ *nm,f* electrician. **électricité** *nf* electricity.

électrifier /elɛktrifje/ [45] *vt* electrify.

électrique /elɛktrik/ *adj* electric; (*installation*) electrical.

électrocuter /elɛktrɔkyte/ [1] *vt* electrocute.

électroménager /elɛktrɔmenaʒe/ *nm* **l'**~ household appliances (+ *pl*).

électron /elɛktrɔ̃/ *nm* electron. **électronicien**, ~**ne** *nm,f* electronics engineer.

électronique /elɛktrɔnik/ *adj* electronic. ● *nf* electronics.

élégance /elegãs/ *nf* elegance. **élégant**, ~**e** *adj* elegant.

élément /elemã/ *nm* element; (*meuble*) unit. **élémentaire** *adj* elementary.

éléphant /elefã/ *nm* elephant.

élevage /ɛlvaʒ/ *nm* (stock-) breeding.

élévation /elevasjɔ̃/ *nf* rise; (hausse) rise; (plan) elevation; ~ **de terrain** rise in the ground.

élève /elɛv/ *nmf* pupil.

élevé, ~**e** /elve/ *adj* high; (noble) elevated; **bien** ~ well-mannered.

élever /elve/ [6] *vt* (lever) raise; (enfants) bring up, raise; (animal) breed. □ **s'**~ *vpr* rise; (dans le ciel) soar up; **s'**~ **à** amount to. **éleveur**, -**euse** *nm,f* (stock-)breeder.

éligible /eliʒibl/ *adj* eligible.

élimination /eliminasjɔ̃/ *nf* elimination.

éliminatoire /eliminatwaʀ/ *adj* qualifying. ● *nf* (Sport) heat.

éliminer /elimine/ [1] *vt* eliminate.

élire /eliʀ/ [39] *vt* elect.

elle /ɛl/ *pron* she; (complément) her; (chose) it. **elle-même** *pron* herself; itself. **elles** *pron* they; (complément) them. **elles-mêmes** *pron* themselves.

élocution /elɔkysjɔ̃/ *nf* diction.

éloge /elɔʒ/ *nm* praise; **faire l'**~ **de** praise; ~**s** praise (+ *sg*).

éloigné, ~**e** /elwaɲe/ *adj* distant; ~ **de** far away from; **parent** ~ distant relative.

éloigner /elwaɲe/ [1] *vt* take away *ou* remove (**de** from); (danger) ward off; (visite) put off. □ **s'**~ *vpr* go *ou* move away (**de** from); (affectivement) become estranged (**de** from).

élongation /elɔ̃gasjɔ̃/ *nf* strained muscle.

éloquent, ~**e** /elɔkɑ̃, -t/ *adj* eloquent.

élu, ~**e** /ely/ *adj* elected. ● *nm,f* (Pol) elected representative.

élucider /elyside/ [1] *vt* elucidate.

éluder /elyde/ [1] *vt* evade.

émacié, ~**e** /emasje/ *adj* emaciated.

émail (*pl* -**aux**) /emaj, -o/ *nm* enamel.

émanciper /emɑ̃sipe/ [1] *vt* emancipate. □ **s'**~ *vpr* become emancipated.

émaner /emane/ [1] *vi* emanate.

emballage /ɑ̃balaʒ/ *nm* (dur) packaging; (souple) wrapping.

emballer /ɑ̃bale/ [1] *vt* pack; (en papier) wrap; **ça ne m'emballe pas** 🄸 I'm not really taken by it. □ **s'**~ *vpr* (moteur) race; (cheval) bolt; (personne) get carried away; (prices) shoot up.

embarcadère /ɑ̃baʀkadɛʀ/ *nm* landing-stage.

embarcation /ɑ̃baʀkasjɔ̃/ *nf* boat.

embardée /ɑ̃baʀde/ *nf* swerve.

embarquement /ɑ̃baʀkəmɑ̃/ *nm* (de passagers) boarding; (de fret) loading.

embarquer /ɑ̃baʀke/ [1] *vt* take on board; (fret) load; (emporter 🄸) cart off. ● *vi* board. □ **s'**~ *vpr* board; **s'**~ **dans** embark upon.

embarras /ɑ̃baʀa/ *nm* (gêne) embarrassment; (difficulté) difficulty.

embarrasser /ɑ̃baʀase/ [1] *vt* (encombrer) clutter (up); (fig) embarrass. □ **s'**~ **de** *vpr* burden oneself with.

embauche /ɑ̃boʃ/ *nf* hiring. **embaucher** [1] *vt* hire, take on.

embaumer /ɑ̃bome/ [1] *vt* (pièce) fill; (cadavre) embalm. ● *vi* be fragrant.

embellir /ɑ̃beliʀ/ [2] *vt* make more attractive; (récit) embellish.

embêtant, ~**e** /ɑ̃betɑ̃, -t/ *adj* 🄸 annoying.

embêter /ɑ̃bete/ [1] *vt* bother. □ **s'**~ *vpr* be bored.

emblée: d'~ /dɑ̃ble/ *loc* right away.

emblème /ɑ̃blɛm/ *nm* emblem.

emboîter /ɑ̃bwate/ [1] *vt* fit together; ~ **le pas à qn** (imiter) follow suit. □ **s'**~ *vpr* fit together; (**s'**)~ **dans** fit into.

embonpoint /ɑ̃bɔ̃pwɛ̃/ *nm* stoutness.

embouchure /ɑ̃buʃyʀ/ *nf* (de fleuve) mouth; (Mus) mouthpiece.

embourber (**s'**) /(s)ɑ̃buʀbe/ [1] *vpr* get stuck in the mud; (fig) get bogged down.

embouteillage /ɑ̃butɛjaʒ/ *nm* traffic jam.

emboutir /ɑ̃butiʀ/ [2] *vt* (Auto) crash into.

embraser (**s'**) /(s)ābʀaze/ [1] *vpr* catch fire.

embrasser /ābʀase/ [1] *vt* kiss; (*adopter, contenir*) embrace. □ **s'**~ *vpr* kiss.

embrayage /ābʀɛjaʒ/ *nm* clutch. **embrayer** [31] *vi* engage the clutch.

embrouiller /ābʀuje/ [1] *vt* confuse; (*fils*) tangle. □ **s'**~ *vpr* become confused.

embryon /ābʀijɔ̃/ *nm* embryo.

embûches /ābyʃ/ *nfpl* traps.

embuer (**s'**) /(s)ābɥe/ [1] *vpr* mist up.

embuscade /ābyskad/ *nf* ambush.

émeraude /ɛmʀod/ *nf* emerald.

émerger /emɛʀʒe/ [40] *vi* emerge; (*fig*) stand out.

émeri /ɛmʀi/ *nm* emery.

émerveillement /emɛʀvɛjmā/ *nm* amazement, wonder.

émerveiller /emɛʀveje/ [1] *vt* fill with wonder. □ **s'**~ *vpr* marvel at.

émetteur /emɛtœʀ/ *nm* transmitter.

émettre /emɛtʀ/ [42] *vt* (*son*) produce; (*message*) send out; (*timbre, billet*) issue; (*opinion*) express.

émeute /emøt/ *nf* riot.

émietter /emjete/ [1] *vt* crumble. □ **s'**~ *vpr* crumble.

émigrant, ~**e** /emigʀā, -t/ *nm,f* emigrant. **émigration** *nf* emigration. **émigrer** [1] *vi* emigrate.

émincer /emɛ̃se/ [10] *vt* cut into thin slices.

éminent, ~**e**/eminā, -t/ *adj* eminent.

émissaire /emisɛʀ/ *nm* emissary.

émission /emisjɔ̃/ *nf* (*programme*) programme; (*de chaleur, gaz*) emission; (*de timbre*) issue.

emmagasiner /āmagazine/ [1] *vt* store.

emmanchure /āmāʃyʀ/ *nf* armhole.

emmêler /āmele/ [1] *vt* tangle. □ **s'**~ *vpr* get mixed up.

emménager /āmenaʒe/ [40] *vi* move in; ~ **dans** move into.

emmener /āmne/ [6] *vt* take; (*comme prisonnier*) take away.

emmerder /āmɛʀde/ [1] ✖ *vt* ~ **qn** get on sb's nerves. □ **s'**~ *vpr* be bored.

emmitoufler /āmitufle/ [1] *vt* wrap up warmly. □ **s'**~ *vpr* wrap oneself up warmly.

émoi /emwa/ *nm* turmoil; (*plaisir*) excitement.

émotif, -**ive** /emɔtif, -v/ *adj* emotional. **émotion** *nf* emotion; (*peur*) fright. **émotionnel**, ~**le** *adj* emotional.

émousser /emuse/ [1] *vt* blunt.

émouvant, ~**e** /emuvā, -t/ *adj* moving.

empailler /āpaje/ [1] *vt* stuff.

empaqueter /āpakte/ [38] *vt* package.

emparer (**s'**) /(s)āpaʀe/ [1] *vpr* **s'**~ **de** get hold of.

empêchement /āpɛʃmā/ *nm* avoir un ~ to be held up.

empêcher /āpeʃe/ [1] *vt* prevent; ~ **de faire** prevent *ou* stop (from) doing; (**il**) **n'empêche que** still. □ **s'**~ *vpr* **il ne peut pas s'en** ~ he cannot help it.

empereur /āpʀœʀ/ *nm* emperor.

empester /āpeste/ [1] *vt* stink out; (*essence*) stink of. ● *vi* stink.

empêtrer (**s'**) /(s)āpetʀe/ [1] *vpr* become entangled.

empiéter /āpjete/ [14] *vi* ~ **sur** encroach upon.

empiffrer (**s'**) /(s)āpifʀe/ [1] *vpr* ▣ stuff oneself.

empiler /āpile/ [1] *vt* pile up. □ **s'**~ *vpr* pile up.

empire /āpiʀ/ *nm* empire.

emplacement /āplasmā/ *nm* site.

emplâtre /āplatʀ/ *nm* (Méd) plaster.

emploi /āplwa/ *nm* (*travail*) job; (*embauche*) employment; (*utilisation*) use; **un** ~ **de chauffeur** a job as a driver; ~ **du temps** timetable. **employé**, ~**e** *nm,f* employee.

employer /āplwaje/ [31] *vt* (*personne*) employ; (*utiliser*) use. □ **s'**~ *vpr* be used; **s'**~ **à** devote oneself to. **employeur**, -**euse** *nm,f* employer.

empoigner /āpwaɲe/ [1] *vt* grab. □ **s'**~ *vpr* come to blows.

empoisonnement /ɑ̃pwazɔnmɑ̃/
nm poisoning.

empoisonner /ɑ̃pwazɔne/ [1] *vt*
poison; (embêter 🆃) annoy. □ **s'~** *vpr*
to poison oneself.

emporter /ɑ̃pɔrte/ [1] *vt* take
(away); (entraîner) sweep away;
(arracher) tear off. □ **s'~** *vpr* lose
one's temper; **l'~** get the upper hand
(**sur** of); **plat à ~** take-away.

empoté, **~e** /ɑ̃pɔte/ *adj* clumsy.

empreinte /ɑ̃pʀɛ̃t/ *nf* mark; **~**
(**digitale**) fingerprint; **~ de pas**
footprint.

empressé, **~e** /ɑ̃pʀese/ *adj* eager,
attentive.

empresser (s') /(s)ɑ̃pʀese/ [1] *vpr*
s'~ de hasten to; **s'~ auprès de** be
attentive to.

emprise /ɑ̃pʀiz/ *nf* influence.

emprisonnement /ɑ̃pʀizɔnmɑ̃/
nm imprisonment. **emprisonner**
[1] *vt* imprison.

emprunt /ɑ̃pʀœ̃/ *nm* loan; **faire un
~** take out a loan.

emprunté, **~e** /ɑ̃pʀœ̃te/ *adj*
awkward.

emprunter /ɑ̃pʀœ̃te/ [1] *vt* borrow
(**à** from); (*route*) take; (fig) assume.
emprunteur, **-euse** *nm,f*
borrower.

ému, **~e** /emy/ *adj* moved; (intimidé)
nervous.

émule /emyl/ *nmf* imitator.

....

en /ɑ̃/

⟹ Pour les expressions comme
en principe, **en train de**, **s'en
aller**, etc. ⟹**principe**, **train**,
aller, etc.

●*préposition*

····▶ (lieu) in.

····▶ (avec mouvement) to.

····▶ (temps) in.

····▶ (manière, état) in; **~ faisant** by *ou*
while doing; **je t'appelle ~ rentrant** I
will call you when I get back.

····▶ (en qualité de) as.

····▶ (transport) by.

····▶ (composition) made of; **table ~ bois**
wooden table.

●*pronom*

····▶ **~ avoir/vouloir** have/want some;
ne pas ~ avoir/vouloir not have/
want any; **j'~ ai deux** I've got two;
prends-~ plusieurs take several; **il
m'~ reste un** I have one left; **j'~ suis
content** I am pleased with him/her/
it/them; **je m'~ souviens** I
remember it.

····▶ **~ êtes-vous sûr?** are you sure?

....

encadrement /ɑ̃kadʀəmɑ̃/ *nm*
framing; (de porte) frame. **encadrer**
[1] *vt* frame; (entourer d'un trait) circle;
(superviser) supervise.

encaisser /ɑ̃kese/ [1] *vt* (*argent*)
collect; (*chèque*) cash; (*coups* 🆃) take.

encart /ɑ̃kaʀ/ *nm* **~ publicitaire**
(advertising) insert.

en-cas /ɑ̃ka/ *nm* (stand-by) snack.

encastré, **~e** /ɑ̃kastʀe/ *adj*
built-in.

encaustique /ɑ̃kɔstik/ *nf* wax
polish.

enceinte /ɑ̃sɛ̃t/ *af* pregnant; **~ de 3
mois** 3 months pregnant. ●*nf*
enclosure; **~ (acoustique)** speaker.

encens /ɑ̃sɑ̃/ *nm* incense.

encercler /ɑ̃sɛʀkle/ [1] *vt* surround.

enchaînement /ɑ̃ʃɛnmɑ̃/ *nm*
(suite) chain; (d'idées) sequence.

enchaîner /ɑ̃ʃene/ [1] *vt* chain (up);
(*phrases*) link (up). ●*vi* continue.
□ **s'~** *vpr* follow on.

enchanté, **~e** /ɑ̃ʃɑ̃te/ *adj* (ravi)
delighted. **enchanter** [1] *vt* delight;
(ensorceler) enchant.

enchère /ɑ̃ʃɛʀ/ *nf* bid; **mettre** *ou*
vendre aux ~s sell by auction.

enchevêtrer /ɑ̃ʃəvetʀe/ [1] *vt*
tangle. □ **s'~** *vpr* become tangled.

enclave /ɑ̃klav/ *nf* enclave.

enclencher /ɑ̃klɑ̃ʃe/ [1] *vt* engage.

enclin, **~e** /ɑ̃klɛ̃, -in/ *adj* **~ à**
inclined to.

enclos /ɑ̃klo/ *nm* enclosure.

enclume /ɑ̃klym/ *nf* anvil.

encoche /ɑ̃kɔʃ/ *nf* notch.

encolure /ɑ̃kɔlyʀ/ *nf* neck.

encombrant, **~e** /ɑ̃kɔ̃bʀɑ̃, -t/ *adj*
cumbersome.

encombre /ɑ̃kɔ̃bʀ/ *nm* **sans ~**
without any problems.

encombrement /ãkɔ̃brəmã/ nm (Auto) traffic congestion; (volume) bulk.

encombrer /ãkɔ̃bre/ [1] vt clutter (up); (obstruer) obstruct. □ s'~ de vpr burden oneself with.

encontre: à l'~ de /alãkɔ̃trədə/ loc against.

encore /ãkɔr/ adv (toujours) still; (de nouveau) again; (de plus) more; (aussi) also; ~ plus grand even larger; ~ un café another coffee; pas ~ not yet; si ~ if only; et puis quoi ~? ⊞ what next?

encouragement /ãkuraʒmã/ nm encouragement. **encourager** [40] vt encourage.

encourir /ãkurir/ [20] vt incur.

encrasser /ãkrase/ [1] vt clog up (with dirt).

encre /ãkr/ nf ink. **encrier** nm ink-well.

encyclopédie /ãsiklɔpedi/ nf encyclopaedia.

endettement /ãdɛtmã/ nm debt.

endetter /ãdɛte/ [1] vt put into debt. □ s'~ vpr get into debt.

endiguer /ãdige/ [1] vt dam; (fig) curb.

endimanché, ~e /ãdimãʃe/ adj in one's Sunday best.

endive /ãdiv/ nf chicory.

endoctriner /ãdɔktrine/ [1] vt indoctrinate.

endommager /ãdɔmaʒe/ [40] vt damage.

endormi, ~e /ãdɔrmi/ adj asleep; (apathique) sleepy.

endormir /ãdɔrmir/ [46] vt send to sleep; (médicalement) put to sleep; (duper) dupe (avec with). □ s'~ vpr fall asleep.

endosser /ãdose/ [1] vt (vêtement) put on; (assumer) take on; (Comm) endorse.

endroit /ãdrwa/ nm place; (de tissu) right side; à l'~ the right way round; par ~s in places.

enduire /ãdɥir/ [17] vt coat. **enduit** nm coating.

endurance /ãdyrãs/ nf endurance. **endurant**, ~e adj tough.

endurcir /ãdyrsir/ [2] vt strengthen. □ s'~ vpr become hard (ened).

endurer /ãdyre/ [1] vt endure.

énergétique /enɛrʒetik/ adj energy; (food) high-calorie. **énergie** nf energy; (Tech) power. **énergique** adj energetic.

énervant, ~e /enɛrvã, -t/ adj irritating, annoying.

énerver /enɛrve/ [1] vt irritate. □ s'~ vpr get worked up.

enfance /ãfãs/ nf childhood; la petite ~ infancy.

enfant /ãfã/ nmf child. **enfantillage** nm childishness. **enfantin**, ~e adj simple, easy; (puéril) childish; (jeu, langage) children's.

enfer /ãfɛr/ nm (Relig) Hell; (fig) hell.

enfermer /ãfɛrme/ [1] vt shut up. □ s'~ vpr shut oneself up.

enfiler /ãfile/ [1] vt (aiguille) thread; (vêtement) slip on; (rue) take.

enfin /ãfɛ̃/ adv (de soulagement) at last; (en dernier lieu) finally; (résignation, conclusion) well; ~ presque well nearly.

enflammé, ~e /ãflame/ adj (Méd) inflamed; (discours) fiery; (lettre) passionate.

enflammer /ãflame/ [1] vt set fire to. □ s'~ vpr catch fire.

enfler /ãfle/ [1] vt (histoire) exaggerate. ● vi (partie du corps) swell (up); (mer) swell; (rumeur, colère) spread. □ s'~ vpr (colère) mount; (rumeur) grow.

enfoncer /ãfɔ̃se/ [10] vt (épingle) push ou drive in; (chapeau) push down; (porte) break down. ● vi sink. □ s'~ vpr sink (dans into).

enfouir /ãfwir/ [2] vt bury.

enfourcher /ãfurʃe/ [1] vt mount.

enfreindre /ãfrɛ̃dr/ [22] vt infringe, break.

enfuir (s') /(s)ãfɥir/ [35] vpr run away.

enfumé, ~e /ãfyme/ adj filled with smoke.

engagé, ~e /ãgaʒe/ adj committed.

engagement /ɑ̃gaʒmɑ̃/ *nm*
(promesse) promise; (Pol, Comm)
commitment.

engager /ɑ̃gaʒe/ [40] *vt* (lier) bind,
commit; (embaucher) take on;
(commencer) start; (introduire) insert;
(investir) invest. □ **s'~** *vpr* (promettre)
commit oneself; (commencer) start;
(*soldat*) enlist; (*concurrent*) enter;
s'~ à faire undertake to do; **s'~
dans** (*voie*) enter.

engelure /ɑ̃ʒlyʀ/ *nf* chilblain.

engendrer /ɑ̃ʒɑ̃dʀe/ [1] *vt* (causer)
generate.

engin /ɑ̃ʒɛ̃/ *nm* device; (véhicule)
vehicle; (missile) missile.

engloutir /ɑ̃glutiʀ/ [2] *vt* swallow
(up).

engouement /ɑ̃gumɑ̃/ *nm* passion.

engouffrer /ɑ̃gufʀe/ [1] *vt* ⊞ gobble
up. □ **s'~ dans** *vpr* rush in.

engourdir /ɑ̃guʀdiʀ/ [2] *vt* numb.
□ **s'~** *vpr* go numb.

engrais /ɑ̃gʀɛ/ *nm* manure;
(chimique) fertilizer.

engrenage /ɑ̃gʀənaʒ/ *nm* gears (+
pl); (fig) spiral.

engueuler /ɑ̃gœle/ [1] ⊠ *vt* shout
at. □ **s'~** *vpr* have a row.

enhardir (**s'**) /(s)ɑ̃aʀdiʀ/ [2] *vpr*
become bolder.

énième /ɛnjɛm/ *adj* umpteenth.

énigmatique /enigmatik/ *adj*
enigmatic. **énigme** *nf* enigma;
(devinette) riddle.

enivrer /ɑ̃nivʀe/ [1] *vt* intoxicate.
□ **s'~** *vpr* get intoxicated.

enjambée /ɑ̃ʒɑ̃be/ *nf* stride.
enjamber [1] *vt* step over; (*pont*)
span.

enjeu (*pl* **~x**) /ɑ̃ʒø/ *nm* stake.

enjoué, **~e** /ɑ̃ʒwe/ *adj* cheerful.

enlacer /ɑ̃lase/ [10] *vt* entwine.

enlèvement /ɑ̃lɛvmɑ̃/ *nm* (de colis)
removal; (d'ordures) collection; (rapt)
kidnapping.

enlever /ɑ̃lve/ [6] *vt* remove (à
from); (*vêtement*) take off; (*tache,
organe*) take out, remove; (kidnapper)
kidnap; (gagner) win.

enliser (**s'**) /(s)ɑ̃lize/ [1] *vpr* get
bogged down.

enneigé, **~e** /ɑ̃neʒe/ *adj* snow-
covered.

ennemi, **~e** /ɛnmi/ *a & nm* enemy;
~ de (fig) hostile to.

ennui /ɑ̃nɥi/ *nm* problem; (tracas)
boredom; **s'attirer des ~s** run into
trouble.

ennuyer /ɑ̃nɥije/ [31] *vt* bore; (irriter)
annoy; (préoccuper) worry; **si cela ne
t'ennuie pas** if you don't mind.
□ **s'~** *vpr* get bored.

ennuyeux, **-euse** /ɑ̃nɥijø, -z/ *adj*
boring; (fâcheux) annoying.

énoncé /enɔ̃se/ *nm* wording, text;
(Gram) utterance.

énoncer /enɔ̃se/ [10] *vt* express,
state.

enorgueillir (**s'**) /(s)ɑ̃nɔʀgœjiʀ/ [2]
vpr **s'~ de** pride oneself on.

énorme /enɔʀm/ *adj* enormous.

enquête /ɑ̃kɛt/ *nf* (Jur)
investigation, inquiry; (sondage)
survey; **mener l'~** lead the inquiry.
enquêter [1] *vi* **~** (**sur**) investigate.
enquêteur, **-euse** *nm, f*
investigator.

enquiquinant, **~e** /ɑ̃kikinɑ̃, -t/
adj ⊞ irritating.

enraciné, **~e** /ɑ̃ʀasine/ *adj* deep-
rooted.

enragé, **~e** /ɑ̃ʀaʒe/ *adj* furious;
(*chien*) rabid; (fig) fanatical.

enrager /ɑ̃ʀaʒe/ [40] *vi* be furious;
faire ~ qn annoy sb.

enregistrement /ɑ̃ʀ(ə)ʒistʀəmɑ̃/
nm recording; (des bagages) check-in.
enregistrer [1] *vt* (Mus, TV) record;
(mémoriser) take in; (*bagages*) check
in.

enrhumer (**s'**) /(s)ɑ̃ʀyme/ [1] *vpr*
catch a cold.

enrichir /ɑ̃ʀiʃiʀ/ [2] *vt* enrich. □ **s'~**
vpr grow rich(er). **enrichissant**,
~e *adj* (*expérience*) rewarding.

enrober /ɑ̃ʀɔbe/ [1] *vt* coat (**de**
with).

enrôler /ɑ̃ʀole/ [1] *vt* recruit. □ **s'~**
vpr enlist, enrol.

enroué, **~e** /ɑ̃ʀwe/ *adj* hoarse.

enrouler /ɑ̃ʀule/ [1] *vt* wind, wrap.
□ **s'~** *vpr* wind; **s'~ dans une
couverture** roll oneself up in a
blanket.

ensanglanté, ~e /ãsãglãte/ *adj* bloodstained.

enseignant, ~e /ãsɛɲã, -t/ *nm, f* teacher. ● *adj* teaching.

enseigne /ãsɛɲ/ *nf* sign.

enseignement /ãsɛɲəmã/ *nm* (profession) teaching; (instruction) education.

enseigner /ãsɛɲe/ [1] *vt/i* teach; ~ qch à qn teach sb sth.

ensemble /ãsãbl/ *adv* together. ● *nm* group; (Mus) ensemble; (vêtements) outfit; (cohésion) unity; (maths) set; **dans l'~** on the whole; **d'~** (idée) general; **l'~ de** (totalité) all of, the whole of.

ensevelir /ãsəvlir/ [2] *vt* bury.

ensoleillé, ~e /ãsɔleje/ *adj* sunny.

ensorceler /ãsɔrsəle/ [38] *vt* bewitch.

ensuite /ãsɥit/ *adv* next, then; (plus tard) later.

ensuivre (s') /(s)ãsɥivr/ [57] *vpr* follow; **et tout ce qui s'ensuit** and all the rest of it.

entaille /ãtaj/ *nf* cut; (profonde) gash; (encoche) notch.

entamer /ãtame/ [1] *vt* start; (inciser) cut into; (ébranler) shake.

entasser /ãtase/ [1] *vt* (livres) pile; (argent) hoard; (personnes) cram (dans into). □ **s'~** *vpr* (objets) pile up (dans into); (personnes) squeeze (dans into).

entendement /ãtãdmã/ *nm* understanding; **ça dépasse l'~** it's beyond belief.

entendre /ãtãdr/ [3] *vt* hear; (comprendre) understand; (vouloir dire) mean; ~ **parler de** hear of; ~ **dire que** hear that. □ **s'~** *vpr* (être d'accord) agree; **s'~** (**bien**) get on (**avec** with); **cela s'entend** of course.

entendu, ~e /ãtãdy/ *adj* (convenu) agreed; (sourire, air) knowing; **bien** ~ of course; (**c'est**) ~! all right!

entente /ãtãt/ *nf* understanding; **bonne** ~ good relationship.

enterrement /ãtɛrmã/ *nm* funeral.

enterrer /ãtere/ [1] *vt* bury.

en-tête /ãtɛt/ *nm* heading; **à** ~ headed.

entêté, ~e /ãtete/ *adj* stubborn.
entêtement *nm* stubbornness.
entêter (s') [1] *vpr* persist (**à, dans** in).

enthousiasme /ãtuzjasm/ *nm* enthusiasm. **enthousiasmer** [1] *vt* fill with enthusiasm. **enthousiaste** *adj* enthusiastic.

enticher (s') /(s)ãtiʃe/ [1] *vpr* **s'~ de** become infatuated with.

entier, -**ière** /ãtje, -jɛr/ *adj* whole; (absolu) absolute; (entêté) unyielding. ● *nm* whole; **en** ~ entirely.

entonnoir /ãtɔnwar/ *nm* funnel; (trou) crater.

entorse /ãtɔrs/ *nf* sprain; (fig) ~ **à** (loi) infringement of.

entortiller /ãtɔrtije/ [1] *vt* wind, wrap (**autour** around); (duper ▯) get round.

entourage /ãturaʒ/ *nm* circle of family and friends; (bordure) surround.

entouré, ~e /ãture/ *adj* (personne) supported.

entourer /ãture/ [1] *vt* surround (**de** with); (réconforter) rally round; ~ **qch de mystère** shroud sth in mystery.

entracte /ãtrakt/ *nm* interval.

entraide /ãtrɛd/ *nf* mutual aid.
entraider (s') [1] *vpr* help each other.

entrain /ãtrɛ̃/ *nm* zest, spirit.

entraînement /ãtrɛnmã/ *nm* (Sport) training.

entraîner /ãtrene/ [1] *vt* (emporter) carry away; (provoquer) lead to; (Sport) train; (actionner) drive. □ **s'~** *vpr* train. **entraîneur** *nm* trainer.

entrave /ãtrav/ *nf* hindrance.
entraver [1] *vt* hinder.

entre /ãtr(ə)/ *prép* between; (parmi) among(st); ~ **autres** among other things; **l'un d'~ nous/eux** one of us/ them.

entrebâillé, ~e /ãtrəbaje/ *adj* ajar, half-open.

entrechoquer (s') /(s)ãtrəʃɔke/ [1] *vpr* knock against each other.

entrecôte /ãtrəkot/ *nf* rib steak.

entrecouper /ãtrəkupe/ [1] *vt* ~ **de** intersperse with.

entrecroiser (s') /(s)ɑ̃trəkrwaze/ [1] *vpr* (routes) intertwine.

entrée /ɑ̃tre/ *nf* entrance; (vestibule) hall; (accès) admission, entry; (billet) ticket; (Culin) starter; (Ordinat) **tapez sur E~** press Enter; '~ **interdite**' 'no entry'.

entrejambes /ɑ̃trəʒɑ̃b/ *nm* crotch.

entremets /ɑ̃trəmɛ/ *nm* dessert.

entremise /ɑ̃trəmiz/ *nf* intervention; **par l'~ de** through.

entreposer /ɑ̃trəpoze/ [1] *vt* store.

entrepôt /ɑ̃trəpo/ *nm* warehouse.

entreprenant, ~**e** /ɑ̃trəprənɑ̃, -t/ *adj* (actif) enterprising; (séducteur) forward.

entreprendre /ɑ̃trəprɑ̃dr/ [50] *vt* start on, undertake; (personne) buttonhole; ~ **de faire** undertake to do.

entrepreneur /ɑ̃trəprənœr/ *nm* (de bâtiment) contractor; (chef d'entreprise) firm manager.

entreprise /ɑ̃trəpriz/ *nf* (projet) undertaking; (société) firm, business, company.

entrer /ɑ̃tre/ [1] *vi* (aux être) go in, enter; (venir) come in, enter; ~ **dans** go *ou* come into, enter; (club) join; ~ **en collision** collide (**avec** with); **faire ~** (personne) show in; **laisser ~** let in; ~ **en guerre** go to war. ● *vt* (données) enter.

entre-temps /ɑ̃trətɑ̃/ *adv* meanwhile.

entretenir /ɑ̃trət(ə)nir/ [58] *vt* (appareil) maintain; (vêtement) look after; (alimenter) (feu) keep going; (amitié) keep alive; ~ **qn de** converse with sb about. □ **s'~** *vpr* speak (**de** about; **avec** to). **entretien** *nm* maintenance; (discussion) talk; (pour un emploi) interview.

entrevoir /ɑ̃trəvwar/ [63] *vt* make out; (brièvement) glimpse.

entrevue /ɑ̃trəvy/ *nf* meeting.

entrouvert, ~**e** /ɑ̃truvɛr, -t/ *adj* ajar, half-open.

énumération /enymerasjɔ̃/ *nf* enumeration. **énumérer** [14] *vt* enumerate.

envahir /ɑ̃vair/ [2] *vt* invade, overrun; (douleur, peur) overcome.

enveloppe /ɑ̃vlɔp/ *nf* envelope; (emballage) wrapping; ~ **budgétaire** budget. **envelopper** [1] *vt* wrap (up); (fig) envelop.

envergure /ɑ̃vɛrgyr/ *nf* wingspan; (importance) scope; (qualité) calibre.

envers /ɑ̃vɛr/ *prep* toward(s), to. ● *nm* (de tissu) wrong side; **à l'~** (tableau) upside down; (devant derrière) back to front; (chaussette) inside out.

envie /ɑ̃vi/ *nf* urge; (jalousie) envy; **avoir ~ de qch** feel like sth; **avoir ~ de faire** want to do; (moins urgent) feel like doing; **faire ~ à qn** make sb envious.

envier /ɑ̃vje/ [45] *vt* envy. **envieux**, **-ieuse** *adj* envious.

environ /ɑ̃virɔ̃/ *adv* about.

environnant, ~**e** /ɑ̃virɔnɑ̃, -t/ *adj* surrounding.

environnement /ɑ̃virɔnmɑ̃/ *nm* environment.

environs /ɑ̃virɔ̃/ *nmpl* vicinity; **aux ~ de** (lieu) in the vicinity of; (heure) round about.

envisager /ɑ̃vizaʒe/ [40] *vt* consider; (imaginer) envisage; ~ **de faire** consider doing.

envoi /ɑ̃vwa/ *nm* dispatch; (paquet) consignment; **faire un ~** send; **coup d'~** (Sport) kick-off.

envoler (s') /(s)ɑ̃vɔle/ [1] *vpr* fly away; (avion) take off; (papiers) blow away.

envoyé, ~**e** /ɑ̃vwaje/ *nm,f* envoy; ~ **spécial** special correspondent.

envoyer /ɑ̃vwaje/ [32] *vt* send; (lancer) throw; ~ **promener qn** Ⓘ send sb packing Ⓘ.

épais, ~**se** /epɛ, -s/ *adj* thick. **épaisseur** *nf* thickness.

épaissir /epesir/ [2] *vt/i* thicken. □ **s'~** *vpr* thicken; (mystère) deepen.

épanoui, ~**e** /epanwi/ *adj* (personne) beaming, radiant.

épanouir (s') /(s)epanwir/ [2] *vpr* (fleur) open out; (visage) beam; (personne) blossom. **épanouissement** *nm* (éclat) blossoming, full bloom.

épargne /eparɲ/ *nf* savings.

épargner /eparɲe/ [1] *vt/i* save; (ne pas tuer) spare; ~ **qch à qn** spare sb sth.

éparpiller /epaʀpije/ [1] vt scatter. □ s'~ vpr scatter; (fig) dissipate one's efforts.

épars, ~e /epaʀ, -s/ adj scattered.

épatant, ~e /epatɑ̃, -t/ adj 🄸 amazing.

épaule /epol/ nf shoulder.

épave /epav/ nf wreck.

épée /epe/ nf sword.

épeler /ɛple/ [6] vt spell.

éperdu, ~e /epɛʀdy/ adj wild, frantic.

éperon /epʀɔ̃/ nm spur.

éphémère /efemɛʀ/ adj ephemeral.

épi /epi/ nm (de blé) ear; (mèche) tuft of hair; ~ de maïs corn cob.

épice /epis/ nf spice. **épicé**, ~e adj spicy.

épicerie /episʀi/ nf grocery shop; (produits) groceries. **épicier**, **-ière** nm,f grocer.

épidémie /epidemi/ nf epidemic.

épiderme /epidɛʀm/ nm skin.

épier /epje/ [45] vt spy on.

épilepsie /epilɛpsi/ nf epilepsy. **épileptique** a & nmf epileptic.

épiler /epile/ [1] vt remove unwanted hair from; (sourcils) pluck.

épilogue /epilɔg/ nm epilogue; (fig) outcome.

épinard /epinaʀ/ nm ~s spinach (+ sg).

épine /epin/ nf thorn, prickle; (d'animal) prickle, spine; ~ dorsale backbone. **épineux**, **-euse** adj thorny.

épingle /epɛ̃gl/ nf pin; ~ de nourrice, ~ de sûreté safety-pin.

épisode /epizɔd/ nm episode; à ~s serialized.

épitaphe /epitaf/ nf epitaph.

épluche-légumes /eplyʃlegym/ nm inv (potato) peeler.

éplucher /eplyʃe/ [1] vt peel; (examiner: fig) scrutinize.

épluchure /eplyʃyʀ/ nf ~s peelings.

éponge /epɔ̃ʒ/ nf sponge. **éponger** [40] vt (liquide) mop up; (surface, front) mop; (fig) (dettes) wipe out.

épopée /epɔpe/ nf epic.

époque /epɔk/ nf time, period; à l'~ at the time; d'~ period.

épouse /epuz/ nf wife.

épouser /epuze/ [1] vt marry; (forme, idée) adopt.

épousseter /epuste/ [38] vt dust.

épouvantable /epuvɑ̃tabl/ adj appalling.

épouvantail /epuvɑ̃taj/ nm scarecrow.

épouvante /epuvɑ̃t/ nf terror. **épouvanter** [1] vt terrify.

époux /epu/ nm husband; les ~ the married couple.

éprendre (s') /(s)epʀɑ̃dʀ/ [50] vpr s'~ de fall in love with.

épreuve /epʀœv/ nf test; (Sport) event; (malheur) ordeal; (Photo, d'imprimerie) proof; mettre à l'~ put to the test.

éprouver /epʀuve/ [1] vt (ressentir) experience; (affliger) distress; (tester) test.

éprouvette /epʀuvɛt/ nf test-tube.

EPS abrév f (éducation physique et sportive) PE.

épuisé, ~e /epɥize/ adj exhausted; (livre) out of print. **épuisement** nm exhaustion.

épuiser /epɥize/ [1] vt (fatiguer, user) exhaust. □ s'~ vpr become exhausted.

épuration /epyʀasjɔ̃/ nf purification; (Pol) purge. **épurer** [1] vt purify; (Pol) purge.

équateur /ekwatœʀ/ nm equator.

équilibre /ekilibʀ/ nm balance; être ou se tenir en ~ (personne) balance; (objet) be balanced. **équilibré**, ~e adj well-balanced.

équilibrer /ekilibʀe/ [1] vt balance. □ s'~ vpr balance each other.

équilibriste /ekilibʀist/ nmf acrobat.

équipage /ekipaʒ/ nm crew.

équipe /ekip/ nf team; ~ de nuit/ jour night/day shift.

équipé, ~e /ekipe/ adj equipped; cuisine ~e fitted kitchen.

équipement /ekipmɑ̃/ nm equipment; ~s (installations) amenities, facilities.

équiper /ekipe/ [1] vt equip (de with). □ s'~ vpr equip oneself.

équipier, -ière /ekipje, -jɛʀ/ *nm,f*
team member.

équitable /ekitabl/ *adj* fair.

équitation /ekitasjɔ̃/ *nf* (horse-)
riding.

équivalence /ekivalɑ̃s/ *nf*
equivalence. **équivalent, ~e** *adj*
equivalent.

équivaloir /ekivalwaʀ/ [60] *vi* ~ à
be equivalent to.

équivoque /ekivɔk/ *adj* equivocal;
(louche) questionable. ● *nf* ambiguity.

érable /eʀabl/ *nm* maple.

érafler /eʀafle/ [1] *vt* scratch.
éraflure *nf* scratch.

éraillé, ~e /eʀaje/ *adj* (*voix*)
raucous.

ère /ɛʀ/ *nf* era.

éreintant, ~e /eʀɛ̃tɑ̃, -t/ *adj*
exhausting. **éreinter (s')** [1] *vpr*
wear oneself out.

ériger /eʀiʒe/ [40] *vt* erect. □ s'~ en
vpr set (oneself) up as.

éroder /eʀɔde/ [1] *vt* erode. **érosion**
nf erosion.

errer /eʀe/ [1] *vi* wander.

erreur /eʀœʀ/ *nf* mistake, error;
dans l'~ mistaken; **par ~** by
mistake; ~ **judiciaire** miscarriage of
justice.

erroné, ~e /eʀɔne/ *adj* erroneous.

érudit, ~e /eʀydi, -t/ *adj* scholarly.
● *nm,f* scholar.

éruption /eʀypsjɔ̃/ *nf* eruption;
(Méd) rash.

es /ɛ/ ⇒ÊTRE [4].

escabeau (*pl* ~x) /ɛskabo/ *nm*
step-ladder.

escadron /ɛskadʀɔ̃/ *nm* (Mil)
company.

escalade /ɛskalad/ *nf* climbing;
(Pol, Comm) escalation. **escalader**
[1] *vt* climb.

escale /ɛskal/ *nf* (d'avion) stopover;
(port) port of call; **faire ~ à** (*avion,
passager*) stop over at; (*navire,
passager*) put in at.

escalier /ɛskalje/ *nm* stairs (+ *pl*);
~ **mécanique** *ou* **roulant** escalator.

escalope /ɛskalɔp/ *nf* escalope.

escargot /ɛskaʀgo/ *nm* snail.

escarpé, ~e /ɛskaʀpe/ *adj* steep.

escarpin /ɛskaʀpɛ̃/ *nm* court shoe;
(US) pump.

escient: à bon ~ /abɔnesjɑ̃/ *loc*
wisely.

esclandre /ɛsklɑ̃dʀ/ *nm* scene.

esclavage /ɛsklavaʒ/ *nm* slavery.
esclave *nmf* slave.

escompte /ɛskɔ̃t/ *nm* discount.
escompter [1] *vt* expect; (Comm)
discount.

escorte /ɛskɔʀt/ *nf* escort.

escrime /ɛskʀim/ *nf* fencing.

escroc /ɛskʀo/ *nm* swindler.

escroquer /ɛskʀɔke/ [1] *vt* swindle;
~ **qch à qn** swindle sb out of sth.
escroquerie *nf* swindle.

espace /ɛspas/ *nm* space; ~**s verts**
gardens and parks.

espacer /ɛspase/ [10] *vt* space out.
□ s'~ *vpr* become less frequent.

espadrille /ɛspadʀij/ *nf* rope
sandal.

Espagne /ɛspaɲ/ *nf* Spain.

espagnol, ~e /ɛspaɲɔl/ *adj*
Spanish. ● *nm* (Ling) Spanish. **E~,
~e** *nm,f* Spaniard.

espèce /ɛspɛs/ *nf* kind, sort; (race)
species; **en ~s** (*argent*) in cash; ~
d'idiot! 🖪 you idiot! 🖪.

espérance /ɛspeʀɑ̃s/ *nf* hope.

espérer /ɛspeʀe/ [14] *vt* hope for; ~
faire/que hope to do/that. ● *vi* hope.

espiègle /ɛspjɛgl/ *adj* mischievous.

espion, ~ne /ɛspjɔ̃, -ɔn/ *nm,f* spy.
espionnage *nm* espionage, spying.
espionner [1] *vt* spy (on).

espoir /ɛspwaʀ/ *nm* hope; **reprendre
~** feel hopeful again.

esprit /ɛspʀi/ *nm* (intellect) mind;
(humour) wit; (fantôme) spirit; (ambiance) atmosphere; **perdre l'~** lose
one's mind; **reprendre ses ~s** come
to; **faire de l'~** try to be witty.

esquimau, ~de (*mpl* ~x) /ɛskimo,
-d/ *nm,f* Eskimo.

esquinter /ɛskɛ̃te/ [1] *vt* 🖪 ruin.

esquisse /ɛskis/ *nf* sketch; (fig)
outline.

esquiver /ɛskive/ [1] *vt* dodge.
□ s'~ *vpr* slip away.

essai /esɛ/ *nm* (épreuve) test, trial;
(tentative) try; (article) essay; (au rugby)

try; ~s (Auto) qualifying round (+ sg); à l'~ on trial.

essaim /esɛ̃/ nm swarm.

essayage /esɛjaʒ/ nm fitting; **salon d'~** fitting room.

essayer /eseje/ [31] vt/i try; (vêtement) try (on); (voiture) try (out); ~ **de faire** try to do.

essence /esɑ̃s/ nf (carburant) petrol; (nature, extrait) essence; ~ **sans plomb** unleaded petrol.

essentiel, **~le** /esɑ̃sjɛl/ adj essential. ● nm l'~ the main thing; (quantité) the main part.

essieu (pl ~**x**) /esjø/ nm axle.

essor /esɔR/ nm expansion; **prendre son ~** expand.

essorage /esɔRaʒ/ nm spin-drying.

essorer [1] vt (linge) spin-dry; (en tordant) wring.

essoreuse /esɔRøz/ nf spin-drier; ~ **à salade** salad spinner.

essoufflé, **~e** /esufle/ adj out of breath.

essuie-glace /esɥiglas/ nm inv windscreen wiper.

essuie-mains /esɥimɛ̃/ nm inv hand-towel.

essuie-tout /esɥitu/ nm inv kitchen paper.

essuyer /esɥije/ [31] vt wipe; (subir) suffer. □ **s'~** vpr dry ou wipe oneself.

est¹ /ɛ/ ⇒ÊTRE [4].

est² /ɛst/ nm east. ● a inv east; (partie) eastern; (direction) easterly.

estampe /ɛstɑ̃p/ nf print.

esthète /ɛstɛt/ nmf aesthete.

esthéticienne /ɛstetisjɛn/ nf beautician.

esthétique /ɛstetik/ adj aesthetic.

estimation /ɛstimasjɔ̃/ nf (de coûts) estimate; (valeur) valuation.

estime /ɛstim/ nf esteem.

estimer /ɛstime/ [1] vt (tableau) value; (calculer) estimate; (respecter) esteem; (considérer) consider (**que** that).

estival, **~e** (mpl -**aux**) /ɛstival, -o/ adj summer. **estivant**, **~e** nm,f summer visitor.

estomac /ɛstɔma/ nm stomach.

estomaqué, **~e** /ɛstɔmake/ adj 🛈 stunned.

Estonie /ɛstɔni/ nf Estonia.

estrade /ɛstRad/ nf platform.

estragon /ɛstRagɔ̃/ nm tarragon.

estropié, **~e** /ɛstRɔpje/ nm,f cripple. ● adj crippled.

estuaire /ɛstɥɛR/ nm estuary.

et /e/ conj and; ~ **moi?** what about me?; ~ **alors?** so what?

étable /etabl/ nf cow-shed.

établi, **~e** /etabli/ adj established; **un fait bien ~** a well-established fact. ● nm work-bench.

établir /etabliR/ [2] vt establish; (liste, facture) draw up; (personne, camp, record) set up. □ **s'~** vpr (personne) settle; **s'~ à son compte** set up on one's own.

établissement /etablismɑ̃/ nm (entreprise) organization; (institution) establishment; ~ **scolaire** school.

étage /etaʒ/ nm floor, storey; (de fusée) stage; **à l'~** upstairs; **au premier ~** on the first floor.

étagère /etaʒɛR/ nf shelf; (meuble) shelving unit.

étain /etɛ̃/ nm pewter.

étais, **était** /etɛ/ ⇒ÊTRE [4].

étalage /etalaʒ/ nm display; (vitrine) shop-window; **faire ~ de** flaunt.

étalagiste /etalaʒist/ nmf window-dresser.

étaler /etale/ [1] vt spread; (journal) spread (out); (pâte) roll out; (exposer) display; (richesse) flaunt. □ **s'~** vpr (prendre de la place) spread out; (tomber 🛈) fall flat; **s'~ sur** (paiement) be spread over.

étalon /etalɔ̃/ nm (cheval) stallion; (modèle) standard.

étanche /etɑ̃ʃ/ adj watertight; (montre) waterproof.

étancher /etɑ̃ʃe/ [1] vt (soif) quench.

étang /etɑ̃/ nm pond.

étant /etɑ̃/ ⇒ÊTRE [4].

étape /etap/ nf stage; (lieu d'arrêt) stopover; (fig) stage.

état /eta/ nm state; (liste) statement; (métier) profession; **en bon/mauvais ~** in good/bad condition; **en ~ de** in a position to; **en ~ de marche** in working order; **faire ~ de** (citer) mention; **être dans tous ses** ~**s** be in a state; ~ **civil** civil status; ~ **des lieux** inventory of fixtures. **État** *nm* State.

état-major (*pl* **états-majors**) /etamaʒɔʀ/ *nm* (officiers) staff (+ *pl*).

États-Unis /etazyni/ *nmpl* ~ (**d'Amérique**) United States (of America).

étau (*pl* ~**x**) /eto/ *nm* vice.

étayer /eteje/ [31] *vt* prop up.

été[1] /ete/ ⇒**ÊTRE** [4].

été[2] /ete/ *nm* summer.

éteindre /etɛ̃dʀ/ [22] *vt* (*feu*) put out; (*lumière, radio*) turn off. □ **s'**~ *vpr* (*feu, lumière*) go out; (*appareil*) go off; (*mourir*) die. **éteint**, ~**e** *adj* (*feu*) out; (*volcan*) extinct.

étendard /etɑ̃daʀ/ *nm* standard.

étendre /etɑ̃dʀ/ [3] *vt* (*nappe*) spread (out); (*bras, jambes*) stretch (out); (*linge*) hang out; (*agrandir*) extend. □ **s'**~ *vpr* (s'allonger) lie down; (se propager) spread; (*plaine*) stretch; **s'**~ **sur** (*sujet*) dwell on.

étendu, ~**e** /etɑ̃dy/ *adj* extensive. **étendue** *nf* area; (d'eau) stretch; (importance) extent.

éternel, ~**le** /etɛʀnɛl/ *adj* (*vie*) eternal; (fig) endless.

éterniser (**s'**) /(s)etɛʀnize/ [1] *vpr* (durer) drag on.

éternité /etɛʀnite/ *nf* eternity.

éternuement /etɛʀnymɑ̃/ *nm* sneeze. **éternuer** /etɛʀnɥe/ [1] *vi* sneeze.

êtes /ɛt/ ⇒**ÊTRE** [4].

éthique /etik/ *adj* ethical. ● *nf* ethics (+ *sg*).

ethnie /ɛtni/ *nf* ethnic group. **ethnique** *adj* ethnic.

étincelant, ~**e** /etɛ̃slɑ̃, -t/ *adj* sparkling. **étinceler** [38] *vi* sparkle. **étincelle** *nf* spark.

étiqueter /etikte/ [38] *vt* label. **étiquette** *nf* label; (protocole) etiquette.

étirer /etiʀe/ [1] *vt* stretch. □ **s'**~ *vpr* stretch.

étoffe /etɔf/ *nf* fabric.

étoffer /etɔfe/ [1] *vt* expand. □ **s'**~ *vpr* fill out.

étoile /etwal/ *nf* star; **à la belle** ~ in the open; ~ **filante** shooting star; ~ **de mer** starfish.

étonnant, ~**e** /etɔnɑ̃, -t/ *adj* (curieux) surprising; (formidable) amazing. **étonnement** *nm* surprise; (plus fort) amazement.

étonner /etɔne/ [1] *vt* amaze. □ **s'**~ *vpr* be amazed (de at).

étouffant, ~**e** /etufɑ̃, -t/ *adj* stifling.

étouffer /etufe/ [1] *vt/i* suffocate; (*sentiment, révolte*) stifle; (*feu*) smother; (*bruit*) muffle; **on étouffe** it is stifling. □ **s'**~ *vpr* suffocate; (en mangeant) choke.

étourderie /etuʀdeʀi/ *nf* thoughtlessness; (acte) careless mistake.

étourdi, ~**e** /etuʀdi/ *adj* absent-minded. ● *nm, f* scatterbrain.

étourdir /etuʀdiʀ/ [2] *vt* stun; (fatiguer) make sb's head spin. **étourdissant**, ~**e** *adj* stunning.

étourneau (*pl* ~**x**) /etuʀno/ *nm* starling.

étrange /etʀɑ̃ʒ/ *adj* strange.

étranger, **-ère** /etʀɑ̃ʒe, -ɛʀ/ *adj* (inconnu) strange, unfamiliar; (d'un autre pays) foreign. ● *nm, f* foreigner; (inconnu) stranger; **à l'**~ abroad; **de l'**~ from abroad.

étrangler /etʀɑ̃gle/ [1] *vt* strangle; (*col*) throttle. □ **s'**~ *vpr* choke.

être /ɛtʀ/ [4]

● *verbe auxiliaire*

····➤ (du passé) have; **elle est partie/venue hier** she left/came yesterday.

····➤ (de la voix passive) be.

● *verbe intransitif* (*aux avoir*)

····➤ be; ~ **médecin** be a doctor; **je suis à vous** I'm all yours; **j'en suis à me demander si…** I'm beginning to wonder whether…; **qu'en est-il de…?** what's the news about…?

····➤ (appartenance) be, belong to.

····➤ (heure, date) be; **nous sommes le 3 mars** it's March 3.

····➤ (aller) be; **je n'y ai jamais été** I've never been; **il a été le voir** he went to see him.

····▸ c'est it is *or* it's; **c'est moi qui l'ai fait** I did it; **est-ce que tu veux du thé?** do you want some tea?

● *nom masculin*

····▸ being; ~ **humain** human being.

····▸ (personne) person; **un ~ cher** a loved one.

étreindre /etʀɛ̃dʀ/ [22] *vt* embrace. **étreinte** *nf* embrace.

étrennes /etʀɛn/ *nfpl* (New Year's) gift (+ *sg*); (argent) money.

étrier /etʀije/ *nm* stirrup.

étriqué, ~**e** /etʀike/ *adj* tight.

étroit, ~**e** /etʀwa, -t/ *adj* narrow; (*vêtement*) tight; (*liens, surveillance*) close; **à l'~** cramped. **étroitement** *adv* closely. **étroitesse** *nf* narrowness.

étude /etyd/ *nf* study; (enquête) survey; (bureau) office; (salle d')~ (Scol) prep room; **à l'~** under consideration; **faire des ~s (de)** study; **il n'a pas fait d'~s** he didn't go to university; ~ **de marché** market research.

étudiant, ~**e** /etydjã, -t/ *nm,f* student.

étudier /etydje/ [45] *vt/i* study.

étui /etɥi/ *nm* case.

étuve /etyv/ *nf* steam room.

eu, ~**e** /y/ ⇒AVOIR [5].

euro /øʀo/ *nm* euro.

Europe /øʀɔp/ *nf* Europe.

européen, ~**ne** /øʀɔpeɛ̃, -eɛn/ *adj* European. **E~**, ~**ne** *nm,f* European.

euthanasie /øtanazi/ *nf* euthanasia.

eux /ø/ *pron* they; (complément) them. **eux-mêmes** *pron* themselves.

évacuation /evakɥasjɔ̃/ *nf* evacuation; (d'eaux usées) discharge. **évacuer** [1] *vt* evacuate.

évadé, ~**e** /evade/ *adj* escaped. ● *nm,f* escaped prisoner. **évader** (s') [1] *vpr* escape.

évaluation /evalɥasjɔ̃/ *nf* assessment. **évaluer** [1] *vt* assess.

évangile /evɑ̃ʒil/ *nm* gospel; **l'É~** the Gospel.

évanouir (s') /(s)evanwiʀ/ [2] *vpr* faint; (disparaître) vanish.

évaporation /evapɔʀasjɔ̃/ *nf* evaporation. **évaporer** (s') [1] *vpr* evaporate.

évasif, -**ive** /evazif, -v/ *adj* evasive.

évasion /evazjɔ̃/ *nf* escape.

éveil /evɛj/ *nm* awakening; **en ~** alert.

éveillé, ~**e** /eveje/ *adj* awake; (intelligent) alert.

éveiller /eveje/ [1] *vt* awake(n); (susciter) arouse. □ **s'~** *vpr* awake.

événement /evenmɑ̃/ *nm* event.

éventail /evɑ̃taj/ *nm* fan; (gamme) range.

éventrer /evɑ̃tʀe/ [1] *vt* (sac) rip open.

éventualité /evɑ̃tɥalite/ *nf* possibility; **dans cette ~** in that event.

éventuel, ~**le** /evɑ̃tɥɛl/ *adj* possible. **éventuellement** *adv* possibly.

évêque /evɛk/ *nm* bishop.

évertuer (s') /(s)evɛʀtɥe/ [1] *vpr* **s'~ à** struggle hard to.

éviction /eviksjɔ̃/ *nf* eviction.

évidemment /evidamɑ̃/ *adv* obviously; (bien sûr) of course.

évidence /evidɑ̃s/ *nf* obviousness; (fait) obvious fact; **être en ~** be conspicuous; **mettre en ~** (fait) highlight. **évident**, ~**e** *adj* obvious, evident.

évier /evje/ *nm* sink.

évincer /evɛ̃se/ [10] *vt* oust.

éviter /evite/ [1] *vt* avoid (**de faire** doing); ~ **qch à qn** (dérangement) save sb sth.

évocateur, -**trice** /evɔkatœʀ, -tʀis/ *adj* evocative. **évocation** *nf* evocation.

évolué, ~**e** /evɔlɥe/ *adj* highly developed.

évoluer /evɔlɥe/ [1] *vi* evolve; (situation) develop; (se déplacer) glide. **évolution** *nf* evolution; (d'une situation) development.

évoquer /evɔke/ [1] *vt* call to mind, evoke.

exacerber /ɛgzasɛʀbe/ [1] *vt* exacerbate.

exact, ~**e** /ɛgza(kt), -akt/ *adj* (précis) exact, accurate; (juste) correct;

(*personne*) punctual. **exactement**
adv exactly. **exactitude** *nf*
exactness; punctuality.

ex æquo /ɛgzeko/ *adv* être ~ tie
(avec qn with sb).

exagération /ɛgzaʒeʀasjɔ̃/ *nf*
exaggeration. **exagéré**, ~**e** *adj*
excessive.

exagérer /ɛgzaʒeʀe/ [14] *vt/i*
exaggerate; (abuser) go too far.

exalté, ~**e** /ɛgzalte/ *nm,f* fanatic.
exalter [1] *vt* excite; (glorifier) exalt.

examen /ɛgzamɛ̃/ *nm* examination;
(Scol) exam. **examinateur, -trice**
nm,f examiner. **examiner** [1] *vt*
examine.

exaspération /ɛgzaspeʀasjɔ̃/ *nf*
exasperation. **exaspérer** [14] *vt*
exasperate.

exaucer /ɛgzose/ [10] *vt* grant;
(*personne*) grant the wish(es) of.

excédent /ɛksedã/ *nm* surplus; ~
de bagages excess luggage; ~ **de la
balance commerciale** trade surplus.
excédentaire *adj* excess, surplus.

excéder /ɛksede/ [14] *vt* (dépasser)
exceed; (agacer) irritate.

excellence /ɛksɛlɑ̃s/ *nf* excellence.
excellent, ~**e** *adj* excellent.
exceller [1] *vi* excel (dans in).

excentricité /ɛksɑ̃tʀisite/ *nf*
eccentricity. **excentrique** *a & nmf*
eccentric.

excepté, ~**e** /ɛksɛpte/ *a & prép*
except.

excepter /ɛksɛpte/ [1] *vt* except.

exception /ɛksɛpsjɔ̃/ *nf* exception;
à l'~ de except for; d'~ exceptional;
faire ~ be an exception.
exceptionnel, ~**le** *adj* exceptional. **exceptionnellement**
adv exceptionally.

excès /ɛksɛ/ *nm* excess; ~ **de
vitesse** speeding.

excessif, -ive /ɛksesif, -v/ *adj*
excessive.

excitant, ~**e** /ɛksitã, -t/ *adj*
stimulating; (palpitant) exciting. ● *nm*
stimulant.

exciter /ɛksite/ [1] *vt* excite; (irriter)
get excited. □ **s'**~ *vpr* get excited.

exclamer (s') /(s)ɛksklame/ [1] *vpr*
exclaim.

exclure /ɛksklyʀ/ [16] *vt* exclude;
(expulser) expel; (empêcher) preclude.

exclusif, -ive /ɛksklyzif, -v/ *adj*
exclusive.

exclusion /ɛksklyzjɔ̃/ *nf* exclusion.

exclusivité /ɛksklyzivite/ *nf* (Comm)
exclusive rights (+ *pl*); projeter en ~
show exclusively.

excursion /ɛkskyʀsjɔ̃/ *nf*
excursion; (à pied) hike.

excuse /ɛkskyz/ *nf* excuse; ~**s**
apology (+ *sg*); faire des ~**s**
apologize.

excuser /ɛkskyze/ [1] *vt* excuse;
excusez-moi excuse me. □ **s'**~ *vpr*
apologize (de for).

exécrable /ɛgzekʀabl/ *adj*
dreadful. **exécrer** [14] *vt* loathe.

exécuter /ɛgzekyte/ [1] *vt* carry
out, execute; (Mus) perform; (tuer)
execute.

exécutif, -ive /ɛgzekytif, -v/ *a &
nm* (Pol) executive.

exécution /ɛgzekysjɔ̃/ *nf*
execution; (Mus) performance.

exemplaire /ɛgzɑ̃plɛʀ/ *adj*
exemplary. ● *nm* copy.

exemple /ɛgzɑ̃pl/ *nm* example; par
~ for example; donner l'~ set an
example.

exempt, ~**e** /ɛgzã, -t/ *adj* ~ **de**
exempt (de from).

exempter /ɛgzãte/ [1] *vt* exempt (de
from). **exemption** *nf* exemption.

exercer /ɛgzɛʀse/ [10] *vt* exercise;
(*influence, contrôle*) exert; (former)
train, exercise; ~ **un métier** have a
job; ~ **le métier de...** work as a...
□ **s'**~ *vpr* practise.

exercice /ɛgzɛʀsis/ *nm* exercise; (de
métier) practice; **en** ~ in office;
(*médecin*) in practice.

exhaler /ɛgzale/ [1] *vt* emit.

exhaustif, -ive /ɛgzostif, -v/ *adj*
exhaustive.

exhiber /ɛgzibe/ [1] *vt* exhibit.

exhorter /ɛgzɔʀte/ [1] *vt* exhort (à
to).

exigeant, ~**e** /ɛgziʒã, -t/ *adj*
demanding; être ~ avec qn demand
a lot of sb. **exigence** *nf* demand.
exiger [40] *vt* demand.

exigu, ~**ë** /ɛgzigy/ *adj* tiny.

exil /ɛgzil/ nm exile. **exilé, ~e** nm, f exile.

exiler /ɛgzile/ [1] vt exile. □ **s'~** vpr go into exile.

existence /ɛgzistãs/ nf existence. **exister** [1] vi exist.

exode /ɛgzɔd/ nm exodus.

exonérer /ɛgzɔnere/ [14] vt exempt (de from).

exorbitant, ~e /ɛgzɔrbitã, -t/ adj exorbitant.

exorciser /ɛgzɔrsize/ [1] vt exorcize.

exotique /ɛgzɔtik/ adj exotic.

expansé, ~e /ɛkspãse/ adj (Tech) expanded.

expansif, -ive /ɛkspãsif, -v/ adj expansive. **expansion** nf expansion.

expatrié, ~e /ɛkspatrije/ nm, f expatriate.

expectative /ɛkspɛktativ/ nf **être dans l'~** wait and see.

expédient /ɛkspedjã/ nm expedient; **vivre d'~s** live by one's wits; **user d'~s** resort to expedients.

expédier /ɛkspedje/ [45] vt send, dispatch; (tâche 🔢) polish off. **expéditeur, -trice** nm, f sender.

expéditif, -ive /ɛkspeditif, -v/ adj quick.

expédition /ɛkspedisjõ/ nf (envoi) dispatching; (voyage) expedition.

expérience /ɛksperjãs/ nf experience; (scientifique) experiment.

expérimental, ~e (mpl **-aux**) /ɛksperimãtal, o/ adj experimental. **expérimentation** nf experimentation. **expérimenté, ~e** adj experienced. **expérimenter** [1] vt test, experiment with.

expert, ~e /ɛkspɛr, -t/ adj expert. ● nm expert; (d'assurances) adjuster. **expert-comptable** (pl **experts-comptables**) nm accountant.

expertise /ɛkspɛrtiz/ nf valuation; (de dégâts) assessment. **expertiser** [1] vt value; (dégâts) assess.

expier /ɛkspje/ [45] vt atone for.

expiration /ɛkspirasjõ/ nf expiry.

expirer /ɛkspire/ [1] vi breathe out; (finir, mourir) expire.

explicatif, -ive /ɛksplikatif, -v/ adj explanatory.

explication /ɛksplikasjõ/ nf explanation; (fig) discussion; **~ de texte** (Scol) literary commentary.

explicite /ɛksplisit/ adj explicit.

expliquer /ɛksplike/ [1] vt explain. □ **s'~** vpr explain oneself; (discuter) discuss things; (être explicable) be understandable.

exploit /ɛksplwa/ nm exploit.

exploitant, ~e /ɛksplwatã, -t/ nm, f **~ (agricole)** farmer.

exploitation /ɛksplwatasjõ/ nf exploitation; (d'entreprise) running; (ferme) farm.

exploiter /ɛksplwate/ [1] vt exploit; (ferme) run; (mine) work.

explorateur, -trice /ɛksplɔratœr, -tris/ nm, f explorer. **exploration** nf exploration. **explorer** [1] vt explore.

exploser /ɛksploze/ [1] vi explode; **faire ~** explode; (bâtiment) blow up.

explosif, -ive /ɛksplozif, -v/ a & nm explosive. **explosion** nf explosion.

exportateur, -trice /ɛkspɔrtatœr, -tris/ nm, f exporter. ● adj exporting. **exportation** nf export. **exporter** [1] vt export.

exposant, ~e /ɛkspozã, -t/ nm, f exhibitor.

exposé, ~e /ɛkspoze/ nm talk (sur on); (d'une action) account; **faire l'~ de la situation** give an account of the situation. ● adj **~ au nord** facing north.

exposer /ɛkspoze/ [1] vt display, show; (expliquer) explain; (soumettre, mettre en danger) expose (à to); (vie) endanger. □ **s'~ à** vpr expose oneself to.

exposition /ɛkspozisjõ/ nf (d'art) exhibition; (de faits) exposition; (géographique) aspect.

exprès¹ /ɛksprɛ/ adv specially; (délibérément) on purpose.

exprès², -esse /ɛksprɛs/ adj express.

express /ɛksprɛs/ a & nm inv **(café) ~** espresso; **(train) ~** fast train.

expressif, -ive /ɛkspresif, -v/ adj expressive. **expression** nf expression.

exprimer /ɛkspʀime/ [1] *vt* express.
□ **s'~** *vpr* express oneself.

expulser /ɛkspylse/ [1] *vt* expel;
(*locataire*) evict; (*joueur*) send off.

expulsion *nf* (d'élève) expulsion; (de
locataire) eviction; (d'immigré)
deportation.

exquis, **~e** /ɛkski, -z/ *adj* exquisite.

extase /ɛkstɑz/ *nf* ecstasy.

extasier (**s'**) /(s)ɛkstazje/ [45] *vpr*
s'~ **sur** be ecstatic about.

extensible /ɛkstãsibl/ *adj* (*tissu*)
stretch.

extension /ɛkstãsjɔ̃/ *nf* extension;
(expansion) expansion.

exténuer /ɛkstenɥe/ [1] *vt* exhaust.

extérieur, **~e** /ɛksteʀjœʀ/ *adj*
outside; (*signe, gaieté*) outward;
(*politique*) foreign. ● *nm* outside,
exterior; (de personne) exterior; **à l'~**
(**de**) outside. **extérioriser** [1] *vt*
show, externalize.

extermination /ɛkstɛʀminasjɔ̃/ *nf*
extermination. **exterminer** [1] *vt*
exterminate.

externe /ɛkstɛʀn/ *adj* external.
● *nmf* (Scol) day pupil.

extincteur /ɛkstɛ̃ktœʀ/ *nm* fire
extinguisher.

extinction /ɛkstɛ̃ksjɔ̃/ *nf*
extinction; **avoir une ~ de voix** have
lost one's voice.

extorquer /ɛkstɔʀke/ [1] *vt* extort.

extra /ɛkstʀa/ *a inv* first-rate. ● *nm
inv* (repas) (special) treat.

extraction /ɛkstʀaksjɔ̃/ *nf*
extraction.

extrader /ɛkstʀade/ [1] *vt* extradite.

extraire /ɛkstʀɛʀ/ [29] *vt* extract.
extrait *nm* extract.

extraordinaire /ɛkstʀaɔʀdinɛʀ/
adj extraordinary.

extravagance /ɛkstʀavagãs/ *nf*
extravagance. **extravagant**, **~e**
adj extravagant.

extraverti, **~e** /ɛkstʀavɛʀti/ *nm,f*
extrovert.

extrême /ɛkstʀɛm/ *a & nm*
extreme. **extrêmement** *adv*
extremely.

Extrême-Orient /ɛkstʀɛmɔʀjã/
nm Far East.

extrémiste /ɛkstʀemist/ *nmf*
extremist.

extrémité /ɛkstʀemite/ *nf* end;
(mains, pieds) extremity.

exubérance /ɛgzybeʀãs/ *nf*
exuberance. **exubérant**, **~e** *adj*
exuberant.

Ff

F *abrév f* (**franc, francs**) franc,
francs.

fabricant, **~e** /fabʀikã, -t/ *nm,f*
manufacturer. **fabrication** *nf*
making; manufacture.

fabrique /fabʀik/ *nf* factory.
fabriquer [1] *vt* make;
(industriellement) manufacture; (fig)
make up.

fabuler /fabyle/ [1] *vi* fantasize.

fabuleux, **-euse** /fabylø, -z/ *adj*
fabulous.

fac /fak/ *nf* Ⅰ university.

façade /fasad/ *nf* front; (fig) façade.

face /fas/ *nf* face; (d'un objet) side; **en
~ (de)**, **d'en ~** opposite; **en ~ de** (fig)
faced with; **~ à** facing; (fig) faced
with; **faire ~ à** face. **face-à-face**
nm inv (débat) one-to-one debate.

fâcher /faʃe/ [1] *vt* anger; **fâché**
angry; (désolé) sorry. □ **se ~** *vpr* get
angry; (se brouiller) fall out.

facile /fasil/ *adj* easy; (*caractère*)
easygoing.

facilité /fasilite/ *nf* easiness;
(aisance) ease; (aptitude) ability; **~s**
(possibilités) facilities, opportunities;
~s d'importation import
opportunities; **~s de paiement** easy
terms.

faciliter /fasilite/ [1] *vt* facilitate,
make easier.

façon /fasɔ̃/ *nf* way; (de vêtement) cut;
de cette ~ in this way; **de ~ à** so as
to; **de toute ~** anyway; **~s** (chichis)
fuss; **faire des ~s** stand on
ceremony; **sans ~s** (*repas*) informal;

(*personne*) unpretentious. **façonner** [1] *vt* shape; (faire) make.

fac-similé (*pl* ~**s**) /faksimile/ *nm* facsimile.

facteur, -trice /faktœʀ, -tʀis/ *nm, f* postman, postwoman. ● *nm* (élément) factor.

facture /faktyʀ/ *nf* bill; (Comm) invoice; ~ **détaillée** itemized bill. **facturer** [1] *vt* invoice. **facturette** *nf* credit card slip.

facultatif, -ive /fakyltatif, -v/ *adj* optional.

faculté /fakylte/ *nf* faculty; (possibilité) power; (Univ) faculty.

fade /fad/ *adj* insipid.

faible /fɛbl/ *adj* weak; (*espoir, quantité, écart*) slight; (*revenu, intensité*) low; ~ **d'esprit** feeble-minded. ● *nm* (personne) weakling; (penchant) weakness. **faiblesse** *nf* weakness. **faiblir** [2] *vi* weaken.

faïence /fajɑ̃s/ *nf* earthenware.

faillir /fajiʀ/ [2] *vi* **j'ai failli acheter** I almost bought.

faillite /fajit/ *nf* bankruptcy; (fig) collapse.

faim /fɛ̃/ *nf* hunger; **avoir** ~ be hungry; **rester sur sa** ~ (fig) be left wanting more.

fainéant, ~e /feneɑ̃, -t/ *adj* idle. ● *nm, f* idler.

....

faire /fɛʀ/ [33]

⟹ Pour les expressions comme **faire attention, faire la cuisine**, etc. ⇒**attention, cuisine**, etc.

● *verbe transitif*

····▸ (préparer, créer) make; ~ **une tarte/ une erreur** make a tart/a mistake.

····▸ (se livrer à une activité) do; ~ **du droit** do law; ~ **du foot/du violon** play football/the violin; **qu'est-ce qu'elle fait?** (dans la vie) what does she do?; (en ce moment précis) what is she doing?

····▸ (dans les calculs, mesures, etc.) **10 et 10 font 20** 10 and 10 make 20; **ça fait 25 francs** that's 25 francs; ~ **60 kilos** weigh 60 kilos; **il fait 1,75 m** he's 1.75 m tall.

····▸ (dans les expressions de temps) **ça fait une heure que j'attends** I have been waiting for an hour.

····▸ (imiter) ~ **le clown** act the clown; **faire le malade** pretend to be ill.

····▸ (parcourir) ~ **10 km** do *ou* cover 10 km; ~ **les musées** go round the museums.

····▸ (entraîner, causer) **ça ne fait rien** it doesn't matter; **l'accident a fait 8 morts** 8 people died in the accident.

····▸ (dire) say; **'excusez-moi', fit-elle** 'excuse me', she said.

● *verbe auxiliaire*

····▸ (**faire** + infinitif + qn) make; ~ **pleurer qn** make sb cry.

····▸ (**faire** + infinitif + qch) have, get; ~ **réparer sa voiture** have *ou* get one's car mended.

····▸ (**ne faire que** + infinitif) (continuellement) **ne** ~ **que pleurer** do nothing but cry; (seulement) **je ne fais qu'obéir** I'm only following orders.

● *verbe intransitif*

····▸ (agir) do, act; ~ **vite** act quickly; **fais comme tu veux** do as you please; **fais comme chez toi** make yourself at home.

····▸ (paraître) look; ~ **joli** look pretty; **ça fait cher** it's expensive.

····▸ (en parlant du temps) **il fait chaud/ gris** it's hot/overcast.

□ **se faire** *verbe pronominal*

····▸ (obtenir, confectionner) make; **se** ~ **des amis** make friends; **se** ~ **un thé** make (oneself) a cup of tea.

····▸ (**se faire** + infinitif) **se** ~ **gronder** be scolded; **se** ~ **couper les cheveux** have one's hair cut.

····▸ (devenir) **il se fait tard** it's getting late.

····▸ (être d'usage) **ça ne se fait pas** it's not the done thing.

····▸ (emploi impersonnel) **comment se fait-il que tu sois ici?** how come you're here?

····▸ □ **se faire à** get used to; **je ne m'y fais pas** I can't get used to it.

····▸ □ **s'en faire** worry; **ne t'en fais pas** don't worry.

! Lorsque **faire** remplace un
verbe plus précis, on traduira
quelquefois par ce dernier:
faire une visite *pay a visit*,
faire un nid *build a nest*.

faire-part /fɛʀpaʀ/ *nm inv*
announcement.

fais /fɛ/ ⇒FAIRE [33].

faisan /fəzã/ *nm* pheasant.

faisceau (*pl* ~x) /fɛso/ *nm* (rayon)
beam; (fagot) bundle.

fait, ~e /fɛ, fɛt/ *adj* done; (*fromage*)
ripe; ~ **pour** made for; **tout** ~ ready
made; **c'est bien** ~ **pour toi** it serves
you right. ● *nm* fact; (événement)
event; **au** ~ (de) informed (of); **de ce**
~ therefore; **du** ~ **de** on account of;
~ **divers** (trivial) news item; ~
nouveau new development; **prendre
qn sur le** ~ catch sb in the act.
● ⇒FAIRE [33].

faîte /fɛt/ *nm* top; (fig) peak.

faites /fɛt/ ⇒FAIRE [33].

falaise /falɛz/ *nf* cliff.

falloir /falwaʀ/ [34] *vi* il faut qch/qn
we/you *etc.* need sth/so; **il lui faut du
pain** he needs bread; **il faut rester**
we/you *etc.* have to *ou* must stay; **il
faut que j'y aille** I have to *ou* must
go; **il faudrait que tu partes** you
should leave; **il aurait fallu le faire**
we/you *etc.* should have done it;
comme il faut (*manger, se tenir*)
properly; (*personne*) respectable,
proper. □ **s'en** ~ *vpr* **il s'en est fallu
de peu qu'il gagne** he nearly won; **il
s'en faut de beaucoup que je sois** I
am far from being.

falsifier /falsifje/ [45] *vt* falsify;
(*signature, monnaie*) forge.

famé, ~e /fame/ *adj* **mal** ~
disreputable, seedy.

fameux, -**euse** /famø, -z/ *adj*
famous; (excellent ▣) first-rate.

familial, ~e (*mpl* -**iaux**) /familjal,
-jo/ *adj* family.

familiale /familjal/ *nf* estate car;
(US) station wagon.

familiariser /familjaʀize/ [1] *vt*
familiarize (**avec** with). □ **se** ~ *vpr*
familiarize oneself.

familier, -**ière** /familje, -jɛʀ/ *adj*
familiar; (amical) informal.

famille /famij/ *nf* family; **en** ~ with
one's family.

famine /famin/ *nf* famine.

fanatique /fanatik/ *adj* fanatical.
● *nmf* fanatic.

fanfare /fãfaʀ/ *nf* brass band;
(musique) fanfare.

fantaisie /fãtezi/ *nf* imagination,
fantasy; (caprice) whim; (de) ~
(*boutons etc.*) fancy. **fantaisiste** *adj*
unorthodox; (*personne*) eccentric.

fantasme /fãtasm/ *nm* fantasy.

fantastique /fãtastik/ *adj*
fantastic.

fantôme /fãtom/ *nm* ghost; **cabi-
net(-)~** (Pol) shadow cabinet.

faon /fã/ *nm* fawn.

FAQ *abrév f* (**Foire aux questions**)
(Internet) FAQ, Frequently Asked
Questions.

farce /faʀs/ *nf* (practical) joke;
(Théât) farce; (hachis) stuffing.

farcir /faʀsiʀ/ [2] *vt* stuff.

fard /faʀ/ *nm* make-up; ~ **à
paupières** eye-shadow; **piquer un** ~
blush.

fardeau (*pl* ~x) /faʀdo/ *nm* burden.

farfelu, ~e /faʀfəly/ *a* & *nm,f*
eccentric.

farine /faʀin/ *nf* flour. **farineux**,
-**euse** *adj* floury. **farineux** *nmpl*
starchy food.

farouche /faʀuʃ/ *adj* shy; (peu sociable) unsociable; (violent) fierce.

fascicule /fasikyl/ *nm* (brochure)
booklet; (partie d'un ouvrage) fascicule.

fasciner /fasine/ [1] *vt* fascinate.

fascisme /faʃism/ *nm* fascism.

fasse /fas/ ⇒FAIRE [33].

fast-food /fastfud/ *nm* fast-food
place.

fastidieux, -**ieuse** /fastidjø, -z/ *adj*
tedious.

fatal, ~e (*mpl* ~s) /fatal/ *adj*
inevitable; (mortel) fatal. **fatalité** *nf*
(destin) fate.

fatigant, ~e /fatigã, -t/ *adj* tiring;
(ennuyeux) tiresome.

fatigue /fatig/ *nf* fatigue, tiredness.

fatigué, ~e /fatige/ *adj* tired.

fatiguer /fatige/ [1] *vt* tire; (*yeux, moteur*) strain. ● *vi* (*moteur*) labour. □ **se ~** *vpr* get tired, tire (**de** of).

faubourg /fobur/ *nm* suburb.

faucher /foʃe/ [1] *vt* (*herbe*) mow; (voler 🅸) pinch; **~ qn** (*véhicule, tir*) mow sb down.

faucon /fokɔ̃/ *nm* falcon, hawk.

faudra, faudrait /fodra, fodrɛ/ ⇨FALLOIR [34].

faufiler (se) /(sə)fofile/ [1] *vpr* edge one's way, squeeze.

faune /fon/ *nf* wildlife, fauna.

faussaire /fosɛr/ *nmf* forger.

fausse /fos/ ⇨FAUX².

fausser /fose/ [1] *vt* buckle; (fig) distort; **~ compagnie à qn** give sb the slip.

faut /fo/ ⇨FALLOIR [34].

faute /fot/ *nf* mistake; (responsabilité) fault; (délit) offence; (péché) sin; **en ~** at fault; **~ de** for want of; **~ de quoi** failing which; **sans ~** without fail; **~ de frappe** typing error; **~ de goût** bad taste; **~ professionnelle** professional misconduct.

fauteuil /fotœj/ *nm* armchair; (de président) chair; (Théât) seat; **~ roulant** wheelchair.

fautif, -ive /fotif, -v/ *adj* guilty; (faux) faulty. ● *nm,f* guilty party.

fauve /fov/ *adj* (couleur) fawn, tawny. ● *nm* wild cat.

faux¹ /fo/ *nf* scythe.

faux², fausse /fo, fos/ *adj* false; (falsifié) fake, forged; (numéro, calcul) wrong; (voix) out of tune; **c'est ~!** that is wrong!; **~ témoignage** perjury; **faire ~ bond à qn** stand sb up; **fausse couche** miscarriage; **~ frais** incidental expenses. ● *adv* (chanter) out of tune. ● *nm* forgery. **faux-filet** (*pl* **~s**) *nm* sirloin.

faveur /favœr/ *nf* favour; **de ~** (régime) preferential; **en ~ de** in favour of.

favorable /favɔrabl/ *adj* favourable.

favori, ~te /favɔri, -t/ *a & nm,f* favourite. **favoriser** [1] *vt* favour.

fax /faks/ *nm* fax. **faxer** [1] *vt* fax.

fébrile /febril/ *adj* feverish.

fécond, ~e /fekɔ̃, -d/ *adj* fertile. **féconder** [1] *vt* fertilize. **fécondité** *nf* fertility.

fédéral, ~e (*mpl* **-aux**) /federal, -o/ *adj* federal. **fédération** *nf* federation.

fée /fe/ *nf* fairy. **féerie** *nf* magical spectacle. **féerique** *adj* magical.

feindre /fɛ̃dr/ [22] *vt* feign; **~ de** pretend to.

fêler /fele/ [1] *vt* crack. □ **se ~** *vpr* crack.

félicitations /felisitasjɔ̃/ *nfpl* congratulations (**pour** on). **féliciter** [1] *vt* congratulate (**de** on).

félin, ~e /felɛ̃, -in/ *a & nm* feline.

femelle /fəmɛl/ *a & nf* female.

féminin, ~e /feminɛ̃, -in/ *adj* feminine; (sexe) female; (mode, équipe) women's. ● *nm* feminine. **féministe** *nmf* feminist.

femme /fam/ *nf* woman; (épouse) wife; **~ au foyer** housewife; **~ de chambre** chambermaid; **~ de ménage** cleaning lady.

fémur /femyr/ *nm* thigh-bone.

fendre /fɑ̃dr/ [3] *vt* (couper) split; (fissurer) crack. □ **se ~** *vpr* crack.

fenêtre /fənɛtr/ *nf* window.

fenouil /fənuj/ *nm* fennel.

fente /fɑ̃t/ *nf* (ouverture) slit, slot; (fissure) crack.

féodal, ~e (*mpl* **-aux**) /feodal, -o/ *adj* feudal.

fer /fɛr/ *nm* iron; **~ (à repasser)** iron; **~ à cheval** horseshoe; **~ de lance** spearhead; **~ forgé** wrought iron.

fera, ferait /fəra, fərɛ/ ⇨FAIRE [33].

férié, ~e /ferje/ *adj* **jour ~** public holiday.

ferme /fɛrm/ *nf* farm; (maison) farm (house). ● *adj* firm. ● *adv* (travailler) hard.

fermé, ~e /fɛrme/ *adj* closed; (gaz, radio) off.

fermenter /fɛrmɑ̃te/ [1] *vi* ferment.

fermer /fɛrme/ [1] *vt/i* close, shut; (cesser d'exploiter) close *ou* shut down; (gaz, robinet) turn off. □ **se ~** *vpr* close, shut.

fermeté /fɛrməte/ *nf* firmness.

fermeture /fɛrmətyr/ *nf* closing; (dispositif) catch; **~ annuelle** annual closure; ~ **éclair®** zip(-fastener); (US) zipper.

fermier, -ière /fɛʀmje, -jɛʀ/ adj farm. ● nm farmer. **fermière** nf farmer's wife.

féroce /feʀɔs/ adj ferocious.

ferraille /feʀaj/ nf scrap-iron.

ferrer /feʀe/ [1] vt (cheval) shoe.

ferroviaire /feʀɔvjɛʀ/ adj rail(way).

ferry /feʀi/ nm ferry.

fertile /fɛʀtil/ adj fertile; ~ **en** (fig) rich in. **fertiliser** [1] vt fertilize. **fertilité** nf fertility.

fervent, -e /fɛʀvã, -t/ adj fervent. ● nm, f enthusiast (**de** of).

fesse /fɛs/ nf buttock. **fessée** nf spanking, smack.

festin /fɛstɛ̃/ nm feast.

festival (pl ~s) /fɛstival/ nm festival.

fêtard, ~e /fɛtaʀ, -d/ nm, f 🄸 party animal.

fête /fɛt/ nf holiday; (religieuse) feast; (du nom) name-day; (réception) party; (en famille) celebration; (foire) fair; (folklorique) festival; ~ **des Mères** Mother's Day; ~ **foraine** fun-fair; **faire la** ~ live it up; **les ~s** (de fin d'année) the Christmas season. **fêter** [1] vt celebrate; (personne) give a celebration for.

fétiche /fetiʃ/ nm fetish; (fig) mascot.

feu¹ (pl ~x) /fø/ nm fire; (lumière) light; (de réchaud) burner; **à** ~ **doux/vif** on a low/high heat; ~ **rouge/vert/orange** red/green/amber light; **aux** ~x, **tournez à droite** turn right at the traffic lights; **avez-vous du** ~? (pour cigarette) have you got a light?; **au** ~! fire!; **mettre le** ~ **à** set fire to; **prendre** ~ catch fire; **jouer avec le** ~ play with fire; **ne pas faire long** ~ not last; ~ **d'artifice** firework display; ~ **de joie** bonfire; ~ **de position** sidelight.

feu² /fø/ a inv (mort) late.

feuillage /fœjaʒ/ nm foliage.

feuille /fœj/ nf leaf; (de papier) sheet; (formulaire) form; ~ **d'impôts** tax return; ~ **de paie** payslip.

feuilleté, ~e /fœjte/ adj **pâte** ~e puff pastry. ● nm savoury pasty.

feuilleter /fœjte/ [1] vt leaf through.

feuilleton /fœjtɔ̃/ nm (à suivre) serial; (histoire complète) series.

feutre /føtʀ/ nm felt; (chapeau) felt hat; (crayon) felt-tip (pen).

fève /fɛv/ nf broad bean.

février /fevʀije/ nm February.

fiable /fjabl/ adj reliable.

fiançailles /fjɑ̃saj/ nfpl engagement.

fiancé, ~e /fjɑ̃se/ adj engaged. ● nm fiancé. **fiancée** nf fiancée. **fiancer (se)** [10] vpr become engaged (**avec** to).

fibre /fibʀ/ nf fibre; ~ **de verre** fibreglass.

ficeler /fisle/ [38] vt tie up.

ficelle /fisɛl/ nf string.

fiche /fiʃ/ nf (index) card; (formulaire) form, slip; (Électr) plug.

ficher¹ /fiʃe/ [1] vt (enfoncer) drive (**dans** into).

ficher² /fiʃe/ [1] 🄸 vt (faire) do; (donner) give; (mettre) put; ~ **le camp** clear off. □ **se** ~ vpr make fun of; **il s'en fiche** he couldn't care less.

fichier /fiʃje/ nm file.

fichu, ~e /fiʃy/ adj 🄸 (mauvais) rotten; (raté) done for; **mal** ~ terrible.

fictif, -ive /fiktif, -v/ adj fictitious. **fiction** nf fiction.

fidèle /fidɛl/ adj faithful. ● nmf (client) regular; (Relig) believer; ~**s** (à l'église) congregation. **fidélité** nf fidelity.

fier¹, fière /fjɛʀ/ adj proud (**de** of).

fier² (se) /(sə)fje/ [45] vpr **se** ~ **à** trust.

fierté /fjɛʀte/ nf pride.

fièvre /fjɛvʀ/ nf fever; **avoir de la** ~ have a temperature. **fiévreux, -euse** adj feverish.

figer /fiʒe/ [40] vi (graisse) congeal; (sang) clot; **figé sur place** frozen to the spot. □ **se** ~ vpr (personne, sourire) freeze; (graisse) congeal; (sang) clot.

figue /fig/ nf fig.

figurant, ~e /figyʀã, -t/ nm, f (au cinéma) extra.

figure /figyʀ/ nf face; (forme, personnage) figure; (illustration) picture.

figuré, ~e /figyʀe/ adj (sens) figurative.

figurer /figyʀe/ [1] vi appear. ● vt represent. □ se ~ vpr imagine.

fil /fil/ nm thread; (métallique, électrique) wire; (de couteau) edge; (à coudre) cotton; au ~ de with the passing of; au ~ de l'eau with the current; ~ de fer wire; au bout du ~ 🄣 on the phone.

file /fil/ nf line; (voie: Auto) lane; ~ (d'attente) queue; (US) line; en ~ indienne in single file.

filer /file/ [1] vt spin; (suivre) shadow; ~ qch à qn 🄣 slip sb sth. ● vi (bas) ladder, run; (liquide) run; (aller vite 🄣) speed along, fly by; (partir 🄣) dash off; (disparaître 🄣) ~ entre les mains slip through one's fingers; ~ doux do as one's told; ~ à l'anglaise take French leave.

filet /file/ nm net; (d'eau) trickle; (de viande) fillet; ~ (à bagages) (luggage) rack; ~ à provisions string bag (for shopping).

filiale /filjal/ nf subsidiary (company).

filière /filjɛʀ/ nf (official) channels; (de trafiquants) network; passer par ou suivre la ~ (employé) work one's way up.

fille /fij/ nf girl; (opposé à fils) daughter. **fillette** nf little girl.

filleul /fijœl/ nm godson.

filleule /fijœl/ nf god-daughter.

film /film/ nm film; ~ d'épouvante/ muet/parlant horror/silent/talking film; ~ dramatique drama. **filmer** [1] vt film.

filon /filɔ̃/ nm (Géol) seam; (travail lucratif 🄣) money spinner; avoir trouvé le bon ~ be onto a good thing.

fils /fis/ nm son.

filtre /filtʀ/ nm filter. **filtrer** [1] vt/i filter; (personne) screen.

fin¹ /fɛ̃/ nf end; à la ~ finally; en ~ de compte all things considered; ~ de semaine weekend; mettre ~ à put an end to; prendre ~ come to an end.

fin², ~e /fɛ̃, in/ adj fine; (tranche, couche) thin; (taille) slim; (plat) exquisite; (esprit, vue) sharp; ~es herbes mixed herbs. ● adv (couper) finely.

final, ~e (mpl -aux) /final, -o/ adj final.

finale /final/ nm (Mus) finale. ● nf (Sport) final; (Gram) final syllable. **finalement** adv finally; (somme toute) after all. **finaliste** nmf finalist.

finance /finɑ̃s/ nf finance. **financer** [10] vt finance.

financier, -ière /finɑ̃sje, -jɛʀ/ adj financial. ● nm financier.

finesse /finɛs/ nf fineness; (de taille) slimness; (acuité) sharpness; ~s (de langue) niceties.

finir /finiʀ/ [2] vt/i finish, end; (arrêter) stop; (manger) finish (up); en ~ avec have done with; ~ par faire end up doing; ça va mal ~ it will turn out badly.

finlandais, ~e /fɛ̃lɑ̃dɛ, -z/ adj Finnish. **F~, ~e** nm, f Finn.

Finlande /fɛ̃lɑ̃d/ nf Finland.

finnois, ~e /finwa/ adj Finnish. ● nm (Ling) Finnish.

firme /firm/ nf firm.

fisc /fisk/ nm tax authorities. **fiscal, ~e** (mpl -aux) adj tax, fiscal. **fiscalité** nf tax system.

fissure /fisyʀ/ nf crack.

fixe /fiks/ adj fixed; (stable) steady; à heure ~ at a set time; menu à prix ~ set menu. ● nm basic pay.

fixer /fikse/ [1] vt fix; ~ (du regard) stare at; être fixé (personne) have made up one's mind. □ se ~ vpr (s'attacher) be attached; (s'installer) settle down.

flacon /flakɔ̃/ nm bottle.

flagrant, ~e /flagʀɑ̃, -t/ adj flagrant, blatant; en ~ délit in the act.

flair /flɛʀ/ nm (sense of) smell; (fig) intuition.

flamand, ~e /flamɑ̃, -d/ adj Flemish. ● nm (Ling) Flemish. **F~, ~e** nm, f Fleming.

flamant /flamɑ̃/ nm flamingo.

flambeau (pl ~x) /flɑ̃bo/ nm torch.

flambée /flɑ̃be/ nf blaze; (fig) explosion.

flamber /flɑ̃be/ [1] vi blaze; (prix) shoot up. ● vt (aiguille) sterilize; (volaille) singe.

flamme /flam/ *nf* flame; (fig) ardour; **en ~s** ablaze.

flan /flɑ̃/ *nm* custard tart.

flanc /flɑ̃/ *nm* side; (d'animal, d'armée) flank.

flâner /flɑne/ [1] *vi* stroll. **flânerie** *nf* stroll.

flanquer /flɑ̃ke/ [1] *vt* flank; (jeter 🄸) chuck; (donner 🄸) give; **~ à la porte** kick out.

flaque /flak/ *nf* (d'eau) puddle; (de sang) pool.

flash (*pl* **~es**) /flaʃ/ *nm* (Photo) flash; (information) news flash; **~ publicitaire** commercial.

flatter /flate/ [1] *vt* flatter. □ **se ~ de** *vpr* pride oneself on.

flatteur, -euse /flatœʀ, -øz/ *adj* flattering. ● *nm, f* flatterer.

fléau (*pl* **~x**) /fleo/ *nm* (désastre) scourge; (personne) pest.

flèche /flɛʃ/ *nf* arrow; (de clocher) spire; **monter en ~** spiral; **partir en ~** shoot off.

flécher /fleʃe/ [14] *vt* mark *ou* signpost (with arrows). **fléchette** *nf* dart.

fléchir /fleʃiʀ/ [2] *vt* bend; (*personne*) move, sway. ● *vi* (faiblir) weaken; (*prix*) fall; (*poutre*) sag, bend.

flemme /flɛm/ *nf* 🄸 laziness; **j'ai la ~ de faire** I can't be bothered doing.

flétrir (se) /(sə)fletʀiʀ/ [2] *vpr* (*plante*) wither; (*fruit*) shrivel; (*beauté*) fade.

fleur /flœʀ/ *nf* flower; **à ~ de terre/ d'eau** just above the ground/water; **à ~s** flowery; **~ de l'âge** prime of life; **en ~s** in flower.

fleurir /flœʀiʀ/ [2] *vi* flower; (*arbre*) blossom; (fig) flourish. ● *vt* decorate with flowers. **fleuriste** *nmf* florist.

fleuve /flœv/ *nm* river.

flic /flik/ *nm* 🄸 cop.

flipper /flipœʀ/ *nm* pinball (machine).

flirter /flœʀte/ [1] *vi* flirt.

flocon /flɔkɔ̃/ *nm* flake.

flore /flɔʀ/ *nf* flora.

florissant, ~e /flɔʀisɑ̃, -t/ *adj* flourishing.

flot /flo/ *nm* flood, stream; **être à ~** be afloat; **les ~s** the waves.

flottant, ~e /flɔtɑ̃, -t/ *adj* (*vêtement*) loose; (indécis) indecisive.

flotte /flɔt/ *nf* fleet; (pluie 🄸) rain; (eau 🄸) water.

flottement /flɔtmɑ̃/ *nm* (incertitude) indecision.

flotter /flɔte/ [1] *vi* float; (*drapeau*) flutter; (*nuage, parfum, pensées*) drift; (pleuvoir 🄸) rain. **flotteur** *nm* float.

flou, ~e /flu/ *adj* out of focus; (fig) vague.

fluctuer /flyktɥe/ [1] *vi* fluctuate.

fluet, ~te /flyɛ, -t/ *adj* thin.

fluide /flɥid/ *a & nm* fluid.

fluor /flyɔʀ/ *nm* (pour les dents) fluoride.

fluorescent, ~e /flyɔʀɛsɑ̃, -t/ *adj* fluorescent.

flûte /flyt/ *nf* flute; (verre) champagne glass.

fluvial, ~e (*mpl* **-iaux**) /flyvjal, -jo/ *adj* river.

flux /fly/ *nm* flow; **~ et reflux** ebb and flow.

FM *abrév f* (**frequency modulation**) FM.

fœtus /fetys/ *nm* foetus.

foi /fwa/ *nf* faith; **être de bonne/ mauvaise ~** be acting in good/bad faith; **ma ~!** well (indeed)!

foie /fwa/ *nm* liver.

foin /fwɛ̃/ *nm* hay.

foire /fwaʀ/ *nf* fair; **faire la ~** 🄸 live it up.

fois /fwa/ *nf* time; **une ~** once; **deux ~** twice; **à la ~** at the same time; **des ~** (parfois) sometimes; **une ~ pour toutes** once and for all.

fol /fɔl/ ⇒FOU.

folie /fɔli/ *nf* madness; (bêtise) foolish thing, folly; **faire une ~, faire des ~s** be extravagant.

folklore /fɔlklɔʀ/ *nm* folklore. **folklorique** *adj* folk; 🄸 eccentric.

folle /fɔl/ ⇒FOU.

foncé, ~e /fɔ̃se/ *adj* dark.

foncer /fɔ̃se/ [10] *vt* darken. ● *vi* (s'assombrir) darken; (aller vite 🄸) dash along; **~ sur** 🄸 charge at.

foncier, -ière /fɔ̃sje, -jɛʀ/ *adj* fundamental; (Comm) real estate.

fonction /fɔ̃ksjɔ̃/ nf function; (emploi) position; ~s (obligations) duties; en ~ de according to; ~ publique civil service; voiture de ~ company car. **fonctionnaire** nmf civil servant. **fonctionnement** nm working.

fonctionner /fɔ̃ksjɔne/ [1] vi work; faire ~ work.

fond /fɔ̃/ nm bottom; (de salle, magasin, etc.) back; (essentiel) basis; (contenu) content; (plan) background; (Sport) long-distance running; à ~ thoroughly; au ~ basically; de ~ (bruit) background; de ~ en comble from top to bottom; au ou dans le ~ really; ~ de teint foundation, make-up base.

fondamental, ~e (mpl -aux) /fɔ̃damɑ̃tal, -o/ adj fundamental.

fondateur, -trice /fɔ̃datœr, -tris/ nm, f founder. **fondation** nf foundation.

fonder /fɔ̃de/ [1] vt found; (baser) base (sur on); (bien) fondé well-founded. ☐ se ~ sur vpr be guided by, be based on.

fonderie /fɔ̃dri/ nf foundry.

fondre /fɔ̃dr/ [3] vt/i melt; (dans l'eau) dissolve; (mélanger) merge; faire ~ melt; dissolve; ~ en larmes burst into tears; ~ sur swoop on. ☐ se ~ vpr merge.

fonds /fɔ̃/ nm fund; ~ de commerce business. ● nmpl (capitaux) funds.

fondu, ~e /fɔ̃dy/ adj melted; (métal) molten.

font /fɔ̃/ ⇒FAIRE [33].

fontaine /fɔ̃tɛn/ nf fountain; (source) spring.

fonte /fɔ̃t/ nf melting; (fer) cast iron; ~ des neiges thaw.

foot /fut/ nm 🔲 football.

football /futbol/ nm football.

footing /futiŋ/ nm jogging.

forain /fɔrɛ̃/ nm fairground entertainer; marchand ~ stall-holder.

forçat /fɔrsa/ nm convict.

force /fɔrs/ nf force; (physique) strength; (hydraulique etc.) power; ~s (physiques) strength; à ~ de by sheer force of; de ~, par la ~ by force; ~ de dissuasion deterrent; ~ de frappe

strike force, deterrent; ~ de l'âge prime of life; ~s de l'ordre police (force); ~s de marché market forces.

forcé, ~e /fɔrse/ adj forced; (inévitable) inevitable; c'est ~ qu'il fasse 🔲 he's bound to do. **forcément** adv necessarily; (évidemment) obviously.

forcené, ~e /fɔrsəne/ adj frenzied. ● nm, f maniac.

forcer /fɔrse/ [10] vt force (à faire to do); (voix) strain; ~ la dose 🔲 overdo it. ● vi force; (exagérer) overdo it. ☐ se ~ vpr force oneself.

forer /fɔre/ [1] vt drill.

forestier, -ière /fɔrɛstje, -jɛr/ adj forest. ● nm, f forestry worker.

forêt /fɔrɛ/ nf forest.

forfait /fɔrfɛ/ nm (Comm) (prix fixe) fixed price; (offre promotionnelle) package. **forfaitaire** adj (prix) fixed.

forger /fɔrʒe/ [40] vt forge; (inventer) make up.

forgeron /fɔrʒərɔ̃/ nm blacksmith.

formaliser (se) /(sə)fɔrmalize/ [1] vpr take offence (de at).

formalité /fɔrmalite/ nf formality.

format /fɔrma/ nm format. **formater** [1] vt (Ordinat) format.

formation /fɔrmasjɔ̃/ nf formation; (professionnelle) training; (culture) education; ~ permanente ou continue continuing education.

forme /fɔrm/ nf form; (contour) shape, form; ~s (de femme) figure; être en ~ be in good shape, be on form; en ~ de in the shape of; en bonne et due ~ in due form.

formel, ~le /fɔrmɛl/ adj formal; (catégorique) positive.

former /fɔrme/ [1] vt form; (instruire) train. ☐ se ~ vpr form.

formidable /fɔrmidabl/ adj fantastic.

formulaire /fɔrmylɛr/ nm form.

formule /fɔrmyl/ nf formula; (expression) expression; (feuille) form; ~ de politesse polite phrase, letter ending. **formuler** [1] vt formulate.

fort, ~e /fɔr, -t/ adj strong; (grand) big; (pluie) heavy; (bruit) loud; (pente) steep; (élève) clever; au plus ~ de at the height of; c'est une ~e tête she/he's headstrong. ● adv (*frapper*) hard; (*parler*) loud; (très) very; (beaucoup) very much. ● *nm* (atout) strong point; (Mil) fort.

fortifiant /fɔʀtifjɑ̃/ *nm* tonic. **fortifier** [45] *vt* fortify.

fortune /fɔʀtyn/ *nf* fortune; de ∼ (improvisé) makeshift; **faire** ∼ make one's fortune.

forum /fɔʀɔm/ *nm* forum; ∼ **de discussion** (Internet) newsgroup.

fosse /fos/ *nf* pit; (tombe) grave; ∼ **d'orchestre** orchestra pit; ∼ **septique** septic tank.

fossé /fose/ *nm* ditch; (fig) gulf.

fossette /fosɛt/ *nf* dimple.

fossile /fosil/ *nm* fossil.

fou (**fol** *before vowel or mute h*), **folle** /fu, fɔl/ *adj* mad; (*course, regard*) wild; (énorme ⊠) tremendous; ∼ **de** crazy about; **le** ∼ **rire** the giggles. ● *nm* madman; (bouffon) jester. **folle** *nf* madwoman.

foudre /fudʀ/ *nf* lightning.

foudroyant, ∼**e** /fudʀwajɑ̃, -t/ *adj* (*mort, maladie*) violent.

foudroyer /fudʀwaje/ [31] *vt* (*orage*) strike; (*maladie etc.*) strike down; ∼ **qn du regard** look daggers at sb.

fouet /fwɛ/ *nm* whip; (Culin) whisk.

fougère /fuʒɛʀ/ *nf* fern.

fougue /fug/ *nf* ardour. **fougueux, -euse** *adj* ardent.

fouille /fuj/ *nf* search; (Archéol) excavation.

fouiller /fuje/ [1] *vt/i* search; (creuser) dig; ∼ **dans** (*tiroir*) rummage through.

fouillis /fuji/ *nm* jumble.

foulard /fulaʀ/ *nm* scarf.

foule /ful/ *nf* crowd; **une** ∼ **de** (fig) a mass of.

foulée /fule/ *nf* stride; **il l'a fait dans la** ∼ he did it while he was at *ou* about it.

fouler /fule/ [1] *vt* (*raisin*) press; (*sol*) set foot on; ∼ **qch aux pieds** trample sth underfoot; (fig) ride roughshod over sth. □ **se** ∼ *vpr* se ∼ **le poignet/le pied** sprain one's wrist/foot; **ne pas se** ⊠ not strain oneself.

four /fuʀ/ *nm* oven; (de potier) kiln; (Théât) flop; ∼ **à micro-ondes**

microwave oven; ∼ **crématoire** crematorium.

fourbe /fuʀb/ *adj* deceitful.

fourche /fuʀʃ/ *nf* fork; (à foin) pitchfork. **fourchette** *nf* fork; (Comm) bracket, range.

fourgon /fuʀgɔ̃/ *nm* van; (wagon) wagon; ∼ **mortuaire** hearse.

fourmi /fuʀmi/ *nf* ant; **avoir des** ∼**s** have pins and needles.

fourmiller /fuʀmije/ [1] *vi* swarm (**de** with).

fourneau (*pl* ∼**x**) /fuʀno/ *nm* stove.

fourni, ∼**e** /fuʀni/ *adj* (épais) thick.

fournir /fuʀniʀ/ [2] *vt* supply, provide; (*client*) supply; (*effort*) put in; ∼ **à qn** supply sb with. □ **se** ∼ **chez** *vpr* shop at.

fournisseur /fuʀnisœʀ/ *nm* supplier; ∼ **d'accès à l'Internet** Internet service provider.

fourniture /fuʀnityʀ/ *nf* supply.

fourrage /fuʀaʒ/ *nm* fodder.

fourré, ∼**e** /fuʀe/ *adj* (*vêtement*) fur-lined; (*gâteau etc.*) filled (*with* jam, cream, etc.). ● *nm* thicket.

fourre-tout /fuʀtu/ *nm inv* (sac) holdall.

fourreur /fuʀœʀ/ *nm* furrier.

fourrière /fuʀjɛʀ/ *nf* (lieu) pound.

fourrure /fuʀyʀ/ *nf* fur.

foutre /futʀ/ [3] *vt* ⊠ = **ficher²** [1].

foutu, ∼**e** /futy/ *adj* ⊠ = **fichu**.

foyer /fwaje/ *nm* home; (âtre) hearth; (club) club; (d'étudiants) hostel; (Théât) foyer; (Photo) focus; (centre) centre.

fracas /fʀaka/ *nm* din; (de train) roar; (d'objet qui tombe) crash. **fracassant**, ∼**e** *adj* (bruyant) deafening; (violent) shattering.

fraction /fʀaksjɔ̃/ *nf* fraction.

fracture /fʀaktyʀ/ *nf* fracture; ∼ **du poignet** fractured wrist.

fragile /fʀaʒil/ *adj* fragile; (*peau*) sensitive; (*cœur*) weak. **fragilité** *nf* fragility.

fragment /fʀagmɑ̃/ *nm* bit, fragment. **fragmenter** [1] *vt* split, fragment.

fraîchement /fʀɛʃmɑ̃/ *adv* (récemment) freshly; (avec froideur) coolly. **fraîcheur** *nf* coolness;

(nouveauté) freshness. **fraîchir** [2] *vi* freshen, become colder.

frais¹, fraîche /fʀɛ, -ʃ/ *adj* fresh; (*temps, accueil*) cool; (*peinture*) wet; ~ **et dispos** fresh; **il fait** ~ it is cool. ● *adv* (*récemment*) newly, freshly. ● *nm* **mettre au** ~ put in a cool place; **prendre le** ~ get some fresh air.

frais² /fʀɛ/ *nmpl* expenses; (droits) fees; **aux** ~ **de** at the expense of; **faire des** ~ spend a lot of money; ~ **généraux** (Comm) overheads, running expenses; ~ **de scolarité** school fees.

fraise /fʀɛz/ *nf* strawberry. **fraisier** *nm* strawberry plant; (gâteau) strawberry gateau.

framboise /fʀɑ̃bwaz/ *nf* raspberry. **framboisier** *nm* raspberry bush.

franc, franche /fʀɑ̃, -ʃ/ *adj* frank; (*regard*) frank, candid; (*cassure*) clean; (*net*) clear; (*libre*) free; (*véritable*) downright. ● *nm* franc.

français, ~e /fʀɑ̃sɛ, -z/ *adj* French. ● *nm* (Ling) French. **F~, ~e** *nm,f* Frenchman, Frenchwoman.

France /fʀɑ̃s/ *nf* France.

franchement /fʀɑ̃ʃmɑ̃/ *adv* frankly; (nettement) clearly; (tout à fait) really.

franchir /fʀɑ̃ʃiʀ/ [2] *vt* (obstacle) get over; (distance) cover; (limite) exceed; (traverser) cross.

franchise /fʀɑ̃ʃiz/ *nf* (qualité) frankness; (Comm) franchise; (exemption) exemption; ~ **douanière** exemption from duties.

franc-maçon (*pl* **francs-maçons**) /fʀɑ̃masɔ̃/ *nm* Freemason. **franc-maçonnerie** *nf* Freemasonry.

franco /fʀɑ̃ko/ *adv* postage paid.

francophone /fʀɑ̃kɔfɔn/ *adj* French-speaking. ● *nmf* French speaker.

franc-parler /fʀɑ̃paʀle/ *nm inv* outspokenness.

frange /fʀɑ̃ʒ/ *nf* fringe.

frappe /fʀap/ *nf* (de texte) typing.

frappé, ~e /fʀape/ *adj* chilled.

frapper /fʀape/ [1] *vt/i* strike; (battre) hit, strike; (monnaie) mint; (à la porte) knock, bang; **frappé de panique** panic-stricken.

fraternel, ~le /fʀatɛʀnɛl/ *adj* brotherly. **fraternité** *nf* brotherhood.

fraude /fʀod/ *nf* fraud; (à un examen) cheating; **passer qch en** ~ smuggle sth in. **frauder** [1] *vt/i* cheat. **frauduleux, -euse** *adj* fraudulent.

frayer /fʀeje/ [31] *vt* open up. □ **se** ~ *vpr* **se** ~ **un passage** force one's way (à travers, dans through).

frayeur /fʀejœʀ/ *nf* fright.

fredonner /fʀədɔne/ [1] *vt* hum.

free-lance /fʀilɑ̃s/ *a & nmf* freelance.

freezer /fʀizœʀ/ *nm* freezer.

frein /fʀɛ̃/ *nm* brake; **mettre un** ~ **à** curb; ~ **à main** hand brake.

freiner /fʀene/ [1] *vt* slow down; (modérer, enrayer) curb. ● *vi* (Auto) brake.

frêle /fʀɛl/ *adj* frail.

frelon /fʀəlɔ̃/ *nm* hornet.

frémir /fʀemiʀ/ [2] *vi* shudder, shake; (feuille, eau) quiver.

frêne /fʀɛn/ *nm* ash.

frénésie /fʀenezi/ *nf* frenzy. **frénétique** *adj* frenzied.

fréquemment /fʀekamɑ̃/ *adv* frequently. **fréquence** *nf* frequency. **fréquent, ~e** *adj* frequent. **fréquentation** *nf* frequenting.

fréquentations /fʀekɑ̃tasjɔ̃/ *nfpl* acquaintances; **avoir de mauvaises** ~ keep bad company.

fréquenter /fʀekɑ̃te/ [1] *vt* frequent; (école) attend; (personne) see.

frère /fʀɛʀ/ *nm* brother.

fret /fʀɛt/ *nm* freight.

friand, ~e /fʀijɑ̃, -d/ *adj* ~ **de** very fond of.

friandise /fʀijɑ̃diz/ *nf* sweet; (US) candy; (gâteau) cake.

fric /fʀik/ *nm* 🗉 money.

friction /fʀiksjɔ̃/ *nf* friction; (massage) rub-down.

frigidaire® /fʀiʒidɛʀ/ *nm* refrigerator.

frigo /fʀigo/ *nm* 🗉 fridge. **frigorifique** *adj* (vitrine etc.) refrigerated.

frileux, -euse /fʀilø, -z/ *adj* sensitive to cold.

frime /fʀim/ nf 🗆 c'est de la ~ it's all pretence; **pour la ~** for show.

frimousse /fʀimus/ nf face.

fringale /fʀɛ̃gal/ nf 🗆 ravenous appetite.

fringant, ~e /fʀɛ̃gɑ̃, -t/ adj dashing.

fringues /fʀɛ̃g/ nfpl 🗆 gear.

friper /fʀipe/ [1] vt crumple, crease. 🗆 **se ~** vpr crumple, crease.

fripon, ~ne /fʀipɔ̃, -ɔn/ nm,f rascal. ● adj mischievous.

fripouille /fʀipuj/ nf rogue.

frire /fʀiʀ/ [56] vt/i fry; **faire ~** fry.

frise /fʀiz/ nf frieze.

friser /fʀize/ [1] vt/i (cheveux) curl; (personne) curl the hair of; **frisé** curly.

frisson /fʀisɔ̃/ nm (de froid) shiver; (de peur) shudder. **frissonner** [1] vi shiver; shudder.

frit, ~e /fʀi, -t/ adj fried.

frite /fʀit/ nf chip; **avoir la ~** 🗆 feel good.

friteuse /fʀitøz/ nf chip pan; (électrique) (deep) fryer.

friture /fʀityʀ/ nf fried fish; (huile) (frying) oil ou fat.

frivole /fʀivɔl/ adj frivolous.

froid, ~e /fʀwa, -d/ a & nm cold; **avoir/prendre ~** be/catch cold; **il fait ~** it is cold. **froidement** adv coldly; (calculer) coolly. **froideur** nf coldness.

froisser /fʀwase/ [1] vt crumple; (fig) offend. 🗆 **se ~** vpr crumple; (fig) take offence; **se ~ un muscle** strain a muscle.

frôler /fʀole/ [1] vt brush against, skim; (fig) come close to.

fromage /fʀɔmaʒ/ nm cheese.

fromager, -ère /fʀɔmaʒe, -ɛʀ/ adj cheese. ● nm,f (fabricant) cheese-maker; (marchand) cheesemonger.

froment /fʀɔmɑ̃/ nm wheat.

froncer /fʀɔ̃se/ [10] vt gather; **~ les sourcils** frown.

front /fʀɔ̃/ nm forehead; (Mil, Pol) front; **de ~** at the same time; (de face) head-on; (côte à côte) abreast; **faire ~ à** face up to. **frontal, ~e** (mpl **-aux**) adj frontal; (Ordinat) front-end.

frontalier, -ière /fʀɔ̃talje, -jɛʀ/ adj border; **travailleur ~** commuter from across the border.

frontière /fʀɔ̃tjɛʀ/ nf border, frontier.

frottement /fʀɔtmɑ̃/ nm rubbing; (Tech) friction. **frotter** [1] vt/i rub; (allumette) strike.

frottis /fʀɔti/ nm ~ **vaginal** cervical smear.

frousse /fʀus/ nf 🗆 fear; **avoir la ~** 🗆 be scared.

fructifier /fʀyktifje/ [45] vi **faire ~** put to work.

fructueux, -euse /fʀyktyø, -z/ adj fruitful.

frugal, ~e (mpl **-aux**) /fʀygal, -o/ adj frugal.

fruit /fʀɥi/ nm fruit; **des ~s** (some) fruit; **~s de mer** seafood. **fruité, ~e** adj fruity.

frustrant, ~e /fʀystʀɑ̃, -t/ adj frustrating. **frustrer** [1] vt frustrate.

fuel /fjul/ nm fuel oil.

fugitif, -ive /fyʒitif, -v/ adj (passager) fleeting. ● nm,f fugitive.

fugue /fyg/ nf (Mus) fugue; **faire une ~** run away.

fuir /fɥiʀ/ [35] vi flee, run away; (eau, robinet, etc.) leak. ● vt (quitter) flee; (éviter) shun.

fuite /fɥit/ nf flight; (de liquide, d'une nouvelle) leak; **en ~** on the run; **mettre en ~** put to flight; **prendre la ~** take flight.

fulgurant, ~e /fylgyʀɑ̃, -t/ adj (vitesse) lightning.

fumé, ~e /fyme/ adj (poisson, verre) smoked.

fumée /fyme/ nf smoke; (vapeur) steam.

fumer /fyme/ [1] vt/i smoke.

fumeur, -euse /fymœʀ, -øz/ nm,f smoker; **zone non-~s** no smoking area.

fumier /fymje/ nm manure.

funambule /fynɑ̃byl/ nmf tightrope walker.

funèbre /fynɛbʀ/ adj funeral; (fig) gloomy.

funérailles /fyneʀaj/ nfpl funeral.

funéraire /fyneʀɛʀ/ adj funeral.

funeste /fynɛst/ adj fatal.

fur: au ∼ et à mesure /ofyʀea-
məzyʀ/ *loc* as one goes along,
progressively; au ∼ et à mesure que
as.

furet /fyʀɛ/ *nm* ferret.

fureur /fyʀœʀ/ *nf* fury; (passion)
passion; avec ∼ furiously;
passionately; mettre en ∼ infuriate;
faire ∼ be all the rage.

furieux, -ieuse /fyʀjø, -z/ *adj*
furious.

furoncle /fyʀɔ̃kl/ *nm* boil.

furtif, -ive /fyʀtif, -v/ *adj* furtive.

fuseau (*pl* ∼x) /fyzo/ *nm* ski
trousers; (pour filer) spindle; ∼ horaire
time zone.

fusée /fyze/ *nf* rocket.

fusible /fyzibl/ *nm* fuse.

fusil /fyzi/ *nm* rifle, gun; (de chasse)
shotgun; ∼ mitrailleur machine-gun.

fusion /fyzjɔ̃/ *nf* fusion; (Comm)
merger. **fusionner** [1] *vt/i* merge.

fut /fy/ ⇒ÊTRE [5].

fût /fy/ *nm* (tonneau) barrel; (d'arbre)
trunk.

futé, ∼e /fyte/ *adj* cunning.

futile /fytil/ *adj* futile.

futur, ∼e /fytyʀ/ *adj* future; ∼e
femme-/maman wife-/mother-to-be.
● *nm* future.

fuyant, ∼e /fɥijɑ̃, -t/ *adj* (*front,
ligne*) receding; (*personne*) evasive.

fuyard, ∼e /fɥijaʀ, -d/ *nm,f*
runaway.

Gg

gabardine /gabaʀdin/ *nf* raincoat.

gabarit /gabaʀi/ *nm* size; (patron)
template; (fig) calibre.

gâcher /gɑʃe/ [1] *vt* (gâter) spoil;
(gaspiller) waste.

gâchette /gɑʃɛt/ *nf* trigger.

gâchis /gɑʃi/ *nm* waste.

gaffe /gaf/ *nf* 🖾 blunder; faire ∼ be
careful (à of).

gage /gaʒ/ *nm* security; (de bonne foi)
pledge; (de jeu) forfeit; ∼s (salaire)

wages; en ∼ de as a token of; mettre
en ∼ pawn; tueur à ∼s hired killer.

gageure /gaʒyʀ/ *nf* challenge.

gagnant, ∼e /gaɲɑ̃, -t/ *adj* winning.
● *nm,f* winner.

gagne-pain /gaɲpɛ̃/ *nm inv* job.

gagner /gaɲe/ [1] *vt* (match, prix)
win; (argent, pain) earn; (terrain)
gain; (temps) save; (atteindre) reach;
(convaincre) win over; ∼ sa vie earn
one's living. ● *vi* win; (fig) gain.

gai, ∼e /ge/ *adj* cheerful; (ivre)
merry. **gaiement** *adv* cheerfully.
gaieté *nf* cheerfulness.

gain /gɛ̃/ *nm* (salaire) earnings;
(avantage) gain; (économie) saving; ∼s
(Comm) profits; (au jeu) winnings.

gaine /gɛn/ *nf* (corset) girdle; (étui)
sheath.

galant, ∼e /galɑ̃, -t/ *adj* courteous;
(amoureux) romantic.

galaxie /galaksi/ *nf* galaxy.

gale /gal/ *nf* (de chat etc.) mange.

galère /galɛʀ/ *nf* (navire) galley; c'est
la ∼! 🖾 what an ordeal!

galérer /galeʀe/ [14] *vi* 🖾 (peiner)
have a hard time.

galerie /galʀi/ *nf* gallery; (Théât)
circle; (de voiture) roof-rack; ∼
marchande shopping arcade.

galet /galɛ/ *nm* pebble.

galette /galɛt/ *nf* flat cake; ∼ des
Rois Twelfth Night cake.

Galles /gal/ *nfpl* le pays de ∼
Wales.

gallois, ∼e /galwa, -z/ *adj* Welsh.
● *nm* (Ling) Welsh. G∼, ∼e *nm,f*
Welshman, Welshwoman.

galon /galɔ̃/ *nm* braid; (Mil) stripe;
prendre du ∼ be promoted.

galop /galo/ *nm* canter; aller au ∼
canter; grand ∼ gallop; ∼ d'essai
trial run. **galoper** [1] *vi* (cheval)
canter; (au grand galop) gallop;
(personne) run.

galopin /galɔpɛ̃/ *nm* 🖾 rascal.

gambader /gɑ̃bade/ [1] *vi* leap
about.

gamelle /gamɛl/ *nf* (de soldat) mess
kit; (d'ouvrier) lunch-box.

gamin, ∼e /gamɛ̃, -in/ *adj* childish;
(air) youthful. ● *nm,f* 🖾 kid.

gamme /gam/ *nf* (Mus) scale; (série) range; **haut de ~** up-market, top of the range; **bas de ~** down-market, bottom of the range.

gang /gɑ̃g/ *nm* 🔲 gang.

ganglion /gɑ̃glijɔ̃/ *nm* ganglion.

gangster /gɑ̃gstɛʀ/ *nm* gangster; (escroc) crook.

gant /gɑ̃/ *nm* glove; **~ de ménage** rubber glove; **~ de toilette** face-flannel, face-cloth.

garage /gaʀaʒ/ *nm* garage. **garagiste** *nmf* garage owner; (employé) car mechanic.

garant, **~e** /gaʀɑ̃, -t/ *nm,f* guarantor. ● *adj* **se porter ~ de** vouch for.

garanti, **~e** /gaʀɑ̃ti/ *adj* guaranteed.

garantie /gaʀɑ̃ti/ *nf* guarantee; **~s** (de police d'assurance) cover. **garantir** [2] *vt* guarantee; (protéger) protect (**de** from).

garçon /gaʀsɔ̃/ *nm* boy; (jeune homme) young man; (célibataire) bachelor; **~ (de café)** waiter; **~ d'honneur** best man. **garçonnière** *nf* bachelor flat.

garde¹ /gaʀd/ *nf* guard; (d'enfants, de bagages) care; (service) guard (duty); (infirmière) nurse; **de ~** on duty; **~ à vue** (police) custody; **mettre en ~** warn; **prendre ~** be careful (**à** of); **(droit de) ~** custody (**de** of).

garde² /gaʀd/ *nm* guard; (de propriété, parc) warden; **~ champêtre** village policeman; **~ du corps** bodyguard.

garde-à-vous /gaʀdavu/ *nm inv* (Mil) **se mettre au ~** stand to attention.

garde-chasse (*pl* **~s**) /gaʀdəʃas/ *nm* gamekeeper.

garde-manger /gaʀdmɑ̃ʒe/ *nm inv* meat safe; (placard) larder.

garder /gaʀde/ [1] *vt* (conserver, maintenir) keep; (vêtement) keep on; (surveiller) look after; (défendre) guard; **~ le lit** stay in bed. □ **se ~** *vpr* (denrée) keep; **se ~ de faire** be careful not to do.

garderie /gaʀdəʀi/ *nf* day nursery.

garde-robe (*pl* **~s**) /gaʀdərɔb/ *nf* wardrobe.

gardien, **~ne** /gaʀdjɛ̃, -ɛn/ *nm,f* (de locaux) security guard; (de prison, réserve) warden; (d'immeuble) caretaker; (de musée) attendant; (de zoo) keeper; (de traditions) guardian; **~ de but** goalkeeper; **~ de la paix** policeman; **~ de nuit** night watchman; **gardienne d'enfants** childminder.

gare /gaʀ/ *nf* (Rail) station; **~ routière** coach station; (US) bus station. ● *interj* **~ (à toi)** watch out!

garer /gaʀe/ [1] *vt* park. □ **se ~** *vpr* park; (s'écarter) move out of the way.

gargouille /gaʀguj/ *nf* water-spout; (sculptée) gargoyle. **gargouiller** [1] *vi* gurgle; (stomach) rumble.

garni, **~e** /gaʀni/ *adj* (plat) served with vegetables; **bien ~** (rempli) well-filled.

garnir /gaʀniʀ/ [2] *vt* (remplir) fill; (décorer) decorate; (couvrir) cover; (doubler) line; (Culin) garnish. **garniture** *nf* (légumes) vegetables; (ornement) trimming; (de voiture) trim.

gars /gɑ/ *nm* 🔲 lad; (adulte) guy, bloke.

gas-oil /gazwal/ *nm* diesel (oil).

gaspillage /gaspijaʒ/ *nm* waste. **gaspiller** [1] *vt* waste.

gastrique /gastʀik/ *adj* gastric.

gastronome /gastʀɔnɔm/ *nmf* gourmet.

gâteau (*pl* **~x**) /gɑto/ *nm* cake; **~ sec** biscuit; (US) cookie; **un papa ~** a doting dad.

gâter /gɑte/ [1] *vt* spoil. □ **se ~** *vpr* (viande) go bad; (dent) rot; (temps) get worse.

gâterie /gɑtʀi/ *nf* little treat.

gâteux, **-euse** /gɑtø, -z/ *adj* senile.

gauche /goʃ/ *adj* left; (maladroit) awkward. ● *nf* left; **à ~** on the left; (direction) (to the) left; **la ~** the left (side); (Pol) the left (wing).

gaucher, **-ère** /goʃe, -ɛʀ/ *adj* left-handed.

gaufre /gofʀ/ *nf* waffle. **gaufrette** *nf* wafer.

gaulois, **~e** /golwa, -z/ *adj* Gallic; (fig) bawdy. **G~**, **~e** *nm,f* Gaul.

gaver /gave/ [1] *vt* force-feed; (fig) cram. □ **se ~ de** *vpr* gorge oneself with; (fig) devour.

gaz /gɑz/ *nm inv* gas; ~
d'échappement exhaust fumes; ~
lacrymogène tear-gas.

gaze /gɑz/ *nf* gauze.

gazer /gɑze/ [1] *vi* ⚠ ça gaze? how's
things?

gazette /gazɛt/ *nf* newspaper.

gazeux, -euse /gazø, -z/ *adj*
(boisson) fizzy; (eau) sparkling.

gazoduc /gazɔdyk/ *nm* gas pipeline.

gazon /gazɔ̃/ *nm* lawn, grass.

gazouiller /gazuje/ [1] *vi* (oiseau)
chirp; (bébé) babble.

GDF *abrév m* (**Gaz de France**)
French gas board.

géant, ~e /ʒeɑ̃, -t/ *adj* giant. ● *nm*
giant. **géante** *nf* giantess.

geindre /ʒɛ̃dʀ/ [22] *vi* groan, moan.

gel /ʒɛl/ *nm* frost; (produit) gel; (Comm)
freeze; ~ coiffant hair gel.

gelée /ʒ(ə)le/ *nf* frost; (Culin) jelly; ~
blanche hoarfrost.

geler /ʒəle/ [6] *vt/i* freeze; **on gèle** (on
a froid) it's freezing; **il** *ou* **ça gèle** (il fait
froid) it's freezing.

gélule /ʒelyl/ *nf* (Méd) capsule.

Gémeaux /ʒemo/ *nmpl* Gemini.

gémir /ʒemiʀ/ [2] *vi* groan.

gênant, ~e /ʒɛnɑ̃, -t/ *adj*
embarrassing; (irritant) annoying;
(incommode) cumbersome.

gencive /ʒɑ̃siv/ *nf* gum.

gendarme /ʒɑ̃daʀm/ *nm* policeman,
gendarme. **gendarmerie** *nf* police
force; (local) police station.

gendre /ʒɑ̃dʀ/ *nm* son-in-law.

gène /ʒɛn/ *nm* gene.

gêne /ʒɛn/ *nf* discomfort; (confusion)
embarrassment; (dérangement)
trouble, inconvenience; (pauvreté)
poverty.

gêné, ~e /ʒene/ *adj* embarrassed;
(désargenté) short of money.

généalogie /ʒenealɔʒi/ *nf*
genealogy.

gêner /ʒene/ [1] *vt* bother, disturb;
(troubler) embarrass; (entraver) block;
(faire mal) hurt.

général, ~e (*mpl* **-aux**) /ʒeneʀal,
-o/ *adj* general; **en** ~ in general.
● *nm* (*pl* **-aux**) general.

généralement /ʒeneʀalmɑ̃/ *adv*
generally.

généraliser /ʒeneʀalize/ [1] *vt*
make general. ● *vi* generalize. □ **se**
~ *vpr* become widespread *ou*
general.

généraliste /ʒeneʀalist/ *nmf*
general practitioner, GP.

généralité /ʒeneʀalite/ *nf* general
point.

génération /ʒeneʀasjɔ̃/ *nf*
generation.

généreux, ~euse /ʒeneʀø, -z/ *adj*
generous.

générique /ʒeneʀik/ *nm* (au cinéma)
credits. ● *adj* generic.

générosité /ʒeneʀozite/ *nf*
generosity.

génétique /ʒenetik/ *adj* genetic.
● *nf* genetics.

Genève /ʒənɛv/ *npr* Geneva.

génial, ~e (*mpl* **-iaux**) /ʒenjal, -jo/
adj brilliant; (fantastique ⚠) fantastic.

génie /ʒeni/ *nm* genius; ~ **civil** civil
engineering.

génital, ~e (*mpl* **-aux**) /ʒenital, -o/
adj genital.

génocide /ʒenɔsid/ *nm* genocide.

génoise /ʒenwaz/ *nf* sponge (cake).

génothèque /ʒenɔtɛk/ *nf* gene
bank.

genou (*pl* ~**x**) /ʒənu/ *nm* knee; **être
à** ~**x** be kneeling.

genre /ʒɑ̃ʀ/ *nm* sort, kind; (Gram)
gender; (allure) **avoir bon/mauvais** ~
to look nice/disreputable;
(comportement) **c'est bien son** ~ it's
just like him/her; ~ **de vie** life-style.

gens /ʒɑ̃/ *nmpl* people.

gentil, ~le /ʒɑ̃ti, -j/ *adj* kind, nice;
(sage) good. **gentillesse** *nf*
kindness. **gentiment** *adv* kindly.

géographie /ʒeɔgʀafi/ *nf*
geography.

geôlier, -ière /ʒolje, -jɛʀ/ *nm,f*
gaoler, jailer.

géologie /ʒeɔlɔʒi/ *nf* geology.

géomètre /ʒeɔmɛtʀ/ *nm* surveyor.

géométrie /ʒeɔmetʀi/ *nf* geometry.
géométrique *adj* geometric.

gérance /ʒeʀɑ̃s/ *nf* management.

gérant, ~e /ʒeʀɑ̃, -t/ *nm,f* manager,
manageress; ~ **d'immeuble**
landlord's agent.

gerbe /ʒɛʁb/ *nf* (de fleurs) bunch, bouquet; (d'eau) spray; (de blé) sheaf.

gercer /ʒɛʁse/ [10] *vt* chap; **avoir les lèvres gercées** have chapped lips. ● *vi* become chapped. **gerçure** *nf* crack, chap.

gérer /ʒeʁe/ [14] *vt* manage, run; (traiter: fig) (crise, situation) handle.

germe /ʒɛʁm/ *nm* germ; ~**s de soja** bean sprouts.

germer /ʒɛʁme/ [1] *vi* germinate.

gestation /ʒɛstasjɔ̃/ *nf* gestation.

geste /ʒɛst/ *nm* gesture.

gesticuler /ʒɛstikyle/ [1] *vi* gesticulate.

gestion /ʒɛstjɔ̃/ *nf* management. **gestionnaire** *nmf* administrator.

ghetto /gɛto/ *nm* ghetto.

gibier /ʒibje/ *nm* (animaux) game.

giboulée /ʒibule/ *nf* shower.

gicler /ʒikle/ [1] *vi* squirt; **faire** ~ squirt.

gifle /ʒifl/ *nf* slap in the face. **gifler** [1] *vt* slap.

gigantesque /ʒigɑ̃tɛsk/ *adj* gigantic.

gigot /ʒigo/ *nm* leg (of lamb).

gigoter /ʒigote/ [1] *vi* wriggle; (nerveusement) fidget.

gilet /ʒilɛ/ *nm* waistcoat; (cardigan) cardigan; ~ **de sauvetage** life-jacket.

gingembre /ʒɛ̃ʒɑ̃bʁ/ *nm* ginger.

girafe /ʒiʁaf/ *nf* giraffe.

giratoire /ʒiʁatwaʁ/ *adj* **sens** ~ roundabout.

girofle /ʒiʁɔfl/ *nm* **clou de** ~ clove.

girouette /ʒiʁwɛt/ *nf* weathercock, weathervane.

gisement /ʒizmɑ̃/ *nm* deposit.

gitan, ~**e** /ʒitɑ̃, -an/ *nm, f* gypsy.

gîte /ʒit/ *nm* (maison) home; (abri) shelter; ~ **rural** holiday cottage.

givre /ʒivʁ/ *nm* frost; (sur pare-brise) ice.

givré, ~**e** /ʒivʁe/ *adj* 🔲 crazy.

glace /glas/ *nf* ice; (crème) ice-cream; (vitre) window; (miroir) mirror; (verre) glass.

glacé, ~**e** /glase/ *adj* (vent, accueil) icy; (hands) frozen; (gâteau) iced.

glacer /glase/ [10] *vt* freeze; (gâteau, boisson) chill; (pétrifier) chill. ◻ **se** ~ *vpr* freeze.

glacier /glasje/ *nm* (Géog) glacier; (vendeur) ice-cream seller. **glacière** *nf* coolbox. **glaçon** *nm* ice-cube.

glaïeul /glajœl/ *nm* gladiolus.

glaise /glɛz/ *nf* clay.

gland /glɑ̃/ *nm* acorn; (ornement) tassel.

glande /glɑ̃d/ *nf* gland.

glander /glɑ̃de/ [1] *vi* 🔲 laze around.

glaner /glane/ [1] *vt* glean.

glauque /glok/ *adj* (fig) murky; (street) squalid.

glissade /glisad/ *nf* (jeu) slide; (dérapage) skid.

glissant, ~**e** /glisɑ̃, -t/ *adj* slippery.

glissement /glismɑ̃/ *nm* sliding; gliding; (fig) shift; ~ **de terrain** landslide.

glisser /glise/ [1] *vi* slide; (être glissant) be slippery; (sur l'eau) glide; (déraper) slip; (véhicule) skid. ● *vt* (objet) slip (dans into); (remarque) slip in. ◻ **se** ~ *vpr* slip (dans into).

glissière /glisjɛʁ/ *nf* slide; **porte à** ~ sliding door; ~ **de sécurité** (Auto) crash-barrier; **fermeture à** ~ zip.

global, ~**e** (*mpl* **-aux**) /glɔbal, -o/ *adj* (entier, général) overall. **globalement** *adv* as a whole.

globe /glɔb/ *nm* globe; ~ **oculaire** eyeball; ~ **terrestre** globe.

globule /glɔbyl/ *nm* (du sang) corpuscle.

gloire /glwaʁ/ *nf* glory, fame. **glorieux**, **-ieuse** *adj* glorious. **glorifier** [45] *vt* glorify.

glose /gloz/ *nf* gloss.

glossaire /glɔsɛʁ/ *nm* glossary.

gloussement /glusmɑ̃/ *nm* chuckle; (de poule) cluck.

glouton, ~**ne** /glutɔ̃, -ɔn/ *adj* gluttonous. ● *nm, f* glutton.

gluant, ~**e** /glyɑ̃, -t/ *adj* sticky.

glucose /glykoz/ *nm* glucose.

glycérine /gliseʁin/ *nf* glycerin(e).

GO *abrév fpl* (**grandes ondes**) long wave.

goal /gol/ *nm* 🔲 goalkeeper.

gobelet /gɔblɛ/ *nm* cup; (en verre) tumbler.

gober /gɔbe/ [1] *vt* swallow (whole); **je ne peux pas le ~** 🔟 I can't stand him.

goéland /gɔelã/ *nm* (sea)gull.

gogo: **à ~** /agɔgo/ *loc* 🔟 galore, in abundance.

goinfre /gwɛ̃fʀ/ *nm* (glouton 🔟) pig. **goinfrer (se)** [1] *vpr* 🔟 stuff oneself (de with).

golf /gɔlf/ *nm* golf; (terrain) golf course.

golfe /gɔlf/ *nm* gulf.

gomme /gɔm/ *nf* rubber; (US) eraser; (résine) gum. **gommer** [1] *vt* rub out.

gond /gɔ̃/ *nm* hinge; **sortir de ses ~s** 🔟 go mad.

gondoler (se) /(sə)gɔ̃dɔle/ [1] *vpr* (bois) warp; (métal) buckle.

gonflé, ~e /gɔ̃fle/ *adj* swollen; **il est ~** 🔟 he's got a nerve.

gonflement /gɔ̃flamã/ *nm* swelling.

gonfler /gɔ̃fle/ [1] *vt* (ballon, pneu) pump up, blow up; (augmenter) increase; (exagérer) inflate. ● *vi* swell.

gorge /gɔʀʒ/ *nf* throat; (poitrine) breast; (vallée) gorge.

gorgée /gɔʀʒe/ *nf* sip, gulp.

gorger /gɔʀʒe/ [40] *vt* fill (de with); **gorgé de** full of. □ **se ~** *vpr* gorge oneself (de with).

gorille /gɔʀij/ *nm* gorilla; (garde 🔟) bodyguard.

gosier /gozje/ *nm* throat.

gosse /gɔs/ *nmf* 🔟 kid.

gothique /gɔtik/ *adj* Gothic.

goudron /gudʀɔ̃/ *nm* tar. **goudronner** [1] *vt* tarmac.

gouffre /gufʀ/ *nm* abyss, gulf.

goujat /guʒa/ *nm* lout, boor.

goulot /gulo/ *nm* neck; **boire au ~** drink from the bottle.

goulu, ~e /guly/ *adj* gluttonous. ● *nm, f* glutton.

gourde /guʀd/ *nf* (à eau) flask; (idiot 🔟) fool.

gourer (se) /(sə)guʀe/ [1] *vpr* 🔟 make a mistake.

gourmand, ~e /guʀmã, -d/ *adj* greedy. ● *nm, f* glutton.

gourmandise /guʀmãdiz/ *nf* greed; **~s** sweets.

gourmet /guʀmɛ/ *nm* gourmet.

gourmette /guʀmɛt/ *nf* chain bracelet.

gousse /gus/ *nf* **~ d'ail** clove of garlic.

goût /gu/ *nm* taste; (gré) liking; **prendre ~ à** develop a taste for; **avoir bon ~** (aliment) taste nice; (personne) have good taste; **donner du ~ à** give flavour.

goûter /gute/ [1] *vt* taste; (apprécier) enjoy; **~ à** ou **de** taste. ● *vi* have tea. ● *nm* tea, snack.

goutte /gut/ *nf* drop; (Méd) gout. **goutte-à-goutte** *nm inv* drip. **goutter** [1] *vi* drip.

gouttière /gutjɛʀ/ *nf* gutter.

gouvernail /guvɛʀnaj/ *nm* rudder; (barre) helm.

gouvernement /guvɛʀnəmã/ *nm* government.

gouverner /guvɛʀne/ [1] *vt/i* govern; (dominer) control. **gouverneur** *nm* governor.

grâce /gʀɑs/ *nf* (charme) grace; (faveur) favour; (volonté) grace; (Jur) pardon; (Relig) grace; **~ à** thanks to; **rendre ~(s) à** give thanks to.

gracier /gʀasje/ [45] *vt* pardon.

gracieusement /gʀasjøzmã/ *adv* gracefully; (gratuitement) free (of charge).

gracieux, -ieuse /gʀasjø, -z/ *adj* graceful.

grade /gʀad/ *nm* rank; **monter en ~** be promoted.

gradin /gʀadɛ̃/ *nm* tier, step; **en ~s** terraced; **les ~s** terraces.

gradué, ~e /gʀadɥe/ *adj* graded, graduated; **verre ~** measuring jug.

graffiti /gʀafiti/ *nmpl* graffiti.

grain /gʀɛ̃/ *nm* grain; (Naut) squall; **~ de beauté** beauty spot; **~ de café** coffee bean; **~ de poivre** pepper corn; **~ de raisin** grape.

graine /gʀɛn/ *nf* seed.

graisse /gʀɛs/ *nf* fat; (lubrifiant) grease. **graisser** [1] *vt* grease. **graisseux, -euse** *adj* greasy.

grammaire /gʀam(m)ɛʀ/ *nf* grammar.

gramme /gʀam/ *nm* gram.

grand, ~e /gʀã, -d/ *adj* big, large; (haut) tall; (intense, fort) great; (brillant)

great; (principal) main; (plus âgé) big,
elder; (adulte) grown-up; **au ~ air** in
the open air; **au ~ jour** in broad
daylight; (fig) in the open; **en ~e
partie** largely; **~e banlieue** outer
suburbs; **~ ensemble** housing estate;
~es lignes (Rail) main lines; **~
magasin** department store; **~e
personne** grown-up; **~ public**
general public; **~e surface**
hypermarket; **~es vacances** summer
holidays. ● *adv* (*ouvrir*) wide; **~
ouvert** wide open; **voir ~** think big.
● *nm, f* (adulte) grown-up; (enfant) big
boy, big girl; (Scol) senior.

Grande-Bretagne /gʀɑ̃dbʀətaɲ/
nf Great Britain.

grand-chose /gʀɑ̃ʃoz/ *pron* **pas ~**
not much, not a lot.

grandeur /gʀɑ̃dœʀ/ *nf* greatness;
(dimension) size; **folie des ~s**
delusions of grandeur.

grandir /gʀɑ̃diʀ/ [2] *vi* grow; (bruit)
grow louder. ● *vt* (talons) make
taller; (loupe) magnify.

grand-mère (*pl* **grands-mères**)
/gʀɑ̃mɛʀ/ *nf* grandmother.

grand-père (*pl* **grands-pères**)
/gʀɑ̃pɛʀ/ *nm* grandfather.

grands-parents /gʀɑ̃paʀɑ̃/ *nmpl*
grandparents.

grange /gʀɑ̃ʒ/ *nf* barn.

granulé /gʀanyle/ *nm* granule.

graphique /gʀafik/ *adj* graphic;
(Ordinat) graphics; **informatique ~**
computer graphics. ● *nm* graph.

graphologie /gʀafɔlɔʒi/ *nf*
graphology.

grappe /gʀap/ *nf* cluster; **~ de
raisin** bunch of grapes.

gras, ~se /gʀɑ, -s/ *adj* (gros) fat;
(aliment) fatty; (surface, peau,
cheveux) greasy; (épais) thick;
(caractères) bold; **faire la ~se
matinée** sleep late. ● *nm* (Culin) fat.

gratifiant, ~e /gʀatifjɑ̃, -t/ *adj*
gratifying; (travail) rewarding.

gratifier /gʀatifje/ [45] *vt* favour,
reward (**de** with).

gratin /gʀatɛ̃/ *nm* gratin (*baked dish
with cheese topping*); (élite 🔟) upper
crust.

gratis /gʀatis/ *adv* free.

gratitude /gʀatityd/ *nf* gratitude.

gratte-ciel /gʀatsjɛl/ *nm inv*
skyscraper.

gratter /gʀate/ [1] *vt/i* scratch; (avec
un outil) scrape; **ça me gratte** 🔟 it
itches. □ **se ~** *vpr* scratch oneself;
se ~ la tête scratch one's head.

gratuiciel /gʀatɥisjɛl/ *nm* (Internet)
freeware.

gratuit, ~e /gʀatɥi, -t/ *adj* free;
(acte) gratuitous. **gratuitement**
adv free (of charge).

grave /gʀav/ *adj* (maladie, accident,
problème) serious; (solennel) grave;
(voix) deep; (accent) grave.
gravement *adv* seriously; gravely.

graver /gʀave/ [1] *vt* engrave; (sur
bois) carve.

gravier /gʀavje/ *nm* **du ~** gravel.

gravité /gʀavite/ *nf* gravity.

graviter /gʀavite/ [1] *vi* revolve.

gravure /gʀavyʀ/ *nf* engraving; (de
tableau, photo) print, plate.

gré /gʀe/ *nm* (volonté) will; (goût) taste;
à son ~ (agir) as one likes; **de bon
~** willingly; **bon ~ mal ~** like it or
not; **je vous en saurais ~** I'd be
grateful for that.

grec, ~que /gʀɛk/ *adj* Greek. ● *nm*
(Ling) Greek. **G~, ~que** *nm, f* Greek.

Grèce *nf* /gʀɛs/ Greece.

greffe /gʀɛf/ *nf* graft; (d'organe)
transplant. **greffer** [1] *vt* graft;
transplant.

greffier, -ière /gʀɛfje, -jɛʀ/ *nm, f*
clerk of the court.

grêle /gʀɛl/ *adj* (maigre) spindly;
(voix) shrill. ● *nf* hail.

grêler /gʀele/ [1] *vi* hail; **il grêle** it's
hailing. **grêlon** *nm* hailstone.

grelot /gʀəlo/ *nm* (little) bell.

grelotter /gʀələte/ [1] *vi* shiver.

grenade /gʀənad/ *nf* (fruit)
pomegranate; (explosif) grenade.

grenat /gʀəna/ *a inv* dark red.

grenier /gʀənje/ *nm* attic; (pour grain)
loft.

grenouille /gʀənuj/ *nf* frog.

grès /gʀɛ/ *nm* sandstone; (poterie)
stoneware.

grésiller /gʀezije/ [1] *vi* sizzle;
(radio) crackle.

grève /gʀɛv/ *nf* (rivage) shore;
(cessation de travail) strike; **faire ~, être**

en ~ be on strike; **se mettre en** ~ go on strike. **gréviste** *nmf* striker.

gribouiller /gʀibuje/ [1] *vt/i* scribble.

grief /gʀijɛf/ *nm* grievance.

grièvement /gʀijɛvmɑ̃/ *adv* seriously.

griffe /gʀif/ *nf* claw; (de couturier) label; **coup de** ~ scratch.

griffé, ~e /gʀife/ *adj* (vêtement, article) designer.

griffer /gʀife/ [1] *vt* scratch, claw.

grignoter /gʀiɲɔte/ [1] *vt/i* nibble.

gril /gʀil/ *nm* (de cuisinière) grill; (plaque) grill pan.

grillade /gʀijad/ *nf* (viande) grill.

grillage /gʀijaʒ/ *nm* wire netting.

grille /gʀij/ *nf* railings; (portail) (metal) gate; (de fenêtre) bars; (de cheminée) grate; (fig) grid. **grille-pain** *nm inv* toaster.

griller /gʀije/ [1] *vt* (pain) toast; (viande) grill; (ampoule) blow; (feu rouge) go through; (appareil) burn out. ● *vi* (ampoule) blow; (Culin) faire ~ (viande) grill; (pain) toast.

grillon /gʀijɔ̃/ *nm* cricket.

grimace /gʀimas/ *nf* (funny) face; (de douleur, dégoût) grimace; faire des ~s make faces; **faire la** ~ pull a face, grimace.

grimper /gʀɛ̃pe/ [1] *vt* climb. ● *vi* climb; ~ **sur** *ou* **dans un arbre** climb a tree.

grincement /gʀɛ̃smɑ̃/ *nm* creak (ing).

grincer /gʀɛ̃se/ [10] *vi* creak; ~ **des dents** grind one's teeth.

grincheux, -euse /gʀɛ̃ʃø, -z/ *adj* grumpy.

grippe /gʀip/ *nf* influenza, flu.

grippé, ~e /gʀipe/ *adj* **être** ~ have (the) flu; (mécanisme) be seized up *ou* jammed.

gris, ~e /gʀi, -z/ *adj* grey; (saoul) tipsy.

grivois, ~e /gʀivwa, -z/ *adj* bawdy.

grog /gʀɔg/ *nm* hot toddy.

grogner /gʀɔɲe/ [1] *vi* (animal) growl; (personne) grumble.

grognon /gʀɔɲɔ̃/ *am* grumpy.

groin /gʀwɛ̃/ *nm* snout.

gronder /gʀɔ̃de/ [1] *vi* (tonnerre, volcan) rumble; (chien) growl; (conflit) be brewing. ● *vt* scold.

groom /gʀum/ *nm* bellboy.

gros, ~se /gʀo, -s/ *adj* big, large; (gras) fat; (important) big; (épais) thick; (lourd) heavy; (buveur, fumeur) heavy; ~ **bonnet** 🖃 bigwig; ~ **lot** jackpot; ~ **mot** swear word; ~ **plan** close-up; ~**se caisse** bass drum; ~ **titre** headline. ● *nm, f* fat man, fat woman. ● *adv* (écrire) big; (risquer, gagner) a lot. ● *nm* **le** ~ **de** the bulk of; **de** ~ (Comm) wholesale; **en** ~ roughly; (Comm) wholesale.

groseille /gʀozɛj/ *nf* redcurrant; ~ **à maquereau** gooseberry.

grossesse /gʀosɛs/ *nf* pregnancy.

grosseur /gʀosœʀ/ *nf* (volume) size; (enflure) lump.

grossier, -ière /gʀosje, -jɛʀ/ *adj* (sans finesse) coarse, rough; (rudimentaire) crude; (vulgaire) coarse; (impoli) rude; (erreur) gross.

grossièrement *adv* (sommairement) roughly; (vulgairement) coarsely.

grossièreté *nf* coarseness; crudeness; rudeness; (mot) rude word.

grossir /gʀosiʀ/ [2] *vt* (faire augmenter) increase, boost; (agrandir) enlarge; (exagérer) exaggerate; ~ **les rangs** *ou* **la foule** swell the ranks. ● *vi* (personne) put on weight; (augmenter) grow.

grossiste /gʀosist/ *nmf* wholesaler.

grosso modo /gʀosomodo/ *adv* roughly.

grotesque /gʀɔtɛsk/ *adj* grotesque; (ridicule) ludicrous.

grotte /gʀɔt/ *nf* cave; grotto.

grouiller /gʀuje/ [1] *vi* swarm; ~ **de** be swarming with.

groupe /gʀup/ *nm* group; (Mus) group, band; ~ **électrogène** generating set; ~ **scolaire** school; ~ **de travail** working party.

groupement /gʀupmɑ̃/ *nm* grouping.

grouper /gʀupe/ [1] *vt* put together. □ **se** ~ *vpr* group (together).

grue /gʀy/ *nf* (machine, oiseau) crane.

gruyère /gʀyjɛʀ/ *nm* gruyère (cheese).

gué /ge/ *nm* ford; **passer** *ou* **traverser à ~** ford.

guenon /gənɔ̃/ *nf* female monkey.

guépard /gepaʀ/ *nm* cheetah.

guêpe /gɛp/ *nf* wasp.

guère /gɛʀ/ *adv* **ne ~** hardly; **il n'y a ~ d'espoir** there is no hope; **elle n'a ~ dormi** she didn't sleep much, she hardly slept.

guérilla /geʀija/ *nf* guerrilla warfare; (groupe) guerillas.

guérir /geʀiʀ/ [2] *vt* (*personne, maladie, mal*) cure (**de** of); (*plaie, membre*) heal. ● *vi* get better; (*blessure*) heal; **~ de** recover from. **guérison** *nf* curing; healing; (de personne) recovery.

guerre /gɛʀ/ *nf* war; **en ~** at war; **faire la ~** wage war (**à** against); **~ civile** civil war; **~ mondiale** world war.

guerrier, -ière /gɛʀje, -jɛʀ/ *adj* warlike. ● *nm,f* warrior.

guet /ge/ *nm* watch; **faire le ~** be on the watch. **guet-apens** (*pl* **guets-apens**) *nm* ambush.

guetter /gete/ [1] *vt* watch; (attendre) watch out for.

gueule /gœl/ *nf* mouth; (figure 🖫) face; **ta ~!** 🗵 shut up!; **~ de bois** 🖫 hangover.

gueuleton /gœltɔ̃/ *nm* 🖫 blow-out, slap-up meal.

gui /gi/ *nm* mistletoe.

guichet /giʃɛ/ *nm* window, counter; (de gare) ticket-office; (Théât) box-office; **jouer à ~s fermés** (*pièce*) be sold out; **~ automatique** cash dispenser.

guide /gid/ *nm* guide. ● *nf* (fille scout) girl guide.

guider /gide/ [1] *vt* guide.

guidon /gidɔ̃/ *nm* handlebars.

guignol /giɲɔl/ *nm* puppet; (personne) clown; (spectacle) puppet-show.

guillemets /gijmɛ/ *nmpl* quotation marks, inverted commas; **entre ~** in inverted commas.

guillotine /gijɔtin/ *nf* guillotine.

guimauve /gimov/ *nf* marshmallow; **c'est de la ~** 🖫 it's slushy *ou* schmaltzy 🖫.

guindé, ~e /gɛ̃de/ *adj* stiff, formal; (*style*) stilted.

guirlande /giʀlɑ̃d/ *nf* garland; tinsel.

guitare /gitaʀ/ *nf* guitar.

gym /ʒim/ *nf* gymnastics; (Scol) physical education, PE.

gymnase /ʒimnɑz/ *nm* gym-(nasium). **gymnastique** *nf* gymnastics.

gynécologie /ʒinekɔlɔʒi/ *nf* gynaecology.

Hh

habile /abil/ *adj* skilful, clever.

habillé, ~e /abije/ *adj* (*vêtement*) smart; (*soirée*) formal.

habillement /abijmɑ̃/ *nm* clothing.

habiller /abije/ [1] *vt* dress (**de** in); (équiper) clothe; (recouvrir) cover (**de** with). □ **s'~** *vpr* get dressed; (élégamment) dress up.

habit /abi/ *nm* (de personnage) outfit; (de cérémonie) tails; **~s** clothes.

habitant, ~e /abitɑ̃, -t/ *nm,f* (de maison, quartier) resident; (de pays) inhabitant.

habitat /abita/ *nm* (mode de peuplement) settlement; (conditions) housing.

habitation /abitasjɔ̃/ *nf* (logement) house.

habité, ~e /abite/ *adj* (*terre*) inhabited.

habiter /abite/ [1] *vi* live. ● *vt* live in.

habitude /abityd/ *nf* habit; **avoir l'~ de** be used to; **d'~** usually; **comme d'~** as usual.

habitué, ~e /abitɥe/ *nm,f* (client) regular.

habituel, ~le /abitɥɛl/ *adj* usual. **habituellement** *adv* usually.

habituer /abitɥe/ [1] *vt* **~ qn à** get sb used to. □ **s'~ à** *vpr* get used to.

hache /'aʃ/ *nf* axe.

haché, **~e** /'aʃe/ *adj* (viande) minced; (phrases) jerky.

hacher /'aʃe/ [1] *vt* mince; (au couteau) chop.

hachis /'aʃi/ *nm* minced meat; (US) ground meat; **~ Parmentier** ≈ *shepherd's pie*.

hachisch /'aʃiʃ/ *nm* hashish.

hachoir /'aʃwaʀ/ *nm* (appareil) mincer; (couteau) chopper; (planche) chopping board.

haie /'ɛ/ *nf* hedge; (de personnes) line; **course de ~s** hurdle race.

haillon /'ajɔ̃/ *nm* rag.

haine /'ɛn/ *nf* hatred.

haïr /'aiʀ/ [36] *vt* hate.

hâlé /'ɑle/ *adj* (sun-)tanned.

haleine /alɛn/ *nf* breath; **travail de longue ~** long job.

haleter /'alte/ [6] *vi* pant.

hall /'ol/ *nm* hall; (de gare) concourse.

halle /'al/ *nf* market hall; **~s** covered market.

halte /'alt/ *nf* stop; **faire ~** stop. ● *interj* stop; (Mil) halt.

haltère /altɛʀ/ *nm* dumbbell; **faire des ~s** to do weightlifting.

hameau (*pl* **~x**) /'amo/ *nm* hamlet.

hameçon /amsɔ̃/ *nm* hook.

hanche /'ɑ̃ʃ/ *nf* hip.

handicap /'ɑ̃dikap/ *nm* handicap. **handicapé**, **~e** *a & nm,f* disabled (person).

hangar /'ɑ̃gaʀ/ *nm* shed; (pour avions) hangar.

hanter /'ɑ̃te/ [1] *vt* haunt.

hantise /'ɑ̃tiz/ *nf* dread; **avoir la ~ de** dread.

haras /'aʀɑ/ *nm* stud-farm.

harasser /'aʀase/ [1] *vt* exhaust.

harcèlement /'aʀsɛlmɑ̃/ *nm* **~ sexuel** sexual harassment.

harceler /'aʀsəle/ [6] *vt* harass.

hardi, **~e** /'aʀdi/ *adj* bold.

hareng /'aʀɑ̃/ *nm* herring.

hargne /'aʀɲ/ *nf* (aggressive) bad temper.

haricot /'aʀiko/ *nm* bean; **~ vert** French bean; (US) green bean.

harmonie /aʀmɔni/ *nf* harmony. **harmonieux**, **-ieuse** *adj* harmonious.

harmoniser /aʀmɔnize/ [1] *vt* harmonize. □ **s'~** *vpr* harmonize.

harnacher /'aʀnaʃe/ [1] *vt* harness.

harnais /'aʀnɛ/ *nm* harness.

harpe /'aʀp/ *nf* harp.

harpon /'aʀpɔ̃/ *nm* harpoon.

hasard /'azaʀ/ *nm* chance; (coïncidence) coincidence; **les ~s de** the fortunes of; **au ~** (choisir etc.) at random; (flâner) aimlessly. **hasardeux**, **-euse** *adj* risky.

hasarder /'azaʀde/ [1] *vt* risk; (remarque) venture.

hâte /'ɑt/ *nf* haste; **à la ~**, **en ~** hurriedly; **avoir ~ de** look forward to.

hâter /'ɑte/ [1] *vt* hasten. □ **se ~** *vpr* hurry (de to).

hâtif, **-ive** /'ɑtif, -v/ *adj* hasty; (précoce) early.

hausse /'os/ *nf* rise (de in); **~ des prix** price rise; **en ~** rising.

hausser /'ose/ [1] *vt* raise; (épaules) shrug.

haut, **~e** /'o, 'ot/ *adj* high; (de taille) tall; **à voix ~e** aloud; **en couleur** colourful; **plus ~** higher up; (dans un texte) above; **en ~ lieu** in high places. ● *adv* high; **tout ~** out loud. ● *nm* top; **des ~s et des bas** ups and downs; **en ~** (regarder) up; (à l'étage) upstairs; **en ~ (de)** at the top (of).

hautbois /'obwa/ *nm* oboe.

haut-de-forme /'odfɔʀm/ (*pl* **hauts-de-forme**) *nm* top hat.

hauteur /'otœʀ/ *nf* height; (colline) hill; (arrogance) haughtiness; **être à la ~** be up to it; **à la ~ de** (ville) near; **être à la ~ de la situation** be equal to the situation.

haut-le-cœur /'olkœʀ/ *nm inv* nausea.

haut-parleur (*pl* **~s**) /'opaʀlœʀ/ *nm* loudspeaker.

havre /'ɑvʀ/ *nm* haven (de of).

hayon /'ajɔ̃/ *nm* (Auto) hatchback.

hebdomadaire /ɛbdɔmadɛʀ/ *a & nm* weekly.

hébergement /ebɛʀʒəmɑ̃/ *nm* accommodation.

héberger /ebɛʀʒe/ [40] *vt* (ami) put up; (réfugiés) take in.

hébreu (pl ~x) /ebRø/ am Hebrew.
● nm (Ling) Hebrew; **c'est de l'~!** it's all Greek to me!

Hébreu (pl ~x) /ebRø/ nm Hebrew; **les ~x** the Hebrews.

hécatombe /ekatɔ̃b/ nf slaughter.

hectare /ɛktaR/ nm hectare (= 10,000 square metres).

hélas /'elas/ interj alas. ● adv sadly.

hélice /elis/ nf propeller.

hélicoptère /elikɔptɛR/ nm helicopter.

helvétique /ɛlvetik/ adj Swiss.

hématome /ematom/ nm bruise.

hémorragie /emɔRaʒi/ nf haemorrhage.

hémorroïdes /emɔRɔid/ nfpl piles, haemorrhoids.

hennir /'eniR/ [2] vi neigh.

hépatite /epatit/ nf hepatitis.

herbe /ɛRb/ nf grass; (Méd, Culin) herb; **en ~** in the blade; (fig) budding.

héréditaire /eReditɛR/ adj hereditary.

hérédité /eRedite/ nf heredity.

hérisser /'eRise/ [1] vt bristle; **~ qn** (fig) ruffle sb. □ **se ~** vpr bristle.

hérisson /'eRisɔ̃/ nm hedgehog.

héritage /eRitaʒ/ nm inheritance; (spirituel) heritage.

hériter /eRite/ [1] vt/i inherit (de from); **~ de qch** inherit sth.
héritier, -ière nm,f heir, heiress.

hermétique /ɛRmetik/ adj airtight; (fig) unfathomable.

hernie /'ɛRni/ nf hernia.

héroïne /eRɔin/ nf (femme) heroine; (drogue) heroin.

héroïque /eRɔik/ adj heroic.

héros /'eRo/ nm hero.

hésiter /ezite/ [1] vi hesitate (à to); **j'hésite** I'm not sure.

hétérogène /eteRɔʒɛn/ adj heterogeneous.

hétérosexuel, ~le /eteRɔseksɥɛl/ nm/f & a heterosexual.

hêtre /'ɛtR/ nm beech.

heure /œR/ nf time; (soixante minutes) hour; **quelle ~ est-il?** what time is it?; **il est dix ~s** it is ten o'clock; **à l'~** (venir, être) on time; **d'~ en ~** by the hour; **toutes les deux ~s** every two hours; **~ de pointe** rush-hour; **~ de cours** (Scol) period; **~ indue** ungodly hour; **~s creuses** off-peak periods; **~s supplémentaires** overtime.

heureusement /œRøzmɑ̃/ adv fortunately, luckily.

heureux, -euse /œRø, -z/ adj happy; (chanceux) lucky, fortunate.

heurt /'œR/ nm collision; (conflit) clash; **sans ~** smoothly.

heurter /'œRte/ [1] vt (cogner) hit; (mur) bump into, hit; (choquer) offend. □ **se ~ à** vpr bump into, hit; (fig) come up against.

hexagone /ɛgzagon/ nm hexagon; **l'~** France.

hiberner /ibɛRne/ [1] vi hibernate.

hibou (pl ~x) /'ibu/ nm owl.

hier /jɛR/ adv yesterday; **~ soir** last night, yesterday evening.

hiérarchie /'jeRaRʃi/ nf hierarchy.

hilare /ilaR/ adj (visage) merry; **être ~** be laughing.

hindou, ~e /ɛ̃du/ a & nm,f Hindu.
H~, ~e nm,f Hindu.

hippique /ipik/ adj equestrian; **le concours ~** showjumping.

hippodrome /ipɔdRom/ nm racecourse.

hippopotame /ipɔpɔtam/ nm hippopotamus.

hirondelle /iRɔ̃dɛl/ nf swallow.

hisser /'ise/ [1] vt hoist, haul. □ **se ~** vpr heave oneself up.

histoire /istwaR/ nf (récit) story; (étude) history; (affaire) business; **~(s)** (chichis) fuss; (ennuis) trouble.
historique adj historical.

hiver /ivɛR/ nm winter. **hivernal, ~e** (mpl -aux) adj winter; (glacial) wintry.

H.L.M. abbrév m ou f (**habitation à loyer modéré**) block of council flats; (US) low-rent apartment building.

hocher /'ɔʃe/ [1] vt **~ la tête** (pour dire oui) nod; (pour dire non) shake one's head.

hochet /'ɔʃɛ/ nm rattle.

hockey /'ɔkɛ/ nm hockey; **~ sur glace** ice hockey.

hollandais, ~e /ɔlɑ̃dɛ, -z/ adj Dutch. ● nm (Ling) Dutch. **H~, ~e** nm, f Dutchman, Dutchwoman.

Hollande /ˈɔlɑ̃d/ nf Holland.

homard /ˈɔmar/ nm lobster.

homéopathie /ɔmeɔpati/ nf homoeopathy.

homicide /ɔmisid/ nm homicide; ~ **involontaire** manslaughter.

hommage /ɔmaʒ/ nm tribute; ~s (salutations) respects; **rendre ~ à** pay tribute to.

homme /ɔm/ nm man; (espèce) man (kind); ~ **d'affaires** businessman; ~ **de la rue** man in the street; ~ **d'État** statesman; ~ **politique** politician.

homogène /ɔmɔʒɛn/ adj homogeneous.

homonyme /ɔmɔnim/ nm (personne) namesake.

homosexualité /ɔmɔsɛksɥalite/ nf homosexuality.

homosexuel, ~le /ɔmɔsɛksɥɛl/ a & nm, f homosexual.

Hongrie /ˈɔ̃gri/ nf Hungary.

hongrois, ~e /ˈɔ̃grwa, -z/ adj Hungarian. ● nm (Ling) Hungarian. **H~, ~e** nm, f Hungarian.

honnête /ɔnɛt/ adj honest; (juste) fair. **honnêteté** nf honesty.

honneur /ɔnœr/ nm honour; (mérite) credit; **d'~** (invité, place) of honour; **en l'~ de** in honour of; **en quel ~?** ⊞ why?; **faire ~ à** (équipe, famille) bring credit to.

honorable /ɔnɔrabl/ adj honourable; (convenable) respectable.

honoraire /ɔnɔrɛr/ adj honorary. **honoraires** nmpl fees.

honorer /ɔnɔre/ [1] vt honour; (faire honneur à) do credit to.

honte /ˈɔ̃t/ nf shame; **avoir ~** be ashamed (de of); **faire ~ à** make ashamed. **honteux, -euse** adj (personne) ashamed (de of); (action) shameful.

hôpital (pl -aux) /ɔpital, -o/ nm hospital.

hoquet /ˈɔkɛ/ nm **le ~** (the) hiccups.

horaire /ɔrɛr/ adj hourly. ● nm timetable; ~s **libres** flexitime.

horizon /ɔrizɔ̃/ nm horizon; (Fig) outlook.

horizontal, ~e (mpl -aux) /ɔrizɔ̃tal, -o/ adj horizontal.

horloge /ɔrlɔʒ/ nf clock.

hormis /ˈɔrmi/ prép save.

hormonal, ~e (mpl -aux) /ɔrmɔnal, -o/ adj hormonal, hormone.

hormone /ɔrmon/ nf hormone.

horreur /ɔrœr/ nf horror; **avoir ~ de** hate.

horrible /ɔribl/ adj horrible.

horrifier /ɔrifje/ [45] vt horrify.

hors /ˈɔr/ prép ~ **de** outside, (avec mouvement) out of; ~ **d'atteinte** out of reach; ~ **d'haleine** out of breath; ~ **de prix** extremely expensive; ~ **pair** outstanding; ~ **de soi** beside oneself. **hors-bord** nm inv speedboat. **hors-d'œuvre** nm inv hors-d'œuvre. **hors-jeu** a inv offside. **hors-la-loi** nm inv outlaw. **hors-piste** nm off-piste skiing. **hors-taxe** a inv duty-free.

horticulteur, -trice /ɔrtikyltœr, -tris/ nm, f horticulturist.

hospice /ɔspis/ nm home.

hospitalier, -ière /ɔspitalje, -jɛr/ adj hospitable; (Méd) hospital. **hospitaliser** [1] vt take to hospital. **hospitalité** nf hospitality.

hostile /ɔstil/ adj hostile. **hostilité** nf hostility.

hôte /ot/ nm (maître) host; (invité) guest.

hôtel /otɛl/ nm hotel; ~ (particulier) (private) mansion; ~ **de ville** town hall.

hôtelier, -ière /otəlje, -jɛr/ adj hotel. ● nm, f hotel keeper. **hôtellerie** nf hotel business.

hôtesse /otɛs/ nf hostess; ~ **de l'air** stewardess.

hotte /ˈɔt/ nf basket; ~ **aspirante** extractor (hood), (US) ventilator.

houblon /ˈublɔ̃/ nm **le ~** hops.

houille /ˈuj/ nf coal; ~ **blanche** hydroelectric power.

houle /ˈul/ nf swell. **houleux, -euse** adj (mer) rough; (débat) stormy.

housse /ˈus/ nf cover; ~ **de siège** seat cover.

houx /ˈu/ nm holly.

huées /'ɥe/ *nfpl* boos. **huer** [1] *vt* boo.

huile /ɥil/ *nf* oil; (personne 🄵) bigwig. **huiler** [1] *vt* oil. **huileux, -euse** *adj* oily.

huis /'ɥi/ *nm* **à ~ clos** in camera.

huissier /ɥisje/ *nm* (Jur) bailiff; (portier) usher.

huit /'ɥi(t)/ *adj* eight; **~ jours** a week; **lundi en ~** a week on Monday. ● *nm* eight. **huitième** *a & nmf* eighth.

huître /ɥitʀ/ *nf* oyster.

humain, ~e /ymɛ̃, -ɛn/ *adj* human; (compatissant) humane. **humanitaire** *adj* humanitarian. **humanité** *nf* humanity.

humble /œ̃bl/ *adj* humble.

humeur /ymœʀ/ *nf* mood; (tempérament) temper; **de bonne/ mauvaise ~** in a good/bad mood.

humide /ymid/ *adj* damp; (*chaleur, climat*) humid; (*lèvres, yeux*) moist. **humidité** *nf* humidity.

humilier /ymilje/ [45] *vt* humiliate.

humoristique /ymɔʀistik/ *adj* humorous.

humour /ymuʀ/ *nm* humour; **avoir de l'~** have a sense of humour.

hurlement /'yʀləmã/ *nm* howl(ing). **hurler** [1] *vt/i* howl.

hutte /'yt/ *nf* hut.

hydratant, ~e /idʀatã, -t/ *adj* (*lotion*) moisturizing.

hydravion /idʀavjɔ̃/ *nm* seaplane.

hydroélectrique /idʀoelɛktʀik/ *adj* hydroelectric.

hydrogène /idʀɔʒɛn/ *nm* hydrogen.

hygiène /iʒjɛn/ *nf* hygiene. **hygiénique** *adj* hygienic.

hymne /imn/ *nm* hymn; **~ national** national anthem.

hyperlien /ipɛʀljɛ̃/ *nm* (Internet) hyperlink.

hypermarché /ipɛʀmaʀʃe/ *nm* (supermarché) hypermarket.

hypertension /ipɛʀtãsjɔ̃/ *nf* high blood-pressure.

hypertexte /ipɛʀtɛkst/ *nm* (Internet) hypertext.

hypnotiser /ipnɔtize/ [1] *vt* hypnotize.

hypocrisie /ipɔkʀizi/ *nf* hypocrisy.

hypocrite /ipɔkʀit/ *adj* hypocritical. ● *nmf* hypocrite.

hypothèque /ipɔtɛk/ *nf* mortgage.

hypothèse /ipɔtɛz/ *nf* hypothesis.

hystérie /isteʀi/ *nf* hysteria.

ici /isi/ *adv* (dans l'espace) here; (dans le temps) now; **d'~ demain** by tomorrow; **d'~ là** in the meantime; **d'~ peu** shortly; **~ même** in this very place; **jusqu'~** until now; (dans le passé) until then.

idéal, ~e (*mpl* **-aux**) /ideal, -o/ *a & nm* ideal. **idéaliser** [1] *vt* idealize.

idée /ide/ *nf* idea; (esprit) mind; **avoir dans l'~ de faire** plan to do; **il ne me viendrait jamais à l'~ de faire** it would never occur to me to do; **~ fixe** obsession; **~ reçue** conventional opinion.

identification /idãtifikasjɔ̃/ *nf* identification. **identifier** [45] *vt*, **s'identifier** *vpr* identify (à with).

identique /idãtik/ *adj* identical.

identité /idãtite/ *nf* identity.

idéologie /ideɔlɔʒi/ *nf* ideology.

idiome /idjom/ *nm* idiom.

idiot, ~e /idjo, -ɔt/ *adj* idiotic. ● *nm,f* idiot. **idiotie** *nf* idiocy; (acte, parole) idiotic thing.

idole /idɔl/ *nf* idol.

if /if/ *nm* yew.

ignare /iɲaʀ/ *adj* ignorant. ● *nmf* ignoramus.

ignoble /iɲɔbl/ *adj* vile.

ignorance /iɲɔʀãs/ *nf* ignorance.

ignorant, ~e /iɲɔʀã, -t/ *adj* ignorant. ● *nm,f* ignoramus.

ignorer /iɲɔʀe/ [1] *vt* not know; **je l'ignore** I don't know; (*personne*) ignore.

il /il/ *pron* (personne, animal familier) he; (chose, animal) it; (impersonnel) it; **~ est vrai que** it is true that; **~ neige/pleut** it is snowing/raining; **~ y a** there is; (pluriel) there are; (temps) ago; (durée) for; ~ **y a 2 ans** 2 years ago; ~ **y a plus d'une heure que j'attends** I've been waiting for over an hour.

île /il/ nf island; ~ **déserte** desert island; ~**s anglo-normandes** Channel Islands; ~**s Britanniques** British Isles.

illégal, ~**e** (mpl ~**aux**) /ilegal, -o/ adj illegal.

illégitime /ileʒitim/ adj illegitimate.

illettré, ~**e** /iletʀe/ a & nm,f illiterate.

illicite /ilisit/ adj illicit; (Jur) unlawful.

illimité, ~**e** /ilimite/ adj unlimited.

illisible /ilizibl/ adj illegible; (livre) unreadable.

illogique /ilɔʒik/ adj illogical.

illuminé, ~**e** /ilymine/ adj lit up; (monument) floodlit.

illusion /ilyzjɔ̃/ nf illusion; **se faire des** ~**s** delude oneself. **illusoire** adj illusory.

illustre /ilystʀ/ adj illustrious.

illustré, ~**e** /ilystʀe/ adj illustrated. ● nm comic.

illustrer /ilystʀe/ [1] vt illustrate. □ **s'**~ vpr become famous.

îlot /ilo/ nm islet; (de maisons) block.

ils /il/ pron they.

image /imaʒ/ nf picture; (métaphore) image; (reflet) reflection. **imagé**, ~**e** adj full of imagery.

imaginaire /imaʒinɛʀ/ adj imaginary. **imaginatif, -ive** adj imaginative. **imagination** nf imagination.

imaginer /imaʒine/ [1] vt imagine; (inventer) think up. □ **s'**~ vpr (se représenter) imagine (**que** that); (croire) think (**que** that).

imbécile /ɛ̃besil/ adj idiotic. ● nmf idiot.

imbiber /ɛ̃bibe/ [1] vt soak (**de** with). □ **s'**~ vpr become soaked (**de** with).

imbriqué, ~**e** /ɛ̃bʀike/ adj (lié) interlinked, interlocking; (tuiles) overlapping.

imbu, ~**e** /ɛ̃by/ adj ~ **de** full of.

imitateur, -trice /imitatœʀ, -tʀis/ nm,f imitator; (comédien) impersonator. **imiter** [1] vt imitate; (personnage) impersonate; (signature) forge; (faire comme) do the same as.

immatriculation /imatʀikylasjɔ̃/ nf registration.

immatriculer /imatʀikyle/ [1] vt register; **se faire** ~ register; **faire** ~ **une voiture** have a car registered.

immédiat, ~**e** /imedja, -t/ adj immediate. ● nm **dans l'**~ for the time being.

immense /imɑ̃s/ adj huge, immense.

immerger /imɛʀʒe/ [40] vt immerse. □ **s'**~ vpr immerse oneself (**dans** in).

immeuble /imœbl/ nm block of flats, building; ~ **de bureaux** office building ou block.

immigrant, ~**e** /imigʀɑ̃, -t/ a & nm,f immigrant. **immigration** nf immigration. **immigré**, ~**e** a & nm,f immigrant. **immigrer** [1] vi immigrate.

imminent, ~**e** /iminɑ̃, -t/ adj imminent.

immobile /imɔbil/ adj still, motionless.

immobilier, -ière /imɔbilje, -jɛʀ/ adj property; **agence immobilière** estate agent's office; (US) real estate office; **agent** ~ estate agent; (US) real estate agent. ● nm **l'**~ property; (US) real estate.

immobiliser /imɔbilize/ [1] vt immobilize; (stopper) stop. □ **s'**~ vpr stop.

immonde /imɔ̃d/ adj filthy.

immoral, ~**e** (mpl -**aux**) /imɔʀal, -o/ adj immoral.

immortel, ~**le** /imɔʀtɛl/ adj immortal.

immuable /imɥabl/ adj unchanging.

immuniser /imynize/ [1] vt immunize; **immunisé contre** (à l'abri de) immune to. **immunité** nf immunity.

impact /ɛ̃pakt/ nm impact.

impair, ~**e** /ɛ̃pɛʀ/ adj (numéro) odd. ● nm blunder, faux pas.

imparfait, ~**e** /ɛ̃paʀfɛ, -t/ a & nm imperfect.

impasse /ɛ̃pas/ nf (rue) dead end; (situation) deadlock.

impatient, ~e /ɛ̃pasjɑ̃, -t/ adj impatient.

impatienter /ɛ̃pasjɑ̃te/ [1] vt annoy. □ s'~ vpr get impatient (contre qn with sb).

impayé, ~e /ɛ̃peje/ adj unpaid.

impeccable /ɛ̃pekabl/ adj (propre) impeccable, spotless; (soigné) perfect.

impensable /ɛ̃pɑ̃sabl/ adj unthinkable.

impératif, **-ive** /ɛ̃peratif, -v/ adj imperative. ● nm (Gram) imperative; (contrainte) imperative; ~s (exigences) requirements, demands (de of).

impératrice /ɛ̃peratʀis/ nf empress.

impérial, ~e (mpl **-iaux**) /ɛ̃peʀjal, -jo/ adj imperial.

impérieux, **-ieuse** /ɛ̃peʀjø, -z/ adj imperious; (pressant) pressing.

imperméable /ɛ̃pɛʀmeabl/ adj impervious (à to); (manteau, tissu) waterproof. ● nm raincoat.

impersonnel, **-le** /ɛ̃pɛʀsɔnɛl/ adj impersonal.

impertinent, ~e /ɛ̃pɛʀtinɑ̃, -t/ adj impertinent.

imperturbable /ɛ̃pɛʀtyʀbabl/ adj unshakeable, unruffled.

impétueux, **-euse** /ɛ̃petɥø, -z/ adj impetuous.

impitoyable /ɛ̃pitwajabl/ adj merciless.

implant /ɛ̃plɑ̃/ nm implant.

implanter /ɛ̃plɑ̃te/ [1] vt establish, set up. □ s'~ vpr become established.

implication /ɛ̃plikasjɔ̃/ nf (conséquence) implication; (participation) involvement.

impliquer /ɛ̃plike/ [1] vt (mêler) implicate (dans in); (signifier) imply, mean (que that); (nécessiter) involve (de faire doing).

implorer /ɛ̃plɔʀe/ [1] vt implore, beg for.

impoli, ~e /ɛ̃pɔli/ adj impolite, rude.

importance /ɛ̃pɔʀtɑ̃s/ nf importance; (taille) size; (ampleur) extent; sans ~ unimportant.

important, ~e /ɛ̃pɔʀtɑ̃, -t/ adj important; (en quantité) considerable,

sizeable, big; (air) self-important. ● nm l'~ the important thing.

importateur, **-trice** /ɛ̃pɔʀtatœʀ, -tʀis/ nm, f importer. ● adj importing. **importation** nf import.

importer /ɛ̃pɔʀte/ [1] vt (Comm) import. ● vi matter, be important (à to); il importe que it is important that; n'importe, peu importe it does not matter; n'importe comment anyhow; n'importe où anywhere; n'importe qui anybody; n'importe quoi anything.

importun, ~e /ɛ̃pɔʀtœ̃, -yn/ adj troublesome. ● nm, f nuisance.

imposer /ɛ̃poze/ [1] vt impose (à on); (taxer) tax; en ~ à qn impress sb. □ s'~ vpr (action) be essential; (se faire reconnaître) stand out; (s'astreindre à) s'~ de faire force oneself to do.

imposition /ɛ̃pozisjɔ̃/ nf taxation; ~ des mains laying-on of hands.

impossible /ɛ̃posibl/ adj impossible. ● nm faire l'~ do one's utmost.

impôt /ɛ̃po/ nm tax; ~s (contributions) tax(ation), taxes; ~ sur le revenu income tax.

impotent, ~e /ɛ̃pɔtɑ̃, -t/ adj disabled.

imprécis, ~e /ɛ̃pʀesi, -z/ adj imprecise.

imprégner /ɛ̃pʀeɲe/ [14] vt fill (de with); (imbiber) impregnate (de with). □ s'~ de vpr (fig) immerse oneself in.

impression /ɛ̃pʀesjɔ̃/ nf impression; (de livre) printing. **impressionnant** adj impressive; (choquant) disturbing. **impressionner** [1] vt impress; (choquer) disturb.

imprévisible /ɛ̃pʀevizibl/ adj unpredictable.

imprévu, ~e /ɛ̃pʀevy/ adj unexpected. ● nm unexpected incident; sauf ~ unless anything unexpected happens.

imprimante /ɛ̃pʀimɑ̃t/ nf (Ordinat) printer; ~ à jet d'encre ink-jet printer; ~ (à) laser laser printer.

imprimé, ~e /ɛ̃pʀime/ adj printed. ● nm printed form.

imprimer /ɛ̃pʀime/ [1] *vt* print; (marquer) imprint. **imprimerie** *nf* (art) printing; (lieu) printing works. **imprimeur** *nm* printer.

improbable /ɛ̃pʀɔbabl/ *adj* unlikely, improbable.

impropre /ɛ̃pʀɔpʀ/ *adj* incorrect; ∼ à unfit for.

improviste: à l'∼ /alɛ̃pʀɔvist/ *loc* unexpectedly.

imprudence /ɛ̃pʀydɑ̃s/ *nf* carelessness; (acte) careless action.

imprudent, ∼e /ɛ̃pʀydɑ̃, -t/ *adj* careless; **il est** ∼ **de** it is unwise to.

impudent, ∼e /ɛ̃pydɑ̃, -t/ *adj* impudent.

impuissant, ∼e /ɛ̃pɥisɑ̃, -t/ *adj* helpless; (Méd) impotent; ∼ à faire powerless to do.

impulsif, **-ive** /ɛ̃pylsif, -v/ *adj* impulsive. **impulsion** *nf* (poussée, influence) impetus; (instinct, mouvement) impulse.

impur, ∼e /ɛ̃pyʀ/ *adj* impure.

imputer /ɛ̃pyte/ [1] *vt* ∼ à attribute to, impute to.

inabordable /inabɔʀdabl/ *adj* (*prix*) prohibitive.

inacceptable /inaksɛptabl/ *adj* unacceptable.

inactif, **-ive** /inaktif, -v/ *adj* inactive.

inadapté, ∼e /inadapte/ *adj* maladjusted. ● *nm,f* (Psych) maladjusted person.

inadmissible /inadmisibl/ *adj* unacceptable.

inadvertance /inadvɛʀtɑ̃s/ *nf* par ∼ by mistake.

inanimé, ∼e /inanime/ *adj* (évanoui) unconscious; (mort) lifeless; (*matière*) inanimate.

inaperçu, ∼e /inapɛʀsy/ *adj* unnoticed.

inapte /inapt/ *adj* unsuited (à to); ∼ à faire incapable of doing; ∼ au service militaire unfit for military service.

inattendu, ∼e /inatɑ̃dy/ *adj* unexpected.

inaugurer /inogyʀe/ [1] *vt* inaugurate.

incapable /ɛ̃kapabl/ *adj* incapable (de qch of sth); ∼ de faire unable to do, incapable of doing. ● *nmf* incompetent.

incapacité /ɛ̃kapasite/ *nf* inability, incapacity; **être dans l'**∼ **de faire** be unable to do.

incarcérer /ɛ̃kaʀseʀe/ [14] *vt* imprison, incarcerate.

incarnation /ɛ̃kaʀnasjɔ̃/ *nf* embodiment, incarnation. **incarné**, ∼e *adj* (*ongle*) ingrowing.

incassable /ɛ̃kasabl/ *adj* unbreakable.

incendiaire /ɛ̃sɑ̃djɛʀ/ *adj* incendiary; (*propos*) inflammatory. ● *nmf* arsonist.

incendie /ɛ̃sɑ̃di/ *nm* fire; ∼ **criminel** arson. **incendier** [45] *vt* set fire to.

incertain, ∼e /ɛ̃sɛʀtɛ̃, -ɛn/ *adj* uncertain; (*contour*) vague; (*temps*) unsettled. **incertitude** *nf* uncertainty.

inceste /ɛ̃sɛst/ *nm* incest.

incidence /ɛ̃sidɑ̃s/ *nf* effect.

incident /ɛ̃sidɑ̃/ *nm* incident; ∼ **technique** technical hitch.

incinérer /ɛ̃sineʀe/ [14] *vt* incinerate; (*mort*) cremate.

inciser /ɛ̃size/ [1] *vt* make an incision in; (*abcès*) lance. **incisif**, **-ive** *adj* incisive. **incision** *nf* incision; (d'abcès) lancing.

incitation /ɛ̃sitasjɔ̃/ *nf* (Jur) incitement (à to); (encouragement) incentive. **inciter** [1] *vt* incite (à to); (encourager) encourage.

inclinaison /ɛ̃klinɛzɔ̃/ *nf* incline; (de la tête) tilt.

inclination /ɛ̃klinasjɔ̃/ *nf* (penchant) inclination; (geste) (du buste) bow; (de la tête) nod.

incliner /ɛ̃kline/ [1] *vt* tilt, lean; (courber) bend; (inciter) encourage (à to); ∼ **la tête** (approuver) nod; (révérence) bow. ● *vi* ∼ à be inclined to. □ **s'**∼ *vpr* lean forward; (se courber) bow down (**devant** before); (céder) give in, yield (**devant** to); (*chemin*) slope.

inclure /ɛ̃klyʀ/ [16] *vt* include; (enfermer) enclose; **jusqu'au lundi inclus** up to and including Monday.

incohérence /ɛ̃kɔeRɑ̃s/ *nf*
incoherence; (contradiction)
discrepancy. **incohérent**, ~e *adj*
incoherent, inconsistent.

incolore /ɛ̃kɔlɔR/ *adj* colourless;
(*verre*) clear.

incommoder /ɛ̃kɔmɔde/ [1] *vt*
inconvenience, bother. .

incompatible /ɛ̃kɔ̃patibl/ *adj*
incompatible.

incompétent, ~e /ɛ̃kɔ̃petɑ̃, -t/ *adj*
incompetent.

incomplet, **-ète** /ɛ̃kɔ̃plɛ, -t/ *adj*
incomplete.

incompréhension /ɛ̃kɔ̃pReɑ̃sjɔ̃/
nf lack of understanding.

incompris, ~e /ɛ̃kɔ̃pRi, -z/ *adj*
misunderstood.

inconcevable /ɛ̃kɔ̃svabl/ *adj*
inconceivable.

incongru, ~e /ɛ̃kɔ̃gRy/ *adj*
unseemly.

inconnu, ~e /ɛ̃kɔny/ *adj* unknown
(à to). ● *nm*, *f* stranger. ● *nm* l'~ the
unknown.

inconscience /ɛ̃kɔ̃sjɑ̃s/ *nf*
unconsciousness; (folie) madness.

inconscient, ~e /ɛ̃kɔ̃sjɑ̃, -t/ *adj*
unconscious (de of); (fou) mad. ● *nm*
(Psych) subconscious.

incontestable /ɛ̃kɔ̃tɛstabl/ *adj*
indisputable.

incontrôlable /ɛ̃kɔ̃tRolabl/ *adj*
unverifiable; (non maîtrisé)
uncontrollable.

inconvenant, ~e /ɛ̃kɔ̃vnɑ̃, -t/ *adj*
improper.

inconvénient /ɛ̃kɔ̃venjɑ̃/ *nm*
disadvantage, drawback; (objection)
objection.

incorporer /ɛ̃kɔRpɔRe/ [1] *vt*
incorporate; (Culin) blend (à into);
(Mil) enlist.

incorrect, ~e /ɛ̃kɔRɛkt/ *adj* (faux)
incorrect; (malséant) improper; (impoli)
impolite; (déloyal) unfair.

incrédule /ɛ̃kRedyl/ *adj*
incredulous.

incriminer /ɛ̃kRimine/ [1] *vt*
(*personne*) incriminate; (*conduite*,
action) attack.

incroyable /ɛ̃kRwajabl/ *adj*
incredible.

incruster /ɛ̃kRyste/ [1] *vt* inlay (**de**
with).

incubateur /ɛ̃kybatœR/ *nm*
incubator.

inculpation /ɛ̃kylpasjɔ̃/ *nf* charge
(**de**, **pour** of). **inculpé**, ~e *nm*, *f*
accused. **inculper** [1] *vt* charge (**de**
with).

inculquer /ɛ̃kylke/ [1] *vt* instil (**à**
into).

inculte /ɛ̃kylt/ *adj* uncultivated;
(*personne*) uneducated.

incurver /ɛ̃kyRve/ [1] *vt* curve,
bend. □ s'~ *vpr* curve, bend.

Inde /ɛ̃d/ *nf* India.

indécent, ~e /ɛ̃desɑ̃, -t/ *adj*
indecent.

indécis, ~e /ɛ̃desi, -z/ *adj* (de nature)
indecisive; (temporairement) undecided.

indéfini, ~e /ɛ̃defini/ *adj* (Gram)
indefinite; (vague) undefined; (sans
limites) indeterminate.

indemne /ɛ̃dɛmn/ *adj* unharmed.

indemniser /ɛ̃dɛmnize/ [1] *vt*
compensate (**de** for).

indemnité /ɛ̃dɛmnite/ *nf*
indemnity, compensation; (allocation)
allowance; ~**s de licenciement**
redundancy payment.

indépendance /ɛ̃depɑ̃dɑ̃s/ *nf*
independence. **indépendant**, ~e
adj independent.

indéterminé, ~e /ɛ̃detɛRmine/ *adj*
unspecified.

index /ɛ̃dɛks/ *nm* forefinger; (liste)
index.

indicateur, **-trice** /ɛ̃dikatœR, -tRis/
nm, *f* (police) informer. ● *nm* (livre)
guide; (Tech) indicator.

indicatif, **-ve** /ɛ̃dikatif, -v/ *adj*
indicative (**de** of). ● *nm* (à la radio)
signature tune; (téléphonique) dialling
code; (Gram) indicative.

indication /ɛ̃dikasjɔ̃/ *nf* indication;
(renseignement) information; (directive)
instruction.

indice /ɛ̃dis/ *nm* sign; (dans une
enquête) clue; (des prix) index; (évaluation) rating; ~ **d'écoute** audience
ratings.

indifférence /ɛ̃difeRɑ̃s/ *nf*
indifference.

indifférent, **~e** /ɛ̃diferɑ̃, -t/ *adj* indifferent (à to); **ça m'est ~** it makes no difference to me.

indigène /ɛ̃diʒɛn/ *a & nmf* native, indigenous; (du pays) local. ● *nmf* native.

indigent, **~e** /ɛ̃diʒɑ̃, -t/ *adj* destitute.

indigeste /ɛ̃diʒɛst/ *adj* indigestible. **indigestion** *nf* indigestion.

indigne /ɛ̃diɲ/ *adj* unworthy (**de** of); (*acte*) vile. **indigner** (**s'**) [1] *vpr* become indignant (**de** at).

indiqué, **~e** /ɛ̃dike/ *adj* (*heure*) appointed; (*opportun*) appropriate; (*conseillé*) recommended.

indiquer /ɛ̃dike/ [1] *vt* (montrer) show, indicate; (renseigner sur) point out, tell; (déterminer) give, state, appoint; **~ du doigt** point to *ou* out *ou* at.

indirect, **~e** /ɛ̃dirɛkt/ *adj* indirect.

indiscipliné, **~e** /ɛ̃disipline/ *adj* unruly.

indiscret, **-ète** /ɛ̃diskrɛ, -t/ *adj* (*personne*) inquisitive; (*question*) indiscreet.

indiscutable /ɛ̃diskytabl/ *adj* unquestionable.

indispensable /ɛ̃dispɑ̃sabl/ *adj* indispensable; **il est ~ qu'il vienne** it is essential that he comes.

individu /ɛ̃dividy/ *nm* individual.

individuel, **~le** /ɛ̃dividɥɛl/ *adj* (pour une personne) individual; (qui concerne l'individu) personal; **chambre ~le** single room; **maison ~le** detached house.

indolore /ɛ̃dɔlɔr/ *adj* painless.

Indonésie /ɛ̃dɔnezi/ *nf* Indonesia.

indu, **~e** /ɛ̃dy/ *adj* **à une heure ~e** at some ungodly hour.

induire /ɛ̃dɥir/ [17] *vt* infer (**de** from); (inciter) induce (**à faire** to do); **~ en erreur** mislead.

indulgence /ɛ̃dylʒɑ̃s/ *nf* indulgence; (de jury) leniency. **indulgent**, **~e** *adj* indulgent; (clément) lenient.

industrialisé, **~e** /ɛ̃dystrijalize/ *adj* industrialized.

industrie /ɛ̃dystri/ *nf* industry.

industriel, **~le** /ɛ̃dystrijɛl/ *adj* industrial. ● *nm* industrialist.

inédit, **~e** /inedi, -t/ *adj* unpublished; (fig) original.

inefficace /inefikas/ *adj* (remède, mesure) ineffective; (appareil, système) inefficient.

inégal, **~e** (*mpl* **-aux**) /inegal, -o/ *adj* unequal; (irrégulier) uneven. **inégalable** *adj* matchless. **inégalité** *nf* (injustice) inequality; (irrégularité) unevenness; (disproportion) disparity.

inéluctable /inelyktabl/ *adj* inescapable.

inepte /inɛpt/ *adj* inept, absurd.

inerte /inɛrt/ *adj* inert; (immobile) lifeless; (sans énergie) apathetic. **inertie** *nf* inertia; (fig) apathy.

inespéré, **~e** /inɛspere/ *adj* unhoped for.

inestimable /inɛstimabl/ *adj* priceless; (aide) invaluable.

inexact, **~e** /inɛgza(kt), -kt/ *adj* (imprécis) inaccurate; (incorrect) incorrect.

in extremis /inɛkstremis/ *adv* (par nécessité) as a last resort; (au dernier moment) at the last minute. ● *adj* last-minute.

infaillible /ɛ̃fajibl/ *adj* infallible.

infâme /ɛ̃fɑm/ *adj* vile.

infantile /ɛ̃fɑ̃til/ *adj* (puéril) infantile; (maladie) childhood; (mortalité) infant.

infarctus /ɛ̃farktys/ *nm* coronary, heart attack.

infatigable /ɛ̃fatigabl/ *adj* tireless.

infect, **~e** /ɛ̃fɛkt/ *adj* revolting.

infecter /ɛ̃fɛkte/ [1] *vt* infect. □ **s'~** *vpr* become infected. **infectieux**, **-ieuse** *adj* infectious. **infection** *nf* infection.

inférieur, **~e** /ɛ̃ferjœr/ *adj* (plus bas) lower; (moins bon) inferior (**à** to); **~ à** (plus petit que) smaller than; (plus bas que) lower than. ● *nm,f* inferior. **infériorité** *nf* inferiority.

infernal, **~e** (*mpl* **-aux**) /ɛ̃fɛrnal, -o/ *adj* infernal.

infester /ɛ̃fɛste/ [1] *vt* infest.

infidèle /ɛ̃fidɛl/ *adj* unfaithful (à to).
infidélité *nf* unfaithfulness; (acte)
infidelity.

infiltrer (s') /sɛ̃filtre/ [1] *vpr* s'~
(dans) (*personnes, idées*) infiltrate;
(*liquide*) seep through.

infime /ɛ̃fim/ *adj* tiny, minute.

infini, ~e /ɛ̃fini/ *adj* infinite. ● *nm*
infinity; à l'~ endlessly.

infinité /ɛ̃finite/ *nf* l'~ infinity; une
~ de an endless number of.

infinitif /ɛ̃finitif/ *nm* infinitive.

infirme /ɛ̃fiʀm/ *adj* disabled. ● *nmf*
disabled person. **infirmerie** *nf*
sickbay, infirmary. **infirmier** *nm*
(male) nurse. **infirmière** *nf* nurse.
infirmité *nf* disability.

inflammable /ɛ̃flamabl/ *adj* inflammable.

inflation /ɛ̃flasjɔ̃/ *nf* inflation.

infliger /ɛ̃fliʒe/ [40] *vt* inflict;
(*sanction*) impose.

influence /ɛ̃flyɑ̃s/ *nf* influence.
influencer [10] *vt* influence.
influent, ~e *adj* influential.

influer /ɛ̃flye/ [1] *vi* ~ sur influence.

informateur, **-trice** /ɛ̃fɔʀmatœʀ,
-tʀis/ *nm, f* informant; (pour la police)
informer.

informaticien, ~ne /ɛ̃fɔʀmatisjɛ̃,
-ɛn/ *nm, f* computer scientist.

information /ɛ̃fɔʀmasjɔ̃/ *nf*
information; (Jur) inquiry; une ~
(some) information; (nouvelle) (some)
news; les ~s the news.

informatique /ɛ̃fɔʀmatik/ *nf*
computer science; (techniques)
information technology.
informatiser [1] *vt* computerize.

informer /ɛ̃fɔʀme/ [1] *vt* inform (de
about, of). □ s'~ *vpr* enquire (de
about).

inforoute /ɛ̃fɔʀut/ *nf* (Ordinat)
information highway.

infortune /ɛ̃fɔʀtyn/ *nf* misfortune.

infraction /ɛ̃fʀaksjɔ̃/ *nf* offence; ~
à (*loi, règlement*) breach of.

infrastructure /ɛ̃fʀastʀyktyʀ/ *nf*
infrastructure; (équipements) facilities.

infructueux, **-euse** /ɛ̃fʀyktɥø, -z/
adj fruitless.

infuser /ɛ̃fyze/ [1] *vt/i* infuse, brew.
infusion *nf* herbal tea, infusion.

ingénier (s') /(s)ɛ̃ʒenje/ [45] *vpr*
s'~ à strive to.

ingénieur /ɛ̃ʒenjœʀ/ *nm* engineer.

ingénieux, **-ieuse** /ɛ̃ʒenjø, -z/ *adj*
ingenious. **ingéniosité** *nf*
ingenuity.

ingénu, ~e /ɛ̃ʒeny/ *adj* naïve.

ingérence /ɛ̃ʒeʀɑ̃s/ *nf* interference.

ingérer (s') /sɛ̃ʒeʀe/ [14] *vpr* s'~
dans interfere in.

ingrat, ~e /ɛ̃gʀa, -t/ *adj* (*personne*)
ungrateful; (*travail*) unrewarding,
thankless; (*visage*) unattractive.

ingrédient /ɛ̃gʀedjɑ̃/ *nm*
ingredient.

ingurgiter /ɛ̃gyʀʒite/ [1] *vt* swallow.

inhabité, ~e /inabite/ *adj*
uninhabited.

inhabituel, ~le /inabitɥɛl/ *adj*
unusual.

inhumain, ~e /inymɛ̃, -ɛn/ *adj*
inhuman.

inhumation /inymasjɔ̃/ *nf* burial.

initial, ~e (*mpl* **-iaux**) /inisjal, -jo/
adj initial. **initiale** *nf* initial.

initialisation /inisjalizasjɔ̃/ *nf*
(Ordinat) formatting. **initialiser** [1] *vt*
format.

initiation /inisjasjɔ̃/ *nf* initiation;
(formation) introduction (à to); cours
d'~ introductory course.

initiative /inisjativ/ *nf* initiative.

initier /inisje/ [45] *vt* initiate (à
into); (faire découvrir) introduce (à to).
□ s'~ *vpr* s'~ à qch learn sth.

injecter /ɛ̃ʒɛkte/ [1] *vt* inject; injecté
de sang bloodshot. **injection** *nf*
injection.

injure /ɛ̃ʒyʀ/ *nf* insult. **injurier** [45]
vt insult. **injurieux**, **-ieuse** *adj*
insulting.

injuste /ɛ̃ʒyst/ *adj* unjust, unfair.
injustice *nf* injustice.

inné, ~e /inne/ *adj* innate, inborn.

innocence /inɔsɑ̃s/ *nf* innocence.
innocent, ~e *a* & *nm, f* innocent.
innocenter [1] *vt* clear, prove
innocent.

innombrable /inɔ̃bʀabl/ *adj*
countless.

innovateur, **-trice** /inɔvatœʀ,
-tʀis/ *nm, f* innovator. **innovation**

nf innovation. **innover** [1] *vi*
innovate.

inodore /inɔdɔʀ/ *adj* odourless.

inoffensif, -ive /inɔfɑ̃sif, -v/ *adj*
harmless.

inondation /inɔ̃dasjɔ̃/ *nf* flood;
(action) flooding.

inonder /inɔ̃de/ [1] *vt* flood; (mouiller)
soak; (envahir) inundate (**de** with);
inondé de soleil bathed in sunlight.

inopiné, ~e /inɔpine/ *adj*
unexpected; (mort) sudden.

inopportun, ~e /inɔpɔʀtœ̃, -yn/
adj inopportune, ill-timed.

inoubliable /inublijabl/ *adj*
unforgettable.

inouï, ~e /inwi/ *adj* incredible;
(événement) unprecedented.

inox® /inɔks/ *nm* stainless steel.

inoxydable /inɔksidabl/ *adj* **acier
~** stainless steel.

inqualifiable /ɛ̃kalifjabl/ *adj*
unspeakable.

inquiet, -iète /ɛ̃kjɛ, -t/ *adj* worried.
inquiétant, ~e *adj* worrying.

inquiéter /ɛ̃kjete/ [14] *vt* worry.
□ **s'~** *vpr* worry (**de** about).
inquiétude *nf* anxiety, worry.

insaisissable /ɛ̃sezizabl/ *adj*
(personne) elusive; (nuance)
indefinable.

insalubre /ɛ̃salybʀ/ *adj* unhealthy.

insatisfaisant, ~e /ɛ̃satisfəzɑ̃, -t/
adj unsatisfactory. **insatisfait, ~e**
adj (mécontent) dissatisfied; (frustré)
unfulfilled.

inscription /ɛ̃skʀipsjɔ̃/ *nf*
inscription; (immatriculation)
enrolment.

inscrire /ɛ̃skʀiʀ/ [30] *vt* write
(down); (graver, tracer) inscribe;
(personne) enrol; (sur une liste) put
down. □ **s'~** *vpr* put one's name
down; **s'~ à** (école) enrol at; (club,
parti) join; (examen) enter for.

insecte /ɛ̃sɛkt/ *nm* insect.

insécurité /ɛ̃sekyʀite/ *nf*
insecurity.

insensé, ~e /ɛ̃sɑ̃se/ *adj* mad.

insensibilité /ɛ̃sɑ̃sibilite/ *nf*
insensitivity. **insensible** *adj*
insensitive (**à** to); (graduel)
imperceptible.

insérer /ɛ̃seʀe/ [14] *vt* insert. □ **s'~**
vpr be inserted; **s'~ dans** be part of.

insigne /ɛ̃siɲ/ *nm* badge; **~s** (d'une
fonction) insignia.

insignifiant, ~e /ɛ̃siɲifjɑ̃, -t/ *adj*
insignificant.

insinuation /ɛ̃sinɥasjɔ̃/ *nf*
insinuation.

insinuer /ɛ̃sinɥe/ [1] *vt* insinuate.
□ **s'~** *vpr* (socialement) ingratiate
oneself (**auprès de qn** with sb); **s'~
dans** (se glisser) slip into; (idée,
nuance) creep into.

insipide /ɛ̃sipid/ *adj* insipid.

insistance /ɛ̃sistɑ̃s/ *nf* insistence.
insistant, ~e *adj* insistent.

insister /ɛ̃siste/ [1] *vi* insist (**pour
faire** on doing); **~ sur** stress.

insolation /ɛ̃sɔlasjɔ̃/ *nf* (Méd)
sunstroke.

insolent, ~e /ɛ̃sɔlɑ̃, -t/ *adj* insolent.

insolite /ɛ̃sɔlit/ *adj* unusual.

insolvable /ɛ̃sɔlvabl/ *adj* insolvent.

insomnie /ɛ̃sɔmni/ *nf* insomnia.

insonoriser /ɛ̃sɔnɔʀize/ [1] *vt*
soundproof.

insouciance /ɛ̃susjɑ̃s/ *nf* lack of
concern. **insouciant, ~e** *adj*
carefree.

insoutenable /ɛ̃sutnabl/ *adj*
unbearable; (argument) untenable.

inspecter /ɛ̃spɛkte/ [1] *vt* inspect.
inspecteur, -trice *nm, f* inspector.
inspection *nf* inspection.

inspiration /ɛ̃spiʀasjɔ̃/ *nf*
inspiration; (respiration) breath.

inspirer /ɛ̃spiʀe/ [1] *vt* inspire; **~ la
méfiance à qn** inspire distrust in sb.
● *vi* breathe in. □ **s'~ de** *vpr* be
inspired by.

instabilité /ɛ̃stabilite/ *nf*
instability; unsteadiness. **instable**
adj unstable; (temps) unsettled.

installation /ɛ̃stalasjɔ̃/ *nf*
installation; (de local) fitting out; (de
locataire) settling in. **installations**
nfpl facilities.

installer /ɛ̃stale/ [1] *vt* install;
(meuble) put in; (étagère) put up;
(gaz, téléphone) connect; (équiper) fit
out. □ **s'~** *vpr* settle (down);
(emménager) settle in; **s'~ comme** set
oneself up as.

instance /ɛ̃stɑ̃s/ *nf* authority; (prière) entreaty; **avec ~** with insistence; **en ~** pending; **en ~ de** in the course of, on the point of.

instant /ɛ̃stɑ̃/ *nm* moment, instant; **à l'~** this instant.

instantané, ~e /ɛ̃stɑ̃tane/ *adj* instantaneous; (*café*) instant.

instar: à l'~ de /alɛ̃staRdə/ *loc* like.

instaurer /ɛ̃stoRe/ [1] *vt* institute.

instigateur, -trice /ɛ̃stigatœR, -tRis/ *nm,f* instigator.

instinct /ɛ̃stɛ̃/ *nm* instinct; **d'~** instinctively. **instinctif, -ive** *adj* instinctive.

instituer /ɛ̃stitɥe/ [1] *vt* establish.

institut /ɛ̃stity/ *nm* institute; **~ de beauté** beauty parlour.

instituteur, -trice /ɛ̃stitytœR, -tRis/ *nm,f* primary-school teacher.

institution /ɛ̃stitysjɔ̃/ *nf* institution; (école) private school.

instructif, -ive /ɛ̃stRyktif, -v/ *adj* instructive.

instruction /ɛ̃stRyksjɔ̃/ *nf* (formation) education; (Mil) training; (document) directive; **~s** (ordres, mode d'emploi) instructions; (Ordinat) (énoncé) instruction; (pas de séquence) statement.

instruire /ɛ̃stRɥiR/ [17] *vt* teach, educate; **~ de** inform of. □ **s'~** *vpr* learn, educate oneself; **s'~ de** enquire about. **instruit, ~e** *adj* educated.

instrument /ɛ̃stRymɑ̃/ *nm* instrument; (outil) tool; (moyen: fig) instrument; **~ de gestion** management tool; **~s de bord** (Aviat) controls.

insu: à l'~ de /alɛ̃sydə/ *loc* without the knowledge of.

insuffisance /ɛ̃syfizɑ̃s/ *nf* (pénurie) shortage; (médiocrité) inadequacy. **insuffisant, ~e** *adj* inadequate; (en nombre) insufficient.

insulaire /ɛ̃sylɛR/ *adj* island. ● *nmf* islander.

insuline /ɛ̃sylin/ *nf* insulin.

insulte /ɛ̃sylt/ *nf* insult. **insulter** [1] *vt* insult.

insupportable /ɛ̃sypɔRtabl/ *adj* unbearable.

insurger (s') /(s)ɛ̃syRʒe/ [40] *vpr* rebel.

intact, ~e /ɛ̃takt/ *adj* intact.

intangible /ɛ̃tɑ̃ʒibl/ *adj* intangible; (*principe*) inviolable.

intarissable /ɛ̃taRisabl/ *adj* inexhaustible.

intégral, ~e (*mpl* **-aux**) /ɛ̃tegRal, -o/ *adj* complete; (*texte, édition*) unabridged; (*paiement*) full, in full. **intégralement** *adv* in full. **intégralité** *nf* whole.

intègre /ɛ̃tɛgR/ *adj* upright.

intégrer /ɛ̃tegRe/ [14] *vt* integrate. □ **s'~** *vpr* (*personne*) integrate; (*maison*) fit in.

intégriste /ɛ̃tegRist/ *nmf* fundamentalist.

intégrité /ɛ̃tegRite/ *nf* integrity.

intellect /ɛ̃telɛkt/ *nm* intellect. **intellectuel, ~le** *a* & *nm,f* intellectual.

intelligence /ɛ̃teliʒɑ̃s/ *nf* intelligence; (compréhension) understanding; (complicité) agreement; **agir d'~ avec qn** act in agreement with sb. **intelligent, ~e** *adj* intelligent.

intempéries /ɛ̃tɑ̃peRi/ *nfpl* severe weather.

intempestif, -ive /ɛ̃tɑ̃pɛstif, -v/ *adj* untimely.

intenable /ɛ̃tnabl/ *adj* unbearable; (*enfant*) impossible.

intendance /ɛ̃tɑ̃dɑ̃s/ *nf* (Scol) bursar's office.

intendant, ~e /ɛ̃tɑ̃dɑ̃, -t/ *nm* (Mil) quartermaster. ● *nm,f* (Scol) bursar.

intense /ɛ̃tɑ̃s/ *adj* intense; (*circulation*) heavy. **intensif, -ive** *adj* intensive. **intensité** *nf* intensity.

intenter /ɛ̃tɑ̃te/ [1] *vt* **~ un procès** *ou* **une action** institute proceedings (à, contre against).

intention /ɛ̃tɑ̃sjɔ̃/ *nf* intention (de faire of doing); **à l'~ de qn** for sb. **intentionnel, ~le** *adj* intentional.

interactif, -ive /ɛ̃teRaktif, -v/ *adj* (*TV, vidéo*) interactive.

interaction /ɛ̃teRaksjɔ̃/ *nf* interaction.

intercaler /ɛ̃teRkale/ [1] *vt* insert.

intercéder /ɛ̃tɛʁsede/ [14] *vi*
intercede (**en faveur de** on behalf of).

intercepter /ɛ̃tɛʁsɛpte/ [1] *vt*
intercept.

interdiction /ɛ̃tɛʁdiksjɔ̃/ *nf* ban; ∼
de fumer no smoking.

interdire /ɛ̃tɛʁdiʁ/ [37] *vt* forbid;
(officiellement) ban, prohibit; ∼ **à qn de
faire** forbid sb to do.

interdit, ∼**e** /ɛ̃tɛʁdi, -t/ *adj*
prohibited, forbidden; (étonné)
dumbfounded.

intéressant, ∼**e** /ɛ̃teʁesɑ̃, -t/ *adj*
interesting; (avantageux) attractive.

intéressé, ∼**e** /ɛ̃teʁese/ *adj* (en
cause) concerned; (pour profiter) self-
interested. ● *nm, f* person concerned.

intéresser /ɛ̃teʁese/ [1] *vt* interest;
(concerner) concern. □ **s'**∼ **à** *vpr* be
interested in.

intérêt /ɛ̃teʁɛ/ *nm* interest; (égoïsme)
self-interest; ∼**(s)** (Comm) interest;
vous avez ∼ **à** it is in your interest
to.

interface /ɛ̃tɛʁfas/ *nf* (Ordinat)
interface.

intérieur, ∼**e** /ɛ̃teʁjœʁ/ *adj* inner,
inside; (mur, escalier) internal; (vol,
politique) domestic; (vie, calme)
inner. ● *nm* interior; (de boîte, tiroir)
inside; **à l'**∼ **(de)** inside; (fig) within.
intérieurement *adv* inwardly.

intérim /ɛ̃teʁim/ *nm* interim;
assurer l'∼ deputize (**de** for); **par** ∼
on an interim basis; **président par** ∼
acting president; **faire de l'**∼ temp.

intérimaire /ɛ̃teʁimɛʁ/ *adj*
temporary, interim. ● *nmf* (secrétaire)
temp; (médecin) locum.

interjection /ɛ̃tɛʁʒɛksjɔ̃/ *nf*
interjection.

interlocuteur, **-trice**
/ɛ̃tɛʁlɔkytœʁ, -tʁis/ *nm, f* **son** ∼ the
person one is speaking to.

interloqué, ∼**e** /ɛ̃tɛʁlɔke/ *adj* **être**
∼ be taken aback.

intermède /ɛ̃tɛʁmɛd/ *nm* interlude.

intermédiaire /ɛ̃tɛʁmedjɛʁ/ *adj*
intermediate. ● *nmf* intermediary.
● *nm* **sans** ∼ without an
intermediary, direct; **par l'**∼ **de**
through.

interminable /ɛ̃tɛʁminabl/ *adj*
endless.

intermittence /ɛ̃tɛʁmitɑ̃s/ *nf* **par**
∼ intermittently.

internat /ɛ̃tɛʁna/ *nm* boarding-
school.

international, ∼**e** (*mpl* **-aux**)
/ɛ̃tɛʁnasjɔnal, -o/ *adj* international.

internaute /ɛ̃tɛʁnot/ *nmf* (Ordinat)
Netsurfer, Internet user.

interne /ɛ̃tɛʁn/ *adj* internal; (cours,
formation) in-house. ● *nmf* (Scol)
boarder; (Méd) house officer; (US)
intern.

internement /ɛ̃tɛʁnəmɑ̃/ *nm* (Pol)
internment. **interner** [1] *vt* (Pol)
intern; (Méd) commit.

Internet /ɛ̃tɛʁnet/ *nm* Internet.

interpellation /ɛ̃tɛʁpelasjɔ̃/ *nf*
(Pol) questioning. **interpeller** [1] *vt*
shout to; (apostropher) shout at;
(interroger) question.

interphone /ɛ̃tɛʁfɔn/ *nm* intercom;
(d'immeuble) entry phone.

interposer (**s'**) /(s)ɛ̃tɛʁpoze/ [1] *vpr*
intervene.

interprétariat /ɛ̃tɛʁpretaʁja/ *nm*
interpreting. **interprétation** *nf*
interpretation; (d'artiste) performance.
interprète *nmf* interpreter; (artiste)
performer. **interpréter** [14] *vt*
interpret; (jouer) play; (chanter) sing.

interrogateur, **-trice** /ɛ̃tɛʁɔgatœʁ,
-tʁis/ *adj* questioning. **interrogatif**,
-ive *adj* interrogative.
interrogation *nf* question; (action)
questioning; (épreuve) test.
interrogatoire *nm* interrogation.
interroger [40] *vt* question; (élève)
test.

interrompre /ɛ̃tɛʁɔ̃pʁ/ [3] *vt* break
off, interrupt; (personne) interrupt.
□ **s'**∼ *vpr* break off. **interrupteur**
nm switch. **interruption** *nf*
interruption; (arrêt) break.

interurbain, ∼**e** /ɛ̃tɛʁyʁbɛ̃, -ɛn/ *adj*
long-distance, trunk.

intervalle /ɛ̃tɛʁval/ *nm* space;
(temps) interval; **dans l'**∼ in the
meantime.

intervenir /ɛ̃tɛʁvəniʁ/ [58] *vi* (agir)
intervene (**auprès de qn** with sb);
(survenir) occur, take place; (Méd)
operate. **intervention** *nf*
intervention; (Méd) operation.

intervertir /ɛ̃tɛʀvɛʀtiʀ/ [2] *vt*
invert; (*rôles*) reverse.

interview /ɛ̃tɛʀvju/ *nf* interview.
interviewer [1] *vt* interview.

intestin /ɛ̃tɛstɛ̃/ *nm* intestine.

intime /ɛ̃tim/ *adj* intimate; (*fête, vie*)
private; (*dîner*) quiet. ● *nmf* intimate
friend.

intimider /ɛ̃timide/ [1] *vt*
intimidate.

intimité /ɛ̃timite/ *nf* intimacy; (vie
privée) privacy.

intituler /ɛ̃tityle/ [1] *vt* call, entitle.
□ **s'~** *vpr* be called *ou* entitled.

intolérable /ɛ̃tɔleʀabl/ *adj*
intolerable. **intolérance** *nf*
intolerance. **intolérant**, **~e** *adj*
intolerant.

intonation /ɛ̃tɔnasjɔ̃/ *nf* intonation.

intox /ɛ̃tɔks/ *nf* Ⓘ brainwashing.

intoxication /ɛ̃tɔksikasjɔ̃/ *nf*
poisoning; (fig) brainwashing; **~**
alimentaire food poisoning.
intoxiquer [1] *vt* poison; (fig)
brainwash.

intraitable /ɛ̃tʀɛtabl/ *adj* inflexible.

Intranet /ɛ̃tʀanɛt/ *nm* (Ordinat)
Intranet.

intransigeant, **~e** /ɛ̃tʀɑ̃ziʒɑ̃, -t/
adj intransigent.

intransitif, **-ive** /ɛ̃tʀɑ̃zitif, -v/ *adj*
intransitive.

intraveineux, **-euse** /ɛ̃tʀavɛnø, -z/
adj intravenous.

intrépide /ɛ̃tʀepid/ *adj* fearless.

intrigue /ɛ̃tʀig/ *nf* intrigue; (scénario)
plot.

intrinsèque /ɛ̃tʀɛ̃sɛk/ *adj* intrinsic.

introduction /ɛ̃tʀɔdyksjɔ̃/ *nf*
introduction; (insertion) insertion.

introduire /ɛ̃tʀɔduiʀ/ [17] *vt*
introduce, bring in; (insérer) put in,
insert; **~ qn** show sb in. □ **s'~** *vpr*
get in; **s'~ dans** get into, enter.

introuvable /ɛ̃tʀuvabl/ *adj* that
cannot be found.

introverti, **~e** /ɛ̃tʀɔvɛʀti/ *nm,f*
introvert. ● *adj* introverted.

intrus, **~e** /ɛ̃tʀy, -z/ *nm,f* intruder.
intrusion *nf* intrusion.

intuitif, **-ive** /ɛ̃tuitif, -iv/ *adj*
intuitive. **intuition** *nf* intuition.

inusable /inyzabl/ *adj* hard-
wearing.

inusité, **~e** /inyzite/ *adj* little used.

inutile /inytil/ *adj* useless; (vain)
needless. **inutilement** *adv*
needlessly. **inutilisable** *adj*
unusable.

invalide /ɛ̃valid/ *a & nmf* disabled
(person).

invariable /ɛ̃vaʀjabl/ *adj*
invariable.

invasion /ɛ̃vazjɔ̃/ *nf* invasion.

invectiver /ɛ̃vɛktive/ [1] *vt* abuse.

inventaire /ɛ̃vɑ̃tɛʀ/ *nm* inventory;
(Comm) stocklist; **faire l'~** draw up
an inventory; (Comm) do a stocktake.

inventer /ɛ̃vɑ̃te/ [1] *vt* invent.
inventeur, **-trice** *nm,f* inventor.
inventif, **-ive** *adj* inventive.
invention *nf* invention.

inverse /ɛ̃vɛʀs/ *adj* opposite; (ordre)
reverse; **en sens ~** in *ou* from the
opposite direction. ● *nm* reverse;
c'est l'~ it's the other way round.
inversement *adv* conversely.
inverser [1] *vt* reverse, invert.

investir /ɛ̃vɛstiʀ/ [2] *vt* invest.
investissement *nm* investment.

investiture /ɛ̃vɛstityʀ/ *nf* (de
candidat) nomination; (de président)
investiture.

invétéré, **~e** /ɛ̃vetere/ *adj*
inveterate; (*menteur*) compulsive;
(enraciné) deep-rooted.

invisible /ɛ̃vizibl/ *adj* invisible.

invitation /ɛ̃vitasjɔ̃/ *nf* invitation.
invité, **~e** *nm,f* guest. **inviter** [1]
vt invite (**à** to).

involontaire /ɛ̃vɔlɔ̃tɛʀ/ *adj*
involuntary; (*témoin, héros*)
unwitting.

invoquer /ɛ̃vɔke/ [1] *vt* call upon,
invoke.

invraisemblable /ɛ̃vʀɛsɑ̃blabl/
adj improbable, unlikely; (incroyable)
incredible. **invraisemblance** *nf*
improbability.

iode /jɔd/ *nm* iodine.

ira, irait /iʀa, iʀɛ/ ⇒ALLER [8].

Irak /iʀak/ *nm* Iraq.

Iran /iʀɑ̃/ *nm* Iran.

iris /iʀis/ *nm* iris.

irlandais, **~e** /iʀlɑ̃dɛ, -z/ adj Irish. **I~**, **~e** nm, f Irishman, Irishwoman.

Irlande /iʀlɑ̃d/ nf Ireland.

ironie /iʀɔni/ nf irony. **ironique** adj ironic.

irrationnel, **~le** /iʀasjɔnɛl/ adj irrational.

irréalisable /iʀealizabl/ adj (idée, rêve) unachievable; (projet) unworkable.

irrécupérable /iʀekypeʀabl/ adj irretrievable; (capital) irrecoverable.

irréel, **~le** /iʀeɛl/ adj unreal.

irréfléchi, **~e** /iʀefleʃi/ adj thoughtless.

irrégulier, **-ière** /iʀegylje, -jɛʀ/ adj irregular.

irrémédiable /iʀemedjabl/ adj irreparable.

irremplaçable /iʀɑ̃plasabl/ adj irreplaceable.

irréparable /iʀepaʀabl/ adj (objet) beyond repair; (tort, dégâts) irreparable.

irréprochable /iʀepʀɔʃabl/ adj flawless.

irrésistible /iʀezistibl/ adj irresistible; (drôle) hilarious.

irrésolu, **~e** /iʀezɔly/ adj indecisive; (problème) unsolved.

irrespirable /iʀɛspiʀabl/ adj stifling.

irresponsable /iʀɛspɔ̃sabl/ adj irresponsible.

irrigation /iʀigasjɔ̃/ nf irrigation. **irriguer** [1] vt irrigate.

irritable /iʀitabl/ adj irritable.

irriter /iʀite/ [1] vt irritate. □ **s'~** vpr get annoyed (**de** at).

irruption /iʀypsjɔ̃/ nf **faire ~ dans** burst into.

Islam /islam/ nm Islam. **islamique** adj Islamic.

islandais, **~e** /islɑ̃dɛ, -z/ adj Icelandic. ● nm (Ling) Icelandic. **I~**, **~e** nm, f Icelander.

Islande /islɑ̃d/ nf Iceland.

isolant /izɔlɑ̃/ nm insulating material. **isolation** nf insulation.

isolé, **~e** /izɔle/ adj isolated. **isolement** nm isolation.

isoler /izɔle/ [1] vt isolate; (Électr) insulate. □ **s'~** vpr isolate oneself.

isoloir /izɔlwaʀ/ nm polling booth.

Isorel® /izɔʀɛl/ nm hardboard.

Israël /isʀaɛl/ nm Israel. **israélien**, **~ne** adj Israeli.

israélite /isʀaelit/ adj Jewish. ● nmf Jew.

issu, **~e** /isy/ adj **être ~ de** (personne) come from; (résulter de) result ou stem from.

issue /isy/ nf (sortie) exit; (résultat) outcome; (fig) solution; **à l'~ de** at the conclusion of; **~ de secours** emergency exit; **rue** ou **voie sans ~** dead end.

Italie /itali/ nf Italy.

italien, **~ne** /italjɛ̃, -ɛn/ adj Italian. ● nm (Ling) Italian. **I~**, **~ne** nm, f Italian.

italique /italik/ nm italics.

itinéraire /itineʀɛʀ/ nm itinerary, route.

I.U.T. abrév m (**Institut universitaire de technologie**) university institute of technology.

I.V.G. abrév f (**interruption volontaire de grossesse**) abortion.

ivoire /ivwaʀ/ nm ivory.

ivre /ivʀ/ adj drunk. **ivresse** nf drunkenness; (fig) exhilaration. **ivrogne** nmf drunk(ard).

j' /ʒ/ ⇒JE.

jacinthe /ʒasɛ̃t/ nf hyacinth.

jadis /ʒadis/ adv long ago.

jaillir /ʒajiʀ/ [2] vi (liquide) spurt (out); (lumière) stream out; (apparaître) burst forth, spring out.

jalonner /ʒalɔne/ [1] vt mark (out).

jalousie /ʒaluzi/ nf jealousy; (store) (venetian) blind. **jaloux**, **-ouse** adj jealous.

jamais /ʒamɛ/ adv ever; **ne ~** never; **il ne boit ~** he never drinks; **à ~** for ever; **si ~** if ever.

jambe /ʒɑ̃b/ nf leg.

jambon /ʒɑ̃bɔ̃/ *nm* ham.
jambonneau (*pl* ~x) *nm* knuckle of ham.

janvier /ʒɑ̃vje/ *nm* January.

Japon /ʒapɔ̃/ *nm* Japan.

japonais, ~e /ʒapɔnɛ, -z/ *adj* Japanese. ● *nm* (Ling) Japanese. **J~, ~e** *nm, f* Japanese.

japper /ʒape/ [1] *vi* yap.

jaquette /ʒakɛt/ *nf* (de livre, femme) jacket; (d'homme) morning coat.

jardin /ʒaʀdɛ̃/ *nm* garden; ~ d'enfants nursery (school); ~ public public park. **jardinage** *nm* gardening. **jardiner** [1] *vi* do some gardening, garden. **jardinier, -ière** *nm, f* gardener.

jardinière /ʒaʀdinjɛʀ/ *nf* (meuble) plant-stand; ~ de légumes mixed vegetables.

jarretelle /ʒaʀtɛl/ *nf* suspender; (US) garter.

jarretière /ʒaʀtjɛʀ/ *nf* garter.

jatte /ʒat/ *nf* bowl.

jauge /ʒoʒ/ *nf* capacity; (de navire) tonnage; (compteur) gauge; ~ d'huile dipstick.

jaune /ʒon/ *a & nm* yellow; (péj) scab; ~ d'œuf (egg) yolk; **rire** ~ give a forced laugh. **jaunir** [2] *vt/i* turn yellow. **jaunisse** *nf* jaundice.

javelot /ʒavlo/ *nm* javelin.

jazz /dʒɑz/ *nm* jazz.

J.C. *abrév m* (**Jésus-Christ**) 500 avant/après ~ 500 B.C./A.D.

je, j' /ʒə, ʒ/ *pron* I.

jean /dʒin/ *nm* jeans; **un** ~ a pair of jeans.

jet¹ /ʒɛ/ *nm* throw; (de liquide, vapeur) jet; ~ d'eau fountain.

jet² /dʒɛt/ *nm* (avion) jet.

jetable /ʒətabl/ *adj* disposable.

jetée /ʒəte/ *nf* pier.

jeter /ʒəte/ [38] *vt* throw; (au rebut) throw away; (regard, ancre, lumière) cast; (cri) utter; (bases) lay; ~ **un coup d'œil** have *ou* take a look (**à** at). □ **se** ~ *vpr* **se** ~ **contre** crash *ou* bash into; **se** ~ **dans** (fleuve) flow into; **se** ~ **sur** (se ruer sur) rush at.

jeton /ʒətɔ̃/ *nm* token; (pour compter) counter; (au casino) chip.

jeu (*pl* ~x) /ʒø/ *nm* game; (amusement) play; (au casino) gambling; (Théât) acting; (série) set; (de lumière, ressort) play; **en** ~ (honneur) at stake; (forces) at work; ~ **de cartes** (paquet) pack of cards; ~ **d'échecs** (boîte) chess set; ~ **de mots** pun; ~ **télévisé** television quiz; ~x **de grattage** scratch cards.

jeudi /ʒødi/ *nm* Thursday.

jeun: à ~ /aʒœ̃/ *loc* on an empty stomach.

jeune /ʒœn/ *adj* young; ~ **fille** girl; ~s **mariés** newlyweds. ● *nmf* young person; **les** ~s young people.

jeûne /ʒøn/ *nm* fast.

jeunesse /ʒœnɛs/ *nf* youth; (apparence) youthfulness; **la** ~ (jeunes) the young.

joaillerie /ʒɔajʀi/ *nf* jewellery; (magasin) jeweller's shop.

joie /ʒwa/ *nf* joy.

joindre /ʒwɛ̃dʀ/ [22] *vt* join (**à** to); (mains, pieds) put together; (efforts) combine; (contacter) enclose; (dans une enveloppe) enclose. □ **se** ~ **à** *vpr* join.

joint, ~e /ʒwɛ̃, -t/ *adj* (efforts) joint; (pieds) together. ● *nm* joint; (de robinet) washer.

joli, ~e /ʒɔli/ *adj* pretty, nice; (somme, profit) nice; **c'est du** ~! (ironique) charming! **c'est bien** ~ **mais** that is all very well but.

joncher /ʒɔ̃ʃe/ [1] *vt* litter, be strewn over; **jonché de** littered with.

jonction /ʒɔ̃ksjɔ̃/ *nf* junction.

jongleur, -euse /ʒɔ̃glœʀ, øz/ *nm, f* juggler.

jonquille /ʒɔ̃kij/ *nf* daffodil.

joue /ʒu/ *nf* cheek.

jouer /ʒwe/ [1] *vt/i* play; (Théât) act; (au casino) gamble; (fonctionner) work; (film, pièce) put on; (cheval) back; (être important) count; ~ **à** (jeu, Sport) play; ~ **de** (Mus) play; ~ **la comédie** put on an act; **bien joué!** well done!

jouet /ʒwɛ/ *nm* toy; (personne: fig) plaything; (victime) victim.

joueur, -euse /ʒwœʀ, -øz/ *nm, f* player; (parieur) gambler.

joufflu, ~e /ʒufly/ *adj* chubby-cheeked; (visage) chubby.

jouir /ʒwiʀ/ [2] *vi* (sexe) come; ~ **de** (droit, avantage) enjoy; (bien,

concession) enjoy the use of.
jouissance *nf* pleasure; (usage) use
(**de qch** of sth).

joujou (*pl* ~**x**) /ʒuʒu/ *nm* 🔲 toy.

jour /ʒuʀ/ *nm* day; (opposé à nuit) day
(time); (lumière) daylight; (aspect)
light; (ouverture) gap; **de nos ~s**
nowadays; **du ~ au lendemain**
overnight; **il fait ~** it is (day)light; ~
chômé *ou* **férié** public holiday; ~ **de**
fête holiday; ~ **ouvrable**, ~ **de travail**
working day; **mettre à ~** update;
mettre au ~ uncover; **au grand ~** in
the open; **donner le ~** give birth;
voir le ~ be born; **vivre au ~ le jour**
live from day to day.

journal (*pl* -**aux**) /ʒuʀnal, -o/ *nm*
(news)paper; (spécialisé) journal;
(intime) diary; (à la radio) news; ~ **de**
bord log-book.

journalier, -ière /ʒuʀnalje, -jɛʀ/
adj daily.

journalisme /ʒuʀnalism/ *nm*
journalism. **journaliste** *nmf*
journalist.

journée /ʒuʀne/ *nf* day.

jovial, ~e (*mpl* -**iaux**) /ʒɔvjal, -jo/
adj jovial.

joyau (*pl* ~**x**) /ʒwajo/ *nm* gem.

joyeux, -euse /ʒwajø, -z/ *a* merry,
joyful; ~ **anniversaire** happy
birthday.

jubiler /ʒybile/ [1] *vi* be jubilant.

jucher /ʒyʃe/ [1] *vt* perch. ☐ **se ~**
vpr perch.

judaïsme /ʒydaism/ *nm* Judaism.

judiciaire /ʒydisjɛʀ/ *adj* judicial.

judicieux, -ieuse /ʒydisjø, -z/ *adj*
judicious.

judo /ʒydo/ *nm* judo.

juge /ʒyʒ/ *nm* judge; (arbitre) referee;
~ **de paix** Justice of the Peace; ~ **de**
touche linesman.

jugé: au ~ /oʒyʒe/ *loc* by guesswork.

jugement /ʒyʒmã/ *nm* judgement;
(criminel) sentence.

juger /ʒyʒe/ [40] *vt/i* judge; (estimer)
consider (**que** that); ~ **de** judge.

juguler /ʒygyle/ [1] *vt* stamp out;
curb.

juif, -ive /ʒyif, -v/ *adj* Jewish. ● *nm,f*
Jew.

juillet /ʒyijɛ/ *nm* July.

juin /ʒyɛ̃/ *nm* June.

jumeau, -elle (*mpl* ~**x**) /ʒymo, -ɛl/
a & nm,f twin. **jumeler** [38] *vt*
(*villes*) twin.

jumelles /ʒymɛl/ *nfpl* binoculars.

jument /ʒymã/ *nf* mare.

junior /ʒynjɔʀ/ *a & nmf* junior.

jupe /ʒyp/ *nf* skirt.

jupon /ʒypõ/ *nm* slip, petticoat.

juré, ~e /ʒyʀe/ *nm,f* juror. ● *adj*
sworn.

jurer /ʒyʀe/ [1] *vt* swear (**que** that).
● *vi* (pester) swear; (contraster) clash
(**avec** with).

juridiction /ʒyʀidiksjõ/ *nf*
jurisdiction; (tribunal) court of law.

juridique /ʒyʀidik/ *adj* legal.

juriste /ʒyʀist/ *nmf* legal expert.

juron /ʒyʀõ/ *nm* swear-word.

jury /ʒyʀi/ *nm* (Jur) jury; (examinateurs)
panel of judges.

jus /ʒy/ *nm* juice; (de viande) gravy; ~
de fruit fruit juice.

jusque /ʒysk(ə)/ *prép* **jusqu'à** (up)
to, as far as; (temps) until, till; (limite)
up to; (y compris) even; **jusqu'à ce que**
until; **jusqu'à présent** until now;
jusqu'en until; **jusqu'où?** how far?;
~ **dans**, ~ **sur** as far as.

juste /ʒyst/ *adj* fair, just; (légitime)
just; (correct, exact) right; (vrai) true;
(*vêtement*) tight; (*quantité*) on the
short side; **le ~ milieu** the happy
medium. ● *adv* rightly, correctly;
(*chanter*) in tune; (seulement,
exactement) just; (**un peu**) ~ (*calculer,
mesurer*) a bit fine *ou* close; **au ~**
exactly; **c'était ~** (presque raté) it was
a close thing. **justement** *adv*
(précisément) precisely; (à l'instant) just;
(avec justesse) correctly; (légitimement)
justifiably.

justesse /ʒystɛs/ *nf* accuracy; **de ~**
just, narrowly.

justice /ʒystis/ *nf* justice; (autorités)
law; (tribunal) court.

justifier /ʒystifje/ [45] *vt* justify. ● *vi*
~ **de** prove. ☐ **se ~** *vpr* justify
oneself.

juteux, -euse /ʒytø, -z/ *adj* juicy.

juvénile /ʒyvenil/ *adj* youthful; (*délinquance, mortalité*) juvenile.

Kk

kaki /kaki/ *a inv & nm* khaki.

kangourou /kɑ̃guʀu/ *nm* kangaroo.

karaté /kaʀate/ *nm* karate.

kart /kaʀt/ *nm* go-cart.

kascher /kaʃɛʀ/ *a inv* kosher.

kayak /kajak/ *nm* kayak.

képi /kepi/ *nm* kepi.

kermesse /kɛʀmɛs/ *nf* fête.

kidnapper /kidnape/ [1] *vt* kidnap.

kilo /kilo/ *nm* kilo.

kilogramme /kilogʀam/ *nm* kilogram.

kilométrage /kilɔmetʀaʒ/ *nm* ≈ mileage. **kilomètre** *nm* kilometre.

kinésithérapeute /kineziteʀapøt/ *nmf* physiotherapist. **kinésithérapie** *nf* physiotherapy.

kiosque /kjɔsk/ *nm* kiosk; ~ à musique bandstand.

kit /kit/ *nm* kit.

kiwi /kiwi/ *nm* kiwi.

klaxon® /klaksɔn/ *nm* (Auto) horn. **klaxonner** [1] *vi* sound one's horn.

Ko *abrév m* (**kilo-octet**) (Ordinat) KB.

KO *abrév m* (**knock-out**) KO 🄴.

K-way® /kawɛ/ *nm inv* windcheater.

kyste /kist/ *nm* cyst.

Ll

l', la /l, la/ ⇒LE.

là /la/

● *adverbe*

····➤ (dans ce lieu) there; (ici) here; (chez soi) in; **c'est** ~ **que** this is where; ~ où where; **par** ~ (dans cette direction) this way; (dans cette zone) around there; **de** ~ hence.

····➤ (à ce moment) then; **c'est** ~ **que** that's when.

····➤ **cet homme-**~ that man; **ces maisons-**~ those houses.

● *interjection*

····➤ ~! **c'est fini** there (now), it's all over!

là-bas /labɑ/ *adv* there; (à l'endroit que l'on indique) over there.

label /labɛl/ *nm* seal, label.

laboratoire /labɔʀatwaʀ/ *nm* laboratory.

laborieux, -ieuse /labɔʀjø, -z/ *adj* laborious; (*personne*) industrious; **classes laborieuses** working classes.

labour /labuʀ/ *nm* ploughing; (US) plowing. **labourer** [1] *vt* plough; (US) plow; (déchirer) rip at.

labyrinthe /labiʀɛ̃t/ *nm* maze, labyrinth.

lac /lak/ *nm* lake.

lacer /lase/ [10] *vt* lace up.

lacet /lasɛ/ *nm* (de chaussure) (shoe-)lace; (de route) sharp bend.

lâche /lɑʃ/ *adj* cowardly; (détendu) loose; (sans rigueur) lax. ● *nmf* coward.

lâcher /lɑʃe/ [1] *vt* let go of; (laisser tomber) drop; (abandonner) give up; (laisser) leave; (libérer) release; (flèche, balle) fire; (juron, phrase) come out with; (desserrer) loosen; ~ **prise** let go. ● *vi* give way.

lâcheté /lɑʃte/ *nf* cowardice.

lacrymogène /lakʀimɔʒɛn/ *adj* **gaz** ~ tear gas.

lacune /lakyn/ *nf* gap.

là-dedans /lad(ə)dɑ̃/ *adv* (près) in here; (plus loin) in there.

là-dessous /lad(ə)su/ *adv* (près) under here; (plus loin) under there.

là-dessus /lad(ə)sy/ *adv* (sur une surface) on here; (plus loin) on there; (sur ce) with that; (quelque temps après) after that; **qu'avez-vous à dire** ~? what have you got to say about it?

ladite /ladit/ ⇒LEDIT.

lagune /lagyn/ *nf* lagoon.

là-haut /lao/ *adv* (en hauteur) up here; (plus loin) up there; (à l'étage) upstairs.

laïc /laik/ *nm* layman.

laid, **~e** /lɛ, lɛd/ *adj* ugly; (*action*) vile. **laideur** *nf* ugliness.

lainage /lɛnaʒ/ *nm* woollen garment.

laine /lɛn/ *nf* wool; **de ~** woollen.

laïque /laik/ *adj* (*état, loi*) secular; (*habit, personne*) lay; (*école*) nondenominational. ● *nmf* layman, laywoman.

laisse /lɛs/ *nf* lead, leash; **tenir en ~** keep on a lead.

laisser /lese/ [1] *vt* (déposer) leave, drop off; (confier) leave (**à qn** with sb); (abandonner) leave; (rendre) **~ qn perplexe/froid** leave sb puzzled/cold; **~ qch à qn** (céder, prêter) let sb have sth; (donner) (*choix, temps*) give sb sth. □ **se ~** *vpr* **se ~ persuader/insulter** let oneself be persuaded/insulted; **elle ne se laisse pas faire** she won't be pushed around; **laisse-toi faire** leave it to me/him/her *etc.*; **se ~ aller** let oneself go. ● *v aux* **~ qn/qch faire** let sb/sth do; **laisse-moi faire** (ne m'aide pas) let me do it; (je m'en occupe) leave it to me; **laisse faire!** so what! **laisser-aller** *nm inv* carelessness; (dans la tenue) scruffiness. **laissez-passer** *nm inv* pass.

lait /lɛ/ *nm* milk; **~ longue conservation** long-life *ou* UHT milk; **frère/sœur de ~** foster-brother/-sister. **laitage** *nm* milk product. **laiterie** *nf* dairy. **laiteux**, **-euse** *adj* milky.

laitier, **-ière** /letje, -jɛʀ/ *adj* dairy. ● *nm, f* (livreur) milkman, milkwoman.

laiton /lɛtɔ̃/ *nm* brass.

laitue /lety/ *nf* lettuce.

lama /lama/ *nm* llama.

lambeau (*pl* **~x**) /lɑ̃bo/ *nm* shred; **en ~x** in shreds.

lame /lam/ *nf* blade; (lamelle) strip; (vague) wave; **~ de fond** ground swell; **~ de rasoir** razor blade.

lamentable /lamɑ̃tabl/ *adj* deplorable. **lamenter (se)** [1] *vpr* moan (**sur** about, over).

lampadaire /lɑ̃padɛʀ/ *nm* standard lamp; (de rue) street lamp.

lampe /lɑ̃p/ *nf* lamp; (ampoule) bulb; (de radio) valve; **~ (de poche)** torch; (US) flashlight; **~ à souder** blowlamp; **~ de chevet** bedside lamp; **~ solaire**, **~ à bronzer** sunlamp.

lance /lɑ̃s/ *nf* spear; (de tournoi) lance; (tuyau) hose; **~ d'incendie** fire hose.

lancement /lɑ̃smɑ̃/ *nm* throwing; (de navire, de missile, mise sur le marché) launch.

lance-missiles /lɑ̃smisil/ *nm inv* missile launcher.

lance-pierres /lɑ̃spjɛʀ/ *nm inv* catapult.

lancer /lɑ̃se/ [10] *vt* throw; (avec force) hurl; (*navire, idée, artiste*) launch; (émettre) give out; (*regard*) cast; (*moteur*) start. □ **se ~** *vpr* (Sport) gain momentum; (se précipiter) rush; **se ~ dans** (*explication*) launch into; (*passe-temps*) take up. ● *nm* throw; (action) throwing.

lancinant, **~e** /lɑ̃sinɑ̃, -t/ *adj* (*douleur*) shooting; (*problème*) nagging.

landau /lɑ̃do/ *nm* pram; (US) baby carriage.

lande /lɑ̃d/ *nf* heath, moor.

langage /lɑ̃gaʒ/ *nm* language; **~ machine/de programmation** machine/programming language.

langouste /lɑ̃gust/ *nf* spiny lobster. **langoustine** *nf* Dublin Bay prawn.

langue /lɑ̃g/ *nf* (Anat) tongue; (Ling) language; **il m'a tiré la ~** he stuck his tongue out at me; **de ~ anglaise** (*personne*) English-speaking; (*journal*) English-language; **~ maternelle** mother tongue; **~ vivante** modern language.

lanière /lanjɛʀ/ *nf* strap.

lanterne /lɑ̃tɛʀn/ *nf* lantern; (électrique) lamp; (de voiture) sidelight.

lapin /lapɛ̃/ *nm* rabbit; **poser un ~ à qn** Ⅰ stand sb up; **le coup du ~** rabbit punch; (en voiture) whiplash injury.

lapsus /lapsys/ *nm* slip (of the tongue).

laque /lak/ *nf* lacquer; (pour cheveux) hairspray; (peinture) gloss paint.

laquelle /lakɛl/ ⇒LEQUEL.

lard /laʀ/ nm streaky bacon.

large /laʀʒ/ adj wide, broad; (grand) large; (généreux) generous; **avoir les idées ~s** be broad-minded; **~ d'esprit** broad-minded. ● adv (calculer, mesurer) on the generous side; **voir ~** think big. ● nm **faire 10 cm de ~** be 10 cm wide; **le ~** (mer) the open sea; **au ~ de** (Naut) off.

largement adv widely; (ouvrir) wide; (amplement) amply; (généreusement) generously; (au moins) easily.

largesse /laʀʒɛs/ nf generous gift.

largeur /laʀʒœʀ/ nf width, breadth; **~ d'esprit** broad-mindedness.

larguer /laʀɡe/ [1] vt drop; **~ les amarres** cast off.

larme /laʀm/ nf tear; (goutte 🔲) drop; **en ~s** in tears.

larmoyant, **~e** /laʀmwajɑ̃, -t/ adj full of tears. **larmoyer** /31/ vi (yeux) water; (pleurnicher) whine.

larynx /laʀɛ̃ks/ nm larynx.

las, **~se** /lɑ, lɑs/ adj weary.

lasagnes /lazaɲ/ nfpl lasagna.

laser /lazɛʀ/ nm laser.

lasser /lɑse/ [1] vt weary. □ **se ~** vpr grow tired, get weary (**de** of).

latéral, **~e** (mpl **-aux**) /lateʀal, -o/ adj lateral.

latin, **~e** /latɛ̃, -in/ adj Latin. ● nm (Ling) Latin.

latte /lat/ nf lath; (de plancher) board; (de siège) slat; (de mur, plafond) lath.

lauréat, **~e** /lɔʀea, -t/ adj prize-winning. ● nm, f prize-winner.

laurier /lɔʀje/ nm (Bot) laurel; (Culin) bay-leaves.

lavable /lavabl/ adj washable.

lavabo /lavabo/ nm wash-basin; **~s** toilet(s).

lavage /lavaʒ/ nm washing; **~ de cerveau** brainwashing.

lavande /lavɑ̃d/ nf lavender.

lave /lav/ nf lava.

lave-glace (pl **~s**) /lavɡlas/ nm windscreen washer.

lave-linge /lavlɛ̃ʒ/ nm inv washing machine.

laver /lave/ [1] vt wash; **~ qn de** (fig) clear sb of. □ **se ~** vpr wash

(oneself); **se ~ les mains** wash one's hands.

laverie /lavʀi/ nf **~ (automatique)** launderette; (US) laundromat.

lave-vaisselle /lavvɛsɛl/ nm inv dishwasher.

laxatif, **-ive** /laksatif, -v/ a & nm laxative.

layette /lɛjɛt/ nf baby clothes.

le, **la**, **l'** (pl **les**) /lə, la, l, le/

l' before vowel or mute h.

● déterminant

••••▶ the.

••••▶ (notion générale) **aimer la musique** like music; **l'amour** love.

••••▶ (possession) **avoir les yeux verts** have green eyes; **il s'est cassé la jambe** he broke his leg.

••••▶ (prix) **10 francs ~ kilo** 10 francs a kilo.

••••▶ (temps) **~ lundi** on Mondays; **tous les mardis** every Tuesday.

••••▶ (avec nom propre) **les Dury** the Durys; **la reine Margot** Queen Margot; **la Belgique** Belgium.

••••▶ (avec adjectif) the; **je veux la rouge** I want the red one; **les riches** the rich.

● pronom

••••▶ (homme) him; (femme) her; (chose, animal) it; (au pluriel) them.

••••▶ (remplaçant une phrase) **je te l'avais bien dit** I told you so; **je ~ croyais aussi** I thought so too.

lécher /leʃe/ [14] vt lick; (flamme) lick; (mer) lap.

lèche-vitrines /lɛʃvitʀin/ nm inv **faire du ~** go window-shopping.

leçon /ləsɔ̃/ nf lesson; **faire la ~ à** lecture; **~ particulière** private lesson; **~s de conduite** driving lessons.

lecteur, **-trice** /lɛktœʀ, -tʀis/ nm, f reader; (Univ) foreign language assistant; **~ de cassettes** cassette player; **~ de disquettes** (disk) drive; **~ laser** CD player; **~ optique** optical scanner.

lecture /lɛktyʀ/ nf reading.

ledit, ladite (*pl* **lesdit(e)s**) / lədi, ladit, ledi(t)/ *adj* the aforementioned.

légal, ~e (*mpl* **-aux**) /legal, -o/ *adj* legal. **légaliser** [1] *vt* legalize. **légalité** *nf* legality; (loi) law.

légendaire /leʒɑ̃dɛʀ/ *adj* legendary. **légende** *nf* (histoire, inscription) legend; (de carte) key; (d'illustration) caption.

léger, -ère /leʒe, -ɛʀ/ *adj* light; (*bruit, faute, maladie*) slight; (*café, argument*) weak; (imprudent) thoughtless; (frivole) fickle; **à la légère** thoughtlessly. **légèrement** *adv* lightly; (*agir*) thoughtlessly; (un peu) slightly. **légèreté** *nf* lightness; thoughtlessness.

légion /leʒjɔ̃/ *nf* legion.

législatif, -ive /leʒislatif, -v/ *adj* legislative; **élections législatives** general election.

législature /leʒislatyʀ/ *nf* term of office.

légitime /leʒitim/ *adj* (Jur) legitimate; (fig) rightful; **agir en état de ~ défense** act in self-defence. **légitimité** *nf* legitimacy.

legs /lɛg/ *nm* legacy; (d'effets personnels) bequest.

léguer /lege/ [14] *vt* bequeath.

légume /legym/ *nm* vegetable.

lendemain /lɑ̃dmɛ̃/ *nm* **le ~ the** next day; (fig) the future; **le ~ de** the day after; **le ~ matin/soir** the next morning/evening; **du jour au ~** from one day to the next.

lent, ~e /lɑ̃, -t/ *adj* slow. **lentement** *adv* slowly. **lenteur** *nf* slowness.

lentille /lɑ̃tij/ *nf* (Culin) lentil; (verre) lens; **~s de contact** contact lenses.

léopard /leɔpaʀ/ *nm* leopard.

lèpre /lɛpʀ/ *nf* leprosy.

....

lequel, laquelle (*pl* **les-quel(le)s**), **auquel** (*pl* **auxquel(le)s**), **duquel** (*pl* **desquel(le)s**) /lakɛl, lakɛl, lekɛl, ɔkɛl, dykɛl, dekɛl/

à + lequel	= auquel,
à + lesquel(le)s	= auxquel(le)s;
de + lequel	= duquel,

de + lesquel(le)s = desquel(le)s

● *pronom*

····▸ (relatif) (personne) who; (complément indirect) whom; (autres cas) which; **l'ami auquel tu as écrit** the friend to whom you wrote; **les voisins chez lesquels Sophie est allée** the neighbours whose house Sophie went to.

····▸ (interrogatif) which; **~ tu veux?** which one do you want?

● *adjectif*

····▸ **auquel cas** in which case.

....

les /le/ ⇨LE.

lesbienne /lɛsbjɛn/ *nf* lesbian.

léser /leze/ [14] *vt* wrong.

lésiner /lezine/ [1] *vi* **ne pas ~ sur** not stint on.

lesquels, lesquelles /lekɛl/ ⇨LEQUEL.

lessive /lesiv/ *nf* (poudre) washing-powder; (liquide) washing liquid; (linge, action) washing.

leste /lɛst/ *adj* agile, nimble; (grivois) coarse.

Lettonie /letɔni/ *nf* Latvia.

lettre /lɛtʀ/ *nf* letter; **à la ~, au pied de la ~** literally; **en toutes ~s** in full; **~s** (Univ) (the) arts.

leucémie /løsemi/ *nf* leukaemia.

....

leur (*pl* **~s**) /lœʀ/

● *pronom personnel invariable*

····▸ them; **donne-le ~** give it to them; **je ~ fais confiance** I trust them.

● *adjectif possessif*

····▸ their; **~s enfants** their children; **à ~ arrivée** when they arrived.

● **le leur, la leur**, (*pl* **les leurs**) *pronom possessif*

····▸ theirs; **chacun le ~** one each; **je suis des ~s** I am one of them.

....

levain /ləvɛ̃/ *nm* leaven.

levé, ~e /ləve/ *adj* (debout) up.

levée /ləve/ *nf* (de peine, de sanctions) lifting; (de courrier) collection; (de troupes, d'impôts) levying.

lever /ləve/ [6] *vt* lift (up), raise; (*interdiction*) lift; (*séance*) close; (*armée, impôts*) levy. ● *vi* (*pâte*) rise. □ **se ~** *vpr* get up; (*soleil, rideau*) rise; (*jour*) break. ● *nm* **au ~** on getting up; **~ du jour** daybreak; **~ de rideau** (Théât) curtain (up); **~ du soleil** sunrise.

levier /ləvje/ *nm* lever; **~ de changement de vitesse** gear lever.

lèvre /lɛvʀ/ *nf* lip.

lévrier /levʀije/ *nm* greyhound.

levure /ləvyʀ/ *nf* yeast; **~ chimique** baking powder.

lexique /lɛksik/ *nm* vocabulary; (*glossaire*) lexicon.

lézard /lezaʀ/ *nm* lizard.

lézarde /lezaʀd/ *nf* crack.

liaison /ljɛzɔ̃/ *nf* connection; (transport, Ordinat) link; (contact) contact; (Gram, Mil) liaison; (amoureuse) affair; **être en ~ avec** be in contact with; **assurer la ~ entre** liaise between.

liane /ljan/ *nf* creeper.

Liban /libɑ̃/ *nm* Lebanon.

libeller /libele/ [1] *vt* (*chèque*) write; (*contrat*) draw up; **libellé à l'ordre de** made out to.

libellule /libelyl/ *nf* dragonfly.

libéral, ~e (*mpl* **-aux**) /libeʀal, -o/ *adj* liberal; **les professions ~es** the professions.

libérateur, -trice /libeʀatœʀ, -tʀis/ *adj* liberating. ● *nm, f* liberator.

libération *nf* release; (de pays) liberation.

libérer /libeʀe/ [14] *vt* (*personne*) free, release; (*pays*) liberate, free; (*bureau, lieux*) vacate; (*gaz*) release. □ **se ~** *vpr* free oneself.

liberté /libɛʀte/ *nf* freedom, liberty; (loisir) free time; **être/mettre en ~** be/ set free; **~ conditionnelle** parole; **~ provisoire** provisional release (*pending trial*); **~ surveillée** probation; **~s publiques** civil liberties.

Libertel /libɛʀtɛl/ *nm* (Internet) Freenet.

libraire /libʀɛʀ/ *nmf* bookseller. **librairie** *nf* bookshop.

libre /libʀ/ *adj* free; (*place, pièce*) vacant, free; (*passage*) clear; (*école*)

private (*usually religious*); **~ de qch/ de faire** free from sth/to do. **libre-échange** *nm* free trade. **libre-service** (*pl* **libres-services**) *nm* (magasin) self-service shop; (restaurant) self-service restaurant.

licence /lisɑ̃s/ *nf* licence; (Univ) degree.

licencié, ~e /lisɑ̃sje/ *nm, f* graduate; **~ ès lettres/sciences** Bachelor of Arts/Science.

licenciements /lisɑ̃simɑ̃/ *nm* redundancy; (pour faute) dismissal. **licencier** [45] *vt* make redundant; (pour faute) dismiss.

licorne /likɔʀn/ *nf* unicorn.

liège /ljɛʒ/ *nm* cork.

lien /ljɛ̃/ *nm* (rapport) link; (attache) bond, tie; (corde) rope; **~s affectifs/de parenté** emotional/family ties.

lier /lje/ [45] *vt* tie (up), bind; (relier) link; (engager, unir) bind; **~ conversation** strike up a conversation; **ils sont très liés** they are very close. □ **se ~ avec** *vpr* make friends with.

lierre /ljɛʀ/ *nm* ivy.

lieu (*pl* **~x**) /ljø/ *nm* place; **~x** (locaux) premises; (d'un accident) scene; **sur les ~x** at the scene; **au ~ de** instead of; **avoir ~** take place; **donner ~ à** give rise to; **tenir ~ de** serve as; **s'il y a ~** if necessary; **en premier ~** firstly; **en dernier ~** lastly; **~ commun** commonplace; **~ de rencontre** meeting place.

lièvre /ljɛvʀ/ *nm* hare.

lifting /liftiŋ/ *nm* face-lift.

ligne /liɲ/ *nf* line; (trajet) route; (de métro, train) line; (formes) lines; (de femme) figure; **en ~** (joueurs) lined up; (au téléphone) on the phone; (Ordinat) on line; **~ spécialisée** (Internet) dedicated line.

ligoter /ligɔte/ [1] *vt* tie up.

ligue /lig/ *nf* league. **liguer (se)** [1] *vpr* join forces (**contre** against).

lilas /lila/ *nm & a inv* lilac.

limace /limas/ *nf* slug.

limande /limɑ̃d/ *nf* (poisson) dab.

lime /lim/ *nf* file; **~ à ongles** nail file.

limitation /limitasjɔ̃/ *nf* limitation; **~ de vitesse** speed limit.

limite /limit/ *nf* limit; (de jardin, champ) boundary; **à la ~ de** (fig) verging on, bordering on; **à la ~** if it comes to it, at a pinch; **dans une certaine ~** up to a point; **dans la ~ du possible** as far as possible. ● *adj* (*vitesse, âge*) maximum; **cas ~** borderline case; **date ~** deadline; **date ~ de vente** sell-by date.

limiter /limite/ [1] *vt* limit; (délimiter) form the border of. □ **se ~** *vpr* limit oneself (à to).

limonade /limɔnad/ *nf* lemonade.

limpide /lɛ̃pid/ *adj* limpid, clear.

lin /lɛ̃/ *nm* (tissu) linen.

linge /lɛ̃ʒ/ *nm* linen; (lessive) washing; (torchon) cloth; **~ (de corps)** underwear. **lingerie** *nf* underwear. **lingette** *nf* wipe.

lingot /lɛ̃go/ *nm* ingot.

linguistique /lɛ̃gɥistik/ *adj* linguistic. ● *nf* linguistics.

lion /ljɔ̃/ *nm* lion; **le L~** Leo. **lionceau** (*pl* **~x**) *nm* lion cub. **lionne** *nf* lioness.

liquidation /likidasjɔ̃/ *nf* liquidation; (vente) (clearance) sale; **entrer en ~** go into liquidation.

liquide /likid/ *adj* liquid. ● *nm* (argent) **~** ready money; **payer en ~** pay cash; **~ de frein** brake fluid.

liquider /likide/ [1] *vt* liquidate; (vendre) sell.

lire /liʁ/ [39] *vt/i* read. ● *nf* lira.

lis¹ /li/ ⇒LIRE[39].

lis² /lis/ *nm* (fleur) lily.

lisible /lizibl/ *adj* legible; (roman) readable.

lisière /lizjɛʁ/ *nf* edge.

lisse /lis/ *adj* smooth.

liste /list/ *nf* list; **~ d'attente** waiting list; **~ électorale** register of voters; **être sur (la) ~ rouge** be ex-directory.

listing /listiŋ/ *nm* printout.

lit /li/ *nm* bed; **se mettre au ~** get into bed; **~ de camp** camp-bed; **~ d'enfant** cot; **~ d'une personne** single bed; **~ de deux personnes**, **grand ~** double bed.

literie /litʁi/ *nf* bedding.

litière /litjɛʁ/ *nf* litter.

litige /litiʒ/ *nm* dispute.

litre /litʁ/ *nm* litre.

littéraire /liteʁɛʁ/ *adj* literary; (études, formation) arts.

littéral, **~e** (*mpl* **-aux**) /literal, -o/ *adj* literal.

littérature /literatyʁ/ *nf* literature.

littoral (*pl* **-aux**) /litɔral, -o/ *nm* coast.

Lituanie /litɥani/ *nf* Lithuania.

livide /livid/ *adj* deathly pale.

livraison /livʁɛzɔ̃/ *nf* delivery.

livre /livʁ/ *nf* (monnaie, poids) pound. ● *nm* book; **~ de bord** log-book; **~ de compte** books; **~ de poche** paperback.

livrer /livʁe/ [1] *vt* (Comm) deliver; (abandonner) give over (à to); (remettre) (coupable, document) hand over (à to); **livré à soi-même** left to oneself. □ **se ~** *vpr* (se rendre) give oneself up (à to); **se ~ à** (boisson, actes) indulge in; (ami) confide in.

livret /livʁɛ/ *nm* book; (Mus) libretto; **~ de caisse d'épargne** savings book; **~ scolaire** school report (book).

livreur, **-euse** /livʁœʁ, -øz/ *nm,f* delivery man, delivery woman.

local¹, **~e** (*mpl* **-aux**) /lɔkal, -o/ *adj* local.

local² (*pl* **-aux**) /lɔkal, -o/ *nm* premises; **locaux** premises.

localement /lɔkalmɑ̃/ *adv* locally.

localiser /lɔkalize/ [1] *vt* (repérer) locate; (circonscrire) localize.

locataire /lɔkatɛʁ/ *nmf* tenant; (de chambre) lodger.

location /lɔkasjɔ̃/ *nf* (de maison) renting; (de voiture, de matériel) hire, rental; (de place) booking, reservation; (par propriétaire) renting out; hiring out; **en ~** (voiture) on hire, rented; (habiter) in rented accommodation.

locomotive /lɔkɔmɔtiv/ *nf* engine, locomotive.

locution /lɔkysjɔ̃/ *nf* phrase.

loge /lɔʒ/ *nf* (de concierge, de franc-maçons) lodge; (d'acteur) dressing-room; (de spectateur) box.

logement /lɔʒmɑ̃/ *nm* accommodation; (appartement) flat; (habitat) housing.

loger /lɔʒe/ [40] *vt* (réfugié, famille) house; (ami) put up; (client) accommodate. ● *vi* live. ◻ **se** ~ *vpr* live; **trouver à se** ~ find accommodation; **se** ~ **dans** (*balle*) lodge itself in.

logiciel /lɔʒisjɛl/ *nm* software; ~ **contributif** shareware; ~ **d'application** application software; ~ **de groupe** groupware; ~ **de jeux** games software; ~ **de navigation** browser; ~ **public** freeware.

logique /lɔʒik/ *adj* logical. ● *nf* logic.

logis /lɔʒi/ *nm* dwelling.

logistique /lɔʒistik/ *nf* logistics.

loi /lwa/ *nf* law.

loin /lwɛ̃/ *adv* far (away); **au** ~ far away; **de** ~ from far away; (de beaucoup) by far; ~ **de là** far from it; **plus** ~ further; **il revient de** ~ (fig) he had a close shave.

lointain, ~**e** /lwɛ̃tɛ̃, -ɛn/ *adj* distant. ● *nm* distance; **dans le** ~ in the distance.

loir /lwaʀ/ *nm* dormouse.

loisir /lwaziʀ/ *nm* (spare) time; ~**s** (temps libre) leisure, spare time; (distractions) leisure activities; **à** ~ at one's leisure; **avoir le** ~ **de faire** have time to do.

londonien, ~**ne** /lɔ̃dɔnjɛ̃, -ɛn/ *adj* London. **L**~, ~**e** *nm, f* Londoner.

Londres /lɔ̃dʀ/ *npr* London.

long, longue /lɔ̃, lɔ̃g/ *adj* long; **à** ~ **terme** long-term; **être** ~ **à faire** be a long time doing. ● *nm* **de** ~ (mesure) long; **de** ~ **en large** back and forth; (tout) **le** ~ **de** (all) along. ● *adv* **en dire** ~ **sur qn/qch** say a lot about sb/sth; **en savoir plus** ~ **sur** know more about.

longer /lɔ̃ʒe/ [40] *vt* go along; (limiter) border.

longitude /lɔ̃ʒityd/ *nf* longitude.

longtemps /lɔ̃tɑ̃/ *adv* a long time; **avant** ~ before long; **trop** ~ too long; **ça prendra** ~ it will take a long time; **prendre plus** ~ **que prévu** take longer than anticipated.

longuement /lɔ̃gmɑ̃/ *adv* (longtemps) for a long time; (en détail) at length.

longueur /lɔ̃gœʀ/ *nf* length; ~**s** (de texte) over-long parts; **à** ~ **de journée**

all day long; **en** ~ lengthwise; ~ **d'onde** wavelength.

lopin /lɔpɛ̃/ *nm* ~ **de terre** patch of land.

loque /lɔk/ *nf* ~**s** rags; ~ (**humaine**) (human) wreck.

loquet /lɔkɛ/ *nm* latch.

lors de /lɔʀdə/ *prép* (au moment de) at the time of; (pendant) during.

lorsque /lɔʀsk(ə)/ *conj* when.

losange /lɔzɑ̃ʒ/ *nm* diamond.

lot /lo/ *nm* (portion) share; (aux enchères) lot; (Ordinat) batch; (destin) lot; **gagner le gros** ~ hit the jackpot.

loterie /lɔtʀi/ *nf* lottery.

lotion /losjɔ̃/ *nf* lotion.

lotissement /lɔtismɑ̃/ *nm* (à construire) building plot; (construit) (housing) development.

louable /luabl/ *adj* praiseworthy. **louange** *nf* praise.

louche /luʃ/ *adj* shady, dubious. ● *nf* ladle.

loucher /luʃe/ [1] *vi* squint.

louer /lwe/ [1] *vt* (approuver) praise (**de** for); (prendre en location) (*maison*) rent; (*voiture, matériel*) hire, rent; (*place*) book, reserve; (donner en location) (*maison*) rent out; (*matériel*) rent out, hire out; **à** ~ to let, for rent (US).

loufoque /lufɔk/ *adj* 🄸 crazy.

loup /lu/ *nm* wolf.

loupe /lup/ *nf* magnifying glass.

louper /lupe/ [1] *vt* 🄸 miss; (*examen*) flunk 🄸.

lourd, ~**e** /luʀ, -d/ *adj* heavy; (*faute*) serious; ~ **de dangers** fraught with danger; **il fait** ~ it's close *ou* muggy.

loutre /lutʀ/ *nf* otter.

louveteau (*pl* ~**x**) /luvto/ *nm* wolf cub; (scout) Cub (Scout).

loyal, ~**e** (*mpl* -**aux**) /lwajal, -o/ *adj* loyal, faithful; (honnête) fair. **loyauté** *nf* loyalty; fairness.

loyer /lwaje/ *nm* rent.

lu /ly/ ⇒LIRE [39].

lubrifiant /lybʀifjɑ̃/ *nm* lubricant.

lucide /lysid/ *adj* lucid. **lucidité** *nf* lucidity.

lucratif, -**ive** /lykʀatif, -v/ *adj* lucrative; **à but non** ~ non-profit-making.

ludiciel /lydisjɛl/ *nm* (Ordinat) games software.

lueur /lɥœʀ/ *nf* (faint) light, glimmer; (fig) glimmer, gleam.

luge /lyʒ/ *nf* toboggan.

lugubre /lygybʀ/ *adj* gloomy.

lui /lɥi/

● *pronom*

···▸ (masculin) (sujet) he; ∼, **il est à l'étranger** he's abroad; **c'est** ∼**!** it's him!; (objet) him; (animal) it; **c'est à** ∼ it's his; **elle conduit mieux que** ∼ she's a better driver than he is.

···▸ (féminin) her; **je** ∼ **ai annoncé** I told her.

···▸ (masculin/féminin) **donne-le-**∼ give it to him/her.

lui-même /lɥimɛm/ *pron* himself; (animal) itself.

luire /lɥiʀ/ [17] *vi* shine; (reflet humide) glisten; (reflet chaud, faible) glow.

lumière /lymjɛʀ/ *nf* light; ∼**s** (connaissances) knowledge; **faire (toute) la** ∼ **sur une affaire** clear a matter up.

luminaire /lyminɛʀ/ *nm* lamp.

lumineux, -euse /lyminø, -z/ *adj* luminous; (éclairé) illuminated; (*rayon*) of light; (radieux) radiant; **source lumineuse** light source.

lunaire /lynɛʀ/ *adj* lunar.

lunatique /lynatik/ *adj* temperamental.

lunch /lœnʃ/ *nm* buffet lunch.

lundi /lœdi/ *nm* Monday.

lune /lyn/ *nf* moon; ∼ **de miel** honeymoon.

lunettes /lynɛt/ *nfpl* glasses; (de protection) goggles; ∼ **de ski/natation** ski/swimming goggles; ∼ **noires** dark glasses; ∼ **de soleil** sun-glasses.

lustre /lystʀ/ *nm* (éclat) lustre; (objet) chandelier.

lutin /lytɛ̃/ *nm* goblin.

lutte /lyt/ *nf* fight, struggle; (Sport) wrestling. **lutter** [1] *vi* fight, struggle; (Sport) wrestle. **lutteur, -euse** *nm, f* fighter; (Sport) wrestler.

luxe /lyks/ *nm* luxury; **de** ∼ luxury; (*produit*) de luxe.

Luxembourg /lyksãbuʀ/ *nm* Luxemburg.

luxer (se) /(sə)lykse/ [1] *vpr* **se** ∼ **le genou** dislocate one's knee.

luxueux, -euse /lyksɥø, -z/ *adj* luxurious.

lycée /lise/ *nm* (secondary) school. **lycéen, ∼ne** *nm, f* pupil (at secondary school).

lyophilisé, ∼e /ljɔfilize/ *adj* freeze-dried.

lyrique /liʀik/ *adj* (*poésie*) lyric; (passionné) lyrical; **artiste/théâtre** ∼ opera singer/house.

lys /lis/ *nm* lily.

Mm

m' /m/ ⇒ME.

ma /ma/ ⇒MON.

macabre /makabʀ/ *adj* macabre.

macadam /makadam/ *nm* Tarmac®.

macaron /makaʀɔ̃/ *nm* (gâteau) macaroon; (insigne) badge.

macédoine /masedwan/ *nf* mixed diced vegetables; ∼ **de fruits** fruit salad.

macérer /maseʀe/ [14] *vt/i* soak; (dans du vinaigre) pickle.

mâcher /maʃe/ [1] *vt* chew; **ne pas** ∼ **ses mots** not mince one's words.

machin /maʃɛ̃/ *nm* 🄸 (chose) thing; (dont on ne trouve pas le nom) whatsit 🄸.

machinal, ∼e (*mpl* **-aux**) /maʃinal, -o/ *adj* automatic. **machinalement** *adv* mechanically, automatically.

machination /maʃinasjɔ̃/ *nf* plot; **des** ∼**s** machinations.

machine /maʃin/ *nf* machine; (d'un train, navire) engine; ∼ **à écrire** typewriter; ∼ **à laver/coudre** washing-/sewing-machine; ∼ **à sous** fruit machine; (US) slot-machine. **machine-outil** (*pl* **machines-**

outils) *nf* machine tool.
machinerie *nf* machinery.
machiniste /maʃinist/ *nm* (Théât)
stage-hand; (conducteur) driver.
mâchoire /maʃwaʀ/ *nf* jaw.
mâchonner /maʃɔne/ [1] *vt* chew.
maçon /masɔ̃/ *nm* (entrepreneur)
builder; (poseur de briques) bricklayer;
(qui construit en pierre) mason.
maçonnerie *nf* (briques) brickwork;
(pierres) stonework, masonry; (travaux)
building.
madame (*pl* **mesdames**)
/madam, medam/ *nf* (à une inconnue)
(dans une lettre) **M~** Dear Madam;
bonjour, ~ good morning; **mesdames
et messieurs** ladies and gentlemen;
(à une femme dont on connaît le nom)
(dans une lettre) **Chère M~** Dear Mrs
ou Ms X; **bonjour, ~** good morning
Mrs *ou* Ms X; **oui M~ le Ministre** yes
Minister; (formule de respect) **oui M~**
yes madam.
mademoiselle (*pl*
mesdemoiselles) /madmwazɛl,
medmwazɛl/ *nf* (à une inconnue) (dans
une lettre) **M~** Dear Madam; **bonjour,
~** good morning; **entrez
mesdemoiselles** come in (ladies); (à
une jeune fille dont on connaît le nom)
(dans une lettre) **Chère M~** Dear Ms *ou*
Miss X; **bonjour, ~** good morning
Miss *ou* Ms X.
magasin /magazɛ̃/ *nm* shop, store;
(entrepôt) warehouse; (d'une arme)
magazine; **en ~** in stock.
magazine /magazin/ *nm* magazine;
(émission) programme.
Maghreb /magʀɛb/ *nm* North
Africa.
magicien, ~ne /maʒisjɛ̃, -ɛn/ *nm,f*
magician.
magie /maʒi/ *nf* magic. **magique**
adj magic; (mystérieux) magical.
magistral, ~e (*mpl* -**aux**)
/maʒistʀal, -o/ *adj* masterly; (grand:
hum) tremendous; **cours ~** lecture.
magistrat /maʒistʀa/ *nm*
magistrate.
magistrature /maʒistʀatyʀ/ *nf*
judiciary; (fonction) public office.
magner (se) /(sə)maɲe/ [1] *upr* 🔲
get a move on.

magnétique /maɲetik/ *adj*
magnetic. **magnétiser** [1] *vt*
magnetize. **magnétisme** *nm*
magnetism.
magnétophone /maɲetɔfɔn/ *nm*
tape recorder; (à cassettes) cassette
recorder.
magnétoscope /maɲetɔskɔp/ *nm*
video recorder.
magnificence /maɲifisɑ̃s/ *nf*
magnificence. **magnifique** *adj*
magnificent.
magot /mago/ *nm* 🔲 hoard (of
money).
magouille /maguj/ *nf* 🔲 scheming,
skulduggery.
magret /magʀɛ/ *nm* **~ de canard**
duck breast.
mai /mɛ/ *nm* May.
maigre /mɛgʀ/ *adj* thin; (viande)
lean; (yaourt) low-fat; (fig) poor,
meagre; **faire ~** abstain from meat.
maigreur *nf* thinness; leanness; (fig)
meagreness.
maigrir /megʀiʀ/ [2] *vi* get thin-
(ner); (en suivant un régime) slim. ● *vt*
make thin(ner).
maille /maj/ *nf* stitch; (de filet) mesh;
~ qui file ladder, run; **avoir ~ à
partir avec qn** have a brush with sb.
maillet /majɛ/ *nm* mallet.
maillon /majɔ̃/ *nm* link.
maillot /majo/ *nm* (Sport) shirt,
jersey; **~ (de corps)** vest; (US)
undershirt; **~ (de bain)** (swimming)
costume.
main /mɛ̃/ *nf* hand; **donner la ~ à qn**
hold sb's hand; **se donner la ~** hold
hands; **en ~s propres** in person; **en
bonnes ~s** in good hands; **~
courante** handrail; **se faire la ~** get
the hang of it; **perdre la ~** lose one's
touch; **sous la ~** to hand; **vol à ~
armée** armed robbery; **fait (à la) ~**
handmade; **haut les ~s!** hands up!
main-d'œuvre (*pl* **mains-
d'œuvre**) *nf* labour; (ouvriers) labour
force.
main-forte /mɛ̃fɔʀt/ *nf inv* **prêter ~
à qn** come to sb's aid.
maint, ~e /mɛ̃, mɛ̃t/ *adj* many a (+
sg); **~s** many; **à ~es reprises** many
times.

maintenant /mɛ̃t(ə)nɑ̃/ *adv* now; (de nos jours) nowadays; (l'époque actuelle) today.

maintenir /mɛ̃t(ə)niʀ/ [58] *vt* keep, maintain; (soutenir) support, hold up; (affirmer) maintain; (*decision*) stand by. □ **se** ~ *vpr* (tendance) persist; (*prix, malade*) remain stable.

maintien /mɛ̃tjɛ̃/ *nm* (attitude) bearing; (conservation) maintenance.

maire /mɛʀ/ *nm* mayor.

mairie /meʀi/ *nf* town hall; (administration) town council.

mais /mɛ/ *conj* but; ~ **oui** of course; ~ **non** of course not.

maïs /mais/ *nm* maize, corn; (Culin) sweetcorn.

maison /mɛzɔ̃/ *nf* house; (foyer) home; (immeuble) building; ~ **(de commerce)** firm; **à la** ~ at home; **rentrer** *ou* **aller à la** ~ go home; ~ **des jeunes (et de la culture)** youth club; ~ **de repos** rest home; ~ **de convalescence** convalescent home; ~ **de retraite** old people's home; ~ **mère** parent company. ● *a inv* (Culin) home-made.

maître, -esse /mɛtʀ, -ɛs/ *adj* (qui contrôle) **être** ~ **de soi** be one's own master; ~ **de la situation** in control of the situation; (principal) (*idée, qualité*) key, main. ● *nm, f* (Scol) teacher; (d'animal) owner, master. ● *nm* (expert, guide) master; (dirigeant) leader; ~ **de conférences** senior lecturer; ~ **d'hôtel** head waiter; (domestique) butler. **maître-assistant**, ~ **e** (*pl* **maîtres-assistants**) *nm, f* lecturer. **maître-chanteur** (*pl* **maîtres-chanteurs**) *nm* blackmailer. **maître-nageur** (*pl* **maîtres-nageurs**) *nm* swimming instructor. **maîtresse** *nf* (amante) mistress.

maîtrise /mɛtʀiz/ *nf* mastery; (contrôle) control; (Mil) supremacy; (Univ) master's degree; ~ **(de soi)** self-control.

maîtriser /mɛtʀize/ [1] *vt* (*sujet, technique*) master; (*incendie, sentiment, personne*) control. □ **se** ~ *vpr* have self-control.

maïzena® /maizena / *nf* cornflour.

majesté /maʒɛste/ *nf* majesty.

majestueux, -euse /maʒɛstɥø, z/ *adj* majestic.

majeur, ~ **e** /maʒœʀ/ *adj* major, main; (Jur) of age; **en** ~ **e partie** mostly; **la** ~ **e partie de** most of. ● *nm* middle finger.

majoration /maʒɔʀasjɔ̃/ *nf* increase (**de** in). **majorer** [1] *vt* increase.

majoritaire /maʒɔʀitɛʀ/ *adj* majority; **être** ~ be in the majority. **majorité** *nf* majority; **en** ~ chiefly.

Majorque /maʒɔʀk/ *nf* Majorca.

majuscule /maʒyskyl/ *adj* capital. ● *nf* capital letter.

mal[1] /mal/ *adv* badly; (incorrectement) wrong(ly); **aller** ~ (*personne*) be unwell; (*affaires*) go badly; ~ **entendre/comprendre** not hear/understand properly; ~ **en point** in a bad state; **pas** ~ quite a lot. ● *a inv* bad, wrong; **c'est** ~ **de** it is wrong *ou* bad to; **ce n'est pas** ~ 🔟 it's not bad; **Nick n'est pas** ~ 🔟 Nick is not bad-looking.

mal[2] (*pl* **maux**) /mal, mo/ *nm* evil; (douleur) pain, ache; (maladie) disease; (effort) trouble; (dommage) harm; (malheur) misfortune; **avoir** ~ **à la tête/à la gorge** have a headache/a sore throat; **avoir le** ~ **de mer/du pays** be seasick/homesick; **faire** ~ hurt; **se faire** ~ hurt oneself; **j'ai** ~ it hurts; **faire du** ~ **à** hurt, harm; **se donner du** ~ **pour faire qch** go to a lot of trouble to do sth.

malade /malad/ *adj* sick, ill; (*bras, œil*) bad; (*plante, poumons, côlon*) diseased; **tomber** ~ fall ill; (*fou* 🔟) mad. ● *nmf* sick person; (d'un médecin) patient; ~ **mental** mentally ill person.

maladie /maladi/ *nf* illness, disease; (manie 🔟) mania.

maladif, -ive /maladif, -v/ *adj* sickly; (*jalousie, peur*) pathological.

maladresse /maladʀɛs/ *nf* clumsiness; (erreur) blunder.

maladroit, ~ **e** /maladʀwa, -t/ *adj* clumsy; (sans tact) tactless.

malaise /malɛz/ *nm* feeling of faintness; (gêne) uneasiness; (état de crise) unrest.

malaisé, ~ **e** /maleze/ *adj* difficult.

Malaisie /malɛzi/ *nf* Malaysia.

malaria /malaʀja/ *nf* malaria.

malaxer /malakse/ [1] *vt* (pétrir) knead; (mêler) mix.

malchance /malʃɑ̃s/ *nf* misfortune. **malchanceux, -euse** *adj* unlucky.

mâle /mɑl/ *adj* male; (viril) manly. ● *nm* male.

malédiction /malediksjɔ̃/ *nf* curse.

maléfice /malefis/ *nm* evil spell. **maléfique** *adj* evil.

malentendant, ~e /malɑ̃tɑ̃dɑ̃, -t/ *adj* hard of hearing.

malentendu /malɑ̃tɑ̃dy/ *nm* misunderstanding.

malfaçon /malfasɔ̃/ *nf* defect.

malfaisant, ~e /malfəzɑ̃, -t/ *adj* harmful; (*personne*) evil.

malfaiteur /malfɛtœʀ/ *nm* criminal.

malformation /malfɔʀmasjɔ̃/ *nf* malformation.

malgré /malgʀe/ *prép* in spite of, despite; ~ **tout** nevertheless.

malheur /malœʀ/ *nm* misfortune; (accident) accident; **par ~** unfortunately; **faire un ~** 🇮 be a big hit; **porter ~** be *ou* bring bad luck.

malheureusement /malœʀøzmɑ̃/ *adv* unfortunately.

malheureux, -euse /malœʀø, -z/ *adj* unhappy; (regrettable) unfortunate; (sans succès) unlucky; (insignifiant) paltry, pathetic. ● *nm,f* (poor) wretch.

malhonnête /malɔnɛt/ *adj* dishonest. **malhonnêteté** *nf* dishonesty.

malice /malis/ *nf* mischief; **sans ~** harmless; **avec ~** mischievously. **malicieux, -ieuse** *adj* mischievous.

malignité /maliɲite/ *nf* malignancy. **malin, -igne** *adj* clever, smart; (méchant) malicious; (*tumeur*) malignant; (difficile 🇮) difficult.

malingre /malɛ̃gʀ/ *adj* puny.

malle /mal/ *nf* (valise) trunk; (Auto) boot; (US) trunk.

mallette /malɛt/ *nf* (small) suitcase; (pour le bureau) briefcase.

malmener /malməne/ [6] *vt* manhandle; (fig) give a rough ride to.

malnutrition /malnytʀisjɔ̃/ *nf* malnutrition.

malodorant, ~e /malɔdɔʀɑ̃, -t/ *adj* smelly, foul-smelling.

malpoli, ~e /malpɔli/ *adj* rude, impolite.

malpropre /malpʀɔpʀ/ *adj* dirty.

malsain, ~e /malsɛ̃, -ɛn/ *adj* unhealthy.

malt /malt/ *nm* malt.

Malte /malt/ *nf* Malta.

maltraiter /maltʀete/ [1] *vt* ill-treat.

malveillance /malvɛjɑ̃s/ *nf* malice. **malveillant, ~e** *adj* malicious.

maman /mamɑ̃/ *nf* mum(my), mother; (US) mom(my).

mamelle /mamɛl/ *nf* teat.

mamelon /mamlɔ̃/ *nm* (Anat) nipple; (colline) hillock.

mamie /mami/ *nf* 🇮 granny.

mammifère /mamifɛʀ/ *nm* mammal.

manche /mɑ̃ʃ/ *nf* sleeve; (Sport, Pol) round. ● *nm* (d'un instrument) handle; **~ à balai** broomstick; (Aviat) joystick. **M~** *nf* **la M~** the Channel; **le tunnel sous la M~** the Channel tunnel.

manchette /mɑ̃ʃɛt/ *nf* cuff; (de journal) headline.

manchot, ~te /mɑ̃ʃo, -ɔt/ *nm,f* one-armed person; (sans bras) armless person. ● *nm* (oiseau) penguin.

mandarine /mɑ̃daʀin/ *nf* tangerine, mandarin (orange).

mandat /mɑ̃da/ *nm* (postal) money order; (Pol) mandate; (procuration) proxy; (de police) warrant; **~ d'arrêt** arrest warrant.

mandataire /mɑ̃datɛʀ/ *nm* representative; (Jur) proxy.

manège /manɛʒ/ *nm* riding school; (à la foire) merry-go-round; (manœuvre) trick, ploy.

manette /manɛt/ *nf* lever; (de jeu) joystick.

mangeable /mɑ̃ʒabl/ *adj* edible.

mangeoire /mɑ̃ʒwaʀ/ *nf* trough; (pour oiseaux) feeder.

manger /mɑ̃ʒe/ [40] *vt* eat; (*fortune*) go through; (*profits*) eat away at;

(économies) use up; *(ronger)* eat into.
● *vi* eat; **donner à ~ à** feed. ● *nm* food.

mangue /mãg/ *nf* mango.

maniable /manjabl/ *adj* easy to handle.

maniaque /manjak/ *adj* fussy.
● *nmf* fusspot; *(fou)* maniac; *(fanatique)* fanatic; **un ~ de l'ordre** a stickler for tidiness.

manie /mani/ *nf* habit; *(marotte)* obsession.

maniement /manimã/ *nm* handling. **manier** [45] *vt* handle.

manière /manjɛʀ/ *nf* way, manner; **~s** *(politesse)* manners; *(chichis)* fuss; **à la ~ de** in the style of; **de ~ à** so as to; **de toute ~** anyway, in any case.

maniéré, ~e /manjeʀe/ *adj* affected.

manif /manif/ *nf* 🄵 demo.

manifestant, ~e /manifɛstã, -t/ *nm,f* demonstrator.

manifestation /manifɛstasjõ/ *nf* expression, manifestation; *(de maladie, phénomène)* appearance; *(Pol)* demonstration; *(événement)* event; **~ culturelle** cultural event.

manifeste /manifɛst/ *adj* obvious.
● *nm* manifesto.

manifester /manifɛste/ [1] *vt* show, manifest; *(désir, crainte)* express.
● *vi* *(Pol)* demonstrate. ☐ **se ~** *vpr* *(sentiment)* show itself; *(apparaître)* appear; *(répondre à un appel)* come forward.

manigance /manigãs/ *nf* little plot. **manigancer** [10] *vt* plot.

manipulation /manipylasjõ/ *nf* handling; *(péj)* manipulation.

manivelle /manivɛl/ *nf* handle, crank.

mannequin /mankɛ̃/ *nm* *(personne)* model; *(statue)* dummy.

manœuvrer /manœvʀe/ [1] *vt* manoeuvre; *(machine)* operate. ● *vi* manoeuvre.

manoir /manwaʀ/ *nm* manor.

manque /mãk/ *nm* lack **(de** of); *(lacune)* gap; **~ à gagner** loss of earnings; **en (état de) ~** having withdrawal symptoms.

manqué, ~e /mãke/ *adj* *(écrivain)* failed; **garçon ~** tomboy.

manquement /mãkmã/ *nm* **~ à** breach of.

manquer /mãke/ [1] *vt* miss; *(gâcher)* spoil; **~ à** *(devoir)* fail in; **~ de** be short of, lack; **il/ça lui manque** he misses him/it; **~ (de) faire** *(faillir)* nearly do; **ne manquez pas de** be sure to; **~ à sa parole** break one's word. ● *vi* be short *ou* lacking; *(être absent)* be absent; *(en moins, disparu)* be missing; **il me manque 20 francs** I'm 20 francs short.

mansarde /mãsaʀd/ *nf* attic (room).

manteau *(pl* **~x**) /mãto/ *nm* coat.

manucure /manykyʀ/ *nmf* manicurist. ● *nf* *(soins)* manicure.

manuel, ~le /manɥɛl/ *adj* manual.
● *nm* *(livre)* manual; *(Scol)* textbook.

manufacture /manyfaktyʀ/ *nf* factory; *(fabrication)* manufacture. **manufacturer** [1] *vt* manufacture.

manuscrit, ~e /manyskʀi, -t/ *adj* handwritten. ● *nm* manuscript.

mappemonde /mapmõd/ *nf* world map; *(sphère)* globe.

maquereau *(pl* **~x**) /makʀo/ *nm* *(poisson)* mackerel; 🄵 pimp.

maquette /makɛt/ *nf* *(scale)* model; **~ (de mise en page)** paste-up.

maquillage /makijaʒ/ *nm* make-up.

maquiller /makije/ [1] *vt* make up; *(truquer)* doctor, fake. ☐ **se ~** *vpr* make (oneself) up.

maquis /maki/ *nm* *(paysage)* scrub; *(Mil)* Maquis, underground.

maraîcher, -ère /maʀeʃe, -ɛʀ/ *nm,f* market gardener; *(US)* truck farmer.

marais /maʀɛ/ *nm* marsh.

marasme /maʀasm/ *nm* slump, stagnation; **dans le ~** in the doldrums.

marbre /maʀbʀ/ *nm* marble.

marc /maʀ/ *nm* *(eau-de-vie)* marc; **~ de café** coffee grounds.

marchand, ~e /maʀʃã, -d/ *adj* *(valeur)* market. ● *nm,f* trader; *(de charbon, vins)* merchant; **~ de couleurs** ironmonger; *(US)* hardware merchant; **~ de journaux** newsagent; **~ de légumes** greengrocer; **~ de poissons** fishmonger.

marchander /maʀʃɑ̃de/ [1] *vt*
haggle over. ● *vi* haggle.

marchandise /maʀʃɑ̃diz/ *nf*
goods.

marche /maʀʃ/ *nf* (démarche, trajet)
walk; (rythme) pace; (Mil, Mus, Pol)
march; (d'escalier) step; (Sport)
walking; (de véhicule) operation,
working; (de véhicule) running; **en ~**
(*train*) moving; (*moteur, machine*)
running; **faire ~ arrière** (*véhicule*)
reverse; **mettre en ~** start (up); **se
mettre en ~** start moving.

marché /maʀʃe/ *nm* market; (contrat)
deal; **faire son ~** do one's shopping;
~ aux puces flea market; **~ noir**
black market.

marchepied /maʀʃəpje/ *nm* (de
train, camion) step.

marcher /maʀʃe/ [1] *vi* walk; (poser
le pied) tread (**sur** on); (aller) go;
(fonctionner) work, run; (prospérer) go
well; (*film, livre*) do well; (consentir
🄙) agree; **faire ~ qn** 🄙 pull sb's leg.

mardi /maʀdi/ *nm* Tuesday; **M~
gras** Shrove Tuesday.

mare /maʀ/ *nf* (étang) pond; (flaque)
pool.

marécage /maʀekaʒ/ *nm* marsh;
(sous les tropiques) swamp.

maréchal (*pl* **-aux**) /maʀeʃal, -o/
nm field marshal.

maréchal-ferrant (*pl* **-aux-
ferrants** /maʀeʃalferɑ̃/ *nm*
blacksmith.

marée /maʀe/ *nf* tide; (poissons) fresh
fish; **~ haute/basse** high/low tide; **~
noire** oil slick.

marelle /maʀɛl/ *nf* hopscotch.

margarine /maʀgaʀin/ *nf*
margarine.

marge /maʀʒ/ *nf* margin; **en ~ de** (à
l'écart de) on the fringe(s) of; **~
bénéficiaire** profit margin.

marginal, ~e (*mpl* **-aux**) /maʀʒinal,
-o/ *adj* marginal. ● *nm, f* drop-out.

marguerite /maʀgəʀit/ *nf* daisy;
(qui imprime) daisy-wheel.

mari /maʀi/ *nm* husband.

mariage /maʀjaʒ/ *nm* marriage;
(cérémonie) wedding.

marié, ~e /maʀje/ *adj* married.
● *nm, f* (bride)groom, bride; **les ~s**
the bride and groom.

marier /maʀje/ [45] *vt* marry. □ **se
~** *vpr* get married, marry; **se ~
avec** marry, get married to.

marin, ~e /maʀɛ̃, -in/ *adj* sea. ● *nm*
sailor.

marine /maʀin/ *nf* navy; **~
marchande** merchant navy. ● *a inv*
navy (blue).

marionnette /maʀjɔnɛt/ *nf* puppet;
(à fils) marionette.

maritalement /maʀitalmɑ̃/ *adv*
(*vivre*) as husband and wife.

maritime /maʀitim/ *adj* maritime,
coastal; (*agent, compagnie*) shipping.

marmaille /maʀmaj/ *nf* 🄙 brats.

marmelade /maʀməlad/ *nf* stewed
fruit; **~ d'oranges** (orange)
marmalade.

marmite /maʀmit/ *nf* (cooking-)pot.

marmonner /maʀmɔne/ [1] *vt*
mumble.

marmot /maʀmo/ *nm* 🄙 kid.

Maroc /maʀɔk/ *nm* Morocco.

maroquinerie /maʀɔkinʀi/ *nf*
(magasin) leather goods shop.

marquant, ~e /maʀkɑ̃, -t/ *adj*
(remarquable) outstanding; (qu'on
n'oublie pas) memorable.

marque /maʀk/ *nf* mark; (de produits)
brand, make; (décompte) score; **à vos
~s!** (Sport) on your marks!; **de ~**
(Comm) brand name; (fig) important;
~ de fabrique trademark; **~ déposée**
registered trademark.

marquer /maʀke/ [1] *vt* mark;
(indiquer) show, say; (écrire) note down;
(*point, but*) score; (*joueur*) mark;
(influencer) leave its mark on; (exprimer)
(*volonté, sentiment*) show. ● *vi* (laisser
une trace) leave a mark; (*événement*)
stand out; (Sport) score.

marquis, ~e /maʀki, -z/ *nm, f*
marquis, marchioness.

marraine /maʀɛn/ *nf* godmother.

marrant, ~e /maʀɑ̃, -t/ *adj* 🄙
funny.

marre /maʀ/ *adv* **en avoir ~** 🄙 be
fed up (**de** with).

marrer (se) /(sə)maʀe/ [1] *vpr* 🄙
laugh, have a (good) laugh.

marron /maʀɔ̃/ *nm* chestnut; (couleur)
brown; (coup 🄙) thump; **~ d'Inde**
horse chestnut. ● *a inv* brown.

mars /maRs/ nm March.

marteau (pl ~x) /maRto/ nm
hammer; ~ (de porte) (door)
knocker; ~ piqueur ou pneumatique
pneumatic drill; être ~ 🄵 be mad.

marteler /maRtəle/ [6] vt hammer;
(poings, talons) pound; (scander) rap
out.

martial, ~e (mpl -iaux) /maRsjal,
-jo/ adj military; (art) martial.

martien, ~ne /maRsjɛ̃, -ɛn/ a & nm,
f Martian.

martyr, ~e /maRtiR/ nm, f martyr.
● adj martyred; (enfant) battered.

martyre /maRtiR/ nm (Relig)
martyrdom; (fig) agony, suffering.

martyriser /maRtiRize/ [1] vt (Relig)
martyr; (torturer) torture; (enfant)
batter.

marxisme /maRksism/ nm
Marxism. **marxiste** a & nmf
Marxist.

masculin, ~e /maskylɛ̃, -in/ adj
masculine; (sexe) male; (mode,
équipe) men's. ● nm masculine.

masochisme /mazoʃism/ nm
masochism.

masochiste /mazoʃist/ nmf
masochist. ● adj masochistic.

masque /mask/ nm mask; ~ de
beauté face pack. **masquer** [1] vt
(cacher) hide, conceal (à from);
(lumière) block (off).

massacre /masakR/ nm massacre.
massacrer [1] vt massacre; (abîmer
🄵) ruin.

massage /masaʒ/ nm massage.

masse /mas/ nf (volume) mass; (gros
morceau) lump, mass; (outil) sledge-
hammer; en ~ (vendre) in bulk;
(venir) in force; produire en ~ mass-
produce; la ~ (foule) the masses; une
~ de 🄵 masses of; la ~ de the
majority of.

masser /mase/ [1] vt (assembler)
assemble; (pétrir) massage. □ se ~
vpr (gens, foule) mass.

massif, -ive /masif, -v/ adj massive;
(or, argent) solid. ● nm (de fleurs)
clump; (parterre) bed; (Géog) massif.
massivement adv (en masse) in
large numbers.

massue /masy/ nf club, bludgeon.

mastic /mastik/ nm putty; (pour
trous) filler.

mastiquer /mastike/ [1] vt (mâcher)
chew.

mat /mat/ adj (couleur) matt; (bruit)
dull; (teint) olive; être ~ (aux échecs)
be in checkmate.

mât /mɑ/ nm mast; (pylône) pole; ~
de drapeau flagpole.

match /matʃ/ nm match; (US) game;
faire ~ nul tie, draw; ~ aller first
leg; ~ retour return match.

matelas /matla/ nm mattress; ~
pneumatique air bed.

matelassé, ~e /matlase/ adj
padded; (tissu) quilted.

matelot /matlo/ nm sailor.

mater /mate/ [1] vt (révolte) put
down; (personne) bring into line.

matérialiser (se) /(sə)
mateRjalize/ [1] vpr materialize.

matérialiste /mateRjalist/ adj
materialistic. ● nmf materialist.

matériau (pl ~x) /mateRjo/ nm
material.

matériel, ~le /mateRjɛl/ adj
material. ● nm equipment,
materials; ~ informatique hardware.

maternel, ~le /matɛRnɛl/ adj
maternal; (comme d'une mère)
motherly. **maternelle** nf nursery
school.

maternité /matɛRnite/ nf maternity
hospital; (état de mère) motherhood;
de ~ maternity.

mathématicien, ~ne
/matematisjɛ̃, -ɛn/ nm, f
mathematician.

mathématique /matematik/ adj
mathematical. **mathématiques**
nfpl mathematics (+ sg).

maths /mat/ nfpl 🄵 maths (+ sg).

matière /matjɛR/ nf matter; (produit)
material; (sujet) subject; en ~ de as
regards; ~ plastique plastic; ~s
grasses fat content; ~s premières
raw materials.

matin /matɛ̃/ nm morning; de bon ~
early in the morning.

matinal, ~e (mpl -aux) /matinal,
-o/ adj morning; (de bonne heure)
early; être ~ be up early; (d'habitude)
be an early riser.

matinée /matine/ *nf* morning;
(spectacle) matinée.

matou /matu/ *nm* tomcat.

matraque /matʀak/ *nf* (de police)
truncheon; (US) billy (club).
matraquer [1] *vt* club, beat;
(*produit, chanson*) plug.

matrimonial, **~e** (*mpl* **-iaux**)
/matʀimɔnjal, -jo/ *adj* matrimonial;
agence ~e marriage bureau.

maturité /matyʀite/ *nf* maturity.

maudire /modiʀ/ [41] *vt* curse.

maudit, **~e** /modi, -t/ *adj* 🔳
blasted, damned.

maugréer /mogʀee/ [15] *vi*
grumble.

mausolée /mozɔle/ *nm* mausoleum.

maussade /mosad/ *adj* gloomy.

mauvais, **~e** /mɔvɛ, -z/ *adj* bad;
(erroné) wrong; (malveillant) evil;
(désagréable) nasty, bad; (mer) rough;
le ~ moment the wrong time; **~e
herbe** weed; **~e langue** gossip; **~e
passe** tight spot; **~ traitements** ill-
treatment. ● *adv* (sentir) bad; **il fait
~** the weather is bad. ● *nm* **le bon et
le ~** the good and the bad.

mauve /mov/ *a & nm* mauve.

mauviette /movjɛt/ *nf* weakling,
wimp.

maux /mo/ ⇨ MAL².

maximal, **~e** (*mpl* **-aux**)
/maksimal, -o/ *adj* maximum.

maxime /maksim/ *nf* maxim.

maximum /maksimɔm/ *adj*
maximum. ● *nm* maximum; **au ~ as**
much as possible; (tout au plus) at
most; **faire le ~** do one's utmost.

mazout /mazut/ *nm* (fuel) oil.

me, **m'** /mə, m/ *pron* me; (indirect) (to)
me; (réfléchi) myself.

méandre /meɑ̃dʀ/ *nm* meander.

mec /mek/ *nm* 🔳 bloke, guy.

mécanicien, **~ne** /mekanisjɛ̃,
-jɛn/ *nm, f* mechanic. ● *nm* train
driver.

mécanique /mekanik/ *adj*
mechanical; (jouet) clockwork;
problème ~ engine trouble. ● *nf*
mechanics (+ *sg*); (mécanisme)
mechanism. **mécaniser** [1] *vt*
mechanize.

mécanisme /mekanism/ *nm*
mechanism.

méchamment /meʃamɑ̃/ *adv*
spitefully. **méchanceté** *nf*
nastiness; (action) wicked action.

méchant, **~e** /meʃɑ̃, -t/ *adj* (cruel)
wicked; (désagréable, grave) nasty;
(enfant) naughty; (chien) vicious;
(sensationnel 🔳) terrific. ● *nm, f* (enfant)
naughty child.

mèche /mɛʃ/ *nf* (de cheveux) lock; (de
bougie) wick; (d'explosif) fuse; (outil)
drill bit; **de ~ avec** in league with.

méconnaissable /mekɔnɛsabl/
adj unrecognizable.

méconnaître /mekɔnɛtʀ/ [18] *vt*
misunderstand, misread; (mésestimer)
underestimate.

méconnu, **~e** /mekɔny/ *adj*
unrecognized; (artiste) neglected.

mécontent, **~e** /mekɔ̃tɑ̃, -t/ *adj*
dissatisfied (**de** with); (irrité) annoyed
(**de** at, with). **mécontentement**
nm dissatisfaction; annoyance.
mécontenter [1] *vt* dissatisfy;
(irriter) annoy.

médaille /medaj/ *nf* medal; (insigne)
badge; (bijou) medallion. **médaillé**,
~e *nm, f* medallist.

médaillon /medajɔ̃/ *nm* medallion;
(bijou) locket.

médecin /medsɛ̃/ *nm* doctor.

médecine /medsin/ *nf* medicine.

média /medja/ *nm* medium; **les ~s**
the media.

médiateur, **-trice** /medjatœʀ,
-tʀis/ *nm, f* mediator.

médiatique /medjatik/ *adj*
(événement, personnalité) media.

médical, **~e** (*mpl* **-aux**) /medikal,
-o/ *adj* medical.

médicament /medikamɑ̃/ *nm*
medicine, drug.

médico-légal, **~e** (*mpl* **-aux**)
/medikɔlegal, -o/ *adj* forensic.

médiéval, **~e** (*mpl* **-aux**)
/medjeval, -o/ *adj* medieval.

médiocre /medjɔkʀ/ *adj* mediocre,
poor. **médiocrité** *nf* mediocrity.

médire /mediʀ/ [37] *vi* **~ de** speak
ill of, malign.

médisance /medizɑ̃s/ *nf* **~(s)**
malicious gossip.

méditer /medite/ [1] *vi* meditate (**sur** on). ● *vt* contemplate; (*paroles, conseils*) mull over; ~ **de** plan to.

Méditerranée /mediterane/ *nf* la ~ the Mediterranean.

méditerranéen, ~**ne** /mediteraneɛ̃, -ɛn/ *adj* Mediterranean.

médium /medjɔm/ *nm* (personne) medium.

méduse /medyz/ *nf* jellyfish.

meeting /mitiŋ/ *nm* meeting.

méfait /mefɛ/ *nm* misdeed; **les** ~**s de** (conséquences) the ravages of.

méfiance /mefjɑ̃s/ *nf* suspicion, distrust. **méfiant**, ~**e** *adj* suspicious, distrustful.

méfier (se) /(sə)mefje/ [45] *vpr* be wary *ou* careful; **se** ~ **de** distrust, be wary of.

mégaoctet /megaɔkte/ *nm* (Ordinat) megabyte.

mégère /meʒɛr/ *nf* (femme) shrew.

mégot /mego/ *nm* cigarette end.

meilleur, ~**e** /mɛjœr/ *adj* (comparatif) better (**que** than); (superlatif) best; **le** ~ **livre** the best book; **mon** ~ **ami** my best friend; ~ **marché** cheaper. ● *nm, f* **le** ~, **la** ~**e** the best (one). ● *adv* (sentir) better; **il fait** ~ the weather is better.

mél /mel/ *nm* e-mail; **envoyer un** ~ send an e-mail.

mélancolie /melɑ̃kɔli/ *nf* melancholy.

mélange /melɑ̃ʒ/ *nm* mixture, blend.

mélanger /melɑ̃ʒe/ [40] *vt* mix; (*thés, parfums*) blend. □ **se** ~ *vpr* mix; (*thés, parfums*) blend; (*idées*) get mixed up.

mélasse /melas/ *nf* black treacle; (US) molasses.

mêlée /mele/ *nf* free for all; (au rugby) scrum.

mêler /mele/ [1] *vt* mix (**à** with); (*qualités*) combine; (embrouiller) mix up; ~ **qn à** (impliquer dans) involve sb in. □ **se** ~ *vpr* mix; combine; **se** ~ **à** (se joindre à) mingle with; (participer à) join in; **se** ~ **de** meddle in; **mêle-toi de ce qui te regarde** mind your own business.

méli-mélo (*pl* **mélis-mélos**) /melimelo/ *nm* jumble.

mélo /melo/ 🔲 *nm* melodrama. ● *a inv* slushy, schmaltzy 🔲.

mélodie /melɔdi/ *nf* melody.

mélodieux, **-ieuse** *adj* melodious.

mélodique *adj* melodic.

mélodramatique /melɔdramatik/ *adj* melodramatic. **mélodrame** *nm* melodrama.

mélomane /melɔman/ *nmf* music lover.

melon /məlɔ̃/ *nm* melon; (chapeau) ~ bowler (hat).

membrane /mɑ̃bran/ *nf* membrane.

membre /mɑ̃br/ *nm* (Anat) limb; (adhérent) member.

même /mɛm/ *adj* same; **ce livre** ~ this very book; **la bonté** ~ kindness itself; **en** ~ **temps** at the same time. ● *pron* **le** ~, **la** ~ the same (one). ● *adv* even; **à** ~ (sur) directly on; **à** ~ **de** in a position to; **de** ~ (aussi) too; (de la même façon) likewise; **de** ~ **que** just as; ~**si** even if.

mémé /meme/ *nf* 🔲 granny.

mémo /memo/ *nm* note, memo.

mémoire /memwar/ *nm* (rapport) memorandum; (Univ) dissertation; ~**s** (souvenirs écrits) memoirs. ● *nf* memory; **à la** ~ **de** to the memory of; **de** ~ from memory; ~ **morte/vive** (Ordinat) ROM/RAM.

mémorable /memɔrabl/ *adj* memorable.

menace /mənas/ *nf* threat. **menacer** [10] *vt* threaten (**de faire** to do).

ménage /menaʒ/ *nm* (couple) couple; (travail) housework; (famille) household; **se mettre en** ~ set up house.

ménagement /menaʒmɑ̃/ *nm* **avec** ~**s** gently; **sans** ~**s** (dire) bluntly; (jeter, pousser) roughly.

ménager[1], **-ère** /menaʒe, -ɛr/ *adj* household, domestic; **travaux** ~**s** housework.

ménager[2] /menaʒe/ [40] *vt* be gentle with, handle carefully; (utiliser) be careful with; (organiser) prepare (carefully); **ne pas** ~ **ses efforts** spare no effort.

ménagère /menaʒɛʀ/ *nf* housewife.

ménagerie /menaʒʀi/ *nf*
menagerie.

mendiant, ∼e /mɑ̃djɑ̃, -t/ *nm,f*
beggar.

mendier /mɑ̃dje/ [45] *vt* beg for. ● *vi*
beg.

mener /məne/ [6] *vt* lead; (*entreprise,
pays*) run; (*étude, enquête*) carry out;
(*politique*) pursue; ∼ **à** (accompagner
à) take to; (faire aboutir) lead to; ∼ **à
bien** see through. ● *vi* lead.

méningite /menɛ̃ʒit/ *nf* meningitis.

menotte /mənɔt/ *nf* 🔲 hand; ∼s
handcuffs.

mensonge /mɑ̃sɔ̃ʒ/ *nm* lie; (action)
lying. **mensonger, -ère** *adj*
untrue, false.

mensualité /mɑ̃sɥalite/ *nf*
monthly payment.

mensuel, ∼le /mɑ̃sɥɛl/ *adj*
monthly. ● *nm* monthly (magazine).
mensuellement *adv* monthly.

mensurations /mɑ̃syʀasjɔ̃/ *nfpl*
measurements.

mental, ∼e (*mpl* -**aux**) /mɑ̃tal, -o/
adj mental; **malade** ∼ mentally ill
person; **handicapé** ∼ mentally
handicapped person.

mentalité /mɑ̃talite/ *nf* mentality.

menteur, -**euse** /mɑ̃tœʀ, -øz/ *nm,f*
liar. ● *adj* untruthful.

menthe /mɑ̃t/ *nf* mint.

mention /mɑ̃sjɔ̃/ *nf* mention;
(annotation) note; (Scol) grade; **rayer la**
∼ **inutile** delete as appropriate.
mentionner [1] *vt* mention.

mentir /mɑ̃tiʀ/ [46] *vi* lie.

menton /mɑ̃tɔ̃/ *nm* chin.

menu, ∼e /məny/ *adj* (petit) tiny; (fin)
fine; (insignifiant) minor. ● *adv* (*couper*)
fine. ● *nm* (carte) menu; (repas) meal;
(Ordinat) menu; ∼ **déroulant** pull-
down menu.

menuiserie /mənɥizʀi/ *nf*
carpentry, joinery. **menuisier** *nm*
carpenter, joiner.

méprendre (se) /(sə)mepʀɑ̃dʀ/
[50] *vpr* se ∼ **sur** be mistaken about.

mépris /mepʀi/ *nm* contempt, scorn
(de for); **au** ∼ **de** regardless of.

méprisable /mepʀizabl/ *adj*
contemptible, despicable.

méprise /mepʀiz/ *nf* mistake.

méprisant, ∼e /mepʀizɑ̃, -t/ *adj*
scornful. **mépriser** [1] *vt* scorn,
despise.

mer /mɛʀ/ *nf* sea; (marée) tide; **en
pleine** ∼ out at sea.

mercenaire /mɛʀsənɛʀ/ *nm & a*
mercenary.

mercerie /mɛʀs(ə)ʀi/ *nf*
haberdashery; (US) notions store.
mercier, -ière *nm,f* haberdasher;
(US) notions seller.

merci /mɛʀsi/ *interj* thank you,
thanks (**de, pour** for); ∼ **beaucoup,**
∼ **bien** thank you very much. ● *nm*
thank you. ● *nf* mercy.

mercredi /mɛʀkʀədi/ *nm*
Wednesday; ∼ **des Cendres** Ash
Wednesday.

merde /mɛʀd/ *nf* 🗙 shit 🗙.

mère /mɛʀ/ *nf* mother; ∼ **de famille**
mother.

méridional, ∼e (*mpl* -**aux**)
/meʀidjɔnal, -o/ *adj* southern.
● *nm,f* Southerner.

mérite /meʀit/ *nm* merit; **avoir du** ∼
à faire deserve credit for doing.

mériter /meʀite/ [1] *vt* deserve; ∼
d'être lu be worth reading.

méritoire /meʀitwaʀ/ *adj*
commendable.

merlan /mɛʀlɑ̃/ *nm* whiting.

merle /mɛʀl/ *nm* blackbird.

merveille /mɛʀvɛj/ *nf* wonder,
marvel; **à** ∼ wonderfully; **faire des**
∼s work wonders.

merveilleux, -euse /mɛʀvɛjø, -z/
adj wonderful, marvellous.

mes /me/ ⇒MON.

mésange /mezɑ̃ʒ/ *nf* tit(mouse).

mésaventure /mezavɑ̃tyʀ/ *nf*
misadventure; **par** ∼ by some
misfortune.

mesdames /medam/ ⇒MADAME.

mesdemoiselles /medmwazɛl/
⇒MADEMOISELLE.

mésentente /mezɑ̃tɑ̃t/ *nf*
disagreement.

mesquin, ∼e /mɛskɛ̃, -in/ *adj*
mean-minded, petty; (chiche) mean.
mesquinerie *nf* meanness.

mess /mɛs/ *nm* (Mil) mess.

message /mesaʒ/ *nm* message; **un ~ électronique** an e-mail.

messager, -ère /mesaze, -ɛʁ/ *nm, f* messenger. ● *nm* **~ de poche** pager.

messagerie /mesaʒʁi/ *nf* (transports) freight forwarding; (télécommunications) messaging; **~ électronique** electronic mail; **~ vocale** voice mail.

messe /mɛs/ *nf* (Relig) mass.

messieurs /mesjø/ ⇒MONSIEUR.

mesure /məzyʁ/ *nf* measurement; (quantité, unité) measure; (disposition) measure, step; (cadence) time; **en ~** in time; (modération) moderation; **à ~ que** as; **dans la ~ où** in so far as; **dans une certaine ~** to some extent; **en ~ de** in a position to; **sans ~** to excess; (fait) **sur ~** made-to-measure.

mesuré, ~e /məzyʁe/ *adj* measured; (attitude) moderate.

mesurer /məzyʁe/ [1] *vt* measure; (juger) assess; (argent, temps) ration. ● *vi* **~ 15 mètres de long** be 15 metres long. □ **se ~ avec** *vpr* pit oneself against.

met /mɛ/ ⇒METTRE [42].

métal (*pl* **-aux**) /metal, -o/ *nm* metal. **métallique** *adj* (objet) metal; (éclat) metallic.

métallurgie /metalyʁʒi/ *nf* (industrie) metalworking industry.

métamorphoser /metamɔʁfoze/ [1] *vt* transform. □ **se ~** *vpr* be transformed; **se ~ en** metamorphose into.

métaphore /metafɔʁ/ *nf* metaphor.

météo /meteo/ *nf* (bulletin) weather forecast.

météore /meteɔʁ/ *nm* meteor.

météorologie /meteɔʁɔlɔʒi/ *nf* meteorology.

météorologique /meteɔʁɔlɔʒik/ *adj* meteorological; **conditions ~s** weather conditions.

méthode /metɔd/ *nf* method; (ouvrage) course, manual. **méthodique** *adj* methodical.

méticuleux, -euse /metikylø, -z/ *adj* meticulous.

métier /metje/ *nm* job; (manuel) trade; (intellectuel) profession; (expérience) experience, skill; **~ (à**

tisser) loom; **remettre qch sur le ~** rework sth.

métis, ~se /metis/ *adj* mixed race. ● *nm, f* person of mixed race.

métrage /metʁaʒ/ *nm* length; **court ~** short (film); **long ~** feature-length film.

mètre /mɛtʁ/ *nm* metre; (règle) rule; **~ ruban** tape-measure.

métreur, -euse /metʁœʁ, -øz/ *nm, f* quantity surveyor.

métrique /metʁik/ *adj* metric.

métro /metʁo/ *nm* underground; (US) subway.

métropole /metʁɔpɔl/ *nf* metropolis; (pays) mother country. **métropolitain, ~e** *adj* metropolitan.

mets /mɛ/ *nm* dish. ● ⇒METTRE [42].

mettable /metabl/ *adj* wearable.

metteur /metœʁ/ *nm* **~ en scène** director.

mettre /mɛtʁ/ [42] *vt* put; (radio, chauffage) put *ou* switch on; (réveil) set; (installer) put in; (revêtir) put on; (porter habituellement) (vêtement, lunettes) wear; (prendre) take; (investir, dépenser) put; (écrire) write, say; **elle a mis deux heures** it took her two hours; **~ la table** lay the table; **~ en question** question; **~ en valeur** highlight; (terrain) develop; **mettons que** let's suppose that. ● *vi* **~ bas** (animal) give birth. □ **se ~** *vpr* (vêtement, maquillage) put on; (se placer) (objet) go; (personne) (debout) stand; (assis) sit; (couché) lie; **se ~ en short** put shorts on; **se ~ debout** stand up; **se ~ au lit** go to bed; **se ~ à table** sit down at table; **se ~ en ligne** line up; **se ~ du sable dans les yeux** get sand in one's eyes; **se ~ au chinois/ tennis** take up Chinese/tennis; **se ~ au travail** set to work; **se ~ à faire** start to do.

meuble /mœbl/ *nm* piece of furniture; **~s** furniture.

meublé /møble/ *nm* furnished flat.

meubler /møble/ [1] *vt* furnish; (fig) fill. □ **se ~** *vpr* buy furniture.

meugler /møgle/ [1] *vi* moo.

meule /møl/ *nf* millstone; **~ de foin** haystack.

meunier, -ière /mønje, -jɛʀ/ *nm,f* miller.

meurs, meurt /mœʀ/ ⇒MOURIR [43].

meurtre /mœʀtʀ/ *nm* murder.

meurtrier, -ière /mœʀtʀije, -jɛʀ/ *adj* deadly. ● *nm,f* murderer, murderess.

meurtrir /mœʀtʀiʀ/ [2] *vt* bruise.

meute /møt/ *nf* pack of hounds.

Mexique /mɛksik/ *nm* Mexico.

mi- /mi/ *préf* mid-, half-; **à mi-chemin** half-way; **à mi-pente** half-way up the hill; **à la mi-juin** in mid-June.

miauler /mjole/ [1] *vi* miaow.

micro /mikʀo/ *nm* microphone, mike; (Ordinat) micro.

microbe /mikʀɔb/ *nm* germ.

microfilm /mikʀofilm/ *nm* microfilm.

micro-onde /mikʀɔɔ̃d/ *nf* microwave; **un four à ~s** microwave (oven). **micro-ondes** *nm inv* microwave (oven).

micro-ordinateur (*pl* ~s) /mikʀɔɔʀdinatœʀ/ *nm* personal computer.

microphone /mikʀofɔn/ *nm* microphone.

microprocesseur /mikʀɔpʀɔsɛsœʀ/ *nm* microprocessor.

microscope /mikʀɔskɔp/ *nm* microscope.

midi /midi/ *nm* twelve o'clock, midday, noon; (déjeuner) lunch-time; (sud) south. **Midi** *nm* **le M~** the South of France.

mie /mi/ *nf* soft part (of the loaf); **un pain de ~** a sandwich loaf.

miel /mjɛl/ *nm* honey.

mielleux, -euse /mjɛlø, -z/ *adj* unctuous.

mien, ~ne /mjɛ̃, -ɛn/ *pron* **le ~, la ~ne, les ~(ne)s** mine.

miette /mjɛt/ *nf* crumb; (fig) scrap; **en ~s** in pieces.

mieux /mjø/ *a inv* better (**que** than); **le** *ou* **la** *ou* **les ~** (the) best. ● *nm* best; (progrès) improvement; **faire de son ~** do one's best; **le ~ serait de** the best thing would be to. ● *adv* better; **le** *ou* **la** *ou* **les ~** (**de deux**) the better; (de plusieurs) the best; **elle va**

~ she is better; **j'aime ~ rester** I'd rather stay; **il vaudrait ~ partir** it would be best to leave; **tu ferais ~ de faire** you would be best to do.

mièvre /mjɛvʀ/ *adj* insipid.

mignon, ~ne /miɲɔ̃, -ɔn/ *adj* cute; (gentil) kind.

migraine /migʀɛn/ *nf* headache; (plus fort) migraine.

migration /migʀasjɔ̃/ *nf* migration.

mijoter /miʒɔte/ [1] *vt/i* simmer; (tramer 🗓) cook up.

mil /mil/ *nm* a thousand.

milice /milis/ *nf* militia.

milieu (*pl* ~x) /miljø/ *nm* middle; (environnement) environment; (appartenance sociale) background; (groupe) circle; (voie) middle way; (criminel) underworld; **au ~ de** in the middle of; **en plein** *ou* **au beau ~ de** right in the middle (of).

militaire /militɛʀ/ *adj* military. ● *nm* soldier, serviceman.

militant, ~e /militɑ̃, -t/ *nm,f* militant.

militer /milite/ [1] *vi* be a militant; **~ pour** militate in favour of.

mille¹ /mil/ *a & nm inv* a thousand; **deux ~** two thousand; **mettre dans le ~** (fig) hit the nail on the head.

mille² /mil/ *nm* **~ (marin)** (nautical) mile.

millénaire /milenɛʀ/ *nm* millennium. ● *adj* a thousand years old.

mille-pattes /milpat/ *nm inv* centipede.

millésime /milezim/ *nm* date; (de vin) vintage.

millet /mijɛ/ *nm* millet.

milliard /miljaʀ/ *nm* thousand million, billion. **milliardaire** *nmf* multimillionaire.

millième /miljɛm/ *a & nmf* thousandth.

millier /milje/ *nm* thousand; **un ~ (de)** about a thousand.

millimètre /milimɛtʀ/ *nm* millimetre.

million /miljɔ̃/ *nm* million; **deux ~s (de)** two million. **millionnaire** *nmf* millionaire.

mime /mim/ *nmf* mime-artist. ● *nm*
(art) mime. **mimer** [1] *vt* mime;
(imiter) mimic.

mimique /mimik/ *nf* expressions
and gestures.

minable /minabl/ *adj* ▣ (*logement*)
shabby; (*médiocre*) pathetic, crummy.

minauder /minode/ [1] *vi* simper.

mince /mɛ̃s/ *adj* thin; (svelte) slim;
(faible) (*espoir, majorité*) slim. ● *interj*
▣ blast ▣, darn it ▣. **minceur** *nf*
thinness; slimness.

mincir /mɛ̃siʀ/ [2] *vi* get slimmer; **ça
te mincit** it makes you look slimmer.

mine /min/ *nf* expression; (allure)
appearance; **avoir bonne ~** look
well; **faire ~ de** make as if to;
(exploitation, explosif) mine; (de crayon)
lead; **~ de charbon** coal-mine.

miner /mine/ [1] *vt* (saper)
undermine; (garnir d'explosifs) mine.

minerai /minʀe/ *nm* ore.

minéral, **~e** (*mpl* **-aux**) /mineʀal,
-o/ *adj* mineral. ● *nm* (*pl* **-aux**)
mineral.

minéralogique /mineʀalɔʒik/ *adj*
plaque ~ numberplate; (US) license
plate.

minet, **~te** /mine, -t/ *nm,f* (chat ▣)
pussy(cat).

mineur, **~e** /minœʀ/ *adj* minor;
(Jur) under age. ● *nm,f* (Jur) minor.
● *nm* (ouvrier) miner.

miniature /minjatyʀ/ *nf & a*
miniature.

minier, **-ière** /minje, -jɛʀ/ *adj*
mining.

minimal, **~e** (*mpl* **-aux**)
/minimal,o/ *adj* minimal, minimum.

minime /minim/ *adj* minimal,
minor. ● *nmf* (Sport) junior.

minimum /minimɔm/ *adj*
minimum. ● *nm* minimum; **au ~**
(pour le moins) at the very least; **en
faire un ~** do as little as possible.

ministère /ministɛʀ/ *nm* ministry;
(gouvernement) government; **~ public**
public prosecutor's office.
ministériel, **~le** *adj* ministerial,
government.

ministre /ministʀ/ *nm* minister; (au
Royaume-Uni) Secretary of State; (US)
Secretary.

Minitel® /minitɛl/ *nm* Minitel
(*telephone videotext system*).

minorer /minɔʀe/ [1] *vt* reduce.

minoritaire /minɔʀitɛʀ/ *adj*
minority; **être ~** be in the minority.
minorité *nf* minority.

minuit /minɥi/ *nm* midnight.

minuscule /minyskyl/ *adj* minute.
● *nf* (lettre) **~** lower case.

minute /minyt/ *nf* minute; **'talons
~'** 'heels repaired while you wait'.

minuterie /minytʀi/ *nf* time-switch.

minutie /minysi/ *nf* meticulousness.

minutieux, **-ieuse** /minysjø, -z/
adj meticulous.

mioche /mjɔʃ/ *nm,f* ▣ kid.

mirabelle /miʀabɛl/ *nf* (mirabelle)
plum.

miracle /miʀakl/ *nm* miracle; **par ~**
miraculously.

miraculeux, **-euse** /miʀakylø, -z/
adj miraculous.

mirage /miʀaʒ/ *nm* mirage.

mire /miʀ/ *nf* (fig) centre of
attraction; (TV) test card.

mirobolant, **~e** /miʀɔbɔlɑ̃, -t/ *adj*
▣ marvellous.

miroir /miʀwaʀ/ *nm* mirror.

miroiter /miʀwate/ [1] *vi* shimmer,
sparkle.

mis, **~e** /mi, miz/ *adj* **bien ~** well-
dressed. ● ⇒METTRE [42].

mise /miz/ *nf* (argent) stake; (tenue)
attire; **~ à feu** blast-off; **~ au point**
adjustment; (fig) clarification; **~ de
fonds** capital outlay; **~ en garde**
warning; **~ en plis** set; **~ en scène**
direction.

miser /mize/ [1] *vt* (argent) bet, stake
(sur on). ● *vi* **~ sur** (parier) place a
bet on; (compter sur) bank on.

misérable /mizeʀabl/ *adj*
miserable, wretched; (indigent)
destitute; (minable) seedy, squalid.

misère /mizɛʀ/ *nf* destitution;
(malheur) trouble, woe. **miséreux**,
-euse *nm,f* destitute person.

miséricorde /mizeʀikɔʀd/ *nf*
mercy.

missel /misɛl/ *nm* missal.

missile /misil/ *nm* missile.

mission /misjɔ̃/ *nm* mission.
missionnaire *nmf* missionary.

missive /misiv/ *nf* missive.

mistral /mistral/ *nm* (vent) mistral.

mitaine /mitɛn/ *nf* fingerless mitt.

mite /mit/ *nf* (clothes-)moth.

mi-temps /mitɑ̃/ *nf inv* (arrêt) half-time; (période) half. ● *nm inv* part-time work; à ~ part-time.

miteux, -euse /mitø, -z/ *adj* shabby.

mitigé, ~e /mitiʒe/ *adj* (modéré) lukewarm; (succès) qualified.

mitonner /mitɔne/ [1] *vt* cook slowly with care; (fig) cook up.

mitoyen, ~ne /mitwajɛ̃, -ɛn/ *adj* mur ~ party wall.

mitrailler /mitraje/ [1] *vt* machine-gun; (fig) bombard.

mitraillette /mitrajɛt/ *nf* submachine gun. **mitrailleuse** *nf* machine gun.

mi-voix: à ~ /amivwa/ *loc* in a low voice.

mixeur /miksœr/ *nm* liquidizer, blender; (batteur) mixer.

mixte /mikst/ *adj* mixed; (commission) joint; (école) coeducational; (peau) combination.

mobile /mɔbil/ *adj* mobile; (pièce) moving; (feuillet) loose. ● *nm* (art) mobile; (raison) motive.

mobilier /mɔbilje/ *nm* furniture.

mobilisation /mɔbilizasjɔ̃/ *nf* mobilization. **mobiliser** [1] *vt* mobilize.

mobilité /mɔbilite/ *nf* mobility.

mobylette® /mɔbilɛt/ *nf* moped.

moche /mɔʃ/ *adj* 🅸 (laid) ugly; (mauvais) lousy.

modalités /mɔdalite/ *nfpl* (conditions) terms; (façon de fonctionner) practical details.

mode /mɔd/ *nf* fashion; (coutume) custom; à la ~ fashionable. ● *nm* method, mode; (genre) way; ~ d'emploi directions (for use).

modèle /mɔdɛl/ *adj* model. ● *nm* model; (exemple) example; (Comm) (type) model; (taille) size; (style) style; ~ familial family size; ~ réduit (small-scale) model.

modeler /mɔdle/ [6] *vt* model (sur on). □ se ~ sur *vpr* model oneself on.

modem /mɔdɛm/ *nm* modem.

modérateur, -trice /mɔderatœr, -tris/ *adj* moderating. **modération** *nf* moderation.

modéré, ~e /mɔdere/ *a & nm, f* moderate.

modérer /mɔdere/ [14] *vt* (propos) moderate; (désirs, sentiments) curb. □ se ~ *vpr* restrain oneself.

moderne /mɔdɛrn/ *adj* modern. **moderniser** [1] *vt* modernize.

modeste /mɔdɛst/ *adj* modest. **modestie** *nf* modesty.

modification /mɔdifikasjɔ̃/ *nf* modification.

modifier /mɔdifje/ [45] *vt* change, modify. □ se ~ *vpr* change, alter.

modique /mɔdik/ *adj* modest.

modiste /mɔdist/ *nf* milliner.

moduler /mɔdyle/ [1] *vt* modulate; (adapter) adjust.

moelle /mwal/ *nf* marrow; ~ épinière spinal cord; ~ osseuse bone marrow.

moelleux, -euse /mwalø, -z/ *adj* soft; (onctueux) smooth.

mœurs /mœr(s)/ *nfpl* (morale) morals; (usages) customs; (manières) habits, ways.

moi /mwa/ *pron* me; (indirect) (to) me; (sujet) I. ● *nm* self.

moignon /mwaɲɔ̃/ *nm* stump.

moi-même /mwamɛm/ *pron* myself.

moindre /mwɛ̃dr/ *adj* (moins grand) lesser; le *ou* la ~, les ~s the slightest, the least.

moine /mwan/ *nm* monk.

moineau (*pl* ~x) /mwano/ *nm* sparrow.

moins /mwɛ̃/ *prép* minus; (pour dire l'heure) to; une heure ~ dix ten to one. ● *adv* less (que than); le *ou* la *ou* les ~ the least; le ~ grand/haut the smallest/lowest; ~ de (avec un nom non dénombrable) less (que than); ~ de dix francs less than ten francs; ~ de livres fewer books; au ~, du ~ at least; à ~ que unless; de ~ less; de ~ en ~ less and less; en ~ less; (manquant) missing.

mois /mwa/ *nm* month.

moisi, ~e /mwazi/ *adj* mouldy.
● *nm* mould; **de ~** (*odeur*) musty.

moisir [2] *vi* go mouldy.

moisissure *nf* mould.

moisson /mwasɔ̃/ *nf* harvest.

moissonner /mwasɔne/ [1] *vt* harvest, reap. **moissonneur, -euse** *nm,f* harvester.

moite /mwat/ *adj* sticky, clammy.

moitié /mwatje/ *nf* half; (milieu) halfway mark; **s'arrêter à la ~** stop halfway through; **à ~ vide** half empty; **à ~ prix** (at) half-price; **la ~ de** half (of). **moitié-moitié** *adv* half-and-half.

mol /mɔl/ ⇨MOU.

molaire /mɔlɛʀ/ *nf* molar.

molécule /mɔlekyl/ *nf* molecule.

molester /mɔlɛste/ [1] *vt* manhandle, rough up.

molle /mɔl/ ⇨MOU.

mollement /mɔlmɑ̃/ *adv* softly; (faiblement) feebly. **mollesse** *nf* softness; (faiblesse) feebleness; (apathie) listlessness.

mollet /mɔlɛ/ *nm* (de jambe) calf.

mollir /mɔliʀ/ [2] *vi* soften; (céder) yield.

môme /mom/ *nmf* 🄵 kid.

moment /mɔmɑ̃/ *nm* moment; (période) time; **(petit) ~** short while; **au ~ où** when; **par ~s** now and then; **du ~ où** *ou* **que** (pourvu que) as long as, provided that; (puisque) since; **en ce ~** at the moment.

momentané, ~e /mɔmɑ̃tane/ *adj* momentary. **momentanément** *adv* momentarily; (en ce moment) at present.

momie /mɔmi/ *nf* mummy.

mon, ma (**mon** *before vowel or mute h*) (*pl* **mes**) /mɔ̃, ma, mɔ̃, me/ *adj* my.

Monaco /mɔnako/ *npr* Monaco.

monarchie /mɔnaʀʃi/ *nf* monarchy.

monarque /mɔnaʀk/ *nm* monarch.

monastère /mɔnastɛʀ/ *nm* monastery.

monceau (*pl* **~x**) /mɔ̃so/ *nm* heap, pile.

mondain, ~e /mɔ̃dɛ̃, -ɛn/ *adj* society, social.

monde /mɔ̃d/ *nm* world; **du ~** (a lot of) people; (quelqu'un) somebody; **le (grand) ~** (high) society; **se faire (tout) un ~ de qch** make a great deal of fuss about sth; **pas le moins du ~** not in the least.

mondial, ~e (*mpl* **-iaux**) /mɔ̃djal, -jo/ *adj* world; (*influence*) worldwide. **mondialement** *adv* the world over.

monétaire /mɔnetɛʀ/ *adj* monetary.

moniteur, -trice /mɔnitœʀ, -tʀis/ *nm,f* instructor; (de colonie de vacances) group leader; (US) (camp) counselor.

monnaie /mɔnɛ/ *nf* currency; (pièce) coin; (appoint) change; **faire la ~ de** get change for; **faire de la ~ à qn** give sb change; **menue** *ou* **petite ~** small change.

monnayer /mɔneje/ [31] *vt* convert into cash.

mono /mɔno/ *a inv* mono.

monologue /mɔnɔlɔg/ *nm* monologue.

monopole /mɔnɔpɔl/ *nm* monopoly. **monopoliser** [1] *vt* monopolize.

monospace /mɔnɔspas/ *nm* (Auto) people carrier.

monotone /mɔnɔtɔn/ *adj* monotonous. **monotonie** *nf* monotony.

Monseigneur (*pl* **Messeigneurs**) /mɔ̃sɛɲœʀ/ *nm* (à un duc, archevêque) Your Grace; (à un prince) Your Highness.

monsieur (*pl* **messieurs**) /məsjø, mesjø/ *nm* (à un inconnu) (dans une lettre) **M~** Dear Sir; **bonjour, ~** good morning; **~** (high) society; **mesdames et messieurs** ladies and gentlemen; (à un homme dont on connaît le nom) (dans une lettre) **Cher M~** Dear Mr X; **bonjour, ~** good morning Mr X; **M~ le curé** Father X; **oui M~ le ministre** yes Minister; (homme) man; (formule de respect) sir.

monstre /mɔ̃stʀ/ *nm* monster. ● *adj* 🄵 colossal.

monstrueux, -euse /mɔ̃stʀyø, -z/ *adj* monstrous. **monstruosité** *nf* monstrosity.

mont /mɔ̃/ *nm* mountain; **le ~ Everest** Mount Everest; **être toujours par ~s et par vaux** be always on the move.

montage /mɔ̃taʒ/ *nm* (assemblage) assembly; (au cinéma) editing.

montagne /mɔ̃taɲ/ *nf* mountain; (région) mountains; **~s russes** roller-coaster. **montagneux, -euse** *adj* mountainous.

montant, ~e /mɔ̃tɑ̃, -t/ *adj* rising; (col) high; (chemin) uphill. ● *nm* amount; (pièce de bois) upright.

mont-de-piété (*pl* **monts-de-piété**) /mɔ̃dpjete/ *nm* pawnshop.

monte-charge /mɔ̃tʃaʒ/ *nm inv* goods lift.

montée /mɔ̃te/ *nf* ascent, climb; (de prix) rise; (de coûts, risques) increase; (côte) hill.

monter /mɔ̃te/ [1] *vt* (aux. avoir) take up; (à l'étage) take upstairs; (escalier, rue, pente) go up; (assembler) assemble; (tente, échafaudage) put up; (col, manche) set in; (organiser) (pièce) stage; (société) set up; (attaque, garde) mount. ● *vi* (aux. être) go *ou* come up; (à l'étage) go *ou* come upstairs; (avion) climb; (route) go uphill, climb; (augmenter) rise; (marée) come up; **~ sur** (trottoir, toit) get up on; (cheval, bicyclette) get on; **~ à l'échelle/l'arbre** climb the ladder/tree; **~ dans** (voiture) get in; (train, bus, avion) get on; **~ à bord** climb on board; **~ (à cheval)** ride; **~ à bicyclette/moto** ride a bike/motorbike.

monteur, -euse /mɔ̃tœʀ, -øz/ *nm,f* (Tech) fitter; (au cinéma) editor.

montre /mɔ̃tʀ/ *nf* watch; **faire ~ de** show.

montrer /mɔ̃tʀe/ [1] *vt* show (à to); **~ du doigt** point to. □ **se ~** *vpr* show oneself; (être) be; (s'avérer) prove to be.

monture /mɔ̃tyʀ/ *nf* (cheval) mount; (de lunettes) frames (+ *pl*); (de bijou) setting.

monument /mɔnymɑ̃/ *nm* monument; **~ aux morts** war memorial. **monumental** (*mpl* **-aux**) *adj* monumental.

moquer (se) /(sə)mɔke/ [1] *vpr* **se ~ de** make fun of; **je m'en moque** 🄳 I couldn't care less. **moquerie** *nf* mockery. **moqueur, -euse** *adj* mocking.

moquette /mɔkɛt/ *nf* fitted carpet; (US) wall-to-wall carpeting.

moral, ~e (*mpl* **-aux**) /mɔʀal, -o/ *adj* moral. ● *nm* (*pl* **-aux**) morale; **ne pas avoir le ~** feel down; **avoir le ~** be in good spirits; **ça m'a remonté le ~** it gave me a boost.

morale /mɔʀal/ *nf* moral code; (mœurs) morals; (de fable) moral; **faire la ~ à** lecture. **moralité** *nf* (de personne) morals (+ *pl*); (d'action, œuvre) morality; (de fable) moral.

moralisateur, -trice /mɔʀalizatœʀ, -tʀis/ *adj* moralizing.

morbide /mɔʀbid/ *adj* morbid.

morceau (*pl* **~x**) /mɔʀso/ *nm* piece, bit; (de sucre) lump; (de viande) cut; (passage) passage; **manger un ~** 🄳 have a bite to eat; **mettre en ~x** smash *ou* tear to bits.

morceler /mɔʀsəle/ [6] *vt* divide up.

mordant, ~e /mɔʀdɑ̃, -t/ *adj* scathing; (froid) biting. ● *nm* vigour, energy.

mordiller /mɔʀdije/ [1] *vt* nibble at.

mordre /mɔʀdʀ/ [3] *vi* bite (dans into); **~ sur** (ligne) go over; (territoire) encroach on; **~ à l'hameçon** bite. ● *vt* bite.

mordu, ~e /mɔʀdy/ 🄳 *nm,f* fan. ● *adj* smitten; **~ de** crazy about.

morfondre (se) /(sə)mɔʀfɔ̃dʀ/ [3] *vpr* wait anxiously; (languir) mope.

morgue /mɔʀg/ *nf* morgue, mortuary; (attitude) arrogance.

moribond, ~e /mɔʀibɔ̃, -d/ *adj* dying.

morne /mɔʀn/ *adj* dull.

morphine /mɔʀfin/ *nf* morphine.

mors /mɔʀ/ *nm* (de cheval) bit.

morse /mɔʀs/ *nm* (animal) walrus; (code) Morse code.

morsure /mɔʀsyʀ/ *nf* bite.

mort¹ /mɔʀ/ *nf* death.

mort², ~e /mɔʀ, -t/ *adj* dead; **~ de fatigue** dead tired. ● *nm,f* dead man, dead woman; **les ~s** the dead.

mortalité /mɔʀtalite/ *nf* mortality; (taux de) ~ death rate.

mortel, **~le** /mɔʀtɛl/ *adj* mortal; (*accident*) fatal; (*poison, silence*) deadly. ● *nm, f* mortal.
mortellement *adv* mortally.

mortifié, **~e** /mɔʀtifje/ *adj* mortified.

mort-né, **~e** /mɔʀne/ *adj* stillborn.

mortuaire /mɔʀtɥɛʀ/ *adj* (*cérémonie*) funeral.

morue /mɔʀy/ *nf* cod.

mosaïque /mɔzaik/ *nf* mosaic.

mosquée /mɔske/ *nf* mosque.

mot /mo/ *nm* word; (lettre, message) note; ~ **d'ordre** watchword; ~ **de passe** password; **~s croisés** crossword (puzzle).

motard /mɔtaʀ/ *nm* biker; (policier) police motorcyclist.

moteur, **-trice** /mɔtœʀ, -tʀis/ *adj* (Méd) motor; (*force*) driving; **à 4 roues motrices** 4-wheel drive. ● *nm* engine, motor; **barque à ~** motor launch; ~ **de recherche** (Internet) search engine.

motif /mɔtif/ *nm* (raisons) grounds (+ *pl*); (*cause*) reason; (Jur) motive; (dessin) pattern.

motion /mɔsjɔ̃/ *nf* motion.

motivation /mɔtivasjɔ̃/ *nf* motivation. **motiver** [1] *vt* motivate.

moto /mɔto/ *nf* motor cycle.
motocycliste *nmf* motorcyclist.

motorisé, **~e** /mɔtɔʀize/ *adj* motorized.

motrice /mɔtʀis/ *nf* ⇒MOTEUR.

motte /mɔt/ *nf* lump; (de beurre) slab; (de terre) clod; ~ **de gazon** turf.

mou (**mol** *before vowel or mute h*), **molle** /mu, mɔl/ *adj* soft; (*ventre*) flabby; (sans conviction) feeble; (apathique) sluggish, listless. ● *nm* slack; **avoir du ~** be slack.

mouchard, **~e** /muʃaʀ, -d/ *nm, f* informer; (Scol) sneak.

mouche /muʃ/ *nf* fly; (de cible) bull's eye.

moucher (**se**) /(sə)muʃe/ [1] *vpr* blow one's nose.

moucheron /muʃʀɔ̃/ *nm* midge.

moucheté, **~e** /muʃte/ *adj* speckled.

mouchoir /muʃwaʀ/ *nm* handkerchief, hanky; ~ **en papier** tissue.

moue /mu/ *nf* pout; **faire la ~** pout.

mouette /mwɛt/ *nf* (sea)gull.

moufle /mufl/ *nf* (gant) mitten.

mouillé, **~e** /muje/ *adj* wet.

mouiller /muje/ [1] *vt* wet, make wet; ~ **l'ancre** drop anchor. □ **se ~** *vpr* get (oneself) wet.

moulage /mulaʒ/ *nm* cast.

moule /mul/ *nf* (coquillage) mussel. ● *nm* mould; ~ **à gâteau** cake tin; ~ **à tarte** flan dish. **mouler** [1] *vt* mould; (*statue*) cast.

moulin /mulɛ̃/ *nm* mill; ~ **à café** coffee grinder; ~ **à poivre** pepper mill; ~ **à vent** windmill.

moulinet /mulinɛ/ *nm* (de canne à pêche) reel; **faire des ~s avec qch** twirl sth around.

moulinette® /mulinɛt/ *nf* vegetable mill.

moulu, **~e** /muly/ *adj* ground; (fatigué 🆃) worn out.

moulure /mulyʀ/ *nf* moulding.

mourant, **-e** /muʀɑ̃, -t/ *adj* dying. ● *nm, f* dying person.

mourir /muʀiʀ/ [43] *vi* (aux. être) die; ~ **d'envie de** be dying to; ~ **de faim** be starving; ~ **d'ennui** be dead bored.

mousquetaire /muskətɛʀ/ *nm* musketeer.

mousse /mus/ *nf* moss; (écume) froth, foam; (de savon) lather; (dessert) mousse; ~ **à raser** shaving foam. ● *nm* ship's boy.

mousseline /muslin/ *nf* muslin; (de soie) chiffon.

mousser /muse/ [1] *vi* froth, foam; (*savon*) lather.

mousseux, **-euse** /musø, -z/ *adj* frothy. ● *nm* sparkling wine.

mousson /musɔ̃/ *nf* monsoon.

moustache /mustaʃ/ *nf* moustache; **~s** (d'animal) whiskers.

moustique /mustik/ *nm* mosquito.

moutarde /mutaʀd/ *nf* mustard.

mouton /mutɔ̃/ *nm* sheep; (peau) sheepskin; (viande) mutton.

mouvant, ~e /muvɑ̃, -t/ *adj*
changing; (*terrain*) shifting,
unstable.

mouvement /muvmɑ̃/ *nm*
movement; (agitation) bustle; (en
gymnastique) exercise; (impulsion)
impulse; (tendance) tend, tendency; **en**
~ in motion.

mouvementé, ~e /muvmɑ̃te/ *adj*
eventful.

moyen, ~ne /mwajɛ̃, -ɛn/ *adj*
average; (médiocre) poor; **de taille
moyenne** medium-sized. ● *nm*
means, way; ~s means; (dons)
ability; **au** ~ **de** by means of; **il n'y a
pas** ~ **de** it is not possible to.
Moyen Âge *nm* Middle Ages (+ *pl*).

moyennant /mwajɛnɑ̃/ *prép* (pour)
for; (grâce à) with.

moyenne /mwajɛn/ *nf* average;
(Scol) pass-mark; **en** ~ on average; ~
d'âge average age. **moyennement**
adv moderately.

Moyen-Orient /mwajɛnɔrjɑ̃/ *nm*
Middle East.

moyeu (*pl* ~**x**) /mwajø/ *nm* hub.

mû, **mue** /my/ *adj* driven (**par** by).

mucoviscidose /mykɔvisidoz/ *nf*
cystic fibrosis.

mue /my/ *nf* moulting; (de voix)
breaking of the voice.

muer /mɥe/ [1] *vi* moult; (*voix*)
break. □ **se** ~ **en** *vpr* change into.

muet, ~**te** /mɥɛ, -t/ *adj* (Méd) dumb;
(fig) speechless (**de** with); (silencieux)
silent. ● *nm*, *f* mute.

mufle /myfl/ *nm* nose, muzzle;
(personne Ⓘ) boor, lout.

mugir /myʒir/ [2] *vi* (*vache*) moo;
(*bœuf*) bellow; (fig) howl.

muguet /mygɛ/ *nm* lily of the
valley.

mule /myl/ *nf* (female) mule;
(pantoufle) mule.

mulet /mylɛ/ *nm* (male) mule.

multicolore /myltikɔlɔr/ *adj*
multicoloured.

multimédia /myltimedja/ *a & nm*
multimedia.

multinational, ~e (*mpl* -**aux**)
/myltinasjɔnal, -o/ *adj*
multinational. **multinationale** *nf*
multinational (company).

multiple /myltipl/ *nm* multiple.
● *adj* numerous, many; (naissances)
multiple.

multiplication /myltiplikasjɔ̃/ *nf*
multiplication.

multiplicité /myltiplisite/ *nf*
multiplicity.

multiplier /myltiplije/ [45] *vt*
multiply; (*risques*) increase. □ **se** ~
vpr multiply; (*accidents*) be on the
increase; (*difficultés*) increase.

multitude /myltityd/ *nf* multitude,
mass.

municipal, ~e (*mpl* -**aux**)
/mynisipal, -o/ *adj* municipal;
conseil ~ town council.

municipalité *nf* (ville) municipality;
(conseil) town council.

munir /mynir/ [2] *vt* ~ **de** provide
with. □ **se** ~ **de** *vpr* (apporter) bring;
(emporter) take.

munitions /mynisjɔ̃/ *nfpl*
ammunition.

mur /myr/ *nm* wall; ~ **du son** sound
barrier.

mûr, ~**e** /myr/ *adj* ripe; (*personne*)
mature.

muraille /myrɑj/ *nf* (high) wall.

mural, ~**e** (*mpl* -**aux**) /myral, -o/
adj wall; **peinture** ~**e** mural.

mûre /myr/ *nf* blackberry.

mûrir /myrir/ [2] *vi* ripen; (*abcès*)
come to a head; (*personne*, *projet*)
mature. ● *vt* (*fruit*) ripen; (*personne*)
mature.

murmure /myrmyr/ *nm* murmur.

musc /mysk/ *nm* musk.

muscade /myskad/ *nf* **noix** ~
nutmeg.

muscle /myskl/ *nm* muscle.
musclé, ~**e** *adj* muscular.
musculaire *adj* muscular.

musculation /myskylasjɔ̃/ *nf*
bodybuilding.

musculature /myskylatyr/ *nf*
muscles (+ *pl*).

museau (*pl* ~**x**) /myzo/ *nm* muzzle;
(de porc) snout.

musée /myze/ *nm* museum; (de
peinture) art gallery.

muselière /myzəljɛr/ *nf* muzzle.

musette /myzɛt/ *nf* haversack.

muséum /myzeɔm/ *nm* natural history museum.

musical, ~e (*mpl* -aux) /myzikal, -o/ *adj* musical.

musicien, ~ne /myzisjɛ̃, -ɛn/ *adj* musical. ● *nm, f* musician.

musique /myzik/ *nf* music; (orchestre) band.

musulman, ~e /myzylmɑ̃, -an/ *a* & *nm,f* Muslim.

mutation /mytasjɔ̃/ *nf* change; (biologique) mutation; (d'un employé) transfer.

muter /myte/ [1] *vt* transfer. ● *vi* mutate.

mutilation /mytilasjɔ̃/ *nf* mutilation. **mutiler** [1] *vt* mutilate. **mutilé**, ~e *nm, f* disabled person.

mutin, ~e /mytɛ̃, -in/ *adj* mischievous. ● *nm* mutineer; (prisonnier) rioter.

mutinerie /mytinʀi/ *nf* mutiny; (de prisonniers) riot.

mutisme /mytism/ *nm* silence.

mutuel, ~le /mytɥɛl/ *adj* mutual. **mutuelle** *nf* mutual insurance company. **mutuellement** *adv* mutually; (l'un l'autre) each other.

myope /mjɔp/ *adj* short-sighted. **myopie** *nf* short-sightedness.

myosotis /mjozɔtis/ *nm* forget-me-not.

myrtille /miʀtij/ *nf* bilberry, blueberry.

mystère /mistɛʀ/ *nm* mystery.

mystérieux, -ieuse /misteʀjø, -z/ *adj* mysterious.

mystification /mistifikasjɔ̃/ *nf* hoax.

mysticisme /mistisism/ *nm* mysticism.

mystique /mistik/ *adj* mystic(al). ● *nmf* mystic. ● *nf* mystique.

mythe /mit/ *nm* myth. **mythique** *adj* mythical.

mythologie /mitɔlɔʒi/ *nf* mythology.

Nn

n' /n/ ⇒NE.

nacre /nakʀ/ *nf* mother-of-pearl.

nage /naʒ/ *nf* swimming; (manière), stroke; **traverser à la** ~ swim across; **en** ~ sweating.

nageoire /naʒwaʀ/ *nf* fin; (de mammifère) flipper.

nager /naʒe/ [40] *vt/i* swim. **nageur**, -euse *nm, f* swimmer.

naguère /nagɛʀ/ *adv* (autrefois) formerly.

naïf, -ive /naif, -v/ *adj* naïve.

nain, ~e /nɛ̃, nɛn/ *nm,f* & *a* dwarf.

naissance /nɛsɑ̃s/ *nf* birth; **donner** ~ **à** give birth to; (fig) give rise to.

naître /nɛtʀ/ [44] *vi* be born; (résulter) arise (**de** from); **faire** ~ (susciter) give rise to.

naïveté /naivte/ *nf* naïvety.

nappe /nap/ *nf* tablecloth; (de pétrole, gaz) layer; ~ **phréatique** ground water.

napperon /napʀɔ̃/ *nm* (cloth) tablemat.

narco-dollars /naʀkodɔlaʀ/ *nmpl* drug money.

narcotique /naʀkɔtik/ *a* & *nm* narcotic. **narco(-)trafiquant**, ~e (*pl* ~s) *nm,f* drug trafficker.

narguer /narge/ [1] *vt* taunt; (*autorité*) flout.

narine /naʀin/ *nf* nostril.

nasal, ~e (*mpl* -aux) /nazal, -o/ *adj* nasal.

naseau (*pl* ~x) /nazo/ *nm* nostril.

natal, ~e (*mpl* ~s) /natal/ *adj* native.

natalité /natalite/ *nf* birth rate.

natation /natasjɔ̃/ *nf* swimming.

natif, -ive /natif, -v/ *adj* native.

nation /nasjɔ̃/ *nf* nation.

national, ~e (*mpl* -aux) /nasjonal, -o/ *adj* national. **nationale** *nf* A road; (US) highway. **nationaliser** [1] *vt* nationalize.

nationalité /nasjɔnalite/ *nf* nationality.

natte /nat/ *nf* (de cheveux) plait; (US) braid; (tapis de paille) mat.

nature /natyʀ/ *nf* nature; ~ **morte** still life; **de** ~ **à** likely to; **payer en** ~ pay in kind. ● *a inv* plain; (yaourt) natural; (thé) black.

naturel, ~**le** /natyʀɛl/ *adj* natural. ● *nm* nature; (simplicité) naturalness; (Culin) **au** ~ plain; (thon) in brine. **naturellement** *adv* naturally; (bien sûr) of course.

naufrage /nofʀaʒ/ *nm* shipwreck; **faire** ~ be shipwrecked; (bateau) be wrecked.

nauséabond, ~**e** /nozeabɔ̃, -d/ *adj* nauseating.

nausée /noze/ *nf* nausea.

nautique /notik/ *adj* nautical; **sports** ~**s** water sports.

naval, ~**e** (*mpl* ~**s**) /naval/ *adj* naval; **chantier** ~ shipyard.

navet /navɛ/ *nm* turnip; (film: péj) flop; (US) turkey.

navette /navɛt/ *nf* shuttle (service); **faire la** ~ shuttle back and forth.

navigateur, **-trice** /navigatœʀ, -tʀis/ *nm, f* sailor; (qui guide) navigator; (Internet) browser. **navigation** *nf* navigation; (trafic) shipping; (Internet) browsing.

naviguer /navige/ [1] *vi* sail; (piloter) navigate; (Internet) browse; ~ **dans l'Internet** surf the Internet.

navire /naviʀ/ *nm* ship.

navré, ~**e** /navʀe/ *adj* sorry (de to).

ne, **n'** /nə, n/

n' before vowel or mute h.

● *adverbe*

····▶ **je n'ai que 10 francs** I've only got 10 francs.

····▶ **tu n'avais qu'à le dire!** you only had to say so!

····▶ **je crains qu'il** ~ **parte** I am afraid he will leave.

! Pour les expressions comme **ne… guère, ne… jamais, ne…**
■ **pas, ne… plus**, etc. ⇒**guère, jamais, pas, plus**, etc.

né, ~**e** /ne/ *adj* born; ~**e Martin** née Martin; (dans composés) **dernier-**~ last-born. ● ⇒NAÎTRE [44].

néanmoins /neãmwɛ̃/ *adv* nevertheless.

néant /neã/ *nm* nothingness; **réduire à** ~ (effet, efforts) negate, nullify; (espoir) dash; '**revenus:** ~' 'income: nil'.

nécessaire /neseseʀ/ *adj* necessary. ● *nm* (sac) bag; (trousse) kit; **le** ~ (l'indispensable) the necessities *ou* essentials; **faire le** ~ do what is necessary.

nécessité /nesesite/ *nf* necessity; **de première** ~ vital.

nécessiter /nesesite/ [1] *vt* necessitate.

néerlandais, ~**e** /neeʀlãdɛ, -z/ *adj* Dutch. ● *nm* (Ling) Dutch. **N**~, ~**e** *nm, f* Dutchman, Dutchwoman.

néfaste /nefast/ *adj* harmful (à to).

négatif, **-ive** /negatif, -v/ *a & nm* negative.

négligé, ~**e** /negliʒe/ *adj* (travail) careless; (tenue) scruffy. ● *nm* (tenue) negligee.

négligent, ~**e** /negliʒã, -t/ *adj* careless, negligent.

négliger /negliʒe/ [40] *vt* neglect; (ne pas tenir compte de) ignore, disregard; ~ **de faire** fail to do. □ **se** ~ *vpr* neglect oneself.

négoce /negɔs/ *nm* business, trade. **négociant**, ~**e** *nm, f* merchant.

négociation /negɔsjasjɔ̃/ *nf* negotiation. **négocier** [45] *vt/i* negotiate.

nègre /nɛgʀ/ *adj* (musique, art) Negro. ● *nm* (écrivain) ghost writer.

neige /nɛʒ/ *nf* snow. **neiger** [40] *vi* snow.

nénuphar /nenyfaʀ/ *nm* waterlily.

nerf /nɛʀ/ *nm* nerve; (vigueur) stamina; **être sur les** ~**s** be on edge.

nerveux, **-euse** /nɛʀvø, -z/ *adj* nervous; (irritable) nervy; (centre, cellule) nerve; (voiture) responsive.

nervosité *nf* nervousness; (irritabilité) touchiness.

net, ~te /nɛt/ *adj* (clair, distinct) clear; (propre) clean; (notable) marked; (soigné) neat; (*prix, poids*) net. ● *adv* (*s'arrêter*) dead; (*refuser*) flatly; (*parler*) plainly; (*se casser*) cleanly; (*tuer*) outright. **nettement** *adv* (*expliquer*) clearly; (*augmenter, se détériorer*) markedly; (indiscutablement) distinctly, decidedly. **netteté** *nf* clearness.

nettoyage /nɛtwajaʒ/ *nm* cleaning; **~ à sec** dry-cleaning; **produit de ~** cleaner.

nettoyer /nɛtwaje/ [31] *vt* clean.

neuf¹ /nœf/ (/nœv/ *before vowels and mute h*) *a inv* & *nm* nine.

neuf², -euve /nœf, -v/ *adj* new; **tout ~** brand new. ● *nm* new; **remettre à ~** brighten up; **du ~** a new development; **quoi de ~?** what's new?

neutre /nøtʀ/ *adj* neutral; (Gram) neuter. ● *nm* (Gram) neuter.

neutron /nøtʀɔ̃/ *nm* neutron.

neuve /nœv/ ⇒NEUF².

neuvième /nœvjɛm/ *a* & *nm, f* ninth.

neveu (*pl* **~x**) /nəvø/ *nm* nephew.

névrose /nevʀoz/ *nf* neurosis. **névrosé, ~e** *a* & *nm,f* neurotic.

nez /ne/ *nm* nose; **~ à ~** face to face; **~ retroussé** turned-up nose; **avoir du ~** have flair.

ni /ni/ *conj* neither, nor; **~ grand ~ petit** neither big nor small; **~ l'un ~ l'autre ne fument** neither (one nor the other) smokes; **sortir sans manteau ~ chapeau** go without a coat or hat; **elle n'a dit ~ oui ~ non** she didn't say either yes or no.

niais, ~e /njɛ, -z/ *adj* silly.

niche /niʃ/ *nf* (de chien) kennel; (cavité) niche.

nicher /niʃe/ [1] *vi* nest. □ **se ~** *vpr* nest; (se cacher) hide.

nicotine /nikɔtin/ *nf* nicotine.

nid /ni/ *nm* nest; **faire un ~** build a nest. **nid-de-poule** (*pl* **nids-de-poule**) *nm* pot-hole.

nièce /njɛs/ *nf* niece.

nier /nje/ [45] *vt* deny.

nigaud, ~e /nigo, -d/ *nm, f* silly idiot.

nippon, ~ne /nipɔ̃, -ɔn/ *adj* Japanese. **N~, ~ne** *nm, f* Japanese.

niveau (*pl* **~x**) /nivo/ *nm* level; (compétence) standard; (étage) storey; (US) story; **au ~** up to standard; **mettre à ~** (Ordinat) upgrade; **~ à bulle** (d'air) spirit-level; **~ de vie** standard of living.

niveler /nivle/ [6] *vt* level.

noble /nɔbl/ *adj* noble. ● *nm, f* nobleman, noblewoman. **noblesse** *nf* nobility.

noce /nɔs/ *nf* (fête 🔲) party; (invités) wedding guests; **~s** wedding; **faire la ~** 🔲 live it up, party.

nocif, -ive /nɔsif, -v/ *adj* harmful.

noctambule /nɔktɑ̃byl/ *nmf* late-night reveller.

nocturne /nɔktyʀn/ *adj* nocturnal. ● *nm* (Mus) nocturne. ● *nf* (Sport) evening fixture; (de magasin) late-night opening.

Noël /nɔɛl/ *nm* Christmas.

nœud /nø/ *nm* (Naut) knot; (pour lier) knot; (pour orner) bow; **~s** (fig) ties; **~ coulant** slipknot, noose; **~ papillon** bow-tie.

noir, ~e /nwaʀ/ *adj* black; (obscur, sombre) dark; (triste) gloomy. ● *nm* black; (obscurité) dark; **travail au ~** moonlighting. ● *nm, f* (personne) Black.

noircir /nwaʀsiʀ/ [2] *vt* blacken; **~ la situation** paint a black picture of the situation. ● *vi* (banane) go black; (mur) get dirty; (métal) tarnish. □ **se ~** *vpr* (ciel) darken.

noire /nwaʀ/ *nf* (Mus) crotchet.

noisette /nwazɛt/ *nf* hazelnut; (de beurre) knob.

noix /nwa/ *nf* nut; (du noyer) walnut; (de beurre) knob; **~ de cajou** cashew nut; **~ de coco** coconut; **à la ~** 🔲 useless.

nom /nɔ̃/ *nm* name; (Gram) noun; **au ~ de** on behalf of; **~ et prénom** full name; **~ déposé** registered trademark; **~ de famille** surname; **~ de jeune fille** maiden name; **~ de plume** pen name; **~ propre** proper noun.

nomade /nɔmad/ *adj* nomadic.
● *nmf* nomad.

nombre /nɔ̃bʀ/ *nm* number; **au ~ de** (parmi) among; (l'un de) one of; **en (grand) ~** in large numbers; **sans ~** countless.

nombreux, -euse /nɔ̃bʀø, -z/ *adj* (en grand nombre) many, numerous; (important) large; **de ~ enfants** many children; **nous étions très ~** there were a great many of us.

nombril /nɔ̃bʀil/ *nm* navel.

nomination /nɔminasjɔ̃/ *nf* appointment.

nommer /nɔme/ [1] *vt* name; (élire) (à un poste) appoint; (à un lieu) post. □ **se ~** *vpr* (s'appeler) be called.

non /nɔ̃/ *adv* no; (pas) not; **~ (pas) que** not that; **il vient, ~?** he is coming, isn't he?; **moi ~ plus** neither am/do/can/*etc.* I. ● *nm inv* no.

non- /nɔ̃/ *préf* non-; **~-fumeur** non-smoker.

nonante /nɔnɑ̃t/ *a & nm* ninety.

non-sens /nɔ̃sɑ̃s/ *nm inv* absurdity.

nord /nɔʀ/ *a inv* (façade, côte) north; (frontière, zone) northern. ● *nm* north; **le ~ de l'Europe** northern Europe; **vent de ~** northerly (wind); **aller vers le ~** go north; **le Nord** the North; **du Nord** northern. **nord-est** *nm* north-east.

nordique /nɔʀdik/ *adj* Scandinavian.

nord-ouest /nɔʀwɛst/ *nm* north-west.

normal, ~e (*mpl* **-aux**) /nɔʀmal, -o/ *adj* normal. **normale** *nf* normality; (norme) norm; (moyenne) average.

normand, ~e /nɔʀmɑ̃, -d/ *adj* Norman. **N~, ~e** *nm, f* Norman.

Normandie /nɔʀmɑ̃di/ *nf* Normandy.

norme /nɔʀm/ *nf* norm; (de production) standard; **~s de sécurité** safety standards.

Norvège /nɔʀvɛʒ/ *nf* Norway.

norvégien, ~ne /nɔʀveʒjɛ̃, -ɛn/ *adj* Norwegian. **N~, ~ne** *nm, f* Norwegian.

nos /no/ ⇒NOTRE.

nostalgie /nɔstalʒi/ *nf* nostalgia; **avoir la ~ de son pays** be homesick. **nostalgique** *adj* nostalgic.

notaire /nɔtɛʀ/ *nm* notary public.

notamment /nɔtamɑ̃/ *adv* notably.

note /nɔt/ *nf* (remarque) note; (chiffrée) mark, grade; (facture) bill; (Mus) note; **~ (de service)** memorandum; **prendre ~ de** take note of.

noter /nɔte/ [1] *vt* note, notice; (écrire) note (down); (devoir) grade; (US) grade; **bien/mal noté** (employé) highly/poorly rated.

notice /nɔtis/ *nf* note; (mode d'emploi) instructions, directions.

notifier /nɔtifje/ [45] *vt* notify (à to).

notion /nosjɔ̃/ *nf* notion; **avoir des ~s de** have a basic knowledge of.

notoire /nɔtwaʀ/ *adj* well-known; (criminel) notorious.

notre (*pl* **nos**) /nɔtʀ/, /no/ *adj* our.

nôtre /notʀ/ *pron* **le** *ou* **la ~, les ~s** ours.

nouer /nwe/ [1] *vt* tie, knot; (relations) strike up.

nouille /nuj/ *nf* (Culin) noodle; **des ~s** noodles, pasta; (idiot 🆃) idiot.

nounours /nunuʀs/ *nm* 🆃 teddy bear.

nourri, ~e /nuʀi/ *adj* **être logé ~** have bed and board; **~ au sein** breastfed.

nourrice /nuʀis/ *nf* childminder.

nourrir /nuʀiʀ/ [2] *vt* feed; (espoir, crainte) harbour; (projet) nurture; (passion) fuel. ● *vi* be nourishing. □ **se ~** *vpr* eat; **se ~ de** feed on.

nourrissant, ~e *adj* nourishing.

nourrisson /nuʀisɔ̃/ *nm* infant.

nourriture /nuʀityʀ/ *nf* food.

nous /nu/ *pron* (sujet) we; (complément) us; (indirect) (to) us; (réfléchi) ourselves; (l'un l'autre) each other; **la voiture est à ~** the car is ours. **nous-mêmes** *pron* ourselves.

nouveau (**nouvel** before vowel or mute h), **nouvelle** (*mpl* **~x**) /nuvo, nuvɛl/ *adj* new; **nouvel an** new year; **~x mariés** newly-weds; **~ venu, nouvelle venue** newcomer. ● *nm, f* (élève) new boy, new girl. ● *nm* **du ~** (fait nouveau) a new development; **de ~, à ~** again. **nouveau-né** (*pl* **~s**) *nm* newborn baby.

nouveauté /nuvote/ *nf* novelty; (chose) new thing; (livre) new publication; (disque) new release.

nouvelle /nuvɛl/ *nf* (piece of) news; (récit) short story; ~s news.

Nouvelle-Zélande /nuvɛlzelɑ̃d/ *nf* New Zealand.

novembre /nɔvɑ̃bʀ/ *nm* November.

noyade /nwajad/ *nf* drowning.

noyau (*pl* ~**x**) /nwajo/ *nm* (de fruit) stone; (US) pit; (de cellule) nucleus; (groupe) group; (centre: fig) core.

noyer /nwaje/ [31] *vt* drown; (inonder) flood. □ **se** ~ *vpr* drown; (volontairement) drown oneself; **se** ~ **dans un verre d'eau** make a mountain out of a molehill. ● *nm* walnut-tree.

nu, ~**e** /ny/ *adj* (corps, personne) naked; (mains, mur, fil) bare; **à l'œil** ~ to the naked eye. ● *nm* nude; **mettre à** ~ expose.

nuage /nɥaʒ/ *nm* cloud.

nuance /nɥɑ̃s/ *nf* shade; (de sens) nuance; (différence) difference. **nuancer** [10] *vt* (opinion) qualify.

nucléaire /nykleɛʀ/ *adj* nuclear. ● *nm* **le** ~ nuclear energy.

nudisme /nydism/ *nm* nudism.

nudité /nydite/ *nf* nudity; (de lieu) bareness.

nuée /nɥe/ *nf* swarm, host.

nues /ny/ *nfpl* **tomber des** ~ be amazed; **porter qn aux** ~ praise sb to the skies.

nuire /nɥiʀ/ [17] *vi* ~ **à** harm.

nuisible /nɥizibl/ *adj* harmful (à to).

nuit /nɥi/ *nf* night; **cette** ~ tonight; (hier) last night; **il fait** ~ it is dark; ~ **blanche** sleepless night; **la** ~, **de** ~ at night; ~ **de noces** wedding night.

nul, ~**le** /nyl/ *adj* (aucun) no; (zéro) nil; (qui ne vaut rien) useless; (non valable) null; (contrat) void; (testament) invalid; **match** ~ draw; ~ **en sciences** no good at science; **nulle part** nowhere; ~ **autre** no one else. ● *pron* no one. **nullement** *adv* not at all. **nullité** *nf* uselessness; (personne) nonentity.

numérique /nymeʀik/ *adj* numerical; (montre, horloge) digital.

numéro /nymeʀo/ *nm* number; (de journal) issue; (spectacle) act; ~ **de téléphone** telephone number; ~ **vert** freephone number. **numéroter** [1] *vt* number.

nuque /nyk/ *nf* nape (of the neck).

nurse /nœʀs/ *nf* nanny.

nutritif, **-ive** /nytʀitif, -v/ *adj* nutritious; (valeur) nutritional.

oasis /ɔazis/ *nf* oasis.

obéir /ɔbeiʀ/ [2] *vt* ~ **à** obey. ● *vi* obey. **obéissance** *nf* obedience. **obéissant**, ~**e** *adj* obedient.

obèse /ɔbɛz/ *adj* obese.

objecter /ɔbʒɛkte/ [1] *vt* object.

objectif, **-ive** /ɔbʒɛktif, -v/ *adj* objective. ● *nm* objective; (Photo) lens.

objection /ɔbʒɛksjɔ̃/ *nf* objection; **soulever des** ~**s** raise objections.

objet /ɔbʒɛ/ *nm* (chose) object; (sujet) subject; (but) purpose, object; **être ou faire l'**~ **de** be the subject of; ~ **d'art** objet d'art; ~**s trouvés** lost property; (US) lost and found.

obligation /ɔbligasjɔ̃/ *nf* obligation; (Comm) bond; **être dans l'**~ **de** be under obligation to.

obligatoire /ɔbligatwaʀ/ *adj* compulsory. **obligatoirement** *adv* (par règlement) of necessity; (inévitablement) inevitably.

obligeance /ɔbliʒɑ̃s/ *nf* **avoir l'**~ **de faire** be kind enough to do.

obliger /ɔbliʒe/ [40] *vt* compel, force (à faire to do); (aider) oblige; **être obligé de** have to (**de** for).

oblique /ɔblik/ *adj* oblique; **regard** ~ sidelong glance; **en** ~ at an angle.

oblitérer /ɔblitere/ [14] *vt* (timbre) cancel.

obnubilé, ~**e** /ɔbnybile/ *adj* obsessed.

obscène /ɔpsɛn/ *adj* obscene.

obscur, ∼e /ɔpskyʀ/ *adj* dark; (confus, humble) obscure; (vague) vague.

obscurcir /ɔpskyʀsiʀ/ [2] *vt* make dark; (fig) obscure. □ **s'**∼ *vpr* (*ciel*) darken.

obscurité /ɔpskyʀite/ *nf* dark-(ness); (de passage, situation) obscurity.

obsédant, ∼e /ɔpsedã, -t/ *adj* (*problème*) nagging; (*musique, souvenir*) haunting.

obsédé, ∼e /ɔpsede/ *nm,f* ∼ (sexuel) sex maniac; ∼ **du ski/jazz** ski/jazz freak.

obséder /ɔpsede/ [14] *vt* obsess.

obsèques /ɔpsɛk/ *nfpl* funeral.

observateur, -trice /ɔpsɛʀvatœʀ, -tʀis/ *adj* observant. ● *nm,f* observer.

observation /ɔpsɛʀvasjõ/ *nf* observation; (remarque) remark, comment; (reproche) criticism; (obéissance) observance; **en** ∼ under observation.

observer /ɔpsɛʀve/ [1] *vt* (regarder) observe; (surveiller) watch, observe; (remarquer) notice, observe; **faire** ∼ **qch** point sth out (**à** to).

obsession /ɔpsesjõ/ *nf* obsession.

obstacle /ɔpstakl/ *nm* obstacle; (pour cheval) fence, jump; (pour athlète) hurdle; **faire** ∼ **à** stand in the way of, obstruct.

obstétrique /ɔpstetʀik/ *nf* obstetrics (+ *sg*).

obstiné, ∼e /ɔpstine/ *adj* stubborn, obstinate.

obstiner (**s'**) /(s)ɔpstine/ [1] *vpr* persist (**à** in).

obstruction /ɔpstʀyksjõ/ *nf* obstruction; (de conduit) blockage.

obstruer /ɔpstʀye/ [1] *vt* obstruct, block.

obtenir /ɔptəniʀ/ [58] *vt* get, obtain. **obtention** *nf* obtaining.

obus /ɔby/ *nm* shell.

occasion /ɔkazjõ/ *nf* opportunity (**de faire** of doing); (circonstance) occasion; (achat) bargain; (article non neuf) second-hand buy; **à l'**∼ sometimes; **d'**∼ second-hand. **occasionnel**, ∼**le** *adj* occasional.

occasionner /ɔkazjɔne/ [1] *vt* cause.

occident /ɔksidã/ *nm* (direction) west; **l'O**∼ the West.

occidental, ∼e (*mpl* -aux) /ɔksidãtal, -o/ *adj* western. **O**∼, ∼e (*mpl* -aux) *nm,f* westerner.

occulte /ɔkylt/ *adj* occult.

occupant, ∼e /ɔkypã, -t/ *nm,f* occupant. ● *nm* (Mil) forces of occupation.

occupation /ɔkypasjõ/ *nf* occupation.

occupé, ∼e /ɔkype/ *adj* busy; (*place, pays*) occupied; (*téléphone*) engaged, busy; (*toilettes*) engaged.

occuper /ɔkype/ [1] *vt* occupy; (*poste*) hold; (*espace, temps*) take up. □ **s'**∼ *vpr* (s'affairer) keep busy (**à faire** doing); **s'**∼ **de** (*personne, problème*) take care of; (*bureau, firme*) be in charge of; (se mêler) **occupe-toi de tes affaires** mind your own business.

occurrence: **en l'**∼ /ãlɔkyʀãs/ *loc* in this case.

océan /ɔseã/ *nm* ocean.

Océanie /ɔseani/ *nf* Oceania.

ocre /ɔkʀ/ *a inv* ochre.

octante /ɔktãt/ *adj* eighty.

octet /ɔktɛ/ *nm* byte.

octobre /ɔktɔbʀ/ *nm* October.

octogone /ɔktɔgɔn/ *nm* octagon.

octroyer /ɔktʀwaje/ [31] *vt* grant.

oculaire /ɔkylɛʀ/ *adj* **témoin** ∼ eye-witness; **troubles** ∼**s** eye trouble.

oculiste /ɔkylist/ *nmf* ophthalmologist.

odeur /ɔdœʀ/ *nf* smell.

odieux, -ieuse /ɔdjø, -z/ *adj* odious.

odorant, ∼e /ɔdɔʀã, -t/ *adj* sweet-smelling.

odorat /ɔdɔʀa/ *nm* sense of smell.

œil (*pl* **yeux**) /œj, jø/ *nm* eye; **à l'**∼ 🅵 for free; **à mes yeux** in my view; **faire de l'**∼ **à** make eyes at; **faire les gros yeux à** glare at; **ouvrir l'**∼ keep one's eyes open; ∼ **poché** black eye; **fermer les yeux** shut one's eyes; (fig) turn a blind eye.

œillères /œjɛʀ/ *nfpl* blinkers.

œillet /œjɛ/ *nm* (plante) carnation; (trou) eyelet.

œuf (*pl* ~s) /œf, ø/ *nm* egg; ~ à la coque/dur/sur le plat boiled/hard-boiled/fried egg.

œuvre /œvʀ/ *nf* (ouvrage, travail) work; ~ d'art work of art; ~ (de bienfaisance) charity; être à l'~ be at work; mettre en ~ (*réforme, moyens*) implement; mise en ~ implementation. ● *nm* (ensemble spécifié) l'~ sculpté de X the sculptures of X; l'~ entier de Beethoven the complete works of Beethoven.

œuvrer /œvʀe/ [1] *vi* work.

off /ɔf/ *a inv* voix ~ voice-over.

offense /ɔfɑ̃s/ *nf* insult.

offenser /ɔfɑ̃se/ [1] *vt* offend. □ s'~ *vpr* take offence (**de** at).

offensive /ɔfɑ̃siv/ *nf* offensive.

offert, ~e /ɔfɛʀ, -t/ ⇒OFFRIR [21].

office /ɔfis/ *nm* office; (Relig) service; (de cuisine) pantry; **faire** ~ **de** act as; **d'**~ without consultation, automatically; ~ **du tourisme** tourist information office.

officiel, ~le /ɔfisjɛl/ *adj* official. ● *nm* official.

officier /ɔfisje/ [45] *vi* (Relig) officiate. ● *nm* officer.

officieux, -**ieuse** /ɔfisjø, -z/ *adj* unofficial.

offre /ɔfʀ/ *nf* offer; (aux enchères) bid; **l'~ et la demande** supply and demand; **'~s d'emploi**' 'situations vacant'.

offrir /ɔfʀiʀ/ [21] *vt* offer (**de faire** to do); (*cadeau*) give; (acheter) buy; ~ **à boire à** (chez soi) give a drink to; (au café) buy a drink for. □ s'~ *vpr* (se proposer) offer oneself (**comme** as); (*solution*) present itself; (s'acheter) treat oneself to.

ogive /ɔʒiv/ *nf* ~ **nucléaire** nuclear warhead.

oie /wa/ *nf* goose.

oignon /ɔɲɔ̃/ *nm* (légume) onion; (de fleur) bulb.

oiseau (*pl* ~x) /wazo/ *nm* bird.

oisif, -**ive** /wazif, -v/ *adj* idle.

olive /ɔliv/ *nf & a inv* olive. **olivier** *nm* olive tree.

olympique /ɔlɛ̃pik/ *adj* Olympic.

ombrage /ɔ̃bʀaʒ/ *nm* shade; **prendre** ~ **de** take offence at. **ombragé**, ~e

adj shady. **ombrageux**, -**euse** *adj* easily offended.

ombre /ɔ̃bʀ/ *nf* (pénombre) shade; (contour) shadow; (soupçon: fig) hint, shadow; **dans l'**~ (*agir, rester*) behind the scenes; **faire de l'**~ **à qn** be in sb's light.

ombrelle /ɔ̃bʀɛl/ *nf* parasol.

omelette /ɔmlɛt/ *nf* omelette.

omettre /ɔmɛtʀ/ [42] *vt* omit, leave out.

omnibus /ɔmnibys/ *nm* stopping *ou* local train.

omoplate /ɔmɔplat/ *nf* shoulder blade.

on /ɔ̃/ *pron* (tu, vous) you; (nous) we; (ils, elles) they; (les gens) people, they; (quelqu'un) someone; (indéterminé) one, you; ~ **dit** people say, they say, it is said; ~ **m'a demandé mon avis** I was asked for my opinion.

oncle /ɔ̃kl/ *nm* uncle.

onctueux, -**euse** /ɔ̃ktɥø, -z/ *adj* smooth.

onde /ɔ̃d/ *nf* wave; ~**s courtes**/ **longues** short/long wave; **sur les** ~**s** on the air.

on-dit /ɔ̃di/ *nm inv* **les** ~ hearsay.

onduler /ɔ̃dyle/ [1] *vi* undulate; (*cheveux*) be wavy.

onéreux, -**euse** /ɔneʀø, -z/ *adj* costly.

ongle /ɔ̃gl/ *nm* (finger)nail; ~ **de pied** toenail; **se faire les** ~**s** do one's nails.

ont /ɔ̃/ ⇒AVOIR [5].

ONU *abrév f* (**Organisation des Nations unies**) UN.

onze /ɔ̃z/ *a & nm* eleven. **onzième** *a & nmf* eleventh.

OPA *abrév f* (**offre publique d'achat**) takeover bid.

opéra /ɔpeʀa/ *nm* opera; (édifice) opera house. **opéra-comique** (*pl* **opéras-comiques**) *nm* light opera.

opérateur, -**trice** /ɔpeʀatœʀ, -tʀis/ *nm, f* operator; ~ (**de prise de vue**) cameraman.

opération /ɔpeʀasjɔ̃/ *nf* operation; (Comm) deal; (calcul) calculation.

opératoire /ɔpeʀatwaʀ/ *adj* (Méd) surgical; **bloc** ~ operating suite.

opérer /ɔpere/ [14] *vt* (*personne*)
operate on; (exécuter) carry out,
make; ~ **qn d'une tumeur** operate on
sb to remove a tumour; **se faire ~**
have surgery *ou* an operation. ● *vi*
(Méd) operate; (faire effet) work. □ **s'~**
vpr (se produire) occur.

opiniâtre /ɔpinjɑtʀ/ *adj* tenacious.

opinion /ɔpinjɔ̃/ *nf* opinion.

opportuniste /ɔpɔʀtynist/ *nmf*
opportunist.

opposant, ~**e** /ɔpozɑ̃, -t/ *nm, f*
opponent.

opposé, ~**e** /ɔpoze/ *adj* (*sens, angle,
avis*) opposite; (*factions*) opposing;
(*intérêts*) conflicting; **être ~ à** be
opposed to. ● *nm* opposite; **à l'~ de**
(contrairement à) contrary to, unlike.

opposer /ɔpoze/ [1] *vt* (*objets*) place
opposite each other; (*personnes*)
match, oppose; (*contraster*) contrast;
(*résistance, argument*) put up. □ **s'~**
vpr (*personnes*) confront each other;
(*styles*) contrast; **s'~ à** oppose.

opposition /ɔpozisjɔ̃/ *nf* opposition;
par ~ à in contrast with; **entrer en ~**
avec come into conflict with; **faire ~**
à un chèque stop a cheque.

oppressant, ~**e** /ɔpʀesɑ̃, -t/ *adj*
oppressive.

opprimer /ɔpʀime/ [1] *vt* oppress.

opter /ɔpte/ [1] *vi* ~ **pour** opt for.

opticien, ~**ne** /ɔptisjɛ̃, -ɛn/ *nm, f*
optician.

optimisme /ɔptimism/ *nm*
optimism.

optimiste /ɔptimist/ *nmf* optimist.
● *adj* optimistic.

option /ɔpsjɔ̃/ *nf* option.

optique /ɔptik/ *adj* (*verre*) optical.
● *nf* (science) optics (+ *sg*); (perspective)
perspective.

or¹ /ɔʀ/ *nm* gold; **d'~** golden; **en ~**
gold; (*occasion*) golden.

or² /ɔʀ/ *conj* now, well; (indiquant une
opposition) and yet.

orage /ɔʀaʒ/ *nm* (thunder)storm.
orageux, -**euse** *adj* stormy.

oral, ~**e** (*mpl* -**aux**) /ɔʀal/ *adj*
oral. ● *nm* (*pl* -**aux**) oral.

orange /ɔʀɑ̃ʒ/ *a inv* orange; (Aut)
(*feu*) amber; (US) yellow. ● *nf*
orange. **orangeade** *nf* orangeade.
oranger *nm* orange tree.

orateur, -**trice** /ɔʀatœʀ, -tʀis/ *nm, f*
speaker.

orbite /ɔʀbit/ *nf* orbit; (d'œil) socket.

orchestre /ɔʀkɛstʀ/ *nm* orchestra;
(de jazz) band; (parterre) stalls.

ordinaire /ɔʀdinɛʀ/ *adj* ordinary;
(habituel) usual; (*qualité*) standard;
(médiocre) very average. ● *nm* **l'~** the
ordinary; (nourriture) the standard
fare; **d'~**, **à l'~** usually.
ordinairement *adv* usually.

ordinateur /ɔʀdinatœʀ/ *nm*
computer; ~ **personnel/de bureau**
personal/desktop computer; ~
portable laptop (computer); ~ **hôte**
(Internet) host.

ordonnance /ɔʀdɔnɑ̃s/ *nf* (ordre,
décret) order; (de médecin)
prescription.

ordonné, ~**e** /ɔʀdɔne/ *adj* tidy.

ordonner /ɔʀdɔne/ [1] *vt* order (**à qn**
de sb to); (agencer) arrange; (Méd)
prescribe; (*prêtre*) ordain.

ordre /ɔʀdʀ/ *nm* order; (propreté)
tidiness; **aux ~s de** qn at sb's
disposal; **avoir de l'~** be tidy; **en ~**
tidy, in order; **de premier ~** first-
rate; **d'~ officiel** of an official
nature; **l'~ du jour** (programme)
agenda; **mettre de l'~ dans** tidy up;
jusqu'à nouvel ~ until further
notice; **un ~ de grandeur** an
approximate idea.

ordure /ɔʀdyʀ/ *nf* filth; ~**s** (détritus)
rubbish; (US) garbage; ~**s**
ménagères household refuse.

oreille /ɔʀɛj/ *nf* ear.

oreiller /ɔʀeje/ *nm* pillow.

oreillons /ɔʀejɔ̃/ *nmpl* mumps.

orfèvre /ɔʀfɛvʀ/ *nm* goldsmith.

organe /ɔʀgan/ *nm* organ.

organigramme /ɔʀganigʀam/ *nm*
organization chart; (Ordinat)
flowchart.

organique /ɔʀganik/ *adj* organic.

organisateur, -**trice**
/ɔʀganizatœʀ, -tʀis/ *nm, f* organizer.

organisation /ɔʀganizasjɔ̃/ *nf*
organization.

organiser /ɔʀganize/ [1] *vt*
organize. □ **s'~** *vpr* organize oneself,
get organized.

organisme /ɔʀganism/ *nm* body,
organism.

orge /ɔʀʒ/ *nf* barley.

orgelet /ɔʀʒəlɛ/ *nm* sty.

orgue /ɔʀg/ *nm* organ; ~ de Barbarie barrel-organ. **orgues** *nfpl* organ.

orgueil /ɔʀgœj/ *nm* pride. **orgueilleux, -euse** *adj* proud.

orient /ɔʀjɑ̃/ *nm* (direction) east; **l'O~** the Orient.

oriental, ~e (*mpl* -aux) /ɔʀjɑ̃tal, -o/ *adj* eastern; (de l'Orient) oriental. **O~, ~e** (*mpl* -aux) *nm,f* Asian.

orientation /ɔʀjɑ̃tasjɔ̃/ *nf* direction; (tendance politique) leanings (+ *pl*); (de maison) aspect; (Sport) orienteering; ~ **professionnelle** careers advice; ~ **scolaire** curriculum counselling.

orienter /ɔʀjɑ̃te/ [1] *vt* position; (*personne*) direct. □ **s'~** *vpr* (se repérer) find one's bearings; **s'~ vers** turn towards.

origan /ɔʀigɑ̃/ *nm* oregano.

originaire /ɔʀiʒinɛʀ/ *adj* **être ~ de** be a native of.

original, ~e (*mpl* -aux) /ɔʀiʒinal, -o/ *adj* original; (curieux) eccentric. ● *nm* (œuvre) original. ● *nm,f* eccentric. **originalité** *nf* originality; eccentricity.

origine /ɔʀiʒin/ *nf* origin; **à l'~** originally; **d'~** (*pièce, pneu*) original; **être d'~ noble** come from a noble background.

originel, ~le /ɔʀiʒinɛl/ *adj* original.

orme /ɔʀm/ *nm* elm.

ornement /ɔʀnəmɑ̃/ *nm* ornament.

orner /ɔʀne/ [1] *vt* decorate.

orphelin, ~e /ɔʀfəlɛ̃, -in/ *nm,f* orphan. ● *adj* orphaned. **orphelinat** *nm* orphanage.

orteil /ɔʀtɛj/ *nm* toe.

orthodoxe /ɔʀtɔdɔks/ *adj* orthodox.

orthographe /ɔʀtɔgʀaf/ *nf* spelling.

ortie /ɔʀti/ *nf* nettle.

os /ɔs, o/ *nm inv* bone.

OS *abrév m* ⇒OUVRIER SPÉCIALISÉ.

osciller /ɔsile/ [1] *vi* sway; (Tech) oscillate; (hésiter) waver; (fluctuer) fluctuate.

osé, ~e /oze/ *adj* daring.

oseille /ozɛj/ *nf* (plante) sorrel.

oser /oze/ [1] *vi* dare.

osier /ozje/ *nm* wicker.

ossature /ɔsatyʀ/ *nf* skeleton, frame.

ossements /ɔsmɑ̃/ *nmpl* bones, remains.

osseux, -euse /ɔsø, -z/ *adj* bony; (Méd) bone.

otage /ɔtaʒ/ *nm* hostage.

OTAN /ɔtɑ̃/ *abrév f* (**Organisation du traité de l'Atlantique Nord**) NATO.

otarie /ɔtaʀi/ *nf* eared seal.

ôter /ote/ [1] *vt* remove (**à qn** from sb); (déduire) take away.

otite /ɔtit/ *nf* ear infection.

ou /u/ *conj* or; ~ **bien** or else; ~ (**bien**)... ~ (**bien**)... either... or...; **vous ~ moi** either you or me.

où /u/ *pron* where; (dans lequel) in which; (sur lequel) on which; (auquel) at which; **d'~** from which; (pour cette raison) hence; **par ~** through which; ~ **qu'il soit** wherever he may be; **juste au moment ~** just as; **le jour ~** the day when. ● *adv* where; **d'~?** where from?

ouate /wat/ *nf* cotton wool; (US) absorbent cotton.

oubli /ubli/ *nm* forgetfulness; (trou de mémoire) lapse of memory; (négligence) oversight; **tomber dans l'~** sink into oblivion.

oublier /ublije/ [45] *vt* forget; (omettre) leave out, forget. □ **s'~** *vpr* (*chose*) be forgotten.

ouest /wɛst/ *a inv* (*façade, côte*) west; (*frontière, zone*) western. ● *nm* west; **l'~ de l'Europe** western Europe; **vent d'~** westerly (wind); **aller vers l'~** go west; **l'O~** the West; **de l'O~** western.

oui /wi/ *adv & nm inv* yes.

ouï-dire: par ~ /paʀwidiʀ/ *loc* by hearsay.

ouïe /wi/ *nf* hearing; (de poisson) gill.

ouragan /uʀagɑ̃/ *nm* hurricane.

ourlet /uʀlɛ/ *nm* hem.

ours /uʀs/ *nm* bear; ~ **blanc** polar bear; ~ **en peluche** teddy bear.

outil /uti/ *nm* tool. **outillage** *nm* tools (+ *pl*). **outiller** [1] *vt* equip.

outrage /utʀaʒ/ *nm* (grave) insult.

outrance /utʀɑ̃s/ *nf* à ~
excessively. **outrancier, -ière** *adj*
extreme.

outre /utʀ/ *prép* besides. ● *adv*
passer ~ pay no heed; ~ **mesure**
unduly; **en** ~ in addition. **outre-**
mer *adv* overseas.

outrepasser /utʀəpase/ [1] *vt*
exceed.

outrer /utʀe/ [1] *vt* exaggerate;
(indigner) incense.

ouvert, ~e /uvɛʀ, -t/ *adj* open; (*gaz*,
radio) on. ● ⇒OUVRIR [21].

ouverture /uvɛʀtyʀ/ *nf* opening;
(Mus) overture; (Photo) aperture; ~s
(offres) overtures; ~ **d'esprit** open-
mindedness.

ouvrable /uvʀabl/ *adj* jour ~
working day; **aux heures** ~s during
business hours.

ouvrage /uvʀaʒ/ *nm* (travail, livre)
work; (couture) (piece of) needlework.

ouvre-boîtes /uvʀəbwat/ *nm inv*
tin-opener.

ouvre-bouteilles /uvʀəbutɛj/ *nm*
inv bottle-opener.

ouvreur, -euse /uvʀœʀ, -øz/ *nm,f*
usherette.

ouvrier, -ière /uvʀije, -jɛʀ/ *nm,f*
worker; ~ **qualifié/spécialisé** skilled/
unskilled worker. ● *adj* working-
class; (*conflit*) industrial; **syndicat** ~
trade union.

ouvrir /uvʀiʀ/ [21] *vt* open (up); (*gaz*,
robinet) turn *ou* switch on. ● *vi* open
(up). □ **s'**~ *vpr* open (up); **s'**~ **à qn**
open one's heart to sb.

ovaire /ɔvɛʀ/ *nm* ovary.

ovale /ɔval/ *a & nm* oval.

ovni /ɔvni/ *abrév m* (**objet volant**
non-identifié) UFO.

ovule /ɔvyl/ *nm* (à féconder) ovum;
(gynécologique) pessary.

oxygène /ɔksiʒɛn/ *nm* oxygen.

oxygéner (s') /(s)ɔksiʒene/ [14] *vpr*
get some fresh air.

ozone /ozon/ *nf* ozone; **la couche**
d'~ the ozone layer.

Pp

pacifique /pasifik/ *adj* peaceful;
(*personne*) peaceable; (Géog) Pacific.
P~ *nm* **le P~** the Pacific (Ocean).

pacotille /pakɔtij/ *nf* junk, rubbish.

pagaie /pagɛ/ *nf* paddle.

pagaille /pagaj/ *nf* 🔲 mess,
shambles (+ *sg*).

page /paʒ/ *nf* page; **mise en** ~
layout; **tourner la** ~ turn over a new
leaf; **être à la** ~ be up to date; ~
d'accueil (Internet) home page.

paie /pɛ/ *nf* pay.

paiement /pɛmɑ̃/ *nm* payment.

païen, ~ne /pajɛ̃, -ɛn/ *a & nm,f*
pagan.

paillasson /pajasɔ̃/ *nm* doormat.

paille /pɑj/ *nf* straw. ● *adj* (*cheveux*)
straw-coloured; **jaune** ~ straw
yellow.

paillette /pajɛt/ *nf* (sur robe) sequin;
(de savon) flake; **robe à** ~s sequined
dress.

pain /pɛ̃/ *nm* bread; (miche) loaf (of
bread); (de savon, cire) bar; ~ **d'épices**
gingerbread; ~ **grillé** toast.

pair, ~e /pɛʀ/ *adj* (*nombre*) even.
● *nm* (personne) peer; **aller de** ~ go
together (**avec** with); **au** ~ (*jeune*
fille) au pair. **paire** *nf* pair.

paisible /pezibl/ *adj* peaceful.

paître /pɛtʀ/ [44] *vi* graze.

paix /pɛ/ *nf* peace; **fiche-moi la** ~! 🔲
leave me alone!

Pakistan /pakistɑ̃/ *nm* Pakistan.

palace /palas/ *nm* luxury hotel.

palais /palɛ/ *nm* palace; (Anat)
palate; ~ **de Justice** law courts; ~
des sports sports stadium.

pâle /pɑl/ *adj* pale.

Palestine /palɛstin/ *nf* Palestine.

palier /palje/ *nm* (d'escalier) landing;
(étape) stage.

pâlir /pɑliʀ/ [2] *vt/i* (turn) pale.

palissade /palisad/ *nf* fence.

pallier /palje/ [45] *vt* compensate for.

palmarès /palmarɛs/ *nm* list of prize-winners.

palme /palm/ *nf* palm leaf; (de nageur) flipper. **palmé**, **~e** *adj* (*patte*) webbed.

palmier /palmje/ *nm* palm (tree).

palper /palpe/ [1] *vt* feel.

palpiter /palpite/ [1] *vi* (battre) pound; (frémir) quiver.

paludisme /palydism/ *nm* malaria.

pamplemousse /pɑ̃pləmus/ *nm* grapefruit.

panaché, **~e** /panaʃe/ *adj* (bariolé, mélangé) motley; **glace ~e** mixed-flavour ice cream. ● *nm* shandy.

pancarte /pɑ̃kart/ *nf* sign; (de manifestant) placard.

pané, **~e** /pane/ *adj* breaded.

panier /panje/ *nm* basket; (de basket-ball) basket; **mettre au ~** 🔲 throw out; **~ à salade** salad shaker; (fourgon 🔲) police van.

panique /panik/ *nf* panic. **paniquer** [1] *vi* panic.

panne /pan/ *nf* breakdown; **être en ~** have broken down; **être en ~ sèche** have run out of petrol; **~ d'électricité** *ou* **de courant** power failure.

panneau (*pl* **~x**) /pano/ *nm* sign; (publicitaire) hoarding; (de porte) panel; **~ (d'affichage)** notice board; **~ (de signalisation)** road sign.

panoplie /panɔpli/ *nf* (jouet) outfit; (gamme) range.

pansement /pɑ̃smɑ̃/ *nm* dressing; **~ adhésif** plaster. **panser** [1] *vt* (*plaie*) dress; (*personne*) dress the wound(s) of; (*cheval*) groom.

pantalon /pɑ̃talɔ̃/ *nm* trousers (+ *pl*).

panthère /pɑ̃tɛr/ *nf* panther.

pantin /pɑ̃tɛ̃/ *nm* puppet.

pantomime /pɑ̃tɔmim/ *nf* mime; (spectacle) mime show.

pantoufle /pɑ̃tufl/ *nf* slipper.

paon /pɑ̃/ *nm* peacock.

papa /papa/ *nm* dad(dy).

pape /pap/ *nm* pope.

paperasse /papras/ *nf* (péj) bumf.

papeterie /papetri/ *nf* (magasin) stationer's shop.

papier /papje/ *nm* paper; (formulaire) form; **~s (d'identité)** (identity) papers; **~ absorbant** kitchen paper; **~ aluminium** tin foil; **~ buvard** blotting paper; **~ cadeau** wrapping paper; **~ calque** tracing paper; **~ carbone** carbon paper; **~ collant** adhesive tape; **~ hygiénique** toilet paper; **~ journal** newspaper; **~ à lettres** writing paper; **~ mâché** papier mâché; **~ peint** wallpaper; **~ de verre** sandpaper.

papillon /papijɔ̃/ *nm* butterfly; (contravention 🔲) parking-ticket; **~ de nuit** moth.

papoter /papɔte/ [1] *vi* 🔲 chatter.

paquebot /pakbo/ *nm* liner.

pâquerette /pɑkrɛt/ *nf* daisy.

Pâques /pɑk/ *nfpl* & *nm* Easter.

paquet /pakɛ/ *nm* packet; (de cartes) pack; (colis) parcel; **un ~ de** (beaucoup 🔲) a mass of.

par /par/ *prép* by; (à travers) through; (motif) out of, from; (provenance) from; **commencer/finir ~ qch** begin/end with sth; **commencer/finir ~ faire** begin by/end up (by) doing; **~ an/mois** a *ou* per year/month; **~ jour** a day; **~ personne** each, per person; **~ avion** (lettre) (by) airmail; **~-ci**, **~-là** here and there; **~ contre** on the other hand; **~ ici/là** this/that way.

parachute /paraʃyt/ *nm* parachute. **parachutiste** *nmf* parachutist; (Mil) paratrooper.

parader /parade/ [1] *vi* show off.

paradis /paradi/ *nm* (Relig) heaven; (lieu idéal) paradise; **~ fiscal** tax haven.

paradoxal, **~e** (*mpl* **-aux**) /paradɔksal, -o/ *adj* paradoxical.

paraffine /parafin/ *nf* paraffin wax.

parages /paraʒ/ *nmpl* **dans les ~** around.

paragraphe /paragraf/ *nm* paragraph.

paraître /parɛtr/ [18] *vi* (se montrer) appear; (sembler) seem, appear; (*ouvrage*) be published, come out; **faire ~** (*ouvrage*) bring out; **il paraît qu'ils...** apparently they...; **oui, il paraît** so I hear.

parallèle /paʀalɛl/ *adj* parallel; (illégal) unofficial. ● *nm* parallel; **faire le ~** make a connection. ● *nf* parallel (line).

paralyser /paʀalize/ [1] *vt* paralyse. **paralysie** *nf* paralysis.

parapente /paʀapɑ̃t/ *nm* paraglider; (activité) paragliding.

parapher /paʀafe/ [1] *vi* initial; (signer) sign.

parapluie /paʀaplɥi/ *nm* umbrella.

parasite /paʀazit/ *nm* parasite; **~s** (radio) interference (+ *sg*).

parasol /paʀasɔl/ *nm* sunshade.

paratonnerre /paʀatɔnɛʀ/ *nm* lightning conductor *ou* rod.

paravent /paʀavɑ̃/ *nm* screen.

parc /paʀk/ *nm* park; (de bétail) pen; (de bébé) play-pen; (entrepôt) depot; **~ relais** park and ride; **~ de stationnement** car park.

parce que /paʀsk(ə)/ *conj* because.

parchemin /paʀʃəmɛ̃/ *nm* parchment.

parcmètre /paʀkmɛtʀ/ *nm* parking meter.

parcourir /paʀkuʀiʀ/ [20] *vt* travel *ou* go through; (*distance*) travel; (*des yeux*) glance at *ou* over.

parcours /paʀkuʀ/ *nm* route; (voyage) journey.

par-delà /paʀdəla/ *prép* beyond.

par-derrière /paʀdɛʀjɛʀ/ *adv* (*attaquer*) from behind; (*critiquer*) behind sb's back.

par-dessous /paʀdəsu/ *prép & adv* under(neath).

pardessus /paʀdəsy/ *nm* overcoat.

par-dessus /paʀdəsy/ *prép & adv* over; **~ bord** overboard; **~ le marché** Ⓕ into the bargain; **~ tout** above all.

par-devant /paʀdəvɑ̃/ *adv* (*passer*) by the front.

pardon /paʀdɔ̃/ *nm* forgiveness; (je vous demande) **~!** (I am) sorry!; (pour demander qch) excuse me.

pardonner /paʀdɔne/ [1] *vt* forgive; **~ qch à qn** forgive sb for sth.

pare-brise /paʀbʀiz/ *nm inv* windscreen.

pare-chocs /paʀʃɔk/ *nm inv* bumper.

pareil, ~le /paʀɛj/ *adj* similar (à to); (tel) such (a); **c'est ~** it's the same; **ce n'est pas ~** it's not the same thing. ● *nm, f* equal. ● *adv* Ⓕ the same.

parent, ~e /paʀɑ̃, -t/ *adj* related (de to). ● *nm, f* relative, relation; **~s** (père et mère) parents; **~ isolé** single parent; **réunion de ~s d'élèves** parents' evening.

parenté /paʀɑ̃te/ *nf* relationship.

parenthèse /paʀɑ̃tɛz/ *nf* bracket, parenthesis; (fig) digression.

parer /paʀe/ [1] *vt* (esquiver) parry; (orner) adorn. ● *vi* **~ à** deal with; **~ au plus pressé** tackle the most urgent things first.

paresse /paʀɛs/ *nf* laziness.

paresseux, -euse /paʀɛsø, -z/ *adj* lazy. ● *nm, f* lazy person.

parfait, ~e /paʀfɛ, -t/ *adj* perfect. **parfaitement** *adv* perfectly; (bien sûr) absolutely.

parfois /paʀfwa/ *adv* sometimes.

parfum /paʀfœ̃/ *nm* (senteur) scent; (substance) perfume, scent; (goût) flavour. **parfumé, ~e** *adj* fragrant; (*savon*) scented; (*thé*) flavoured.

parfumer /paʀfyme/ [1] *vt* (embaumer) scent; (*gâteau*) flavour. □ **se ~** *vpr* put on one's perfume. **parfumerie** *nf* (produits) perfumes; (boutique) perfume shop.

pari /paʀi/ *nm* bet.

Paris /paʀi/ *npr* Paris.

parisien, ~ne /paʀizjɛ̃, -ɛn/ *adj* Parisian; (banlieue) Paris. **P~, ~ne** *nm, f* Parisian.

parking /paʀkiŋ/ *nm* car park.

parlement /paʀləmɑ̃/ *nm* parliament.

parlementaire /paʀləmɑ̃tɛʀ/ *adj* parliamentary. ● *nmf* Member of Parliament.

parlementer /paʀləmɑ̃te/ [1] *vi* negotiate.

parler /paʀle/ [1] *vi* talk (à to); **~ de** talk about; **tu parles d'un avantage!** call that a benefit!; **de quoi ça parle?** what is it about? ● *vt* (*langue*) speak; (*politique, affaires*) talk. □ **se ~** *vpr* (*personnes*) talk (to each other); (*langue*) be spoken. ● *nm* speech; (dialecte) dialect.

parmi /paʀmi/ *prép* among(st).

paroi /paʀwa/ *nf* wall; ~ **rocheuse** rock face.

paroisse /paʀwas/ *nf* parish.

parole /paʀɔl/ *nf* (mot, promesse) word; (langage) speech; **demander la** ~ ask to speak; **prendre la** ~ (begin to) speak; **tenir** ~ keep one's word; **croire qn sur** ~ take sb's word for it.

parquet /paʀkɛ/ *nm* (parquet) floor; **lame de** ~ floorboard; **le** ~ (Jur) prosecution.

parrain /paʀɛ̃/ *nm* godfather; (fig) sponsor.

parsemer /paʀsəme/ [6] *vt* strew (**de** with).

part /paʀ/ *nf* share, part; **à** ~ (de côté) aside; (séparément) separate; (excepté) apart from; **d'une** ~ on the one hand; **d'autre** ~ on the other hand; (de plus) moreover; **de la** ~ **de** from; **de toutes** ~s from all sides; **de** ~ **et d'autre** on both sides; **faire** ~ **à qn** inform sb (**de** of); **faire la** ~ **des choses** make allowances; **prendre** ~ **à** take part in; (*joie, douleur*) share; **pour ma** ~ as for me.

partage /paʀtaʒ/ *nm* (division) dividing; (répartition) sharing out; **recevoir qch en** ~ be left sth in a will.

partager /paʀtaʒe/ [40] *vt* divide; (distribuer) share out; (avoir en commun) share. □ **se** ~ **qch** *vpr* share sth.

partenaire /paʀtənɛʀ/ *nmf* partner.

parterre /paʀtɛʀ/ *nm* flower-bed; (Théât) stalls.

parti /paʀti/ *nm* (Pol) party; (décision) decision; (en mariage) match; ~ **pris** bias; **prendre** ~ get involved; **prendre** ~ **pour qn** side with sb; **j'en ai pris mon** ~ I've come to terms with that.

partial, ~e (*mpl* **-iaux**) /paʀsjal, -jo/ *adj* biased.

participe /paʀtisip/ *nm* (Gram) participle.

participant, ~e /paʀtisipɑ̃, -t/ *nm,f* participant (**à** in).

participation /paʀtisipasjɔ̃/ *nf* participation; (financière) contribution; (d'un artiste) appearance.

participer /paʀtisipe/ [1] *vi* ~ **à** take part in, participate in; (*profits, frais*) share.

particule /paʀtikyl/ *nf* particle.

particulier, -ière /paʀtikylje, -jɛʀ/ *adj* (spécifique) particular; (bizarre) unusual; (privé) private; **rien de** ~ nothing special. ● *nm* private individual; **en** ~ in particular, particularly. **particulièrement** *adv* particularly.

partie /paʀti/ *nf* part; (cartes, Sport) game; (Jur) party; **une** ~ **de pêche** a fishing trip; **en** ~ partly, in part; **en grande** ~ largely; **faire** ~ **de** be part of; (adhérer à) be a member of; **faire** ~ **intégrante de** be an integral part of.

partiel, ~le /paʀsjɛl/ *adj* partial. ● *nm* (Univ) exam based on a module.

partir /paʀtiʀ/ [46] *vi* (aux être) go; (quitter un lieu) leave, go; (*tache*) come out; (*bouton*) come off; (*coup de feu*) go off; (commencer) start; ~ **pour le Brésil** leave for Brazil; ~ **du principe que** work on the assumption that; **à** ~ **de** from; **à** ~ **de maintenant** from now on.

partisan, ~e /paʀtizɑ̃, -an/ *nm,f* supporter. ● *nm* (Mil) partisan; **être** ~ **de** be in favour of.

partition /paʀtisjɔ̃/ *nf* (Mus) score.

partout /paʀtu/ *adv* everywhere; ~ **où** wherever.

paru /paʀy/ ⇒PARAÎTRE [18].

parure /paʀyʀ/ *nf* finery; (bijoux) set of jewels; (de draps) set.

parution /paʀysjɔ̃/ *nf* publication.

parvenir /paʀvəniʀ/ [58] *vi* (aux être) ~ **à** reach; ~ **à faire** manage to do; **faire** ~ send.

parvenu, ~e /paʀvəny/ *nm,f* upstart.

----

pas¹ /pɑ/

Pour les expressions comme **pas encore**, **pas mal**, etc. ⇒**encore**, **mal**, etc.

● *adverbe*

····▸ not; **ne** ~ not; **je ne sais** ~ I don't know; **je ne pense** ~ I don't think so; **il a aimé, moi** ~ he liked it, I didn't; ~ **cher/poli** cheap/impolite.

····➤ ~ **du tout** not at all; ~ **de chance!** tough luck!

····➤ **on a bien ri,** ~ **vrai?** 🔟 we had a good laugh, didn't we?

> ❗ In spoken colloquial French **ne... pas** is often shortened to **pas.** You will often hear **j'ai pas compris** instead of **je n'ai pas compris** (I didn't understand). Note that this would not be correct in written French.

pas² /pɑ/ *nm* step; (*bruit*) footstep; (*trace*) footprint; (*vitesse*) pace; **à deux** ~ (**de**) a step away (from); **marcher au** ~ march; **rouler au** ~ move very slowly; **à** ~ **de loup** stealthily; **faire les cent** ~ walk up and down; **faire le premier** ~ make the first move; ~ **de porte** doorstep; ~ **de vis** (Tech) thread.

passage /pɑsaʒ/ *nm* (*traversée*) crossing; (*visite*) visit; (*chemin*) way, passage; (*d'une œuvre*) passage; **de** ~ (*voyageur*) visiting; (*amant*) casual; **la tempête a tout emporté sur son** ~ the storm swept everything away; ~ **clouté** pedestrian crossing; ~ **interdit** (*panneau*) no thoroughfare; ~ **à niveau** level crossing; ~ **souterrain** subway.

passager, -ère /pɑsaʒe, -ɛʀ/ *adj* temporary. ● *nm,f* passenger; ~ **clandestin** stowaway.

passant, ~e /pɑsɑ̃, -t/ *adj* (*rue*) busy. ● *nm,f* passer-by. ● *nm* (*anneau*) loop.

passe /pɑs/ *nf* pass; **bonne/mauvaise** ~ good/bad patch; **en** ~ **de** on the road to.

passé, ~e /pɑse/ *adj* (*révolu*) past; (*dernier*) last; (*fané*) faded; ~ **de mode** out of fashion. ● *nm* past. ● *prép* after.

passe-partout /pɑspɑʀtu/ *nm inv* master-key. ● *a inv* for all occasions.

passeport /pɑspɔʀ/ *nm* passport.

passer /pɑse/ [1] *vi* (*aux être ou avoir*) go past, pass; (*aller*) go; (*venir*) come; (*temps, douleur*) pass; (*film*) be on; (*couleur*) fade; **laisser** ~ let through; (*occasion*) miss; ~ **devant** (à pied) walk past; (en voiture) drive past;

~ **par** go through; **où est-il passé?** where did he get to?; ~ **outre** take no notice; **passons!** let's forget about it!; **passons aux choses sérieuses** let's turn to serious matters; ~ **dans la classe supérieure** go up a year; ~ **pour un idiot** look a fool. ● *vt* (*aux avoir*) (*franchir*) pass, cross; (*donner*) pass, hand; (*temps*) spend; (*enfiler*) slip on; (*vidéo, disque*) put on; (*examen*) take, sit; (*commande*) place; (*faire*) ~ **le temps** while away the time; ~ **l'aspirateur** hoover; ~ **un coup de fil à qn** give sb a ring; **je vous passe Mme X** (par le standard) I'll put you through to Mrs X; (en donnant l'appareil) I'll pass you over to Mrs X; ~ **qch en fraude** smuggle sth. □ **se** ~ *vpr* happen, take place; (*s'écouler*) go by; **se** ~ **de** go ou do without.

passerelle /pɑsʀɛl/ *nf* footbridge; (*de navire*) gangway; (*d'avion*) (passenger) footbridge; (Internet) gateway.

passe-temps /pɑstɑ̃/ *nm inv* pastime.

passif, -ive /pɑsif, -v/ *adj* passive. ● *nm* (Comm) liabilities.

passion /pɑsjɔ̃/ *nf* passion.

passionnant, ~e *adj* fascinating.

passionné, ~e /pɑsjɔne/ *adj* passionate; **être** ~ **de** have a passion for.

passionner /pɑsjɔne/ [1] *vt* fascinate. □ **se** ~ **pour** *vpr* have a passion for.

passoire /pɑswaʀ/ *nf* (à thé) strainer; (à légumes) colander.

pastèque /pɑstɛk/ *nf* watermelon.

pasteur /pɑstœʀ/ *nm* (Relig) minister.

pastille /pɑstij/ *nf* (*médicament*) pastille, lozenge.

patate /patat/ *nf* 🔟 spud; ~ (**douce**) sweet potato.

patauger /patoʒe/ [40] *vi* splash about.

pâte /pɑt/ *nf* paste; (à gâteau) dough; (à tarte) pastry; (à frire) batter; ~**s** (*alimentaires*) pasta (+ *sg*); ~ **à modeler** Plasticine®; ~ **d'amandes** marzipan.

pâté /pɑte/ *nm* (Culin) pâté; (*d'encre*) blot; (*de sable*) sandpie; ~ **en croûte**

≈ pie; ~ de maisons block (of houses).

pâtée /pate/ *nf* feed, mash.

patente /patɑ̃t/ *nf* trade licence.

paternel, ~le /patɛʀnɛl/ *adj* paternal. **paternité** *nf* paternity.

pathétique /patetik/ *adj* moving.

patience /pasjɑ̃s/ *nf* patience. **patient, ~e** *a & nm,f* patient. **patienter** [1] *vi* wait.

patin /patɛ̃/ *nm* skate; **~ à roulettes** roller-skate.

patinage /patinaʒ/ *nm* skating. **patiner** [1] *vi* skate; (*roue*) spin. **patinoire** *nf* ice rink.

pâtisserie /pɑtisʀi/ *nf* cake shop; (*gâteau*) pastry; (*secteur*) cake making. **pâtissier, -ière** *nm,f* confectioner, pastry-cook.

patrie /patʀi/ *nf* homeland.

patrimoine /patʀimwan/ *nm* heritage.

patriote /patʀijɔt/ *adj* patriotic. ● *nmf* patriot.

patron, ~ne /patʀɔ̃, -ɔn/ *nm,f* employer, boss; (*propriétaire*) owner, boss; (*saint*) patron saint. ● *nm* (*couture*) pattern. **patronal, ~e** (*mpl* **-aux**) *adj* employers'. **patronat** *nm* employers (+ *pl*).

patrouille /patʀuj/ *nf* patrol.

patte /pat/ *nf* leg; (*pied*) foot; (*de chat*) paw; **~s** (*favoris*) sideburns; **marcher à quatre ~s** walk on all fours; (*bébé*) crawl; **~s de derrière** hind legs.

paume /pom/ *nf* (de main) palm.

paumé, ~e /pome/ *nm,f* 🔲 misfit.

paupière /popjɛʀ/ *nf* eyelid.

pause /poz/ *nf* pause; (*halte*) break.

pauvre /povʀ/ *adj* poor. ● *nmf* poor man, poor woman. **pauvreté** *nf* poverty.

pavé /pave/ *nm* cobblestone.

pavillon /pavijɔ̃/ *nm* (maison) house; (*drapeau*) flag.

payant, ~e /pejɑ̃, -t/ *adj* (*hôte*) paying; **c'est ~** you have to pay to get in.

payer /peje/ [31] *vt/i* pay; (*service, travail*) pay for; **~ qch à qn** buy sb sth; **faire ~ qn** charge sb; **il me le paiera!** he'll pay for this. ◻ **se ~** *vpr*

se ~ qch buy oneself sth; **se ~ la tête de** make fun of.

pays /pei/ *nm* country; (*région*) region; **du ~** local.

paysage /peizaʒ/ *nm* landscape.

paysan, ~ne /peizɑ̃, -an/ *nm,f* farmer, country person; (*péj*) peasant. ● *adj* (*agricole*) farming; (*rural*) country.

Pays-Bas /peibɑ/ *nmpl* **les ~** the Netherlands.

PCV *abrév m* (**paiement contre vérification**) **téléphoner en ~** reverse the charges.

PDG *abrév m* (**président-directeur général**) chairman and managing director.

péage /peaʒ/ *nm* toll; (*lieu*) tollgate.

peau (*pl* **~x**) /po/ *nf* skin; (*cuir*) hide; **~ de chamois** shammy (leather); **~ de mouton** sheepskin; **être bien/mal dans sa ~** be/not be at ease with oneself.

pêche /pɛʃ/ *nf* (fruit) peach; (*activité*) fishing; (*poissons*) catch; **~ à la ligne** angling.

péché /peʃe/ *nm* sin.

pêcher /peʃe/ *vt* (*poisson*) catch; (*dénicher* 🔲) dig up. ● *vi* fish. **pêcheur** *nm* fisherman; (à la ligne) angler.

pécuniaire /pekynjɛʀ/ *adj* financial.

pédagogie /pedagɔʒi/ *nf* education.

pédale /pedal/ *nf* pedal.

pédalo® /pedalo/ *nm* pedal boat.

pédant, ~e /pedɑ̃, -t/ *adj* pedantic.

pédestre /pedɛstʀ/ *adj* **faire de la randonnée ~** go walking *ou* hiking.

pédiatre /pedjatʀ/ *nmf* paediatrician.

pédicure /pedikyʀ/ *nmf* chiropodist.

peigne /pɛɲ/ *nm* comb.

peigner /peɲe/ [1] *vt* comb; (*personne*) comb the hair of. ◻ **se ~** *vpr* comb one's hair.

peignoir /pɛɲwaʀ/ *nm* dressing-gown.

peindre /pɛ̃dʀ/ [22] *vt* paint.

peine /pɛn/ *nf* sadness, sorrow; (effort, difficulté) trouble; (Jur) sentence; **avoir de la ~** feel sad; **faire de la ~ à**

hurt; **ce n'est pas la ~ de sonner**
you don't need to ring the bell; **j'ai
de la ~ à le croire** I find it hard to
believe; **se donner** *ou* **prendre la ~
de faire** go to the trouble of doing; **~
de mort** death penalty. ● *adv* **à ~**
hardly.
peiner /pene/ [1] *vi* struggle. ● *vt*
sadden.
peintre /pɛ̃tʀ/ *nm* painter; **~ en
bâtiment** house painter.
peinture /pɛ̃tyʀ/ *nf* painting;
(*matière*) paint; **~ à l'huile** oil
painting.
péjoratif, -ive /peʒɔʀatif, -v/ *adj*
pejorative.
pelage /pəlaʒ/ *nm* coat, fur.
pêle-mêle /pɛlmɛl/ *adv* in a
jumble.
peler /pəle/ [6] *vt/i* peel.
pèlerinage /pɛlʀinaʒ/ *nm*
pilgrimage.
pelle /pɛl/ *nf* shovel; (d'enfant) spade.
pellicule /pelikyl/ *nf* film; **~s**
(cheveux) dandruff.
pelote /pəlɔt/ *nf* (of wool) ball.
peloton /p(ə)lɔtɔ̃/ *nm* platoon; (Sport)
pack; **~ d'exécution** firing squad.
pelotonner (se) /(sə)plɔtɔne/ [1]
vpr curl up.
pelouse /p(ə)luz/ *nf* lawn.
peluche /p(ə)lyʃ/ *nf* (matière) plush;
(jouet) cuddly toy; **en ~** (lapin, chien)
fluffy.
pénal, ~e (*mpl* **-aux**) /penal, -o/ *adj*
penal. **pénaliser** [1] *vt* penalize.
pénalité *nf* penalty.
penchant /pɑ̃ʃɑ̃/ *nm* inclination;
(goût) liking (**pour** for).
pencher /pɑ̃ʃe/ [1] *vt* tilt; **~ pour**
favour. ● *vi* lean (over), tilt. ❑ **se ~**
vpr lean (forward); **se ~ sur**
(*problème*) examine.
pendaison /pɑ̃dɛzɔ̃/ *nf* hanging.
pendant¹ /pɑ̃dɑ̃/ *prép* (au cours de)
during; (durée) for; **~ que** while.
pendant², ~e /pɑ̃dɑ̃, -t/ *adj*
hanging; **jambes ~es** with one's legs
dangling. ● *nm* (contrepartie) matching
piece (de to); **~ d'oreille** drop earring.
pendentif /pɑ̃dɑ̃tif/ *nm* pendant.
penderie /pɑ̃dʀi/ *nf* wardrobe.

pendre /pɑ̃dʀ/ [3] *vt/i* hang. ❑ **se ~**
vpr hang (à from); (se tuer) hang
oneself.
pendule /pɑ̃dyl/ *nf* clock. ● *nm*
pendulum.
pénétrer /penetʀe/ [14] *vi* **~ (dans)**
enter; **faire ~ une crème** rub a
cream in. ● *vt* penetrate.
pénible /penibl/ *adj* (travail) hard;
(*nouvelle*) painful; (*enfant*) tiresome.
péniche /peniʃ/ *nf* barge.
pénitence /penitɑ̃s/ *nf* (Relig)
penance; (punition) punishment; **faire
~** repent.
pénitentiaire /penitɑ̃sjɛʀ/ *adj*
(*établissement*) penal.
pénombre /penɔ̃bʀ/ *nf* half-light.
pensée /pɑ̃se/ *nf* (idée) thought;
(fleur) pansy.
penser /pɑ̃se/ [1] *vt/i* think; **~ à**
(réfléchir à) think about; (se souvenir de,
prévoir) think of; **~ faire** think of
doing; **faire ~ à** remind one of.
pensif, -ive /pɑ̃sif, -v/ *adj* pensive.
pension /pɑ̃sjɔ̃/ *nf* (Scol) boarding
school; (repas, somme) board;
(allocation) pension; **~ (de famille)**
guest house; **~ alimentaire** (Jur)
alimony. **pensionnaire** *nmf* (Scol)
boarder; (d'hôtel) guest. **pensionnat**
nm boarding school.
pente /pɑ̃t/ *nf* slope; **en ~** sloping.
Pentecôte /pɑ̃tkot/ *nf* **la ~**
Whitsun.
pénurie /penyʀi/ *nf* shortage.
pépin /pepɛ̃/ *nm* (graine) pip; (ennui 🎓)
hitch.
pépinière /pepinjɛʀ/ *nf* (tree)
nursery.
perçant, ~e /pɛʀsɑ̃, -t/ *adj* (cri)
shrill; (*regard*) piercing.
perce-neige /pɛʀsənɛʒ/ *nm or f
inv* snowdrop.
percepteur /pɛʀsɛptœʀ/ *nm* tax
inspector.
percer /pɛʀse/ [10] *vt* pierce; (avec
perceuse) drill; (*mystère*) penetrate.
● *vi* break through; (*dent*) come
through. **perceuse** *nf* drill.
percevoir /pɛʀsəvwaʀ/ [52] *vt*
perceive; (impôt) collect.
perche /pɛʀʃ/ *nf* (bâton) pole.

percher (se) /(sə)pɛʀʃe/ [1] *vpr* perch.

percolateur /pɛʀkɔlatœʀ/ *nm* coffee machine.

percuter /pɛʀkyte/ [1] *vt* (*véhicule*) crash into.

perdant, ~e /pɛʀdɑ̃, -t/ *adj* losing. ● *nm, f* loser.

perdre /pɛʀdʀ/ [3] *vt/i* lose; (*gaspiller*) waste; ~ **ses poils** (*chat*) moult. □ **se ~** *vpr* get lost; (*rester inutilisé*) go to waste.

perdrix /pɛʀdʀi/ *nf* partridge.

perdu, ~e /pɛʀdy/ *adj* lost; (*endroit*) isolated; (*balle*) stray; **c'est du temps ~** it's a waste of time.

père /pɛʀ/ *nm* father; ~ **de famille** father, family man; ~ **spirituel** father figure; **le ~ Noël** Santa Claus.

perfection /pɛʀfɛksjɔ̃/ *nf* perfection.

perfectionner /pɛʀfɛksjɔne/ [1] *vt* (*technique*) perfect; (*art*) refine. □ **se ~** *vpr* improve; **se ~ en anglais** improve one's English.

perforer /pɛʀfɔʀe/ [1] *vt* perforate; (*billet, bande*) punch.

performance /pɛʀfɔʀmɑ̃s/ *nf* performance.

perfusion /pɛʀfyzjɔ̃/ *nf* drip; **sous ~** on a drip.

péridurale /peʀidyʀal/ *nf* epidural.

péril /peʀil/ *nm* peril; **à tes risques et ~s** at your own risk.

périlleux, -euse /peʀijø, -z/ *adj* perilous.

périmé, ~e /peʀime/ *adj* (*produit*) past its use-by date; (*désuet*) outdated.

période /peʀjɔd/ *nf* period.

périodique /peʀjɔdik/ *adj* periodic(al). ● *nm* (*journal*) periodical.

péripétie /peʀipesi/ *nf* (*unexpected*) event, adventure.

périphérique /peʀifeʀik/ *adj* peripheral. ● *nm* (**boulevard**) ~ ring road.

périple /peʀipl/ *nm* journey.

périr /peʀiʀ/ [2] *vi* perish, die.

perle /pɛʀl/ *nf* (d'huître) pearl; (de verre) bead.

permanence /pɛʀmanɑ̃s/ *nf* permanence; (Scol) study room; **de ~**

on duty; **en ~** permanently; **assurer une ~** keep the office open.

permanent, ~e /pɛʀmanɑ̃, -t/ *adj* permanent; (*constant*) constant; **formation ~e** continuous education. **permanente** *nf* (coiffure) perm.

permettre /pɛʀmɛtʀ/ [42] *vt* allow; ~ **à qn de** allow sb to. □ **se ~** *vpr* (*achat*) afford; **se ~ de faire** take the liberty of doing.

permis, ~e /pɛʀmi, -z/ *adj* allowed. ● *nm* licence, permit; ~ (**de conduire**) driving licence.

permission /pɛʀmisjɔ̃/ *nf* permission; **en ~** (Mil) on leave.

Pérou /peʀu/ *nm* Peru.

perpendiculaire /pɛʀpɑ̃dikylɛʀ/ *a* & *nf* perpendicular.

perpétuité /pɛʀpetɥite/ *nf* **à ~** for life.

perplexe /pɛʀplɛks/ *adj* perplexed.

perquisition /pɛʀkizisjɔ̃/ *nf* (police) search.

perron /pɛʀɔ̃/ *nm* (front) steps.

perroquet /pɛʀɔkɛ/ *nm* parrot.

perruche /peʀyʃ/ *nf* budgerigar.

perruque /peʀyk/ *nf* wig.

persécuter /pɛʀsekyte/ [1] *vt* persecute.

persévérance /pɛʀseveʀɑ̃s/ *nf* perseverance. **persévérer** [14] *vi* persevere.

persienne /pɛʀsjɛn/ *nf* (outside) shutter.

persil /pɛʀsi/ *nm* parsley.

persistance /pɛʀsistɑ̃s/ *nf* persistence. **persistant, ~e** *adj* persistent; (*feuillage*) evergreen.

persister /pɛʀsiste/ [1] *vi* persist (**à faire** in doing).

personnage /pɛʀsɔnaʒ/ *nm* character; (*personne célèbre*) personality.

personnalité /pɛʀsɔnalite/ *nf* personality.

personne /pɛʀsɔn/ *nf* person; ~**s** people. ● *pron* nobody, no-one; **je n'ai vu ~** I didn't see anybody.

personnel, ~le /pɛʀsɔnɛl/ *adj* personal; (*égoïste*) selfish. ● *nm* staff.

perspective /pɛʀspɛktiv/ *nf* (art, point de vue) perspective; (vue) view; (*éventualité*) prospect.

perspicace /pɛʀspikas/ *adj*
shrewd. **perspicacité** *nf*
shrewdness.

persuader /pɛʀsɥade/ [1] *vt*
persuade (**de faire** to do).

persuasif, -ive /pɛʀsɥazif, -v/ *adj*
persuasive.

perte /pɛʀt/ *nf* loss; (ruine) ruin; **à ~
de vue** as far as the eye can see; **~
de** (*temps, argent*) waste of; **~ sèche**
total loss; **~s** (Méd) discharge.

pertinent, ~e /pɛʀtinɑ̃, -t/ *adj*
pertinent.

perturbateur, -trice /pɛʀtyʀ-
batœʀ, -tʀis/ *nm, f* disruptive
element. **perturbation** *nf*
disruption. **perturber** [1] *vt* disrupt;
(*personne*) perturb.

pervers, ~e /pɛʀvɛʀ, -s/ *adj*
(*dépravé*) perverted; (*méchant*) wicked.

pervertir /pɛʀvɛʀtiʀ/ [2] *vt* pervert.

pesant, ~e /pəzɑ̃, -t/ *adj* heavy.

pesanteur /pəzɑ̃tœʀ/ *nf* heaviness;
la ~ (force) gravity.

pesée /pəze/ *nf* weighing; (effort)
pressure.

pèse-personne (*pl ~s*) /pɛzpɛʀ-
sɔn/ *nm* (bathroom) scales.

peser /pəze/ [6] *vt/i* weigh; **~ sur**
bear upon.

pessimiste /pesimist/ *adj*
pessimistic. ● *nmf* pessimist.

peste /pɛst/ *nf* plague; (personne 🔲)
pest.

pet /pɛ/ *nm* 🔲 fart 🔲.

pétale /petal/ *nm* petal.

pétard /petaʀ/ *nm* banger.

péter /pete/ [14] *vi* 🔲 fart 🔲, go
bang; (casser) snap.

pétillant, ~e /petijɑ̃, -t/ *adj*
(*boisson*) sparkling; (*personne*)
bubbly.

pétiller /petije/ [1] *vi* (*feu*) crackle;
(*champagne, yeux*) sparkle; **~
d'intelligence** sparkle with
intelligence.

petit, ~e /p(ə)ti, -t/ *adj* small; (avec
nuance affective) little; (jeune) young,
small; (*défaut*) minor; (mesquin) petty;
en ~ in miniature; **~ à ~** little by
little; **un ~ peu** a little bit; **~ ami**
boyfriend; **~e amie** girlfriend; **~es
annonces** small ads; **~e cuillère**

teaspoon; **~ déjeuner** breakfast; **~
pois** garden pea. ● *nm, f* little child;
(Scol) junior; **~s** (de chat) kittens; (de
chien) pups. **petite-fille** (*pl
petites-filles*) *nf* granddaughter.
petit-fils (*pl petits-fils*) *nm*
grandson.

pétition /petisjɔ̃/ *nf* petition.

petits-enfants /pətizɑ̃fɑ̃/ *nmpl*
grandchildren.

pétrin /petʀɛ̃/ *nm* **dans le ~** 🔲 in a
fix 🔲.

pétrir /petʀiʀ/ [2] *vt* knead.

pétrole /petʀɔl/ *nm* oil; **~ brut**
crude oil.

pétrolier, -ière /petʀɔlje, -jɛʀ/ *adj*
oil. ● *nm* (navire) oil-tanker.

peu /pø/ *adv* **~ (de)** (quantité) little,
not much; (nombre) few, not many; **~
intéressant** not very interesting; **il
mange ~** he doesn't eat very much.
● *pron* few. ● *nm* little; **un ~ (de)** a
little; **à ~ près** more or less; **de ~**
only just; **~ à ~** gradually; **~ après/
avant** shortly after/before; **~ de
chose** not much; **~ nombreux** few;
~ souvent seldom; **pour ~ que** if.

peuple /pœpl/ *nm* people. **peupler**
[1] *vt* populate.

peuplier /pøplije/ *nm* poplar.

peur /pœʀ/ *nf* fear; **avoir ~** be afraid
(**de** of); **de ~ de** for fear of; **faire ~ à**
frighten. **peureux, -euse** *adj*
fearful.

peut /pø/ ⇒POUVOIR [49].

peut-être /pøtɛtʀ/ *adv* perhaps,
maybe; **~ qu'il viendra** he might
come.

peux /pø/ ⇒POUVOIR [49].

phare /faʀ/ *nm* (tour) lighthouse; (de
véhicule) headlight; **~ antibrouillard**
fog lamp.

pharmacie /faʀmasi/ *nf* (magasin)
chemist's (shop), pharmacy; (science)
pharmacy; (armoire) medicine cabinet.
pharmacien, ~ne *nm, f* chemist,
pharmacist.

phénomène /fenɔmɛn/ *nm*
phenomenon; (personne 🔲) eccentric.

philosophe /filɔzɔf/ *nmf*
philosopher. ● *adj* philosophical.
philosophie *nf* philosophy.
philosophique *adj* philosophical.

phobie /fɔbi/ *nf* phobia.

phonétique /fɔnetik/ *adj* phonetic.
● *nf* phonetics.

phoque /fɔk/ *nm* (animal) seal.

photo /fɔto/ *nf* photo; (art)
photography; **prendre en** ~ take a
photo of; ~ **d'identité** passport
photograph.

photocopie /fɔtɔkɔpi/ *nf*
photocopy. **photocopier** [45] *vt*
photocopy.

photographe /fɔtɔgRaf/ *nmf*
photographer. **photographie** *nf*
photograph; (art) photography.
photographier [45] *vt* take a photo
of.

phrase /fRɑz/ *nf* sentence.

physicien, ~**ne** /fizisjɛ̃, -ɛn/ *nm,f*
physicist.

physique /fizik/ *adj* physical. ● *nm*
physique; **au** ~ physically. ● *nf*
physics (+ *sg*).

piano /pjano/ *nm* piano.

pianoter /pjanɔte/ [1] *vi* tinkle; ~
sur (*ordinateur*) tap at.

PIB *abrév m* (**produit intérieur
brut**) GDP.

pic /pik/ *nm* (outil) pickaxe; (sommet)
peak; (oiseau) woodpecker; **à** ~
(*falaise*) sheer; (*couler*) straight to
the bottom; **tomber à** ~ Ⓘ come just
at the right time.

pichet /piʃɛ/ *nm* jug.

picorer /pikɔre/ [1] *vt/i* peck.

picotement /pikɔtmɑ̃/ *nm*
tingling. **picoter** [1] *vt* sting; (*yeux*)
sting.

pie /pi/ *nf* magpie.

pièce /pjɛs/ *nf* (d'habitation) room; (de
monnaie) coin; (Théât) play; (pour
raccommoder) patch; (écrit) document;
(morceau) piece; ~ (**de théâtre**) play;
dix francs (la) ~ ten francs each; ~
détachée part; ~ **d'identité** identity
paper; ~**s jointes** enclosures; (courrier
électronique) attachments; ~**s
justificatives** written proof; ~
montée tiered cake; ~ **de rechange**
spare part; **un deux-**~**s** a two-room
flat.

pied /pje/ *nm* foot; (de meuble) leg; (de
lampe) base; (de verre) stem; (d'appareil
photo) stand; **être** ~**s nus** be bare-
foot; **à** ~ on foot; **au** ~ **de la lettre**
literally; **avoir** ~ be able to touch the

bottom; **jouer au tennis comme un** ~
Ⓘ be hopeless at tennis; **mettre sur**
~ set up; **sur un** ~ **d'égalité** on an
equal footing; **mettre les** ~**s dans le
plat** Ⓘ put one's foot in it; **c'est le** ~
Ⓘ it's great. **pied-bot** (*pl* **pieds-
bots**) *nm* club-foot.

piédestal /pjedɛstal/ *nm* pedestal.

piège /pjɛʒ/ *nm* trap.

piéger /pjeʒe/ [14] [40] *vt* trap; **lettre/
voiture piégée** letter/car bomb.

pierre /pjɛR/ *nf* stone; ~ **précieuse**
precious stone; ~ **tombale**
tombstone.

piétiner /pjetine/ [1] *vi* (avancer
lentement) shuffle along; (fig) make no
headway; ~ **d'impatience** hop up and
down with impatience. ● *vt* trample
(on).

piéton /pjetɔ̃/ *nm* pedestrian.

pieu (*pl* ~**x**) /pjø/ *nm* post, stake.

pieuvre /pjœvR/ *nf* octopus.

pieux, **-ieuse** /pjø, -z/ *adj* pious.

pigeon /piʒɔ̃/ *nm* pigeon.

piger /piʒe/ [40] *vt/i* Ⓘ understand,
get (it).

pile /pil/ *nf* (tas) pile; (Électr) battery;
~ **ou face?** heads or tails? ● *adv*
(s'arrêter) Ⓘ dead; **à dix heures** ~ Ⓘ
at ten on the dot.

pilier /pilje/ *nm* pillar.

pillage /pijaʒ/ *nm* looting. **pillard**,
~**e** *nm,f* looter. **piller** [1] *vt* loot.

pilote /pilɔt/ *nm* (Aviat, Naut) pilot;
(Auto) driver. ● *adj* pilot. **piloter** [1]
vt (Aviat, Naut) pilot; (Auto) drive; (fig)
guide.

pilule /pilyl/ *nf* pill; **la** ~ the pill.

piment /pimɑ̃/ *nm* hot pepper; (fig)
spice. **pimenté**, ~**e** *adj* spicy.

pin /pɛ̃/ *nm* pine.

pinard /pinaR/ *nm* Ⓘ plonk Ⓘ,
cheap wine.

pince /pɛ̃s/ *nf* (outil) pliers (+ *pl*);
(levier) crowbar; (de crabe) pincer; (à
sucre) tongs (+ *pl*); ~ **à épiler**
tweezers (+ *pl*); ~ **à linge** clothes
peg.

pinceau (*pl* ~**x**) /pɛ̃so/ *nm*
paintbrush.

pincée /pɛ̃se/ *nf* pinch (**de** of).

pincer /pɛ̃se/ [10] *vt* pinch; (attraper 🔟) catch. □ **se** ~ *vpr* catch oneself; **se** ~ **le doigt** catch one's finger.

pince-sans-rire /pɛ̃ssɑ̃rir/ *nmf inv* **c'est un** ~ he has a deadpan sense of humour.

pingouin /pɛ̃gwɛ̃/ *nm* penguin.

pingre /pɛ̃gr/ *adj* stingy.

pintade /pɛ̃tad/ *nf* guinea fowl.

piocher /pjɔʃe/ [1] *vt/i* dig; (étudier 🔟) study hard, slog away (at).

pion /pjɔ̃/ *nm* (de jeu) counter; (aux échecs) pawn; (Scol 🔟) supervisor.

pipe /pip/ *nf* pipe; **fumer la** ~ smoke a pipe.

piquant, ~**e** /pikɑ̃, -t/ *adj* (barbe) prickly; (goût) pungent; (remarque) cutting. ● *nm* prickle.

pique /pik/ *nm* (aux cartes) spades.

pique-nique (*pl* ~**s**) /piknik/ *nm* picnic.

piquer /pike/ [1] *vt* (épine) prick; (épice) burn, sting; (abeille, ortie) sting; (serpent, moustique) bite; (enfoncer) stick; (coudre) (machine-) stitch; (curiosité) excite; (voler 🔟) pinch. ● *vi* (avion) dive; (goût) be hot. □ **se** ~ *vpr* prick oneself.

piquet /pike/ *nm* stake; (de tente) peg; (de parasol) pole; ~ **de grève** (strike) picket.

piqûre /pikyr/ *nf* prick; (d'abeille) sting; (de serpent) bite; (point) stitch; (Méd) injection, jab; **faire une** ~ **à qn** give sb an injection.

pirate /pirat/ *nm* pirate; ~ **informatique** computer hacker; ~ **de l'air** hijacker.

pire /pir/ *adj* worse (que than); **les** ~**s mensonges** the most wicked lies. ● *nm* **le** ~ the worst; **au** ~ at worst.

pis /pi/ *nm* (de vache) udder. ● *a inv & adv* worse; **aller de mal en** ~ go from bad to worse.

piscine /pisin/ *nf* swimming-pool; ~ **couverte** indoor swimming-pool.

pissenlit /pisɑ̃li/ *nm* dandelion.

pistache /pistaʃ/ *nf* pistachio.

piste /pist/ *nf* track; (de personne, d'animal) track, trail; (Aviat) runway; (de cirque) ring; (de ski) slope; (de danse) floor; (Sport) racetrack; ~ **cyclable** cycle lane.

pistolet /pistɔlɛ/ *nm* gun, pistol; (de peintre) spray-gun.

piteux, -**euse** /pitø, -z/ *adj* pitiful.

pitié /pitje/ *nf* pity; **il me fait** ~ I feel sorry for him.

piton /pitɔ̃/ *nm* (à crochet) hook; (sommet pointu) peak.

pitoyable /pitwajabl/ *adj* pitiful.

pitre /pitr/ *nm* clown; **faire le** ~ clown around.

pittoresque /pitɔrɛsk/ *adj* picturesque.

pivot /pivo/ *nm* pivot. **pivoter** [1] *vi* revolve; (personne) swing round.

placard /plakar/ *nm* cupboard; (affiche) poster. **placarder** [1] *vt* (affiche) post up; (mur) cover with posters.

place /plas/ *nf* place; (espace libre) room, space; (siège) seat, place; (prix d'un trajet) fare; (esplanade) square; (emploi) position; (de parking) space; **à la** ~ **de** instead of; **en** ~, **à sa** ~ in its place; **faire** ~ **à** give way to; **sur** ~ on the spot; **remettre qn à sa** ~ put sb in his place; **ça prend de la** ~ it takes up a lot of room; **se mettre à la** ~ **de qn** put oneself in sb's shoes *ou* place.

placement /plasmɑ̃/ *nm* (d'argent) investment.

placer /plase/ [10] *vt* place; (invité, spectateur) seat; (argent) invest. □ **se** ~ *vpr* (personne) take up a position.

plafond /plafɔ̃/ *nm* ceiling.

plage /plaʒ/ *nf* beach; ~ **horaire** time slot.

plagiat /plaʒja/ *nm* plagiarism.

plaider /plede/ [1] *vt/i* plead. **plaidoirie** *nf* (defence) speech. **plaidoyer** *nm* plea.

plaie /plɛ/ *nf* wound; (personne 🔟) nuisance.

plaignant, ~**e** /plɛɲɑ̃, -t/ *nm,f* plaintiff.

plaindre /plɛ̃dr/ [22] *vt* pity. □ **se** ~ *vpr* complain (de about); **se** ~ **de** (souffrir de) complain of.

plaine /plɛn/ *nf* plain.

plainte /plɛ̃t/ *nf* complaint; (gémissement) groan. **plaintif**, -**ive** *adj* plaintive.

plaire /plɛʀ/ [47] *vi* ~ à please; ça lui plaît he likes it; elle lui plaît he likes her; ça me plaît de faire I like *ou* enjoy doing; s'il vous plaît please. □ se ~ *vpr* il se plaît ici he likes it here.

plaisance /plɛzɑ̃s/ *nf* la (navigation de) ~ boating.

plaisant, ~e /plɛzɑ̃, -t/ *adj* pleasant; (drôle) amusing.

plaisanter /plɛzɑ̃te/ [1] *vi* joke. **plaisanterie** *nf* joke. **plaisantin** *nm* joker.

plaisir /pleziʀ/ *nm* pleasure; faire ~ à please; pour le ~ for fun *ou* pleasure.

plan /plɑ̃/ *nm* plan; (de ville) map; (de livre) outline; ~ d'eau artificial lake; premier ~ foreground.

planche /plɑ̃ʃ/ *nf* board, plank; (gravure) plate; ~ à repasser ironing-board; ~ à voile windsurfing board; (Sport) windsurfing.

plancher /plɑ̃ʃe/ *nm* floor.

planer /plane/ [1] *vi* glide; ~ sur (*mystère, danger*) hang over.

planète /planɛt/ *nf* planet.

planeur /planœʀ/ *nm* (avion) glider.

planifier /planifje/ [45] *vt* plan.

plant /plɑ̃/ *nm* seedling; (de légumes) patch.

plante /plɑ̃t/ *nf* plant; ~ d'appartement houseplant; ~ des pieds sole (of the foot).

planter /plɑ̃te/ [1] *vt* (*plante*) plant; (enfoncer) drive in; (*tente*) put up; rester planté Ⅰ stand still, remain standing.

plaque /plak/ *nf* plate; (de marbre) slab; (insigne) badge; ~ chauffante hotplate; ~ commémorative plaque; ~ minéralogique numberplate; ~ de verglas patch of ice.

plaquer /plake/ [1] *vt* (*bois*) veneer; (aplatir) flatten; (rugby) tackle; (abandonner Ⅰ) ditch Ⅰ; tout ~ chuck it all.

plastique /plastik/ *a* & *nm* plastic; en ~ plastic.

plastiquer /plastike/ [1] *vt* blow up.

plat, ~e /pla, -t/ *adj* flat. ● *nm* (Culin) dish; (partie de repas) course; (de la main) flat. ● à plat *adv* (*poser*) flat;

(*batterie, pneu*) flat; à ~ ventre flat on one's face.

platane /platan/ *nm* plane tree.

plateau (*pl* ~x) /plato/ *nm* tray; (de cinéma) set; (de balance) pan; (Géog) plateau; ~ de fromages cheeseboard; ~ de fruits de mer seafood platter.

plate-bande (*pl* plates-bandes) *nf* flower-bed.

platine /platin/ *nm* platinum. ● *nf* (tourne-disque) turntable; ~ laser compact disc player.

plâtre /plɑtʀ/ *nm* plaster; (Méd) (plaster) cast.

plein, ~e /plɛ̃, -ɛn/ *adj* full (de of); (total) complete. ● *nm* faire le ~ (d'essence) fill up (the tank); à ~ fully; à ~ temps full-time; en ~ air in the open air; en ~ milieu/visage right in the middle/the face; en ~e nuit in the middle of the night. ● *adv* avoir des idées ~ la tête be full of ideas. **pleinement** *adv* fully.

pleurer /plœʀe/ [1] *vi* cry, weep (sur over); (*yeux*) water. ● *vt* mourn.

pleurnicher /plœʀniʃe/ [1] *vi* Ⅰ snivel.

pleurs /plœʀ/ *nmpl* tears; en ~ in tears.

pleuvoir /pløvwaʀ/ [48] *vi* rain; (fig) rain *ou* shower down; il pleut it is raining; il pleut à verse *ou* des cordes it is pouring.

pli /pli/ *nm* fold; (de jupe) pleat; (de pantalon) crease; (lettre) letter; (habitude) habit; (faux) ~ crease.

pliant, ~e /plijɑ̃, -t/ *adj* folding. ● *nm* folding stool, camp-stool.

plier /plije/ [45] *vt* fold; (courber) bend; (soumettre) submit (à to). ● *vi* bend. □ se ~ *vpr* fold; se ~ à submit to.

plinthe /plɛ̃t/ *nf* skirting-board.

plissé, ~e /plise/ *adj* (*jupe*) pleated.

plisser /plise/ [1] *vt* crease; (*yeux*) screw up.

plomb /plɔ̃/ *nm* lead; (fusible) fuse; ~s (de chasse) lead shot; de *ou* en ~ lead. **plombage** *nm* filling.

plomberie /plɔ̃bʀi/ *nf* plumbing. **plombier** *nm* plumber.

plongée /plɔ̃ʒe/ *nf* diving; en ~ (*sous-marin*) submerged.

plongeoir /plɔ̃ʒwaʀ/ *nm* diving-board.

plonger /plɔ̃ʒe/ [40] *vi* dive; (*route*) plunge. ● *vt* plunge. □ **se ~** *vpr* plunge into; **se ~ dans** (*fig*) (*lecture*) bury oneself in. **plongeur, -euse** *nm, f* diver; (de restaurant) dishwasher.

plu /ply/ ⇒PLAIRE [47], PLEUVOIR [48].

pluie /plɥi/ *nf* rain; (averse) shower; **~ battante/diluvienne** driving/ torrential rain.

plume /plym/ *nf* feather; (pointe) nib.

plumeau (*pl* **~x**) /plymo/ *nm* feather duster.

plumier /plymje/ *nm* pencil box.

plupart: **la ~** /laplypaʀ/ *loc* **la ~ des** (*gens, cas*) most; **la ~ du temps** most of the time; **pour la ~** for the most part.

pluriel, **~le** /plyʀjɛl/ *a & nm* plural.

- -

plus /ply, plys, plyz/

● *adverbe de comparaison*

••••▸ more (que than); **~ âgé/tard** older/later; **~ beau** more beautiful; **~ j'y pense...** the more I think about it...; **deux fois ~** twice as much; **deux fois ~ cher** twice as expensive.

••••▸ **le ~** the most; **le ~ grand** the biggest; (de deux) the bigger.

••••▸ **~ de** (*pain*) more; (*dix jours*) more than; **il est ~ de 8 heures** it is after 8 o'clock.

••••▸ **de ~** more (que than); (en outre) moreover; **les enfants de ~ de 10 ans** children over 10 years old; **de ~ en ~** more and more.

••••▸ **en ~** on top of that; **c'est en ~** it's extra; **en ~ de** in addition to.

••••▸ **~ ou moins** more or less.

••••▸ **au ~ tard** at the latest.

● *adverbe de négation*

••••▸ **ne ~** (*temps*) no longer, not any more; **je n'y vais ~** I don't go there any longer *ou* any more.

••••▸ **ne ~ de** (quantité) no more; **il n'y a ~ de pain** there is no more bread.

••••▸ **~ que deux jours!** only two days left!

● *préposition & nom masculin*

••••▸ (maths) plus.

plusieurs /plyzjœʀ/ *a & pron* several.

plus-value (*pl* **~s**) /plyvaly/ *nf* (bénéfice) profit.

plutôt /plyto/ *adv* rather (**que** than).

pluvieux, -ieuse /plyvjø, -z/ *adj* rainy.

PME *abrév f* (**petites et moyennes entreprises**) SME.

PNB *abrév m* (**produit national brut**) GNP.

pneu (*pl* **~s**) /pnø/ *nm* tyre. **pneumatique** *adj* inflatable.

poche /pɔʃ/ *nf* pocket; (sac) bag; **~s** (sous les yeux) bags.

pocher /pɔʃe/ [1] *vt* (œuf) poach.

pochette /pɔʃɛt/ *nf* (de documents) folder; (sac) bag, pouch; (d'allumettes) book; (de disque) sleeve; (mouchoir) pocket handkerchief.

poêle /pwal/ *nf* **~** (à frire) frying-pan. ● *nm* stove.

poème /pɔɛm/ *nm* poem. **poésie** *nf* poetry; (poème) poem. **poète** *nm* poet. **poétique** *adj* poetic.

poids /pwa/ *nm* weight; **~ coq/ lourd/plume** bantam weight/ heavyweight/featherweight; **~ lourd** (camion) lorry, juggernaut; (US) truck.

poignard /pwaɲaʀ/ *nm* dagger. **poignarder** [1] *vt* stab.

poigne /pwaɲ/ *nf* **avoir de la ~** have a strong grip.

poignée /pwaɲe/ *nf* (de porte) handle; (quantité) handful; **~ de main** handshake.

poignet /pwaɲɛ/ *nm* wrist; (de chemise) cuff.

poil /pwal/ *nm* hair; (pelage) fur; (de brosse) bristle; **~s** (de tapis) pile; **à ~** 🆃 naked; **~ à gratter** itching powder. **poilu, ~e** *adj* hairy.

poinçon /pwɛ̃sɔ̃/ *nm* awl; (marque) hallmark. **poinçonner** [1] *vt* (billet) punch.

poing /pwɛ̃/ *nm* fist.

point /pwɛ̃/ *nm* (endroit, Sport) point; (marque visible) spot, dot; (de couture) stitch; (pour évaluer) mark; **enlever un ~ par faute** take a mark off for each mistake; **à ~** (Culin) medium; (*arriver*) at the right time; **faire le ~** take stock; **mettre au ~** (*photo*) focus; (*technique*) develop; **mettre les**

choses au ∼ get things clear; **Camille n'est pas encore au ∼ pour ses examens** Camille is not ready for her exams; **sur le ∼ de** about to; **au ∼ que** to the extent that; **∼ (final)** full stop, period; **deux ∼s** colon; **∼ d'interrogation/d'exclamation** question/exclamation mark; **∼s de suspension** suspension points; **∼ virgule** semicolon; **∼ culminant** peak; **∼ du jour** daybreak; **∼ mort** (Auto) neutral; **∼ de repère** landmark; **∼ de suture** (Méd) stitch; **∼ de vente** point of sale; **∼ de vue** point of view. ● *adv* (ne) ∼ not.

pointe /pwɛ̃t/ *nf* point, tip; (clou) tack; (de grille) spike; (fig) touch (**de** of); **de ∼** (*industrie*) high-tech; **en ∼** pointed; **heure de ∼** peak hour; **sur la ∼ des pieds** on tiptoe.

pointer /pwɛte/ [1] *vt* (cocher) tick off; (diriger) point, aim. ● *vi* (*employé*) (en arrivant) clock in; (en sortant) clock out. □ **se ∼** 🄴 turn up.

pointillé /pwɛ̃tije/ *nm* dotted line.

pointilleux, -euse /pwɛ̃tijø, -z/ *adj* fastidious, particular.

pointu, ∼e /pwɛ̃ty/ *adj* pointed; (aiguisé) sharp.

pointure /pwɛ̃tyʀ/ *nf* size.

poire /pwaʀ/ *nf* pear.

poireau (*pl* ∼**x**) /pwaʀo/ *nm* leek.

poirier /pwaʀje/ *nm* pear tree.

pois /pwa/ *nm* pea; (motif) dot; **robe à ∼** polka dot dress.

poison /pwazɔ̃/ *nm* poison.

poisseux, -euse /pwasø, -z/ *adj* sticky.

poisson /pwasɔ̃/ *nm* fish; **∼ rouge** goldfish; **∼ d'avril** April fool; **les P∼s** Pisces. **poissonnerie** *nf* fish shop. **poissonnier, -ière** *nm,f* fishmonger.

poitrine /pwatʀin/ *nf* chest; (seins) bosom.

poivre /pwavʀ/ *nm* pepper. **poivré, ∼e** *adj* peppery. **poivrière** *nf* pepper-pot.

poivron /pwavʀɔ̃/ *nm* sweet pepper.

polaire /pɔlɛʀ/ *adj* polar. ● *nf* (veste) fleece.

pôle /pol/ *nm* pole.

polémique /pɔlemik/ *nf* debate. ● *adj* controversial.

poli, ∼e /pɔli/ *adj* (personne) polite.

police /pɔlis/ *nf* (force) police (+ *pl*); (discipline) (law and) order; (d'assurance) policy.

policier, -ière /pɔlisje, -jɛʀ/ *adj* police; (*roman*) detective. ● *nm* policeman.

polir /pɔliʀ/ [2] *vt* polish.

politesse /pɔlitɛs/ *nf* politeness; (parole) polite remark.

politicien, ∼ne /pɔlitisjɛ̃, -ɛn/ *nm,f* (péj) politician.

politique /pɔlitik/ *adj* political; **homme ∼** politician. ● *nf* politics; (ligne de conduite) policy.

pollen /pɔlɛn/ *nm* pollen.

polluant, ∼e /pɔlɥɑ̃, -t/ *adj* polluting. ● *nm* pollutant.

polluer /pɔlɥe/ [1] *vt* pollute. **pollution** *nf* pollution.

polo /pɔlo/ *nm* (Sport) polo; (vêtement) polo shirt.

Pologne /pɔlɔɲ/ *nf* Poland.

polonais, ∼e /pɔlɔnɛ, -z/ *adj* Polish. ● *nm* (Ling) Polish. **P∼, ∼e** *nm,f* Pole.

poltron, ∼ne /pɔltʀɔ̃, -ɔn/ *adj* cowardly. ● *nm,f* coward.

polygame /pɔligam/ *nmf* polygamist.

polyvalent, ∼e /pɔlivalɑ̃, -t/ *adj* varied; (personne) versatile.

pommade /pɔmad/ *nf* ointment.

pomme /pɔm/ *nf* apple; (d'arrosoir) rose; **∼ d'Adam** Adam's apple; **∼ de pin** pine cone; **∼ de terre** potato; **∼s frites** chips; (US) French fries; **tomber dans les ∼s** 🄴 pass out.

pommette /pɔmɛt/ *nf* cheekbone.

pommier /pɔmje/ *nm* apple tree.

pompe /pɔ̃p/ *nf* pump; (splendeur) pomp; **∼ à incendie** fire-engine; **∼s funèbres** undertaker's (+ *sg*).

pomper /pɔ̃pe/ [1] *vt* pump; (copier) 🄴 copy, crib; **∼ l'air à qn** 🄴 get on sb's nerves.

pompier /pɔ̃pje/ *nm* fireman.

pomponner (se) /(sə)pɔ̃pɔne/ [1] *vpr* get dolled up.

poncer /pɔ̃se/ [10] *vt* sand.

ponctuation /pɔ̃ktɥasjɔ̃/ *nf* punctuation.

ponctuel, **~le** /pɔ̃ktɥɛl/ *adj* punctual.

pondre /pɔ̃dʀ/ [3] *vt/i* lay.

poney /pɔnɛ/ *nm* pony.

pont /pɔ̃/ *nm* bridge; (de navire) deck; (de graissage) ramp; **faire le ~** get an extended weekend; **~ aérien** airlift. **pont-levis** (*pl* **ponts-levis**) *nm* drawbridge.

populaire /pɔpylɛʀ/ *adj* popular; (*expression*) colloquial; (*quartier, origine*) working-class. **popularité** *nf* popularity.

population /pɔpylasjɔ̃/ *nf* population.

porc /pɔʀ/ *nm* pig; (viande) pork.

porcelaine /pɔʀsəlɛn/ *nf* china, porcelain.

porc-épic (*pl* **porcs-épics**) /pɔʀkepik/ *nm* porcupine.

porcherie /pɔʀʃəʀi/ *nf* pigsty.

pornographie /pɔʀnɔgʀafi/ *nf* pornography.

port /pɔʀ/ *nm* port, harbour; **à bon ~** safely; **~ maritime** seaport; (transport) carriage; (d'armes) carrying; (de barbe) wearing.

portable /pɔʀtabl/ *nm* (Ordinat) laptop (computer); (telephone) mobile (phone).

portail /pɔʀtaj/ *nm* gate.

portatif, **-ive** /pɔʀtatif, -v/ *adj* portable.

porte /pɔʀt/ *nf* door; (passage) doorway; (de jardin, d'embarquement) gate; **mettre à la ~** throw out; **~ d'entrée** front door.

porté, **~e** /pɔʀte/ *adj* **~ à** inclined to; **~ sur** keen on.

porte-avions /pɔʀtavjɔ̃/ *nm inv* aircraft carrier.

porte-bagages /pɔʀtbagaʒ/ *nm inv* (de vélo) carrier.

porte-bonheur /pɔʀtbɔnœʀ/ *nm inv* lucky charm.

porte-clefs /pɔʀtəkle/ *nm inv* key ring.

porte-documents /pɔʀtdɔkymɑ̃/ *nm inv* briefcase.

portée /pɔʀte/ *nf* (d'une arme) range; (de voûte) span; (d'animaux) litter; (impact) significance; (Mus) stave; **à ~ de (la) main** within (arm's) reach;

hors de ~ (de) out of reach (of); **à la ~ de qn** at sb's level.

porte-fenêtre (*pl* **portes-fenêtres**) /pɔʀtfənɛtʀ/ *nf* French window.

portefeuille /pɔʀtəfœj/ *nm* wallet; (de ministre) portfolio.

porte-jarretelles /pɔʀtʒaʀtɛl/ *nm inv* suspender belt.

portemanteau (*pl* **~x**) /pɔʀt-mɑ̃to/ *nm* coat *ou* hat stand.

porte-monnaie /pɔʀtmɔnɛ/ *nm inv* purse.

porte-parole /pɔʀtpaʀɔl/ *nm inv* spokesperson.

porter /pɔʀte/ [1] *vt* carry; (vêtement, bague) wear; (fruits, responsabilité, nom) bear; (coup) strike; (amener) bring; (inscrire) enter. ● *vi* (bruit) carry; (coup) hit home; **~ sur** rest on; (concerner) be about. □ **se ~** *vpr* **bien se ~** be *ou* feel well; **se ~ candidat** stand as a candidate.

porteur, **-euse** /pɔʀtœʀ, -øz/ *nm,f* (de nouvelles) bearer; (Méd) carrier. ● *nm* (Rail) porter.

portier /pɔʀtje/ *nm* doorman.

portière /pɔʀtjɛʀ/ *nf* door.

porto /pɔʀto/ *nm* port (wine).

portrait /pɔʀtʀɛ/ *nm* portrait. **portrait-robot** (*pl* **portraits-robots**) *nm* identikit®, photofit®.

portuaire /pɔʀtɥɛʀ/ *adj* port.

portugais, **~e** /pɔʀtygɛ, -z/ *adj* Portuguese. ● *nm* (Ling) Portuguese. **P~**, **~e** *nm,f* Portuguese.

Portugal /pɔʀtygal/ *nm* Portugal.

pose /poz/ *nf* installation; (attitude) pose; (Photo) exposure.

posé, **~e** /poze/ *adj* calm, serious.

poser /poze/ [1] *vt* put (down); (installer) install, put in; (fondations) lay; (question) ask; (problème) pose; **~ sa candidature** apply (**à** for). ● *vi* (modèle) pose. □ **se ~** *vpr* (avion, oiseau) land; (regard) fall; (se présenter) arise.

positif, **-ive** /pozitif, -v/ *adj* positive.

position /pozisjɔ̃/ *nf* position; **prendre ~** take a stand.

posologie /pozolɔʒi/ *nf* dosage.

posséder /pɔsede/ [14] *vt*
(*propriété*) own, possess; (*diplôme*)
have.

possessif, -ive /pɔsesif, -v/ *adj*
possessive.

possession /pɔsesjɔ̃/ *nf*
possession; **prendre ~ de** take
possession of.

possibilité /pɔsibilite/ *nf*
possibility.

possible /pɔsibl/ *adj* possible; **dès
que ~** as soon as possible; **le plus
tard ~** as late as possible. ● *nm* **le ~**
what is possible; **faire son ~** do
one's utmost.

postal, ~e (*mpl* **-aux**) /pɔstal, -o/
adj postal.

poste /pɔst/ *nf* (service) post; (bureau)
post office; **~ aérienne** airmail;
mettre à la ~ post; **~ restante** poste
restante. ● *nm* (lieu, emploi) post; (de
radio, télévision) set; (téléphone)
extension (number); **~ d'essence**
petrol station; **~ d'incendie** fire
point; **~ de pilotage** cockpit; **~ de
police** police station; **~ de secours**
first-aid post.

poster¹ /pɔste/ [1] *vt* (*lettre,
personne*) post.

poster² /pɔstɛʀ/ *nm* poster.

postérieur, ~e /pɔsteʀjœʀ/ *adj*
later; (*partie*) back; **~ à** after. ● *nm*
🇫 posterior.

posthume /pɔstym/ *adj*
posthumous.

postiche /pɔstiʃ/ *adj* false.

postier, -ière /pɔstje, -jɛʀ/ *nm,f*
postal worker.

post-scriptum /pɔstskʀiptɔm/ *nm
inv* postscript.

postuler /pɔstyle/ [1] *vt/i* apply (à
for); (*principe*) postulate.

pot /po/ *nm* pot; (en plastique) carton;
(en verre) jar; (chance 🇫) luck; (boisson
🇫) drink; **~ catalytique** catalytic
converter; **~ d'échappement** exhaust
pipe.

potable /pɔtabl/ *adj* **eau ~** drinking
water.

potage /pɔtaʒ/ *nm* soup.

potager, -ère /pɔtaʒe, -ɛʀ/ *adj*
vegetable. ● *nm* vegetable garden.

pot-au-feu /pɔtofø/ *nm inv* (plat)
stew.

pot-de-vin (*pl* **pots-de-vin**)
/podvɛ̃/ *nm* bribe.

poteau (*pl* **~x**) /pɔto/ *nm* post;
(télégraphique) pole; **~ indicateur**
signpost.

potelé, ~e /pɔtle/ *adj* plump.

potentiel, ~le /pɔtɑ̃sjɛl/ *a & nm*
potential.

poterie /pɔtʀi/ *nf* pottery; (objet)
piece of pottery. **potier** *nm* potter.

potins /pɔtɛ̃/ *nmpl* gossip (+ *sg*).

potiron /pɔtiʀɔ̃/ *nm* pumpkin.

pou (*pl* **~x**) /pu/ *nm* louse.

poubelle /pubɛl/ *nf* dustbin.

pouce /pus/ *nm* thumb; (de pied) big
toe; (mesure) inch.

poudre /pudʀ/ *nf* powder; **~** (à
canon) gunpowder; **en ~** (*lait*)
powdered; (*chocolat*) drinking.

poudrier /pudʀije/ *nm* (powder)
compact.

pouf /puf/ *nm* pouffe.

poulailler /pulaje/ *nm* hen house.

poulain /pulɛ̃/ *nm* foal; (protégé)
protégé.

poule /pul/ *nf* hen; (Culin) fowl;
(femme 🇫) tart.

poulet /pulɛ/ *nm* chicken.

pouliche /puliʃ/ *nf* filly.

poulie /puli/ *nf* pulley.

pouls /pu/ *nm* pulse.

poumon /pumɔ̃/ *nm* lung.

poupe /pup/ *nf* stern.

poupée /pupe/ *nf* doll.

pour /puʀ/ *prép* for; (envers) to; (à la
place de) on behalf of; (comme) as; **~
cela** for that reason; **~ cent** per cent;
~ de bon for good; **~ faire** (in order)
to do; **~ que** so that; **~ moi** (à mon
avis) as for me; **trop poli ~** too polite
to; **~ ce qui est de** as for; **être ~** be
in favour. ● *nm inv* **le ~ et le contre**
the pros and cons.

pourboire /puʀbwaʀ/ *nm* tip.

pourcentage /puʀsɑ̃taʒ/ *nm*
percentage.

pourparlers /puʀpaʀle/ *nmpl* talks.

pourpre /puʀpʀ/ *a & nm* crimson;
(violet) purple.

pourquoi /puʀkwa/ *conj & adv* why.
● *nm inv* **le ~ et le comment** the
why and the wherefore.

pourra, pourrait /puʀa, puʀɛ/
⇒POUVOIR [49].

pourri, **~e** /puʀi/ adj rotten.
pourrir [2] vt/i rot. **pourriture** nf
rot.

poursuite /puʀsɥit/ nf pursuit (de
of); **~s** (Jur) legal action (+ sg).

poursuivre /puʀsɥivʀ/ [57] vt
pursue; (continuer) continue (with); ~
(en justice) take to court; (droit civil)
sue. ● vi continue. □ **se ~** vpr
continue.

pourtant /puʀtɑ̃/ adv yet.

pourvoir /puʀvwaʀ/ [63] vi ~ à
provide for; **pourvu de** supplied
with.

pourvu que /puʀvyk(ə)/ conj
(condition) provided (that); (souhait) let
us hope (that).

pousse /pus/ nf growth; (bourgeon)
shoot.

poussé, **~e** /puse/ adj (études)
advanced; (enquête) thorough.

poussée /puse/ nf pressure; (coup)
push; (de prix) upsurge; (Méd) attack.

pousser /puse/ [1] vt push; (cri) let
out; (soupir) heave; (continuer)
continue; (exhorter) urge (à to); (forcer)
drive (à to). ● vi push; (grandir) grow;
faire ~ (cheveux) let grow; (plante)
grow. □ **se ~** vpr move over ou up;
pousse-toi! move over!

poussette /puset/ nf pushchair.

poussière /pusjɛʀ/ nf dust.
poussiéreux, **-euse** adj dusty.

poussin /pusɛ̃/ nm chick.

poutre /putʀ/ nf beam; (en métal)
girder.

pouvoir /puvwaʀ/ [49] v aux
(possibilité) can, be able; (permission,
éventualité) may, can; **il peut/pouvait/
pourrait venir** he can/could/might
come; **je n'ai pas pu** I couldn't; **j'ai pu
faire** (réussi à) I managed to do; **je
n'en peux plus** I am exhausted; **il se
peut que** it may be that. ● nm
power; (gouvernement) government; **au
~ in power; ~s publics** authorities.

prairie /pʀeʀi/ nf meadow.

praticien, **~ne** /pʀatisjɛ̃, -ɛn/ nm,f
practitioner.

pratiquant, **~e** /pʀatikɑ̃, -t/ adj
practising. ● nm,f churchgoer.

pratique /pʀatik/ adj practical. ● nf
practice; (expérience) experience; **la ~
du golf/du cheval** golfing/riding.
pratiquement adv (en pratique) in
practice; (presque) practically.

pratiquer /pʀatike/ [1] vt/i practise;
(Sport) play; (faire) make.

pré /pʀe/ nm meadow.

préalable /pʀealabl/ adj
preliminary, prior. ● nm
precondition; **au ~** first.

préambule /pʀeɑ̃byl/ nm preamble.

préavis /pʀeavi/ nm notice.

précaire /pʀekɛʀ/ adj precarious.
précarité nf (d'emploi) insecurity.

précaution /pʀekosjɔ̃/ nf (mesure)
precaution; (prudence) caution.

précédent, **~e** /pʀesedɑ̃, -t/ adj
previous. ● nm precedent.

précéder /pʀesede/ [14] vt/i
precede.

précepteur, **-trice** /pʀesɛptœʀ,
-tʀis/ nm,f (private) tutor.

prêcher /pʀeʃe/ [1] vt/i preach.

précieux, **-ieuse** /pʀesjø, -z/ adj
precious.

précipitamment /pʀesipitamɑ̃/
adv hastily. **précipitation** nf haste.

précipiter /pʀesipite/ [1] vt throw,
precipitate; (hâter) hasten. □ **se ~**
vpr (se dépêcher) rush (sur at, on to);
(se jeter) throw oneself; (s'accélérer)
speed up.

précis, **~e** /pʀesi, -z/ adj precise,
specific; (mécanisme) accurate; **dix
heures ~es** ten o'clock sharp. ● nm
summary.

préciser /pʀesize/ [1] vt specify;
précisez votre pensée could you be
more specific. □ **se ~** vpr become
clear(er). **précision** nf precision;
(détail) detail.

précoce /pʀekɔs/ adj (enfant)
precocious.

préconiser /pʀekɔnize/ [1] vt
advocate.

précurseur /pʀekyʀsœʀ/ nm
forerunner.

prédicateur /pʀedikatœʀ/ nm
preacher.

prédilection /pʀedilɛksjɔ̃/ nf
preference.

prédire /pʀediʀ/ [37] vt predict.

prédominer /pʀedɔmine/ [1] *vi*
predominate.

préface /pʀefas/ *nf* preface.

préfecture /pʀefɛktyʀ/ *nf*
prefecture; ~ **de police** police
headquarters.

préféré, ~**e** /pʀefeʀe/ *a & nm,f*
favourite.

préférence /pʀefeʀɑ̃s/ *nf*
preference; **de** ~ preferably.

préférentiel, ~**le** /pʀefeʀɑ̃sjɛl/ *adj*
preferential.

préférer /pʀefeʀe/ [14] *vt* prefer (**à**
to); ~ **faire** prefer to do; **je ne préfère
pas** I'd rather not; **j'aurais préféré ne
pas savoir** I wish I hadn't found out.

préfet /pʀefɛ/ *nm* prefect; ~ **de
police** prefect *ou* chief of police.

préfixe /pʀefiks/ *nm* prefix.

préhistorique /pʀeistɔʀik/ *adj*
prehistoric.

préjudice /pʀeʒydis/ *nm* harm,
prejudice; **porter** ~ **à** harm.

préjugé /pʀeʒyʒe/ *nm* prejudice;
être plein de ~**s** be very prejudiced.

prélasser (se) /(sə)pʀelase/ [1] *vpr*
loll (about).

prélèvement /pʀelɛvmɑ̃/ *nm*
deduction; (de sang) sample. **prélever** [6] *vt* deduct (**sur** from); (*sang*)
take.

préliminaire /pʀeliminɛʀ/ *a & nm*
preliminary; ~**s** (sexuels) foreplay.

prématuré, ~**e** /pʀematyʀe/ *adj*
premature. ● *nm* premature baby.

premier, -**ière** /pʀəmje, -jɛʀ/ *adj*
first; (*rang*) front, first; (*enfance*)
early; (*nécessité, souci*) prime;
(*qualité*) top, prime; **de** ~ **ordre** first-
rate; ~ **ministre** Prime Minister.
● *nm,f* first (one). ● *nm* (date) first;
(étage) first floor; **en** ~ first.
première *nf* (Rail) first class; (exploit
jamais vu) first; (cinéma, Théât)
première; (Aut) (vitesse) first (gear).
premièrement *adv* firstly.

prémunir /pʀemyniʀ/ [2] *vt* protect
(**contre** against).

prenant, ~**e** /pʀənɑ̃, -t/ *adj*
(*activité*) engrossing; (*enfant*)
demanding.

prénatal, ~**e** (*mpl* ~**s**) /pʀenatal/
adj antenatal.

prendre /pʀɑ̃dʀ/ [50] *vt* take;
(attraper) catch, get; (acheter) get;
(*repas*) have; (engager, adopter) take
on; (*poids*) put on; (chercher) pick up;
qu'est-ce qui te prend? what's the
matter with you? ● *vi* (*liquide*) set;
(*feu*) catch; (*vaccin*) take. □ **se** ~
vpr **se** ~ **pour** think one is; **s'en** ~ **à**
attack; (rendre responsable) blame; **s'y**
~ set about (it).

preneur, -**euse** /pʀənœʀ, -øz/ *nm,f*
buyer; **être** ~ be willing to buy;
trouver ~ find a buyer.

prénom /pʀenɔ̃/ *nm* first name.

prénommer /pʀenɔme/ [1] *vt* call.
□ **se** ~ *vpr* be called.

préoccupation /pʀeɔkypasjɔ̃/ *nf*
(souci) worry; (idée fixe)
preoccupation.

préoccuper /pʀeɔkype/ [1] *vt*
worry; (absorber) preoccupy. □ **se** ~
de *vpr* think about.

préparation /pʀepaʀasjɔ̃/ *nf*
preparation. **préparatoire** *adj*
preparatory.

préparer /pʀepaʀe/ [1] *vt* prepare;
(*repas, café*) make; **plats préparés**
ready-cooked meals. □ **se** ~ *vpr*
prepare oneself (**à** for); (s'apprêter) get
ready; (être proche) be brewing.

préposé, ~**e** /pʀepoze/ *nm,f*
employee; (des postes) postman,
postwoman.

préposition /pʀepozisjɔ̃/ *nf*
preposition.

préretraite /pʀeʀətʀɛt/ *nf* early
retirement.

près /pʀɛ/ *adv* near, close; ~ **de** near
(to), close to; (presque) nearly; **à cela**
~ except that; **de** ~ closely.

présage /pʀezaʒ/ *nm* omen.

presbyte /pʀɛsbit/ *adj* long-sighted,
far-sighted.

prescrire /pʀɛskʀiʀ/ [30] *vt*
prescribe.

préséance /pʀeseɑ̃s/ *nf*
precedence.

présence /pʀezɑ̃s/ *nf* presence;
(Scol) attendance.

présent, ~**e** /pʀezɑ̃, -t/ *adj* present.
● *nm* (temps, cadeau) present; **à** ~
now.

présentateur, -**trice** /pʀezɑ̃tatœʀ,
-tʀis/ *nm,f* presenter.

présentation /pʀezɑ̃tasjɔ̃/ *nf* (de personne) introduction; (exposé) presentation.

présenter /pʀezɑ̃te/ [1] *vt* present; (*personne*) introduce (à to); (montrer) show. ● *vi* ~ **bien** have a pleasing appearance. □ **se** ~ *vpr* introduce oneself (à to); (aller) go; (apparaître) appear; (*candidat*) come forward; (*occasion*) arise; **se** ~ **à** (*examen*) sit for; (*élection*) stand for; **se** ~ **bien** look good.

préservatif /pʀezɛʀvatif/ *nm* condom.

préserver /pʀezɛʀve/ [1] *vt* protect.

présidence /pʀezidɑ̃s/ *nf* (d'État) presidency; (de société) chairmanship.

président, ~e /pʀezidɑ̃, -t/ *nm,f* president; (de société, comité) chairman, chairwoman; ~-**directeur général** managing director.

présidentiel, ~le /pʀezidɑ̃sjɛl/ *adj* presidential.

présider /pʀezide/ [1] *vt* preside.

présomptueux, -euse /pʀezɔ̃ptɥø, -z/ *adj* presumptuous.

presque /pʀɛsk(ə)/ *adv* almost, nearly; ~ **jamais** hardly ever; ~ **rien** hardly anything; ~ **pas (de)** hardly any.

presqu'île /pʀɛskil/ *nf* peninsula.

pressant, ~e /pʀɛsɑ̃, -t/ *adj* pressing, urgent.

presse /pʀɛs/ *nf* (journaux, appareil) press.

pressentiment /pʀɛsɑ̃timɑ̃/ *nm* premonition. **pressentir** [46] *vt* have a premonition of.

pressé, ~e /pʀese/ *adj* in a hurry; (*orange, citron*) freshly squeezed.

presser /pʀese/ [1] *vt* squeeze, press; (appuyer sur, harceler) press; (hâter) hasten; (inciter) urge (**de** to). ● *vi* (*temps*) press; (*affaire*) be pressing. □ **se** ~ *vpr* (se hâter) hurry; (se grouper) crowd.

pressing /pʀesiŋ/ *nm* (teinturerie) dry-cleaner's.

pression /pʀesjɔ̃/ *nf* pressure; (bouton) press-stud.

prestance /pʀɛstɑ̃s/ *nf* (imposing) presence.

prestation /pʀɛstasjɔ̃/ *nf* allowance; (d'artiste) performance.

prestidigitation /pʀɛstidiʒitasjɔ̃/ *nf* conjuring.

prestige /pʀɛstiʒ/ *nm* prestige. **prestigieux**, -ieuse *adj* prestigious.

présumer /pʀezyme/ [1] *vt* presume; ~ **que** assume that; ~ **de** overrate.

prêt, ~e /pʀɛ, -t/ *adj* ready (à qch for sth, à faire to do). ● *nm* loan. **prêt-à-porter** *nm inv* ready-to-wear clothes.

prétendre /pʀetɑ̃dʀ/ [3] *vt* claim (que that); (vouloir) intend; **on le prétend riche** he is said to be very rich. **prétendu**, ~e *adj* so-called. **prétendument** *adv* supposedly, allegedly.

prétentieux, -ieuse /pʀetɑ̃sjø, -z/ *adj* pretentious.

prêter /pʀete/ [1] *vt* lend (à to); (*attribuer*) attribute; ~ **son aide à qn** give sb some help; ~ **attention** pay attention; ~ **serment** take an oath. ● *vi* ~ **à** lead to.

prêteur, -euse /pʀetœʀ, -øz/ *nm,f* (money-)lender; ~ **sur gages** pawnbroker.

prétexte /pʀetɛkst/ *nm* pretext, excuse.

prêtre /pʀetʀ/ *nm* priest.

preuve /pʀœv/ *nf* proof; **des** ~s evidence (+ *sg*); **faire** ~ **de** show; **faire ses** ~s prove oneself.

prévaloir /pʀevalwaʀ/ [60] *vi* prevail.

prévenant, ~e /pʀevnɑ̃, -t/ *adj* thoughtful.

prévenir /pʀevniʀ/ [58] *vt* (menacer) warn; (informer) tell; (*médecin*) call; (éviter, anticiper) prevent.

préventif, -ive /pʀevɑ̃tif, -v/ *adj* preventive.

prévention /pʀevɑ̃sjɔ̃/ *nf* prevention; **faire de la** ~ take preventive action; ~ **routière** road safety.

prévenu, ~e /pʀevny/ *nm,f* defendant.

prévisible /pʀevizibl/ *adj* predictable. **prévision** *nf* prediction; (météorologique) forecast.

prévoir /pʀevwaʀ/ [63] *vt* foresee; (*temps*) forecast; (organiser) plan (for), provide for; (envisager) allow (for); **prévu pour** (*jouet*) designed for; **comme prévu** as planned.

prévoyance /pʀevwajɑ̃s/ *nf* foresight. **prévoyant, ~e** *adj* far-sighted.

prier /pʀije/ [45] *vi* pray. ● *vt* pray to; (demander à) ask (de to); **je vous en prie** please; (il n'y a pas de quoi) don't mention it.

prière /pʀijɛʀ/ *nf* prayer; (demande) request; **~ de** (vous êtes prié de) will you please.

primaire /pʀimɛʀ/ *adj* primary.

prime /pʀim/ *nf* free gift; (d'employé) bonus; (subvention) subsidy; (d'assurance) premium.

primé, ~e /pʀime/ *adj* prize-winning.

primeurs /pʀimœʀ/ *nfpl* early fruit and vegetables.

primevère /pʀimvɛʀ/ *nf* primrose.

primitif, -ive /pʀimitif, -v/ *adj* primitive; (d'origine) original. ● *nm, f* primitive.

primordial, ~e (*mpl* **-iaux**) /pʀimɔʀdjal, -jo/ *adj* essential.

prince /pʀɛ̃s/ *nm* prince. **princesse** *nf* princess. **princier, -ière** *adj* princely.

principal, ~e (*mpl* **-aux**) /pʀɛ̃sipal, -o/ *adj* main, principal. ● *nm* headmaster; (chose) main thing.

principe /pʀɛ̃sip/ *nm* principle; **en ~** in theory; (d'habitude) as a rule.

printanier, -ière /pʀɛ̃tanje, -jɛʀ/ *adj* spring(-like).

printemps /pʀɛ̃tɑ̃/ *nm* spring.

prioritaire /pʀijɔʀitɛʀ/ *adj* priority; **être ~** have priority. **priorité** *nf* priority; (Auto) right of way.

pris, ~e /pʀi, -z/ *adj* (*place*) taken; (*personne, journée*) busy; (*nez*) stuffed up; (*de peur, fièvre*) stricken with; **~ de panique** panic-stricken. ● ⇒PRENDRE [50].

prise /pʀiz/ *nf* hold, grip; (animal attrapé) catch; (Mil) capture; **~ (de courant)** (mâle) plug; (femelle) socket; **~ multiple** multiplug adapter; **avoir ~ sur qn** have a hold over sb; **aux ~s avec** to grips with; **~ de conscience** awareness; **~ de contact** first contact, initial meeting; **~ de position** stand; **~ de sang** blood test.

prisé, ~e /pʀize/ *adj* popular.

prison /pʀizɔ̃/ *nf* prison, jail; (réclusion) imprisonment. **prisonnier, -ière** *nm, f* prisoner.

privation /pʀivasjɔ̃/ *nf* deprivation; (sacrifice) hardship.

privatiser /pʀivatize/ [1] *vt* privatize.

privé /pʀive/ *adj* private. ● *nm* (Comm) private sector; (Scol) private schools (+ *pl*); **en ~** in private.

priver /pʀive/ [1] *vt* **~ de** deprive of. □ **se ~ (de)** *vpr* go without.

privilège /pʀivilɛʒ/ *nm* privilege. **privilégié, ~e** *nm, f* privileged person.

prix /pʀi/ *nm* price; (récompense) prize; **à tout ~** at all costs; **au ~ de** (fig) at the expense of; **~ coûtant, ~ de revient** cost price; **à ~ fixe** set price.

probabilité /pʀɔbabilite/ *nf* probability. **probable** *adj* probable, likely. **probablement** *adv* probably.

probant, ~e /pʀɔbɑ̃, -t/ *adj* convincing, conclusive.

problème /pʀɔblɛm/ *nm* problem.

procédé /pʀɔsede/ *nm* process; (manière d'agir) practice.

procéder /pʀɔsede/ [14] *vi* proceed; **~ à** carry out.

procès /pʀɔsɛ/ *nm* (criminel) trial; (civil) lawsuit, proceedings (+ *pl*).

processus /pʀɔsesys/ *nm* process.

procès-verbal (*pl* **procès-verbaux**) /pʀɔsevɛʀbal, -o/ *nm* minutes (+ *pl*); (contravention) ticket.

prochain, ~e /pʀɔʃɛ̃, -ɛn/ *adj* (suivant) next; (proche) imminent; (avenir) near. ● *nm* fellow man. **prochainement** *adv* soon.

proche /pʀɔʃ/ *adj* near, close; (avoisinant) neighbouring; (*parent, ami*) close; **~ de** close ou near to; **de ~ en ~** gradually; **dans un ~ avenir** in the near future; **être ~** (imminent) be approaching. ● *nm* close relative; (ami) close friend.

Proche-Orient /pʀɔʃɔʀjɑ̃/ *nm* Near East.

proclamation /prɔklamasjɔ̃/ nf declaration, proclamation. **proclamer** [1] vt declare, proclaim.

procuration /prɔkyrasjɔ̃/ nf proxy.

procurer /prɔkyre/ [1] vt bring (à to). □ se ~ vpr obtain.

procureur /prɔkyrœr/ nm public prosecutor.

prodige /prɔdiʒ/ nm (fait) marvel; (personne) prodigy; **enfant/musicien** ~ child/musical prodigy. **prodigieux, -ieuse** adj tremendous, prodigious.

prodigue /prɔdig/ adj wasteful; **fils** ~ prodigal son.

producteur, -trice /prɔdyktœr, -tris/ adj producing. ● nm,f producer. **productif, -ive** adj productive. **production** nf production; (produit) product. **productivité** nf productivity.

produire /prɔdɥir/ [17] vt produce. □ se ~ vpr (survenir) happen; (acteur) perform.

produit /prɔdɥi/ nm product; ~s (de la terre) produce (+ sg); ~ **chimique** chemical; ~s **alimentaires** foodstuffs; ~ **de consommation** consumer goods; ~ **intérieur brut** gross domestic product; ~ **national brut** gross national product.

proéminent, ~e /prɔeminɑ̃, -t/ adj prominent.

profane /prɔfan/ adj secular. ● nmf lay person.

proférer /prɔfere/ [14] vt utter.

professeur /prɔfesœr/ nm teacher; (Univ) lecturer; (avec chaire) professor.

profession /prɔfesjɔ̃/ nf occupation; ~ **libérale** profession. **professionnel, ~le** /prɔfesjɔnɛl/ adj professional; (école) vocational. ● nm,f professional.

profil /prɔfil/ nm profile.

profit /prɔfi/ nm profit; **au** ~ **de** in aid of. **profitable** adj profitable.

profiter /prɔfite/ [1] vi ~ **à** benefit; ~ **de** take advantage of.

profond, ~e /prɔfɔ̃, -d/ adj deep; (sentiment, intérêt) profound; (causes) underlying; **au plus** ~ **de** in the depths of. **profondément** adv deeply; (différent, triste) profoundly; (dormir) soundly. **profondeur** nf depth.

progéniture /prɔʒenityr/ nf offspring.

progiciel /prɔʒisjɛl/ nm (Ordinat) package.

programmation /prɔgramasjɔ̃/ nf programming.

programme /prɔgram/ nm programme; (Scol) (d'une matière) syllabus; (général) curriculum; (Ordinat) program. **programmer** [1] vt (ordinateur, appareil) program; (émission) schedule. **programmeur, -euse** nm,f computer programmer.

progrès /prɔgrɛ/ nm & nmpl progress; **faire des** ~ make progress. **progresser** [1] vi progress. **progressif, -ive** adj progressive. **progression** nf progression.

prohibitif, -ive /prɔibitif, -v/ adj prohibitive.

proie /prwa/ nf prey; **en** ~ **à** tormented by.

projecteur /prɔʒɛktœr/ nm floodlight; (Mil) searchlight; (cinéma) projector.

projectile /prɔʒɛktil/ nm missile.

projection /prɔʒɛksjɔ̃/ nf projection; (séance) show.

projet /prɔʒɛ/ nm plan; (ébauche) draft; ~ **de loi** bill.

projeter /prɔʒte/ [38] vt (prévoir) plan (de to); (film) project, show; (jeter) hurl, project.

prolétaire /prɔletɛr/ nmf proletarian.

prologue /prɔlɔg/ nm prologue.

prolongation /prɔlɔ̃gasjɔ̃/ nf extension; ~s (football) extra time.

prolonger /prɔlɔ̃ʒe/ [40] vt extend. □ se ~ vpr go on.

promenade /prɔmnad/ nf walk; (à bicyclette, à cheval) ride; (en auto) drive, ride; **faire une** ~ go for a walk.

promener /prɔmne/ [6] vt take for a walk; ~ **son regard sur** cast an eye over. □ se ~ vpr walk; (aller) se ~ go for a walk. **promeneur, -euse** nm,f walker.

promesse /prɔmɛs/ nf promise.

prometteur, -euse /prɔmɛtœr, -øz/ adj promising.

promettre /prɔmɛtr/ [42] vt/i promise. ● vi be promising. □ se ~ **de** vpr resolve to.

promoteur /prɔmɔtœr/ nm
(immobilier) property developer.

promotion /prɔmɔsjɔ̃/ nf
promotion; (Univ) year; (Comm)
special offer.

prompt, ~e /prɔ̃, -t/ adj swift.

promu, ~e /prɔmy/ adj être ~ be
promoted.

prôner /prone/ [1] vt extol.

pronom /prɔnɔ̃/ nm pronoun.
pronominal, ~e (mpl -aux) adj
pronominal.

prononcé, ~e /prɔnɔ̃se/ adj
strong.

prononcer /prɔnɔ̃se/ [10] vt
pronounce; (discours) make. □ se ~
vpr (mot) be pronounced; (personne)
make a decision (pour in favour of).
prononciation nf pronunciation.

pronostic /prɔnɔstik/ nm forecast;
(Méd) prognosis.

propagande /prɔpagɑ̃d/ nf
propaganda.

propager /prɔpaʒe/ [40] vt spread.
□ se ~ vpr spread.

prophète /prɔfɛt/ nm prophet.
prophétie nf prophecy.

propice /prɔpis/ adj favourable.

proportion /prɔpɔrsjɔ̃/ nf
proportion; (en mathématiques) ratio;
toutes ~s **gardées** relatively
speaking. **proportionné**, ~e adj
proportionate (à to).
proportionnel, ~le adj
proportional.
proportionnellement adv
proportionately.

propos /prɔpo/ nm intention; (sujet)
subject; **à** ~ at the right time; (dans
un dialogue) by the way; **à** ~ **de** about;
à tout ~ at every possible occasion.
● nmpl (paroles) remarks.

proposer /prɔpoze/ [1] vt suggest,
propose; (offrir) offer. □ se ~ vpr
volunteer (pour to). **proposition** nf
proposal; (affirmation) proposition;
(Gram) clause.

propre /prɔpr/ adj (non sali) clean;
(soigné) neat; (honnête) decent; (à soi)
own; (sens) literal; ~ **à** (qui convient)
suited to; (spécifique) particular to.
● nm mettre au ~ write out again
neatly; **c'est du** ~! (ironique) well
done!

proprement /prɔprəmɑ̃/ adv (avec
soin) neatly; (au sens strict) strictly; **le
bureau** ~ **dit** the office itself.

propreté /prɔprəte/ nf cleanliness.

propriétaire /prɔprijetɛr/ nmf
owner; (Comm) proprietor; (qui loue)
landlord, landlady.

propriété /prɔprijete/ nf property;
(droit) ownership.

propulser /prɔpylse/ [1] vt propel.

proroger /prɔrɔʒe/ [40] vt (contrat)
defer; (passeport) extend.

proscrire /prɔskrir/ [30] vt
proscribe.

proscrit, ~e /prɔskri, -t/ adj
proscribed. ● nm, f (exilé) exile.

prose /proz/ nf prose.

prospectus /prɔspɛktys/ nm
leaflet.

prospère /prɔspɛr/ adj flourishing,
thriving. **prospérer** [14] vi thrive,
prosper. **prospérité** nf prosperity.

prosterner (se) /(sə)prɔstɛrne/ [1]
vpr prostrate oneself; **prosterné
devant** prostrate before.

prostituée /prɔstitɥe/ nf
prostitute. **prostitution** nf
prostitution.

protecteur, **-trice** /prɔtɛktœr,
-tris/ nm, f protector. ● adj
protective.

protection /prɔtɛksjɔ̃/ nf
protection.

protégé, ~e /prɔteʒe/ nm, f
protégé.

protéger /prɔteʒe/ [40] vt protect.
□ se ~ vpr protect oneself.

protéine /prɔtein/ nf protein.

protestant, ~e /prɔtɛstɑ̃, -t/ a &
nm, f Protestant.

protestation /prɔtɛstasjɔ̃/ nf
protest. **protester** [1] vt/i protest.

protocole /prɔtɔkɔl/ nm protocol.

protubérant, ~e /prɔtyberɑ̃/ adj
protruding.

proue /pru/ nf bow, prow.

prouesse /prues/ nf feat, exploit.

prouver /pruve/ [1] vt prove.

provenance /prɔvnɑ̃s/ nf origin;
en ~ **de** from.

provençal, ~e (mpl -aux) /prɔ-
vɑ̃sal, -o/ a & nm, f Provençal.

provenir /pʀɔvniʀ/ [58] *vi* ~ de come from.

proverbe /pʀɔvɛʀb/ *nm* proverb.

province /pʀɔvɛ̃s/ *nf* province; de ~ provincial; **la** ~ the provinces (+ *pl*). **provincial**, ~**e** (*mpl* **-iaux**) *a* & *nm*, *f* provincial.

proviseur /pʀɔvizœʀ/ *nm* headmaster, principal.

provision /pʀɔvizjɔ̃/ *nf* supply, store; (sur un compte) credit (balance); (acompte) deposit; ~**s** (vivres) food shopping.

provisoire /pʀɔvizwaʀ/ *adj* provisional.

provocant, ~**e** /pʀɔvɔkɑ̃, -t/ *adj* provocative. **provocation** *nf* provocation. **provoquer** [1] *vt* cause; (sexuellement) arouse; (défier) provoke.

proxénète /pʀɔksenɛt/ *nm* pimp, procurer.

proximité /pʀɔksimite/ *nf* proximity; **à** ~ **de** close to.

prude /pʀyd/ *adj* prudish.

prudemment /pʀydamɑ̃/ *adv* (*conduire*) carefully; (*attendre*) cautiously. **prudence** *nf* caution. **prudent**, ~**e** *adj* (au volant) careful; (à agir) cautious; (sage) wise.

prune /pʀyn/ *nf* plum.

pruneau (*pl* ~**x**) /pʀyno/ *nm* prune.

prunelle /pʀynɛl/ *nf* (pupille) pupil; (fruit) sloe.

prunier /pʀynje/ *nm* plum tree.

psaume /psom/ *nm* psalm.

pseudonyme /psødɔnim/ *nm* pseudonym.

psychanalyse /psikanaliz/ *nf* psychoanalysis. **psychanalyste** *nmf* psychoanalyst.

psychiatre /psikjatʀ/ *nmf* psychiatrist. **psychiatrie** *nf* psychiatry. **psychiatrique** *adj* psychiatric.

psychique /psiʃik/ *adj* mental, psychological.

psychologie /psikɔlɔʒi/ *nf* psychology. **psychologique** *adj* psychological. **psychologue** *nmf* psychologist.

pu /py/ ⇒POUVOIR [49].

puant, ~**e** /pɥɑ̃, -t/ *adj* stinking.

pub /pyb/ *nf* 🗓 **la** ~ advertising; **une** ~ an advert.

puberté /pybɛʀte/ *nf* puberty.

public, -que /pyblik/ *adj* public. ● *nm* public; (assistance) audience; (Scol) state schools (+ *pl*); **en** ~ in public.

publication /pyblikasjɔ̃/ *nf* publication.

publicitaire /pyblisitɛʀ/ *adj* publicity. **publicité** *nf* publicity, advertising; (annonce) advertisement.

publier /pyblije/ [45] *vt* publish.

publiquement /pyblikmɑ̃/ *adv* publicly.

puce /pys/ *nf* flea; (électronique) chip; **marché aux** ~**s** flea market.

pudeur /pydœʀ/ *nf* modesty.

pudibond, ~**e** /pydibɔ̃, -d/ *adj* prudish.

pudique /pydik/ *adj* modest.

puer /pɥe/ [1] *vi* stink. ● *vt* stink of.

puéricultrice /pɥeʀikyltʀis/ *nf* pediatric nurse.

puéril, ~**e** /pɥeʀil/ *adj* puerile.

puis /pɥi/ *adv* then.

puiser /pɥize/ [1] *vt* draw (dans from). ● *vi* ~ dans qch dip into sth.

puisque /pɥisk(ə)/ *conj* since, as.

puissance /pɥisɑ̃s/ *nf* power; **en** ~ potential.

puissant, ~**e** /pɥisɑ̃, -t/ *adj* powerful.

puits /pɥi/ *nm* well; (de mine) shaft.

pull(-over) /pyl(ɔvɛʀ)/ *nm* pullover, jumper.

pulpe /pylp/ *nf* pulp.

pulsation /pylsasjɔ̃/ *nf* (heart-)beat.

pulvériser /pylveʀize/ [1] *vt* pulverize; (*liquide*) spray.

punaise /pynɛz/ *nf* (insecte) bug; (clou) drawing-pin.

punch¹ /pɔ̃ʃ/ *nm* (boisson) punch.

punch² /pœnʃ/ *nm* **avoir du** ~ have drive.

punir /pyniʀ/ [2] *vt* punish. **punition** *nf* punishment.

pupille /pypij/ *nf* (de l'œil) pupil. ● *nmf* (enfant) ward.

pupitre /pypitʀ/ *nm* (Scol) desk; ~ **à musique** music stand.

pur /pyʀ/ *adj* pure; (*whisky*) neat.

purée /pyʀe/ *nf* purée; (de pommes de terre) mashed potatoes (+ *pl*).

pureté /pyʀte/ *nf* purity.

purgatoire /pyʀgatwaʀ/ *nm* purgatory.

purge /pyʀʒ/ *nf* purge. **purger** [40] *vt* (Pol, Méd) purge; (*peine*: Jur) serve.

purifier /pyʀifje/ [45] *vt* purify.

puritain, ~**e** /pyʀitɛ̃, -ɛn/ *nm,f* puritan. ● *adj* puritanical.

pur-sang /pyʀsɑ̃/ *nm inv* (cheval) thoroughbred.

pus /py/ *nm* pus.

putain /pytɛ̃/ *nf* ✕ whore.

puzzle /pœzl/ *nm* jigsaw (puzzle).

P-V *abrév m* (**procès-verbal**) ticket, traffic fine.

pyjama /piʒama/ *nm* pyjamas (+ *pl*); **un** ~ a pair of pyjamas.

pylône /pilon/ *nm* pylon.

Pyrénées /piʀene/ *nfpl* **les** ~ the Pyrenees.

pyromane /piʀɔman/ *nmf* arsonist.

....

Qq

....

QG *abrév m* (**quartier général**) HQ.

QI *abrév m* (**quotient intellectuel**) IQ.

qu' /k/ ⇨QUE.

quadriller /kadʀije/ [1] *vt* (*armée*) take control of; (*police*) spread one's net over; **papier quadrillé** squared paper.

quadrupède /kadʀypɛd/ *nm* quadruped.

quadruple /kadʀypl/ *adj* quadruple. ● *nm* **le** ~ **de** four times. **quadrupler** [1] *vt/i* quadruple.

quai /ke/ *nm* (de gare) platform; (de port) quay; (de rivière) bank.

qualification /kalifikasjɔ̃/ *nf* qualification; (compétence pratique) skills (+ *pl*).

qualifié, ~**e** /kalifje/ *adj* (diplômé) qualified; (main-d'œuvre) skilled.

qualifier /kalifje/ [45] *vt* qualify; (décrire) describe (**de** as). ◻ **se** ~ *vpr* qualify (**pour** for).

qualité /kalite/ *nf* quality; (titre) occupation; (fonction) position; **en sa** ~ **de** in his *ou* her capacity as.

quand /kɑ̃/ *adv* when; ~ **même** all the same. ● *conj* when; (toutes les fois que) whenever; ~ **bien même** even if.

quant à /kɑ̃ta/ *prép* as for.

quantité /kɑ̃tite/ *nf* quantity; **une** ~ **de** a lot of; **des** ~**s** (**de**) masses *ou* lots (of).

quarantaine /kaʀɑ̃tɛn/ *nf* (Méd) quarantine; **une** ~ (**de**) about forty; **avoir la** ~ be in one's forties.

quarante /kaʀɑ̃t/ *a & nm* forty.

quart /kaʀ/ *nm* quarter; (Naut) watch; **onze heures moins le** ~ quarter to eleven; ~ (**de litre**) quarter litre; ~ **de finale** quarter-final; ~ **d'heure** quarter of an hour; ~ **de tour** ninety-degree turn.

quartier /kaʀtje/ *nm* area, district; (zone ethnique) quarter; (de lune, pomme, bœuf) quarter; (d'une orange) segment; ~**s** (Mil) quarters; **de** ~, **du** ~ local; ~ **général** headquarters; **avoir** ~ **libre** be free.

quasiment /kazimɑ̃/ *adv* almost, practically.

quatorze /katɔʀz/ *a & nm* fourteen.

quatre /katʀ(ə)/ *a & nm* four. **quatre-vingt(s)** *a & nm* eighty. **quatre-vingt-dix** *a & nm* ninety.

quatrième /katʀijɛm/ *a & nmf* fourth. ● *nf* (Auto) fourth gear.

quatuor /kwatɥɔʀ/ *nm* quartet.

....

que, **qu'** /kə, k/
        qu' before vowel or mute h.

● *conjonction*

····▸ that; **je crains** ~... I'm worried that...

····▸ (souhait, volonté) **je veux** ~ **tu viennes** I want you to come; ~ **tu viennes ou non** whether you come or not; **qu'il entre** let him come in.

····▸ (comparaison) than; **plus grand** ~ **toi** taller than you.

● *pronom interrogatif*

····▸ what; ~ **voulez-vous manger?** what would you like to eat?

● *pronom relatif*

····▸ (personne) whom, that; **l'homme ~ j'ai rencontré** the man (whom) I met.

····▸ (chose) that, which; **le cheval ~ Nick m'a offert** the horse (which) Nick gave me.

● *adverbe*

····▸ ~ **c'est joli!** it's so pretty!; ~ **de monde!** what a lot of people!

Québec /kebɛk/ *nm* Quebec.

quel, quelle (*pl* **quel(le)s**) /kɛl/

● *adjectif interrogatif*

····▸ which, what; ~ **auteur a écrit...?** which writer wrote...?; ~ **jour sommes-nous?** what day is it today?

● *adjectif exclamatif*

····▸ what; ~ **idiot!** what an idiot!; **quelle horreur!** that's horrible!

● *adjectif relatif*

····▸ ~ **que soit son âge** whatever his age; **quelles que soient tes raisons** whatever your reasons; ~ **que soit le gagnant** whoever the winner is.

quelconque /kɛlkɔ̃k/ *adj* any, some; (banal) ordinary; (médiocre) poor, second rate.

quelque /kɛlkə/ *adj* some; ~**s** a few, some. ● *adv* (environ) about, some; **et ~** 🔢 and a bit; ~ **chose** something; (dans les phrases interrogatives) anything; ~ **part** somewhere; ~ **peu** somewhat.

quelquefois /kɛlkəfwa/ *adv* sometimes.

quelques-uns, -unes /kɛlkəzœ̃, -yn/ *pron* some, a few.

quelqu'un /kɛlkœ̃/ *pron* someone, somebody; (dans les phrases interrogatives) anyone, anybody.

querelle /kərɛl/ *nf* quarrel. **quereller (se)** [1] *vpr* quarrel. **querelleur, -euse** *adj* quarrelsome.

question /kɛstjɔ̃/ *nf* question; (affaire) matter, question; **poser une ~** ask a question; **en ~** in question;

il est ~ de (cela concerne) it is about; (on parle de) there is talk of; **il n'en est pas ~** it is out of the question; **pas ~!** no way!

questionnaire /kɛstjɔnɛr/ *nm* questionnaire.

questionner /kɛstjɔne/ [1] *vt* question.

quête /kɛt/ *nf* (Relig) collection; (recherche) search; **en ~ de** in search of.

queue /kø/ *nf* tail; (de poêle) handle; (de fruit) stalk; (de fleur) stem; (file) queue; (US) line; (de train) rear; **faire la ~** queue (up); (US) line up; ~ **de cheval** pony-tail; **faire une ~ de poisson à qn** (Auto) cut in front of sb.

qui /ki/

● *pronom interrogatif*

····▸ (sujet) who; ~ **a fait ça?** who did that?

····▸ (complément) whom; **à ~ est ce livre?** whose book is this?

● *pronom relatif*

····▸ (personne sujet) who; **c'est Isabelle qui vient d'appeler** it's Isabelle who's just called.

····▸ (autres cas) that, which; **qu'est-ce ~ te prend?** what is the matter with you?; **invite ~ tu veux** invite whoever you want; ~ **que ce soit** whoever it is, anybody.

quiche /kiʃ/ *nf* quiche.

quiconque /kikɔ̃k/ *pron* whoever; (n'importe qui) anyone.

quille /kij/ *nf* (de bateau) keel; (jouet) skittle.

quincaillerie /kɛ̃kɑjri/ *nf* hardware; (magasin) hardware shop. **quincaillier, -ière** *nm, f* hardware dealer.

quintal (*pl* **-aux**) /kɛ̃tal, -o/ *nm* quintal, one hundred kilos.

quinte /kɛ̃t/ *nf* ~ **de toux** coughing fit.

quintuple /kɛ̃typl/ *adj* quintuple. ● *nm* **le ~ de** five times. **quintupler** [1] *vt/i* quintuple, increase fivefold.

quinzaine /kɛ̃zɛn/ *nf* **une ~ (de)** about fifteen.

quinze /kɛ̃z/ a & nm inv fifteen; ~
jours two weeks.

quiproquo /kipʀoko/ nm
misunderstanding.

quittance /kitɑ̃s/ nf receipt.

quitte /kit/ adj quits (**envers** with);
~ **à faire** even if it means doing.

quitter /kite/ [1] vt leave; (vêtement)
take off; **ne quittez pas!** hold the line,
please! □ **se** ~ vpr part.

qui-vive /kiviv/ nm inv **être sur le**
~ be alert.

quoi /kwa/ pron what; (après une
préposition) which; **de** ~ **vivre** (assez)
enough to live on; **de** ~ **écrire**
something to write with; ~ **qu'il dise**
whatever he says; ~ **que ce soit**
anything; **il n'y a pas de** ~ my
pleasure; **il n'y a pas de** ~ **s'inquiéter**
there's nothing to worry about.

quoique /kwak(ə)/ conj although,
though.

quota /kɔta/ nm quota.

quote-part (pl **quotes-parts**)
/kɔtpaʀ/ nf share.

quotidien, **~ne** /kɔtidjɛ̃, -ɛn/ adj
daily; (banal) everyday. ● nm daily
(paper); (vie quotidienne) everyday life.
quotidiennement adv daily.

Rr

rabâcher /ʀabɑʃe/ [1] vt keep
repeating.

rabais /ʀabɛ/ nm reduction,
discount. **rabaisser** [1] vt (déprécier)
belittle; (réduire) reduce.

rabat-joie /ʀabaʒwa/ nm inv killjoy.

rabattre /ʀabatʀ/ [11] vt (chapeau,
visière) pull down; (refermer) shut;
(diminuer) reduce; (déduire) take off;
(col, drap) turn down. □ **se** ~ vpr
(se refermer) close; (véhicule) cut
back in; **se** ~ **sur** make do with.

rabot /ʀabo/ nm plane.

rabougri, **~e** /ʀabugʀi/ adj stunted.

racaille /ʀakɑj/ nf rabble.

raccommoder /ʀakɔmɔde/ [1] vt
mend; (personnes 🔟) reconcile.

raccompagner /ʀakɔ̃paɲe/ [1] vt
see ou take back (home).

raccord /ʀakɔʀ/ nm link; (de papier
peint) join; (retouche) touch-up.
raccorder [1] vt connect, join.

raccourci /ʀakuʀsi/ nm short cut;
en ~ in short.

raccourcir /ʀakuʀsiʀ/ [2] vt
shorten. ● vi get shorter.

raccrocher /ʀakʀɔʃe/ [1] vt hang
back up; (passant) grab hold of;
(relier) connect; ~ **le combiné** ou **le
téléphone** hang up. ● vi hang up.
□ **se** ~ **à** vpr cling to; (se relier à) be
connected to ou with.

race /ʀas/ nf race; (animale) breed; **de**
~ (chien) pedigree; (cheval)
thoroughbred.

racheter /ʀaʃte/ [6] vt buy (back);
(acheter encore) buy more; (nouvel
objet) buy another; (société) buy out;
~ **des chaussettes** buy new socks.
□ **se** ~ vpr make amends.

racial, **~e** (mpl **-iaux**) /ʀasjal, -o/
adj racial.

racine /ʀasin/ nf root; ~ **carrée**/
cubique square/cube root.

racisme /ʀasism/ nm racism.
raciste a & nmf racist.

racket /ʀakɛt/ nm racketeering.

raclée /ʀɑkle/ nf 🔟 thrashing.

racler /ʀɑkle/ [1] vt scrape. □ **se** ~
vpr **se** ~ **la gorge** clear one's throat.

racolage /ʀakɔlaʒ/ nm soliciting.

raconter /ʀakɔ̃te/ [1] vt (histoire)
tell; (vacances) tell about; (vie,
épisode) describe; ~ **à qn** tell sb
that, say to sb that; **qu'est-ce que tu
racontes?** what are you talking
about?

radar /ʀadaʀ/ nm radar.

radeau (pl ~**x**) /ʀado/ nm raft.

radiateur /ʀadjatœʀ/ nm radiator;
(électrique) heater.

radiation /ʀadjasjɔ̃/ nf radiation.

radical, **~e** (mpl **-aux**) /ʀadikal, -o/
adj radical. ● nm (pl **-aux**) radical.

radieux, **-ieuse** /ʀadjø, -z/ adj
radiant.

radin, **~e** /ʀadɛ̃, -in/ adj 🔟 stingy
🔟.

radio /ʀadjo/ *nf* radio; **à la ~** on the radio; (*radiographie*) X-ray.

radioactif, -ive /ʀadjɔaktif, -v/ *adj* radioactive. **radioactivité** *nf* radioactivity.

radiocassette /ʀadjɔkasɛt/ *nf* radio cassette player.

radiodiffuser /ʀadjɔdifyze/ [1] *vt* broadcast.

radiographie /ʀadjɔgʀafi/ *nf* (*photographie*) X-ray.

radiomessageur /ʀadjɔmesaʒœʀ/ *nm* pager.

radis /ʀadi/ *nm* radish; **ne pas avoir un ~** ⓘ be broke.

radoter /ʀadɔte/ [1] *vi* ⓘ talk drivel.

radoucir (se) /(sə)ʀadusiʀ/ [2] *vpr* (*humeur*) improve; (*temps*) become milder.

rafale /ʀafal/ *nf* (de vent) gust; (de mitraillette) burst.

raffermir /ʀafɛʀmiʀ/ [2] *vt* strengthen. □ **se ~** *vpr* become stronger.

raffiné, ~e /ʀafine/ *adj* refined. **raffinement** *nm* refinement.

raffiner /ʀafine/ [1] *vt* refine. **raffinerie** *nf* refinery.

raffoler /ʀafɔle/ [1] *vt* ⓘ **~ de** be crazy about ⓘ.

raffut /ʀafy/ *nm* ⓘ din.

rafle /ʀafl/ *nf* (police) raid.

rafraîchir /ʀafʀeʃiʀ/ [2] *vt* cool (down); (*mur*) give a fresh coat of paint to; (*personne, mémoire*) refresh. □ **se ~** *vpr* (boire) refresh oneself; (*temps*) get cooler. **rafraîchissant, ~e** *adj* refreshing.

rafraîchissement /ʀafʀeʃismã/ *nm* (boisson) cold drink; **~s** refreshments.

ragaillardir /ʀagajaʀdiʀ/ [2] *vt* ⓘ cheer up.

rage /ʀaʒ/ *nf* rage; (maladie) rabies; **faire ~** (*bataille, incendie*) rage; (*maladie*) be rife; **~ de dents** raging toothache. **rageant, ~e** *adj* infuriating.

ragots /ʀago/ *nmpl* ⓘ gossip.

ragoût /ʀagu/ *nm* stew.

raid /ʀɛd/ *nm* (Mil) raid; (Sport) trek.

raide /ʀɛd/ *adj* stiff; (*côte*) steep; (*corde*) tight; (*cheveux*) straight.

● *adv* (monter, descendre) steeply. **raideur** *nf* stiffness; steepness.

raidir /ʀediʀ/ [2] *vt* (*corps*) tense. □ **se ~** *vpr* tense up; (*position*) harden; (*corde*) tighten.

raie /ʀɛ/ *nf* (ligne) line; (bande) strip; (de cheveux) parting; (poisson) skate.

raifort /ʀɛfɔʀ/ *nm* horseradish.

rail /ʀɑj/ *nm* rail, track; **le ~** (transport) rail.

raisin /ʀezɛ̃/ *nm* **le ~** grapes; **~ sec** raisin; **un grain de ~** a grape.

raison /ʀezɔ̃/ *nf* reason; **à ~ de** at the rate of; **avec ~** rightly; **avoir ~** be right (**de faire** to do); **avoir ~ de** qn get the better of sb; **donner ~ à** prove right; **en ~ de** because of; **~ de plus** all the more reason; **perdre la ~** lose one's mind.

raisonnable /ʀezɔnabl/ *adj* reasonable, sensible.

raisonnement /ʀezɔnmã/ *nm* reasoning; (*propositions*) argument.

raisonner /ʀezɔne/ [1] *vi* think. ● *vt* (*personne*) reason with.

rajeunir /ʀaʒœniʀ/ [2] *vt* **~ qn** make sb (look) younger; (*moderniser*) modernize; (Méd) rejuvenate. ● *vi* (*personne*) look younger.

rajuster /ʀaʒyste/ [1] *vt* straighten; (*salaires*) (re)adjust.

ralenti, ~e /ʀalãti/ *adj* slow. ● *nm* (au cinéma) slow motion; **tourner au ~** tick over, idle.

ralentir /ʀalãtiʀ/ [2] *vt/i* slow down. □ **se ~** *vpr* slow down.

ralentisseur /ʀalãtisœʀ/ *nm* speed ramp.

râler /ʀɑle/ [1] *vi* groan; (protester ⓘ) moan.

rallier /ʀalje/ [45] *vt* rally; (rejoindre) rejoin. □ **se ~** *vpr* rally; **se ~ à** (*avis*) come round to; (*parti*) join.

rallonge /ʀalɔ̃ʒ/ *nf* (de table) leaf; (de fil électrique) extension lead.

rallonger /ʀalɔ̃ʒe/ [40] *vt* lengthen; (*séjour, fil, table*) extend.

rallumer /ʀalyme/ [1] *vt* (*feu*) relight; (*lampe*) switch on again; (ranimer: fig) revive.

rallye /ʀali/ *nm* rally.

ramassage /ʀamasaʒ/ *nm* (cueillette) gathering; (d'ordures) collection; **~ scolaire** school bus service.

ramasser /Ramase/ [1] *vt* pick up; (*récolter*) gather; (*recueillir, rassembler*) collect. □ **se ~** *vpr* huddle up, curl up.

rame /Ram/ *nf* (*aviron*) oar; (*train*) train.

ramener /Ramne/ [1] *vt* (*rapporter, faire revenir*) bring back; (*reconduire*) take back; **~ à** (*réduire à*) reduce to. □ **se ~** *vpr* Ⅱ turn up; **se ~ à** (*problème*) come down to.

ramer /Rame/ [1] *vi* row.

ramollir /RamɔliR/ [2] *vt* soften. □ **se ~** *vpr* become soft.

ramoneur /RamɔnœR/ *nm* (chimney) sweep.

rampe /Rɑ̃p/ *nf* banisters; (*pente*) ramp; **~ d'accès** (Auto) slip road; **~ de lancement** launching pad.

ramper /Rɑ̃pe/ [1] *vi* crawl.

rancard /Rɑ̃kaR/ *nm* Ⅱ date.

rancart /Rɑ̃kaR/ *nm* **mettre** *ou* **jeter au ~** Ⅱ scrap.

rance /Rɑ̃s/ *adj* rancid.

rancœur /Rɑ̃kœR/ *nf* resentment.

rançon /Rɑ̃sɔ̃/ *nf* ransom. **rançonner** [1] *vt* rob, extort money from.

rancune /Rɑ̃kyn/ *nf* grudge; **sans ~!** no hard feelings! **rancunier, -ière** *adj* vindictive.

randonnée /Rɑ̃dɔne/ *nf* walk, ramble; **la ~ à cheval** pony trekking; **faire une ~** go walking *ou* rambling.

rang /Rɑ̃/ *nm* row; (*hiérarchie, condition*) rank; **se mettre en ~** line up; **au premier ~** in the first row; (fig) at the forefront; **de second ~** (péj) second-rate.

rangée /Rɑ̃ʒe/ *nf* row.

rangement /Rɑ̃ʒmɑ̃/ *nm* (*de pièce*) tidying (up); (*espace*) storage space.

ranger /Rɑ̃ʒe/ [40] *vt* put away; (*chambre*) tidy (up); (*disposer*) place. □ **se ~** *vpr* (*véhicule*) park; (*s'écarter*) stand aside; (*conducteur*) pull over; (*s'assagir*) settle down; **se ~ à** (*avis*) accept.

ranimer /Ranime/ [1] *vt* revive; (Méd) resuscitate. □ **se ~** *vpr* come round.

rapace /Rapas/ *nm* bird of prey. ● *adj* grasping.

rapatriement /RapatRimɑ̃/ *nm* repatriation. **rapatrier** [45] *vt* repatriate.

râpe /Rɑp/ *nf* (Culin) grater; (lime) rasp.

râpé, ~e /Rɑpe/ *adj* (*vêtement*) threadbare; (*fromage*) grated.

râper /Rɑpe/ [1] *vt* grate; (*bois*) rasp.

rapide /Rapid/ *adj* fast, rapid. ● *nm* (train) express (train); (cours d'eau) rapids (+ *pl*). **rapidement** *adv* fast, rapidly. **rapidité** *nf* speed.

rappel /Rapɛl/ *nm* recall; (deuxième avis) reminder; (de salaire) back pay; (Méd) booster; (de diplomate) recall; (de réservistes) call-up; (Théât) curtain call.

rappeler /Raple/ [38] *vt* (par téléphone) call back; (*réserviste*) call up; (*diplomate*) recall; (évoquer) recall; **~ qch à qn** remind sb of sth. □ **se ~** *vpr* remember, recall.

rapport /RapɔR/ *nm* connection; (compte-rendu) report; (profit) yield; **~s** (relations) relations; **en ~ avec** (accord) in keeping with; **mettre/se mettre en ~ avec** put/get in touch with; **par ~ à** (comparé à) compared with; (vis-à-vis de) with regard to; **~s** (sexuels) intercourse.

rapporter /RapɔRte/ [1] *vt* (ici) bring back; (là-bas) take back, return; (profit) bring in; (dire, répéter) report. ● *vi* (Comm) bring in a good return; (moucharder Ⅱ) tell tales. □ **se ~ à** *vpr* relate to; **s'en ~ à** rely on.

rapporteur, -euse /RapɔRtœR, -øz/ *nm, f* (mouchard) tell-tale. ● *nm* protractor.

rapprochement /RapRɔʃmɑ̃/ *nm* reconciliation; (Pol) rapprochement; (rapport) connection; (comparaison) parallel.

rapprocher /RapRɔʃe/ *vt* move closer (de to); (réconcilier) bring together; (comparer) compare; (date, rendez-vous) bring forward. □ **se ~** *vpr* get *ou* come closer (de to); (personnes, pays) come together; (s'apparenter) be close (de to).

rapt /Rapt/ *nm* abduction.

raquette /Rakɛt/ *nf* (de tennis) racket; (de ping-pong) bat.

rare /RaR/ *adj* rare; (insuffisant) scarce. **rarement** *adv* rarely, seldom.

rareté *nf* rarity; scarcity; (objet) rarity.

ras, **~e** /ʀɑ, ʀɑz/ *adv* coupé ~ cut short. ● *adj* (herbe, poil) short; **à ~ de terre** very close to the ground; **en avoir ~ le bol** 🔲 be really fed up; **~e campagne** open country; **à ~ bord** to the brim.

raser /ʀɑze/ [1] *vt* shave; (cheveux, barbe) shave off; (frôler) skim; (abattre) raze; (ennuyer 🔲) bore. □ **se ~** *vpr* shave.

rasoir /ʀɑzwaʀ/ *nm* razor. ● *a inv* 🔲 boring.

rassasier /ʀɑsɑzje/ [45] *vt* satisfy, fill up; **être rassasié de** have had enough of.

rassemblement /ʀɑsɑ̃bləmɑ̃/ *nm* gathering; (manifestation) rally.

rassembler /ʀɑsɑ̃ble/ [1] *vt* gather; (forces, courage) summon up; (idées) collect. □ **se ~** *vpr* gather.

rassis, **~e** /ʀɑsi, -z/ *adj* (pain) stale.

rassurer /ʀɑsyʀe/ [1] *vt* reassure. □ **se ~** *vpr* reassure oneself; **rassure-toi** don't worry.

rat /ʀɑ/ *nm* rat.

rate /ʀɑt/ *nf* spleen.

raté, **~e** /ʀɑte/ *nm,f* (personne) failure. ● *nm* **avoir des ~s** (voiture) backfire.

râteau (pl **~x**) /ʀɑto/ *nm* rake.

râtelier /ʀɑtəlje/ *nm* hayrack; (dentier 🔲) dentures.

rater /ʀɑte/ [1] *vt* (train, rendez-vous, cible) miss; (gâcher) make a mess of, spoil; (examen) fail. ● *vi* fail.

ratio /ʀɑsjo/ *nm* ratio.

rationaliser /ʀɑsjɔnalize/ [1] *vt* rationalize.

rationnel, **~le** /ʀɑsjɔnɛl/ *adj* rational.

rationnement /ʀɑsjɔnmɑ̃/ *nm* rationing.

ratisser /ʀɑtise/ [1] *vt* rake; (fouiller) comb.

rattacher /ʀɑtaʃe/ [1] *vt* (lacets) tie up again; (ceinture de sécurité, collier) refasten; (relier) link; (incorporer) join.

rattrapage /ʀɑtʀɑpaʒ/ *nm* (Comm) adjustment; **cours de ~** remedial lesson.

rattraper /ʀɑtʀɑpe/ [1] *vt* catch; (rejoindre) catch up with; (retard, erreur) make up for. □ **se ~** *vpr* catch up; (se dédommager) make up for it; **se ~ à** catch hold of.

rature /ʀɑtyʀ/ *nf* deletion.

rauque /ʀok/ *adj* raucous, harsh.

ravager /ʀɑvaʒe/ [40] *vt* devastate, ravage.

ravages /ʀɑvaʒ/ *nmpl* **faire des ~** wreak havoc.

ravaler /ʀɑvale/ [1] *vt* (façade) clean; (colère) swallow.

ravi, **~e** /ʀɑvi/ *adj* delighted (que that).

ravin /ʀɑvɛ̃/ *nm* ravine.

ravir /ʀɑviʀ/ [2] *vt* delight; **~ qch à qn** rob sb of sth.

ravissant, **~e** /ʀɑvisɑ̃, -t/ *adj* beautiful.

ravisseur, **-euse** /ʀɑvisœʀ, -øz/ *nm,f* kidnapper.

ravitaillement /ʀɑvitɑjmɑ̃/ *nm* provision of supplies (de to); (denrées) supplies; **~ en essence** refuelling.

ravitailler /ʀɑvitɑje/ [1] *vt* provide with supplies; (avion) refuel. □ **se ~** *vpr* stock up.

raviver /ʀɑvive/ [1] *vt* revive; (feu, colère) rekindle.

rayé, **~e** /ʀeje/ *adj* striped.

rayer /ʀeje/ [31] *vt* scratch; (biffer) cross out; **'~ la mention inutile'** 'delete as appropriate'.

rayon /ʀɛjɔ̃/ *nm* ray; (étagère) shelf; (de magasin) department; (de roue) spoke; (de cercle) radius; **~ d'action** range; **~ de miel** honeycomb; **~ X** X-ray; **en connaître un ~** 🔲 know one's stuff 🔲.

rayonnement /ʀɛjɔnmɑ̃/ *nm* (éclat) radiance; (influence) influence; (radiations) radiation. **rayonner** [1] *vi* radiate; (de joie) beam; (se déplacer) tour around (from a central point).

rayure /ʀɛjyʀ/ *nf* scratch; (dessin) stripe; **à ~s** striped.

raz-de-marée /ʀɑdmaʀe/ *nm inv* tidal wave; **~ électoral** electoral landslide.

réacteur /ʀeaktœʀ/ *nm* jet engine; (nucléaire) reactor.

réaction /Reaksjɔ̃/ nf reaction; ∼ en chaîne chain reaction; **moteur à** ∼ **jet** engine.

réagir /ReaʒiR/ [2] vi react; ∼ **sur** have an effect on.

réalisateur, **-trice** /Realizatœr, -tris/ nm,f (au cinéma) director; (TV) producer.

réalisation /Realizasjɔ̃/ nf (de rêve) fulfilment; (œuvre) achievement; (TV, cinéma) production; **projet en** ∼ project in progress.

réaliser /Realize/ [1] vt carry out; (effort, bénéfice, achat) make; (rêve) fulfil; (film) direct; (capital) realize; (se rendre compte de) realize. □ **se** ∼ vpr be fulfilled.

réalisme /Realism/ nm realism.

réaliste /Realist/ adj realistic. ● nmf realist.

réalité /Realite/ nf reality.

réanimation /Reanimasjɔ̃/ nf resuscitation; **service de** ∼ intensive care. **réanimer** [1] vt resuscitate.

réarmement /ReaRməmɑ̃/ nm rearmament.

rébarbatif, **-ive** /RebaRbatif, -v/ adj forbidding, off-putting.

rebelle /Rəbɛl/ adj rebellious; (soldat) rebel; ∼ **à** resistant to. ● nmf rebel.

rébellion /Rebeljɔ̃/ nf rebellion.

rebondir /Rəbɔ̃diR/ [2] vi bounce; rebound; (fig) get moving again.

rebondissement /Rəbɔ̃dismɑ̃/ nm (new) development.

rebord /RəbɔR/ nm edge; ∼ **de la fenêtre** window ledge ou sill.

rebours: **à** ∼ /aRəbuR/ loc (compter, marcher) backwards.

rebrousse-poil: **à** ∼ /aRəbruspwal/ loc the wrong way; (fig) **prendre qn à** ∼ **rub** sb up the wrong way.

rebrousser /Rəbruse/ [1] vt ∼ **chemin** turn back.

rebut /Rəby/ nm **mettre** ou **jeter au** ∼ scrap.

rebutant, ∼**e** /Rəbytɑ̃, -t/ adj off-putting.

recaler /Rəkale/ [1] vt 🗉 fail; **se faire** ∼, **être recalé** fail.

recel /Rəsɛl/ nm receiving. **receler** [6] vt (objet volé) receive; (cacher) conceal.

récemment /Resamɑ̃/ adv recently.

recensement /Rəsɑ̃smɑ̃/ nm census; (inventaire) inventory. **recenser** [1] vt (population) take a census of; (objets) list.

récent, ∼**e** /Resɑ̃, -t/ adj recent.

récépissé /Resepise/ nm receipt.

récepteur /Resɛptœr/ nm receiver.

réception /Resɛpsjɔ̃/ nf reception; (de courrier) receipt. **réceptionniste** nmf receptionist.

récession /Resesjɔ̃/ nf recession.

recette /Rəsɛt/ nf (Culin) recipe; (argent) takings; ∼**s** (Comm) receipts.

receveur, **-euse** /Rəs(ə)vœr, -øz/ nm,f (de bus) conductor; ∼ **des contributions** tax collector.

recevoir /Rəs(ə)vwaR/ [52] vt receive, get; (client, malade) see; (invités) welcome, receive; **être reçu à un examen** pass an exam.

rechange: **de** ∼ /dəRəʃɑ̃ʒ/ loc (roue, vêtements) spare; (solution) alternative.

réchapper /Reʃape/ [1] vt/i ∼ **de** come through, survive.

recharge /RəʃaRʒ/ nf (de stylo) refill.

réchaud /Reʃo/ nm stove.

réchauffement /Reʃofmɑ̃/ nm (de température) rise (**de** in); **le** ∼ **de la planète** global warming.

réchauffer /Reʃofe/ [1] vt warm up. □ **se** ∼ vpr warm oneself up; (temps) get warmer.

rêche /Rɛʃ/ adj rough.

recherche /RəʃɛRʃ/ nf search (**de** for); (raffinement) meticulousness; ∼(**s**) (Univ) research; ∼**s** (enquête) investigations; ∼ **d'emploi** job-hunting.

recherché, ∼**e** /RəʃɛRʃe/ adj in great demand; (style) original, recherché (péj); ∼ **pour meurtre** wanted for murder.

rechercher /RəʃɛRʃe/ [1] vt search for.

rechute /Rəʃyt/ nf (Méd) relapse; **faire une** ∼ have a relapse.

récidiver /Residive/ [1] *vi* commit a second offence.

récif /Resif/ *nm* reef.

récipient /Resipjã/ *nm* container.

réciproque /ResipRɔk/ *adj* mutual, reciprocal.

réciproquement /ResipRɔkmã/ *adv* each other; **et ~** and vice versa.

récit /Resi/ *nm* (compte-rendu) account, story; (histoire) story.

réciter /Resite/ [1] *vt* recite.

réclamation /Reklamasjõ/ *nf* complaint; (demande) claim.

réclame /Reklam/ *nf* advertisement; **faire de la ~** advertise; **en ~** on offer.

réclamer /Reklame/ [1] *vt* call for, demand. ● *vi* complain.

reclus, **~e** /Rəkly, -z/ *nm,f* recluse. ● *adj* reclusive.

réclusion /Reklyzjõ/ *nf* imprisonment.

récolte /Rekɔlt/ *nf* (action) harvest; (produits) crop, harvest; (fig) crop.

récolter [1] *vt* harvest, gather; (fig) collect, get.

recommandation /Rekɔmãdasjõ/ *nf* recommendation.

recommandé /Rəkɔmãde/ *nm* registered letter; **envoyer en ~** send by registered post.

recommander /Rəkɔmãde/ [1] *vt* recommend.

recommencer /Rəkɔmãse/ [10] *vt* (reprendre) begin *ou* start again; (refaire) repeat. ● *vi* start *ou* begin again; **ne recommence pas** don't do it again.

récompense /Rekõpãs/ *nf* reward; (prix) award. **récompenser** [1] *vt* reward (**de** for).

réconcilier /Rekõsilje/ [45] *vt* reconcile. □ **se ~** *vpr* become reconciled (**avec** with).

reconduire /RəkõdɥiR/ [17] *vt* see home; (à la porte) show out; (renouveler) renew.

réconfort /RekõfɔR/ *nm* comfort.

reconnaissance /Rekɔnɛsãs/ *nf* gratitude; (fait de reconnaître) recognition; (Mil) reconnaissance. **reconnaissant**, **~e** *adj* grateful (**de** for).

reconnaître /RəkɔnɛtR/ [18] *vt* recognize; (admettre) admit (**que** that); (Mil) reconnoitre; (enfant, tort) acknowledge. □ **se ~** *vpr* (s'orienter) know where one is; (l'un l'autre) recognize each other.

reconstituer /Rəkõstitɥe/ [1] *vt* reconstitute; (crime) reconstruct; (époque) recreate.

reconversion /RəkõvɛRsjõ/ *nf* (de main-d'œuvre) redeployment.

recopier /Rəkɔpje/ [45] *vt* copy out.

record /RəkɔR/ *nm & a inv* record.

recouper /Rəkupe/ [1] *vt* confirm. □ **se ~** *vpr* check, tally, match up.

recourbé, **~e** /RəkuRbe/ *adj* curved; (nez) hooked.

recourir /RəkuRiR/ [20] *vi* **~ à** (expédient, violence) resort to; (remède, méthode) have recourse to.

recours /RəkuR/ *nm* resort; **avoir ~ à** have recourse to, resort to; **avoir ~ à qn** turn to sb.

recouvrer /RəkuvRe/ [1] *vt* recover.

recouvrir /RəkuvRiR/ [21] *vt* cover.

récréation /RekReasjõ/ *nf* recreation; (Scol) break; (US) recess.

recroqueviller (**se**) /(sə) RəkRɔkvije/ [1] *vpr* curl up.

recrudescence /RəkRydesãs/ *nf* new outbreak.

recrue /RəkRy/ *nf* recruit.

recrutement /RəkRytmã/ *nm* recruitment. **recruter** [1] *vt* recruit.

rectangle /Rɛktãgl/ *nm* rectangle. **rectangulaire** *adj* rectangular.

rectifier /Rɛktifje/ [45] *vt* correct, rectify.

recto /Rɛkto/ *nm* **au ~** on the front of the page.

reçu, **~e** /Rəsy/ *adj* accepted; (candidat) successful. ● *nm* receipt. ● ⇒RECEVOIR [52].

recueil /Rəkœj/ *nm* collection.

recueillement /Rəkœjmã/ *nm* meditation.

recueillir /RəkœjiR/ [25] *vt* collect; (prendre chez soi) take in. □ **se ~** *vpr* meditate.

recul /Rəkyl/ *nm* retreat; (éloignement) distance; (déclin) decline; **avoir un mouvement de ~** recoil; **être en ~** be on the decline; **avec le ~** with hindsight.

reculé, ~e /Rəkyle/ *adj* (*région*) remote.

reculer /Rəkyle/ [1] *vt* move back; (*véhicule*) reverse; (*différer*) postpone. ● *vi* move back; (*voiture*) reverse; (*armée*) retreat; (*régresser*) fall; (*céder*) back down; **~ devant** (fig) shrink from. □ **se ~** *vpr* move back.

récupération /RekypeRasjɔ̃/ *nf* (de l'organisme, de dette) recovery; (d'objets) salvage.

récupérer /RekypeRe/ [14] *vt* recover; (*vieux objets*) salvage. ● *vi* recover.

récurer /RekyRe/ [1] *vt* scour; **poudre à ~** scouring powder.

récuser /Rekyze/ [1] *vt* challenge. □ **se ~** *vpr* state that one is not qualified to judge.

recyclage /Rəsiklaʒ/ *nm* (de personnel) retraining; (de matériau) recycling.

recycler /Rəsikle/ [1] *vt* (*personne*) retrain; (*chose*) recycle. □ **se ~** *vpr* retrain.

rédacteur, -trice /RedaktœR, -tRis/ *nm, f* author, writer; (de journal, magazine) editor.

rédaction /Redaksjɔ̃/ *nf* writing; (Scol) essay, composition; (personnel) editorial staff.

redevable /Rədvabl/ *adj* **être ~ à qn de** (*argent*) owe sb; (fig) be indebted to sb for.

redevance /Rədvɑ̃s/ *nf* (de télévision) licence fee; (de téléphone) rental charge.

rédiger /Rediʒe/ [40] *vt* write; (*contrat*) draw up.

redire /RədiR/ [27] *vt* repeat; **avoir** *ou* **trouver à ~ à** find fault with.

redondant, ~e /Rədɔ̃dɑ̃, -t/ *adj* superfluous.

redonner /Rədɔne/ [1] *vt* (rendre) give back; (donner davantage) give more; (donner de nouveau) give again.

redoubler /Rəduble/ [1] *vt* increase; (*classe*) repeat; **~ de prudence** be even more careful. ● *vi* (Scol) repeat a year; (s'intensifier) intensify.

redoutable /Rədutabl/ *adj* formidable.

redouter /Rədute/ [1] *vt* dread.

redressement /RədREsmɑ̃/ *nm* (reprise) recovery; **~ judiciaire** receivership.

redresser /Rədrese/ [1] *vt* straighten (out *ou* up); (*situation*) right, redress; (*économie, entreprise*) turn around. □ **se ~** *vpr* (*personne*) straighten (oneself) up; (se remettre debout) stand up; (*pays, économie*) recover.

réduction /Redyksjɔ̃/ *nf* reduction.

réduire /RedɥiR/ [17] *vt* reduce (à to). □ **se ~** *vpr* be reduced *ou* cut; **se ~ à** (revenir à) come down to.

réduit, ~e /Redɥi, -t/ *adj* (*objet*) small-scale; (limité) limited. ● *nm* cubbyhole.

rééducation /Reedykasjɔ̃/ *nf* (de handicapé) rehabilitation; (Méd) physiotherapy. **rééduquer** [1] *vt* (*personne*) rehabilitate; (*membre*) restore normal movement to.

réel, ~le /Reɛl/ *adj* real. ● *nm* reality. **réellement** *adv* really.

réexpédier /Reɛkspedje/ [45] *vt* forward; (retourner) send back.

refaire /RəfɛR/ [33] *vt* do again; (*erreur, voyage*) make again; (réparer) do up, redo.

réfectoire /RefɛktwaR/ *nm* refectory.

référence /RefeRɑ̃s/ *nf* reference.

référendum /RefeRɛ̃dɔm/ *nm* referendum.

référer /RefeRe/ [14] *vi* **en ~ à** consult. □ **se ~ à** *vpr* refer to, consult.

refermer /RəfɛRme/ [1] *vt* close (again). □ **se ~** *vpr* close (again).

réfléchi, ~e /Refleʃi/ *adj* (*personne*) thoughtful; (*verbe*) reflexive.

réfléchir /RefleʃiR/ [2] *vi* think (à, sur about). ● *vt* reflect. □ **se ~** *vpr* be reflected.

reflet /Rəflɛ/ *nm* reflection; (nuance) sheen.

refléter /Rəflete/ [14] *vt* reflect. □ **se ~** *vpr* be reflected.

réflexe /Reflɛks/ *adj* reflex. ● *nm* reflex; (réaction) reaction.

réflexion /Reflɛksjɔ̃/ *nf* (pensée) thought, reflection; (remarque) remark, comment; **à la ~** on second thoughts.

refluer /Rəflye/ [1] *vi* flow back; (*foule*) retreat; (*inflation*) go down.

reflux /Rəfly/ *nm* (marée) ebb, tide.

réforme /RefɔRm/ *nf* reform. **réformer** [1] *vt* reform; (*soldat*) invalid out.

refouler /Rəfule/ [1] *vt* (*larmes*) hold back; (*désir*) repress; (*souvenir*) suppress.

refrain /Rəfrɛ̃/ *nm* chorus; **le même ~** the same old story.

refréner /Rəfrene/ [14] *vt* curb, check.

réfrigérateur /RefRiʒeRatœR/ *nm* refrigerator.

refroidir /RəfRwadiR/ [2] *vt/i* cool (down). □ **se ~** *vpr* (*personne, temps*) get cold. **refroidissement** *nm* cooling; (rhume) chill.

refuge /Rəfyʒ/ *nm* refuge; (chalet) mountain hut.

réfugié, ~e /Refyʒje/ *nm,f* refugee. **réfugier (se)** [45] *vpr* take refuge.

refus /Rəfy/ *nm* refusal; **ce n'est pas de ~** 🔲 I wouldn't say no.

refuser /Rəfyze/ [1] *vt* refuse (**de** to); (*client, spectateur*) turn away; (recaler) fail; (à un poste) turn down. □ **se ~ à** *vpr* (*évidence*) reject; **se ~ à faire** refuse to do.

regain /Rəgɛ̃/ *nm* **~ de** renewal *ou* revival of; (Comm) rise.

régal (*pl* **~s**) /Regal/ *nm* treat, delight.

régaler /Regale/ [1] *vt* **~ qn de** treat sb to. □ **se ~** *vpr* (de nourriture) **je me régale** it's delicious.

regard /RəgaR/ *nm* (expression, coup d'œil) look; (vue) eye; (yeux) eyes; **~ fixe** stare; **au ~ de** with regard to; **en ~ de** compared with.

regardant, ~e /Rəgaʀdɑ̃, -t/ *adj* **~ avec son argent** careful with money; **peu ~ (sur)** not fussy (about).

regarder /Rəgaʀde/ [1] *vt* look at; (observer) watch; (considérer) consider; (concerner) concern; **~ fixement** stare at; **~ à** think about, pay attention to. ● *vi* look. □ **se ~** *vpr* (soi-même) look at oneself; (*personnes*) look at each other.

régate /Regat/ *nf* regatta.

régie /Reʒi/ *nf* **~ d'État** public corporation; (radio, TV) control room; (au cinéma) production; (Théât) stage management.

régime /Reʒim/ *nm* (organisation) system; (Pol) regime; (Méd) diet; (de moteur) speed; (de bananes) bunch; **se mettre au ~** go on a diet; **à ce ~** at this rate.

régiment /Reʒimɑ̃/ *nm* regiment.

région /Reʒjɔ̃/ *nf* region. **régional, ~e** (*mpl* **-aux**) *adj* regional.

régir /ReʒiR/ [2] *vt* govern.

régisseur /ReʒisœR/ *nm* (Théât) stage manager; **~ de plateau** (TV) floor manager; (au cinéma) studio manager.

registre /RəʒistR/ *nm* register.

réglage /Reglaʒ/ *nm* adjustment; (de moteur) tuning.

règle /Regl/ *nf* rule; (instrument) ruler; **~s** (de femme) period; **en ~** in order.

réglé, ~e /Regle/ *adj* (vie) ordered; (arrangé) settled; (*papier*) ruled.

règlement /Regləmɑ̃/ *nm* (règles) regulations; (solution) settlement; (paiement) payment. **réglementaire** *adj* (uniforme) regulation. **réglementation** *nf* regulation, rules. **réglementer** [1] *vt* regulate, control.

régler /Regle/ [14] *vt* settle; (*machine*) adjust; (programmer) set; (*facture*) settle; (*personne*) settle up with; **~ son compte à** 🔲 settle a score with.

réglisse /Reglis/ *nf* liquorice.

règne /Rɛɲ/ *nm* reign; (végétal, animal, minéral) kingdom.

regret /RəgRɛ/ *nm* regret; **à ~** with regret.

regretter /RəgRete/ [1] *vt* regret; (*personne*) miss; (pour s'excuser) be sorry.

regrouper /RəgRupe/ [1] *vt* group *ou* bring together. □ **se ~** *vpr* gather *ou* group together.

régularité /RegylaRite/ *nf* regularity; (de rythme, progrès) steadiness; (de surface, écriture) evenness.

régulier, -ière /Regylje, -jɛR/ *adj* regular; (*qualité, vitesse*) steady, even; (*ligne, paysage*) even; (*légal*) legal; (*honnête*) honest.

rehausser /Rəose/ [1] *vt* raise; (faire valoir) enhance.

rein /Rɛ̃/ *nm* kidney; ~s (dos) small of the back.

reine /Rɛn/ *nf* queen.

réinsertion /Reɛ̃sɛRsjɔ̃/ *nf* reintegration.

réintégrer /Reɛ̃tegRe/ [14] *vt* (*lieu*) return to; (Jur) reinstate; (*personne*) reintegrate.

réitérer /Reitere/ [14] *vt* repeat.

rejaillir /RəʒajiR/ [2] *vi* ~ sur splash back onto; ~ sur qn (*succès*) reflect on sb.

rejet /Rəʒɛ/ *nm* rejection; ~s (déchets) waste.

rejeter /Rəʒte/ [38] *vt* throw back; (refuser) reject; (déverser) discharge; ~ une faute sur qn shift the blame for a mistake onto sb.

rejeton /Rəʒtɔ̃/ *nm* (enfant 🅸) offspring (*inv*).

rejoindre /Rəʒwɛ̃dR/ [22] *vt* go back to, rejoin; (rattraper) catch up with; (rencontrer) join, meet up with. □ **se** ~ *vpr* (*personnes*) meet up; (*routes*) join, meet.

réjoui, ~**e** /Reʒwi/ *adj* joyful.

réjouir /ReʒwiR/ [2] *vt* delight. □ **se** ~ *vpr* be delighted (de at). **réjouissances** *nfpl* festivities. **réjouissant**, ~**e** *adj* cheering.

relâche /Rəlɑʃ/ *nm* (repos) break, rest; faire ~ (Théât) be closed.

relâcher /Rəlɑʃe/ [1] *vt* slacken; (*personne*) release; (*discipline*) relax. □ **se** ~ *vpr* slacken.

relais /Rəlɛ/ *nm* (Sport) relay; (hôtel) hotel; (intermédiaire) intermediary; prendre le ~ de take over from.

relancer /Rəlɑ̃se/ [10] *vt* boost, revive; (renvoyer) throw back.

relatif, -ive /Rəlatif, -v/ *adj* relative; ~ à relating to.

relation /Rəlasjɔ̃/ *nf* relationship; (ami) acquaintance; (personne puissante) connection; ~s relations; ~s extérieures foreign affairs; en ~ avec qn in touch with sb.

relativement /Rəlativmɑ̃/ *adv* relatively; ~ à in relation to.

relativité /Rəlativite/ *nf* relativity.

relax /Rəlaks/ *a inv* 🅸 laid-back.

relaxer (se) /(sə)Rəlakse/ [1] *vpr* relax.

relayer /Rəleje/ [31] *vt* relieve; (*émission*) relay. □ **se** ~ *vpr* take over from one another.

reléguer /Rəlege/ [14] *vt* relegate.

relent /Rəlɑ̃/ *nm* stink; (fig) whiff.

relève /Rəlɛv/ *nf* relief; prendre *ou* assurer la ~ take over (de from).

relevé, ~**e** /Rəlve/ *adj* spicy. ● *nm* (de compteur) reading; (facture) bill; ~ bancaire, ~ de compte bank statement; faire le ~ de list.

relever /Rəlve/ [6] *vt* pick up; (*personne tombée*) help up; (remonter) raise; (*col*) turn up; (*compteur*) read; (*défi*) accept; (relayer) relieve; (remarquer, noter) note; (*plat*) spice up; (rebâtir) rebuild; ~ **de** come within the competence of; (Méd) recover from. □ **se** ~ *vpr* (*personne*) get up (again); (*pays, économie*) recover.

relief /Rəljɛf/ *nm* relief; mettre en ~ highlight.

relier /Rəlje/ [45] *vt* link (up) (à to); (*livre*) bind.

religieux, -ieuse /Rəliʒjø, -z/ *adj* religious. ● *nm, f* monk, nun.

religion /Rəliʒjɔ̃/ *nf* religion.

reliure /RəljyR/ *nf* binding.

reluire /RəlɥiR/ [17] *vi* shine.

remaniement /Rəmanimɑ̃/ *nm* revision; ~ ministériel cabinet reshuffle.

remarquable /RəmaRkabl/ *adj* remarkable.

remarque /Rəmark/ *nf* remark; (par écrit) comment.

remarquer /RəmaRke/ [1] *vt* notice; (dire) say; faire ~ point out (à to); se faire ~ draw attention to oneself; remarque(z) mind you.

remblai /Rɑ̃blɛ/ *nm* embankment.

remboursement /Rɑ̃buRsəmɑ̃/ *nm* (d'emprunt, dette) repayment; (Comm) refund.

rembourser /Rɑ̃buRse/ [1] *vt* (dette, emprunt) repay; (billet, frais) refund; (client) give a refund to; (ami) pay back.

remède /Rəmɛd/ *nm* remedy; (*médicament*) medicine.

remédier /Rəmedje/ [45] *vi* ~ à remedy.

remerciements /RəmɛRsimã/ *nmpl* thanks. **remercier** [45] *vt* thank (**de** for); (*licencier*) dismiss.

remettre /RəmɛtR/ [42] *vt* put back; (*vêtement*) put back on; (*donner*) hand over; (*devoir, démission*) hand in; (*faire fonctionner*) switch back on; (*restituer*) give back; (*différer*) put off; (*ajouter*) add; (*se rappeler*) remember; ~ **en cause** *ou* **en question** call into question. □ **se** ~ *vpr* (*guérir*) recover; **se** ~ **au tennis** take up tennis again; **se** ~ **au travail** get back to work; ~ **à faire** start doing again; **s'en** ~ **à** leave it to.

remise /Rəmiz/ *nf* (*abri*) shed; (*rabais*) discount; (*transmission*) handing over; (*ajournement*) postponement; ~ **en cause** *ou* **en question** calling into question; ~ **des prix** prizegiving; ~ **des médailles** medals ceremony; ~ **de peine** remission.

remontant /Rəmõtã/ *nm* tonic.

remontée /Rəmõte/ *nf* ascent; (*d'eau, de prix*) rise; ~ **mécanique** ski lift.

remonte-pente (*pl* ~**s**) /Rəmõt-pãt/ *nm* ski tow.

remonter /Rəmõte/ [1] *vi* go *ou* come (back) up; (*prix, niveau*) rise (again); (*revenir*) go back (**à** to); ~ **dans le temps** go back in time. ● *vt* (*rue, escalier*) go *ou* come (back) up; (*relever*) raise; (*montre*) wind up; (*objet démonté*) put together again; (*personne*) buck up.

remontoir /RəmõtwaR/ *nm* winder.

remords /RəmɔR/ *nm* remorse; **avoir du** *or* **des** ~ feel remorse.

remorque /RəmɔRk/ *nf* trailer; **en** ~ **on** tow. **remorquer** [1] *vt* tow.

remous /Rəmu/ *nm* eddy; (*de bateau*) backwash; (*fig*) turmoil.

rempart /RãpaR/ *nm* rampart.

remplaçant, ~**e** /Rãplasã, -t/ *nm,f* replacement; (*joueur*) reserve, substitute.

remplacement /Rãplasmã/ *nm* replacement; **faire des** ~**s** do supply teaching. **remplacer** [10] *vt* replace.

rempli, ~**e** /Rãpli/ *adj* full (**de** of); (*journée*) busy.

remplir /RãpliR/ [2] *vt* fill (up); (*formulaire*) fill in *ou* out; (*condition*) fulfil; (*devoir, tâche, rôle*) carry out. □ **se** ~ *vpr* fill (up). **remplissage** *nm* filling; (*de texte*) padding.

remporter /RãpɔRte/ [1] *vt* take back; (*victoire*) win.

remuant, ~**e** /Rəmɥã, -t/ *adj* boisterous.

remue-ménage /Rəmymena3/ *nm inv* commotion, bustle.

remuer /Rəmɥe/ [1] *vt* move; (*thé, café*) stir; (*passé*) rake up. ● *vi* move; (*gigoter*) fidget. □ **se** ~ *vpr* move.

rémunération /RemyneRasjõ/ *nf* payment.

renaissance /Rənɛsãs/ *nf* rebirth.

renard /RənaR/ *nm* fox.

renchérir /RãʃeRiR/ [2] *vi* (*dans une vente*) raise the bidding; ~ **sur** go one better than. ● *vt* increase, put up.

rencontre /RãkõtR/ *nf* meeting; (*de routes*) junction; (Mil) encounter; (*match*) match; (US) game.

rencontrer /RãkõtRe/ [1] *vt* meet; (*heurter*) hit; (*trouver*) find. □ **se** ~ *vpr* meet.

rendement /Rãdmã/ *nm* yield; (*travail*) output.

rendez-vous /Rãdevu/ *nm* appointment; (*d'amoureux*) date; (*lieu*) meeting-place; **prendre** ~ (**avec**) make an appointment (with).

rendormir (se) /(sə)RãdɔRmiR/ [46] *vpr* go back to sleep.

rendre /RãdR/ [3] *vt* give back, return; (*donner en retour*) return; (*monnaie*) give; (*justice*) dispense; (*jugement*) pronounce; ~ **heureux**/**possible** make happy/possible; (vomir □) vomit; ~ **compte de** report on; ~ **service (à)** help; ~ **visite à** visit. ● *vi* (*terres*) yield; (*activité*) be profitable. □ **se** ~ *vpr* (*capituler*) surrender; (*aller*) go (**à** to); **se** ~ **utile** make oneself useful.

rêne /Rɛn/ *nf* rein.

renfermé, ~**e** /RãfɛRme/ *adj* withdrawn. ● *nm* **sentir le** ~ smell musty.

renflé, ~**e** /Rãfle/ *adj* bulging.

renforcer /ʀɑ̃fɔʀse/ [10] vt
reinforce.

renfort /ʀɑ̃fɔʀ/ nm reinforcement; **à
grand ~ de** with a great deal of.

renier /ʀənje/ [45] vt (*personne,
œuvre*) disown; (*foi*) renounce.

renifler /ʀənifle/ [1] vt/i sniff.

renne /ʀɛn/ nm reindeer.

renom /ʀənɔ̃/ nm renown; (*réputation*)
reputation. **renommé, ~e** adj
famous. **renommée** nf (*célébrité*)
fame; (*réputation*) reputation.

renoncement /ʀənɔ̃smɑ̃/ nm
renunciation.

renoncer /ʀənɔ̃se/ [10] vi ~ à
(*habitude, ami*) give up, renounce;
(*projet*) abandon; ~ **à faire** abandon
the idea of doing.

renouer /ʀənwe/ [1] vt tie up
(again); (*amitié*) renew; ~ **avec qn**
get back in touch with sb; (*après une
dispute*) make up with sb.

renouveau (*pl ~x*) /ʀənuvo/ nm
revival.

renouveler /ʀənuvle/ [38] vt renew;
(*réitérer*) repeat; (*remplacer*) replace.
□ **se ~** vpr be renewed; (*incident*)
recur, happen again.

renouvellement /ʀənuvɛlmɑ̃/ nm
renewal.

rénovation /ʀenɔvasjɔ̃/ nf (*d'édifice*)
renovation; (*d'institution*) reform.

renseignement /ʀɑ̃sɛɲ(ə)mɑ̃/ nm
~(s) information; (**bureau des**) ~s
information desk; (**service des**) ~s
téléphoniques directory enquiries.

renseigner /ʀɑ̃seɲe/ [1] vt inform,
give information to. □ **se ~** vpr
enquire, make enquiries, find out.

rentabilité /ʀɑ̃tabilite/ nf
profitability. **rentable** adj
profitable.

rente /ʀɑ̃t/ nf (*private*) income;
(*pension*) annuity. **rentier, -ière**
nm, f person of private means.

rentrée /ʀɑ̃tʀe/ nf return; (*revenu*)
income; **la ~ parlementaire** the
reopening of Parliament; **la ~ (des
classes)** the start of the new school
year; **faire sa ~** make a comeback.

rentrer /ʀɑ̃tʀe/ [1] vi (*aux être*) go ou
come back home, return home;
(entrer) go ou come in; (entrer à
nouveau) go ou come back in; (*revenu*)

come in; (*élèves*) go back (to school);
~ **dans** (heurter) smash into; **tout est
rentré dans l'ordre** everything is
back to normal; ~ **dans ses frais**
break even. ● vt (*aux avoir*) bring in;
(*griffes*) draw in; (*vêtement*) tuck in.

renverser /ʀɑ̃vɛʀse/ [1] vt knock
over ou down; (*piéton*) knock down;
(*liquide*) upset, spill; (mettre à l'envers)
turn upside down; (*gouvernement*)
overthrow; (inverser) reverse. □ **se ~**
vpr (*véhicule*) overturn; (*verre, vase*)
fall over.

renvoi /ʀɑ̃vwa/ nm return;
(d'employé) dismissal; (d'élève)
expulsion; (report) postponement;
(dans un livre, fichier) cross-reference;
(rot) burp.

renvoyer /ʀɑ̃vwaje/ [32] vt send
back, return; (*employé*) dismiss;
(*élève*) expel; (ajourner) postpone;
(référer) refer; (réfléchir) reflect.

repaire /ʀəpɛʀ/ nm den.

répandre /ʀepɑ̃dʀ/ [3] vt (liquide)
spill; (étendre, diffuser) spread; (*odeur*)
give off. □ **se ~** vpr spread; (*liquide*)
spill; **se ~ en injures** let out a
stream of abuse.

répandu, ~e /ʀepɑ̃dy/ adj
widespread.

réparateur, -trice /ʀepaʀatœʀ,
-tʀis/ nm engineer. **réparation** nf
repair; (compensation) compensation.
réparer [1] vt repair, mend; (*faute*)
make amends for; (remédier à) put
right.

repartie /ʀəpaʀti/ nf retort; **avoir de
la ~** always have a ready reply.

repartir /ʀəpaʀtiʀ/ [46] vi start
again; (*voyageur*) set off again; (s'en
retourner) go back; (*secteur
économique*) pick up again.

répartir /ʀepaʀtiʀ/ [2] vt distribute;
(partager) share out; (étaler) spread.
répartition nf distribution.

repas /ʀəpɑ/ nm meal.

repassage /ʀəpasaʒ/ nm ironing.

repasser /ʀəpase/ [1] vi come ou go
back; ~ **devant qch** go past sth
again. ● vt (*linge*) iron; (*examen*)
retake, resist; (*film*) show again.

repêcher /ʀəpeʃe/ [1] vt recover,
fish out; (*candidat*) allow to pass.

repentir¹ /ʀəpɑ̃tiʀ/ nm repentance.

repentir² (se) /(sə)ʀəpɑ̃tiʀ/ [2] *vpr* (Relig) repent (de of); se ~ de (regretter) regret.

répercuter /ʀepɛʀkyte/ [1] *vt* (*bruit*) send back. □ se ~ *vpr* echo; se ~ sur have repercussions on.

repère /ʀəpɛʀ/ *nm* mark; (jalon) marker; (événement) landmark; (référence) reference point.

repérer /ʀəpeʀe/ [14] *vt* locate, spot. □ se ~ *vpr* get one's bearings.

répertoire /ʀepɛʀtwaʀ/ *nm* (artistique) repertoire; (liste) directory; ~ **téléphonique** telephone directory; (personnel) telephone book. **répertorier** [45] *vt* index.

répéter /ʀepete/ [14] *vt* repeat; (Théât) rehearse. ● *vi* rehearse. □ se ~ *vpr* be repeated; (*personne*) repeat oneself.

répétition /ʀepetisjɔ̃/ *nf* repetition; (Théât) rehearsal.

répit /ʀepi/ *nm* respite, break.

replier /ʀəplije/ [45] *vt* fold (up); (*ailes, jambes*) tuck in. □ se ~ *vpr* withdraw (sur soi-même into oneself).

réplique /ʀeplik/ *nf* reply; (riposte) retort; (objection) objection; (Théât) line; (copie) replica. **répliquer** [1] *vt/ i* reply; (riposter) retort; (objecter) answer back.

répondeur /ʀepɔ̃dœʀ/ *nm* answering machine.

répondre /ʀepɔ̃dʀ/ [3] *vt* (*injure, bêtise*) reply with; ~ que answer *ou* reply that; ~ à (être conforme à) answer; (*affection, sourire*) return; (*avances, appel, critique*) respond to; ~ de answer for. ● *vi* answer, reply; (être insolent) answer back; (réagir) respond (à to).

réponse /ʀepɔ̃s/ *nf* answer, reply; (fig) response.

report /ʀəpɔʀ/ *nm* (transcription) transfer; (renvoi) postponement.

reportage /ʀəpɔʀtaʒ/ *nm* report; (par écrit) article.

reporter¹ /ʀəpɔʀte/ [1] *vt* take back; (ajourner) put off; (transcrire) transfer. □ se ~ à *vpr* refer to.

reporter² /ʀəpɔʀtɛʀ/ *nm* reporter.

repos /ʀəpo/ *nm* rest; (paix) peace. **reposant**, ~e *adj* restful.

reposer /ʀəpoze/ [1] *vt* put down again; (délasser) rest. ● *vi* rest (sur on); **laisser** ~ (*pâte*) leave to stand. □ se ~ *vpr* rest; se ~ sur rely on.

repousser /ʀəpuse/ [1] *vt* push back; (écarter) push away; (dégoûter) repel; (décliner) reject; (ajourner) postpone, put back. ● *vi* grow again.

reprendre /ʀəpʀɑ̃dʀ/ [50] *vt* take back; (confiance, conscience) regain; (souffle) get back; (évadé) recapture; (recommencer) resume; (redire) repeat; (modifier) alter; (blâmer) reprimand; ~ **du pain** take some more bread; **on ne m'y reprendra pas** I won't be caught out again. ● *vi* (recommencer) resume; (affaires) pick up. □ se ~ *vpr* (se ressaisir) pull oneself together; (se corriger) correct oneself.

représailles /ʀəpʀezaj/ *nfpl* reprisals.

représentant, ~e /ʀəpʀezɑ̃tɑ̃, -t/ *nm, f* representative.

représentation /ʀəpʀezɑ̃tasjɔ̃/ *nf* representation; (Théât) performance.

représenter /ʀəpʀezɑ̃te/ [1] *vt* represent; (figures) depict, show; (pièce de théâtre) perform. □ se ~ *vpr* (s'imaginer) imagine.

répression /ʀepʀesjɔ̃/ *nf* repression; (d'élan) suppression.

réprimande /ʀepʀimɑ̃d/ *nf* reprimand.

réprimer /ʀepʀime/ [1] *vt* (*peuple*) repress; (*sentiment*) suppress; (*fraude*) crack down on.

reprise /ʀəpʀiz/ *nf* resumption; (Théât) revival; (TV) repeat; (de tissu) darn, mend; (essor) recovery; (Comm) part-exchange, trade-in; **à plusieurs** ~**s** on several occasions.

repriser /ʀəpʀize/ [1] *vt* darn, mend.

reproche /ʀəpʀɔʃ/ *nm* reproach; **faire des** ~**s à** find fault with.

reprocher /ʀəpʀɔʃe/ [1] *vt* ~ **qch à qn** reproach *ou* criticize sb for sth.

reproducteur, -trice /ʀəpʀɔdyktœʀ, -tʀis/ *adj* reproductive.

reproduire /ʀəpʀɔdɥiʀ/ [17] *vt* reproduce; (répéter) repeat. □ se ~ *vpr* reproduce; (se répéter) recur.

reptile /ʀɛptil/ *nm* reptile.

repu, ~e /ʀəpy/ *adj* satiated, replete.

républicain, **~e** /ʀepyblikɛ̃, -ɛn/ a
& nm, f republican.

république /ʀepyblik/ nf republic;
~ populaire people's republic.

répudier /ʀepydje/ [45] vt repudiate;
(droit) renounce.

répugnance /ʀepynɑ̃s/ nf
repugnance; (hésitation) reluctance;
avoir de la ~ pour loathe.
répugnant, **~e** adj repulsive.

répugner /ʀepyne/ [1] vt be
repugnant to, disgust; **~ à** (effort,
violence) be averse to; **~ à faire** be
reluctant to.

répulsion /ʀepylsjɔ̃/ nf repulsion.

réputation /ʀepytasjɔ̃/ nf
reputation.

réputé, **~e** /ʀepyte/ adj renowned
(pour for); (école, compagnie)
reputable; **~ pour être** reputed to be.

requérir /ʀəkeʀiʀ/ [7] vt require,
demand.

requête /ʀəkɛt/ nf request; (Jur)
petition.

requin /ʀəkɛ̃/ nm shark.

requis, **~e** /ʀəki, -z/ adj (exigé)
required; (nécessaire) necessary.

RER abrév m (**réseau express
régional**) Parisian rapid transit
rail system.

rescapé, **~e** /ʀɛskape/ nm, f
survivor. ● adj surviving.

rescousse /ʀɛskus/ nf **à la ~** to
the rescue.

réseau (pl **~x**) /ʀezo/ nm network;
~ local local area network, LAN; **le
~ des ~x** (Ordinat) Internet.

réservation /ʀezɛʀvasjɔ̃/ nf
reservation, booking.

réserve /ʀezɛʀv/ nf reserve; (restriction) reservation, reserve; (indienne)
reservation; (entrepôt) store-room; **en
~** in reserve; **les ~s** (Mil) the
reserves.

réserver /ʀezɛʀve/ [1] vt reserve;
(place) book, reserve. □ **se ~** vpr **se
~ qch** save sth for oneself; **se ~
pour** save oneself for; **se ~ le droit
de** reserve the right to.

réservoir /ʀezɛʀvwaʀ/ nm tank;
(lac) reservoir.

résidence /ʀezidɑ̃s/ nf residence;
~ secondaire second home; **~
universitaire** hall of residence.

résident, **~e** /ʀezidɑ̃, -t/ nm, f
resident; (étranger) foreign resident.

résider /ʀezide/ [1] vi reside; **~
dans qch** (difficulté) lie in.

résigner (se) /(sə)ʀezine/ [1] vpr
se ~ à faire resign oneself to doing.

résilier /ʀezilje/ [45] vt terminate.

résine /ʀezin/ nf resin.

résistance /ʀezistɑ̃s/ nf resistance;
(fil électrique) element. **résistant**, **~e**
adj tough.

résister /ʀeziste/ [1] vi resist; **~ à**
(agresseur, assaut, influence,
tentation) resist; (corrosion, chaleur)
withstand.

résolu, **~e** /ʀezɔly/ adj resolute; **~
à faire** determined to do.
● ⇒RÉSOUDRE [53].

résolution /ʀezɔlysjɔ̃/ nf (fermeté)
resolution; (d'un problème) solving.

résonner /ʀezɔne/ [1] vi resound.

résorber /ʀezɔʀbe/ [1] vt reduce.
□ **se ~** vpr be reduced.

résoudre /ʀezudʀ/ [53] vt solve;
(crise, conflit) resolve. □ **se ~ à** vpr
(se décider) resolve to; (se résigner)
resign oneself to.

respect /ʀɛspɛ/ nm respect.
respectabilité nf respectability.

respecter /ʀɛspɛkte/ [1] vt respect;
faire ~ (loi, décision) enforce.

respectueux, **-euse** /ʀɛspɛktɥø,
-z/ adj respectful; **~ de**
l'environnement environmentally
friendly.

respiration /ʀɛspiʀasjɔ̃/ nf
breathing; (haleine) breath.
respiratoire adj respiratory,
breathing.

respirer /ʀɛspiʀe/ [1] vi breathe; (se
reposer) catch one's breath. ● vt
breathe (in); (exprimer) radiate.

resplendir /ʀɛsplɑ̃diʀ/ [2] vi shine
(de with). **resplendissant**, **~e** adj
brilliant, radiant.

responsabilité /ʀɛspɔ̃sabilite/ nf
responsibility; (légale) liability.

responsable /ʀɛspɔ̃sabl/ adj
responsible (de for); **~ de** (chargé de)
in charge of. ● nmf person in charge;
(coupable) person responsible.

resquiller /ʀɛskije/ [1] vi Ⓕ (dans le
train) fare-dodge; (au spectacle) get in

without paying; (dans la queue) jump the queue.

ressaisir (se) /(sə)Rəseziʀ/ [2] *vpr* pull oneself together; (*équipe sportive, valeurs boursières*) make a recovery.

ressemblance /Rəsãblãs/ *nf* resemblance.

ressemblant, **∼e** /Rəsãblã, -t/ *adj* être ∼ (*portrait*) be a good likeness.

ressembler /Rəsãble/ [1] *vi* ∼ à resemble, look like. □ **se** ∼ *vpr* be alike; (*physiquement*) look alike.

ressentiment /Rəsãtimã/ *nm* resentment.

ressentir /Rəsãtiʀ/ [46] *vt* feel. □ **se** ∼ *vpr* feel the effects of.

resserrer /Rəseʀe/ [1] *vt* tighten; (*contracter*) compress; (*vêtement*) take in. □ **se** ∼ *vpr* tighten; (*route*) narrow; (*se regrouper*) move closer together.

ressort /RəsɔR/ *nm* (*objet*) spring; (fig) energy; **être du** ∼ **de** be the province of; (*Jur*) be within the jurisdiction of; **en dernier** ∼ as a last resort.

ressortir /RəsɔRtiʀ/ [46] *vi* go *ou* come back out; (*se voir*) stand out; (*film, disque*) be re-released; **faire** ∼ bring out; **il ressort que** it emerges that. ● *vt* take out again; (*redire*) come out with again; (*disque, film*) re-release.

ressortissant, **∼e** /RəsɔRtisã, -t/ *nm,f* national.

ressource /RəsuRs/ *nf* resource; ∼**s** resources; **à bout de** ∼ at one's wits' end.

ressusciter /Resysite/ [1] *vi* come back to life. ● *vt* bring back to life; (fig) revive.

restant, **∼e** /Rəstã, -t/ *adj* remaining. ● *nm* remainder.

restaurant /RəstoRã/ *nm* restaurant.

restauration /RəstoRasjɔ̃/ *nf* restoration; (*hôtellerie*) catering.

restaurer /RəstɔRe/ [1] *vt* restore. □ **se** ∼ *vpr* eat.

reste /Rεst/ *nm* rest; (d'une soustraction) remainder; ∼**s** remains (de of); (nourriture) leftovers; **un** ∼ **de poulet** some left-over chicken; **au** ∼, **du** ∼ moreover, besides.

rester /Rεste/ [1] *vi* (aux être) stay, remain; (subsister) be left, remain; **il reste du pain** there is some bread left (over); **il me reste du pain** I have some bread left (over); **il me reste à** it remains for me to; **en** ∼ **à** go no further than; **en** ∼ **là** stop there.

restituer /Rεstitɥe/ [1] *vt* (rendre) return; (recréer) reproduce; (rétablir) reconstruct.

restreindre /RεstRɛ̃dR/ [22] *vt* restrict. □ **se** ∼ *vpr* (dans les dépenses) cut back.

résultat /Rezylta/ *nm* result.

résulter /Rezylte/ [1] *vi* ∼ **de** result from, be the result of.

résumé /Rezyme/ *nm* summary; **en** ∼ in short; (pour finir) to sum up.

résumer [1] *vt* summarize.

résurrection /RezyRεksjɔ̃/ *nf* resurrection; (renouveau) revival.

rétablir /Retabliʀ/ [2] *vt* restore; (*personne*) restore to health. □ **se** ∼ *vpr* (ordre, silence) be restored; (guérir) recover. **rétablissement** *nm* restoration; (de malade, monnaie) recovery.

retard /RətaR/ *nm* lateness; (sur un programme) delay; (infériorité) backwardness; **avoir du** ∼ be late; (*montre*) be slow; **en** ∼ late; (retardé) behind; **en** ∼ **sur l'emploi du temps** behind schedule; **rattraper** *ou* **combler son** ∼ catch up; **prendre du** ∼ fall behind.

retardataire /RətaRdatεR/ *nmf* latecomer. ● *adj* late.

retarder /RətaRde/ [1] *vt* ∼ **qn/qch** delay sb/sth, hold sb/sth up; (par rapport à une heure convenue) make sb/ sth late; (*montre*) put back. ● *vi* (*montre*) be slow; (*personne*) be out of touch.

retenir /RətniʀR/ [58] *vt* hold back; (souffle, attention, prisonnier) hold; (eau, chaleur) retain, hold; (larmes) hold back; (garder) keep; (retarder) detain, hold up; (réserver) book; (se rappeler) remember; (déduire) deduct; (accepter) accept. □ **se** ∼ *vpr* (se contenir) restrain oneself; **se** ∼ **à** hold on to; **se** ∼ **de faire** stop oneself from doing.

rétention /Retãsjɔ̃/ *nf* retention.

retentir /ʀətɑ̃tiʀ/ [2] *vi* ring out, resound; ∼ **sur** have an impact on.
retentissant, ∼**e** *adj* resounding.
retentissement *nm* (effet) effect.

retenue /ʀətny/ *nf* restraint; (somme) deduction; (Scol) detention.

réticent, ∼**e** /ʀetisɑ̃, -t/ *adj* (hésitant) hesitant; (qui rechigne) reluctant; (réservé) reticent.

rétine /ʀetin/ *nf* retina.

retiré, ∼**e** /ʀətiʀe/ *adj* (vie) secluded; (lieu) remote.

retirer /ʀətiʀe/ [1] *vt* (sortir) take out; (ôter) take off; (argent, offre, candidature) withdraw; (écarter) (main, pied) withdraw; (billet, bagages) collect, pick up; (avantage) derive; ∼ **à qn** take away from sb. □ **se** ∼ *vpr* withdraw, retire.

retombées /ʀətɔ̃be/ *nfpl* (conséquences) effects; ∼ **radioactives** nuclear fall-out.

retomber /ʀətɔ̃be/ [1] *vi* (faire une chute) fall again; (retourner au sol) land, come down; ∼ **dans** (erreur) fall back into.

retouche /ʀətuʃ/ *nf* alteration; (de photo, tableau) retouch.

retour /ʀətuʀ/ *nm* return; **être de** ∼ be back (**de** from); ∼ **en arrière** flashback; **par** ∼ **du courrier** by return of post; **en** ∼ in return.

retourner /ʀətuʀne/ [1] *vt* (aux avoir) turn over; (vêtement) turn inside out; (maison) turn upside down; (lettre, compliment) return; (émouvoir 🟊) shake, upset. ● *vi* (aux être) go back, return. □ **se** ∼ *vpr* turn round; (dans son lit) twist and turn; **s'en** ∼ go back; **se** ∼ **contre** turn against.

retrait /ʀətʀɛ/ *nm* withdrawal; (des eaux) receding; **être** (**situé**) **en** ∼ (**de**) be set back (from).

retraite /ʀətʀɛt/ *nf* retirement; (pension) (retirement) pension; (fuite, refuge) retreat; **mettre à la** ∼ pension off; **prendre sa** ∼ retire.

retraité, ∼**e** /ʀətʀete/ *adj* retired. ● *nm, f* (old-age) pensioner.

retrancher /ʀətʀɑ̃ʃe/ [1] *vt* remove; (soustraire) deduct, subtract. □ **se** ∼ *vpr* (Mil) entrench oneself; **se** ∼ **derrière** take refuge behind.

retransmettre /ʀətʀɑ̃smɛtʀ/ [42] *vt* broadcast.

rétrécir /ʀetʀesiʀ/ [2] *vt* make narrower; (vêtement) take in. ● *vi* (tissu) shrink. □ **se** ∼ *vpr* (rue) narrow.

rétribution /ʀetʀibysjɔ̃/ *nf* payment.

rétroactif, -**ive** /ʀetʀɔaktif, -v/ *adj* retrospective; **augmentation à effet** ∼ backdated pay rise.

retrousser /ʀətʀuse/ [1] *vt* pull up; (manche) roll up.

retrouvailles /ʀətʀuvɑj/ *nfpl* reunion.

retrouver /ʀətʀuve/ [1] *vt* find (again); (rejoindre) meet (again); (forces, calme) regain; (lieu) be back in; (se rappeler) remember. □ **se** ∼ *vpr* find oneself (back); (se réunir) meet (again); (être présent) be found; **s'y** ∼ (s'orienter, comprendre) find one's way; (rentrer dans ses frais 🟊) break even.

rétroviseur /ʀetʀɔvizœʀ/ *nm* (Auto) (rear-view) mirror.

réunion /ʀeynjɔ̃/ *nf* meeting; (rencontre) gathering; (après une séparation) réunion; (d'objets) collection.

réunir /ʀeyniʀ/ [2] *vt* gather, collect; (rapprocher) bring together; (convoquer) call together; (raccorder) join; (qualités) combine. □ **se** ∼ *vpr* meet.

réussi, ∼**e** /ʀeysi/ *adj* successful.

réussir /ʀeysiʀ/ [2] *vi* succeed, be successful; ∼ **à faire** succeed in doing, manage to do; ∼ **à un examen** pass an exam; ∼ **à qn** (méthode) work well for sb; (climat, mode de vie) agree with sb. ● *vt* (vie) make a success of.

réussite /ʀeysit/ *nf* success; (jeu) patience.

revaloir /ʀəvalwaʀ/ [60] *vt* **je vous revaudrai cela** (en mal) I'll pay you back for this; (en bien) I'll repay you some day.

revanche /ʀəvɑ̃ʃ/ *nf* revenge; (Sport) return *ou* revenge match; **en** ∼ on the other hand.

rêvasser /ʀɛvase/ [1] *vi* daydream.

rêve /ʀɛv/ *nm* dream; **faire un** ∼ have a dream.

réveil /Revɛj/ nm waking up, (fig) awakening; (pendule) alarm clock.

réveillé, ~e /Reveje/ adj awake.

réveille-matin /Revɛjmatɛ̃/ nm inv alarm clock.

réveiller /Reveje/ [1] vt wake (up); (sentiment, souvenir) awaken; (curiosité) arouse. □ se ~ vpr wake up.

réveillon /Revɛjɔ̃/ nm (Noël) Christmas Eve; (nouvel an) New Year's Eve. **réveillonner** [1] vi see Christmas ou the New Year in.

révéler /Revele/ [14] vt reveal. □ se ~ vpr be revealed; se ~ facile turn out to be easy, prove easy.

revendeur, -euse /Revɑ̃dœr, -øz/ nm, f dealer, stockist; ~ de drogue drug dealer.

revendication /Revɑ̃dikasjɔ̃/ nf claim. **revendiquer** [1] vt claim.

revendre /Rəvɑ̃dʀ/ [3] vt sell (again); **avoir de l'énergie à ~** have energy to spare.

revenir /Rəvnir/ [58] vi (aux être) come back, return (à to); ~ à (activité) go back to; (se résumer à) come down to; (échoir à) fall to; ~ à 100 francs cost 100 francs; ~ de (maladie, surprise) get over; ~ sur ses pas retrace one's steps; faire ~ (Culin) brown; ça me revient! now I remember!; je n'en reviens pas! Ⓘ I can't get over it!

revenu /Rəvny/ nm income; (de l'État) revenue.

rêver /Reve/ [1] vt/i dream (à of; de faire of doing).

réverbère /Reverber/ nm street lamp.

révérence /Reverɑ̃s/ nf reverence; (salut d'homme) bow; (salut de femme) curtsy.

rêverie /Revri/ nf daydream; (activité) daydreaming.

revers /Rəver/ nm reverse; (de main) back; (d'étoffe) wrong side; (de veste) lapel; (de pantalon) turn-up; (de manche) cuff; (tennis) backhand; (fig) set-back.

revêtement /Rəvetmɑ̃/ nm covering; (de route) surface; ~ de sol floor covering. **revêtir** [61] vt cover; (habit) put on; (prendre, avoir) assume.

rêveur, -euse /Revœr, -øz/ adj dreamy. ● nm, f dreamer.

réviser /Revize/ [1] vt revise; (machine, véhicule) service. **révision** nf revision; service.

revivre /Rəvivr/ [62] vi come alive again. ● vt relive.

révocation /Revɔkasjɔ̃/ nf repeal; (d'un fonctionnaire) dismissal.

revoir[1] /Rəvwar/ [63] vt see (again); (réviser) revise.

revoir[2] /Rəvwar/ nm au ~ goodbye.

révolte /Revɔlt/ nf revolt. **révolté**, ~e nm, f rebel.

révolter /Revɔlte/ [1] vt appal, revolt. □ se ~ vpr revolt.

révolu, ~e /Revɔly/ adj past; **avoir 21 ans** ~s be over 21 years of age.

révolution /Revɔlysjɔ̃/ nf revolution. **révolutionnaire** a & nmf revolutionary. **révolutionner** [1] vt revolutionize.

revolver /Revɔlver/ nm revolver, gun.

révoquer /Revɔke/ [1] vt repeal; (fonctionnaire) dismiss.

revue /Rəvy/ nf (examen, défilé) review; (magazine) magazine; (spectacle) variety show.

rez-de-chaussée /Redʃose/ nm inv ground floor; (US) first floor.

RF abrév f (**République Française**) French Republic.

rhinocéros /Rinɔseʀɔs/ nm rhinoceros.

rhubarbe /Rybarb/ nf rhubarb.

rhum /Rɔm/ nm rum.

rhumatisme /Rymatism/ nm rheumatism.

rhume /Rym/ nm cold; ~ des foins hay fever.

ri /Ri/ ⇒RIRE [54].

ricaner /Rikane/ [1] vi snigger.

riche /Riʃ/ adj rich (en in). ● nmf rich man, rich woman.

richesse /Riʃɛs/ nf wealth; (de sol, décor) richness; ~s wealth; (ressources) resources.

ride /Rid/ nf wrinkle; (sur l'eau) ripple.

rideau (pl ~x) /Rido/ nm curtain; (métallique) shutter; (fig) screen.

ridicule /Ridikyl/ adj ridiculous. ● nm (d'une situation) absurdity; (le grotesque; **le** ~ ridicule. **ridiculiser** [1] *vt* ridicule.

rien /ʀjɛ̃/ *pron* nothing; (quoi que ce soit) anything; **de** ~**!** I don't mention it!; ~ **de bon** nothing good; **elle n'a** ~ **dit** she didn't say anything; ~ **d'autre/de plus** nothing else/more; ~ **du tout** nothing at all; ~ **que** (seulement) just, only; **trois fois** ~ next to nothing; **il n'y est pour** ~ he has nothing to do with it; ~ **à faire!** (c'est impossible) it's no good!; (refus) no way! Ⓘ. ● *nm* **un** ~ **de** a touch of; **être puni pour un** ~ be punished for the slightest thing; **se disputer pour un** ~ fight over nothing; **en un** ~ **de temps** in next to no time.

rieur, -euse /ʀijœʀ, -øz/ *adj* cheerful; (*yeux*) laughing.

rigide /ʀiʒid/ *adj* rigid.

rigolade /ʀigɔlad/ *nf* fun.

rigoler /ʀigɔle/ [1] *vi* laugh; (s'amuser) have some fun; (plaisanter) joke.

rigolo, ~te /ʀigɔlo, -ɔt/ *adj* Ⓘ funny. ● *nm, f* Ⓘ joker.

rigoureux, -euse /ʀiguʀø, -z/ *adj* rigorous; (*hiver*) harsh; (sévère) strict; (*travail, recherches*) meticulous.

rigueur /ʀigœʀ/ *nf* rigour; **à la** ~ at a pinch; **être de** ~ be obligatory; **tenir** ~ **à qn de qch** bear sb a grudge for sth.

rime /ʀim/ *nf* rhyme.

rimer /ʀime/ [1] *vi* rhyme (**avec** with); **cela ne rime à rien** it makes no sense.

rinçage /ʀɛ̃saʒ/ *nm* rinse; (action) rinsing.

rincer /ʀɛ̃se/ [10] *vt* rinse.

riposte /ʀipɔst/ *nf* retort.

riposter /ʀipɔste/ [1] *vi* retaliate; ~ **à** (*attaque*) counter; (*insulte*) reply to. ● *vt* retort (**que** that).

rire /ʀiʀ/ [54] *vi* laugh (**de** at); (plaisanter) joke; (s'amuser) have fun; **c'était pour** ~ it was a joke. ● *nm* laugh; **des** ~**s** laughter.

risée /ʀize/ *nf* **la** ~ **de** the laughing-stock of.

risque /ʀisk/ *nm* risk. **risqué, ~e** *adj* risky; (osé) daring.

risquer /ʀiske/ [1] *vt* risk (**de faire** of doing); (être passible de) face; **il risque**

de pleuvoir it might rain; **tu risques de te faire mal** you might hurt yourself. ◻ **se** ~ **à/dans** *vpr* venture to/into.

ristourne /ʀistuʀn/ *nf* discount.

rite /ʀit/ *nm* rite; (habitude) ritual. **rituel, ~le** *a & nm* ritual.

rivage /ʀivaʒ/ *nm* shore.

rival, ~e (*mpl* **-aux**) /ʀival, -o/ *a & nm, f* rival. **rivaliser** [1] *vi* compete (**avec** with). **rivalité** *nf* rivalry.

rive /ʀiv/ *nf* (de fleuve) bank; (de lac) shore.

riverain, ~e /ʀivʀɛ̃, -ɛn/ *adj* riverside. ● *nm, f* riverside resident; (d'une rue) resident.

rivière /ʀivjɛʀ/ *nf* river.

riz /ʀi/ *nm* rice. **rizière** *nf* paddy field.

robe /ʀɔb/ *nf* (de femme) dress; (de juge) robe; (de cheval) coat; ~ **de chambre** dressing-gown.

robinet /ʀɔbinɛ/ *nm* tap; (US) faucet.

robot /ʀɔbo/ *nm* robot; ~ **ménager** food processor.

robuste /ʀɔbyst/ *adj* robust.

roche /ʀɔʃ/ *nf* rock.

rocher /ʀɔʃe/ *nm* rock.

rock /ʀɔk/ *nm* (Mus) rock.

rodage /ʀɔdaʒ/ *nm* **en** ~ (Auto) running in.

roder /ʀɔde/ [1] *vt* (Auto) run in; **être rodé** (*personne*) have got the hang of things.

rôder /ʀode/ [1] *vi* roam; (*suspect*) prowl.

rogne /ʀɔɲ/ *nf* Ⓘ anger; **en** ~ in a temper.

rogner /ʀɔɲe/ [1] *vt* trim; ~ **sur** cut down on.

rognon /ʀɔɲɔ̃/ *nm* (Culin) kidney.

roi /ʀwa/ *nm* king; **les R**~ **mages** the Magi; **la fête des R**~ Twelfth Night.

rôle /ʀol/ *nm* role, part.

romain, ~e /ʀɔmɛ̃, -ɛn/ *adj* Roman. **R**~, **~e** *nm, f* Roman. **romaine** *nf* (laitue) cos.

roman /ʀɔmɑ̃/ *nm* novel; (genre) fiction.

romance /ʀɔmɑ̃s/ *nf* ballad.

romancier, -ière /ʀɔmɑ̃sje, -jɛʀ/ *nm, f* novelist.

romanesque /ʀɔmanɛsk/ *adj*
romantic; (*fantastique*) fantastic; (*récit*)
fictional; œuvres ∼s novels, fiction.

romantique /ʀɔmɑ̃tik/ *a & nmf*
romantic. **romantisme** *nm*
romanticism.

rompre /ʀɔ̃pʀ/ [3] *vt* break;
(*relations*) break off. ● *vi* (se *séparer*)
break up; ∼ avec (*fiancé*) break up
with; (*parti*) break away from;
(*tradition*) break with. □ se ∼ *vpr*
break.

ronce /ʀɔ̃s/ *nf* bramble.

rond, ∼e /ʀɔ̃, -d/ *adj* round; (gras)
plump; (ivre 🅿) drunk. ● *nm* (cercle)
ring; (tranche) slice; en ∼ in a circle;
il n'a pas un ∼ 🅿 he hasn't got a
penny.

ronde /ʀɔ̃d/ *nf* (de policier) beat; (de
soldat, gardien) watch; (Mus) semibreve.

rondelle /ʀɔ̃dɛl/ *nf* (Tech) washer;
(tranche) slice.

rondement /ʀɔ̃dmɑ̃/ *adv* promptly;
(franchement) frankly.

rondeur /ʀɔ̃dœʀ/ *nf* roundness;
(franchise) frankness; (embonpoint)
plumpness.

rondin /ʀɔ̃dɛ̃/ *nm* log.

rond-point (*pl* ronds-points)
/ʀɔ̃pwɛ̃/ *nm* roundabout; (US) traffic
circle.

ronfler /ʀɔ̃fle/ [1] *vi* snore; (*moteur*)
purr.

ronger /ʀɔ̃ʒe/ [40] *vt* gnaw (at); (*vers,
acide*) eat into. □ se ∼ *vpr* se ∼ les
ongles bite one's nails.

rongeur /ʀɔ̃ʒœʀ/ *nm* rodent.

ronronner /ʀɔ̃ʀɔne/ [1] *vi* purr.

rosbif /ʀɔsbif/ *nm* roast beef.

rose /ʀoz/ *nf* rose. ● *a & nm* pink.

rosé, ∼e /ʀoze/ *adj* pinkish. ● *nm*
rosé.

roseau (*pl* ∼x) /ʀozo/ *nm* reed.

rosée /ʀoze/ *nf* dew.

rosier /ʀozje/ *nm* rose bush.

rossignol /ʀɔsiɲɔl/ *nm* nightingale.

rotatif, -ive /ʀɔtatif, -v/ *adj* rotary.

roter /ʀɔte/ [1] *vi* 🅿 burp.

rôti /ʀɔti/ *nm* joint; (cuit) roast; ∼ de
porc roast pork.

rotin /ʀɔtɛ̃/ *nm* (rattan) cane.

rôtir /ʀɔtiʀ/ [2] *vt* roast.

rôtissoire /ʀɔtiswaʀ/ *nf* roasting
spit.

rotule /ʀɔtyl/ *nf* kneecap.

rouage /ʀwaʒ/ *nm* (Tech) wheel; les
∼s the works; (d'une organisation: fig)
wheels.

roucouler /ʀukule/ [1] *vi* coo.

roue /ʀu/ *nf* wheel; ∼ dentée cog
(wheel); ∼ de secours spare wheel.

rouer /ʀwe/ [1] *vt* ∼ de coups
thrash.

rouge /ʀuʒ/ *adj* red; (*fer*) red-hot.
● *nm* red; (vin) red wine; (fard)
blusher; ∼ à lèvres lipstick. ● *nmf*
(Pol) red. **rouge-gorge** (*pl* rouges-
gorges) *nm* robin.

rougeole /ʀuʒɔl/ *nf* measles (+ *sg*).

rouget /ʀuʒɛ/ *nm* red mullet.

rougeur /ʀuʒœʀ/ *nf* redness; (tache)
red blotch.

rougir /ʀuʒiʀ/ [2] *vi* turn red; (de
honte) blush.

rouille /ʀuj/ *nf* rust. **rouillé, ∼e** *adj*
rusty.

rouiller /ʀuje/ [1] *vi* rust. □ se ∼
vpr get rusty.

rouleau (*pl* ∼x) /ʀulo/ *nm* roll;
(outil, vague) roller; ∼ à pâtisserie
rolling pin; ∼ compresseur
steamroller.

roulement /ʀulmɑ̃/ *nm* rotation;
(bruit) rumble; (alternance) rotation; (de
tambour) roll; ∼ à billes ball-bearing;
travailler par ∼ work in shifts.

rouler /ʀule/ [1] *vt* roll; (*ficelle,
manches*) roll up; (*pâte*) roll out;
(duper 🅿) cheat. ● *vi* (*véhicule, train*)
go, travel; (*conducteur*) drive. □ se
∼ dans *vpr* (*herbe*) roll in;
(*couverture*) roll oneself up in.

roulette /ʀulɛt/ *nf* (de meuble) castor;
(de dentiste) drill; (jeu) roulette;
comme sur des ∼s very smoothly.

roulotte /ʀulɔt/ *nf* caravan.

roumain, ∼e /ʀumɛ̃, -ɛn/ *adj*
Romanian. R∼, ∼e *nm, f* Romanian.

Roumanie /ʀumani/ *nf* Romania.

rouquin, ∼e /ʀukɛ̃, -in/ 🅿 *adj* red-
haired. ● *nm, f* redhead.

rouspéter /ʀuspete/ [14] *vi* 🅿
grumble, moan.

rousse /ʀus/ ⇒ROUX.

roussir /ʀusiʀ/ [2] *vt* scorch. ● *vi* turn brown.

route /ʀut/ *nf* road; (Naut, Aviat) route; (direction) way; (voyage) journey; (chemin: fig) path; **en ~** on the way; **en ~!** let's go!; **mettre en ~** start; **~ nationale** trunk road, main road; **se mettre en ~** set out; **il y a une heure de ~** it's an hour's journey.

routier, -ière /ʀutje, -jɛʀ/ *adj* road. ● *nm* long-distance lorry *ou* truck driver; (restaurant) transport café; (US) truck stop.

routine /ʀutin/ *nf* routine.

roux, rousse /ʀu, ʀus/ *adj* red, russet; (*personne*) red-haired; (*chat*) ginger. ● *nm, f* redhead.

royal, ~e (*mpl* **-aux**) /ʀwajal, -jo/ *adj* royal; (*cadeau*) fit for a king.

royaume /ʀwajom/ *nm* kingdom.

Royaume-Uni /ʀwajomyni/ *nm* United Kingdom.

royauté /ʀwajote/ *nf* royalty.

ruban /ʀybɑ̃/ *nm* ribbon; (de chapeau) band; **~ adhésif** sticky tape; **~ magnétique** magnetic tape.

rubéole /ʀybeɔl/ *nf* German measles (+ *sg*).

rubis /ʀybi/ *nm* ruby; (de montre) jewel.

rubrique /ʀybʀik/ *nf* heading; (article) column.

ruche /ʀyʃ/ *nf* beehive.

rude /ʀyd/ *adj* (au toucher) rough; (pénible) tough; (grossier) coarse; (fameux 🔢) tremendous.

rudement /ʀydmɑ̃/ *adv* (frapper) hard; (traiter) harshly; (très 🔢) really.

rudimentaire /ʀydimɑ̃tɛʀ/ *adj* rudimentary.

rue /ʀy/ *nf* street.

ruée /ʀɥe/ *nf* rush.

ruer /ʀɥe/ [1] *vi* (cheval) buck. □ **se ~** *vpr* rush (**dans** into; **vers** towards); **se ~ sur** pounce on.

rugby /ʀygbi/ *nm* rugby.

rugir /ʀyʒiʀ/ [2] *vi* roar.

rugueux, -euse /ʀygø, -z/ *adj* rough.

ruine /ʀɥin/ *nf* ruin; **en ~(s)** in ruins. **ruiner** [1] *vt* ruin.

ruisseau (*pl* **~x**) /ʀɥiso/ *nm* stream; (rigole) gutter.

rumeur /ʀymœʀ/ *nf* (nouvelle) rumour; (son) murmur, hum.

ruminer /ʀymine/ [1] *vi* (animal) ruminate; (méditer) meditate.

rupture /ʀyptyʀ/ *nf* break; (action) breaking; (de contrat) breach; (de pourparlers) breakdown; (de relations) breaking off; (de couple, coalition) break-up.

rural, ~e (*mpl* **-aux**) /ʀyʀal, -o/ *adj* rural.

ruse /ʀyz/ *nf* cunning; **une ~** a trick, a ruse. **rusé, ~e** *adj* cunning.

russe /ʀys/ *adj* Russian. ● *nm* (Ling) Russian. **R~** *nmf* Russian.

Russie /ʀysi/ *nf* Russia.

rustique /ʀystik/ *adj* rustic.

rythme /ʀitm/ *nm* rhythm; (vitesse) rate; (de la vie) pace. **rythmique** *adj* rhythmical.

Ss

s' /s/ ⇒SE.

sa /sa/ ⇒SON[1].

SA *abrév f* (**société anonyme**) PLC.

sabbatique /sabatik/ *adj* (année) sabbatical year.

sable /sɑbl/ *nm* sand; **~s mouvants** quicksands. **sabler** *vt* [1] grit.

sablier /sablije/ *nm* (Culin) eggtimer.

sablonneux, -euse /sablɔnø, -z/ *adj* sandy.

sabot /sabo/ *nm* (de cheval) hoof; (chaussure) clog; (de frein) shoe; **~ de Denver®** (wheel) clamp.

saboter /sabɔte/ [1] *vt* sabotage; (bâcler) botch.

sac /sak/ *nm* bag; (grand, en toile) sack; **mettre à ~** (maison) ransack; (ville) sack; **~ à dos** rucksack; **~ à main** handbag; **~ de couchage** sleeping-bag; **mettre dans le même ~** lump together.

saccadé, ~e /sakade/ *adj* jerky.

saccager /sakaʒe/ [40] vt (abîmer) wreck; (maison) ransack; (ville, pays) sack.

saccharine /sakaʀin/ nf saccharin.

sachet /saʃɛ/ nm (small) bag; (d'aromates) sachet; ~ de thé tea-bag.

sacoche /sakɔʃ/ nf bag; (de vélo) saddlebag.

sacre /sakʀ/ nm (de roi) coronation; (d'évêque) consecration. **sacré**, ~e adj sacred; (maudit 🔢) damned. **sacrement** nm sacrament. **sacrer** [1] vt crown; consecrate.

sacrifice /sakʀifis/ nm sacrifice.

sacrifier /sakʀifje/ [45] vt sacrifice; ~ à conform to. □ se ~ vpr sacrifice oneself.

sacrilège /sakʀilɛʒ/ nm sacrilege. ● adj sacrilegious.

sadique /sadik/ adj sadistic. ● nmf sadist.

sage /saʒ/ adj wise; (docile) good, well behaved. ● nm wise man.

sage-femme (pl **sages-femmes**) /saʒfam/ nf midwife.

sagesse /saʒɛs/ nf wisdom.

Sagittaire /saʒitɛʀ/ nm le ~ Sagittarius.

saignant, ~e /sɛɲɑ̃, -t/ adj (Culin) rare.

saigner /seɲe/ [1] vt/i bleed; ~ du nez have a nosebleed.

saillant, ~e /sajɑ̃, -t/ adj prominent.

sain, ~e /sɛ̃, sɛn/ adj healthy; (moralement) sane; ~ et sauf safe and sound.

saindoux /sɛ̃du/ nm lard.

saint, ~e /sɛ̃, -t/ adj holy; (bon, juste) saintly. ● nm, f saint. **Saint-Esprit** nm Holy Spirit. **sainteté** nf holiness; (d'un lieu) sanctity. **Sainte Vierge** nf Blessed Virgin. **Saint-Sylvestre** nf New Year's Eve.

sais /sɛ/ ⇒SAVOIR [55].

saisie /sezi/ nf (Jur) seizure; (Comput) keyboarding; ~ de données data capture.

saisir /seziʀ/ [2] vt grab (hold of); (proie) seize; (occasion, biens) seize; (comprendre) grasp; (frapper) strike; (Ordinat) keyboard, capture; **saisi de** (peur) stricken by, overcome by. □ se ~ de vpr seize. **saisissant**, ~e adj (spectacle) gripping.

saison /sɛzɔ̃/ nf season; la morte ~ the off season. **saisonnier**, -ière adj seasonal.

sait /sɛ/ ⇒SAVOIR [55].

salade /salad/ nf (plat) salad; (plante) lettuce. **saladier** nm salad bowl.

salaire /salɛʀ/ nm wages (+ pl), salary.

salarié, ~e /salaʀje/ adj wage-earning. ● nm, f wage earner.

sale /sal/ adj dirty; (mauvais) nasty.

salé, ~e /sale/ adj (goût) salty; (plat) salted; (opposé à sucré) savoury; (grivois 🔢) spicy; (excessif 🔢) steep. **saler** [1] vt salt.

saleté /salte/ nf dirtiness; (crasse) dirt; (obscénité) obscenity; ~(s) (camelote) rubbish; (détritus) mess.

salir /saliʀ/ [2] vt (make) dirty; (réputation) tarnish. □ se ~ vpr get dirty. **salissant**, ~e adj dirty; (étoffe) easily dirtied.

salive /saliv/ nf saliva.

salle /sal/ nf room; (grande, publique) hall; (de restaurant) dining room; (Théât, cinéma) auditorium; **cinéma à trois** ~s three-screen cinema; ~ à **manger** dining room; ~ **d'attente** waiting room; ~ **de bains** bathroom; ~ **de séjour** living room; ~ **de classe** classroom; ~ **d'embarquement** departure lounge; ~ **d'opération** operating theatre; ~ **des ventes** saleroom.

salon /salɔ̃/ nm lounge; (de coiffure, beauté) salon; (exposition) show; ~ **de thé** tea-room.

salopette /salɔpɛt/ nf dungarees (+ pl); (d'ouvrier) overalls (+ pl).

saltimbanque /saltɛ̃bɑ̃k/ nmf (street) acrobat.

salubre /salybʀ/ adj healthy.

saluer /salɥe/ [1] vt greet; (en partant) take one's leave of; (de la tête) nod to; (de la main) wave to; (Mil) salute; (accueillir favorablement) welcome.

salut /saly/ nm greeting; (de la tête) nod; (de la main) wave; (Mil) salute; (rachat) salvation. ● interj (bonjour 🔢) hello; (au revoir 🔢) bye.

salutation /salytasjɔ̃/ nf greeting.

samedi /samdi/ *nm* Saturday.

SAMU /samy/ *abrév m* (**Service d'assistance médicale d'urgence**) ≈ mobile accident unit.

sanction /sɑ̃ksjɔ̃/ *nf* sanction. **sanctionner** [1] *vt* sanction; (*punir*) punish.

sandale /sɑ̃dal/ *nf* sandal.

sang /sɑ̃/ *nm* blood; **se faire du mauvais ~ ou un ~ d'encre** be worried stiff. **sang-froid** *nm inv* self-control. **sanglant, ~e** *adj* bloody.

sangle /sɑ̃gl/ *nf* strap.

sanglier /sɑ̃glije/ *nm* wild boar.

sanglot /sɑ̃glo/ *nm* sob. **sangloter** [1] *vi* sob.

sanguin, ~e /sɑ̃gɛ̃, -in/ *adj* (*groupe*) blood.

sanguinaire /sɑ̃ginɛʀ/ *adj* bloodthirsty.

sanisette® /sanizɛt/ *nf* automatic public toilet.

sanitaire /sanitɛʀ/ *adj* (*directives*) health; (*conditions*) sanitary; (*appareils, installations*) bathroom, sanitary. **sanitaires** *nmpl* bathroom.

sans /sɑ̃/ *prép* without; **~ ça, ~ quoi** otherwise; **~ arrêt** nonstop; **~ encombre/faute/tarder** without incident/fail/delay; **~ fin/goût/limite** endless/tasteless/limitless; **~ importance/pareil/précédent/travail** unimportant/unparalleled/unprecedented/unemployed; **j'ai aimé mais ~ plus** it was good, it wasn't great.

sans-abri /sɑ̃zabʀi/ *nmf inv* homeless person.

sans-gêne /sɑ̃ʒɛn/ *a inv* inconsiderate, thoughtless. ● *nm inv* thoughtlessness.

sans-papiers /sɑ̃papje/ *nm inv* illegal immigrant.

santé /sɑ̃te/ *nf* health; **à ta ou votre ~!** cheers!

saoul, ~e /su, sul/ ⇒SOÛL.

sapin /sapɛ̃/ *nm* fir(tree); **~ de Noël** Christmas tree.

sarcasme /saʀkasm/ *nm* sarcasm. **sarcastique** *adj* sarcastic.

sardine /saʀdin/ *nf* sardine.

sas /sɑs/ *nm* (Naut, Aviat) airlock.

satané, ~e /satane/ *adj* 🅸 damned.

satellite /satelit/ *nm* satellite.

satin /satɛ̃/ *nm* satin.

satire /satiʀ/ *nf* satire.

satisfaction /satisfaksjɔ̃/ *nf* satisfaction.

satisfaire /satisfɛʀ/ [33] *vt* satisfy. ● *vi* **~ à** fulfil. **satisfaisant, ~e** *adj* (*acceptable*) satisfactory. **satisfait, ~e** *adj* satisfied (**de** with).

saturer /satyʀe/ [1] *vt* saturate.

sauce /sos/ *nf* sauce; **~ tartare** tartar sauce. **saucière** *nf* sauceboat.

saucisse /sosis/ *nf* sausage.

saucisson /sosisɔ̃/ *nm* (slicing) sausage.

sauf¹ /sof/ *prép* except; **~ erreur** if I'm not mistaken; **~ imprévu** unless anything unforeseen happens; **~ avis contraire** unless otherwise stated.

sauf², -ve /sof, sov/ *adj* safe, unharmed.

sauge /soʒ/ *nf* (Culin) sage.

saule /sol/ *nm* willow; **~ pleureur** weeping willow.

saumon /somɔ̃/ *nm* salmon. ● *a inv* salmon-(pink).

sauna /sona/ *nm* sauna.

saupoudrer /sopudʀe/ [1] *vt* sprinkle (**de** with).

saut /so/ *nm* jump; **faire un ~ chez qn** pop round to sb's (place); **le ~** (Sport) jumping; **~ en hauteur/longueur** high/long jump; **~ périlleux** somersault; **au ~ du lit** on getting up.

sauté, ~e /sote/ *a & nm* (Culin) sauté.

saute-mouton /sotmutɔ̃/ *nm inv* leap-frog.

sauter /sote/ [1] *vi* jump; (*exploser*) blow up; (*fusible*) blow; (*se détacher*) come off; **faire ~** (*détruire*) blow up; (*fusible*) blow; (*casser*) break; **~ à la corde** skip; **~ aux yeux** be obvious; **~ au cou de qn** fling one's arms round sb; **~ sur une occasion** jump at an opportunity. ● *vt* jump (over); (*page, classe*) skip.

sauterelle /sotʀɛl/ *nf* grasshopper.
sautiller /sotije/ [1] *vi* hop.
sauvage /sovaʒ/ *adj* wild; (primitif, cruel) savage; (farouche) unsociable; (illégal) unauthorized. ● *nmf* unsociable person; (brute) savage.
sauve /sov/ ⇒SAUF[2].
sauvegarder /sovgaʀde/ [1] *vt* safeguard; (Ordinat) back up.
sauver /sove/ [1] *vt* save; (d'un danger) rescue, save; (matériel) salvage. □ **se ∼** *vpr* (fuir) run away; (partir 🔢) be off. **sauvetage** *nm* rescue. **sauveteur** *nm* rescuer. **sauveur** *nm* saviour.
savant, **∼e** /savã, -t/ *adj* learned; (habile) skilful. ● *nm* scientist.
saveur /savœʀ/ *nf* flavour; (fig) savour.
savoir /savwaʀ/ [55] *vt* know; **elle sait conduire/nager** she can drive/ swim; **faire ∼ à qn que** inform sb that; **(pas) que je sache** (not) as far as I know; **à ∼** namely. ● *nm* learning.
savon /savõ/ *nm* soap; **passer un ∼ à qn** 🔢 give sb a telling-off. **savonnette** *nf* bar of soap. **savonneux**, **-euse** *adj* soapy.
savourer /savuʀe/ [1] *vt* savour. **savoureux**, **-euse** *adj* tasty; (fig) spicy.
scandale /skãdal/ *nm* scandal; (tapage) uproar; (en public) noisy scene; **faire ∼** shock people; **faire un ∼** make a scene. **scandaleux**, **-euse** *adj* scandalous. **scandaliser** [1] *vt* scandalize, shock.
scander /skãde/ [1] *vt* (vers) scan; (slogan) chant.
scandinave /skãdinav/ *adj* Scandinavian. **S∼** *nmf* Scandinavian.
Scandinavie /skãdinavi/ *nf* Scandinavia.
scarabée /skaʀabe/ *nm* beetle.
sceau (*pl* **∼x**) /so/ *nm* seal.
scélérat /seleʀa/ *nm* scoundrel.
sceller /sele/ [1] *vt* seal; (fixer) cement.
scène /sɛn/ *nf* scene; (estrade, art dramatique) stage; **mettre en ∼** (pièce) stage; (film) direct; **mise en ∼**

direction; **∼ de ménage** domestic dispute.
scepticisme /sɛptisism/ *nm* scepticism.
sceptique /sɛptik/ *adj* sceptical. ● *nmf* sceptic.
schéma /ʃema/ *nm* diagram. **schématique** *adj* schematic; (sommaire) sketchy. **schématiser** [1] *vt* simplify.
schizophrène /skizofʀɛn/ *a* & *nmf* schizophrenic.
sciatique /sjatik/ *adj* (nerf) sciatic. ● *nf* sciatica.
scie /si/ *nf* saw.
sciemment /sjamã/ *adv* knowingly.
science /sjãs/ *nf* science; (savoir) knowledge.
science-fiction /sjãsfiksjõ/ *nf* science fiction.
scientifique /sjãtifik/ *adj* scientific. ● *nmf* scientist.
scier /sje/ [45] *vt* saw.
scintiller /sɛ̃tije/ [1] *vi* glitter; (étoile) twinkle.
scission /sisjõ/ *nf* split.
sclérose /skleʀoz/ *nf* sclerosis; **∼ en plaques** multiple sclerosis.
scolaire /skɔlɛʀ/ *adj* school. **scolarisé**, **∼e** *adj* going to school. **scolarité** *nf* schooling.
score /skɔʀ/ *nm* score.
scorpion /skɔʀpjõ/ *nm* scorpion; **le S∼** Scorpio.
scotch /skɔtʃ/ *nm* (boisson) Scotch (whisky); (ruban adhésif)® Sellotape®.
scout, **∼e** /skut/ *nm* & *a* scout.
scrupule /skʀypyl/ *nm* scruple. **scrupuleux**, **-euse** *adj* scrupulous.
scruter /skʀyte/ [1] *vt* examine, scrutinize.
scrutin /skʀytɛ̃/ *nm* (vote) ballot; (élections) polls (+ *pl*).
sculpter /skylte/ [1] *vt* sculpt, carve. **sculpteur** *nm* sculptor. **sculpture** *nf* sculpture.

....

se, **s'** /sə, s/

s' before vowel or mute h.

● *pronom*

····▸ himself, (féminin) herself; (indéfini) oneself; (non humain) itself; (au pluriel) themselves; ~ **laver les mains** wash one's hands; (réciproque) each other, one another; **ils se détestent** they hate each other.

! The translation of **se** will vary according to which verb it is associated with. You should therefore refer to the verb to find it. For example, **se promener**, **se taire** will be treated respectively under **promener** and **taire**.

séance /seɑ̃s/ *nf* session; (Théât, cinéma) show; ~ **de pose** sitting; ~ **tenante** forthwith.

seau (*pl* ~**x**) /so/ *nm* bucket, pail.

sec, sèche /sɛk, sɛʃ/ *adj* dry; (*fruits*) dried; (*coup, bruit*) sharp; (*cœur*) hard; (*whisky*) neat. ● *nm* à ~ (sans eau) dry; (sans argent) broke; **au** ~ in a dry place.

sèche-cheveux /sɛʃʃəvø/ *nm inv* hairdrier.

sèchement /sɛʃmɑ̃/ *adv* drily.

sécher /seʃe/ [14] *vt/i* dry; (*cours:* Ⅰ) skip; (ne pas savoir Ⅰ) be stumped. □ **se** ~ *vpr* dry oneself. **sécheresse** *nf* (de climat) dryness; (temps sec) drought. **séchoir** *nm* drier.

second, ~e /səɡɔ̃, -d/ *a & nm,f* second. ● *nm* (adjoint) second in command; (étage) second floor. **secondaire** *adj* secondary. **seconde** *nf* (instant) second; (vitesse) second gear.

seconder /səɡɔ̃de/ [1] *vt* assist.

secouer /səkwe/ [1] *vt* shake; (*poussière, torpeur*) shake off. □ **se** ~ *vpr* Ⅰ (se dépêcher) get a move on; (réagir) shake oneself up.

secourir /səkuʀiʀ/ [20] *vt* assist, help. **secouriste** *nmf* first-aid worker.

secours /səkuʀ/ *nm* assistance, help; **au** ~! help!; **de** ~ (*sortie*) emergency; (*équipe, opération*) rescue. ● *nmpl* (Méd) first aid.

secousse /səkus/ *nf* jolt, jerk; (séisme) tremor.

secret, -ète /səkʀɛ, -t/ *adj* secret. ● *nm* secret; (discrétion) secrecy; **le** ~ **professionnel** professional confidentiality; ~ **de Polichinelle** open secret; **en** ~ in secret, secretly.

secrétaire /səkʀetɛʀ/ *nmf* secretary; ~ **de direction** personal assistant. ● *nm* (meuble) writing-desk; ~ **d'État** junior minister.

secrétariat /səkʀetaʀja/ *nm* secretarial work; (bureau) secretariat.

sectaire /sɛktɛʀ/ *adj* sectarian.

secte /sɛkt/ *nf* sect.

secteur /sɛktœʀ/ *nm* area; (Comm) sector; (circuit: Électr) mains (+ *pl*).

section /sɛksjɔ̃/ *nf* section; (Scol) stream; (Mil) platoon. **sectionner** [1] *vt* sever.

sécuriser /sekyʀize/ [1] *vt* reassure.

sécurité /sekyʀite/ *nf* security; (absence de danger) safety; **en** ~ safe, secure. **Sécurité sociale** *nf* social services, social security services.

sédatif /sedatif/ *nm* sedative.

sédentaire /sedɑ̃tɛʀ/ *adj* sedentary.

séducteur, -trice /sedyktœʀ, -tʀis/ *adj* seductive. ● *nm, f* seducer. **séduction** *nf* seduction; (charme) charm.

séduire /seduiʀ/ [17] *vt* charm; (plaire à) appeal to; (sexuellement) seduce. **séduisant, ~e** *adj* attractive.

ségrégation /seɡʀeɡasjɔ̃/ *nf* segregation.

seigle /sɛɡl/ *nm* rye.

seigneur /sɛɲœʀ/ *nm* lord; **le S**~ the Lord.

sein /sɛ̃/ *nm* breast; **au** ~ **de** within.

séisme /seism/ *nm* earthquake.

seize /sɛz/ *a & nm* sixteen.

séjour /seʒuʀ/ *nm* stay; (pièce) living room. **séjourner** [1] *vi* stay.

sel /sɛl/ *nm* salt; (piquant) spice.

sélectif, -ive /selɛktif, -v/ *adj* selective.

sélection /selɛksjɔ̃/ *nf* selection. **sélectionner** [1] *vt* select.

selle /sɛl/ *nf* saddle; **aller à la** ~ have a bowel movement; ~**s** (Méd) stools.

sellette /sɛlɛt/ *nf* sur la ~
(*personne*) in the hot seat.

selon /səlɔ̃/ *prép* according to; ~
que depending on whether.

semaine /sɔmɛn/ *nf* week; en ~
during the week.

sémantique /semãtik/ *adj*
semantic. ● *nf* semantics.

semblable /sãblabl/ *adj* similar (à
to). ● *nm* fellow (creature).

semblant /sãblã/ *nm* faire ~ de
pretend to; un ~ de a semblance of.

sembler /sãble/ [1] *vi* seem (à to;
que that); il me semble que it seems
to me that.

semelle /səmɛl/ *nf* sole; ~
compensée wedge heel.

semence /s(ə)mãs/ *nf* seed.

semer /s(ə)me/ [6] *vt* (*graine, doute*)
sow; (jeter, parsemer) strew; (*personne*
🅵) lose; ~ la panique spread panic.

semestre /səmɛstʀ/ *nm* half-year;
(Univ) semester. **semestriel**, ~le
adj (revue) biannual; (examen) end-of-
semester.

séminaire /seminɛʀ/ *nm* (Relig)
seminary; (Univ) seminar.

semi-remorque /s(ə)miʀ(ə)mɔʀk/
nm articulated lorry.

semis /s(ə)mi/ *nm* (terrain) seedbed;
(plant) seedling.

semoule /s(ə)mul/ *nf* semolina.

sénat /sena/ *nm* senate. **sénateur**
nm senator.

sénile /senil/ *adj* senile.

sens /sãs/ *nm* (Méd) sense;
(signification) meaning, sense; (direction)
direction; à mon ~ to my mind; à ~
unique (*rue*) one-way; ça n'a pas de
~ it doesn't make sense; ~ commun
common sense; ~ giratoire
roundabout; ~ interdit no-entry sign;
(rue) one-way street; dans le ~ des
aiguilles d'une montre clockwise;
dans le ~ inverse des aiguilles d'une
montre anticlockwise; ~ dessus
dessous upside down; ~ devant
derrière back to front.

sensation /sãsasjɔ̃/ *nf* feeling,
sensation; faire ~ create a sensation.
sensationnel, ~le *adj* sensational.

sensé, ~e /sãse/ *adj* sensible.

sensibiliser /sãsibilize/ [1] *vt* ~
l'opinion increase people's
awareness (à qch to sth).

sensibilité /sãsibilite/ *nf*
sensitivity. **sensible** *adj* sensitive
(à to); (appréciable) noticeable.
sensiblement *adv* noticeably; (à
peu près) more or less.

sensoriel, ~le /sãsɔʀjɛl/ *adj*
sensory.

sensualité /sãsɥalite/ *nf*
sensuousness; sensuality. **sensuel**,
~le *adj* sensual.

sentence /sãtãs/ *nf* sentence.

senteur /sãtœʀ/ *nf* scent.

sentier /sãtje/ *nm* path.

sentiment /sãtimã/ *nm* feeling;
faire du ~ sentimentalize; j'ai le ~
que... I get the feeling that...
sentimental, ~e (*mpl* -aux) *adj*
sentimental.

sentir /sãtir/ [46] *vt* feel; (*odeur*)
smell; (pressentir) sense; ~ la lavande
smell of lavender; je ne peux pas le
~ 🅵 I can't stand him. ● *vi* smell.
□ se ~ *vpr* se ~ fier/mieux feel
proud/better.

séparation /separasjɔ̃/ *nf*
separation.

séparatiste /separatist/ *a & nmf*
separatist.

séparé, ~e /separe/ *adj* separate;
(*conjoints*) separated.

séparer /separe/ [1] *vt* separate; (en
deux) split. □ se ~ *vpr* separate, part
(de from); (se détacher) split; se ~ de
(se défaire de) part with.

sept /sɛt/ *a & nm* seven.

septante /sɛptãt/ *a & nm* seventy.

septembre /sɛptãbʀ/ *nm*
September.

septentrional, ~e (*mpl* -aux)
/sɛptãtʀijɔnal, -o/ *adj* northern.

septième /sɛtjɛm/ *a & nmf*
seventh.

sépulture /sepyltyʀ/ *nf* burial; (lieu)
burial place.

séquelles /sekɛl/ *nfpl* (maladie)
aftereffects; (fig) aftermath (+ sg).

séquence /sekãs/ *nf* sequence.

séquestrer /sekɛstʀe/ [1] *vt* confine
(illegally).

sera, serait /səʀa, səʀɛ/ →ÊTRE [4].

serbe /sɛrb/ adj Serbian. **S~** nmf
Serbian.

Serbie /sɛrbi/ nf Serbia.

serein, **~e** /sərɛ̃, -ɛn/ adj serene.

sérénité /serenite/ nf serenity.

sergent /sɛrʒɑ̃/ nm sergeant.

série /seri/ nf series (+ sg); (d'objets)
set; de **~** (véhicule etc.) standard;
fabrication ou **production en ~** mass
production.

sérieusement /serjøzmɑ̃/ adv
seriously.

sérieux, **-ieuse** /serjø, -z/ adj
serious; (digne de confiance) reliable;
(chances, raison) good. ● nm
seriousness; **garder son ~** keep a
straight face; **prendre au ~** take
seriously.

serin /sərɛ̃/ nm canary.

seringue /sərɛ̃g/ nf syringe.

serment /sɛrmɑ̃/ nm oath;
(promesse) vow.

sermon /sɛrmɔ̃/ nm sermon.
sermonner [1] vt lecture.

séropositif, **-ive** /seropozitif, -v/
adj HIV positive.

serpent /sɛrpɑ̃/ nm snake; **~ à
sonnettes** rattlesnake.

serpillière /sɛrpijɛr/ nf floorcloth.

serre /sɛr/ nf (de jardin) greenhouse;
(griffe) claw.

serré, **~e** /sere/ adj (habit, nœud,
écrou) tight; (personnes) packed,
crowded; (lutte, mailles) close;
(écriture) cramped; (cœur) heavy.

serrer /sere/ [1] vt (saisir) grip;
(presser) squeeze; (vis, corde, ceinture)
tighten; (poing, dents) clench; **~ qn
dans ses bras** hug sb; **~ les rangs**
close ranks; **~ qn** (vêtement) be tight
on sb; **~ qn de près** follow sb
closely; **~ la main à** shake hands
with. ● vi **~ à droite** keep over to
the right. □ **se ~** vpr (se rapprocher)
squeeze (up) (**contre** against).

serrure /seryr/ nf lock. **serrurier**
nm locksmith.

servante /sɛrvɑ̃t/ nf (maid) servant.

serveur, **-euse** /sɛrvœr, -øz/ nm, f
(homme) waiter; (femme) waitress.
● nm (Ordinat) server.

serviable /sɛrvjabl/ adj helpful.

service /sɛrvis/ nm service; (fonction,
temps de travail) duty; (pourboire) service
(charge); (dans une société)
department; **~ (non) compris** service
(not) included; **être de ~** be on duty;
pendant le ~ (when) on duty; **rendre
~ à qn** be a help to sb; **~ à thé** tea
set; **~ d'ordre** stewards (+ pl); **~
après-vente** after-sales service; **~
militaire** military service; **les ~s
secrets** the secret service (+ sg).

serviette /sɛrvjɛt/ nf (de toilette)
towel; (cartable) briefcase; **~ (de
table)** serviette, napkin; **~
hygiénique** sanitary towel.

servir /sɛrvir/ [46] vt/i serve; (être
utile) be of use, serve; **~ qn** (à table)
wait on sb; **ça sert à** (outil, récipient) it
is used for; **ça me sert à/de** I use it
to/as; **ça ne sert à rien** (action) it's
pointless; **~ de** serve as, be used as; **
~ à qn de guide** act as a guide for
sb. □ **se ~** vpr (à table) help oneself
(**de** to); **se ~ de** use. **serviteur** nm
servant.

ses /se/ ⇒SON¹.

session /sesjɔ̃/ nf session.

seuil /sœj/ nm doorstep; (entrée)
doorway; (fig) threshold.

seul, **~e** /sœl/ adj alone, on one's
own; (unique) only; **un ~ exemple**
only one example; **pas un ~ ami** not
a single friend; **lui ~ le sait** only he
knows; **dans le ~ but de** with the
sole aim of; **parler tout ~** talk to
oneself; **faire qch tout ~** do sth on
one's own. ● nm, f **le ~**, **la ~e** the
only one. **seulement** adv only.

sève /sɛv/ nf sap.

sévère /sevɛr/ adj severe. **sévérité**
nf severity.

sévices /sevis/ nmpl physical abuse
(+ sg).

sévir /sevir/ [2] vi (fléau) rage; **~
contre** punish.

sevrer /səvre/ [6] vt wean.

sexe /sɛks/ nm sex; (organes) genitals
(+ pl). **sexiste** adj sexist.
sexualité nf sexuality. **sexuel**,
~le adj sexual.

shampooing /ʃɑ̃pwɛ̃/ nm shampoo.

shérif /ʃerif/ nm sheriff.

short /ʃɔrt/ nm shorts (+ pl).

si (**s'** before il, ils) /si, s/ conj if; (interrogation indirecte) if, whether; ∼ **on allait se promener?** what about a walk?; **s'il vous** ou **te plaît** please; ∼ **oui** if so; ∼ **seulement** if only. ● adv (tellement) so; (oui) yes; **un** ∼ **bon repas** such a good meal; ∼ **habile qu'il soit** however skilful he may be; ∼ **bien que** with the result that.

sida /sida/ nm (Méd) Aids.

sidérurgie /sideryrʒi/ nf steel industry.

siècle /sjɛkl/ nm century; (époque) age.

siège /sjɛʒ/ nm seat; (Mil) siege; ∼ **éjectable** ejector seat; ∼ **social** head office, headquarters (+ pl). **siéger** [14] [40] vi (assemblée) sit.

sien, ∼**ne** /sjɛ̃, -ɛn/ pron **le** ∼, **la** ∼**ne, les** ∼(**ne**)**s** (homme) his; (femme) hers; (chose) its; **les** ∼**s** (famille) one's family.

sieste /sjɛst/ nf nap, siesta.

sifflement /sifləmɑ̃/ nm whistling; **un** ∼ a whistle.

siffler /sifle/ [1] vi whistle; (avec un sifflet) blow one's whistle; (serpent, gaz) hiss. ● vt (air) whistle; (chien) whistle to ou for; (acteur) hiss.

sifflet /siflɛ/ nm whistle; ∼**s** (huées) boos.

sigle /sigl/ nm acronym.

signal (pl **-aux**) /siɲal, -o/ nm signal; ∼ **sonore** (de répondeur) tone.

signalement /siɲalmɑ̃/ nm description.

signaler /siɲale/ [1] vt indicate; (par une sonnerie, un écriteau) signal; (dénoncer, mentionner) report; (faire remarquer) point out.

signalisation /siɲalizasjɔ̃/ nf signalling, signposting; (signaux) signals (+ pl).

signataire /siɲatɛr/ nmf signatory.

signature /siɲatyr/ nf signature; (action) signing.

signe /siɲ/ nm sign; (de ponctuation) mark; **faire** ∼ **à qn** wave at sb; (contacter) contact; **faire** ∼ **à qn de** beckon sb to; **faire** ∼ **que non** shake one's head; **faire** ∼ **que oui** nod.

signer /siɲe/ [1] vt sign. □ **se** ∼ vpr (Relig) cross oneself.

signet /siɲɛ/ nm (pour livre, Internet) bookmark; ∼**s favoris** (Internet) hotlist.

significatif, -ive /siɲifikatif, -v/ adj significant.

signification /siɲifikasjɔ̃/ nf meaning. **signifier** [45] vt mean, signify; (faire connaître) make known (à to).

silence /silɑ̃s/ nm silence; (Mus) rest; **garder le** ∼ keep silent.

silencieux, -ieuse /silɑ̃sjø, -z/ adj silent. ● nm silencer.

silex /silɛks/ nm inv flint.

silhouette /silwɛt/ nf outline, silhouette.

sillon /sijɔ̃/ nm furrow; (de disque) groove.

sillonner /sijɔne/ [1] vt crisscross.

similaire /similɛr/ adj similar. **similitude** nf similarity.

simple /sɛ̃pl/ adj simple; (non double) single. ● nm ∼ **dames/messieurs** ladies'/men's singles (+ pl). **simple d'esprit** nmf simpleton. **simplement** adv simply. **simplicité** nf simplicity; (naïveté) simpleness.

simplification /sɛ̃plifikasjɔ̃/ nf simplification. **simplifier** [45] vt simplify.

simpliste /sɛ̃plist/ adj simplistic.

simulacre /simylakr/ nm pretence, sham.

simulation /simylasjɔ̃/ nf simulation. **simuler** [1] vt simulate.

simultané, ∼**e** /simyltane/ adj simultaneous.

sincère /sɛ̃sɛr/ adj sincere. **sincérité** nf sincerity.

singe /sɛ̃ʒ/ nm monkey; (grand) ape. **singer** [40] vt mimic, ape.

singulier, -ière /sɛ̃gylje, -jɛr/ adj peculiar, remarkable; (Gram) singular. ● nm (Gram) singular.

sinistre /sinistr/ adj sinister. ● nm disaster; (incendie) blaze; (dommages) damage.

sinistré, ∼**e** /sinistre/ adj stricken. ● nm, f disaster victim.

sinon /sinɔ̃/ conj (autrement) otherwise; (sauf) except (**que** that);

difficile ~ impossible difficult if not impossible.

sinueux, -euse /sinuø, -z/ *adj* winding; (fig) tortuous.

sirène /siʀɛn/ *nf* (appareil) siren; (femme) mermaid.

sirop /siʀo/ *nm* (de fruits, Méd) syrup; (boisson) cordial.

sis, ~e /si, siz/ *adj* situated.

sismique /sismik/ *adj* seismic.

site /sit/ *nm* site; **~ touristique** place of interest; **~ Internet** *or* **Web** Web site.

sitôt /sito/ *adv* **~ entré** immediately after coming in; **~ que** as soon as; **pas de ~** not for a while.

situation /sitɥasjõ/ *nf* situation; (emploi) job, position; **~ de famille** marital status.

situé, ~e /sitɥe/ *adj* situated.

situer /sitɥe/ [1] *vt* situate, locate. □ **se ~** *vpr* (se trouver) be situated.

six /sis/ (/si/ *before consonant*, /siz/ *before vowel*) *a & nm* six. **sixième** *a & nmf* sixth.

sketch (*pl* **~es**) /skɛtʃ/ *nm* (Théât) sketch.

ski /ski/ *nm* (matériel) ski; (Sport) skiing; **faire du ~** ski; **~ de fond** cross-country skiing; **~ nautique** water skiing. **skier** [45] *vi* ski.

slave /slav/ *adj* Slav; (Ling) Slavonic.

slip /slip/ *nm* (d'homme) underpants (+ *pl*); (de femme) knickers (+ *pl*); **~ de bain** (swimming) trunks (+ *pl*); (du bikini) bikini bottom.

slogan /slɔgã/ *nm* slogan.

Slovaquie /slɔvaki/ *nf* Slovakia.

Slovénie /slɔveni/ *nf* Slovenia.

smoking /smɔkiŋ/ *nm* dinner jacket.

SNCF *abrév f* (**Société nationale des Chemins de fer français**) *French national railway company.*

snob /snɔb/ *nmf* snob. ● *adj* snobbish. **snobisme** *nm* snobbery.

sobre /sɔbʀ/ *adj* sober.

social, ~e (*mpl* **-iaux**) /sɔsjal, -jo/ *adj* social.

socialisme /sɔsjalism/ *nm* socialism. **socialiste** *nmf & a* socialist.

société /sɔsjete/ *nf* society; (entreprise) company.

socle /sɔkl/ *nm* (de colonne, statue) plinth; (de lampe) base.

socquette /sɔkɛt/ *nf* ankle sock.

soda /sɔda/ *nm* fizzy drink.

sœur /sœʀ/ *nf* sister.

soi /swa/ *pron* oneself; **derrière ~** behind one; **en ~** in itself; **aller de ~** be obvious.

soi-disant /swadizã/ *a inv* so-called. ● *adv* supposedly.

soie /swa/ *nf* silk.

soif /swaf/ *nf* thirst; **avoir ~** be thirsty; **donner ~** make one thirsty.

soigné, ~e /swaɲe/ *adj* (apparence) tidy, neat; (travail) carefully done.

soigner /swaɲe/ [1] *vt* (s'occuper de) look after, take care of; (tenue, style) take care over; (maladie) treat. □ **se ~** *vpr* look after oneself.

soigneusement /swaɲøzmã/ *adv* carefully. **soigneux, -euse** *adj* careful (de about); (ordonné) tidy.

soi-même /swamɛm/ *pron* oneself.

soin /swẽ/ *nm* care; (ordre) tidiness; **~s** care; (Méd) treatment; **avec ~** carefully; **avoir** *ou* **prendre ~ de qn/ de faire** take care of sb/to do; **premiers ~s** first aid (+ *sg*).

soir /swaʀ/ *nm* evening; **à ce ~** see you tonight.

soirée /swaʀe/ *nf* evening; (réception) party.

soit /swa/ *conj* (à savoir) that is to say; **~ ... ~** either ... or. ● ⇒ÊTRE [4].

soixante /swasãt/ *a & nm* sixty. **soixante-dix** *a & nm* seventy.

soja /sɔʒa/ *nm* (graines) soya beans (+ *pl*); (plante) soya.

sol /sɔl/ *nm* ground; (de maison) floor; (terrain agricole) soil.

solaire /sɔlɛʀ/ *adj* solar; (huile, filtre) sun.

soldat /sɔlda/ *nm* soldier.

solde¹ /sɔld/ *nf* (salaire) pay.

solde² /sɔld/ *nm* (Comm) balance; **les ~s** the sales; **~s** (écrit en vitrine) sale; **en ~** (acheter) at sale price.

solder /sɔlde/ [1] *vt* sell off at sale price; (compte) settle. □ **se ~ par** *vpr* (aboutir à) end in.

sole /sɔl/ *nf* (poisson) sole.

soleil /sɔlɛj/ nm sun; (fleur) sunflower; **il y a du ~** it's sunny.

solennel, ~le /sɔlanɛl/ adj solemn.

solfège /sɔlfɛʒ/ nm musical theory.

solidaire /sɔlidɛR/ adj (mécanismes) interdependent; (collègues) (mutually) supportive; **être ~ de qn** support sb. **solidarité** nf solidarity.

solide /sɔlid/ adj solid; (personne) strong. ● nm solid.

solidifier /sɔlidifje/ [45] vt solidify. □ **se ~** vpr solidify.

solitaire /sɔlitɛR/ adj solitary. ● nmf (personne) loner. **solitude** nf solitude.

solliciter /sɔlisite/ [1] vt seek; (faire appel à) call upon; **être très sollicité** be very much in demand.

sollicitude /sɔlisityd/ nf concern.

solo /sɔlo/ nm & a inv (Mus) solo.

solution /sɔlysjɔ̃/ nf solution.

solvable /sɔlvabl/ adj solvent.

solvant /sɔlvɑ̃/ nm solvent.

sombre /sɔ̃bR/ adj dark; (triste) sombre.

sombrer /sɔ̃bRe/ [1] vi sink (dans into).

sommaire /sɔmɛR/ adj (exécution) summary; (description) rough. ● nm contents (+ pl); **au ~** on the programme.

sommation /sɔmasjɔ̃/ nf (Mil) warning; (Jur) notice.

somme /sɔm/ nf sum; **en ~, ~ toute** in short; **faire la ~ de** add (up), total (up). ● nm nap.

sommeil /sɔmɛj/ nm sleep; **avoir ~** be ou feel sleepy; **en ~** (projet) put on ice. **sommeiller** [1] vi doze; (fig) lie dormant.

sommelier /sɔməlje/ nm wine steward.

sommer /sɔme/ [1] vt summon.

sommes /sɔm/ ⇒ÊTRE [4].

sommet /sɔmɛ/ nm top; (de montagne) summit; (de triangle) apex; (gloire) height.

sommier /sɔmje/ nm bed base.

somnambule /sɔmnɑ̃byl/ nm sleepwalker.

somnifère /sɔmnifɛR/ nm sleeping pill.

somnolent, ~e /sɔmnɔlɑ̃, -t/ adj drowsy. **somnoler** [1] vi doze.

somptueux, -euse /sɔ̃ptɥø, -z/ adj sumptuous.

son¹, sa (**son** before vowel or mute h) (pl **ses**) /sɔ̃, sa, sɔ̃, se/ adj (homme) his; (femme) her; (chose) its; (indéfini) one's.

son² /sɔ̃/ nm (bruit) sound; (de blé) bran; **baisser le ~** turn the volume down.

sondage /sɔ̃daʒ/ nm **~ (d'opinion)** (opinion) poll.

sonde /sɔ̃d/ nf (de forage) drill; (Méd) (d'évacuation) catheter; (d'examen) probe.

sonder /sɔ̃de/ [1] vt (population) poll; (explorer) sound; (terrain) drill; (intentions) sound out.

songe /sɔ̃ʒ/ nm dream.

songer /sɔ̃ʒe/ [40] vt **~ que** think that; **~ à** think about. **songeur, -euse** adj pensive.

sonné, ~e /sɔne/ adj (étourdi) groggy; ⏚ crazy.

sonner /sɔne/ [1] vt/i ring; (clairon, glas) sound; (heure) strike; (domestique) ring for; **midi sonné** well past noon; **~ de** (clairon) sound, blow.

sonnerie /sɔnRi/ nf ringing; (de clairon) sounding; (sonnette) bell.

sonnet /sɔnɛ/ nm sonnet.

sonnette /sɔnɛt/ nf bell.

sonore /sɔnɔR/ adj resonant; (onde, effets) sound; (rire) resounding.

sonorisation /sɔnɔRizasjɔ̃/ nf (matériel) public address system.

sonorité /sɔnɔRite/ nf resonance; (d'un instrument) tone.

sont /sɔ̃/ ⇒ÊTRE [4].

sophistiqué, ~e /sɔfistike/ adj sophisticated.

sorcellerie /sɔRsɛlRi/ nf witchcraft. **sorcier** nm (guérisseur) witch doctor; (maléfique) sorcerer. **sorcière** nf witch.

sordide /sɔRdid/ adj sordid; (lieu) squalid.

sort /sɔR/ nm (destin, hasard) fate; (condition) lot; (maléfice) spell; **tirer (qch) au ~** draw lots (for sth).

sortant, **~e** /sɔʀtɑ̃, -t/ *adj* (*président etc.*) outgoing.

sorte /sɔʀt/ *nf* sort, kind; **de ~ que** so that; **en quelque ~** in a way; **de la ~** in this way; **faire en ~ que** make sure that.

sortie /sɔʀti/ *nf* exit; (promenade, dîner) outing; (*déclaration* ⬛) remark; (parution) publication; (de disque, film) release; (d'un ordinateur) output; **~s** (argent) outgoings.

sortilège /sɔʀtilɛʒ/ *nm* (magic) spell.

sortir /sɔʀtiʀ/ [46] *vi* (*aux être*) go out, leave; (venir) come out; (aller au spectacle) go out; (*livre, film*) come out; (*plante*) come up; **~ de** (*pièce*) leave; (*milieu social*) come from; (*limites*) go beyond; **~ du commun ou de l'ordinaire** be out of the ordinary. ● *vt* (*aux avoir*) take out; (*livre, modèle*) bring out; (dire ⬛) come out with; **~ qn de** get sb out of; **être sorti d'affaire** be in the clear. □ **s'en ~** *vpr* cope, manage.

sosie /sozi/ *nm* double.

sot, **~te** /so, sɔt/ *adj* silly.

sottise /sɔtiz/ *nf* silliness; (action, remarque) foolish thing; **faire des ~s** be naughty.

sou /su/ *nm* ⬛ **~s** money; **sans le ~** without a penny; **près de ses ~s** tight-fisted.

soubresaut /subʀəso/ *nm* (sudden) start.

souche /suʃ/ *nf* (d'arbre) stump; (de famille) stock; (de carnet) counterfoil.

souci /susi/ *nm* (inquiétude) worry; (préoccupation) concern; (plante) marigold; **se faire du ~** worry.

soucier (se) /(sə)susje/ [45] *vpr* se **~ de** care about. **soucieux**, **-ieuse** *adj* concerned (**de** about).

soucoupe /sukup/ *nf* saucer; **~ volante** flying saucer.

soudain, **~e** /sudɛ̃, -ɛn/ *adj* sudden. ● *adv* suddenly.

soude /sud/ *nf* soda.

souder /sude/ [1] *vt* weld, solder; **famille très soudée** close-knit family. □ **se ~** *vpr* (os) knit (together).

⸺udoyer /sudwaje/ [31] *vt* bribe.

⸺fle /sufl/ *nm* (haleine) breath; (⸺tion) breathing; (explosion) blast;

(vent) breath of air; **le ~ coupé** out of breath; **à couper le ~** breathtaking.

souffler /sufle/ [1] *vi* blow; (haleter) puff. ● *vt* (*bougie*) blow out; (*poussière, fumée*) blow; (*verre*) blow; (par explosion) destroy; (chuchoter) whisper; **~ la réplique à** prompt. **souffleur**, **-euse** *nm,f* (Théât) prompter.

souffrance /sufʀɑ̃s/ *nf* suffering; **en ~** (*affaire*) pending. **souffrant**, **~e** *adj* unwell.

souffrir /sufʀiʀ/ [21] *vi* suffer (**de** from). ● *vt* (endurer) suffer; **il ne peut pas le ~** he cannot stand *ou* bear him.

soufre /sufʀ/ *nm* sulphur.

souhait /swɛ/ *nm* wish; **à tes ~s!** bless you!; **paisible à ~** incredibly peaceful. **souhaitable** *adj* desirable.

souhaiter /swete/ [1] *vt* **~ qch à qn** wish sb sth; **~ que/faire** hope that/to do; **~ la bienvenue à qn** welcome sb.

soûl, **~e** /su, sul/ *adj* drunk. ● *nm* **tout son ~** as much as one can.

soulagement /sulaʒmɑ̃/ *nm* relief. **soulager** [40] *vt* relieve.

soûler /sule/ [1] *vt* make drunk. □ **se ~** *vpr* get drunk.

soulèvement /sulɛvmɑ̃/ *nm* uprising.

soulever /sulve/ [6] *vt* lift, raise; (*question, poussière*) raise; (*enthousiasme*) arouse; (*foule*) stir up. □ **se ~** *vpr* lift *ou* raise oneself up; (se révolter) rise up.

soulier /sulje/ *nm* shoe.

souligner /suliɲe/ [1] *vt* underline; (*yeux*) outline; (taille) emphasize.

soumettre /sumɛtʀ/ [42] *vt* (assujettir) subject (**à** to); (présenter) submit (**à** to). □ **se ~** *vpr* submit (**à** to). **soumis**, **~e** *adj* submissive. **soumission** *nf* submission.

soupape /supap/ *nf* valve.

soupçon /supsɔ̃/ *nm* suspicion; **un ~ de** (un peu de) a touch of. **soupçonner** [1] *vt* suspect. **soupçonneux**, **-euse** *adj* suspicious.

soupe /sup/ *nf* soup.

souper /supe/ [6] *vi* have supper. ● *nm* supper.

soupeser /supəze/ [1] *vt* judge the weight of; (fig) weigh up.

soupière /supjɛʀ/ *nf* (soup) tureen.

soupir /supiʀ/ *nm* sigh; **pousser un** ∼ heave a sigh.

soupirer /supiʀe/ [1] *vi* sigh.

souple /supl/ *adj* supple; (*règlement, caractère*) flexible. **souplesse** *nf* suppleness; (de règlement) flexibility.

source /suʀs/ *nf* (de rivière, origine) source; (eau) spring; **prendre sa** ∼ **à** rise in; **de** ∼ **sûre** from a reliable source; ∼ **thermale** hot spring.

sourcil /suʀsi/ *nm* eyebrow.

sourciller /suʀsije/ [1] *vi* **sans** ∼ without batting an eyelid.

sourd, ∼e /suʀ, -d/ *adj* deaf; (*bruit, douleur*) dull; **faire la** ∼**e oreille** turn a deaf ear. ● *nm, f* deaf person.

sourd-muet (*pl* **sourds-muets**), **sourde-muette** (*pl* **sourdes-muettes**) /suʀmɥe, suʀdmɥɛt/ *adj* deaf and dumb. ● *nm, f* deaf-mute.

souricière /suʀisjɛʀ/ *nf* mousetrap; (fig) trap.

sourire /suʀiʀ/ [54] *vi* smile (**à** at); ∼ **à** (fortune) smile on. ● *nm* smile; **garder le** ∼ keep smiling.

souris /suʀi/ *nf* mouse; **des** ∼ mice.

sournois, ∼e /suʀnwa, -z/ *adj* sly, underhand.

sous /su/ *prép* under, beneath; ∼ **la main** handy; ∼ **la pluie** in the rain; ∼ **peu** shortly; ∼ **terre** underground.

sous-alimenté, ∼e /suzalimɑ̃te/ *adj* undernourished.

souscription /suskʀipsjɔ̃/ *nf* subscription. **souscrire** /30/ *vi* ∼ **à** subscribe to.

sous-entendre /suzɑ̃tɑ̃dʀ/ [3] *vt* imply. **sous-entendu** *nm* innuendo, insinuation.

sous-estimer /suzɛstime/ [1] *vt* underestimate.

sous-jacent, ∼e /suʒasɑ̃, -t/ *adj* underlying.

sous-marin, ∼e /sumaʀɛ̃, -in/ *adj* underwater; (*plongée*) deep-sea. ● *nm* submarine.

soussigné, ∼e /susiɲe/ *a & nm,f* undersigned.

sous-sol /susɔl/ *nm* (cave) basement.

sous-titre /sutitʀ/ *nm* subtitle.

soustraction /sustʀaksjɔ̃/ *nf* (déduction) subtraction.

soustraire /sustʀɛʀ/ [29] *vt* (déduire) subtract; (retirer) take away (**à** from). ▫ **se** ∼ **à** *vpr* escape from.

sous-traitant /sutʀɛtɑ̃/ *nm* subcontractor.

sous-verre /suvɛʀ/ *nm inv* glass mount.

sous-vêtement /suvɛtmɑ̃/ *nm* underwear.

soute /sut/ *nf* (de bateau) hold; ∼ **à charbon** coal-bunker.

soutenir /sutniʀ/ [59] *vt* support; (*effort, rythme*) sustain; (résister à) withstand; ∼ **que** maintain that.

soutenu, ∼e /sutny/ *adj* (constant) sustained; (style) formal.

souterrain, ∼e /sutɛʀɛ̃, -ɛn/ *adj* underground. ● *nm* underground passage.

soutien /sutjɛ̃/ *nm* support.

soutien-gorge (*pl* **soutiens-gorge**) /sutjɛ̃gɔʀʒ/ *nm* bra.

soutirer /sutiʀe/ [1] *vt* ∼ **à qn** extract from sb.

souvenir¹ /suvniʀ/ *nm* memory, recollection; (objet) memento; (cadeau) souvenir; **en** ∼ **de** in memory of.

souvenir² (se) /(sə)suvniʀ/ [59] *vpr* **se** ∼ **de** remember; **se** ∼ **que** remember that.

souvent /suvɑ̃/ *adv* often.

souverain, ∼e /suvʀɛ̃, -ɛn/ *adj* sovereign. ● *nm, f* sovereign.

soviétique /sɔvjetik/ *adj* Soviet.

soyeux, -euse /swajø, -z/ *adj* silky.

spacieux, -ieuse /spasjø, -z/ *adj* spacious.

sparadrap /spaʀadʀa/ *nm* (sticking) plaster.

spatial, ∼e (*mpl* **-iaux**) /spasjal, -jo/ *adj* space.

speaker, ∼ine /spikœʀ, -kʀin/ *nm, f* announcer.

spécial, ∼e (*mpl* **-iaux**) /spesjal, -jo/ *adj* special; (bizarre) odd. **spécialement** *adv* (exprès) specially; (très) especially.

spécialiser (se) /səspesjalize/ [1] *vpr* specialize (**dans** in). **spécialiste** *nmf* specialist. **spécialité** *nf* speciality; (US) specialty.

spécifier /spesifje/ [45] *vt* specify.

spécifique /spesifik/ *adj* specific.

spécimen /spesimɛn/ *nm* specimen.

spectacle /spɛktakl/ *nm* show; (vue) sight, spectacle.

spectaculaire /spɛktakylɛʀ/ *adj* spectacular.

spectateur, -trice /spɛktatœʀ, -tʀis/ *nm, f* (Sport) spectator; (témoin oculaire) onlooker; **les ~s** (Théât) the audience (+ *sg*).

spectre /spɛktʀ/ *nm* (revenant) spectre; (images) spectrum.

spéculateur, -trice /spekylatœʀ, -tʀis/ *nm, f* speculator. **spéculation** *nf* speculation. **spéculer** [1] *vi* speculate.

spéléologie /speleɔlɔʒi/ *nf* cave exploration, pot-holing.

spermatozoïde /spɛʀmatozoid/ *nm* spermatozoon. **sperme** *nm* sperm.

sphère /sfɛʀ/ *nf* sphere.

spirale /spiʀal/ *nf* spiral.

spirituel, ~le /spiʀitɥel/ *adj* spiritual; (amusant) witty.

spiritueux /spiʀitɥø/ *nm* (alcool) spirit.

splendeur /splɑ̃dœʀ/ *nf* splendour. **splendide** *adj* splendid.

sponsoriser /spɔ̃sɔʀize/ [1] *vt* sponsor.

spontané, ~e /spɔ̃tane/ *adj* spontaneous. **spontanéité** *nf* spontaneity.

sport /spɔʀ/ *a inv* (vêtements) casual. ● *nm* sport; **veste/voiture de ~** sports jacket/car.

sportif, -ive /spɔʀtif, -v/ *adj* (personne) sporty; (physique) athletic; (résultats) sports. ● *nm, f* sportsman, sportswoman.

spot /spɔt/ *nm* spotlight; **~ (publicitaire)** ad.

square /skwaʀ/ *nm* small public garden.

squatter /skwate/ [1] *vt* squat in.

squelette /skəlɛt/ *nm* skeleton. **squelettique** *adj* skeletal; (maigre) all skin and bone; (rapport) sketchy.

stabiliser /stabilize/ [1] *vt* stabilize. **stable** *adj* stable.

stade /stad/ *nm* (Sport) stadium; (phase) stage.

stage /staʒ/ *nm* (cours) course; (professionnel) placement. **stagiaire** *nmf* course member; (apprenti) trainee.

stagner /stagne/ [1] *vi* stagnate.

stand /stɑ̃d/ *nm* stand; (de fête foraine) stall; **~ de tir** shooting range.

standard /stɑ̃daʀ/ *nm* switchboard. ● *a inv* standard. **standardiser** [1] *vt* standardize.

standardiste /stɑ̃daʀdist/ *nmf* switchboard operator.

standing /stɑ̃diŋ/ *nm* status, standing; **de ~** (hôtel) luxury.

starter /staʀtɛʀ/ *nm* (Auto) choke.

station /stasjɔ̃/ *nf* station; (halte) stop; **~ debout** standing position; **~ de taxis** taxi rank; **~ balnéaire/de ski** seaside/ski resort; **~ thermale** spa.

stationnaire /stasjɔnɛʀ/ *adj* stationary.

stationnement /stasjɔnmɑ̃/ *nm* parking. **stationner** [1] *vi* park.

station-service (*pl* **stations-service**) /stasjɔ̃sɛʀvis/ *nf* service station.

statique /statik/ *adj* static.

statistique /statistik/ *nf* statistic; (science) statistics (+ *sg*). ● *adj* statistical.

statue /staty/ *nf* statue.

statuer /statɥe/ [1] *vi* **~ sur** give a ruling on.

statut /staty/ *nm* status. **statutaire** *adj* statutory.

sténo /steno/ *nf* (sténographie) shorthand. **sténodactylo** *nf* shorthand typist. **sténographie** *nf* shorthand.

stéréo /steʀeo/ *nf & a inv* stereo.

stéréotype /steʀeɔtip/ *nm* stereotype.

stérile /steʀil/ *adj* sterile.

stérilet /steʀilɛ/ *nm* coil, IUD.

stérilisation /steʀilizasjɔ̃/ *nf* sterilization. **stériliser** [1] *vt* sterilize.

stéroïde /steʀɔid/ *a & nm* steroid.

stimulant /stimylɑ̃/ *nm* stimulus; (médicament) stimulant.

stimulateur /stimylatœʀ/ *nm* ~ **cardiaque** (Méd) pacemaker.

stimuler /stimyle/ [1] *vt* stimulate.

stipuler /stipyle/ [1] *vt* stipulate.

stock /stɔk/ *nm* stock. **stocker** [1] *vt* stock.

stoïque /stɔik/ *adj* stoical. ● *nmf* stoic.

stop /stɔp/ *interj* stop. ● *nm* stop sign; (feu arrière) brake light; **faire du** ~ 🚗 hitch-hike. **stopper** [1] *vt/i* stop.

store /stɔʀ/ *nm* blind; (de magasin) awning.

strapontin /stʀapɔ̃tɛ̃/ *nm* folding seat, jump seat.

stratégie /stʀateʒi/ *nf* strategy. **stratégique** *adj* strategic.

stress /stʀɛs/ *nm* stress. **stressant**, ~**e** *adj* stressful. **stressé**, ~**e** *adj* stressed. **stresser** [1] *vt* put under stress.

strict /stʀikt/ *adj* strict; (tenue, vérité) plain; **le** ~ **minimum** the bare minimum. **strictement** *adv* strictly.

strident, ~**e** /stʀidɑ̃, -t/ *adj* shrill.

strophe /stʀɔf/ *nf* stanza, verse.

structure /stʀyktyʀ/ *nf* structure.

studieux, -**ieuse** /stydjø, -z/ *adj* studious.

studio /stydjo/ *nm* (d'artiste, de télévision) studio; (logement) studio flat.

stupéfaction /stypefaksjɔ̃/ *nf* amazement. **stupéfait**, ~**e** *adj* amazed.

stupéfiant, ~**e** /stypefjɑ̃, -t/ *adj* astounding. ● *nm* drug, narcotic.

stupéfier /stypefje/ [45] *vt* amaze.

stupeur /stypœʀ/ *nf* amazement; (Méd) stupor.

stupide /stypid/ *adj* stupid. **stupidité** *nf* stupidity.

style /stil/ *nm* style.

styliste /stilist/ *nmf* fashion designer.

stylo /stilo/ *nm* pen; ~ **(à) bille** ball-point pen; ~ **(à) encre** fountain pen.

su /sy/ ⇒SAVOIR [55].

suave /sɥav/ *adj* sweet.

subalterne /sybaltɛʀn/ *a & nmf* subordinate.

subconscient /sypkɔ̃sjɑ̃/ *nm* subconscious.

subir /sybiʀ/ [2] *vt* be subjected to; (traitement, expériences) undergo.

subit, ~**e** /sybi, -t/ *adj* sudden.

subjectif, -**ive** /sybʒɛktif, -v/ *adj* subjective.

subjonctif /sybʒɔ̃ktif/ *nm* subjunctive.

subjuguer /sybʒyge/ [1] *vt* (charmer) captivate.

sublime /syblim/ *adj* sublime.

submerger /sybmɛʀʒe/ [40] *vt* submerge; (fig) overwhelm.

subordonné, ~**e** /sybɔʀdɔne/ *a & nm, f* subordinate.

subside /sybzid/ *nm* grant.

subsidiaire /sybzidjɛʀ/ *adj* subsidiary; **question** ~ tiebreaker.

subsistance /sybzistɑ̃s/ *nf* subsistence. **subsister** [1] *vi* subsist; (durer, persister) exist.

substance /sypstɑ̃s/ *nf* substance.

substantiel, ~**le** /sypstɑ̃sjɛl/ *adj* substantial.

substantif /sypstɑ̃tif/ *nm* noun.

substituer /sypstitɥe/ [1] *vt* substitute (à for). □ **se** ~ **à** *vpr* (remplacer) substitute for. **substitut** *nm* substitute; (Jur) deputy public prosecutor.

subtil, ~**e** /syptil/ *adj* subtle.

subtiliser /syptilize/ [1] *vt* ~ **qch (à qn)** steal sth.

subvenir /sybvəniʀ/ [59] *vi* ~ **à** provide for.

subvention /sybvɑ̃sjɔ̃/ *nf* subsidy. **subventionner** [1] *vt* subsidize.

subversif, -**ive** /sybvɛʀsif, -v/ *adj* subversive.

suc /syk/ *nm* juice.

succédané /syksedane/ *nm* substitute (de for).

succéder /syksede/ [14] *vi* ~ **à** succeed. □ **se** ~ *vpr* succeed one another.

succès /syksɛ/ nm success; **à ~** (film, livre,) successful; **avoir du ~** be a success.

successeur /syksesœr/ nm successor. **successif, -ive** adj successive. **succession** nf succession; (Jur) inheritance.

succinct, ~e /syksɛ̃, -t/ adj succinct.

succomber /sykɔ̃be/ [1] vi die; **~ à** succumb to.

succulent, ~e /sykylɑ̃, -t/ adj delicious.

succursale /sykyrsal/ nf (Comm) branch.

sucer /syse/ [10] vt suck.

sucette /sysɛt/ nf (bonbon) lollipop; (tétine) dummy; (US) pacifier.

sucre /sykr/ nm sugar; **~ d'orge** barley sugar; **~ en poudre** caster sugar; **~ glace** icing sugar; **~ roux** brown sugar.

sucré /sykre/ adj sweet; (additionné de sucre) sweetened. **sucrer** [1] vt sugar, sweeten. **sucreries** nfpl sweets.

sucrier, -ière /sykrije, -jɛr/ adj sugar. ● nm (récipient) sugar-bowl.

sud /syd/ nm south. ● a inv south; (partie) southern.

sud-est /sydɛst/ nm south-east.

sud-ouest /sydwɛst/ nm south-west.

Suède /sɥɛd/ nf Sweden.

suédois, ~e /sɥedwa, -z/ adj Swedish. ● nm (Ling) Swedish. **S~, ~e** nm,f Swede.

suer /sɥe/ [1] vt/i sweat; **faire ~ qn** 🄣 get on sb's nerves.

sueur /sɥœr/ nf sweat; **en ~** covered in sweat.

suffire /syfir/ [57] vi be enough (**à qn** for sb); **il suffit de compter** all you have to do is count; **une goutte suffit** a drop is enough; **~ à** (besoin) satisfy. ◻ **se ~** vpr **se ~ à soi-même** be self-sufficient.

suffisamment /syfizamɑ̃/ adv sufficiently; **~ de qch** enough of sth. **suffisance** nf (vanité) conceit. **suffisant, ~e** adj sufficient; (vaniteux) conceited.

suffixe /syfiks/ nm suffix.

suffoquer /syfɔke/ [1] vt/i choke, suffocate.

suffrage /syfraʒ/ nm (voix: Pol) vote; (système) suffrage.

suggérer /sygʒere/ [14] vt suggest. **suggestion** nf suggestion.

suicidaire /sɥisidɛr/ adj suicidal. **suicide** nm suicide. **suicider (se)** [1] vpr commit suicide.

suinter /sɥɛ̃te/ [1] vi ooze.

suis /sɥi/ ⇒ÊTRE [4], SUIVRE [57].

Suisse /sɥis/ nf Switzerland. ● nmf Swiss. **suisse** adj Swiss.

suite /sɥit/ nf continuation, rest; (d'un film) sequel; (série) series; (appartement, escorte) suite; (résultat) consequence; **à la ~, de ~** (successivement) in a row; **à la ~ de** (derrière) behind; **à la ~ de, par ~ de** (en conséquence) as a result of; **faire ~ (à)** follow; **par la ~** afterwards; **~ à votre lettre du** further to your letter of the; **des ~s de** as a result of.

suivant¹, ~e /sɥivɑ̃, -t/ adj following, next. ● nm,f following ou next person.

suivant² /sɥivɑ̃/ prép (selon) according to.

suivi, ~e /sɥivi/ adj (effort) steady, sustained; (cohérent) consistent; **peu/ très ~** (cours) poorly/well attended.

suivre /sɥivr/ [57] vt/i follow; (comprendre) follow; **faire ~** (courrier) forward. ◻ **se ~** vpr follow each other.

sujet, ~te /syʒɛ, -t/ adj **~ à** liable ou subject to. ● nm (d'un royaume) subject; (question) subject; (motif) cause; (Gram) subject; **au ~ de** about.

super /sypɛr/ nm (essence) four-star. ● a inv 🄣 (très) great. ● adv 🄣 ultra, really.

superbe /sypɛrb/ adj superb.

supérette /sypɛrɛt/ nf minimarket.

superficie /sypɛrfisi/ nf area.

superficiel, ~le /sypɛrfisjɛl/ adj superficial.

superflu /sypɛrfly/ adj superfluous. ● nm (excédent) surplus.

supérieur, ~e /syperjœr/ adj (plus haut) upper; (quantité, nombre) greater (**à** than); (études, principe) higher (**à** than); (meilleur, hautain)

superior (à to). ● *nm,f* superior.
supériorité *nf* superiority.
superlatif, -ive /sypɛʀlatif, -v/ *a* &
nm superlative.
supermarché /sypɛʀmaʀʃe/ *nm*
supermarket.
superposer /sypɛʀpoze/ [1] *vt*
superimpose; **lits superposés** bunk
beds.
superproduction
/sypɛʀpʀɔdyksjɔ̃/ *nf* (film)
blockbuster.
superpuissance /sypɛʀpɥisɑ̃s/ *nf*
superpower.
superstitieux, -ieuse /sypɛʀs-
tisjø, -z/ *adj* superstitious.
superviser /sypɛʀvize/ [1] *vt*
supervise.
suppléant, ~e /sypleɑ̃, -t/ *nmf* & *a*
(professeur) ~ supply teacher; (juge)
~ deputy (judge).
suppléer /syplee/ [15] *vt* (remplacer)
fill in for. ● *vi* ~ **à** (compenser) make
up for.
supplément /syplemɑ̃/ *nm* (argent)
extra charge; (de frites, légumes) extra
portion; **en** ~ extra; **un** ~ **de** (travail)
additional; **payer un** ~ pay a
supplement. **supplémentaire** *adj*
extra, additional.
supplice /syplis/ *nm* torture.
supplier /syplije/ [45] *vt* beg,
beseech (de to).
support /sypɔʀ/ *nm* support;
(Ordinat) medium.
supportable /sypɔʀtabl/ *adj*
bearable.
supporter¹ /sypɔʀte/ [1] *vt*
(*privations*) bear; (*personne*) put up
with; (*structure*: Ordinat) support; **il ne
supporte pas les enfants/de perdre**
he can't stand children/losing.
supporter² /sypɔʀtɛʀ/ *nm* (Sport)
supporter.
supposer /sypoze/ [1] *vt* suppose;
(impliquer) imply; **à** ~ **que** supposing
that.
suppression /sypʀesjɔ̃/ *nf* (de taxe)
abolition; (de sanction) lifting; (de mot)
deletion. **supprimer** [1] *vt*
(*allocation*) withdraw; (*contrôle*) lift;
(*train*) cancel; (*preuve*) suppress.
suprématie /sypʀemasi/ *nf*
supremacy.

suprême /sypʀɛm/ *adj* supreme.
sur /syʀ/ *prép* on, upon; (par-dessus)
over; (au sujet de) about, on; (proportion)
out of; (mesure) by; ~ **la photo** in the
photograph; **mettre/jeter** ~ put/
throw on to; ~ **mesure** made to
measure; ~ **place** on the spot; ~ **ce,
je pars** with that, I must go; ~ **le
moment** at the time.
sûr /syʀ/ *adj* certain, sure; (sans
danger) safe; (digne de confiance)
reliable; (*main*) steady; (*jugement*)
sound; **être** ~ **de soi** be self-
confident; **j'en étais** ~**I** I knew it!
surabondance /syʀabɔ̃dɑ̃s/ *nf*
overabundance.
surcharge /syʀʃaʀʒ/ *nf*
overloading; (poids) excess load.
surcharger [1] *vt* overload; (*texte*)
alter.
surchauffer /syʀʃofe/ [1] *vt*
overheat.
surcroît /syʀkʀwa/ *nm* increase (de
in); **de** ~ in addition.
surdité /syʀdite/ *nf* deafness.
surélever /syʀelve/ [6] *vt* raise.
sûrement /syʀmɑ̃/ *adv* certainly;
(sans danger) safely; **il a** ~ **oublié** he
must have forgotten.
surenchère /syʀɑ̃ʃɛʀ/ *nf* higher
bid. **surenchérir** [2] *vi* bid higher
(**sur** than).
surestimer /syʀɛstime/ [1] *vt*
overestimate.
sûreté /syʀte/ *nf* safety; (de pays)
security; (d'un geste) steadiness; **être
en** ~ be safe; **S**~ **(nationale)** police
(+ *pl*).
surexcité, ~e /syʀɛksite/ *adj* very
excited.
surf /sœʀf/ *nm* surfing.
surface /syʀfas/ *nf* surface; **faire** ~
(*sous-marin*, fig) surface; **en** ~ on the
surface.
surfait, ~e /syʀfɛ, -t/ *adj* overrated.
surfer /sœʀfe/ [1] *vi* go surfing; ~
sur l'Internet surf the Internet.
surgelé, ~e /syʀʒale/ *adj* (deep-)
frozen; **aliments** ~**s** frozen food (+
sg).
surgir /syʀʒiʀ/ [2] *vi* appear
(suddenly); (*difficulté*) crop up.
sur-le-champ /syʀləʃɑ̃/ *adv* right
away.

surlendemain /syʀlɑ̃dmɛ̃/ nm le ~ two days later; le ~ de two days after.

surligneur /syʀliɲœʀ/ nm highlighter (pen).

surmenage /syʀmənaʒ/ nm overwork.

surmonter /syʀmɔ̃te/ [1] vt (vaincre) overcome, surmount; (être au-dessus de) surmount, top.

surnaturel, **~le** /syʀnatyʀɛl/ adj supernatural.

surnom /syʀnɔ̃/ nm nickname. **surnommer** [1] vt nickname.

surpeuplé, **~e** /syʀpœple/ adj overpopulated.

surplomber /syʀplɔ̃be/ [1] vt/i overhang.

surplus /syʀply/ nm surplus.

suprenant, **~e** /syʀpʀənɑ̃, -t/ adj surprising. **surprendre** [50] vt (étonner) surprise; (prendre au dépourvu) catch, surprise; (entendre) overhear. **surpris**, **~e** adj surprised (de at).

surprise /syʀpʀiz/ nf surprise.

surréaliste /syʀʀealist/ a & nmf surrealist.

sursaut /syʀso/ nm start, jump; en ~ with a start; ~ de (regain) burst of. **sursauter** [1] vi start, jump.

sursis /syʀsi/ nm reprieve; (Mil) deferment; **deux ans (de prison) avec** ~ a two-year suspended sentence.

surtaxe /syʀtaks/ nf surcharge.

surtout /syʀtu/ adv especially; (avant tout) above all; ~ **pas** certainly not.

surveillance /syʀvɛjɑ̃s/ nf watch; (d'examen) supervision; (de la police) surveillance. **surveillant**, **~e** nm,f (de prison) warder; (au lycée) supervisor (in charge of discipline). **surveiller** [1] vt watch; (travaux, élèves) supervise.

survenir /syʀvəniʀ/ [59] vi occur, take place; (personne) turn up.

survêtement /syʀvɛtmɑ̃/ nm (Sport) tracksuit.

survie /syʀvi/ nf survival.

survivant, **~e** /syʀvivɑ̃, -t/ adj surviving. ● nm,f survivor.

survivre /syʀvivʀ/ [63] vi survive; ~ à (conflit) survive; (personne) outlive.

survoler /syʀvɔle/ [1] vt fly over; (livre) skim through.

sus: en ~ /ɑ̃sys/ loc in addition.

susceptible /syseptibl/ adj touchy; ~ **de faire** likely to do.

susciter /sysite/ [1] vt (éveiller) arouse; (occasionner) create.

suspect, **~e** /syspɛ, -ɛkt/ adj (individu, faits) suspicious; (témoignage) suspect; ~ **de** suspected of. ● nm,f suspect. **suspecter** [1] vt suspect.

suspendre /syspɑ̃dʀ/ [3] vt (accrocher) hang (up); (interrompre, destituer) suspend; **suspendu à** hanging from. □ se ~ à vpr hang from.

suspens: en ~ /ɑ̃syspɑ̃/ loc (affaire) outstanding; (dans l'indécision) in suspense.

suspense /syspɛns/ nm suspense.

suture /sytyʀ/ nf **point de** ~ stitch.

svelte /svɛlt/ adj slender.

S.V.P. abrév (**s'il vous plaît**) please.

syllabe /silab/ nf syllable.

symbole /sɛ̃bɔl/ nm symbol. **symboliser** [1] vt symbolize.

symétrie /simetʀi/ nf symmetry.

sympa /sɛ̃pa/ a inv Ⓘ nice; **sois** ~ be a pal.

sympathie /sɛ̃pati/ nf (goût) liking; (compassion) sympathy; **avoir de la** ~ **pour** like. **sympathique** adj nice, pleasant. **sympathisant**, **~e** nm,f sympathizer. **sympathiser** [1] vi get on well (avec with).

symphonie /sɛ̃fɔni/ nf symphony.

symptôme /sɛ̃ptom/ nm symptom.

synagogue /sinagɔg/ nf synagogue.

synchroniser /sɛ̃kʀɔnize/ [1] vt synchronize.

syncope /sɛ̃kɔp/ nf (Méd) blackout.

syndic /sɛ̃dik/ nm ~ (**d'immeuble**) property manager.

syndicaliste /sɛ̃dikalist/ nmf (trade-)unionist. ● adj (trade-)union.

syndicat /sɛ̃dika/ nm (trade) union; ~ **d'initiative** tourist office.

syndiqué, **~e** /sɛ̃dike/ adj **être** ~ be a (trade-)union member.

synonyme /sinɔnim/ adj synonymous. ● nm synonym.

syntaxe /sɛ̃taks/ nf syntax.

synthèse /sɛ̃tɛz/ nf synthesis.
synthétique adj synthetic.

synthé(tiseur) /sɛ̃te(tizœʀ)/ nm
synthesizer.

systématique /sistematik/ adj
systematic.

système /sistɛm/ nm system; le ~
D 🔲 resourcefulness.

....

Tt

....

t' /t/ ⇒TE.

ta /ta/ ⇒TON¹.

tabac /taba/ nm tobacco; (magasin)
tobacconist's shop.

table /tabl/ nf table; à ~! dinner is
ready!; ~ de nuit bedside table; ~
des matières table of contents; ~ à
repasser ironing board; ~ roulante
(tea-)trolley; (US) (serving) cart.

tableau (pl ~x) /tablo/ nm picture;
(peinture) painting; (panneau) board;
(graphique) chart; (Scol) blackboard; ~
d'affichage notice-board; ~ de bord
dashboard.

tablette /tablɛt/ nf shelf; ~ de
chocolat bar of chocolate.

tableur /tablœʀ/ nm spreadsheet.

tablier /tablije/ nm apron; (de pont)
platform; (de magasin) shutter.

tabou /tabu/ nm & a taboo.

tabouret /tabuʀɛ/ nm stool.

tache /taʃ/ nf mark, spot; (salissure)
stain; faire ~ d'huile spread; ~ de
rousseur freckle.

tâche /taʃ/ nf task, job.

tacher /taʃe/ [1] vt stain. □ se ~
vpr (personne) get oneself dirty.

tâcher /taʃe/ [1] vi ~ de faire try to
do.

tacheté, ~e /taʃte/ adj spotted.

tact /takt/ nm tact.

tactique /taktik/ adj tactical. ● nf
(Mil) tactics; une ~ a tactic.

taie /tɛ/ nf ~ (d'oreiller) pillowcase.

taille /tɑj/ nf (milieu du corps) waist;
(hauteur) height; (grandeur) size; de ~

sizeable; être de ~ à faire be up to
doing.

taille-crayons /tajkʀɛjɔ̃/ nm inv
pencil-sharpener.

tailler /taje/ [1] vt cut; (arbre) prune;
(crayon) sharpen; (vêtement) cut out.
□ se ~ vpr 🔀 clear off.

tailleur /tajœʀ/ nm (costume)
woman's suit; (couturier) tailor; en ~
cross-legged; ~ de pierre stone-
cutter.

taire /tɛʀ/ [47] vt not to reveal; faire
~ silence. □ se ~ vpr be silent ou
quiet; (devenir silencieux) fall silent.

talc /talk/ nm talcum powder.

talent /talɑ̃/ nm talent.
talentueux, **-euse** adj talented,
gifted.

talon /talɔ̃/ nm heel; (de chèque) stub.

tambour /tɑ̃buʀ/ nm drum; (d'église)
vestibule.

Tamise /tamiz/ nf Thames.

tampon /tɑ̃pɔ̃/ nm (de bureau) stamp;
(ouate) wad, pad; ~ (hygiénique)
tampon.

tamponner /tɑ̃pɔne/ [1] vt
(document) stamp; (véhicule) crash
into; (plaie) swab.

tandem /tɑ̃dɛm/ nm (vélo) tandem;
(personnes: fig) duo.

tandis que /tɑ̃dik(ə)/ conj while.

tanière /tanjɛʀ/ nf den.

tant /tɑ̃/ adv (travailler, manger) so
much; ~ de (quantité) so much;
(nombre) so many; ~ que as long as;
en ~ que as; ~ mieux! all the
better!; ~ pis! too bad!

tante /tɑ̃t/ nf aunt.

tantôt /tɑ̃to/ adv sometimes.

tapage /tapaʒ/ nm din.

tape /tap/ nf slap. **tape-à-l'œil** a
inv flashy, tawdry.

taper /tape/ [1] vt hit; (prendre 🔲)
scrounge; ~ (à la machine) type. ● vi
(cogner) bang; (soleil) beat down; ~
dans (puiser dans) dig into; ~ sur hit;
~ sur l'épaule de qn tap sb on the
shoulder. □ se ~ vpr (corvée 🔲) get
stuck with 🔲.

tapis /tapi/ nm carpet; (petit) rug; ~
de bain bathmat; ~ roulant (pour
objets) conveyor belt; (pour piétons)
moving walkway.

tapisser /tapise/ [1] *vt* (wall)paper; (fig) cover (**de** with). **tapisserie** *nf* tapestry; (papier peint) wallpaper.

taquin, **~e** /takɛ̃, -in/ *adj* fond of teasing. ● *nm,f* tease(r).

tard /taʀ/ *adv* late; **au plus ~** at the latest; **plus ~** later; **sur le ~** late in life.

tarder /taʀde/ [1] *vi* (être lent à venir) be a long time coming; **~ (à faire)** take a long time (doing), delay (doing); **sans (plus) ~** without (further) delay; **il me tarde de** I'm longing to.

tardif, **-ive** /taʀdif, -v/ *adj* late.

tare /taʀ/ *nf* (défaut) defect.

tarif /taʀif/ *nm* rate; (de train, taxi) fare; **plein ~** full price.

tarir /taʀiʀ/ [2] *vt/i* dry up. □ **se ~** *vpr* dry up.

tarte /taʀt/ *nf* tart. ● *a inv* (ridicule Ⓘ) ridiculous.

tartine /taʀtin/ *nf* slice of bread; **~ de beurre** slice of bread and butter. **tartiner** [1] *vt* spread.

tartre /taʀtʀ/ *nm* (de bouilloire) fur, scale; (sur les dents) tartar.

tas /tɑ/ *nm* pile, heap; **un** *ou* **des ~ de** Ⓘ lots of.

tasse /tɑs/ *nf* cup; **~ à thé** teacup.

tasser /tɑse/ [1] *vt* pack, squeeze; (*terre*) pack (down). □ **se ~** *vpr* (*terrain*) sink; (se serrer) squeeze up.

tâter /tɑte/ [1] *vt* feel; (opinion: fig) sound out. ● *vi* **~ de** try out.

tatillon, **~ne** /tatijɔ̃, -jɔn/ *adj* finicky.

tâtonnements /tɑtɔnmɑ̃/ *nmpl* (essais) trial and error (+ *sg*).

tâtons: **à ~** /atɑtɔ̃/ *loc* **avancer à ~** grope one's way along.

tatouage /tatwaʒ/ *nm* (dessin) tattoo.

taupe /top/ *nf* mole.

taureau (*pl* **~x**) /tɔʀo/ *nm* bull; **le T~** Taurus.

taux /to/ *nm* rate.

taxe /taks/ *nf* tax.

taxi /taksi/ *nm* taxi(-cab); (personne Ⓘ) taxi driver.

taxiphone® /taksifɔn/ *nm* pay phone.

Tchécoslovaquie /tʃekɔslɔvaki/ *nf* Czechoslovakia.

tchèque /tʃɛk/ *adj* Czech; **République ~** Czech Republic. **T~** *nmf* Czech.

te, **t'** /tə, t/ *pron* you; (indirect) (to) you; (réfléchi) yourself.

technicien, **~ne** /tɛknisjɛ̃, -ɛn/ *nm,f* technician.

technique /tɛknik/ *adj* technical. ● *nf* technique.

techno /tɛkno/ *nf* (Mus) techno.

technologie /tɛknɔlɔʒi/ *nf* technology.

teindre /tɛ̃dʀ/ [22] *vt* dye. □ **se ~** *vpr* **se ~ les cheveux** dye one's hair.

teint /tɛ̃/ *nm* complexion.

teinte /tɛ̃t/ *nf* shade. **teinter** [1] *vt* (*verre*) tint; (*bois*) stain.

teinture /tɛ̃tyʀ/ *nf* (produit) dye.

teinturier, **-ière** /tɛ̃tyʀje, -jɛʀ/ *nm,f* dry-cleaner.

tel, **~le** /tɛl/ *adj* such; **un ~ livre** such a book; **~ que** such as, like; (ainsi que) (just) as; **~ ou ~** such-and-such; **~ quel** (just) as it is.

télé /tele/ *nf* Ⓘ TV.

télécharger /teleʃaʀʒe/ [40] *vt* (Ordinat) download.

télécommande /telekɔmɑ̃d/ *nf* remote control.

télécommunications /telekɔmynikasjɔ̃/ *nfpl* telecommunications.

téléconférence /telekɔ̃feʀɑ̃s/ *nf* teleconferencing.

télécopie /telekɔpi/ *nf* fax. **télécopieur** *nm* fax machine.

téléfilm /telefilm/ *nm* TV film.

télégramme /telegʀam/ *nm* telegram.

télégraphier /telegʀafje/ [45] *vt/i* **~ (à)** cable.

téléguidé, **~e** /telegide/ *adj* radio-controlled.

télématique /telematik/ *nf* telematics (+ *sg*).

téléphérique /teleferik/ *nm* cable car.

téléphone /telefɔn/ *nm* (tele-) phone; **~ à carte** cardphone. **téléphoner** [1] *vt/i* **~ (à)** (tele)

phone. **téléphonique** adj (tele)
phone.

téléserveur /telesɛʀvœʀ/ nm
(Internet) remote server.

télésiège /telesjɛʒ/ nm chairlift.

téléski /teleski/ nm ski tow.

téléspectateur, -trice /tele-
spɛktatœʀ, -tʀis/ nm, f (television)
viewer.

télévente /televãt/ nf telesales (+
pl).

télévisé, ~e /televize/ adj (débat)
televised; **émission** ~e television
programme. **télévision** nf
television.

télex /telɛks/ nm telex.

tellement /tɛlmã/ adv (tant) so
much; (si) so; ~ **de** (quantité) so much;
(nombre) so many.

téméraire /temeʀɛʀ/ adj (personne)
reckless.

témoignage /temwaɲaʒ/ nm
testimony, evidence; (récit) account;
~ **de** (marque) token of.

témoigner /temwaɲe/ [1] vi testify
(de to). ● vt (montrer) show; ~ **que**
testify that.

témoin /temwɛ̃/ nm witness; (Sport)
baton; **être ~ de** witness; ~ **oculaire**
eyewitness.

tempe /tãp/ nf (Anat) temple.

tempérament /tãpeʀamã/ nm
temperament, disposition.

température /tãpeʀatyʀ/ nf
temperature.

tempête /tãpɛt/ nf storm; ~ **de
neige** snowstorm.

temple /tãpl/ nm temple; (protestant)
church.

temporaire /tãpɔʀɛʀ/ adj
temporary.

temps /tã/ nm (notion) time; (Gram)
tense; (étape) stage; **à ~ partiel/plein**
part-/full-time; **ces derniers ~** lately;
dans le ~ at one time; **dans quelque
~** in a while; **de ~ en ~** from time
to time; ~ **d'arrêt** pause; **avoir tout
son ~** have plenty of time; (météo)
weather; ~ **de chien** filthy weather;
quel ~ fait-il? what's the weather
like?

tenace /tənas/ adj stubborn.

tenaille /tənaj/ nf pincers (+ pl).

tendance /tãdãs/ nf tendency;
(évolution) trend; **avoir ~ à** tend to.

tendon /tãdɔ̃/ nm tendon.

tendre¹ /tãdʀ/ [3] vt stretch; (piège)
set; (bras) stretch out; (main) hold
out; (cou) crane; ~ **qch à qn** hold sth
out to sb; ~ **l'oreille** prick up one's
ears. ● vi ~ **à** tend to.

tendre² /tãdʀ/ adj tender; (couleur,
bois) soft. **tendresse** nf tenderness.

tendu, ~e /tãdy/ adj (corde) tight;
(personne, situation) tense.

ténèbres /tenɛbʀ/ nfpl darkness (+
sg).

teneur /tənœʀ/ nf content.

tenir /təniʀ/ [59] vt hold; (pari,
promesse, hôtel) keep; (place) take
up; (propos) utter; (rôle) play; ~ **de**
(avoir reçu de) have got from; ~ **pour**
regard as; ~ **chaud** keep warm; ~
compte de take into account; ~ **le
coup** hold out; ~ **tête à** stand up to.
● vi hold; ~ **à** be attached to; ~ **à
faire** be anxious to do; ~ **bon** stand
firm; ~ **dans** fit into; ~ **de qn** take
after sb; **tiens!** (surprise) hey! □ **se ~**
vpr (debout) stand; (avoir lieu) be held;
se ~ à hold on to; **s'en ~ à** (se limiter
à) confine oneself to.

tennis /tenis/ nm tennis; ~ **de table**
table tennis. ● nmpl (chaussures)
sneakers.

ténor /tenɔʀ/ nm tenor.

tension /tãsjɔ̃/ nf tension; **avoir de
la ~** have high blood-pressure.

tentation /tãtasjɔ̃/ nf temptation.

tentative /tãtativ/ nf attempt.

tente /tãt/ nf tent.

tenter /tãte/ [1] vt (allécher) tempt;
(essayer) try (**de faire** to do).

tenture /tãtyʀ/ nf curtain; ~s
draperies.

tenu, ~e /təny/ adj **bien ~** well
kept; ~ **de** required. ● ⇒TENIR [58].

tenue /təny/ nf (habillement) dress; (de
maison) upkeep; (conduite) (good)
behaviour; (maintien) posture; ~ **de
soirée** evening dress.

Tergal® /tɛʀgal/ nm Terylene®.

terme /tɛʀm/ nm (mot) term; (date
limite) time-limit; (fin) end; **né avant ~**
premature; **à long/court ~** long-/
short-term; **en bons ~s** on good
terms (**avec** with).

terminaison /tɛʀminɛzɔ̃/ *nf* (Gram) ending.

terminal, ~**e** (*mpl* -**aux**) /tɛʀminal, -o/ *adj* terminal. ● *nm* terminal.
terminale *nf* (Scol) ≈ sixth form; (US) twelfth grade.

terminer /tɛʀmine/ [1] *vt/i* finish; (*discours*) end), finish. □ **se** ~ *vpr* end (**par** with).

terne /tɛʀn/ *adj* dull, drab.

ternir /tɛʀniʀ/ [2] *vt/i* tarnish. □ **se** ~ *vpr* tarnish.

terrain /tɛʀɛ̃/ *nm* ground; (*parcelle*) piece of land; (à bâtir) plot; ~ **d'aviation** airfield; ~ **de camping** campsite; ~ **de golf** golf course; ~ **de jeu** playground; ~ **vague** waste ground.

terrasse /tɛʀas/ *nf* terrace; **à la** ~ (d'un café) outside (a café).

terrasser /tɛʀase/ [1] *vt* (*adversaire*) knock down; (*maladie*) strike down.

terre /tɛʀ/ *nf* (planète, matière) earth; (étendue, pays) land; (sol) ground; **à** ~ (Naut) ashore; **par** ~ (dehors) on the ground; (dedans) on the floor; ~ (**cuite**) terracotta; **la** ~ **ferme** dry land; ~ **glaise** clay. **terreau** (*pl* ~**x**) *nm* compost. **terre-plein** (*pl* **terres-pleins**) *nm* platform; (de route) central reservation.

terrestre /tɛʀɛstʀ/ *adj* (*animaux*) land; (de notre planète) of the Earth.

terreur /tɛʀœʀ/ *nf* terror.

terrible /tɛʀibl/ *adj* terrible; (formidable 🗊) terrific.

terrier /tɛʀje/ *nm* (trou) burrow; (chien) terrier.

terrifier /tɛʀifje/ [45] *vt* terrify.

territoire /tɛʀitwaʀ/ *nm* territory.

terroir /tɛʀwaʀ/ *nm* land; **du** ~ local.

terroriser /tɛʀɔʀize/ [1] *vt* terrorize.

terrorisme /tɛʀɔʀism/ *nm* terrorism. **terroriste** *nmf* terrorist.

tertiaire /tɛʀsjɛʀ/ *adj* (*secteur*) service.

tes /te/ ⇒**TON**[1].

test /tɛst/ *nm* test.

testament /tɛstamɑ̃/ *nm* (Jur) will; (politique, artistique) testament; **Ancien/ Nouveau T**~ Old/New Testament.

tétanos /tetanos/ *nm* tetanus.

têtard /tɛtaʀ/ *nm* tadpole.

tête /tɛt/ *nf* head; (visage) face; (cheveux) hair; **à la** ~ **de** at the head of; **à** ~ **reposée** at one's leisure; **de** ~ (*calculer*) in one's head; **faire la** ~ sulk; **tenir** ~ **à qn** stand up to sb; **il n'en fait qu'à sa** ~ he does just as he pleases; **en** ~ (Sport) in the lead; **faire une** ~ (au football) head the ball; **une forte** ~ a rebel; **la** ~ **la première** head first; **de la** ~ **aux pieds** from head to toe.

tête-à-tête /tɛtatɛt/ *nm inv* tête-à-tête; **en** ~ in private.

tétée /tete/ *nf* feed. **téter** [14] *vt/i* suck.

tétine /tetin/ *nf* (de biberon) teat; (sucette) dummy; (US) pacifier.

têtu, ~**e** /tety/ *adj* stubborn.

texte /tɛkst/ *nm* text; (de leçon) subject; (morceau choisi) passage.

texteur /tɛkstœʀ/ *nm* (Ordinat) word-processor.

textile /tɛkstil/ *nm* & *a* textile.

TGV *abrév m* (**train à grande vitesse**) TGV, high-speed train.

thé /te/ *nm* tea.

théâtre /teatʀ/ *nm* theatre; (d'un crime) scene; **faire du** ~ act.

théière /tejɛʀ/ *nf* teapot.

thème /tɛm/ *nm* theme; (traduction: Scol) prose.

théorie /teɔʀi/ *nf* theory. **théorique** *adj* theoretical.

thérapie /teʀapi/ *nf* therapy.

thermique /tɛʀmik/ *adj* thermal.

thermomètre /tɛʀmɔmɛtʀ/ *nm* thermometer.

thermos® /tɛʀmos/ *nm ou f* Thermos® (flask).

thermostat /tɛʀmɔsta/ *nm* thermostat.

thèse /tɛz/ *nf* thesis.

thon /tɔ̃/ *nm* tuna.

thym /tɛ̃/ *nm* thyme.

tibia /tibja/ *nm* shinbone.

tic /tik/ *nm* (contraction) tic, twitch; (manie) habit.

ticket /tikɛ/ *nm* ticket.

tiède /tjɛd/ *adj* lukewarm; (*nuit*) warm.

tiédir /tjediʀ/ [2] *vt/i* (faire) ~ warm up.

tien, **~ne** /tjɛ̃, -ɛn/ *pron* le ~, la ~ne, les ~(ne)s yours; à la ~ne! cheers!

tiens, **tient** /tjɛ̃/ ⇒TENIR [59].

tiercé /tjɛʀse/ *nm* place-betting.

tiers, **tierce** /tjɛʀ, tjɛʀs/ *adj* third. ● *nm* (fraction) third; (personne) third party. **tiers-monde** *nm* Third World.

tige /tiʒ/ *nf* (Bot) stem, stalk; (en métal) shaft, rod.

tigre /tigʀ/ *nm* tiger.

tigresse /tigʀɛs/ *nf* tigress.

tilleul /tijœl/ *nm* lime tree, linden tree; (infusion) linden tea.

timbre /tɛ̃bʀ/ *nm* stamp; (sonnette) bell; (de voix) tone. ~ **poste** (*pl* ~s **poste**) *nm* postage stamp. **timbrer** [1] *vt* stamp.

timide /timid/ *adj* shy, timid. **timidité** *nf* shyness.

timoré, **~e** /timɔʀe/ *adj* timorous.

tintement /tɛ̃tmɑ̃/ *nm* (de sonnette) ringing; (de clés) jingling.

tique /tik/ *nf* tick.

tir /tiʀ/ *nm* (Sport) shooting; (action de tirer) firing; (feu, rafale) fire; ~ **à l'arc** archery; ~ **au pigeon** clay pigeon shooting.

tirage /tiʀaʒ/ *nm* (de photo) printing; (de journal) circulation; (de livre) edition; (Ordinat) hard copy; (de cheminée) draught; ~ **au sort** draw.

tire-bouchon (*pl* ~s) /tiʀbuʃɔ̃/ *nm* corkscrew.

tirelire /tiʀliʀ/ *nf* piggy bank.

tirer /tiʀe/ [1] *vt* pull; (langue) stick out; (conclusion, trait, rideaux) draw; (coup de feu) fire; (gibier) shoot; (photo) print; ~ **de** (sortir) take *ou* get out of; (extraire) extract from; (plaisir, nom) derive from; ~ **parti de** take advantage of; ~ **profit de** profit from; **se faire** ~ **l'oreille** get told off. ● *vi* shoot, fire (**sur** at); ~ **sur** (corde) pull at; (couleur) verge on; ~ **à sa fin** be drawing to a close; ~ **au clair** clarify; ~ **au sort** draw lots (for). □ **se** ~ *vpr* 🔁 clear off; **se** ~ **de** get out of; **s'en** ~ (en réchapper) pull through; (réussir 🔁) cope.

tiret /tiʀe/ *nm* dash.

tireur /tiʀœʀ/ *nm* gunman; ~ **d'élite** marksman; ~ **isolé** sniper.

tiroir /tiʀwaʀ/ *nm* drawer. **tiroir-caisse** (*pl* **tiroirs-caisses**) *nm* till, cash register.

tisane /tizan/ *nf* herbal tea.

tissage /tisaʒ/ *nm* weaving. **tisser** [1] *vt* weave. **tisserand** *nm* weaver.

tissu /tisy/ *nm* fabric, material; (biologique) tissue; **un** ~ **de mensonges** (fig) a pack of lies. **tissu-éponge** (*pl* **tissus-éponge**) *nm* towelling.

titre /titʀ/ *nm* title; (diplôme) qualification; (Comm) bond; ~**s** (droits) claims; (gros) ~**s** headlines; **à** ~ **d'exemple** as an example; **à juste** ~ rightly; **à** ~ **privé** in a private capacity; **à double** ~ on two accounts; ~ **de propriété** title deed.

tituber /titybe/ [1] *vi* stagger.

titulaire /titylɛʀ/ *adj* **être** ~ be a permanent staff member; **être** ~ **de** hold. ● *nmf* (de permis) holder. **titulariser** [1] *vt* give permanent status to.

toast /tost/ *nm* (pain) piece of toast; (canapé, allocution) toast.

toboggan /tɔbɔgɑ̃/ *nm* (de jeu) slide; (Auto) flyover.

toi /twa/ *pron* you; (réfléchi) yourself; **dépêche-**~ hurry up.

toile /twal/ *nf* cloth; (tableau) canvas; ~ **d'araignée** cobweb; ~ **de fond** (fig) backdrop; **la** ~ (Internet) the Web.

toilette /twalɛt/ *nf* (habillement) outfit; ~**s** (cabinets) toilet(s); **de** ~ (articles, savon) toilet; **faire sa** ~ have a wash.

toi-même /twamɛm/ *pron* yourself.

toit /twa/ *nm* roof; ~ **ouvrant** (Auto) sunroof.

toiture /twatyʀ/ *nf* roof.

tôle /tol/ *nf* (plaque) iron sheet; ~ **ondulée** corrugated iron.

tolérant, **~e** /tɔleʀɑ̃, -t/ *adj* tolerant. **tolérer** [14] *vt* tolerate.

tomate /tɔmat/ *nf* tomato.

tombe /tɔ̃b/ *nf* grave; (pierre) gravestone.

tombeau (*pl* ~**x**) /tɔ̃bo/ *nm* tomb.

tomber /tɔ̃be/ [1] *vi* (aux être) fall; (fièvre, vent) drop; **faire** ~ knock over; (gouvernement) bring down; **laisser** ~ (objet, amoureux) drop; (collègue) let down; (activité) give up;

laisse ∼! 🔲 forget it!; ∼ **à l'eau** (*projet*) fall through; ∼ **bien** *ou* **à point** come at the right time; ∼ **en panne** break down; ∼ **en syncope** faint; ∼ **sur** (trouver) run across.

tombola /tɔ̃bɔla/ *nf* tombola; (US) lottery.

tome /tɔm/ *nm* volume.

ton¹, ta (**ton** *before vowel or mute h*) (*pl* **tes**) /tɔ̃, ta, tɔ̃n, te/ *adj* your.

ton² /tɔ̃/ *nm* (hauteur de voix) pitch; **d'un** ∼ **sec** drily; **de bon** ∼ in good taste.

tonalité /tɔnalite/ *nf* (Mus) key; (de téléphone) dialling tone; (US) dial tone.

tondeuse /tɔ̃døz/ *nf* (à moutons) shears (+ *pl*); (à cheveux) clippers (+ *pl*); ∼ **à gazon** lawn-mower. **tondre** [3] *vt* (*herbe*) mow; (*mouton*) shear; (*cheveux*) clip.

tonne /tɔn/ *nf* tonne.

tonneau (*pl* ∼**x**) /tɔno/ *nm* barrel; (en voiture) somersault.

tonnerre /tɔnɛʀ/ *nm* thunder.

tonton /tɔ̃tɔ̃/ *nm* 🔲 uncle.

tonus /tɔnys/ *nm* energy.

torche /tɔʀʃ/ *nf* torch.

torchon /tɔʀʃɔ̃/ *nm* (pour la vaisselle) tea towel.

tordre /tɔʀdʀ/ [3] *vt* twist. □ **se** ∼ *vpr* **se** ∼ **la cheville** twist one's ankle; **se** ∼ **de douleur** writhe in pain; **se** ∼ (**de rire**) split one's sides.

tordu, ∼e /tɔʀdy/ *adj* twisted, bent; (*esprit*) warped, twisted.

torpille /tɔʀpij/ *nf* torpedo.

torrent /tɔʀã/ *nm* torrent.

torride /tɔʀid/ *adj* torrid; (*chaleur*) scorching.

torse /tɔʀs/ *nm* chest; (Anat) torso.

tort /tɔʀ/ *nm* wrong; **avoir** ∼ be wrong (**de faire** to do); **donner** ∼ **à** prove wrong; **être dans son** ∼ be in the wrong; **faire (du)** ∼ **à** harm; **à** ∼ wrongly; **à** ∼ **et à travers** without thinking.

torticolis /tɔʀtikɔli/ *nm* stiff neck.

tortiller /tɔʀtije/ [1] *vt* twist, twirl. □ **se** ∼ *vpr* wriggle.

tortionnaire /tɔʀsjɔnɛʀ/ *nm* torturer.

tortue /tɔʀty/ *nf* tortoise; (d'eau) turtle.

tortueux, -euse /tɔʀtɥø, -z/ *adj* (*chemin*) twisting; (*explication*) tortuous.

torture /tɔʀtyʀ/ *nf* torture. **torturer** [1] *vt* torture.

tôt /to/ *adv* early; **au plus** ∼ at the earliest; **le plus** ∼ **possible** as soon as possible; ∼ **ou tard** sooner or later; **ce n'est pas trop** ∼! it's about time!

total, ∼e (*mpl* **-aux**) /tɔtal, -o/ *adj* total. ● *nm* (*pl* **-aux**) total; **au** ∼ all in all. **totalement** *adv* totally. **totaliser** [1] *vt* total. **totalitaire** *adj* totalitarian.

totalité /tɔtalite/ *nf* **la** ∼ **de** all of.

touche /tuʃ/ *nf* (de piano) key; (de peinture) touch; (**ligne de**) ∼ (Sport) touchline.

toucher /tuʃe/ [1] *vt* touch; (émouvoir) move, touch; (contacter) get in touch with; (*cible*) hit; (*argent*) draw; (*chèque*) cash; (concerner) affect. ● *vi* **à** touch; (*question*) touch on; (*fin, but*) approach; **je vais lui en** ∼ **deux mots** I'll talk to him about it. □ **se** ∼ *vpr* (*lignes*) touch. ● *nm* (sens) touch.

touffe /tuf/ *nf* (de poils, d'herbe) tuft; (de plantes) clump.

toujours /tuʒuʀ/ *adv* always; (encore) still; (de toute façon) anyway; **pour** ∼ for ever; ∼ **est-il que** the fact remains that.

toupet /tupɛ/ *nm* (culot 🔲) cheek, nerve.

tour /tuʀ/ *nf* tower; (immeuble) tower block; (échecs) rook; ∼ **de contrôle** control tower. ● *nm* (mouvement, succession, tournure) turn; (excursion) trip; (à pied) walk; (en auto) drive; (artifice) trick; (circonférence) circumference; (Tech) lathe; ∼ (**de piste**) lap; **à** ∼ **de rôle** in turn; **à mon** ∼ when it is my turn; **c'est mon** ∼ **de** it is my turn to; **faire le** ∼ **de** go round; (*question*) survey; ∼ **d'horizon** survey; ∼ **de potier** potter's wheel; ∼ **de taille** waist measurement; (ligne) waistline.

tourbillon /tuʀbijɔ̃/ *nm* whirlwind; (d'eau) whirlpool; (fig) swirl.

tourisme /tuʀism/ *nm* tourism; **faire du** ∼ do some sightseeing.

touriste /tuʀist/ *nmf* tourist.
touristique *adj* tourist; (*route*)
scenic.

tourmenter /tuʀmɑ̃te/ *vt* torment.
□ **se ~** *vpr* worry.

tournant, ~e /tuʀnɑ̃, -t/ *adj* (qui
pivote) revolving. ● *nm* bend; (fig)
turning-point.

tourne-disque (*pl* ~s)
/tuʀnədisk/ *nm* record-player.

tournée /tuʀne/ *nf* (de facteur, au café)
round; **c'est ma ~** I'll buy this
round; (d'artiste) tour.

tourner /tuʀne/ [1] *vt* turn; (*film*)
shoot, make; **~ le dos à** turn one's
back on; **~ en dérision** mock. ● *vi*
turn; (*toupie, tête*) spin; (*moteur,
usine*) run; **~ autour de** go round;
(*personne, maison*) hang around;
(*terre*) revolve round; (*question*)
centre on; **~ de l'œil** 🔲 faint; **mal ~**
(*affaire*) turn out badly. □ **se ~** *vpr*
turn.

tournesol /tuʀnəsɔl/ *nm* sunflower.

tournevis /tuʀnəvis/ *nm*
screwdriver.

tournoi /tuʀnwa/ *nm* tournament.

tourte /tuʀt/ *nf* pie.

tourterelle /tuʀtəʀɛl/ *nf* turtle
dove.

Toussaint /tusɛ̃/ *nf* **la ~** All Saints'
Day.

tousser /tuse/ [1] *vi* cough.

tout, ~e (*pl* **tous, toutes**) /tu, tut/
nm (ensemble) whole; **en ~** in all; **pas
du ~** not at all! ● *adj* all; (n'importe
quel) any; **~ le pays** the whole
country, all the country; **~e la nuit/
journée** the whole night/day; **~ un
paquet** a whole pack; **tous les jours**
every day; **tous les deux ans** every
two years; **~ le monde** everyone;
tous les deux, toutes les deux both
of them; **tous les trois** all three (of
them). ● *pron* everything; all;
anything; **tous** /tus/, **toutes** all; **tous
ensemble** all together; **prends ~** take
everything; **~ ce que tu veux**
everything you want. ● *adv* (très)
very; (entièrement) all; **~ au bout/
début** right at the end/beginning; **~
en marchant** while walking; **~ à
coup** all of a sudden; **~ à fait** quite,
completely; **~ à l'heure** in a moment;

(passé) a moment ago; **~ au ou le
long de** throughout; **~ au plus/
moins** at most/least; **~ de même** all
the same; **~ de suite** straight away;
~ entier whole; **~ neuf** brand new;
~ nu stark naked. **tout-à-l'égout**
nm inv main drainage.

toutefois /tutfwa/ *adv* however.

tout(-)terrain /tutɛʀɛ̃/ *a inv* all
terrain.

toux /tu/ *nf* cough.

toxicomane /tɔksikɔman/ *nmf*
drug addict.

toxique /tɔksik/ *adj* toxic.

trac /tʀak/ *nm* **le ~** nerves; (Théât)
stage fright.

tracas /tʀaka/ *nm* worry.

trace /tʀas/ *nf* (traînée, piste) trail;
(d'animal, de pneu) tracks; **~s de pas**
footprints.

tracer /tʀase/ [10] *vt* draw; (écrire)
write; (route) open up.

trachée-artère /tʀaʃeaʀtɛʀ/ *nf*
windpipe.

tracteur /tʀaktœʀ/ *nm* tractor.

tradition /tʀadisjɔ̃/ *nf* tradition.
traditionnel, ~le *adj* traditional.

traducteur, -trice /tʀadyktœʀ,
-tʀis/ *nm, f* translator. **traduction**
nf translation.

traduire /tʀadɥiʀ/ [17] *vt* translate;
~ en justice take to court.

trafic /tʀafik/ *nm* (commerce,
circulation) traffic.

trafiquant, ~e /tʀafikɑ̃, -t/ *nm, f*
trafficker; (d'armes, de drogues) dealer.

trafiquer /tʀafike/ [1] *vi* traffic. ● *vt*
🔲 (moteur) fiddle with.

tragédie /tʀaʒedi/ *nf* tragedy.
tragique *adj* tragic.

trahir /tʀaiʀ/ [2] *vt* betray. **trahison**
nf betrayal; (Mil) treason.

train /tʀɛ̃/ *nm* (Rail) train; (allure)
pace; **aller bon ~** walk briskly; **en ~
de faire** (busy) doing; **~
d'atterrissage** undercarriage; **~
électrique** (jouet) electric train set; **~
de vie** lifestyle.

traîne /tʀɛn/ *nf* (de robe) train; **à la ~**
lagging behind.

traîneau (*pl* ~**x**) /tʀeno/ *nm* sleigh.

traînée /tʀene/ *nf* (trace) trail;
(longue) streak; (femme: péj) slut.

traîner /tʀene/ [1] vt drag (along); ~
les pieds drag one's feet. ● vi (pendre)
trail; (rester en arrière) trail behind;
(flâner) hang about; (papiers, affaires)
lie around; ~ (en longueur) drag on;
ça n'a pas traîné! that didn't take
long! □ **se** ~ vpr (par terre) crawl.

traire /tʀɛʀ/ [29] vt milk.

trait /tʀɛ/ nm line; (en dessinant)
stroke; (caractéristique) feature, trait;
~**s** (du visage) features; **avoir** ~ **à**
relate to; **d'un** ~ (boire) in one gulp;
~ **d'union** hyphen; (fig) link.

traite /tʀɛt/ nf (de vache) milking;
(Comm) draft; **d'une (seule)** ~ in one
go, at a stretch.

traité /tʀete/ nm (pacte) treaty;
(ouvrage) treatise.

traitement /tʀɛtmã/ nm treatment;
(salaire) salary; ~ **de données** data
processing; ~ **de texte** word
processing.

traiter /tʀete/ [1] vt treat; (affaire)
deal with; (données, produit) process;
~ **qn de lâche** call sb a coward. ● vi
deal (avec with); ~ **de** (sujet) deal
with.

traiteur /tʀetœʀ/ nm caterer;
(boutique) delicatessen.

traître, -esse /tʀɛtʀ, -ɛs/ adj
treacherous. ● nm, f traitor.

trajectoire /tʀaʒɛktwaʀ/ nf path.

trajet /tʀaʒɛ/ nm (voyage) journey;
(itinéraire) route.

trame /tʀam/ nf (de tissu) weft; (de
récit) framework.

tramway /tʀamwɛ/ nm tram; (US)
streetcar.

tranchant, ~e /tʀãʃã, -t/ adj
sharp; (fig) cutting. ● nm cutting
edge; **à double** ~ two-edged.

tranche /tʀãʃ/ nf (rondelle) slice;
(bord) edge; (d'âge, de revenu) bracket.

tranchée /tʀãʃe/ nf trench.

trancher /tʀãʃe/ [1] vt cut;
(question) decide; (contraster) contrast
(**sur** with).

tranquille /tʀãkil/ adj quiet;
(esprit) at rest; (conscience) clear;
être/laisser ~ be/leave in peace;
tiens-toi ~! be quiet!

tranquillisant nm tranquillizer.

tranquilliser [1] vt reassure.

tranquillité nf (peace and) quiet;
(d'esprit) peace of mind.

transcription /tʀãskʀipsjõ/ nf
transcription; (copie) transcript.

transcrire [30] vt transcribe.

transe /tʀãs/ nf **en** ~ in a trance.

transférer /tʀãsfeʀe/ [14] vt
transfer.

transfert /tʀãsfɛʀ/ nm transfer; ~
d'appel (au téléphone) call diversion.

transformateur /tʀãsfɔʀmatœʀ/
nm transformer.

transformation /tʀãsfɔʀmasjõ/ nf
change; transformation.

transformer /tʀãsfɔʀme/ [1] vt
change; (radicalement) transform;
(vêtement) alter. □ **se** ~ vpr change;
(radicalement) be transformed; (se) ~
en turn into.

transiger /tʀãsiʒe/ [40] vi
compromise.

transiter /tʀãzite/ vt/i ~ **par**
pass through.

transitif, -ive /tʀãzitif, -v/ adj
transitive.

translucide /tʀãslysid/ adj
translucent.

transmettre /tʀãsmɛtʀ/ [42] vt
(savoir, maladie) pass on; (ondes)
transmit; (à la radio) broadcast.

transmission nf transmission;
(radio) broadcasting.

transparence /tʀãspaʀãs/ nf
transparency. **transparent, ~e** adj
transparent.

transpercer /tʀãspɛʀse/ [10] vt
pierce.

transpiration /tʀãspiʀasjõ/ nf
perspiration. **transpirer** [1] vi
perspire.

transplanter /tʀãsplãte/ [1] vt (Bot,
Méd) transplant.

transport /tʀãspɔʀ/ nm transport
(ation); **durant le** ~ in transit; **les**
~**s** transport (+ sg); **les** ~**s en
commun** public transport (+ sg).

transporter /tʀãspɔʀte/ [1] vt
transport; (à la main) carry.

transporteur nm haulier; (US)
trucker.

transversal, ~e (mpl **-aux**)
/tʀãsvɛʀsal, -o/ adj cross, transverse.

trapu, ~e /tʀapy/ adj stocky.

traumatisant, **~e** /tʀomatizɑ̃, -t/ *adj* traumatic. **traumatiser** *vt* [1] traumatize. **traumatisme** *nm* trauma.

travail (*pl* **-aux**) /tʀavaj, -o/ *nm* work; (emploi, tâche) job; (façonnage) working; **travaux** work (+ *sg*); (routiers) roadworks; **~ à la chaîne** production line work; **travaux dirigés** (Scol) practical; **travaux forcés** hard labour; **travaux manuels** handicrafts; **travaux ménagers** housework.

travailler /tʀavaje/ [1] *vi* work; (se déformer) warp. ● *vt* (façonner) work; (étudier) work at *ou* on.

travailleur, **-euse** /tʀavajœʀ, -øz/ *nm, f* worker. ● *adj* hardworking.

travailliste /tʀavajist/ *adj* Labour. ● *nmf* Labour party member.

travers /tʀavɛʀ/ *nm* (défaut) failing; **à ~** through; **au ~** (**de**) through; **de ~** (chapeau, nez) crooked; (regarder) askance; **j'ai avalé de ~** it went the wrong way; **en ~** (**de**) across.

traversée /tʀavɛʀse/ *nf* crossing.

traverser /tʀavɛʀse/ [1] *vt* cross; (transpercer) go (right) through; (période, forêt) go *ou* pass through.

traversin /tʀavɛʀsɛ̃/ *nm* bolster.

travesti /tʀavesti/ *nm* transvestite.

trébucher /tʀebyʃe/ [1] *vi* stumble, trip (over); **faire ~** trip (up).

trèfle /tʀɛfl/ *nm* (plante) clover; (cartes) clubs.

treillis /tʀeji/ *nm* trellis; (en métal) wire mesh; (tenue militaire) combat uniform.

treize /tʀɛz/ *a & nm* thirteen.

tréma /tʀema/ *nm* diaeresis.

tremblement /tʀɑ̃bləmɑ̃/ *nm* shaking; **~ de terre** earthquake. **trembler** [1] *vi* shake, tremble; (lumière, voix) quiver.

tremper /tʀɑ̃pe/ [1] *vt/i* soak; (plonger) dip; (acier) temper; **faire ~** soak; **~ dans** (fig) be mixed up. □ **se ~** *vpr* (se baigner) have a dip.

tremplin /tʀɑ̃plɛ̃/ *nm* springboard.

trente /tʀɑ̃t/ *a & nm* thirty; **se mettre sur son ~ et un** dress up; **tous les ~-six du mois** once in a blue moon.

trépied /tʀepje/ *nm* tripod.

très /tʀɛ/ *adv* very; **~ aimé/estimé** much liked/esteemed.

trésor /tʀezɔʀ/ *nm* treasure; **le T~** public the revenue department.

trésorerie /tʀezɔʀʀi/ *nf* (bureaux) accounts department; (du Trésor public) revenue office; (argent) funds (+ *pl*); (gestion) accounts (+ *pl*). **trésorier**, **-ière** *nm, f* treasurer.

tressaillement /tʀesajmɑ̃/ *nm* quiver; start.

tresse /tʀɛs/ *nf* braid, plait.

trêve /tʀɛv/ *nf* truce; (fig) respite; **~ de plaisanteries** that's enough joking.

tri /tʀi/ *nm* (classement) sorting; (sélection) selection; **faire le ~ de** (classer) sort; (choisir) select; **centre de ~** sorting office.

triangle /tʀijɑ̃gl/ *nm* triangle.

tribal, **~e** (*mpl* **-aux**) /tʀibal, -o/ *adj* tribal.

tribord /tʀibɔʀ/ *nm* starboard.

tribu /tʀiby/ *nf* tribe.

tribunal (*mpl* **-aux**) /tʀibynal, -o/ *nm* court.

tribune /tʀibyn/ *nf* (de stade) grandstand; (d'orateur) rostrum; (débat) forum; (d'église) gallery.

tribut /tʀiby/ *nm* tribute.

tributaire /tʀibytɛʀ/ *adj* **~ de** dependent on.

tricher /tʀiʃe/ [1] *vi* cheat. **tricheur**, **-euse** *nm, f* cheat.

tricolore /tʀikɔlɔʀ/ *adj* three-coloured; (écharpe) red, white and blue; (équipe) French.

tricot /tʀiko/ *nm* (activité) knitting; (pull) sweater; **en ~** knitted; **~ de corps** vest; (US) undershirt. **tricoter** [1] *vt/i* knit.

trier /tʀije/ [45] *vt* (classer) sort; (choisir) select.

trimestre /tʀimɛstʀ/ *nm* quarter; (Scol) term. **trimestriel**, **~le** *adj* quarterly; (bulletin) end-of-term.

tringle /tʀɛ̃gl/ *nf* rail.

trinquer /tʀɛ̃ke/ [1] *vi* clink glasses.

triomphant, **~e** /tʀijɔ̃fɑ̃, -t/ *adj* triumphant. **triomphe** *nm* triumph. **triompher** [1] *vi* triumph (**de** over); (jubiler) be triumphant.

tripes /tʀip/ *nfpl* (mets) tripe (+ *sg*); (entrailles 🔲) guts.

triple /tʀipl/ *adj* triple, treble. ● *nm* le ~ three times as much (**de** as). **triplés, -es** *nm, fpl* triplets.

tripot /tʀipo/ *nm* gambling den.

tripoter /tʀipɔte/ [1] *vt* 🔲 (*personne*) grope; (*objet*) fiddle with.

trisomique /tʀizɔmik/ *adj* être ~ have Down's syndrome.

triste /tʀist/ *adj* sad; (*rue, temps, couleur*) dreary; (lamentable) dreadful. **tristesse** *nf* sadness; dreariness.

trivial, ~**e** (*mpl* **-iaux**) /tʀivjal, -jo/ *adj* coarse.

troc /tʀɔk/ *nm* exchange; (Comm) barter.

trognon /tʀɔɲɔ̃/ *nm* (de fruit) core.

trois /tʀwɑ/ *a* & *nm* three; **hôtel** ~ **étoiles** three-star hotel. **troisième** *a* & *nmf* third.

trombone /tʀɔ̃bɔn/ *nm* (Mus) trombone; (agrafe) paperclip.

trompe /tʀɔ̃p/ *nf* (d'éléphant) trunk; (Mus) horn.

tromper /tʀɔ̃pe/ [1] *vt* deceive, mislead; (déjouer) elude. □ **se** ~ *vpr* be mistaken; **se** ~ **de route/d'heure** take the wrong road/get the time wrong.

trompette /tʀɔ̃pɛt/ *nf* trumpet.

trompeur, -euse /tʀɔ̃pœʀ, -øz/ *adj* (*apparence*) deceptive.

tronc /tʀɔ̃/ *nm* trunk; (boîte) collection box.

tronçon /tʀɔ̃sɔ̃/ *nm* section.

tronçonneuse /tʀɔ̃sɔnøz/ *nf* chain saw.

trône /tʀon/ *nm* throne. **trôner** [1] *vi* (*vase*) have pride of place (**sur** on).

trop /tʀo/ *adv* (*grand, loin*) too; (*boire, marcher*) too much; ~ (**de**) (quantité) too much; (nombre) too many; **ce serait** ~ **beau** one should be so lucky; **de** ~, **en** ~ too much; too many; **il a bu un verre de** ~ he's had one too many; **se sentir de** ~ feel one is in the way.

trophée /tʀɔfe/ *nm* trophy.

tropical, ~**e** (*mpl* **-aux**) /tʀɔpikal, -o/ *adj* tropical. **tropique** *nm* tropic.

trop-plein (*pl* ~**s**) /tʀoplɛ̃/ *nm* excess; (dispositif) overflow.

troquer /tʀɔke/ [1] *vt* exchange; (Comm) barter (**contre** for).

trot /tʀo/ *nm* trot; **aller au** ~ trot. **trotter** [1] *vi* trot.

trotteuse /tʀɔtøz/ *nf* (de montre) second hand.

trottoir /tʀɔtwaʀ/ *nm* pavement; (US) sidewalk; ~ **roulant** moving walkway.

trou /tʀu/ *nm* hole; (moment) gap; (lieu: péj) dump; ~ (**de mémoire**) memory lapse; ~ **de serrure** keyhole; **faire son** ~ carve one's niche.

trouble /tʀubl/ *adj* (*eau, image*) unclear; (louche) shady. ● *nm* (émoi) emotion; ~**s** (Pol) disturbances; (Méd) disorder (+ *sg*).

troubler /tʀuble/ [1] *vt* disturb; (*eau*) make cloudy; (inquiéter) trouble. □ **se** ~ *vpr* (*personne*) become flustered.

trouer /tʀue/ [1] *vt* make a hole *ou* holes in; **mes chaussures sont trouées** my shoes have got holes in them.

troupe /tʀup/ *nf* troop; (d'acteurs) company.

troupeau (*pl* ~**x**) /tʀupo/ *nm* herd; (de moutons) flock.

trousse /tʀus/ *nf* case, bag; **aux** ~**s de** hot on sb's heels; ~ **de toilette** toilet bag.

trousseau (*pl* ~**x**) /tʀuso/ *nm* (de clefs) bunch; (de mariée) trousseau.

trouver /tʀuve/ [1] *vt* find; (penser) think; **il est venu me** ~ he came to see me. □ **se** ~ *vpr* (être) be; (se sentir) feel; **il se trouve que** it happens that; **si ça se trouve** maybe; **se** ~ **mal** faint.

truand /tʀyɑ̃/ *nm* gangster.

truc /tʀyk/ *nm* (moyen) way; (artifice) trick; (chose 🔲) thing. **trucage** *nm* (cinéma) special effect.

truffe /tʀyf/ *nf* (champignon, chocolat) truffle; (de chien) nose.

truffer /tʀyfe/ [1] *vt* (fig) fill, pack (**de** with).

truie /tʀyi/ *nf* (animal) sow.

truite /tʀyit/ *nf* trout.

truquer /tʀyke/ [1] *vt* fix, rig; (*photo*) fake; (*résultats*) fiddle.

tsar /tsaʀ/ nm tsar, czar.

tu /ty/ pron (parent, ami, enfant) you.
● ⇒TAIRE [47].

tuba /tyba/ nm (Mus) tuba; (Sport)
snorkel.

tube /tyb/ nm tube.

tuberculose /tybɛʀkylɔz/ nf
tuberculosis.

tuer /tɥe/ [1] vt kill; (d'une balle) shoot,
kill; (épuiser) exhaust; ~ **par balles**
shoot dead. □ **se** ~ vpr kill oneself;
(accident) be killed.

tuerie /tyʀi/ nf killing.

tue-tête: à ~ /atytɛt/ loc at the top
of one's voice.

tuile /tɥil/ nf tile; (malchance 🄸)
(stroke of) bad luck.

tulipe /tylip/ nf tulip.

tumeur /tymœʀ/ nf tumour.

tumulte /tymylt/ nm commotion;
(désordre) turmoil.

tunique /tynik/ nf tunic.

Tunisie /tynizi/ nf Tunisia.

tunnel /tynɛl/ nm tunnel.

turbo /tyʀbo/ adj turbo. ● nf (voiture)
turbo.

turbulent, ~**e** /tyʀbylɑ̃, -t/ adj
boisterous, turbulent.

turc, -que /tyʀk/ adj Turkish. ● nm
(Ling) Turkish. **T~, ~que** Turk.

turfiste /tyʀfist/ nmf racegoer.

Turquie /tyʀki/ nf Turkey.

tutelle /tytɛl/ nf (Jur) guardianship;
(fig) protection.

tuteur, -trice /tytœʀ, -tʀis/ nm,f
(Jur) guardian. ● nm (bâton) stake.

tutoiement /tytwamɑ̃/ nm use of
the 'tu' form. **tutoyer** [31] vt
address using the 'tu' form.

tuyau (pl ~**x**) /tɥijo/ nm pipe;
(conseil 🄸) tip; ~ **d'arrosage**
hosepipe.

TVA abrév f (**taxe à la valeur
ajoutée**) VAT.

tympan /tɛ̃pɑ̃/ nm ear-drum.

type /tip/ nm (genre, traits) type;
(individu 🄸) bloke, guy; **le** ~ **même de**
a classic example of. ● a inv typical.

typique /tipik/ adj typical.

tyran /tiʀɑ̃/ nm tyrant. **tyrannie** nf
tyranny. **tyranniser** [1] vt oppress,
tyrannize.

Uu

UE abrév f (**Union européenne**)
European Union.

Ukraine /ykʀɛn/ nf Ukraine.

ulcère /ylsɛʀ/ nm (Méd) ulcer.

ULM abrév m (**ultraléger
motorisé**) microlight.

ultérieur, ~**e** /ylteʀjœʀ/ adj later.
ultérieurement adv later.

ultime /yltim/ adj final.

un, une /œ̃, yn/

● déterminant

····▸ a; (devant voyelle) an; ~ **animal** an
animal; ~ **jour** one day; **pas** ~ **arbre**
not a single tree; **il fait** ~ **froid!** it's
so cold!

● pronom

····▸ one; **l'**~ **d'entre nous** one of us;
les ~**s croient que…** some believe…

····▸ **la une** the front page.

····▸ **j'en veux une** I want one.

● adjectif

····▸ one, a, an; **j'ai** ~ **garçon et deux
filles** I have a ou one boy and two
girls; **il est une heure** it is one
o'clock.

● nom masculin & féminin

····▸ ~ **par** ~ one by one.

unanime /ynanim/ adj unanimous.

unanimité /ynanimite/ nf
unanimity; **à l'**~ unanimously.

uni, ~**e** /yni/ adj united; (couple)
close; (surface) smooth; (tissu) plain.

unième /ynjɛm/ adj -first; **vingt et** ~
twenty-first; **cent** ~ one hundred
and first.

unifier /ynifje/ [45] vt unify.

uniforme /ynifɔʀm/ nm uniform.
● adj uniform. **uniformiser** [1] vt standardize. **uniformité** nf uniformity.

unilatéral, ~e (mpl -aux) /ynilateʀal, -o/ adj unilateral.

union /ynjɔ̃/ nf union; l'U~ européenne the European Union.

unique /ynik/ adj (seul) only; (prix, voie) one; (incomparable) unique; enfant ~ only child; sens ~ one-way street. **uniquement** adv only, solely.

unir /yniʀ/ [2] vt unite. □ s'~ vpr unite, join.

unité /ynite/ nf unit; (harmonie) unity.

univers /ynivɛʀ/ nm universe.

universel, ~le /ynivɛʀsɛl/ adj universal.

universitaire /ynivɛʀsitɛʀ/ adj (résidence) university; (niveau) academic. ● nmf academic.

université /ynivɛʀsite/ nf university.

uranium /yʀanjɔm/ nm uranium.

urbain, ~e /yʀbɛ̃, -ɛn/ adj urban. **urbanisme** nm town planning.

urgence /yʀʒɑ̃s/ nf (cas) emergency; (de situation, tâche) urgency; d'~ (mesure) emergency; (transporter) urgently; les ~s casualty (+ sg). **urgent**, ~e adj urgent.

urine /yʀin/ nf urine. **urinoir** nm urinal.

urne /yʀn/ nf (électorale) ballot box; (vase) urn; aller aux ~s go to the polls.

urticaire /yʀtikɛʀ/ nf hives (+ pl), urticar.

us /ys/ nmpl les ~ et coutumes habits and customs.

usage /yzaʒ/ nm use; (coutume) custom; (de langage) usage; à l'~ de for; d'~ (habituel) customary; faire ~ de make use of.

usagé, ~e /yzaʒe/ adj worn.

usager /yzaʒe/ nm user.

usé, ~e /yze/ adj worn (out); (banal) trite.

user /yze/ [1] vt wear (out). ● vi ~ de use. □ s'~ vpr (tissu) wear (out).

usine /yzin/ nf factory, plant; ~ sidérurgique ironworks (+ pl).

usité, ~e /yzite/ adj common.

ustensile /ystɑ̃sil/ nm utensil.

usuel, ~le /yzɥɛl/ adj ordinary, everyday.

usure /yzyʀ/ nf (détérioration) wear (and tear).

utérus /yteʀys/ nm womb, uterus.

utile /ytil/ adj useful.

utilisable /ytilizabl/ adj usable. **utilisation** nf use. **utiliser** [1] vt use.

utopie /ytɔpi/ nf Utopia; (idée) Utopian idea. **utopique** adj Utopian.

UV[1] abrév f (**unité de valeur**) course unit.

UV[2] abrév mpl (**ultraviolets**) ultraviolet rays; faire des ~ use a sunbed.

Vv

va /va/ ⇒ALLER [8].

vacance /vakɑ̃s/ nf (poste) vacancy.

vacances /vakɑ̃s/ nfpl holiday(s); (US) vacation; en ~ on holiday; ~ d'été, grandes ~ summer holidays. **vacancier**, -ière nm,f holidaymaker; (US) vacationer.

vacant, ~e /vakɑ̃, -t/ adj vacant.

vacarme /vakaʀm/ nm din.

vaccin /vaksɛ̃/ nm vaccine. **vacciner** [1] vt vaccinate.

vache /vaʃ/ nf cow. ● adj (méchant 🔟) nasty.

vaciller /vasije/ [1] vi sway, wobble; (lumière) flicker; (hésiter) falter; (santé, mémoire) fail.

vadrouiller /vadʀuje/ [1] vi 🔟 wander about.

va-et-vient /vaevjɛ̃/ nm inv toing and froing; (de personnes) comings and goings; faire le ~ go to and fro; (interrupteur) two-way switch.

vagabond, ~e /vagabɔ̃, -d/ nm,f vagrant.

vagin /vaʒɛ̃/ nm vagina.

vague /vag/ *adj* vague. ● *nm*
regarder dans le ~ stare into space;
il est resté dans le ~ he was vague
about it. ● *nf* wave; ~ de fond
ground swell; ~ de froid cold spell;
~ de chaleur heatwave.

vaillant, ~e /vajã, -t/ *adj* brave;
(*vigoureux*) strong.

vaille /vaj/ ⇒VALOIR [60].

vain, ~e /vɛ̃, vɛn/ *adj* vain, futile; en
~ in vain.

vaincre /vɛ̃kʀ/ [59] *vt* defeat;
(*surmonter*) overcome. **vaincu**, ~e
nm,f (Sport) loser. **vainqueur** *nm*
victor; (Sport) winner.

vais /vɛ/ ⇒ALLER [8].

vaisseau (*pl* ~x) /vɛso/ *nm* ship;
(veine) vessel; ~ spatial spaceship.

vaisselle /vɛsɛl/ *nf* crockery; (à
laver) dishes; faire la ~ do the
washing-up, wash the dishes; liquide
~ washing-up liquid.

valable /valabl/ *adj* valid; (de qualité)
worthwhile.

valet /valɛ/ *nm* (aux cartes) jack; ~
(de chambre) manservant.

valeur /valœʀ/ *nf* value; (mérite)
worth, value; ~s (Comm) stocks and
shares; avoir de la ~ be valuable;
prendre/perdre de la ~ go up/down
in value; objets de ~ valuables; sans
~ worthless.

valide /valid/ *adj* (*personne*) fit;
(*billet*) valid. **valider** [1] *vt* validate.

valise /valiz/ *nf* (suit)case; faire ses
~s pack (one's bags).

vallée /vale/ *nf* valley.

valoir /valwaʀ/ [60] *vi* (mériter) be
worth; (égaler) be as good as; (être
valable) (*règle*) apply; faire ~ (mérite,
qualité) emphasize; (*terrain*)
cultivate; (*droit*) assert; se faire ~
put oneself forward; ~ cher/100
francs be worth a lot/100 francs; que
vaut ce vin? what's this wine like?;
ne rien ~ be useless *ou* no good; ça
ne me dit rien qui vaille I don't like
the sound of that; ~ la peine *or* le
coup 🛈 be worth it; il vaut/vaudrait
mieux faire it is/would be better to
do. ● *vt* ~ qch à qn (*éloges, critiques*)
earn sb sth; (*admiration*) win sb sth.
◻ se ~ *vpr* (être équivalents) be as

good as each other; ça se vaut it's all
the same.

valoriser /valɔʀize/ [1] *vt* add value
to; (*produit*) promote; (*profession*)
make attractive; (*région, ressources*)
develop.

valse /vals/ *nf* waltz.

vandale /vãdal/ *nmf* vandal.

vanille /vanij/ *nf* vanilla.

vanité /vanite/ *nf* vanity.
vaniteux, **-euse** *adj* vain,
conceited.

vanne /van/ *nf* (d'écluse) sluice-gate;
(propos 🛈) dig 🛈.

vantard, ~e /vãtaʀ, -d/ *adj*
boastful. ● *nm,f* boaster.

vanter /vãte/ [1] *vt* praise. ◻ se ~
vpr boast (de about); se ~ de faire
pride oneself on doing.

vapeur /vapœʀ/ *nf* (eau) steam;
(brume, émanation) vapour; ~s fumes;
à ~ (*bateau, locomotive*) steam; faire
cuire à la ~ steam.

vaporisateur /vapɔʀizatœʀ/ *nm*
spray, atomizer. **vaporiser** [1] *vt*
spray.

varappe /vaʀap/ *nf* rock-climbing.

variable /vaʀjabl/ *adj* variable;
(*temps*) changeable.

varicelle /vaʀisɛl/ *nf* chickenpox.

varié, ~e /vaʀje/ *adj* (non monotone,
étendu) varied; (divers) various;
sandwichs ~s a selection of
sandwiches.

varier /vaʀje/ [45] *vt/i* vary.

variété /vaʀjete/ *nf* variety;
spectacle de ~s variety show.

vase /vɑz/ *nm* vase. ● *nf* silt, mud.

vaseux, **-euse** /vɑzø, -z/ *adj* (confus
🛈) woolly, hazy.

vaste /vast/ *adj* vast, huge.

vaurien, ~ne /voʀjɛ̃, -ɛn/ *nm,f*
good-for-nothing.

vautour /votuʀ/ *nm* vulture.

vautrer (se) /(sə)votʀe/ [1] *vpr*
sprawl; se ~ dans (*vice, boue*)
wallow in.

veau (*pl* ~x) /vo/ *nm* calf; (viande)
veal; (cuir) calfskin.

vécu, ~e /veky/ *adj* (réel) true, real.
● ⇒VIVRE [62].

vedette /vədɛt/ *nf* (artiste) star; en ~
(*objet*) in a prominent position;

(*personne*) in the limelight; **joueur ~** star player; (bateau) launch.

végétal (*mpl* **-aux**) /veʒetal, -o/ *adj* plant. ● *nm* (*pl* **-aux**) plant.

végétalien, **~ne** /veʒetaljɛ̃, -ɛn/ *a* & *nm,f* vegan.

végétarien, **~ne** /veʒetaʀjɛ̃, -ɛn/ *a* & *nm,f* vegetarian.

végétation /veʒetasjɔ̃/ *nf* vegetation; **~s** (Méd) adenoids.

véhicule /veikyl/ *nm* vehicle.

veille /vɛj/ *nf* (état) wakefulness; (jour précédent) **la ~ (de)** the day before; **la ~ de Noël** Christmas Eve; **à la ~ de** on the eve of; **la ~ au soir** the previous evening.

veillée /veje/ *nf* evening (gathering).

veiller /veje/ [1] *vi* stay up; (monter la garde) be on watch. ● *vt* (*malade*) watch over; **~ à** attend to; **~ sur** watch over.

veilleur /vɛjœʀ/ *nm* **~ de nuit** night-watchman.

veilleuse /vɛjøz/ *nf* night light; (de véhicule) sidelight; (de réchaud) pilot light; **mettre qch en ~** put sth on the back burner.

veine /vɛn/ *nf* (Anat) vein; (nervure, filon) vein; (chance 🔢) luck; **avoir de la ~** 🔢 be lucky.

véliplanchiste /veliplɑ̃ʃist/ *nmf* windsurfer.

vélo /velo/ *nm* bike; (activité) cycling; **faire du ~** go cycling; **~ tout terrain** mountain bike.

vélomoteur /velɔmɔtœʀ/ *nm* moped.

velours /v(ə)luʀ/ *nm* velvet; **~ côtelé** corduroy.

velouté, **~e** /vəlute/ *adj* smooth. ● *nm* (Culin) **~ d'asperges** cream of asparagus soup.

vendanges /vɑ̃dɑ̃ʒ/ *nfpl* grape harvest.

vendeur, **-euse** /vɑ̃dœʀ, -øz/ *nm,f* shop assistant; (marchand) salesman, saleswoman; (Jur) vendor, seller.

vendre /vɑ̃dʀ/ [3] *vt* sell; **à ~** for sale. □ **se ~** *vpr* (être vendu) be sold; (trouver acquéreur) sell; **se ~ bien** sell well.

vendredi /vɑ̃dʀədi/ *nm* Friday; **V~ saint** Good Friday.

vénéneux, **-euse** /venenø, -z/ *adj* poisonous.

vénérer /veneʀe/ [14] *vt* revere.

vénérien, **~ne** /veneʀjɛ̃, -ɛn/ *adj* **maladie ~ne** venereal disease.

vengeance /vɑ̃ʒɑ̃s/ *nf* revenge, vengeance.

venger /vɑ̃ʒe/ [40] *vt* avenge. □ **se ~** *vpr* take *ou* get one's revenge (**de qch** for sth; **de qn** on sb).

vengeur, **-eresse** /vɑ̃ʒœʀ, -əʀɛs/ *adj* vengeful. ● *nm,f* avenger.

venimeux, **-euse** /vənimø, -z/ *adj* poisonous, venomous.

venin /vənɛ̃/ *nm* venom.

venir /vəniʀ/ [58] *vi* (*aux être*) come (**de** from); **faire ~ qn** send for sb, call sb; **en ~ à** come to; **en ~ aux mains** come to blows; **où veut-elle en ~?** what is she driving at?; **il m'est venu à l'esprit** *or* **à l'idée que** it occurred to me that; **s'il venait à pleuvoir** if it should rain; **dans les jours à ~** in the next few days. ● *v aux* **~ de faire** have just done; **il vient/venait d'arriver** he has/had just arrived; **~ faire** come to do; **viens voir** come and see.

vent /vɑ̃/ *nm* wind; **il fait du ~** it is windy; **être dans le ~** 🔢 be trendy.

vente /vɑ̃t/ *nf* sale; **~ (aux enchères)** auction; **en ~ on ou** for sale; **mettre qch en ~** put sth up for sale; **~ de charité** (charity) bazaar; **~ au détail/ en gros** retailing/wholesaling; **équipe de ~** sales team.

ventilateur /vɑ̃tilatœʀ/ *nm* fan, ventilator. **ventiler** [1] *vt* ventilate.

ventouse /vɑ̃tuz/ *nf* suction pad; (pour déboucher) plunger.

ventre /vɑ̃tʀ/ *nm* stomach; (d'animal) belly; (utérus) womb; **avoir du ~** have a paunch.

venu, **~e** /vəny/ *adj* **bien ~** (à propos) apt, timely; **mal ~** badly timed; **il serait mal ~ de faire** it wouldn't be a good idea to do. ● ⇒VENIR [59].

venue /vəny/ *nf* coming.

ver /vɛʀ/ *nm* worm; (dans la nourriture) maggot; (du bois) woodworm; **~ luisant** glow-worm; **~ à soie** silkworm; **~ solitaire** tapeworm; **~ de terre** earthworm.

verbal, **~e** (*mpl* **-aux**) /vɛRbal, -o/ *adj* verbal.

verbe /vɛRb/ *nm* verb.

verdir /vɛRdiR/ [2] *vi* turn green.

véreux, **-euse** /veRø, -z/ *adj* wormy; (*malhonnête*) shady.

verger /vɛRʒe/ *nm* orchard.

verglas /vɛRgla/ *nm* black ice.

véridique /veRidik/ *adj* true.

vérification /veRifikasjɔ̃/ *nf* check (ing), verification.

vérifier /veRifje/ [45] *vt* check, verify; (*confirmer*) confirm.

véritable /veRitabl/ *adj* true, real; (*authentique*) real.

vérité /veRite/ *nf* truth; (*de tableau, roman*) realism; **en ~** in fact, actually.

vermine /vɛRmin/ *nf* vermin.

verni, **~e** /vɛRni/ *adj* (*chaussures*) patent (leather); (*chanceux* 🎨) lucky.

vernir /vɛRniR/ [2] *vt* varnish. □ **se ~** *vpr* se **~ les ongles** apply nail polish.

vernis /vɛRni/ *nm* varnish; (*de poterie*) glaze; **~ à ongles** nail polish.

verra, **verrait** /vɛRa, vɛRɛ/ ⇒VOIR [64].

verre /vɛR/ *nm* glass; (*de lunettes*) lens; **~ à vin** wine glass; **prendre** *ou* **boire un ~** have a drink; **~ de contact** contact lens; **~ dépoli** frosted glass.

verrière /vɛRjɛR/ *nf* (*toit*) glass roof; (*paroi*) glass wall.

verrou /vɛRu/ *nm* bolt; **sous les ~s** behind bars.

verrouillage /vɛRujaz/ *nm* **~ central** *or* **centralisé** (**des portes**) central locking.

verrue /vɛRy/ *nf* wart; **~ plantaire** verruca.

vers[1] /vɛR/ *prép* towards; (*aux environs de*) (*temps*) about; (*lieu*) near, around; (*période*) towards; **~ le soir** towards evening.

vers[2] /vɛR/ *nm* (*poésie*) line of verse.

versatile /vɛRsatil/ *adj* unpredictable, volatile.

verse: **à ~** /avɛRs/ *loc* in torrents.

Verseau /vɛRso/ *nm* le **~** Aquarius.

versement /vɛRsəmã/ *nm* payment; (*échelonné*) instalment.

verser /vɛRse/ [1] *vt/i* pour; (*larmes, sang*) shed; (*payer*) pay. ● *vi* pour; (*voiture*) overturn; **~ dans** (fig) lapse into.

version /vɛRsjɔ̃/ *nf* version; (*traduction*) translation.

verso /vɛRso/ *nm* back (of the page); **voir au ~** see overleaf.

vert, **~e** /vɛR, -t/ *adj* green; (*vieillard*) sprightly. ● *nm* green; **les ~s** the Greens.

vertèbre /vɛRtɛbR/ *nf* vertebra; **se déplacer une ~** slip a disc.

vertical, **~e** (*mpl* **-aux**) /vɛRtikal, -o/ *adj* vertical.

vertige /vɛRtiʒ/ *nm* dizziness; **~s** dizzy spells; **avoir le ~** feel dizzy.

vertigineux, **-euse** *adj* dizzy; (*très grand*) staggering.

vertu /vɛRty/ *nf* virtue; **en ~ de** in accordance with. **vertueux**, **-euse** *adj* virtuous.

verveine /vɛRvɛn/ *nf* verbena.

vessie /vesi/ *nf* bladder.

veste /vɛst/ *nf* jacket.

vestiaire /vɛstjɛR/ *nm* cloakroom; (Sport) changing-room; (US) locker-room.

vestibule /vɛstibyl/ *nm* hall; (Théât, d'hôtel) foyer.

vestige /vɛstiʒ/ *nm* (*objet*) relic; (*trace*) vestige.

veston /vɛstɔ̃/ *nm* jacket.

vêtement /vɛtmã/ *nm* article of clothing; **~s** clothes, clothing.

vétéran /veteRã/ *nm* veteran.

vétérinaire /veteRinɛR/ *nmf* vet, veterinary surgeon, (US) veterinarian.

vêtir /vetiR/ [61] *vt* dress. □ **se ~** *vpr* dress.

veto /veto/ *nm inv* veto.

vêtu, **~e** /vety/ *adj* dressed (**de** in).

veuf, **veuve** /vœf, -v/ *adj* widowed. ● *nm, f* widower, widow.

veuille /vœj/ ⇒VOULOIR [64].

veut, **veux** /vø/ ⇒VOULOIR [64].

vexation /vɛksasjɔ̃/ *nf* humiliation.

vexer /vɛkse/ [1] *vt* upset, hurt. □ **se ~** *vpr* be upset, be hurt.

viable /vjabl/ *adj* viable; (*projet*) feasible.

viande /vjãd/ *nf* meat.

vibrer /vibʀe/ [1] *vi* vibrate; **faire ~** (*âme, foules*) stir.

vicaire /vikɛʀ/ *nm* curate.

vice /vis/ *nm* (moral) vice; (physique) defect.

vicier /visje/ [45] *vt* contaminate; (*air*) pollute.

vicieux, -ieuse /visjø, -z/ *adj* depraved. ● *nm, f* pervert.

victime /viktim/ *nf* victim; (d'un accident) casualty.

victoire /viktwaʀ/ *nf* victory; (Sport) win. **victorieux, -ieuse** *adj* victorious; (*équipe*) winning.

vidange /vidɑ̃ʒ/ *nf* emptying; (Auto) oil change; (tuyau) waste pipe *ou* outlet.

vide /vid/ *adj* empty. ● *nm* (absence, manque) vacuum, void; (espace) space; (trou) gap; (sans air) vacuum; **à ~** empty; **emballé sous ~** vacuum packed; **suspendu dans le ~** dangling in space.

vidéo /video/ *a inv* video; **jeu ~** video game. ● *nf* video. **vidéocassette** *nf* video(tape). **vidéoclip** *nm* music video. **vidéoconférence** *nf* videoconferencing; (séance) videoconference. **vidéodisque** *nm* videodisc.

vide-ordures /vidɔʀdyʀ/ *nm inv* rubbish chute.

vidéothèque /videotɛk/ *nf* video library.

vider /vide/ [1] *vt* empty; (*poisson*) gut; (expulser 🔲) throw out; **~ les lieux** leave. □ **se ~** *vpr* empty.

vie /vi/ *nf* life; (durée) lifetime; **à ~, pour la ~** for life; **donner la ~ à** give birth to; **en ~** alive; **la ~ est chère** the cost of living is high.

vieil /vjɛj/ ⇒VIEUX.

vieillard /vjɛjaʀ/ *nm* old man.

vieille /vjɛj/ ⇒VIEUX.

vieillesse /vjɛjɛs/ *nf* old age.

vieillir /vjejiʀ/ [2] *vi* grow old, age; (*mot, idée*) become old-fashioned. ● *vt* age. **vieillissement** *nm* ageing.

viens, vient /vjɛ̃/ ⇒VENIR [59].

vierge /vjɛʀʒ/ *nf* virgin; **la V~** Virgo. ● *adj* virgin; (*feuille, cassette*) blank; (*cahier, pellicule*) unused, new.

vieux (**vieil** before vowel or mute *h*), **vieille** (*mpl* **vieux**) /vjø, vjɛj/ *adj* old. ● *nm, f* old man, old woman; **petit ~** little old man; **les ~** old people; **vieille fille** (péj) spinster; **~ garçon** old bachelor. **vieux jeu** *a inv* old-fashioned.

vif, vive /vif, viv/ *adj* (animé) lively; (*émotion, vent*) keen; (*froid*) biting; (*lumière*) bright; (*douleur, contraste, parole*) sharp; (*souve-nir, style, teint*) vivid; (*succès, impatience*) great; **brûler/enterrer ~** burn/bury alive; **de vive voix** personally. ● *nm* **à ~** (*plaie*) open; **avoir les nerfs à ~** be on edge; **blessé au ~** cut to the quick.

vigie /viʒi/ *nf* lookout.

vigilant, ~e /viʒilɑ̃, -t/ *adj* vigilant.

vigne /viɲ/ *nf* (plante) vine; (vignoble) vineyard. **vigneron, ~ne** *nm, f* wine-grower.

vignette /viɲɛt/ *nf* (étiquette) label; (Auto) road tax disc.

vignoble /viɲɔbl/ *nm* vineyard.

vigoureux, -euse /viguʀø, -z/ *adj* vigorous, sturdy.

vigueur /viguœʀ/ *nf* vigour; **être/ entrer en ~** (*loi*) be/come into force; **en ~** current.

VIH *abrév m* (**virus immunodé-ficitaire humain**) HIV.

vilain, ~e /vilɛ̃, -ɛn/ *adj* (mauvais) nasty; (laid) ugly. ● *nm, f* naughty boy, naughty girl.

villa /villa/ *nf* detached house.

village /vilaʒ/ *nm* village.

villageois, ~e /vilaʒwa, -z/ *adj* village. ● *nm, f* villager.

ville /vil/ *nf* town; (importante) city; **~ d'eaux** spa.

vin /vɛ̃/ *nm* wine; **~ d'honneur** reception.

vinaigre /vinɛgʀ/ *nm* vinegar. **vinaigrette** *nf* oil and vinegar dressing, vinaigrette.

vingt /vɛ̃/ (/vɛ̃t/ before vowel and in numbers 22-29) *a & nm* twenty.

vingtaine /vɛ̃tɛn/ *nf* **une ~ (de)** about twenty.

vingtième /vɛ̃tjɛm/ *a & nmf* twentieth.

vinicole /vinikɔl/ *adj* wine(-producing).

viol /vjɔl/ *nm* (de femme) rape; (de lieu, loi) violation.

violemment /vjɔlamɑ̃/ *adv* violently.

violence /vjɔlɑ̃s/ *nf* violence; (acte) act of violence. **violent, ~e** *adj* violent.

violer /vjɔle/ [1] *vt* rape; (lieu, loi) violate.

violet, ~te /vjɔlɛ, -t/ *adj* purple. ● *nm* purple. **violette** *nf* violet.

violon /vjɔlɔ̃/ *nm* violin; ~ **d'Ingres** hobby.

violoncelle /vjɔlɔ̃sɛl/ *nm* cello.

vipère /vipɛʀ/ *nf* viper, adder.

virage /viʀaʒ/ *nm* bend; (en ski) turn; (changement d'attitude: fig) change of course.

virée /viʀe/ *nf* 🄵 trip, tour; (en voiture) drive; (à vélo) ride.

virement /viʀmɑ̃/ *nm* (Comm) (credit) transfer; ~ **automatique** standing order.

virer /viʀe/ [1] *vi* turn; ~ **de bord** tack; (fig) do a U-turn; ~ **au rouge** turn red. ● *vt* (argent) transfer; (expulser 🄵) throw out; (élève) expel; (licencier 🄵) fire.

virgule /viʀgyl/ *nf* comma; (dans un nombre) (decimal) point.

viril, ~e /viʀil/ *adj* virile.

virtuel, ~le /viʀtɥɛl/ *adj* (potentiel) potential; (mémoire, réalité) virtual.

virulent, ~e /viʀylɑ̃, -t/ *adj* virulent.

virus /viʀys/ *nm* virus.

vis¹ /vi/ ⇒VIVRE [62], VOIR [63].

vis² /vis/ *nf* screw.

visa /viza/ *nm* visa.

visage /vizaʒ/ *nm* face.

vis-à-vis /vizavi/ *prép* ~ **de** (en face de) opposite; (à l'égard de) in relation to; (comparé à) compared to, beside. ● *nm inv* (personne) person opposite; **en** ~ opposite each other.

visée /vize/ *nf* aim; **avoir des** ~**s sur** have designs on.

viser /vize/ [1] *vt* (cible, centre) aim at; (poste, résultats) aim for; (concerner) be aimed at; (document) stamp; ~ **à** aim at; (mesure, propos) be aimed at; ~ **à faire** aim to do. ● *vi* aim.

viseur /vizœʀ/ *nm* (d'arme) sights (+ *pl*); (Photo) viewfinder.

visière /vizjɛʀ/ *nf* (de casquette) peak; (de casque) visor.

vision /vizjɔ̃/ *nf* vision.

visite /vizit/ *nf* visit; (pour inspecter) inspection; (personne) visitor; **heures de** ~ visiting hours; ~ **guidée** guided tour; ~ **médicale** medical; **rendre** ~ **à, faire une** ~ **à** pay a visit; **être en** ~ **(chez qn)** be visiting (sb); **avoir de la** ~ have visitors.

visiter /vizite/ [1] *vt* visit; (appartement) view. **visiteur, -euse** *nm,f* visitor.

visser /vise/ *vt* screw (on).

visuel, ~le /vizɥɛl/ *adj* visual. ● *nm* (Ordinat) visual display unit, VDU.

vit /vi/ ⇒VIVRE [62], VOIR [63].

vital, ~e (mpl **-aux**) /vital, -o/ *adj* vital.

vitamine /vitamin/ *nf* vitamin.

vite /vit/ *adv* fast, quickly; (tôt) soon; ~**!** quick!; **faire** ~ be quick; **au plus** ~, **le plus** ~ **possible** as quickly as possible.

vitesse /vitɛs/ *nf* speed; (régime: Auto) gear; **à toute** ~ at top speed; **en** ~ in a hurry, quickly; **boîte à cinq** ~**s** five-speed gearbox.

viticole /vitikɔl/ *adj* (industrie) wine; (région) wine-producing. **viticulteur** *nm* wine-grower.

vitrage /vitʀaʒ/ *nm* (vitres) windows; **double** ~ double glazing.

vitrail (pl **-aux**) /vitʀaj, -o/ *nm* stained-glass window.

vitre /vitʀ/ *nf* (window) pane; (de véhicule) window.

vitrine /vitʀin/ *nf* (shop) window; (meuble) display cabinet.

vivace /vivas/ *adj* (plante) perennial; (durable) enduring.

vivacité /vivasite/ *nf* liveliness; (agilité) quickness; (d'émotion, d'intelligence) keenness; (de souvenir, style, teint) vividness.

vivant, ~e /vivɑ̃, -t/ *adj* (example, symbole) living; (en vie) alive, living; (actif, vif) lively. ● *nm* **un bon** ~ a bon viveur; **de son** ~ in his lifetime; **les** ~**s** the living.

vive¹ /viv/ ⇒VIF.

vive² /viv/ *interj* ∼ **le roi!** long live the king!

vivement /vivmɑ̃/ *adv* (fortement) strongly; (vite, sèchement) sharply; (avec éclat) vividly; (beaucoup) greatly; ∼ **la fin!** I'll be glad when it's the end!

vivier /vivje/ *nm* fish pond; (artificiel) fish tank.

vivifier /vivifje/ [45] *vt* invigorate.

vivre /vivʀ/ [63] *vi* live; ∼ **de** (nourriture) live on; ∼ **encore** be still alive; **faire** ∼ (famille) support. ● *vt* (vie) live; (période, aventure) live through.

vivres /vivʀ/ *nmpl* supplies.

VO *abrév f* (**version originale**) en ∼ in the original language.

vocabulaire /vɔkabylɛʀ/ *nm* vocabulary.

vocal, ∼**e** (*mpl* -**aux**) /vɔkal, -o/ *adj* vocal.

vœu (*pl* ∼**x**) /vø/ *nm* (souhait) wish; (promesse) vow; **meilleurs** ∼**x** best wishes.

vogue /vɔg/ *nf* fashion, vogue; **en** ∼ in fashion *ou* vogue.

voguer /vɔge/ [1] *vi* sail.

voici /vwasi/ *prép* here is, this is; (au pluriel) here are, these are; **me** ∼ here I am; ∼ **un an** (temps passé) a year ago; ∼ **un an que** it is a year since.

voie /vwa/ *nf* (route) road; (partie de route) lane; (chemin) way; (moyen) means, way; (rails) track; (quai) platform; **en** ∼ **de** in the process of; **en** ∼ **de développement** (pays) developing; **espèce en** ∼ **de disparition** endangered species; **par la** ∼ **des airs** by air; **par** ∼ **orale** orally; **sur la bonne/mauvaise** ∼ (fig) on the right/wrong track; **montrer la** ∼ lead the way; ∼ **de dégagement** slip-road; ∼ **ferrée** railway; (US) railroad; **V**∼ **lactée** Milky Way; ∼ **navigable** waterway; ∼ **publique** public highway; ∼ **sans issue** (sur panneau) no through road; (fig) dead end.

voilà /vwala/ *prép* there is, that is; (au pluriel) there are, those are; (voici) here is, here are; **le** ∼ there he is; ∼**!** right!; (en offrant qch) there you are!; ∼ **un an** (temps passé) a year

ago; ∼ **un an que** it is a year since; **tu en veux? en** ∼ do you want some? here you are; **en** ∼ **des histoires!** what a fuss!; **et** ∼ **que** and then.

voilage /vwalaʒ/ *nm* net curtain.

voile /vwal/ *nf* (de bateau) sail; (Sport) sailing. ● *nm* veil; (tissu léger) net.

voilé, ∼**e** /vwale/ *adj* (allusion, femme) veiled; (flou) hazy.

voiler /vwale/ [1] *vt* (dissimuler) veil; (déformer) buckle. □ **se** ∼ *vpr* (devenir flou) become hazy; (se déformer) (roue) buckle.

voilier /vwalje/ *nm* sailing ship.

voir /vwaʀ/ [64] *vt* see; **faire** ∼ **qch à qn** show sth to sb; **laisser** ∼ show; **avoir quelque chose à** ∼ **avec** have something to do with; **ça n'a rien à** ∼ that's got nothing to do with it; **je ne peux pas le** ∼ 🔲 I can't stand him. ● *vi* **y** ∼ be able to see; **je n'y vois rien** I cannot see; ∼ **trouble** have blurred vision; **voyons** let's see now; **voyons, soyez sages!** come on now, behave yourselves! □ **se** ∼ *vpr* (dans la glace) see oneself; (être visible) show; (se produire) be seen; (se trouver) find oneself; (se fréquenter, se rencontrer) see each other; (être vu) be seen.

voire /vwaʀ/ *adv* or even, not to say.

voirie /vwaʀi/ *nf* (service) highway maintenance.

voisin, ∼**e** /vwazɛ̃, -in/ *adj* (de voisinage) neighbouring; (proche) nearby; (adjacent) next (**de** to); (semblable) similar (**de** to). ● *nm,f* neighbour; **le** ∼ the man next door, the neighbour.

voisinage *nm* neighbourhood; (proximité) proximity.

voiture /vwatyʀ/ *nf* (motor) car; (wagon) coach, carriage; **en** ∼**!** all aboard!; ∼ **bélier** ramraiding car; ∼ **à cheval** horse-drawn carriage; ∼ **de course** racing car; ∼ **école** driving school car; ∼ **d'enfant** pram; (US) baby carriage; ∼ **de tourisme** saloon car.

voix /vwa/ *nf* voice; (suffrage) vote; **à** ∼ **basse** in a whisper.

vol /vɔl/ *nm* (d'avion, d'oiseau) flight; (groupe d'oiseaux) flock, flight; (délit) theft; (hold-up) robbery; ∼ **à l'étalage** shoplifting; ∼ **à la tire** pickpocketing; **à** ∼ **d'oiseau** as the crow flies; **de haut ~** high-ranking; **~ libre** hang-gliding; **~ à voile** gliding.

volaille /vɔlaj/ *nf* **la ~ (poules)** poultry; **une ~ a** fowl.

volant /vɔlɑ̃/ *nm* (steering-)wheel; (de jupe) flounce; (de badminton) shuttlecock; **donner un coup de ~** turn the wheel sharply.

volcan /vɔlkɑ̃/ *nm* volcano.

volée /vɔle/ *nf* flight; (oiseaux) flight, flock; (de coups, d'obus, au tennis) volley; **à toute ~** hard; **à la ~** in flight, in mid-air.

voler /vɔle/ [1] *vi* (oiseau) fly; (dérober) steal (à from). ● *vt* steal; **~ qn** rob sb; **il ne l'a pas volé** he deserved it.

volet /vɔlɛ/ *nm* (de fenêtre) shutter; (de document) (folded *ou* tear-off) section; **trié sur le ~** hand-picked.

voleur, -euse /vɔlœʀ, -øz/ *nm,f* thief; **au ~!** stop thief! ● *adj* thieving.

volley-ball /vɔlɛbol/ *nm* volleyball.

volontaire /vɔlɔ̃tɛʀ/ *adj* (délibéré) voluntary; (opiniâtre) determined. ● *nmf* volunteer. **volontairement** *adv* voluntarily; (exprès) intentionally.

volonté /vɔlɔ̃te/ *nf* (faculté, intention) will; (souhait) wish; (énergie) will-power; **à ~** (comme on veut) as required; **du vin à ~** unlimited wine; **bonne ~** goodwill; **mauvaise ~** ill will.

volontiers /vɔlɔ̃tje/ *adv* (de bon gré) with pleasure, willingly, gladly; (admettre) readily.

volt /vɔlt/ *nm* volt.

volte-face /vɔltəfas/ *nf inv* (fig) U-turn; **faire ~** do a U-turn.

voltige /vɔltiʒ/ *nf* acrobatics (+ *pl*).

volume /vɔlym/ *nm* volume.

volumineux, -euse /vɔlyminø, -z/ *adj* bulky; (livre, dossier) thick.

volupté /vɔlypte/ *nf* voluptuousness.

vomi /vɔmi/ *nm* vomit.

vomir /vɔmiʀ/ [2] *vt* vomit; (fig) belch out. ● *vi* be sick, vomit.

vomissement /vɔmismɑ̃/ *nm* vomiting; **~s du matin** morning sickness.

vont /vɔ̃/ ⇒ALLER [8].

vorace /vɔʀas/ *adj* voracious.

vos /vo/ ⇒VOTRE.

votant, ~e /vɔtɑ̃, -t/ *nm,f* voter.

vote /vɔt/ *nm* (action) voting; (suffrage) vote; **~ d'une loi** passing of a bill; **~ par correspondance/procuration** postal/proxy vote.

voter /vɔte/ [1] *vi* vote. ● *vt* vote for; (adopter) pass; (crédits) vote.

votre (*pl* **vos**) /vɔtʀ, vo/ *adj* your.

vôtre /votʀ/ *pron* **le** *ou* **la ~, les ~s** yours.

vouer /vwe/ [1] *vt* (vie, temps) dedicate (à to); **voué à l'échec** doomed to failure.

vouloir /vulwaʀ/ [64] *vt* (exiger) want (**faire** to do); (souhaiter) want; **que veux-tu boire?** what would you like to drink?; **je voudrais bien y aller** I'd really like to go; **je veux bien venir** I'm happy to come; **comme tu voudras** as you wish; (accepter) **veuillez vous asseoir** please sit down; **veuillez patienter** (au téléphone) please hold the line; (signifier) **~ dire** mean; **qu'est-ce que cela veut dire?** what does that mean?; **en ~ à qn** bear a grudge against sb. □ **s'en ~** *vpr* regret; **je m'en veux de lui avoir dit** I really regret having told her.

voulu, ~e /vuly/ *adj* (délibéré) intentional; (requis) required.

vous /vu/ *pron* (sujet, complément) you; (indirect) (to) you; (réfléchi) yourself; (pluriel) yourselves; (l'un l'autre) each other. **vous-même** *pron* yourself. **vous-mêmes** *pron* yourselves.

voûte /vut/ *nf* (plafond) vault; (porche) archway.

vouvoiement /vuvwamɑ̃/ *nm* use of the 'vous' form. **vouvoyer** [31] *vt* address using the 'vous' form.

voyage /vwajaʒ/ *nm* trip; (déplacement) journey; (par mer) voyage; **~(s)** (action) travelling; **~ d'affaires** business trip; **~ d'études** study trip; **~ de noces** honeymoon; **~ organisé** (package) tour.

voyager /vwajaʒe/ [40] *vi* travel.

voyageur, -euse /vwajaʒœʀ, -øz/ *nm,f* traveller; (passager) passenger; **~ de commerce** travelling salesman.

voyant, ~e /vwajã, -t/ *adj* gaudy.
● *nm* (signal) (warning) light.

voyelle /vwajɛl/ *nf* vowel.

voyou /vwaju/ *nm* hooligan.

vrac: **en** ~ /ãvʀak/ *loc* (pêle-mêle) haphazardly; (sans emballage) loose; (en gros) in bulk.

vrai, ~e /vʀɛ/ *adj* true; (authentique) real. ● *nm* truth; **à** ~ **dire** to tell the truth; **pour de** ~ for real. **vraiment** *adv* really.

vraisemblable /vʀɛsãblabl/ *adj* (probable) likely; (*excuse, histoire*) plausible. **vraisemblablement** *adv* probably. **vraisemblance** *nf* likelihood, plausibility.

vrombir /vʀɔ̃biʀ/ [2] *vi* roar.

VRP *abrév m* (**voyageur représentant placier**) rep, representative.

VTT *abrév m* (**vélo tout terrain**) mountain bike.

vu, ~e /vy/ *adj* **bien** ~ well thought of; **ce serait plutôt mal** ~ it wouldn't go down well; **bien** ~! good point! ● *prép* in view of; ~ **que** seeing that. ● ⇒VOIR [64].

vue /vy/ *nf* (spectacle) sight; (vision) (eye)sight; (panorama, idée, image, photo) view; **avoir en** ~ have in mind; **à** ~ (*tirer*) on sight; (*payable*) at sight; **de** ~ by sight; **perdre de** ~ lose sight of; **en** ~ (proche) in sight; (célèbre) in the public eye; **en** ~ **de faire** with a view to doing; **à** ~ **d'œil** visibly; **avoir des** ~**s sur** have designs on.

vulgaire /vylgɛʀ/ *adj* (grossier) vulgar; (ordinaire) common.

vulnérable /vylneʀabl/ *adj* vulnerable.

wagon /vagɔ̃/ *nm* (de voyageurs) carriage; (de marchandises) wagon. **wagon-lit** (*pl* **wagons-lits**) *nm* sleeper. **wagon-restaurant** (*pl* **wagons-restaurants**) *nm* restaurant car.

walkman® /wokman/ *nm* personal stereo, walkman®.

waters /watɛʀ/ *nmpl* toilets.

watt /wat/ *nm* watt.

wc /(dublə)vese/ *nmpl* toilet (+ *sg*).

Web /wɛb/ *nm* Web; **un site** ~ a Web site.

week-end /wikɛnd/ *nm* weekend.

whisky (*pl* **-ies**) /wiski/ *nm* whisky.

xénophobe /gzenɔfɔb/ *adj* xenophobic. ● *nmf* xenophobe.

xérès /gzeʀɛs/ *nm* sherry.

xylophone /ksilɔfon/ *nm* xylophone.

y /i/

● *adverbe*

····▸ there; (dessus) on it; (pluriel) on them; (dedans) in it; (pluriel) in them; **j'**~ **vais** I'm on my way; **n'**~ **va pas** don't go; **du lait? il n'**~ **en a pas** milk? there's none; **tu n'**~ **arriveras jamais** you'll never manage it.

● *pronom*

····▸ **s'**~ **habituer** get used to it.

····▸ **s'**~ **attendre** expect it.

····▸ ~ **penser** think about it.

····▸ ~ **être pour qch** have sth to do with it.

yaourt /'jauʀ(t)/ *nm* yoghurt. **yaourtière** *nf* yoghurt-maker.

yard /'jaʀd/ *nm* yard (= *91,44 cm*).

yen /'jɛn/ *nm* yen.

yeux /jø/ ⇒ŒIL.

yoga /'jɔga/ *nm* yoga.

yougoslave /'jugɔslav/ *adj*
Yugoslav. **Y~** *nmf* Yugoslav.

Yougoslavie /'jugɔslavi/ *nf*
Yugoslavia.

yo-yo® /'jojo/ *nm inv* yo-yo®.

Zz

zèbre /zɛbʀ/ *nm* zebra.

zèle /zɛl/ *nm* zeal.

zéro /zeʀo/ *nm* nought, zero;
(température) zero; (Sport) nil; (tennis)
love; (personne) nonentity; **partir de ~**
start from scratch; **repartir à ~** start
all over again.

zeste /zɛst/ *nm* peel; **un ~ de** (fig) a
touch of.

zézayer /zezeje/ [31] *vi* lisp.

zigzag /zigzag/ *nm* zigzag; **en ~**
winding.

zinc /zɛ̃g/ *nm* (métal) zinc; (comptoir 🅱)
bar.

zizanie /zizani/ *nf* discord; **semer la
~** put the cat among the pigeons.

zizi /zizi/ *nm* 🅱 willy.

zodiaque /zɔdjak/ *nm* zodiac.

zona /zona/ *nm* (Méd) shingles (+ *sg*).

zone /zon/ *nf* zone, area; (banlieue
pauvre) slums; **~ bleue** restricted
parking zone.

zoo /zo(o)/ *nm* zoo.

zoom /zum/ *nm* zoom lens.

zut /zyt/ *interj* 🅱 damn 🅱.

Aa

a *determiner*

an avant voyelle ou h muet.

➡ For expressions such as **make a noise, make a fortune** ⇒**noise, fortune**.

····▸ un/une; ∼ **tree** un arbre; ∼ **chair** une chaise.

····▸ (per) **ten francs** ∼ **kilo** dix francs le kilo; **three times** ∼ **day** trois fois par jour.

❗ When talking about what people do or are, **a** is not translated into French: **she's a teacher** *elle est professeur*; **he's a widower** *il est veuf*.

aback *adv* **taken** ∼ déconcerté.

abandon *vt* abandonner. ● *n* abandon *m*.

abate *vi* (*flood, fever*) baisser; (*storm*) se calmer. ● *vt* diminuer.

abbey *n* abbaye *f*.

abbot *n* abbé *m*.

abbreviate *vt* abréger. **abbreviation** *n* abréviation *f*.

abdicate *vt/i* abdiquer.

abdomen *n* abdomen *m*.

abduct *vt* enlever. **abductor** *n* ravisseur/-euse *m/f*.

abhor *vt* (*pt* **abhorred**) exécrer.

abide *vt* supporter; ∼ **by** respecter.

ability *n* capacité *f* (**to do** à faire); (*talent*) talent *m*.

abject *adj* (*state*) misérable; (*coward*) abject.

ablaze *adj* en feu.

able *adj* (*skilled*) compétent; **be** ∼ **to do** pouvoir faire; (*know how to*) savoir faire. **ably** *adv* avec compétence.

abnormal *adj* anormal. **abnormality** *n* anomalie *f*.

aboard *adv* à bord. ● *prep* à bord de.

abode *n* demeure *f*; **of no fixed** ∼ sans domicile fixe.

abolish *vt* abolir.

Aborigine *n* aborigène *mf* (d'Australie).

abort *vt* faire avorter; (*Comput*) abandonner. ● *vi* avorter.

abortion *n* avortement *m*; **have an** ∼ se faire avorter.

abortive *adj* (*attempt*) avorté; (*coup*) manqué.

about *adv* (approximately) environ; ∼ **the same** à peu près pareil; **there was no-one** ∼ il n'y avait personne. ● *prep* **it's** ∼ … il s'agit de …; **what I like** ∼ **her is** ce que j'aime chez elle c'est; **to wander** ∼ **the streets** errer dans les rues; **how/what** ∼ **some tea?** et si on prenait un thé?; **what** ∼ **you?** et toi? ● *adj* **be** ∼ **to do** être sur le point de faire; **be up and** ∼ être debout. ∼**-face**, ∼**-turn** *n* (fig) volte-face *f inv*.

above *prep* au-dessus de; **he is not** ∼ **lying** il n'est pas incapable de mentir; ∼ **all** surtout. ● *adv* **the apartment** ∼ l'appartement du dessus; **see** ∼ voir ci-dessus. ∼**-board** *adj* honnête. ∼**-mentioned** *adj* susmentionné.

abrasive *adj* abrasif; (*manner*) mordant. ● *n* abrasif *m*.

abreast *adv* de front; **keep** ∼ **of** se tenir au courant de.

abroad *adv* à l'étranger.

abrupt *adj* (sudden, curt) brusque; (steep) abrupt. **abruptly** *adv* (suddenly) brusquement; (curtly) avec brusquerie.

abscess *n* abcès *m*.

abseil *vi* descendre en rappel.

absence *n* absence *f*; (*lack*) manque *m*; **in the** ∼ **of** faute de.

absent *adj* absent.

absentee *n* absent/-e *m/f*.

absent-minded *adj* distrait.

absolute *adj* (*monarch, majority*) absolu; (*chaos, idiot*) véritable. **absolutely** *adv* absolument.

absolve *vt* ∼ **sb of sth** décharger qn de qch.

absorb *vt* absorber.

abstain *vi* s'abstenir (**from** de).

abstract[1] *adj* abstrait. ● *n* (*summary*) résumé *m*; **in the ~** dans l'abstrait.

abstract[2] *vt* tirer.

absurd *adj* absurde.

abundance *n* abondance *f*. **abundant** *adj* abondant. **abundantly** *adv* (*entirely*) tout à fait.

abuse[1] *vt* (*position*) abuser de; (*person*) maltraiter; (*insult*) injurier.

abuse[2] *n* (*misuse*) abus *m* (**of** de); (*cruelty*) mauvais traitement *m*; (*insults*) injures *fpl*.

abusive *adj* (*person*) grossier; (*language*) injurieux.

abysmal *adj* épouvantable.

abyss *n* abîme *m*.

academic *adj* (*career*) universitaire; (*year*) académique; (*scholarly*) intellectuel; (*theoretical*) théorique. ● *n* universitaire *mf*.

academy *n* (*school*) école *f*; (*society*) académie *f*.

accelerate *vi* (*speed up*) s'accélérer; (*Auto*) accélérer. **accelerator** *n* accélérateur *m*.

accent[1] *n* accent *m*.

accent[2] *vt* accentuer.

accept *vt* accepter. **acceptable** *adj* acceptable. **acceptance** *n* (*of offer*) acceptation *f*; (*of proposal*) approbation *f*.

access *n* accès *m*. **accessible** *adj* accessible.

accessory *adj* accessoire. ● *n* (*Jur*) complice *mf* (**to** de).

accident *n* accident *m*; (*chance*) hasard *m*; **by ~** par hasard. **accidental** *adj* (*death*) accidentel; (*meeting*) fortuit. **accidentally** *adv* accidentellement; (*by chance*) par hasard.

acclaim *vt* applaudir. ● *n* louanges *fpl*.

acclimatize *vt/i* (s')acclimater (**to** à).

accommodate *vt* loger; (*adapt to*) s'adapter à; (*satisfy*) satisfaire. **accommodating** *adj* accommodant. **accommodation** *n* logement *m*.

accompaniment *n* accompagnement *m*. **accompany** *vt* accompagner.

accomplice *n* complice *mf* (**in, to** de).

accomplish *vt* accomplir; (*objective*) réaliser. **accomplished** *adj* très compétent. **accomplishment** *n* (*feat*) réussite *f*; (*talent*) talent *m*.

accord *vi* concorder (**with** avec). ● *vt* accorder (**sb sth** qch à qn). ● *n* accord *m*; **of my own ~** de moi-même.

accordance *n* **in ~ with** conformément à.

according *adv* **~ to** (*principle, law*) selon; (*person, book*) d'après. **accordingly** *adv* en conséquence.

accordion *n* accordéon *m*.

accost *vt* aborder.

account *n* (*Comm*) compte *m*; (*description*) compte-rendu *m*; **on ~ of** à cause de; **on no ~** en aucun cas; **take into ~** tenir compte de; **it's of no ~** peu importe. □ **~ for** (*explain*) expliquer; (*represent*) représenter. **accountability** *n* responsabilité *f*. **accountable** *adj* responsable (**for** de; **to** envers).

accountancy *n* comptabilité *f*. **accountant** *n* comptable *mf*. **accounts** *npl* comptabilité *f*, comptes *mpl*.

accumulate *vt/i* (s')accumuler.

accuracy *n* (*of figures*) justesse *f*; (*of aim*) précision *f*; (*of forecast*) exactitude *f*. **accurate** *adj* juste, précis. **accurately** *adv* exactement, précisément.

accusation *n* accusation *f*.

accuse *vt* accuser; **the ~d** l'accusé/-e *m/f*.

accustomed *adj* accoutumé; **become ~ to** s'accoutumer à.

ace *n* (*card, person*) as *m*.

ache *n* douleur *f*. ● *vi* (*person*) avoir mal; **my leg ~s** ma jambe me fait mal.

achieve *vt* (*aim*) atteindre; (*result*) obtenir; (*ambition*) réaliser. **achievement** *n* (*feat*) réussite *f*; (*fulfilment*) réalisation *f* (**of** de).

acid *a* & *n* acide (*m*). **acidity** *n* acidité *f*. ~ **rain** *n* pluies *fpl* acides.

acknowledge *vt* (*error, authority*) reconnaître; (*letter*) accuser réception de. **acknowledgement** *n* reconnaissance *f*.

acne *n* acné *f*.

acorn *n* (Bot) gland *m*.

acoustic *adj* acoustique.
acoustics *npl* acoustique *f*.

acquaint *vt* ~ sb with sth mettre qn au courant de qch; be ~ed with (*person*) connaître; (*fact*) savoir. **acquaintance** *n* connaissance *f*.

acquire *vt* acquérir; (*habit*) prendre.

acquit *vt* (*pt* **acquitted**) (Jur) acquitter. **acquittal** *n* acquittement *m*.

acre *n* acre *f*, ≈ demi-hectare *m*.

acrid *adj* âcre.

acrimonious *adj* acrimonieux.

acrobat *n* acrobate *mf*. **acrobatics** *npl* acrobaties *fpl*.

acronym *n* acronyme *m*.

across *adv* & *prep* (side to side) d'un côté à l'autre (de); (on other side) de l'autre côté (from de); go *or* walk ~ traverser; lie ~ the bed se coucher en travers du lit; ~ the world partout dans le monde.

act *n* acte *m*; (Jur, Pol) loi *f*; put on an ~ jouer la comédie. ● *vi* agir; (Theat) jouer; ~ as servir de. ● *vt* (*part, role*) jouer.

acting *n* (Theat) jeu *m*. ● *adj* (temporary) intérimaire.

action *n* action *f*; (Mil) combat *m*; out of ~ hors service; take ~ agir.

activate *vt* (*machine*) faire démarrer; (*alarm*) déclencher.

active *adj* actif; (*volcano*) en activité; take an ~ interest in s'intéresser activement à. **activist** *n* activiste *mf*. **activity** *n* activité *f*.

actor *n* acteur *m*. **actress** *n* actrice *f*.

actual *adj* réel; the ~ words les mots exacts; in the ~ house (the house itself) dans la maison elle-même. **actuality** *n* réalité *f*. **actually** *adv* (in fact) en fait; (really) vraiment.

acute *adj* (*anxiety*) vif; (*illness*) aigu; (*shortage*) grave; (*mind*) pénétrant.

ad *n* (TV) pub *f* 🄵; small ~ petite annonce *f*.

AD *abbr* (**Anno Domini**) ap. J.-C.

adamant *adj* catégorique.

adapt *vt/i* (s')adapter (to à). **adaptability** *n* adaptabilité *f*. **adaptable** *adj* souple. **adaptation** *n* adaptation *f*. **adaptor** *n* (Electr) adaptateur *m*.

add *vt/i* ajouter (to à); (in maths) additionner. □ ~ up (*facts, figures*) s'accorder; ~ sth up additionner qch; ~ up to s'élever à.

adder *n* vipère *f*.

addict *n* toxicomane *mf*; (fig) accro *mf* 🄵.

addicted *adj* be ~ avoir une dépendance (to à); (fig) être accro 🄵 (to à). **addiction** *n* (Med) dépendance *f* (to à); passion *f* (to pour). **addictive** *adj* qui crée une dépendance.

addition *n* (item) ajout *m*; (in maths) addition *f*; in ~ en plus. **additional** *adj* supplémentaire.

additive *n* additif *m*.

address *n* adresse *f*; (speech) discours *m*. ● *vt* (*letter*) mettre l'adresse sur; (*crowd*) s'adresser à; ~ sth to adresser qch à. **addressee** *n* destinataire *mf*.

adequate *adj* suffisant; (satisfactory) satisfaisant.

adhere *vi* (lit, fig) adhérer (to à); ~ to (*policy*) observer.

adjacent *adj* contigu; ~ to attenant à.

adjective *n* adjectif *m*.

adjoin *vt* être contigu à. **adjoining** *adj* (*room*) voisin.

adjourn *vt* (*trial*) ajourner; the session was ~ed la séance a été levée. ● *vi* s'arrêter; (*Parliament*) lever la séance; ~ to passer à.

adjust *vt* (*level, speed*) régler; (*price*) ajuster; (*clothes*) rajuster. ● *vt/i* ~ (oneself) to s'adapter à. **adjustable** *adj* réglable. **adjustment** *n* (of rates) rajustement *m*; (of control) réglage *m*; (of person) adaptation *f*.

ad lib *vt/i* (*pt* **ad libbed**) improviser.

administer *vt* administrer.

administration *n* administration *f*. **administrative** *adj* administratif. **administrator** *n* administrateur/-trice *m/f*.

admiral *n* amiral *m*.

admiration *n* admiration *f*. **admire** *vt* admirer. **admirer** *n* admirateur/-trice *m/f*.

admission *n* (to a place) entrée *f*; (confession) aveu *m*.

admit *vt* (*pt* **admitted**) (acknowledge) reconnaître, admettre; (*crime*) avouer; (*new member*) admettre; ~ **to** reconnaître. **admittance** *n* entrée *f*. **admittedly** *adv* il est vrai.

ado *n* without more ~ sans plus de cérémonie.

adolescence *n* adolescence *f*. **adolescent** *n* & *a* adolescent/-e (*m/f*).

adopt *vt* adopter. **adopted** *adj* (*child*) adoptif. **adoption** *n* adoption *f*. **adoptive** *adj* adoptif.

adorable *adj* adorable. **adoration** *n* adoration *f*. **adore** *vt* adorer.

adorn *vt* orner.

adrift *a* & *adv* à la dérive.

adult *a* & *n* adulte (*mf*).

adultery *n* adultère *m*.

adulthood *n* âge *m* adulte.

advance *vt* (*sum*) avancer; (*tape, career*) faire avancer; (*interests*) servir. ● *vi* (lit) avancer; (progress) progresser. ● *n* avance *f*; (progress) progrès *m*; **in** ~ à l'avance. **advanced** *adj* avancé; (*studies*) supérieur.

advantage *n* avantage *m*; **take** ~ **of** profiter de; (*person*) exploiter. **advantageous** *adj* avantageux.

adventure *n* aventure *f*. **adventurer** *n* aventurier/-ière *m/f*. **adventurous** *adj* aventureux.

adverb *n* adverbe *m*.

adverse *adj* défavorable.

advert *n* annonce *f*; (TV) pub *f* 🔲.

advertise *vt* faire de la publicité pour; (*car, house, job*) mettre une annonce pour. ● *vi* faire de la publicité; (for staff) passer une annonce. **advertisement** *n* publicité *f*; (in newspaper) annonce *f*. **advertiser** *n* annonceur *m*. **advertising** *n* publicité *f*.

advice *n* conseils *mpl*; **some** ~, **a piece of** ~ un conseil.

advise *vt* conseiller; (inform) aviser; ~ **against** déconseiller. **adviser** *n* conseiller/-ère *m/f*. **advisory** *adj* consultatif.

advocate[1] *n* (Jur) avocat *m*; (supporter) partisan *m*.

advocate[2] *vt* recommander.

aerial *adj* aérien. ● *n* antenne *f*.

aerobics *n* aérobic *m*.

aeroplane *n* avion *m*.

aerosol *n* bombe *f* aérosol.

aesthetic *adj* esthétique.

afar *adv* **from** ~ de loin.

affair *n* (matter) affaire *f*; (romance) liaison *f*.

affect *vt* affecter.

affection *n* affection *f*. **affectionate** *adj* affectueux.

affinity *n* affinité *f*.

afflict *vt* affliger. **affliction** *n* affection *f*.

affluence *n* richesse *f*.

afford *vt* avoir les moyens d'acheter; (provide) fournir; **can you** ~ **the time?** avez-vous le temps?

afloat *adj* & *adv* (boat) à flot.

afoot *adv* **sth is** ~ il se prépare qch.

afraid *adj* **be** ~ (frightened) avoir peur (of, to de; that que); (worried) craindre (that que); **I'm** ~ **I can't come** je suis désolé mais je ne peux pas venir.

Africa *n* Afrique *f*.

African *n* Africain/-e *m/f*. ● *adj* africain.

after *adv* & *prep* après; **soon** ~ peu après; **be** ~ **sth** rechercher qch; ~ **all** après tout. ● *conj* après que; ~ **doing** après avoir fait.

aftermath *n* conséquences *fpl* (of de).

afternoon *n* après-midi *m or f inv*; **in the** ~ (dans) l'après-midi.

after: ~**shave** *n* après-rasage *m*. ~**thought** *n* pensée *f* après coup.

afterwards *adv* après, par la suite.

again *adv* encore; ~ **and** ~ à plusieurs reprises; **start** ~ recommencer; **she never saw him** ~ elle ne l'a jamais revu.

against *prep* contre; ~ **the law** illégal.

age *n* âge *m*; (era) ère *f*, époque *f*; **I've been waiting for ~s** j'attends depuis des heures. ● *vt/i* (*pres p* **ageing**) vieillir.

aged¹ *adj* **~ six** âgé de six ans.

aged² *adj* âgé.

agency *n* agence *f*.

agenda *n* ordre *m* du jour; (fig) programme *m*.

agent *n* agent *m*.

aggravate *vt* (make worse) aggraver; (annoy) exaspérer. **aggravation** *n* (worsening) aggravation *f*; (annoyance) ennuis *mpl*.

aggression *n* agression *f*.
aggressive *adj* agressif.
aggressiveness *n* agressivité *f*.
aggressor *n* agresseur *m*.

agitate *vt* agiter.

ago *adv* il y a; **a month ~** il y a un mois; **long ~** il y a longtemps; **how long ~?** il y a combien de temps?

agonize *vi* se tourmenter (**over** à propos de). **agonized** *adj* angoissé. **agonizing** *adj* déchirant. **agony** *n* douleur *f* atroce; (mental) angoisse *f*.

agree *vi* être d'accord (**on** sur; **with** avec); **~ to** consentir à; **~ with** (approve of) approuver. ● *vt* être d'accord (**that** sur le fait que); (admit) convenir (**that** que); (*date, solution*) se mettre d'accord sur.

agreeable *adj* agréable; **be ~** (willing) être d'accord.

agreed *adj* (*time, place*) convenu; **we're ~** nous sommes d'accord.

agreement *n* accord *m*; **in ~** d'accord.

agricultural *adj* agricole.
agriculture *n* agriculture *f*.

aground *adv* **run ~** (*ship*) s'échouer.

ahead *adv* (in front) en avant, devant; (in advance) à l'avance; **be 10 points ~** avoir 10 points d'avance; **~ of time** en avance; **go ~!** allez-y!

aid *vt* aider. ● *n* aide *f*; **in ~ of** au profit de.

aide *n* aide *mf*.

Aids *n* (Med) sida *m*.

aim *vt* (*gun*) braquer (**at** sur); **be ~ed at sb** (*campaign, remark*) viser qn. ● *vi* **~ for/at sth** viser qch; **~ to do**

avoir l'intention de faire. ● *n* but *m*; **take ~** viser. **aimless** *adj* sans but.

air *n* air *m*; **by ~** par avion; **on the ~** à l'antenne. ● *vt* aérer; (*views*) exprimer. ● *adj* (*base, disaster*) aérien; (*pollution, pressure*) atmosphérique. **~-bed** *n* matelas *m* pneumatique. **~-conditioning** *n* climatisation *f*. **~craft** *n inv* avion *m*. **~craft carrier** *n* porte-avions *m inv*. **~field** *n* terrain *m* d'aviation. **~ force** *n* armée *f* de l'air. **~ freshener** *n* désodorisant *m* d'atmosphère. **~ hostess** *n* hôtesse *f* de l'air. **~lift** *vt* transporter par pont aérien. **~line** *n* compagnie *f* aérienne. **~liner** *n* avion *m* de ligne. **~lock** *n* (in pipe) bulle *f* d'air; (chamber) sas *m*. **~mail** *n* (by) **~mail** par avion. **~plane** *n* (US) avion *m*. **~port** *n* aéroport *m*. **~ raid** *n* attaque *f* aérienne. **~tight** *adj* hermétique. **~ traffic controller** *n* contrôleur/-euse *m/f* aérien/-ne. **~waves** *npl* ondes *fpl*.

airy *adj* (**-ier, -iest**) (*room*) clair et spacieux.

aisle *n* (of church) allée *f* centrale; (in train) couloir *m*.

ajar *adv & a* entrouvert.

akin *adj* **~ to** semblable à.

alarm *n* alarme *f*; (clock) réveil *m*; (feeling) frayeur *f*. ● *vt* inquiéter. **~-clock** *n* réveil *m*.

alas *interj* hélas.

Albania *n* Albanie *f*.

album *n* album *m*.

alcohol *n* alcool *m*.

alcoholic *adj* alcoolique; (*drink*) alcoolisé. ● *n* alcoolique *mf*.

ale *n* bière *f*.

alert *adj* alerte; (watchful) vigilant. ● *n* alerte *f*; **on the ~** sur le qui-vive. ● *vt* alerter; **~ sb to** prévenir qn de. **alertness** *n* vivacité *f*; vigilance *f*.

A-level *n* ≈ baccalauréat *m*.

algebra *n* algèbre *f*.

Algeria *n* Algérie *f*.

alias *n* (*pl* **~es**) faux nom *m*. ● *prep* alias.

alibi *n* alibi *m*.

alien *n & a* étranger/-ère (*m/f*) (**to** à).

alienate *vt* éloigner.

alight *adj* en feu, allumé.

alike *adj* semblable. ● *adv* de la même façon; **look ~** se ressembler.

alive *adj* vivant; **~ to** conscient de; **~ with** grouillant de.

all

● *pronoun*

····▸ (everything) tout; **is that ~?** c'est tout?; **that was ~ (that) he said** c'est tout ce qu'il a dit; **I ate it ~** j'ai tout mangé.

❚ Use the translation **tous** for a group of masculine or mixed gender people or objects and **toutes** for a group of feminine gender: **we were all delighted** *nous étions tous ravis*; **'where are the cups?'—'they're all in the kitchen'** *'où sont les tasses?'—'elles sont toutes dans la cuisine'.*

● *determiner*

····▸ tout/toute/tous/toutes; **~ the time** tout le temps; **~ his life** toute sa vie; **~ of us** nous tous; **~ (the) women** toutes les femmes.

● *adverb*

····▸ (completely) tout; **they were ~ alone** ils étaient tout seuls; **tell me ~ about it** raconte-moi tout; **~ for** tout à fait pour; **not ~ that well** pas si bien que ça; **~ too** bien trop.

❚ When the adjective that follows is in the feminine and begins with a consonant, the translation is *toute/toutes*: **she was all alone** *elle était toute seule.*

allege *vt* prétendre. **allegedly** *adv* prétendument.

allergic *adj* allergique (**to** à). **allergy** *n* allergie *f.*

alleviate *vt* alléger.

alley *n* (street) ruelle *f.*

alliance *n* alliance *f.*

allied *adj* allié.

alligator *n* alligator *m.*

allocate *vt* (*funds*) affecter; (*time*) accorder; (*task*) assigner.

allot *vt* (*pt* **allotted**) (*money*) attribuer; (*task*) assigner. **allotment** *n* attribution *f;* (land) parcelle *f* de terre.

all-out *adj* (*effort*) acharné; (*strike*) total.

allow *vt* (authorize) autoriser à; (let) laisser; (enable) permettre; (concede) accorder; **~ for** tenir compte de.

allowance *n* allocation *f;* **make ~s for sth** tenir compte de qch; **make ~s for sb** essayer de comprendre qn.

alloy *n* alliage *m.*

all right *adj* (not bad) pas mal; **are you ~?** ça va?; **is it ~ if …?** est-ce que ça va si …? ● *adv* (*see*) bien; (*function*) comme il faut. ● *interj* d'accord.

ally[1] *n* allié/-e *m/f.*

ally[2] *vt* allier; **~ oneself with** s'allier avec.

almighty *adj* tout-puissant; (very great) formidable.

almond *n* amande *f.* **~ tree** *n* amandier *m.*

almost *adv* presque; **he ~ died** il a failli mourir.

alone *a & adv* seul.

along *prep* le long de; **walk ~ the beach** marcher sur la plage. ● *adv* **come ~** venir; **walk ~** marcher; **push/pull sth ~** pousser/tirer qch; **all ~** (time) depuis le début; **~ with** avec.

alongside *adv* à côté; **come ~** (Naut) accoster. ● *prep* (next to) à côté de; (all along) le long de.

aloof *adj* distant.

aloud *adv* à haute voix.

alphabet *n* alphabet *m.* **alphabetical** *adj* alphabétique.

alpine *adj* (*landscape*) alpestre; (*climate*) alpin.

already *adv* déjà.

alright *a & adv* = ALL RIGHT.

Alsatian *n* (dog) berger *m* allemand.

also *adv* aussi.

altar *n* autel *m.*

alter *vt/i* changer; (*building*) transformer; (*garment*) retoucher. **alteration** *n* changement *m;* (to building) transformation *f;* (to garment) retouche *f.*

alternate[1] *vt/i* alterner.

alternate[2] *adj* en alternance; **on ~ days** un jour sur deux. **alternately** *adv* alternativement.

alternative *adj* autre; (*solution*) de rechange. ● *n* (specified option) alternative *f*; (possible option) choix *m*. **alternatively** *adv* sinon.

alternator *n* alternateur *m*.

although *conj* bien que.

altitude *n* altitude *f*.

altogether *adv* (completely) tout à fait; (on the whole) tout compte fait.

aluminium *n* aluminium *m*.

always *adv* toujours.

am ⇒BE.

a.m. *adv* du matin.

amalgamate *vt/i* (merge) fusionner; (*metals*) (s')amalgamer.

amateur *n & a* amateur (*m*).

amaze *vt* stupéfaire. **amazed** *adj* stupéfait. **amazement** *n* stupéfaction *f*. **amazing** *adj* stupéfiant; (great) exceptionnel.

ambassador *n* ambassadeur *m*.

amber *n* ambre *m*; (Auto) orange *m*.

ambiguity *n* ambiguïté *f*. **ambiguous** *adj* ambigu.

ambition *n* ambition *f*. **ambitious** *adj* ambitieux.

ambulance *n* ambulance *f*.

ambush *n* embuscade *f*. ● *vt* tendre une embuscade à.

amenable *adj* obligeant; **~ to** (responsive) sensible à.

amend *vt* modifier. **amendment** *n* (to rule) amendement *m*.

amends *npl* **make ~** réparer son erreur.

amenities *npl* équipements *mpl*.

America *n* Amérique *f*.

American *n* Américain/-e *m/f*. ● *adj* américain.

amiable *adj* aimable.

amicable *adj* amical.

amid(st) *prep* au milieu de.

amiss *adj* **there is something ~** il y a quelque chose qui ne va pas.

ammonia *n* (gas) ammoniac *m*; (solution) ammoniaque *f*.

ammunition *n* munitions *fpl*.

amnesty *n* amnistie *f*.

among(st) *prep* parmi; (affecting a group) chez; **be ~ the poorest** être un des plus pauvres; **be ~ the first** être dans les premiers.

amorous *adj* amoureux.

amount *n* quantité *f*; (total) montant *m*; (sum of money) somme *f*. ● *vi* **~ to** (add up to) s'élever à; (be equivalent to) revenir à.

amp *n* ampère *m*.

amphibian *n* amphibie *m*.

ample *adj* (*resources*) largement suffisant; (*proportions*) généreux.

amplifier *n* amplificateur *m*.

amputate *vt* amputer.

amuse *vt* amuser.

amusement *n* (mirth) amusement *m*; (diversion) distraction *f*. **~ arcade** *n* salle *f* de jeux.

an ⇒A.

anaemia *n* anémie *f*.

anaesthetic *n* anesthésique *m*.

analyse *vt* analyser. **analysis** *n* (*pl* **-yses**) analyse *f*. **analyst** *n* analyste *mf*.

anarchist *n* anarchiste *mf*.

anatomical *adj* anatomique. **anatomy** *n* anatomie *f*.

ancestor *n* ancêtre *m*.

anchor *n* ancre *f*. ● *vt* mettre à l'ancre. ● *vi* jeter l'ancre.

anchovy *n* anchois *m*.

ancient *adj* ancien.

ancillary *adj* auxiliaire.

and *conj* et; **two hundred ~ sixty** deux cent soixante; **go ~ see him** allez le voir; **richer ~ richer** de plus en plus riche.

anew *adv* (once more) encore, de nouveau; (in a new way) à nouveau.

angel *n* ange *m*.

anger *n* colère *f*. ● *vt* mettre en colère, fâcher.

angle *n* angle *m*. ● *vi* pêcher (à la ligne); **~ for** (fig) quêter. **angler** *n* pêcheur/-euse *m/f*.

Anglo-Saxon *adj* anglo-saxon. ● *n* Anglo-Saxon/-ne *m/f*.

angry *adj* (**-ier, -iest**) fâché, en colère; **get ~** se fâcher, se mettre en colère (**with** contre); **make sb ~** mettre qn en colère.

anguish *n* angoisse *f*.

animal *n & a* animal (*m*).

animate[1] *adj* (*person*) vivant; (*object*) animé.

animate[2] *vt* animer.

aniseed *n* anis *m*.

ankle *n* cheville *f*. ~ **sock** *n* socquette *f*.

annex *vt* annexer.

anniversary *n* anniversaire *m*.

announce *vt* annoncer (**that** que). **announcement** *n* (spoken) annonce *f*; (written) avis *m*. **announcer** *n* (radio, TV) speaker/-ine *m/f*.

annoy *vt* agacer, ennuyer. **annoyance** *n* contrariété *f*. **annoyed** *adj* fâché (**with** contre); **get** ~**ed** se fâcher. **annoying** *adj* ennuyeux.

annual *adj* annuel. ● *n* publication *f* annuelle. **annually** *adv* (*earn, produce*) par an; (*do, inspect*) tous les ans.

annul *vt* (*pt* **annulled**) annuler.

anonymity *n* anonymat *m*.

anonymous *adj* anonyme.

anorak *n* anorak *m*.

another *det & pron* un/-e autre; ~ **coffee** (one more) encore un café; ~ **ten minutes** encore dix minutes, dix minutes de plus; **can I have** ~**?** est-ce que je peux en avoir un autre?

answer *n* réponse *f*; (solution) solution *f*; (phone) **there's no** ~ ça ne répond pas. ● *vt* répondre à; (*prayer*) exaucer; ~ **the door** ouvrir la porte. ● *vi* répondre. □ ~ **back** répondre; ~ **for** répondre de; ~ **to** (*superior*) dépendre de; (*description*) répondre à. **answerable** *adj* responsable (**for** de; **to** devant). **answering machine** *n* répondeur *m*.

ant *n* fourmi *f*.

antagonism *n* antagonisme *m*. **antagonize** *vt* provoquer l'hostilité de.

Antarctic *n* **the** ~ l'Antarctique *m*. ● *adj* antarctique.

antenatal *adj* prénatal.

antenna *n* (*pl* **-ae**) (of insect) antenne *f*; (*pl* **-as**; aerial: US) antenne *f*.

anthem *n* (Relig) motet *m*; (of country) hymne *m* national.

antibiotic *n & a* antibiotique (*m*).

antibody *n* anticorps *m*.

anticipate *vt* (foresee, expect) prévoir, s'attendre à; (forestall) devancer.

anticipation *n* attente *f*; **in** ~ **of** en prévision *or* attente de.

anticlimax *n* (let-down) déception *f*.

anticlockwise *adv & a* dans le sens inverse des aiguilles d'une montre.

antics *npl* pitreries *fpl*.

antifreeze *n* antigel *m*.

antiquated *adj* (idea) archaïque; (*building*) vétuste.

antique *adj* (old) ancien; (old-style) à l'ancienne. ● *n* objet *m* ancien, antiquité *f*. ~ **dealer** *n* antiquaire *mf*. ~ **shop** *n* magasin *m* d'antiquités.

anti-Semitic *adj* antisémite.

antiseptic *a & n* antiseptique (*m*).

antisocial *adj* asocial, antisocial; (reclusive) sauvage.

antlers *npl* bois *mpl*.

anxiety *n* (worry) anxiété *f*; (eagerness) impatience *f*.

anxious *adj* (troubled) anxieux; (eager) impatient (**to** de).

any *det* (some) du, de l', de la, des; (after negative) de, d'; (every) tout; (no matter which) n'importe quel; **at** ~ **moment** à tout moment; **have you** ~ **water?** avez-vous de l'eau? ● *pron* (no matter which one) n'importe lequel; (any amount of it or them) en; **I do not have** ~ je n'en ai pas; **did you see** ~ **of them?** en avez-vous vu? ● *adv* (a little) un peu; **do you have** ~ **more?** en avez-vous encore?; **do you have** ~ **more tea?** avez-vous encore du thé?; **I don't do it** ~ **more** je ne le fais plus.

anybody *pron* (no matter who) n'importe qui; (somebody) quelqu'un; (after negative) personne; **he did not see** ~ il n'a vu personne.

anyhow *adv* (anyway) de toute façon; (carelessly) n'importe comment.

anyone *pron* = ANYBODY.

anything *pron* (no matter what) n'importe quoi; (something) quelque chose; (after negative) rien; **he did not see** ~ il n'a rien vu; ~ **but**

nullement; ~ **you do** tout ce que tu fais.

anyway *adv* de toute façon.

anywhere *adv* (no matter where) n'importe où; (somewhere) quelque part; (after negative) nulle part; **he does not go** ~ il ne va nulle part; ~ **you go** partout où tu vas, où que tu ailles; ~ **else** partout ailleurs.

apart *adv* (on or to one side) à part; (separated) séparé; (into pieces) en pièces; ~ **from** à part, excepté; **ten metres** ~ à dix mètres l'un de l'autre; **come** ~ (break) tomber en morceaux; (*machine*) se démonter; **legs** ~ les jambes écartées; **keep** ~ séparer; **take** ~ démonter.

apartment *n* (US) appartement *m*.

ape *n* singe *m*. ● *vt* singer.

aperitif *n* apéritif *m*.

apex *n* sommet *m*.

apologetic *adj* (*tone*) d'excuse; **be** ~ s'excuser. **apologetically** *adv* en s'excusant.

apologize *vi* s'excuser (**for** de; **to** auprès de).

apology *n* excuses *fpl*.

apostrophe *n* apostrophe *f*.

appal *vt* (*pt* **appalled**) horrifier. **appalling** *adj* épouvantable.

apparatus *n* appareil *m*.

apparent *adj* apparent. **apparently** *adv* apparemment.

appeal *n* appel *m*; (attractiveness) attrait *m*, charme *m*. ● *vi* (Jur) faire appel; ~ **to sb** (beg) faire appel à qn; (attract) plaire à qn; ~ **to sb for sth** demander qch à qn. **appealing** *adj* (attractive) attirant.

appear *vi* apparaître; (arrive) se présenter; (seem, be published) paraître; (Theat) jouer; ~ **on TV** passer à la télé. **appearance** *n* apparition *f*; (aspect) apparence *f*.

appease *vt* apaiser.

appendix *n* (*pl* **-ices**) appendice *m*.

appetite *n* appétit *m*.

appetizer *n* (snack) amuse-gueule *m inv*; (drink) apéritif *m*.

appetizing *adj* appétissant.

applaud *vt/i* applaudir; (*decision*) applaudir à. **applause** *n* applaudissements *mpl*.

apple *n* pomme *f*. ~**-tree** *n* pommier *m*.

appliance *n* appareil *m*.

applicable *adj* valable; **if** ~ le cas échéant.

applicant *n* candidat/-e *m/f* (**for** à).

application *n* application *f*; (request, form) demande *f*; (for job) candidature *f*.

apply *vt* appliquer. ● *vi* ~ **to** (refer) s'appliquer à; (ask) s'adresser à; ~ **for** (*job*) postuler pour; (*grant*) demander; ~ **oneself to** s'appliquer à.

appoint *vt* (to post) nommer; (fix) désigner; **well-**~**ed** bien équipé.

appointment *n* nomination *f*; (meeting) rendez-vous *m inv*; (job) poste *m*; **make an** ~ prendre rendez-vous (**with** avec).

appraisal *n* évaluation *f*. **appraise** *vt* évaluer.

appreciate *vt* (like) apprécier; (understand) comprendre; (be grateful for) être reconnaissant de. ● *vi* prendre de la valeur. **appreciation** *n* appréciation *f*; (gratitude) reconnaissance *f*; (rise) augmentation *f*. **appreciative** *adj* reconnaissant; (*audience*) enthousiaste.

apprehend *vt* (arrest) appréhender; (understand) comprendre. **apprehension** *n* (arrest) appréhension *f*; (fear) crainte *f*.

apprehensive *adj* inquiet; **be** ~ **of** craindre.

apprentice *n* apprenti *m*. ● *vt* mettre en apprentissage.

approach *vt* (s')approcher de; (accost) aborder; (with request) s'adresser à. ● *vi* (s')approcher. ● *n* approche *f*; **an** ~ **to** (*problem*) une façon d'aborder; (*person*) une démarche auprès de. **approachable** *adj* abordable.

appropriate[1] *vt* s'approprier.

appropriate[2] *adj* approprié, propre. **appropriately** *adv* à propos.

approval *n* approbation *f*; **on** ~ à *or* sous condition.

approve *vt* approuver. ● *vi* ~ **of** approuver. **approving** *adj* approbateur.

approximate¹ *vi* ~ **to** se rapprocher de.

approximate² *adj* approximatif. **approximately** *adv* environ. **approximation** *n* approximation *f*.

apricot *n* abricot *m*.

April *n* avril *m*. ~ **Fools Day** *n* le premier avril.

apron *n* tablier *m*.

apt *adj* (suitable) approprié; **be** ~ **to** avoir tendance à.

aptitude *n* aptitude *f*.

aptly *adv* à propos.

Aquarius *n* Verseau *m*.

aquatic *adj* aquatique; (Sport) nautique.

Arab *n* Arabe *mf*. ● *adj* arabe.

Arabian *adj* d'Arabie.

Arabic *a & n* (Ling) arabe (*m*).

arbitrary *adj* arbitraire.

arbitrate *vi* arbitrer. **arbitration** *n* arbitrage *m*. **arbitrator** *n* médiateur/-trice *m/f*.

arcade *n* (shops) galerie *f*; (arches) arcades *fpl*.

arch *n* arche *f*; (of foot) voûte *f* plantaire. ● *vt/i* (s')arquer. ● *adj* (playful) malicieux.

archaeological *adj* archéologique. **archaeologist** *n* archéologue *mf*. **archaeology** *n* archéologie *f*.

archbishop *n* archevêque *m*.

archery *n* tir *m* à l'arc.

architect *n* architecte *mf*; (of plan) artisan *m*. **architectural** *adj* architectural. **architecture** *n* architecture *f*.

archives *npl* archives *fpl*.

archway *n* voûte *f*.

Arctic *n* **the** ~ l'Arctique *m*. ● *adj* (climate) arctique; (expedition) polaire; (conditions) glacial.

ardent *adj* ardent.

are ⇒BE.

area *n* (region) région *f*; (district) quartier *m*; (fig) domaine *m*; (in geometry) aire *f*; **parking/picnic** ~ aire *f* de parking/de pique-nique.

arena *n* arène *f*.

aren't = ARE NOT.

Argentina *n* Argentine *f*.

arguable *adj* discutable. **arguably** *adv* selon certains.

argue *vi* (quarrel) se disputer; (reason) argumenter. ● *vt* (debate) discuter; ~ **that** alléguer que.

argument *n* dispute *f*; (reasoning) argument *m*; (discussion) débat *m*. **argumentative** *adj* ergoteur.

Aries *n* Bélier *m*.

arise *vi* (*pt* **arose**; *pp* **arisen**) (problem) survenir; (question) se poser; ~ **from** résulter de.

aristocrat *n* aristocrate *mf*.

arithmetic *n* arithmétique *f*.

ark *n* (Relig) arche *f*.

arm *n* bras *m*; ~ **in arm** bras dessus bras dessous. ● *vt* armer; ~**ed robbery** vol *m* à main armée.

armament *n* armement *m*.

arm: ~**-band** *n* brassard *m*. ~**chair** *n* fauteuil *m*.

armour *n* armure *f*. **armoured** *adj* blindé. **armoury** *n* arsenal *m*.

armpit *n* aisselle *f*.

arms *npl* (weapons) armes *fpl*. ~ **dealer** *n* trafiquant *m* d'armes.

army *n* armée *f*.

aroma *n* arôme *m*. **aromatic** *adj* aromatique.

arose ⇒ARISE.

around *adv* (tout) autour; (here and there) çà et là. ● *prep* autour de; ~ **here** par ici.

arouse *vt* (awaken, cause) éveiller; (excite) exciter.

arrange *vt* arranger; (time, date) fixer; ~ **to** s'arranger pour.

arrangement *n* arrangement *m*; (agreement) entente *f*; **make** ~**s** prendre des dispositions.

array *n* **an** ~ **of** (display) un étalage impressionnant de.

arrears *npl* arriéré *m*; **in** ~ (rent) arriéré; **he is in** ~ il a des retards dans ses paiements.

arrest *vt* arrêter; (attention) retenir. ● *n* arrestation *f*; **under** ~ en état d'arrestation.

arrival *n* arrivée *f*; **new** ~ nouveau venu *m*, nouvelle venue *f*.

arrive *vi* arriver; ~ **at** (destination) arriver à; (decision) parvenir à.

arrogance *n* arrogance *f*.

arrow *n* flèche *f*.

arse *n* 🗙 cul *m* 🗙.

arson *n* incendie *m* criminel.
arsonist *n* incendiaire *mf*.

art *n* art *m*; (fine arts) beaux-arts *mpl*.

artery *n* artère *f*.

art gallery *n* (public) musée *m*
(d'art); (private) galerie *f* (d'art).

arthritis *n* arthrite *f*.

artichoke *n* artichaut *m*.

article *n* article *m*; ~ **of clothing**
vêtement *m*.

articulate *adj* (person) capable de
s'exprimer clairement; (speech)
distinct.

articulated lorry *n* semi-
remorque *m*.

artificial *adj* artificiel.

artist *n* artiste *mf*.

arts *npl* the ~ les arts *mpl*; (Univ)
lettres *fpl*.

artwork *n* (of book) illustrations *fpl*.

as *conj* comme; (while) pendant que;
(over gradual period of time) au fur et à
mesure que; ~ **she grew older** au fur
et à mesure qu'elle vieillissait; **do** ~
I say fais ce que je dis; ~ **usual**
comme d'habitude. ● *prep* ~ **a**
mother en tant que mère; ~ **a gift** un
cadeau; ~ **from Monday** à partir de
lundi; ~ **for**, ~ **to** quant à; ~ **if**
comme si; **you look** ~ **if you're tired**
vous avez l'air (d'être) fatigué. ● *adv*
~ **tall** ~ aussi grand que; ~ **much**
~, ~ **many** ~ autant que; ~ **soon** ~
aussitôt que; ~ **well** ~ aussi bien
que; ~ **wide** ~ **possible** aussi large
que possible.

asbestos *n* amiante *f*.

ascend *vt* gravir. ● *vi* monter.

ascertain *vt* établir (that que).

ash *n* cendre *f*; ~(-tree) frêne *m*.

ashamed *adj* be ~ avoir honte (of
de).

ashore *adv* à terre.

ashtray *n* cendrier *m*.

Asia *n* Asie *f*.

Asian *n* Asiatique *mf*. ● *adj*
asiatique.

aside *adv* de côté; ~ **from** à part. ● *n*
aparté *m*.

ask *vt/i* demander; (a question) poser;
(invite) inviter; ~ **sb sth** demander

qch à qn; ~ **sb to do** demander à qn
de faire; ~ **about** (thing) se
renseigner sur; (person) demander
des nouvelles de; ~ **for** demander.

asleep *adj* endormi; (numb)
engourdi. ● *adv* fall ~ s'endormir.

asparagus *n* (plant) asperge *f*; (Culin)
asperges *fpl*.

aspect *n* aspect *m*; (direction)
orientation *f*.

asphyxiate *vt/i* (s')asphyxier.

aspire *vi* aspirer (to à; to do à faire).

aspirin *n* aspirine® *f*.

ass *n* âne *m*; (person 🗓) idiot/-e *m/f*.

assail *vt* attaquer. **assailant** *n*
agresseur *m*.

assassin *n* assassin *m*.
assassinate *vt* assassiner.
assassination *n* assassinat *m*.

assault *n* (Mil) assaut *m*; (Jur)
agression *f*. ● *vt* (person: Jur)
agresser.

assemble *vt* (construct) assembler;
(gather) rassembler. ● *vi* se
rassembler.

assembly *n* assemblée *f*. ~ **line** *n*
chaîne *f* de montage.

assent *n* assentiment *m*. ● *vi*
consentir.

assert *vt* affirmer; (rights)
revendiquer. **assertion** *n*
affirmation *f*. **assertive** *adj* assuré.

assess *vt* évaluer; (payment)
déterminer le montant de.
assessment *n* évaluation *f*
assessor *n* (valuer) expert *m*.

asset *n* (advantage) atout *m*; (financial)
bien *m*; ~**s** (Comm) actif *m*.

assign *vt* (allot) assigner; ~ **sb to**
(appoint) affecter qn à.

assignment *n* (task) mission *f*;
(diplomatic) poste *m*; (academic) devoir
m.

assist *vt/i* aider. **assistance** *n*
aide *f*.

assistant *n* aide *mf*; (in shop)
vendeur/-euse *m/f*. ● *adj* (manager)
adjoint.

associate¹ *n & a* associé/-e (*m/f*).

associate² *vt* associer. ● *vi* ~ **with**
fréquenter. **association** *n*
association *f*.

assorted *adj* divers; (foods) assorti.

assortment *n* assortiment *m*; (of people) mélange *m*.

assume *vt* supposer; (*power, attitude*) prendre; (*role, burden*) assumer.

assurance *n* assurance *f*.

assure *vt* assurer.

asterisk *n* astérisque *m*.

asthma *n* asthme *m*.

astonish *vt* étonner.

astound *vt* stupéfier.

astray *adv* go ~ s'égarer; lead ~ égarer.

astride *adv & prep* à califourchon (sur).

astrologer *n* astrologue *mf*. **astrology** *n* astrologie *f*.

astronaut *n* astronaute *mf*.

astronomer *n* astronome *mf*.

asylum *n* asile *m*.

at *preposition*

➡ For expressions such as **laugh at, look at** ⇒**laugh, look**.

····➤ (in position or place) à; **he's ~ his desk** il est à son bureau; **she's ~ work/school** elle est au travail/à l'école.

····➤ (at someone's house or business) chez; **~ Mary's/the dentist's** chez Mary/le dentiste.

····➤ (in times, ages) à; **~ four o'clock** à quatre heures; **~ two years of age** à l'âge de deux ans.

ate ⇒EAT.

atheist *n* athée *mf*.

athlete *n* athlète *mf*. **athletic** *adj* athlétique. **athletics** *npl* athlétisme *m*; (US) sports *mpl*.

Atlantic *adj* atlantique. ● *n* the ~ (Ocean) l'Atlantique *m*.

atlas *n* atlas *m*.

atmosphere *n* (air) atmosphère *f*; (mood) ambiance *f*. **atmospheric** *adj* atmosphérique; d'ambiance.

atom *n* atome *m*.

atrocious *adj* atroce.

atrocity *n* atrocité *f*.

attach *vt/i* (s')attacher; (*letter*) joindre (**to** à).

attaché *n* (Pol) attaché/-e *m/f*. ~ **case** *n* attaché-case *m*.

attached *adj* be ~ to (like) être attaché à; **the ~ letter** la lettre ci-jointe.

attachment *n* (accessory) accessoire *m*; (affection) attachement *m*; (e-mail) pièces *fpl* jointes.

attack *n* attaque *f*; (Med) crise *f*. ● *vt* attaquer.

attain *vt* atteindre (à); (gain) acquérir.

attempt *vt* tenter. ● *n* tentative *f*; **an ~ on sb's life** un attentat contre qn.

attend *vt* assister à; (*class*) suivre; (*school, church*) aller à. ● *vi* assister; **~ (to)** (look after) s'occuper de.

attendance *n* présence *f*; (people) assistance *f*.

attendant *n* employé/-e *m/f*. ● *adj* associé.

attention *n* attention *f*; **~!** (Mil) garde-à-vous!; **pay ~** faire *or* prêter attention (**to** à).

attentive *adj* attentif; (considerate) attentionné. **attentively** *adv* attentivement. **attentiveness** *n* attention *f*.

attest *vt/i* ~ (**to**) attester.

attic *n* grenier *m*.

attitude *n* attitude *f*.

attorney *n* (US) avocat/-e *m/f*.

attract *vt* attirer. **attraction** *n* attraction *f*; (charm) attrait *m*.

attractive *adj* attrayant, séduisant. **attractively** *adv* agréablement. **attractiveness** *n* attrait *m*, beauté *f*.

attribute¹ *vt* ~ to attribuer à.

attribute² *n* attribut *m*.

aubergine *n* aubergine *f*.

auction *n* vente *f* aux enchères. ● *vt* vendre aux enchères. **auctioneer** *n* commissaire-priseur *m*.

audacious *adj* audacieux.

audience *n* (theatre, radio) public *m*; (interview) audience *f*.

audiovisual *adj* audiovisuel.

audit *n* vérification *f* des comptes. ● *vt* vérifier.

audition *n* audition *f*. ● *vt/i* auditionner (**for** pour).

auditor *n* commissaire *m* aux comptes.

August *n* août *m*.

aunt *n* tante *f*.

auspicious *adj* favorable.

Australia *n* Australie *f*.

Australian *n* Australien/-ne *m*/*f*. ● *adj* australien.

Austria *n* Autriche *f*.

Austrian *n* Autrichien/-ne *m*/*f*. ● *adj* autrichien.

authentic *adj* authentique.

author *n* auteur *m*.

authoritarian *adj* autoritaire.

authoritative *adj* (credible) qui fait autorité; (*manner*) autoritaire.

authority *n* autorité *f*; (permission) autorisation *f*.

authorization *n* autorisation *f*. **authorize** *vt* autoriser.

autistic *adj* (*person*) autiste; (*response*) autistique.

autograph *n* autographe *m*. ● *vt* signer, dédicacer.

automate *vt* automatiser.

automatic *adj* automatique. ● *n* (Auto) voiture *f* automatique.

automobile *n* (US) auto(mobile) *f*.

autonomous *adj* autonome.

autumn *n* automne *m*.

auxiliary *a* & *n* auxiliaire (*mf*); ∼ (verb) auxiliaire *m*.

avail *vt* ∼ oneself of profiter de. ● *n* of no ∼ inutile; to no ∼ sans résultat.

availability *n* disponibilité *f*. **available** *adj* disponible.

avenge *vt* venger; ∼ oneself se venger (on de).

avenue *n* avenue *f*; (line of approach: fig) voie *f*.

average *n* moyenne *f*; on ∼ en moyenne. ● *adj* moyen. ● *vt* faire la moyenne de; (produce, do) faire en moyenne.

aviary *n* volière *f*.

avocado *n* avocat *m*.

avoid *vt* éviter. **avoidance** *n* (of injuries) prévention *f*; (of responsibility) refus *m*.

await *vt* attendre.

awake *vt*/*i* (*pt* awoke; *pp* awoken) (s')éveiller. ● *adj* be ∼ ne pas dormir, être (r)éveillé.

award *vt* (*grant*) attribuer; (*prize*) décerner; (*points*) accorder. ● *n* récompense *f*, prix *m*; (scholarship) bourse *f*; **pay** ∼ augmentation *f* (de salaire).

aware *adj* (well-informed) averti; **be** ∼ **of** (*danger*) être conscient de; (*fact*) savoir; **become** ∼ **of** prendre conscience de. **awareness** *n* conscience *f*.

away *adv* (far) (au) loin; (absent) absent, parti; ∼ **from** loin de; **move** ∼ s'écarter; (to new home) déménager; **six kilometres** ∼ à six kilomètres (de distance); **take** ∼ emporter; **he was snoring** ∼ il ronflait. ● *a* & *n* ∼ (match) match *m* à l'extérieur.

awe *n* crainte *f* (révérencielle).

awe-inspiring *adj* impressionnant.

awesome *adj* redoutable.

awful *adj* affreux. **awfully** *adv* (badly) affreusement; (very 🔢) rudement.

awkward *adj* difficile; (inconvenient) inopportun; (clumsy) maladroit; (embarrassing) gênant; (embarrassed) gêné. **awkwardly** *adv* maladroitement; avec gêne. **awkwardness** *n* maladresse *f*; (discomfort) gêne *f*.

awning *n* auvent *m*; (of shop) store *m*.

awoke, awoken ⇒AWAKE.

axe *n* hache *f*. ● *vt* (*pres p* axing) réduire; (eliminate) supprimer; (employee) renvoyer.

axis *n* (*pl* axes) axe *m*.

axle *n* essieu *m*.

Bb

BA *abbr* ⇒BACHELOR OF ARTS.

babble *vi* babiller; (*stream*) gazouiller. ● *n* babillage *m*.

baby *n* bébé *m*. ∼ **carriage** *n* (US) voiture *f* d'enfant. ∼**-sit** *vi* faire du babysitting, garder des enfants. **∼-sitter** n baby-sitter mf.

bachelor n célibataire m. **B∼ of Arts** licencié/-e m/f ès lettres.

back n (of person, hand, page, etc.) dos m; (of house) derrière m; (of vehicle) arrière m; (of room) fond m; (of chair) dossier m; (in football) arrière m; **at the ∼ of the book** à la fin du livre; **in ∼** of (US) derrière. ● adj (leg, wheel) arrière inv; (door, gate) de derrière; (taxes) arriéré. ● adv en arrière; (returned) de retour, rentré; **come ∼** revenir; **give ∼** rendre; **take ∼** reprendre; **I want it ∼** je veux le récupérer. ● vt (support) appuyer; (bet on) miser sur; (vehicle) faire reculer. ● vi (of person, vehicle) reculer. □ ∼ **down** céder; ∼ **out** se désister; (Auto) sortir en marche arrière; ∼ **up** (support) appuyer. **∼ache** n mal m de dos. **∼-bencher** n (Pol) député m. **∼bone** n colonne f vertébrale. **∼date** vt antidater. **∼fire** vi (Auto) pétarader; (fig) mal tourner. **∼gammon** n trictrac m.

background n fond m, arrière-plan m; (context) contexte m; (environment) milieu m; (experience) formation f. ● adj (music, noise) de fond.

backhand n revers m. **backhander** n (bribe) pot-de-vin m.

backing n soutien m.

back: **∼lash** n retour m de bâton; réaction f violente (**against** contre). **∼log** n retard m. ∼ **number** n vieux numéro m. **∼pack** n sac m à dos. **∼side** n (buttocks 🔲) derrière m. **∼stage** a & adv dans les coulisses. **∼stroke** n dos m crawlé. **∼track** vi rebrousser chemin; (change one's opinion) faire marche arrière.

back-up n soutien m; (Comput) sauvegarde f. ● adj de secours; (Comput) de sauvegarde.

backward adj (step etc.) en arrière; (retarded) arriéré.

backwards adv en arrière; (walk) à reculons; (read) à l'envers; **go ∼ and forwards** aller et venir.

bacon n lard m; (in rashers) bacon m.

bacteria npl bactéries fpl.

bad adj (**worse**, **worst**) mauvais; (wicked) méchant; (ill) malade; (accident) grave; (food) gâté; **feel ∼** se sentir mal; **go ∼** se gâter; ∼ **language** gros mots mpl; **too ∼!** tant pis!; (I'm sorry) dommage!

badge n badge m; (coat of arms) insigne m.

badger n blaireau m. ● vt harceler.

badly adv mal; (hurt) gravement; **want ∼** avoir grande envie de.

badminton n badminton m.

bad-tempered adj irritable.

baffle vt déconcerter.

bag n sac m; ∼**s** (luggage) bagages mpl; (under eyes 🔲) valises fpl; ∼**s of** plein de.

baggage n bagages mpl; ∼ **reclaim** réception f des bagages.

baggy adj large.

bagpipes npl cornemuse f.

bail n caution f; **on ∼** sous caution; (cricket) bâtonnet m. ● vt mettre en liberté provisoire.

bailiff n huissier m.

bait n appât m. ● vt appâter; (fig) tourmenter.

bake vt faire cuire au four; ∼ **a cake** faire un gâteau. ● vi cuire; (person) faire du pain. **baked beans** npl haricots mpl blancs à la tomate. **baked potato** n pomme f de terre en robe des champs. **baker** n boulanger/-ère m/f. **bakery** n boulangerie f.

balance n équilibre m; (scales) balance f; (outstanding sum: Comm) solde m; (of payments, of trade) balance f; (remainder) restant m. ● vt mettre en équilibre; (weigh up also Comm) balancer; (budget) équilibrer; (to compensate) contrebalancer. ● vi être en équilibre.

balcony n balcon m.

bald adj chauve; (tyre) lisse; (fig) simple.

balk vt contrecarrer. ● vi ∼ **at** reculer devant.

ball n (golf, tennis, etc.) balle f; (football) ballon m; (billiards) bille f; (of wool) pelote f; (sphere) boule f; (dance) bal m.

ballet n ballet m.

balloon n ballon m.

ballot n scrutin m. ● vt consulter par vote (on sur). ∼-**box** n urne f. ∼-**paper** n bulletin m de vote.

ballpoint pen n stylo m (à) bille.

ban vt (pt **banned**) interdire; ∼ sb from exclure qn de; ∼ sb from doing interdire à qn de faire. ● n interdiction f (on de).

banal adj banal.

banana n banane f.

band n (strip, group of people) bande f; (pop group) groupe m; (brass band) fanfare f. ● vi ∼ **together** se réunir.

bandage n bandage m. ● vt bander.

B and B abbr ⇨BED AND BREAKFAST.

bandit n bandit m.

bandstand n kiosque m à musique.

bang n (blow, noise) coup m; (explosion) détonation f; (of door) claquement m. ● vt/i taper; (door) claquer; ∼ one's head se cogner la tête. ● interj vlan. ● adv 🄸 ∼ **in the middle** en plein milieu; ∼ **on time** à l'heure pile.

banger n (firework) pétard m; (Culin) saucisse f; (old) ∼ (car 🄸) guimbarde f.

banish vt bannir.

banister n rampe f d'escalier.

bank n (Comm) banque f; (of river) rive f; (of sand) banc m. ● vt mettre en banque. ● vi (Aviat) virer; ∼ **with** avoir un compte à; ∼ **on** compter sur. ∼ **account** n compte m en banque. ∼ **card** n carte f bancaire. ∼ **holiday** n jour m férié.

banking n opérations fpl bancaires; (as career) la banque.

banknote n billet m de banque.

bankrupt adj be ∼ être en faillite; go ∼ faire faillite. ● n failli/-e m/f. ● vt mettre en faillite. **bankruptcy** n faillite f.

bank statement n relevé m de compte.

banner n bannière f.

baptism n baptême m. **baptize** vt baptiser.

bar n (of metal) barre f; (on window, cage) barreau m; (of chocolate) tablette f; (pub) bar m; (counter) comptoir m; (Mus) mesure f; (fig) obstacle m; ∼ **of soap** savonnette f; **the** ∼ (Jur) le barreau. ● vt (pt **barred**) (obstruct) barrer; (prohibit) interdire; (exclude) exclure. ● prep sauf.

barbecue n barbecue m. ● vt faire au barbecue.

barbed wire n fil m de fer barbelé.

barber n coiffeur m (pour hommes).

bar code n code m (à) barres.

bare adj nu; (cupboard) vide. ● vt mettre à nu. ∼**foot** adj nu-pieds inv, pieds nus. **barely** adv à peine.

bargain n (deal) marché m; (cheap thing) occasion f. ● vi négocier; (haggle) marchander; **not** ∼ **for** ne pas s'attendre à.

barge n péniche f. ● vi ∼ **in** interrompre; (into room) faire irruption.

bark n (of tree) écorce f; (of dog) aboiement m. ● vi aboyer.

barley n orge f.

bar: ∼**maid** n serveuse f. ∼**man** n (pl -**men**) barman m.

barn n grange f.

barracks npl caserne f.

barrel n tonneau m; (of oil) baril m; (of gun) canon m.

barren adj stérile.

barricade n barricade f. ● vt barricader.

barrier n barrière f; **ticket** ∼ guichet m.

barrister n avocat m.

bartender n (US) barman m.

barter n troc m. ● vt troquer (**for** contre).

base n base f. ● vt baser (**on** sur; **in** à). ● adj ignoble. **baseball** n baseball m.

basement n sous-sol m.

bash 🄸 vt cogner; ∼**ed in** enfoncé. ● n coup m violent; **have a** ∼ **at** s'essayer à.

basic adj fondamental, élémentaire; **the** ∼**s** l'essentiel m. **basically** adv au fond.

basil n basilic m.

basin n (for liquids) cuvette f; (for food) bol m; (for washing) lavabo m; (of river) bassin m.

basis n (pl **bases**) base f.

bask vi se prélasser (**in** à).

basket n corbeille f; (with handle) panier m. **basketball** n basket(-ball) m.

Basque n (person) Basque mf; (Ling) basque m. ● adj basque.

bass¹ adj (voice, part) de basse; (sound, note) grave. ● n (pl **basses**) basse f.

bass² n inv (freshwater fish) perche f; (sea) bar m.

bassoon n basson m.

bastard n (illegitimate) bâtard/-e m/f; (insult 🅧) salaud m 🅧.

bat n (cricket etc.) batte f; (table tennis) raquette f; (animal) chauve-souris f. ● vt (pt **batted**) (ball) frapper; not ~ an eyelid ne pas sourciller.

batch n (of cakes, people) fournée f; (of goods, text also Comput) lot m.

bath n (pl -**s**) bain m; (tub) baignoire f; have a ~ prendre un bain; (swimming) ~s piscine f. ● vt donner un bain à.

bathe vt baigner. ● vi se baigner; (US) prendre un bain.

bathing n baignade f. ~-**costume** n maillot m de bain.

bath: ~**robe** n (US) robe f de chambre. ~**room** n salle f de bains.

baton n (policeman's) matraque f; (Mus) baguette f.

batter vt battre. ● n (Culin) pâte f (à frire).

battery n (Mil, Auto) batterie f; (of torch, radio) pile f.

battle n bataille f; (fig) lutte f. ● vi se battre. ~**field** n champ m de bataille.

baulk vt/i = BALK.

bay n (Bot) laurier m; (Geog, Archit) baie f; (area) aire f; (bark) aboiement m; keep or hold at ~ tenir à distance. ● vi aboyer. ~-**leaf** n feuille f de laurier. ~ **window** n fenêtre f en saillie.

bazaar n (shop, market) bazar m; (sale) vente f.

BC abbr (**before Christ**) avant J.-C.

BBS abbr (**Bulletin Board System**) (Internet) babillard m électronique, BBS m.

be

present **am**, **is**, **are**; past **was**, **were**; past participle **been**.

● intransitive verb

····▸ être; **I am tired** je suis fatigué; **it's me** c'est moi.

····▸ (feelings) avoir; **I am hot** j'ai chaud; **he is hungry/thirsty** il a faim/soif; **her hands are cold** elle a froid aux mains.

····▸ (age) avoir; **I am 15** j'ai 15 ans.

····▸ (weather) faire; **it's warm** il fait chaud; **it's 25** il fait 25.

····▸ (health) aller; **how are you?** comment allez-vous or comment vas-tu?

····▸ (visit) aller; **I've never been to Italy** je ne suis jamais allé en Italie.

● auxiliary verb

····▸ (in tenses) **I am working** je travaille; **he was writing to his mother** il écrivait à sa mère; **she is to do it at once** (obligation) elle doit le faire tout de suite.

····▸ (in passives) **he was killed** il a été tué; **the window has been fixed** on a réparé la fenêtre.

····▸ (in tag questions) **their house is lovely, isn't it?** leur maison est très jolie, n'est-ce pas?

····▸ (in short answers) **'I am a painter'— 'are you?'** 'je suis peintre'—'ah oui?'; **'are you a doctor?'—'yes, I am'** 'êtes-vous médecin?'—'oui'; **'you're not going out'—'yes I am'** 'tu ne sors pas'—'si'.

beach n plage f.

beacon n (lighthouse) phare m; (marker) balise f.

bead n perle f.

beak n bec m.

beaker n gobelet m.

beam n (timber) poutre f; (of light) rayon m; (of torch) faisceau m. ● vi rayonner. ● vt (broadcast) transmettre.

bean n haricot m.

bear n ours m. ● vt (pt **bore**; pp **borne**) (carry, show, feel) porter;

(endure, sustain) supporter; (*child*) mettre au monde. ● *vi* ~ **left** (go) prendre à gauche; ~ **in mind** tenir compte de. □ ~ **out** confirmer; ~ **up** tenir le coup. **bearable** *adj* supportable.

beard *n* barbe *f.*

bearer *n* porteur/-euse *m/f.*

bearing *n* (behaviour) maintien *m*; (relevance) rapport *m*; **get one's** ~**s** s'orienter.

beast *n* bête *f*; (*person*) brute *f.*

beat *vt/i* (*pt* **beat**; *pp* **beaten**) battre; ~ **a retreat** battre en retraite; ~ **it!** dégage! 🄸; **it** ~**s me** 🄸 ça me dépasse. ● *n* (of drum, heart) battement *m*; (Mus) mesure *f*; (of policeman) ronde *f.* □ ~ **off** repousser; ~ **up** tabasser. **beating** *n* raclée *f.*

beautiful *adj* beau.

beauty *n* beauté *f.* ~ **parlour** *n* institut *m* de beauté. ~ **spot** *n* grain *m* de beauté; (place) site *m* pittoresque.

beaver *n* castor *m.*

became ⇒BECOME.

because *conj* parce que; ~ **of** à cause de.

become *vt/i* (*pt* **became**; *pp* **become**) devenir; (befit) convenir à; **what has** ~ **of her?** qu'est-ce qu'elle est devenue?

bed *n* lit *m*; (layer) couche *f*; (of sea) fond *m*; (of flowers) parterre *m*; **go to** ~ (aller) se coucher. ● *vi* (*pt* **bedded**) ~ **down** se coucher. **bed and breakfast** *n* chambre *f* avec petit déjeuner, chambre *f* d'hôte. ~**bug** *n* punaise *f.* ~**clothes** *npl* couvertures *fpl.*

bedding *n* literie *f.*

bed: ~**ridden** *adj* cloué au lit. ~**room** *n* chambre *f* (à coucher). ~**side** *n* chevet *m.* ~**sit**, ~**sitter** *n* chambre *f* meublée, studio *m.* ~**spread** *n* dessus *m* de lit. ~**time** *n* heure *f* du coucher.

bee *n* abeille *f*; **make a** ~**-line for** aller tout droit vers.

beech *n* hêtre *m.*

beef *n* bœuf *m.* ~**burger** *n* hamburger *m.*

beehive *n* ruche *f.*

been ⇒BE.

beer *n* bière *f.*

beetle *n* scarabée *m.*

beetroot *n inv* betterave *f.*

before *prep* (time) avant; (place) devant; **the day** ~ **yesterday** avant-hier. ● *adv* avant; (already) déjà; **the day** ~ la veille. ● *conj* ~ **leaving** avant de partir; ~ **I forget** avant que j'oublie. **beforehand** *adv* à l'avance.

beg *vt* (*pt* **begged**) (*food, money, favour*) demander (**from** à); ~ **sb to do** supplier qn de faire. ● *vi* mendier; **it is going** ~**ging** personne n'en veut.

began ⇒BEGIN.

beggar *n* mendiant/-e *m/f.*

begin *vt/i* (*pt* **began**, *pp* **begun**, *pres p* **beginning**) commencer (**to do** à faire). **beginner** *n* débutant/-e *m/f.* **beginning** *n* commencement *m*, début *m.*

begun ⇒BEGIN.

behalf *n* **on** ~ **of** (*act, speak, campaign*) pour; (*phone, write*) de la part de.

behave *vi* se conduire; ~ (**oneself**) se conduire bien.

behaviour, (US) **behavior** *n* comportement *m* (**towards** envers).

behead *vt* décapiter.

behind *prep* derrière; (in time) en retard sur. ● *adv* derrière; (late) en retard; **leave** ~ oublier. ● *n* (buttocks 🄸) derrière *m* 🄸.

beige *a* & *n* beige (*m*).

being *n* (person) être *m.*

belch *vi* avoir un renvoi. ● *vt* ~ **out** (*smoke*) s'échapper. ● *n* renvoi *m.*

Belgian *n* Belge *mf.* ● *adj* belge. **Belgium** *n* Belgique *f.*

belief *n* conviction *f*; (trust) confiance *f*; (faith: Relig) foi *f.*

believe *vt/i* croire; ~ **in** croire à; (*deity*) croire en. **believer** *n* croyant/-e *m/f.*

bell *n* cloche *f*; (small) clochette *f*; (on door) sonnette *f.*

belly *n* ventre *m.* ~ **button** *n* nombril *m.*

belong *vi* ~ **to** appartenir à; (*club*) être membre de.

belongings *npl* affaires *fpl.*

beloved *a & n* bien-aimé/-e (*m/f*).

below *prep* sous, au-dessous de; (fig) indigne de. ● *adv* en dessous; (on page) ci-dessous.

belt *n* ceinture *f*; (Tech) courroie *f*; (fig) zone *f*. ● *vt* (hit 🔢) rosser. ● *vi* (rush 🔢) ~ **in/out** entrer/sortir à toute vitesse.

beltway *n* (US) périphérique *m*.

bemused *adj* perplexe.

bench *n* banc *m*; **the** ~ (Jur) la magistrature (assise).

bend *vt* (*pt* **bent**) (*knee, arm, wire*) plier; (*head, back*) courber. ● *vi* (*road*) tourner; (*person*) ~ **down/over** se pencher. ● *n* courbe *f*; (in road) virage *m*; (of arm, knee) pli *m*.

beneath *prep* sous, au-dessous de; (fig) indigne de. ● *adv* en dessous.

benefactor *n* bienfaiteur/-trice *m/f*.

beneficial *adj* bénéfique.

benefit *n* avantage *m*; (allowance) allocation *f*. ● *vt* (be useful to) profiter à; (do good to) faire du bien à. ● *vi* profiter; ~ **from** tirer profit de.

benign *adj* (kindly) bienveillant; (Med) bénin.

bent ⇒BEND. ● *n* (talent) aptitude *f*; (inclination) penchant *m*. ● *adj* tordu; 🔣 corrompu; ~ **on doing** décidé à faire.

bequest *n* legs *m*.

bereaved *adj* endeuillé; **the** ~ la famille endeuillée. **bereavement** *n* deuil *m*.

berry *n* baie *f*.

berserk *adj* fou furieux.

berth *n* (in train, ship) couchette *f*; (anchorage) mouillage *m*; **give a wide** ~ **to** éviter. ● *vi* mouiller.

beside *prep* à côté de; ~ **oneself** hors de soi; ~ **the point** sans rapport.

besides *prep* en plus de. ● *adv* en plus.

besiege *vt* assiéger.

best *adj* meilleur; **the** ~ **book** le meilleur livre; **the** ~ **part of** la plus grande partie de; **the** ~ **thing is to** le mieux est de. ● *adv* (the) ~ (*behave, play*) le mieux. ● *n* **the** ~ le meilleur, la meilleure; **do one's** ~

faire de son mieux; **make the** ~ **of** s'accommoder de. ~ **man** *n* témoin. ~**-seller** *n* bestseller *m*, livre *m* à succès.

bet *n* pari *m*. ● *vt/i* (*pt* **bet** or **betted**, *pres p* **betting**) parier (**on** sur).

betray *vt* trahir.

better *adj* meilleur; **the** ~ **part of** la plus grande partie de; **get** ~ s'améliorer; (recover) se remettre. ● *adv* mieux; **I had** ~ **go** je ferais mieux de partir. ● *vt* (improve) améliorer; (do better than) surpasser. ● *n* **get the** ~ **of** l'emporter sur; **so much the** ~ tant mieux. ~ **off** *adj* (richer) plus riche; **he is/would be** ~ **off at home** il est/serait mieux chez lui.

betting-shop *n* bureau *m* du PMU.

between *prep* entre. ● *adv* **in** ~ au milieu.

beverage *n* boisson *f*.

beware *vi* prendre garde (**of** à).

bewilder *vt* déconcerter.

beyond *prep* au-delà de; (*control, reach*) hors de; (besides) excepté. ● *adv* au-delà; **it is** ~ **me** ça me dépasse.

bias *n* (inclination) tendance *f*; (prejudice) parti *m* pris. ● *vt* (*pt* **biased**) influer sur. **biased** *adj* partial.

bib *n* bavoir *m*.

Bible *n* Bible *f*.

biceps *n* biceps *m*.

bicycle *n* vélo *m*, bicyclette *f*. ● *adj* (*bell, chain*) de vélo; (*pump, clip*) à vélo.

bid *n* (at auction) enchère *f*; (attempt) tentative *f*. ● *vt/i* (*pt* **bade**, *pp* **bidden** or **bid**, *pres p* **bidding**) (offer) offrir, mettre une enchère (de) (**for** pour); ~ **sb good morning** dire bonjour à qn; ~ **sb farewell** faire ses adieux à qn.

bidding *n* (at auction) enchères *fpl*; **he did my** ~ il a fait ce que je lui ai dit.

bifocals *npl* verres *mpl* à double foyer.

big *adj* (**bigger, biggest**) grand; (in bulk) gros.

bike *n* vélo *m*.

bikini *n* bikini *m*.

bilberry *n* myrtille *f*.

bilingual *adj* bilingue.

bill *n* (invoice) facture *f*; (in hotel, for gas) note *f*; (in restaurant) addition *f*; (of sale) acte *m*; (Pol) projet *m* de loi; (banknote: US) billet *m* de banque; (Theat) **on the** ~ à l'affiche; (of bird) bec *m*. ● *vt* (person: Comm) envoyer la facture à. ~**board** *n* panneau *m* d'affichage.

billet *n* cantonnement *m*. ● *vt* (*pt* **billeted**) cantonner (**on** chez).

billiards *n* billard *m*.

billion *n* billion *m*; (US) milliard *m*.

bin *n* (for rubbish) poubelle *f*; (for storage) casier *m*.

bind *vt* (*pt* **bound**) attacher; (book) relier; **be bound by** être tenu par. ● *n* (bore) corvée *f*.

binding *n* reliure *f*. ● *adj* (*agreement*, *contract*) qui lie.

binge *n* (drinking) beuverie *f*; (eating) gueuleton *m*.

binoculars *npl* jumelles *fpl*.

biochemistry *n* biochimie *f*.

biodegradable *adj* biodégradable.

biographer *n* biographe *mf*.
biography *n* biographie *f*.

biological *adj* biologique.

biologist *n* biologiste *mf*.

biology *n* biologie *f*.

birch *n* (tree) bouleau *m*; (whip) fouet *m*.

bird *n* oiseau *m*; (girl 🔢) nana *f*.

Biro® *n* stylo *m* à bille, bic® *m*.

birth *n* naissance *f*; **give** ~ accoucher. ~ **certificate** *n* acte *m* de naissance. ~-**control** *n* contraception *f*. ~**day** *n* anniversaire *m*. ~**mark** *n* tache *f* de naissance. ~-**rate** *n* taux *m* de natalité.

biscuit *n* biscuit *m*; (US) petit pain *m* (au lait).

bisect *vt* couper en deux.

bishop *n* évêque *m*.

bit ⇒BITE. ● *n* morceau *m*; (of horse) mors *m*; (of tool) mèche *f*; **a** ~ (a little) un peu; (Comput) bit *m*.

bitch *n* chienne *f*; (woman 🔢) garce *f* 🔢. ● *vi* dire du mal (**about** de).

bite *vt/i* (*pt* **bit**; *pp* **bitten**) mordre; ~ **one's nails** se ronger les ongles.

● *n* morsure *f*; (by insect) piqûre *f*; (mouthful) bouchée *f*; **have a** ~ manger un morceau.

bitter *adj* amer; (weather) glacial. ● *n* bière *f*. **bitterly** *adv* amèrement; **it is** ~**ly cold** il fait un temps glacial.

bizarre *adj* bizarre.

black *adj* noir; ~ **and blue** couvert de bleus. ● *n* (colour) noir *m*; B~ (person) Noir/-e *m/f* . ● *vt* noircir; (goods) boycotter. ~**berry** *n* mûre *f*. ~**bird** *n* merle *m*. ~**board** *n* tableau *m* noir. ~**currant** *n* cassis *m*.

blacken *vt/i* noircir.

black: ~ **eye** *n* œil *m* poché. ~**head** *n* point *m* noir. ~ **ice** *n* verglas *m*. ~**leg** *n* jaune *m*.

blacklist *n* liste *f* noire. ● *vt* mettre à l'index.

blackmail *n* chantage *m*. ● *vt* faire chanter. **blackmailer** *n* maître-chanteur *m*.

black: ~ **market** *n* marché *m* noir. ~**out** *n* panne *f* de courant; (Med) syncope *f*. ~ **pudding** *n* boudin *m*. ~ **sheep** *n* brebis *f* galeuse. ~**smith** *n* forgeron *m*. ~ **spot** *n* point *m* noir.

bladder *n* vessie *f*.

blade *n* (of knife) lame *f*; (of propeller, oar) pale *f*; ~ **of grass** brin *m* d'herbe.

blame *vt* accuser; ~ **sb for sth** reprocher qch à qn; **he is to** ~ il est responsable (**for** de). ● *n* responsabilité *f* (**for** de).

bland *adj* (insipid) fade.

blank *adj* (*page*) blanc; (*screen*) vide; (*cheque*) en blanc; **to look** ~ avoir l'air ébahi. ● *n* blanc *m*; ~ (cartridge) cartouche *f* à blanc.

blanket *n* couverture *f*; (layer) couche *f*.

blasphemous *adj* blasphématoire; (*person*) blasphémateur.

blast *n* explosion *f*; (wave of air) souffle *m*; (of wind) rafale *f*; (noise from siren etc.) coup *m*. ● *vt* (blow up) faire sauter. □ ~ **off** décoller. ~ **furnace** *n* haut-fourneau *m*. ~ **off** *n* lancement *m*.

blatant *adj* (obvious) flagrant; (shameless) éhonté.

blaze n feu m; (accident) incendie m.
● vt ～ **a trail** faire œuvre de
pionnier. ● vi (fire) brûler; (sky,
eyes) flamboyer.

bleach n (for cleaning) eau f de Javel;
(for hair, fabric) décolorant m. ● vt/i
blanchir; (hair) décolorer.

bleak adj (landscape) désolé;
(outlook, future) sombre.

bleed vt/i (pt **bled**) saigner.

bleep n bip m.

blemish n imperfection f; (on fruit,
reputation) tache f. ● vt entacher.

blend vt mélanger. ● vi se fondre
ensemble; **to ～ with** se marier à. ● n
mélange m. **blender** n mixeur n,
mixer n.

bless vt bénir; **be ～ed with** jouir de;
～ you! à vos souhaits! **blessed** adj
(holy) saint; (damned 🅸) sacré.
blessing n bénédiction f; (benefit)
avantage m; (stroke of luck) chance f.

blew ⇨BLOW.

blight n (disease: Bot) rouille f; (fig)
plaie f.

blind adj aveugle (**to** à); (corner,
bend) sans visibilité. ● vt aveugler.
● n (on window) store m; **the ～** les
aveugles mpl.

blindfold adj **be ～** avoir les yeux
bandés. ● adv les yeux bandés. ● n
bandeau m. ● vt bander les yeux à.

blindness n (Med) cécité f; (fig)
aveuglement m.

blind spot n (Auto) angle m mort.

blink vi cligner des yeux; (light)
clignoter.

bliss n délice m. **blissful** adj
délicieux.

blister n ampoule f; (on paint) cloque
f. ● vi cloquer.

blitz n (Aviat) raid m éclair. ● vt
bombarder.

blob n (drop) (grosse) goutte f; (stain)
tache f.

block n bloc m; (buildings) pâté m de
maisons; (in pipe) obstruction f; ～ (**of
flats**) immeuble m; ～ **letters**
majuscules fpl. ● vt bloquer.

blockade n blocus m. ● vt bloquer.

blockage n obstruction f.

block-buster n gros succès m.

bloke n 🅸 type m.

blond a & n blond (m).

blonde a & n blonde (f).

blood n sang m. ● adj (donor, bath)
de sang; (bank, poisoning) du sang;
(group, vessel) sanguin.
～-pressure n tension f artérielle.
～shed n effusion f de sang. **～shot**
adj injecté de sang. **～stream** n
sang m. **～ test** n prise f de sang.

bloody adj (-ier, -iest) sanglant;
⊠ sacré. ● adv ⊠ vachement 🅸.
～-minded adj 🅸 hargneux,
obstiné.

bloom n fleur f. ● vi fleurir; (person)
s'épanouir.

blossom n fleur(s) f(pl). ● vi fleurir;
(person) s'épanouir.

blot n tache f. ● vt (pt **blotted**)
tacher; (dry) sécher; ～ **out** effacer.

blotch n tache f.

blouse n chemisier m.

blow vt/i (pt **blew**; pp **blown**)
souffler; (fuse) (faire) sauter;
(squander ⊠) claquer; (opportunity)
rater; ～ **one's nose** se moucher; ～ **a
whistle** siffler. ● n coup m. □ ～
away or **off** emporter; ～ **out**
souffler; ～ **over** passer; ～ **up**
(faire) sauter; (tyre) gonfler; (Photo)
agrandir.

blow-dry n brushing m. ● vt faire
un brushing à.

blown ⇨BLOW.

bludgeon n matraque f. ● vt
matraquer.

blue adj bleu; (movie) porno. ● n bleu
m; **come out of the ～** être inattendu;
have the ～s avoir le cafard. **～bell** n
jacinthe f des bois. **～print** n projet
m.

bluff vt/i bluffer. ● n bluff m; **call
sb's ～** dire chiche à qn. ● adj
(person) carré.

blunder vi faire une bourde; (move)
avancer à tâtons. ● n gaffe f.

blunt adj (knife) émoussé; (person)
brusque. ● vt émousser. **bluntly** adv
carrément.

blur n image f floue. ● vt (pt
blurred) brouiller.

blurb n résumé m publicitaire.

blush vi rougir. ● n rougeur f.
blusher n fard m à joues.

blustery adj ～ **wind** bourrasque f.

boar n sanglier m.

board n planche f; (for notices) tableau m; (food) pension f; **full ~** pension f complète; **half ~** demi-pension f; (committee) conseil m; **~ of directors** conseil m d'administration; **go by the ~** tomber à l'eau; **on ~** à bord. ● vt/i (bus, train) monter dans; (Naut) monter à bord (de); **~ with** être en pension chez.

boarding-school n école f privée avec internat.

boast vi se vanter (about de). ● vt s'enorgueillir de. ● n vantardise f.

boat n bateau m; (small) canot m; **in the same ~** logé à la même enseigne.

bode vi **~ well/ill** être de bon/ mauvais augure.

bodily adj (need, well-being) physique; (injury) corporel. ● adv physiquement; (in person) en personne.

body n corps m; (mass) masse f; (organization) organisme m; **~(work)** (Auto) carrosserie f; **the main ~ of** le gros de. **~-building** n culturisme m. **~guard** n garde m du corps.

bog n marais m. ● vt (pt **bogged**) **get ~ged down** s'enliser dans.

bogus adj faux.

boil n furoncle m; **bring to the ~** porter à ébullition. ● vt/i bouillir. □ **~ down to** se ramener à; **~ over** déborder. **boiled** adj (egg) à la coque; (potatoes) à l'eau.

boiler n chaudière f; **~ suit** bleu m (de travail).

boisterous adj tapageur; (child) turbulent.

bold adj hardi; (cheeky) effronté; (type) gras.

Bolivia n Bolivie f.

bollard n (on road) balise f.

bolt n (on door) verrou m; (for nut) boulon m; (lightning) éclair m. ● vt (door) verrouiller; (food) engouffrer. ● vi s'emballer.

bomb n bombe f; **~ scare** alerte f à la bombe. ● vt bombarder.

bomber n (aircraft) bombardier m; (person) plastiqueur m.

bombshell n **be a ~** tomber comme une bombe.

bond n (agreement) engagement m; (link) lien m; (Comm) obligation f, bon m; **in ~** (entreposé) en douane.

bone n os m; (of fish) arête f. ● vt désosser. **~-dry** adj tout à fait sec.

bonfire n feu m; (for celebration) feu m de joie.

bonnet n (hat) bonnet m; (of vehicle) capot m.

bonus n prime f.

bony adj (-ier, -iest) (thin) osseux; (fish) plein d'arêtes.

boo interj hou. ● vt/i huer. ● n huée f.

booby-trap n mécanisme m piégé. ● vt (pt **-trapped**) piéger.

book n livre m; (exercise) cahier m; (of tickets etc.) carnet m; **~s** (Comm) comptes mpl. ● vt (reserve) réserver; (driver) dresser un PV à; (player) prendre le nom de; (write down) inscrire. ● vi retenir des places; (fully) **~ed** complet. **~case** n bibliothèque f. **booking-office** n guichet m. **~keeping** n comptabilité f. **booklet** n brochure f. **~maker** n bookmaker m. **~mark** n (for book, Internet) signet m. **~seller** n libraire mf. **~shop** n librairie f. **~stall** n kiosque m (à journaux).

boom vi (gun, wind, etc.) gronder; (trade) prospérer. ● n grondement m; (Comm) boom m, prospérité f.

boost vt stimuler; (morale) remonter; (price) augmenter; (publicize) faire de la réclame pour.

boot n (knee-length) botte f; (ankle-length) chaussure f (montante); (for walking) chaussure f de marche; (Sport) chaussure f de sport; (of vehicle) coffre m; **get the ~** 🖾 se faire virer. ● vt/i **~ up** (Comput) amorcer.

booth n (for telephone) cabine f; (at fair) baraque f.

booze vi 🗍 boire (beaucoup). ● n 🗍 alcool m.

border n (edge) bord m; (frontier) frontière f; (in garden) bordure f. ● vi **~ on** être voisin de, avoisiner.

bore vt ennuyer; **be ~d** s'ennuyer; ⇒BEAR. ● vi (Tech) forer. ● n raseur/ -euse m/f; (thing) ennui m. **boredom** n ennui m. **boring** adj ennuyeux.

born adj né; **be ~** naître.

borne ⇒BEAR.

borough n municipalité f.

borrow vt emprunter (**from** à).

Bosnia n Bosnie f.

Bosnian adj bosniaque. ● n Bosniaque.

bosom n poitrine f; ~ **friend** ami/-e m/f intime.

boss n 🔟 patron/-ne m/f. ● vt ~ (**about**) 🔟 mener par le bout du nez.

bossy adj autoritaire.

botch vt bâcler, saboter.

both det les deux; ~ **the books** les deux livres. ● pron tous/toutes (les) deux, l'un/-e et l'autre; **we** ~ **agree** nous sommes tous les deux d'accord; **I bought** ~ (**of them**) j'ai acheté les deux; **I saw** ~ **of you** je vous ai vus tous les deux; ~ **Paul and Anne** (et) Paul et Anne. ● adv à la fois.

bother vt (annoy, worry) ennuyer; (disturb) déranger. ● vi se déranger; **don't** ~ (**calling**) ce n'est pas la peine (d'appeler); **don't** ~ **about us** ne t'inquiète pas pour nous; **I can't be** ~**ed** j'ai la flemme 🔟. ● n ennui m; (effort) peine f; **it's no** ~ ce n'est rien.

bottle n bouteille f; (for baby) biberon m. ● vt mettre en bouteille. □ ~ **up** contenir. ~ **bank** n collecteur m (de verre usagé). ~**neck** n (traffic jam) embouteillage m. ~**opener** n ouvre-bouteilles m inv.

bottom n fond m; (of hill, page, etc.) bas m; (buttocks) derrière m 🔟. ● adj inférieur, du bas.

bought ⇒BUY.

bounce vi rebondir; (person) faire des bonds, bondir; (cheques ⊠) être refusé. ● vt faire rebondir. ● n rebond m.

bound vi (leap) bondir; ~**ed by** limité par; ⇒BIND. ● n bond m. ● adj **be** ~ **for** être en route pour, aller vers; ~ **to** (obliged) obligé de; (certain) sûr de.

boundary n limite f.

bounds npl limites fpl; **out of** ~ être interdit d'accès.

bout n période f; (Med) accès m; (boxing) combat m.

bow[1] n (weapon) arc m; (of violin) archet m; (knot) nœud m.

bow[2] n salut m; (of ship) proue f. ● vt/i (s')incliner.

bowels npl intestins mpl; (fig) profondeurs fpl.

bowl n (for washing) cuvette f; (for food) bol m; (for soup) assiette f creuse. ● vt/i (cricket) lancer; ~ **over** bouleverser.

bowler n (cricket) lanceur m; ~ (**hat**) (chapeau) melon m.

bowling n (ten-pin) bowling m; (on grass) jeu m de boules. ~**-alley** n bowling m.

bow-tie n nœud m papillon.

box n boîte f; (cardboard) carton m; (Theat) loge f; **the** ~ 🔟 la télé. ● vt mettre en boîte; (Sport) boxer; ~ **sb's ears** gifler qn; ~ **in** enfermer.

boxing n boxe f. ● adj de boxe. **B**~ **Day** n le lendemain de Noël.

box office n guichet m.

boy n garçon m.

boycott vt boycotter. ● n boycottage m.

boyfriend n (petit) ami m.

bra n soutien-gorge m.

brace n (fastener) attache f; (dental) appareil m; (tool) vilbrequin m; ~**s** (for trousers) bretelles fpl. ● vt soutenir; ~ **oneself** rassembler ses forces.

bracket n (for shelf etc.) tasseau m, support m; (group) tranche f; **in** ~**s** entre parenthèses. ● vt mettre entre parenthèses or crochets.

braid n (trimming) galon m; (of hair) tresse f.

brain n cerveau m; ~**s** (fig) intelligence f. ● vt assommer. **brainless** adj stupide. ~**wash** vt faire subir un lavage de cerveau à. ~**wave** n idée f géniale, trouvaille f. **brainy** adj (**-ier, -iest**) doué.

brake n (Auto also fig) frein m. ● vt/i freiner. ~ **light** n feu m stop.

bran n son m.

branch n (of tree) branche f; (of road) embranchement m; (Comm) succursale f; (of bank) agence f. ● vi ~ (**off**) bifurquer.

brand n marque f. ● vt ~ **sb as** désigner qn comme qch.

brand-new adj tout neuf.

brandy n cognac m.

brass n cuivre m; **get down to ~ tacks** en venir aux choses sérieuses; **the ~** (Mus) les cuivres mpl; **top ~** ⊠ galonnés mpl.

brat n ⚀ môme mf ⚀.

brave adj courageux; (smile) brave. ● n (American Indian) brave m. ● vt braver. **bravery** n courage m.

brawl n bagarre f. ● vi se bagarrer.

Brazil n Brésil m.

breach n (of copyright, privilege) violation f; (in relationship) rupture f; (gap) brèche f. ● vt ouvrir une brèche dans.

bread n pain m; **~ and butter** tartine f. **~-bin**, (US) **~-box** n boîte f à pain. **~crumbs** npl chapelure f.

breadth n largeur f.

bread-winner n soutien m de famille.

break vt (pt **broke**, pp **broken**) casser; (smash into pieces) briser; (vow, silence, rank, etc.) rompre; (law) violer; (a record) battre; (news) révéler; (journey) interrompre; (heart, strike, ice) briser; **~ one's arm** se casser le bras. ● vi (se) casser; se briser. ● n cassure f, rupture f; (in relationship, continuity) rupture f; (interval) interruption f; (at school) récréation f, récré f; (for coffee) pause f; (luck ⚀) chance f. □ **~ away from** se détacher; **~ down** vi (collapse) s'effondrer; (negotiations) échouer; (machine) tomber en panne; vt (door) enfoncer; (analyse) analyser; **~ even** rentrer dans ses frais; **~ into** cambrioler; **~ off** (se) détacher; (suspend) rompre; (stop talking) s'interrompre; **~ out** (fire, war, etc.) éclater; **~ up** (end) (faire) cesser; (couple) rompre; (marriage) (se) briser; (crowd) (se) disperser; (schools) être en vacances. **breakable** adj fragile. **breakage** n casse f.

breakdown n (Tech) panne f; (Med) dépression f; (of figures) analyse f. ● adj (Auto) de dépannage.

breakfast n petit déjeuner m.

break: **~-in** n cambriolage m. **~through** n percée f.

breast n sein m; (chest) poitrine f. **~-feed** vt (pt **-fed**) allaiter. **~-stroke** n brasse f.

breath n souffle m, haleine f; **out of ~** à bout de souffle; **under one's ~** tout bas.

breathalyser® n alcootest m.

breathe vt/i respirer. □ **~ in** inspirer; **~ out** expirer.

breathless adj à bout de souffle.

breathtaking adj à vous couper le souffle.

bred ⇒BREED.

breed vt (pt **bred**) élever; (give rise to) engendrer. ● vi se reproduire. ● n race f.

breeze n brise f.

brew vt (beer) brasser; (tea) faire infuser. ● vi (beer) fermenter; (tea) infuser; (fig) se préparer. ● n décoction f. **brewer** n brasseur m. **brewery** n brasserie f.

bribe n pot-de-vin m. ● vt soudoyer. **bribery** n corruption f.

brick n brique f. **~layer** n maçon m.

bridal adj (dress) de mariée; (car, chamber) des mariés.

bride n mariée f. **~groom** n marié m. **~smaid** n demoiselle f d'honneur.

bridge n pont m; (Naut) passerelle f; (of nose) arête f; (card game) bridge m. ● vt **~ a gap** combler une lacune.

bridle n bride f. ● vt brider. **~-path** n piste f cavalière.

brief adj bref. ● n instructions fpl; (Jur) dossier m. ● vt donner des instructions à.

briefcase n serviette f.

briefs npl slip m.

bright adj brillant, vif; (day, room) clair; (cheerful) gai; (clever) intelligent.

brighten vt égayer. ● vi (weather) s'éclaircir; (face) s'éclairer.

brilliant adj (student, career) brillant; (light) éclatant; (very good ⚀) super.

brim n bord m. ● vi (pt **brimmed**); **~ over** déborder (**with** de).

bring vt (pt **brought**) (thing) apporter; (person, vehicle) amener; **~ to bear** (pressure etc.) exercer. □ **~**

about provoquer; ∼ **back** (return with) rapporter; (*colour, shine*) redonner; ∼ **down** faire tomber; (shoot down, knock down) abattre; ∼ **forward** avancer; ∼ **off** réussir; ∼ **out** (take out) sortir; (show) faire ressortir; (book) publier; ∼ **round** faire revenir à soi; ∼ **up** (*child*) élever; (Med) vomir; (*question*) aborder.

brink *n* bord *m*.

brisk *adj* vif.

bristle *n* poil *m*. ● *vi* se hérisser; bristling with hérissé de.

Britain *n* Grande-Bretagne *f*.

British *adj* britannique; the ∼ les Britanniques *mpl*.

Briton *n* Britannique *mf*.

Brittany *n* Bretagne *f*.

brittle *adj* fragile.

broad *adj* large; (*choice, range*) grand. ∼ **bean** *n* fève.

broadcast *vt/i* (*pt* **broadcast**) diffuser; (person) parler à la télévision *or* à la radio. ● *n* émission *f*.

broadly *adv* en gros.

broad-minded *adj* large d'esprit.

broccoli *n inv* brocoli *m*.

brochure *n* brochure *f*.

broke ⇒BREAK. ● *adj* (penniless ✖) fauché.

broken ⇒BREAK. ● *adj* ∼ English mauvais anglais *m*.

bronchitis *n* bronchite *f*.

bronze *n* bronze *m*. ● *vt/i* (se) bronzer.

brooch *n* broche *f*.

brood *n* nichée *f*, couvée *f*. ● *vi* (*bird*) couver; (fig) méditer tristement.

broom *n* balai *m*.

broth *n* bouillon *m*.

brothel *n* maison *f* close.

brother *n* frère *m*. ∼**hood** *n* fraternité *f*. ∼**-in-law** *n* (*pl* ∼**s-in-law**) beau-frère *m*.

brought ⇒BRING.

brow *n* front *m*; (of hill) sommet *m*.

brown *adj* (*object*) marron; (*hair*) brun; ∼ **bread** pain *m* complet; ∼ **sugar** sucre *m* roux. ● *n* marron *m*;

brun *m*. ● *vt/i* brunir; (Culin) (faire) dorer.

Brownie *n* jeannette *f*.

browse *vi* flâner; (*animal*) brouter. ● *vt* (Comput) naviguer. **browser** *n* (Comput) navigateur *m*.

bruise *n* bleu *m*. ● *vt* (*knee, arm etc.*) faire un bleu à; (*fruit*) abîmer.

brush *n* brosse *f*; (skirmish) accrochage *m*; (bushes) broussailles *fpl*. ● *vt* brosser. □ ∼ **against** frôler; ∼ **aside** (dismiss) repousser; (move) écarter; ∼ **up (on)** se remettre à.

Brussels *n* Bruxelles. ∼ **sprouts** *npl* choux *mpl* de Bruxelles.

brutal *adj* brutal.

brute *n* brute *f*; **by** ∼ **force** par la force.

bubble *n* bulle *f*; **blow** ∼s faire des bulles. ● *vi* bouillonner; ∼ **over** déborder. ∼ **bath** *n* bain *m* moussant.

buck *n* mâle *m*; (US, ✖) dollar *m*; **pass the** ∼ rejeter la responsabilité (to sur). ● *vi* (*horse*) ruer; ∼ **up** ✖ prendre courage; (hurry ✖) se grouiller 🇫.

bucket *n* seau *m* (of de).

buckle *n* boucle *f*. ● *vt/i* (fasten) (se) boucler; (bend) voiler. □ ∼ **down to** s'atteler à.

bud *n* bourgeon *m*. ● *vi* (*pt* **budded**) bourgeonner.

Buddhism *n* bouddhisme *m*.

budding *adj* (*talent*) naissant; (*athlete*) en herbe.

budge *vt/i* (faire) bouger.

budgerigar *n* perruche *f*.

budget *n* budget *m*. ● *vi* ∼ **for** prévoir (dans son budget).

buff *n* (colour) chamois *m*; 🇫 fanatique *mf*.

buffalo *n* (*pl* **-oes** or **-o**) buffle *m*; (US) bison *m*.

buffer *n* tampon *m*; ∼ **zone** zone *f* tampon.

buffet¹ *n* (meal, counter) buffet *m*; ∼ **car** buffet *m*.

buffet² *n* (blow) soufflet *m*. ● *vt* (*pt* **buffeted**) souffleter.

bug *n* (bedbug) punaise *f*; (any small insect) bestiole *f*; (germ) microbe *m*;

(stomachache 🇹) ennuis *mpl*
gastriques; (device) micro *m*; (defect)
défaut *m*; (Comput) bogue *f*, bug *m*.
● *vt* (*pt* **bugged**) mettre des micros
dans; 🇽 embêter.

buggy *n* poussette *f*.

build *vt/i* (*pt* **built**) bâtir, construire.
● *n* carrure *f*. □ ~ **up** (increase)
augmenter, monter; (accumulate) (s')
accumuler. **builder** *n* entrepreneur
m en bâtiment; (workman) ouvrier *m*
du bâtiment.

building *n* (structure) bâtiment *m*;
(dwelling) immeuble *m*. ~ **society** *n*
caisse *f* d'épargne.

build-up *n* accumulation *f*; (fig)
publicité *f*.

built ⇒BUILD.

built-in *adj* encastré.

built-up area *adj* agglomération *f*,
zone *f* urbanisée.

bulb *n* (Bot) bulbe *m*; (Electr) ampoule
f.

Bulgaria *n* Bulgarie *f*.

Bulgarian *n* (person) Bulgare *mf*;
(Ling) bulgare *m*. ● *adj* bulgare.

bulge *n* renflement *m*. ● *vi* se
renfler, être renflé; **be bulging with**
être gonflé *or* bourré de.

bulimia *n* boulimie *f*.

bulk *n* volume *f*; **in** ~ (buy, sell) en
gros; (transport) en vrac; **the** ~ **of** la
majeure partie de.

bull *n* taureau *m*. ~**dog** *n*
bouledogue *m*. ~**doze** *vt* raser au
bulldozer.

bullet *n* balle *f*.

bulletin *n* bulletin *m*.

bullet-proof *adj* (vest) pare-balles
inv; (vehicle) blindé.

bullfight *n* corrida *f*.

bullion *n* or *m* or argent *m* en
lingots.

bullring *n* arène *f*.

bull's-eye *n* mille *m*.

bully *n* (child) petite brute *f*; (adult)
tyran *m*. ● *vt* maltraiter.

bum *n* 🇽 derrière *m* 🇹; (US, 🇽)
vagabond/-e *m/f*.

bumble-bee *n* bourdon *m*.

bump *n* (swelling) bosse *f*; (on road)
bosse *f*. ● *vt/i* cogner, heurter. □ ~

along cahoter; ~ **into** (hit) rentrer
dans; (meet) tomber sur.

bumper *n* pare-chocs *m inv*. ● *adj*
exceptionnel.

bumpy *adj* (road) accidenté.

bun *n* (cake) petit pain *m*; (hair)
chignon *m*.

bunch *n* (of flowers) bouquet *m*; (of
keys) trousseau *m*; (of people) groupe
m; (of bananas) régime *m*; ~ **of grapes**
grappe *f* de raisin.

bundle *n* paquet *m*. ● *vt* mettre en
paquet; (push) fourrer.

bung *n* bouchon *m*. ● *vt* (stop up)
boucher; (throw 🇽) flanquer 🇹.

bunion *n* (Med) oignon *m*.

bunk *n* (on ship, train) couchette *f*.
~**-beds** *npl* lits *mpl* superposés.

buoy *n* bouée *f*. ● *vt* ~ **up** (hearten)
soutenir, encourager.

buoyancy *n* (of floating object)
flottabilité *f*; (cheerfulness) gaieté *f*.

burden *n* fardeau *m*. ● *vt* ennuyer
(with de).

bureau *n* (*pl* **-eaux**) bureau *m*.

bureaucracy *n* bureaucratie *f*.

burglar *n* cambrioleur *m*; ~ **alarm**
alarme *f*. **burglarize** *vt* (US)
cambrioler. **burglary** *n* cambriolage
m. **burgle** *vt* cambrioler.

Burgundy *n* (wine) bourgogne *m*.

burial *n* enterrement *m*.

burn *vt/i* (*pt* **burned** *or* **burnt**)
brûler. ● *n* brûlure *f*. □ ~ **down**
être réduit en cendres. **burning** *adj*
en flammes; (fig) brûlant.

burnt ⇒BURN.

burp *n* 🇹 rot *m*. ● *vi* 🇹 roter.

burrow *n* terrier *m*. ● *vt* creuser.

bursar *n* intendant/-e *m/f*. **bursary**
n bourse *f*.

burst *vt/i* (*pt* **burst**) (balloon,
bubble) crever; (pipe) (faire) éclater.
● *n* explosion *f*; (of laughter) éclat *m*;
(surge) élan *m*. □ ~ **into** (room) faire
interruption dans; ~ **into tears**
fondre en larmes; ~ **out** ~ **out**
laughing éclater de rire; ~ **with** be
~**ing with** déborder de.

bury *vt* (person etc.) enterrer; (hide,
cover) enfouir; (engross, thrust) plonger.

bus n (pl **buses**) (auto)bus m. ● vt transporter en bus. ● vi (pt **bussed**) prendre l'autobus.

bush n (shrub) buisson m; (land) brousse f.

business n (task, concern) affaire f; (commerce) affaires fpl; (line of work) métier m; (shop) commerce m; **he has no ~ to** il n'a pas le droit de; **mean ~** être sérieux; **that's none of your ~!** ça ne vous regarde pas! **~like** adj sérieux. **~man** n homme m d'affaires.

busker n musicien/-ne m/f des rues.

bus-stop n arrêt m d'autobus.

bust n (statue) buste m; (bosom) poitrine f. ● vt/i (pt **busted** or **bust**) (burst ▣) crever; (break ▣) (se) casser. ● adj (broken, finished ▣) fichu; **go ~** ▣ faire faillite.

bustle vi s'affairer. ● n affairement m, remue-ménage m.

busy adj (**-ier**, **-iest**) (person) occupé; (street) animé; (day) chargé. ● vt **~ oneself with** s'occuper à.

but conj mais. ● prep sauf; **~ for** sans; **nobody ~** personne d'autre que; **nothing ~** rien que. ● adv (only) seulement.

butcher n boucher m. ● vt massacrer.

butler n maître m d'hôtel.

butt n (of gun) crosse f; (of cigarette) mégot m; (of joke) cible f; (barrel) tonneau m; (US, ▣) derrière m ▣. ● vi **~ in** interrompre.

butter n beurre m. ● vt beurrer. **~-bean** n haricot m blanc. **~cup** n bouton-d'or m.

butterfly n papillon m.

buttock n fesse f.

button n bouton m. ● vt/i **~ (up)** (se) boutonner.

buttonhole n boutonnière f. ● vt accrocher.

buy vt (pt **bought**) acheter (from à); **~ sth for sb** acheter qch à qn, prendre qch pour qn; (believe ▣) croire, avaler.

buzz n bourdonnement m. ● vi bourdonner. **buzzer** n sonnerie f.

by prep par, de; (near) à côté de; (before) avant; (means) en, à, par; **~ bike** à vélo; **~ car** en auto; **~ day** de jour; **~ the kilo** au kilo; **~ running** en courant; **~ sea** par mer; **~ that time** à ce moment-là; **~ the way** à propos; **~ oneself** tout seul. ● adv **close ~** tout près; **~ and large** dans l'ensemble.

bye(-bye) interj ▣ au revoir, salut ▣.

by-election n élection f partielle.

Byelorussia n Biélorussie f.

by-law n arrêté m municipal.

bypass n (Auto) rocade f; (Med) pontage m. ● vt contourner.

by-product n dérivé m; (fig) conséquence f.

byte n octet m.

Cc

cab n taxi m; (of lorry, train) cabine f.

cabbage n chou m.

cabin n (hut) cabane f; (in ship, aircraft) cabine f.

cabinet n petit placard m; (glass-fronted) vitrine f; (Pol) cabinet m.

cable n câble m. ● vt câbler. **~-car** n téléphérique m. **~ television** n télévision f par câble.

cache n (hoard) cache f; (place) cachette f.

cackle n (of hen) caquet m; (laugh) ricanement m. ● vi caqueter; (laugh) ricaner.

cactus n (pl **-ti** or **~es**) cactus m.

cadet n élève m officier.

Caesarean adj **~ (section)** césarienne f.

café n café m, snack-bar m.

caffeine n caféine f.

cage n cage f. ● vt mettre en cage.

cagey adj réticent.

cagoule n K-way® m.

cajole vt **~ sb into doing sth** amener qn à faire qch par la cajolerie.

cake n gâteau m; (of soap) pain m. ● vi former une croûte (**on** sur).

calculate *vt* calculer; (estimate) évaluer. **calculated** *adj* délibéré; (*risk*) calculé. **calculating** *adj* calculateur. **calculation** *n* calcul *m*. **calculator** *n* calculatrice *f*.

calculus *n* (*pl* **-li** *or* ~**es**) calcul *m*.

calendar *n* calendrier *m*.

calf *n* (*pl* **calves**) (young cow or bull) veau *m*; (of leg) mollet *m*.

calibre *n* calibre *m*.

call *vt/i* appeler; (loudly) crier; **he's ~ed John** il s'appelle John; ~ **sb stupid** traiter qn d'imbécile. ● *n* appel *m*; (of bird) cri *m*; (visit) visite *f*; **make/pay a ~ on** rendre visite à; **be on ~** être de garde; ~ **box** cabine *f* téléphonique. □ ~ **back** rappeler; (visit) repasser; ~ **for** (*help*) appeler à; (demand) demander; (require) exiger; (collect) passer prendre; ~ **in** passer; ~ **off** annuler; ~ **on** (visit) rendre visite à; (urge) demander à (**to do** de faire); ~ **out** (to) appeler; ~ **round** venir; ~ **up** appeler.

calling *n* vocation *f*.

callous *adj* inhumain.

calm *adj* calme. ● *n* calme *m*. ● *vt/i* ~ (**down**) (se) calmer.

calorie *n* calorie *f*.

camcorder *n* caméscope® *m*.

came ⇒COME.

camel *n* chameau *m*.

camera *n* appareil(-photo) *m*; (TV, cinema) caméra *f*; **in ~** à huis clos. ~**man** *n* (*pl* -**men**) cadreur *m*, cameraman *m*.

camouflage *n* camouflage *m*. ● *vt* camoufler.

camp *n* camp *m*. ● *vi* camper.

campaign *n* campagne *f*. ● *vi* faire campagne.

camper *n* campeur/-euse *m/f*. ~(-**van**) *n* camping-car *m*.

camping *n* camping *m*; **go ~** faire du camping.

campsite *n* camping *m*.

campus *n* (*pl* ~**es**) campus *m*.

infinitive **be able to**; *present* **can**; *present negative* **can't**, **cannot**

(formal); *past* **could**; *past participle* **been able to**

● *auxiliary verb*

····▸ pouvoir; **where ~ I buy stamps?** où est-ce que je peux acheter des timbres?; **she can't come** elle ne peut pas venir.

····▸ (be allowed to) pouvoir; ~ **I smoke?** est-ce que je peux fumer?

····▸ (know how to) savoir; **she ~ swim** elle sait nager; **he can't drive** il ne sait pas conduire.

····▸ (with verbs of perception) **I ~ hear you** je t'entends; ~ **they see us?** est-ce qu'ils nous voient?

can² *n* (for food) boîte *f*; (of petrol) bidon *m*. ● *vt* (*pt* **canned**) mettre en conserve.

Canada *n* Canada *m*.

Canadian *n* Canadien/-ne *m/f*. ● *adj* canadien.

canal *n* canal *m*.

canary *n* canari *m*.

cancel *vt/i* (*pt* **cancelled**) (call off, revoke) annuler; (cross out) barrer; (a stamp) oblitérer; ~ **out** (se) neutraliser. **cancellation** *n* annulation *f*.

cancer *n* cancer *m*; **have ~** avoir un cancer.

Cancer *n* Cancer *m*.

cancerous *adj* cancéreux.

candid *adj* franc.

candidate *n* candidat/-e *m/f*.

candle *n* bougie *f*; (in church) cierge *m*. ~**stick** *n* bougeoir *m*.

candy *n* (US) bonbon(s) *m(pl)*. ~-**floss** *n* barbe *f* à papa.

cane *n* canne *f*; (for baskets) rotin *m*; (for punishment) badine *f*. ● *vt* donner des coups de badine à.

canister *n* boîte *f*.

cannabis *n* cannabis *m*.

cannibal *n* cannibale *mf*.

cannon *n* (*pl* ~ *or* ~**s**) canon *m*. ~-**ball** *n* boulet *m* de canon.

cannot = CAN NOT.

canoe *n* canoë *m*. ● *vi* faire du canoë. **canoeist** *n* canoéiste *mf*.

canon *n* (clergyman) chanoine *m*; (rule) canon *m*.

can-opener *n* ouvre-boîtes *m inv.*

canopy *n* dais *m*; (for bed) baldaquin *m.*

can't = CAN NOT.

canteen *n* (restaurant) cantine *f*; (flask) bidon *m.*

canter *n* petit galop *m.* ● *vi* aller au petit galop.

canvas *n* toile *f.*

canvass *vt/i* (Comm, Pol) faire du démarchage (auprès de); ~ **opinion** sonder l'opinion.

canyon *n* cañon *m.*

cap *n* (hat) casquette *f*; (of bottle, tube) bouchon *m*; (of beer or milk bottle) capsule *f*; (of pen) capuchon *m*; (for toy gun) amorce *f.* ● *vt* (*pt* **capped**) couronner.

capability *n* capacité *f.*

capable *adj* (person) compétent; ~ **of doing** capable de faire.

capacity *n* capacité *f*; **in my ~ as a doctor** en ma qualité de médecin.

cape *n* (cloak) cape *f*; (Geog) cap *m.*

caper *vi* gambader. ● *n* (leap) cabriole *f*; (funny film) comédie *f*; (Culin) câpre *f.*

capital *adj* (*letter*) majuscule; (*offence*) capital. ● *n* (town) capitale *f*; (money) capital *m*; ~ (**letter**) majuscule *f.*

capitalism *n* capitalisme *m.*

capitalize *vi* ~ **on** tirer parti de.

capitulate *vi* capituler.

Capricorn *n* Capricorne *m.*

capsize *vt/i* (faire) chavirer.

capsule *n* capsule *f.*

captain *n* capitaine *m.*

caption *n* (under photo) légende *f*; (subtitle) sous-titre *m.*

captivate *vt* captiver.

captive *a & n* captif/-ive (*m/f*). **captivity** *n* captivité *f.*

capture *vt* (*person, animal*) capturer; (*moment, likeness*) saisir. ● *n* capture *f.*

car *n* voiture *f.* ● *adj* (*industry, insurance*) automobile; (*accident, phone*) de voiture; (*journey, chase*) en voiture.

caravan *n* caravane *f.*

carbohydrate *n* hydrate *m* de carbone.

carbon *n* carbone *m.*

carburettor *n* carburateur *m.*

card *n* carte *f.*

cardboard *n* carton *m.*

cardiac *adj* cardiaque; ~ **arrest** arrêt *m* du cœur.

cardigan *n* cardigan *m.*

cardinal *adj* (sin) capital; (rule) fondamental; (*number*) cardinal. ● *n* cardinal *m.*

card-index *n* fichier *m.*

care *n* (attention) soin *m*, attention *f*; (worry) souci *m*; (looking after) soins *mpl*; **take ~ of** (deal with) s'occuper de; (be careful with) prendre soin de; **take ~ to do sth** faire bien attention à faire qch. ● *vi* ~ **about** s'intéresser à; ~ **for** s'occuper de; (invalid) soigner; ~ **to do** vouloir faire; **I don't ~** ça m'est égal.

career *n* carrière *f.* ● *vi* ~ **in/out** entrer/sortir à toute vitesse.

carefree *adj* insouciant.

careful *adj* prudent; (*research, study*) méticuleux; (**be**) ~! (fais) attention! **carefully** *adv* avec soin; (cautiously) prudemment.

careless *adj* négligent; (work) bâclé.

caress *n* caresse *f.* ● *vt* caresser.

caretaker *n* concierge *mf.* ● *adj* (*president*) par intérim.

car ferry *n* ferry *m.*

cargo *n* (*pl* ~**es**) chargement *m*; (Naut) cargaison *f.*

Caribbean *adj* des Caraïbes, des Antilles. ● *n* **the** ~ (sea) la mer des Antilles; (islands) les Antilles *fpl.*

caring *adj* affectueux. ● *n* affection *f.*

carnal *adj* charnel.

carnation *n* œillet *m.*

carnival *n* carnaval *m.*

carol *n* chant *m* de Noël.

carp *n inv* carpe *f.* ● *vi* maugréer.

car-park *n* parc *m* de stationnement, parking *m.*

carpenter *n* (joiner) menuisier *m*; (builder) charpentier *m.* **carpentry** *n* menuiserie *f*; (structural) charpenterie *f.*

carpet *n* (fitted) moquette *f*; (loose) tapis *m.* ● *vt* (*pt* **carpeted**) mettre de la moquette dans.

carriage n (rail) wagon m; (ceremonial) carrosse m; (of goods) transport m; (cost) port m.

carriageway n chaussée f.

carrier n transporteur m; (Med) porteur/-euse m/f; ~ (bag) sac m en plastique.

carrot n carotte f.

carry vt/i porter; (goods) transporter; (involve) comporter; (motion) voter; **be carried away** s'emballer. □ ~ **off** emporter; (prize) remporter; ~ **on** (continue) continuer; (business) conduire; (conversation) mener; ~ **out** (order, plan) exécuter; (duty) remplir; (experiment, operation, repair) effectuer. ~**-cot** n porte-bébé m.

car sharing n covoiturage m.

cart n charrette f. ● vt (heavy bag 🔳) trimballer 🔳.

carton n (box) boîte f; (of yoghurt, cream) pot m; (of cigarettes) cartouche f.

cartoon n dessin m humoristique; (cinema) dessin m animé; (strip cartoon) bande f dessinée.

cartridge n cartouche f.

carve vt tailler; (meat) découper.

car-wash n lavage m automatique.

cascade n cascade f. ● vi tomber en cascade.

case n cas m; (Jur) affaire f; (suitcase) valise f; (crate) caisse f; (for spectacles) étui m; (just) in ~ au cas où; in ~ he comes au cas où il viendrait; in ~ of fire en cas d'incendie; in any ~ de toute façon; the ~ for sth les arguments mpl en faveur de qch; the ~ for the defence la défense.

cash n espèces fpl, argent m; in ~ en espèces. ● adj (price) comptant. ● vt encaisser; ~ **in** (on) profiter (de). ~ **desk** n caisse f. ~ **dispenser** n distributeur m de billets.

cashew n cajou m.

cash-flow n marge f brute d'autofinancement.

cashier n caissier/-ière m/f.

cashmere n cachemire m.

cash: ~ **point** n distributeur m de billets. ~ **point card** n carte f de retrait. ~ **register** n caisse f enregistreuse.

casino n casino m.

casket n (box) coffret m; (coffin) cercueil m.

casserole n (pan) daubière f; (food) ragoût m.

cassette n cassette f.

cast vt (pt **cast**) (object, glance) jeter; (shadow) projeter; (metal) couler; ~ (**off**) (shed) se dépouiller de; ~ **one's vote** voter; ~ **iron** fonte f. ● n (cinema, Theat, TV) distribution f; (mould) moule m; (Med) plâtre m.

castaway n naufragé/-e m/f.

cast-iron adj de fonte; (fig) en béton.

castle n château m; (chess) tour f.

cast-offs npl vieux vêtements mpl.

castor n (wheel) roulette f.

castrate vt châtrer.

casual adj (informal) décontracté; (remark) désinvolte; (acquaintance) de passage; (work) temporaire.

casually adv (remark) d'un air détaché; (dress) simplement.

casualty n victime f; (part of hospital) urgences fpl.

cat n chat m; (feline) félin m.

catalogue n catalogue m. ● vt dresser un catalogue de.

catalyst n catalyseur m.

catalytic adj ~ **converter** pot m catalytique.

catapult n lance-pierres m inv. ● vt projeter.

cataract n (Med, Geog) cataracte f.

catarrh n catarrhe m.

catastrophe n catastrophe f.

catch vt (pt **caught**) attraper; (bus, plane) prendre; (understand) saisir; ~ **sb doing** surprendre qn en train de faire; ~ **fire** prendre feu; ~ **sight of** apercevoir; ~ **sb's attention/eye** attirer l'attention de qn. ● vi (get stuck) se prendre (**in** dans); (start to burn) prendre. ● n (fastening) fermeture f; (drawback) piège m; (in sport) prise f. □ ~ **on** devenir populaire; ~ **out** prendre de court; ~ **up** rattraper son retard; ~ **up with sb** rattraper qn.

catching adj contagieux.

catchment n ~ **area** (School) secteur m.

catch-phrase n formule f favorite.

catchy adj entraînant.

category n catégorie f.

cater vi organiser des réceptions; ~ **for/to** (guests) accueillir; (needs) pourvoir à; (reader) s'adresser à. **caterer** n traiteur m.

caterpillar n chenille f.

cathedral n cathédrale f.

catholic adj éclectique. **Catholic** a & n catholique (mf). **Catholicism** n catholicisme m.

Catseye® n plot m rétroréfléchissant.

cattle npl bétail m.

catty adj méchant.

caught ⇒CATCH.

cauliflower n chou-fleur m.

cause n cause f; (reason) raison f, motif m. ● vt causer; ~ **sth to grow/move** faire pousser/bouger qch.

causeway n chaussée f.

caution n prudence f; (warning) avertissement m. ● vt avertir. **cautious** adj prudent. **cautiously** adv prudemment.

cave n grotte f. ● vi ~ **in** s'effondrer; (agree) céder. ~**man** n (pl -**men**) homme m des cavernes.

cavern n caverne f.

caviare n caviar m.

caving n spéléologie f.

CD abbr (**compact disc**) disque m compact, CD m.

CD-ROM n disque m optique compact, CD-ROM m.

cease vt/i cesser. ~-**fire** n cessez-le-feu m inv.

cedar n cèdre m.

cedilla n cédille f.

ceiling n plafond m.

celebrate vt (occasion) fêter; (Easter, mass) célébrer. ● vi faire la fête. **celebrated** adj célèbre. **celebration** n fête f.

celebrity n célébrité f.

celery n céleri m.

cell n cellule f; (Electr) élément m.

cellar n cave f.

cellist n violoncelliste mf. **cello** n violoncelle m.

Celt n Celte mf.

cement n ciment m. ● vt cimenter. ~-**mixer** n bétonnière f.

cemetery n cimetière m.

censor n censeur m. ● vt censurer.

censure n censure f. ● vt critiquer.

census n recensement m.

cent n (coin) cent m.

centenary n centenaire m.

centigrade adj centigrade.

centilitre, (US) **centiliter** n centilitre m.

centimetre, (US) **centimeter** n centimètre m.

centipede n millepattes m inv.

central adj central; ~ **heating** chauffage m central; ~ **locking** fermeture f centralisée des portes. **centralize** vt centraliser. **centrally** adv (situated) au centre.

centre, (US) **center** n centre m. ● vt (pt **centred**) centrer. ● vi ~ **on** tourner autour de.

century n siècle m.

ceramic adj (art) céramique; (object) en céramique.

cereal n céréale f.

ceremonial adj (dress) de cérémonie. ● n cérémonial m. **ceremony** n cérémonie f.

certain adj certain; for ~ avec certitude; make ~ of s'assurer de. **certainly** adv certainement. **certainty** n certitude f.

certificate n certificat m.

certify vt certifier.

cesspit, **cesspool** n fosse f d'aisances.

chafe vt/i frotter (contre).

chagrin n dépit m.

chain n chaîne f; ~ **reaction** réaction f en chaîne; ~ **store** magasin m à succursales multiples. ● vt enchaîner. ~-**smoke** vi fumer sans arrêt.

chair n chaise f; (armchair) fauteuil m; (Univ) chaire f; (chairperson) président/-e m/f. ● vt (preside over) présider. ~**man** n (pl -**men**) président/-e m/f. ~**woman** n (pl -**women**) présidente f.

chalk n craie f.

challenge n défi m; (opportunity) challenge m. ● vt (summon) défier (**to do** de faire); (question truth of) contester. **challenger** n (Sport)

challenger m. **challenging** adj
stimulant.

chamber n (old use) chambre f.
~**maid** n femme f de chambre. ~
music n musique f de chambre.
~**-pot** n pot m de chambre.

champagne n champagne m.

champion n champion/-ne m/f. ● vt
défendre. **championship** n
championnat m.

chance n (luck) hasard m; (opportunity)
occasion f; (likelihood) chances fpl;
(risk) risque m; **by** ~ par hasard; **by
any** ~ par hasard; ~**s are that** il est
probable que. ● adj fortuit. ● vt ~
doing prendre le risque de faire; ~ **it**
tenter sa chance.

chancellor n chancelier m; **C**~ **of
the Exchequer** Chancelier de
l'Échiquier.

chandelier n lustre m.

change vt (alter) changer; (exchange)
échanger (**for** contre); (money)
changer; ~ **trains/one's dress**
changer de train/de robe; ~ **one's
mind** changer d'avis. ● vi changer;
(change clothes) se changer; ~ **into** se
transformer en; ~ **over** passer (**to** à).
● n changement m; (money) monnaie
f; **a** ~ **for the better** une
amélioration; **a** ~ **for the worse** un
changement en pire; **a** ~ **of clothes**
des vêtements de rechange; **for a** ~
pour changer. **changeable** adj
changeant. **changing room** n (in
shop) cabine f d'essayage; (Sport)
vestiaire m.

channel n (for liquid, information) canal
m; (TV) chaîne f; (groove) rainure f.
● vt (pt **channelled**) canaliser. **C**~
n **the (English) C**~ la Manche; **the
C**~ **tunnel** le tunnel sous la Manche;
the C~ **Islands** les îles fpl Anglo-
Normandes.

chant n (Relig) mélopée f; (of
demonstrators) chant m scandé. ● vt/i
scander; (Relig) psalmodier.

chaos n chaos m.

chap n (man 🇬🇧) type m 🇬🇧.

chapel n chapelle f.

chaplain n aumônier m.

chapped adj gercé.

chapter n chapitre m.

char vt (pt **charred**) carboniser.

character n caractère m; (in novel,
play) personnage m; **of good** ~ de
bonne réputation.

characteristic a & n
caractéristique (f).

charcoal n charbon m de bois; (art)
fusain m.

charge n (fee) frais mpl; (Mil) charge
f; (Jur) inculpation f; (task, custody)
charge f; **in** ~ **of** responsable de; **take**
~ **of** prendre en charge, se charger
de. ● vt (customer) faire payer;
(enemy, gun) charger; (Jur) inculper
(**with** de); ~ **£20 an hour** prendre 20
livres de l'heure; ~ **card** carte f
d'achat. ● vi faire payer; (bull)
foncer; (person) se précipiter.

charisma n charisme m.
charismatic adj charismatique.

charitable adj charitable. **charity**
n charité f; (organization) organisation
f caritative.

charm n charme m; (trinket) amulette
f. ● vt charmer. **charming** adj
charmant.

chart n (graph) graphique m; (table)
tableau m; (map) carte f. ● vt (route)
porter sur la carte.

charter n charte f; ~ (**flight**) charter
m. ● vt affréter; ~**ed accountant**
expert-comptable m.

chase vt poursuivre; ~ **away** or **off**
chasser. ● vi courir (**after** après). ● n
chasse f.

chassis n châssis m.

chastise vt châtier.

chastity n chasteté f.

chat n conversation f; **have a** ~
bavarder; ~ **show** talk-show m; ~
mode (Internet) mode m causerie. ● vi
(pt **chatted**) bavarder. □ ~ **up**
🇬🇧 draguer 🇬🇧.

chatter n bavardage m. ● vi
bavarder; **his teeth are** ~**ing** il
claque des dents. ~**box** n bavard/-e
m/f.

chatty adj bavard.

chauffeur n chauffeur m.

chauvinist n chauvin/-e m/f;
macho m.

cheap adj bon marché inv; (fare,
rate) réduit; (joke, gimmick) facile;
~**er** meilleur marché inv. **cheapen**

vt déprécier. **cheaply** *adv* à bas prix. **cheapness** *n* bas prix *m*.

cheat *vi* tricher. ● *vt* tromper. ● *n* tricheur/-euse *m/f*.

check *vt/i* vérifier; (*tickets, rises, inflation*) contrôler; (stop) arrêter; (tick off: US) cocher. ● *n* contrôle *m*; (curb) frein *m*; (chess) échec *m*; (pattern) carreaux *mpl*; (bill: US) addition *f*; (cheque: US) chèque *m*. □ ∼ **in** remplir la fiche; (at airport) enregistrer; ∼ **out** partir; ∼ **sth out** vérifier qch; ∼ **up** vérifier; ∼ **up on** (*story*) vérifier; (*person*) faire une enquête sur.

check: ∼**-in** *n* enregistrement *m*. **checking account** *n* (US) compte *m* courant. ∼**-list** *n* liste *f* de contrôle. ∼**mate** *n* échec *m* et mat. ∼**-out** *n* caisse *f*. ∼**-point** *n* contrôle *m*. ∼**-up** *n* examen *m* médical.

cheek *n* joue *f*; (impudence) culot *m* ⊞. **cheeky** *adj* effronté.

cheer *n* gaieté *f*; ∼s acclamations *fpl*; (when drinking) à la vôtre. ● *vt/i* applaudir; ∼ **sb** (**up**) (gladden) remonter le moral à qn; ∼ **up** prendre courage. **cheerful** *adj* joyeux. **cheerfulness** *n* gaieté *f*.

cheerio *interj* ⊞ salut ⊞.

cheese *n* fromage *m*.

cheetah *n* guépard *m*.

chef *n* chef *m*.

chemical *adj* chimique. ● *n* produit *m* chimique.

chemist *n* pharmacien/-ne *m/f*; (scientist) chimiste *mf*; ∼'s (**shop**) pharmacie *f*. **chemistry** *n* chimie *f*.

cheque *n* chèque *m*. ∼**-book** *n* chéquier *m*. ∼ **card** *n* carte *f* bancaire.

chequered *adj* (pattern) à damiers; (fig) en dents de scie.

cherish *vt* chérir; (hope) caresser.

cherry *n* cerise *f*; (tree, wood) cerisier *m*.

chess *n* échecs *mpl*. ∼**-board** *n* échiquier *m*.

chest *n* (Anat) poitrine *f*; (box) coffre *m*; ∼ **of drawers** commode *f*.

chestnut *n* (nut) marron *m*, châtaigne *f*; (tree) marronnier *m*; (sweet) châtaignier *m*.

chew *vt* mâcher.

chic *adj* chic *inv*.

chick *n* poussin *m*.

chicken *n* poulet *m*. ● *adj* ⊠ froussard. ● *vi* ∼ **out** ⊠ se dégonfler. ∼**-pox** *n* varicelle *f*.

chick-pea *n* pois *m* chiche.

chicory *n* (for salad) endive *f*; (in coffee) chicorée *f*.

chief *n* chef *m*. ● *adj* principal. **chiefly** *adv* principalement.

chilblain *n* engelure *f*.

child *n* (*pl* **children**) enfant *mf*. ∼**birth** *n* accouchement *m*. **childhood** *n* enfance *f*. **childish** *adj* puéril. **childless** *adj* sans enfants. **childlike** *adj* enfantin. ∼**-minder** *n* nourrice *f*.

Chile *n* Chili *m*.

chill *n* froid *m*; (Med) refroidissement *m*. ● *adj* froid. ● *vt* (person) faire frissonner; (wine) rafraîchir; (food) mettre à refroidir.

chilli *n* (*pl* ∼**es**) piment *m*.

chilly *adj* froid; **it's** ∼ il fait froid.

chime *n* carillon *m*. ● *vt/i* carillonner.

chimney *n* cheminée *f*. ∼**-sweep** *n* ramoneur *m*.

chimpanzee *n* chimpanzé *m*.

chin *n* menton *m*.

china *n* porcelaine *f*.

China *n* Chine *f*.

Chinese *n* (person) Chinois/-e *m/f*; (Ling) chinois *m*. ● *adj* chinois.

chip *n* (on plate) ébréchure *f*; (piece) éclat *m*; (of wood) copeau *m*; (Culin) frite *f*; (Comput) puce *f*; (**potato**) ∼s (US) chips *fpl*. ● *vt/i* (*pt* **chipped**) (s')ébrécher; ∼ **in** ⊞ dire son mot; (with money) contribuer.

chiropodist *n* pédicure *mf*.

chirp *n* pépiement *m*. ● *vi* pépier. **chirpy** *adj* gai.

chisel *n* ciseau *m*. ● *vt* (*pt* **chiselled**) ciseler.

chit *n* note *f*; (voucher) bon *m*.

chitchat *n* ⊞ bavardage *m*.

chivalrous *adj* galant.

chives *npl* ciboulette *f*.

chlorine *n* chlore *m*.

choc-ice *n* esquimau *m*.

chock-a-block *adj* plein à craquer.

chocolate *n* chocolat *m*.

choice *n* choix *m*. ● *adj* de choix.

choir *n* chœur *m*. ~**boy** *n* jeune choriste *m*.

choke *vt/i* (s')étrangler; ~ (up) boucher. ● *n* starter *m*.

cholesterol *n* cholestérol *m*.

choose *vt/i* (*pt* **chose**; *pp* **chosen**) choisir; ~ to do décider de faire. **choosy** *adj* difficile.

chop *vt/i* (*pt* **chopped**) (*wood*) couper; (*food*) hacher; **chopping board** planche *f* à découper; ~ **down** abattre. ● *n* (meat) côtelette *f*. **chopper** *n* hachoir *m*; Ⓘ hélico *m* Ⓘ.

choppy *adj* (*sea*) agité.

chopstick *n* baguette *f* (*chinoise*).

chord *n* (Mus) accord *m*.

chore *n* (routine) tâche *f*; (*unpleasant*) corvée *f*.

chortle *n* gloussement *m*. ● *vi* glousser.

chorus *n* chœur *m*; (of song) refrain *m*.

chose, chosen ⇨CHOOSE.

Christ *n* le Christ.

christen *vt* baptiser. **christening** *n* baptême *m*.

Christian *a* & *n* chrétien/-ne (*m/f*); ~ name nom *m* de baptême. **Christianity** *n* christianisme *m*.

Christmas *n* Noël *m*; ~ Day/Eve le jour/la veille de Noël. ● *adj* (*card, tree*) de Noël.

chronic *adj* (*situation, disease*) chronique; (bad Ⓘ) nul.

chronicle *n* chronique *f*.

chronological *adj* chronologique.

chrysanthemum *n* chrysanthème *m*.

chubby *adj* (**-ier, -iest**) potelé.

chuck *vt* Ⓘ lancer; ~ **away** *or* **out** Ⓘ balancer.

chuckle *n* gloussement *m*. ● *vi* glousser.

chuffed *adj* Ⓘ vachement content Ⓘ.

chunk *n* morceau *m*. **chunky** *adj* (*sweater, jewellery*) gros; (*person*) costaud.

church *n* église *f*. ~**goer** *n* pratiquant/-e *m/f*. ~**yard** *n* cimetière *m*.

churn *n* baratte *f*; (milk-can) bidon *m*. ● *vt* baratter; ~ **out** produire en série.

chute *n* toboggan *m*; (for rubbish) vide-ordures *m inv*.

chutney *n* condiment *m* aigre-doux.

cider *n* cidre *m*.

cigar *n* cigare *m*.

cigarette *n* cigarette *f*; ~ **end** mégot *m*.

cinder *n* cendre *f*.

cinema *n* cinéma *m*.

cinnamon *n* cannelle *f*.

circle *n* cercle *m*; (Theat) balcon *m*. ● *vt* (go round) tourner autour de; (word, error) encercler. ● *vi* tourner en rond.

circuit *n* circuit *m*. ~ **board** *n* carte *f* de circuit imprimé. ~**breaker** *n* disjoncteur *m*.

circuitous *adj* indirect.

circular *a* & *n* circulaire (*f*).

circulate *vt/i* (faire) circuler. **circulation** *n* circulation *f*; (of newspaper) tirage *m*.

circumcise *vt* circoncire.

circumference *n* circonférence *f*.

circumflex *n* circonflexe *m*.

circumstance *n* circonstance *f*; ~**s** (financial) situation *f*; **under no** ~**s** en aucun cas.

circus *n* cirque *m*.

cistern *n* réservoir *m*.

citation *n* citation *f*. **cite** *vt* citer.

citizen *n* citoyen/-ne *m/f*; (of town) habitant/-e *m/f*. **citizenship** *n* nationalité *f*.

citrus *adj* ~ **fruit(s)** agrumes *mpl*; ~ **tree** citrus *m*.

city *n* (grande) ville *f*.

civic *adj* (*official*) municipal; (*pride, duty*) civique.

civil *adj* civil. ~ **disobedience** *n* résistance *f* passive. ~ **engineer** *n* ingénieur *m* des travaux publics.

civilian *a* & *n* civil/-e (*m/f*).

civilization *n* civilisation *f*. **civilize** *vt* civiliser.

civil: ~ **law** *n* droit *m* civil. ~ **liberties** *npl* libertés *fpl* individuelles. ~ **rights** *npl* droits *mpl* civils. ~ **servant** *n* fonctionnaire *mf*. ~ **service** *n* fonction *f* publique. ~ **war** *n* guerre *f* civile.

clad *adj* ~ **in** vêtu de.

claim *vt* (demand) revendiquer; (assert) prétendre. ● *n* revendication *f*; (assertion) affirmation *f*; (for insurance) réclamation *f*; (right) droit *m*. **claimant** *n* (of benefits) demandeur/-euse *m/f*.

clairvoyant *n* voyant/-e *m/f*.

clam *n* palourde *f*.

clamber *vi* grimper.

clammy *adj* (**-ier, -iest**) moite.

clamour *n* clameur *f*. ● *vi* ~ **for** réclamer.

clamp *n* valet *m*; (Med) pince *f*; (wheel) ~ sabot *m* de Denver. ● *vt* cramponner; (*jaw*) serrer; (*car*) mettre un sabot de Denver à; ~ **down on** faire de la répression contre.

clan *n* clan *m*.

clang *n* son *m* métallique.

clap *vt/i* (*pt* **clapped**) applaudir; (put forcibly) mettre; ~ **one's hands** frapper dans ses mains. ● *n* applaudissement *m*; (of thunder) coup *m*.

claret *n* bordeaux *m* rouge.

clarification *n* clarification *f*. **clarify** *vt/i* (se) clarifier.

clarinet *n* clarinette *f*.

clarity *n* clarté *f*.

clash *n* choc *m*; (fig) conflit *m*. ● *vi* (*metal objects*) s'entrechoquer; (*armies*) s'affronter; (*interests*) être incompatibles; (*meetings*) avoir lieu en même temps; (*colours*) jurer.

clasp *n* (fastener) fermoir *m*. ● *vt* serrer.

class *n* classe *f*. ● *vt* classer; ~ **sb/ sth as** assimiler qn/qch à.

classic *a & n* classique (*m*); ~**s** (Univ) lettres *fpl* classiques. **classical** *adj* classique.

classified *adj* (*information*) secret; ~ (**ad**) petite annonce *f*.

classroom *n* salle *f* de classe.

clatter *n* cliquetis *m*. ● *vi* cliqueter.

clause *n* clause *f*; (Gram) proposition *f*.

claw *n* (of animal, small bird) griffe *f*; (of bird of prey) serre *f*; (of lobster) pince *f*. ● *vt* griffer.

clay *n* argile *f*.

clean *adj* propre; (shape, stroke) net. ● *adv* complètement. ● *vt* nettoyer; ~ **one's teeth** se brosser les dents. ● *vi* ~ **up** faire le nettoyage.

cleaner *n* (at home) femme *f* de ménage; (industrial) agent *m* de nettoyage; (of clothes) teinturier/-ière *m/f*. **cleanliness** *n* propreté *f*.

cleanly *adv* proprement; (sharply) nettement.

cleanse *vt* nettoyer; (fig) purifier.

clean-shaven *adj* glabre.

clear *adj* (*explanation*) clair; (*need, sign*) évident; (*glass*) transparent; (*profit*) net; (*road*) dégagé; **make sth** ~ être très clair sur qch; ~ **of** (away from) à l'écart de. ● *adv* complètement; **stand** ~ **of** s'éloigner de. ● *vt* (free) dégager (**of** de); (*table*) débarrasser; (*building*) évacuer; (*cheque*) compenser; (jump over) franchir; (*debt*) liquider; (Jur) disculper. ● *vi* (*fog*) se dissiper; (*cheque*) être compensé. □ ~ **away** *or* **off** (remove) enlever; ~ **off** *or* **out** ① décamper; ~ **out** (clean) nettoyer; ~ **up** (tidy) ranger; (*mystery*) éclaircir; (*weather*) s'éclaircir.

clearance *n* (permission) autorisation *f*; (space) espace *m*; ~ **sale** liquidation *f*.

clear-cut *adj* net.

clearing *n* clairière *f*.

clearly *adv* clairement.

clef *n* (Mus) clé *f*.

cleft *n* fissure *f*.

clench *vt* serrer.

clergy *n* clergé *m*. ~**man** *n* (*pl* **-men**) ecclésiastique *m*.

cleric *n* clerc *m*. **clerical** *adj* (Relig) clérical; (*staff, work*) de bureau.

clerk *n* employé/-e *m/f* de bureau; (US) (*sales*) ~ vendeur/-euse *m/f*.

clever *adj* intelligent; (skilful) habile.

click *n* déclic *m*. ● *vi* faire un déclic; (people ①) sympathiser. ● *vt* (*heels, tongue*) faire claquer.

client *n* client/-e *m/f*.

clientele *n* clientèle *f*.

cliff *n* falaise *f*.

climate *n* climat *m*.

climax *n* (of story, contest) point *m* culminant; (sexual) orgasme *m*.

climb *vt* grimper; (*steps*) monter; (*tree, ladder*) grimper à; (*mountain*) faire l'ascension de. ● *vi* grimper; ∼ **into** (*car*) monter dans; ∼ **into bed** se mettre au lit. ● *n* (of mountain) escalade *f*; (steep hill, rise) montée *f*. □ ∼ **down** (fig) reculer. **climber** *n* (Sport) alpiniste *mf*.

clinch *vt* (*deal*) conclure; (*victory, order*) décrocher.

cling *vi* (*pt* **clung**) se cramponner (**to** à); (stick) coller. ∼**-film** *n* scellofrais® *m*.

clinic *n* centre *m* médical; (private) clinique *f*. **clinical** *adj* clinique.

clink *n* tintement *m*. ● *vt/i* (faire) tinter.

clip *n* (for paper) trombone *m*; (for hair) barrette *f*; (for tube) collier *m*; (of film) extrait *m*. ● *vt* (*pt* **clipped**) (fasten) attacher (**to** à); (cut) couper.

clippers *npl* tondeuse *f*; (for nails) coupe-ongles *m inv*.

clipping *n* (from press) coupure *f* de presse.

cloak *n* cape *f*; (man's) houppelande *f*. ∼**room** *n* vestiaire *m*; (toilet) toilettes *fpl*.

clobber *n* 🗊 attirail *m*. ● *vt* (hit 🗊) tabasser 🗊.

clock *n* pendule *f*; (large) horloge *f*. ● *vi* ∼ **on/in** *or* **off/out** pointer; ∼ **up** (*miles*) faire. ∼**-tower** *n* beffroi *m*. ∼**wise** *a* & *adv* dans le sens des aiguilles d'une montre.

clockwork *n* mécanisme *m*. ● *adj* mécanique.

clog *n* sabot *m*. ● *vt/i* (*pt* **clogged**) (se) boucher.

cloister *n* cloître *m*.

close¹ *adj* (*friend, relative*) proche (**to** de); (*link, collaboration*) étroit; (*examination*) minutieux; (*result, match*) serré; (*weather*) lourd; ∼ **together** (crowded) serrés; ∼ **by**, ∼ **at hand** tout près; **have a** ∼ **shave** l'échapper belle; **keep a** ∼ **watch on** surveiller de près. ● *adv* près. ● *n* (street) impasse *f*.

close² *vt* fermer; (*meeting, case*) mettre fin à. ● *vi* se fermer; (*shop*) fermer; (*meeting, play*) prendre fin. ● *n* fin *f*.

closely *adv* (follow) de près.

closeness *n* proximité *f*.

closet *n* (US) placard *m*.

close-up *n* gros plan *m*.

closure *n* fermeture *f*.

clot *n* (of blood) caillot *m*; (in sauce) grumeau. ● *vt/i* (*pt* **clotted**) (se) coaguler.

cloth *n* (fabric) tissu *m*; (duster) chiffon *m*; (table-cloth) nappe *f*.

clothe *vt* vêtir.

clothes *npl* vêtements *mpl*. ∼**-hanger** *n* cintre *m*. ∼**-line** *n* corde *f* à linge.

clothing *n* vêtements *mpl*.

cloud *n* nuage *m*. ● *vi* ∼ (**over**) se couvrir (de nuages); (*face*) s'assombrir. **cloudy** *adj* (*sky*) couvert; (*liquid*) trouble.

clout *n* (blow) coup *m* de poing; (power) influence *f*. ● *vt* frapper.

clove *n* clou *m* de girofle; ∼ **of garlic** gousse *f* d'ail.

clover *n* trèfle *m*.

clown *n* clown *m*. ● *vi* faire le clown.

club *n* (group) club *m*; (weapon) massue *f*; (**golf**) ∼ **club** *m* (de golf); ∼**s** (cards) trèfle *m*. ● *vt/i* (*pt* **clubbed**) matraquer. □ ∼ **together** cotiser.

cluck *vi* glousser.

clue *n* indice *m*; (in crossword) définition *f*; **I haven't a** ∼ 🗊 je n'en ai pas la moindre idée.

clump *n* massif *m*.

clumsy *adj* (**-ier, -iest**) maladroit; (*tool*) peu commode.

clung ⇒CLING.

cluster *n* (of people, islands) groupe *m*; (of flowers, berries) grappe *f*. ● *vi* se grouper.

clutch *vt* (hold) serrer fort; (grasp) saisir. ● *vi* ∼ **at** (try to grasp) essayer de saisir. ● *n* (Auto) embrayage *m*; (of eggs) couvée *f*; (of people) groupe *m*.

clutter *n* désordre *m*. ● *vt* ∼ (**up**) encombrer.

coach n autocar m; (of train) wagon m; (horse-drawn) carrosse m; (Sport) entraîneur/-euse m/f. ● vt (team) entraîner; (pupil) donner des leçons particulières à.

coal n charbon m. **~field** n bassin m houiller. **~-mine** n mine f de charbon.

coarse adj grossier.

coast n côte f. ● vi (car, bicycle) descendre en roue libre. **coastal** adj côtier.

coast: **~guard** n (person) gardecôte m; (organization) gendarmerie f maritime. **~line** n littoral m.

coat n manteau m; (of animal) pelage m; (of paint) couche f; **~ of arms** armoiries fpl. ● vt enduire, couvrir; (with chocolate) enrober (**with** de). **coating** n couche f.

coax vt cajoler.

cob n (of corn) épi m.

cobbler n cordonnier m.

cobblestones npl pavés mpl.

cobweb n toile f d'araignée.

cocaine n cocaïne f.

cock n (rooster) coq m; (oiseau) mâle m. ● vt (gun) armer; (ears) dresser.

cockerel n jeune coq m.

cockle n (Culin) coque f.

cock: **~pit** n poste m de pilotage. **~roach** n cafard m. **~tail** n cocktail m.

cocky adj (-ier, -iest) trop sûr de soi.

cocoa n cacao m.

coconut n noix f de coco.

COD abbr (**cash on delivery**) envoi m contre remboursement.

cod n inv morue f; **~-liver oil** huile f de foie de morue.

code n code m. ● vt coder.

coerce vt contraindre.

coexist vi coexister.

coffee n café m. **~ bar** n café m. **~ bean** n grain m de café. **~pot** n cafetière f. **~-table** n table f basse.

coffin n cercueil m.

cog n pignon m; (fig) rouage m.

cognac n cognac m.

coil vt/i (s')enrouler. ● n (of rope) rouleau m; (of snake) anneau m; (contraceptive) stérilet m.

coin n pièce f (de monnaie). ● vt (word) inventer.

coincide vi coïncider.

coincidence n coïncidence f.

coincidental adj dû à une coïncidence.

colander n passoire f.

cold adj froid; (person) be or feel **~** avoir froid; **it is ~** il fait froid; **get ~ feet** avoir les jetons 🔢; **~-blooded** (lit) à sang froid; (fig) sans pitié. ● n froid m; (Med) rhume m; **~ sore** bouton m de fièvre. **coldness** n froideur f.

coleslaw n salade f de chou cru.

colic n coliques fpl.

collaborate vi collaborer.

collapse vi s'effondrer; (person) s'écrouler; (fold) se plier. ● n effondrement m.

collar n col m; (of dog) collier m. **~-bone** n clavicule f.

collateral n nantissement m.

colleague n collègue mf.

collect vt rassembler; (pick up) ramasser; (call for) passer prendre; (money, fare) encaisser; (taxes, rent) percevoir; (as hobby) collectionner. ● vi se rassembler; (dust) s'amasser. ● adv call **~** (US) appeler en PCV. **collection** n collection f; (of money) collecte f; (in church) quête f; (of mail) levée f.

collective adj collectif.

collector n (as hobby) collectionneur/-euse m/f; (of taxes) percepteur m; (of rent, debt) encaisseur m.

college n (for higher education) établissement m d'enseignement supérieur; (within university) collège m; **be at ~** faire des études supérieures.

collide vi entrer en collision (**with** avec).

colliery n houillère f.

collision n collision f.

colloquial adj familier. **colloquialism** n expression f familière.

Colombia n Colombie f.

colon n (Gram) deux-points m inv; (Anat) côlon m.

colonel n colonel m.

colonial *a & n* colonial/-e (*m/f*).

colour, (US) **color** *n* couleur *f*;
~-**blind** daltonien. ● *adj* (*photo*) en
couleur; (*TV set*) couleur *inv*. ● *vt*
colorer; (*with crayon*) colorier.
  coloured *adj* de couleur.
  colourful *adj* aux couleurs vives;
(*fig*) haut en couleur. **colouring** *n*
(*of skin*) teint *m*; (*in food*) colorant *m*.

colt *n* poulain *m*.

column *n* colonne *f*.

coma *n* coma *m*.

comb *n* peigne *m*. ● *vt* peigner; ~
one's hair se peigner; ~ **a place**
passer un lieu au peigne fin.

combat *n* combat *m*. ● *vt* (*pt*
combated) combattre.

combination *n* combinaison *f*.

combine¹ *vt/i* (se) combiner, (s')
unir.

combine² *n* (Comm) groupe *m*; ~
(*harvester*) moissonneuse-batteuse *f*.

come *vi* (*pt* **came**; *pp* **come**)
venir; (*bus, letter*) arriver; (*postman*)
passer; ~ **and look!** viens voir!; ~ **in**
(*size, colour*) exister en; **when it** ~**s**
to lorsqu'il s'agit de. □ ~ **about**
survenir; ~ **across** (*meaning*)
passer; ~ **across sth** tomber sur qch;
~ **away** (*leave*) partir; (*come off*) se
détacher; ~ **back** revenir; ~ **by**
obtenir; ~ **down** descendre; (*price*)
baisser; ~ **forward** se présenter; ~
in entrer; ~ **in useful** être utile; ~
in for recevoir; ~ **into** (*money*)
hériter de; ~ **off** (*succeed*) réussir;
(*fare*) s'en tirer; (*detach*) se détacher;
~ **on** (*actor*) entrer en scène; (*light*)
s'allumer; (*improve*) faire des progrès;
~ **on!** allez!; ~ **out** sortir; ~ **round**
reprendre connaissance; (*change mind*)
changer d'avis; ~ **through** s'en
tirer; ~ **to** reprendre connaissance;
~ **to sth** (*amount*) revenir à qch;
(*decision, conclusion*) arriver à qch;
~ **up** (*problem*) être soulevé;
(*opportunity*) se présenter; (*sun*) se
lever; ~ **up against** se heurter à;
~ **up with** trouver.

comedian *n* comique *m*.

comedy *n* comédie *f*.

comfort *n* confort *m*; (*consolation*)
réconfort *m*. ● *vt* consoler.
  comfortable *adj* (*chair, car*)
confortable; (*person*) à l'aise; (*wealthy*)
aisé.

comfortably *adv* confortablement;
~ **off** aisé.

comfy *adj* ① = COMFORTABLE.

comic *adj* comique. ● *n* (*person*)
comique *m*; ~ (*book*), ~ **strip** bande
f dessinée.

coming *n* arrivée *f*; ~**s and goings**
allées et venues *fpl*. ● *adj* à venir.

comma *n* virgule *f*.

command *n* (*authority*)
commandement *m*; (*order*) ordre *m*;
(*mastery*) maîtrise *f*. ● *vt* ordonner à
(**to do** de faire); (*be able to use*)
disposer de; (*respect*) inspirer.
  commandeer *vt* réquisitionner.
  commander *n* commandant *m*.
  commanding *adj* imposant.
  commandment *n* commandement
m.

commando *n* commando *m*.

commemorate *vt* commémorer.

commence *vt/i* commencer.

commend *vt* (*praise*) louer; (*entrust*)
confier.

commensurate *adj* proportionné.

comment *n* commentaire *m*. ● *vi*
faire des commentaires; ~ **on**
commenter. **commentary** *n*
commentaire *m*; (*radio, TV*) reportage
m. **commentate** *vi* faire un
reportage. **commentator** *n*
commentateur/-trice *m/f*.

commerce *n* commerce *m*.

commercial *adj* commercial;
(*traveller*) de commerce. ● *n*
publicité *f*.

commiserate *vi* compatir (**with**
avec).

commission *n* commission *f*; (*order
for work*) commande *f*; **out of** ~ hors
service. ● *vt* (*order*) commander; (*Mil*)
nommer officier; ~ **to do** charger de
faire. **commissioner** *n* préfet *m*
(de police); (*in EC*) membre *m* de la
Commission européenne.

commit *vt* (*pt* **committed**)
commettre; (*entrust*) confier; ~
oneself s'engager; ~ **perjury** se
parjurer; ~ **suicide** se suicider; ~ **to**
memory apprendre par cœur.
  commitment *n* engagement *m*.

committee *n* comité *m*.

commodity *n* article *m*.

common *adj* (shared by all) commun (to à); (usual) courant; (vulgar) vulgaire, commun; in ∼ en commun; ∼ **people** le peuple; ∼ **sense** bon sens *m*. ● *n* terrain *m* communal; the C∼s Chambre *f* des Communes.

commoner *n* roturier/-ière *m/f*.

common law *n* droit *m* coutumier.

commonly *adv* communément.

commonplace *adj* banal. ● *n* banalité *f*.

common-room *n* salle *f* de détente.

Commonwealth *n* the ∼ le Commonwealth *m*.

commotion *n* (noise) vacarme *m*; (disturbance) agitation *f*.

communal *adj* (shared) commun; (life) collectif.

commune *n* (group) communauté *f*.

communicate *vt/i* communiquer. **communication** *n* communication *f*. **communicative** *adj* communicatif.

communion *n* communion *f*.

Communism *n* communisme *m*. **Communist** *a* & *n* communiste (*mf*).

community *n* communauté *f*.

commute *vi* faire la navette. ● *vt* (Jur) commuer. **commuter** *n* navetteur/-euse *m/f*.

compact *adj* compact; (lady's case) poudrier *m*.

compact disc *n* disque *m* compact. ∼ **player** *n* platine *f* laser.

companion *n* compagnon/-agne *m/ f*. **companionship** *n* camaraderie *f*.

company *n* (companionship, firm) compagnie *f*; (guests) invités/-es *m/ fpl*.

comparative *adj* (study, form) comparatif; (comfort) relatif.

compare *vt* comparer (with, to à); ∼d with par rapport à. ● *vi* être comparable. **comparison** *n* comparaison *f*.

compartment *n* compartiment *m*.

compass *n* (for direction) boussole *f*; (scope) portée *f*; a pair of ∼es compas *m*.

compassionate *adj* compatissant.

compatible *adj* compatible.

compel *vt* (*pt* **compelled**) contraindre. **compelling** *adj* irrésistible.

compensate *vt/i* (financially) dédommager (for de); ∼ for sth compenser qch. **compensation** *n* compensation *f*; (financial) dédommagement *m*.

compete *vi* concourir; ∼ with rivaliser avec.

competent *adj* compétent.

competition *n* (contest) concours *m*; (Sport) compétition *f*; (Comm) concurrence *f*.

competitive *adj* (prices) compétitif; (person) qui a l'esprit de compétition.

competitor *n* concurrent/-e *m/f*.

compile *vt* (list) dresser; (book) rédiger.

complacency *n* suffisance *f*.

complain *vi* se plaindre (about, of de). **complaint** *n* plainte *f*; (official) réclamation *f*; (illness) maladie *f*.

complement *n* complément *m*. ● *vt* compléter. **complementary** *adj* complémentaire.

complete *adj* complet; (finished) achevé; (downright) parfait. ● *vt* achever; (a form) remplir. **completely** *adv* complètement. **completion** *n* achèvement *m*.

complex *adj* complexe. ● *n* (Psych) complexe *m*.

complexion *n* (of face) teint *m*; (fig) caractère *m*.

compliance *n* (agreement) conformité *f*.

complicate *vt* compliquer. **complicated** *adj* compliqué. **complication** *n* complication *f*.

compliment *n* compliment *m*. ● *vt* complimenter. **complimentary** *adj* (offert) à titre gracieux; (praising) flatteur.

comply *vi* ∼ with se conformer à, obéir à.

component *n* (of machine) pièce *f*; (chemical substance) composant *m*; (element: fig) composante *f*. ● *adj* constituant.

compose vt composer; ~ oneself se calmer. **composed** adj calme. **composer** n (Mus) compositeur m. **composition** n composition f.

composure n calme m.

compound n (substance, word) composé m; (enclosure) enclos m. ● adj composé.

comprehend vt comprendre. **comprehension** n compréhension f.

comprehensive adj étendu, complet; (insurance) tous risques inv. ~ **school** n collège m d'enseignement secondaire.

compress vt comprimer.

comprise vt comprendre, inclure.

compromise n compromis m. ● vt compromettre. ● vi transiger, arriver à un compromis.

compulsive adj (Psych) compulsif; (liar, smoker) invétéré.

compulsory adj obligatoire.

computer n ordinateur m; ~ **science** informatique f. **computerize** vt informatiser.

comrade n camarade mf.

con[1] vt (pt **conned**) 🅇 rouler 🅣, escroquer (out of de). ● n 🅇 escroquerie f.

con[2] ⇨PRO.

conceal vt dissimuler (from à).

concede vt concéder. ● vi céder.

conceited adj vaniteux.

conceive vt/i concevoir; ~ of concevoir.

concentrate vt/i (se) concentrer. **concentration** n concentration f.

concept n concept m.

conception n conception f.

concern n (interest, business) affaire f; (worry) inquiétude f; (firm: Comm) entreprise f, affaire f. ● vt concerner; ~ oneself with, be ~ed with s'occuper de. **concerned** adj inquiet. **concerning** prep en ce qui concerne.

concert n concert m.

concession n concession f.

conciliation n conciliation f.

concise adj concis.

conclude vt conclure. ● vi se terminer. **conclusion** n conclusion f. **conclusive** adj concluant.

concoct vt confectionner; (invent: fig) fabriquer. **concoction** n mélange m.

concourse n (Rail) hall m.

concrete n béton m. ● adj de béton; (fig) concret. ● vt bétonner.

concur vi (pt **concurred**) être d'accord.

concurrently adv simultanément.

concussion n commotion f (cérébrale).

condemn vt condamner.

condensation n (on walls) condensation f; (on windows) buée f. **condense** vt/i (se) condenser.

condition n condition f; on ~ that à condition que. ● vt conditionner. **conditional** adj conditionnel.

conditioner n après-shampooing m.

condolences npl condoléances fpl.

condom n préservatif m.

condone vt pardonner, fermer les yeux sur.

conducive adj ~ to favorable à.

conduct[1] n conduite f.

conduct[2] vt conduire; (orchestra) diriger. **conductor** n chef m d'orchestre; (of bus) receveur m; (on train: US) chef m de train; (Electr) conducteur m. **conductress** n receveuse f.

cone n cône m; (of ice-cream) cornet m.

confectioner n confiseur/-euse m/ f. **confectionery** n confiserie f.

confer vt/i (pt **conferred**) conférer.

conference n conférence f.

confess vt/i avouer; (Relig) (se) confesser. **confession** n confession f; (of crime) aveu m.

confide vt confier. ● vi ~ in se confier à.

confidence n (trust) confiance f; (boldness) confiance f en soi; (secret) confidence f; in ~ en confidence. **confident** adj sûr.

confidential adj confidentiel.

confine vt enfermer; (limit) limiter; ∼d space espace m réduit; ∼d to limité à.

confirm vt confirmer. **confirmed** adj (bachelor) endurci; (smoker) invétéré.

confiscate vt confisquer.

conflict¹ n conflit m.

conflict² vi (statements, views) être en contradiction (with avec); (appointments) tomber en même temps (with que). **conflicting** adj contradictoire.

conform vt/i (se) conformer.

confound vt confondre.

confront vt affronter; ∼ with confronter avec.

confuse vt (bewilder) troubler; (mistake, confound) confondre; **become** ∼d s'embrouiller; **I am** ∼d je m'y perds. **confusing** adj déroutant. **confusion** n confusion f.

congeal vt/i (se) figer.

congested adj (road) embouteillé; (passage) encombré; (Med) congestionné. **congestion** n (traffic) encombrement(s) m(pl); (Med) congestion f.

congratulate vt féliciter (on de). **congratulations** npl félicitations fpl.

congregate vi se rassembler. **congregation** n assemblée f.

congress n congrès m; **C∼** (US) le Congrès.

conjugate vt conjuguer. **conjugation** n conjugaison f.

conjunction n (Ling) conjonction f; **in ∼ with** conjointement avec.

conjunctivitis n conjonctivite f.

conjure vi faire des tours de passe-passe. ● vt ∼ **up** faire apparaître. **conjuror** n prestidigitateur/-trice m/f.

con man n ⊠ escroc m.

connect vt/i (se) relier; (in mind) faire le rapport entre; (install, wire up to mains) brancher; ∼ **with** (of train) assurer la correspondance avec; ∼**ed** (idea, event) lié; **be** ∼**ed with** avoir rapport à.

connection n rapport m; (Rail) correspondance f; (phone call) communication f; (Electr) contact m;

(joining piece) raccord m; ∼**s** (Comm) relations fpl.

connive vi ∼ **at** se faire le complice de.

conquer vt vaincre; (country) conquérir. **conqueror** n conquérant m.

conquest n conquête f.

conscience n conscience f. **conscientious** adj consciencieux.

conscious adj conscient; (deliberate) voulu. **consciously** adv consciemment. **consciousness** n conscience f; (Med) connaissance f.

conscript n appelé m.

consecutive adj consécutif.

consensus n consensus m.

consent vi consentir (to à). ● n consentement m.

consequence n conséquence f. **consequently** adv par conséquent.

conservation n préservation f; ∼ **area** zone f protégée. **conservationist** n défenseur m de l'environnement.

conservative adj conservateur; (estimate) minimal.

Conservative Party n parti m conservateur.

conservatory n (greenhouse) serre f; (room) véranda f.

conserve vt conserver; (energy) économiser.

consider vt considérer; (allow for) tenir compte de; (possibility) envisager (doing de faire).

considerable adj considérable; (much) beaucoup de.

considerate adj prévenant, attentionné. **consideration** n considération f; (respect) égard(s) m(pl).

considering prep compte tenu de.

consignment n envoi m.

consist vi consister (of en; in doing à faire).

consistency n (of liquids) consistance f; (of argument) cohérence f.

consistent adj cohérent; ∼ **with** conforme à.

consolation n consolation f.

consolidate vt/i (se) consolider.

consonant *n* consonne *f*.

conspicuous *adj* (easily seen) en évidence; (showy) voyant; (noteworthy) remarquable.

conspiracy *n* conspiration *f*.

constable *n* agent *m* de police, gendarme *m*.

constant *adj* (*questions*) incessant; (unchanging) constant; (*friend*) fidèle. ● *n* constante *f*. **constantly** *adv* constamment.

constellation *n* constellation *f*.

constipation *n* constipation *f*.

constituency *n* circonscription *f* électorale.

constituent *adj* constitutif. ● *n* élément *m* constitutif; (Pol) électeur/-trice *m/f*.

constitution *n* constitution *f*.

constrain *vt* contraindre. **constraint** *n* contrainte *f*.

constrict *vt* (*flow*) comprimer; (*movement*) gêner.

construct *vt* construire. **construction** *n* construction *f*. **constructive** *adj* constructif.

consulate *n* consulat *m*.

consult *vt* consulter. ● *vi* ~ **with** conférer avec. **consultant** *n* conseiller/-ère *m/f*; (Med) spécialiste *mf*. **consultation** *n* consultation *f*.

consume *vt* consommer; (destroy) consumer. **consumer** *n* consommateur/-trice *m/f*.

consummate *vt* consommer.

consumption *n* consommation *f*; (Med) phtisie *f*.

contact *n* contact *m*; (person) relation *f*. ● *vt* contacter. ~ **lenses** *npl* lentilles *fpl* (de contact).

contagious *adj* contagieux.

contain *vt* contenir; ~ **oneself** se contenir. **container** *n* récipient *m*; (for transport) container *m*.

contaminate *vt* contaminer.

contemplate *vt* (gaze at) contempler; (think about) envisager.

contemporary *a & n* contemporain/-e (*m/f*).

contempt *n* mépris *m*. **contemptible** *adj* méprisable. **contemptuous** *adj* méprisant.

contend *vt* soutenir. ● *vi* ~ **with** (compete) rivaliser avec; (face) faire face à. **contender** *n* adversaire *mf*.

content[1] *n* (of letter) contenu *m*; (amount) teneur *f*; ~**s** contenu *m*.

content[2] *adj* satisfait. ● *vt* contenter. **contented** *adj* satisfait. **contentment** *n* contentement *m*.

contest[1] *n* (competition) concours *m*; (struggle) lutte *f*.

contest[2] *vt* contester; (compete for or in) disputer. **contestant** *n* concurrent/-e *m/f*.

context *n* contexte *m*.

continent *n* continent *m*; the C~ l'Europe *f* (continentale). **continental** *adj* continental; européen. **continental quilt** *n* couette *f*.

contingency *n* éventualité *f*; ~ **plan** plan *m* d'urgence.

continual *adj* continuel.

continuation *n* continuation *f*; (after interruption) reprise *f*; (new episode) suite *f*.

continue *vt/i* continuer; (resume) reprendre. **continued** *adj* continu.

continuous *adj* continu. **continuously** *adv* (without a break) sans interruption; (repeatedly) continuellement.

contort *vt* tordre; ~ **oneself** se contorsionner.

contour *n* contour *m*.

contraband *n* contrebande *f*.

contraception *n* contraception *f*. **contraceptive** *a & n* contraceptif (*m*).

contract[1] *n* contrat *m*.

contract[2] *vt/i* (se) contracter. **contraction** *n* contraction *f*.

contractor *n* entrepreneur/-euse *m/f*.

contradict *vt* contredire. **contradictory** *adj* contradictoire.

contrary[1] *adj* contraire (to à). ● *n* contraire *m*; on the ~ au contraire. ● *adv* ~ to contrairement à.

contrary[2] *adj* entêté.

contrast[1] *n* contraste *m*.

contrast[2] *vt/i* contraster.

contravention *n* infraction *f*.

contribute vt donner. ● vi ~ to contribuer à; (take part) participer à; (newspaper) collaborer à.
contribution n contribution f.
contributor n collaborateur/-trice m/f.

contrive vt imaginer; ~ to do trouver moyen de faire.

control vt (pt **controlled**) (firm) diriger; (check) contrôler; (restrain) maîtriser. ● n contrôle m; (mastery) maîtrise f; ~s commandes fpl; (knobs) boutons mpl; have under ~ (event) avoir en main; in ~ of maître de. ~ **tower** n tour f de contrôle.

controversial adj discutable, discuté. **controversy** n controverse f.

conurbation n agglomération f, conurbation f.

convalesce vi être en convalescence.

convene vt convoquer. ● vi se réunir.

convenience n commodité f; ~s toilettes fpl; all modern ~s tout le confort moderne; at your ~ quand cela vous conviendra, à votre convenance. ~ **foods** npl plats mpl tout préparés.

convenient adj commode, pratique; (time) bien choisi; be ~ for convenir à.

convent n couvent m.

convention n (assembly, agreement) convention f; (custom) usage m. **conventional** adj conventionnel.

conversation n conversation f. **conversational** adj (tone) de la conversation; (French) de tous les jours.

converse[1] vi s'entretenir, converser (with avec).

converse[2] a & n inverse (m). **conversely** adv inversement.

conversion n conversion f.

convert[1] vt convertir; (house) aménager. ● vi ~ into se transformer en.

convert[2] n converti/-e m/f.

convertible adj convertible. ● n (car) décapotable f.

convey vt (wishes, order) transmettre; (goods, people) transporter; (idea, feeling) communiquer. **conveyor belt** n tapis m roulant.

convict[1] vt déclarer coupable.

convict[2] n prisonnier/-ière m/f.

conviction n (Jur) condamnation f; (opinion) conviction f.

convince vt convaincre.

convoke vt convoquer.

convoy n convoi m.

convulse vt convulser; (fig) bouleverser; be ~d with laughter se tordre de rire.

cook vt/i (faire) cuire; (of person) faire la cuisine; ~ up ▣ fabriquer. ● n cuisinier/-ière m/f. **cooker** n (stove) cuisinière f. **cookery** n cuisine f.

cookie n (US) biscuit m.

cooking n cuisine f. ● adj de cuisine.

cool adj frais; (calm) calme; (unfriendly) froid. ● n fraîcheur f; (calmness ▣) sang-froid m; in the ~ au frais. ● vt/i rafraîchir. ~ **box** n glacière f.

coolly adv calmement; froidement.

coop n poulailler m. ● vt ~ up enfermer.

co-operate vi coopérer. **co-operation** n coopération f.

co-operative adj coopératif. ● n coopérative f.

co-ordinate vt coordonner.

cop vt (pt **copped**) ▣ piquer. ● n (policeman ▣) flic m. □ ~ **out** ▣ se dérober.

cope vi s'en sortir ▣, se débrouiller; ~ with (problem) faire face à.

copper n cuivre m; (coin) sou m; ▣ flic m. ● adj de cuivre.

copulate vi s'accoupler.

copy n copie f; (of book, newspaper) exemplaire m; (print: Photo) épreuve f. ● vt/i copier.

copyright n droit m d'auteur, copyright m.

copy-writer n rédacteur-concepteur m, rédactrice-conceptrice f.

cord n (petite) corde f; (of curtain, pyjamas) cordon m; (Electr) cordon m électrique; (fabric) velours m côtelé.

cordial adj cordial. ● n (drink) sirop m.

corduroy n velours m côtelé.

core n (of apple) trognon m; (of problem) cœur m; (Tech) noyau m. ● vt (apple) évider.

cork n liège m; (for bottle) bouchon m. ● vt boucher. **corkscrew** n tire-bouchon m.

corn n blé m; (maize: US) maïs m; (seed) grain m; (hard skin) cor m.

cornea n cornée f.

corner n coin m; (bend in road) virage m; (football) corner m. ● vt coincer, acculer; (market) accaparer. ● vi prendre un virage.

cornflour n farine f de maïs.

cornice n corniche f.

corny adj (-ier, -iest) (joke) éculé.

corollary n corollaire m.

coronary n infarctus m.

coronation n couronnement m.

corporal n caporal m. ~ **punishment** n châtiment m corporel.

corporate adj (ownership) en commun; (body) constitué.

corporation n (Comm) société f.

corpse n cadavre m.

corpuscle n globule m.

correct adj (right) exact, juste, correct; (proper) correct; **you are** ~ vous avez raison. ● vt corriger.

correction n correction f.

correlate vt/i (faire) correspondre.

correspond vi correspondre. **correspondence** n correspondance f.

corridor n couloir m.

corrode vt/i (se) corroder.

corrugated adj ondulé; ~ **iron** tôle f ondulée.

corrupt adj corrompu. ● vt corrompre. **corruption** n corruption f.

Corsica n Corse f.

cosh n matraque f. ● vt matraquer.

cosmetic n produit m de beauté. ● adj cosmétique; (fig, pej) superficiel. ~ **surgery** n chirurgie f esthétique

cosmopolitan a & n cosmopolite (mf).

cosmos n cosmos m.

cost vt (pt **cost**) coûter; (pt **costed**) établir le prix de. ● n coût m; ~**s** (Jur) dépens mpl; **at all** ~**s** à tout prix; **to one's** ~ à ses dépens; ~ **price** prix m de revient; ~ **of living** coût m de la vie. ~-**effective** adj rentable.

costly adj (-ier, -iest) coûteux; (valuable) précieux.

costume n costume m; (for swimming) maillot m. ~ **jewellery** npl bijoux mpl de fantaisie.

cosy adj (-ier, -iest) confortable, intime.

cot n lit m d'enfant; (camp-bed: US) lit m de camp.

cottage n petite maison f de campagne; (thatched) chaumière f. ~ **pie** n hachis m Parmentier.

cotton n coton m; (for sewing) fil m (à coudre). ● vi ~ **on** ⊠ piger. ~ **wool** n coton m hydrophile.

couch n canapé m. ● vt (express) formuler.

cough vi tousser. ● n toux f. □ ~ **up** ⊠ cracher, payer.

could ⇒CAN¹.

couldn't = COULD NOT.

council n conseil m. ~ **house** n maison f louée par la municipalité, ≈ H.L.M. m or f.

councillor n conseiller/-ère m/f municipal/-e.

counsel n conseil m. ● n inv (Jur) avocat/-e m/f. **counsellor** n conseiller/-ère m/f.

count vt/i compter. ● n (numerical record) décompte m; (nobleman) comte m. □ ~ **on** compter sur.

counter n comptoir m; (in bank) guichet m; (token) jeton m. ● adv ~ **to** à l'encontre de. ● adj opposé. ● vt opposer; (blow) parer. ● vi riposter.

counteract vt neutraliser.

counterbalance n contrepoids m. ● vt contrebalancer.

counterfeit a & n faux (m). ● vt contrefaire.

counterfoil n souche f.

counter-productive adj qui produit l'effet contraire.

countess n comtesse f.

countless adj innombrable.

country n (land, region) pays m; (homeland) patrie f; (countryside) campagne f.

countryman n (pl -men) campagnard m; (fellow citizen) compatriote m.

countryside n campagne f.

county n comté m.

coup n (achievement) joli coup m; (Pol) coup m d'état.

couple n (people, animals) couple m; a ~ (of) (two or three) deux ou trois. ● vt/i (s')accoupler.

coupon n coupon m; (for shopping) bon m or coupon m de réduction.

courage n courage m.

courgette n courgette f.

courier n messager/-ère m/f; (for tourists) guide m.

course n cours m; (for training) stage m; (series) série f; (Culin) plat m; (for golf) terrain m; (at sea) itinéraire m; **change ~** changer de cap; **~ (of action)** façon f de faire; **during the ~ of** pendant; **in due ~** en temps utile; **of ~** bien sûr.

court n cour f; (tennis) court m; **go to ~** aller devant les tribunaux. ● vt faire la cour à; (danger) rechercher.

courteous adj courtois.

courtesy n courtoisie f; **by ~ of** avec la permission de.

court-house n (US) palais m de justice.

court-martial vt (pt -martialled) faire passer en conseil de guerre. ● n cour f martiale.

court: **~room** n salle f de tribunal. **~shoe** n escarpin m. **~yard** n cour f.

cousin n cousin/-e m/f; **first ~** cousin/-e m/f germain/-e.

cove n anse f, crique f.

covenant n convention f.

cover vt couvrir. ● n (for bed, book) couverture f; (lid) couvercle m; (for furniture) housse f; (shelter) abri m; **take ~** se mettre à l'abri. □ **~ up** cacher; (crime) couvrir; **~ up for** couvrir.

coverage n reportage m.

covering n enveloppe f; **~ letter** lettre f d'accompagnement.

covert adj (activity) secret; (threat) voilé; (look) dérobé.

cover-up n opération f de camouflage.

cow n vache f.

coward n lâche mf.

cowboy n cow-boy m.

cowshed n étable f.

coy adj (faussement) timide, qui fait le or la timide.

cozy US = cosy.

crab n crabe m. **~-apple** n pomme f sauvage.

crack n fente f; (in glass) fêlure f; (noise) craquement m; (joke 🗷) plaisanterie f. ● adj 🗉 d'élite. ● vt/i (break partially) (se) fêler; (split) (se) fendre; (nut) casser; (joke) raconter; (problem) résoudre; **get ~ing** 🗉 s'y mettre. □ **~ down on** 🗉 sévir contre; **~ up** 🗉 craquer.

cracker n (Culin) biscuit m (salé); (for Christmas) diablotin f.

crackle vi crépiter. ● n crépitement m.

cradle n berceau m. ● vt bercer.

craft n métier m artisanal; (technique) art m; (boat) bateau m. **craftsman** n (pl -men) artisan m. **craftsmanship** n art m.

crafty adj (-ier, -iest) rusé.

crag n rocher m à pic.

cram vt/i (pt crammed); (for an exam) bachoter (for pour); **~ into** (pack) (s')entasser dans; **~ with** (fill) bourrer de.

cramp n crampe f.

cramped adj à l'étroit.

cranberry n canneberge f.

crane n grue f. ● vt (neck) tendre.

crank n excentrique mf; (Tech) manivelle f.

crap n (nonsense 🗷) conneries fpl 🗷; (faeces 🗷) merde f 🗷.

crash n accident m; (noise) fracas m; (of thunder) coup m; (of firm) faillite f. ● vt/i avoir un accident (avec); (of plane) s'écraser; (two vehicles) se percuter; **~ into** rentrer dans. **~ course** n cours m intensif. **~-helmet** n casque m (anti-choc). **~-land** vi atterrir en catastrophe.

crate n cageot m.

cravat n foulard m.

crave vt/i ~ **(for)** désirer ardemment. **craving** n envie f irrésistible.

crawl vi (insect) ramper; (vehicle) se traîner; **be ~ing with** grouiller de. ● n (pace) pas m; (swimming) crawl m.

crayfish n inv écrevisse f.

crayon n craie f grasse.

craze n engouement m.

crazy adj (-ier, -iest) fou; ~ **about** (person) fou de; (thing) fana or fou de.

creak n grincement m. ● vi grincer.

cream n crème f. ● adj crème inv. ● vt écrémer.

crease n pli m. ● vt/i (se) froisser.

create vt créer. **creation** n création f. **creative** adj (person) créatif; (process) créateur. **creator** n créateur/-trice m/f.

creature n créature f.

crèche n garderie f.

credentials npl (identity) pièces fpl d'identité; (competence) références fpl.

credibility n crédibilité f.

credit n (credence) crédit m; (honour) honneur m; **in** ~ créditeur; ~**s** (cinema) générique m. ● adj (balance) créditeur. ● vt croire; (Comm) créditer; ~ **sb with** attribuer à qn. ~ **card** n carte f de crédit. ~ **note** n avoir m.

creditor n créancier/-ière m/f.

credit-worthy adj solvable.

creed n credo m.

creek n (US) ruisseau m; **up the** ~ 🗙 dans le pétrin 🅸.

creep vi (pt **crept**) (insect, cat) ramper; (fig) se glisser. ● n (person 🗙) pauvre type m 🅸; **give sb the** ~**s** faire frissonner qn. **creeper** n liane f.

cremate vt incinérer. **cremation** n incinération f. **crematorium** n (pl **-ia**) crématorium m.

crêpe n crêpe m. ~ **paper** n papier m crépon.

crept ⇒CREEP.

crescent n croissant m; (of houses) rue f en demi-lune.

cress n cresson m.

crest n crête f; (coat of arms) armoiries fpl.

cretin n crétin/-e m/f.

crevice n fente f.

crew n (of plane, ship) équipage m; (gang) équipe f. ~ **cut** n coupe f en brosse. ~ **neck** n (col) ras du cou m.

crib n lit m d'enfant. ● vt/i (pt **cribbed**) copier.

cricket n (Sport) cricket m; (insect) grillon m.

crime n crime m; (minor) délit m; (acts) criminalité f.

criminal a & n criminel/-le (m/f).

crimson a & n cramoisi (m).

cringe vi reculer; (fig) s'humilier.

crinkle vt/i (se) froisser. ● n pli m.

cripple n infirme mf. ● vt estropier; (fig) paralyser.

crisis n (pl **crises**) crise f.

crisp adj (Culin) croquant; (air, reply) vif. **crisps** npl chips fpl.

criss-cross adj entrecroisé. ● vt/i (s')entrecroiser.

criterion n (pl **-ia**) critère m.

critic n critique m. **critical** adj critique. **critically** adv d'une manière critique; (ill) gravement.

criticism n critique f.

criticize vt/i critiquer.

croak n (bird) croassement m; (frog) coassement m. ● vi croasser; coasser.

Croatia n Croatie f.

Croatian n Croate mf. ● adj Croate.

crochet n crochet m. ● vt faire du crochet.

crockery n vaisselle f.

crocodile n crocodile m.

crook n (criminal 🅸) escroc m; (stick) houlette f.

crooked adj tordu; (winding) tortueux; (askew) de travers; (dishonest: fig) malhonnête.

crop n récolte f; (fig) quantité f. ● vt (pt **cropped**) couper. ● vi ~ **up** se présenter.

cross n croix f; (hybrid) hybride m. ● vt/i traverser; (legs, animals) croiser; (cheque) barrer; (paths) se croiser; ~ **sb's mind** venir à l'esprit de qn. ● adj en colère, fâché (**with** contre); **talk at** ~ **purposes** parler sans se comprendre. □ ~ **off** or **out**

rayer. **~-check** *vt* vérifier (pour confirmer). **~-country (running)** *n* cross *m*. **~-examine** *vt* faire subir un contre-interrogatoire à. **~-eyed** *adj* be **~-eyed** loucher. **~fire** *n* feux *mpl* croisés.

crossing *n* (by boat) traversée *f*; (on road) passage *m* clouté.

crossly *adv* avec colère.

cross: **~-reference** *n* renvoi *m*. **~roads** *n* carrefour *m*. **~word** *n* mots *mpl* croisés.

crotch *n* (of garment) entrejambes *m inv*.

crouch *vi* s'accroupir.

crow *n* corbeau *m*; as the **~** flies à vol d'oiseau. ● *vi* (of cock) chanter; (fig) jubiler. **~bar** *n* pied-de-biche *m*.

crowd *n* foule *f*. **crowded** *adj* plein.

crown *n* couronne *f*; (top part) sommet *m*. ● *vt* couronner.

Crown Court *n* Cour *f* d'assises.

crucial *adj* crucial.

crucifix *n* crucifix *m*.

crucify *vt* crucifier.

crude *adj* (raw) brut; (rough, vulgar) grossier.

cruel *adj* (**crueller**, **cruellest**) cruel.

cruise *n* croisière *f*. ● *vi* (ship) croiser; (tourists) faire une croisière; (vehicle) rouler; **cruising speed** vitesse *f* de croisière.

crumb *n* miette *f*.

crumble *vt/i* (s')effriter; (bread) (s')émietter; (collapse) s'écrouler.

crumple *vt/i* (se) froisser.

crunch *vt* croquer. ● *n* (event) moment *m* critique; **when it comes to the ~** quand ça devient sérieux.

crusade *n* croisade *f*. **crusader** *n* (knight) croisé *m*; (fig) militant/-e *m/f*.

crush *vt* écraser; (clothes) froisser. ● *n* (crowd) presse *f*; **a ~ on** 🖾 le béguin pour.

crust *n* croûte *f*. **crusty** *adj* croustillant.

crutch *n* béquille *f*; (crotch) entrejambes *m inv*.

crux *n* the **~** of (problem) le point crucial de.

cry *n* cri *m*. ● *vi* (weep) pleurer; (call out) crier. ▫ **~ off** se décommander.

crying *adj* (need) urgent; **a ~ shame** une vraie honte. ● *n* pleurs *mpl*.

cryptic *adj* énigmatique.

crystal *n* cristal *m*. **~-clear** *adj* parfaitement clair.

cub *n* petit *m*; **Cub (Scout)** louveteau *m*.

Cuba *n* Cuba *f*.

cube *n* cube *m*. **cubic** *adj* cubique; (metre) cube.

cubicle *n* (in room, hospital) box *m*; (at swimming-pool) cabine *f*.

cuckoo *n* coucou *m*.

cucumber *n* concombre *m*.

cuddle *vt* câliner. ● *vi* (kiss and) **~** s'embrasser. ● *n* caresse *f*. **cuddly** *adj* câlin; **cuddly toy** peluche *f*.

cue *n* signal *m*; (Theat) réplique *f*; (billiards) queue *f*.

cuff *n* manchette *f*; (US: on trousers) revers *m*; **off the ~** impromptu. ● *vt* gifler. **~-link** *n* bouton *m* de manchette.

cul-de-sac *n* (*pl* **culs-de-sac**) impasse *f*.

cull *vt* (select) choisir; (kill) massacrer.

culminate *vi* **~ in** se terminer par. **culmination** *n* point *m* culminant.

culprit *n* coupable *mf*.

cult *n* culte *m*.

cultivate *vt* cultiver. **cultivation** *n* culture *f*.

cultural *adj* culturel.

culture *n* culture *f*. **cultured** *adj* cultivé.

cumbersome *adj* encombrant.

cunning *adj* rusé. ● *n* astuce *f*, ruse *f*.

cup *n* tasse *f*; (prize) coupe *f*; **Cup final** finale *f* de la coupe.

cupboard *n* placard *m*.

cup-tie *n* match *m* de coupe.

curate *n* vicaire *m*.

curator *n* (of museum) conservateur *m*.

curb *n* (restraint) frein *m*; (of path) (US) bord *m* du trottoir. ● *vt* (desires) refréner; (price increase) freiner.

cure *vt* guérir; (fig) éliminer; (Culin) fumer; (in brine) saler. ● *n* (recovery) guérison *f*; (remedy) remède *m*.

curfew n couvre-feu m.

curiosity n curiosité f. **curious** adj curieux.

curl vt/i (hair) boucler. ● n boucle f. □ ~ **up** se pelotonner; (shrivel) se racornir.

curler n bigoudi m.

curly adj (-ier, -iest) bouclé.

currant n raisin m de Corinthe.

currency n (money) monnaie f; (of word) fréquence f; **foreign** ~ devises fpl étrangères.

current adj (term, word) usité; (topical) actuel; (year) en cours. ● n courant m. ~ **account** n compte m courant. ~ **events** npl l'actualité f.

currently adv actuellement.

curriculum n (pl **-la**) programme m scolaire. ~ **vitae** n curriculum vitae m.

curry n curry m. ● vt ~ **favour with** chercher les bonnes grâces de.

curse n (spell) malédiction f; (swearword) juron m. ● vt maudire. ● vi (swear) jurer.

cursor n curseur m.

curt adj brusque.

curtain n rideau m.

curve n courbe f. ● vi (line) s'incurver; (edge) se recourber; (road) faire une courbe. ● vt courber.

cushion n coussin m. ● vt (a blow) amortir; (fig) protéger.

custard n crème f anglaise; (set) flan m.

custody n (of child) garde f; (Jur) détention f préventive.

custom n coutume f; (patronage: Comm) clientèle f. **customary** adj habituel.

customer n client/-e m/f; (person 🄸) type m.

customize vt personnaliser.

custom-made adj fait sur mesure.

customs npl douane f. ● adj douanier. ~ **officer** n douanier m.

cut vt/i (pt cut; pres p **cutting**) vt couper; (hedge) tailler; (prices) réduire. ● vi couper. ● n (wound) coupure f; (of clothes) coupe f; (in surgery) incision f; (share) part f; (in prices) réduction f. □ ~ **back** vi faire des économies. vt réduire. ~ **down** (on) réduire; ~ **in** (in conversation) intervenir; ~ **off** couper; (tide, army) isoler; ~ **out** vt découper; (leave out) supprimer; vi (engine) s'arrêter. ~ **short** (visit) écourter; ~ **up** couper; (carve) découper.

cut-back n réduction f.

cute adj 🄸 mignon.

cutlery n couverts mpl.

cutlet n côtelette f.

cut-price adj à prix réduit.

cutting adj cinglant. ● n (from newspaper) coupure f; (plant) bouture f.

CV abbr ⇒CURRICULUM VITAE.

cyanide n cyanure m.

cycle n cycle m; (bicycle) vélo m. ● vi aller à vélo.

cycling n cyclisme m. ~ **shorts** npl cycliste m.

cyclist n cycliste mf.

cylinder n cylindre m.

cymbal n cymbale f.

cynic n cynique mf. **cynical** adj cynique. **cynicism** n cynisme m.

cypress n cyprès m.

Cypriot n Cypriote mf. ● adj cypriote.

Cyprus n Chypre f.

cyst n kyste m.

czar n tsar m.

Czech n (person) Tchèque mf; (Ling) tchèque m. ~ **Republic** n République f tchèque.

Dd

dab vt (pt **dabbed**) tamponner; ~ **sth on** appliquer qch par petites touches. ● n touche f.

dabble vi ~ **in sth** faire qch en amateur.

dad n 🄸 papa m. **daddy** n 🄸 papa m.

daffodil n jonquille f.

daft adj bête.

dagger n poignard m.

daily *adj* quotidien. ● *adv* tous les jours. ● *n* (newspaper) quotidien *m*.

dainty *adj* (**-ier, -iest**) (*lace, food*) délicat; (*shoe, hand*) mignon.

dairy *n* (on farm) laiterie *f*; (shop) crémerie *f*. ● *adj* (*farm, cow, product*) laitier; (*butter*) fermier.

daisy *n* pâquerette *f*; (Comput) ∼ **wheel** marguerite *f*.

dale *n* vallée *f*.

dam *n* barrage *m*.

damage *n* (to property) dégâts *mpl*; (Med) lésions *fpl*; **to do sth** ∼ (cause, trade) porter atteinte à; ∼**s** (Jur) dommages-intérêts *mpl*. ● *vt* (*property*) endommager; (*health*) nuire à; (*reputation*) porter atteinte à. **damaging** *adj* (to health) nuisible; (to reputation) préjudiciable.

damn *vt* (Relig) damner; (condemn: fig) condamner. ● *interj* 🄴 zut 🄴, merde 🅇. ● *n* not give/care a ∼ about se ficher de 🄴. ● *adj* fichu 🄴. ● *adv* franchement.

damp *n* humidité *f*. ● *adj* humide. **dampen** *vt* (lit) humecter; (fig) refroidir. **dampness** *n* humidité *f*.

dance *vt/i* danser. ● *n* danse *f*; (gathering) bal *m*; ∼ **hall** dancing *m*. **dancer** *n* danseur/-euse *m/f*.

dandelion *n* pissenlit *m*.

dandruff *n* pellicules *fpl*.

Dane *n* Danois/-e *m/f*.

danger *n* danger *m*; (risk) risque *m*; **be in** ∼ **of** risquer de. **dangerous** *adj* dangereux.

dangle *vt* (*object*) balancer; (*legs*) laisser pendre. ● *vi* (*object*) se balancer (**from** à).

Danish *n* (Ling) danois *m*. ● *adj* danois.

dare *vt* oser (**(to) do** faire); ∼ **sb to do** défier qn de faire. ● *n* défi *m*. **daring** *adj* audacieux.

dark *adj* (*day, colour, suit, mood, warning*) sombre; (*hair, eyes, skin*) brun; (*secret, thought*) noir. ● *n* noir *m*; (nightfall) tombée *f* de la nuit; **in the** ∼ (fig) dans le noir. **darken** *vt/i* (*sky*) (s')obscurcir; (*colour*) (se) foncer; (*mood*) (s')assombrir. **darkness** *n* obscurité *f*. ∼**-room** *n* chambre *f* noire.

darling *a* & *n* chéri/-e (*m/f*).

dart *n* fléchette *f*; ∼**s** (game) fléchettes *fpl*. ● *vi* ∼ **in/away** entrer/ filer comme une flèche.

dash *vi* se précipiter; ∼ **off** se sauver. ● *vt* (hope) anéantir; ∼ **sth against** projeter qch contre. ● *n* course *f* folle; (of liquid) goutte *f*; (of colour) touche *f*; (in punctuation) tiret *m*.

dashboard *n* tableau *m* de bord.

data *npl* données *fpl*. ∼**base** *n* base *f* de données. ∼ **capture** *n* saisie *f* de données. ∼ **processing** *n* traitement *m* des données. ∼ **protection** *n* protection *f* de l'information.

date *n* date *f*; (meeting) rendez-vous *m*; (fruit) datte *f*; **out of** ∼ (old-fashioned) démodé; (*passport*) périmé; **to** ∼ à ce jour; **up to** ∼ (modern) moderne; (*list*) à jour. ● *vt/i* dater; (go out with) sortir avec; ∼ **from** dater de. **dated** *adj* démodé.

daughter *n* fille *f*. ∼**-in-law** *n* (*pl* ∼**s-in-law**) belle-fille *f*.

daunt *vt* décourager.

dawdle *vi* flâner, traînasser 🄴.

dawn *n* aube *f*. ● *vi* (day) se lever; **it** ∼**ed on me that** je me suis rendu compte que.

day *n* jour *m*; (whole day) journée *f*; (period) époque *f*; **the** ∼ **before** la veille; **the following** *or* **next** ∼ le lendemain. ∼**break** *n* aube *f*.

daydream *n* rêves *mpl*. ● *vi* rêvasser (**about** de).

day: ∼**light** *n* jour *m*. ∼**time** *n* journée *f*.

daze *n* **in a** ∼ (from blow) étourdi; (from drug) hébété. **dazed** *adj* (by blow) abasourdi; (by news) ahuri.

dazzle *vt* éblouir.

dead *adj* mort; (numb) engourdi. ● *adv* complètement; **in** ∼ **centre** au beau milieu; **stop** ∼ s'arrêter net. ● *n* **in the** ∼ **of** au cœur de; **the** ∼ les morts. **deaden** *vt* (*sound, blow*) amortir; (*pain*) calmer. ∼ **end** *n* impasse *f*. ∼**line** *n* date *f* limite. ∼**lock** *n* impasse *f*.

deadly *adj* (**-ier, -iest**) mortel; (*weapon*) meurtrier.

deaf *adj* sourd. **deafen** *vt* assourdir. **deafness** *n* surdité *f*.

deal vt (pt **dealt**) donner; (blow) porter. ● vi (trade) être en activité; ~ **in** être dans le commerce de. ● n affaire f; (cards) donne f; **a great** or **good** ~ beaucoup (of de). □ ~ **with** (handle, manage) s'occuper de; (be about) traiter de. **dealer** n marchand/-e m/f; (agent) concessionnaire mf. **dealings** npl relations fpl.

dear adj cher; ~ **Sir/Madam** Monsieur/Madame. ● n (my) ~ mon chéri/ma chérie m/f. ● adv cher. ● interj oh ~! oh mon Dieu!

death n mort f; ~ **penalty** peine f de mort. **deathly** adj de mort, mortel.

debase vt avilir.

debatable adj discutable.

debate n (formal) débat m; (informal) discussion f. ● vt (formally) débattre de; (informally) discuter.

debit n débit m. ● adj (balance) débiteur. ● vt (pt **debited**) débiter.

debris n débris mpl; (rubbish) déchets mpl.

debt n dette f; **be in** ~ avoir des dettes.

debug vt (Comput) déboguer.

decade n décennie f.

decadent adj décadent.

decaffeinated adj décaféiné.

decay vi (vegetation) pourrir; (tooth) se carier; (fig) décliner. ● n pourriture f; (of tooth) carie f; (fig) déclin m.

deceased adj décédé. ● n défunt/-e m/f.

deceit n tromperie f. **deceitful** adj trompeur. **deceitfully** adv d'une manière trompeuse.

deceive vt tromper.

December n décembre m.

decent adj (respectable) comme il faut; (adequate) convenable; (good) bon; (kind) gentil; (not indecent) décent. **decently** adv convenablement.

deception n tromperie f. **deceptive** adj trompeur.

decide vt/i décider (**to do** de faire); (question) régler; ~ **on** se décider pour. **decided** adj (firm) résolu; (clear) net. **decidedly** adv nettement.

decimal adj décimal. ● n décimale f; ~ **point** virgule f.

decipher vt déchiffrer.

decision n décision f.

decisive adj (conclusive) décisif; (firm) décidé.

deck n pont m; (of cards: US) jeu m; (of bus) étage m. ~-**chair** n chaise f longue.

declaration n déclaration f. **declare** vt déclarer.

decline vt/i refuser; (fall) baisser. ● n (waning) déclin m; (drop) baisse f; **in** ~ sur le déclin.

decode vt décoder.

decompose vt/i (se) décomposer.

decor n décor m.

decorate vt décorer; (room) refaire, peindre. **decoration** n décoration f. **decorative** adj décoratif.

decorator n peintre m; (interior) ~ décorateur/-trice m/f.

decoy n (person, vehicle) leurre m; (for hunting) appeau m.

decrease¹ vt/i diminuer.

decrease² n diminution f.

decree n (Pol, Relig) décret m; (Jur) jugement m. ● vt (pt **decreed**) décréter.

decrepit adj (building) délabré; (person) décrépit.

dedicate vt dédier; ~ **oneself to** se consacrer à.

dedicated adj dévoué; ~ **line** (Internet) ligne f spécialisée.

dedication n dévouement m; (in book) dédicace f.

deduce vt déduire.

deduct vt déduire; (from wages) retenir.

deed n acte m.

deem vt considérer.

deep adj profond; (mud, carpet) épais. ● adv profondément; ~ **in** **thought** absorbé dans ses pensées. **deepen** vt/i (admiration, concern) augmenter; (colour) foncer.

deep-freeze n congélateur m. ● vt congeler.

deer n inv cerf m; (doe) biche f.

deface vt dégrader.

default vi (Jur) ~ (**on payments**) ne pas régler ses échéances. ● n (on

payments) non-remboursement *m*; **by
~** par défaut; **win by ~** gagner par
forfait. ● *adj* (Comput) par défaut.

defeat *vt* vaincre; (thwart) faire
échouer. ● *n* défaite *f*; (of plan) échec
m.

defect¹ *n* défaut *m*.

defect² *vi* faire défection; **~ to**
passer à.

defective *adj* défectueux.

defector *n* transfuge *mf*.

defence *n* défense *f*.

defend *vt* défendre. **defendant** *n*
(Jur) accusé/-e *m/f*. **defender**
défenseur *m*.

defensive *adj* défensif. ● *n*
défensive *f*.

defer *vt* (*pt* **deferred**) (postpone)
reporter; (*judgement*) suspendre;
(*payment*) différer.

deference *n* déférence *f*.
deferential *adj* déférent.

defiance *n* défi *m*; **in ~ of** contre.
defiant *adj* rebelle. **defiantly** *adv*
avec défi.

deficiency *n* insuffisance *f*; (fault)
défaut *m*.

deficient *adj* insuffisant; **be ~ in**
manquer de.

deficit *n* déficit *m*.

define *vt* définir.

definite *adj* (exact) précis; (obvious)
net; (firm) ferme; (certain) certain.
definitely *adv* certainement; (clearly)
nettement.

definition *n* définition *f*.

deflate *vt* dégonfler.

deflect *vt* (*missile*) dévier; (*criticism*)
détourner.

deforestation *n* déforestation *f*.

deform *vt* déformer.

defraud *vt* (*client, employer*)
escroquer; (*state, customs*) frauder;
~ sb of sth escroquer qch à qn.

defrost *vt* dégivrer.

deft *adj* adroit.

defunct *adj* défunt.

defuse *vt* désamorcer.

defy *vt* défier; (*attempts*) résister à.

degenerate¹ *vi* dégénérer (**into**
en).

degenerate² *a & n* dégénéré/-e (*m/
f*).

degrade *vt* (humiliate) humilier;
(damage) dégrader.

degree *n* degré *m*; (Univ) diplôme *m*
universitaire; (Bachelor's degree)
licence *f*; **to such a ~ that** à tel point
que.

dehydrate *vt/i* (se) déshydrater.

deign *vt* **~ to do** daigner faire.

dejected *adj* découragé.

delay *vt* (*flight*) retarder; (*decision*)
différer; **~ doing** attendre pour
faire. ● *n* (of plane, post) retard *m*;
(time lapse) délai *m*.

delegate¹ *n* délégué/-e *m/f*.

delegate² *vt* déléguer. **delegation**
n délégation *f*.

delete *vt* supprimer; (Comput)
effacer; (with pen) barrer. **deletion** *n*
suppression *f*; (with line) rature *f*.

deliberate¹ *vi* délibérer.

deliberate² *adj* délibéré; (*steps,
manner*) mesuré. **deliberately** *adv*
(*do, say*) exprès; (*sarcastically,
provocatively*) délibérément.

delicacy *n* délicatesse *f*; (food) mets
m raffiné.

delicate *adj* délicat.

delicatessen *n* épicerie *f* fine.

delicious *adj* délicieux.

delight *n* joie *f*, plaisir *m*. ● *vt* ravir.
● *vi* **~ in** prendre plaisir à.
delighted *adj* ravi. **delightful** *adj*
charmant/-e.

delinquent *a & n* délinquant/-e (*m/
f*).

delirious *adj* délirant.

deliver *vt* (*message*) remettre;
(*goods*) livrer; (*speech*) faire; (*baby*)
mettre au monde; (rescue) délivrer.
delivery *n* (of goods) livraison *f*; (of
mail) distribution *f*; (of baby)
accouchement *m*.

delude *vt* tromper; **~ oneself** se
faire des illusions.

deluge *n* déluge *m*. ● *vt* submerger
(**with** de).

delusion *n* illusion *f*.

delve *vi* fouiller.

demand *vt* (request, require)
demander; (forcefully) exiger. ● *n*
(request) demande *f*; (pressure)
exigence *f*; **in ~** très demandé; **on ~**

à la demande. **demanding** *adj*
exigeant.

demean *vt* ~ oneself s'abaisser.

demeanour, (US) **demeanor** *n*
comportement *m*.

demented *adj* fou.

demise *n* disparition *f*.

demo *n* (demonstration Ⓘ) manif *f* Ⓘ.

democracy *n* démocratie *f*.

democrat *n* démocrate *mf*.
democratic *adj* démocratique.

demolish *vt* démolir.

demon *n* démon *m*.

demonstrate *vt* démontrer;
(*concern, skill*) manifester. ● *vi* (Pol)
manifester. **demonstration** *n*
démonstration *f*; (Pol) manifestation
f. **demonstrative** *adj* démonstratif.
demonstrator *n* manifestant/-e *m*/
f.

demoralize *vt* démoraliser.

demote *vt* rétrograder.

den *n* (of lion) antre *m*; (room) tanière
f.

denial *n* (of rumour) démenti *m*; (of
rights) négation *f*; (of request) rejet *m*.

denim *n* jean *m*; ~s (jeans) jean *m*.

Denmark *n* Danemark *m*.

denomination *n* (Relig) confession
f; (money) valeur *f*.

denounce *vt* dénoncer.

dense *adj* dense. **densely** *adv*
(*packed*) très. **density** *n* densité *f*.

dent *n* bosse *f*. ● *vt* cabosser.

dental *adj* dentaire; ~ floss fil *m*
dentaire; ~ surgeon chirurgien-
dentiste *m*.

dentist *n* dentiste *mf*. **dentistry** *n*
médecine *f* dentaire.

dentures *npl* dentier *m*.

deny *vt* nier (that que); (*rumour*)
démentir; ~ sb sth refuser qch à qn.

deodorant *n* déodorant *m*.

depart *vi* partir; ~ from (deviate)
s'éloigner de.

department *n* (in shop) rayon *m*; (in
hospital, office) service *m*; (Univ)
département *m*; D~ of Health
ministère *m* de la santé; ~ store
grand magasin *m*.

departure *n* départ *m*; a ~ from
(*custom, truth*) une entorse à.

depend *vi* dépendre (on de); ~ on
(rely on) compter sur; it (all) ~s ça
dépend; ~ing on the season suivant
la saison. **dependable** *adj* (*person*)
digne de confiance. **dependant** *n*
personne *f* à charge. **dependence**
n dépendance *f*.

dependent *adj* dépendant; be ~ on
dépendre de.

depict *vt* (describe) dépeindre; (in
picture) représenter.

deplete *vt* réduire.

deport *vt* expulser.

depose *vt* déposer.

deposit *vt* (*pt* **deposited**) déposer.
● *n* (in bank) dépôt *m*; (on house)
versement *m* initial; (on holiday)
acompte *m*; (against damage) caution *f*;
(on bottle) consigne *f*; (of mineral)
gisement *m*; ~ account compte *m* de
dépôt. **depositor** *n* (Comm)
déposant/-e *m*/*f*.

depot *n* dépôt *m*; (US) gare *f*.

depreciate *vt*/*i* (se) déprécier.

depress *vt* déprimer. **depressing**
adj déprimant. **depression** *n*
dépression *f*; (Econ) récession *f*.

deprivation *n* privation *f*.

deprive *vt* ~ of priver de.
deprived *adj* démuni.

depth *n* profondeur *f*; (of knowledge,
ignorance) étendue *f*; (of colour, emotion)
intensité *f*.

deputize *vi* ~ for remplacer.

deputy *n* adjoint/-e *m*/*f*. ● *adj*
adjoint; ~ chairman vice-président
m.

derail *vt* faire dérailler.
derailment *n* déraillement *m*.

deranged *adj* dérangé.

derelict *adj* abandonné.

deride *vt* ridiculiser. **derision** *n*
moqueries *fpl*. **derisory** *adj*
dérisoire.

derivative *a* & *n* dérivé (*m*).

derive *vt* ~ sth from tirer qch de.
● *vi* ~ from découler de.

derogatory *adj* (*word*) péjoratif;
(*remark*) désobligeant.

descend *vt*/*i* descendre; be ~ed
from descendre de. **descendant** *n*
descendant/-e *m*/*f*. **descent** *n*
descente *f*; (lineage) origine *f*.

describe *vt* décrire; ~ **sb as sth** qualifier qn de qch. **description** *n* description *f*. **descriptive** *adj* descriptif.

desert[1] *n* désert *m*.

desert[2] *vt/i* abandonner; (*cause*) déserter. **deserted** *adj* désert. **deserter** *n* déserteur *m*.

deserts *npl* **get one's** ~ avoir ce qu'on mérite.

deserve *vt* mériter (**to** de). **deservedly** *adv* à juste titre. **deserving** *adj* (*person*) méritant; (*action*) louable.

design *n* (*sketch*) plan *m*; (*idea*) conception *f*; (*pattern*) motif *m*; (*art of designing*) design *m*; (*aim*) dessein *m*. ● *vt* (*sketch*) dessiner; (*devise, intend*) concevoir.

designate *vt* désigner.

designer *n* concepteur/-trice *m/f*; (of fashion, furniture) créateur/-trice *m/f*. ● *adj* (*clothes*) de haute couture; (*sunglasses, drink*) de dernière mode.

desirable *adj* (*outcome*) souhaitable; (*person*) désirable.

desire *n* désir *m*. ● *vt* désirer.

desk *n* bureau *m*; (of pupil) pupitre *m*; (in hotel) réception *f*; (in bank) caisse *f*.

desolate *adj* (*place*) désolé; (*person*) affligé.

despair *n* désespoir *m*. ● *vi* désespérer (**of** de).

desperate *adj* désespéré; (criminal) prêt à tout; **be** ~ **for** avoir désespérément besoin de. **desperately** *adv* désespérément; (*worried*) terriblement; (*ill*) gravement.

desperation *n* désespoir *m*; **in** ~ en désespoir de cause.

despicable *adj* méprisable.

despise *vt* mépriser.

despite *prep* malgré.

despondent *adj* découragé.

dessert *n* dessert *m*. ~**spoon** *n* cuillère *f* à dessert.

destination *n* destination *f*.

destiny *n* destin *m*.

destitute *adj* sans ressources.

destroy *vt* détruire; (*animal*) abattre. **destroyer** *n* (warship) contre-torpilleur *m*.

destruction *n* destruction *f*. **destructive** *adj* destructeur.

detach *vt* détacher; ~**ed house** maison *f* (individuelle).

detail *n* détail *m*; **go into** ~ entrer dans les détails. ● *vt* (*plans*) exposer en détail.

detain *vt* retenir; (in prison) placer en détention. **detainee** *n* détenu/-e *m/ f*.

detect *vt* (*error, trace*) déceler; (*crime, mine, sound*) détecter. **detection** *n* détection *f*. **detective** *n* inspecteur/-trice *m/f*; (private) détective *m*.

detention *n* détention *f*; (School) retenue *f*.

deter *vt* (*pt* **deterred**) dissuader (**from** de).

detergent *a & n* détergent (*m*).

deteriorate *vi* se détériorer.

determine *vt* déterminer; ~ **to do** résoudre de faire. **determined** *adj* (*person*) décidé; (*air*) résolu.

deterrent *n* moyen *m* de dissuasion. ● *adj* (*effect*) dissuasif.

detest *vt* détester.

detonate *vt/i* (faire) détoner. **detonation** *n* détonation *f*. **detonator** *n* détonateur *m*.

detour *n* détour *m*.

detract *vi* ~ **from** (*success, value*) porter atteinte à; (*pleasure*) diminuer.

detriment *n* **to the** ~ **of** au détriment de. **detrimental** *adj* nuisible (**to** à).

devalue *vt* dévaluer.

devastate *vt* (*place*) ravager; (*person*) accabler.

develop *vt* (*plan*) élaborer; (*mind, body*) développer; (*land*) mettre en valeur; (*illness*) attraper; (*habit*) prendre. ● *vi* (*child, country, plot, business*) se développer; (*hole, crack*) se former.

development *n* développement *m*; (housing) ~ lotissement *m*; (new) ~ fait *m* nouveau.

deviate *vi* dévier; ~ **from** (*norm*) s'écarter de.

device *n* appareil *m*; (means) moyen *m*; (bomb) engin *m* explosif.

devil n diable m.

devious adj (person) retors.

devise vt (scheme) concevoir; (product) inventer.

devoid adj ~ of dépourvu de.

devolution n (Pol) régionalisation f.

devote vt consacrer (to à). **devoted** adj dévoué. **devotion** n dévouement m; (Relig) dévotion f.

devour vt dévorer.

devout adj fervent.

dew n rosée f.

diabetes n diabète m.

diabolical adj diabolique; (bad 🎧) atroce.

diagnose vt diagnostiquer. **diagnosis** n (pl -oses) diagnostic m.

diagonal adj diagonal. ● n diagonale f.

diagram n schéma m.

dial n cadran m. ● vt (pt dialled) (number) faire; (person) appeler; **dialling code** indicatif m; **dialling tone** tonalité f.

dialect n dialecte m.

dialogue n dialogue m.

diameter n diamètre m.

diamond n diamant m; (shape) losange m; (baseball) terrain m; ~s (cards) carreau m.

diaper n (US) couche f.

diaphragm n diaphragme m.

diarrhoea, (US) **diarrhea** n diarrhée f.

diary n (for appointments) agenda m; (journal) journal m intime.

dice n inv dé m. ● vt (food) couper en dés.

dictate vt/i dicter.

dictation n dictée f.

dictator n dictateur m. **dictatorship** n dictature f.

dictionary n dictionnaire m.

did ⇒DO.

didn't = DID NOT.

die vi (pres p **dying**) mourir; (plant) crever; **be dying to do** mourir d'envie de faire. □ ~ **down** diminuer; ~ **out** disparaître.

diesel n gazole m; ~ **engine** moteur m diesel.

diet n (usual food) alimentation f; (restricted) régime m. ● vi être au régime. **dietary** adj alimentaire. **dietician** n diététicien/-ne m/f.

differ vi différer (from de).

difference n différence f; (disagreement) différend m. **different** adj différent (from, to de).

differentiate vt différencier. ● vi faire la différence (between entre).

differently adv différemment (from de).

difficult adj difficile. **difficulty** n difficulté f.

diffuse¹ adj diffus.

diffuse² vt diffuser.

dig vt/i (pt **dug**; pres p **digging**) (excavate) creuser; (in garden) bêcher. ● n (poke) coup m de coude; (remark) pique f 🎧; (Archeol) fouilles fpl. □ ~ **up** déterrer.

digest vt/i digérer. **digestible** adj digestible. **digestion** n digestion f.

digger n excavateur m.

digit n chiffre m.

digital adj (clock) à affichage numérique; (display, recording) numérique. ~ **audio tape** n cassette f audionumérique.

dignified adj digne.

dignitary n dignitaire m.

dignity n dignité f.

digress vi faire une digression.

dilapidated adj délabré.

dilate vt/i (se) dilater.

dilemma n dilemme m.

diligent adj appliqué.

dilute vt diluer.

dim adj (dimmer, dimmest) (weak) faible; (dark) sombre; (indistinct) vague; 🎧 stupide. ● vt/i (pt **dimmed**) (light) baisser.

dime n (US) (pièce f de) dix cents.

dimension n dimension f.

diminish vt/i diminuer.

dimple n fossette f.

din n vacarme m.

dine vi dîner. **diner** n dîneur/-euse m/f; (Rail) wagon-restaurant m; (US) restaurant m à service rapide.

dinghy n dériveur m.

dingy adj (-ier, -iest) miteux, minable.

dining room *n* salle *f* à manger.

dinner *n* (evening meal) dîner *m*; (lunch) déjeuner *m*; **have ∼** dîner. **∼-jacket** *n* smoking *m*. **∼ party** *n* dîner *m*.

dinosaur *n* dinosaure *m*.

dip *vt/i* (*pt* **dipped**) plonger; **∼ into** (*book*) feuilleter; (*savings*) puiser dans; **∼ one's headlights** se mettre en code. ● *n* (slope) déclivité *f*; (in sea) bain *m* rapide.

diploma *n* diplôme *m* (**in** en).

diplomacy *n* diplomatie *f*.

diplomat *n* diplomate *mf*.

diplomatic *adj* (Pol) diplomatique; (tactful) diplomate.

dire *adj* affreux; (*need, poverty*) extrême.

direct *adj* direct. ● *adv* directement. ● *vt* diriger; (*letter, remark*) adresser; (*a play*) mettre en scène; **∼ sb to** indiquer à qn le chemin de; (order) signifier à qn de.

direction *n* direction *f*; (Theat) mise *f* en scène; **∼s** indications *fpl*; **ask ∼s** demander le chemin; **∼s for use** mode *m* d'emploi.

directly *adv* directement; (at once) tout de suite. ● *conj* dès que.

director *n* directeur/-trice *m/f*; (Theat) metteur *m* en scène.

directory *n* (phone book) annuaire *m*. **∼ enquiries** *npl* renseignements *mpl* téléphoniques.

dirt *n* saleté *f*; (earth) terre *f*; **∼ cheap** ⊠ très bon marché *inv*. **∼-track** *n* (Sport) cendrée *f*.

dirty *adj* (**-ier, -iest**) sale; (word) grossier; **get ∼** se salir. ● *vt/i* (se) salir.

disability *n* handicap *m*.

disable *vt* rendre infirme. **disabled** *adj* handicapé.

disadvantage *n* désavantage *m*. **disadvantaged** *adj* défavorisé.

disagree *vi* ne pas être d'accord (with avec); **∼ with sb** (*food, climate*) ne pas convenir à qn. **disagreement** *n* désaccord *m*; (quarrel) différend *m*.

disappear *vi* disparaître. **disappearance** *n* disparition *f* (of de).

disappoint *vt* décevoir. **disappointment** *n* déception *f*.

disapproval *n* désapprobation *f* (of de).

disapprove *vi* **∼ (of)** désapprouver.

disarm *vt/i* désarmer. **disarmament** *n* désarmement *m*.

disarray *n* désordre *m*.

disaster *n* désastre *m*. **disastrous** *adj* désastreux.

disband *vi* disperser. ● *vt* dissoudre.

disbelief *n* incrédulité *f*.

disc *n* disque *m*; (Comput) = DISK.

discard *vt* se débarrasser de; (*beliefs*) abandonner.

discharge *vt* (unload) décharger; (*liquid*) déverser; (*duty*) remplir; (dismiss) renvoyer; (*prisoner*) libérer. ● *vi* (of pus) s'écouler.

disciple *n* disciple *m*.

disciplinary *adj* disciplinaire.

discipline *n* discipline *f*. ● *vt* discipliner; (punish) punir.

disc jockey *n* disc-jockey *m*, animateur *m*.

disclaimer *n* démenti *m*.

disclose *vt* révéler. **disclosure** *n* révélation *f* (of de).

disco *n* (club 🔳) discothèque *f*; (event) soirée *f* disco.

discolour *vt/i* (se) décolorer.

discomfort *n* gêne *f*.

disconcert *vt* déconcerter.

disconnect *vt* détacher; (unplug) débrancher; (cut off) couper.

discontent *n* mécontentement *m*.

discontinue *vt* (*service*) supprimer; (*production*) arrêter.

discord *n* discorde *f*; (Mus) discordance *f*.

discount¹ *n* remise *f*; (on minor purchase) rabais *m*.

discount² *vt* (*advice*) ne pas tenir compte de; (*possibility*) écarter.

discourage *vt* décourager.

discourse *n* discours *m*.

discourteous *adj* peu courtois.

discover *vt* découvrir. **discovery** *n* découverte *f*.

discreet *adj* discret.

discrepancy *n* divergence *f*.

discretion n discrétion f.

discriminate vt/i distinguer; ~ against faire de la discrimination contre. **discriminating** adj qui a du discernement. **discrimination** n discernement m; (bias) discrimination f.

discus n disque m.

discuss vt (talk about) discuter de; (in writing) examiner. **discussion** n discussion f.

disdain n dédain m.

disease n maladie f.

disembark vt/i débarquer.

disenchanted adj désabusé.

disentangle vt démêler.

disfigure vt défigurer.

disgrace n (shame) honte f; (disfavour) disgrâce f. ● vt déshonorer. **disgraced** adj (in disfavour) disgracié. **disgraceful** adj honteux.

disgruntled adj mécontent.

disguise vt déguiser. ● n déguisement m; in ~ déguisé.

disgust n dégoût m. ● vt dégoûter.

dish n plat m; the ~es (crockery) la vaisselle. ● vt ~ out ⊞ distribuer; ~ up servir.

dishcloth n lavette f; (for drying) torchon m.

dishearten vt décourager.

dishevelled adj échevelé.

dishonest adj malhonnête.

dishonour, (US) **dishonor** n déshonneur m.

dishwasher n lave-vaisselle m inv.

disillusion vt désabuser. **disillusionment** n désillusion f.

disincentive n be a ~ to décourager.

disinclined adj ~ to peu disposé à.

disinfect vt désinfecter. **disinfectant** n désinfectant m.

disintegrate vt/i (se) désintégrer.

disinterested adj désintéressé.

disjointed adj (talk) décousu.

disk n (US) = DISC; (Comput) disque m. ~ **drive** n drive m, lecteur m de disquettes.

diskette n disquette f.

dislike n aversion f. ● vt ne pas aimer.

dislocate vt (limb) disloquer.

dislodge vt (move) déplacer; (drive out) déloger.

disloyal adj déloyal (to envers).

dismal adj morne, triste.

dismantle vt démonter, défaire.

dismay n consternation f (at devant). ● vt consterner.

dismiss vt renvoyer; (appeal) rejeter; (from mind) écarter. **dismissal** n renvoi m.

dismount vi descendre, mettre pied à terre.

disobedient adj désobéissant.

disobey vt désobéir à. ● vi désobéir.

disorder n désordre m; (ailment) trouble(s) m(pl). **disorderly** adj désordonné.

disorganized adj désorganisé.

disown vt renier.

disparaging adj désobligeant.

dispassionate adj impartial; (unemotional) calme.

dispatch vt (send, complete) expédier; (troops) envoyer. ● n expédition f; envoi m; (report) dépêche f.

dispel vt (pt dispelled) dissiper.

dispensary n (in hospital) pharmacie f, (in chemist's) officine f.

dispense vt distribuer; (medicine) préparer. ● vi ~ with se passer de. **dispenser** n (container) distributeur m.

disperse vt/i (se) disperser.

display vt montrer, exposer; (feelings) manifester. ● n exposition f; manifestation f; (Comm) étalage m; (of computer) visuel m.

displeased adj mécontent (with de).

disposable a jetable.

disposal n (of waste) évacuation f; at sb's ~ à la disposition de qn.

dispose vt disposer. ● vi ~ of se débarrasser de; well ~d to bien disposé envers.

disposition n disposition f; (character) naturel m.

disprove vt réfuter.

dispute vt contester. ● n discussion f; (Pol) conflit m; in ~ contesté.

disqualify vt rendre inapte; (Sport) disqualifier; ~ **from driving** retirer le permis à.

disquiet n inquiétude f. **disquieting** adj inquiétant.

disregard vt ne pas tenir compte de. ● n indifférence f (**for** à).

disrepair n délabrement m.

disreputable adj peu recommandable.

disrepute n discrédit m.

disrespect n manque m de respect. **disrespectful** adj irrespectueux.

disrupt vt (disturb, break up) perturber; (plans) déranger. **disruption** n perturbation f. **disruptive** adj perturbateur.

dissatisfied adj mécontent.

dissect vt disséquer.

disseminate vt diffuser.

dissent vi différer (**from** de). ● n dissentiment m.

dissertation n mémoire m.

disservice n do a ~ **to sb** rendre un mauvais service à qn.

dissident a & n dissident/-e (m/f).

dissimilar adj dissemblable, différent.

dissipate vt/i (se) dissiper. **dissipated** adj (person) dissolu.

dissolve vt/i (se) dissoudre.

dissuade vt dissuader.

distance n distance f; **from a** ~ de loin; **in the** ~ au loin. **distant** adj éloigné, lointain; (relative) éloigné; (aloof) distant.

distaste n dégoût m. **distasteful** adj désagréable.

distil vt (pt distilled) distiller.

distinct adj distinct; (definite) net; **as** ~ **from** par opposition à. **distinction** n distinction f; (in exam) mention f très bien. **distinctive** adj distinctif.

distinguish vt/i distinguer.

distort vt déformer. **distortion** n distorsion f; (of facts) déformation f.

distract vt distraire. **distracted** adj (distraught) éperdu. **distracting** adj gênant. **distraction** n (lack of attention, entertainment) distraction f.

distraught adj éperdu.

distress n douleur f; (poverty, danger) détresse f. ● vt peiner. **distressing** adj pénible.

distribute vt distribuer.

district n région f; (of town) quartier m.

distrust n méfiance f. ● vt se méfier de.

disturb vt déranger; (alarm, worry) troubler. **disturbance** n dérangement m (of de); (noise) tapage m. **disturbances** npl (Pol) troubles mpl. **disturbed** adj troublé; (psychologically) perturbé. **disturbing** adj troublant.

disused adj désaffecté.

ditch n fossé m. ● vt 🗷 abandonner.

ditto adv idem.

dive vi plonger; (rush) se précipiter. ● n plongeon m; (of plane) piqué m; (place 🗷) bouge m. **diver** n plongeur/-euse m/f.

diverge vi diverger. **divergent** adj divergent.

diverse adj divers.

diversion n détournement m; (distraction) diversion f; (of traffic) déviation f. **divert** vt détourner; (traffic) dévier.

divide vt/i (se) diviser.

dividend n dividende m.

divine adj divin.

diving: ~**-board** n plongeoir m. ~**-suit** n scaphandre m.

division n division f.

divorce n divorce m (**from** avec). ● vt/i divorcer (d'avec).

divulge vt divulguer.

DIY abbr ⇒DO-IT-YOURSELF.

dizziness n vertige m.

dizzy adj (-ier, -iest) vertigineux; **be** or **feel** ~ avoir le vertige.

···

do

present **do, does**; present negative **don't, do not**; past **did**; past participle **done**

● transitive and intransitive verb

····▶ faire; **she is doing her homework** elle fait ses devoirs.

····➤ (progress, be suitable) aller; **how are you doing?** comment ça va?

····➤ (be enough) suffire; **will five dollars ~?** cinq dollars, ça suffira?

● *auxiliary verb*

····➤ (in questions) **~ you like Mozart?** aimes-tu Mozart?, est-ce que tu aimes Mozart?; **did your sister phone?** est-ce que ta sœur a téléphoné?, ta sœur a-t-elle téléphoné?

····➤ (in negatives) **I don't like Mozart** je n'aime pas Mozart.

····➤ (emphatic uses) **I ~ like your dress** j'aime beaucoup ta robe; **I ~ think you should go** je pense vraiment que tu devrais y aller.

····➤ (referring back to another verb) **I live in Oxford and so does Lily** j'habite à Oxford et Lily aussi; **she gets paid more than I ~** elle est payée plus que moi; **'I don't like carrots'—'neither ~ I'** 'je n'aime pas les carottes'—'moi non plus'.

····➤ (imperatives) **don't shut the door** ne ferme pas la porte; **~ be quiet** tais-toi!

····➤ (short questions and answers) **you like fish, don't you?** tu aimes le poisson, n'est-ce pas?; **Lola didn't phone, did she?** Lola n'a pas téléphoné par hasard?; **'does he play tennis?'—'no he doesn't/yes he does'** 'est-ce qu'il joue au tennis?'—'non/oui'; **'Marion didn't say that'—'yes she did'** 'Marion n'a pas dit ça'—'si'.

□ **do away with** supprimer;

do up (fasten) fermer; (*house*) refaire;

do with it's to ~ with c'est à propos de; **it's nothing to ~ with** ça n'a rien à voir avec;

do without se passer de.

docile *adj* docile.

dock *n* (Jur) banc *m* des accusés; dock *m*. ● *vi* arriver au port. ● *vt* mettre à quai; (*wages*) faire une retenue sur.

doctor *n* médecin *m*, docteur *m*; (Univ) docteur *m*. ● *vt* (*cat*) châtrer; (fig) altérer.

doctorate *n* doctorat *m*.

document *n* document *m*.
documentary *a* & *n* documentaire (*m*). **documentation** *n* documentation *f*.

dodge *vt* esquiver. ● *vi* faire un saut de côté. ● *n* mouvement *m* de côté.

dodgems *npl* autos *fpl* tamponneuses.

dodgy *adj* (**-ier, -iest**) (Ⓔ: difficult) épineux, délicat; (untrustworthy) louche Ⓔ.

doe *n* (deer) biche *f*.

does ⇨DO.

doesn't = DOES NOT.

dog *n* chien *m*. ● *vt* (*pt* **dogged**) poursuivre. **~-collar** *n* col *m* romain. **~-eared** *adj* écorné.

dogged *adj* obstiné.

dogma *n* dogme *m*. **dogmatic** *adj* dogmatique.

dogsbody *n* bonne *f* à tout faire.

do-it-yourself *n* bricolage *m*.

doldrums *npl* **be in the ~** (person) avoir le cafard.

dole *vt* **~ out** distribuer. ● *n* Ⓔ indemnité *f* de chômage; **on the ~** Ⓔ au chômage.

doll *n* poupée *f*. ● *vt* **~ up** Ⓔ bichonner.

dollar *n* dollar *m*.

dollop *n* (of food Ⓔ) gros morceau *m*.

dolphin *n* dauphin *m*.

domain *n* domaine *m*.

dome *n* dôme *m*.

domestic *adj* familial; (*trade, flights*) intérieur; (*animal*) domestique. **domesticated** *adj* (*animal*) domestiqué.

domesticity *n* vie *f* de famille.

domestic science *n* arts *mpl* ménagers.

dominant *adj* dominant.

dominate *vt/i* dominer. **domination** *n* domination *f*.

domineering *adj* dominateur.

domino *n* (*pl* **~es**) domino *m*; **~es** (game) dominos *mpl*.

donate *vt* faire don de. **donation** *n* don *m*.

done ⇨DO.

donkey *n* âne *m*. **~ work** *n* travail *m* pénible.

donor n donateur/-trice m/f; (of blood) donneur/-euse m/f.

don't = DO NOT.

doodle vi griffonner.

doom n (ruin) ruine f; (fate) destin m.
● vt be ~ed to être destiné or condamné à; ~ed (to failure) voué à l'échec.

door n porte f; (of vehicle) portière f, porte f. ~**bell** n sonnette f. ~**man** n (pl -**men**) portier m. ~**mat** n paillasson m. ~**step** n pas m de (la) porte, seuil m. ~**way** n porte f.

dope n ⊞ cannabis m; (idiot ⊠) imbécile mf. ● vt doper. **dopey** adj (foolish ⊠) imbécile.

dormant adj en sommeil.

dormitory n dortoir m; (Univ, US) résidence f.

dosage n dose f; (on label) posologie f.

dose n dose f.

doss vi ⊠ roupiller.

dot n point m; on the ~ ⊞ à l'heure pile. ~**com** n société f en ligne or point com.

dote vi ~ on adorer.

dotted adj (fabric) à pois; ~ **line** pointillé m; ~ **with** parsemé de.

double adj double; (room, bed) pour deux personnes; ~ **the size** deux fois plus grand. ● adv deux fois; **pay** ~ payer le double. ● n double m; (stuntman) doublure f; ~**s** (tennis) double m; **at** or **on the** ~ au pas de course. ● vt/i doubler; (fold) plier en deux. ~**bass** n (Mus) contrebasse f. ~**check** vt revérifier. ~ **chin** n double menton m. ~**cross** vt tromper. ~**decker** n autobus m à impériale. ~ **Dutch** n de l'hébreu m.

doubt n doute m. ● vt douter de; ~ **if** or **that** douter que. **doubtful** adj incertain, douteux; (person) qui a des doutes. **doubtless** adv sans doute.

dough n pâte f; (money ⊠) fric m ⊞.

doughnut n beignet m.

douse vt arroser; (light, fire) éteindre.

dove n colombe f.

Dover n Douvres.

dowdy adj (-**ier**, -**iest**) (clothes) sans chic, monotone; (person) sans élégance.

down adv en bas; (of sun) couché; (lower) plus bas; **come** or **go** ~ descendre; **go** ~ **to the post office** aller à la poste; ~ **under** aux antipodes; ~ **with** à bas. ● prep en bas de; (along) le long de. ● vt (knock down, shoot down) abattre; (drink) vider.
● n (fluff) duvet m.

down: ~-**and-out** n clochard/-e m/f.
~**cast** adj démoralisé. ~**fall** n chute f. ~**grade** vt déclasser.
~-**hearted** adj découragé.

downhill adv **go** ~ descendre; (pej) baisser.

down: ~**load** n (Comput) télécharger.
~-**market** adj bas de gamme. ~ **payment** n acompte m. ~**pour** n grosse averse f.

downright adj (utter) véritable; (honest) franc. ● adv carrément.

downstairs adv en bas. ● adj d'en bas.

down: ~**stream** adv en aval. ~-**to-earth** adj pratique.

downtown adj (US) du centre-ville; ~ **Boston** le centre de Boston.

downtrodden adj tyrannisé.

downward adj & adv, **downwards** adv vers le bas.

doze vi somnoler; ~ **off** s'assoupir.
● n somme m.

dozen n douzaine f; **a** ~ **eggs** une douzaine d'œufs; ~**s of** ⊞ des dizaines de.

Dr abbr (**Doctor**) Docteur.

drab adj terne.

draft n (outline) brouillon m; (Comm) traite f; **the** ~ (Mil, US) la conscription; **a** ~ **treaty** un projet de traité; (US) = DRAUGHT. ● vt faire le brouillon de; (draw up) rédiger.

drag vt/i (pt **dragged**) trainer; (river) draguer; (pull away) arracher; ~ **on** s'éterniser. ● n (task ⊞) corvée f; (person ⊞) raseur/-euse m/f; **in** ~ en travesti.

dragon n dragon m.

drain vt (land) drainer; (vegetables) égoutter; (tank, glass) vider; (use up) épuiser; ~ (**off**) (liquid) faire écouler. ● vi ~ (**off**) (of liquid) s'écouler. ● n (sewer) égout m; ∼(-pipe) tuyau m d'écoulement; **a ∼ on** une ponction sur. **draining-board** n égouttoir m.

drama n art m dramatique, théâtre m; (play, event) drame m. **dramatic** adj (situation) dramatique; (increase) spectaculaire. **dramatist** n dramaturge m. **dramatize** vt adapter pour la scène; (fig) dramatiser.

drank ⇒DRINK.

drape vt draper. **drapes** npl (US) rideaux mpl.

drastic adj sévère.

draught n courant m d'air; ∼s (game) dames fpl. ∼ **beer** n bière f pression.

draughty adj plein de courants d'air.

draw vt (pt **drew**; pp **drawn**) (picture) dessiner; (line) tracer; (pull) tirer; (attract) attirer. ● vi dessiner; (Sport) faire match nul; (come, move) venir. ● n (Sport) match m nul; (in lottery) tirage m au sort. □ ∼ **back** reculer; ∼ **near** (s')approcher (to de); ∼ **out** (money) retirer; ∼ **up** vi (stop) s'arrêter; vt (document) dresser; (chair) approcher.

drawback n inconvénient m.

drawbridge n pont-levis m.

drawer n tiroir m.

drawing n dessin m. ∼-**board** n planche f à dessin. ∼-**pin** n punaise f. ∼-**room** n salon m.

drawl n voix f traînante.

drawn ⇒DRAW. ● adj (features) tiré; (match) nul.

dread n terreur f, crainte f. ● vt redouter. **dreadful** adj épouvantable, affreux. **dreadfully** adv terriblement.

dream n rêve m. ● vt/i (pt **dreamed** or **dreamt**) rêver; ∼ **up** imaginer. ● adj (ideal) de ses rêves.

dreary adj (-ier, -iest) triste; (boring) monotone.

dredge vt (river) draguer; ∼ **sth up** (fig) exhumer.

dregs npl lie f.

drench vt tremper.

dress n robe f; (clothing) tenue f. ● vt/i (s')habiller; (food) assaisonner;

(wound) panser; ∼ **up as** se déguiser en; **get ∼ed** s'habiller. ∼ **circle** n premier balcon m.

dresser n (furniture) buffet m; **be a stylish ∼** s'habiller avec chic.

dressing n (sauce) assaisonnement m; (bandage) pansement m. ∼-**gown** n robe f de chambre. ∼-**room** n (Sport) vestiaire m; (Theat) loge f. ∼-**table** n coiffeuse f.

dressmaker n couturière f. **dressmaking** n couture f.

dress rehearsal n répétition f générale.

dressy adj (-ier, -iest) chic inv.

drew ⇒DRAW.

dribble vi (liquid) dégouliner; (person) baver; (football) dribbler.

dried adj (fruit) sec.

drier n séchoir m.

drift vi aller à la dérive; (pile up) s'amonceler; ∼ **towards** glisser vers. ● n dérive f; amoncellement m; (of events) tournure f; (meaning) sens m; **snow ∼** congère f. **driftwood** n bois m flotté.

drill n (tool) perceuse f; (for teeth) roulette f; (training) exercice m; (procedure ⚠) marche f à suivre; (pneumatic) ∼ marteau m piqueur. ● vt percer; (train) entraîner. ● vi être à l'exercice.

drink vt/i (pt **drank**; pp **drunk**) boire. ● n (liquid) boisson f; (glass of alcohol) verre m; **a ∼ of water** un verre d'eau. **drinking water** n eau f potable.

drip vi (pt **dripped**) (é)goutter; (washing) s'égoutter. ● n goutte f; (person ⚠) lavette f.

drip-dry vt laisser égoutter. ● adj sans essorage.

drive vt (pt **drove**; pp **driven**) (vehicle) conduire; (sb somewhere) chasser, pousser; (machine) actionner; ∼ **mad** rendre fou. ● vi conduire. ● n promenade f en voiture; (private road) allée f; (fig) énergie f; (Psych) instinct m; (Pol) campagne f; (Auto) traction f; (golf, Comput) drive m; **it's a two-hour ∼** il y a deux heures de route; **left-hand ∼** conduite f à gauche. □ ∼ **at** en venir à.

drivel n bêtises fpl.

driver n conducteur/-trice m/f, chauffeur m. **~'s license** n (US) permis m de conduire.

driving n conduite f; take one's ~ test passer son permis. ● adj (rain) battant; (wind) cinglant. ~ **licence** n permis m de conduire. ~ **school** n auto-école f.

drizzle n bruine f. ● vi bruiner.

drone n (of engine) ronronnement m; (of insects) bourdonnement m. ● vi ronronner; bourdonner.

drool vi baver (over sur).

droop vi pencher, tomber.

drop n goutte f; (fall, lowering) chute f. ● vt/i (pt **dropped**) (laisser) tomber; (decrease, lower) baisser; ~ **off** (person from car) déposer; ~ **a line** écrire un mot (to à). □ ~ **in** passer (on chez); ~ **off** (doze) s'assoupir; ~ **out** se retirer (of de); (of student) abandonner.

drop-out n marginal/-e m/f, raté/-e m/f.

droppings npl crottes fpl.

drought n sécheresse f.

drove ⇒DRIVE.

droves npl foules fpl.

drown vt/i (se) noyer.

drowsy adj somnolent; be or feel ~ avoir envie de dormir.

drug n drogue f; (Med) médicament m. ● vt (pt **drugged**) droguer. ~ **addict** n drogué/-e m/f. **drugstore** n (US) drugstore m.

drum n tambour m; (for oil) bidon m; ~**s** batterie f. ● vi (pt **drummed**) tambouriner. ● vt ~ **into sb** répéter sans cesse à qn; ~ **up** (support) susciter; (business) créer. **drummer** n tambour m; (in pop group) batteur m.

drumstick n baguette f de tambour; (of chicken) pilon m.

drunk ⇒DRINK. ● adj ivre; get ~ s'enivrer. ● n ivrogne/-esse m/f. **drunkard** n ivrogne/-esse m/f. **drunken** adj ivre; (habitually) ivrogne. **drunkenness** n ivresse f.

dry adj (**drier**, **driest**) sec; (day) sans pluie; be or feel ~ avoir soif. ● vt/i (faire) sécher; ~ **up** (dry dishes) essuyer la vaisselle; (of supplies) (se)

tarir; (be silent 🎲) se taire. ~**clean** vt nettoyer à sec. ~**-cleaner** n teinturier m. ~ **run** n galop m d'essai.

dual adj double. ~ **carriageway** n route f à quatre voies. ~**-purpose** adj qui fait double emploi.

dub vt (pt **dubbed**) (film) doubler (into en); (nickname) surnommer.

dubious adj (pej) douteux; be ~ **about sth** (person) avoir des doutes sur qch.

duck n canard m. ● vi se baisser subitement. ● vt (head) baisser; (person) plonger dans l'eau.

duct n conduit m.

dud adj (tool 🎲) mal fichu; (coin 🎲) faux; (cheque 🎲) sans provision. ● n be a ~ (not work 🎲) ne pas marcher.

due adj (owing) dû; (expected) attendu; (proper) qui convient; ~ **to** à cause de; (caused by) dû à; she's ~ **to leave** now il est prévu qu'elle parte maintenant; **in ~ course** (at the right time) en temps voulu; (later) plus tard. ● adv ~ **east** droit vers l'est. ● n dû m; ~**s** droits mpl; (of club) cotisation f.

duel n duel m.

duet n duo m.

dug ⇒DIG.

duke n duc m.

dull adj ennuyeux; (colour) terne; (weather) maussade; (sound) sourd. ● vt (pain) atténuer; (shine) ternir.

duly adv comme il convient; (as expected) comme prévu.

dumb adj muet; (stupid 🎲) bête.

dumbfound vt sidérer, ahurir.

dummy n (of tailor) mannequin m; (of baby) sucette f. ● adj factice. ~ **run** n galop m d'essai.

dump vt déposer; (get rid of 🎲) se débarrasser de. ● n tas m d'ordures; (refuse tip) décharge f; (Mil) dépôt m; (dull place 🎲) trou m 🎲; be in the ~**s** 🎲 avoir le cafard.

dune n dune f.

dung n (excrement) bouse f, crotte f; (manure) fumier m.

dungarees npl salopette f.

dungeon n cachot m.

duplicate¹ n double m. ● adj identique.

duplicate² vt faire un double de; (on machine) polycopier.

durable adj (tough) résistant; (enduring) durable.

duration n durée f.

during prep pendant.

dusk n crépuscule m.

dusky adj (-ier, -iest) foncé.

dust n poussière f. ● vt/i épousseter; (sprinkle) saupoudrer (**with** de). ~**bin** n poubelle f.

duster n chiffon m.

dust: ~**man** n (pl -**men**) éboueur m. ~**pan** n pelle f (à poussière).

dusty adj (-ier, -iest) poussiéreux.

Dutch adj néerlandais; **go** ~ partager les frais. ● n (Ling) néerlandais m. ~**man** n Néerlandais m. ~**woman** n Néerlandaise f.

dutiful adj obéissant.

duty n devoir m; (tax) droit m; (of official) fonction f; **on** ~ de service. ~**free** adj hors-taxe.

duvet n couette f.

dwarf n nain/-e m/f. ● vt rapetisser.

dwell vi (pt **dwelt**) demeurer; ~ **on** s'étendre sur. **dweller** n habitant/-e m/f. **dwelling** n habitation f.

dwindle vi diminuer.

dye vt teindre. ● n teinture f.

dying adj mourant; (art) qui se perd.

dynamic adj dynamique.

dynamite n dynamite f.

dysentery n dysenterie f.

dyslexia n dyslexie f. **dyslexic** a & n dyslexique (mf).

Ee

each det chaque inv; ~ **one** chacun/ -e m/f. ● pron chacun/-e m/f; oranges at 30p ~ des oranges à 30 pence pièce.

each other pron l'un/l'une l'autre, les uns/les unes les autres; **know** ~ se connaître; **love** ~ s'aimer.

eager adj impatient (**to** de); (person, acceptance) enthousiaste; ~ **for** avide de.

eagle n aigle m.

ear n oreille f; (of corn) épi m. ~**ache** n mal m à l'oreille. ~**drum** n tympan m.

earl n comte m.

early (-ier, -iest) adv tôt, de bonne heure; (ahead of time) en avance; **as I said earlier** comme je l'ai déjà dit. ● adj (attempt, years) premier; (hour) matinal; (fruit) précoce; (retirement) anticipé; **have an** ~ **dinner** dîner tôt; **in** ~ **summer** au début de l'été; **at the earliest** au plus tôt.

earmark vt désigner (**for** pour).

earn vt gagner; (interest: Comm) rapporter.

earnest adj sérieux; **in** ~ sérieusement.

earnings npl salaire m; (profits) gains mpl.

ear: ~**phones** npl casque m. ~**ring** n boucle f d'oreille. ~**shot** n **within/ in** ~**shot** à portée de voix.

earth n terre f; **why/how/where on** ~...? pourquoi/comment/où diable...? ● vt (Electr) mettre à la terre. **earthenware** n faïence f. ~**quake** n tremblement m de terre.

ease n facilité f; (comfort) bien-être m; **at** ~ à l'aise; (Mil) au repos; **with** ~ facilement. ● vt (pain, pressure) atténuer; (congestion) réduire; (transition) faciliter. ● vi (pain, pressure) s'atténuer; (congestion, rain) diminuer.

easel n chevalet m.

east n est m; **the E**~ (Orient) l'Orient m. ● adj (side, coast) est; (wind) d'est. ● adv à l'est.

Easter n Pâques m; ~ **egg** œuf m de Pâques.

easterly adj (wind) d'est; (direction) de l'est.

eastern de l'est; ~ **France** l'est de la France.

eastward adj (side) est inv; (journey) vers l'est.

easy adj (**-ier, -iest**) facile; go ∼ with 🔢 y aller doucement avec; **take it** ∼ ne te fatigue pas. ∼**going** adj accommodant.

eat vt/i (pt **ate**; pp **eaten**) manger; ∼ **into** ronger.

eavesdrop vi (pt **-dropped**) écouter aux portes.

ebb n reflux m. ● vi descendre; (fig) décliner.

ebony n ébène f.

EC abbr (**European Community**) CE f.

eccentric a & n excentrique (mf).

echo n (pl **-oes**) écho m. ● vt répercuter; (idea, opinion) reprendre. ● vi retentir, résonner (**to, with** de).

eclipse n éclipse f. ● vt éclipser.

ecological adj écologique.

ecology n écologie f.

economic adj économique; (profitable) rentable. **economical** adj économique; (person) économe. **economics** n économie f, sciences fpl économiques. **economist** n économiste mf.

economize vi ∼ (**on**) économiser.

economy n économie f.

ecosystem n écosystème m.

ecstasy n extase f; (drug) ecstasy m.

ECU n écu m.

eczema n eczéma m.

edge n bord m; (of town) abords mpl; (of knife) tranchant m; **have the** ∼ **on** 🔢 l'emporter sur; **on** ∼ énervé. ● vt (trim) border. ● vi ∼ **forward** avancer doucement.

edgeways adv I can't get a word in ∼ je n'arrive pas à placer un mot.

edgy adj énervé.

edible adj comestible; (pleasant) mangeable.

edit vt (pt **edited**) (newspaper, page) être le rédacteur/la rédactrice de; (check) réviser; (cut) couper; (TV, cinema) monter.

edition n édition f.

editor n (writer) rédacteur/-trice m/f; (of works, anthology) éditeur/-trice m/f; (TV, cinema) monteur/-teuse m/f; **the** ∼ (**in chief**) le rédacteur en chef.

editorial adj de la rédaction. ● n éditorial m.

educate vt instruire; (mind, public) éduquer. **educated** adj instruit. **education** n éducation f; (schooling) études fpl. **educational** adj éducatif; (establishment, method) d'enseignement.

eel n anguille f.

eerie adj (**-ier, -iest**) sinistre.

effect n effet m; **come into** ∼ entrer en vigueur; **in** ∼ effectivement; **take** ∼ agir. ● vt effectuer.

effective adj efficace; (actual) effectif. **effectively** adv efficacement; (in effect) en réalité. **effectiveness** n efficacité f.

effeminate adj efféminé.

effervescent adj effervescent.

efficiency n efficacité f; (of machine) rendement m. **efficient** adj efficace. **efficiently** adv efficacement.

effort n efforts mpl; **make an** ∼ faire un effort; **be worth the** ∼ en valoir la peine. **effortless** adj facile.

effusive adj expansif.

e.g. abbr par ex.

egg n œuf m. ● vt ∼ **on** pousser. ∼**-cup** n coquetier m. ∼**-plant** n (US) aubergine f. ∼**shell** n coquille f d'œuf.

ego n amour-propre m; (Psych) moi m. **egotism** n égotisme m. **egotist** n égotiste mf.

Egypt n Égypte f.

eiderdown n édredon m.

eight a & n huit (m). **eighteen** a & n dix-huit (m). **eighth** a & n huitième (mf). **eighty** a & n quatre-vingts (m).

either det & pron l'un/une ou l'autre; (with negative) ni l'un/une ni l'autre; **you can take** ∼ tu peux prendre n'importe lequel/laquelle. ● adv non plus. ● conj ∼...**or** ou (bien)...ou (bien); (with negative) ni...ni.

eject vt (troublemaker) expulser; (waste) rejeter.

elaborate[1] adj compliqué.

elaborate[2] vt élaborer. ● vi préciser; ∼ **on** s'étendre sur.

elastic a & n élastique (m); ∼ **band** élastique m. **elasticity** n élasticité f.

elated *adj* transporté de joie.

elbow *n* coude *m*; ~ **room** espace *m* vital.

elder *a* & *n* aîné/-e (*m/f*); (tree) sureau *m*.

elderly *adj* âgé; **the** ~ les personnes *fpl* âgées.

eldest *a* & *n* aîné/-e (*m/f*).

elect *vt* élire; ~ **to do** choisir de faire. ● *adj* (president etc.) futur. **election** *n* élection *f*. **elector** *n* électeur/-trice *m/f*. **electoral** *adj* électoral. **electorate** *n* électorat *m*.

electric *adj* électrique; ~ **blanket** couverture *f* chauffante. **electrical** *adj* électrique. **electrician** *n* électricien/-ne *m/f*. **electricity** *n* électricité *f*. **electrify** *vt* électrifier; (excite) électriser. **electrocute** *vt* électrocuter.

electronic *adj* électronique. ~ **publishing** *n* éditique *f*. **electronics** *n* électronique *f*.

elegance *n* élégance *f*.

element *n* élément *m*; (of heater etc.) résistance *f*. **elementary** *adj* élémentaire.

elephant *n* éléphant *m*.

elevate *vt* élever. **elevation** *n* élévation *f*. **elevator** *n* (US) ascenseur *m*.

eleven *a* & *n* onze (*m*). **eleventh** *a* & *n* onzième (*mf*).

elicit *vt* obtenir (**from** de).

eligible *adj* admissible (**for** à); **be** ~ **for** (entitled to) avoir droit à.

eliminate *vt* éliminer.

elm *n* orme *m*.

elongate *vt* allonger.

elope *vi* s'enfuir (**with** avec). **elopement** *n* fugue *f* (amoureuse).

eloquence *n* éloquence *f*.

else *adv* d'autre; **somebody/nothing** ~ quelqu'un/rien d'autre; **everybody** ~ tous les autres; **somewhere/ something** ~ autre part/chose; **or** ~ ou bien. **elsewhere** *adv* ailleurs.

elude *vt* échapper à.

elusive *adj* insaisissable.

emaciated *adj* émacié.

e-mail *n* e-mail *m*, mél *m*.

emancipate *vt* émanciper.

embankment *n* (of river) quai *m*; (of railway) remblai *m*.

embark *vt* embarquer. ● *vi* (Naut) embarquer; ~ **on** (*journey*) entreprendre; (*campaign, career*) se lancer dans.

embarrass *vt* plonger dans l'embarras; **be/feel** ~**ed** être/se sentir gêné. **embarrassment** *n* confusion *f*, gêne *f*.

embassy *n* ambassade *f*.

embed *vt* (*pt* **embedded**) enfoncer (**in** dans).

embellish *vt* embellir.

embers *npl* braises *fpl*.

embezzle *vt* détourner (**from** de). **embezzlement** *n* détournement *m* de fonds. **embezzler** *n* escroc *m*.

embitter *vt* aigrir; **become** ~**ed** s'aigrir.

emblem *n* emblème *m*.

embodiment *n* incarnation *f*. **embody** *vt* incarner; (legally) incorporer.

emboss *vt* (metal) repousser; (paper) gaufrer.

embrace *vt* (*person*) étreindre; (*religion*) embrasser; (include) comprendre. ● *n* étreinte *f*.

embroider *vt* broder. **embroidery** *n* broderie *f*.

embryo *n* embryon *m*.

emerald *n* émeraude *f*.

emerge *vi* (*person*) sortir (**from** de); **it** ~**d that** il est apparu que. **emergence** *n* apparition *f*.

emergency *n* (crisis) crise *f*; (urgent case: Med) urgence *f*; **in an** ~ en cas d'urgence. ● *adj* d'urgence; ~ **exit** sortie *f* de secours; ~ **landing** atterrissage *m* forcé.

emigrant *n* émigrant/-e *m/f*. **emigrate** *vi* émigrer.

eminence *n* éminence *f*. **eminent** *adj* éminent.

emission *n* émission *f*.

emit *vt* (*pt* **emitted**) émettre.

emotion *n* émotion *f*. **emotional** *adj* (*development*) émotif; (*reaction*) émotionel; (*film, scène*) émouvant.

emotive *adj* qui soulève les passions.

emperor *n* empereur *m*.

emphasis n accent m; lay ~ on mettre l'accent sur. **emphasize** vt mettre l'accent sur. **emphatic** adj catégorique; (manner) énergique.

empire n empire m.

employ vt employer. **employee** n employé/-e m/f. **employer** n employeur/-euse m/f.

employment n emploi m; find ~ trouver du travail.

empower vt autoriser (to do à faire).

empty adj (-ier, -iest) vide; (street) désert; (promise) vain; on an ~ stomach à jeun. ● vt/i (se) vider. **~-handed** adj les mains vides.

emulate vt imiter.

enable vt ~ sb to permettre à qn de.

enamel n émail m. ● vt (pt **enamelled**) émailler.

encampment n campement m.

encase vt revêtir, recouvrir (in de).

enchant vt enchanter.

enclose vt entourer; (land) clôturer; (with letter) joindre. **enclosed** adj (space) clos; (with letter) ci-joint. **enclosure** n enceinte f; (with letter) pièce f jointe.

encompass vt inclure.

encore interj & n bis (m).

encounter vt rencontrer. ● n rencontre f.

encourage vt encourager.

encroach vi ~ upon empiéter sur.

encyclopaedia n encyclopédie f. **encyclopaedic** adj encyclopédique.

end n fin f; (farthest part) bout m; come to an ~ prendre fin; ~-product produit m fini; in the ~ finalement; no ~ of 🅸 énormément de; on ~ (upright) debout; (in a row) de suite; put an ~ to mettre fin à. ● vt (marriage) mettre fin à; ~ one's days finir ses jours. ● vi se terminer; ~ up doing finir par faire.

endanger vt mettre en danger.

endearing adj attachant.

endeavour, (US) **endeavor** n (attempt) tentative f; (hard work) effort m. ● vi faire tout son possible (to do pour faire).

ending n fin f.

endive n chicorée f.

endless adj interminable; (supply) inépuisable; (patience) infini.

endorse vt (candidate, decision) appuyer; (product, claim) approuver; (cheque) endosser.

endurance n endurance f.

endure vt supporter. ● vi durer. **enduring** adj durable.

enemy n & a ennemi/-e (m/f).

energetic adj énergique. **energy** n énergie f.

enforce vt (rule, law) appliquer, faire respecter; (silence, discipline) imposer (on à); ~d forcé.

engage vt (staff) engager; (attention) retenir; be ~d in se livrer à. ● vi ~ in se livrer à. **engaged** adj fiancé; (busy) occupé; get ~d se fiancer. **engagement** n fiançailles fpl; (meeting) rendez-vous m; (undertaking) engagement m.

engaging adj attachant, engageant.

engine n moteur m; (of train) locomotive f; (of ship) machines fpl. **~-driver** n mécanicien m.

engineer n ingénieur m; (repairman) technicien m; (on ship) mécanicien m. ● vt (contrive) manigancer.

engineering n ingénierie f; (industry) mécanique f; civil ~ génie m civil.

England n Angleterre f.

English adj anglais. ● n (Ling) anglais m; the ~ les Anglais mpl. **~man** n Anglais m. **~-speaking** adj anglophone. **~woman** n Anglaise f.

engrave vt graver.

engrossed adj absorbé (in dans).

engulf vt engouffrer.

enhance vt (prospects, status) améliorer; (price, value) augmenter.

enjoy vt aimer (doing faire); (benefit from) jouir de; ~ oneself s'amuser; ~ your meal! bon appétit! **enjoyable** adj agréable. **enjoyment** n plaisir m.

enlarge vt agrandir. ● vi s'agrandir; (pupil) se dilater; ~ on s'étendre sur. **enlargement** n agrandissement m.

enlighten vt éclairer (on sur).
enlightenment n instruction f;
(information) éclaircissement m.

enlist vt (person) recruter; (fig)
obtenir. ● vi s'engager.

enmity n inimitié f.

enormous adj énorme.
enormously adv énormément.

enough adv & n assez; have ∼ of en
avoir assez de. ● det assez de; ∼
glasses/time assez de verres/de
temps.

enquire ⇒INQUIRE. **enquiry**
⇒INQUIRY.

enrage vt mettre en rage, rendre
furieux.

enrol vt/i (pt **enrolled**) (s')inscrire.
enrolment n inscription f.

ensure vt garantir; ∼ that (ascertain)
s'assurer que.

entail vt entraîner.

entangle vt emmêler.

enter vt (room, club, phase) entrer
dans; (note down, register) inscrire;
(data) entrer, saisir. ● vi entrer (into
dans); ∼ for s'inscrire à.

enterprise n entreprise f; (boldness)
initiative f. **enterprising** adj
entreprenant.

entertain vt amuser, divertir;
(guests) recevoir; (ideas) considérer.
entertainer n artiste mf.
entertaining adj divertissant.
entertainment n divertissement
m; (performance) spectacle m.

enthral vt (pt **enthralled**) captiver.

enthusiasm n enthousiasme m (for
pour).

enthusiast n passionné/-e m/f (for
de). **enthusiastic** adj (supporter)
enthousiaste; be ∼ic about être
enthousiasmé par. **enthusiastically**
adv avec enthousiasme.

entice vt attirer; ∼ to do entraîner
à faire.

entire adj entier. **entirely** adv
entièrement. **entirety** n in its ∼ty
en entier.

entitle vt donner droit à (to sth à
qch; to do de faire); ∼d (book)
intitulé; be ∼d to sth avoir droit à
qch.

entrance[1] n (entering, way in) entrée f
(to de); (right to enter) admission f.
● adj (charge, exam) d'entrée.

entrance[2] vt transporter.

entrant n (Sport) concurrent/-e m/f;
(in exam) candidat/-e m/f.

entrenched adj (opinion)
inébranlable; (Mil) retranché.

entrepreneur n entrepreneur/
-euse m/f.

entrust vt confier; ∼ sb with sth
confier qch à qn.

entry n entrée f; ∼ form fiche f
d'inscription.

envelop vt (pt **enveloped**)
envelopper.

envelope n enveloppe f.

envious adj envieux (of de).

environment n (ecological)
environnement m; (social) milieu m.
environmental adj du milieu; de
l'environnement.
environmentalist n écologiste mf.

envisage vt prévoir (doing de
faire).

envoy n envoyé/-e m/f.

envy n envie f. ● vt envier; ∼ sb sth
envier qch à qn.

epic n épopée f. ● adj épique.

epidemic n épidémie f.

epilepsy n épilepsie f.

episode n épisode m.

epitome n modèle m. **epitomize** vt
incarner.

equal a & n égal/-e (m/f); ∼
opportunities/rights égalité f des
chances/droits; ∼ to (task) à la
hauteur de. ● vt (pt **equalled**)
égaler. **equality** n égalité f.
equalize vt/i égaliser. **equalizer** n
(goal) but m égalisateur. **equally**
adv (divide) en parts égales; (just as)
tout aussi.

equanimity n sérénité f.

equate vt assimiler (with à).
equation n équation f.

equator n équateur m.

equilibrium n équilibre m.

equip vt (pt **equipped**) équiper (with
de). **equipment** n équipement m.

equity n équité f.

equivalence n équivalence f.

era n ère f, époque f.
eradicate vt éliminer; (*disease*) éradiquer.
erase vt effacer. **eraser** n (rubber) gomme f.
erect adj droit. ● vt ériger. **erection** n érection f.
erode vt éroder; (fig) saper. **erosion** n érosion f.
erotic adj érotique.
errand n commission f, course f.
erratic adj (*behaviour, person*) imprévisible; (*performance*) inégal.
error n erreur f.
erupt vi (volcano) entrer en éruption; (fig) éclater.
escalate vt intensifier. ● vi (*conflict*) s'intensifier; (*prices*) monter en flèche. **escalation** n intensification f. **escalator** n escalier m mécanique, escalator® m.
escapade n frasque f.
escape vt échapper à. ● vi s'enfuir, s'évader; (*gas*) fuir. ● n fuite f, évasion f; (of gas etc.) fuite f; **have a lucky** or **narrow ~** l'échapper belle.
escapism n évasion f (*du réel*).
escort¹ n (guard) escorte f; (companion) compagnon/compagne m/f.
escort² vt escorter.
Eskimo n Esquimau/-de m/f.
especially adv en particulier.
espionage n espionnage m.
espresso n (café) express m.
essay n (in literature) essai m; (School) rédaction f; (Univ) dissertation f.
essence n essence f.
essential adj essentiel; **the ~s** l'essentiel m. **essentially** adv essentiellement.
establish vt établir; (business) fonder.
establishment n (process) instauration f; (institution) établissement m; **the E~** l'ordre m établi.
estate n (house and land) domaine m; (possessions) biens mpl; (housing estate) cité f. **~ agent** n agent m immobilier. **~ car** n break m.
esteem n estime f.
esthetic adj (US) = AESTHETIC.

estimate¹ n (calculation) estimation f; (Comm) devis m.
estimate² vt évaluer; **~ that** estimer que. **estimation** n (esteem) estime f; (judgment) opinion f.
Estonia n Estonie f.
estuary n estuaire m.
etc. adv etc.
eternal adj éternel.
eternity n éternité f.
ethic n éthique f; **~s** moralité f. **ethical** adj éthique.
ethnic adj ethnique.
ethos n philosophie f.
etymology n étymologie f.
EU abbr (**European Union**) UE f, Union f européenne.
euphoria n euphorie f.
Euro n euro m.
Europe n Europe f.
European a & n européen/-ne (m/f); **~ Community** Communauté f Européenne.
euthanasia n euthanasie f.
evacuate vt évacuer.
evade vt (*blow*) esquiver; (*question*) éluder.
evaporate vi s'évaporer; **~d milk** lait m condensé.
evasion n fuite f (of devant); (excuse) faux-fuyant m; **tax ~** évasion f fiscale. **evasive** adj évasif.
eve n veille f (of de).
even adj (*surface, voice, contest*) égal; (*teeth, hem*) régulier; (number) pair; **get ~ with** se venger de. ● adv même; **~ better**/*etc.* (still) encore mieux/*etc.*; **~ so** quand même. □ **~ out** (*differences*) s'atténuer; **~ sth out** (*inequalities*) réduire qch; **~ up** équilibrer.
evening n soir m; (whole evening, event) soirée f.
evenly adv (spread, apply) uniformément; (*breathe*) régulièrement; (equally) en parts égales.
event n événement m; (Sport) épreuve f; **in the ~ of** en cas de. **eventful** adj mouvementé.
eventual adj (*outcome, decision*) final; (*aim*) à long terme. **eventuality** n éventualité f.

eventually *adv* finalement; (in future) un jour ou l'autre.

ever *adv* jamais; (at all times) toujours.

evergreen *n* arbre *m* à feuilles persistantes.

everlasting *adj* éternel.

ever since *prep & adv* depuis.

every *adj* ~ house/window toutes les maisons/les fenêtres; ~ time/minute chaque fois/minute; ~ day tous les jours; ~ other day tous les deux jours. **everybody** *pron* tout le monde. **everyday** *adj* quotidien. **everyone** *pron* tout le monde. **everything** *pron* tout. **everywhere** *adv* partout; ~where he goes partout où il va.

evict *vt* expulser (from de).

evidence *n* (proof) preuves *fpl* (that que; of, for de); (testimony) témoignage *m*; (traces) trace *f* (of de); give ~ témoigner; be in ~ être visible.

evident *adj* manifeste. **evidently** *adv* (apparently) apparemment; (obviously) manifestement.

evil *adj* malfaisant. ●*n* mal *m*.

evoke *vt* évoquer.

evolution *n* évolution *f*.

evolve *vi* évoluer. ●*vt* élaborer.

ewe *n* brebis *f*.

ex- *pref* ex-, ancien.

exact *adj* exact; the ~ opposite exactement le contraire. ●*vt* exiger (from de). **exactly** *adv* exactement.

exaggerate *vt/i* exagérer.

exalted *adj* élevé.

exam *n* 🄵 examen *m*.

examination *n* examen *m*.

examine *vt* examiner; (witness) interroger. **examiner** *n* examinateur/-trice *m/f*.

example *n* exemple *m*; for ~ par exemple; make an ~ of punir pour l'exemple.

exasperate *vt* exaspérer.

excavate *vt* fouiller. **excavations** *npl* fouilles *fpl*.

exceed *vt* dépasser. **exceedingly** *adv* extrêmement.

excel *vi* (*pt* **excelled**) exceller (at, in en; at doing à faire). ●*vt* surpasser.

excellence *n* excellence *f*. **excellent** *adj* excellent.

except *prep* sauf, excepté; ~ for à part. ●*vt* excepter. **excepting** *prep* sauf, excepté.

exception *n* exception *f*; take ~ to s'offusquer. **exceptional** *adj* exceptionnel.

excerpt *n* extrait *m*.

excess¹ *n* excès *m*.

excess² *adj* ~ weight excès *m* de poids; ~ baggage excédent *m* de bagages.

excessive *adj* excessif.

exchange *vt* échanger (for contre). ●*n* échange *m*; (between currencies) change *m*; ~ rate taux *m* de change; telephone ~ central *m* téléphonique.

Exchequer *n* (Pol) ministère *m* britannique des finances.

excise *n* excise *f*, taxe *f*.

excite *vt* exciter; (enthuse) enthousiasmer. **excited** *adj* excité; get ~d s'exciter. **excitement** *n* excitation *f*. **exciting** *adj* passionnant.

exclaim *vt* s'exclamer.

exclamation *n* exclamation *f*; ~ mark *or* point (US) point *m* d'exclamation.

exclude *vt* exclure.

exclusive *adj* (club) fermé; (rights) exclusif; (news item) en exclusivité; ~ of meals repas non compris. **exclusively** *adv* exclusivement.

excruciating *adj* atroce.

excursion *n* excursion *f*.

excuse¹ *vt* excuser; ~ from (exempt) dispenser de; ~ me! excusez-moi!, pardon!

excuse² *n* (reason) excuse *f*; (pretext) prétexte *m* (for sth à qch; for doing pour faire).

ex-directory *adj* sur liste rouge.

execute *vt* exécuter. **executioner** *n* bourreau *m*.

executive *n* (person) cadre *m*; (committee) exécutif *m*. ●*adj* exécutif.

exemplary *adj* exemplaire.

exemplify *vt* illustrer.

exempt *adj* exempt (from de). ●*vt* exempter.

exercise n exercice m; ~ **book**
cahier m. ● vt exercer; (restraint,
patience) faire preuve de. ● vi faire
de l'exercice.

exert vt exercer; ~ **oneself** se
fatiguer. **exertion** n effort m.

exhaust vt épuiser. ● n (Auto) pot m
d'échappement.

exhaustive adj exhaustif.

exhibit vt exposer; (fig) manifester.
● n objet m exposé.

exhibition n exposition f; (of skill)
démonstration f. **exhibitionist** n
exhibitionniste mf.

exhibitor n exposant/-e m/f.

exhilarate vt griser.

exile n exil m; (person) exilé/-e m/f.
● vt exiler.

exist vi exister. **existence** n
existence f; be in ~ence exister.
existing adj actuel.

exit n sortie f. ● vt/i (also Comput)
sortir (de).

exodus n exode m.

exonerate vt disculper.

exotic adj exotique.

expand vt développer; (workforce)
accroître. ● vi se développer;
(population) s'accroître; (metal) se
dilater.

expanse n étendue f.

expansion n développement m;
(Pol, Comm) expansion f.

expatriate a & n expatrié/-e (m/f).

expect vt s'attendre à; (suppose)
supposer; (demand) exiger; (baby)
attendre.

expectancy n attente f.

expectant adj ~ **mother** future
maman f.

expectation n (assumption)
prévision f; (hope) aspiration f;
(demand) exigence f.

expedient adj opportun. ● n
expédient m.

expedition n expédition f.

expel vt (pt **expelled**) expulser;
(pupil) renvoyer.

expend vt consacrer.

expenditure n dépenses fpl.

expense n frais mpl; at sb's ~ aux
frais de qn; ~ **account** frais mpl de
représentation. **expensive** adj

cher; (tastes) de luxe. **expensively**
adv luxueusement.

experience n expérience f. ● vt
(undergo) connaître; (feel) éprouver;
~d expérimenté.

experiment n expérience f. ● vi
expérimenter, faire des essais.

expert n spécialiste mf. ● adj
spécialisé, expert. **expertise** n
compétence f. **expertly** adv de
manière experte.

expire vi expirer; ~d périmé.
expiry n expiration f.

explain vt expliquer. **explanation**
n explication f. **explanatory** adj
explicatif.

explicit adj explicite.

explode vt/i (faire) exploser.

exploit[1] n exploit m.

exploit[2] vt exploiter.

exploration n exploration f.
exploratory adj (talks)
exploratoire. **explore** vt explorer;
(fig) étudier. **explorer** n
explorateur/-trice m/f.

explosion n explosion f.
explosive a & n explosif (m).

exponent n avocat/-e m/f (of de).

export[1] vt exporter.

export[2] n (process) exportation f;
(product) produit m d'exportation.

expose vt exposer; (disclose) révéler.

exposure n révélation f; (Photo)
pose f; die of ~ mourir de froid.

express vt exprimer. ● adj exprès.
● adv send sth ~ envoyer qch en
exprès. ● n (train) rapide m.
expression n expression f.
expressive adj expressif.
expressly adv expressément.

exquisite adj exquis.

extend vt (visit) prolonger; (house)
agrandir; (range) élargir; (arm, leg)
étendre. ● vi (stretch) s'étendre; (in
time) se prolonger. **extension** n (of
line, road) prolongement m; (of visa,
loan) prorogation f; (building) addition
f; (phone number) poste m; (cable)
rallonge f.

extensive adj vaste; (study)
approfondi; (damage) considérable.
extensively adv (much) beaucoup;
(very) très.

extent n (size, scope) étendue f;
(degree) mesure f; **to some ~** dans
une certaine mesure; **to such an ~
that** à tel point que.

extenuating adj atténuant.

exterior a & n extérieur (m).

exterminate vt exterminer.

external adj extérieur; (cause,
medical use) externe.

extinct adj (species) disparu; (volcano,
passion) éteint.

extinguish vt éteindre.
  extinguisher n extincteur m.

extol vt (pt **extolled**) louer, chanter
les louanges de.

extort vt extorquer (**from** à).
  extortion n (Jur) extorsion f.
  extortionate adj exorbitant.

extra adj supplémentaire; **~ charge**
supplément m; **~ time** (football)
prolongation f; **~ strong** extra-fort.
● adv encore; plus. ● n supplément
m; (cinema) figurant/-e m/f.

extract¹ vt sortir (**from** de); (tooth)
extraire; (promise) arracher.

extract² n extrait m.

extra-curricular adj parascolaire.

extradite vt extrader.

extramarital adj extraconjugal.

extramural adj (Univ) hors faculté.

extraordinary adj extraordinaire.

extravagance n prodigalité f.
  extravagant adj (person)
dépensier; (claim) extravagant.

extreme a & n extrême (m).
  extremely adv extrêmement.
  extremist n extrémiste mf.
  extremity n extrémité f.

extricate vt dégager.

extrovert n extraverti/-e m/f.

exuberance n exubérance f.

exude vt (charm) respirer; (smell)
exhaler.

eye n œil m (pl yeux); **keep an ~ on**
surveiller. ● vt (pt **eyed**; pres p
eyeing) regarder. **~ball** n globe m
oculaire. **~brow** n sourcil m.
~-catching adj attrayant. **~lash**
n cil m. **~lid** n paupière f.
~-opener n révélation f.

~-shadow n ombre f à paupières.
~sight n vue f. **~sore** n horreur f.
~witness n témoin m oculaire.

fable n fable f.

fabric n (cloth) tissu m.

fabulous adj fabuleux; (marvellous 🔢)
formidable.

face n visage m, figure f; (expression)
air m; (appearance, dignity) face f; (of
clock) cadran m; (Geol) face f; (of rock)
paroi f; **in the ~ of** face à; **make a
(funny) ~** faire la grimace; **to ~
face** à face. ● vt être en face de;
(risk) devoir affronter; (confront) faire
face à; (deal with) **I can't ~ him** je n'ai
pas le courage de le voir. ● vi
(person) regarder; (chair) être tourné
vers; (window) donner sur; **~ up to**
faire face à; **~d with** face à.

face-lift n lifting m; **give a ~ to**
donner un coup de neuf à.

face value n valeur f nominale;
take sth at ~ prendre qch au pied de
la lettre.

facial adj (hair) du visage; (injury)
au visage. ● n soin m du visage.

facility n (building) complexe m;
(feature) fonction f; **facilities**
(equipment) équipements mpl.

facsimile n fac-similé m.

fact n fait m; **as a matter of ~, in ~**
en fait; **know for a ~ that** savoir de
source sûre que; **owing/due to the ~
that** étant donné que.

factor n facteur m.

factory n usine f.

factual adj (account, description)
basé sur les faits; (evidence) factuel.

faculty n faculté f.

fade vi (sound) s'affaiblir; (memory)
s'effacer; (flower) se faner;
(material) se décolorer; (colour)
passer.

fail vi échouer; (grow weak) (s'af)
faiblir; (run short) manquer; (engine)

tomber en panne. ● vt (exam)
échouer à; ~ **to do** (not do) ne pas
faire; (not be able) ne pas réussir à
faire; **without** ~ à coup sûr.

failing n défaut m; ~ **that/this** sinon.

failure n échec m; (person) raté/-e m/
f; (breakdown) panne f; ~ **to do**
(inability) incapacité f de faire.

faint adj léger, faible; **feel** ~ (ill) se
sentir mal; **I haven't the ~est idea** je
n'en ai pas la moindre idée. ● vi
s'évanouir. ● n évanouissement m.
~-hearted adj timide.

fair n foire f. ● adj (hair, person)
blond; (skin) clair; (weather) beau;
(amount, quality) raisonnable; (just)
juste, équitable. ● adv (play)
loyalement.

fair-ground n champ m de foire.

fairly adv (justly) équitablement;
(rather) assez.

fairness n justice f.

fairy n fée f. ~ **story**, **~-tale** n
conte m de fées.

faith n (belief) foi f; (confidence)
confiance f.

faithful adj fidèle.

fake n (forgery) faux m; (person)
imposteur m; **it is a** ~ c'est un faux.
● adj faux. ● vt (signature)
contrefaire; (results) falsifier;
(illness) feindre.

falcon n faucon m.

fall vi (pt **fell**; pp **fallen**) tomber; ~
short être insuffisant. ● n chute f;
(autumn: US) automne m; **Niagara F~s**
chutes fpl du Niagara. □ ~ **back on**
se rabattre sur; ~ **behind** prendre
du retard; ~ **down** or **off** tomber;
~ **for** (person 🔲) tomber amoureux
de; (a trick 🔲) se laisser prendre à;
~ **in** (Mil) se mettre en rangs; ~ **off**
(decrease) diminuer; ~ **out** se
brouiller (with avec); ~ **over** tomber
(par terre); ~ **through** (plans)
tomber à l'eau.

fallacy n erreur f.

false adj faux. ~ **teeth** npl dentier
m.

falter vi (economy) fléchir; (courage)
faiblir; (when speaking) bafouiller 🔲.

fame n renommée f. **famed** adj
célèbre (for pour).

familiar adj familier; **be** ~ **with**
connaître.

family n famille f. ● adj de famille,
familial.

famine n famine f.

famished adj affamé.

famous adj célèbre (for pour).

fan n (mechanical) ventilateur m; (hand-
held) éventail m; (of person) fan mf 🔲,
admirateur/-trice m/f; (enthusiast)
fervent/-e m/f, passionné/-e m/f. ● vt
(pt **fanned**) (face) éventer; (fig)
attiser; ● vi ~ **out** se déployer en
éventail.

fanatic n fanatique mf.

fan belt n courroie f de ventilateur.

fancy n (whim, fantasy) fantaisie f; **take
a** ~ **to sb** se prendre d'affection pour
qn; **it took my** ~ ça m'a plu. ● adj
(buttons etc.) fantaisie inv; (prices)
extravagant; (impressive)
impressionnant. ● vt s'imaginer;
(want 🔲) avoir envie de; (like 🔲)
aimer. ~ **dress** n déguisement m.

fang n (of dog) croc m; (of snake)
crochet m.

fantasize vi fantasmer.

fantastic adj fantastique.

fantasy n fantaisie f; (daydream)
fantasme m.

FAQ abbr (**Frequently Asked
Questions**) (Internet) FAQ f, foire f
aux questions.

far adv loin; (much) beaucoup; (very)
très; ~ **away**, ~ **off** au loin; **as** ~ **as**
(up to) jusqu'à; **as** ~ **as I know** autant
que je sache; **by** ~ de loin; ~ **from**
loin de. ● adj lointain; (end, side)
autre. **~away** adj lointain.

farce n farce f.

fare n (prix du) billet m; (food)
nourriture f. ● vi (progress) aller;
(manage) se débrouiller.

Far East n Extrême-Orient m.

farewell interj & n adieu (m).

farm n ferme f. ● vt cultiver; ~ **out**
céder en sous-traitance. ● vi être
fermier. **farmer** n fermier m.
~house n ferme f. **farming** n
agriculture f. **~yard** n basse-cour f.

fart 🔲 vi péter 🔲. ● n pet m 🔲.

farther adv plus loin. ● adj plus
éloigné.

farthest *adv* le plus loin. ● *adj* le plus éloigné.

fascinate *vt* fasciner.

Fascism *n* fascisme *m*.

fashion *n* (current style) mode *f*; (manner) façon *f*; **in** ~ à la mode; **out of** ~ démodé. ● *vt* façonner. **fashionable** *adj* à la mode.

fast *adj* rapide; (colour) grand teint *inv*; (firm) fixe, solide; **be** ~ (of a clock) avancer. ● *adv* vite; (firmly) ferme; **be** ~ **asleep** dormir d'un sommeil profond. ● *vi* jeûner. ● *n* jeûne *m*.

fasten *vt/i* (s')attacher. **fastener**, **fastening** *n* attache *f*, fermeture *f*.

fast food *n* fast-food *m*; restauration *f* rapide.

fat *n* graisse *f*; (on meat) gras *m*. ● *adj* (**fatter**, **fattest**) gros, gras; (meat) gras; (profit) gros; **a** ~ **lot** 🆒 bien peu (of de).

fatal *adj* mortel; (fateful, disastrous) fatal. **fatality** *n* mort *m*. **fatally** *adv* mortellement.

fate *n* sort *m*. **fateful** *adj* fatidique.

father *n* père *m*. ~**hood** *n* paternité *f*. ~**-in-law** *n* (*pl* ~**s-in-law**) beau-père *m*.

fathom *n* brasse *f* (=1.8 m). ● *vt* ~ (**out**) comprendre.

fatigue *n* épuisement *m*; (Tech) fatigue *f*. ● *vt* fatiguer.

fatten *vt/i* engraisser. **fattening** *adj* qui fait grossir.

fatty *adj* (food) gras; (tissue) adipeux.

faucet *n* (US) robinet *m*.

fault *n* (defect, failing) défaut *m*; (blame) faute *f*; (Geol) faille *f*; **at** ~ fautif; **find** ~ **with** critiquer. ● *vt* ~ **sth/sb** prendre en défaut qn/qch. **faulty** *adj* défectueux.

favour, (US) **favor** *n* faveur *f*; **do sb a** ~ rendre service à qn; **in** ~ **of** pour. ● *vt* favoriser; (support) être en faveur de; (prefer) préférer. **favourable** *adj* favorable.

favourite *a* & *n* favori/-te (*m/f*).

fawn *n* (animal) faon *m*; (colour) beige *m* foncé. ● *vi* ~ **on** flagorner.

fax *n* fax *m*, télécopie *f*. ● *vt* faxer, envoyer par télécopie. ~ **machine** *n* fax *m*; télécopieur *m*; (for public use) Publifax® *m*.

FBI *abbr* (**Federal Bureau of Investigation**) (US) Police *f* judiciaire fédérale.

fear *n* crainte *f*, peur *f*; (fig) risque *m*; **for** ~ **of/that** de peur de/que. ● *vt* craindre.

feasible *adj* faisable; (likely) plausible.

feast *n* festin *m*; (Relig) fête *f*. ● *vi* festoyer. ● *vt* régaler (on de).

feat *n* exploit *m*.

feather *n* plume *f*. ● *vt* ~ **one's nest** s'enrichir.

feature *n* caractéristique *f*; (of person, face) trait *m*; (film) long métrage *m*; (article) article *m* de fond. ● *vt* (advert) représenter; (give prominence to) mettre en vedette. ● *vi* figurer (in dans).

February *n* février *m*.

fed ⇒FEED. ● *adj* **be** ~ **up** 🆒 en avoir marre 🆒 (with de).

federal *adj* fédéral.

fee *n* (for entrance) prix *m*; ~(**s**) (of doctor) honoraires *mpl*; (of actor, artist) cachet *m*; (for tuition) frais *mpl*; (for enrolment) droits *mpl*.

feeble *adj* faible.

feed *vt* (*pt* **fed**) nourrir, donner à manger à; (suckle) allaiter; (supply) alimenter. ● *vi* se nourrir (on de); ~ **in information** rentrer des données. ● *n* nourriture *f*; (of baby) tétée *f*.

feedback *n* réaction(s) *f(pl)*; (Med, Tech) feed-back *m*.

feel *vt* (*pt* **felt**) (touch) tâter; (be conscious of) sentir; (emotion) ressentir; (experience) éprouver; (think) estimer. ● *vi* (tired, lonely) se sentir; ~ **hot/thirsty** avoir chaud/soif; ~ **as if** avoir l'impression que; ~ **awful** (ill) se sentir malade; ~ **like** (want 🆒) avoir envie de.

feeler *n* antenne *f*; **put out** ~**s** tâter le terrain.

feeling *n* (emotion) sentiment *m*; (physical) sensation *f*; (impression) impression *f*.

feet ⇒FOOT.

feign *vt* feindre.

fell ⇒FALL. ● *vt* (cut down) abattre.

fellow *n* compagnon *m*, camarade *m*; (of society) membre *m*; (man 🆒) type *m* 🆒. ~**-countryman** *n* compatriote *m.* **~-passenger** *n* compagnon *m* de voyage.

fellowship *n* camaraderie *f*; (group) association *f*.

felony *n* crime *m*.

felt ⇒FEEL. ● *n* feutre *m*. **~-tip** *n* feutre *m*.

female *adj* (*animal*) femelle; (*voice, sex*) féminin. ● *n* femme *f*; (animal) femelle *f*.

feminine *a* & *n* féminin (*m*). **femininity** *n* féminité *f*. **feminist** *n* féministe *mf*.

fence *n* barrière *f*; sit on the ~ ne pas prendre position. ● *vt* ~ (in) clôturer. ● *vi* (Sport) faire de l'escrime. **fencing** *n* escrime *f*.

fend *vi* ~ for oneself se débrouiller tout seul. ● *vt* ~ off (blow, attack) parer.

fender *n* (for fireplace) garde-cendre *m*; (mudguard: US) garde-boue *m inv*.

ferment¹ *n* ferment *m*; (excitement: fig) agitation *f*.

ferment² *vt/i* (faire) fermenter.

fern *n* fougère *f*.

ferocious *adj* féroce.

ferret *n* (animal) furet *m*. ● *vi* ~ about fureter. ● *vt* ~ out dénicher.

ferry *n* (long-distance) ferry *m*; (short-distance) bac *m*. ● *vt* transporter.

fertile *adj* fertile; (*person, animal*) fécond. **fertilizer** *n* engrais *m*.

festival *n* festival *m*; (Relig) fête *f*.

festive *adj* de fête, gai; ~ season période *f* des fêtes. **festivity** *n* réjouissances *fpl*.

fetch *vt* (go for) aller chercher; (bring person) amener; (bring thing) apporter; (be sold for) rapporter.

fête *n* fête *f*; (church) kermesse *f*. ● *vt* fêter.

fetish *n* (object) fétiche *m*; (Psych) obsession *f*.

feud *n* querelle *f*.

fever *n* fièvre *f*. **feverish** *adj* fiévreux.

few *det* peu de; a ~ houses quelques maisons; quite a ~ people un bon nombre de personnes. ● *pron* quelques-uns/quelques-unes.

fewer *det* moins de; be ~ être moins nombreux (**than** que). **fewest** *det* le moins de.

fiancé *n* fiancé *m*. **fiancée** *n* fiancée *f*.

fibre, (US) **fiber** *n* fibre *f*. **~glass** *n* fibre *f* de verre.

fiction *n* fiction *f*; (works of) ~ romans *mpl*. **fictional** *adj* fictif.

fiddle *n* 🔳 violon *m*; (swindle 🔳) combine *f*. ● *vi* 🔳 frauder. ● *vt* 🔳 falsifier; ~ with 🔳 tripoter 🔳.

fidget *vi* gigoter sans cesse.

field *n* champ *m*; (Sport) terrain *m*; (fig) domaine *m*. ● *vt* (*ball*: cricket) bloquer.

fierce *adj* féroce; (*storm, attack*) violent.

fiery *adj* (**-ier**, **-iest**) (hot) ardent; (spirited) fougueux.

fifteen *a* & *n* quinze (*m*).

fifth *a* & *n* cinquième (*mf*).

fifty *a* & *n* cinquante (*m*).

fig *n* figue *f*.

fight *vi* (*pt* **fought**) se battre; (struggle: fig) lutter; (quarrel) se disputer. ● *vt* se battre avec; (*evil*: fig) lutter contre. ● *n* (struggle) lutte *f*; (quarrel) dispute *f*; (brawl) bagarre *f*; (Mil) combat *m*. □ ~ **back** se défendre (**against** contre); ~ **off** surmonter; ~ **over** se disputer qch. **fighter** *n* (determined person) lutteur/-euse *m/f*; (plane) avion *m* de chasse. **fighting** *n* combats *mpl*.

figment *n* a ~ of the imagination un produit de l'imagination.

figure *n* (number) chiffre *m*; (diagram) figure *f*; (shape) forme *f*; (body) ligne *f*; ~s arithmétique *f*. ● *vt* s'imaginer. ● *vi* (appear) figurer; that ~s (US, 🔳) c'est logique; ~ **out** comprendre. ~ **of speech** *n* façon *f* de parler.

file *n* (tool) lime *f*; dossier *m*, classeur *m*; (Comput) fichier *m*; (row) file *f*. ● *vt* limer; (*papers*) classer; (Jur) déposer. □ ~ **in** entrer en file; ~ **past** défiler devant.

filing cabinet *n* classeur *m*.

fill *vt/i* (se) remplir; **have had one's** ~ en avoir assez. □ ~ **in** (*form*) remplir; ~ **out** prendre du poids; ~ **up** (Auto) faire le plein (de carburant); (*bath, theatre*) (se) remplir.

fillet *n* filet *m*. ● *vt* découper en filets.

filling *n* (of tooth) plombage *m*; (of sandwich) garniture *f*. ~ **station** *n* station-service *f*.

film *n* film *m*; (Photo) pellicule *f*. ● *vt* filmer. ~-**goer** *n* cinéphile *mf*. ~ **star** *n* vedette *f* de cinéma.

filter *n* filtre *m*; (traffic signal) flèche *f*. ● *vt/i* filtrer; (of traffic) suivre la flèche. ~ **coffee** *n* café *m* filtre.

filth *n* crasse *f*. **filthy** *adj* crasseux.

fin *n* (of fish, seal) nageoire *f*; (of shark) aileron *m*.

final *adj* dernier; (conclusive) définitif. ● *n* (Sport) finale *f*.

finale *n* (Mus) finale *m*.

finalize *vt* mettre au point, fixer.

finally *adv* (lastly, at last) enfin, finalement; (once and for all) définitivement.

finance *n* finance *f*. ● *adj* financier. ● *vt* financer. **financial** *adj* financier.

find *vt* (*pt* **found**) trouver; (sth lost) retrouver. ● *n* trouvaille *f*. ~ **out** *vt* découvrir; *vi* se renseigner (**about** sur). **findings** *npl* conclusions *fpl*.

fine *adj* fin; (excellent) beau; ~ **arts** beaux-arts *mpl*. ● *n* amende *f*. ● *vt* condamner à une amende.

finger *n* doigt *m*. ● *vt* palper. ~-**nail** *n* ongle *m*. ~**print** *n* empreinte *f* digitale. ~-**tip** *n* bout *m* du doigt.

finish *vt/i* finir; ~ **doing** finir de faire; ~ **up doing** finir par faire; ~ **up in** se retrouver à. ● *n* fin *f*; (of race) arrivée *f*; (appearance) finition *f*.

finite *adj* fini.

Finland *n* Finlande *f*. **Finn** *n* Finlandais/-e *m/f*.

Finnish *adj* finlandais. ● *n* (Ling) finnois *m*.

fir *n* sapin *m*.

fire *n* (element) feu *m*; (blaze) incendie *m*; (heater) radiateur *m*; **set** ~ **to** mettre le feu à. ● *vt* (bullet) tirer; (dismiss) renvoyer; (fig) enflammer. ● *vi* tirer (**at** sur); ~ **a gun** tirer un coup de revolver/de fusil. ~ **alarm** *n* alarme *f* incendie. ~**arm** *n* arme *f* à feu. ~ **brigade** *n* pompiers *mpl*.

~ **engine** *n* voiture *f* de pompiers. ~ **escape** *n* escalier *m* de secours. ~ **extinguisher** *n* extincteur *m*. ~**man** *n* (*pl* -**men**) pompier *m*. ~**place** *n* cheminée *f*. ~ **station** *n* caserne *f* de pompiers. ~**wall** *n* mur *m* coupe-feu; (Internet) pare-feu *m inv*. ~**wood** *n* bois *m* de chauffage. ~**work** *n* feu *m* d'artifice.

firing-squad *n* peloton *m* d'exécution.

firm *n* entreprise *f*, société *f*. ● *adj* ferme; (belief) solide.

first *adj* premier; **at** ~ **hand** de première main; **at** ~ **sight** à première vue; ~ **of all** tout d'abord. ● *n* premier/-ière *m/f*. ● *adv* d'abord, premièrement; (arrive) le premier, la première; **at** ~ d'abord. ~ **aid** *n* premiers soins *mpl*. ~-**class** *adj* de première classe. ~ **floor** *n* premier étage *m*; (US) rez-de-chaussée *m inv*. ~ **gear** *n* première (vitesse) *f*. **F**~ **Lady** *n* (US) épouse *f* du Président.

firstly *adv* premièrement.

first name *n* prénom *m*.

fish *n* poisson *m*; ~ **shop** poissonnerie *f*. ● *vi* pêcher; ~ **for** (cod) pêcher; ~ **out** (from water) repêcher; (take out 🔲) sortir. **fisherman** *n* (*pl* -**men**) *n* pêcheur *m*.

fishing *n* pêche *f*; **go** ~ aller à la pêche. ~ **rod** *n* canne *f* à pêche.

fishmonger *n* poissonnier/-ière *m/f*.

fist *n* poing *m*.

fit *n* accès *m*, crise *f*; **be a good** ~ (dress) être à la bonne taille. ● *adj* (**fitter, fittest**) en bonne santé; (proper) convenable; (good enough) bon; (able) capable; **in no** ~ **state to do** pas en état de faire. ● *vt/i* (*pt* **fitted**) (into space) aller; (install) poser. □ ~ **in** *vt* caser; *vi* (newcomer) s'intégrer; ~ **out**, ~ **up** équiper.

fitness *n* forme *f*; (of remark) justesse *f*.

fitted *adj* (wardrobe) encastré. ~ **carpet** *n* moquette *f*.

fitting *adj* approprié. ● *n* essayage *m*. ~ **room** *n* cabine *f* d'essayage.

five *a* & *n* cinq (*m*).

fix *vt* (make firm, attach, decide) fixer; (mend) réparer; (deal with) arranger; ∼ **sb up with sth** trouver qch à qn.

fixture *n* (Sport) match *m*; ∼**s** (in house) installations *fpl*.

fizz *vi* pétiller. ● *n* pétillement *m*. **fizzy** *adj* gazeux.

flabbergast *vt* sidérer.

flabby *adj* flasque.

flag *n* drapeau *m*; (Naut) pavillon *m*. ● *vt* (*pt* **flagged**) ∼ (**down**) faire signe de s'arrêter à. ● *vi* (weaken) faiblir; (*sick person*) s'affaiblir. ∼**-pole** *n* mât *m*. ∼**stone** *n* dalle *f*.

flake *n* flocon *m*; (of paint, metal) écaille *f*. ● *vi* s'écailler.

flamboyant *adj* (*colour*) éclatant; (*manner*) extravagant.

flame *n* flamme *f*; **burst into** ∼**s** exploser; **go up in** ∼**s** brûler. ● *vi* flamber.

flamingo *n* flamant *m* (rose).

flammable *adj* inflammable.

flan *n* tarte *f*; (custard tart) flan *m*.

flank *n* flanc *m*. ● *vt* flanquer.

flannel *n* (material) flannelle *f*; (for face) gant *m* de toilette.

flap *vi* (*pt* **flapped**) battre. ● *vt* ∼ **its wings** battre des ailes. ● *n* (of pocket) rabat *m*; (of table) abattant *m*.

flare *vi* ∼ **up** (fighting) éclater. ● *n* flamboiement *m*; (Mil) fusée *f* éclairante; (in skirt) évasement *m*. **flared** *adj* évasé.

flash *vi* briller; (on and off) clignoter; ∼ **past** passer à toute vitesse. ● *vt* faire briller; (aim torch) diriger (**at** sur); (flaunt) étaler; ∼ **one's headlights** faire un appel de phares. ● *n* (of news, camera) flash *m*; **in a** ∼ en un éclair. ∼**back** *n* retour *m* en arrière. ∼**light** *n* lampe *f* de poche.

flask *n* (for chemicals) flacon *m*; (for drinks) thermos® *m or f inv*.

flat *adj* (**flatter**, **flattest**) plat; (*tyre*) à plat; (*refusal*) catégorique; (*fare*, *rate*) fixe. ● *adv* (say) carrément. ● *n* (rooms) appartement *m*; (tyre 🇬🇧) crevaison *f*; (Mus) bémol *m*.

flat out *adv* (*drive*) à toute vitesse; (*work*) d'arrache-pied.

flatten *vt/i* (s')aplatir.

flatter *vt* flatter.

flaunt *vt* étaler, afficher.

flavour, (US) **flavor** *n* goût *m*; (of ice-cream) parfum *m*. ● *vt* parfumer (**with** à), assaisonner (**with** de). **flavouring** *n* arôme *m* artificiel.

flaw *n* défaut *m*.

flea *n* puce *f*. ∼ **market** *n* marché *m* aux puces.

fleck *n* petite tache *f*.

fled ⇒FLEE.

flee *vt/i* (*pt* **fled**) fuir.

fleece *n* toison *f*; (garment) polaire *f*. ● *vt* plumer.

fleet *n* (Naut, Aviat) flotte *f*; **a** ∼ **of vehicles** (in reserve) parc *m*; (on road) convoi *m*.

fleeting *adj* très bref.

Flemish *adj* flamand. ● *n* (Ling) flamand *m*.

flesh *n* chair *f*; **one's (own)** ∼ **and blood** la chair de sa chair.

flew ⇒FLY.

flex *vt* (knee) fléchir; (*muscle*) faire jouer. ● *n* (Electr) fil *m*.

flexible *adj* flexible.

flexitime *n* horaire *m* variable.

flick *n* petit coup *m*. ● *vt* donner un petit coup à; ∼ **through** feuilleter.

flight *n* (of bird, plane) vol *m*; ∼ **of stairs** escalier *m*; (fleeing) fuite *f*; **take** ∼ prendre la fuite. ∼**-deck** *n* poste *m* de pilotage.

flimsy *adj* (**-ier**, **-iest**) (pej) mince, peu solide.

flinch *vi* (wince) broncher; (draw back) reculer.

fling *vt* (*pt* **flung**) jeter.

flint *n* (rock) silex *m*.

flip *vt* (*pt* **flipped**) donner un petit coup à; ∼ **through** feuilleter. ● *n* chiquenaude *f*.

flippant *adj* désinvolte.

flipper *n* (of seal) nageoire *f*; (of swimmer) palme *f*.

flirt *vi* flirter. ● *n* flirteur/-euse *m/f*.

float *vt/i* (faire) flotter. ● *n* flotteur *m*; (cart) char *m*.

flock *n* (of sheep) troupeau *m*; (of people) foule *f*. ● *vi* affluer.

flog *vt* (*pt* **flogged**) (beat) fouetter; (sell 🇬🇧) vendre.

flood *n* inondation *f*; (fig) flot *m*. ● *vt* inonder. ● *vi* (*building*) être inondé; (*river*) déborder; (*people*: fig) affluer.

floodlight *n* projecteur *m*. ● *vt* (*pt* **floodlit**) illuminer.

floor *n* sol *m*, plancher *m*; (for dancing) piste *f*; (storey) étage *m*. ● *vt* (knock down) terrasser; (baffle) stupéfier. **~-board** *n* planche *f*.

flop *vi* (*pt* **flopped**) (drop) s'affaler; (fail 🗷) échouer; (*head*) tomber. ● *n* 🗓 échec *m*, fiasco *m*.

floppy *adj* lâche, flasque. **~** (**disk**) *n* disquette *f*.

florist *n* fleuriste *mf*.

flounder *vi* (*animal, person*) se débattre (**in** dans); (*economy*) stagner. ● *n* flet *m*; (US) poisson *m* plat.

flour *n* farine *f*.

flourish *vi* prospérer. ● *vt* brandir. ● *n* geste *m* élégant; (curve) fioriture *f*.

flout *vt* se moquer de.

flow *vi* couler; (circulate) circuler; (*traffic*) s'écouler; (hang loosely) flotter; **~ in** affluer; **~ into** (of river) se jeter dans. ● *n* (of liquid, traffic) écoulement *m*; (of tide) flux *m*; (of orders, words: fig) flot *m*. **~ chart** *n* organigramme *m*.

flower *n* fleur *f*. ● *vi* fleurir.

flown ⇒FLY.

flu *n* grippe *f*.

fluctuate *vi* varier.

fluent *adj* (*style*) aisé; **be ~** (**in a language**) parler (une langue) couramment.

fluff *n* peluche(s) *f(pl)*; (down) duvet *m*.

fluid *a* & *n* fluide (*m*).

fluke *n* coup *m* de chance.

flung ⇒FLING.

fluoride *n* fluor *m*.

flush *vi* rougir. ● *vt* nettoyer à grande eau; **~ the toilet** tirer la chasse d'eau. ● *n* (blush) rougeur *f*; (fig) excitation *f*. ● *adj* **~ with** (level with) au ras du. □ **~ out** chasser.

fluster *vt* énerver.

flute *n* flûte *f*.

flutter *vi* voleter; (of wings) battre. ● *n* (wings) battement *m*; (fig) agitation *f*; (bet 🗓) pari *m*.

flux *n* changement *m* continuel.

fly *n* mouche *f*; (of trousers) braguette *f*. ● *vi* (*pt* **flew**; *pp* **flown**) voler; (*passengers*) voyager en avion; (*flag*) flotter; (rush) filer. ● *vt* (*aircraft*) piloter; (*passengers, goods*) transporter par avion; (*flag*) arborer. □ **~ off** s'envoler.

flyer *n* (person) aviateur *m*; (circular) prospectus *m*.

flying *adj* (*saucer*) volant; **with ~ colours** haut la main; **~ start** excellent départ *m*; **~ visit** visite *f* éclair (*a inv*). ● *n* (activity) aviation *f*.

flyover *n* pont *m* (routier).

foal *n* poulain *m*.

foam *n* écume *f*, mousse *f*; **~ (rubber)** caoutchouc *m* mousse. ● *vi* écumer, mousser.

focus *n* (*pl* **~es** or **-ci**) foyer *m*; (fig) centre *m*; **be in/out of ~** être/ne pas être au point. ● *vt/i* (faire) converger; (*instrument*) mettre au point; (with camera) faire la mise au point (**on** sur); (fig) (se) concentrer.

fodder *n* fourrage *m*.

foe *n* ennemi/-e *m/f*.

foetus *n* fœtus *m*.

fog *n* brouillard *m*. ● *vt/i* (*pt* **fogged**) (*window*) (s')embuer.

foggy *adj* brumeux; **it is ~** il fait du brouillard.

foil *n* (tin foil) papier *m* d'aluminium; (deterrent) repoussoir *m*. ● *vt* (thwart) déjouer.

fold *vt/i* (*paper, clothes*) (se) plier; (*arms*) croiser; (fail) s'effondrer. ● *n* pli *m*; (for sheep) parc *m* à moutons; (Relig) bercail *m*. **folder** *n* (file) chemise *f*; (leaflet) dépliant *m*. **folding** *adj* pliant.

foliage *n* feuillage *m*.

folk *n* gens *mpl*; **~s** parents *mpl*. ● *adj* (dance) folklorique; (music) folk.

folklore *n* folklore *m*.

follow *vt/i* suivre; **it ~s that** il s'ensuit que; **~ suit** faire autant; **~ up** (letter) donner suite à. **follower** *n* partisan *m*.

following *n* partisans *mpl*. ● *adj* suivant; **~ day** lendemain *m*. ● *prep* à la suite de.

fond adj (loving) affectueux; (hope)
cher; be ~ of aimer.

fondle vt caresser.

fondness n affection f; (for things)
attachement m.

food n nourriture f; **French** ~ la
cuisine française. ● adj alimentaire.
~ **processor** n robot m (ménager).

fool n idiot/-e m/f. ● vt duper. ● vi ~
around faire l'idiot. **foolish** adj
idiot.

foot n (pl **feet**) pied m; (measure)
pied m (=30.48 cm); (of stairs, page)
bas m; **on** ~ à pied; **on** or **to one's
feet** debout; **under sb's feet** dans les
jambes de qn. ● vt (bill) payer.

footage n (of film) métrage m.

football n (ball) ballon m; (game)
football m. **footballer** n footballeur
m.

foot: ~**bridge** n passerelle f.
~**hold** n prise f.

footing n **on an equal** ~ sur un pied
d'égalité; **be on a friendly** ~ **with sb**
avoir des rapports amicaux avec qn;
lose one's ~ perdre pied.

foot: ~**note** n note f (en bas de la
page). ~**path** n (in countryside) sentier
m; (in town) chemin m. ~**print** n
empreinte f (de pied). ~**step** n pas
m. ~**wear** n chaussures fpl.

---

for

● preposition

····➤ pour; ~ **me** pour moi; **music** ~
dancing de la musique pour danser;
what is it ~? ça sert à quoi?

····➤ (with a time period that is still continuing)
depuis; **I've been waiting** ~ **two
hours** j'attends depuis deux heures; **I
haven't seen him** ~ **ten years** je ne
l'ai pas vu depuis dix ans.

····➤ (with a time period that has ended)
pendant; **I waited** ~ **two hours** j'ai
attendu pendant deux heures.

····➤ (with a future time period) pour; **I'm
going to Paris** ~ **six weeks** je vais à
Paris pour six semaines.

····➤ (with distances) pendant; **I drove** ~
50 kilometres j'ai roulé pendant 50
kilomètres.

forbade ⇒FORBID.

forbid vt (pt **forbade**; pp
forbidden) interdire, défendre (**sb
to do** à qn de faire); ~ **sb sth**
interdire or défendre qch à qn; **you
are forbidden to leave** il vous est
interdit de partir. **forbidding** adj
menaçant.

force n force f; **come into** ~ entrer
en vigueur; **the** ~**s** les forces fpl
armées. ● vt forcer. □ ~ **into** faire
entrer de force; ~ **on** imposer à.
forced adj forcé.

force-feed vt (pt **-fed**) (person)
nourrir de force; (animal) gaver.

forceful adj énergique.

ford n gué m. ● vt passer à gué.

forearm n avant-bras m inv.

forecast vt (pt **forecast**) prévoir.
● n **weather** ~ météo f.

forecourt n (of garage) devant m; (of
station) cour f.

forefinger n index m.

forefront n **at/in the** ~ **of** à la
pointe de.

foregone adj **it's a** ~ **conclusion**
c'est couru d'avance.

foreground n premier plan m.

forehead n front m.

foreign adj étranger; (trade)
extérieur; (travel) à l'étranger.
foreigner n étranger/-ère m/f.

foreman n (pl **-men**) contremaître
m.

foremost adj le plus éminent.
● adv **first and** ~ tout d'abord.

forensic adj médico-légal; ~
medicine médecine f légale.

foresee vt (pt **-saw**; pp **-seen**)
prévoir.

forest n forêt f. **forestry** n
sylviculture f.

foretaste n avant-goût m.

forever adv toujours.

foreword n avant-propos m inv.

forfeit n (penalty) peine f; (in game)
gage m. ● vt perdre.

forgave ⇒FORGIVE.

forge n forge f. ● vt (metal,
friendship) forger; (copy) contrefaire,
falsifier. ● vi ~ **ahead** aller de
l'avant, avancer. **forger** n faussaire
m. **forgery** n faux m, contrefaçon f.

forget vt/i (pt **forgot**; pp **forgotten**) oublier; ~ **oneself** s'oublier. **forgetful** adj distrait. ~**-me-not** n myosotis m.

forgive vt (pt **forgave**; pp **forgiven**) pardonner (**sb for sth** qch à qn).

fork n fourchette f; (for digging) fourche f; (in road) bifurcation f. ● vi (road) bifurquer; ~ **out** 🔲 payer. **forked** adj fourchu. ~**-lift truck** n chariot m élévateur.

form n forme f; (document) formulaire m; (School) classe f; **on** ~ en forme. ● vt/i (se) former.

formal adj officiel, en bonne et due forme; (person) compassé, cérémonieux; (dress) de cérémonie; (denial, grammar) formel; (language) soutenu. **formality** n cérémonial m; (requirement) formalité f.

format n format m. ● vt (pt **formatted**) (disk) formater.

former adj ancien; (first of two) premier. ● n the ~ celui-là, celle-là. **formerly** adv autrefois.

formula n (pl **-ae** or **-as**) formule f. **formulate** vt formuler.

fort n (Mil) fort m; **to hold the** ~ s'occuper de tout.

forth adv **from this day** ~ à partir d'aujourd'hui; **and so** ~ et ainsi de suite; **go back and** ~ aller et venir.

forthcoming adj à venir, prochain; (sociable 🔲) communicatif.

forthright adj direct.

forthwith adv sur-le-champ.

fortnight n quinze jours mpl, quinzaine f.

fortnightly adj bimensuel. ● adv tous les quinze jours.

fortunate adj heureux; **be** ~ avoir de la chance. **fortunately** adv heureusement.

fortune n fortune f; **make a** ~ faire fortune; **have the good** ~ **to** avoir la chance de. ~**-teller** n diseur/-euse m/f de bonne aventure.

forty a & n quarante (m); ~ **winks** un petit somme.

forward adj en avant; (advanced) précoce; (bold) effronté. ● n (Sport) avant m. ● adv en avant; **come** ~ se présenter; **go** ~ avancer. ● vt (letter, e-mail) faire suivre; (goods) expédier; (fig) favoriser. **forwardness** n précocité f. **forwards** adv en avant.

fossil n & a fossile (m).

foster vt (promote) encourager; (child) élever. ● adj (child, parent) adoptif; (family, home) de placement.

fought ⇒FIGHT.

foul adj (smell, weather) infect; (place, action) immonde; (language) ordurier. ● n (football) faute f. ● vt souiller, encrasser; ~ **up** 🔲 gâcher. ~**-mouthed** adj grossier.

found ⇒FIND. ● vt fonder. **foundation** n fondation f; (basis) fondement m; (make-up) fond m de teint. **founder** n fondateur/-trice m/f.

fountain n fontaine f. ~**-pen** n stylo m à encre.

four a & n quatre (m).

fourteen a & n quatorze (m).

fourth a & n quatrième (mf).

four-wheel drive n (car) quatre-quatre m.

fowl n (one bird) poulet m; (group) volaille f.

fox n renard m. ● vt (baffle) mystifier; (deceive) tromper.

fraction n fraction f.

fracture n fracture f. ● vt/i (se) fracturer.

fragile adj fragile.

fragment n fragment m.

fragrance n parfum m.

frail adj frêle.

frame n (of building, boat) charpente f; (of picture) cadre m; (of window) châssis m; (of spectacles) monture f; ~ **of mind** humeur f. ● vt encadrer; (fig) formuler; (Jur, 🔲) monter un coup contre. ~**work** n structure f; (context) cadre m.

France n France f.

franchise n (Pol) droit m de vote; (Comm) franchise f.

frank adj franc. ● vt affranchir. **frankly** adv franchement.

frantic adj frénétique; ~ **with** fou de.

fraternity n (bond) fraternité f; (group, club) confrérie f.

fraud n (deception) fraude f; (person) imposteur m. **fraudulent** adj frauduleux.

fray n the ~ la bataille. ● vt/i (s') effilocher.

freckle n tache f de rousseur.

free adj libre; (gratis) gratuit; (lavish) généreux; ~ **(of charge)** gratuit (ement); **a ~ hand** carte f blanche. ● vt (pt **freed**) libérer; (clear) dégager.

freedom n liberté f.

free: ~ **enterprise** n la libre entreprise. ~ **kick** n coup m franc. **~lance** a & n free-lance (mf), indépendant/-e (m/f).

freely adv librement.

Freemason n franc-maçon m.

Freenet n (Comput) Libertel m.

free: ~ **phone,** ~ **number** n numéro m vert. **~-range** adj (eggs) de ferme.

Freeware n (Comput) Gratuiciel m.

freeway n (US) autoroute f.

freeze vt/i (pt **froze**; pp **frozen**) geler; (Culin) (se) congeler; (wages) bloquer. ● n gel m; blocage m. **~-dried** adj lyophilisé.

freezer n congélateur m.

freezing adj glacial; **below ~** au-dessous de zéro.

freight n fret m.

French adj français. ● n (Ling) français m; **the ~** les Français mpl. ~ **bean** n haricot m vert. ~ **fries** npl frites fpl. **~man** n Français m. **~-speaking** adj francophone. ~ **window** n porte-fenêtre f. **~woman** n Française f.

frenzied adj frénétique. **frenzy** n frénésie f.

frequent¹ adj fréquent.

frequent² vt fréquenter.

fresco n fresque f.

fresh adj frais; (different, additional) nouveau; (cheeky 🆃) culotté.

freshen vi (weather) fraîchir; ~ **up** (person) se rafraîchir.

freshly adv nouvellement.

freshness n fraîcheur f.

freshwater adj d'eau douce.

friction n friction f.

Friday n vendredi m.

fridge n frigo m.

fried ⇨FRY. ● adj frit; ~ **eggs** œufs mpl sur le plat.

friend n ami/-e m/f. **friendly** adj (**-ier, -iest**) amical, gentil. **friendship** n amitié f.

frieze n frise f.

fright n peur f; (person, thing) horreur f.

frighten vt effrayer; ~ **off** faire fuir; **frightened** adj effrayé; **be ~ed** avoir peur (**of** de). **frightening** adj effrayant.

frill n (trimming) fanfreluche f; **with no ~s** très simple.

fringe n (edging, hair) frange f; (of area) bordure f; (of society) marge f. ~ **benefits** npl avantages mpl sociaux.

frisk vt (search) fouiller.

fritter n beignet m. ● vt ~ **away** gaspiller.

frivolity n frivolité f.

frizzy adj crépu.

fro ⇨TO AND FRO.

frog n grenouille f; **a ~ in one's throat** un chat dans la gorge.

frolic vi (pt **frolicked**) s'ébattre. ● n ébats mpl.

from prep de; (with time, prices) à partir de, de; (habit, conviction) par; (according to) d'après; **take ~ sb** prendre à qn; **take ~ one's pocket** prendre dans sa poche.

front n (of car, train) avant m; (of garment, building) devant m; (Mil, Pol) front m; (of book, pamphlet) début m; (appearance: fig) façade f. ● adj de devant, avant inv; (first) premier; ~ **door** porte f d'entrée; **in ~ (of)** devant. **frontage** n façade f.

frontier n frontière f.

frost n gel m, gelée f; (on glass) givre m. ● vt/i (se) givrer. **~-bite** n gelure f.

frosty adj (weather, welcome) glacial; (window) givré.

froth n (on beer) mousse f; (on water) écume f. ● vi mousser, écumer.

frown vi froncer les sourcils; ~ **on** désapprouver. ● n froncement m de sourcils.

froze ⇨FREEZE.

frozen ⇨FREEZE. ● adj congelé.

fruit n fruit m; (collectively) fruits mpl. **fruitful** adj (discussions) fructueux. ~ **machine** n machine f à sous.

frustrate vt (plan) faire échouer; (person: Psych) frustrer; (upset 🔢) exaspérer. **frustration** n (Psych) frustration f; (disappointment) déception f.

fry vt/i (pt **fried**) (faire) frire. **frying-pan** n poêle f (à frire).

FTP abbr (**File Transfer Protocol**) (Internet) protocole m FTP.

fudge n caramel m mou. ● vt (issue) esquiver.

fuel n combustible m; (for car engine) carburant m. ● vt (pt **fuelled**) alimenter en combustible.

fugitive n & a fugitif/-ive (m/f).

fulfil vt (pt **fulfilled**) accomplir, réaliser; (condition) remplir; ~ **oneself** s'épanouir. **fulfilling** adj satisfaisant. **fulfilment** n réalisation f; épanouissement m.

full adj plein (of de); (bus, hotel) complet; (programme) chargé; (skirt) ample; **be** ~ (**up**) n'avoir plus faim; **at** ~ **speed** à toute vitesse. ● n **in** ~ intégralement; **to the** ~ complètement. ~ **back** n (Sport) arrière m. ~ **moon** n pleine lune f. ~ **name** n nom m et prénom m. ~**-scale** adj (drawing etc.) grandeur nature inv; (fig) de grande envergure. ~ **stop** n point m. ~**-time** a & adv à plein temps.

fully adv complètement; ~ **fledged** (member, citizen) à part entière.

fume vi rager. **fumes** npl émanations fpl, vapeurs fpl.

fun n amusement m; **be** ~ être chouette; **for** ~ pour rire; **make** ~ **of** se moquer de.

function n (purpose, duty) fonction f; (event) réception f. ● vi fonctionner.

fund n fonds m. ● vt fournir les fonds pour.

fundamental adj fondamental. **fundamentalist** n intégriste mf.

funeral n enterrement m. ● adj funèbre.

fun-fair n fête f foraine.

fungus n (pl **-gi**) (plant) champignon m; (mould) moisissure f.

funnel n (for pouring) entonnoir m; (of ship) cheminée f.

funny adj (**-ier**, **-iest**) drôle; (odd) bizarre.

fur n (for garment) fourrure f; (on animal) poils mpl; (in kettle) tartre m.

furious adj furieux.

furnace n fourneau m.

furnish vt (room) meubler; (supply) fournir. **furnishings** npl ameublement m.

furniture n meubles mpl, mobilier m.

furry adj (animal) à fourrure; (toy) en peluche.

further adj plus éloigné; (additional) supplémentaire. ● adv plus loin; (more) davantage. ● vt avancer. ~ **education** n formation f continue.

furthermore adv en outre, de plus.

furthest adj le plus éloigné. ● adv le plus loin.

fury n fureur f.

fuse vt/i (melt) fondre; (unite: fig) fusionner; ~ **the lights** faire sauter les plombs. ● n (of plug) fusible m; (of bomb) amorce f.

fuss n (when upset) histoire(s) f(pl); (when excited) agitation f; **make a** ~ faire des histoires; s'agiter; (about food) faire des chichis; **make a** ~ **of** faire grand cas de. ● vi s'agiter. **fussy** adj (finicky) tatillon; (hard to please) difficile.

future adj futur. ● n avenir m; (Gram) futur m; **in** ~ à l'avenir.

fuzzy adj (hair) crépu; (photograph) flou; (person 🔢) à l'esprit confus.

Gg

Gaelic n gaélique m.

gag n (on mouth) bâillon m; (joke) blague f. ● vt (pt **gagged**) bâillonner.

gain vt (respect, support) gagner; (speed, weight) prendre. ● vi (of clock) avancer. ● *n* (increase) augmentation *f* (**in** de); (profit) gain *m*.

galaxy *n* galaxie *f*.

gale *n* tempête *f*.

gallery *n* galerie *f*; (art) ∼ musée *m*.

Gallic *adj* français.

gallon *n* gallon *m* (*imperial = 4.546 litres; Amer. = 3.785 litres*).

gallop *n* galop *m*. ● *vi* (*pt* **galloped**) galoper.

galore *adv* (*prizes, bargains*) en abondance; (*drinks, sandwiches*) à gogo Ⅰ.

gamble *vt/i* jouer; ∼ **on** miser sur. ● *n* (venture) entreprise *f* risquée; (bet) pari *m*; (risk) risque *m*. **gambling** *n* jeu *m*.

game *n* jeu *m*; (football) match *m*; (tennis) partie *f*; (animals, birds) gibier *m*. ● *adj* (brave) courageux; ∼ **for** prêt à. ∼**keeper** *n* garde-chasse *m*.

gammon *n* jambon *m*.

gang *n* (of youths) bande *f*; (of workmen) équipe *f*. ● *vi* ∼ **up** se liguer (**on**, **against** contre).

gangway *n* passage *m*; (aisle) allée *f*; (of ship) passerelle *f*.

gaol *n* & *vt* = JAIL.

gap *n* trou *m*, vide *m*; (in time) intervalle *m*; (in education) lacune *f*; (difference) écart *m*.

gape *vi* rester bouche bée. **gaping** *adj* béant.

garage *n* garage *m*. ● *vt* mettre au garage.

garbage *n* (US) ordures *fpl*.

garden *n* jardin *m*. ● *vi* jardiner. **gardener** *n* jardinier/-ière *m/f*. **gardening** *n* jardinage *m*.

gargle *vi* se gargariser.

garish *adj* (*clothes*) tape-à-l'œil; (*light*) cru.

garland *n* guirlande *f*.

garlic *n* ail *m*.

garment *n* vêtement *m*.

garnish *vt* garnir (**with** de). ● *n* garniture *f*.

garter *n* jarretière *f*.

gas *n* (*pl* ∼**es**) gaz *m*; (Med) anesthésie *m*; (petrol: US) essence *f*. ● *adj* (*mask, pipe*) à gaz. ● *vt* asphyxier; (Mil) gazer. ● *vi* Ⅰ bavarder.

gash *n* entaille *f*. ● *vt* entailler.

gasoline *n* (petrol: US) essence *f*.

gasp *vi* haleter; (in surprise: fig) avoir le souffle coupé. ● *n* halètement *m*.

gate *n* (in garden, airport) porte *f*; (of field, level crossing) barrière *f*. ∼**way** *n* porte *f*; (Internet) passerelle *f*.

gather *vt* (*people, objects*) rassembler; (pick up) ramasser; (*flowers*) cueillir; (fig) comprendre; ∼ **speed** prendre de la vitesse; (sewing) froncer. ● *vi* (*people*) se rassembler; (pile up) s'accumuler. **gathering** *n* réunion *m*.

gauge *n* jauge *f*, indicateur *m*. ● *vt* (*speed, distance*) jauger; (*reaction, mood*) évaluer.

gaunt *adj* décharné.

gauze *n* gaze *f*.

gave ⇒GIVE.

gay *adj* (joyful) gai; (homosexual) gay *inv*. ● *n* gay *mf*.

gaze *vi* ∼ (**at**) regarder (fixement). ● *n* regard *m* (fixe).

gazette *n* journal *m* (officiel).

GB *abbr* ⇒GREAT BRITAIN.

gear *n* (equipment) matériel *m*; (Tech) engrenage *m*; (Auto) vitesse *f*; **in** ∼ en prise; **out of** ∼ au point mort. ● *vt* **to be geared to** s'adresser à. ∼**box** *n* (Auto) boîte *f* de vitesses. ∼**-lever**, (US) ∼**-shift** *n* levier *m* de vitesse.

geese ⇒GOOSE.

gel *n* (for hair) gel *m*.

gem *n* pierre *f* précieuse.

Gemini *n* Gémeaux *mpl*.

gender *n* (Ling) genre *m*; (of person) sexe *m*.

gene *n* gène *m*. ∼ **library** *n* génothèque *f*.

general *adj* général. ● *n* général *m*; **in** ∼ en général.

general election *n* élections *fpl* législatives.

generalization *n* généralisation *f*. **generalize** *vt/i* généraliser.

general practitioner *n* (Med) généraliste *m*.

generate *vt* produire.

generation *n* génération *f*.

generator *n* (Electr) groupe *m* électrogène.

generosity n générosité f.
generous adj généreux; (plentiful) copieux.
genetics n génétique f.
Geneva n Genève.
genial adj affable, sympathique.
genitals npl organes mpl génitaux.
genius n (pl ~es) génie m.
gentle adj (mild, kind) doux; (pressure, breeze) léger; (reminder, hint) discret.
gentleman n (pl -men) (man) monsieur m; (well-bred) gentleman m.
gently adv doucement.
gents npl (toilets) toilettes fpl; (on sign) 'Messieurs'.
genuine adj (reason, motive) vrai; (jewel, substance) véritable; (person, belief) sincère.
geography n géographie f.
geology n géologie f.
geometry n géométrie f.
geriatric adj gériatrique.
germ n (Med) microbe m.
German n (person) Allemand/-e m/f; (Ling) allemand m. ● adj allemand.
Germanic adj germanique.
German measles n rubéole f.
Germany n Allemagne f.
gesture n geste m.

····································

get

past **got**; *past participle* **got**, **gotten** (US); *present participle* **getting**

● *transitive verb*
····▶ recevoir; **we got a letter** nous avons reçu une lettre.
····▶ (obtain) **I got a job in Paris** j'ai trouvé un travail à Paris; **I'll ~ sth to eat at the airport** je mangerai qch à l'aéroport.
····▶ (buy) acheter; **~ sb a present** acheter un cadeau à qn.
····▶ (achieve) obtenir; **he got it right** il a obtenu le bon résultat; **~ good grades** avoir de bonnes notes.
····▶ (fetch) chercher; **go and ~ a chair** va chercher une chaise.
····▶ (transport) prendre; **we can ~ the bus** on peut prendre le bus.

····▶ (understand 🔢) comprendre; **now let me ~ this right** alors si je comprends bien…
····▶ (experience) **~ a surprise** être surpris; **~ a shock** avoir un choc.
····▶ (illness) **~ measles** attraper la rougeole; **~ a cold** s'enrhumer.
····▶ (ask or persuade) **~ him to call me** dis-lui de m'appeler; **I'll ~ her to help me** je lui demanderai de m'aider.
····▶ (cause to be done) **~ a TV repaired** faire réparer une télévision; **~ one's hair cut** se faire couper les cheveux.

● *intransitive verb*
····▶ devenir; **he's getting old** il vieillit; **it's getting late** il se fait tard.
····▶ (in passives) **~ married** se marier; **~ hurt** être blessé.
····▶ (arrive) arriver; **~ to the airport** arriver à l'aéroport.
□ **get about** (person) se déplacer.
get along (manage) se débrouiller; (progress) avancer.
get along with s'entendre avec.
get at (reach) atteindre; (imply) vouloir dire.
get away partir; (escape) s'échapper.
get back vi revenir. vt récupérer.
get by vi (manage) se débrouiller. vt (pass) passer.
get down vt/i descendre. vt (depress) déprimer.
get in entrer.
get into (car) monter dans; (dress) mettre.
get off vt (bus) descendre; (remove) enlever. vi (from bus) descendre; (leave) partir; (Jur) être acquitté.
get on vi (to bus) monter; (succeed) réussir. vt (bus) monter.
get on with (person) s'entendre avec; (job) attaquer.
get out sortir.
get out of (fig) se soustraire.
get over (illness) se remettre de.
get round (rule) contourner; (person) entortiller.
get through vi passer; (on phone) **~ through to sb** avoir qn. vt traverser.
get up se lever.

get up to faire.

getaway n fuite f.
ghastly adj (**-ier, -iest**) affreux.
gherkin n cornichon m.
ghetto n ghetto m.
ghost n fantôme m.
giant n & a géant (m).
gibberish n baragouin m, charabia m.
giblets npl abats mpl.
giddy adj (**-ier, -iest**) vertigineux; be or feel ~ avoir le vertige.
gift n (present) cadeau m; (ability) don m.
gifted adj doué.
gift-wrap n paquet-cadeau m.
gigantic adj gigantesque.
giggle vi ricaner (sottement), glousser. ● n ricanement m; the ~s le fou rire.
gimmick n truc m.
gin n gin m.
ginger n gingembre m. ● adj (hair) roux. ~ **beer** n boisson f gazeuse au gingembre. ~**bread** n pain m d'épices.
gingerly adv avec précaution.
giraffe n girafe f.
girl n (child) (petite) fille f; (young woman) (jeune) fille f. ~**friend** n amie f; (of boy) petite amie f.
giro n virement m bancaire; (cheque) mandat m.
gist n essentiel m.
give vt (pt **gave**; pp **given**) donner; (gesture) faire; (laugh, sigh) pousser; ~ **sb sth** donner qch à qn. ● vi donner; (yield) céder; (stretch) se détendre. ● n élasticité f. □ ~ **away** donner; (secret) trahir; ~ **back** rendre; ~ **in** (yield) céder (to à); ~ **off** (heat, fumes) dégager; (signal, scent) émettre; ~ **out** vt distribuer; ~ **over** (devote) consacrer; (stop 🆇) cesser; ~ **up** vt/i (renounce) renoncer (à); (yield) céder; ~ **oneself up** se rendre; ~ **way** céder; (collapse) s'effondrer.
given ⇒GIVE. ● adj donné. ~ **name** n prénom m.
glad adj content. **gladly** adv avec plaisir.

glamorous adj séduisant, ensorcelant.
glamour, (US) **glamor** n enchantement m, séduction f.
glance n coup m d'œil. ● vi ~ **at** jeter un coup d'œil à.
gland n glande f.
glare vi briller très fort; ~ **at** regarder d'un air furieux. ● n (of lights) éclat m (aveuglant); (stare: fig) regard m furieux. **glaring** adj (dazzling) éblouissant; (obvious) flagrant.
glass n verre m. **glasses** npl (spectacles) lunettes fpl.
glaze vt (door) vitrer; (pottery) vernisser. ● n vernis m.
gleam n lueur f. ● vi luire.
glide vi glisser; (of plane) planer. **glider** n planeur m.
glimpse n (insight) aperçu m; **catch a** ~ **of** entrevoir.
glitter vi scintiller. ● n scintillement m.
global adj (world-wide) mondial; (all-embracing) global. ~ **warming** n réchauffement m de la planète.
globe n globe m.
gloom n obscurité f; (sadness: fig) tristesse f. **gloomy** adj triste; (pessimistic) pessimiste.
glorious adj splendide; (deed, hero) glorieux.
glory n gloire f; (beauty) splendeur f. ● vi ~ **in** être très fier de.
gloss n lustre m, brillant m. ● adj brillant. ● vi ~ **over** (make light of) glisser sur; (cover up) dissimuler.
glossary n glossaire m.
glossy adj brillant.
glove n gant m. ~ **compartment** n (Auto) boîte f à gants.
glow vi (fire) rougeoyer; (person, eyes) rayonner. ● n rougeoiement m, éclat m. **glowing** adj (report) enthousiaste.
glucose n glucose m.
glue n colle f. ● vt (pres p **gluing**) coller.
glutton n glouton/-ne m/f.
gnaw vt/i ronger.

GNP *abbr* (**Gross National Product**) produit *m* national brut, PNB *m*.

go

⇒ *present* go, goes; *past* went; *past participle* gone

● *intransitive verb*

····▸ aller; ∼ to school/town/market aller à l'école/en ville/au marché; ∼ for a swim/walk/coffee aller nager/se promener/prendre un café.

····▸ (leave) s'en aller; I must be ∼ing il faut que je m'en aille.

····▸ (vanish) the money's gone il n'y a plus d'argent; my bike's gone mon vélo n'est plus là.

····▸ (work, function) marcher; is the car ∼ing? est-ce que la voiture marche?

····▸ (become) devenir; ∼ blind devenir aveugle; ∼ pale/red pâlir/rougir.

····▸ (turn out, progress) aller; how's it going? comment ça va?; how did the exam ∼? comment s'est passé l'examen?

····▸ (in future tenses) be ∼ing to do aller faire.

● *noun*

····▸ (turn) tour *m*; (try) essai *m*; have a ∼! essaie!; full of ∼ 🄸 dynamique.

❑ **go across** traverser.

go after poursuivre.

go away partir; ∼ away! va-t'en!, allez-vous-en!

go back retourner; ∼ back in rentrer; ∼ back to work reprendre le travail.

go down (*quality, price*) baisser; (*person*) descendre; (*sun*) se coucher.

go in entrer.

go in for (*exam*) se présenter à.

go off (leave) partir; (*bomb*) exploser; (*alarm clock*) sonner; (*milk*) tourner; (*light*) s'éteindre.

go on (continue) continuer; (*light*) s'allumer; ∼ on doing continuer à faire; what's ∼ing on? qu'est-ce qui se passe?

go out sortir; (*light, fire*) s'éteindre.

go over vérifier.

go round (be enough) être assez; ∼ round to see sb passer voir qn.

go through (check) examiner; (search) fouiller; ∼ through a difficult time traverser une période difficile.

go together aller ensemble.

go under (sink) couler; (fail) échouer.

go up (*person*) monter; (*price, salary*) augmenter.

go without se passer de.

go-ahead *n* feu *m* vert. ● *adj* dynamique.

goal *n* but *m*. ∼**keeper** *n* gardien *m* de but. ∼**post** *n* poteau *m* de but.

goat *n* chèvre *f*.

gobble *vt* engouffrer.

go-between *n* intermédiaire *mf*.

god *n* dieu *m*. ∼**child** *n* (*pl* -children) filleul/-e *m/f*. ∼**daughter** *n* filleule *f*.

goddess *n* déesse *f*.

god: ∼**father** *n* parrain *m*. ∼**mother** *n* marraine *f*. ∼**send** *n* aubaine *f*. ∼**son** *n* filleul *m*.

goggles *npl* lunettes *fpl* (protectrices).

going *n* it is slow/hard ∼ c'est lent/difficile. ● *adj* (*price, rate*) actuel.

go-kart *n* kart *m*.

gold *n* or *m*. ● *adj* en or, d'or.

golden *adj* en or, d'or; (in colour) doré; (opportunity) unique.

gold: ∼**fish** *n* poisson *m* rouge. ∼**-plated** *adj* plaqué or. ∼**smith** *n* orfèvre *m*.

golf *n* golf *m*. ∼**-course** *n* terrain *m* de golf.

gone ⇒GO. ● *adj* parti; ∼ six o'clock six heures passées; the butter's all ∼ il n'y a plus de beurre.

good *adj* (**better, best**) bon; (weather) beau; (well-behaved) sage; as ∼ as (almost) pratiquement; that's ∼ of you c'est gentil (de ta part); be ∼ with savoir s'y prendre avec; feel ∼ se sentir bien; it is ∼ for you ça vous fait du bien. ● *n* bien *m*; do ∼ faire du bien; is it any ∼? est-ce que c'est bien?; it's no ∼ ça ne vaut rien; it is no ∼ shouting ça ne sert à rien de crier; for ∼ pour toujours. ∼ **afternoon** *interj* bonjour. ∼**bye** *interj* & *n* au revoir (*m inv*). ∼ **evening** *interj* bonsoir. **G**∼ **Friday**

n Vendredi *m* saint. **~-looking** *adj* beau. **~ morning** *interj* bonjour. **~-natured** *adj* gentil.

goodness *n* bonté *f*; **my ~!** mon Dieu!

good-night *interj* bonsoir, bonne nuit.

goods *npl* marchandises *fpl*.

goodwill *n* bonne volonté *f*.

goose *n* (*pl* **geese**) oie *f*. **gooseberry** *n* groseille *f* à maquereau. **~-pimples** *npl* chair *f* de poule.

gorge *n* (Geog) gorge *f*. ● *vt* **~ oneself** se gaver (**on** de).

gorgeous *adj* magnifique, splendide, formidable.

gorilla *n* gorille *m*.

gory *adj* (**-ier**, **-iest**) sanglant; (horrific: fig) horrible.

gospel *n* évangile *m*; **the G~** l'Évangile *m*.

gossip *n* bavardages *mpl*, commérages *mpl*; (person) bavard/-e *m/f*. ● *vi* bavarder.

got ⇒GET. ● **have ~** avoir; **have ~ to do** devoir faire.

govern *vt/i* gouverner. **governess** *n* gouvernante *f*. **government** *n* gouvernement *m*. **governor** *n* gouverneur *m*.

gown *n* robe *f*; (of judge, teacher) toge *f*.

GP *abbr* ⇒GENERAL PRACTITIONER.

grab *vt* (*pt* **grabbed**) saisir.

grace *n* grâce *f*. ● *vt* (honour) honorer; (adorn) orner. **graceful** *adj* gracieux.

gracious *adj* (kind) bienveillant; (elegant) élégant.

grade *n* catégorie *f*; (of goods) qualité *f*; (on scale) grade *m*; (school mark) note *f*; (class: US) classe *f*. ● *vt* classer; (school work) noter. **~ school** *n* (US) école *f* primaire.

gradual *adj* progressif, graduel. **gradually** *adv* progressivement, peu à peu.

graduate[1] *n* (Univ) diplômé/-e *m/f*.

graduate[2] *vi* obtenir son diplôme. ● *vt* graduer. **graduation** *n* remise *f* des diplômes.

graffiti *npl* graffiti *mpl*.

graft *n* (Med, Bot) greffe *f*; (work) boulot *m*. ● *vt* greffer (**on to** sur); (work) trimer.

grain *n* (seed, quantity, texture) grain *m*; (in wood) fibre *f*.

gram *n* gramme *m*.

grammar *n* grammaire *f*.

grand *adj* magnifique; (*duke, chorus*) grand.

grandad *n* 🎩 papy *m*.

grand: ~child *n* (girl) petite-fille *f*; (boy) petit-fils *m*; **her ~children** ses petits-enfants *mpl*. **~daughter** *n* petite-fille *f*. **~father** *n* grand-père *m*. **~ma** *n* = GRANNY. **~mother** *n* grand-mère *f*. **~parents** *npl* grands-parents *mpl*. **~ piano** *n* piano *m* à queue. **~son** *n* petit-fils *m*. **~stand** *n* tribune *f*.

granny *n* 🎩 mémé *f*, mamie *f*.

grant *vt* (*permission*) accorder; (*request*) accéder à; (admit) admettre (**that** que); **take sth for ~ed** considérer qch comme une chose acquise. ● *n* subvention *f*; (Univ) bourse *f*.

granule *n* (*of sugar, salt*) grain *m*; (*of coffee*) granulé *m*.

grape *n* grain *m* de raisin; **~s** raisin (s) *m*(*pl*).

grapefruit *n* *inv* pamplemousse *m*.

graph *n* graphique *m*.

graphic *adj* (*arts*) graphique; (fig) vivant, explicite. **graphics** *npl* (Comput) graphiques *mpl*.

grasp *vt* saisir. ● *n* (hold) prise *f*; (strength of hand) poigne *f*; (reach) portée *f*; (fig) compréhension *f*.

grass *n* herbe *f*. **~hopper** *n* sauterelle *f*. **~land** *n* prairie *f*.

grass roots *npl* peuple *m*. ● *adj* (*movement*) populaire; (*support*) de base.

grate *n* (hearth) âtre *m*; (fire basket) grille *f*. ● *vt* râper. ● *vi* grincer.

grateful *adj* reconnaissant.

grater *n* râpe *f*.

gratified *adj* très heureux. **gratify** *vt* faire plaisir à.

grating *n* (bars) grille *f*; (noise) grincement *m*.

gratitude *n* reconnaissance *f*.

gratuity *n* (tip) pourboire *m*; (bounty: Mil) prime *f*.

grave¹ *n* (tombe *f*. ● *adj* (serious) grave.

grave² *adj* ~ **accent** accent *m* grave.

gravel *n* graviers *mpl*.

grave: ~**stone** *n* pierre *f* tombale. ~**yard** *n* cimetière *m*.

gravity *n* (seriousness) gravité *f*; (force) pesanteur *f*.

gravy *n* jus *m* (de viande).

gray (US) *a* & *n* = GREY.

graze *vi* (eat) paître. ● *vt* (touch) frôler; (scrape) écorcher. ● *n* écorchure *f*.

grease *n* graisse *f*. ● *vt* graisser. **greasy** *adj* graisseux.

great *adj* grand; (very good 🗓) génial 🗓, formidable 🗓, (*grandfather, grandmother*) arrière.

Great Britain *n* Grande-Bretagne *f*.

greatly *adv* (very) très; (much) beaucoup.

Greece *n* Grèce *f*.

greed *n* avidité *f*; (for food) gourmandise *f*. **greedy** *adj* avide; gourmand.

Greek *n* (person) Grec/-que *m/f*; (Ling) grec *m*. ● *adj* grec.

green *adj* vert; (fig) naïf. ● *n* vert *m*; (grass) pelouse *f*; (golf) green *m*; ~**s** légumes *mpl* verts. ~**grocer** *n* marchand/-e *m/f* de fruits et légumes.

green house *n* serre *f*; ~ **effect** effet *m* de serre.

greet *vt* (welcome) accueillir; (address politely) saluer. **greeting** *n* accueil *m*.

greetings *interj* salutations! ● *npl* (*Christmas*) vœux *mpl*. ~ **card** *n* carte *f* de vœux.

grew ⇒GROW.

grey *adj* gris; (fig) triste; **go** ~ (*hair, person*) grisonner. ● *n* gris *m*. ~**hound** *n* lévrier *m*.

grid *n* grille *f*; (network: Electr) réseau *m*.

grief *n* chagrin *m*; **come to** ~ (*person*) avoir un malheur; (fail) tourner mal.

grievance *n* griefs *mpl*.

grieve *vt/i* (s')affliger; ~ **for** pleurer.

grill *n* (cooking device) gril *m*; (food) grillade *f*; (Auto) calandre *f*. ● *vt/i* (faire) griller; (interrogate) mettre sur la sellette.

grim *adj* sinistre.

grimace *n* grimace *f*. ● *vi* grimacer.

grime *n* crasse *f*.

grin *vi* (*pt* **grinned**) sourire. ● *n* (large) sourire *m*.

grind *vt* (*pt* **ground**) (*grain*) écraser; (*coffee*) moudre; (sharpen) aiguiser; ~ **one's teeth** grincer des dents. ● *vi* ~ **to a halt** s'immobiliser. ● *n* corvée *f*.

grip *vt* (*pt* **gripped**) saisir; (interest) passionner. ● *n* prise *f*; (strength of hand) poigne *f*; **come to** ~**s with** en venir aux prises avec.

grisly *adj* (**-ier, -iest**) (*remains*) macabre; (*sight*) horrible.

gristle *n* cartilage *m*.

grit *n* (for roads) sable *m*; (fig) courage *m*. ● *vt* (*pt* **gritted**) (*road*) sabler; (*teeth*) serrer.

groan *vi* gémir. ● *n* gémissement *m*.

grocer *n* (person) épicier/-ière *m/f*; (shop) épicerie *f*. **groceries** *npl* (shopping) courses *fpl*; (goods) épicerie *f*. **grocery** *n* (shop) épicerie *f*.

groin *n* aine *f*.

groom *n* marié *m*; (for horses) palefrenier/-ière *m/f*. ● *vt* (*horse*) panser; (fig) préparer.

groove *n* (for door etc.) rainure *f*; (in record) sillon *m*.

grope *vi* tâtonner; ~ **for** chercher à tâtons.

gross *adj* (*behaviour*) vulgaire; (Comm) brut. ● *n inv* grosse *f*.

grotto *n* (*pl* ~**es**) grotte *f*.

grouch *vi* (grumble 🗓) rouspéter, râler.

ground¹ *n* terre *f*, sol *m*; (area) terrain *m*; (reason) raison *f*; (Electr, US) masse *f*; ~**s** terres *fpl*, parc *m*; (of coffee) marc *m*; **on the** ~ par terre; **lose** ~ perdre du terrain. ● *vt/i* (Naut) échouer; (aircraft) retenir au sol.

ground² ⇒GRIND. ● *adj* ~ **beef** (US) bifteck *m* haché.

ground: ~ **floor** n rez-de-chaussée m inv. ~**work** n travail m préparatoire.

group n groupe m. ● vt/i (se) grouper. ~**ware** n (Comput) logiciel m de groupe.

grovel vi (pt **grovelled**) ramper.

grow vi (pt **grew**; pp **grown**) (person) grandir; (plant) pousser; (become) devenir; (crime) augmenter. ● vt cultiver; ~ **up** devenir adulte, grandir. **grower** n cultivateur/-trice m/f.

growl vi (dog) gronder; (person) grogner. ● n grognement m.

grown ⇒GROW. ● adj adulte. ~**-up** a & n adulte (mf).

growth n (of person, plant) croissance f; (in numbers) accroissement m; (of hair, tooth) pousse f; (Med) grosseur f, tumeur f.

grudge vt ~ **doing** faire à contrecœur; ~ **sb sth** (success, wealth) en vouloir à qn de qch. ● n rancune f; **have a ~ against** en vouloir à.

grumble vi ronchonner, grogner (at après).

grumpy adj (-**ier**, -**iest**) grincheux, grognon.

grunt vi grogner. ● n grognement m.

guarantee n garantie f. ● vt garantir.

guard vt protéger; (watch) surveiller. ● vi ~ **against** se protéger contre. ● n (Mil) garde f; (person) garde m; (on train) chef m de train.

guardian n gardien/-ne m/f; (of orphan) tuteur/-trice m/f.

guess vt/i deviner; (suppose) penser. ● n conjecture f.

guest n invité/-e m/f; (in hotel) client/ -e m/f. ~**-house** n pension f. ~**-room** n chambre f d'amis.

guidance n (advice) conseils mpl; (information) information f.

guide n (person, book) guide m; (girl) guide f. ● vt guider. ~**book** n guide m. ~**-dog** n chien m d'aveugle. ~**line** n indication f; (advice) conseils mpl.

guillotine n (for execution) guillotine f; (for paper) massicot m.

guilt n culpabilité f. **guilty** adj coupable.

guinea-pig n (animal) cochon m d'Inde; (fig) cobaye m.

guitar n guitare f.

gulf n (part of sea) golfe m; (hollow) gouffre m.

gull n mouette f, (larger) goéland m.

gullible adj crédule.

gully n (ravine) ravin m; (drain) rigole f.

gulp vt ~ (**down**) avaler en vitesse. ● vi (from fear etc.) avoir la gorge serrée. ● n gorgée f.

gum n (Anat) gencive f; (glue) colle f; (for chewing) chewing-gum m. ● vt (pt **gummed**) gommer.

gun n (pistol) revolver m; (rifle) fusil m; (large) canon m. ● vt (pt **gunned**) ~ **down** abattre. ~**fire** n fusillade f. ~**powder** n poudre f à canon. ~**shot** n coup m de feu.

gurgle n (of water) gargouillement m; (of baby) gazouillis m. ● vi (water) gargouiller; (baby) gazouiller.

gush vi ~ (**out**) jaillir. ● n jaillissement m.

gust n rafale f; (of smoke) bouffée f.

gut n (belly 🗔) ventre m. ● vt (pt **gutted**) (fish) vider; (of fire) dévaster.

guts npl 🗔 (insides of human) tripes fpl 🗔; (insides of animal, building) entrailles fpl; (courage) cran m 🗔.

gutter n (on roof) gouttière f; (in street) caniveau m.

guy n (man 🗔) type m.

gym n (place) gymnase m; (activity) gym(nastique) f.

gymnasium n gymnase m.

gymnastics npl gymnastique f.

gynaecologist n gynécologue mf.

gypsy n bohémien/-ne m/f.

Hh

habit *n* habitude *f*; (costume: Relig) habit *m*; **be in/get into the ~ of** avoir/prendre l'habitude de.

habitual *adj* (usual) habituel; (*smoker, liar*) invétéré.

hack *n* (writer) écrivaillon *m*. ● *vi* (Comput) pirater; **~ into** s'introduire dans. ● *vt* tailler. **hacker** *n* (Comput) pirate *m* informatique.

hackneyed *adj* rebattu.

had ⇨HAVE.

haddock *n inv* églefin *m*.

haemorrhage *n* hémorragie *f*.

haggard *adj* (*person*) exténué; (*face, look*) défait.

haggle *vi* marchander; **~ over sth** discuter du prix de qch.

hail *n* grêle *f*. ● *vt* (greet) saluer; (*taxi*) héler. ● *vi* grêler; **~ from** venir de. **~stone** *n* grêlon *m*.

hair *n* (on head) cheveux *mpl*; (on body, of animal) poils *mpl*; (single strand on head) cheveu *m*; (on body) poil *m*. **~brush** *n* brosse *f* à cheveux. **~cut** *n* coupe *f* de cheveux. **~do** *n* Ⓕ coiffure *f*. **~dresser** *n* coiffeur/ -euse *m/f*. **~drier** *n* séchoir *m* (à cheveux). **~pin** *n* épingle *f* à cheveux. **~ remover** *n* dépilatoire *m*. **~style** *n* coiffure *f*.

hairy *adj* (-ier, -iest) poilu; (terrifying Ⓕ) horrifiant.

half *n* (*pl* **halves**) (part) moitié *f*; (fraction) demi *m*; **~ a dozen** une demi-douzaine; **~ an hour** une demi-heure; **four and a ~** quatre et demi; **an hour and a ~** une heure et demie; **~ and half** moitié moitié; **in ~** en deux. ● *adj* demi; **~ price** à moitié prix. ● *adv* à moitié. **~-back** *n* (Sport) demi *m*. **~-hearted** *adj* tiède. **~-mast** *n* **at ~-mast** en berne. **~-term** *n* vacances *fpl* de demi-trimestre. **~-time** *n* mi-temps *f*. **~-way** *adv* à mi-chemin. **~-wit** *n* imbécile *mf*.

hall *n* (in house) entrée *f*; (corridor) couloir *m*; (in airport) hall *m*; (for events) salle *f*; **~ of residence** résidence *f* universitaire.

hallmark *n* (on gold) poinçon *m*; (fig) caractéristique *f*.

hallo = HELLO.

Hallowe'en *n* la veille de la Toussaint.

halt *n* arrêt *m*; (temporary) suspension *f*; (Mil) halte *f*. ● *vt* (*proceedings*) interrompre; (*arms sales, experiments*) mettre fin à. ● *vi* (*vehicle*) s'arrêter; (*army*) faire halte.

halve *vt* (*time*) réduire de moitié; (*fruit*) couper en deux.

ham *n* jambon *m*.

hamburger *n* hamburger *m*.

hammer *n* marteau *m*. ● *vt/i* marteler; **~ sth into sth** enfoncer qch dans qch; **~ sth out** (*agreement*) parvenir à qch.

hammock *n* hamac *m*.

hamper *n* panier *m*. ● *vt* gêner.

hamster *n* hamster *m*.

hand *n* main *f*; (of clock) aiguille *f*; (writing) écriture *f*; (worker) ouvrier/ -ière *m/f*; (cards) jeu *m*; **give sb a ~** donner un coup de main à qn; **at ~** proche; **on ~** disponible; **on the one ~...on the other ~** d'une part...d'autre part; **to ~** à portée de la main. ● *vt* **~ sb sth, ~ sth to sb** donner qch à qn. □ **~ in** *or* **over** remettre; **~ out** distribuer. **~bag** *n* sac *m* à main. **~baggage** *n* bagages *mpl* à main. **~book** *n* manuel *m*. **~brake** *n* frein *m* à main. **~cuffs** *npl* menottes *fpl*.

handicap *n* handicap *m*. ● *vt* (*pt* **handicapped**) handicaper.

handkerchief *n* (*pl* **~s**) mouchoir *m*.

handle *n* (of door, bag) poignée *f*; (of implement) manche *m*; (of cup, bucket) anse *f*; (of frying pan) queue *f*. ● *vt* (manage) manier; (deal with) traiter; (touch) manipuler.

hand: **~-out** *n* document *m*; (leaflet) prospectus *m*; (money) aumône *f*. **~shake** *n* poignée *f* de main.

handsome *adj* (good looking) beau; (generous) généreux.

handwriting *n* écriture *f*.

handy *adj* (-ier, -iest) (*book, skill*) utile; (*size, shape, tool*) pratique;

(*person*) doué. **~man** *n* (*pl* **-men**) bricoleur *m*, homme *m* à tout faire.

hang *vt* (*pt* **hung**) (from hook, hanger) accrocher; (from rope) suspendre; (*pt* **hanged**) (*person*) pendre. ● *vi* (from hook) être accroché; (from rope) être suspendu; (*person*) être pendu. ● *n* get the **~ of doing** 🔲 piger comment faire 🔲. □ **~about** traîner; **~ on** 🔲 (hold out) tenir; (wait) attendre; **~ on to sth** s'agripper à qch; **~ out** *vi* 🔲 (live) crécher 🔲; (spend time) passer son temps; *vt* (*washing*) étendre; **~ up** (telephone) raccrocher.

hanger *n* (for clothes) cintre *m*.

hang-gliding *n* vol *m* libre.

hangover *n* gueule *f* de bois 🔲.

hang-up *n* 🔲 complexe *m*.

hankering *n* envie *f*.

haphazard *adj* peu méthodique.

happen *vi* arriver, se passer; **~ to sb** arriver à qn; **it so ~s that** il se trouve que.

happily *adv* joyeusement; (fortunately) heureusement.

happiness *n* bonheur *m*.

happy *adj* (**-ier, -iest**) heureux; **I'm not ~ about it** je ne suis pas content; **~ with sth** satisfait de qch; **~ medium** juste milieu *m*.

harass *vt* harceler. **harassment** *n* harcèlement *m*.

harbour, (US) **harbor** *n* port *m*. ● *vt* (shelter) héberger.

hard *adj* dur; (difficult) difficile, dur; (*evidence, fact*) solide; **find it ~ to do** avoir du mal à faire; **~ on sb** dur envers qn. ● *adv* (work) dur; (pull, hit, cry) fort; (think, study) sérieusement. **~board** *n* aggloméré *m*. **~ copy** *n* (Comput) tirage *m*. **~ disk** *n* disque *m* dur.

hardly *adv* à peine; (*expect, hope*) difficilement; **~ ever** presque jamais.

hardship *n* (poverty) privations *fpl*; (ordeal) épreuve *f*.

hard: **~ shoulder** *n* bande *f* d'arrêt d'urgence. **~ up** *adj* 🔲 fauché 🔲. **~ware** *n* (Comput) matériel *m*, hardware *m*; (goods) quincaillerie *f*. **~-working** *adj* travailleur.

hardy *adj* (**-ier, -iest**) résistant.

hare *n* lièvre *m*. ● *vi* **~ around** courir partout.

harm *n* mal *m*; **there is no ~ in** il n'y a pas de mal à. ● *vt* (*person*) faire du mal à; (*object*) endommager. **harmful** *adj* nuisible. **harmless** *adj* inoffensif.

harmony *n* harmonie *f*.

harness *n* harnais *m*. ● *vt* (*horse*) harnacher; (use) exploiter.

harp *n* harpe *f*. ● *vi* **~ on (about)** rabâcher.

harrowing *adj* (*experience*) atroce; (*story*) déchirant.

harsh *adj* (*punishment*) sévère; (*person*) dur; (*light*) cru; (*voice*) rude; (*chemical*) corrosif. **harshness** *n* dureté *f*.

harvest *n* récolte *f*; **the wine ~** les vendanges *fpl*. ● *vt* (*corn*) moissonner; (*vegetables*) récolter.

has ⇒HAVE.

hassle *n* complications *fpl*. ● *vt* 🔲 talonner (**about** à propos de); (worry) stresser.

haste *n* hâte *f*; **in ~** à la hâte; **make ~** se dépêcher.

hasty *adj* (**-ier, -iest**) précipité.

hat *n* chapeau *m*.

hatch *n* (Aviat) panneau *m* mobile; (Naut) écoutille *f*; (for food) passe-plats *m inv*. ● *vt/i* (*eggs*) (faire) éclore.

hate *n* haine *f*. ● *vt* détester; (violently) haïr; (*sport, food*) avoir horreur de.

hatred *n* haine *f*.

haughty *adj* (**-ier, -iest**) hautain.

haul *vt* tirer. ● *n* (by thieves) butin *m*; (by customs) saisie *f*; **it will be a long ~** l'étape sera longue; **long/short ~** (*transport*) long/court courrier *m*. **haulage** *n* transport *m* routier. **haulier** *n* (firm) société *f* de transports routiers.

haunt *vt* hanter. ● *n* lieu *m* de prédilection.

have

present **have, has**; *past* **had**; *past participle* **had**

● *transitive verb*

⋯▶ (possess) avoir; **I ~ (got) a car** j'ai une voiture; **they ~ (got) problems** ils ont des problèmes.

····▶ (do sth) ∼ **a try** essayer; ∼ **a bath** prendre un bain.

····▶ ∼ **sth done** faire faire qch; ∼ **your hair cut** se faire couper les cheveux.

● *auxiliary verb*

····▶ (in perfect tenses) avoir; être; **I** ∼ **seen him** je l'ai vu; **she had fallen** elle était tombée.

····▶ (in tag questions) **you've seen her, haven't you?** tu l'as vue, n'est-ce pas?; **you haven't seen her,** ∼ **you?** tu ne l'as pas vue, par hasard?

····▶ (in short answers) **'you've never met him'—'yes I** ∼**'** 'tu ne l'as jamais rencontré'—'mais si!'

····▶ (must) ∼ **to** devoir; **I** ∼ **to go** je dois partir; **you don't** ∼ **to do it** tu n'es pas obligé de le faire.

▭▶ For expressions such as **have a walk, have dinner** ⇒**walk, dinner.**

haven *n* refuge *m*; (fig) havre *m*.

havoc *n* dévastation *f*.

hawk *n* faucon *m*.

hay *n* foin *m*; ∼ **fever** rhume *m* des foins.

haywire *adj* go ∼ (*plans*) dérailler; (*machine*) se détraquer.

hazard *n* risque *m*; ∼ (**warning**) **lights** feux *mpl* de détresse. ● *vt* hasarder.

haze *n* brume *f*.

hazel *n* (bush) noisetier *m*. ∼**nut** *n* noisette *f*.

hazy *adj* (**-ier, -iest**) (misty) brumeux; (fig) vague.

he *pron* il; (emphatic) lui; **here** ∼ **is** le voici.

head *n* tête *f*; (leader) chef *m*; (of beer) mousse *f*; ∼**s or tails?** pile ou face? ● *vt* (*list*) être en tête de; (*team*) être à la tête de; (*chapter*) intituler; ∼ **the ball** faire une tête. ● *vi* ∼ **for** se diriger vers.

headache *n* mal *m* de tête; **have a** ∼ avoir mal à la tête.

heading *n* titre *m*; (subject category) rubrique *f*.

head: ∼**lamp,** ∼**light** *n* phare *m*. ∼**line** *n* gros titre *m*. ∼**master** *n*

directeur *m*. ∼**mistress** *n* directrice *f*. ∼ **office** *n* siège *m* social. ∼**-on** *a* & *adv* de front. ∼**phones** *npl* casque *m*. ∼**quarters** *npl* siège *m* social; (Mil) quartier *m* général. ∼ **rest** *n* (Auto) repose-tête *m inv.* ∼**strong** *adj* têtu.

heal *vt/i* guérir.

health *n* santé *f*. ∼ **centre** *n* centre *m* médico-social. ∼ **food** *n* produits *mpl* diététiques. ∼ **insurance** *n* assurance *f* maladie.

healthy *adj* (*person, plant, skin, diet*) sain; (*air*) salutaire.

heap *n* tas *m*; ∼**s of** 🄸 un tas de. ● *vt* ∼ (**up**) entasser.

hear *vt* (*pt* **heard**) entendre; (*news, rumour*) apprendre; (*lecture, broadcast*) écouter. ● *vi* entendre; ∼ **from** recevoir des nouvelles de; ∼ **of** *or* **about** entendre parler de.

hearing *n* ouïe *f*; (of case) audience *f*; **give sb a** ∼ écouter qn. ∼**-aid** *n* prothèse *f* auditive.

hearse *n* corbillard *m*.

heart *n* cœur *m*; ∼**s** (cards) cœur *m*; **at** ∼ au fond; **by** ∼ par cœur; **be** ∼**-broken** avoir le cœur brisé; **lose** ∼ perdre courage. ∼ **attack** *n* crise *f* cardiaque. ∼**burn** *n* brûlures *fpl* d'estomac. ∼**felt** *adj* sincère.

hearth *n* foyer *m*.

heartily *adv* (*greet*) chaleureusement; (*laugh, eat*) de bon cœur.

hearty *adj* (**-ier, -iest**) (sincere) chaleureux; (*meal*) solide.

heat *n* chaleur *f*; (contest) épreuve *f* éliminatoire. ● *vt* (*house*) chauffer; ∼ (**up**) (*food*) faire chauffer; (reheat) réchauffer. **heated** *adj* (fig) passionné; (lit) (*pool*) chauffé.

heater *n* appareil *m* de chauffage.

heather *n* bruyère *f*.

heating *n* chauffage *m*.

heave *vt* (lift) hisser; (pull) traîner péniblement; ∼ **a sigh** pousser un soupir. ● *vi* (pull) tirer de toutes ses forces; (retch) avoir un haut-le-cœur.

heaven *n* ciel *m*.

heavily *adv* lourdement; (smoke, drink) beaucoup.

heavy *adj* (**-ier, -iest**) lourd; (*cold, work*) gros; (*traffic*) dense.

~ **goods vehicle** n poids m lourd. ~**-handed** adj maladroit. ~**weight** n poids m lourd.

Hebrew n (person) Hébreu m; (Ling) hébreu m. ● adj hébreu; (Ling) hébraïque.

hectic adj (activity) intense; (period, day) mouvementé.

hedge n haie f. ● vi (in answering) se dérober.

hedgehog n hérisson m.

heel n talon m.

hefty adj (-ier, -iest) (person) costaud ⊞; (object) pesant.

height n hauteur f; (of person) taille f; (of plane, mountain) altitude f; (of fame, glory) apogée m; (of joy, folly, pain) comble m.

heir n héritier/-ière m/f. **heiress** n héritière f. **heirloom** n objet m de famille.

held ⇨HOLD.

helicopter n hélicoptère m.

hell n enfer m.

hello interj bonjour!; (on phone) allô!

helmet n casque m.

help vt/i aider (**to do** à faire); ~ (**sb**) **with a bag/the housework** aider qn à porter un sac/à faire le ménage; ~ **oneself** se servir; **he can't** ~ **it** ce n'est pas de sa faute. ● n aide f. ● interj au secours! **helper** n aide mf. **helpful** adj utile; (person) serviable. **helping** n portion f. **helpless** adj impuissant.

hem n ourlet m. ● vt (pt **hemmed**) faire un ourlet à; ~ **in** cerner.

hen n poule f.

hence adv (for this reason) d'où; (from now) d'ici. **henceforth** adv désormais.

hepatitis n hépatite f.

her pron la, l'; (indirect object) lui; **it's** ~ c'est elle; **for** ~ pour elle. ● adj son, sa; pl ses.

herb n herbe f; ~**s** (Culin) fines herbes fpl.

herd n troupeau m.

here adv ici; ~**!** (take this) tiens!; tenez!; ~ **is**, ~ **are** voici; **I'm** ~ je suis là. **hereabouts** adv par ici. **hereafter** adv après; (in book) ci-

après. **hereby** adv par le présent acte; (in letter) par la présente.

herewith adv ci-joint.

heritage n patrimoine m.

hernia n hernie f.

hero n (pl ~**es**) héros m.

heroic adj héroïque.

heroin n héroïne f.

heroine n héroïne f.

heron n héron m.

herring n hareng m.

hers pron le sien, la sienne, les sien (ne)s; **it is** ~ c'est à elle or le sien or la sienne.

herself pron (emphatic) elle-même; (reflexive) se; **proud of** ~ fière d'elle; **by** ~ toute seule.

hesitate vi hésiter. **hesitation** n hésitation f.

heterosexual a & n hétérosexuel/ -le (m/f).

hexagon n hexagone m.

heyday n apogée m.

HGV abbr ⇨HEAVY GOODS VEHICLE.

hi interj ⊞ salut! ⊞.

hiccup n hoquet m; (the) ~**s** le hoquet. ● vi hoqueter.

hide vt (pt **hid**; pp **hidden**) cacher (**from** à). ● vi se cacher (**from** de); **go into hiding** se cacher. ● n (skin) peau f.

hideous adj (monster, object) hideux; (noise) affreux.

hiding n **go into** ~ se cacher; **give sb a** ~ administrer une correction à qn.

hierarchy n hiérarchie f.

hi-fi n (chaîne f) hi-fi f inv.

high adj haut; (price, number) élevé; (priest, speed) grand; (voice) aigu; **in the** ~ **season** en pleine saison. ● n a (new) ~ un niveau record. ● adv haut. ~**brow** a & n intellectuel/-le (m/f). ~ **chair** f haute. ~ **court** n cour f suprême. **higher education** n enseignement m supérieur. ~**jump** n saut m en hauteur. ~**level** adj à haut niveau.

highlight n (best moment) point m fort; ~**s** (in hair) reflet m; (artificial) mèches fpl; (Sport) résumé m. ● vt (emphasize) souligner.

highly *adv* extrêmement; (paid) très bien; **speak/think ~ of** dire/penser beaucoup de bien de.

Highness *n* Altesse *f*.

high: **~-rise (building)** *n* tour *f*. **~ school** *n* lycée *m*. **~-speed** *adj* (*train*) à grande vitesse; (*film*) ultrarapide. **~ street** *n* rue *f* principale. **~-tech** *adj* de pointe.

highway *n* route *f* nationale; (US) autoroute *f*; **~ code** code *m* de la route.

hijack *vt* détourner. ● *n* détournement *m*. **hijacker** *n* pirate *m* (de l'air).

hike *n* randonnée *f*; **price ~** hausse *f* de prix. ● *vi* faire de la randonnée.

hilarious *adj* désopilant.

hill *n* colline *f*; (slope) côte *f*. **hilly** *adj* vallonné.

him *pron* le, l'; (indirect object) lui; **it's ~** c'est lui; **for ~** pour lui.

himself *pron* (emphatic) lui-même; (reflexive) se; **proud of ~** fier de lui; **by ~** tout seul.

hind *adj* de derrière.

hinder *vt* (hamper) gêner; (prevent) empêcher. **hindrance** *n* obstacle *m*, gêne *f*.

hindsight *n* **with ~** rétrospectivement.

Hindu *n* Hindou/-e *m/f*. ● *adj* hindou.

hinge *n* charnière *f*. ● *vi* **~ on** dépendre de.

hint *n* allusion *f*; (of spice, accent) pointe *f*; (of colour) touche *f*; (advice) conseil *m*. ● *vt* laisser entendre. ● *vi* **~ at** faire allusion à.

hip *n* hanche *f*.

hippopotamus *n* (*pl* ~**es**) hippopotame *m*.

hire *vt* (thing) louer; (person) engager. ● *n* location *f*. **~-car** *n* voiture *f* de location. **~-purchase** *n* achat *m* à crédit.

his *adj* son, sa, *pl* ses. ● *pron* le sien, la sienne, *pl* les sien(ne)s; **it is ~** c'est à lui *or* le sien *or* la sienne.

hiss *n* sifflement *m*. ● *vt/i* siffler.

history *n* histoire *f*; **make ~** entrer dans l'histoire.

hit *vt* (*pt* **hit**; *pres p* **hitting**) frapper; (collide with) heurter; (find) trouver; (affect, reach) toucher. ● *vi* **~ on** (find) tomber sur; **~ it off** s'entendre bien (with avec). ● *n* (blow) coup *m*; (fig) succès *m*; (song) tube *m* 🆃.

hitch *vt* (fasten) accrocher; **~ up** remonter. ● *n* (snag) anicroche *f*. **~-hike** *vi* faire du stop 🆃. **~-hiker** *n* auto-stoppeur/-euse *m/f*.

hi-tech *a & n* = HIGH-TECH.

hitherto *adv* jusqu'ici.

HIV *abbr* (**human immunodeficiency virus**) VIH *m*.

hive *n* ruche *f*. ● *vt* **~ off** séparer; (industry) céder.

HIV-positive *adj* séropositif.

hoard *vt* amasser; (supplies) stocker. ● *n* trésor *m*; (of provisions) provisions *fpl*.

hoarse *adj* enroué.

hoax *n* canular *m*.

hobby *n* passe-temps *m inv*. **~-horse** *n* (fig) dada *m*.

hockey *n* hockey *m*.

hog *n* cochon *m*. ● *vt* (*pt* **hogged**) 🆃 monopoliser.

hold *vt* (*pt* **held**) tenir; (contain) contenir; (conversation, opinion) avoir; (shares, record, person) détenir; **~ (the line), please** ne quittez pas. ● *vi* (rope, weather) tenir. ● *n* prise *f*; **get ~ of** attraper; (ticket) se procurer; (person) (by phone) joindre; **on ~** en attente. □ **~ back** (contain) retenir; (hide) cacher; **~ down** (job) garder; (person) tenir; (costs) limiter; **~ on** (stand firm) tenir bon; (wait) attendre; **~ on to** (keep) garder; (cling to) se cramponner à; **~ out** *vt* (offer) offrir; *vi* (resist) tenir le coup; **~ up** (support) soutenir; (delay) retarder; (rob) attaquer.

holder *n* détenteur/-trice *m/f*; (of passport, post) titulaire *mf*; (for object) support *m*.

hold-up *n* retard *m*; (of traffic) embouteillage *m*; (robbery) hold-up *m inv*.

hole *n* trou *m*.

holiday *n* vacances *fpl*; (public) jour *m* férié; (time off) congé *m*. ● *vi* passer ses vacances. ● *adj* de vacances. **~maker** *n* vacancier/-ière *m/f*.

Holland *n* Hollande *f*.

hollow *adj* creux; (fig) faux. ● *n* creux *m*. ● *vt* creuser.

holly *n* houx *m*.

holy *adj* (**-ier, -iest**) saint; (water) bénit; H~ Ghost, H~ Spirit Saint-Esprit *m*.

homage *n* hommage *m*.

home *n* (place to live) logement *m*; maison *f*; (institution) maison *f*; (family base) foyer *m*; (country) pays *m*. ● *adj* de la maison, du foyer; (of family) de famille; (Pol) intérieur; (*match, visit*) à domicile. ● *adv* (at) ~ à la maison, chez soi; **come** *or* **go** ~ rentrer; (from abroad) rentrer dans son pays; **feel at** ~ **with** être à l'aise avec. **~ computer** *n* ordinateur *m*, PC *m*.

homeless *adj* sans abri. ● **the** ~ les sans-abri *mpl*.

homely *adj* (**-ier, -iest**) (cosy) accueillant; (simple) sans prétention; (person: US) sans attraits.

home: **~-made** *adj* (fait) maison. **H~ Office** *n* ministère *m* de l'Intérieur. ~ **page** *n* (Internet) page *f* d'accueil. **H~ Secretary** *n* Ministre *m* de l'Intérieur. **~sick** *adj* **be ~sick** avoir le mal du pays. **~work** *n* devoirs *mpl*.

homosexual *a & n* homosexuel/-le (*m/f*).

honest *adj* (truthful) intègre; (trustworthy) honnête; (sincere) franc. **honestly** *adv* honnêtement; franchement. **honesty** *n* honnêteté *f*.

honey *n* miel *m*; (person ⚠) chéri/-e *m/f*. **~moon** *n* voyage *m* de noces; (fig) lune *f* de miel.

honk *vi* klaxonner.

honorary *adj* (*person*) honoraire; (*degree*) honorifique.

honour, (US) **honor** *n* honneur *m*. ● *vt* honorer.

hood *n* capuchon *m*; (on car, pram) capote *f*; (car engine cover: US) capot *m*.

hoof *n* (*pl* **~s**) sabot *m*.

hook *n* crochet *m*; (on garment) agrafe *f*; (for fishing) hameçon *m*; **off the** ~ tiré d'affaire; (phone) décroché. ● *vt* accrocher.

hoot *n* (of owl) (h)ululement *m*; (of car) coup *m* de klaxon. ● *vi* (*owl*) (h)ululer; (*car*) klaxonner; (jeer) huer.

hoover *vt* ~ **a room** passer l'aspirateur dans une pièce.

Hoover® *n* aspirateur *m*.

hop *vi* (*pt* **hopped**) sauter (à cloche-pied); ~ **in!** ⚠ vas-y, monte! ● *n* bond *m*; ~**s** houblon *m*.

hope *n* espoir *m*. ● *vt/i* espérer; ~ **for** espérer avoir; **I** ~ **so** je l'espère.

hopeful *adj* (*news, sign*) encourageant; (*person*) plein d'espoir; (*mood*) optimiste. **hopefully** *adv* (with luck) avec un peu de chance; (with hope) avec optimisme.

hopeless *adj* désespéré; (useless: fig) nul ⚠.

horizon *n* horizon *m*.

horizontal *adj* horizontal.

hormone *n* hormone *f*.

horn *n* corne *f*; (of car) klaxon® *m*; (Mus) cor *m*.

horoscope *n* horoscope *m*.

horrible *adj* horrible.

horrid *adj* horrible.

horrific *adj* horrifiant.

horrify *vt* horrifier.

horror *n* horreur *f*. ● *adj* (*film, story*) d'épouvante.

horse *n* cheval *m*. **~back** *n* **on ~back** à cheval. **~chestnut** *n* marron *m* (d'Inde). **~man** *n* (*pl* **-men**) cavalier *m*. **~power** *n* puissance *f* (en chevaux). **~race** *n* course *f* de chevaux. **~radish** *n* raifort *m*. **~shoe** *n* fer *m* à cheval. **~show** *n* concours *m* hippique.

hose *n* tuyau *m*. ● *vt* arroser. **~pipe** *n* tuyau *m*.

hospitable *adj* hospitalier.

hospital *n* hôpital *m*.

host *n* (to guests) hôte *m*; (on TV) animateur *m*; (Internet) ordinateur *m* hôte; **a** ~ **of** une foule de; (Relig) hostie *f*.

hostage *n* otage *m*; **hold sb** ~ garder qn en otage.

hostel *n* foyer *m*; (youth) ~ auberge *f* (de jeunesse).

hostess *n* hôtesse *f*.

hostile *adj* hostile.

hot adj (**hotter**, **hottest**) chaud; (Culin) épicé; be or feel ~ avoir chaud; it is ~ il fait chaud; in ~ water ⊞ dans le pétrin. ● vt/i (pt **hotted**) ~ **up** ⊞ chauffer. ~ **air balloon** n montgolfière f. ~ **dog** n hot-dog m.

hotel n hôtel m.

hot: ~**headed** adj impétueux. ~ **list** n (Internet) signets mpl favoris. ~**plate** n plaque f chauffante. ~ **water bottle** n bouillotte f.

hound n chien m de chasse. ● vt poursuivre.

hour n heure f.

hourly adj horaire; on an ~ **basis** à l'heure. ● adv toutes les heures.

house[1] n maison f; (Pol) Chambre f; on the ~ aux frais de la maison.

house[2] vt loger; (of building) abriter.

household n (house, family) ménage m. ● adj ménager.

house: ~**keeper** n gouvernante f. ~**-proud** adj méticuleux. ~**-warming** n pendaison f de crémaillère. ~**wife** n (pl -**wives**) ménagère f. ~**work** n travaux mpl ménagers.

housing n logement m; ~ **association** service m de logement; ~ **development** cité f; (smaller) lotissement m.

hover vi (bird) voleter; (vacillate) vaciller. **hovercraft** n aéroglisseur m.

how adv comment; ~ **are you?** comment allez-vous?; ~ **long/tall is...?** quelle est la longueur/hauteur de...?; ~ **many?**, ~ **much?** combien?; ~ **pretty!** comme or que c'est joli!; ~ **about a walk?** si on faisait une promenade?; ~ **do you do?** (greeting) enchanté.

however adv (nevertheless) cependant; ~ **hard I try** j'ai beau essayer; ~ **much it costs** quel que soit le prix; ~ **young/poor he is** si jeune/pauvre soit-il; ~ **you like** comme tu veux.

howl n hurlement m. ● vi hurler.

HP abbr ⇒HIRE-PURCHASE.

hp abbr ⇒HORSEPOWER.

HQ abbr ⇒HEADQUARTERS.

hub n moyeu m; (fig) centre m.

hug vt (pt **hugged**) serrer dans ses bras. ● n étreinte f; give sb a ~ serrer qn dans ses bras.

huge adj énorme.

hull n (of ship) coque f.

hum vt/i (pt **hummed**) (person) fredonner; (insect) bourdonner; (engine) ronronner. ● n bourdonnement m; ronronnement m.

human adj humain. ● n humain m. ~ **being** n être m humain.

humane adj (person) humain; (act) d'humanité; (killing) sans cruauté.

humanitarian adj humanitaire.

humanity n humanité f.

humble adj humble.

humid adj humide.

humiliate vt humilier.

humorous adj humoristique; (person) plein d'humour.

humour, (US) **humor** n humour m; (mood) humeur f. ● vt amadouer.

hump n bosse f. ● vt ⊞ porter.

hunchback n bossu/-e m/f.

hundred a & n cent (m); **two** ~ **and one** deux cent un; ~**s of** des centaines de. **hundredth** a & n centième (mf).

hung ⇒HANG.

Hungarian n (person) Hongrois/-e m/f; (Ling) hongrois m. ● adj hongrois. **Hungary** n Hongrie f.

hunger n faim f. ● vi ~ **for** avoir faim de.

hungry adj (-**ier**, -**iest**) affamé; be ~ avoir faim.

hunt vt/i chasser; ~ **for** chercher. ● n chasse f. **hunter** n chasseur m. **hunting** n chasse f.

hurdle n (Sport) haie f; (fig) obstacle m.

hurricane n ouragan m.

hurry vi se dépêcher; ~ **out** sortir précipitamment. ● vt (work) terminer à la hâte; (person) bousculer. ● n hâte f; in a ~ pressé.

hurt vt/i (pt **hurt**) faire mal (à); (injure, offend) blesser. ● adj blessé. ● n blessure f.

hurtle vi ~ **down** dévaler; ~ **along a road** foncer sur une route.

husband n mari m.

hush *vt* faire taire; ~ **up** (*news*) étouffer. ● *n* silence *m*. ● *interj* chut!

husky *adj* (-**ier**, -**iest**) enroué. ● *n* husky *m*.

hustle *vt* (push, rush) bousculer. ● *vi* (hurry) se dépêcher; (work: US) se démener. ● *n* ~ **and bustle** agitation *f*.

hut *n* cabane *f*.

hyacinth *n* jacinthe *f*.

hydrant *n* (fire) ~ bouche *f* d'incendie.

hydraulic *adj* hydraulique.

hydroelectric *adj* hydroélectrique.

hydrogen *n* hydrogène *m*; ~ **bomb** bombe *f* à hydrogène.

hyena *n* hyène *f*.

hygiene *n* hygiène *f*. **hygienic** *adj* hygiénique.

hymn *n* cantique *m*; (fig) hymne *m*.

hype *n* ⊞ battage *m* publicitaire. ● *vt* ~ (**up**) (*film, book*) faire du battage pour.

hyperactive *adj* hyperactif.

hyperlink *n* hyperlien *m*.

hypermarket *n* hypermarché *m*.

hypertext *n* hypertexte *m*.

hyphen *n* trait *m* d'union.

hypnosis *n* hypnose *f*.

hypocrisy *n* hypocrisie *f*. **hypocrite** *n* hypocrite *mf*. **hypocritical** *adj* hypocrite.

hypothesis *n* (*pl* -**ses**) hypothèse *f*.

hysteria *n* hystérie *f*. **hysterical** *adj* hystérique.

hysterics *npl* crise *f* de nerfs; **be in** ~ rire aux larmes.

I *pron* je, j'; (stressed) moi.

ice *n* glace *f*; (on road) verglas *m*. ● *vt* (*cake*) glacer. ● *vi* ~ (**up**) (*window*) se givrer; (*river*) geler. ~**box** *n* (US) réfrigérateur *m*. ~**-cream** *n* glace *f*.

~**-cube** *n* glaçon *m*. ~ **hockey** *n* hockey *m* sur glace.

Iceland *n* Islande *f*. **Icelander** *n* Islandais/-e *m/f*. **Icelandic** *a* & *n* islandais (*m*).

ice: ~ **lolly** *n* glace *f* (*sur bâtonnet*). ~ **rink** *n* patinoire *f*. ~ **skate** *n* patin *m* à glace.

icicle *n* stalactite *f* (de glace).

icing *n* (sugar) glaçage *m*.

icy *adj* (-**ier**, -**iest**) (*hands, wind*) glacé; (*road*) verglacé; (*manner, welcome*) glacial.

ID *n* pièce *f* d'identité; ~ **card** carte *f* d'identité.

idea *n* idée *f*.

ideal *adj* idéal. ● *n* idéal *m*.

identical *adj* identique.

identification *n* identification *f*; (papers) pièce *f* d'identité.

identify *vt* identifier. ● *vi* ~ **with** s'identifier à.

identikit *n* ~ **picture** portrait-robot *m*.

identity *n* identité *f*.

ideological *adj* idéologique.

idiom *n* (phrase) idiome *m*; (language) parler *m*, langue *f*. **idiomatic** *adj* idiomatique.

idiosyncrasy *n* particularité *f*.

idiot *n* idiot/-e *m/f*. **idiotic** *adj* idiot.

idle *adj* (lazy) paresseux; (doing nothing) oisif; (*boast, threat*) vain. ● *vi* (*engine*) tourner au ralenti. ● *vt* ~ **away** gaspiller.

idol *n* idole *f*. **idolize** *vt* idolâtrer.

idyllic *adj* idyllique.

i.e. *abbr* c-à-d, c'est-à-dire.

if *conj* si.

ignite *vt/i* (s')enflammer.

ignition *n* (Auto) allumage *m*; ~ (switch) contact *m*; ~ **key** clé *f* de contact.

ignorance *n* ignorance *f*. **ignorant** *adj* ignorant (**of** de). **ignorantly** *adv* par ignorance.

ignore *vt* (*person*) ignorer; (*mistake, remark*) ne pas relever; (*feeling, fact*) ne pas tenir compte de.

ill *adj* malade. ● *adv* mal. ● *n* mal *m*. ~**-advised** *adj* malavisé. ~ **at ease** *adj* mal à l'aise. ~**-bred** *adj* mal élevé.

illegal *adj* illégal.

illegible *adj* illisible.

illegitimate *adj* illégitime.

ill: **~-fated** *adj* malheureux. **~ feeling** *n* ressentiment *m*.

illiterate *a & n* analphabète (*mf*).

illness *n* maladie *f*.

ill-treat *vt* maltraiter.

illuminate *vt* éclairer; (decorate with lights) illuminer. **illumination** *n* éclairage *m*; illumination *f*.

illusion *n* illusion *f*.

illustrate *vt* illustrer. **illustration** *n* illustration *f*. **illustrative** *adj* qui illustre.

image *n* image *f*; (of firm, person) image *f* de marque. **imagery** *n* images *fpl*.

imaginable *adj* imaginable. **imaginary** *adj* imaginaire. **imagination** *n* imagination *f*. **imaginative** *adj* plein d'imagination.

imagine *vt* (s')imaginer (**that** que); **~ being rich** s'imaginer riche.

imbalance *n* déséquilibre *m*.

imitate *vt* imiter.

immaculate *adj* impeccable.

immaterial *adj* sans importance (**to** pour; **that** que).

immature *adj* (*person*) immature; (*plant*) qui n'est pas arrivé à maturité.

immediate *adj* immédiat.

immediately *adv* immédiatement. ● *conj* dès que.

immense *adj* immense. **immensely** *adv* extrêmement, immensément. **immensity** *n* immensité *f*.

immerse *vt* plonger (**in** dans). **immersion** *n* immersion *f*; **immersion heater** chauffe-eau *m inv* électrique.

immigrant *n & a* immigré/-e (*m/f*); (newly-arrived) immigrant/-e (*m/f*). **immigrate** *vi* immigrer. **immigration** *n* immigration *f*.

imminent *adj* imminent.

immoral *adj* immoral.

immortal *adj* immortel.

immune *adj* immunisé (**from, to** contre); (*reaction, system*) immunitaire. **immunity** *n* immunité *f*. **immunization** *n* immunisation *f*. **immunize** *vt* immuniser.

impact *n* impact *m*.

impair *vt* (*performance*) affecter; (*ability*) affaiblir.

impart *vt* communiquer, transmettre.

impartial *adj* impartial.

impassable *adj* (*barrier*) infranchissable; (*road*) impraticable.

impassive *adj* impassible.

impatience *n* impatience *f*. **impatient** *adj* impatient; **get impatient** s'impatienter. **impatiently** *adv* impatiemment.

impeccable *adj* impeccable.

impede *vt* entraver.

impediment *n* entrave *f*; **speech ~** défaut *m* d'élocution.

impending *adj* imminent.

imperative *adj* urgent. ● *n* impératif *m*.

imperfect *adj* incomplet; (faulty) défectueux. ● *n* (Gram) imparfait *m*. **imperfection** *n* imperfection *f*.

imperial *adj* impérial; (measure) conforme aux normes britanniques. **imperialism** *n* impérialisme *m*.

impersonal *adj* impersonnel.

impersonate *vt* se faire passer pour; (mimic) imiter.

impertinent *adj* impertinent.

impervious *adj* imperméable (**to** à).

impetuous *adj* impétueux.

impetus *n* impulsion *f*.

impinge *vi* **~ on** affecter; (encroach) empiéter sur.

implement *n* instrument *m*; (tool) outil *m*. ● *vt* exécuter, mettre en application; (*software*) implanter.

implicit *adj* (implied) implicite (**in** dans); (unquestioning) absolu.

imply *vt* (assume, mean) impliquer; (insinuate) laisser entendre.

impolite *adj* impoli.

import¹ *vt* importer.

import² *n* (*article*) importation *f*; (*meaning*) signification *f*.

importance *n* importance *f*.

important *adj* important.

impose vt imposer (**on sb** à qn; **on sth** sur qch). ● vi s'imposer; ~ **on sb** abuser de la bienveillance de qn.
imposing adj imposant.
imposition n dérangement m; (tax) imposition f.
impossible adj impossible. ● n the ~ l'impossible m.
impotent adj impuissant.
impound vt confisquer, saisir.
impoverish vt appauvrir.
impractical adj peu réaliste.
impregnable adj imprenable.
impress vt impressionner; ~ **sth on sb** faire bien comprendre qch à qn.
impression n impression f.
impressionable adj impressionnable. **impressive** adj impressionnant.
imprint¹ n empreinte f.
imprint² vt (fix) graver (**on** dans); (print) imprimer.
imprison vt emprisonner.
improbable adj (not likely) improbable; (incredible) invraisemblable.
improper adj (unseemly) malséant; (dishonest) irrégulier.
improve vt/i (s')améliorer.
improvement n amélioration f.
improvise vt/i improviser.
impudent adj impudent.
impulse n impulsion f; **on** ~ sur un coup de tête. **impulsive** adj impulsif. **impulsively** adv par impulsion.
impurity n impureté f.
in prep (inside, within) dans; (expressing place, position) à, en; (expressing time) en, dans; ~ **the box/garden** dans la boîte/le jardin; ~ **Paris/school** à Paris/l'école; ~ **town** en ville; ~ **the country** à la campagne; ~ **English** en anglais; ~ **India** en Inde; ~ **Japan** au Japon; ~ **winter** en hiver; ~ **spring** au printemps; ~ **an hour** (at end of) au bout d'une heure; ~ **an hour('s time)** dans une heure; ~ (**the space of**) **an hour** en une heure; ~ **doing** en faisant; ~ **the evening** le soir; **one** ~ **ten** un sur dix; ~ **between** entre les deux; (time) entretemps; ~ **a firm voice** d'une voix ferme; ~ **blue** en bleu; ~ **ink** à l'encre; ~ **uniform** en uniforme; ~ **a skirt** en jupe; ~ **a whisper** en chuchotant; ~ **a loud voice** d'une voix forte; **the best** ~ le meilleur de; **we are** ~ **for** on va avoir; **have it** ~ **for sb** Ⓘ avoir qn dans le collimateur. ● adv (inside) dedans; (at home) là, à la maison; (in fashion) à la mode; **come** ~ entrer; **run** ~ entrer en courant.
inability n incapacité f (**to do** de faire).
inaccessible adj inaccessible.
inaccurate adj inexact.
inactive adj inactif. **inactivity** n inaction f.
inadequate adj insuffisant.
inadvertently adv par mégarde.
inadvisable adj inopportun, à déconseiller.
inane adj idiot, débile.
inanimate adj inanimé.
inappropriate adj inopportun; (term) inapproprié.
inarticulate adj qui a du mal à s'exprimer.
inasmuch as adv dans la mesure où; (because) vu que.
inaugurate vt (open, begin) inaugurer; (person) investir.
inborn adj inné.
inbred adj (inborn) inné.
Inc. abbr (**incorporated**) S.A.
incapable adj incapable (**of doing** de faire).
incapacitate vt immobiliser.
incense¹ n encens m.
incense² vt mettre en fureur.
incentive n motivation f; (payment) prime f.
incessant adj incessant.
incessantly adv sans cesse.
incest n inceste m. **incestuous** adj incestueux.
inch n pouce m (=2.54 cm.). ● vi ~ **towards** se diriger petit à petit vers.
incidence n fréquence f.
incident n incident m. **incidental** adj secondaire. **incidentally** adv à propos; (by chance) par la même occasion.
incinerate vt incinérer.
incinerator n incinérateur m.
incite vt inciter, pousser.

inclination *n* (tendency) tendance *f*; (desire) envie *f*.

incline[1] *vt/i* (s')incliner; **be ~d to** avoir tendance à.

incline[2] *n* pente *f*.

include *vt* comprendre, inclure.
 including *prep* (y) compris.
 inclusion *n* inclusion *f*.

inclusive *a & adv* inclus; **~ of** delivery livraison comprise.

income *n* revenus *mpl*; **~ tax** impôt *m* sur le revenu.

incoming *adj* (*tide*) montant; (*tenant, government*) nouveau; (*call*) qui vient de l'extérieur.

incompatible *adj* incompatible.

incompetent *adj* incompétent.

incomplete *adj* incomplet.

incomprehensible *adj* incompréhensible.

inconceivable *adj* inconcevable.

inconclusive *adj* peu concluant.

incongruous *adj* déconcertant, surprenant.

inconsiderate *adj* (*person*) peu attentif à autrui; (*act*) maladroit.

inconsistent *adj* (*argument*) incohérent; (*performance*) inégal; (*behaviour*) changeant; **~ with** en contradiction avec.

inconspicuous *adj* qui passe inaperçu.

incontinent *adj* incontinent.

inconvenience *n* dérangement *m*; (drawback) inconvénient *m*. ● *vt* déranger. **inconvenient** *adj* incommode; **if it's not inconvenient for you** si cela ne vous dérange pas.

incorporate *vt* incorporer (**into** dans); (contain) comporter.

incorrect *adj* incorrect.

increase[1] *n* augmentation *f* (**in, of** de); **be on the ~** être en progression.

increase[2] *vt/i* augmenter.
 increasing *adj* croissant.
 increasingly *adv* de plus en plus.

incredible *adj* incroyable.

incriminate *vt* incriminer.
 incriminating *adj* compromettant.

incubate *vt* (eggs) couver.
 incubation *n* incubation *f*.
 incubator *n* couveuse *f*.

incur *vt* (*pt* **incurred**) (*penalty, anger*) encourir; (*debts*) contracter.

indebted *adj* **~ to sb** redevable à qn (**for** de); (grateful) reconnaissant à qn.

indecent *adj* indécent.

indecisive *adj* indécis; (ending) peu concluant.

indeed *adv* en effet; (emphatic) vraiment.

indefinite *adj* vague; (period, delay) illimité. **indefinitely** *adv* indéfiniment.

indelible *adj* indélébile.

indemnity *n* (protection) assurance *f*; (payment) indemnité *f*.

indent *vt* (text) renfoncer.
 indentation *n* (dent) marque *f*.

independence *n* indépendance *f*.
 independent *adj* indépendant.
 independently *adv* de façon indépendante; **independently of** indépendamment de.

index *n* (*pl* **~es**) (in book) index *m*; (in library) catalogue *m*; (in economy) indice *m*; **~ card** fiche *f*; **~ (finger)** index *m*. ● *vt* classer. **~-linked** *adj* indexé.

India *n* Inde *f*.

Indian *n* Indien/-ne *m/f*. ● *adj* indien.

indicate *vt* indiquer. **indication** *n* indication *f*.

indicative *a & n* indicatif (*m*).

indicator *n* (pointer) aiguille *f*; (on vehicle) clignotant *m*; (board) tableau *m*.

indict *vt* inculper. **indictment** *n* accusation *f*.

indifferent *adj* indifférent; (not good) médiocre.

indigenous *adj* indigène.

indigestible *adj* indigeste.
 indigestion *n* indigestion *f*.

indignant *adj* indigné.

indirect *adj* indirect. **indirectly** *adv* indirectement.

indiscreet *adj* indiscret.
 indiscretion *n* indiscrétion *f*.

indiscriminate *adj* sans distinction. **indiscriminately** *adv* sans distinction.

indisputable *adj* indiscutable.

individual *adj* individuel; (*tuition*)
particulier. ● *n* individu *m*.
individualist *n* individualiste *mf*.
individuality *n* individualité *f*.
individually *adv* individuellement.
indoctrinate *vt* endoctriner.
indoctrination *n* endoctrinement
m.
indolent *adj* indolent.
Indonesia *n* Indonésie *f*.
indoor *adj* (*clothes*) d'intérieur; (*pool,
court*) couvert. **indoors** *adv* à
l'intérieur.
induce *vt* (*influence*) persuader;
(*stronger*) inciter (**to do** à faire).
inducement *n* (*financial*)
récompense *f*; (*incentive*) motivation *f*.
induction *n* (Electr) induction *f*;
(*inauguration*) installation *f*.
indulge *vt* (*person, whim*) céder à;
(*child*) gâter. ● *vi* ~ **in** se livrer à.
indulgence *n* indulgence *f*; (*treat*)
plaisir *m*. **indulgent** *adj* indulgent.
industrial *adj* industriel; (*accident*)
du travail; ~ **action** grève *f*; ~
dispute conflit *m* social.
industrialist *n* industriel/-le *m/f*.
industrialized *adj* industrialisé.
industrious *adj* diligent.
industry *n* industrie *f*; (*zeal*) zèle *m*.
inebriated *adj* ivre.
inedible *adj* immangeable.
ineffective *adj* inefficace.
inefficient *adj* inefficace; (*person*)
incompétent.
ineligible *adj* inéligible; **be** ~ **for**
ne pas avoir droit à.
inept *adj* incompétent; (*tactless*)
maladroit.
inequality *n* inégalité *f*.
inescapable *adj* indéniable.
inevitable *adj* inévitable.
inexcusable *adj* inexcusable.
inexhaustible *adj* inépuisable.
inexpensive *adj* pas cher.
inexperience *n* inexpérience *f*.
inexperienced *adj* inexpérimenté.
infallible *adj* infaillible.
infamous *adj* (*person*) tristement
célèbre; (*deed*) infâme.
infancy *n* petite enfance *f*; **in its** ~
(fig) à ses débuts *mpl*. **infant** *n* (baby)

bébé *m*; (at school) enfant *m*.
infantile *adj* infantile.
infatuated *adj* ~ **with** entiché de.
infatuation *n* engouement *m*.
infect *vt* contaminer; ~ **sb with sth**
transmettre qch à qn. **infection** *n*
infection *f*. **infectious** *adj*
contagieux.
infer *vt* (*pt* **inferred**) (deduce)
déduire.
inferior *adj* inférieur (**to** à); (*work,
product*) de qualité inférieure. ● *n*
inférieur/-e *m/f*. **inferiority** *n*
infériorité *f*.
inferno *n* (hell) enfer *m*; (blaze)
brasier *m*.
infertile *adj* infertile.
infest *vt* infester (**with** de).
infidelity *n* infidélité *f*.
infighting *n* conflits *mpl* internes.
infinite *adj* infini. **infinitely** *adv*
infiniment. **infinitive** *n* infinitif *m*.
infinity *n* infinité *f*.
infirm *adj* infirme. **infirmary** *n*
hôpital *m*; (sick-bay) infirmerie *f*.
infirmity *n* infirmité *f*.
inflame *vt* enflammer.
inflammable *adj* inflammable.
inflammation *n* inflammation *f*.
inflammatory *adj* incendiaire.
inflatable *adj* gonflable. **inflate** *vt*
(lit, fig) gonfler.
inflation *n* inflation *f*.
inflection *n* (of word root) flexion *f*;
(of vowel, voice) inflexion *f*.
inflict *vt* infliger (**on** à).
influence *n* influence *f*; **under the**
~ (drunk 🅸) éméché. ● *vt* (*person*)
influencer; (*choice*) influer sur.
influential *adj* (powerful) influent;
(*theory, artist*) très suivi.
influenza *n* grippe *f*.
influx *n* afflux *m*.
inform *vt* informer (**of** de); **keep** ~**ed**
tenir au courant.
informal *adj* (simple) simple, sans
façons; (unofficial) officieux; (colloquial)
familier. **informality** *n* simplicité *f*.
informally *adv* (*dress*) en tenue
décontractée; (*speak*) en toute
simplicité.
informant *n* indicateur/-trice *m/f*.

information *n* renseignements *mpl*, informations *fpl*; some ~ un renseignement. ~ **superhighway** *n* autoroute *f* de l'information. ~ **technology** *n* informatique *f*.

informative *adj* (*book*) riche en renseignements; (*visit*) instructif.

informer *n* indicateur/-trice *m/f*.

infrequent *adj* rare.

infringe *vt* (*rule*) enfreindre; (*rights*) ne pas respecter. **infringement** *n* infraction *f*.

infuriate *vt* exaspérer.

ingenuity *n* ingéniosité *f*.

ingot *n* lingot *m*.

ingrained *adj* (*hatred*) enraciné; (*dirt*) bien incrusté.

ingratiate *vt* ~ oneself with se faire bien voir de.

ingredient *n* ingrédient *m*.

inhabit *vt* habiter. **inhabitable** *adj* habitable. **inhabitant** *n* habitant/-e *m/f*.

inhale *vt* inhaler; (*smoke*) avaler. **inhaler** *n* inhalateur *m*.

inherent *adj* inhérent (**in** à). **inherently** *adv* en soi, par sa nature.

inherit *vt* hériter de; ~ sth from sb hériter qch de qn. **inheritance** *n* héritage *m*.

inhibit *vt* (*restrain*) inhiber; (*prevent*) entraver.

inhospitable *adj* inhospitalier.

inhuman *adj* inhumain.

initial *n* initiale *f*. ● *vt* (*pt* **initialled**) parapher. ● *adj* initial.

initiate *vt* (*project*) mettre en œuvre; (*talks*) amorcer; (*person*) initier (**into** à). **initiation** *n* initiation *f*; (*start*) amorce *f*.

initiative *n* initiative *f*.

inject *vt* injecter (**into** dans); (*new element*: fig) insuffler (**into** à). **injection** *n* injection *f*, piqûre *f*.

injure *vt* blesser; (*damage*) nuire à. **injury** *n* blessure *f*.

injustice *n* injustice *f*.

ink *n* encre *f*.

inkling *n* petite idée *f*.

inland *adj* intérieur; I~ Revenue service *m* des impôts britannique.

in-laws *npl* (parents) beaux-parents *mpl*; (family) belle-famille *f*.

inlay[1] *vt* (*pt* **inlaid**) incruster (**with** de); (on wood) marqueter.

inlay[2] *n* incrustation *f*; (on wood) marqueterie *f*.

inlet *n* bras *m* de mer; (Tech) arrivée *f*.

inmate *n* (of asylum) interné/-e *m/f*; (of prison) détenu/-e *m/f*.

inn *n* auberge *f*.

innate *adj* inné.

inner *adj* intérieur; ~ **city** quartiers *mpl* déshérités; ~ **tube** chambre *f* à air.

innocent *a* & *n* innocent/-e (*m/f*).

innocuous *adj* inoffensif.

innovate *vi* innover.

innuendo *n* (*pl* ~es) insinuations *fpl*; (sexual) allusions *fpl* grivoises.

innumerable *adj* innombrable.

inoculate *vt* vacciner (**against** contre).

inopportune *adj* inopportun.

in-patient *n* malade *mf* hospitalisé/-e.

input *n* (of energy) alimentation *f* (**of** en); (contribution) contribution *f*; (data) données *fpl*; (computer process) saisie *f* des données. ● *vt* (*data*) saisir.

inquest *n* enquête *f*.

inquire *vi* se renseigner (**about, into** sur). ● *vt* demander.

inquiry *n* demande *f* de renseignements; (inquest) enquête *f*.

inquisitive *adj* curieux.

inroad *n* make ~s into faire une avancée sur.

insane *adj* fou; (Jur) aliéné.

insanity *n* folie *f*; (Jur) aliénation *f* mentale.

inscribe *vt* inscrire. **inscription** *n* inscription *f*.

inscrutable *adj* énigmatique.

insect *n* insecte *m*. **insecticide** *n* insecticide *m*.

insecure *adj* (*person*) qui manque d'assurance; (job) précaire; (*lock, property*) peu sûr. **insecurity** *n* (of person) manque *m* d'assurance; (of situation) insécurité *f*.

insensitive *adj* insensible; (*remark*) indélicat.

inseparable adj inséparable (**from** de).

insert vt insérer (**in** dans).

in-service adj (training) continu.

inshore adj côtier.

inside n intérieur m; ∼**s**
⊞ entrailles fpl. ● adj intérieur.
● adv à l'intérieur; **go** ∼ entrer.
● prep à l'intérieur de; (of time) en
moins de; ∼ **out** à l'envers;
(thoroughly) à fond.

insight n (perception) perspicacité f;
(idea) aperçu m.

insignia npl insigne m.

insignificant adj (cost, difference)
négligeable; (person) insignifiant.

insincere adj peu sincère.

insinuate vt insinuer.

insist vt/i insister (**that** pour que); ∼
on exiger; ∼ **on doing** vouloir à tout
prix faire. **insistence** n insistance
f. **insistent** adj insistant.
insistently adv avec insistance.

insofar as adv dans la mesure où.

insolent adj insolent.

insolvent adj insolvable.

insomnia n insomnie f.
insomniac n insomniaque mf.

inspect vt (school, machinery)
inspecter; (tickets) contrôler.
inspection n inspection f; (of
passport, ticket) contrôle m. **inspector**
n inspecteur/-trice m/f; (on bus)
contrôleur/-euse m/f.

inspiration n inspiration f.
inspire vt inspirer.

install vt installer.

instalment n (payment) versement
m; (of serial) épisode m.

instance n exemple m; (case) cas m;
for ∼ par exemple; **in the first** ∼ en
premier lieu.

instant adj immédiat; (food)
instantané. ● n instant m.
instantaneous adj instantané.
instantly adv immédiatement.

instead adv plutôt; ∼ **of doing** au
lieu de faire; ∼ **of sb** à la place de
qn.

instep n cou-de-pied m.

instigate vt (attack) lancer;
(proceedings) engager.

instil vt (pt **instilled**) inculquer;
(fear) insuffler.

instinct n instinct m. **instinctive**
adj instinctif.

institute n institut m. ● vt
instituer; (proceedings) engager.
institution n institution f; (school,
hospital) établissement m.

instruct vt (teach) instruire; (order)
ordonner; ∼ **sb in sth** enseigner qch
à qn; ∼ **sb to do** donner l'ordre à qn
de faire. **instruction** n instruction
f. **instructions** npl (for use) mode m
d'emploi. **instructive** adj
instructif. **instructor** n (skiing,
driving) moniteur/-trice m/f.

instrument n instrument m.

instrumental adj instrumental; **be**
∼ **in** contribuer à. **instrumentalist**
n instrumentaliste mf.

insubordinate adj insubordonné.

insufficient adj insuffisant.

insular adj (Geog) insulaire; (mind,
person: fig) borné.

insulate vt (room, wire) isoler.

insulin n insuline f.

insult¹ vt insulter.

insult² n insulte f.

insurance n assurance f (**against**
contre).

insure vt assurer; ∼ **that** (US)
s'assurer que.

intact adj intact.

intake n (of food) consommation f;
(School, Univ) admissions fpl.

integral adj intégral (**to** à).

integrate vt/i (s')intégrer (**with** à;
into dans).

integrity n intégrité f.

intellect n intelligence f.
intellectual a & n intellectuel/-le
(m/f).

intelligence n intelligence f; (Mil)
renseignements mpl. **intelligent**
adj intelligent. **intelligently** adv
intelligemment.

intend vt (outcome) vouloir; ∼ **to do**
avoir l'intention de faire. **intended**
adj (result) voulu; (visit) projeté.

intense adj intense; (person) sérieux.
intensely adv (very) extrêmement.

intensify vt/i (s')intensifier.

intensive *adj* intensif; **in ~ care** en réanimation.

intent *n* intention *f.* ● *adj* absorbé; **~ on doing** résolu à faire.

intention *n* intention *f.*
intentional *adj* intentionnel.

intently *adv* attentivement.

interact *vi* (*factors*) agir l'un sur l'autre; (*people*) communiquer.
interactive *adj* (*TV, video*) interactif.

intercept *vt* intercepter.

interchange *n* (road junction) échangeur *m*; (exchange) échange *m*.

interchangeable *adj* interchangeable.

intercom *n* interphone® *m.*

interconnected *adj* (*parts*) raccordé; (*problems*) lié.

intercourse *n* rapports *mpl.*

interest *n* intérêt *m*; **~ rate** taux *m* d'intérêt. ● *vt* intéresser (**in** à).
interested *adj* intéressé; **be ~ed in** s'intéresser à. **interesting** *adj* intéressant.

interfere *vi* se mêler des affaires des autres; **~ in** se mêler de; **~ with** (*freedom*) empiéter sur; (tamper with) toucher. **interference** *n* ingérence *f*; (sound, light waves) brouillage *m*; (radio) parasites *mpl.*

interim *n* **in the ~** entre-temps. ● *adj* (*government*) provisoire; (*payment*) intermédiaire.

interior *n* intérieur *m*. ● *adj* intérieur.

interjection *n* interjection *f.*

interlock *vt/i* (Tech) (s')emboîter, (s')enclencher.

interlude *n* intervalle *m*; (Theat, Mus) intermède *m.*

intermediary *a & n* intermédiaire (*mf*).

intermediate *adj* intermédiaire; (*exam, level*) moyen.

intermission *n* (Theat) entracte *m.*

intermittent *adj* intermittent.

intern¹ *vt* interner.

intern² *n* (US) stagiaire *mf*; (Med) interne *mf.*

internal *adj* interne; (domestic: Pol) intérieur; **I~ Revenue** (US) service *m* des impôts américain.

international *adj* international.

Internet *n* Internet *m*; **on the ~** sur l'Internet; **~ service provider** fournisseur *m* d'accès à l'Internet.

interpret *vt* interpréter (**as** comme). ● *vi* faire l'interprète.
interpretation *n* interprétation *f.*
interpreter *n* interprète *mf.*

interrelated *adj* interdépendant, lié.

interrogate *vt* interroger.
interrogative *a & n* (Ling) interrogatif (*m*).

interrupt *vt/i* interrompre.
interruption *n* interruption *f.*

intersect *vt/i* (lines, roads) (se) croiser. **intersection** *n* intersection *f.*

interspersed *adj* parsemé (**with** de).

intertwine *vt/i* (s')entrelacer.

interval *n* intervalle *m*; (Theat) entracte *m.*

intervene *vi* intervenir; (of time) s'écouler (**between** entre); (happen) arriver.

interview *n* (for job) entretien *m*; (by a journalist) interview *f*. ● *vt* (*candidate*) faire passer un entretien à; (*celebrity*) interviewer.

intestine *n* intestin *m.*

intimacy *n* intimité *f.*

intimate¹ *vt* (state) annoncer; (hint) laisser entendre.

intimate² *adj* intime. **intimately** *adv* intimement.

intimidate *vt* intimider.

into *prep* (put, go, fall) dans; (divide, translate, change) en; **be ~ jazz** être fana du jazz ⊞; **8 ~ 24 is 3** 24 divisé par 8 égale 3.

intolerant *adj* intolérant.

intonation *n* intonation *f.*

intoxicate *vt* enivrer.
intoxicated *adj* ivre.
intoxication *n* ivresse *f.*

intractable *adj* (*person*) intraitable; (*problem*) rebelle.

Intranet *n* (Comput) Intranet *m.*

intransitive *adj* intransitif.

intravenous *adj* (Med) intraveineux.

intricate *adj* complexe.

intrigue vt intriguer. ● n intrigue f.
  intriguing adj fascinant; (curious)
  curieux.
intrinsic adj intrinsèque (**to** à).
introduce vt (person, idea,
  programme) présenter; (object, law)
  introduire (**into** dans).
  introduction n introduction f; (of
  person) présentation f. **introductory**
  adj (words) préliminaire.
introvert n introverti-e m/f.
intrude vi (person) s'imposer (**on sb** à
  qn), déranger. **intruder** n intrus/-e
  m/f. **intrusion** n intrusion f.
intuition n intuition f. **intuitive**
  adj intuitif.
inundate vt inonder (**with** de).
invade vt envahir.
invalid[1] n malade mf; (disabled)
  infirme mf.
invalid[2] adj (passport) pas valable;
  (claim) sans fondement. **invalidate**
  vt (argument) infirmer; (claim)
  annuler.
invaluable adj inestimable.
invariable adj invariable.
  invariably adv invariablement.
invasion n invasion f.
invent vt inventer. **invention** n
  invention f. **inventive** adj inventif.
  inventor n inventeur/-trice m/f.
inventory n inventaire m.
invert vt (order) intervertir; (image,
  values) renverser; **~ed commas**
  guillemets mpl.
invest vt investir; (time, effort)
  consacrer. ● vi faire un
  investissement; **~ in** (buy) s'acheter.
investigate vt examiner; (crime)
  enquêter sur. **investigation** n
  investigation f. **investigator** n
  (police) enquêteur/-euse m/f.
investment n investissement m;
  emotional **~** engagement m
  personnel. **investor** n investisseur/
  -euse m/f; (in shares) actionnaire mf.
invigilate vi (exam) surveiller.
  invigilator n surveillant/-e m/f.
invigorate vt revigorer.
invisible adj invisible.
invitation n invitation f. **invite** vt
  inviter; (ask for) demander. **inviting**
  adj engageant.

invoice n facture f. ● vt facturer.
involuntary adj involontaire.
involve vt impliquer; (person) faire
  participer (**in** à). **involved** adj
  (complex) compliqué; (at stake) en jeu;
  be ~d in (work) participer à; (crime)
  être mêlé à. **involvement** n
  participation f (**in** à).
inward adj (feeling) intérieur.
  inwardly adv intérieurement.
  inwards adv vers l'intérieur.
iodine n iode m; (antiseptic) teinture f
  d'iode.
iota n iota m; **not one ~ of** pas un
  grain de.
IOU abbr (**I owe you**)
  reconnaissance f de dette.
IQ abbr (**intelligence quotient**) QI
  m.
Iran n Iran m.
Iraq n Irak m.
irate adj furieux.
IRC abbrev (**Internet Relay Chat**)
  (Internet) conversation f IRC.
Ireland n Irlande f.
Irish n & a irlandais (m). **~man** n
  Irlandais m. **~woman** n Irlandaise
  f.
iron n fer m; (appliance) fer m (à
  repasser). ● adj (will) de fer; (bar)
  en fer. ● vt repasser; **~ out** (fig)
  aplanir.
ironic(al) adj ironique.
iron: ironing-board n planche f à
  repasser. **~monger** n quincaillier
  m.
irony n ironie f.
irrational adj irrationnel; (person)
  pas raisonnable.
irregular adj irrégulier.
irrelevant adj hors de propos.
irreplaceable adj irremplaçable.
irresistible adj irrésistible.
irrespective adj **~ of** sans tenir
  compte de.
irresponsible adj irresponsable.
irreverent adj irrévérencieux.
irreversible adj irréversible.
irrigate vt irriguer.
irritable adj irritable.
irritate vt irriter. **irritating** adj
  irritant.
is ⇒BE.

Islam *n* (faith) islam *m*; (Muslims) Islam *m*. **Islamic** *adj* islamique.

island *n* île *f*. **islander** *n* insulaire *mf*.

isle *n* île *f*.

isolate *vt* isoler. **isolation** *n* isolement *m*.

Israel *n* Israël *m*.

Israeli *n* Israélien/-ne *m/f*. ● *adj* israélien.

issue *n* question *f*; (outcome) résultat *m*; (of magazine) numéro *m*; (of stamps) émission *f*; (offspring) descendance *f*; **at ~** en cause. ● *vt* distribuer; (stamps) émettre; (*book*) publier; (*order*) délivrer. ● *vi* **~ from** provenir de.

- - -

it

● *pronoun*

····▸ (subject) il, elle; **'where's the book/chair?'—'~'s in the kitchen'** 'où est le livre/la chaise?'—'il/elle est dans la cuisine'.

····▸ (object) le, la, l'; **~'s my book and I want ~** c'est mon livre et je le veux; **I liked his shirt, did you notice ~?** sa chemise m'a plu, l'as-tu remarquée?; **give ~ to me** donne-le-moi.

····▸ (with preposition) **we talked a lot about ~** on en a beaucoup parlé; **Elliott went to ~** Elliott y est allé.

····▸ (impersonal) il; **~'s raining** il pleut; **~ will snow** il va neiger.

- - -

IT *abbr* ⇒INFORMATION TECHNOLOGY.

Italian *n* (person) Italien/-ne *m/f*; (Ling) italien *m*. ● *adj* italien.

italics *npl* italique *m*.

Italy *n* Italie *f*.

itch *n* démangeaison *f*. ● *vi* démanger; **my arm ~es** j'ai le bras qui me démange; **be ~ing to do** mourir d'envie de faire.

item *n* article *m*; (on agenda) point *m*.

itemize *vt* détailler; **~d bill** facture *f* détaillée.

itinerary *n* itinéraire *m*.

its *det* son, sa; *pl* ses.

it's = IT IS, IT HAS.

itself *pron* lui-même, elle-même; (reflexive) se.

ivory *n* ivoire *m*; **~ tower** tour *f* d'ivoire.

ivy *n* lierre *m*.

- - -

Jj

- - -

jab *vt* (*pt* **jabbed**) **~ sth into sth** planter qch dans qch. ● *n* coup *m*; (injection) piqûre *f*.

jack *n* (Auto) cric *m*; (cards) valet *m*; (Electr) jack *m*. ● *vt* **~ up** soulever avec un cric.

jackal *n* chacal *m*.

jacket *n* veste *f*, veston *m*; (of book) jaquette *f*.

jack-knife *n* couteau *m* pliant. ● *vi* (lorry) se mettre en portefeuille.

jackpot *n* gros lot *m*; **hit the ~** gagner le gros lot.

jade *n* (stone) jade *m*.

jaded *adj* (tired) fatigué; (bored) blasé.

jagged *adj* (*rock*) déchiqueté; (*knife*) dentelé.

jail *n* prison *f*. ● *vt* mettre en prison.

jam *n* confiture *f*; (traffic) **~** embouteillage *m*. ● *vt/i* (*pt* **jammed**) (wedge) (se) coincer; (cram) (s')entasser; (*street*) encombrer; (*radio*) brouiller.

Jamaica *n* Jamaïque *f*.

jam-packed *adj* 🄸 bondé; **~ with** bourré de.

jangle *n* tintement *m*. ● *vt/i* (faire) tinter.

janitor *n* (US) gardien *m*.

January *n* janvier *m*.

Japan *n* Japon *m*.

Japanese *n* (person) Japonais/-e *m/f*; (Ling) japonais *m*. ● *adj* japonais.

jar *n* pot *m*, bocal *m*. ● *vi* (*pt* **jarred**) rendre un son discordant; (*colours*) détonner. ● *vt* ébranler.

jargon *n* jargon *m*.

jaundice *n* jaunisse *f*.

javelin *n* javelot *m*.

jaw *n* mâchoire *f*.

jay *n* geai *m*.

jazz n jazz m. ● vt ~ **up** (dress) rajeunir; (event) ranimer.

jealous adj jaloux. **jealousy** n jalousie f.

jeans npl jean m.

jeer vt/i ~ (at) huer. ● n huée f.

jelly n gelée f. ~**fish** n méduse f.

jeopardize vt (career, chance) compromettre; (lives) mettre en péril.

jerk n secousse f; (fool 🔳) crétin m 🔳. ● vt tirer brusquement. ● vi tressaillir. **jerky** adj saccadé.

jersey n (garment) pull-over m; (fabric) jersey m.

jet n (plane, stream) jet m; (mineral) jais m; ~ **lag** décalage m horaire.

jettison vt jeter par-dessus bord; (Aviat) larguer; (fig) rejeter.

jetty n jetée f.

Jew n juif/juive m/f.

jewel n bijou m. **jeweller** n bijoutier/-ière m/f. **jeweller('s)** n (shop) bijouterie f. **jewellery** n bijoux mpl.

Jewish adj juif.

jibe n moquerie f.

jigsaw n puzzle m.

jingle vt/i (faire) tinter. ● n tintement m; (advertising) refrain m publicitaire, sonal m.

jinx n (person) porte-malheur m inv; (curse) sort m.

jitters npl have the ~ 🔳 être nerveux. **jittery** adj nerveux.

job n emploi m; (post) poste m; out of a ~ sans emploi; **it is a good ~ that** heureusement que; **just the ~** tout à fait ce qu'il faut. ~ **centre** n bureau m des services nationaux de l'emploi. **jobless** adj sans emploi.

jockey n jockey m.

jog n go for a ~ aller faire un jogging. ● vt (pt **jogged**) heurter; (memory) rafraîchir. ● vi faire du jogging. **jogging** n jogging m.

join vt (attach) réunir, joindre; (club) devenir membre de; (company) entrer dans; (army) s'engager dans; (queue) se mettre dans; ~ **sb** (in activity) se joindre à qn; (meet) rejoindre qn. ● vi (become member) adhérer; (pieces) se joindre; (roads) se rejoindre. ● n raccord m. □ ~ **in** participer; ~ **in sth** participer à qch; ~ **up** (Mil) s'engager; ~ **sth up** relier qch. **joiner** n menuisier/-ière m/f.

joint adj (action) collectif; (measures, venture) commun; (winner) ex aequo inv; (account) joint; ~ **author** coauteur m. ● n (join) joint m; (Anat) articulation f; (Culin) rôti m; out of ~ déboîté.

joke n plaisanterie f; (trick) farce f; **it's no ~** ce n'est pas drôle. ● vi plaisanter. **joker** n blagueur/-euse m/f; (cards) joker m.

jolly adj (-**ier**, -**iest**) (person) enjoué; (tune) joyeux. ● adv 🔳 drôlement.

jolt vt secouer. ● vi cahoter. ● n secousse f; (shock) choc m.

jostle vt/i (se) bousculer.

jot vt (pt **jotted**) ~ (**down**) noter.

journal n journal m. **journalism** n journalisme m. **journalist** n journaliste mf.

journey n (trip) voyage m; (short or habitual) trajet m. ● vi voyager.

joy n joie f. **joyful** adj joyeux.

joy: ~**riding** n rodéo m à la voiture volée. ~**stick** n (Comput) manette f; (Aviat) manche m à balai.

jubilant adj (person) exultant; (mood) réjoui.

Judaism n judaïsme m.

judge n juge m. ● vt juger; (distance) estimer; **judging by/from** à en juger par. **judg(e)ment** n jugement m.

judicial adj judiciaire. **judiciary** n magistrature f.

judo n judo m.

jug n (glass) carafe f; (pottery) pichet m.

juggernaut n (lorry) poids m lourd.

juggle vt/i jongler (avec). **juggler** n jongleur/-euse m/f.

juice n jus m. **juicy** adj juteux; (details 🔳) croustillant.

jukebox n juke-box m.

July n juillet m.

jumble vt mélanger. ● n (of objects) tas m; (of ideas) fouillis m; ~ **sale** vente f de charité.

jumbo n (also ~ **jet**) gros-porteur m.

jump vt sauter; ~ **the lights** passer au feu rouge; ~ **the queue** passer devant tout le monde. ● vi sauter; (in

surprise) sursauter; (*price*) monter en
flèche; ∼ **at** (*opportunity*) sauter sur.
● *n* saut *m*, bond *m*; (*increase*) bond
m.

jumper *n* pull(-over) *m*; (dress: US)
robe *f* chasuble.

jump-leads *npl* câbles *mpl* de
démarrage.

jumpy *adj* nerveux.

junction *n* (of roads) carrefour *m*; (on
motorway) échangeur *m*.

June *n* juin *m*.

jungle *n* jungle *f*.

junior *adj* (young) jeune; (in rank)
subalterne; (school) primaire. ● *n*
cadet/-te *m/f*; (School) élève *mf* du
primaire.

junk *n* bric-à-brac *m inv*; (poor quality)
camelote *f*; ∼ **food** nourriture *f*
industrielle.

junkie *n* ⊠ drogué/-e *m/f*.

junk: ∼ **mail** *n* prospectus *mpl*.
∼**-shop** *n* boutique *f* de bric-à-brac.

jurisdiction *n* compétence *f*; (Jur)
juridiction *f*.

juror *n* juré *m*.

jury *n* jury *m*.

just *adj* (fair) juste. ● *adv* (immediately,
slightly) juste; (simply) tout simplement;
(exactly) exactement; **he has/had** ∼
left il vient/venait de partir; **have** ∼
missed avoir manqué de peu; **I'm** ∼
leaving je suis sur le point de partir;
it's ∼ **a cold** ce n'est qu'un rhume;
∼ **as tall/well as** tout aussi grand/
bien que; ∼ **listen!** écoutez donc!; **it's**
∼ **ridiculous** c'est vraiment ridicule.

justice *n* justice *f*; **J**∼ **of the Peace**
juge *m* de paix.

justification *n* justification *f*.

justify *vt* justifier.

jut *vi* (*pt* **jutted**) ∼ **(out)** s'avancer
en saillie.

juvenile *adj* (childish) puéril;
(offender) mineur; (delinquent) jeune.
● *n* jeune *mf*; (Jur) mineur/-e *m/f*.

juxtapose *vt* juxtaposer.

Kk

kangaroo *n* kangourou *m*.

karate *n* karaté *m*.

kebab *n* brochette *f*.

keel *n* (of ship) quille *f*. ● *vi* ∼ **over**
(bateau) chavirer; (person)
s'écrouler.

keen *adj* (*interest, wind, feeling*) vif;
(mind, analysis) pénétrant; (edge,
appetite) aiguisé; (eager)
enthousiaste; **be** ∼ **on** être
passionné de; **be** ∼ **to do** *or* **on doing**
tenir beaucoup à faire. **keenly** *adv*
vivement. **keenness** *n*
enthousiasme *m*.

keep *vt* (*pt* **kept**) garder; (promise,
shop, diary) tenir; (family) faire
vivre; (animals) élever; (rule)
respecter; (celebrate) célébrer; (delay)
retenir; ∼ **sth clean/warm** garder
qch propre/au chaud; ∼ **sb in/out**
empêcher qn de sortir/d'entrer; ∼
sb from doing empêcher qn de faire.
● *vi* (food) se conserver; ∼ **(on)**
continuer (**doing** à faire). ● *n*
pension *f*; (of castle) donjon *m*. □ ∼
down rester allongé; ∼ **sth down**
limiter qch; ∼ **your voice down!**
baisse la voix!; ∼ **to** (road) ne pas
s'écarter de; (rules) respecter; ∼ **up**
(car, runner) suivre; (rain)
continuer; ∼ **up with sb** (in speed)
aller aussi vite que; (class, inflation,
fashion, news) suivre.

keeper *n* gardien/-ne *m/f*.

keepsake *n* souvenir *m*.

kennel *n* niche *f*.

kept ⇒KEEP.

kerb *n* bord *m* du trottoir.

kernel *n* amande *f*; ∼ **of truth** fond
m de vérité.

kettle *n* bouilloire *f*.

key *n* clé *f*; (of computer, piano) touche *f*.
● *adj* (industry, figure) clé (inv). ● *vt*
∼ **(in)** saisir. ∼**board** *n* clavier *m*.

~hole n trou m de serrure. **~pad** n (of telephone) clavier m numérique. **~ring** n porte-clés m inv. **~stroke** n (Comput) frappe f.

khaki adj kaki inv.

kick vt/i donner un coup de pied (à); (horse) botter. ● n coup m de pied; (of gun) recul m; **get a ~ out of doing** 🔲 prendre plaisir à faire. □ **~ out** 🔲 virer 🔲.

kick-off n coup m d'envoi.

kid n (goat, leather) chevreau m; (child 🔲) gosse mf 🔲. ● vt/i (pt **kidded**) blaguer.

kidnap vt (pt **kidnapped**) enlever. **kidnapping** n enlèvement m.

kidney n rein m; (Culin) rognon m.

kill vt tuer; (rumour: fig) arrêter. ● n mise f à mort. **killer** n tueur/-euse m/f. **killing** n meurtre m.

kiln n four m.

kilo n kilo m.

kilobyte n kilo-octet m.

kilogram n kilogramme m.

kilometre, (US) **kilometer** n kilomètre m.

kilowatt n kilowatt m.

kin n parents mpl.

kind n genre m, sorte f; **in ~** en nature; **~ of** (somewhat 🔲) assez. ● adj gentil, bon.

kindergarten n jardin m d'enfants.

kindle vt/i (s')allumer.

kindly adj (-ier, -iest) (person) gentil; (interest) bienveillant. ● adv avec gentillesse; **would you ~ do** auriez-vous l'amabilité de faire.

kindness n bonté f.

king n roi m. **kingdom** n royaume m; (Bot) règne m. **~fisher** n martin-pêcheur m. **~-size(d)** adj géant.

kiosk n kiosque m; **telephone ~** cabine f téléphonique; (Internet) borne f interactive, kiosque m.

kiss n baiser m. ● vt/i (s')embrasser.

kit n (clothing) affaires fpl; (set of tools) trousse f; (for assembly) kit m. ● vt (pt **kitted**) **~ out** équiper.

kitchen n cuisine f.

kite n (toy) cerf-volant m; (bird) milan m.

kitten n chaton m.

kitty n (fund) cagnotte f.

knack n tour m de main (**of doing** pour faire).

knead vt pétrir.

knee n genou m. **~cap** n rotule f.

kneel vi (pt **knelt**) **~ (down)** se mettre à genoux; (in prayer) s'agenouiller.

knew ⇒KNOW.

knickers npl petite culotte f, slip m.

knife n (pl **knives**) couteau m. ● vt poignarder.

knight n chevalier m; (chess) cavalier m. ● vt anoblir. **~hood** n titre m de chevalier.

knit vt/i (pt **knitted** or **knit**) tricoter; (bones) (se) souder. **knitting** n tricot m. **knitwear** n tricots mpl.

knob n bouton m.

knock vt/i cogner; (criticize 🔲) critiquer; **~ sth off/out** faire tomber qch. ● n coup m. □ **~ down** (chair, pedestrian) renverser; (demolish) abattre; (reduce) baisser; **~ off** (stop work 🔲) arrêter de travailler; **~ £10 off** faire une réduction de 10 livres; **~ it off!** 🔲 ça suffit!; **~ out** assommer; **~ over** renverser; **~ up** (meal) préparer en vitesse.

knock-out n (boxing) knock-out m.

knot n nœud m. ● vt (pt **knotted**) nouer.

know vt/i (pt **knew**; pp **known**) (answer, reason, language) savoir (**that** que); (person, place, name, rule, situation) connaître; (recognize) reconnaître; **~ how to do** savoir faire; **~ about** (event) être au courant de; (subject) s'y connaître en; **~ of** (from experience) connaître; (from information) avoir entendu parler de. **~how** n savoir-faire m inv.

knowingly adv (intentionally) délibérément; (meaningfully) d'un air entendu.

knowledge n connaissance f; (learning) connaissances fpl. **knowledgeable** adj savant.

knuckle n jointure f, articulation f.

Koran n Coran m.

Korea n Corée f.

kosher *adj* casher *inv.*

lab *n* 🄸 labo *m.*

label *n* étiquette *f.* ● *vt* (*pt* **labelled**) étiqueter.

laboratory *n* laboratoire *m.*

laborious *adj* laborieux.

labour, (US) **labor** *n* travail *m*; (workers) main-d'œuvre *f*; **in** ∼ en train d'accoucher. ● *vi* peiner (**to do** à faire). ● *vt* trop insister sur.

Labour *n* le parti travailliste. ● *adj* travailliste.

laboured *adj* laborieux.

labourer *n* ouvrier/-ière *m/f*; (on farm) ouvrier/-ière *m/f* agricole.

lace *n* dentelle *f*; (of shoe) lacet *m.* ● *vt* (*shoe*) lacer; (*drink*) arroser.

lacerate *vt* lacérer.

lack *n* manque *m*; **for** ∼ **of** faute de. ● *vt* manquer de; **be** ∼**ing** manquer (**in** de).

lad *n* garçon *m*, gars *m.*

ladder *n* échelle *f*; (in stocking) maille *f* filée. ● *vt/i* (*stocking*) filer.

laden *adj* chargé (**with** de).

ladle *n* louche *f.*

lady *n* (*pl* **ladies**) dame *f*; **ladies and gentlemen** mesdames et messieurs; **young** ∼ jeune femme *or* fille *f.* ∼**bird** *n* coccinelle *f.*

ladylike *adj* distingué.

lag *vi* (*pt* **lagged**) traîner. ● *vt* (*pipes*) calorifuger. ● *n* (interval) décalage *m.*

lager *n* bière *f* blonde.

lagoon *n* lagune *f.*

laid ⇒LAY¹. ∼ **back** *adj* décontracté.

lain ⇒LIE².

lake *n* lac *m.*

lamb *n* agneau *m*; **leg of** ∼ gigot *m* d'agneau.

lame *adj* boiteux.

lament *n* lamentation *f.* ● *vt/i* se lamenter (sur).

laminated *adj* laminé.

lamp *n* lampe *f.* ∼**post** *n* réverbère *m.* ∼**shade** *n* abat-jour *m inv.*

lance *vt* (Med) inciser.

land *n* terre *f*; (plot) terrain *m*; (country) pays *m.* ● *adj* terrestre; (*policy, reform*) agraire. ● *vt/i* débarquer; (*aircraft*) (se) poser; (fall) tomber; (obtain) décrocher; (*a blow*) porter; ∼ **up** se retrouver.

landing *n* débarquement *m*; (Aviat) atterrissage *m*; (top of stairs) palier *m.* ∼**stage** *n* débarcadère *m.*

land: ∼**lady** *n* propriétaire *f*; (of pub) patronne *f.* ∼**lord** *n* propriétaire *m*; (of pub) patron *m.* ∼**mark** *n* (point de) repère *m.* ∼**mine** *n* mine *f* terrestre.

landscape *n* paysage *m.* ● *vt* aménager.

landslide *n* glissement *m* de terrain; (Pol) raz-de-marée *m inv* (électoral).

lane *n* (path, road) chemin *m*; (strip of road) voie *f*; (of traffic) file *f*; (Aviat) couloir *m.*

language *n* langue *f*; (speech, style) langage *m.* ∼ **engineering** *n* ingénierie *f* des langues. ∼ **laboratory** *n* laboratoire *m* de langue.

lank *adj* (*hair*) plat.

lanky *adj* (**-ier**, **-iest**) grand et maigre.

lantern *n* lanterne *f.*

lap *n* genoux *mpl*; (Sport) tour *m* (de piste). ● *vi* (*pt* **lapped**) (*waves*) clapoter. ▢ ∼ **up** laper.

lapel *n* revers *m.*

lapse *vi* (decline) se dégrader; (expire) se périmer; ∼ **into** retomber dans. ● *n* défaillance *f*, erreur *f*; (of time) intervalle *m.*

laptop *n* (Comput) portable *m.*

lard *n* saindoux *m.*

larder *n* garde-manger *m inv.*

large *adj* grand, gros; **at** ∼ en liberté; **by and** ∼ en général. **largely** *adv* en grande mesure.

lark *n* (bird) alouette *f*; (bit of fun 🄸) rigolade *f.* ● *vi* 🄸 rigoler.

larva *n* (*pl* **-vae**) larve *f.*

laryngitis *n* laryngite *f*.

laser *n* laser *m*. ∼ **printer** *n* imprimante *f* laser. ∼ **treatment** *n* (Med) laserothérapie *f*.

lash *vt* fouetter. ● *n* coup *m* de fouet; (eyelash) cil *m*. □ ∼ **out** (spend) dépenser follement; ∼ **out against** attaquer.

lass *n* jeune fille *f*.

lasso *n* lasso *m*.

last *adj* dernier; the ∼ straw le comble; the ∼ word le mot de la fin; on its ∼ legs sur le point de rendre l'âme; ∼ night hier soir. ● *adv* en dernier; (most recently) la dernière fois. ● *n* dernier/-ière *m*/*f*; (remainder) reste *m*; at (long) ∼ enfin. ● *vi* durer. ∼-**ditch** *adj* ultime. **lasting** *adj* durable. **lastly** *adv* en dernier lieu. ∼-**minute** *adj* de dernière minute.

latch *n* loquet *m*.

late *adj* (not on time) en retard; (former) ancien; (hour, fruit) tardif; the ∼ Mrs X feu Mme X. ● *adv* (not early) tard; (not on time) en retard; in ∼ July fin juillet; of ∼ dernièrement. **lately** *adv* dernièrement. **latest** *adj* ⇒LATE; (last) dernier.

lathe *n* tour *m*.

lather *n* mousse *f*. ● *vt* savonner. ● *vi* mousser.

Latin *n* (Ling) latin *m*. ● *adj* latin. ∼ **America** *n* Amérique *f* latine.

latitude *n* latitude *f*.

latter *adj* dernier. ● *n* the ∼ celui-ci, celle-ci.

Latvia *n* Lettonie *f*.

laudable *adj* louable.

laugh *vi* rire (at de). ● *n* rire *m*. **laughable** *adj* ridicule.

laughing stock *n* risée *f*.

laughter *n* (act) rire *m*; (sound of laughs) rires *mpl*.

launch *vt* (rocket) lancer; (boat) mettre à l'eau; ∼ (out) into se lancer dans. ● *n* lancement *m*; (boat) vedette *f*. **launching pad** *n* aire *f* de lancement.

launderette *n* laverie *f* automatique.

laundry *n* (place) blanchisserie *f*; (clothes) linge *m*.

laurel *n* laurier *m*.

lava *n* lave *f*.

lavatory *n* toilettes *fpl*.

lavender *n* lavande *f*.

lavish *adj* (person) généreux; (lush) somptueux. ● *vt* prodiguer (on à). **lavishly** *adv* luxueusement.

law *n* loi *f*; (profession, subject of study) droit *m*; ∼ **and order** l'ordre public. ∼-**abiding** *adj* respectueux des lois. ∼-**court** *n* tribunal *m*.

lawful *adj* légal.

lawn *n* pelouse *f*, gazon *m*. ∼-**mower** *n* tondeuse *f* à gazon.

lawsuit *n* procès *m*.

lawyer *n* avocat *m*.

lax *adj* (government) laxiste; (security) relâché.

laxative *n* laxatif *m*.

lay[1] *adj* (non-clerical) laïque; (worker) non-initié. ● *vt* (pt **laid**) poser, mettre; (trap) tendre; (table) mettre; (plan) former; (eggs) pondre. ● *vi* pondre; ∼ **waste** ravager. □ ∼ **aside** mettre de côté; ∼ **down** (dé)poser; (condition) imposer; ∼ **off** *vt* (worker) licencier; *vi* 🄸 arrêter; ∼ **on** (provide) fournir; ∼ **out** (design) dessiner; (display) disposer; (money) dépenser.

lay[2] ⇒LIE[2].

lay-by *n* (*pl* ∼s) aire *f* de repos.

layer *n* couche *f*.

layman *n* (*pl* -**men**) profane *m*.

layout *n* disposition *f*.

laze *vi* paresser. **laziness** *n* paresse *f*. **lazy** *adj* (-**ier**, -**iest**) paresseux.

lead[1] *vt*/*i* (pt **led**) mener; (team) diriger; (life) mener; (induce) amener; ∼ **to** conduire à, mener à. ● *n* avance *f*; (clue) indice *m*; (leash) laisse *f*; (Theat) premier rôle *m*; (wire) fil *m*; in the ∼ en tête. □ ∼ **away** emmener; ∼ **up to** (come to) en venir à; (precede) précéder.

lead[2] *n* plomb *m*; (of pencil) mine *f*.

leader *n* chef *m*; (of country, club) dirigeant/-e *m*/*f*; (leading article) éditorial *m*. **leadership** *n* direction *f*.

lead-free *adj* (petrol) sans plomb.

leading *adj* principal.

leaf n (pl **leaves**) feuille f; (of table) rallonge f. ● vi ~ **through** feuilleter.

leaflet n prospectus m.

leafy adj feuillu.

league n ligue f; (Sport) championnat m; in ~ **with** de mèche avec.

leak n fuite f. ● vi fuir; (news: fig) s'ébruiter. ● vt répandre; (fig) divulguer.

lean[1] adj maigre. ● n (of meat) maigre m.

lean[2] vt/i (pt **leaned** or **leant**) (rest) (s')appuyer; (slope) pencher. □ ~ **out** se pencher à l'extérieur; ~ **over** (of person) se pencher.

leaning adj penché. ● n tendance f.

leap vi (pt **leaped** or **leapt**) bondir. ● n bond m. ~ **year** n année f bissextile.

learn vt/i (pt **learned** or **learnt**) apprendre (**to do** à faire). **learned** adj érudit. **learner** n débutant/-e m/f.

lease n bail m. ● vt louer à bail.

leash n laisse f.

least adj the ~ (smallest amount of) le moins de; (slightest) le or la moindre. ● n le moins. ● adv le moins; (with adjective) le or la moins; at ~ au moins.

leather n cuir m.

leave vt (pt **left**) laisser; (depart from) quitter; (person) laisser tranquille; **be left** (over) rester. ● n (holiday) congé m; (consent) permission f; **take one's** ~ prendre congé (**of** de); **on** ~ (Mil) en permission. □ ~ **alone** (thing) ne pas toucher; (person) laisser tranquille; ~ **behind** laisser; ~ **out** omettre.

Lebanon n Liban m.

lecture n cours m, conférence f; (rebuke) réprimande f. ● vt/i faire un cours or une conférence (à); (rebuke) réprimander. **lecturer** n conférencier/-ière m/f; (Univ) enseignant/-e m/f.

led ⇨LEAD[1].

ledge n (window) rebord m; (rock) saillie f.

ledger n grand livre m.

leech n sangsue f.

leek n poireau m.

leer vi ~ (**at**) lorgner. ● n regard m sournois.

leeway n (fig) liberté f d'action; (Naut) dérive f.

left ⇨LEAVE. ● adj gauche. ● adv à gauche. ● n gauche f. ~**-hand** adj à or de gauche. ~**-handed** adj gaucher.

left luggage (**office**) n consigne f.

left-overs npl restes mpl.

left-wing adj de gauche.

leg n jambe f; (of animal) patte f; (of table) pied m; (of chicken) cuisse f; (of lamb) gigot m; (of journey) étape f.

legacy n legs m.

legal adj légal; (affairs) juridique.

legend n légende f.

leggings npl (for woman) caleçon m.

legible adj lisible.

legionnaire n légionnaire m.

legislation n (body of laws) législation f; (law) loi f. **legislature** n corps m législatif.

legitimate adj légitime.

leisure n loisirs mpl; **at one's** ~ à tête reposée. ● adj (centre) de loisirs.

leisurely adj lent. ● adv sans se presser.

lemon n citron m.

lemonade n (fizzy) limonade f; (still) citronnade f.

lend vt (pt **lent**) prêter; (credibility) conférer; ~ **itself to** se prêter à.

length n longueur f; (in time) durée f; (section) morceau m; **at** ~ (at last) enfin; **at** (great) ~ longuement.

lengthen vt/i (s')allonger.

lengthways adv dans le sens de la longueur.

lengthy adj long.

lenient adj indulgent.

lens n lentille f; (of spectacles) verre m; (Photo) objectif m.

lent ⇨LEND.

Lent n Carême m.

lentil n lentille f.

Leo n Lion m.

leopard n léopard m.

leotard n body m.

leprosy n lèpre f.

lesbian n lesbienne f. ● adj lesbien.

less adj (in quantity) moins de (than que). ● adv, n & prep moins; ~ than (with numbers) moins de; work ~ than travailler moins que; ten pounds ~ dix livres de moins; ~ and ~ de moins en moins. **lessen** vt/i diminuer. **lesser** adj moindre.

lesson n leçon f.

let vt (pt let; pres p **letting**) laisser; (lease) louer. ● v aux ~ us do, ~'s do faisons; ~ him do qu'il fasse; ~ me know the results informe-moi des résultats. ● n location f. □ ~ **down** baisser; (deflate) dégonfler; (fig) décevoir; ~ **go** vt lâcher; vi lâcher prise; ~ **sb in/out** laisser or faire entrer/sortir qn; ~ **a dress out** élargir une robe; ~ **oneself in for** (task) s'engager à; (trouble) s'attirer; ~ **off** (explode, fire) faire éclater or partir; (excuse) dispenser; (not punish) ne pas punir; ~ **up** ⊞ s'arrêter.

let-down n déception f.

lethal adj mortel; (weapon) meurtrier.

letter n lettre f. ~**-bomb** n lettre f piégée. ~**-box** n boîte f à or aux lettres.

lettering n (letters) caractères mpl.

lettuce n laitue f, salade f.

let-up n répit m.

leukaemia n leucémie f.

level adj plat, uni; (on surface) horizontal; (in height) au même niveau (with que); (in score) à égalité. ● n niveau m; (spirit) ~ niveau m à bulle; **be on the** ~ ⊞ être franc. ● vt (pt **levelled**) niveler; (aim) diriger. ~ **crossing** n passage m à niveau. ~**-headed** adj équilibré.

lever n levier m. ● vt soulever au moyen d'un levier.

leverage n influence f.

levy vt (tax) prélever. ● n impôt m.

lexicon n lexique m.

liability n responsabilité f; ⊞ handicap m; **liabilities** (debts) dettes fpl.

liable adj be ~ to do avoir tendance à faire, pouvoir faire; ~ to (illness) sujet à; (fine) passible de; ~ for responsable de.

liaise vi ⊞ faire la liaison. **liaison** n liaison f.

liar n menteur/-euse m/f.

libel n diffamation f. ● vt (pt **libelled**) diffamer.

liberal adj libéral; (generous) généreux, libéral.

Liberal a & n (Pol) libéral/-e (m/f).

liberate vt libérer.

liberty n liberté f; **at** ~ **to** libre de; **take liberties** prendre des libertés.

Libra n Balance f.

librarian n bibliothécaire mf.

library n bibliothèque f.

libretto n livret m.

lice ⇒LOUSE.

licence, (US) **license** n permis m; (for television) redevance f; (Comm) licence f; (liberty: fig) licence f. ~ **plate** n plaque f minéralogique.

license vt accorder un permis à, autoriser.

lick vt lécher; (defeat ⊞) rosser; (fig) a ~ **of paint** un petit coup de peinture. ● n coup m de langue.

lid n couvercle m.

lie¹ n mensonge m. ● vi (pt **lied**; pres p **lying**) (tell lies) mentir.

lie² vi (pt **lay**; pp **lain**; pres p **lying**) s'allonger; (remain) rester; (be) se trouver, être; (in grave) reposer; **be lying** être allongé. □ ~ **down** s'allonger; ~ **in** faire la grasse matinée; ~ **low** se cacher.

lieutenant n lieutenant m.

life n (pl **lives**) vie f. ~**belt** n bouée f de sauvetage. ~**boat** n canot m de sauvetage. ~**buoy** n bouée f de sauvetage. ~ **cycle** n cycle m de vie. ~**-guard** n sauveteur m. ~ **insurance** n assurance-vie f. ~**-jacket** n gilet m de sauvetage.

lifeless adj inanimé.

lifelike adj très ressemblant.

life: ~**long** adj de toute la vie. ~ **sentence** n condamnation f à perpétuité. ~**-size(d)** adj grandeur nature inv. ~ **story** n vie f. ~**-style** n style m de vie. ~ **support machine** n appareil m de respiration artificielle.

lifetime n vie f; **in one's** ~ de son vivant.

lift vt lever; (steal ⊞) voler. ● vi (of fog) se lever. ● n (in building) ascenseur m;

give a ∼ to emmener (en voiture).
∼-off n (Aviat) décollage m.

light n lumière f; (lamp) lampe f; (for fire, on vehicle) feu m; (headlight) phare m; **bring to ∼** révéler; **come to ∼** être révélé; **have you got a ∼?** vous avez du feu? ● adj (not dark) clair; (not heavy) léger. ● vt (pt **lit** or **lighted**) allumer; (room) éclairer; (match) frotter. □ ∼ **up** vi s'allumer; vt (room) éclairer. ∼ **bulb** n ampoule f.

lighten vt (give light to) éclairer; (make brighter) éclaircir; (make less heavy) alléger.

lighter n briquet m; (for stove) allume-gaz m inv.

light: **∼-headed** adj (dizzy) qui a un vertige; (frivolous) étourdi. **∼-hearted** adj gai. **∼house** n phare m.

lighting n éclairage m.

lightly adv légèrement.

lightning n éclair m, foudre f. ● adj (visit) éclair inv.

lightweight adj léger. ● n (boxing) poids m léger.

light-year n année f lumière.

like¹ adj semblable, pareil; **be ∼-minded** avoir les mêmes sentiments. ● prep comme. ● conj 🄵 comme. ● n pareil m; **the ∼s of you** les gens comme vous.

like² vt aimer (bien); **I should ∼** je voudrais, j'aimerais; **would you ∼?** voudriez-vous?, voudrais-tu?; **∼s** goûts mpl. **likeable** adj sympathique.

likelihood n probabilité f.

likely adj (-ier, -iest) probable. ● adv probablement; **he is ∼ to do** il fera probablement; **not ∼!** 🄵 pas question!

likeness n ressemblance f.

likewise adv également.

liking n (for thing) penchant m; (for person) affection f.

lilac n lilas m. ● adj lilas inv.

Lilo® n matelas m pneumatique.

lily n lis m, lys m. ∼ **of the valley** n muguet m.

limb n membre m.

limber vi ∼ **up** faire des exercices d'assouplissement.

limbo n **be in ∼** (forgotten) être tombé dans l'oubli.

lime n (fruit) citron m vert; **∼(-tree)** tilleul m.

limelight n **in the ∼** en vedette.

limestone n calcaire m.

limit n limite f. ● vt limiter.

limited company n société f anonyme.

limp vi boiter. ● n **have a ∼** boiter. ● adj mou.

line n ligne f; (track) voie f; (wrinkle) ride f; (row) rangée f, file f; (of poem) vers m; (rope) corde f; (of goods) gamme f; (queue: US) queue f; **be in ∼ for** avoir de bonnes chances de; **hold the ∼** ne quittez pas; **in ∼ with** en accord avec; **stand in ∼** faire la queue. ● vt (paper) régler; (streets) border; (garment) doubler; (fill) remplir, garnir. □ ∼ **up** (s')aligner; (in queue) faire la queue; ∼ **sth up** prévoir qch.

linen n (sheets) linge m; (material) lin m.

liner n paquebot m.

linesman n (football) juge m de touche; (tennis) juge m de ligne.

linger vi s'attarder; (smells) persister.

linguist n linguiste mf. **linguistics** n linguistique f.

lining n doublure f.

link n lien m; (of chain) maillon m. ● vt (relate) (re)lier; ∼ **up** (of roads) se rejoindre. **linkage** n lien m. **links** n inv terrain m de golf. **∼-up** n liaison f.

lino n lino m.

lion n lion m. **lioness** n lionne f.

lip n lèvre f; (edge) rebord m; **pay ∼-service to** n'approuver que pour la forme. **∼-read** vt/i lire sur les lèvres. **∼salve** n baume m pour les lèvres. **∼stick** n rouge m (à lèvres).

liquid n & a liquide (m).

liquidation n liquidation f; **go into ∼** déposer son bilan.

liquidize vt passer au mixeur. **liquidizer** n mixeur m.

liquor n alcool m.

liquorice n réglisse f.

lisp n zézaiement m; **with a ∼** en zézayant. ● vi zézayer.

list _n_ liste _f._ ● _vt_ dresser la liste de.
● _vi_ (_ship_) gîter.

listen _vi_ écouter; ~ **to**, ~ **in (to)**
écouter. **listener** _n_ auditeur/-trice
_m/f._

listless _adj_ apathique.

lit ⇒LIGHT.

liter ⇒LITRE.

literal _adj_ (_meaning_) littéral;
(_translation_) mot à mot. **literally**
adv littéralement; mot à mot.

literary _adj_ littéraire.

literate _adj_ qui sait lire et écrire.

literature _n_ littérature _f;_ (brochures)
documentation _f._

Lithuania _n_ Lituanie _f._

litigation _n_ litiges _mpl._

litre, (US) **liter** _n_ litre _m._

litter _n_ (rubbish) détritus _mpl_, papiers
mpl; (animals) portée _f._ ● _vt_ éparpiller;
(make untidy) laisser des détritus dans;
~ed with jonché de. ~-bin _n_
poubelle _f._

little _adj_ petit; (not much) peu de. ● _n_
peu _m;_ a ~ un peu (de). ● _adv_ peu.

live[1] _adj_ vivant; (_wire_) sous tension;
(_broadcast_) en direct; be a ~ wire
être très dynamique.

live[2] _vt/i_ vivre; (reside) habiter, vivre;
~ **it up** mener la belle vie. □ ~
down faire oublier; ~ **on** (feed
oneself on) vivre de; (continue)
survivre; ~ **up to** se montrer à la
hauteur de.

livelihood _n_ moyens _mpl_
d'existence.

lively _adj_ (**-ier, -iest**) vif, vivant.

liven _vt/i_ ~ **up** (s')animer; (cheer up)
(s')égayer.

liver _n_ foie _m._

livestock _n_ bétail _m._

livid _adj_ livide; (angry) furieux.

living _adj_ vivant. ● _n_ vie _f;_ **make a** ~
gagner sa vie; ~ **conditions**
conditions _fpl_ de vie. ~-**room** _n_
salle _f_ de séjour.

lizard _n_ lézard _m._

load _n_ charge _f;_ (loaded goods)
chargement _m_, charge _f;_ (weight, strain)
poids _m;_ ~**s of** 🄣 des tas de 🄣. ● _vt_
charger.

loaf _n_ (_pl_ **loaves**) pain _m._ ● _vi_ ~
(**about**) fainéanter.

loan _n_ prêt _m;_ (money borrowed)
emprunt _m._ ● _vt_ prêter.

loathe _vt_ détester (**doing** faire).
loathing _n_ dégoût _m._

lobby _n_ entrée _f_, vestibule _m;_ (Pol)
lobby _m_, groupe _m_ de pression. ● _vt_
faire pression sur.

lobster _n_ homard _m._

local _adj_ local; (_shops_) du quartier;
~ **government** administration _f_
locale. ● _n_ personne _f_ du coin; (pub
🄑) pub _m_ du coin.

locally _adv_ localement; (nearby) dans
les environs.

locate _vt_ (situate) situer; (find)
repérer.

location _n_ emplacement _m;_ **on** ~
(cinema) en extérieur.

lock _n_ (of door) serrure _f;_ (on canal)
écluse _f;_ (of hair) mèche _f._ ● _vt/i_
fermer à clef; (wheels: Auto) (se)
bloquer. □ ~ **in** _or_ **up** (_person_)
enfermer; ~ **out** (by mistake)
enfermer dehors.

locker _n_ casier _m._

locket _n_ médaillon _m._

locksmith _n_ serrurier _m._

locum _n_ (doctor) remplaçant/-e _m/f._

lodge _n_ (house) pavillon _m_ (de
gardien _or_ de chasse); (of porter) loge
_f._ ● _vt_ (accommodate) loger; (_money,
complaint_) déposer. ● _vi_ être logé
(with chez); (become fixed) se loger.
lodger _n_ locataire _mf_, pensionnaire
_mf._ **lodgings** _n_ logement _m._

loft _n_ grenier _m._

lofty _adj_ (**-ier, -iest**) (tall, noble) élevé;
(haughty) hautain.

log _n_ (of wood) bûche _f;_ ~(-**book**) (Naut)
journal _m_ de bord; (Auto) ≈ carte _f_
grise. ● _vt_ (_pt_ **logged**) noter;
(distance) parcourir. □ ~ **on** (Comput)
se connecter; ~ **off** (Comput) se
déconnecter.

logic _adj_ logique. **logical** _adj_
logique.

logistics _n_ logistique _f._

loin _n_ (Culin) filet _m;_ ~**s** reins _mpl._

loiter _vi_ traîner.

loll _vi_ se prélasser.

lollipop _n_ sucette _f._

London _n_ Londres. **Londoner** _n_
Londonien/-ne _m/f._

lone *adj* solitaire.

lonely (**-ier, -iest**) solitaire; (person) seul, solitaire.

long *adj* long; **how ~ is?** quelle est la longueur de?; (in time) quelle est la durée de?; **how ~?** combien de temps?; **a ~ time** longtemps. ● *adv* longtemps; **he will not be ~** il n'en a pas pour longtemps; **as** *or* **so ~ as** pourvu que; **before ~** avant peu; **I no ~er do** je ne fais plus. ● *vi* avoir bien *or* très envie (**for, to** de); **~ for sb** (pine for) se languir de qn. **~-distance** *adj* (*flight*) sur long parcours; (*phone call*) interurbain; (*runner*) de fond. **~ face** *n* grimace *f*. **~hand** *n* écriture *f* courante.

longing *n* envie *f* (**for** de); (nostalgia) nostalgie *f* (**for** de).

longitude *n* longitude *f*.

long: ~ jump *n* saut *m* en longueur. **~-range** *adj* (*missile*) à longue portée; (*forecast*) à long terme. **~-sighted** *adj* presbyte. **~-standing** *adj* de longue date. **~-term** *adj* à long terme. **~ wave** *n* grandes ondes *fpl*. **~-winded** *adj* verbeux.

loo *n* ⊞ toilettes *fpl*.

look *vi* regarder; (seem) avoir l'air; **~ like** ressembler à, avoir l'air de. ● *n* regard *m*; (appearance) air *m*, aspect *m*; (good) **~s** beauté *f*. □ **~ after** s'occuper de, soigner; **~ at** regarder; **~ back on** repenser à; **~ down on** mépriser; **~ for** chercher; **~ forward to** attendre avec impatience; **~ in on** passer voir; **~ into** examiner; **~ out** faire attention; **~ out for** (*person*) guetter; (*symptoms*) guetter l'apparition de; **~ round** se retourner; **~ up** (*word*) chercher; (visit) passer voir; **~ up to** respecter.

look-out *n* (Mil) poste *m* de guet; (person) guetteur *m*; **be on the ~ for** rechercher.

loom *vi* surgir; (*war*) menacer; (*interview*) être imminent. ● *n* métier *m* à tisser.

loony *n & a* ⊞ fou, folle (*mf*).

loop *n* boucle *f*. ● *vt* boucler. **~hole** *n* lacune *f*.

loose *adj* (*knot*) desserré; (*page*) détaché; (*clothes*) ample, lâche; (*tooth*) qui bouge; (lax) relâché; (not packed) en vrac; (inexact) vague; (pej) immoral; **at a ~ end** désœuvré; **come ~** bouger. **loosely** *adv* sans serrer; (roughly) vaguement. **loosen** *vt* (slacken) desserrer; (untie) défaire.

loot *n* butin *m*. ● *vt* piller.

lord *n* seigneur *m*; (British title) lord *m*; **the L~** le Seigneur; (good) **L~!** mon Dieu!

lorry *n* camion *m*.

lose *vt/i* (*pt* **lost**) perdre; **get lost** se perdre. **loser** *n* perdant/-e *m/f*.

loss *n* perte *f*; **be at a ~** être perplexe; **be at a ~ to** être incapable de; **heat ~** déperdition *f* de chaleur.

lost ⇒LOSE. ● *adj* perdu. **~ property** *n* objets *mpl* trouvés.

lot *n* **the ~** (le) tout *m*; (people) tous *mpl*, toutes *fpl*; **a ~ (of)**, **~s (of)** ⊞ beaucoup (de); **quite a ~ (of)** ⊞ pas mal (de); (fate) sort *m*; (at auction) lot *m*; (land) lotissement *m*.

lotion *n* lotion *f*.

lottery *n* loterie *f*.

loud *adj* bruyant, fort. ● *adv* fort; **out ~** tout haut. **loudly** *adv* fort. **~speaker** *n* haut-parleur *m*.

lounge *vi* paresser. ● *n* salon *m*.

louse *n* (*pl* **lice**) pou *m*.

lousy *adj* (**-ier, -iest**) ⊞ infect.

lout *n* rustre *m*.

lovable *adj* adorable.

love *n* amour *m*; (tennis) zéro *m*; **in ~** amoureux (**with** de); **make ~** faire l'amour. ● *vt* (*person*) aimer; (like greatly) aimer (beaucoup) (**to do** faire). **~ affair** *n* liaison *f* amoureuse. **~ life** *n* vie *f* amoureuse.

lovely *adj* (**-ier, -iest**) joli; (delightful ⊞) très agréable.

lover *n* (male) amant *m*; (female) maîtresse *f*; (devotee) amateur *m* (**of** de).

loving *adj* affectueux.

low *a & adv* bas; **~ in sth** à faible teneur en qch. ● *n* (low pressure) dépression *f*; **reach a (new) ~** atteindre son niveau le plus bas. ● *vi* meugler. **~-calorie** *adj* basses-calories. **~-cut** *adj* décolleté.

lower *a & adv* ⇒LOW. ● *vt* baisser; ~ oneself s'abaisser.

low: ~**-fat** *adj* (*diet*) sans matières grasses; (*cheese*) allégé. ~**-key** *adj* modéré; (discreet) discret. ~**lands** *npl* plaine(s) *f*(*pl*). ~**-lying** *adj* à faible altitude.

loyal *adj* loyal (**to** envers).

lozenge *n* (shape) losange *m*; (tablet) pastille *f*.

LP *n* (disque *m*) 33 tours *m*.

Ltd. *abbr* (**Limited**) SA.

lubricant *n* lubrifiant *m*. **lubricate** *vt* lubrifier.

luck *n* chance *f*; **bad** ~ malchance *f*; **good** ~**!** bonne chance!

luckily *adv* heureusement.

lucky *adj* (**-ier**, **-iest**) qui a de la chance, heureux; (event) heureux; (number) qui porte bonheur; **it's** ~ **that** heureusement que.

ludicrous *adj* ridicule.

lug *vt* (*pt* **lugged**) traîner.

luggage *n* bagages *mpl*. ~**-rack** *n* porte-bagages *m inv*.

lukewarm *adj* tiède.

lull *vt* he ~ed them into thinking that il leur a fait croire que. ● *n* accalmie *f*.

lullaby *n* berceuse *f*.

lumber *n* bois *m* de charpente. ● *vt* Ⅱ ~ sb with (*chore*) coller à qn Ⅱ. ~**jack** *n* bûcheron *m*.

luminous *adj* lumineux.

lump *n* morceau *m*; (swelling on body) grosseur *f*; (in liquid) grumeau *m*. ● *vt* ~ **together** réunir. ~ **sum** *n* somme *f* globale.

lunacy *n* folie *f*.

lunar *adj* lunaire.

lunatic *n* fou/ folle *m/f*.

lunch *n* déjeuner *m*. ● *vi* déjeuner.

luncheon *n* déjeuner *m*. ~ **voucher** *n* chèque-repas *m*.

lung *n* poumon *m*.

lunge *vi* bondir (**at** sur; **forward** en avant).

lurch *n* leave in the ~ planter là, laisser en plan. ● *vi* (*person*) tituber.

lure *vt* appâter, attirer. ● *n* (attraction) attrait *m*, appât *m*.

lurid *adj* choquant, affreux; (gaudy) voyant.

lurk *vi* se cacher; (in ambush) s'embusquer; (prowl) rôder; (*suspicion, danger*) menacer.

luscious *adj* appétissant.

lush *adj* luxuriant. ● *n* (US, Ⅱ) ivrogne/-esse *m/f*.

lust *n* luxure *f*. ● *vi* ~ **after** convoiter.

Luxembourg *n* Luxembourg *m*.

luxurious *adj* luxueux.

luxury *n* luxe *m*. ● *adj* de luxe.

lying ⇒LIE[1], LIE[2]. ● *n* mensonges *mpl*.

lyric *adj* lyrique. **lyrical** *adj* lyrique. **lyrics** *npl* paroles *fpl*.

Mm

MA *abbr* ⇒MASTER OF ARTS.

mac *n* Ⅱ imper *m*.

machine *n* machine *f*. ● *vt* (sew) coudre à la machine; (Tech) usiner. ~**-gun** *n* mitrailleuse *f*.

mackerel *n inv* maquereau *m*.

mackintosh *n* imperméable *m*.

mad *adj* (**madder**, **maddest**) fou; (foolish) insensé; (*dog*) enragé; (angry Ⅱ) furieux; **be** ~ **about** se passionner pour; (*person*) être fou de; **drive sb** ~ exaspérer qn; **like** ~ comme un fou.

madam *n* madame *f*; (unmarried) mademoiselle *f*.

made ⇒MAKE.

madly *adv* (*interested, in love*) follement; (frantically) comme un fou.

madman *n* (*pl* **-men**) fou *m*.

madness *n* folie *f*.

magazine *n* revue *f*, magazine *m*; (of gun) magasin *m*.

maggot *n* (in fruit) ver *m*, (for fishing) asticot *m*.

magic *n* magie *f*. ● *adj* magique.

magician *n* magicien/-ne *m/f*.

magistrate *n* magistrat *m*.

magnet *n* aimant *m*. **magnetic** *adj* magnétique.

magnificent *adj* magnifique.

magnify *vt* grossir; (*sound*) amplifier; (*fig*) exagérer.

magnifying glass *n* loupe *f*.

magpie *n* pie *f*.

mahogany *n* acajou *m*.

maid *n* (servant) bonne *f*; (in hotel) femme *f* de chambre.

maiden *n* (old use) jeune fille *f*. ● *adj* (*aunt*) célibataire; (*voyage*) premier. ~ **name** *n* nom *m* de jeune fille.

mail *n* (postal service) poste *f*; (letters) courrier *m*; (armour) cotte *f* de mailles. ● *adj* (*bag, van*) postal. ● *vt* envoyer par la poste. ~ **box** *n* boîte *f* aux lettres; (Comput) boîte *f* aux lettres électronique. **mailing list** *n* liste *f* d'adresses. ~**man** *n* (*pl* **-men**) (US) facteur *m*. ~ **order** *n* vente *f* par correspondance. ~ **shot** *n* publipostage *m*.

main *adj* principal; **a** ~ **road** une grande route. ● *n* (**water/gas**) ~ conduite *f* d'eau/de gaz; **the** ~**s** (Electr) le secteur; **in the** ~ en général. ~**frame** *n* unité *f* centrale. ~**land** *n* continent *m*. ~**stream** *n* tendance *f* principale, ligne *f*.

maintain *vt* (continue, keep, assert) maintenir; (*house, machine, family*) entretenir; (*rights*) soutenir.

maintenance *n* (care) entretien *m*; (continuation) maintien *m*; (allowance) pension *f* alimentaire.

maisonette *n* duplex *m*.

maize *n* maïs *m*.

majestic *adj* majestueux.

majesty *n* majesté *f*.

major *adj* majeur. ● *n* commandant *m*. ● *vi* ~ **in** (Univ, US) se spécialiser en.

majority *n* majorité *f*; **the** ~ **of people** la plupart des gens. ● *adj* majoritaire.

make *vt/i* (*pt* **made**) faire; (manufacture) fabriquer; (*friends*) se faire; (*money*) gagner; (*decision*) prendre; (*place, position*) arriver à; (cause to be) rendre; ~ **sb do sth** faire faire qch à qn; (force) obliger qn à faire qch; **be made of** être fait de; ~ **oneself at home** se mettre à l'aise; ~ **sb happy** rendre qn heureux; ~ **it** arriver; (succeed) réussir; **I** ~ **it two**

o'clock j'ai deux heures; **I** ~ **it 150** d'après moi, ça fait 150; **I cannot** ~ **anything of it** je n'y comprends rien; **can you** ~ **Friday?** vendredi, c'est possible?; ~ **as if to** faire mine de. ● *n* (brand) marque *f*. □ ~ **do** (manage) se débrouiller (**with** avec); ~ **for** se diriger vers; (cause) tendre à créer; ~ **good** *vi* réussir; *vt* compenser; (repair) réparer; ~ **off** filer (**with** avec); ~ **out** distinguer; (understand) comprendre; (draw up) faire; (assert) prétendre; ~ **up** *vt* faire, former; (*story*) inventer; (*deficit*) combler; *vi* se réconcilier; ~ **up** (one's face) se maquiller; ~ **up for** compenser; (*time*) rattraper; ~ **up one's mind** se décider; ~ **up to** se concilier les bonnes grâces de.

make-believe *adj* feint, illusoire. ● *n* fantaisie *f*.

maker *n* fabricant *m*.

makeshift *adj* improvisé.

make-up *n* maquillage *m*; (of object) constitution *f*; (Psych) caractère *m*.

malaria *n* paludisme *m*.

Malaysia *n* Malaisie *f*.

male *adj* (*voice, sex*) masculin; (Bot, Tech) mâle. ● *n* mâle *m*.

malfunction *n* mauvais fonctionnement *m*. ● *vi* mal fonctionner.

malice *n* méchanceté *f*. **malicious** *adj* méchant.

malignant *adj* malveillant; (*tumour*) malin.

mall *n* (shopping) ~ (in suburbs) centre *m* commercial; (in town) galerie *f* marchande.

malnutrition *n* sous-alimentation *f*.

Malta *n* Malte *f*.

mammal *n* mammifère *m*.

mammoth *n* mammouth *m*. ● *adj* (*task*) gigantesque; (*organization*) géant.

man *n* (*pl* **men**) homme *m*; (in sports team) joueur *m*; (chess) pièce *f*; ~ **to man** d'homme à homme. ● *vt* (*pt* **manned**) (*desk*) tenir; (*ship*) armer; (*guns*) servir; (be on duty at) être de service à.

manage *vt* (*project, organization*) diriger; (*shop, affairs*) gérer; (handle) manier; **I could ∼ another drink** ▣ je prendrais bien encore un verre; **can you ∼ Friday?** vendredi, c'est possible? ● *vi* se débrouiller; **∼ to do** réussir à faire. **manageable** *adj* (*tool, size, person*) maniable; (*job*) faisable.

management *n* (managers) direction *f*; (of shop) gestion *f*.

manager *n* directeur/-trice *m/f*; (of shop) gérant/-e *m/f*; (of actor) impresario *m*.

mandate *n* mandat *m*.

mandatory *adj* obligatoire.

mane *n* crinière *f*.

mango *n* (*pl* ∼**es**) mangue *f*.

manhandle *vt* maltraiter, malmener.

man: ∼**hole** *n* regard *m*. ∼**hood** *n* âge *m* d'homme; (quality) virilité *f*.

maniac *n* maniaque *mf*, fou *m*, folle *f*.

manicure *n* manucure *f*. ● *vt* soigner, manucurer.

manifest *adj* manifeste. ● *vt* manifester.

manipulate *vt* (*tool, person*) manipuler.

mankind *n* genre *m* humain.

manly *adj* viril.

man-made *adj* (*fibre*) synthétique; (*pond*) artificiel; (*disaster*) d'origine humaine.

manned *adj* (*spacecraft*) habité.

manner *n* manière *f*; (attitude) attitude *f*; (kind) sorte *f*; ∼**s** (social behaviour) manières *fpl*.

mannerism *n* particularité *f*; (quirk) manie *f*.

manoeuvre *n* manœuvre *f*. ● *vt/i* manœuvrer.

manor *n* manoir *m*.

manpower *n* main-d'œuvre *f*.

mansion *n* (in countryside) demeure *f*; (in town) hôtel *m* particulier.

manslaughter *n* homicide *m* involontaire.

mantelpiece *n* (manteau *m* de) cheminée.

manual *adj* (*labour*) manuel; (*typewriter*) mécanique. ● *n* (handbook) manuel *m*.

manufacture *vt* fabriquer. ● *n* fabrication *f*.

manure *n* fumier *m*.

many *a & n* beaucoup (de); **a great** *or* **good ∼** un grand nombre (de); **∼ a** bien des.

map *n* carte *f*; (of streets) plan *m*. ● *vt* (*pt* **mapped**) faire la carte de; **∼ out** (*route*) tracer; (arrange) organiser.

mar *vt* (*pt* **marred**) gâcher.

marble *n* marbre *m*; (for game) bille *f*.

March *n* mars *m*.

march *vi* (Mil) marcher (au pas). ● *vt* **∼ off** (lead away) emmener. ● *n* marche *f*.

margin *n* marge *f*.

marginal *adj* marginal; (*increase*) léger, faible; (*seat*: Pol) disputé.

marinate *vt* faire mariner (**in** dans).

marine *adj* marin. ● *n* (shipping) marine *f*; (sailor) fusilier *m* marin.

marital *adj* conjugal. **∼ status** *n* situation *f* de famille.

mark *n* (currency) mark *m*; (stain) tache *f*; (trace) marque *f*; (School) note *f*; (target) but *m*. ● *vt* marquer; (*exam*) corriger; **∼ out** délimiter; (*person*) désigner; **∼ time** marquer le pas.

marker *n* (pen) marqueur *m*; (tag) repère *m*; (School, Univ) examinateur/ -trice *m/f*.

market *n* marché *m*; **on the ∼** en vente. ● *vt* (sell) vendre; (launch) commercialiser. **∼ research** *n* étude *f* de marché.

marmalade *n* confiture *f* d'oranges.

maroon *n* bordeaux *m inv*. ● *adj* bordeaux *inv*.

marooned *adj* abandonné; (snowbound) bloqué.

marquee *n* grande tente *f*; (of circus) chapiteau *m*; (awning: US) auvent *m*.

marriage *n* mariage *m* (**to** avec).

married *adj* marié (**to** à); (life) conjugal; **get ∼** se marier (**to** avec).

marrow *n* (of bone) moelle *f*; (vegetable) courge *f*.

marry *vt* épouser; (give or unite in marriage) marier. ● *vi* se marier.

marsh *n* marais *m*.

marshal *n* maréchal *m*; (at event) membre *m* du service d'ordre. ● *vt* (*pt* **marshalled**) rassembler.

martyr *n* martyr/-e *m*/*f*. ● *vt* martyriser.

marvel *n* merveille *f*. ● *vi* (*pt* **marvelled**) s'émerveiller (**at** de).

marvellous *adj* merveilleux.

marzipan *n* pâte *f* d'amandes.

masculine *a* & *n* masculin (*m*).

mash *n* (potatoes 🔟) purée *f*. ● *vt* écraser. **mashed potatoes** *npl* purée *f* (de pommes de terre).

mask *n* masque *m*. ● *vt* masquer.

Mason *n* franc-maçon *m*.

masonry *n* maçonnerie *f*.

mass *n* (Relig) messe *f*; masse *f*; **the ～es** les masses *fpl*. ● *vt*/*i* (se) masser.

massacre *n* massacre *m*. ● *vt* massacrer.

massage *n* massage *m*. ● *vt* masser.

massive *adj* (large) énorme; (heavy) massif.

mass media *n* médias *mpl*.

mass-produce *vt* fabriquer en série.

mast *n* (on ship) mât *m*; (for radio, TV) pylône *m*.

master *n* maître *m*; (in secondary school) professeur *m*; **M～ of Arts** titulaire *mf* d'une maîtrise ès lettres. ● *vt* maîtriser.

masterpiece *n* chef-d'œuvre *m*.

mastery *n* maîtrise *f*.

mat *n* (petit) tapis *m*; (at door) paillasson *m*.

match *n* (for lighting fire) allumette *f*; (Sport) match *m*; (equal) égal/-e *m*/*f*; (marriage) mariage *m*; (sb to marry) parti *m*; **be a ～ for** pouvoir tenir tête à. ● *vt* opposer; (go with) aller avec; (*cups*) assortir; (equal) égaler. ● *vi* (be alike) être assorti.

matchbox *n* boîte *f* à allumettes.

matching *adj* assorti.

mate *n* camarade *mf*; (of animal) compagnon *m*, compagne *f*; (assistant) aide *mf*; (chess) mat *m*. ● *vt*/*i* (s') accoupler (**with** avec).

material *n* matière *f*; (fabric) tissu *m*; (documents, for building) matériau(x)

m(*pl*); **～s** (equipment) matériel *m*. ● *adj* matériel; (fig) important.

materialistic *adj* matérialiste.

materialize *vi* se matérialiser, se réaliser.

maternal *adj* maternel.

maternity *n* maternité *f*. ● *adj* (*clothes*) de grossesse. **～ hospital** *n* maternité *f*. **～ leave** *n* congé *m* maternité.

mathematics *n* & *npl* mathématiques *fpl*.

maths, (US) **math** *n* maths *fpl*.

mating *n* accouplement *m*.

matrimony *n* mariage *m*.

matron *n* (married, elderly) dame *f* âgée; (in hospital) infirmière *f* en chef.

matt *adj* mat.

matter *n* (substance) matière *f*; (affair) affaire *f*; **as a ～ of fact** en fait; **what is the ～?** qu'est-ce qu'il y a? ● *vi* importer; **it does not ～** ça ne fait rien; **no ～ what happens** quoi qu'il arrive.

mattress *n* matelas *m*.

mature *adj* (psychologically) mûr; (*plant*) adulte. ● *vt*/*i* (se) mûrir. **maturity** *n* maturité *f*.

mauve *a* & *n* mauve (*m*).

maverick *n* non-conformiste *mf*.

maximize *vt* porter au maximum.

maximum *a* & *n* (*pl* **-ima**) maximum (*m*).

---

may

past **might**

● *auxiliary verb*

····➤ (possibility) **they ～ be able to come** ils pourront peut-être venir; **she ～ not have seen him** elle ne l'a peut-être pas vu; **it ～ rain** il risque de pleuvoir; **'will you come?'—'I might'** 'tu viendras?'—'peut-être'.

····➤ (permission) **you ～ leave** vous pouvez partir; **～ I smoke?** puis-je fumer?

····➤ (wish) **～ he be happy** qu'il soit heureux.

May *n* mai *m*.

maybe *adv* peut-être.

mayhem *n* (havoc) ravages *mpl*.

mayonnaise *n* mayonnaise *f*.

mayor *n* maire *m*.

maze *n* labyrinthe *m*.

Mb *abbr* (**megabyte**) (Comput) Mo.

me *pron* me, m'; (after prep.) moi; (indirect object) me, m'; **he knows** ∼ il me connaît.

meadow *n* pré *m*.

meagre *adj* maigre.

meal *n* repas *m*; (grain) farine *f*.

mean *adj* (poor) misérable; (miserly) avare; (unkind) méchant; (average) moyen. ● *n* milieu *m*; (average) moyenne *f*; **in the** ∼ **time** en attendant. ● *vt* (*pt* **meant**) vouloir dire, signifier; (involve) entraîner; **I** ∼ **that!** je suis sérieux; **be meant for** être destiné à; ∼ **to do** avoir l'intention de faire.

meaning *n* sens *m*, signification *f*.

meaningful *adj* significatif.

meaningless *adj* dénué de sens.

means *n* moyen(s) *m*(*pl*); **by** ∼ **of sth** au moyen de qch. ● *npl* (wealth) moyens *mpl* financiers; **by all** ∼ certainement; **by no** ∼ nullement.

meant ⇒MEAN.

meantime, **meanwhile** *adv* en attendant.

measles *n* rougeole *f*.

measure *n* mesure *f*; (ruler) règle *f*. ● *vt/i* mesurer; ∼ **up to** être à la hauteur de.

meat *n* viande *f*. **meaty** *adj* de viande; (fig) substantiel.

mechanic *n* mécanicien/-ne *m/f*.

mechanical *adj* mécanique.

mechanism *n* mécanisme *m*.

medal *n* médaille *f*.

meddle *vi* (interfere) se mêler (**in** de); (tinker) toucher (**with** à).

media *n* ⇒MEDIUM. ● *npl* **the** ∼ les média *mpl*; **talk to the** ∼ parler à la presse.

median *adj* médian. ● *n* médiane *f*.

mediate *vi* servir d'intermédiaire.

medical *adj* médical; (student) en médecine. ● *n* visite *f* médicale.

medication *n* médicaments *mpl*.

medicine *n* (science) médecine *f*; (substance) médicament *m*.

medieval *adj* médiéval.

mediocre *adj* médiocre.

meditate *vt/i* méditer.

Mediterranean *adj* méditerranéen. ● *n* **the** ∼ la Méditerranée *f*.

medium *n* (*pl* **media**) (mid-point) milieu *m*; (for transmitting data) support *m*; (*pl* **mediums**) (person) médium *m*. ● *adj* moyen.

medley *n* mélange *m*; (Mus) pot-pourri *m*.

meet *vt* (*pt* **met**) rencontrer; (see again) retrouver; (be introduced to) faire la connaissance de; (face) faire face à; (*requirement*) satisfaire. ● *vi* se rencontrer; (see each other again) se retrouver; (in session) se réunir.

meeting *n* réunion *f*; (between two people) rencontre *f*.

megabyte *n* (Comput) mégaoctet *m*.

melancholy *n* mélancolie *f*. ● *adj* mélancolique.

mellow *adj* (*fruit*) mûr; (*sound, colour*) moelleux, doux; (*person*) mûri. ● *vt/i* (mature) mûrir; (soften) (s')adoucir.

melody *n* mélodie *f*.

melon *n* melon *m*.

melt *vt/i* (faire) fondre.

member *n* membre *m*. **M**∼ **of Parliament** *n* député *m*. **membership** *n* adhésion *f*; (members) membres *mpl*; (fee) cotisation *f*.

memento *n* (*pl* ∼**es**) (object) souvenir *m*.

memo *n* note *f*.

memoir *n* (record, essay) mémoire *m*.

memorandum *n* note *f*.

memorial *n* monument *m*. ● *adj* commémoratif.

memorize *vt* apprendre par cœur.

memory *n* (mind, in computer) mémoire *f*; (thing remembered) souvenir *m*; **from** ∼ de mémoire; **in** ∼ **of** à la mémoire de.

men ⇒MAN.

menace *n* menace *f*; (nuisance) peste *f*. ● *vt* menacer.

mend *vt* réparer; (darn) raccommoder; ∼ **one's ways** s'amender. ● *n* raccommodage *m*; **on the** ∼ en voie de guérison.

meningitis *n* méningite *f*.

menopause *n* ménopause *f*.

mental *adj* mental; (*hospital*) psychiatrique.

mentality *n* mentalité *f*.

mention *vt* mentionner; **don't ~ it!** il n'y a pas de quoi!, je vous en prie! ● *n* mention *f*.

menu *n* (food, on computer) menu *m*; (list) carte *f*.

MEP *abbr* (**Member of the European Parliament**) député *m* au Parlement européen.

mercenary *a & n* mercenaire (*m*).

merchandise *n* marchandises *fpl*.

merchant *n* marchand *m*. ● *adj* (*ship, navy*) marchand. **~ bank** *n* banque *f* de commerce.

merciful *adj* miséricordieux.

mercury *n* mercure *m*.

mercy *n* pitié *f*; **at the ~ of** à la merci de.

mere *adj* simple. **merest** *adj* moindre.

merge *vt/i* (se) mêler (**with** à); (*companies*: Comm) fusionner. **merger** *n* fusion *f*.

mermaid *n* sirène *f*.

merrily *adv* (happily) joyeusement; (unconcernedly) avec insouciance.

merry *adj* (**-ier, -iest**) gai; **make ~** faire la fête. **~-go-round** *n* manège *m*.

mesh *n* maille *f*; (fabric) tissu *m* à mailles; (network) réseau *m*.

mesmerize *vt* hypnotiser.

mess *n* désordre *m*, gâchis *m*; (dirt) saleté *f*; (Mil) mess *m*; **make a ~ of** gâcher. ● *vt* **~ up** gâcher. ● *vi* **~ about** s'amuser; (dawdle) traîner; **~ with** (tinker with) tripoter.

message *n* message *m*.

messenger *n* messager/-ère *m/f*.

messy *adj* (**-ier, -iest**) en désordre; (dirty) sale.

met ⇒MEET.

metal *n* métal *m*. ● *adj* de métal. **metallic** *adj* métallique; (paint, colour) métallisé.

metallurgy *n* métallurgie *f*.

metaphor *n* métaphore *f*.

meteor *n* météore *m*.

meteorite *n* météorite *m*.

meteorology *n* météorologie *f*.

meter *n* compteur *m*; (US) = METRE.

method *n* méthode *f*.

methylated spirit(s) *n* alcool *m* à brûler.

meticulous *adj* méticuleux.

metre, (US) **meter** *n* mètre *m*.

metric *adj* métrique.

metropolis *n* métropole *f*.

metropolitan *adj* métropolitain.

mew *n* miaulement *m*. ● *vi* miauler.

mews *npl* appartements *mpl* chic aménagés dans d'anciennes écuries.

Mexico *n* Mexique *m*.

miaow *n & vi* = MEW.

mice ⇒MOUSE.

mickey *n* **take the ~ out of** 🄵 se moquer de.

microchip *n* puce *f*; circuit *m* intégré.

microlight *n* ULM *m*.

microprocessor *n* microprocesseur *m*.

microscope *n* microscope *m*.

microwave *n* micro-onde *f*; **~ (oven)** four *m* à micro-ondes. ● *vt* passer au four à micro-ondes.

mid *adj* **in ~ air** en plein ciel; **in ~ March** à la mi-mars; **~ afternoon** milieu *m* de l'après-midi; **he's in his ~ twenties** il a environ vingt-cinq ans.

midday *n* midi *m*.

middle *adj* (*door, shelf*) du milieu; (*size*) moyen. ● *n* milieu *m*; **in the ~ of** au milieu de. **~-aged** *adj* d'âge mûr. **M~ Ages** *n* Moyen Âge *m*. **~ class** *n* classe *f* moyenne. **M~ East** *n* Moyen-Orient *m*.

midge *n* moucheron *m*.

midget *n* nain/-e *m/f*. ● *adj* minuscule.

midnight *n* minuit *f*; **it's ~** il est minuit.

midst *n* **in the ~ of** au beau milieu de; **in our ~** parmi nous.

midsummer *n* milieu *m* de l'été; (solstice) solstice *m* d'été.

midway *adv* **~ between/along** à mi-chemin entre/le long de.

midwife *n* (*pl* **-wives**) sage-femme *f*.

might¹ v aux I ~ have been killed! j'aurais pu être tué; **you ~ try doing sth** vous pourriez faire qch; ⇒MAY.

might² n puissance f.

mighty adj puissant; (huge 🎓) énorme. ● adv 🎓 vachement 🎓.

migrant a & n (bird) migrateur (m); (worker) migrant/-e (m/f).

migrate vi émigrer. **migration** n migration f.

mild adj (surprise, taste, tobacco, attack) léger; (weather, cheese, soap, person) doux; (case, infection) bénin.

mile n mile m (= 1.6 km); **walk for ~s** marcher pendant des kilomètres; **~s better** 🎓 bien meilleur. **mileage** n nombre m de miles, kilométrage m.

milestone n (lit) borne f; (fig) étape f importante.

military adj militaire.

militia n milice f.

milk n lait m. ● vt (cow) traire; (fig) pomper.

milkman n (pl -men) laitier m.

milky adj (skin, colour) laiteux; (tea) au lait; **M~ Way** Voie f lactée.

mill n moulin m; (factory) usine f. ● vt moudre. ● vi ~ **around** grouiller.

millennium n (pl ~s) millénaire m.

millimetre, (US) **millimeter** n millimètre m.

million n million m; **a ~ pounds** un million de livres. **millionaire** n millionnaire m.

millstone n meule f; (fig) boulet m.

mime n (actor) mime mf; (art) mime m. ● vt/i mimer.

mimic vt (pt **mimicked**) imiter. ● n imitateur/-trice m/f.

mince vt hacher; **not to ~ matters** ne pas mâcher ses mots. ● n viande f hachée.

mind n esprit m; (sanity) raison f; (opinion) avis m; **be on sb's ~** préoccuper qn; **bear that in ~** ne l'oubliez pas; **change one's ~** changer d'avis; **make up one's ~** se décider (**to** à). ● vt (have charge of) s'occuper de; (heed) faire attention à; **I do not ~ the noise** le bruit ne me dérange pas; **I don't ~** ça m'est égal;

would you ~ **checking?** je peux vous demander de vérifier?

minder n (bodyguard) garde m de corps; (child) ~ nourrice f.

mindless adj (programme) bête; (work) abrutissant; (vandalism) gratuit.

mine n mine f. ● vt extraire; (Mil) miner. ● pron le mien, la mienne, les mien(ne)s; **the blue car is ~** la voiture bleue est la mienne or à moi.

minefield n (lit) champ m de mines; (fig) terrain m miné.

miner n mineur m.

mineral n & a minéral (m); ~ **water** eau f minérale.

minesweeper n (ship) dragueur m de mines.

mingle vt/i (se) mêler (**with** à).

minibus n minibus m.

minicab n taxi m (non agréé).

minimal adj minimal.

minimize vt minimiser; (Comput) réduire.

minimum a & n (pl -ima) minimum (m).

minister n ministre m. **ministerial** adj ministériel. **ministry** n ministère m.

mink n vison m.

minor adj (change, surgery) mineur; (injury, burn) léger; (road) secondaire. ● n (Jur) mineur/-e m/f.

minority n minorité f; **in the ~** en minorité. ● adj minoritaire.

mint n (Bot, Culin) menthe f; (sweet) bonbon m à la menthe; (fortune 🎓) fortune f. ● vt frapper; **in ~ condition** à l'état neuf.

minus prep moins; (without 🎓) sans. ● n moins m; (drawback) inconvénient m.

minute¹ n minute f; ~**s** (of meeting) compte-rendu m.

minute² adj (object) minuscule; (risk, variation) minime.

miracle n miracle m.

mirror n miroir m, glace f; (Auto) rétroviseur. ● vt refléter.

misbehave vi se conduire mal.

miscalculation n (lit) erreur f de calcul; (fig) mauvais calcul m.

miscarriage n fausse couche f; ∼ of justice erreur f judiciaire.

miscellaneous adj divers.

mischief n (playfulness) espièglerie f; (by children) bêtises fpl. **mischievous** adj espiègle; (malicious) méchant.

misconduct n mauvaise conduite f.

misconstrue vt mal interpréter.

misdemeanour, (US) **misdemeanor** n (Jur) délit m.

miser n avare mf.

miserable adj (sad) malheureux; (wretched) misérable; (performance, result) lamentable.

misery n (unhappiness) souffrance f; (misfortune) misère f; (person □) rabat-joie mf inv.

misfit n inadapté/-e m/f.

misfortune n malheur m.

misgiving n (doubt) doute m; (apprehension) crainte f.

misguided adj (foolish) imprudent; (mistaken) erroné; **be** ∼ (person) se tromper.

mishap n incident m.

misjudge vt (distance, speed) mal évaluer; (person) mal juger.

mislay vt (pt **mislaid**) égarer.

mislead vt (pt **misled**) tromper. **misleading** adj trompeur.

misplace vt mal ranger; (lose) égarer. **misplaced** adj (fear, criticism) déplacé.

misprint n coquille f, faute f typographique.

misread vt (pt **misread**) mal lire; (intentions) mal interpréter.

miss vt/i manquer; (bus) rater; **he** ∼**es her/Paris** elle/Paris lui manque; **you're** ∼**ing the point** tu n'as rien compris; ∼ **sth out** omettre qch; ∼ **out on sth** laisser passer qch. ● n coup m manqué; **it was a near** ∼ on l'a échappé belle.

Miss n Mademoiselle f; ∼ **Smith** (written) Mlle Smith.

misshapen adj difforme.

missile n (Mil) missile m; (thrown) projectile m.

mission n mission f. **missionary** n missionnaire mf.

misspell vt (pt **misspelt** or **misspelled**) mal écrire.

mist n brume f; (on window) buée f. ● vt/i (s')embuer.

mistake n erreur f; **by** ∼ par erreur; **make a** ∼ faire une erreur. ● vt (pt **mistook**; pp **mistaken**) (meaning) mal interpréter; ∼ **for** prendre pour.

mistaken adj (enthusiasm) mal placé; **be** ∼ avoir tort.

mistletoe n gui m.

mistreat vt maltraiter.

mistress n maîtresse f.

misty adj (-ier, -iest) brumeux; (window) embué.

misunderstanding n malentendu m.

misuse vt (word) mal employer; (power) abuser de; (equipment) faire mauvais usage de.

mitten n moufle f.

mix n mélange m. ● vt mélanger; (drink) préparer; (cement) malaxer. ● vi se mélanger (with avec, à); (socially) être sociable; ∼ **with sb** fréquenter qn. □ ∼ **up** (confuse) confondre; (jumble up) mélanger; **get** ∼**ed up in** se trouver mêlé à.

mixed adj (school) mixte; (collection, diet) varié; (nuts, sweets) assorti.

mixer n (Culin) batteur m électrique; **be a good** ∼ être sociable; ∼ **tap** mélangeur m.

mixture n mélange m.

mix-up n confusion f (over sur).

moan n gémissement m. ● vi gémir; (complain □) râler □.

mob n (crowd) foule f; (gang) gang m; **the M**∼ la Mafia. ● vt (pt **mobbed**) assaillir.

mobile adj mobile; ∼ **phone** téléphone m portable. ● n mobile m.

mobilize vt/i mobiliser.

mock vt/i se moquer (de). ● adj faux.

mockery n moquerie f; **a** ∼ **of** une parodie de.

mock-up n maquette f.

mode n mode m.

model n (Comput, Auto) modèle m; (scale representation) maquette f; (person showing clothes) mannequin m. ● adj modèle; (car) modèle réduit inv;

(*railway*) miniature. ● *vt* (*pt* **modelled**) modeler; (*clothes*) présenter. ● *vi* être mannequin; (pose) poser. **modelling** *n* métier *m* de mannequin.

modem *n* modem *m*.

moderate *a & n* modéré/-e (*m/f*).

moderation *n* modération *f*; in ∼ avec modération.

modern *adj* moderne; ∼ **languages** langues *fpl* vivantes. **modernize** *vt* moderniser.

modest *adj* modeste. **modesty** *n* modestie *f*.

modification *n* modification *f*. **modify** *vt* modifier.

module *n* module *m*.

moist *adj* (*soil*) humide; (*skin, palms*) moite; (*cake*) moelleux. **moisten** *vt* humecter. **moisture** *n* humidité *f*. **moisturizer** *n* crème *f* hydratante.

molar *n* molaire *f*.

mold (US) = MOULD.

mole *n* grain *m* de beauté; (animal) taupe *f*.

molecule *n* molécule *f*.

molest *vt* (pester) importuner; (sexually) agresser sexuellement.

moment *n* (short time) instant *m*; (point in time) moment *m*. **momentarily** *adv* momentanément; (soon: US) très bientôt. **momentary** *adj* momentané.

momentum *n* élan *m*.

monarch *n* monarque *m*. **monarchy** *n* monarchie *f*.

Monday *n* lundi *m*.

monetary *adj* monétaire.

money *n* argent *m*; make ∼ (*person*) gagner de l'argent; (*business*) rapporter de l'argent. ∼**-box** *n* tirelire *f*. ∼ **order** *n* mandat *m* postal.

monitor *n* dispositif *m* de surveillance; (Comput) moniteur *m*. ● *vt* surveiller; (*broadcast*) être à l'écoute de.

monk *n* moine *m*.

monkey *n* singe *m*.

monopolize *vt* monopoliser. **monopoly** *n* monopole *m*.

monotonous *adj* monotone. **monotony** *n* monotonie *f*.

monsoon *n* mousson *f*.

monster *n* monstre *m*. **monstrous** *adj* monstrueux.

month *n* mois *m*.

monthly *adj* mensuel. ● *adv* (*pay*) au mois; (*publish*) tous les mois. ● *n* (periodical) mensuel *m*.

monument *n* monument *m*.

moo *vi* meugler.

mood *n* humeur *f*; in a good/bad ∼ de bonne/mauvaise humeur. **moody** *adj* d'humeur changeante.

moon *n* lune *f*.

moonlight *n* clair *m* de lune. **moonlighting** *n* 🅸 travail *m* au noir.

moor *n* lande *f*. ● *vt* amarrer.

mop *n* balai *m* à franges; ∼ of hair crinière *f* 🅸. ● *vt* (*pt* **mopped**) ∼ (up) éponger.

moped *n* vélomoteur *m*.

moral *adj* moral. ● *n* morale *f*; ∼s moralité *f*.

morale *n* moral *m*.

morbid *adj* morbide.

more *adv* plus; ∼ **serious** plus sérieux; work ∼ travailler plus; sleep ∼ and ∼ dormir de plus en plus; once ∼ une fois de plus; I don't go there any ∼ je n'y vais plus; ∼ **or less** plus ou moins. ● *det* plus de; a little ∼ wine un peu plus de vin; ∼ bread encore un peu de pain; there's no ∼ bread il n'y a plus de pain; nothing ∼ rien de plus. ● *pron* plus; cost ∼ than coûter plus cher que; I need ∼ of it il m'en faut davantage.

moreover *adv* de plus.

morning *n* matin *m*; (whole morning) matinée *f*.

Morocco *n* Maroc *m*.

morsel *n* morceau *m*.

mortal *a & n* mortel/-le (*m/f*).

mortgage *n* emprunt-logement *m*. ● *vt* hypothéquer.

mortuary *n* morgue *f*.

mosaic *n* mosaïque *f*.

mosque n mosquée f.

mosquito n (pl ~es) moustique m.

moss n mousse f.

most det (nearly all) la plupart de; ~ **people** la plupart des gens; **the** ~ **votes/money** le plus de voix/ d'argent. ● n le plus. ● pron la plupart; ~ **of us** la plupart d'entre nous; ~ **of the money** la plus grande partie de l'argent; **the** ~ **I can do is** ... tout ce que je peux faire c'est ... ● adv **the** ~ **beautiful house/hotel in Oxford** la maison la plus belle/l'hôtel le plus beau d'Oxford; ~ **interesting** très intéressant; **what I like** ~ **(of all) is** ce que j'aime le plus c'est. **mostly** adv surtout.

moth n papillon m de nuit; (in cloth) mite f.

mother n mère f. ● vt (lit) materner; (fig) dorloter. **motherhood** n maternité f. ~**in-law** n (pl ~s-in-law) belle-mère f. ~**of-pearl** n nacre f. **M~'s Day** n la fête des mères. ~**to-be** n future maman f. ~ **tongue** n langue f maternelle.

motion n mouvement m; (proposal) motion f; ~ **picture** (US) film m. ● vt/ i ~ **(to) sb** to faire signe à qn de. **motionless** adj immobile.

motivate vt motiver.

motive n motif m; (Jur) mobile m.

motor n moteur m; (car) auto f. ● adj (industry, insurance, vehicle) automobile; (activity, disorder: Med) moteur. ~**bike** n moto f. ~ **car** n auto f. ~**cyclist** n motocycliste mf. ~ **home** n auto-caravane f.

motorist n automobiliste mf.

motorway n autoroute f.

mottled adj tacheté.

motto n (pl ~es) devise f.

mould n (shape) moule m; (fungus) moisissure f. ● vt mouler; (influence) former. **moulding** n moulure f. **mouldy** adj moisi.

mount n (hill) mont m; (horse) monture f. ● vt (stairs) gravir; (platform, horse, bike) monter sur; (jewel, picture, campaign, exhibit) monter. ● vi monter; (number, toll) augmenter; (concern) grandir.

mountain n montagne f; ~ **bike** (vélo) tout terrain m, VTT m. **mountaineer** n alpiniste mf.

mourn vt/i ~ **(for)** pleurer. **mournful** adj mélancolique. **mourning** n deuil m.

mouse n (pl **mice**) souris f. ~**trap** n souricière f.

mouth n bouche f; (of dog, cat) gueule f; (of cave, tunnel) entrée f. **mouthful** n bouchée f. ~**wash** n eau f dentifrice. ~**watering** adj appétissant.

move vt (object) déplacer; (limb, head) bouger; (emotionally) émouvoir; ~ **house** déménager. ● vi bouger; (vehicle) rouler; (change address) déménager; (act) agir. ● n mouvement m; (in game) coup m; (player's turn) tour m; (step, act) manœuvre f; (house change) déménagement m; **on the** ~ en mouvement. □ ~ **back** reculer; ~ **in** emménager; ~ **in with** s'installer avec; ~ **on** (person) se mettre en route; (vehicle) repartir; (time) passer; ~ **sth on** faire avancer qch; ~ **sb on** faire circuler qn; ~ **over** or **up** se pousser.

movement n mouvement m.

movie n (US) film m; **the** ~s le cinéma.

moving adj (vehicle) en marche; (part, target) mobile; (staircase) roulant; (touching) émouvant.

mow vt (pp **mowed** or **mown**) (lawn) tondre; (hay) couper; ~ **down** faucher. **mower** n tondeuse f.

MP abbr ⇒MEMBER OF PARLIAMENT.

Mr n (pl **Messrs**) ~ **Smith** Monsieur or M. Smith; ~ **President** Monsieur le Président.

Mrs n (pl **Mrs**) ~ **Smith** Madame or Mme Smith.

Ms n Mme.

much adv beaucoup; **too** ~ trop; **very** ~ beaucoup; **I like them as** ~ **as you (do)** je les aime autant que toi. ● pron beaucoup; **not** ~ pas grand-chose; **he didn't say** ~ il n'a pas dit grand-chose; **I ate so** ~ **that** j'ai tellement mangé que. ● det beaucoup de; **too** ~ **money** trop d'argent; **how**

~ **time is left?** combien de temps reste-t-il?

muck *n* saletés *fpl*; (manure) fumier *m*. □ ~ **about** 🗓 faire l'imbécile. **mucky** *adj* sale.

mud *n* boue *f*.

muddle *n* (mix-up) malentendu *m*; (mess) pagaille *f* 🗓; **get into a** ~ s'embrouiller. □ ~ **through** se débrouiller; ~ **up** embrouiller.

muddy *adj* couvert de boue.

muffle *vt* emmitoufler; (bell) assourdir; (voice) étouffer.

mug *n* grande tasse *f*; (for beer) chope *f*; (face 🗓) gueule *f* 🗓; (fool 🗓) poire *f* 🗓. ● *vt* (pt **mugged**) agresser. **mugger** *n* agresseur *m*.

muggy *adj* lourd.

mule *n* mulet *m*.

multicoloured *adj* multicolore.

multiple *a & n* multiple (*m*); ~ **sclerosis** sclérose *f* en plaques.

multiplication *n* multiplication *f*.

multiply *vt/i* (se) multiplier.

multistorey *adj* (car park) à niveaux multiples.

mum *n* 🗓 maman *f*.

mumble *vt/i* marmonner.

mummy *n* (mother 🗓) maman *f*; (embalmed body) momie *f*.

mumps *n* oreillons *mpl*.

munch *vt* mâcher.

mundane *adj* terre-à-terre.

municipal *adj* municipal.

mural *adj* mural. ● *n* peinture *f* murale.

murder *n* meurtre *m*. ● *vt* assassiner. **murderer** *n* meurtrier *m*, assassin *m*.

murky *adj* (-ier, -iest) (water) glauque; (past) trouble.

murmur *n* murmure *m*. ● *vt/i* murmurer.

muscle *n* muscle *m*. ● *vi* ~ **in** 🗓 s'imposer (on dans).

muscular *adj* (tissue, disease) musculaire; (body, person) musclé.

museum *n* musée *m*.

mushroom *n* champignon *m*. ● *vi* (town) proliférer; (demand) s'accroître rapidement.

music *n* musique *f*.

musical *adj* (person) musicien; (voice) mélodieux; (accompaniment) musical; (instrument) de musique. ● *n* comédie *f* musicale.

musician *n* musicien/-ne *m/f*.

Muslim *n* Musulman/-e *m/f*. ● *adj* musulman.

mussel *n* moule *f*.

must *v aux* devoir; **you** ~ **go** vous devez partir, il faut que vous partiez; **she** ~ **be consulted** il faut la consulter; **he** ~ **be old** il doit être vieux; **I** ~ **have done it** j'ai dû le faire. ● *n* **be a** ~ 🗓 être indispensable.

mustard *n* moutarde *f*.

musty *adj* (-ier, -iest) (room) qui sent le renfermé; (smell) de moisi.

mute *a & n* muet/-te (*m/f*). **muted** *adj* (colour) sourd; (response) tiède; (celebration) mitigé.

mutilate *vt* mutiler.

mutter *vt/i* marmonner.

mutton *n* mouton *m*.

mutual *adj* (reciprocal) réciproque; (common) commun; (consent) mutuel. **mutually** *adv* mutuellement.

muzzle *n* (snout) museau *m*; (device) muselière *f*; (of gun) canon *m*. ● *vt* museler.

my *adj* mon, ma, *pl* mes.

myself *pron* (reflexive) me, m'; **I've hurt** ~ je me suis fait mal; (emphatic) moi-même; **I did it** ~ je l'ai fait moi-même; (after preposition) moi, moi-même; **I am proud of** ~ je suis fier de moi.

mysterious *adj* mystérieux.

mystery *n* mystère *m*.

mystic *a & n* mystique (*mf*). **mystical** *adj* mystique.

myth *n* mythe *m*. **mythical** *adj* mythique. **mythology** *n* mythologie *f*.

Nn

nag *vt/i* (*pt* **nagged**) critiquer; (pester) harceler. **nagging** *adj* persistant.

nail *n* clou *m*; (of finger, toe) ongle *m*; **on the ~** sans tarder, tout de suite. ● *vt* clouer. **~ polish** *n* vernis *m* à ongles.

naïve *adj* naïf.

naked *adj* nu; **to the ~ eye** à l'œil nu.

name *n* nom *m*; (fig) réputation *f*. ● *vt* nommer; (terms) fixer; **be ~d after** porter le nom de.

namely *adv* à savoir.

nanny *n* nurse *f*.

nap *n* somme *m*.

nape *n* nuque *f*.

napkin *n* serviette *f*.

nappy *n* couche *f*.

narcotic *a & n* narcotique (*m*).

narrative *n* récit *m*. **narrator** *n* narrateur/-trice *m/f*.

narrow *adj* étroit. ● *vt/i* (se) rétrécir; (limit) (se) limiter; **~ down the choices** limiter les choix. **~-minded** *adj* à l'esprit étroit; (ideas) étroit.

nasal *adj* nasal.

nasty *adj* (**-ier, -iest**) mauvais, désagréable; (malicious) méchant.

nation *n* nation *f*.

national *adj* national. ● *n* ressortissant/-e *m/f*.

nationality *n* nationalité *f*.

nationalize *vt* nationaliser.

nationally *adv* à l'échelle nationale.

native *n* (local inhabitant) autochtone *mf*; (non-European) indigène *mf*; **be a ~ of** être originaire de. ● *adj* indigène; (country) natal; (inborn) inné; **~ language** langue *f* maternelle; **~ speaker of French** personne *f* de langue maternelle française.

natural *adj* naturel.

naturally *adv* (normally, of course) naturellement; (by nature) de nature.

nature *n* nature *f*.

naughty *adj* (**-ier, -iest**) vilain, méchant; (indecent) grivois.

nausea *n* nausée *f*. **nauseous** *adj* (smell) écœurant.

nautical *adj* nautique.

naval *adj* (battle) naval; (officer) de marine.

navel *n* nombril *m*.

navigate *vt* (sea) naviguer sur; (ship) piloter. ● *vi* naviguer. **navigation** *n* navigation *f*.

navy *n* marine *f*. ● *adj* **~ (blue)** bleu *inv* marine.

near *adv* près; **draw ~** (s')approcher (to de). ● *prep* près de. ● *adj* proche; **~ to** près de. ● *vt* approcher de.

nearby *adj* proche. ● *adv* à proximité.

nearly *adv* presque; **I ~ forgot** j'ai failli oublier; **not ~ as pretty as** loin d'être aussi joli que.

nearness *n* proximité *f*.

nearside *adj* (Auto) du côté du passager.

neat *adj* soigné, net; (room) bien rangé; (clever) habile; (drink) sec. **neatly** *adv* avec soin; habilement. **neatness** *n* netteté *f*.

necessarily *adv* nécessairement.

necessary *adj* nécessaire.

necessitate *vt* nécessiter.

necessity *n* nécessité *f*; (thing) chose *f* indispensable.

neck *n* cou *m*; (of dress) encolure *f*. **~ and neck** *adj* à égalité. **~lace** *n* collier *m*. **~line** *n* encolure *f*. **~tie** *n* cravate *f*.

nectarine *n* brugnon *m*, nectarine *f*.

need *n* besoin *m*. ● *vt* avoir besoin de; (demand) demander; **you ~ not come** vous n'êtes pas obligé de venir.

needle *n* aiguille *f*.

needless *adj* inutile.

needlework *n* couture *f*; (object) ouvrage *m* (à l'aiguille).

needy *adj* (**-ier, -iest**) nécessiteux. ● *n* **the ~** les indigents.

negative *adj* négatif. ● *n* (of photograph) négatif *m*; (word: Gram) négation *f*; in the ∼ (answer) par la négative; (Gram) à la forme négative.

neglect *vt* négliger, laisser à l'abandon; ∼ **to do** négliger de faire. ● *n* manque *m* de soins; (**state of**) ∼ abandon *m*.

negligent *adj* négligent.

negotiate *vt/i* négocier.

negotiation *n* négociation *f*.

neigh *n* hennissement *m*. ● *vi* hennir.

neighbour, (US) **neighbor** *n* voisin/-e *m/f*. **neighbourhood** *n* voisinage *m*, quartier *m*; **in the** ∼**hood of** aux alentours de. **neighbouring** *adj* voisin. **neighbourly** *adj* amical.

neither *a* & *pron* aucun/-e des deux, ni l'un/-e ni l'autre. ● *adv* ni; ∼ **big nor small** ni grand ni petit. ● *conj* (ne) non plus; ∼ **am I coming** je ne viendrai pas non plus.

nephew *n* neveu *m*.

nerve *n* nerf *m*; (courage) courage *m*; (calm) sang-froid *m*; (impudence Ⓣ) culot *m*; ∼**s** (before exams) trac *m*. ∼**-racking** *adj* éprouvant.

nervous *adj* nerveux; **be** *or* **feel** ∼ (afraid) avoir peur; ∼ **breakdown** dépression *f* nerveuse. **nervousness** *n* nervosité *f*; (fear) crainte *f*.

nest *n* nid *m*. ● *vi* nicher. ∼**-egg** *n* pécule *m*.

nestle *vi* se blottir.

net *n* filet *m*; (Comput) net *m*, Internet *m*. ● *vt* (*pt* **netted**) prendre au filet. ● *adj* (weight) net. ∼**ball** *n* netball *m*.

Netherlands *n* **the** ∼ les Pays-Bas *mpl*.

Netsurfer *n* Internaute *mf*.

nettle *n* ortie *f*.

network *n* réseau *m*.

neurotic *a* & *n* névrosé/-e (*m/f*).

neuter *a* & *n* neutre (*m*). ● *vt* (castrate) castrer.

neutral *adj* neutre; ∼ (**gear**) (Auto) point *m* mort.

never *adv* (ne) jamais; **he** ∼ **refuses** il ne refuse jamais; **I** ∼ **saw him** Ⓣ je ne l'ai pas vu; ∼ **again** plus jamais; ∼ **mind** (don't worry) ne vous en faites pas; (it doesn't matter) peu importe.

nevertheless *adv* néanmoins, toutefois.

new *adj* nouveau; (brand-new) neuf. ∼**-born** *adj* nouveau-né. ∼**comer** *n* nouveau venu *m*, nouvelle venue *f*.

newly *adv* nouvellement. ∼**-weds** *npl* jeunes mariés *mpl*.

news *n* nouvelle(s) *f(pl)*; (radio, press) informations *fpl*; (TV) actualités *fpl*, informations *fpl*. ∼ **agency** *n* agence *f* de presse. ∼**agent** *n* marchand/-e *m/f* de journaux. ∼**caster** *n* présentateur/-trice *m/f*. ∼**group** *n* (Internet) forum *m* de discussion. ∼**letter** *n* bulletin *m*. ∼**paper** *n* journal *m*.

new year *n* nouvel an *m*. **New Year's Day** *n* le jour de l'an. **New Year's Eve** *n* la Saint-Sylvestre.

New Zealand *n* Nouvelle-Zélande *f*.

next *adj* prochain; (adjoining) voisin; (following) suivant; ∼ **to** à côté de; ∼ **door** à côté (**to** de). ● *adv* la prochaine fois; (afterwards) ensuite. ● *n* suivant/-e *m/f*; (e-mail) message *m* suivant. ∼**-door** *adj* d'à côté. ∼ **of kin** *n* parent *m* le plus proche.

nib *n* plume *f*.

nibble *vt/i* grignoter.

nice *adj* agréable, bon; (kind) gentil; (pretty) joli; (respectable) bien *inv*; (subtle) délicat. **nicely** *adv* agréablement; gentiment; (well) bien.

nicety *n* subtilité *f*.

niche *n* (recess) niche *f*; (fig) place *f*, situation *f*.

nick *n* petite entaille *f*; **be in good/ bad** ∼ être en bon/mauvais état. ● *vt* (steal, arrest Ⓣ) piquer.

nickel *n* (metal) nickel *m*; (US) pièce *f* de cinq cents.

nickname *n* surnom *m*. ● *vt* surnommer.

nicotine *n* nicotine *f*.

niece *n* nièce *f*.

niggling *adj* (*person*) tatillon; (*detail*) insignifiant.

night *n* nuit *f*; (evening) soir *m*. ● *adj* de nuit. ∼**-cap** *n* boisson *f* (*avant d'aller se coucher*). ∼**-club** *n* boîte *f* de nuit. ∼**-dress** *n* chemise *f* de nuit. ∼**fall** *n* tombée *f* de la nuit. **nightie** *n* chemise *f* de nuit.

nightingale n rossignol m.

nightly a & adv (de) chaque nuit or soir.

night: ~**mare** n cauchemar m. ~**time** n nuit f.

nil n (Sport) zéro m. ● adj (chances, risk) nul.

nimble adj agile.

nine a & n neuf (m).

nineteen a & n dix-neuf (m).

ninety a & n quatre-vingt-dix (m).

ninth a & n neuvième (mf).

nip vt/i (pt nipped) (pinch) pincer; (rush 🔲) courir; ~ **out/back** sortir/ rentrer rapidement. ● n pincement m.

nipple n mamelon m; (of baby's bottle) tétine f.

nippy adj (-ier, -iest) (air) piquant; (car) rapide.

nitrogen n azote m.

no det aucun/-e; pas de; ~ **man** aucun homme; ~ **money/time** pas d'argent/ de temps; ~ **one** = NOBODY; ~ **smoking/entry** défense de fumer/ d'entrer; ~ **way!** 🔲 pas question! ● adv non. ● n(pl noes) non m inv.

nobility n noblesse f.

noble adj noble. ~ **man** n (pl -men) noble m.

nobody pron (ne) personne; he knows ~ il ne connaît personne. ● n nullité f.

nocturnal adj nocturne.

nod vt/i (pt nodded); ~ (one's head) faire un signe de tête; ~ **off** s'endormir. ● n signe m de tête.

noise n bruit m; make a ~ faire du bruit. **noisily** adv. bruyamment. **noisy** adj (-ier, -iest) bruyant.

no man's land n no man's land m.

nominal adj symbolique, nominal; (value) nominal.

nominate vt nommer; (put forward) proposer.

none pron aucun/-e; ~ **of us** aucun/ -e de nous; I have ~ je n'en ai pas.

non-existent adj inexistant.

nonplussed adj perplexe.

nonsense n absurdités fpl.

non-smoker n non-fumeur m.

non-stick adj antiadhésif.

non-stop adj (train, flight) direct. ● adv sans arrêt.

noodles npl nouilles fpl.

noon n midi m.

nor adv ni. ● conj (ne) non plus; ~ **shall I come** je ne viendrai pas non plus.

norm n norme f.

normal adj normal.

Norman n Normand/-e m/f. ● adj (village) normand; (arch) roman.

north n nord m. ● adj nord inv, du nord. ● adv vers le nord.

North America n Amérique f du Nord.

north-east n nord-est m.

northerly adj (wind, area) du nord; (point) au nord.

northern adj (accent) du nord; (coast) nord. **northerner** n habitant/-e m/f du nord.

northward adj (side) nord inv; (journey) vers le nord.

north-west n nord-ouest m.

Norway n Norvège f.

Norwegian n (person) Norvégien/ -ne m/f; (language) norvégien m. ● adj norvégien.

nose n nez m. ● vi ~ **about** fouiner.

nosedive n piqué m. ● vi descendre en piqué.

nostalgia n nostalgie f.

nostril n narine f; (of horse) naseau m.

nosy adj (-ier, -iest) 🔲 curieux, indiscret.

not adv (ne) pas; I do ~ **know** je ne sais pas; ~ **at all** pas du tout; ~ **yet** pas encore; I suppose ~ je suppose que non.

notably adv notamment.

notch n entaille f. ● vt ~ **up** (score) marquer.

note n note f; (banknote) billet m; (short letter) mot m. ● vt noter; (notice) remarquer. ~**book** n carnet m.

nothing pron (ne) rien; he eats ~ il ne mange rien; ~ **else** rien d'autre; ~ **much** pas grand-chose; for ~ pour rien, gratis. ● n rien m; (person) nullité f. ● adv nullement.

notice n avis m, annonce f; (poster) affiche f; (advance) ~ préavis m; at

short ~ dans des délais très brefs;
give in one's ~ donner sa démission;
take ~ faire attention (**of** à). ● *vt*
remarquer, observer. **noticeable**
adj visible. ~**-board** *n* tableau *m*
d'affichage.

notify *vt* (inform) aviser; (make known)
notifier.

notion *n* idée *f*, notion *f*.

notorious *adj* (*criminal*) notoire;
(*district*) mal famé; (*case*) tristement
célèbre.

notwithstanding *prep* malgré.
● *adv* néanmoins.

nought *n* zéro *m*.

noun *n* nom *m*.

nourish *vt* nourrir. **nourishing** *adj*
nourrissant. **nourishment** *n*
nourriture *f*.

novel *n* roman *m*. ● *adj* nouveau.
novelist *n* romancier/-ière *m*/*f*.
novelty *n* nouveauté *f*.

November *n* novembre *m*.

now *adv* maintenant. ● *conj*
maintenant que; **just** ~ maintenant;
(a moment ago) tout à l'heure; ~ **and**
again, ~ **and then** de temps à autre.

nowadays *adv* de nos jours.

nowhere *adv* nulle part.

nozzle *n* (tip) embout *m*; (of hose) jet
m.

nuclear *adj* nucléaire.

nude *adj* nu. ● *n* nu/-e *m*/*f*; **in the** ~
tout nu.

nudge *vt* pousser du coude. ● *n* coup
m de coude.

nudism *n* nudisme *m*. **nudity** *n*
nudité *f*.

nuisance *n* (thing, event) ennui *m*;
(person) peste *f*; **be a** ~ être
embêtant.

null *adj* nul.

numb *adj* engourdi (**with** par). ● *vt*
engourdir.

number *n* nombre *m*; (of ticket, house,
page) numéro *m*; (written figure) chiffre
m; **a** ~ **of people** plusieurs
personnes. ● *vt* numéroter; (count,
include) compter. ~**-plate** *n* plaque *f*
d'immatriculation.

numeral *n* chiffre *m*.

numerate *adj* qui sait compter.

numerical *adj* numérique.

numerous *adj* nombreux.

nun *n* religieuse *f*.

nurse *n* infirmier/-ière *m*/*f*; (nanny)
nurse *f*. ● *vt* soigner; (*hope*) nourrir.

nursery *n* (room) chambre *f*
d'enfants; (for plants) pépinière *f*; (**day**)
~ crèche *f*. ~ **rhyme** *n* comptine *f*.
~ **school** *n* (école) maternelle *f*.

nursing home *n* maison *f* de
retraite.

nut *n* (walnut, Brazil nut) noix *f*; (hazelnut)
noisette *f*; (peanut) cacahuète *f*; (Tech)
écrou *m*. ~**crackers** *npl* casse-noix
m inv.

nutmeg *n* muscade *f*.

nutrient *n* substance *f* nutritive.

nutritious *adj* nutritif.

nuts *adj* (crazy Ⅱ) cinglé.

nutshell *n* coquille *f* de noix; **in a** ~
en un mot.

nylon *n* nylon *m*.

oak *n* chêne *m*.

OAP *abbr* (**old-age pensioner**)
retraité/-e *m*/*f*.

oar *n* rame *f*.

oath *n* (promise) serment *m*; (swear-
word) juron *m*.

oats *npl* avoine *f*.

obedience *n* obéissance *f*.
obedient *adj* obéissant.
obediently *adv* docilement.

obese *adj* obèse.

obey *vt*/*i* obéir (à).

object¹ *n* (thing) objet *m*; (aim) but *m*;
(Gram) complément *m* d'objet; **money**
is no ~ l'argent n'est pas un
problème.

object² *vi* protester. ● *vt* ~ **that**
objecter que; ~ **to** (*behaviour*)
désapprouver; (*plan*) protester
contre. **objection** *n* objection *f*;
(drawback) inconvénient *m*.

objective *a* & *n* objectif (*m*).

obligation *n* devoir *m*.

obligatory *adj* obligatoire.

oblige *vt* obliger (**to do** à faire).

oblivion *n* oubli *m*. **oblivious** *adj* inconscient (**to, of** de).

oblong *adj* oblong. ● *n* rectangle *m*.

obnoxious *adj* odieux.

oboe *n* hautbois *m*.

obscene *adj* obscène.

obscure *adj* obscur. ● *vt* obscurcir; (conceal) cacher.

observance *n* (of law) respect *m*; (of sabbath) observance *f*. **observant** *adj* observateur.

observation *n* observation *f*.

observe *vt* observer; (remark) remarquer.

obsess *vt* obséder. **obsession** *n* obsession *f*. **obsessive** *adj* (*person*) maniaque; (*thought*) obsédant; (*illness*) obsessionnel.

obsolete *adj* dépassé.

obstacle *n* obstacle *m*.

obstinate *adj* obstiné.

obstruct *vt* (road) bloquer; (view) cacher; (*progress*) gêner. **obstruction** *n* (act) obstruction *f*; (thing) obstacle *m*; (in traffic) encombrement *m*.

obtain *vt* obtenir. ● *vi* avoir cours. **obtainable** *adj* disponible.

obvious *adj* évident. **obviously** *adv* manifestement.

occasion *n* occasion *f*; (big event) événement *m*; **on ~** à l'occasion.

occasional *adj* (*event*) qui a lieu de temps en temps; **the ~ letter** une lettre de temps en temps. **occasionally** *adv* de temps à autre.

occupation *n* (activity) occupation *f*; (job) métier *m*, profession *f*. **occupational therapy** *n* ergothérapie *f*.

occupier *n* occupant/-e *m/f*.

occupy *vi* occuper.

occur *vi* (*pt* **occurred**) se produire; (arise) se présenter; **~ to sb** venir à l'esprit de qn.

occurrence *n* (event) fait *m*; (instance) occurrence *f*.

ocean *n* océan *m*.

Oceania *n* Océanie *f*.

o'clock *adv* **it is six ~** il est six heures; **at one ~** à une heure.

October *n* octobre *m*.

octopus *n* (*pl* **~es**) pieuvre *f*.

odd *adj* bizarre; (*number*) impair; (left over) qui reste; (*sock*) dépareillé; **write the ~ article** écrire un article de temps en temps; **~ jobs** menus travaux *mpl*; **twenty ~** vingt et quelques. **oddity** *n* bizarrerie *f*.

odds *npl* chances *fpl*; (in betting) cote *f* (**on** de); **at ~** en désaccord; **it makes no ~** ça ne fait rien; **~ and ends** des petites choses.

odour, (US) **odor** *n* odeur *f*. **odourless** *adj* inodore.

....

of

⇒ For expressions such as **of course**, **consist of** ⇒**course**, **consist**.

● *preposition*

····▸ de; **a photo ~ the dog** une photo du chien; **the king ~ the beasts** le roi des animaux; (made) **~ gold** en or; **it's kind ~ you** c'est très gentil de votre part; **some ~ us** quelques-uns d'entre nous; **~ it/them** en; **have you heard ~ it?** est-ce que tu en as entendu parler?

....

off *adv* **be ~** partir, s'en aller; **I'm ~** je m'en vais; **30 metres ~** à 30 mètres; **a month ~** dans un mois. ● *adj* (*gas, water*) coupé; (*tap*) fermé; (*light, TV*) éteint; (*party, match*) annulé; (bad) (*food*) avarié; (*milk*) tourné; **Friday is my day ~** je ne travaille pas le vendredi; **25% ~** 25% de remise. ● *prep* **3 metres ~ the ground** 3 mètres (au-dessus) du sol; **just ~ the kitchen** juste à côté de la cuisine; **that is ~ the point** là n'est pas la question.

offal *n* abats *mpl*.

offence *n* (Jur) infraction *f*; **give ~ to** offenser; **take ~** s'offenser (**at** de).

offend *vt* offenser; **be ~ed** s'offenser (**at** de). ● *vi* (Jur) commettre une infraction. **offender** *n* délinquant/-e *m/f*.

offensive *adj* (*remark*) injurieux; (*language*) grossier; (*smell*) repoussant; (*weapon*) offensif. ● *n* offensive *f*.

offer *vt* (*pt* **offered**) offrir. ● *n* offre *f*; **on** ~ en promotion.

offhand *adj* désinvolte. ● *adv* à l'improviste.

office *n* bureau *m*; (*duty*) fonction *f*; **in** ~ au pouvoir. ● *adj* de bureau.

officer (*army*) officier *m*; (*police*) ~ policier *m*; (*government*) ~ fonctionnaire *mf*.

official *adj* officiel. ● *n* (civil servant) fonctionnaire *mf*; (of party, union) officiel/-le *m*/*f*; (of police, customs) agent *m*.

off: ~-**licence** *n* magasin *m* de vins et spiritueux. ~-**line** *adj* autonome; (switched off) déconnecté. ~-**load** *vt* (*stock*) écouler; (Comput) décharger. ~-**peak** *adj* (*call*) au tarif réduit; (*travel*) en période creuse. ~-**putting** *adj* rebutant. ~**set** *vt* (*pt* -**set**; *pres p* -**setting**) compenser. ~**shore** *adj* (*waters*) du large; (*funds*) hors-lieu *inv*. ~**side** *adj* (Sport) hors jeu *inv*; (Auto) du côté du conducteur. ~**spring** *n inv* progéniture *f*. ~-**white** *adj* blanc cassé *inv*.

often *adv* souvent; **how** ~ **do you meet?** vous vous voyez tous les combien?; **every so** ~ de temps en temps.

oil *n* (for lubrication, cooking) huile *f*; (for fuel) pétrole *m*; (for heating) mazout *m*. ● *vt* huiler. ~**field** *n* gisement *m* pétrolifère. ~-**painting** *n* peinture *f* à l'huile. ~**skins** *npl* ciré *m*. ~-**tanker** *n* pétrolier *m*.

oily *adj* graisseux.

ointment *n* pommade *f*.

OK, **okay** *adj* d'accord; **is it** ~ **if...?** ça va si...?; **feel** ~ aller bien.

old *adj* vieux; (*person*) vieux, âgé; (former) ancien; **how** ~ **is he?** quel âge a-t-il?; **he is eight years** ~ il a huit ans; ~**er**, ~**est** aîné. ~ **age** *n* vieillesse *f*. ~-**age pensioner** *n* retraité/-e *m*/*f*. ~-**fashioned** *adj* démodé; (person) vieux jeu *inv*. ~ **man** *n* vieillard *m*, vieux *m*. ~ **woman** *n* vieille *f*.

olive *n* olive *f*; ~ **oil** huile *f* d'olive. ● *adj* olive *inv*.

Olympic *adj* olympique. ~ **Games** *npl* Jeux *mpl* olympiques.

omelette *n* omelette *f*.

omen *n* augure *m*.

ominous *adj* (*presence, cloud*) menaçant; (*sign*) de mauvais augure.

omission *n* omission *f*. **omit** *vt* (*pt* **omitted**) omettre.

on *prep* sur; ~ **the table** sur la table; **put the key** ~ **it** mets la clé dessus; ~ **22 March** le 22 mars; ~ **Monday** lundi; ~ **TV** à la télé; ~ **video** en vidéo; **be** ~ **steroids** prendre des stéroïdes; ~ **arriving** en arrivant. ● *adj* (*TV, oven, light*) allumé; (*dishwasher, radio*) en marche; (*tap*) ouvert; (*lid*) mis; **the match is still** ~ le match aura lieu quand même; **the news is** ~ **in 10 minutes** les informations sont dans 10 minutes. ● *adv* **have sth** ~ porter qch; **20 years** ~ 20 ans plus tard; **from that day** ~ à partir de ce jour-là; **further** ~ plus loin; ~ **and off** (occasionally) de temps en temps; **go** ~ **and** ~ (*person*) parler pendant des heures.

once *adv* une fois; (formerly) autrefois. ● *conj* une fois que; **all at** ~ tout d'un coup.

oncoming *adj* (*vehicle*) qui approche.

one *det* & *n* un/-e (*m*/*f*). ● *pron* un/-e *m*/*f*; (impersonal) on; ~ **(and only)** seul (et unique); **a big** ~ un grand/une grande; **this/that** ~ celui-ci/-là, celle-ci/-là; ~ **another** l'un/-e l'autre. ~-**off** *adj* Ⓔ unique, exceptionnel. ~-**self** *pron* soi-même; (reflexive) se. ~-**way** *adj* (*street*) à sens unique; (*ticket*) simple.

ongoing *adj* (*process*) continu; **be** ~ être en cours.

onion *n* oignon *m*.

onlooker *n* spectateur/-trice *m*/*f*.

only *adj* seul; ~ **son** fils unique. ● *adv* & *conj* seulement; **he is** ~ **six** il n'a que six ans; ~ **too** extrêmement.

onset *n* début *m*.

onward(s) *adv* en avant.

open *adj* ouvert; (*view*) dégagé; (free to all) public; (undisguised) manifeste; (*question*) en attente; **in the** ~ **air** en plein air. ● *vt*/*i* (*door*) (s')ouvrir;

(*shop*, *play*) ouvrir; ~ **out** *or* **up** (s') ouvrir. ~**-ended** *adj* (*stay*) de durée indéterminée; (*debate*, *question*) ouvert. ~**-heart** *adj* (*surgery*) à cœur ouvert.

opening *n* (of book) début *m*; (of exhibition, shop) ouverture *f*; (of film) première *f*; (in market) débouché *m*; (job) poste *m* (disponible).

open: ~**-minded** *adj* be ~**-minded** avoir l'esprit ouvert. ~**-plan** *adj* paysagé.

opera *n* opéra *m*.

operate *vt/i* opérer; (Tech) (faire) fonctionner; ~ **on** (Med) opérer; **operating theatre** salle *f* d'opération.

operation *n* opération *f*; **have an** ~ se faire opérer; **in** ~ (*plan*) en vigueur; (*mine*) en service.

operative *n* employé/-e *m/f*. ● *adj* (*law*) en vigueur.

operator *n* opérateur/-trice *m/f*; (telephonist) standardiste *mf*.

opinion *n* opinion *f*, avis *m*. **opinionated** *adj* qui a des avis sur tout.

opponent *n* adversaire *mf*.

opportunity *n* occasion *f* (**to do** de faire).

oppose *vt* s'opposer à; **as** ~**d to** par opposition à. **opposing** *adj* opposé.

opposite *adj* (*direction*, *side*) opposé; (*building*) d'en face. ● *n* contraire *m*. ● *adv* en face. ● *prep* ~ (**to**) en face de.

opposition *n* opposition *f*.

oppress *vt* opprimer. **oppressive** *adj* (*cruel*) oppressif; (*heat*) oppressant.

opt *vi* ~ **for** opter pour; ~ **out** refuser de participer (**of** à); ~ **to do** choisir de faire.

optical *adj* optique. ~ **illusion** *n* illusion *f* d'optique. ~ **scanner** *n* lecteur *m* optique.

optician *n* opticien/-ne *m/f*.

optimism *n* optimisme *m*. **optimist** *n* optimiste *mf*. **optimistic** *adj* optimiste.

option *n* option *f*; (choice) choix *m*.

optional *adj* facultatif; ~ **extras** accessoires *mpl* en option.

or *conj* ou; (with negative) ni.

oral *n* & *a* oral (*m*).

orange *n* (fruit) orange *f*; (*colour*) orange *m*. ● *adj* (colour) orange *inv*.

orbit *n* orbite *f*. ● *vt* décrire une orbite autour de.

orchard *n* verger *m*.

orchestra *n* orchestre *m*.

orchid *n* orchidée *f*.

ordeal *n* épreuve *f*.

order *n* ordre *m*; (Comm) commande *f*; **in** ~ (tidy) en ordre; (*document*) en règle; **in** ~ **that** pour que; **in** ~ **to** pour. ● *vt* ordonner; (*goods*) commander; ~ **sb to** ordonner à qn de.

orderly *adj* (tidy) ordonné; (not unruly) discipliné. ● *n* (Mil) planton *m*; (Med) aide-soignant/-e *m/f*.

ordinary *adj* (usual) ordinaire; (average) moyen.

ore *n* minerai *m*.

organ *n* organe *m*; (Mus) orgue *m*.

organic *adj* organique; (*produce*) biologique.

organization *n* organisation *f*.

organize *vt* organiser.

organizer *n* organisateur/-trice *m/f*; **electronic** ~ agenda *m* électronique.

orgasm *n* orgasme *m*.

Orient *n* **the** ~ l'Orient *m*. **oriental** *adj* oriental.

origin *n* origine *f*.

original *adj* original; (*inhabitant*) premier; (*member*) originaire. **originality** *n* originalité *f*. **originally** *adv* (at the outset) à l'origine.

originate *vi* (plan) prendre naissance; ~ **from** provenir de; (person) venir de. ● *vt* être l'auteur de. **originator** *n* (of idea) auteur *m*; (of invention) créateur/-trice *m/f*.

ornament *n* (decoration) ornement *m*; (object) objet *m* décoratif.

orphan *n* orphelin/-e *m/f*. ● *vt* rendre orphelin. **orphanage** *n* orphelinat *m*.

orthopaedic *adj* orthopédique.

ostentatious *adj* tape-à-l'œil *inv*.

osteopath *n* ostéopathe *mf*.

ostrich *n* autruche *f*.

other *adj* autre; **the** ~ **one** l'autre *mf*. ● *n* & *pron* autre *mf*; (some) ~**s**

d'autres. ● *adv* ~ **than** (apart from) à part; (otherwise than) autrement que. **otherwise** *adv* autrement.

otter *n* loutre *f*.

ouch *interj* aïe!

ought *v aux* devoir; **you ~ to stay** vous devriez rester; **he ~ to succeed** il devrait réussir; **I ~ to have done it** j'aurais dû le faire.

ounce *n* once *f* (= 28.35 g).

our *adj* notre, *pl* nos.

ours *poss* le *or* la nôtre, les nôtres.

ourselves *pron* (reflexive) nous; (emphatic) nous-mêmes; (after preposition) **for ~** pour nous, pour nous-mêmes.

out *adv* dehors; **he's ~** il est sorti; **further ~** plus loin; **be ~** (*book*) être publié; (*light*) être éteint; (*sun*) briller; (*flower*) être épanoui; (*tide*) être bas; (*player*) être éliminé; **~ of** hors de; **go/walk/get ~ of** sortir de; **~ of pity** par pitié; **made ~ of** fait de; **5 ~ of 6** 5 sur 6. **~break** *n* (of war) déclenchement *m*; (of violence, boils) éruption *f*. **~burst** *n* explosion *f*. **~cast** *n* paria *m*. **~class** *vt* surclasser. **~come** *n* résultat *m*. **~cry** *n* tollé *m*. **~dated** *adj* démodé. **~door** *adj* (*activity*) de plein air; (*pool*) en plein air. **~doors** *adv* dehors.

outer *adj* extérieur; **~ space** espace *m* extra-atmosphérique.

outfit *n* (clothes) tenue *f*.

outgoing *adj* (*minister, tenant*) sortant; (sociable) ouvert. **outgoings** *npl* dépenses *fpl*.

outgrow *vt* (*pt* -**grew**; *pp* -**grown**) (*clothes*) devenir trop grand pour; (*habit*) dépasser.

outing *n* sortie *f*.

outlaw *n* hors-la-loi *m inv*. ● *vt* déclarer illégal.

outlet *n* (for water, gas) tuyau *m* de sortie; (for goods) débouché *m*; (for feelings) exutoire *m*.

outline *n* contour *m*; (of plan) grandes lignes *fpl*; (of essay) plan *m*. ● *vt* tracer le contour de; (summarize) exposer brièvement.

out: **~live** *vt* survivre à. **~look** *n* perspective *f*. **~number** *vt* surpasser en nombre. **~ of date** *adj* démodé; (expired) périmé. **~ of hand** *adj* incontrôlable. **~ of order** *adj* en panne. **~ of work** *adj* sans travail. **~patient** *n* malade *mf* externe.

output *n* rendement *m*; (Comput) sortie *f*. ● *vt/i* (Comput) sortir.

outrage *n* (anger) indignation *f*; (atrocity) attentat *m*; (scandal) outrage *m*. ● *vt* (*morals*) outrager; (*person*) scandaliser. **outrageous** *adj* scandaleux.

outright *adv* (completely) catégoriquement; (killed) sur le coup. ● *adj* (majority) absolu; (ban) catégorique; (hostility) pur et simple.

outset *n* début *m*.

outside *n* extérieur *m*. ● *adv* dehors. ● *prep* en dehors de; (in front of) devant. ● *adj* extérieur. **outsider** *n* étranger/-ère *m/f*; (Sport) outsider *m*.

out: **~skirts** *npl* périphérie *f*. **~spoken** *adj* franc. **~standing** *adj* exceptionnel; (not settled) en suspens.

outward *a & adv* vers l'extérieur; (*sign*) extérieur; (*journey*) d'aller. **outwards** *adv* vers l'extérieur.

oval *n & a* ovale (*m*).

ovary *n* ovaire *m*.

oven *n* four *m*.

over *prep* (across) par-dessus; (above) au-dessus de; (covering) sur; (more than) plus de; **it's ~ the road** c'est de l'autre côté de la rue; **~ here/there** par ici/là; **children ~ six** les enfants de plus de six ans; **~ the weekend** pendant le week-end; **all ~ the house** partout dans la maison. ● *a, adv* (*term*) terminé; (*war*) fini; **get sth ~ with** en finir avec qch; **ask sb ~** inviter qn; **~ and ~ (again)** à plusieurs reprises; **five times ~** cinq fois de suite.

overall *adj* global, d'ensemble; (*length*) total. ● *adv* globalement.

overalls *npl* combinaison *f*.

over: **~board** *adv* par-dessus bord. **~cast** *adj* couvert. **~charge** *vt* faire payer trop cher à. **~coat** *n* pardessus *m*.

overcome *vt* (*pt* **-came**; *pp* **-come**) (*enemy*) vaincre; (*difficulty, fear*) surmonter; ~ **by** accablé de.

overcrowded *adj* bondé; (*country*) surpeuplé.

overdo *vt* (*pt* **-did**; *pp* **-done**) (Culin) trop cuire; ~ **it** (overwork) en faire trop.

over: ~**dose** *n* surdose *f*, overdose *f*. ~**draft** *n* découvert *m*. ~**draw** *vt* (*pt* **-drew**; *pp* **-drawn**) faire un découvert sur. ~**due** *adj* en retard; (*bill*) impayé.

overflow[1] *vi* déborder.

overflow[2] *n* (outlet) trop-plein *m*.

overhaul *vt* réviser.

overhead[1] *adv* au-dessus; (in sky) dans le ciel.

overhead[2] *adj* aérien; ~ **projector** rétroprojecteur *m*. **overheads** *npl* frais *mpl* généraux.

over: ~**hear** *vt* (*pt* **-heard**) entendre par hasard. ~**lap** *vt/i* (*pt* **-lapped**) (se) chevaucher. ~**leaf** *adv* au verso. ~**load** *vt* surcharger. ~**look** *vt* (*window*) donner sur; (miss) ne pas voir.

overnight[1] *adv* dans la nuit; (instantly: fig) du jour au lendemain.

overnight[2] *adj* (*train*) de nuit; (*stay*) d'une nuit; (fig) soudain.

over: ~**power** *vt* (*thief*) maîtriser; (*army*) vaincre; (fig) accabler. ~**priced** *adj* trop cher. ~**rate** *vt* surestimer. ~**react** *vi* réagir de façon excessive. ~**riding** *adj* (*consideration*) numéro un; (*importance*) primordial. ~**rule** *vt* (*decision*) annuler.

overrun *vt* (*pt* **-ran**; *pp* **-run**; *pres p* **-running**) (*country*) envahir; (*budget*) dépasser. ● *vi* (meeting) durer plus longtemps que prévu.

overseas *adj* étranger. ● *adv* outremer, à l'étranger.

over: ~**see** *vt* (*pt* **-saw**; *pp* **-seen**) surveiller. ~**sight** *n* omission *f*. ~**sleep** *vi* (*pt* **-slept**) se réveiller trop tard. ~**take** *vt/i* (*pt* **-took**; *pp* **-taken**) dépasser; (fig) frapper. ~**time** *n* heures *fpl* supplémentaires. ~**turn** *vt/i* (se) renverser. ~**weight** *adj* trop gros.

overwhelm *vt* (*enemy*) écraser; (*shame*) accabler. **overwhelmed** *adj* (with offers, calls) submergé (**with, by** de); (with shame, work) accablé; (by sight) ébloui. **overwhelming** *adj* (*heat, grief*) accablant; (*defeat, victory*) écrasant; (*urge*) irrésistible.

overwork *vt/i* (se) surmener. ● *n* surmenage *m*.

owe *vt* devoir. **owing** *adj* dû; **owing to** en raison de.

owl *n* hibou *m*.

own *adj* propre. ● *pron* my ~ le mien, la mienne; **a house of one's** ~ sa propre maison; **on one's** ~ tout seul. ● *vt* posséder; ~ **up (to)** avouer. **owner** *n* propriétaire *mf*. **ownership** *n* propriété *f*; (of land) possession *f*.

oxygen *n* oxygène *m*.

oyster *n* huître *f*.

ozone *n* ozone *m*; ~ **layer** couche *f* d'ozone.

Pp

PA *abbr* ⇒PERSONAL ASSISTANT.

pace *n* pas *m*; (speed) allure *f*; **keep** ~ **with** suivre. ● *vt* (*room*) arpenter. ● *vi* ~ **(up and down)** faire les cent pas.

Pacific *n* ~ **(Ocean)** océan *m* Pacifique.

pack *n* paquet *m*; (Mil) sac *m*; (of hounds) meute *f*; (of thieves) bande *f*; (of lies) tissu *m*. ● *vt* (into case) mettre dans une valise; (into box, crate) emballer; (for sale) conditionner; (*crowd*) remplir complètement; ~ **one's suitcase** faire ses valises. ● *vi* faire ses valises; ~ **into** (cram) s'entasser dans; ~ **off** expédier; **send** ~**ing** envoyer promener.

package *n* paquet *m*; (Comput) progiciel *m*; ~ **deal** offre *f* globale; ~ **holiday** voyage *m* organisé. ● *vt* empaqueter.

packed *adj* (crowded) bondé; ~ **lunch** repas *m* froid.

packet n paquet m.

packing n (action, material) emballage m.

pad n (of paper) bloc m; (to protect) protection f; (for ink) tampon m; (launch) ~ rampe f de lancement. ● vt (pt **padded**) rembourrer; (text: fig) délayer. ● vi (pt **padded**) (walk) marcher à pas feutrés. **padding** n rembourrage m.

paddle n pagaie f. ● vt ~ **a canoe** pagayer. ● vi patauger.

padlock n cadenas m. ● vt cadenasser.

paediatrician n pédiatre mf.

pagan a & n païen/-ne (m/f).

page n (of book) page f. ● vt (on pager) rechercher; (over speaker) faire appeler. **pager** n radiomessageur m.

pain n douleur f; ~s efforts mpl; be in ~ souffrir; take ~s to se donner du mal pour. ● vt (grieve) peiner. **painful** adj douloureux; (laborious) pénible. ~**killer** n analgésique m. **painless** adj (operation) indolore; (death) sans souffrance; (trouble-free) sans peine. **painstaking** adj minutieux.

paint n peinture f; ~s (in tube, box) couleurs fpl. ● vt/i peindre. ~**brush** n pinceau m. **painter** n peintre m. **painting** n peinture f. ~**work** n peintures fpl.

pair n paire f; (of people) couple m; a ~ **of trousers** un pantalon. ● vi ~ **off** former un couple.

pajamas npl (US) = PYJAMAS.

Pakistan n Pakistan m.

palace n palais m.

palatable adj (food) savoureux; (solution) acceptable. **palate** n palais m.

pale adj pâle. ● vi pâlir.

Palestine n Palestine f.

pallid adj pâle.

palm n (of hand) paume f; (tree) palmier m; (symbol) palme f. □ ~ **off** 🗊 ~ sth off as faire passer qch pour; ~ sth off on sb refiler qch à qn 🗊.

palpitate vi palpiter.

paltry adj (**-ier**, **-iest**) dérisoire, piètre.

pamper vt choyer.

pamphlet n brochure f.

pan n casserole f; (for frying) poêle f.

pancake n crêpe f.

pandemonium n tohu-bohu m.

pander vi ~ **to** (person, taste) flatter bassement.

pane n carreau m, vitre f.

panel n (of door) panneau m; (of experts, judges) commission f; (on discussion programme) invités mpl; (instrument) ~ tableau m de bord.

pang n serrement m au cœur; ~s of conscience remords mpl.

panic n panique f. ● vt/i (pt **panicked**) (s')affoler. ~**-stricken** adj pris de panique, affolé.

pansy n (Bot) pensée f.

pant vi haleter.

panther n panthère f.

pantomime n (show) spectacle m de Noël; (mime) mime m.

pantry n garde-manger m inv.

pants npl (underwear) slip m; (trousers: US) pantalon m.

paper n papier m; (newspaper) journal m; (exam) épreuve f; (essay) exposé m; (wallpaper) papier m peint; (identity) ~s papiers mpl (d'identité); on ~ par écrit. ● vt (room) tapisser. ~**back** n livre m de poche. ~**clip** n trombone m. ~ **feed tray** n (Comput) bac m d'alimentation en papier. ~**work** n (work) travail m administratif; (documentation) documents mpl.

par n be below ~ ne pas être en forme; on a ~ with (performance) comparable à; (person) l'égal de; (golf) par m.

parachute n parachute m. ● vi descendre en parachute.

parade n (procession) parade f; (Mil) défilé m. ● vi défiler. ● vt faire étalage de.

paradise n paradis m.

paradox n paradoxe m.

paraffin n pétrole m (lampant); (wax) paraffine f.

paragliding n parapente m.

paragon n modèle m.

paragraph n paragraphe m.

parallel *adj* parallèle. ● *n* parallèle *m*; (maths) parallèle *f*.

paralyse *vt* paralyser. **paralysis** *n* paralysie *f*.

paramedic *n* auxiliaire *mf* médical/-e.

paramount *adj* suprême.

paranoia *n* paranoïa *f*. **paranoid** *adj* paranoïaque; (Psych) paranoïde.

paraphernalia *n* attirail *m*.

parasol *n* ombrelle *f*; (on table, at beach) parasol *m*.

paratrooper *n* (Mil) parachutiste *mf*.

parcel *n* paquet *m*.

parchment *n* parchemin *m*.

pardon *n* pardon *m*; (Jur) grâce *f*; I beg your ~ je vous demande pardon. ● *vt* (*pt* **pardoned**) pardonner (**sb for sth** qch à qn); (Jur) gracier.

parent *n* parent *m*.

parenthesis *n* (*pl* **-theses**) parenthèse *f*.

parenthood *n* (fatherhood) paternité *f*; (motherhood) maternité *f*.

Paris *n* Paris.

parish *n* (Relig) paroisse *f*; (municipal) commune *f*.

park *n* parc *m*. ● *vt/i* (se) garer; (remain parked) stationner. ~ **and ride** *n* parc *m* relais.

parking *n* stationnement *m*; **no** ~ stationnement interdit. ~**-lot** *n* (US) parking *m*. ~**-meter** *n* parcmètre *m*. ~ **ticket** *n* (fine) contravention *f*, PV *m* 🗊.

parliament *n* parlement *m*. **parliamentary** *adj* parlementaire.

parlour, (US) **parlor** *n* salon *m*.

parody *n* parodie *f*. ● *vt* parodier.

parole *n* **on** ~ en liberté conditionnelle.

parrot *n* perroquet *m*.

parry *vt* (Sport) parer; (*question*) éluder. ● *n* parade *f*.

parsley *n* persil *m*.

parsnip *n* panais *m*.

part *n* partie *f*; (of serial) épisode *m*; (of machine) pièce *f*; (Theat) rôle *m*; (side in dispute) parti *m*; **in** ~ en partie; **on the** ~ **of** de la part de; **take** ~ **in** participer à. ● *adj* partiel. ● *adv* en partie. ● *vt/i* (separate) (se) séparer; ~ **with** se séparer de.

part-exchange *n* reprise *f*; **take sth in** ~ reprendre qch.

partial *adj* partiel; (biased) partial; **be** ~ **to** avoir un faible pour.

participant *n* participant/-e *m/f*. **participate** *vi* participer (**in** à). **participation** *n* participation *f*.

participle *n* participe *m*.

particular *n* détail *m*; ~**s** détails *mpl*; **in** ~ en particulier. ● *adj* particulier; (fussy) difficile; (careful) méticuleux; **that** ~ **man** cet homme-là. **particularly** *adv* particulièrement.

parting *n* séparation *f*; (in hair) raie *f*. ● *adj* d'adieu.

partition *n* (of room) cloison *f*; (Pol) partition *f*. ● *vt* (*room*) cloisonner; (*country*) partager.

partly *adv* en partie.

partner *n* (professional) associé/-e *m/f*; (economic, sporting) partenaire *mf*; (spouse) époux/-se *m/f*; (unmarried) partenaire *mf*. **partnership** *n* association *f*.

partridge *n* perdrix *f*.

part-time *a* & *adv* à temps partiel.

party *n* fête *f*; (formal) réception *f*; (group) groupe *m*; (Pol) parti *m*; (Jur) partie *f*.

pass *vt/i* (*pt* **passed**) passer; (overtake) dépasser; (in exam) réussir; (approve) (*candidate*) admettre; (*invoice*) approuver; (*remark*) faire; (*judgement*) prononcer; (*law, bill*) adopter; ~ (**by**) (*building*) passer devant; (*person*) croiser. ● *n* (permit) laisser-passer *m inv*; (ticket) carte *f* d'abonnement; (Geog) col *m*; (Sport) passe *f*; ~ (**mark**) (in exam) moyenne *f*. □ ~ **away** mourir; ~ **out** (faint) s'évanouir; ~ **sth out** distribuer qch; ~ **over** (overlook) délaisser; ~ **up** (forego) laisser passer.

passage *n* (way through, text) passage *m*; (voyage) traversée *f*; (corridor) couloir *m*.

passenger *n* (in car, plane, ship) passager/-ère *m/f*; (in train, bus, tube) voyageur/-euse *m/f*.

passer-by *n* (*pl* **passers-by**) passant/-e *m/f*.

passing adj (motorist) qui passe; (whim) passager; (reference) en passant.

passion n passion f. **passionate** adj passionné.

passive adj passif.

passport n passeport m.

password n mot m de passe.

past adj (times, problems) passé; (president) ancien; **the ~ months** ces derniers mois. ● n passé m. ● prep (beyond) après; **walk/go ~ sth** passer devant qch; **10 ~ 6** six heures dix; **it's ~ 11** il est 11 heures passées. ● adv go/walk ~ passer.

pasta n pâtes fpl (alimentaires).

paste n (glue) colle f; (dough) pâte f; (of fish, meat) pâté m; (jewellery) strass m. ● vt coller.

pasteurize vt pasteuriser.

pastime n passe-temps m inv.

pastry n (dough) pâte f; (tart) pâtisserie f.

pat vt (pt **patted**) tapoter. ● n petite tape f.

patch n pièce f; (over eye) bandeau m; (spot) tache f; (of snow, ice) plaque f; (of vegetables) carré m; **bad ~** période f difficile. □ ~ **up** (trousers) rapiécer; (quarrel) résoudre.

patent adj (obvious) manifeste; (patented) breveté; **~ leather** cuir m verni. ● n brevet m. ● vt faire breveter.

path n (pl **-s**) sentier m, chemin m; (in park) allée f; (of rocket) trajectoire f.

pathetic adj misérable; (bad 🄸) lamentable.

patience n patience f.

patient adj patient. ● n patient/-e m/f. **patiently** adv patiemment.

patriotic adj patriotique; (person) patriote.

patrol n patrouille f; **~ car** voiture f de police. ● vt/i patrouiller (dans).

patron n (of the arts) mécène m; (customer) client/-e m/f. **patronage** n clientèle f; (support) patronage m.

patronize vt (person) traiter avec condescendance; (establishment) fréquenter.

patter n (of steps) bruit m; (of rain) crépitement m.

pattern n motif m, dessin m; (for sewing) patron m; (for knitting) modèle m.

paunch n ventre m.

pause n pause f. ● vi faire une pause; (hesitate) hésiter.

pave vt paver; **~ the way** ouvrir la voie (**for** à).

pavement n trottoir m; (US) chaussée f.

paving stone n pavé m.

paw n patte f. ● vt (animal) donner des coups de patte à; (touch 🄸) peloter 🄸.

pawn n pion m. ● vt mettre en gage. **~broker** n prêteur/-euse m/f sur gages. **~-shop** n mont-de-piété m.

pay vt (pt **paid**) payer; (interest) rapporter; (compliment, attention) faire; (visit, homage) rendre. ● vi payer; (business) rapporter; **~ for sth** payer qch. ● n salaire m; **~ rise** augmentation f (de salaire). □ ~ **back** rembourser; **~ in** déposer; **~ off** (loan) rembourser; (worker) congédier; (succeed) être payant; **~ out** payer, débourser.

payable adj payable; **~ to** (cheque) à l'ordre de.

payment n paiement m; (regular) versement m; (reward) récompense f.

payroll n fichier m des salaires; **be on the ~ of** être employé par.

PC abbr ⇒PERSONAL COMPUTER.

PE abbr (**physical education**) éducation f physique, EPS f.

pea n (petit) pois m.

peace n paix f; **~ of mind** tranquillité f d'esprit. **peaceful** adj (tranquil) paisible; (peaceable) pacifique.

peach n pêche f.

peacock n paon m.

peak n (of mountain) pic m; (of cap) visière f; (maximum) maximum m; (on graph) sommet m; (of career) apogée m; (of fitness) meilleur m; **~ hours** heures fpl de pointe.

peal n (of bells) carillon m; (of laughter) éclat m.

peanut n cacahuète f; **~s** (money 🅇) clopinettes fpl 🄸.

pear n poire f.

pearl n perle f.

peasant n paysan/-ne m/f.

peat n tourbe f.

pebble n caillou m; (on beach) galet m.

peck vt/i (food) picorer; (attack) donner des coups de bec (à). ● n coup m de bec; **a ~ on the cheek** une bise.

peckish adj be ~ 🔲 avoir faim.

peculiar adj (odd) bizarre; (special) particulier (to à). **peculiarity** n bizarrerie f.

pedal n pédale f. ● vi pédaler.

pedantic adj pédant.

peddle vt colporter; (drugs) faire du trafic de.

pedestrian n piéton m. ● adj (precinct, street) piétonnier; (fig) prosaïque; ~ **crossing** passage m pour piétons.

pedigree n (of animal) pedigree m; (of person) ascendance f. ● adj (dog) de pure race.

pee vi 🔲 faire pipi 🔲.

peek vi & n = PEEP.

peel n (on fruit) peau m; (removed) épluchures fpl. ● vt (fruit, vegetables) éplucher; (prawn) décortiquer. ● vi (of skin) peler; (of paint) s'écailler.

peep vi jeter un coup d'œil (furtif) (at à). ● n coup m d'œil (furtif). ~**hole** n judas m.

peer vi ~ (at) regarder fixement. ● n (equal, noble) pair m; (contemporary) personne f de la même génération. **peerage** n pairie f.

peg n (for clothes) pince f à linge; (to hang coats) patère f; (for tent) piquet m. ● vt (pt **pegged**) (clothes) accrocher avec des pinces; (prices) indexer.

pejorative adj péjoratif.

pelican n pélican m; ~ **crossing** passage m pour piétons.

pellet n (round mass) boulette f; (for gun) plomb m.

pelt vt bombarder (with de). ● n (skin) peau f.

pelvis n (Anat) bassin m.

pen n stylo m; (for sheep) enclos m; (for baby, cattle) parc m.

penal adj pénal. **penalize** vt pénaliser.

penalty n peine f; (fine) amende f; (in football) penalty m.

penance n pénitence f.

pence ⇒PENNY.

pencil n crayon m. ● vt (pt **pencilled**) crayonner; ~ **in** noter provisoirement. ~**-sharpener** n taille-crayons m inv.

pending adj (matter) en souffrance; (Jur) en instance. ● prep (until) en attendant.

penetrate vt pénétrer; (silence, defences) percer; (organization) infiltrer. ● vi pénétrer. **penetrating** adj pénétrant.

pen-friend n correspondant/-e m/f.

penguin n manchot m, pingouin m.

pen: ~**knife** n (pl **-knives**) canif m. ~**name** n pseudonyme m.

penniless adj sans le sou.

penny n (pl **pennies** or **pence**) (unit of currency) penny m; (small amount) centime m.

pension n (from state) pension f; (from employer) retraite f; ~ **scheme** plan m de retraite. ● vt ~ **off** mettre à la retraite. **pensioner** n retraité/-e m/f.

pensive adj songeur.

penthouse n appartement m de luxe (au dernier étage).

penultimate adj avant-dernier.

people npl gens mpl, personnes fpl; English ~ les Anglais mpl; ~ **say** on dit. ● n peuple m. ● vt peupler. ~ **carrier** n monospace m.

pepper n poivre m; (vegetable) poivron m. ● vt (Culin) poivrer.

peppermint n (plant) menthe f poivrée; (sweet) bonbon m à la menthe.

per prep par; ~ **annum** par an; ~ **cent** pour cent; ~ **kilo** le kilo; **ten km** ~ **hour** dix km à l'heure.

percentage n pourcentage m.

perception n perception f. **perceptive** adj perspicace.

perch n (of bird) perchoir m. ● vi (se) percher.

perennial adj perpétuel; (plant) vivace.

perfect[1] vt perfectionner.

perfect² adj parfait. ● n (Ling)
parfait m. **perfectly** adv
parfaitement.

perfection n perfection f; **to ~** à la
perfection.

perforate vt perforer.

perform vt (task) exécuter;
(function) remplir; (operation)
procéder à; (play) jouer; (song)
chanter. ● vi (actor, musician, team)
jouer; **~ well/badly** (candidate,
business) avoir de bons/de mauvais
résultats. **performance** n
interprétation f; (of car, team)
performance f; (show) représentation
f; (fuss) histoire f. **performer** n
artiste mf.

perfume n parfum m.

perhaps adv peut-être.

peril n péril m. **perilous** adj
périlleux.

perimeter n périmètre m.

period n période f; (era) époque f;
(lesson) cours m; (Gram) point m; (Med)
règles fpl. ● adj d'époque.
periodical n périodique m.

peripheral adj (vision, suburb)
périphérique; (issue) annexe. ● n
(Comput) périphérique m.

perish vi périr; (rubber) se
détériorer.

perjury n faux témoignage m.

perk n Ⓑ avantage m. ● vt/i **~ up**
Ⓑ (se) remonter. **perky** adj Ⓑ gai.

perm n permanente f. ● vt **have
one's hair ~ed** se faire faire une
permanente.

permanent adj permanent.
permanently adv (happy) en
permanence; (employed) de façon
permanente.

permissible adj permis.

permission n permission f.

permissive adj libéral; (pej)
permissif.

permit¹ vt (pt **permitted**)
permettre (**sb to** à qn de), autoriser
(**sb to** qn à).

permit² n permis m.

perpendicular adj
perpendiculaire.

perpetrator n auteur m.

perpetuate vt perpétuer.

perplexed adj perplexe.

persecute vt persécuter.

perseverance n persévérance f.
persevere vi persévérer.

persist vi persister (**in doing** à
faire). **persistence** n persistance f.
persistent adj (cough, snow)
persistant; (obstinate) obstiné; (noise,
pressure) continuel.

person n personne f; **in ~** en
personne.

personal adj (life, problem, opinion)
personnel; (safety, freedom,
insurance) individuel. **~ ad** n petite
annonce f. **~ assistant** n
secrétaire mf de direction. **~
computer** n ordinateur m
(personnel), micro-ordinateur m.

personality n personnalité f; (star)
vedette f.

personal: ~ organizer n agenda
m. **~ stereo** n baladeur m.

personnel n personnel m.

perspiration n (sweat) sueur f;
(sweating) transpiration f. **perspire**
vi transpirer.

persuade vt persuader (**to** de).
persuasion n persuasion f.
persuasive adj persuasif.

pertinent adj pertinent.

perturb vt troubler.

Peru n Pérou m.

pervasive adj (smell) pénétrant;
(feeling) envahissant.

perverse adj (desire) pervers;
(refusal, attitude) illogique.
perversion n perversion f.

pervert¹ vt (truth) travestir; (values)
fausser; (justice) entraver.

pervert² n pervers/-e m/f.

pessimist n pessimiste mf.
pessimistic adj pessimiste.

pest n (insect) insecte m nuisible;
(animal) animal m nuisible; (person Ⓑ)
enquiquineur/-euse m/f Ⓑ.

pester vt harceler.

pet n animal m de compagnie;
(favourite) chouchou/-te m/f. ● adj
(theory, charity) favori; **~ hate** bête f
noire; **~ name** petit nom m. ● vt (pt
petted) caresser; (spoil) chouchouter
Ⓑ.

petal n pétale m.

peter *vi* ~ **out** (*conversation*) tarir; (*supplies*) s'épuiser.

petite *adj* (*woman*) menue.

petition *n* pétition *f*. ● *vt* adresser une pétition à.

petrol *n* essence *f*. ~ **bomb** *n* cocktail *m* molotov. ~ **station** *n* station-service *f*. ~ **tank** *n* réservoir *m* d'essence.

petticoat *n* jupon *m*.

petty *adj* (**-ier, -iest**) (minor) petit; (mean) mesquin; ~ **cash** petite caisse *f*.

pew *n* banc *m* (d'église).

pharmacist *n* pharmacien/-ne *m/f*. **pharmacy** *n* pharmacie *f*.

phase *n* phase *f*. ● *vt* ~ **in/out** introduire/supprimer peu à peu.

PhD *abbr* (**Doctor of Philosophy**) doctorat *m*.

pheasant *n* faisan/-e *m/f*.

phenomenon *n* (*pl* **-ena**) phénomène *m*.

phew *interj* ouf.

philosopher *n* philosophe *mf*. **philosophical** *adj* philosophique; (resigned) philosophe. **philosophy** *n* philosophie *f*.

phlegm *n* (Med) mucosité *f*.

phobia *n* phobie *f*.

phone *n* téléphone *m*; **on the** ~ au téléphone. ● *vt* (person) téléphoner à; ~ **England** téléphoner en Angleterre. ● *vi* téléphoner; ~ **back** rappeler. ~ **book** *n* annuaire *m*. ~ **booth**, ~ **box** *n* cabine *f* téléphonique. ~ **call** *n* coup *m* de fil 🇬🇧. ~ **card** *n* télécarte *f*. ~**-in** *n* émission *f* à ligne ouverte. ~ **number** *n* numéro *m* de téléphone.

phonetic *adj* phonétique.

phoney *adj* (**-ier, -iest**) 🇬🇧 faux. ● *n* 🇬🇧 (person) charlatan *m*; **it's a** ~ c'est un faux.

photocopier *n* photocopieuse *f*.

photocopy *n* photocopie *f*. ● *vt* photocopier.

photograph *n* photographie *f*. ● *vt* photographier. **photographer** *n* photographe *mf*.

phrase *n* expression *f*; (idiom) locution *f*. ● *vt* exprimer, formuler. ~**-book** *n* guide *m* de conversation.

physical *adj* physique.

physicist *n* physicien/-ne *m/f*.

physics *n* physique *f*.

physiotherapist *n* kinésithérapeute *mf*.

physiotherapy *n* kinésithérapie *f*.

physique *n* physique *m*.

piano *n* piano *m*.

pick *n* choix *m*; (best) meilleur/-e *m/f*; (tool) pioche *f*. ● *vt* choisir; (*flower*) cueillir; (*lock*) crocheter; ~ **a quarrel with** chercher querelle à; ~ **one's nose** se curer le nez. □ ~ **on** harceler; ~ **out** choisir; (identify) distinguer; ~ **up** *vt* ramasser; (*sth fallen*) relever; (*weight*) soulever; (*habit, passenger, speed*) prendre; (learn) apprendre; *vi* s'améliorer.

pickaxe *n* pioche *f*.

picket *n* (striker) gréviste *mf*; (stake) piquet *m*; ~ (**line**) piquet *m* de grève. ● *vt* (*pt* **picketed**) installer un piquet de grève devant.

pickle *n* conserves *fpl* au vinaigre; (gherkin) cornichon *m*. ● *vt* conserver dans du vinaigre.

pick-up *n* (stylus-holder) lecteur *m*; (on guitar) capteur *m*; (collection) ramassage *m*; (improvement) reprise *f*.

picnic *n* pique-nique *m*. ● *vi* (*pt* **picnicked**) pique-niquer.

pictorial *adj* (*magazine*) illustré; (*record*) graphique.

picture *n* image *f*; (painting) tableau *m*; (photograph) photo *f*; (film) film *m*; (fig) description *f*; **the ~s** le cinéma. ● *vt* s'imaginer; **be ~d** (shown) être représenté.

picturesque *adj* pittoresque.

pie *n* (sweet) tarte *f*; (savoury) tourte *f*.

piece *n* morceau *m*; (of string, ribbon) bout *m*; (of currency, machine) pièce *f*; **a** ~ **of advice/furniture** un conseil/meuble; **go to ~s** (fig) s'effondrer; **take to ~s** démonter.

pier *n* jetée *f*.

pierce *vt* percer.

pig *n* porc *m*, cochon *m*.

pigeon *n* pigeon *m*. ~**-hole** *n* casier *m*.

pig-headed *adj* entêté.

pigsty *n* porcherie *f*.

pigtail *n* natte *f*.

pike *n inv* (fish) brochet *m*.

pile *n* (heap) tas *m*; (stack) pile *f*; (of carpet) poil *m*; **~s of** 🔲 un tas de 🔲. ● *vt* **~ (up)** entasser. ● *vi* **~ into** s'engouffrer dans; **~ up** (*snow, leaves*) s'entasser; (*debts, work*) s'accumuler. **~-up** *n* (Auto) carambolage *m*.

pilgrim *n* pèlerin *m*. **pilgrimage** *n* pèlerinage *m*.

pill *n* pilule *f*.

pillar *n* pilier *m*. **~-box** *n* boîte *f* aux lettres.

pillion *n* siège *m* de passager; **ride ~** monter en croupe.

pillow *n* oreiller *m*. **~case** *n* taie *f* d'oreiller.

pilot *n* pilote *m*. ● *adj* pilote. ● *vt* (*pt* **piloted**) piloter. **~-light** *n* veilleuse *f*.

pimple *n* bouton *m*.

pin *n* épingle *f*; (of plug) fiche *f*; (for wood, metal) goujon *m*; (in surgery) broche *f*; **have ~s and needles** avoir des fourmis. ● *vt* (*pt* **pinned**) épingler, attacher; (trap) coincer; **~ sb down** (fig) forcer qn à se décider; **~ up** accrocher.

pinafore *n* tablier *m*.

pincers *npl* tenailles *fpl*.

pinch *vt* pincer; (steal 🔲) piquer. ● *vi* (be too tight) serrer. ● *n* (mark) pinçon *m*; (of salt) pincée *f*; **at a ~** à la rigueur.

pine *n* (tree) pin *m*. ● *vi* **~ (away)** dépérir; **~ for** languir après.

pineapple *n* ananas *m*.

pinecone *n* pomme *f* de pin.

pink *a & n* rose (*m*).

pinpoint *vt* (*problem, cause, location*) indiquer; (*time*) déterminer.

pint *n* pinte *f* (GB = *0.57 litre*; US = *0.47 litre*).

pin-up *n* 🔲 pin-up *f inv* 🔲.

pioneer *n* pionnier *m*. ● *vt* **~ the use of** être le premier à utiliser.

pious *adj* pieux.

pip *n* (seed) pépin *m*; (sound) top *m*.

pipe *n* tuyau *m*; (to smoke) pipe *f*; (Mus) chalumeau *m*; **~s** cornemuse *f*. ● *vt* transporter par tuyau. □ **~ down** se taire.

pipeline *n* oléoduc *m*; **in the ~** en cours.

piping *n* tuyauterie *f*; **~ hot** fumant.

pique *n* dépit *m*.

pirate *n* pirate *m*. ● *vt* pirater.

Pisces *n* Poissons *mpl*.

pistol *n* pistolet *m*.

pit *n* fosse *f*; (mine) puits *m*; (quarry) carrière *f*; (for orchestra) fosse *f*; (of stomach) creux *m*; (of cherry: US) noyau *m*. ● *vt* (*pt* **pitted**) marquer; (fig) opposer; **~ oneself against** se mesurer à.

pitch *n* (Sport) terrain *m*; (of voice, note) hauteur *f*; (degree) degré *m*; (Mus) ton *m*; (tar) brai *m*. ● *vt* jeter; (*tent*) planter. ● *vi* (*ship*) tanguer. □ **~ in** 🔲 contribuer.

pitfall *n* écueil *m*.

pitiful *adj* pitoyable. **pitiless** *adj* impitoyable.

pittance *n* **earn a ~** gagner trois fois rien.

pity *n* pitié *f*; (regrettable fact) dommage *m*; **take ~ on** avoir pitié de; **what a ~!** quel dommage! ● *vt* avoir pitié de.

pivot *n* pivot *m*. ● *vi* (*pt* **pivoted**) pivoter.

placard *n* affiche *f*.

place *n* endroit *m*, lieu *m*; (house) maison *f*; (seat, rank) place *f*; **at** *or* **to my ~** chez moi; **change ~s** changer de place; **in the first ~** d'abord; **out of ~** déplacé; **take ~** avoir lieu. ● *vt* placer; (*order*) passer; (remember) situer; **be ~d** (in race) se placer. **~-mat** *n* set *m*.

placid *adj* placide.

plagiarism *n* plagiat *m*. **plagiarize** *vt/i* plagier.

plague *n* (bubonic) peste *f*; (epidemic) épidémie *f*; (of ants, locusts) invasion *f*. ● *vt* harceler.

plaice *n inv* carrelet *m*.

plain *adj* (obvious) clair; (candid) franc; (simple) simple; (not pretty) sans beauté; (not patterned) uni; **~ chocolate** chocolat *m* noir; **in ~ clothes** en civil. ● *adv* franchement. ● *n* plaine *f*. **plainly** *adv* clairement; franchement; simplement.

plaintiff *n* plaignant/-e *m/f*.

plaintive *adj* plaintif.

plait *vt* tresser. ● *n* natte *f*.

plan *n* projet *m*, plan *m*; (diagram) plan *m*. ● *vt* (*pt* **planned**) projeter (**to do** de faire); (*timetable, day*) organiser; (*economy, work*) planifier. ● *vi* prévoir; ~ **on** s'attendre à.

plane *n* (level) plan *m*; (aeroplane) avion *m*; (tool) rabot *m*. ● *adj* plan. ● *vt* raboter.

planet *n* planète *f*.

plank *n* planche *f*.

planning *n* (of economy, work) planification *f*; (of holiday, party) organisation *f*; (of town) urbanisme *m*; **family** ~ **planning** *m* familial; ~ **permission** permis *m* de construire.

plant *n* plante *f*; (Tech) matériel *m*; (factory) usine *f*. ● *vt* planter; (*bomb*) placer.

plaster *n* plâtre *m*; (adhesive) sparadrap *m*. ● *vt* plâtrer; (cover) couvrir (**with** de).

plastic *adj* en plastique; (*art, substance*) plastique; ~ **surgery** chirurgie *f* esthétique. ● *n* plastique *m*.

plate *n* assiette *f*; (of metal) plaque *f*; (silverware) argenterie *f*; (in book) gravure *f*. ● *vt* (*metal*) plaquer.

plateau *n* (*pl* ~**x**) plateau *m*; (fig) palier *m*.

platform *n* (stage) estrade *f*; (for speaking) tribune *f*; (Rail) quai *m*; (Pol) plate-forme *f*.

platoon *n* (Mil) section *f*.

play *vt/i* jouer; (*instrument*) jouer de; (*record*) mettre; (*game*) jouer à; (*opponent*) jouer contre; (*match*) disputer; ~ **safe** ne pas prendre de risques. ● *n* jeu *m*; (Theat) pièce *f*. □ ~ **down** minimiser; ~ **on** (*fears*) exploiter; ~ **up** 🔢 commencer à faire des siennes 🔢; ~ **up sth** mettre l'accent sur qch.

playful *adj* (*remark*) taquin; (*child*) joueur.

play: ~**ground** *n* cour *f* de récréation. ~**-group**, ~**-school** *n* garderie *f*.

playing *n* (Sport) jeu *m*; (Theat) interprétation *f*. ~**-card** *n* carte *f* à jouer. ~**-field** *n* terrain *m* de sport.

play: ~**-pen** *n* parc *m* (pour bébé). ~**wright** *n* auteur *m* dramatique.

plc *abbr* (**public limited company**) SA.

plea *n* (for mercy, tolerance) appel *m*; (for food, money) demande *f*; (reason) excuse *f*; **make a** ~ **of guilty** plaider coupable.

plead *vt/i* supplier; (Jur) plaider.

pleasant *adj* agréable.

please *vt/i* plaire (à), faire plaisir (à); ~ **oneself, do as one** ~**s** faire ce qu'on veut. ● *adv* s'il vous *or* te plaît. **pleased** *adj* content (**with** de). **pleasing** *adj* agréable.

pleasure *n* plaisir *m*; **with** ~ avec plaisir; **my** ~ je vous en prie.

pleat *n* pli *m*. ● *vt* plisser.

pledge *n* (token) gage *m*; (promise) promesse *f*. ● *vt* promettre; (pawn) mettre en gage.

plentiful *adj* abondant.

plenty *n* abondance *f*; ~ (**of**) (a great deal) beaucoup (de); (enough) assez (de).

pliers *npl* pinces *fpl*.

plight *n* détresse *f*.

plinth *n* socle *m*.

plod *vi* (*pt* **plodded**) avancer péniblement.

plonk *n* 🔢 pinard *m* 🔢.

plot *n* (conspiracy) complot *m*; (of novel) intrigue *f*; ~ (**of land**) terrain *m*. ● *vt/i* (*pt* **plotted**) (plan) comploter; (mark out) tracer.

plough *n* charrue *f*. ● *vt/i* labourer. □ ~ **back** réinvestir; ~ **through** avancer péniblement dans.

plow *n* & *vt/i* (US) = PLOUGH.

ploy *n* stratagème *m*.

pluck *vt* (*flower, fruit*) cueillir; (*bird*) plumer; (*eyebrows*) épiler; (*strings*: Mus) pincer; ~ **up courage** prendre son courage à deux mains. **plucky** *adj* courageux.

plug *n* (for sink) bonde *f*; (Electr) fiche *f*, prise *f*. ● *vt* (*pt* **plugged**) (*hole*) boucher; (publicize 🔢) faire du battage autour de. □ ~ **in** brancher. ~**-hole** *n* bonde *f*.

plum *n* prune *f*; ~ **pudding** (plum-) pudding *m*.

plumber *n* plombier *m*.

plume *n* (of feathers) panache *m*.

plummet *vi* tomber, plonger.

plump *adj* potelé, dodu.

plunge *vt/i* (dive, thrust) plonger; (fall) tomber. ● *n* plongeon *m*; (fall) chute *f*; take the ~ se jeter à l'eau. **plunger** *n* (for sink) ventouse *f*.

plural *adj* pluriel; (*noun*) au pluriel; (*ending*) du pluriel. ● *n* pluriel *m*.

plus *prep* plus; ten ~ plus de dix. ● *adj* (Electr & fig) positif. ● *n* signe *m* plus; (fig) atout *m*.

ply *vt* (*tool*) manier; (*trade*) exercer. ● *vi* faire la navette; ~ sb with drink offrir continuellement à boire à qn.

plywood *n* contreplaqué *m*.

p.m. *adv* de l'après-midi *or* du soir.

pneumatic drill *n* marteau-piqueur *m*.

pneumonia *n* pneumonie *f*.

PO *abbr* ⇒POST OFFICE.

poach *vt/i* (*game*) braconner; (*staff*) débaucher; (Culin) pocher.

PO Box *n* boîte *f* postale.

pocket *n* poche *f*; be out of ~ avoir perdu de l'argent. ● *adj* de poche. ● *vt* empocher. **~-book** *n* (notebook) carnet *m*; (wallet: US) portefeuille *m*; (handbag: US) sac *m* à main. **~-money** *n* argent *m* de poche.

pod *n* (peas) cosse *f*; (vanilla) gousse *f*.

podgy *adj* (**-ier**, **-iest**) dodu.

poem *n* poème *m*. **poet** *n* poète *m*. **poetic** *adj* poétique. **poetry** *n* poésie *f*.

point *n* (position) point *m*; (tip) pointe *f*; (decimal point) virgule *f*; (remark) remarque *f*; good ~s qualités *fpl*; on the ~ of sur le point de; ~ in time moment *m*; ~ of view point *m* de vue; to the ~ pertinent; what is the ~? à quoi bon? ● *vt* (aim) braquer; (show) indiquer; ~ out signaler. ● *vi* indiquer du doigt; ~ out that, make the ~ that faire remarquer que. **~-blank** *a & adv* à bout portant.

pointed *adj* (sharp) pointu; (window) en pointe; (*remark*) lourd de sens.

pointless *adj* inutile.

poise *n* (confidence) assurance *f*; (physical elegance) aisance *f*.

poison *n* poison *m*. ● *vt* empoisonner. **poisonous** *adj*

(*substance*) toxique; (*plant*) vénéneux; (*snake*) venimeux.

poke *vt/i* (push) pousser; (*fire*) tisonner; (thrust) fourrer; ~ fun at se moquer de. ● *n* (petit) coup *m*. □ ~ out (*head*) sortir.

poker *n* (for fire) tisonnier *m*; (cards) poker *m*.

Poland *n* Pologne *f*.

polar *adj* polaire.

pole *n* (stick) perche *f*; (for flag) mât *m*; (Geog) pôle *m*.

Pole *n* Polonais/-e *m/f*.

pole-vault *n* saut *m* à la perche.

police *n* police *f*. ● *vt* faire la police dans. ~ **constable** *n* agent *m* de police. **~man** *n* (*pl* **-men**) agent *m* de police. ~ **station** *n* commissariat *m* de police. **~woman** *n* (*pl* **-women**) femme-agent *f*.

policy *n* politique *f*; (*insurance*) police *f* (d'assurance).

polish *vt* polir; (*shoes, floor*) cirer. ● *n* (for shoes) cirage *m*; (for floor) encaustique *f*; (for nails) vernis *m*; (shine) poli *m*; (fig) raffinement *m*. □ ~ **off** finir en vitesse; ~ **up** (*language*) perfectionner.

Polish *adj* polonais. ● *n* (Ling) polonais *m*.

polished *adj* raffiné.

polite *adj* poli.

political *adj* politique.

politician *n* homme *m* politique, femme *f* politique.

politics *n* politique *f*.

poll *n* (vote casting) scrutin *m*; (survey) sondage *m*; go to the ~s aller aux urnes. ● *vt* (*votes*) obtenir.

pollen *n* pollen *m*.

polling booth *n* isoloir *m*.

polling station *n* bureau *m* de vote.

pollution *n* pollution *f*.

polo *n* polo *m*. ~ **neck** *n* col *m* roulé.

pomegranate *n* grenade *f*.

pomp *n* pompe *f*.

pompous *adj* pompeux.

pond *n* étang *m*; (artificial) bassin *m*; (stagnant) mare *f*.

ponder *vt/i* réfléchir (à), méditer (sur).

pong *n* (stink 🄸) puanteur *f*. ● *vi* 🄸 puer.

pony *n* poney *m*. **∼tail** *n* queue *f* de cheval.

poodle *n* caniche *m*.

pool *n* (puddle) flaque *f*; (pond) étang *m*; (of blood) mare *f*; (for swimming) piscine *f*; (fund) fonds *m* commun; (of ideas) réservoir *m*; (snooker) billard *m* américain; **∼s** pari *m* mutuel sur le football. ● *vt* mettre en commun.

poor *adj* (not wealthy) pauvre; (not good) médiocre, mauvais.

poorly *adj* malade. ● *adv* mal.

pop *n* (noise) pan *m*; (music) pop *m*. ● *adj* pop *inv*. ● *vt/i* (*pt* **popped**) (burst) crever; (put) mettre; **∼ in/out/ off** entrer/sortir/partir. □ **∼ up** surgir.

pope *n* pape *m*.

poppy *n* pavot *m*; (wild) coquelicot *m*.

popular *adj* populaire; (in fashion) en vogue; **be ∼ with** plaire à.

population *n* population *f*.

porcelain *n* porcelaine *f*.

porcupine *n* porc-épic *m*.

pork *n* porc *m*.

pornography *n* pornographie *f*.

port *n* (harbour) port *m*; (left: Naut) bâbord *m*; **∼ of call** escale *f*; (wine) porto *m*.

portable *adj* portable.

porter *n* (carrier) porteur *m*; (door-keeper) portier *m*.

portfolio *n* (Pol, Comm) portefeuille *m*.

portion *n* (at meal) portion *f*; (part) partie *f*.

portrait *n* portrait *m*.

portray *vt* représenter.

Portugal *n* Portugal *m*.

Portuguese *n* (Ling) portugais *m*; (person) Portugais/-e *m/f*. ● *adj* portugais.

pose *vt/i* poser; **∼ as** (expert) se poser en. ● *n* pose *f*.

poser *n* (person) frimeur/-euse *m/f*; (puzzle) colle *f*.

posh *adj* 🄸 chic *inv*.

position *n* position *f*; (job, state) situation *f*. ● *vt* placer.

positive *adj* positif; (sure) sûr, certain; (real) réel, vrai.

possess *vt* posséder.

possession *n* possession *f*; **take ∼ of** prendre possession de.

possessive *adj* possessif.

possible *adj* possible.

possibly *adv* peut-être; **if I ∼ can** si cela m'est possible; **I cannot ∼ leave** il m'est impossible de partir.

post *n* (pole) poteau *m*; (station, job) poste *m*; (mail service) poste *f*; (letters) courrier *m*. ● *adj* postal. ● *vt* (letter) poster; **keep ∼ed** tenir au courant; **∼ (up)** (a notice) afficher; (appoint) affecter.

postage *n* affranchissement *m*; tarif *m* postal.

postal *adj* postal. **∼ order** *n* mandat *m*.

post: **∼box** *n* boîte *f* aux lettres. **∼card** *n* carte *f* postale. **∼ code** *n* code *m* postal.

poster *n* (for information) affiche *f*; (for decoration) poster *m*.

postgraduate *n* étudiant/-e *m/f* de troisième cycle.

posthumous *adj* posthume.

post: **∼man** *n* (*pl* **-men**) facteur *m*. **∼mark** *n* cachet *m* de la poste.

post-mortem *n* autopsie *f*.

post office *n* poste *f*.

postpone *vt* remettre.

postscript *n* (to letter) post-scriptum *m inv*.

posture *n* posture *f*. ● *vi* prendre des poses.

pot *n* pot *m*; (drug 🄸) hasch *m*; **go to ∼** 🄸 aller à la ruine; **take ∼ luck** tenter sa chance. ● *vt* (plants) mettre en pot.

potato *n* (*pl* **∼es**) pomme *f* de terre.

pot-belly *n* bedaine *f*.

potential *a & n* potentiel (*m*).

pot-hole *n* (in rock) caverne *f*; (in road) nid *m* de poule. **pot-holing** *n* spéléologie *f*.

potter *n* potier *m*. ● *vi* bricoler. **pottery** *n* (art) poterie *f*; (objects) poteries *fpl*.

potty *adj* (**-ier**, **-iest**) (crazy 🄳) toqué. ● *n* pot *m*.

pouch n poche f; (for tobacco) blague f.

poultry n volailles fpl.

pounce vi bondir (on sur). ● n bond m.

pound n (weight) livre f (= 454 g); (money) livre f; (for dogs, cars) fourrière f. ● vt (crush) piler; (bombard) pilonner. ● vi frapper fort; (of heart) battre fort; (walk) marcher à pas lourds.

pour vt verser. ● vi couler, ruisseler (from de); (rain) pleuvoir à torrents. □ ~ in/out (people) arriver/sortir en masse; ~ off or out vider. **pouring rain** n pluie f torrentielle.

pout vi faire la moue.

poverty n misère f, pauvreté f.

powder n poudre f. ● vt poudrer.

power n (strength) puissance f; (control) pouvoir m; (energy) énergie f; (Electr) courant m. ● vt (engine) faire marcher; (plane) propulser; ~ed by (engine) propulsé par; (generator) alimenté par. ~ cut n coupure f de courant.

powerful adj puissant.

powerless adj impuissant.

power: ~ **point** n prise f de courant. ~**station** n centrale f électrique.

practical adj pratique. ~ **joke** n farce f.

practice n (procedure) pratique f; (of profession) exercice m; (Sport) entraînement m; **in** ~ (in fact) en pratique; (well-trained) en forme; **out of** ~ rouillé; **put into** ~ mettre en pratique.

practise vt/i (musician, typist) s'exercer (à); (Sport) s'entraîner (à); (put into practice) pratiquer; (profession) exercer.

praise vt faire l'éloge de; (God) louer. ● n éloges mpl, louanges fpl.

pram n landau m.

prance vi caracoler.

prawn n crevette f rose.

pray vi prier. **prayer** n prière f.

preach vt/i prêcher; ~ **at** or **to** prêcher.

precarious adj précaire.

precaution n précaution f.

precede vt précéder.

precedence n (in importance) priorité f; (in rank) préséance f.

precedent n précédent m.

precinct n quartier m commerçant; (pedestrian area) zone f piétonne; (district: US) circonscription f.

precious adj précieux.

precipitate vt (person, event, chemical) précipiter.

précis n résumé m.

precise adj précis; (careful) méticuleux. **precision** n précision f.

precocious adj précoce.

preconceived adj préconçu.

predator n prédateur m.

predicament n situation f difficile.

predict vt prédire. **predictable** adj prévisible. **prediction** n prédiction f.

predispose vt prédisposer (**to do** à faire).

predominant adj prédominant.

pre-empt vt (anticipate) anticiper; (person) devancer.

preface n (to book) préface f; (to speech) préambule m.

prefect n (pupil) élève m/f chargé/-e de la discipline; (official) préfet m.

prefer vt (pt **preferred**) préférer (**to do** faire). **preferably** adv de préférence. **preference** n préférence f. **preferential** adj préférentiel.

prefix n préfixe m.

pregnancy n grossesse f. **pregnant** adj (woman) enceinte; (animal) pleine; (pause) éloquent.

prehistoric adj préhistorique.

prejudge vt (issue) préjuger de; (person) juger d'avance.

prejudice n préjugé(s) m(pl); (harm) préjudice m. ● vt (claim) porter préjudice à; (person) léser. **prejudiced** adj partial; (person) qui a des préjugés.

premature adj prématuré.

premeditated adj prémédité.

premises npl locaux mpl; **on the** ~ sur les lieux.

premium n (insurance) prime f; **be at a** ~ être précieux.

preoccupied *adj* préoccupé.

preparation *n* préparation *f*; ~s préparatifs *mpl*.

preparatory *adj* préparatoire. ~ **school** *n* école *f* primaire privée; (US) école *f* secondaire privée.

prepare *vt/i* (se) préparer (**for** à); **be** ~**d for** (expect) s'attendre à; ~**d to** prêt à.

preposition *n* préposition *f*.

preposterous *adj* absurde, ridicule.

prep school *n* = PREPARATORY SCHOOL.

prerequisite *n* condition *f* préalable.

prescribe *vt* prescrire.

prescription *n* (Med) ordonnance *f*.

presence *n* présence *f*; ~ **of mind** présence *f* d'esprit.

present[1] *adj* présent. ● *n* présent *m*; (gift) cadeau *m*; **at** ~ à présent; **for the** ~ pour le moment.

present[2] *vt* présenter; (*film, concert*) donner; ~ **sb with** offrir à qn. **presentation** *n* présentation *f*. **presenter** *n* présentateur/-trice *m/f*.

preservation *n* (of food) conservation *f*; (of wildlife) préservation *f*.

preservative *n* (Culin) agent *m* de conservation.

preserve *vt* préserver; (Culin) conserver. ● *n* réserve *f*; (fig) domaine *m*; (jam) confiture *f*.

presidency *n* présidence *f*.

president *n* président/-e *m/f*.

press *vt/i* (*button*) appuyer (sur); (squeeze) presser; (iron) repasser; (pursue) poursuivre; **be** ~**ed for** (*time*) manquer de; ~ **for sth** faire pression pour avoir qch; ~ **sb to do sth** pousser qn à faire qch; ~ **on** continuer (**with sth** qch). ● *n* (newspapers, machine) presse *f*; (for wine) pressoir *m*. ~ **cutting** *n* coupure *f* de presse.

pressing *adj* pressant.

press: ~ **release** *n* communiqué *m* de presse. ~**-stud** *n* bouton-pression *m*. ~**-up** *n* pompe *f*.

pressure *n* pression *f*. ● *vt* faire pression sur. ~**-cooker** *n* cocotte-minute *f*. ~ **group** *n* groupe *m* de pression.

pressurize *vt* (*cabin*) pressuriser; (*person*) faire pression sur.

prestige *n* prestige *m*.

presumably *adv* vraisemblablement.

presume *vt* (suppose) présumer.

pretence, (US) **pretense** *n* feinte *f*, simulation *f*; (claim) prétention *f*; (pretext) prétexte *m*.

pretend *vt/i* faire semblant (**to do** de faire); ~ **to** (lay claim to) prétendre à.

pretentious *adj* prétentieux.

pretext *n* prétexte *m*.

pretty *adj* (**-ier**, **-iest**) joli. ● *adv* assez; ~ **much** presque.

prevail *vi* (be usual) prédominer; (win) prévaloir; ~ **on** persuader (**to do** de faire). **prevailing** *adj* actuel; (*wind*) dominant.

prevalent *adj* répandu.

prevent *vt* empêcher (**from doing** de faire). **prevention** *n* prévention *f*. **preventive** *adj* préventif.

preview *n* avant-première *f*; (fig) aperçu *m*.

previous *adj* précédent, antérieur; ~ **to** avant. **previously** *adv* auparavant.

prey *n* proie *f*; **bird of** ~ rapace *m*. ● *vi* ~ **on** faire sa proie de; (worry) préoccuper.

price *n* prix *m*. ● *vt* fixer le prix de. **priceless** *adj* inestimable; (amusing 🔢) impayable 🔢.

prick *vt* (with pin) piquer; ~ **up one's ears** dresser l'oreille. ● *n* piqûre *f*.

prickle *n* piquant *m*.

pride *n* orgueil *m*; (satisfaction) fierté *f*; ~ **of place** place *f* d'honneur. ● *vpr* ~ **oneself on** s'enorgueillir de.

priest *n* prêtre *m*.

prim *adj* (**primmer**, **primmest**) guindé, méticuleux.

primarily *adv* essentiellement.

primary *adj* (*school, elections*) primaire; (chief, basic) premier, fondamental. ● *n* (Pol: US) primaire *f*.

prime adj principal, premier; (first-rate) excellent. ● vt (*pump, gun*) amorcer; (*surface*) apprêter. **P~ Minister** n Premier Ministre m.

primitive adj primitif.

primrose n primevère f (*jaune*).

prince n prince m. **princess** n princesse f.

principal adj principal. ● n (of school) directeur/-trice m/f.

principle n principe m; **in/on ~** en/par principe.

print vt imprimer; (write in capitals) écrire en majuscules; **~ed matter** imprimés mpl. ● n (of foot) empreinte f; (letters) caractères mpl; (photograph) épreuve f; (engraving) gravure f; **in ~** disponible; **out of ~** épuisé. **printer** n (person) imprimeur m; (Comput) imprimante f.

prior adj précédent. ● n (Relig) prieur m. **~ to** prep avant (de).

priority n priorité f; **take ~** avoir la priorité (**over** sur).

prise vt forcer; **~ open** ouvrir en forçant.

prison n prison f. **prisoner** n prisonnier/-ière m/f. **~ officer** n gardien/-ne m/f de prison.

pristine adj **be in ~ condition** être comme neuf.

privacy n intimité f, solitude f.

private adj privé; (confidential) personnel; (*lessons, house*) particulier; (*ceremony*) intime; **in ~** en privé; (of ceremony) dans l'intimité. ● n (soldier) simple soldat m. **privately** adv en privé; dans l'intimité; (inwardly) intérieurement.

privilege n privilège m. **privileged** adj privilégié; **be ~d to** avoir le privilège de.

prize n prix m. ● adj (entry) primé; (*fool*) parfait. ● vt (value) priser.

pro n **the ~s and cons** le pour et le contre.

probable adj probable. **probably** adv probablement.

probation n (testing) essai m; (Jur) liberté f surveillée.

probe n (device) sonde f; (fig) enquête f. ● vt sonder. ● vi **~ into** sonder.

problem n problème m. ● adj difficile. **problematic** adj problématique.

procedure n procédure f; (way of doing sth) démarche f à suivre.

proceed vi (go) aller, avancer; (pass) passer (**to** à); (act) procéder; **~ (with)** continuer; **~ to do** se mettre à faire.

proceedings npl (discussions) débats mpl; (meeting) réunion f; (report) actes mpl; (Jur) poursuites fpl.

proceeds npl (profits) produit m, bénéfices mpl.

process n processus m; (method) procédé m; **in ~** en cours; **in the ~ of doing** en train de faire. ● vt (*material, data*) traiter.

procession n défilé m.

procrastinate vi différer, tergiverser.

procure vt obtenir.

prod vt/i (pt **prodded**) pousser doucement. ● n petit coup m.

prodigy n prodige m.

produce[1] n produits mpl.

produce[2] vt/i produire; (bring out) sortir; (show) présenter; (cause) provoquer; (Theat, TV) mettre en scène; (radio) réaliser; (cinema) produire. **producer** n metteur m en scène; réalisateur m; producteur m.

product n produit m.

production n production f; (Theat, TV) mise f en scène; (radio) réalisation f.

productive adj productif. **productivity** n productivité f.

profession n profession f.

professional adj professionnel; (of high quality) de professionnel; (*person*) qui exerce une profession libérale. ● n professionnel/-le m/f.

professor n professeur m (*titulaire d'une chaire*).

proficient adj compétent.

profile n (of face) profil m; (of body, mountain) silhouette f; (by journalist) portrait m.

profit n profit m, bénéfice m. ● vi **~ by** tirer profit de. **profitable** adj rentable.

profound adj profond.

profusely adv (bleed) abondamment; (apologize) avec effusion. **profusion** n profusion f.

program n (US) = PROGRAMME; (computer) ~ programme m. ● vt (pt **programmed**) programmer.

programme n programme m; (broadcast) émission f.

programmer n programmeur/-euse m/f.

programming n (Comput) programmation f.

progress¹ n progrès m(pl); in ~ en cours; **make** ~ faire des progrès; ~ **report** compte-rendu m.

progress² vi (advance, improve) progresser.

progressive adj progressif; (reforming) progressiste.

prohibit vt interdire (**sb from doing** à qn de faire).

project¹ vt projeter. ● vi (jut out) être en saillie.

project² n (plan) projet m; (undertaking) entreprise f; (School) dossier m.

projection n projection f; saillie f; (estimate) prévision f.

projector n projecteur m.

proliferate vi proliférer.

prolong vt prolonger.

prominent adj (projecting) proéminent; (conspicuous) bien en vue; (fig) important.

promiscuous adj de mœurs faciles.

promise n promesse f. ● vt/i promettre. **promising** adj prometteur; (person) qui promet.

promote vt promouvoir; (advertise) faire la promotion de. **promotion** n promotion f.

prompt adj rapide; (punctual) à l'heure, ponctuel. ● adv (on the dot) pile. ● vt inciter; (cause) provoquer; (Theat) souffler à. ● n (Comput) message m guide-opérateur. **prompter** n souffleur/-euse m/f. **promptly** adv rapidement; ponctuellement.

prone adj ~ **to** sujet à.

pronoun n pronom m.

pronounce vt prononcer.

pronunciation n prononciation f.

proof n (evidence) preuve f; (test, trial copy) épreuve f; (of alcohol) teneur f en alcool. ● adj ~ **against** à l'épreuve de.

prop n support m; (Theat) accessoire m. ● vt (pt **propped**) ~ (**up**) (support) étayer; (lean) appuyer.

propaganda n propagande f.

propel vt (pt **propelled**) (vehicle, ship) propulser; (person) pousser.

propeller n hélice f.

proper adj correct, bon; (adequate) convenable; (real) vrai; (thorough 🔲) parfait. **properly** adv correctement, comme il faut; (adequately) convenablement.

proper noun n nom m propre.

property n (house) propriété f; (things owned) biens mpl, propriété f. ● adj immobilier, foncier.

prophecy n prophétie f.

prophet n prophète m.

proportion n (ratio, dimension) proportion f; (amount) partie f.

proposal n proposition f; (of marriage) demande f en mariage.

propose vt proposer. ● vi faire une demande en mariage; ~ **to do** se proposer de faire.

proposition n proposition f; (matter 🔲) affaire f. ● vt 🔲 faire des propositions malhonnêtes à.

proprietor n propriétaire mf.

propriety n (correct behaviour) bienséance f.

prose n prose f; (translation) thème m.

prosecute vt poursuivre en justice. **prosecution** n poursuites fpl. **prosecutor** n procureur m.

prospect¹ n (outlook) perspective f; (chance) espoir m.

prospect² vt/i prospecter.

prospective adj (future) futur; (possible) éventuel.

prospectus n brochure f; (Univ) livret m de l'étudiant.

prosperity n prospérité f. **prosperous** adj prospère.

prostitute n prostituée f.

prostrate adj (prone) à plat ventre; (exhausted) prostré.

protect *vt* protéger. **protection** *n* protection *f*. **protective** *adj* protecteur; (*clothes*) de protection.

protein *n* protéine *f*.

protest[1] *n* protestation *f*; **under ~** en protestant.

protest[2] *vt/i* protester.

Protestant *a* & *n* protestant/-e (*m/f*).

protester *n* manifestant/-e *m/f*.

protocol *n* protocole *m*.

protrude *vi* dépasser.

proud *adj* fier, orgueilleux.

prove *vt* prouver. ● *vi* ~ **(to be) easy** se révéler facile; **~ oneself** faire ses preuves. **proven** *adj* éprouvé.

proverb *n* proverbe *m*.

provide *vt* fournir (**sb with sth** qch à qn). ● *vi* ~ **for** (allow for) prévoir; (guard against) parer à; (*person*) pourvoir aux besoins de.

provided *conj* ~ **that** à condition que.

providing *conj* = PROVIDED.

province *n* province *f*; (fig) compétence *f*.

provision *n* (stock) provision *f*; (supplying) fourniture *f*; (stipulation) dispositions *fpl*; **~s** (food) provisions *fpl*.

provisional *adj* provisoire.

provocative *adj* provocant.

provoke *vt* provoquer.

prow *n* proue *f*.

prowess *n* prouesses *fpl*.

prowl *vi* rôder.

proxy *n* **by ~** par procuration.

prudish *adj* pudibond, prude.

prune *n* pruneau *m*. ● *vt* (cut) tailler.

pry *vi* ~ **into** mettre son nez dans.

psalm *n* psaume *m*.

pseudonym *n* pseudonyme *m*.

psychiatric *adj* psychiatrique. **psychiatrist** *n* psychiatre *mf*. **psychiatry** *n* psychiatrie *f*.

psychic *adj* (*phenomenon*) métapsychique; (*person*) doué de télépathie.

psychoanalyse *vt* psychanalyser.

psychological *adj* psychologique. **psychologist** *n* psychologue *mf*. **psychology** *n* psychologie *f*.

PTO *abbr* (**please turn over**) TSVP.

pub *n* pub *m*.

puberty *n* puberté *f*.

public *adj* public; (*library*) municipal; **in ~** en public.

publican *n* patron/-ne *m/f* de pub.

publication *n* publication *f*.

public house *n* pub *m*.

publicity *n* publicité *f*.

publicize *vt* faire connaître au public.

public: **~ relations** *n* relations *fpl* publiques. **~ school** *n* école *f* privée; (US) école *f* publique. **~ transport** *n* transports *mpl* en commun.

publish *vt* publier. **publisher** *n* éditeur *m*. **publishing** *n* édition *f*.

pudding *n* dessert *m*; (steamed) pudding *m*.

puddle *n* flaque *f* d'eau.

puff *n* (of smoke) bouffée *f*; (of breath) souffle *m*. ● *vt/i* souffler. □ ~ **at** (*cigar*) tirer sur. ~ **out** (swell) (se) gonfler.

pull *vt/i* tirer; (*muscle*) se froisser; ~ **a face** faire une grimace; ~ **one's weight** faire sa part du travail; ~ **sb's leg** faire marcher qn. ● *n* traction *f*; (fig) attraction *f*; (influence) influence *f*; **give a ~** tirer. □ ~ **away** (Auto) démarrer; ~ **back** or **out** (withdraw) (se) retirer; ~ **down** (*building*) démolir; ~ **in** (enter) entrer; (stop) s'arrêter; ~ **off** enlever; (fig) réussir; ~ **out** (from bag) sortir; (extract) arracher; (Auto) déboîter; ~ **over** (Auto) se ranger (sur le côté); ~ **through** s'en tirer; ~ **oneself together** se ressaisir.

pull-down menu *n* (Comput) menu *m* déroulant.

pulley *n* poulie *f*.

pullover *n* pull(-over) *m*.

pulp *n* (of fruit) pulpe *f*; (for paper) pâte *f* à papier.

pulpit *n* chaire *f*.

pulsate *vi* battre.

pulse *n* (Med) pouls *m*.

pump *n* pompe *f*; (plimsoll) chaussure *f* de sport. ● *vt/i* pomper; (*person*)

soutirer des renseignements à; ~ **up**
gonfler.

pumpkin n citrouille f.

pun n jeu m de mots.

punch vt donner un coup de poing à;
(*ticket*) poinçonner. ● n coup m de
poing; (vigour Ⓣ) punch m; (device)
poinçonneuse f; (drink) punch m.
~**-line** n chute f.

punctual adj à l'heure; (habitually)
ponctuel.

punctuation n ponctuation f.

puncture n crevaison f. ● vt/i
crever.

pungent adj âcre.

punish vt punir (for sth de qch).
punishment n punition f.

punk n (music, fan) punk m; (US: Ⓣ)
voyou m.

punt n (boat) barque f; (Irish pound)
livre f irlandaise.

puny adj (-ier, -iest) chétif.

pupil n (person) élève mf; (of eye)
pupille f.

puppet n marionnette f.

puppy n chiot m.

purchase vt acheter (from sb à qn).
● n achat m.

pure adj pur.

purgatory n purgatoire m.

purge vt purger (of de). ● n purge f.

purification n (of water, air)
épuration f; (Relig) purification f.

purify vt épurer; purifier.

puritan n puritain/-e m/f.

purity n pureté f.

purple a & n violet (m).

purpose n but m; (determination)
résolution f; on ~ exprès; to no ~
sans résultat.

purr n ronronnement m. ● vi
ronronner.

purse n porte-monnaie m inv;
(handbag: US) sac m à main. ● vt (lips)
pincer.

pursue vt poursuivre.

pursuit n poursuite f; (hobby) activité
f, occupation f.

pus n pus m.

push vt/i pousser; (button) appuyer
sur; (thrust) enfoncer; (recommend Ⓣ)
proposer avec insistance; be ~ed for
(*time*) manquer de; be ~ing thirty

Ⓣ friser la trentaine; ~ **sb around**
bousculer qn. ● n poussée f; (effort)
gros effort m; (drive) dynamisme m;
give the ~ **to** Ⓣ flanquer à la porte
Ⓣ. □ ~ **in** resquiller; ~ **on**
continuer; ~ **up** (lift) relever; (*prices*)
faire monter.

pushchair n poussette f.

pusher n revendeur/-euse m/f (de
drogue).

push-up n pompe f.

put vt/i (pt put; pres p putting)
mettre, placer, poser; (*question*)
poser; ~ **the damage at a million**
estimer les dégâts à un million; ~
sth tactfully dire qch avec tact. □ ~
across communiquer; ~ **away**
ranger; (in hospital, prison) enfermer; ~
back (postpone) remettre; (delay)
retarder; ~ **down** (dé)poser; (write)
inscrire; (pay) verser; (suppress)
réprimer; ~ **forward** (*plan*)
soumettre; ~ **in** (insert) introduire;
(fix) installer; (submit) soumettre; ~ **in**
for faire une demande de; ~ **off**
(postpone) renvoyer à plus tard;
(disconcert) déconcerter; (displease)
rebuter; ~ **sb off sth** dégoûter qn de
qch; ~ **on** (*clothes, radio*) mettre;
(*light*) allumer; (*accent, weight*)
prendre; ~ **out** (stretch) (é)
tendre; (extinguish) éteindre; (disconcert)
déconcerter; (inconvenience) déranger; ~
up lever, remonter; (*building*)
construire; (*notice*) mettre; (*price*)
augmenter; (*guest*) héberger; (*offer*)
offrir; ~ **up with** supporter.

putty n mastic m.

puzzle n énigme f; (game) casse-tête
m inv; (jigsaw) puzzle m. ● vt rendre
perplexe. ● vi se creuser la tête.

pyjamas npl pyjama m.

pylon n pylône m.

Qq

quack n (of duck) coin-coin m inv; (doctor) charlatan m.

quadrangle (of college) n cour f.

quadruple a & n quadruple (m). ● vt/i quadrupler.

quail n (bird) caille f.

quaint adj pittoresque; (old) vieillot; (odd) bizarre.

qualification n diplôme m; (ability) compétence f; (fig) réserve f, restriction f.

qualified adj diplômé; (able) qualifié (to do pour faire); (fig) conditionnel.

qualify vt qualifier; (modify) mettre des réserves à; (statement) nuancer. ● vi obtenir son diplôme (as de); (Sport) se qualifier; ~ for remplir les conditions requises pour.

quality n qualité f.

qualm n scrupule m.

quantity n quantité f.

quarantine n quarantaine f.

quarrel n dispute f, querelle f. ● vi (pt **quarrelled**) se disputer.

quarry n (excavation) carrière f; (prey) proie f. ● vt extraire.

quart n ≈ litre m.

quarter n quart m; (of year) trimestre m; (25 cents: US) quart m de dollar; (district) quartier m; ~s logement m; from all ~s de toutes parts. ● vt diviser en quatre; (troops) cantonner.

quarterly adj trimestriel. ● adv tous les trois mois.

quartet n quatuor m.

quartz n quartz m. ● adj (watch) à quartz.

quash vt (suppress) étouffer; (Jur) annuler.

quaver vi trembler, chevroter. ● n (Mus) croche f.

quay n (Naut) quai m.

queasy adj feel ~ avoir mal au cœur.

queen n reine f; (cards) dame f.

queer adj étrange; (dubious) louche; ☒ homosexuel.

quench vt éteindre; (thirst) étancher; (desire) étouffer.

query n question f. ● vt mettre en question.

quest n recherche f.

question n question f; in ~ en question; out of the ~ hors de question. ● vt interroger; (doubt) mettre en question, douter de. ~ **mark** n point m d'interrogation.

questionnaire n questionnaire m.

queue n queue f. ● vi (pres p **queuing**) faire la queue.

quibble vi ergoter.

quick adj rapide; (clever) vif/vive; be ~ (hurry) se dépêcher. ● adv vite. ● n cut to the ~ piquer au vif. **quicken** vt/i (s')accélérer. **quickly** adv rapidement, vite. ~**sand** n sables mpl mouvants.

quid n inv ⒢ livre f sterling.

quiet adj (calm, still) tranquille; (silent) silencieux; (gentle) doux; (discreet) discret; keep ~ se taire. ● n tranquillité f; on the ~ en cachette. **quieten** vt/i (se) calmer. **quietly** adv (speak) doucement; (sit) en silence.

quilt n édredon m; (continental) ~ couette f.

quirk n bizarrerie f.

quit vt (pt **quitted**) quitter; (smoking) arrêter de. ● vi abandonner; (resign) démissionner; ~ **doing** (US) cesser de faire.

quite adv tout à fait, vraiment; (rather) assez; ~ **a few** un bon nombre (de).

quits adj quitte (with envers); call it ~ en rester là.

quiver vi trembler.

quiz n (pl **quizzes**) test m; (game) jeu-concours m. ● vt (pt **quizzed**) questionner.

quotation n citation f; (price) devis m; (stock exchange) cotation f; ~ **marks** guillemets mpl.

quote vt citer; (reference, number) rappeler; (price) indiquer; (share price) coter. ● vi ~ **for** faire un devis

pour; ∼ **from** citer. ● *n* (quotation)
citation *f*; (estimate) devis *m*; **in** ∼**s**
⊞ entre guillemets.

....

Rr

....

rabbi *n* rabbin *m*.

rabbit *n* lapin *m*.

rabies *n* (disease) rage *f*.

race *n* (contest) course *f*; (group) race *f*.
● *adj* racial; ∼ **relations** relations *fpl*
inter-raciales. ● *vt* (compete with) faire
la course avec; (horse) faire courir.
● *vi* courir; (pulse) battre
précipitamment; (engine) s'emballer.
∼**course** *n* champ *m* de courses.
∼**horse** *n* cheval *m* de course.
∼**track** *n* piste *f*; (for horses) champ
m de courses.

racing *n* courses *fpl*; ∼ **car** voiture *f*
de course.

racism *n* racisme *m*. **racist** *a* & *n*
raciste (*mf*).

rack *n* (shelf) étagère *f*; (for clothes)
portant *m*; (for luggage) compartiment
m à bagages; (for dishes) égouttoir *m*.
● *vt* ∼ **one's brains** se creuser la
cervelle.

racket *n* (Sport) raquette *f*; (noise)
vacarme *m*; (swindle) escroquerie *f*;
(crime) trafic *m*.

radar *n* & *a* radar (*m*).

radial *n* ∼ (tyre) pneu *m* radial.

radiate *vt* (happiness) rayonner de;
(heat) émettre. ● *vi* rayonner (**from**
de). **radiation** *n* (radioactivity)
radiation *f*. **radiator** *n* radiateur *m*.

radical *n* & *a* radical/-e (*m*/*f*).

radio *n* radio *f*; **on the** ∼ à la radio.
● *vt* (message) envoyer par radio;
(person) appeler par radio.

radioactive *adj* radioactif.

radiographer *n* manipulateur/
-trice *m*/*f* radiographe.

radish *n* radis *m*.

radius *n* (*pl* **-dii**) rayon *m*.

raffle *n* tombola *f*.

rag *n* chiffon *m*; ∼**s** loques *fpl*.

rage *n* rage *f*, colère *f*; **be all the** ∼
faire fureur. ● *vi* (person) tempêter;
(storm, battle) faire rage.

ragged *adj* (clothes) en loques;
(person) dépenaillé.

raid *n* (Mil, on stock market) raid *m*; (by
police) rafle *f*; (by criminals) hold-up *m*
inv. ● *vt* faire un raid *or* une rafle *or*
un hold-up dans. **raider** *n* (thief)
pillard *m*; (Mil) commando *m*;
(corporate) raider *m*.

rail *n* (on balcony) balustrade *f*; (stairs)
rampe *f*; (for train) rail *m*; (for curtain)
tringle *f*; **by** ∼ par chemin de fer.

railing *n* (also ∼**s**) grille *f*.

railway, (US) **railroad** *n* chemin *m*
de fer. ∼ **line** *n* voie *f* ferrée. ∼
station *n* gare *f*.

rain *n* pluie *f*. ● *vi* pleuvoir. ∼**bow** *n*
arc-en-ciel *m*. ∼**coat** *n* imperméable
m. ∼**fall** *n* précipitation *f*. ∼ **forest**
n forêt *f* tropicale.

rainy *adj* (**-ier, -iest**) pluvieux;
(season) des pluies.

raise *vt* (barrier, curtain) lever;
(child, cattle) élever; (question)
soulever; (price, salary) augmenter.
● *n* (US) augmentation *f*.

raisin *n* raisin *m* sec.

rake *n* râteau *m*. ● *vt* (garden)
ratisser; (search) fouiller dans. ▫ ∼
in (money) amasser; ∼ **up** (past)
remuer.

rally *vt*/*i* (se) rallier; (strength)
reprendre; (after illness) aller mieux;
∼ **round** venir en aide. ● *n*
rassemblement *m*; (Auto) rallye *m*;
(tennis) échange *m*.

ram *n* bélier *m*. ● *vt* (*pt* **rammed**)
(thrust) enfoncer; (crash into) rentrer
dans.

RAM *abbr* (**random access
memory**) RAM *f*.

ramble *n* randonnée *f*. ● *vi* faire une
randonnée. ▫ ∼ **on** discourir.

ramp *n* (slope) rampe *f*; (in garage)
pont *m* de graissage.

rampage[1] *vi* se déchaîner (**through**
dans).

rampage[2] *n* **go on the** ∼ tout
saccager.

ran ⇒RUN.

rancid *adj* rance.

random adj (fait) au hasard. ● n at ~ au hasard.

rang ⇒RING².

range n (of prices, products) gamme f; (of people, beliefs) variété f; (of radar, weapon) portée f; (of aircraft) autonomie f; (of mountains) chaîne f. ● vi aller; (vary) varier.

rank n rang m; (Mil) grade m. ● vt/i ~ among (se) classer parmi.

ransack vt (search) fouiller; (pillage) mettre à sac.

ransom n rançon f.

rap n coup m sec; (Mus) rap m. ● vi (pt **rapped**) donner des coups secs (on sur).

rape vt violer. ● n viol m.

rapid adj rapide.

rapist n violeur m.

rapturous adj (delight) extasié; (welcome) enthousiaste.

rare adj rare; (Culin) saignant. **rarely** adv rarement.

rascal n coquin/-e m/f.

rash n (Med) rougeurs fpl. ● adj irréfléchi.

raspberry n framboise f.

rat n rat m. ● vi (pt **ratted**) ~ on (desert) lâcher; (inform on) dénoncer.

rate n (ratio, level) taux m; (speed) rythme m; (price) tarif m; (of exchange) taux m; **at any** ~ en tout cas. ● vt (value) estimer; (deserve) mériter; ~ **sth highly** admirer beaucoup qch. ● vi ~ **as** être considéré comme.

rather adv (by preference) plutôt; (fairly) assez, plutôt; (a little) un peu; **I would** ~ **go** j'aimerais mieux partir; ~ **than go** plutôt que de partir.

rating n (score, value) cote f; **the** ~**s** (TV) l'indice m d'écoute, l'audimat® m.

ratio n proportion f.

ration n ration f. ● vt rationner.

rational adj rationnel; (person) sensé.

rationalize vt justifier; (organize) rationaliser.

rattle vi (bottles, chains) s'entrechoquer; (window) vibrer. ● vt (bottles, chains) faire s'entrechoquer; (fig, 🔟) énerver. ● n

cliquetis m; (toy) hochet m. ~**snake** n serpent m à sonnette, crotale m.

rave vi (enthuse) s'emballer; (in fever) délirer; (in anger) tempêter.

raven n corbeau m.

ravenous adj **be** ~ avoir une faim de loup.

ravine n ravin m.

raving adj ~ **lunatic** fou m furieux, folle f furieuse.

ravishing adj ravissant.

raw adj cru; (not processed) brut; (wound) à vif; (immature) inexpérimenté; **get a** ~ **deal** être mal traité; ~ **material** matière f première.

ray n (of light) rayon m; ~ **of hope** lueur f d'espoir.

razor n rasoir m. ~**-blade** n lame f de rasoir.

re prep au sujet de; (at top of letter) objet.

reach vt (place, level) atteindre; (decision) arriver à; (contact) joindre; (audience, market) toucher. ● vi ~ **up/down** lever/baisser le bras; ~ **across** étendre le bras. ● n portée f; **within** ~ **of** à portée de; (close to) à proximité de.

react vi réagir. **reaction** n réaction f. **reactor** n réacteur m.

read vt/i (pt **read**) lire; (study) étudier; (instrument) indiquer; ~ **about sb** lire quelque chose sur qn; ~ **out** lire à haute voix. **reader** n lecteur/-trice m/f. **reading** n lecture f; (measurement) indication f; (interpretation) interprétation f.

readjust vt rajuster. ● vi se réadapter (to à).

read-only memory, ROM n mémoire f morte.

ready adj (-ier, -iest) prêt; (quick) prompt. ~**-made** adj tout fait. ~**-to-wear** adj prêt-à-porter.

real adj (not imaginary) véritable, réel; (not artificial) vrai; **it's a** ~ **shame** c'est vraiment dommage. ~ **estate** n biens mpl immobiliers.

realism n réalisme m. **realistic** adj réaliste.

reality n réalité f.

realize *vt* se rendre compte de, comprendre; (*fulfil, turn into cash*) réaliser; (*price*) atteindre.

really *adv* vraiment.

reap *vt* (*crop*) recueillir; (*benefits*) récolter.

reappear *vi* reparaître.

rear *n* arrière *m*; (*of person*) derrière *m* ⚠. ● *adj* (*seat*) arrière *inv*; (*entrance*) de derrière. ● *vt* élever. ● *vi* (*horse*) se cabrer. ~~**view mirror** *n* rétroviseur *m*.

reason *n* raison *f* (**to do, for doing** de faire); **within** ~ dans la limite du raisonnable. ● *vi* ~ **with sb** raisonner qn.

reasonable *adj* raisonnable.

reassurance *n* réconfort *m*.

reassure *vt* rassurer.

rebate *n* (*refund*) remboursement *m*; (*discount*) remise *f*.

rebel[1] *n* & *a* rebelle (*mf*).

rebel[2] *vi* (*pt* **rebelled**) se rebeller. **rebellion** *n* rébellion *f*.

rebound[1] *vi* rebondir; ~ **on** (*backfire*) se retourner contre.

rebound[2] *n* **n** rebond *m*.

rebuke *vt* réprimander. ● *n* réprimande *f*.

recall *vt* (*remember*) se souvenir de; (*call back*) rappeler. ● *n* (*memory*) mémoire *f*; (*Comput, Mil*) rappel *m*.

recap *vt/i* (*pt* **recapped**) récapituler. ● *n* récapitulation *f*.

recede *vi* s'éloigner; **his hair is receding** son front se dégarnit.

receipt *n* (*written*) reçu *m*; (*of letter*) réception *f*; ~**s** (Comm) recettes *fpl*.

receive *vt* recevoir; (*stolen goods*) receler. **receiver** *n* (*telephone*) combiné *m*; (TV) récepteur *m*.

recent *adj* récent. **recently** *adv* récemment.

receptacle *n* récipient *m*.

reception *n* réception *f*; **give sb a warm** ~ donner un accueil chaleureux à.

recess *n* (*alcove*) alcôve *m*; (*for door*) embrasure *f*; (Jur, Pol) vacances *fpl*; (School, US) récréation *f*.

recession *n* récession *f*.

recharge *vt* recharger.

recipe *n* recette *f*.

recipient *n* (*of honour*) récipiendaire *mf*; (*of letter*) destinataire *mf*.

reciprocate *vt* (*compliment*) retourner; (*kindness*) payer de retour. ● *vi* en faire autant.

recite *vi* réciter.

reckless *adj* imprudent.

reckon *vt/i* calculer; (*judge*) considérer; (*think*) penser; ~ **on/with** compter sur/avec. **reckoning** *n* (*guess*) estimation *f*; (*calculation*) calculs *mpl*.

reclaim *vt* récupérer; (*flooded land*) assécher.

recline *vi* s'allonger; (*seat*) s'incliner.

recluse *n* reclus/-e *m/f*.

recognition *n* reconnaissance *f*; **beyond** ~ méconnaissable; **gain** ~ être reconnu.

recognize *vt* reconnaître.

recollect *vt* se souvenir de, se rappeler. **recollection** *n* souvenir *m*.

recommend *vt* recommander. **recommendation** *n* recommandation *f*.

reconcile *vt* (*people*) réconcilier; (*facts*) concilier; ~ **oneself to** se résigner à.

recondition *vt* remettre à neuf.

reconsider *vt* réexaminer. ● *vi* réfléchir.

reconstruct *vt* reconstruire; (*crime*) faire une reconstitution de.

record[1] *vt/i* (*in register, on tape*) enregistrer; (*in diary*) noter; ~ **that** rapporter que.

record[2] *n* (*of events*) compte-rendu *m*; (*official*) procès-verbal *m*; (*personal, administrative*) dossier *m*; (*historical*) archives *fpl*; (*past history*) réputation *f*; (Mus) disque *m*; (Sport) record *m*; (*criminal*) ~ casier *m* judiciaire; **off the** ~ officieusement. ● *adj* record *inv*.

recorder *n* (Mus) flûte *f* à bec.

recording *n* enregistrement *m*.

record-player *n* tourne-disque *m*.

recover *vt* récupérer. ● *vi* se remettre; (*economy*) se redresser. **recovery** *n* (Med) rétablissement *m*; (*of economy*) relance *f*.

recreation *n* récréation *f.*

recruit *n* recrue *f.* ● *vt* recruter. **recruitment** *n* recrutement *m.*

rectangle *n* rectangle *m.*

rectify *vt* rectifier.

recuperate *vt* récupérer. ● *vi* se rétablir.

recur *vi* (*pt* **recurred**) se reproduire.

recycle *vt* recycler.

red *adj* (**redder, reddest**) rouge; (*hair*) roux. ● *n* rouge *m*; in the ∼ en déficit. **R∼ Cross** *n* Croix-Rouge *f.* ∼**currant** *n* groseille *f.*

redecorate *vt* repeindre, refaire.

redeploy *vt* réorganiser; (*troops*) répartir.

red: ∼**-handed** *adj* en flagrant délit. ∼**-hot** *adj* brûlant.

redirect *vt* (*traffic*) dévier; (*letter*) faire suivre.

redness *n* rougeur *f.*

redo *vt* (*pt* **-did**; *pp* **-done**) refaire.

redress *vt* (*wrong*) redresser; (*balance*) rétablir. ● *n* réparation *f.*

reduce *vt* réduire; (*temperature*) faire baisser. **reduction** *n* réduction *f.*

redundancy *n* licenciement *m.*

redundant *adj* superflu; (*worker*) licencié; **make** ∼ licencier.

reed *n* (plant) roseau *m.*

reef *n* récif *m*, écueil *m.*

reel *n* (of thread) bobine *f*; (of film) bande *f*; (winding device) dévidoir *m.* ● *vi* chanceler. ● *vt* ∼ **off** réciter.

refectory *n* réfectoire *m.*

refer *vt/i* (*pt* **referred**) ∼ **to** (allude to) faire allusion à; (concern) s'appliquer à; (consult) consulter; (direct) renvoyer à.

referee *n* (Sport) arbitre *m.* ● *vt* (*pt* **refereed**) arbitrer.

reference *n* référence *f*; (mention) allusion *f*; (person) personne *f* pouvant fournir des références; **in** or **with** ∼ **to** en ce qui concerne; (Comm) suite à.

referendum *n* (*pl* ∼**s**) référendum *m.*

refill¹ *vt* (*glass*) remplir à nouveau; (*pen*) recharger.

refill² *n* recharge *f.*

refine *vt* raffiner.

reflect *vt* refléter; (*heat, light*) renvoyer. ● *vi* réfléchir (**on** à); ∼ **well/badly on sb** faire honneur/du tort à qn.

reflection *n* réflexion *f*; (image) reflet *m*; **on** ∼ à la réflexion.

reflective *adj* (*surface*) réfléchissant; (*person*) réfléchi.

reflector *n* (on car) catadioptre *m.*

reflex *a* & *n* réflexe (*m*).

reflexive *adj* (Gram) réfléchi.

reform *vt* réformer. ● *vi* (*person*) s'amender. ● *n* réforme *f.*

refrain *n* refrain *m.* ● *vi* s'abstenir (**from** de).

refresh *vt* (*drink*) rafraîchir; (*rest*) reposer. **refreshments** *npl* rafraîchissements *mpl.*

refrigerate *vt* réfrigérer. **refrigerator** *n* réfrigérateur *m.*

refuel *vt/i* (*pt* **refuelled**) (se) ravitailler.

refuge *n* refuge *m*; **take** ∼ se réfugier. **refugee** *n* réfugié/-e *m/f.*

refund¹ *vt* rembourser.

refund² *n* remboursement *m.*

refurbish *vt* remettre à neuf.

refuse¹ *vt/i* refuser.

refuse² *n* ordures *fpl.*

regain *vt* retrouver; (*lost ground*) regagner.

regard *vt* considérer; **as** ∼**s** en ce qui concerne. ● *n* égard *m*, estime *f*; **in this** ∼ à cet égard; ∼**s** amitiés *fpl.* **regarding** *prep* en ce qui concerne.

regardless *adv* malgré tout; ∼ **of** sans tenir compte de.

regime *n* régime *m.*

regiment *n* régiment *m.*

region *n* région *f*; **in the** ∼ **of** environ.

register *n* registre *m.* ● *vt* (record) enregistrer; (*vehicle*) faire immatriculer; (*birth*) déclarer; (*letter*) recommander; (indicate) indiquer; (express) exprimer. ● *vi* (enrol) s'inscrire; (at hotel) se présenter; (fig) être compris.

registrar *n* officier *m* de l'état civil; (Univ) responsable *m* du bureau de la scolarité.

registration *n* (of voter, student) inscription *f*; (of birth) déclaration *f*; ∼ **(number)** (Auto) numéro *m* d'immatriculation.

registry office *n* bureau *m* de l'état civil.

regret *n* regret *m*. ● *vt* (*pt* **regretted**) regretter (**to do de** faire). **regretfully** *adv* à regret.

regular *adj* régulier; (usual) habituel. ● *n* habitué/-e *m/f*. **regularity** *n* régularité *f*. **regularly** *adv* régulièrement.

regulate *vt* régler. **regulation** *n* (rule) règlement *m*; (process) réglementation *f*.

rehabilitate *vt* (in public esteem) réhabiliter; (prisoner) réinsérer.

rehearsal *n* répétition *f*. **rehearse** *vt/i* répéter.

reign *n* règne *m*. ● *vi* régner (**over** sur).

reimburse *vt* rembourser.

reindeer *n inv* renne *m*.

reinforce *vt* renforcer. **reinforcement** *n* renforcement *m*; ∼**s** renforts *mpl*.

reinstate *vt* (*person*) réintégrer; (*law*) rétablir.

reject[1] *n* marchandise *f* de deuxième choix.

reject[2] *vt* (*offer, plea*) rejeter; (*goods*) refuser. **rejection** *n* (personal) rejet *m*; (of candidate, work) refus *m*.

rejoice *vi* se réjouir.

relapse *n* rechute *f*. ● *vi* rechuter; ∼ **into** retomber dans.

relate *vt* raconter; (associate) associer. ● *vi* ∼ **to** se rapporter à; (get on with) s'entendre avec. **related** *adj* (*ideas*) lié; **we are** ∼**d** nous sommes parents.

relation *n* rapport *m*; (person) parent/-e *m/f*. **relationship** *n* relations *fpl*; (link) rapport *m*.

relative *n* parent/-e *m/f*. ● *adj* relatif; (respective) respectif.

relax *vt* (grip) relâcher; (*muscle*) décontracter; (*discipline*) assouplir. ● *vi* (*person*) se détendre; (*grip*) se relâcher. **relaxation** *n* détente *f*. **relaxing** *adj* délassant.

relay[1] *n* (also ∼ **race**) course *f* de relais.

relay[2] *vt* relayer.

release *vt* (*prisoner*) libérer; (*fastening*) faire jouer; (*object, hand*) lâcher; (*film*) faire sortir; (*news*) publier. ● *n* libération *f*; (of film) sortie *f*; (new record, film) nouveauté *f*.

relevance *n* pertinence *f*, intérêt *m*.

relevant *adj* pertinent; **be** ∼ **to** avoir rapport à.

reliability *n* (of firm) sérieux *m*; (of car) fiabilité *f*; (of person) honnêteté *f*. **reliable** *adj* (*firm*) sérieux; (*person, machine*) fiable.

reliance *n* dépendance *f*.

relic *n* vestige *m*; (object) relique *f*.

relief *n* soulagement *m* (**from** à); (assistance) secours *m*; (outline) relief *m*; ∼ **road** route *f* de délestage.

relieve *vt* soulager; (help) secourir; (take over from) relayer.

religion *n* religion *f*. **religious** *adj* religieux.

relish *n* plaisir *m*; (Culin) condiment *m*. ● *vt* (*food*) savourer; (*idea*) se réjouir de.

relocate *vt* muter. ● *vi* (*company*) déménager; (*worker*) être muté.

reluctance *n* répugnance *f*.

reluctant *adj* (*person*) peu enthousiaste; (*consent*) accordé à contrecœur; ∼ **to** peu disposé à. **reluctantly** *adv* à contrecœur.

rely *vi* ∼ **on** (count) compter sur; (be dependent) dépendre de.

remain *vi* rester. **remainder** *n* reste *m*.

remand *vt* mettre en détention provisoire. ● *n* **on** ∼ en détention provisoire.

remark *n* remarque *f*. ● *vt* remarquer. ● *vi* ∼ **on** faire des remarques sur. **remarkable** *adj* remarquable.

remedy *n* remède *m*. ● *vt* remédier à.

remember *vt* se souvenir de, se rappeler; ∼ **to do** ne pas oublier de faire. **remembrance** *n* souvenir *m*.

remind *vt* rappeler (**sb of sth** qch à qn); ~ **sb to do** rappeler à qn de faire. **reminder** *n* rappel *m*.

reminisce *vi* évoquer ses souvenirs.

remission *n* (Med) rémission *f*; (Jur) remise *f*.

remnant *n* reste *m*; (trace) vestige *m*; (of cloth) coupon *m*.

remodel *vt* (*pt* **remodelled**) remodeler.

remorse *n* remords *m*.

remote *adj* (*place, time*) lointain; (*person*) distant; (slight) vague; ~ **control** télécommande *f*.

removable *adj* amovible.

removal *n* (of employee) renvoi *m*; (of threat) suppression *f*; (of troops) retrait *m*; (of stain) détachage *m*; (from house) déménagement *m*; ~ **men** déménageurs *mpl*.

remove *vt* enlever; (dismiss) renvoyer; (do away with) supprimer; (Comput) effacer.

remunerate *vt* rémunérer. **remuneration** *n* rémunération *f*.

render *vt* rendre.

renegade *n* renégat/-e *m/f*.

renew *vt* renouveler; (resume) reprendre. **renewable** *adj* renouvelable.

renounce *vt* renoncer à; (disown) renier.

renovate *vt* rénover.

renown *n* renommée *f*.

rent *n* loyer *m*. ● *vt* louer; **for** ~ à louer. **rental** *n* prix *m* de location.

reopen *vt/i* rouvrir.

reorganize *vt* réorganiser.

rep *n* (Comm) représentant/-e *m/f*.

repair *vt* réparer. ● *n* réparation *f*; **in good/bad** ~ en bon/mauvais état.

repatriate *vt* rapatrier. **repatriation** *n* rapatriement *m*.

repay *vt* (*pt* **repaid**) rembourser; (reward) récompenser. **repayment** *n* remboursement *m*.

repeal *vt* abroger. ● *n* abrogation *f*.

repeat *vt/i* répéter; (renew) renouveler; ~ **itself**, ~ **oneself** se répéter. ● *n* répétition *f*; (broadcast) reprise *f*.

repel *vt* (*pt* **repelled**) repousser.

repent *vi* se repentir (**of** de).

repercussion *n* répercussion *f*.

repetition *n* répétition *f*.

replace *vt* (put back) remettre; (take the place of) remplacer. **replacement** *n* remplacement *m* (**of** de); (person) remplaçant/-e *m/f*; (new part) pièce *f* de rechange.

replay *n* (Sport) match *m* rejoué; (recording) répétition *f* immédiate.

replenish *vt* (refill) remplir; (renew) renouveler.

replica *n* copie *f* exacte.

reply *vt/i* répondre. ● *n* réponse *f*.

report *vt* rapporter, annoncer (**that** que); (notify) signaler; (denounce) dénoncer. ● *vi* faire un rapport; ~ (**on**) (*news item*) faire un reportage sur; ~ **to** (go) se présenter chez. ● *n* rapport *m*; (in press) reportage *m*; (School) bulletin *m*. **reporter** *n* reporter *m*.

repossess *vt* reprendre.

represent *vt* représenter.

representation *n* représentation *f*; **make** ~**s to** protester auprès de.

representative *adj* représentatif, typique (**of** de). ● *n* représentant/-e *m/f*.

repress *vt* réprimer.

reprieve *n* (delay) sursis *m*; (pardon) grâce *f*. ● *vt* accorder un sursis à; gracier.

reprimand *vt* réprimander. ● *n* réprimande *f*.

reprisals *npl* représailles *fpl*.

reproach *vt* reprocher (**sb for sth** qch à qn). ● *n* reproche *m*.

reproduce *vt/i* (se) reproduire. **reproduction** *n* reproduction *f*. **reproductive** *adj* reproducteur.

reptile *n* reptile *m*.

republic *n* république *f*. **republican** *a* & *n* républicain/-e (*m/f*).

repudiate *vt* répudier; (*contract*) refuser d'honorer.

reputable *adj* honorable, de bonne réputation.

reputation *n* réputation *f*.

repute *n* réputation *f*.

request *n* demande *f*. ● *vt* demander (**of, from** à).

require vt (of thing) demander; (of person) avoir besoin de; (demand, order) exiger. **required** adj requis. **requirement** n exigence f; (condition) condition f (requise).

rescue vt sauver. ● n sauvetage m (of de); (help) secours m.

research n recherche(s) f(pl). ● vt/i faire des recherches. **researcher** n chercheur/-euse m/f.

resemblance n ressemblance f. **resemble** vt ressembler à.

resent vt être indigné de, s'offenser de. **resentment** n ressentiment m.

reservation n (doubt) réserve f; (booking) réservation f; (US) réserve f (indienne); **make a** ~ réserver.

reserve vt réserver. ● n (stock, land) réserve f; (Sport) remplaçant/-e m/f; **in** ~ en réserve; **the** ~s (Mil) les réserves fpl. **reserved** adj (person, room) réservé.

reshuffle vt (Pol) remanier. ● n (Pol) remaniement m (ministériel).

residence n résidence f; (of students) foyer m; **in** ~ (doctor) résidant.

resident adj résidant; **be** ~ résider. ● n habitant/-e m/f; (foreigner) résident/-e m/f; (in hotel) pensionnaire mf. **residential** adj résidentiel.

resign vt abandonner; (job) démissionner de. ● vi démissionner; ~ **oneself to** se résigner à. **resignation** n résignation f; (from job) démission f. **resigned** adj résigné.

resilience n élasticité f; ressort m.

resin n résine f.

resist vt/i résister (à). **resistance** n résistance f. **resistant** adj (Med) rebelle; (metal) résistant.

resolution n résolution f.

resolve vt résoudre (**to do** de faire). ● n résolution f.

resort vi ~ **to** avoir recours à. ● n (recourse) recours m; (place) station f; **in the last** ~ en dernier ressort.

resource n ressource f; ~s (wealth) ressources fpl. **resourceful** adj ingénieux.

respect n respect m; (aspect) égard m; **with** ~ **to** à l'égard de, relativement à. ● vt respecter.

respectability n respectabilité f. **respectable** adj respectable.

respectful adj respectueux.

respective adj respectif.

respite n répit m.

respond vi répondre (**to** à); ~ **to** (react to) réagir à. **response** n réponse f.

responsibility n responsabilité f. **responsible** adj responsable; (job) qui comporte des responsabilités.

responsive adj réceptif.

rest vt/i (se) reposer; (lean) (s') appuyer (**on** sur); (be buried, lie) reposer; (remain) demeurer. ● n repos m; (support) support m; **have a** ~ se reposer; **the** ~ (remainder) le reste (**of** de); (other people) les autres.

restaurant n restaurant m.

restless adj agité.

restoration n rétablissement m; restauration f.

restore vt rétablir; (building) restaurer; ~ **sth to sb** restituer qch à qn.

restrain vt contenir; ~ **sb from** retenir qn de. **restrained** adj (moderate) mesuré; (in control of self) maître de soi.

restrict vt restreindre.

rest room n (US) toilettes fpl.

result n résultat m. ● vi résulter; ~ **in** aboutir à.

resume vt/i reprendre.

résumé n résumé m; (of career: US) CV m, curriculum vitae m.

resurrect vt ressusciter.

resuscitate vt réanimer.

retail n détail m. ● a & adv au détail. ● vt/i (se) vendre (au détail). **retailer** n détaillant/-e m/f.

retain vt (hold back, remember) retenir; (keep) conserver.

retaliate vi riposter. **retaliation** n représailles fpl.

retch vi avoir un haut-le-cœur.

retire vi (from work) prendre sa retraite; (withdraw) se retirer; (go to bed) se coucher. **retired** adj retraité. **retirement** n retraite f.

retort vt/i répliquer. ● n réplique f.

retrace vt ~ **one's steps** revenir sur ses pas.

retract *vt/i* (se) rétracter.

retrain *vt/i* (se) recycler.

retreat *vi* (Mil) battre en retraite. ● *n* retraite *f*.

retrieval *n* (Comput) extraction *f*.

retrieve *vt* (*object*) récupérer; (*situation*) redresser; (*data*) extraire.

retrospect *n* in ∼ rétrospectivement.

return *vi* (come back) revenir; (go back) retourner; (go home) rentrer. ● *vt* (give back) rendre; (bring back) rapporter; (send back) renvoyer; (put back) remettre. ● *n* retour *m*; (yield) rapport *m*; ∼s (Comm) bénéfices *mpl*; in ∼ for en échange de. ∼ **ticket** *n* aller-retour *m*.

reunion *n* réunion *f*.

reunite *vt* réunir.

rev *n* (Auto 🗊) tour *m*. ● *vt/i* (*pt* **revved**) ∼ (**up**) (engine 🗊) (s') emballer.

reveal *vt* révéler; (allow to appear) laisser voir.

revelation *n* révélation *f*.

revenge *n* vengeance *f*. ● *vt* venger.

revenue *n* revenu *m*.

reverberate *vi* (sound, light) se répercuter.

reverend *adj* révérend.

reversal *n* renversement *m*; (of view) revirement *m*.

reverse *adj* contraire, inverse. ● *n* contraire *m*; (back) revers *m*, envers *m*; (gear) marche *f* arrière. ● *vt* (*situation, bracket*) renverser; (*order*) inverser; (*decision*) annuler; ∼ **the charges** appeler en PCV. ● *vi* (Auto) faire marche arrière.

review *n* (inspection, magazine) revue *f*; (of book) critique *f*. ● *vt* passer en revue; (situation) réexaminer; faire la critique de. **reviewer** *n* critique *m*.

revise *vt* réviser; (*text*) revoir. **revision** *n* révision *f*.

revival *n* (of economy) reprise *f*; (of interest) regain *m*.

revive *vt* (person, hopes) ranimer; (custom) rétablir. ● *vi* se ranimer.

revoke *vt* révoquer.

revolt *vt/i* (se) révolter. ● *n* révolte *f*. **revolting** *adj* dégoûtant.

revolution *n* révolution *f*.

revolve *vi* tourner.

revolver *n* revolver *m*.

revolving door *n* porte *f* à tambour.

reward *n* récompense *f*. ● *vt* récompenser (for de). **rewarding** *adj* rémunérateur; (worthwhile) qui (en) vaut la peine.

rewind *vt* (*pt* **rewound**) rembobiner.

rewire *vt* refaire l'installation électrique de.

rhetorical *adj* (de) rhétorique; (*question*) de pure forme.

rheumatism *n* rhumatisme *m*.

rhinoceros *n* (*pl* ∼**es**) rhinocéros *m*.

rhubarb *n* rhubarbe *f*.

rhyme *n* rime *f*; (poem) vers *mpl*. ● *vt/i* (faire) rimer.

rhythm *n* rythme *m*. **rhythmic-(al)** *adj* rythmique.

rib *n* côte *f*.

ribbon *n* ruban *m*; in ∼s en lambeaux.

rice *n* riz *m*. ∼ **pudding** *n* riz *m* au lait.

rich *adj* riche.

rid *vt* (*pt* **rid**; *pres p* **ridding**) débarrasser (of de); **get** ∼ **of** se débarrasser de.

ridden ⇒RIDE.

riddle *n* énigme *f*. ● *vt* ∼ **with** (*bullets*) cribler de; (*mistakes*) bourrer de.

ride *vi* (*pt* **rode**; *pp* **ridden**) aller (à bicyclette, à cheval); (in car) rouler; (on a horse as sport) monter à cheval. ● *vt* (a particular horse) monter; (distance) parcourir. ● *n* promenade *f*, tour *m*; (distance) trajet *m*; **give sb a** ∼ (US) prendre qn en voiture; **go for a** ∼ aller faire un tour (à bicyclette, à cheval). **rider** *n* cavalier/-ière *m/f*; (in horse race) jockey *m*; (cyclist) cycliste *mf*; (motorcyclist) motocycliste *mf*.

ridge *n* arête *f*, crête *f*.

ridiculous *adj* ridicule.

riding *n* équitation *f*.

rifle *n* fusil *m*. ● *vt* (rob) dévaliser.

rift *n* (crack) fissure *f*; (between people) désaccord *m*.

rig vt (pt **rigged**) (equip) équiper; (election, match) truquer. ● n (for oil) derrick m. □ ~ **out** habiller; ~ **up** (arrange) arranger.

right adj (morally) bon; (fair) juste; (best) bon, qu'il faut; (not left) droit; **be** ~ (person) avoir raison (**to** de); (calculation, watch) être exact; **put** ~ arranger, rectifier. ● n (entitlement) droit m; (not left) droite f; (not evil) le bien; **be in the** ~ avoir raison; **on the** ~ à droite. ● vt (a wrong, sth fallen) redresser. ● adv (not left) à droite; (directly) tout droit; (exactly) bien, juste; (completely) tout (à fait); ~ **away** tout de suite; ~ **now** (at once) tout de suite; (at present) en ce moment.

righteous adj vertueux.

rightful adj légitime.

right-handed adj droitier.

rightly adv correctement; (with reason) à juste titre.

right of way n (Auto) priorité f.

right wing adj de droite.

rigid adj rigide.

rigorous adj rigoureux.

rim n bord m.

rind n (on cheese) croûte f; (on bacon) couenne f; (on fruit) écorce f.

ring[1] n (hoop) anneau m; (jewellery) bague f; (circle) cercle m; (boxing) ring m; (wedding) ~ alliance f. ● vt entourer; (word in text) entourer d'un cercle.

ring[2] vt/i (pt **rang**; pp **rung**) sonner; (of words) retentir; ~ **the bell** sonner. ● n sonnerie f; **give sb a** ~ donner un coup de fil à qn. □ ~ **back** rappeler; ~ **off** raccrocher; ~ **up** téléphoner (à).

ring road n périphérique m.

rink n patinoire f.

rinse vt rincer; ~ **out** rincer. ● n rinçage m.

riot n émeute f; (of colours) profusion f; **run** ~ se déchaîner. ● vi faire une émeute.

rip vt/i (pt **ripped**) (se) déchirer; **let** ~ (not check) laisser courir; ~ **off** ⊠ rouler. ● n déchirure f.

ripe adj mûr. **ripen** vt/i mûrir.

rip-off n 🅸 vol m; arnaque f 🅸.

ripple n ride f, ondulation f. ● vt/i (water) (se) rider.

rise vi (pt **rose**; pp **risen**) (go upwards, increase) monter, s'élever; (stand up, get up from bed) se lever; (rebel) se soulever; (sun) se lever; (water) monter; ~ **up** se soulever. ● n (slope) pente f; (increase) hausse f; (in pay) augmentation f; (progress, boom) essor m; **give** ~ **to** donner lieu à.

risk n risque m; **at** ~ menacé. ● vt risquer; ~ **doing** (venture) se risquer à faire. **risky** adj risqué.

rite n rite m; **last** ~s derniers sacrements mpl.

rival n rival/-e m/f. ● adj rival; (claim) opposé. ● vt (pt **rivalled**) rivaliser avec.

river n rivière f; (flowing into sea) fleuve m. ● adj (fishing, traffic) fluvial.

rivet n (bolt) rivet m. ● vt (pt **riveted**) river, riveter.

Riviera n **the (French)** ~ la Côte d'Azur.

road n route f; (in town) rue f; (small) chemin m; **the** ~ **to** (glory: fig) le chemin de. ● adj (sign, safety) routier. ~**-map** n carte f routière. ~ **rage** n violence f au volant. ~**worthy** adj en état de marche.

roam vi errer. ● vt (streets, seas) parcourir.

roar n hurlement m; (of lion, wind) rugissement m; (of lorry, thunder) grondement m. ● vt/i hurler; (lion, wind) rugir; (lorry, thunder) gronder; ~ **with laughter** rire aux éclats.

roast vt/i rôtir. ● n (meat) rôti m. ● adj rôti. ~ **beef** n rôti m de bœuf.

rob vt (pt **robbed**) voler (**sb of sth** qch à qn); (bank, house) dévaliser; (deprive) priver (**of** de). **robber** n voleur/-euse m/f. **robbery** n vol m.

robe n (of judge) robe f; (dressing-gown) peignoir m.

robin n rouge-gorge m.

robot n robot m.

robust adj robuste.

rock n roche f; (rock face, boulder) rocher m; (hurled stone) pierre f; (sweet) sucre m d'orge; (Mus) rock m;

on the ~s (*drink*) avec des glaçons; (*marriage*) en crise. ● *vt/i* (se) balancer; (shake) (faire) trembler; (*child*) bercer. ~**-climbing** *n* varappe *f*.

rocket *n* fusée *f*.

rocking-chair *n* fauteuil *m* à bascule.

rocky *adj* (**-ier, -iest**) (*ground*) rocailleux; (*hill*) rocheux; (shaky: fig) branlant.

rod *n* (metal) tige *f*; (wooden) baguette *f*; (for fishing) canne *f* à pêche.

rode ⇨RIDE.

roe *n* œufs *mpl* de poisson.

rogue *n* (dishonest) bandit *m*, voleur/ -euse *m/f*; (mischievous) coquin/-e *m/f*.

role *n* rôle *m*.

roll *vt/i* rouler; ~ (**about**) (*child, dog*) se rouler; **be** ~**ing** (**in money**) 🔢 rouler sur l'or. ● *n* rouleau *m*; (list) liste *f*; (bread) petit pain *m*; (of drum, thunder) roulement *m*; (of ship) roulis *m*. □ ~ **out** étendre; ~**over** se retourner; ~ **up** (*sleeves*) retrousser.

roll-call *n* appel *m*.

roller *n* rouleau *m*. ~**-coaster** *n* montagnes *fpl* russes. ~**-skate** *n* patin *m* à roulettes.

ROM (*abbr*) (**read-only memory**) mémoire *f* morte.

Roman *a* & *n* romain/-e (*m/f*). ~ **Catholic** *a* & *n* catholique (*mf*).

romance *n* (novel) roman *m* d'amour; (love) amour *m*; (affair) idylle *f*; (fig) poésie *f*.

Romania *n* Roumanie *f*.

Romanian *adj* roumain. ● *n* (person) Roumain/-e *m/f*; (language) roumain *m*.

romantic *adj* (love) romantique; (of the imagination) romanesque.

roof *n* toit *m*; (of mouth) palais *m*. ● *vt* recouvrir. ~**-rack** *n* galerie *f*. ~**-top** *n* toit *m*.

room *n* pièce *f*; (bedroom) chambre *f*; (large hall) salle *f*; (space) place *f*; ~ **for manoeuvre** marge *f* de manœuvre. ~**-mate** *n* camarade *mf* de chambre.

roomy *adj* spacieux; (*clothes*) ample.

root *n* racine *f*; (source) origine *f*; **take** ~ prendre racine. ● *vt/i* (s') enraciner. □ ~ **about** fouiller; ~ **for** (US 🔢) encourager; ~ **out** extirper.

rope *n* corde *f*; **know the** ~**s** être au courant. ● *vt* attacher; ~ **in** (*person*) enrôler.

rose *n* rose *f*. ● ⇨RISE.

rosé *n* rosé *m*.

rosy *adj* (**-ier, -iest**) rose; (hopeful) plein d'espoir.

rot *vt/i* (*pt* **rotted**) pourrir. ● *n* pourriture *f*.

rota *n* liste *f* (de service).

rotary *adj* rotatif.

rotate *vt/i* (faire) tourner; (change round) alterner.

rotten *adj* pourri; (*tooth*) gâté; (bad 🔢) mauvais, sale.

rough *adj* (manners) rude; (to touch) rugueux; (*ground*) accidenté; (violent) brutal; (bad) mauvais; (*estimate*) approximatif. ● *adv* (live) à la dure; (*play*) brutalement.

roughage *n* fibres *fpl* (alimentaires).

roughly *adv* rudement; (approximately) à peu près.

round *adj* rond. ● *n* (circle) rond *m*; (slice) tranche *f*; (of visits, drinks) tournée *f*; (competition) partie *f*, manche *f*; (boxing) round *m*; (of talks) série *f*; ~ **of applause** applaudissements *mpl*; **go the** ~**s** circuler. ● *prep* autour de; **she lives** ~ **here** elle habite par ici; ~ **the clock** vingt-quatre heures sur vingt-quatre. ● *adv* autour; ~ **about** (nearby) par ici; (fig) à peu près; **go** *or* **come** ~ **to** (*a friend*) passer chez; **enough to go** ~ assez pour tout le monde. ● *vt* (object) arrondir; (*corner*) tourner. □ ~ **off** terminer; ~ **up** rassembler

roundabout *n* (in fairground) manège *m*; (for traffic) rond-point *m* (*à sens giratoire*). ● *adj* indirect.

round trip *n* voyage *m* aller-retour.

round-up *n* rassemblement *m*; (of suspects) rafle *f*.

route *n* itinéraire *m*, parcours *m*; (Naut, Aviat) route *f*.

routine n routine f. ● adj de routine.

row¹ n rangée f, rang m; **in a ~** (consecutive) consécutif. ● vi ramer; (Sport) faire de l'aviron. ● vt **~ a boat up the river** remonter la rivière à la rame.

row² n (noise 🔊) tapage m; (quarrel 🔊) dispute f. ● vi 🔊 se disputer.

rowdy adj (**-ier**, **-iest**) tapageur.

rowing n aviron m. **~-boat** n bateau m à rames.

royal adj royal. **royalty** n famille f royale; **royalties** droits mpl d'auteur.

rub vt/i (pt **rubbed**) frotter; **~ it in** insister, en rajouter. ● n friction f. ◻ **~ out** (s')effacer.

rubber n caoutchouc m; (eraser) gomme f. **~ band** n élastique m. **~ stamp** n tampon m.

rubbish n (refuse) ordures fpl; (junk) saletés fpl; (fig) bêtises fpl.

rubble n décombres mpl.

ruby n rubis m.

rucksack n sac m à dos.

rude adj impoli, grossier; (improper) indécent; (blow) brutal.

ruffle vt (hair) ébouriffer; (clothes) froisser; (person) contrarier. ● n (frill) ruche f.

rug n petit tapis m.

rugby n rugby m.

rugged adj (surface) rude, rugueux; (ground) accidenté; (character, features) rude.

ruin n ruine f. ● vt (destroy) ruiner; (damage) abîmer; (spoil) gâter.

rule n règle f; (regulation) règlement m; (Pol) gouvernement m; **as a ~** en règle générale. ● vt gouverner; (master) dominer; (decide) décider; **~ out** exclure. ● vi régner. **ruler** n dirigeant/-e m/f, gouvernant m; (measure) règle f.

ruling adj (class) dirigeant; (party) au pouvoir. ● n décision f.

rum n rhum m.

rumble vi gronder; (stomach) gargouiller. ● n grondement m; gargouillement m.

rumour, (US) **rumor** n bruit m, rumeur f; **there's a ~ that** le bruit court que.

rump n (of animal) croupe f; (of bird) croupion m; (steak) romsteck m.

run vi (pt **ran**; pp **run**; pres p **running**) courir; (flow) couler; (pass) passer; (function) marcher; (melt) fondre; (extend) s'étendre; (of bus) circuler; (of play) se jouer; (last) durer; (of colour in washing) déteindre; (in election) être candidat. ● vt (manage) diriger; (event) organiser; (risk, race) courir; (house) tenir; (temperature, errand) faire; (Comput) exécuter. ● n course f; (journey) parcours m; (outing) promenade f; (rush) ruée f; (series) série f; (for chickens) enclos m; (in cricket) point m; **in the long ~** avec le temps; **on the ~** en fuite. ◻ **~ across** rencontrer par hasard; **~ away** s'enfuir; **~ down** descendre en courant; (of vehicle) renverser; (production) réduire progressivement; (belittle) dénigrer; **~ into** (hit) heurter; **~ off** (copies) tirer; **~ out** (be used up) s'épuiser; (of lease) expirer; **~ out of** manquer de; **~ over** (of vehicle) écraser; (details) revoir; **~ through** regarder qch rapidement; **~ sth through sth** passer qch à travers qch; **~ up** (bill) accumuler.

runaway n fugitif/-ive m/f. ● adj fugitif; (horse, vehicle) fou; (inflation) galopant.

rung ⇒RING². ● n (of ladder) barreau m.

runner n coureur/-euse m/f. **~ bean** n haricot m d'Espagne. **~-up** n second/-e m/f.

running n course f à pied; (of business) gestion f; (of machine) marche f; **be in the ~ for** être sur les rangs pour. ● adj (commentary) suivi; (water) courant; **four days ~** quatre jours de suite.

runway n piste f.

rural adj rural.

rush vi (move) se précipiter; (be in a hurry) se dépêcher. ● vt (person) bousculer; (Mil) prendre d'assaut; **~ to** envoyer d'urgence à. ● n ruée f; (haste) bousculade f; (plant) jonc m; **in a ~** pressé. **~-hour** n heure f de pointe.

Russia n Russie f.

Russian *adj* russe. ● *n* (person)
Russe *mf*; (language) russe.

rust *n* rouille *f*. ● *vt/i* rouiller.

rustle *vt/i* (*papers*) froisser.

rusty *adj* rouillé.

ruthless *adj* impitoyable.

rye *n* seigle *m*.

Ss

sabbath *n* (Jewish) sabbat *m*;
(Christian) jour *m* du seigneur.

sabbatical *adj* (Univ) sabbatique.

sabotage *n* sabotage *m*. ● *vt*
saboter.

saccharin *n* saccharine *f*.

sack *n* (bag) sac *m*; **get the** ～ 🖪 être
renvoyé. ● *vt* 🖪 renvoyer; (plunder)
saccager. **sacking** *n* (cloth) toile *f* à
sac; (dismissal 🖪) renvoi *m*.

sacrament *n* sacrement *m*.

sacred *adj* sacré.

sacrifice *n* sacrifice *m*. ● *vt*
sacrifier.

sad *adj* (**sadder**, **saddest**) triste.

saddle *n* selle *f*. ● *vt* (*horse*) seller.

sadist *n* sadique *mf*. **sadistic** *adj*
sadique.

sadly *adv* tristement; (unfortunately)
malheureusement.

sadness *n* tristesse *f*.

safe *adj* (not dangerous) sans danger;
(reliable) sûr; (out of danger) en
sécurité; (after accident) sain et sauf; ～
from à l'abri de. ● *n* coffre-fort *m*.

safeguard *n* sauvegarde *f*. ● *vt*
sauvegarder.

safely *adv* sans danger; (in safe place)
en sûreté.

safety *n* sécurité *f*. ～-**belt** *n*
ceinture *f* de sécurité. ～-**pin** *n*
épingle *f* de sûreté. ～-**valve** *n*
soupape *f* de sûreté.

saffron *n* safran *m*.

sag *vi* (*pt* **sagged**) (*beam, mattress*)
s'affaisser; (*flesh*) être flasque.

sage *n* (herb) sauge *f*.

Sagittarius *n* Sagittaire *m*.

said ⇒SAY.

sail *n* voile *f*; (journey) tour *m* en
bateau. ● *vi* (*person*) voyager en
bateau; (as sport) faire de la voile; (set
off) prendre la mer; ～ **across**
traverser. ● *vt* (*boat*) piloter; (*sea*)
traverser. **sailing-boat**, **sailing-ship** *n* voilier *m*.

sailor *n* marin *m*.

saint *n* saint/-e *m/f*.

sake *n* for the ～ of pour.

salad *n* salade *f*.

salaried *adj* salarié.

salary *n* salaire *m*.

sale *n* vente *f*; for ～ à vendre; on ～
en vente; (reduced) en solde; ～s
(reductions) soldes *mpl*; ～s **assistant**,
(US) ～s **clerk** vendeur/-euse *m/f*.

salesman *n* (*pl* -**men**) (in shop)
vendeur *m*; (traveller) représentant *m*.

saline *adj* salin. ● *n* sérum *m*
physiologique.

saliva *n* salive *f*.

salmon *n* *inv* saumon *m*.

salon *n* salon *m*.

saloon *n* (on ship) salon *m*; ～ (**car**)
berline *f*.

salt *n* sel *m*. ● *vt* saler. **salty** *adj*
salé.

salutary *adj* salutaire.

salute *n* salut *m*. ● *vt* saluer. ● *vi*
faire un salut.

salvage *n* sauvetage *m*; (of waste)
récupération *f*. ● *vt* sauver; (for re-use) récupérer.

same *adj* même (as que). ● *pron* the
～ le même, la même, les mêmes; **at
the** ～ **time** en même temps; **the** ～
(thing) la même chose.

sample *n* échantillon *m*; (of blood)
prélèvement *m*. ● *vt* essayer; (*food*)
goûter.

sanctimonious *adj* (pej)
supérieur.

sanction *n* sanction *f*. ● *vt*
sanctionner.

sanctity *n* sainteté *f*.

sanctuary *n* (safe place) refuge *m*;
(Relig) sanctuaire *m*; (for animals)
réserve *f*.

sand *n* sable *m*; ～s (beach) plage *f*.

sandal *n* sandale *f*.

sandpaper n papier m de verre.
● vt poncer.

sandpit n bac m à sable.

sandwich n sandwich m; ~ **course**
cours m avec stage pratique.

sandy adj (beach) de sable; (soil)
sablonneux; (hair) blond roux inv.

sane adj (view) sensé; (person) sain
d'esprit.

sang ⇒SING.

sanitary adj (clean) hygiénique;
(system) sanitaire; ~ **towel** serviette
f hygiénique.

sanitation n installations fpl
sanitaires.

sanity n équilibre m mental; (sense)
bon sens m.

sank ⇒SINK.

Santa (**Claus**) n le père Noël.

sapphire n saphir m.

sarcasm n sarcasme m. **sarcastic**
adj sarcastique.

sash n (on uniform) écharpe f; (on dress)
ceinture f.

sat ⇒SIT.

satchel n cartable m.

satellite n & a satellite (m); ~ **dish**
antenne f parabolique.

satire n satire f. **satirical** adj
satirique.

satisfaction n satisfaction f.

satisfactory adj satisfaisant.

satisfy vt satisfaire; (convince)
convaincre.

saturate vt saturer. **saturated** adj
(wet) trempé.

Saturday n samedi m.

sauce n sauce f.

saucepan n casserole f.

saucer n soucoupe f.

Saudi Arabia n Arabie f saoudite.

sausage n (for cooking) saucisse f;
(ready to eat) saucisson m.

savage adj (blow, temper) violent;
(attack) sauvage. ● n sauvage mf.
● vt attaquer sauvagement.

save vt sauver; (money) économiser;
(time) gagner; (keep) garder; ~ (**sb**)
doing sth éviter (à qn) de faire qch.
● n (football) arrêt m. **saver** n
épargnant/-e m/f. **saving** n
économie f. **savings** npl économies
fpl.

saviour, (US) **savior** n sauveur m.

savour, (US) **savor** n saveur f. ● vt
savourer. **savoury** adj (tasty)
savoureux; (Culin) salé.

saw ⇒SEE. ● n scie f. ● vt (pt
sawed; pp **sawn** or **sawed**) scier.

sawdust n sciure f.

saxophone n saxophone m.

say vt/i (pt **said**) dire; (prayer) faire.
● n have a ~ dire son mot; (in
decision) avoir voix au chapitre.
saying n proverbe m.

scab n croûte f.

scaffolding n échafaudage m.

scald vt (injure, cleanse) ébouillanter.
● n brûlure f.

scale n (for measuring) échelle f;
(extent) étendue f; (Mus) gamme f; (on
fish) écaille f; on a small ~ sur une
petite échelle; ~ **model** maquette f.
● vt (climb) escalader; ~ **down**
réduire. **scales** npl (for weighing)
balance f.

scallop n coquille f Saint-Jacques.

scalp n cuir m chevelu.

scampi npl (fresh) langoustines fpl;
(breaded) scampi mpl.

scan vt (pt **scanned**) scruter;
(quickly) parcourir. ● n (ultrasound)
échographie f; (CAT) scanner m.

scandal n scandale m; (gossip)
potins mpl ⚠.

Scandinavia n Scandinavie f.

scanty adj (-ier, -iest) maigre;
(clothing) minuscule.

scapegoat n bouc m émissaire.

scar n cicatrice f. ● vt (pt **scarred**)
marquer.

scarce adj rare. **scarcely** adv à
peine.

scare vt faire peur à; **be** ~**d** avoir
peur. ● n peur f; **bomb** ~ alerte f à
la bombe. **scarecrow** n
épouvantail m.

scarf n (pl **scarves**) écharpe f; (over
head) foulard m.

scarlet adj écarlate; ~ **fever**
scarlatine f.

scary adj (-ier, -iest) ⚠ qui fait
peur.

scathing adj cinglant.

scatter *vt* (throw) éparpiller, répandre; (disperse) disperser. ● *vi* se disperser.

scavenge *vi* fouiller (dans les ordures). **scavenger** *n* (animal) charognard *m*.

scene *n* scène *f*; (of accident, crime) lieu *m*; (sight) spectacle *m*; **behind the** ∼**s** en coulisse. **scenery** *n* paysage *m*; (Theat) décors *mpl*. **scenic** *adj* panoramique.

scent *n* (perfume) parfum *m*; (trail) piste *f*. ● *vt* flairer; (make fragrant) parfumer.

sceptic *n* sceptique *mf*. **sceptical** *adj* sceptique. **scepticism** *n* scepticisme *m*.

schedule *n* horaire *m*; (for job) planning *m*; **behind** ∼ en retard; **on** ∼ dans les temps. ● *vt* prévoir; ∼**d flight** vol *m* régulier.

scheme *n* projet *m*; (dishonest) combine *f*; **pension** ∼ plan *m* de retraite. ● *vi* comploter.

schizophrenic *a* & *n* schizophrène (*mf*).

scholar *n* érudit/-e *m/f*.

school *n* école *f*; **go to** ∼ aller à l'école. ● *adj* (age, year, holidays) scolaire. ∼**boy** *n* élève *m*. ∼**girl** *n* élève *f*. **schooling** *n* scolarité *f*. ∼**teacher** *n* (primary) instituteur/ -trice *m/f*; (secondary) professeur *m*.

science *n* science *f*; **teach** ∼ enseigner les sciences. **scientific** *adj* scientifique. **scientist** *n* scientifique *mf*.

scissors *npl* ciseaux *mpl*.

scold *vt* gronder.

scoop *n* (shovel) pelle *f*; (measure) mesure *f*; (for ice cream) cuillère *f* à glace; (news) exclusivité *f*.

scooter *n* (child's) trottinette *f*; (motor cycle) scooter *m*.

scope *n* étendue *f*; (competence) compétence *f*; (opportunity) possibilité *f*.

scorch *vt* brûler; (iron) roussir.

score *n* score *m*; (Mus) partition *f*; **on that** ∼ à cet égard. ● *vt* marquer; (success) remporter. ● *vi* marquer un point; (football) marquer un but; (keep score) marquer les points. **scorer** *n* (Sport) marqueur *m*.

scorn *n* mépris *m*. ● *vt* mépriser.

Scorpio *n* Scorpion *m*.

Scot *n* Écossais/-e *m/f*.

Scotland *n* Écosse *f*.

Scottish *adj* écossais.

scoundrel *n* gredin *m*.

scour *vt* (pan) récurer; (search) parcourir. **scourer** *n* tampon *m* à récurer.

scourge *n* fléau *m*.

scout *n* éclaireur *m*. ● *vi* ∼ **around for** rechercher.

scowl *n* air *m* renfrogné. ● *vi* prendre un air renfrogné.

scramble *vi* (clamber) grimper. ● *vt* (eggs) brouiller. ● *n* (rush) course *f*.

scrap *n* petit morceau *m*; ∼**s** (of metal, fabric) déchets *mpl*; (of food) restes *mpl*; (fight ▣) bagarre *f*. ● *vt* (pt **scrapped**) abandonner; (car) détruire.

scrape *vt* gratter; (damage) érafler. ● *vi* ∼ **against** érafler. ● *n* raclement *m*. □ ∼ **through** réussir de justesse.

scrap: ∼**-paper** *n* papier *m* brouillon. ∼ **yard** *n* casse *f*.

scratch *vt/i* (se) gratter; (with claw, nail) griffer; (graze) érafler; (mark) rayer. ● *n* (on body) égratignure *f*; (on surface) éraflure *f*; **start from** ∼ partir de zéro; **up to** ∼ à la hauteur. ∼ **card** *n* jeu *m* de grattage.

scrawl *n* gribouillage *m*. ● *vt/i* gribouiller.

scrawny *adj* (**-ier, -iest**) décharné.

scream *vt/i* crier. ● *n* cri *m* (perçant).

screech *vi* (scream) hurler; (tyres) crisser. ● *n* cri *m* strident; (of tyres) crissement *m*.

screen *n* écran *m*; (folding) paravent *m*. ● *vt* masquer; (protect) protéger; (film) projeter; (candidates) filtrer; (Med) faire subir un test de dépistage. **screening** *n* (cinema) projection *f*; (Med) dépistage *m*.

screen: ∼**play** *n* scénario *m*. ∼ **saver** *n* protecteur *m* d'écran.

screw *n* vis *f*. ● *vt* visser; ∼ **up** (eyes) plisser; (ruin ▣) cafouiller ▣. ∼**driver** *n* tournevis *m*.

scribble *vt/i* griffonner. ● *n* griffonnage *m*.

script *n* script *m*; (of play) texte *m*.

scroll *n* rouleau *m*. ● *vt/i* (Comput) (faire) défiler.

scrounge 🄕 *vt* (*favour*) quémander; (*cigarette*) piquer 🄕; ~ **money from sb** taper de l'argent à qn. ● *vi* ~ **off sb** vivre sur le dos de qn.

scrub *n* (land) broussailles *fpl*. ● *vt/i* (*pt* **scrubbed**) nettoyer (à la brosse), frotter.

scruffy *adj* (**-ier**, **-iest**) 🄕 dépenaillé.

scrum *n* (rugby) mêlée *f*.

scruple *n* scrupule *m*.

scrutinize *vt* scruter. **scrutiny** *n* examen *m* minutieux.

scuba-diving *n* plongée *f* sousmarine.

scuffle *n* bagarre *f*.

sculpt *vt/i* sculpter. **sculptor** *n* sculpteur *m*.

sculpture *n* sculpture *f*.

scum *n* (on liquid) mousse *f*; (people: pej) racaille *f*.

scurry *vi* se précipiter, courir (**for** pour chercher); ~ **off** se sauver.

sea *n* mer *f*; **at** ~ en mer; **by** ~ par mer. ● *adj* (air) marin; (*bird*) de mer; (*voyage*) par mer. ~**food** *n* fruits *mpl* de mer. ~**gull** *n* mouette *f*.

seal *n* (animal) phoque *m*; (insignia) sceau *m*; (with wax) cachet *m*. ● *vt* sceller; cacheter; (stick down) coller. □ ~ **off** (area) boucler.

seam *n* (in cloth) couture *f*; (of coal) veine *f*.

search *vt/i* (examine) fouiller; (seek) chercher; (study) examiner; (Comput) rechercher. ● *n* fouille *f*; (quest) recherches *fpl*; (Comput) recherche *f*; **in** ~ **of** à la recherche de. ~ **engine** *n* (Internet) moteur *m* de recherche. ~**light** *n* projecteur *m*. ~**-warrant** *n* mandat *m* de perquisition.

sea: ~**shell** *n* coquillage *m*. ~**shore** *n* (coast) littoral *m*; (beach) plage *f*.

seasick *adj* **be** ~ avoir le mal de mer.

seaside *n* bord *m* de la mer.

season *n* saison *f*; ~ **ticket** carte *f* d'abonnement. ● *vt* assaisonner.

seasonal *adj* saisonnier.

seasoning *n* assaisonnement *m*.

seat *n* siège *m*; (place) place *f*; (of trousers) fond *m*; **take a** ~ asseyezvous. ● *vt* (put) placer; **the room** ~**s 30** la salle peut accueillir 30 personnes. ~**-belt** *n* ceinture *f* (de sécurité).

seaweed *n* algue *f* marine.

secluded *adj* retiré.

seclusion *n* isolement *m*.

second[1] *adj* deuxième, second; **a** ~ **chance** une nouvelle chance; **have** ~ **thoughts** avoir des doutes. ● *n* deuxième *mf*, second/-e *m/f*; (unit of time) seconde *f*; ~**s** (food) rab *m* 🄕. ● *adv* (in race) deuxième; (secondly) deuxièmement. ● *vt* (*proposal*) appuyer.

second[2] *vt* (transfer) détacher (**to** à).

secondary *adj* secondaire; ~ **school** lycée *m*, école *f* secondaire.

second-best *n* pis-aller *m*.

second-class *adj* (Rail) de deuxième classe; (*post*) au tarif lent.

second hand *n* (on clock) trotteuse *f*.

second-hand *a* & *adv* (*article*) d'occasion; (*information*) de seconde main.

secondly *adv* deuxièmement.

second-rate *adj* médiocre.

secrecy *n* secret *m*.

secret *adj* secret. ● *n* secret *m*; **in** ~ en secret.

secretarial *adj* (*work*) de secrétaire.

secretary *n* secrétaire *mf*; **S**~ **of State** ministre *m*; (US) ministre *m* des Affaires étrangères.

secrete *vt* (Med) sécréter; (hide) cacher.

secretive *adj* secret. **secretly** *adv* secrètement.

sect *n* secte *f*. **sectarian** *adj* sectaire.

section *n* partie *f*; (in store) rayon *m*; (of newspaper) rubrique *f*; (of book) passage *m*.

sector *n* secteur *m*.

secular *adj* (*school*) laïque; (*art, music*) profane.

secure *adj* (*safe*) sûr; (*job, marriage*) stable; (*knot, lock*) solide; (*window*) bien fermé; (*feeling*) de sécurité; (*person*) sécurisé. ● *vt* attacher; (obtain) s'assurer; (ensure) assurer.

security *n* (safety) sécurité *f*; (for loan) caution *f*; ~ **guard** vigile *m*.

sedate *adj* calme. ● *vt* donner un sédatif à. **sedative** *n* sédatif *m*.

seduce *vt* séduire. **seducer** *n* séducteur/-trice *m/f*. **seduction** *n* séduction *f*. **seductive** *adj* séduisant.

see *vt/i* (*pt* **saw**; *pp* **seen**) voir; **see you (soon)!** à bientôt!; ~**ing that** vu que. □ ~ **out** (*person*) raccompagner à la porte; ~ **through** (*deception*) déceler; (*person*) percer à jour; ~ **sth through** mener qch à bonne fin; ~ **to** s'occuper de; ~ **to it that** veiller à ce que.

seed *n* graine *f*; (collectively) graines *fpl*; (origin: fig) germe *m*; (tennis) tête *f* de série. **seedling** *n* plant *m*.

seek *vt* (*pt* **sought**) chercher.

seem *vi* sembler; **he** ~**s to think** il a l'air de croire.

seen ⇒SEE.

seep *vi* suinter; ~ **into** s'infiltrer dans.

see-saw *n* tapecul *m*. ● *vt* osciller.

seethe *vi* ~ **with** (*anger*) bouillir de; (*people*) grouiller de.

segment *n* segment *m*; (of orange) quartier *m*.

segregate *vt* séparer.

seize *vt* saisir; (*territory, prisoner*) s'emparer de. ● *vi* ~ **on** (*chance*) saisir; ~ **up** (*engine*) se gripper.

seizure *n* (Med) crise *f*.

seldom *adv* rarement.

select *vt* sélectionner. ● *adj* privilégié. **selection** *n* sélection *f*. **selective** *adj* sélectif.

self *n* (*pl* **selves**) moi *m*; (on cheque) moi-même. ~**-assured** *adj* plein d'assurance. ~**-catering** *adj* (*holiday*) en location. ~**-centred**, (US) ~**-centered** *adj* égocentrique. ~**-confident** *adj* sûr de soi. ~**-conscious** *adj* timide.

~**-contained** *adj* (*flat*) indépendant. ~**-control** *n* sang-froid *m*. ~**-defence** *n* autodéfense *f*; (Jur) légitime défense *f*. ~**-employed** *adj* qui travaille à son compte. ~**-esteem** *n* amour-propre *m*. ~**-governing** *adj* autonome. ~**-indulgent** *adj* complaisant. ~**-interest** *n* intérêt *m* personnel.

selfish *adj* égoïste.

selfless *adj* désintéressé.

self: ~**-portrait** *n* autoportrait *m*. ~**-reliant** *adj* autosuffisant. ~**-respect** *n* respect *m* de soi. ~**-righteous** *adj* satisfait de soi. ~**-sacrifice** *n* abnégation *f*. ~**-satisfied** *adj* satisfait de soi. ~**-seeking** *adj* égoïste. ~**-service** *n* & *a* libre-service (*m*).

sell *vt/i* (*pt* **sold**) vendre; ~ **well** se vendre bien. □ ~ **off** liquider; ~ **out** (*items*) se vendre; **have sold out** avoir tout vendu.

Sellotape® *n* scotch® *m*.

sell-out *n* (betrayal) 🛈 revirement *m*; **be a** ~ (*show*) afficher complet.

semester *n* (Univ) semestre *m*.

semicircle *n* demi-cercle *m*.

semicolon *n* point-virgule *m*.

semi-detached *adj* ~ **house** maison *f* jumelée.

semifinal *n* demi-finale *f*.

seminar *n* séminaire *m*.

semolina *n* semoule *f*.

senate *n* sénat *m*. **senator** *n* sénateur *m*.

send *vt/i* (*pt* **sent**) envoyer. □ ~ **away** (dismiss) renvoyer; ~ (**away** *or* **off**) **for** commander (par la poste); ~ **back** renvoyer; ~ **for** (*person, help*) envoyer chercher; ~ **up** 🛈 parodier.

senile *adj* sénile.

senior *adj* plus âgé (**to** que); (in rank) haut placé; **be** ~ **to sb** être le supérieur de qn. ● *n* aîné/-e *m/f*. ~ **citizen** *n* personne *f* âgée. ~ **school** *n* lycée *m*.

sensation *n* sensation *f*. **sensational** *adj* sensationnel.

sense *n* sens *m*; (mental impression) sentiment *m*; (common sense) bon sens *m*; ~**s** (mind) raison *f*; **there's no** ~ **in doing** cela ne sert à rien de faire;

make ～ avoir un sens; **make** ～ **of** comprendre. ● *vt* (pres)sentir.

senseless *adj* insensé; (Med) sans connaissance.

sensible *adj* raisonnable; (*clothing*) pratique.

sensitive *adj* sensible (**to** à); (*issue*) difficile.

sensory *adj* sensoriel.

sensual *adj* sensuel. **sensuality** *n* sensualité *f*.

sensuous *adj* sensuel.

sent ⇨SEND.

sentence *n* phrase *f*; (punishment: Jur) peine *f*. ● *vt* ～ **to** condamner à.

sentiment *n* sentiment *m*.

sentimental *adj* sentimental.

sentry *n* sentinelle *f*.

separate[1] *adj* (*piece*) à part; (*issue*) autre; (*sections*) différent; (*organizations*) distinct.

separate[2] *vt/i* (se) séparer.

separately *adv* séparément.

separation *n* séparation *f*.

September *n* septembre *m*.

septic *adj* (*wound*) infecté; ～ **tank** fosse *f* septique.

sequel *n* suite *f*.

sequence *n* (order) ordre *m*; (series) suite *f*; (in film) séquence *f*.

Serb *adj* serbe. ● *n* (person) Serbe *mf*; (Ling) serbe *m*.

Serbia *n* Serbie *f*.

sergeant *n* (Mil) sergent *m*; (policeman) brigadier *m*.

serial *n* feuilleton *m*. ● *adj* (Comput) série *inv*.

series *n* *inv* série *f*.

serious *adj* sérieux; (*accident*, *crime*) grave.

seriously *adv* sérieusement; (*ill*) gravement; **take** ～ prendre au sérieux.

sermon *n* sermon *m*.

serpent *n* serpent *m*.

serrated *adj* dentelé.

serum *n* sérum *m*.

servant *n* domestique *mf*.

serve *vt/i* servir; faire; (*transport*, *hospital*) desservir; ～ **as/to** servir de/à; ～ **a purpose** être utile; ～ **a sentence** (Jur) purger une peine. ● *n* (tennis) service *m*.

server *n* serveur *m*; **remote** ～ téléserveur *m*.

service *n* service *m*; (maintenance) révision *f*; (Relig) office *m*; ～**s** (Mil) forces *fpl* armées. ● *vt* (car) réviser. ～ **area** *n* (Auto) aire *f* de services. ～ **charge** *n* service *m*. ～ **station** *n* station-service *f*.

session *n* séance *f*; **be in** ～ (Jur) tenir séance.

set *vt* (*pt* set; *pres p* **setting**) placer; (*table*) mettre; (*limit*) fixer; (*clock*) mettre à l'heure; (*example*, *task*) donner; (TV, cinema) situer; ～ **fire to** mettre le feu à; ～ **free** libérer; ～ **to music** mettre en musique. ● *vi* (*sun*) se coucher, (*jelly*) prendre; ～ **sail** partir. ● *n* (of chairs, stamps) série *f*; (of knives, keys) jeu *m*; (of people) groupe *m*; (TV, radio) poste *m*; (Theat) décor *m*; (tennis) set *m*; (mathematics) ensemble *m*. ● *adj* (*time, price*) fixe; (*procedure*) bien determiné; (*meal*) à prix fixe; (*book*) au programme; ～ **against sth** opposé à; **be** ～ **on doing** tenir absolument à faire. □ ～ **about** se mettre à; ～ **back** (delay) retarder; (cost 🄴) coûter; ～ **in** (take hold) s'installer, commencer; ～ **off** *or* **out** partir; ～ **off** (*panic, riot*) déclencher; (*bomb*) faire exploser; ～ **out** (state) présenter; (arrange) disposer; ～ **out to do sth** chercher à faire qch; ～ **up** (*stall*) monter; (*equipment*) assembler; (*experiment*) préparer; (*company*) créer; (*meeting*) organiser. ～-**back** *n* revers *m*.

settee *n* canapé *m*.

setting *n* cadre *m*; (on dial) position *f*.

settle *vt* (arrange, pay) régler; (*date*) fixer; (*nerves*) calmer. ● *vi* (come to rest) (*bird*) se poser; (*dust*) se déposer; (live) s'installer. □ ～ **down** se calmer; (marry etc.) se ranger; ～ **for** accepter; ～ **in** s'installer; ～ **up** (**with**) régler.

settlement *n* règlement *m* (of de); (agreement) accord *m*; (place) colonie *f*.

settler *n* colon *m*.

seven *a & n* sept (*m*).

seventeen *a & n* dix-sept (*m*).

seventh *a & n* septième (*mf*).

seventy *a & n* soixante-dix (*m*).

sever vt (cut) couper; (relations) rompre.

several a & pron plusieurs; ~ of us plusieurs d'entre nous.

severe adj (harsh) sévère; (serious) grave.

sew vt/i (pt **sewed**; pp **sewn** or **sewed**) coudre.

sewage n eaux fpl usées.

sewer n égout m.

sewing n couture f. ~**-machine** n machine f à coudre.

sewn ⇒SEW.

sex n sexe m; **have** ~ avoir des rapports (sexuels). ● adj sexuel.

sexist a & n sexiste (mf). **sexual** adj sexuel.

shabby adj (-ier, -iest) (place, object) miteux; (person) habillé de façon miteuse; (treatment) mesquin.

shack n cabane f.

shade n ombre f; (of colour, opinion) nuance f; (for lamp) abat-jour m inv; **a** ~ **bigger** légèrement plus grand. ● vt (tree) ombrager; (hat) projeter une ombre sur.

shadow n ombre f. ● vt (follow) filer. **S**~ **Cabinet** n cabinet m fantôme.

shady adj (-ier, -iest) ombragé; (dubious) véreux.

shaft n (of tool) manche m; (of arrow) tige f; (in machine) axe m; (of mine) puits m; (of light) rayon m.

shake vt (pt **shook**; pp **shaken**) secouer; (bottle) agiter; (belief) ébranler; ~ **hands with** serrer la main à; ~ **one's head** dire non de la tête. ● vi trembler. ● n secousse f; **give sth a** ~ secouer qch. □ ~ **off** se débarrasser de. ~**-up** n (Pol) remaniement m.

shaky adj (-ier, -iest) (hand, voice) tremblant; (ladder) branlant; (weak: fig) instable.

shall v aux I ~ **do** je ferai; **we** ~ **see** nous verrons; ~ **we go…?** si on allait…?

shallow adj peu profond; (fig) superficiel.

shame n honte f; **it's a** ~ c'est dommage. ● vt faire honte à.

shampoo n shampooing m. ● vt faire un shampooing à.

shandy n panaché m.

shan't = SHALL NOT.

shanty n (shack) baraque f; ~ **town** bidonville m.

shape n forme f. ● vt (clay) modeler; (rock) façonner; (future: fig) déterminer; ~ **sth into balls** faire des boules avec qch. ● vi ~ **up** (plan) prendre tournure; (person) faire des progrès.

share n part f; (Comm) action f. ● vt/i partager; (feature) avoir en commun. ~**holder** n actionnaire mf. ~**ware** n (Comput) logiciel m contributif.

shark n requin m.

sharp adj (knife) tranchant; (pin) pointu; (point, angle, cry) aigu; (person, mind) vif; (tone) acerbe. ● adv (stop) net; (sing, play) trop haut; **six o'clock** ~ six heures pile. ● n (Mus) dièse m.

sharpen vt aiguiser; (pencil) tailler.

shatter vt (glass) fracasser; (hope) briser. ● vi (glass) voler en éclats.

shave vt/i (se) raser. ● n **have a** ~ se raser. **shaver** n rasoir m électrique.

shaving n (of wood) copeau m. ● adj (cream, foam, gel) à raser.

shawl n châle m.

she pron elle. ● n (animal) femelle f.

shear vt (pp **shorn** or **sheared**) (sheep) tondre; ~ **off** se détacher.

shears npl cisaille f.

shed n remise f. ● vt (pt **shed**; pres p **shedding**) perdre; (light, tears) répandre.

sheen n lustre m.

sheep n inv mouton m. ~**-dog** n chien m de berger.

sheepish adj penaud.

sheepskin n peau f de mouton.

sheer adj pur; (steep) à pic; (fabric) très fin. ● adv à pic.

sheet n drap m; (of paper) feuille f; (of glass, ice) plaque f.

shelf n (pl **shelves**) étagère f; (in shop, fridge) rayon m; (in oven) plaque f.

shell n coquille f; (on beach) coquillage m; (of building) carcasse f; (explosive) obus m. ● vt (nut) décortiquer; (*peas*) écosser; (Mil) bombarder.

shellfish *npl* (lobster etc.) crustacés *mpl*; (mollusc) coquillages *mpl*.

shelter *n* abri *m*. ● *vt/i* (s')abriter; (give lodging to) donner asile à.

shelve *vt* (*plan*) mettre en suspens.

shepherd *n* berger *m*; ~'s pie hachis *m* Parmentier. ● *vt* (*people*) guider.

sherry *n* xérès *m*.

shield *n* bouclier *m*; (screen) écran *m*. ● *vt* protéger.

shift *vt/i* (se) déplacer, bouger; (exchange, alter) changer de. ● *n* changement *m*; (workers) équipe *f*; (work) poste *m*; ~ **work** travail *m* posté, travail *m* par roulement.

shifty *adj* (-**ier**, -**iest**) louche.

shimmer *vi* chatoyer. ● *n* chatoiement *m*.

shin *n* tibia *m*.

shine *vt* (*pt* **shone**) (*torch*) braquer (on sur). ● *vi* (*light, sun, hair*) briller; (*brass*) reluire. ● *n* lustre *m*.

shingle *n* (pebbles) galets *mpl*; (on roof) bardeau *m*.

shingles *npl* (Med) zona *m*.

shiny *adj* (-**ier**, -**iest**) brillant.

ship *n* bateau *m*, navire *m*. ● *vt* (*pt* **shipped**) transporter. **shipment** *n* (by sea) cargaison *f*; (by air, land) chargement *m*. **shipping** *n* (ships) navigation *f*. ~**wreck** *n* épave *f*; (event) naufrage *m*.

shirt *n* chemise *f*; (woman's) chemisier *m*.

shiver *vi* frissonner. ● *n* frisson *m*.

shock *n* choc *m*; (Electr) décharge *f*; **in** ~ en état de choc; ~ **absorber** amortisseur *m*. ● *adj* (*result*) choc *inv*; (*tactics*) de choc. ● *vt* choquer.

shoddy *adj* (-**ier**, -**iest**) mal fait; (*behaviour*) mesquin.

shoe *n* chaussure *f*; (of horse) fer *m*; (brake) ~ sabot *m* (*de frein*). ● *vt* (*pt* **shod** ; *pres p* **shoeing**) (*horse*) ferrer. ~**lace** *n* lacet *m*. ~ **size** *n* pointure *f*.

shone ⇒SHINE.

shook ⇒SHAKE.

shoot *vt* (*pt* **shot**) (*gun*) tirer un coup de; (*bullet*) tirer; (*missile,*

glance) lancer; (*person*) tirer sur; (kill) abattre; (execute) fusiller; (*film*) tourner. ● *vi* tirer (at sur). ● *n* (Bot) pousse *f*. □ ~ **down** abattre; ~ **out** (rush) sortir en vitesse; ~ **up** (spurt) jaillir; (grow) pousser vite.

shooting *n* (killing) meurtre *m* (*par arme à feu*); **hear** ~ entendre des coups de feu.

shop *n* magasin *m*; (small) boutique *f*; (workshop) atelier *m*. ● *vi* (*pt* **shopped**) faire ses courses; ~ **around** comparer les prix. ~ **assistant** *n* vendeur/-euse *m/f*. ~**floor** *n* (workers) ouvriers *mpl*. ~**keeper** *n* commerçant/-e *m/f*. ~**lifter** *n* voleur/-euse *m/f* à l'étalage.

shopper *n* acheteur/-euse *m/f*.

shopping *n* (goods) achats *mpl*; **go** ~ (for food) faire les courses; (for clothes etc.) faire les magasins. ~ **bag** *n* sac *m* à provisions. ~ **centre**, (US) ~ **center** *n* centre *m* commercial.

shop window *n* vitrine *f*.

shore *n* côte *f*, rivage *m*; **on** ~ à terre.

short *adj* court; (*person*) petit; (brief) court, bref; (curt) brusque; **be** ~ (**of**) manquer (de); **everything** ~ **of** tout sauf; **nothing** ~ **of** rien de moins que; **cut** ~ écourter; **cut sb** ~ interrompre qn; **fall** ~ **of** ne pas arriver à; **he is called Tom for** ~ son diminutif est Tom; **in** ~ en bref. ● *adv* (*stop*) net. ● *n* (Electr) court-circuit *m*; (film) court-métrage *m*; ~**s** (trousers) short *m*.

shortage *n* manque *m*.

short: ~**bread** *n* sablé *m*. ~**change** *vt* (cheat) rouler 🄸. ~ **circuit** *n* court-circuit *m*. ~**coming** *n* défaut *m*. ~ **cut** *n* raccourci *m*.

shorten *vt* raccourcir.

shortfall *n* déficit *m*.

shorthand *n* sténographie *f*; ~ **typist** sténodactylo *f*.

short: ~ **list** *n* liste *f* des candidats choisis. ~**lived** *adj* de courte durée.

shortly *adv* bientôt.

short: **~-sighted** adj myope.
~-staffed adj à court de personnel;
~ story n nouvelle f. **~-term** adj à
court terme.

shot ⇒SHOOT. ● n (firing, attempt) coup
m de feu; (person) tireur m; (bullet)
balle f; (photograph) photo f; (injection)
piqûre f; **like a ~** sans hésiter.
~-gun n fusil m de chasse.

should v aux devoir; **you ~ help me**
vous devriez m'aider; **I ~ have**
stayed j'aurais dû rester; **I ~ like to**
j'aimerais bien; **if he ~ come** s'il
venait.

shoulder n épaule f. ● vt
(responsibility) endosser; (burden) se
charger de. **~-bag** n sac m à
bandoulière. **~-blade** n omoplate f.

shout n cri m. ● vt/i crier (at après);
~ sth out lancer qch à haute voix.

shove n **give sth a ~** pousser qch.
● vt/i pousser; **~ off!** 🗊 tire-toi! 🗊.

shovel n pelle f. ● vt (pt
shovelled) pelleter.

show vt (pt **showed**; pp **shown**)
montrer; (dial, needle) indiquer; (put
on display) exposer; (film) donner;
(conduct) conduire; **~ sb in/out** faire
entrer/sortir qn. ● vi (be visible) se
voir. ● n (exhibition) exposition f,
salon m; (Theat) spectacle m; (cinema)
séance f; (of strength) démonstration f;
for ~ pour l'effet; **on ~** exposé. □ **~**
off faire le fier/la fière; **~ sth/sb off**
exhiber qch/qn; **~ up** se voir;
(appear) se montrer; **~ sb up** 🗊 faire
honte à qn.

shower n douche f; (of rain) averse f.
● vt **~ with** couvrir de. ● vi se
doucher.

showing n performance f; (cinema)
séance f.

show-jumping n concours m
hippique.

shown ⇒SHOW.

show: **~-off** n m'as-tu-vu mf inv 🗊.
~room n salle f d'exposition.

shrank ⇒SHRINK.

shrapnel n éclats mpl d'obus.

shred n lambeau m; (least amount: fig)
parcelle f. ● vt (pt **shredded**)
déchiqueter; (Culin) râper.

shrewd adj (person) habile; (move)
astucieux.

shriek n hurlement m. ● vt/i hurler.

shrill adj (voice) perçant; (tone)
strident.

shrimp n crevette f.

shrine n (place) lieu m de pèlerinage.

shrink vt/i (pt **shrank**; pp **shrunk**)
rétrécir; (lessen) diminuer; **~ from**
reculer devant.

shrivel vt/i (pt **shrivelled**) (se)
ratatiner.

shroud n linceul m. ● vt (veil)
envelopper.

Shrove Tuesday n mardi m gras.

shrub n arbuste m.

shrug vt (pt **shrugged**) **~ one's**
shoulders hausser les épaules; **~ sth**
off ignorer qch.

shrunk ⇒SHRINK.

shudder vi frémir. ● n
frémissement m.

shuffle vt (feet) traîner; (cards)
battre. ● vi traîner les pieds.

shun vt (pt **shunned**) fuir.

shut vt (pt **shut**; pres p **shutting**)
fermer. ● vi (door) se fermer; (shop)
fermer. □ **~ in** or **up** enfermer; **~**
up 🗊 se taire; **~ sb up** faire taire
qn.

shutter n volet m; (Photo) obturateur
m.

shuttle n (bus) navette f; **~ service**
navette f. ● vi faire la navette. ● vt
transporter.

shuttlecock n (badminton) volant m.

shy adj timide. ● vi **~ away from** se
tenir à l'écart de.

sibling n frère/sœur m/f.

sick adj malade; (humour) macabre;
(mind) malsain; **be ~** (vomit) vomir;
be ~ of 🗊 en avoir assez or marre
de 🗊; **feel ~** avoir mal au cœur.
~-leave n congé m de maladie.

sickly adj (-ier, -iest) (person)
maladif; (taste, smell) écœurant.

sickness n maladie f.

sick-pay n indemnité f de maladie.

side n côté m; (of road, river) bord m;
(of hill, body) flanc m; (Sport) équipe f;
(TV 🗊) chaîne f; **~ by ~** côte à côte.
● adj latéral. ● vi **~ with** se ranger
du côté de. **~board** n buffet m.
~-effect n effet m secondaire.
~light n (Auto) feu m de position.

∼line *n* activité *f* secondaire.
∼-show *n* attraction *f*. **∼-step** *vt*
(*pt* **-stepped**) éviter. **∼-street** *n*
rue *f* latérale. **∼-track** *vt* fourvoyer.
∼walk *n* (US) trottoir *m*.

sideways *adj* (*look*) de travers.
● *adv* (*move*) latéralement; (*look at*)
de travers.

siding *n* voie *f* de garage.

sidle *vi* s'avancer furtivement (**up to**
vers).

siege *n* siège *m*.

siesta *n* sieste *f*.

sieve *n* tamis *m*; (for liquids) passoire
f. ● *vt* tamiser.

sift *vt* tamiser. ● *vi* ∼ **through**
examiner.

sigh *n* soupir *m*. ● *vt/i* soupirer.

sight *n* vue *f*; (scene) spectacle *m*; (on
gun) mire *f*; **at** *or* **on** ∼ à vue; **catch**
∼ **of** apercevoir; **in** ∼ visible; **lose** ∼
of perdre de vue. ● *vt* apercevoir.

sightseeing *n* tourisme *m*.

sign *n* signe *m*; (notice) panneau *m*.
● *vt/i* signer. ☐ ∼ **on** (as unemployed)
pointer au chômage; ∼ **up** (s')
engager.

signal *n* signal *m*. ● *vt* (*pt*
signalled) (gesture) faire signe (**that**
que); (indicate) indiquer.

signatory *n* signataire *mf*.

signature *n* signature *f*; ∼ **tune**
indicatif *m*.

significance *n* importance *f*;
(meaning) signification *f*. **significant**
adj important; (meaningful)
significatif. **significantly** *adv*
(much) sensiblement.

signify *vt* signifier.

signpost *n* panneau *m* indicateur.

silence *n* silence *m*. ● *vt* faire taire.

silent *adj* silencieux; (*film*) muet.
silently *adv* silencieusement.

silhouette *n* silhouette *f*. ● *vt* be
∼**d against** se profiler contre.

silicon *n* silicium *m*; ∼ **chip** puce *f*
électronique.

silk *n* soie *f*.

silly *adj* (**-ier**, **-iest**) bête, idiot.

silver *n* argent *m*; (silverware)
argenterie *f*. ● *adj* en argent.

similar *adj* semblable (**to** à).
similarity *n* ressemblance *f*.
similarly *adv* de même.

simile *n* comparaison *f*.

simmer *vt/i* (*soup*) mijoter; (*water*)
(laisser) frémir.

simple *adj* simple.

simplicity *n* simplicité *f*.

simplify *vt* simplifier.

simplistic *adj* simpliste.

simply *adv* simplement; (absolutely)
absolument.

simulate *vt* simuler.

simultaneous *adj* simultané.

sin *n* péché *m*. ● *vi* (*pt* **sinned**)
pécher.

....

since

● *preposition*
····▸ depuis; **I haven't seen him** ∼
Monday je ne l'ai pas vu depuis
lundi; **I've been waiting** ∼ **yesterday**
j'attends depuis hier; **she had been
living in Paris** ∼ **1985** elle habitait
Paris depuis 1985.

● *conjunction*
····▸ (in time expressions) depuis que; ∼
she's been working here depuis
qu'elle travaille ici; ∼ **she left**
depuis qu'elle est partie *or* depuis
son départ.
····▸ (because) comme; ∼ **he was ill, he
couldn't go** comme il était malade, il
ne pouvait pas y aller.

● *adverb*
····▸ depuis; **he hasn't been seen** ∼ on
ne l'a pas vu depuis.
....

sincere *adj* sincère. **sincerely** *adv*
sincèrement. **sincerity** *n* sincérité
f.

sinful *adj* immoral; ∼ **man** pécheur
m.

sing *vt/i* (*pt* **sang**; *pp* **sung**)
chanter.

singe *vt* (*pres p* **singeing**) brûler
légèrement; (with iron) roussir.

singer *n* chanteur/-euse *m/f*.

single *adj* seul; (not double) simple;
(unmarried) célibataire; (*room, bed*)
pour une personne; (*ticket*) simple; **in**

$\sim$ **file** en file indienne. ● *n* (ticket) aller simple *m*; (record) 45 tours *m inv*; $\sim$**s** (tennis) simple *m*. ● *vt* $\sim$ **out** choisir. $\sim$**-handed** *adj* tout seul. $\sim$**-minded** *adj* tenace. $\sim$ **parent** *n* parent *m* isolé.

singular *n* singulier *m*. ● *adj* (strange) singulier; (*noun*) au singulier.

sinister *adj* sinistre.

sink *vt* (*pt* **sank**; *pp* **sunk**) (*boat*) couler; (*well*) forer; (*post*) enfoncer. ● *vi* (*boat*) couler; (*sun, level*) baisser; (*wall*) s'effondrer. ● *n* (in kitchen) évier *m*; (wash-basin) lavabo *m*. □ $\sim$ **in** (*news*) faire son chemin.

sinner *n* pécheur/-eresse *m/f*.

sip *n* petite gorgée *f*. ● *vt* (*pt* **sipped**) boire à petites gorgées.

siphon *n* siphon *m*. ● *vt* $\sim$ **off** siphonner.

sir *n* Monsieur *m*; **Sir** (title) Sir *m*.

siren *n* sirène *f*.

sirloin *n* aloyau *m*.

sister *n* sœur *f*; (nurse) infirmière *f* en chef. $\sim$**-in-law** *n* (*pl* $\sim$**s-in-law**) belle-sœur *f*.

sit *vt/i* (*pt* **sat**; *pres p* **sitting**) (s') asseoir; (*committee*) siéger; $\sim$ **(for)** (exam) se présenter à; **be** $\sim$**ting** être assis. □ $\sim$ **around** ne rien faire; $\sim$ **down** s'asseoir.

site *n* emplacement *m*; (building) $\sim$ chantier *m*. ● *vt* construire.

sitting *n* séance *f*; (in restaurant) service *m*. $\sim$**-room** *n* salon *m*.

situate *vt* situer; **be** $\sim$**d** être situé. **situation** *n* situation *f*.

six *a* & *n* six (*m*).

sixteen *a* & *n* seize (*m*).

sixth *a* & *n* sixième (*mf*).

sixty *a* & *n* soixante (*m*).

size *n* dimension *f*; (of person, garment) taille *f*; (of shoes) pointure *f*; (of sum, salary) montant *m*; (extent) ampleur *f*. □ $\sim$ **up** (*person*) se faire une opinion de; (*situation*) évaluer. **sizeable** *adj* assez grand.

skate *n* patin *m*; (fish) raie *f*. ● *vi* patiner.

skating *n* patinage *m*.

skeletal *adj* squelettique.

skeleton *n* squelette *m*; $\sim$ **staff** effectifs *mpl* minimums.

sketch *n* esquisse *f*; (hasty) croquis *m*; (Theat) sketch *m*. ● *vt* faire une esquisse *or* un croquis de. ● *vi* faire des esquisses.

sketchy *adj* (**-ier**, **-iest**) (*details*) insuffisant; (*memory*) vague.

skewer *n* brochette *f*.

ski *n* ski *m*. ● *adj* de ski. ● *vi* (*pt* **ski'd** *or* **skied**; *pres p* **skiing**) skier; (go skiing) faire du ski.

skid *vi* (*pt* **skidded**) déraper. ● *n* dérapage *m*.

skier *n* skieur/-euse *m/f*.

skiing *n* ski *m*.

ski jump *n* saut *m* à ski.

skilful *adj* habile.

ski lift *n* remontée *f* mécanique.

skill *n* habileté *f*; (craft) compétence *f*; $\sim$**s** connaissances *fpl*. **skilled** *adj* (*worker*) qualifié; (talented) consommé.

skim *vt* (*pt* **skimmed**) écumer; (*milk*) écrémer; (pass over) effleurer. ● *vi* $\sim$ **through** parcourir.

skimpy *adj* (*clothes*) étriqué; (*meal*) chiche.

skin *n* peau *f*. ● *vt* (*pt* **skinned**) (*animal*) écorcher; (*fruit*) éplucher.

skinny *adj* (**-ier**, **-iest**) Ⓘ maigre.

skip *vi* (*pt* **skipped**) sautiller; (with rope) sauter à la corde. ● *vt* (*page, class*) sauter. ● *n* petit saut *m*; (container) benne *f*.

skipper *n* capitaine *m*.

skirmish *n* escarmouche *f*, accrochage *m*.

skirt *n* jupe *f*. ● *vt* contourner. **skirting-board** *n* plinthe *f*.

skittle *n* quille *f*.

skull *n* crâne *m*.

sky *n* ciel *m*. $\sim$**-blue** *a* & *n* bleu ciel *m inv*. $\sim$**scraper** *n* gratte-ciel *m inv*.

slab *n* (of stone) dalle *f*.

slack *adj* (not tight) détendu; (*person*) négligent; (*period*) creux. ● *n* (in rope) mou *m*. ● *vi* se relâcher.

slacken *vt* (*rope*) donner du mou à; (*grip*) relâcher; (*pace*) réduire. ● *vi* (*grip, rope*) se relâcher; (*activity*) ralentir; (*rain*) se calmer.

slam *vt/i* (*pt* **slammed**) (*door*) claquer; (throw) flanquer; (criticize 🅣) critiquer. ● *n* (noise) claquement *m*.

slander *n* (offence) diffamation *f*; (statement) calomnie *f*. ● *vt* calomnier; (Jur) diffamer. **slanderous** *adj* diffamatoire.

slang *n* argot *m*.

slant *vt/i* (faire) pencher; (*news*) présenter sous un certain jour. ● *n* inclinaison *f*; (bias) angle *m*. **slanted** *adj* (biased) orienté; (sloping) en pente.

slap *vt* (*pt* **slapped**) (strike) donner une tape à; (*face*) gifler; (put) flanquer 🅣. ● *n* claque *f*; (on face) gifle *f*. ● *adv* tout droit.

slapdash *adj* (*person*) brouillon 🅣; (*work*) bâclé 🅣.

slash *vt* (*picture, tyre*) taillader; (*face*) balafrer; (*throat*) couper; (fig) réduire (radicalement). ● *n* lacération *f*.

slat *n* (in blind) lamelle *f*; (on bed) latte *f*.

slate *n* ardoise *f*. ● *vt* 🅣 taper sur 🅣.

slaughter *vt* massacrer; (*animal*) abattre. ● *n* massacre *m*; abattage *m*.

slave *n* esclave *mf*. ● *vi* trimer 🅣. **slavery** *n* esclavage *m*.

sleazy *adj* (**-ier, -iest**) 🅣 (*story*) scabreux; (*club*) louche.

sledge *n* luge *f*; (horse-drawn) traîneau *m*.

sleek *adj* (*hair*) lisse, brillant; (*shape*) élégant.

sleep *n* sommeil *m*; go to ∼ s'endormir. ● *vi* (*pt* **slept**) dormir; (spend the night) coucher; ∼ **in** faire la grasse matinée. ● *vt* loger.

sleeper *n* (Rail) (berth) couchette *f*; (on track) traverse *f*.

sleeping-bag *n* sac *m* de couchage.

sleeping-pill *n* somnifère *m*.

sleep-walker *n* somnambule *mf*.

sleepy *adj* (**-ier, -iest**) somnolent; be ∼ avoir sommeil.

sleet *n* neige *f* fondue.

sleeve *n* manche *f*; (of record) pochette *f*; up one's ∼ en réserve.

sleigh *n* traîneau *m*.

slender *adj* (*person*) mince; (*majority*) faible.

slept ⇒SLEEP.

slice *n* tranche *f*. ● *vt* couper (en tranches).

slick *adj* (adept) habile; (insincere) roublard 🅣. ● *n* (oil) ∼ marée *f* noire.

slide *vt/i* (*pt* **slid**) glisser; ∼ **into** (go silently) se glisser dans. ● *n* glissade *f*; (fall: fig) baisse *f*; (in playground) toboggan *m*; (for hair) barrette *f*; (Photo) diapositive *f*.

sliding *adj* (*door*) coulissant; ∼ **scale** échelle *f* mobile.

slight *adj* petit, léger; (slender) mince; (frail) frêle. ● *vt* (insult) offenser. ● *n* affront *m*. **slightest** *adj* moindre. **slightly** *adv* légèrement, un peu.

slim *adj* (**slimmer, slimmest**) mince. ● *vi* (*pt* **slimmed**) maigrir.

slime *n* dépôt *m* gluant; (on river-bed) vase *f*. **slimy** *adj* visqueux; (fig) servile.

sling *n* (weapon, toy) fronde *f*; (bandage) écharpe *f*. ● *vt* (*pt* **slung**) jeter, lancer.

slip *vt/i* (*pt* **slipped**) glisser; ∼**ped disc** hernie *f* discale; ∼ **sb's mind** échapper à qn. ● *n* (mistake) erreur *f*; (petticoat) combinaison *f*; (paper) bout *m* de papier; ∼ **of the tongue** lapsus *m*. □ ∼ **away** s'esquiver; ∼ **into** (go) se glisser dans; (*clothes*) mettre; ∼ **up** 🅣 faire une gaffe 🅣.

slipper *n* pantoufle *f*.

slippery *adj* glissant.

slip road *n* bretelle *f*.

slit *n* fente *f*. ● *vt* (*pt* **slit**; *pres p* **slitting**) déchirer; ∼ **sth open** ouvrir qch; ∼ **sb's throat** égorger qn.

slither *vi* glisser.

sliver *n* (of glass) éclat *m*; (of soap) reste *m*.

slobber *vi* 🅣 baver.

slog 🅣 *vt* (*pt* **slogged**) (hit) frapper dur. ● *vi* (work) bosser 🅣. ● *n* (work) travail *m* dur.

slogan *n* slogan *m*.

slope *vi* être en pente; (*handwriting*) pencher. ● *n* pente *f*; (of mountain) flanc *m*.

sloppy *adj* (**-ier, -iest**) (*food*)
liquide; (*work*) négligé; (*person*)
négligent.

slosh *vt* 🛈 répandre; (hit 🛈) frapper.
● *vi* clapoter.

slot *n* fente *f*. ● *vt/i* (*pt* **slotted**)
(s')insérer.

sloth *n* paresse *f*.

slot-machine *n* distributeur *m*
automatique; (for gambling) machine *f*
à sous.

slouch *vi* être avachi.

Slovakia *n* Slovaquie *f*.

Slovenia *n* Slovénie *f*.

slovenly *adj* débraillé.

slow *adj* lent; **be** ∼ (*clock*) retarder;
in ∼ **motion** au ralenti. ● *adv*
lentement. ● *vt/i* ralentir. **slowly**
adv lentement. **slowness** *n* lenteur
f.

sludge *n* vase *f*.

slug *n* (mollusc) limace *f*; (bullet 🛈)
balle *f*; (blow 🛈) coup *m*.

sluggish *adj* (*person*) léthargique;
(*circulation*) lent.

slum *n* taudis *m*.

slump *n* (Econ) effondrement *m*; (in
support) baisse *f*. ● *vi* (*demand, trade*)
chuter; (*economy*) s'effondrer;
(*person*) s'affaler.

slung ⇒SLING.

slur *vt/i* (*pt* **slurred**) (*words*) mal
articuler. ● *n* calomnie *f* (**on** sur).

slush *n* (snow) neige *f* fondue. ∼
fund *n* caisse *f* noire.

sly *adj* (crafty) rusé; (secretive)
sournois. ● *n* **on the** ∼ en cachette.

smack *n* tape *f*; (on face) gifle *f*. ● *vt*
donner une tape à; gifler. ● *vi* ∼ **of**
sth sentir qch. ● *adv* 🛈 tout droit.

small *adj* petit. ● *n* ∼ **of the back**
creux *m* des reins. ● *adv* (*cut*) menu.
∼ **ad** *n* petite annonce *f*. ∼
business *n* petite entreprise *f*. ∼
change *n* petite monnaie *f*. ∼ **pox**
n variole *f*. ∼ **print** *n* petits
caractères *mpl*. ∼ **talk** *n* banalités
fpl.

smart *adj* élégant; (clever 🛈) malin,
habile; (*restaurant*) chic *inv*; (Comput)
intelligent. ● *vi* (*wound*) brûler.

smarten *vt/i* ∼ (**up**) embellir; ∼
(**oneself**) **up** s'arranger.

smash *vt/i* (se) briser, (se) fracasser;
(*opponent, record*) pulvériser. ● *n*
(noise) fracas *m*; (blow) coup *m*; (car
crash) collision *f*; (hit record 🛈) tube *m*
🛈.

smashing *adj* 🛈 épatant.

SME *abbr* (**small and medium
enterprises**) PME.

smear *vt* (stain) tacher; (coat) enduire;
(discredit: fig) diffamer. ● *n* tache *f*;
(effort to discredit) propos *m*
diffamatoire; ∼ (**test**) frottis *m*.

smell *n* odeur *f*; (sense) odorat *m*.
● *vt/i* (*pt* **smelt** or **smelled**) sentir;
∼ **of** sentir. **smelly** *adj* qui sent
mauvais.

smelt ⇒SMELL.

smile *n* sourire *m*. ● *vi* sourire.

smiley *n* (Internet) þinette *f*.

smirk *n* petit sourire *m* satisfait.

smitten *adj* (in love) fou d'amour.

smog *n* smog *m*.

smoke *n* fumée *f*; **have a** ∼ fumer.
● *vt/i* fumer. **smoked** *adj* fumé.
smokeless *adj* (*fuel*) non polluant.
smoker *n* fumeur/-euse *m/f*.
smoky *adj* (*air*) enfumé.

smooth *adj* lisse; (*movement*) aisé;
(*manners*) onctueux; (*flight*) sans
heurts. ● *vt* lisser; (*process*) faciliter.

smoothly *adv* (*move, flow*)
doucement; (*brake, start*) en
douceur; **go** ∼ marcher bien.

smother *vt* (stifle) étouffer; (cover)
couvrir.

smoulder *vi* (lit) se consumer; (fig)
couver.

smudge *n* trace *f*. ● *vt/i* (*ink*) (s')
étaler.

smug *adj* (**smugger, smuggest**)
suffisant.

smuggle *vt* passer (en
contrebande). **smuggler** *n*
contrebandier/-ière *m/f*. **smuggling**
n contrebande *f*.

smutty *adj* grivois.

snack *n* casse-croûte *m inv*.

snag *n* inconvénient *m*; (in cloth)
accroc *m*.

snail *n* escargot *m*.

snake *n* serpent *m*.

snap *vt/i* (*pt* **snapped**) (*whip,
fingers*) (faire) claquer; (break) (se)

casser net; (say) dire sèchement. ● *n*
claquement *m*; (Photo) photo *f*. ● *adj*
soudain. □ ~ **up** (buy) sauter sur.

snapshot *n* photo *f*.

snare *n* piège *m*.

snarl *vi* gronder (en montrant les
dents). ● *n* grondement *m*. **~-up** *n*
embouteillage *m*.

snatch *vt* (grab) attraper; (steal)
voler; (opportunity) saisir; ~ **sth
from sb** arracher qch à qn. ● *n* (theft)
vol *m*; (short part) fragment *m*.

sneak *vi* aller furtivement. ● *n*
🇬🇧 rapporteur/-euse *m/f*.

sneer *n* sourire *m* méprisant. ● *vi*
sourire avec mépris.

sneeze *n* éternuement *m*. ● *vi*
éternuer.

snide *adj* narquois.

sniff *vt/i* renifler. ● *n* reniflement *m*.

snigger *n* ricanement *m*. ● *vi*
ricaner.

snip *vt* (pt **snipped**) couper.

sniper *n* tireur *m* embusqué.

snippet *n* bribe *f*.

snivel *vi* (pt **snivelled**)
pleurnicher.

snob *n* snob *mf*.

snooker *n* snooker *m*.

snoop *vi* 🇬🇧 fourrer son nez partout.

snooty *adj* (-ier, -iest) 🇬🇧 snob *inv*,
hautain.

snooze *n* petit somme *m*. ● *vi*
sommeiller.

snore *n* ronflement *m*. ● *vi* ronfler.

snorkel *n* tuba *m*.

snort *n* grognement *m*. ● *vi* (person)
grogner; (horse) s'ébrouer.

snout *n* museau *m*.

snow *n* neige *f*. ● *vi* neiger; **be ~ed
under with** être submergé de.

snowball *n* boule *f* de neige. ● *vi*
faire boule de neige.

snow: **~boarding** *n* surf *m* des
neiges. **~-bound** *adj* bloqué par la
neige. **~drift** *n* congère *f*. **~drop** *n*
perce-neige *m or f inv*. **~flake** *n*
flocon *m* de neige. **~man** *n* (pl
-men) bonhomme *m* de neige.
~plough *n* chasse-neige *m inv*.

snub *vt* (pt **snubbed**) rembarrer.
● *n* rebuffade *f*.

snuffle *vi* renifler.

snug *adj* (**snugger, snuggest**)
(cosy) confortable; (tight) bien ajusté.

snuggle *vi* se pelotonner.

so *adv* si, tellement; (thus) ainsi; ~ **am
I** moi aussi; ~ **good as** aussi bon
que; **that is** ~ c'est ça; **I think** ~ je
pense que oui; **five or** ~ environ
cinq; ~ **as to** de manière à; ~ **far**
jusqu'ici; ~ **long!** 🇬🇧 à bientôt!; ~
many, ~ **much** tant (de); ~ **that** pour
que. ● *conj* donc, alors.

soak *vt/i* (faire) tremper (**in** dans).
□ ~ **in** pénétrer; ~ **up** absorber.
soaking *adj* trempé.

soap *n* savon *m*. ● *vt* savonner. ~
opera *n* feuilleton *m*. ~ **powder** *n*
lessive *f*.

soar *vi* monter (en flèche).

sob *n* sanglot *m*. ● *vi* (pt **sobbed**)
sangloter.

sober *adj* qui n'a pas bu d'alcool;
(serious) sérieux. ● *vi* ~ **up** dessoûler.

soccer *n* football *m*.

sociable *adj* sociable.

social *adj* social. ● *n* réunion *f*
(amicale), fête *f*.

socialism *n* socialisme *m*.
socialist *a & n* socialiste (*mf*).

socialize *vi* se mêler aux autres; ~
with fréquenter.

socially *adv* socialement; (meet) en
société.

social: ~ **security** *n* aide *f* sociale.
~ **worker** *n* travailleur/-euse *m/f*
social/-e.

society *n* société *f*.

sociological *adj* sociologique.
sociologist *n* sociologue *mf*.
sociology *n* sociologie *f*.

sock *n* chaussette *f*. ● *vt* (hit 🇬🇧)
flanquer un coup (de poing) à.

socket *n* (for lamp) douille *f*; (Electr)
prise *f* (de courant); (of eye) orbite *f*.

soda *n* soude *f*; ~(**-water**) eau *f* de
Seltz.

sodden *adj* détrempé.

sofa *n* canapé *m*. ~ **bed** *n* canapé-lit
m.

soft *adj* (gentle, lenient) doux; (not hard)
doux, mou; (heart, wood) tendre;
(silly) ramolli. ~ **drink** *n* boisson *f*
non alcoolisée.

soften *vt/i* (se) ramollir; (tone down, lessen) (s')adoucir.

soft spot *n* to have a ~ for sb avoir un faible pour qn.

software *n* logiciel *m*.

soggy *adj* (**-ier, -iest**) (*ground*) détrempé; (*food*) ramolli.

soil *n* sol *m*, terre *f*. ● *vt/i* (se) salir.

sold ⇒SELL. ● *adj* ~ out épuisé.

solder *n* soudure *f*. ● *vt* souder.

soldier *n* soldat *m*. ● *vi* ~ on
🛈 persévérer.

sole *n* (of foot) plante *f*; (of shoe) semelle *f*; (fish) sole *f*. ● *adj* unique, seul. **solely** *adv* uniquement.

solemn *adj* solennel.

solicitor *n* notaire *m*; (for court and police work) ≈ avocat/-e *m/f*.

solid *adj* solide; (not hollow) plein; (*gold*) massif; (*mass*) compact; (*meal*) substantiel. ● *n* solide *m*; ~s (food) aliments *mpl* solides.

solidarity *n* solidarité *f*.

solidify *vt/i* (se) solidifier.

solitary *adj* (alone) solitaire; (only) seul.

solo *n* solo *m*. ● *adj* (Mus) solo *inv*; (*flight*) en solitaire.

soluble *adj* soluble.

solution *n* solution *f*.

solve *vt* résoudre.

solvent *adj* (Comm) solvable. ● *n* (dis)solvant *m*.

---

some

● *determiner*

····▸ (unspecified amount) du/de l'/de la/ des; **I have to buy ~ bread** je dois acheter du pain; **have ~ water** prenez de l'eau; **~ sweets** des bonbons.

····▸ (certain) certains/certaines; **~ people say that** certains disent que.

····▸ (unknown) un/une; **~ man came to the house** un homme est venu à la maison.

····▸ (considerable amount) **we stayed there for ~ time** nous sommes restés là assez longtemps; **it will take ~ doing** ça ne va pas être facile à faire.

! In front of a plural adjective *des* changes to *de*: **some pretty dresses** de jolies robes.

● *pronoun*

····▸ en; **he wants ~** il en veut; **have ~ more** reprenez-en.

····▸ (certain) certains/certaines; **~ are expensive** certains sont chers.

● *adverb*

····▸ environ; **~ 20 people** environ 20 personnes.

---

somebody *pron* quelqu'un. ● *n* be a ~ être quelqu'un.

somehow *adv* d'une manière ou d'une autre; (for some reason) je ne sais pas pourquoi.

someone *pron & n* = SOMEBODY.

someplace *adv* (US) = SOMEWHERE.

somersault *n* roulade *f*. ● *vi* faire une roulade.

something *pron & n* quelque chose (*m*); ~ **good** quelque chose de bon; ~ **like** un peu comme.

sometime *adv* un jour; ~ **in June** en juin. ● *adj* (former) ancien.

sometimes *adv* quelquefois, parfois.

somewhat *adv* quelque peu, un peu.

somewhere *adv* quelque part.

son *n* fils *m*.

song *n* chanson *f*; (of bird) chant *m*.

son-in-law *n* (*pl* **sons-in-law**) gendre *m*.

soon *adv* bientôt; (early) tôt; **I would ~er stay** j'aimerais mieux rester; ~ **after** peu après; ~**er or later** tôt ou tard.

soot *n* suie *f*.

soothe *vt* calmer.

sophisticated *adj* raffiné; (*machine*) sophistiqué.

sopping *adj* trempé.

soppy *adj* (**-ier, -iest**)
🛈 sentimental.

sorcerer *n* sorcier *m*.

sordid *adj* sordide.

sore *adj* douloureux; (vexed) en rogne (at, with contre). ● *n* plaie *f*.

sorely *adv* fortement.

sorrow *n* chagrin *m*.

sorry *adj* (**-ier, -iest**) (regretful) désolé (to de; that que); (wretched) triste; **feel ~ for** plaindre; **~!** pardon!

sort *n* genre *m*, sorte *f*, espèce *f*; (person 🔢) type *m*; **what ~ of?** quel genre de?; **be out of ~s** ne pas être dans son assiette. ● *vt* **~ (out)** (classify) trier; **~ out** (tidy) ranger; (arrange) arranger; (*problem*) régler.

so-so *a & adv* comme ci comme ça.

sought ⇒SEEK.

soul *n* âme *f*.

sound *n* son *m*, bruit *m*. ● *adj* solide; (healthy) sain; (sensible) sensé. ● *vt/i* sonner; (seem) sembler (**as if** que); (test) sonder; **~ out** sonder; **~ a horn** klaxonner; **~ like** sembler être. **~ asleep** *adj* profondément endormi. **~ barrier** *n* mur *m* du son.

soundly *adv* (*sleep*) à poings fermés; (*built*) solidement.

sound-proof *adj* insonorisé. ● *vt* insonoriser.

sound-track *n* bande *f* sonore.

soup *n* soupe *f*, potage *m*.

sour *adj* aigre. ● *vt/i* (s')aigrir.

source *n* source *f*.

south *n* sud *m*. ● *adj* sud *inv*, du sud. ● *adv* vers le sud.

South Africa *n* Afrique *f* du Sud.

South America *n* Amérique *f* du Sud.

south-east *n* sud-est *m*.

southern *adj* du sud. **southerner** *n* habitant/-e *m/f* du sud.

southward *adj* (*side*) sud *inv*; (*journey*) vers le sud.

south-west *n* sud-ouest *m*.

souvenir *n* souvenir *m*.

sovereign *n & a* souverain/-e (*m/f*).

sow¹ *vt* (*pt* **sowed**; *pp* **sowed** or **sown**) (*seed*) semer; (*land*) ensemencer.

sow² *n* (pig) truie *f*.

soya *n* soja *m*. **~ sauce** *n* sauce *f* soja.

spa *n* station *f* thermale.

space *n* espace *m*; (room) place *f*; (period) période *f*. ● *adj* (*research*) spatial. ● *vt* **~ (out)** espacer. **~craft** *n inv*, **~ship** *n* engin *m* spatial. **~suit** *n* combinaison *f* spatiale.

spacious *adj* spacieux.

spade *n* (for garden) bêche *f*; (child's) pelle *f*; (cards) pique *m*. **~work** *n* (fig) travail *m* préparatoire.

spaghetti *n* spaghetti *mpl*.

Spain *n* Espagne *f*.

span *n* (of arch) portée *f*; (of wings) envergure *f*; (of time) durée *f*. ● *vt* (*pt* **spanned**) enjamber; (in time) embrasser.

Spaniard *n* Espagnol/-e *m/f*.

spaniel *n* épagneul *m*.

Spanish *adj* espagnol. ● *n* espagnol *m*.

spank *vt* donner une fessée à.

spanner *n* (tool) clé *f* (plate); (adjustable) clé *f* à molette.

spare *vt* (treat leniently) épargner; (do without) se passer de; (afford to give) donner, accorder. ● *adj* en réserve; (surplus) de trop; (*tyre, shoes*) de rechange; (*room, bed*) d'ami; **are there any ~ tickets?** y a-t-il encore des places? ● *n* **~ (part)** pièce *f* de rechange. **~ time** *n* loisirs *mpl*.

sparing *adj* frugal. **sparingly** *adv* en petite quantité.

spark *n* étincelle *f*. ● *vt* **~ off** (initiate) provoquer.

sparkle *vi* étinceler. ● *n* étincellement *m*. **sparkling** *adj* (*wine*) mousseux, pétillant; (*eyes*) brillant.

spark-plug *n* bougie *f*.

sparrow *n* moineau *m*.

sparse *adj* clairsemé. **sparsely** *adv* (*furnished*) peu.

spasm *n* (of muscle) spasme *m*; (of coughing, anger) accès *m*.

spasmodic *adj* intermittent.

spat ⇒SPIT.

spate *n* **a ~ of** (*letters*) une avalanche de.

spatter *vt* éclabousser (**with** de).

spawn *n* frai *m*, œufs *mpl*. ● *vt* pondre. ● *vi* frayer.

speak *vi* (*pt* **spoke**; *pp* **spoken**) parler. ● *vt* (say) dire; (*language*) parler. □ **~ up** parler plus fort.

speaker *n* (in public) orateur *m*; (Pol) président *m*; (loudspeaker) baffle *m*; **be**

a French/a good ~ parler français/bien.

spear n lance f.

spearmint n menthe f verte.

special adj spécial; (exceptional) exceptionnel.

specialist n spécialiste mf.

speciality, (US) **specialty** n spécialité f.

specialize vi se spécialiser (in en).

specially adv spécialement.

species n inv espèce f.

specific adj précis, explicite.

specification n (of design) spécification f; (of car equipment) caractéristiques fpl. **specify** vt spécifier.

specimen n spécimen m, échantillon m.

speck n (stain) (petite) tache f; (particle) grain m.

specs npl 🄹 lunettes fpl.

spectacle n spectacle m. **spectacles** n lunettes fpl. **spectacular** adj spectaculaire.

spectator n spectateur/-trice m/f.

spectrum n (pl **-tra**) spectre m; (of ideas) gamme f.

speculate vi s'interroger (about sur); (Comm) spéculer. **speculation** n conjectures fpl; (Comm) spéculation f. **speculator** n spéculateur/-trice m/f.

speech n (faculty) parole f; (diction) élocution f; (dialect) langage m; (address) discours m. **speechless** adj muet (with de).

speed n (of movement) vitesse f; (swiftness) rapidité f. ● vi (pt **sped**) aller vite; (pt **speeded**) (drive too fast) aller trop vite. □ ~ **up** accélérer; (of pace) s'accélérer.

speedboat n vedette f.

speeding n excès m de vitesse.

speed limit n limitation f de vitesse.

speedometer n compteur m (de vitesse).

spell n (magic) charme m, sortilège m; (curse) sort m; (of time) (courte) période f. ● vt/i (pt **spelled** or **spelt**) écrire; (mean) signifier; ~ **out** épeler; (explain) expliquer.

~**checker** n correcteur m orthographique.

spelling n orthographe f. ● adj (mistake) d'orthographe.

spend vt (pt **spent**) (money) dépenser (on pour); (time, holiday) passer; (energy) consacrer (on à). ● vi dépenser.

spent ⇒SPEND. ● adj (used) utilisé; (person) épuisé.

sperm n (pl **sperms** or **sperm**) sperme m.

sphere n sphère f.

spice n épice f; (fig) piquant m.

spick-and-span adj impeccable.

spicy adj épicé; piquant.

spider n araignée f.

spike n pointe f.

spill vt (pt **spilled** or **spilt**) renverser, répandre. ● vi se répandre; ~ **over** déborder.

spin vt/i (pt **spun**; pres p **spinning**) (wool, web) filer; (turn) (faire) tourner; (story) débiter; ~ **out** faire durer. ● n (movement, excursion) tour m.

spinach n épinards mpl.

spinal adj vertébral. ~ **cord** n moelle f épinière.

spin-drier n essoreuse f.

spine n colonne f vertébrale; (prickle) piquant m.

spin-off n avantage m accessoire; (by-product) dérivé m.

spinster n célibataire f; (pej) vieille fille f.

spiral adj en spirale; (staircase) en colimaçon. ● n spirale f. ● vi (pt **spiralled**) (prices) monter (en flèche).

spire n flèche f.

spirit n esprit m; (boldness) courage m; ~**s** (morale) moral m; (drink) spiritueux mpl. ● vt ~ **away** faire disparaître. **spirited** adj fougueux. ~**level** n niveau m à bulle.

spiritual adj spirituel.

spit vt/i (pt **spat** or **spit**; pres p **spitting**) cracher; (of rain) crachiner; ~ **out** cracher; the ~**ting** image of le portrait craché or vivant de. ● n crachat(s) m(pl); (for meat) broche f.

spite n rancune f. **in ~ of** malgré.
● vt contrarier.

splash vt éclabousser. ● vi faire des éclaboussures; **~ (about)** patauger.
● n (act, mark) éclaboussure f; (sound) plouf m; (of colour) tache f.

spleen n (Anat) rate f.

splendid adj magnifique, splendide.

splint n (Med) attelle f.

splinter n éclat m; (in finger) écharde f. **~ group** n groupe m dissident.

split vt/i (pt split; pres p splitting) (se) fendre; (tear) (se) déchirer; (divide) (se) diviser; (share) partager; **~ one's sides** se tordre (de rire). ● n fente f; déchirure f; (share 🗊) part f, partage m; (quarrel) rupture f; (Pol) scission f. □ **~ up** (couple) rompre. **~ second** n fraction f de seconde.

splutter vi crachoter; (stammer) bafouiller; (engine) tousser.

spoil vt (pt spoilt or spoiled) (pamper) gâter; (ruin) abîmer; (mar) gâcher, gâter. ● n ~(s) butin m.
~-sport n trouble-fête mf inv.

spoke¹ n rayon m.

spoke², **spoken** ⇒SPEAK.

spokesman n (pl -men) porte-parole m inv.

sponge n éponge f. ● vt éponger.
● vi **~ on** vivre aux crochets de.
~-bag n trousse f de toilette.
~-cake n génoise f.

sponsor n (of concert) parrain m, sponsor m; (surety) garant m; (for membership) parrain m, marraine f.
● vt parrainer, sponsoriser; (member) parrainer. **sponsorship** n patronage m; parrainage m.

spontaneous adj spontané.

spoof n 🗊 parodie f.

spoon n cuiller f, cuillère f.

spoonful n (pl ~s) cuillerée f.

sport n sport m; (good) ~ (person 🗊) chic type m; **~s car/coat** voiture/veste f de sport. ● vt (display) exhiber, arborer.

sporting adj sportif; **a ~ chance** une assez bonne chance.

sportsman n (pl -men) sportif m.

sporty adj 🗊 sportif.

spot n (mark, stain) tache f; (dot) point m; (in pattern) pois m; (drop) goutte f; (place) endroit m; (pimple) bouton m; **a ~ of** 🗊 un peu de; **on the ~** sur place; (without delay) sur le coup. ● vt (pt spotted) 🗊 apercevoir. **~ check** n contrôle m surprise.

spotless adj impeccable.

spotlight n (lamp) projecteur m, spot m.

spotty adj (skin) boutonneux.

spouse n époux m, épouse f.

spout n (of teapot) bec m; (of liquid) jet m; **up the ~** (ruined 🗊) fichu. ● vi jaillir.

sprain n entorse f, foulure f. ● vt ~ **one's wrist** se fouler le poignet.

sprang ⇒SPRING.

sprawl vi (town, person) s'étaler. ● n étalement m.

spray n (of flowers) gerbe f; (water) gerbe f d'eau; (from sea) embruns mpl; (device) bombe f, atomiseur m.
● vt (surface, insecticide, plant) vaporiser; (person) asperger; (crops) traiter.

spread vt/i (pt spread) (stretch, extend) (s')étendre; (news, fear) (se) répandre; (illness) (se) propager; (butter) (s')étaler. ● n propagation f; (of population) distribution f; (paste) pâte f à tartiner; (food) belle table f.
~-eagled adj bras et jambes écartés. **~-sheet** n tableur m.

spree n **go on a ~** (have fun 🗊) faire la noce.

sprig n petite branche f.

sprightly adj (-ier, -iest) alerte, vif.

spring vi (pt sprang; pp sprung) bondir. ● vt ~ **sth on sb** annoncer qch de but en blanc à qn. ● n bond m; (device) ressort m; (season) printemps m; (of water) source f. □ **~ from** provenir de; **~ up** surgir.
~board n tremplin m. **~ onion** n oignon m blanc.

springy adj (-ier, -iest) élastique.

sprinkle vt (with liquid) arroser (**with** de); (with salt, flour) saupoudrer (**with** de); (sand) répandre. **sprinkler** n (in garden) arroseur m; (for fires) extincteur m (à déclenchement) automatique.

sprint vi (Sport) sprinter. ● n sprint m.

sprout vt/i pousser. ● n (on plant) pousse f; (**Brussels**) ~s choux mpl de Bruxelles.

spruce adj pimpant. ● vt ~ **oneself up** se faire beau. ● n (tree) épicéa m.

sprung ⇒SPRING.

spud n 🄸 patate f.

spun ⇒SPIN.

spur n (of rider) éperon m; (stimulus) aiguillon m; **on the** ~ **of the moment** sous l'impulsion du moment. ● vt (pt **spurred**) éperonner.

spurious adj faux.

spurn vt repousser.

spurt vi jaillir; (fig) accélérer. ● n jet m; (of energy) sursaut m.

spy n espion/-ne m/f. ● vi espionner. ● vt apercevoir.

squabble vi se chamailler. ● n chamaillerie f.

squad n (of soldiers) escouade f; (Sport) équipe f.

squadron n (Mil) escadron m; (Aviat) escadrille f.

squalid adj sordide.

squander vt (money, time) gaspiller.

square n carré m; (open space in town) place f. ● adj carré; (honest) honnête; (meal) solide; (boring 🄸) ringard; (all) ~ (quits) quitte; ~ **metre** mètre m carré. ● vt (settle) régler; ~ **up to** faire face à.

squash vt écraser; (crowd) serrer. ● n (game) squash m; (marrow: US) courge f; **lemon** ~ citronnade f; **orange** ~ orangeade f.

squat vi (pt **squatted**) s'accroupir; ~ **in a house** squattériser une maison. ● adj (dumpy) trapu. **squatter** n squatter m.

squawk n cri m rauque. ● vi pousser un cri rauque.

squeak n petit cri m; (of door) grincement m. ● vi crier; grincer.

squeal n cri m aigu. ● vi pousser un cri aigu; ~ **on** (inform on 🄸) dénoncer.

squeamish adj (trop) délicat.

squeeze vt presser; (hand, arm) serrer; (extract) exprimer (**from** de); (extort) soutirer (**from** à). ● vi (force one's way) se glisser. ● n pression f; (Comm) restrictions fpl de crédit.

squid n calmar m.

squint vi loucher; (with half-shut eyes) plisser les yeux. ● n (Med) strabisme m.

squirm vi se tortiller.

squirrel n écureuil m.

squirt vt/i (faire) jaillir. ● n jet m.

stab vt (pt **stabbed**) (with knife) poignarder. ● n coup m (de couteau); **have a** ~ **at sth** essayer de faire qch.

stability n stabilité f. **stabilize** vt stabiliser.

stable adj stable. ● n écurie f. ~-**boy** n lad m.

stack n tas m. ● vt ~ (**up**) entasser, empiler.

stadium n stade m.

staff n personnel m; (in school) professeurs mpl; (Mil) état-major m; (stick) bâton m. ● vt pourvoir en personnel.

stag n cerf m.

stage n (Theat) scène f; (phase) stade m, étape f; (platform in hall) estrade f; **go on the** ~ faire du théâtre. ● vt mettre en scène; (fig) organiser. ~ **door** n entrée f des artistes. ~ **fright** n trac m.

stagger vi chanceler. ● vt (shock) stupéfier; (payments) échelonner. **staggering** adj stupéfiant.

stagnate vi stagner.

stag night n soirée f pour enterrer une vie de garçon.

staid adj sérieux.

stain vt tacher; (wood) colorer. ● n tache f; (colouring) colorant m. **stained glass window** n vitrail m.

stainless steel n acier m inoxydable.

stain remover n détachant m.

stair n marche f; **the** ~s l'escalier m. ~**case**, ~**way** n escalier m.

stake n (post) pieu m; (wager) enjeu m; **at** ~ en jeu. ● vt (area) jalonner; (wager) jouer; ~ **a claim to** revendiquer.

stale adj pas frais; (bread) rassis; (smell) de renfermé.

stalk n (of plant) tige f. ● vi marcher de façon guindée. ● vt (hunter) chasser; (murderer) suivre.

stall n (in stable) stalle f; (in market) éventaire m; ~**s** (Theat) orchestre m. ● vt/i (Auto) caler; ~ (for time) temporiser.

stallion n étalon m.

stamina n résistance f.

stammer vt/i bégayer. ● n bégaiement m.

stamp vt/i ~ (one's foot) taper du pied. ● vt (letter) timbrer. ● n (for postage, marking) timbre m; (mark: fig) sceau m. □ ~ **out** supprimer. ~**-collecting** n philatélie f.

stampede n fuite f désordonnée; (rush: fig) ruée f. ● vi s'enfuir en désordre; se ruer.

stand vi (pt **stood**) être or se tenir (debout); (rise) se lever; (be situated) se trouver; (Pol) être candidat (**for** à); ~ **in line** (US) faire la queue; ~ **to reason** être logique. ● vt mettre (debout); (tolerate) supporter; ~ **a chance** avoir une chance. ● n (stance) position f; (Mil) résistance f; (for lamp) support m; (at fair) stand m; (in street) kiosque m; (for spectators) tribune f; (Jur, US) barre f; **make a** ~ prendre position. □ ~ **back** reculer; ~ **by** or **around** ne rien faire; ~ **by** (be ready) se tenir prêt; (promise, person) rester fidèle à; ~ **down** se désister; ~ **for** représenter; Ⅰ supporter; ~ **in for** remplacer; ~ **out** ressortir; ~ **up** se lever; ~ **up for** défendre; ~ **up to** résister à.

standard n norme f; (level) niveau m (voulu); (flag) étendard m; ~ **of living** niveau m de vie; ~**s** (morals) principes mpl. ● adj ordinaire.

standard of living n niveau m de vie.

stand-by adj de réserve. ● n **be a** ~ être de réserve.

stand-in n remplaçant/-e m/f.

standing adj debout inv. ● n réputation f; (duration) durée f. ~ **order** n prélèvement m bancaire.

standpoint n point m de vue.

standstill n **at a** ~ immobile; **bring/ come to a** ~ (s')immobiliser.

stank ⇒STINK.

staple n agrafe f. ● vt agrafer. ● adj principal, de base. **stapler** n agrafeuse f.

star n étoile f; (person) vedette f. ● vt (pt **starred**) (film) avoir pour vedette. ● vi ~ **in** être la vedette de.

starch n amidon m; (in food) fécule f. ● vt amidonner.

stardom n célébrité f.

stare vi ~ **at** regarder fixement. ● n regard m fixe.

starfish n étoile f de mer.

stark adj (desolate) désolé; (severe) austère; (utter) complet; (fact) brutal. ● adv complètement.

starling n étourneau m.

start vt/i commencer; (machine) (se) mettre en marche; (fashion) lancer; (cause) provoquer; (jump) sursauter; (of vehicle) démarrer; ~ **to do** commencer or se mettre à faire; ~**ing tomorrow** à partir de demain. ● n commencement m, début m; (of race) départ m; (lead) avance f; (jump) sursaut m. □ ~ **off** commencer (**doing** par faire); ~ **out** partir; ~ **up** (business) lancer. **starter** n (Auto) démarreur m; (runner) partant m; (Culin) entrée f.

starting point n point m de départ.

startle vt (make jump) faire tressaillir; (shock) alarmer.

starvation n faim f.

starve vi mourir de faim. ● vt affamer; (deprive) priver.

stash vt cacher.

state n état m; (pomp) apparat m; S~ État m; **the S~s** les États-Unis; **get into a** ~ s'affoler. ● adj d'État, de l'État; (school) public. ● vt affirmer (**that** que); (views) exprimer; (fix) fixer.

stately adj (-ier, -iest) majestueux. ~ **home** n château m.

statement n déclaration f; (of account) relevé m.

statesman n (pl -**men**) homme m d'État.

static adj statique. ● n (radio, TV) parasites mpl.

station n (Rail) gare f; (TV) chaîne f; (Mil) poste m; (rank) condition f. ● vt poster, placer; ~**ed at** or **in** (Mil) en garnison à.

stationary adj immobile, stationnaire; (vehicle) à l'arrêt.

stationery n papeterie f.

station wagon n (US) break m.

statistic n statistique f; ~s statistique f.

statue n statue f.

status n (pl ~es) situation f, statut m; (prestige) standing m.

statute n loi f; ~s (rules) statuts mpl. **statutory** adj statutaire; (holiday) légal.

staunch adj (friend) loyal, fidèle.

stave n (Mus) portée f. ● vt ~ off éviter, conjurer.

stay vi rester; (spend time) séjourner; (reside) loger. ● vt (hunger) tromper. ● n séjour m. □ ~ **away from** (school) ne pas aller à; ~ **behind** or ~ **on** rester; ~ **in** rester à la maison; ~ **up** veiller, se coucher tard.

stead n **stand sb in good** ~ être utile à qn.

steadfast adj ferme.

steady adj (-ier, -iest) stable; (hand, voice) ferme; (regular) régulier; (staid) sérieux. ● vt maintenir, assurer; (calm) calmer.

steak n steak m, bifteck m; (of fish) darne f.

steal vt/i (pt **stole**; pp **stolen**) voler (**from sb** à qn).

steam n vapeur f; (on glass) buée f. ● vt (cook) cuire à la vapeur. ● vi fumer. ~**engine** n locomotive f à vapeur

steamer n (Culin) cuit-vapeur m; (boat) (bateau à) vapeur m.

steel n acier m; ~ **industry** sidérurgie f. ● vpr ~ **oneself** s'endurcir, se cuirasser.

steep adj raide, rapide; (price: 🄵) excessif. ● vt (soak) tremper; ~ed in (fig) imprégné de.

steeple n clocher m.

steer vt diriger; (ship) gouverner; (fig) guider. ● vi (in ship) gouverner; ~ **clear of** éviter.

steering-wheel n volant m.

stem n tige f; (of glass) pied m. ● vi (pt **stemmed**) ~ **from** provenir de. ● vt (pt **stemmed**) (check, stop) endiguer, contenir.

stench n puanteur f.

stencil n pochoir m. ● vt (pt **stencilled**) décorer au pochoir.

step vi (pt **stepped**) marcher, aller. ● n pas m; (stair) marche f; (of train) marchepied m; (action) mesure f; ~s (ladder) escabeau m; **in** ~ au pas; (fig) conforme (**with** à). □ ~ **down** (resign) démissionner; (from ladder) descendre; ~ **forward** faire un pas en avant; ~ **in** (intervene) intervenir; ~ **up** (pressure) augmenter. ~**brother** n demi-frère m. ~**daughter** n belle-fille f. ~**father** n beau-père m. ~**-ladder** n escabeau m. ~**mother** n belle-mère f. **stepping-stone** n (fig) tremplin m. ~**sister** n demi-sœur f. ~**son** n beau-fils m.

stereo n stéréo f; (record-player) chaîne f stéréo. ● adj stéréo inv.

stereotype n stéréotype m. **stereotyped** adj stéréotypé.

sterile adj stérile. **sterility** n stérilité f.

sterilize vt stériliser.

sterling n livre(s) f(pl) sterling. ● adj sterling inv; (silver) fin; (fig) excellent.

stern adj sévère. ● n (of ship) arrière m.

steroid n stéroïde m.

stew vt/i cuire à la casserole; ~ed fruit compote f; ~ed tea thé m trop infusé. ● n ragoût m.

steward n (of club) intendant m; (on ship) steward m. **stewardess** n hôtesse f.

stick vt (pt **stuck**) (glue) coller; (put 🄵) mettre; (endure 🄵) supporter. ● vi (adhere) coller, adhérer; (to pan) attacher; (remain 🄵) rester; (be jammed) être coincé; **be stuck with sb** 🄵 se farcir qn. ● n bâton m; (for walking) canne f. □ ~ **at** persévérer dans; ~ **out** vt (head) sortir; (tongue) tirer; vi (protrude) dépasser; ~ **to** (promise) rester fidèle à; ~ **up for** 🄵 défendre.

sticker n autocollant m.

sticky adj (-ier, -iest) poisseux; (label, tape) adhésif.

stiff adj raide; (limb, joint) ankylosé; (tough) dur; (drink) fort; (price) élevé; (manner) guindé; ~ **neck** torticolis m.

stifle vt/i étouffer.

stiletto a & n ∼s, ∼ **heels** talons mpl aiguille.

still adj immobile; (quiet) calme, tranquille; **keep** ∼**!** arrête de bouger! ● n silence m. ● adv encore, toujours; (even) encore; (nevertheless) tout de même.

stillborn adj mort-né.

still life n nature f morte.

stimulate vt stimuler.

   stimulation n stimulation f.

stimulus n (pl **-li**) (spur) stimulant m.

sting n piqûre f; (of insect) aiguillon m. ● vt/i (pt **stung**) piquer.

stingy adj (**-ier**, **-iest**) avare (with de).

stink n puanteur f. ● vi (pt **stank** or **stunk**; pp **stunk**) ∼ (of) puer.

stipulate vt stipuler.

stir vt/i (pt **stirred**) (move) remuer; (excite) exciter; ∼ **up** (trouble) provoquer. ● n agitation f.

stirrup n étrier m.

stitch n point m; (in knitting) maille f; (Med) point m de suture; (muscle pain) point m de côté; **be in** ∼**es** 🏳 avoir le fou rire. ● vt coudre.

stock n réserve f; (Comm) stock m; (financial) valeurs fpl; (family) souche f; (soup) bouillon m; **we're out of** ∼ il n'y en a plus; **take** ∼ (fig) faire le point; **in** ∼ en stock. ● adj (goods) courant. ● vt (shop) approvisionner; (sell) vendre. ● vi ∼ **up** s'approvisionner (with de). ∼ **broker** n agent m de change. ∼ **cube** n bouillon-cube m. **S**∼ **Exchange** n Bourse f.

stocking n bas m.

stock market n Bourse f.

stockpile n stock m. ● vt stocker; (arms) amasser.

stock-taking n (Comm) inventaire m.

stocky adj (**-ier**, **-iest**) trapu.

stodgy adj lourd.

stole, stolen ⇒STEAL.

stomach n estomac m; (abdomen) ventre m. ● vt (put up with) supporter. ∼**-ache** n mal m à l'estomac or au ventre.

stone n pierre f; (pebble) caillou m; (in fruit) noyau m; (weight) 6,350 kg. ● adj de pierre; ∼**-cold**/**-deaf** complètement froid/sourd. ● vt (throw stones) lapider; (fruit) dénoyauter.

stony adj pierreux.

stood ⇒STAND.

stool n tabouret m.

stoop vi (bend) se baisser; (condescend) s'abaisser. ● n **have a** ∼ être voûté.

stop vt/i (pt **stopped**) arrêter (doing de faire); (moving, talking) s'arrêter; (prevent) empêcher (from de); (hole, leak) boucher; (pain, noise) cesser; (stay 🏳) rester. ● n arrêt m; (full stop) point m; ∼**-over** halte f; (port of call) escale f. □ ∼ **off** s'arrêter; ∼ **up** boucher,

stopgap n bouche-trou m. ● adj intérimaire.

stoppage n arrêt m; (of work) arrêt m de travail; (of pay) retenue f.

stopper n bouchon m.

stop-watch n chronomètre m.

storage n (of goods, food) emmagasinage m. ∼ **heater** n radiateur m électrique à accumulation.

store n réserve f; (warehouse) entrepôt m; (shop) grand magasin m; (US) magasin m; **have in** ∼ **for** réserver à; **set** ∼ **by** attacher du prix à. ● vt (for future) mettre en réserve; (in warehouse, mind) emmagasiner. ∼**-room** n réserve f.

storey n étage m.

stork n cigogne f.

storm n tempête f, orage m. ● vt prendre d'assaut. ● vi (rage) tempêter.

story n histoire f; (in press) article m; (storey: US) étage m. ∼**-teller** n conteur/-euse m/f.

stout adj corpulent; (strong) solide. ● n bière f brune.

stove n cuisinière f.

stow vt ∼ **away** (put away) ranger; (hide) cacher. ● vi voyager clandestinement.

straddle vt être à cheval sur, enjamber.

straggler n traînard/-e m/f.

straight *adj* droit; (tidy) en ordre; (frank) franc; ~ **face** visage *m* sérieux; **get sth** ~ mettre qch au clair. ● *adv* (in straight line) droit; (direct) tout droit; ~ **ahead** *or* **on** tout droit; ~ **away** tout de suite; ~ **off** Ⓣ sans hésiter. ● *n* (Sport) ligne *f* droite.

straighten *vt* (*nail, situation*) redresser; (tidy) arranger.

straightforward *adj* honnête; (easy) simple.

straight off *adj* Ⓣ sans hésiter.

strain *vt* (*rope, ears*) tendre; (*limb*) fouler; (*eyes*) fatiguer; (*muscle*) froisser; (filter) passer; (*vegetables*) égoutter; (fig) mettre à l'épreuve. ● *vi* fournir des efforts. ● *n* tension *f*; (fig) effort *m*; (breed) race *f*; (of virus) variété *f*, ~**s** (tune: Mus) accents *mpl*. **strained** *adj* forcé; (*relations*) tendu. **strainer** *n* passoire *f*.

strait *n* détroit *m*; ~**s** détroit *m*; **be in dire** ~**s** être aux abois. ~**jacket** *n* camisole *f* de force.

strand *n* (thread) fil *m*, brin *m*; (of hair) mèche *f*.

stranded *adj* (*person*) en rade; (*ship*) échoué.

strange *adj* étrange; (unknown) inconnu. **stranger** *n* inconnu/-e *m/f*.

strangle *vt* étrangler.

stranglehold *n* **have a** ~ **on** tenir à la gorge.

strap *n* (of leather) courroie *f*; (of dress) bretelle *f*; (of watch) bracelet *m*. ● *vt* (*pt* **strapped**) attacher.

strategic *adj* stratégique.

strategy *n* stratégie *f*.

straw *n* paille *f*; **the last** ~ le comble.

strawberry *n* fraise *f*.

stray *vi* s'égarer; (deviate) s'écarter. ● *adj* perdu; (isolated) isolé. ● *n* animal *m* perdu.

streak *n* raie *f*, bande *f*; (trace) trace *f*; (period) période *f*; (tendency) tendance *f*. ● *vt* (mark) strier. ● *vi* filer à toute allure.

stream *n* ruisseau *m*; (current) courant *m*; (flow) flot *m*; (in school) classe *f* (de niveau). ● *vi* ruisseler (with de); (*eyes, nose*) couler.

streamline *vt* rationaliser. **streamlined** *adj* (*shape*) aérodynamique.

street *n* rue *f*. ~**car** *n* (US) tramway *m*. ~ **lamp** *n* réverbère *m*. ~ **map** *n* indicateur *m* des rues.

strength *n* force *f*; (of wall, fabric) solidité *f*; **on the** ~ **of** en vertu de. **strengthen** *vt* renforcer, fortifier.

strenuous *adj* (*exercise*) énergique; (*work*) ardu.

stress *n* (emphasis) accent *m*; (pressure) pression *f*; (Med) stress *m*. ● *vt* souligner, insister sur.

stretch *vt* (pull taut) tendre; (*arm, leg*) étendre; (*neck*) tendre; (*clothes*) étirer; (*truth*) forcer; ~ **one's legs** se dégourdir les jambes. ● *vi* s'étendre; (*person*) s'étirer; (*clothes*) se déformer. ● *n* étendue *f*; (period) période *f*; (of road) tronçon *m*; **at a** ~ d'affilée. ● *adj* (*fabric*) extensible.

stretcher *n* brancard *m*.

strew *vt* (*pt* **strewed**; *pp* **strewed** *or* **strewn**) (scatter) répandre; (cover) joncher.

strict *adj* strict.

stride *vi* (*pt* **strode**; *pp* **stridden**) faire de grands pas. ● *n* grand pas *m*.

strife *n* conflit(s) *m(pl)*.

strike *vt* (*pt* **struck**) frapper; (blow) donner; (*match*) frotter; (*gold*) trouver. ● *vi* faire grève; (attack) attaquer; (*clock*) sonner. ● *n* (of workers) grève *f*; (Mil) attaque *f*; (find) découverte *f*; **on** ~ en grève. □ ~ **off** *or* **out** rayer; ~ **up** (*a friendship*) lier amitié (**with** avec). **striker** *n* gréviste *mf*; (football) attaquant/-e *m/f*. **striking** *adj* frappant.

string *n* ficelle *f*; (of violin, racket) corde *f*; (of pearls) collier *m*; (of lies) chapelet *m*; **the** ~**s** (Mus) les cordes; **pull** ~**s** faire jouer ses relations. ● *vt* (*pt* **strung**) (thread) enfiler. **stringed** *adj* (*instrument*) à cordes.

stringent *adj* rigoureux, strict.

stringy *adj* filandreux.

strip *vt/i* (*pt* **stripped**) (undress) (se) déshabiller; (deprive) dépouiller. ● *n* bande *f*.

stripe *n* rayure *f*, raie *f*. **striped** *adj* rayé.

strip light n néon m.

stripper n strip-teaseur/-euse m/f; (solvent) décapant.

strip-tease n strip-tease m.

strive vi (pt **strove**; pp **striven**) s'efforcer (to de).

strode ⇒STRIDE.

stroke vt (with hand) caresser. ● n coup m; (of pen) trait m; (swimming) nage f; (Med) attaque f, congestion f; **at a ~** d'un seul coup.

stroll vi flâner; **~ in** entrer tranquillement. ● n petit tour m.

stroller n (US) poussette f.

strong adj fort; (shoes, fabric) solide; **be fifty ~** être fort de cinquante personnes. **~hold** n bastion m.

strongly adv (greatly) fortement; (with energy) avec force; (deeply) profondément.

strove ⇒STRIVE.

struck ⇒STRIKE.

structure n (of cell, poem) structure f; (building) construction f.

struggle vi lutter, se battre. ● n lutte f; (effort) effort m; **have a ~ to** avoir du mal à.

strum vt (pt **strummed**) gratter de.

strung ⇒STRING. ● adj **~ up** (tense) nerveux.

strut n (support) étai m. ● vi (pt **strutted**) se pavaner.

stub n bout m; (counterfoil) talon m. ● vt (pt **stubbed**) **~ one's toe** se cogner le doigt de pied. □ **~ out** écraser.

stubble n (on chin) barbe f de plusieurs jours; (remains of wheat) chaume m.

stubborn adj obstiné.

stuck ⇒STICK. ● adj (jammed) coincé; **I'm ~** (for answer) je sèche. **~-up** adj 🄸 prétentieux.

stud n (on jacket) clou m; (for collar) bouton m; (stallion) étalon m; (horse farm) haras m. ● vt (pt **studded**) clouter.

student n (Univ) étudiant/-e m/f; (School) élève mf. ● adj (restaurant, life) universitaire.

studio n studio m.

studious adj (person) studieux; (deliberate) étudié.

study n étude f; (office) bureau m. ● vt/i étudier.

stuff n substance f; 🄸 chose(s) f(pl). ● vt rembourrer; (animal) empailler; (cram) bourrer; (Culin) farcir; (block up) boucher; (put) fourrer. **stuffing** n bourre f; (Culin) farce f.

stuffy adj (**-ier, -iest**) mal aéré; (dull 🄸) vieux jeu inv.

stumble vi trébucher; **~ across** or **on** tomber sur. **stumbling-block** n obstacle m.

stump n (of tree) souche f; (of limb) moignon m; (of pencil) bout m.

stumped adj embarrassé.

stun vt (pt **stunned**) étourdir; (bewilder) stupéfier.

stung ⇒STING.

stunk ⇒STINK.

stunning adj (delightful 🄸) sensationnel.

stunt vt (growth) retarder. ● n (feat 🄸) tour m de force; (trick 🄸) truc m; (dangerous) cascade f.

stupid adj stupide, bête. **stupidity** n stupidité f.

sturdy adj (**-ier, -iest**) robuste.

stutter vi bégayer. ● n bégaiement m.

sty n (pigsty) porcherie f; (on eye) orgelet m.

style n style m; (fashion) mode f; (sort) genre m; (pattern) modèle m; **do sth in ~** faire qch avec classe. ● vt (design) créer; **~ sb's hair** coiffer qn.

stylish adj élégant.

stylist n (of hair) coiffeur/-euse m/f.

suave adj (urbane) courtois; (smooth: pej) doucereux.

subconscious a & n inconscient (m), subconscient (m).

subcontract vt sous-traiter.

subdue vt (feeling) maîtriser; (country) subjuguer. **subdued** adj (person, mood) morose; (light) tamisé; (criticism) contenu.

subject[1] adj (state) soumis; **~ to** soumis à; (liable to, dependent on) sujet à. ● n sujet m; (focus) objet m; (School, Univ) matière f; (citizen) ressortissant/-e m/f, sujet/-te m/f.

subject[2] vt soumettre.

subjective adj subjectif.

subject-matter *n* contenu *m*.
subjunctive *a* & *n* subjonctif (*m*).
sublet *vt* sous-louer.
submarine *n* sousmarin *m*.
submerge *vt* submerger. ● *vi* plonger.
submissive *adj* soumis.
submit *vt/i* (*pt* **submitted**) (se) soumettre (**to** à).
subordinate *adj* subalterne; (Gram) subordonné. ● *n* subordonné/-e *m/f*.
subpoena *n* (Jur) citation *f*, assignation *f*.
subscribe *vt/i* verser (de l'argent) (**to** à); ~ **to** (*loan, theory*) souscrire à; (*newspaper*) s'abonner à, être abonné à. **subscriber** *n* abonné/-e *m/f*. **subscription** *n* abonnement *m*; (membership dues) cotisation *f*.
subsequent *adj* (later) ultérieur; (next) suivant. **subsequently** *adv* par la suite.
subside *vi* (land) s'affaisser; (*flood, wind*) baisser.
subsidiary *adj* accessoire. ● *n* (Comm) filiale *f*.
subsidize *vt* subventionner. **subsidy** *n* subvention *f*.
substance *n* substance *f*.
substandard *adj* de qualité inférieure.
substantial *adj* considérable; (*meal*) substantiel.
substitute *n* succédané *m*; (person) remplaçant/-e *m/f*. ● *vt* substituer (**for** à).
subtitle *n* sous-titre *m*.
subtle *adj* subtil.
subtract *vt* soustraire.
suburb *n* faubourg *m*, banlieue *f*; ~**s** banlieue *f*. **suburban** *adj* de banlieue. **suburbia** *n* la banlieue.
subway *n* passage *m* souterrain; (US) métro *m*.
succeed *vi* réussir (**in doing** à faire). ● *vt* (follow) succéder à.
success *n* succès *m*, réussite *f*.
successful *adj* réussi, couronné de succès; (favourable) heureux; (in exam) reçu; **be** ~ **in doing** réussir à faire.
succession *n* succession *f*; **in** ~ de suite.

successive *adj* successif; **six** ~ **days** six jours consécutifs.
successor *n* successeur *m*.
such *det* & *pron* tel(le), tel(le)s; (so much) tant (de). ● *adv* si; ~ **a book** un tel livre; ~ **books** de tels livres; ~ **courage** tant de courage; ~ **a big house** une si grande maison; ~ **as** comme, tel que; **as** ~ en tant que tel; **there's no** ~ **thing** ça n'existe pas. ~**-and-**~ *adj* tel ou tel.
suck *vt* sucer. □ ~ **in** *or* **up** aspirer.
sucker *n* (rubber pad) ventouse *f*; (person 🔳) dupe *f*.
suction *n* succion *f*.
sudden *adj* soudain, subit; **all of a** ~ tout à coup. **suddenly** *adv* subitement, brusquement.
sue *vt* (*pres p* **suing**) poursuivre (en justice).
suede *n* daim *m*.
suffer *vt/i* souffrir; (*loss, attack*) subir. **sufferer** *n* victime *f*, malade *mf*. **suffering** *n* souffrance(s) *f(pl)*.
sufficient *adj* (enough) suffisamment de; (big enough) suffisant.
suffix *n* suffixe *m*.
suffocate *vt/i* suffoquer.
sugar *n* sucre *m*. ● *vt* sucrer.
suggest *vt* suggérer. **suggestion** *n* suggestion *f*.
suicidal *adj* suicidaire.
suicide *n* suicide *m*; **commit** ~ se suicider.
suit *n* (man's) costume *m*; (woman's) tailleur *m*; (cards) couleur *f*. ● *vt* convenir à; (*garment, style*) aller à; (adapt) adapter.
suitable *adj* qui convient (**for** à), convenable. **suitably** *adv* convenablement.
suitcase *n* valise *f*.
suite *n* (rooms) suite *f*; (furniture) mobilier *m*.
suited *adj* (well) ~ (matched) bien assorti; ~ **to** fait pour, apte à.
sulk *vi* bouder.
sullen *adj* maussade.
sultana *n* raisin *m* de Smyrne, raisin *m* sec.
sultry *adj* (**-ier**, **-iest**) étouffant, lourd; (fig) sensuel.

sum n somme f; (in arithmetic) calcul m. ● vt/i (pt **summed**) ~ **up** résumer, récapituler; (assess) évaluer.

summarize vt résumer.

summary n résumé m. ● adj sommaire.

summer n été m. ● adj d'été. ~**time** n (season) été m.

summery adj estival.

summit n sommet m; ~ (**conference**) (Pol) (conférence f au) sommet m.

summon vt appeler; ~ **sb to a meeting** convoquer qn à une réunion; ~ **up** (strength, courage) rassembler.

summons n (Jur) assignation f. ● vt assigner.

sun n soleil m. ● vt (pt **sunned**) ~ **oneself** se chauffer au soleil. ~**burn** n coup m de soleil.

Sunday n dimanche m. ~ **school** n catéchisme m.

sundry adj divers; **sundries** articles mpl divers; **all and** ~ tout le monde.

sunflower n tournesol m.

sung ⇒SING.

sun-glasses npl lunettes fpl de soleil.

sunk ⇒SINK.

sunken adj (ship) submergé; (eyes) creux.

sunlight n soleil m.

sunny adj (-**ier**, -**iest**) ensoleillé.

sun: ~**rise** n lever m du soleil. ~-**roof** n toit m ouvrant. ~ **screen** n filtre m solaire. ~**set** n coucher m du soleil. ~**shine** n soleil m. ~**stroke** n insolation f.

sun-tan n bronzage m. ~ **lotion** n lotion f solaire. ~ **oil** n huile f solaire.

super adj Ⅱ formidable.

superb adj superbe.

superficial adj superficiel.

superfluous adj superflu.

superimpose vt superposer (**on** à).

superintendent n directeur/-trice m/f; (of police) commissaire m.

superior a & n supérieur/-e (m/f).

superlative adj suprême. ● n (Gram) superlatif m.

supermarket n supermarché m.

supersede vt remplacer, supplanter.

superstition n superstition f.

superstitious adj superstitieux.

superstore n hypermarché m.

supervise vt surveiller, diriger.

supervision n surveillance f.

supervisor n surveillant/-e m/f; (shop) chef m de rayon; (firm) chef m de service.

supper n dîner m; (late at night) souper m.

supple adj souple.

supplement[1] n supplément m. **supplementary** adj supplémentaire.

supplement[2] vt compléter.

supplier n fournisseur m.

supply vt fournir; (equip) pourvoir; (feed) alimenter (**with** en). ● n provision f; (of gas) alimentation f; **supplies** (food) vivres mpl; (material) fournitures fpl.

support vt soutenir; (family) assurer la subsistance de. ● n soutien m, appui m; (Tech) support m. **supporter** n partisan/-e m/f; (Sport) supporter m. **supportive** adj qui soutient et encourage.

suppose vt/i supposer; **be** ~**d to do** être censé faire, devoir faire; **supposing he comes** supposons qu'il vienne. **supposedly** adv soi-disant, prétendument.

suppress vt (put an end to) supprimer; (restrain) réprimer; (stifle) étouffer.

supreme adj suprême.

surcharge n supplément m; (tax) surtaxe f.

sure adj sûr; **make** ~ **of** s'assurer de; **make** ~ **that** vérifier que. ● adv (US Ⅱ) pour sûr. **surely** adv sûrement.

surf n ressac m. ● vi faire du surf; (Internet) surfer.

surface n surface f. ● adj superficiel. ● vt revêtir. ● vi faire surface; (fig) réapparaître.

surfer n surfeur/-euse m/f; (Internet) internaute mf.

surge vi (waves, crowd) déferler; (increase) monter. ● n (wave) vague f; (rise) montée f.

surgeon *n* chirurgien *m*.

surgery *n* chirurgie *f*; (office) cabinet *m*; (session) consultation *f*; **need ~** devoir être opéré.

surgical *adj* chirurgical. **~ spirit** *n* alcool *m* à 90 degrés.

surly *adj* (**-ier, -iest**) bourru.

surname *n* nom *m* de famille.

surplus *n* surplus *m*. ● *adj* en surplus.

surprise *n* surprise *f*. ● *vt* surprendre. **surprised** *adj* surpris (at de). **surprising** *adj* surprenant.

surrender *vi* se rendre. ● *vt* (hand over) remettre; (Mil) rendre. ● *n* (Mil) reddition *f*; (of passport) remise *f*.

surround *vt* entourer; (Mil) encercler. **surrounding** *adj* environnant. **surroundings** *npl* environs *mpl*; (setting) cadre *m*.

surveillance *n* surveillance *f*.

survey[1] *vt* (review) passer en revue; (inquire into) enquêter sur; (building) inspecter.

survey[2] *n* (inquiry) enquête *f*; inspection *f*; (general view) vue *f* d'ensemble.

surveyor *n* expert *m* (géomètre).

survival *n* survie *f*.

survive *vt/i* survivre (à). **survivor** *n* survivant/-e *m/f*.

susceptible *adj* sensible (to à); **~ to** (prone to) prédisposé à.

suspect[1] *vt* soupçonner; (doubt) douter de.

suspect[2] *n* & *a* suspect/-e (*m/f*).

suspend *vt* (hang, stop) suspendre; (*licence*) retirer provisoirement. **suspended sentence** *n* condamnation *f* avec sursis.

suspender *n* jarretelle *f*; **~s** (braces: US) bretelles *fpl*. **~ belt** *n* porte-jarretelles *m*.

suspension *n* suspension *f*; retrait *m* provisoire.

suspicion *n* soupçon *m*; (distrust) méfiance *f*.

suspicious *adj* soupçonneux; (causing suspicion) suspect; **be ~ of** se méfier de. **suspiciously** *adv* de façon suspecte.

sustain *vt* supporter; (*effort*) soutenir; (suffer) subir.

sustenance *n* (food) nourriture *f*; (nourishment) valeur *f* nutritive.

swallow *vt/i* avaler; **~ up** (absorb, engulf) engloutir. ● *n* hirondelle *f*.

swam ⇨SWIM.

swamp *n* marais *m*. ● *vt* (flood, overwhelm) submerger.

swan *n* cygne *m*.

swap *vt/i* (*pt* **swapped**) 🔲 échanger. ● *n* 🔲 échange *m*.

swarm *n* essaim *m*. ● *vi* fourmiller; **~ into** *or* **round** (*crowd*) envahir.

swat *vt* (*pt* **swatted**) (*fly*) écraser.

sway *vt/i* (se) balancer; (influence) influencer. ● *n* balancement *m*; (rule) empire *m*.

swear *vt/i* (*pt* **swore**; *pp* **sworn**) jurer (to sth de qch); **~ at** injurier; **~ by sth** 🔲 ne jurer que par qch. **~-word** *n* juron *m*.

sweat *n* sueur *f*. ● *vi* suer.

sweater *n* pull-over *m*.

sweat-shirt *n* sweat-shirt *m*.

swede *n* rutabaga *m*.

Swede *n* Suédois/-e *m/f*. **Sweden** *n* Suède *f*.

Swedish *adj* suédois. ● *n* (Ling) suédois *m*.

sweep *vt/i* (*pt* **swept**) (*floor*) balayer; (carry away) emporter, entraîner; (*chimney*) ramoner. ● *n* coup *m* de balai; (curve) courbe *f*; (mouvement) geste *m*, mouvement *m*; (for chimneys) ramoneur *m*. □ **~ by** passer rapidement *or* majestueusement. **sweeper** *n* (for carpet) balai *m* mécanique; (football) libero *m*.

sweet *adj* (not sour, pleasant) doux; (not savoury) sucré; (charming 🔲) gentil; **have a ~ tooth** aimer les sucreries. ● *n* bonbon *m*; (dish) dessert *m*. **~corn** *n* maïs *m*.

sweeten *vt* sucrer; (fig) adoucir. **sweetener** *n* édulcorant *m*.

sweetheart *n* petit/-e ami/-e *m/f*; (term of endearment) chéri/-e *m/f*.

sweetly *adv* gentiment.

sweetness *n* douceur *f*; goût *m* sucré.

sweet pea *n* pois *m* de senteur.

swell *vt/i* (*pt* **swelled**; *pp* **swollen** *or* **swelled**) (increase) grossir;

(expand) (se) gonfler; (*hand, face*) enfler. ● *n* (of sea) houle *f*. **swelling** *n* (Med) enflure *f*.

sweltering *adj* étouffant.

swept ⇒SWEEP.

swerve *vi* faire un écart.

swift *adj* rapide. ● *n* (bird) martinet *m*.

swim *vi* (*pt* **swam**; *pp* **swum**; *pres p* **swimming**) nager; (be dizzy) tourner. ● *vt* traverser à la nage; (*distance*) nager. ● *n* baignade *f*; **go for a** ~ aller se baigner. **swimmer** *n* nageur/-euse *m/f*. **swimming** *n* natation *f*.

swimming-pool *n* piscine *f*.

swim-suit *n* maillot *m* (de bain).

swindle *vt* escroquer. ● *n* escroquerie *f*.

swine *npl* (pigs) pourceaux *mpl*. ● *n inv* (person 🔲) salaud *m*.

swing *vt/i* (*pt* **swung**) (se) balancer; (turn round) tourner; (*pendulum*) osciller. ● *n* balancement *m*; (seat) balançoire *f*; (of opinion) revirement *m* (**towards** en faveur de); (Mus) rythme *m*; **be in full** ~ battre son plein. ◻ ~ **round** (*person*) se retourner.

swipe *vt* (hit 🔲) frapper; (steal 🔲) piquer.

swirl *vi* tourbillonner. ● *n* tourbillon *m*.

Swiss *adj* suisse. ● *n inv* Suisse *mf*.

switch *n* bouton *m* (électrique), interrupteur *m*; (shift) changement *m*, revirement *m*. ● *vt* (transfer) transférer; (exchange) échanger (**for** contre); (reverse positions of) changer de place; ~ **trains** (change) changer de train. ● *vi* changer. ◻ ~ **off** éteindre; ~ **on** mettre, allumer.

switchboard *n* standard *m*.

Switzerland *n* Suisse *f*.

swivel *vt/i* (*pt* **swivelled**) (faire) pivoter.

swollen ⇒SWELL.

swoop *vi* (bird) fondre; (police) faire une descente, foncer. ● *n* (police raid) descente *f*.

sword *n* épée *f*.

swore ⇒SWEAR.

sworn ⇒SWEAR. ● *adj* (*enemy*) juré; (*ally*) dévoué.

swot *vt/i* (*pt* **swotted**) (study 🔲) bûcher 🔲. ● *n* 🔲 bûcheur/-euse *m/f* 🔲.

swum ⇒SWIM.

swung ⇒SWING.

syllabus *n* (*pl* ~**es**) (School, Univ) programme *m*.

symbol *n* symbole *m*. **symbolic(al)** *adj* symbolique. **symbolize** *vt* symboliser.

symmetrical *adj* symétrique.

sympathetic *adj* compatissant; (fig) compréhensif.

sympathize *vi* ~ **with** (pity) plaindre; (fig) comprendre les sentiments de. **sympathizer** *n* sympathisant/-e *m/f*.

sympathy *n* (pity) compassion *f*; (fig) compréhension *f*; (solidarity) solidarité *f*; (condolences) condoléances *fpl*; (affinity) affinité *f*; **be in** ~ **with** comprendre, être en accord avec.

symptom *n* symptôme *m*.

synagogue *n* synagogue *f*.

synonym *n* synonyme *m*.

synopsis *n* (*pl* -**opses**) résumé *m*.

syntax *n* syntaxe *f*.

synthesis *n* (*pl* -**theses**) synthèse *f*.

synthetic *adj* synthétique.

syringe *n* seringue *f*.

syrup *n* (liquid) sirop *m*; (treacle) mélasse *f* raffinée.

system *n* système *m*; (body) organisme *m*; (order) méthode *f*. **systematic** *adj* systématique.

systems analyst *n* analyste-programmeur/-euse *m/f*.

Tt

tab *n* (on can) languette *f*; (on garment) patte *f*; (label) étiquette *f*; (US 🔲) addition *f*; (Comput) tabulatrice *f*; (setting) tabulation *f*.

table *n* table *f*; **at (the)** ~ à table; **lay** *or* **set the** ~ mettre la table. ● *vt* (*motion*) présenter. ~-**cloth** *n* nappe *f.* ~**mat** *n* set *m* de table. ~**spoon** *n* cuillère *f* de service.

tablet *n* (of stone) plaque *f*; (drug) comprimé *m*.

table tennis *n* tennis *m* de table; ping-pong® *m*.

taboo *n & a* tabou (*m*).

tacit *adj* tacite.

tack *n* (nail) clou *m*; (stitch) point *m* de bâti; (course of action) voie *f*. ● *vt* (nail) clouer; (stitch) bâtir; (add) ajouter. ● *vi* (Naut) louvoyer.

tackle *n* équipement *m*; (in soccer) tacle *m*; (in rugby) plaquage *m*. ● *vt* (problem) s'attaquer à; (player) tacler, plaquer.

tact *n* tact *m*. **tactful** *adj* plein de tact.

tactics *npl* tactique *f*.

tadpole *n* têtard *m*.

tag *n* (label) étiquette *f*. ● *vt* (*pt* **tagged**) (label) étiqueter. ● *vi* ~ **along** 🇬🇧 suivre.

tail *n* queue *f*; ~**s** (coat) habit *m*; ~**s!** (on coin) pile! ● *vt* (follow) filer. ● *vi* ~ **away** *or* **off** diminuer. ~**back** *n* bouchon *m*. ~**gate** *n* hayon *m*.

tailor *n* tailleur *m*. ● *vt* (garment) façonner; (fig) adapter. ~**made** *adj* fait sur mesure.

take *vt/i* (*pt* **took**; *pp* **taken**) prendre (from sb à qn); (carry) emporter, porter (to à); (escort) emmener; (contain) contenir; (tolerate) supporter; (accept) accepter; (prize) remporter; (exam) passer; (precedence) avoir; (view) adopter; ~ **sb home** ramener qn chez lui; **be taken by** *or* **with** être impressionné par; **be taken ill** tomber malade; **it** ~**s time** il faut du temps pour. □ ~ **after** tenir de; ~ **apart** démonter; (fig) descendre en flammes 🇬🇧; ~ **away** (object) enlever; (person) emmener; (pain) supprimer; ~ **back** reprendre; (return) rendre; (accompany) raccompagner; (statement) retirer; ~ **down** (object) descendre; (notes) prendre; ~ **in** (object) rentrer; (include) inclure; (cheat) tromper; ~ **off** (Aviat) décoller; ~ **sth off** enlever qch; ~ **sb off** imiter qn; ~ **on** (task, staff, passenger) prendre; (challenger)

relever le défi de; ~ **out** sortir; (stain) enlever; ~ **over** *vt* (country, firm) prendre le contrôle de; *vi* prendre le pouvoir; ~ **over from** remplacer; ~ **part** participer (in à); ~ **place** avoir lieu; ~ **to** se prendre d'amitié pour; (activity) prendre goût à; ~ **to doing** se mettre à faire; ~ **up** (object) monter; (hobby) se mettre à; (occupy) prendre; (resume) reprendre; ~ **up with** se lier avec. ~**away** *n* (meal) repas *m* à emporter. ~**off** *n* (Aviat) décollage *m*. ~**over** *n* (Pol) prise *f* de pouvoir; (Comm) rachat *m*.

tale *n* conte *m*; (report) récit *m*; (lie) histoire *f*.

talent *n* talent *m*. **talented** *adj* doué.

talk *vt/i* parler; (chat) bavarder; ~ **sb into doing** persuader qn de faire; ~ **sth over** discuter de qch. ● *n* (talking) propos *mpl*; (conversation) conversation *f*; (lecture) exposé *m*.

talkative *adj* bavard.

tall *adj* (high) haut; (person) grand.

tame *adj* apprivoisé; (dull) insipide. ● *vt* apprivoiser; (lion) dompter.

tamper *vi* ~ **with** (lock, machine) tripoter; (accounts, evidence) trafiquer.

tan *vt/i* (*pt* **tanned**) bronzer; (hide) tanner. ● *n* bronzage *m*.

tangerine *n* mandarine *f*.

tangle *vt/i* ~ (**up**) s'emmêler. ● *n* enchevêtrement *m*.

tank *n* réservoir *m*; (vat) cuve *f*; (for fish) aquarium *m*; (Mil) char *m* (de combat).

tanker *n* (lorry) camion-citerne *m*; (ship) navire-citerne *m*; **oil/petrol** ~ pétrolier *m*.

tantrum *n* crise *f* (de colère).

tap *n* (for water) robinet *m*; (knock) petit coup *m*; **on** ~ disponible. ● *vt* (*pt* **tapped**) (knock) taper (doucement); (resources) exploiter; (phone) mettre sur écoute.

tape *n* bande *f* (magnétique); (cassette) cassette *f*; (video) cassette *f* vidéo; (fabric) ruban *m*; (sticky) scotch® *m*. ● *vt* (record) enregistrer; ~ **sth to sth** coller qch à qch.

~-measure *n* mètre *m* ruban. **~ recorder** *n* magnétophone *m*.

tapestry *n* tapisserie *f*.

tar *n* goudron *m*. ● *vt* (*pt* **tarred**) goudronner.

target *n* cible *f*; (objective) objectif *m*. ● *vt* (*city*) prendre pour cible; (*weapon*) diriger; (in marketing) viser.

tariff *n* (price list) tarif *m*; (on imports) droit *m* de douane.

tarmac, Tarmac® *n* macadam *m*; (runway) piste *f*.

tarpaulin *n* bâche *f*.

tarragon *n* estragon *m*.

tart *n* tarte *f*. ● *adj* aigrelet.

task *n* tâche *f*.

taste *n* goût *m*; (experience) aperçu *m*. ● *vt* (eat, enjoy) goûter à; (try) goûter; (perceive taste of) sentir (le goût de). ● *vi* **~ of** *or* **like** avoir un goût de. **tasteful** *adj* de bon goût.

tattoo *vt* tatouer. ● *n* tatouage *m*.

tatty *adj* (**-ier, -iest**) Ⓔ miteux.

taught ⇒TEACH.

taunt *vt* railler. ● *n* raillerie *f*.

Taurus *n* Taureau *m*.

tax *n* (on goods, services) taxe *f*; (on income) impôt *m*. ● *vt* imposer; (put to test: fig) mettre à l'épreuve. **taxable** *adj* imposable. **taxation** *n* imposition *f*; (taxes) impôts *mpl*.

tax: **~-collector** *n* percepteur *m*. **~-deductible** *adj* déductible des impôts. **~ disc** *n* vignette *f*. **~-free** *adj* exempt d'impôts. **~ haven** *n* paradis *m* fiscal.

taxi *n* taxi *m*. **~ rank** *n* station *f* de taxi.

tax: **~payer** *n* contribuable *mf*. **~ relief** *n* dégrèvement *m* fiscal. **~ return** *n* déclaration *f* d'impôts.

tea *n* (drink, meal) thé *m*; (children's snack) goûter *m*; **~ bag** sachet *m* de thé.

teach *vt* (*pt* **taught**) apprendre (**sb sth** qch à qn); (in school) enseigner (**sb sth** qch à qn). ● *vi* enseigner. **teacher** *n* enseignant/-e *m/f*; (secondary) professeur *m*; (primary) instituteur/-trice *m/f*.

team *n* équipe *f*; (of animals) attelage *m*. ● *vi* **~ up** faire équipe (**with** avec).

teapot *n* théière *f*.

tear[1] *vt/i* (*pt* **tore**; *pp* **torn**) (se) déchirer; (snatch) arracher (**from** à); (rush) aller à toute vitesse. ● *n* déchirure *f*.

tear[2] *n* larme *f*; **in ~s** en larmes. **~-gas** *n* gaz *m* lacrymogène.

tease *vt* taquiner. ● *n* taquin/-e *m/f*.

tea: **~-shop** *n* salon *m* de thé. **~spoon** *n* petite cuillère *f*.

teat *n* tétine *f*.

tea-towel *n* torchon *m*.

technical *adj* technique.

technician *n* technicien/-ne *m/f*.

technique *n* technique *f*.

techno *n* (Mus) techno *f*.

technology *n* technologie *f*.

teddy *adj* **~ bear** ours *m* en peluche.

tedious *adj* ennuyeux.

tee *n* (golf) tee *m*.

teenage *adj* (*girl, boy*) adolescent; (*fashion*) des adolescents. **teenager** *n* jeune *mf*, adolescent/-e *m/f*.

teens *npl* **in one's ~** adolescent.

teeth ⇒TOOTH.

teethe *vi* faire ses dents.

teetotaller *n* personne *f* qui ne boit pas d'alcool.

telecommunications *npl* télécommunications *fpl*.

telecommuting *n* télétravail *m*.

teleconferencing *n* téléconférence *f*.

telegram *n* télégramme *m*.

telegraph *n* télégraphe *m*. ● *adj* télégraphique.

telephone *n* téléphone *m*. ● *vt* (*person*) téléphoner à; (*message*) téléphoner. ● *vi* téléphoner. **~ book** annuaire *m*. **~ booth, ~-box** *n* cabine *f* téléphonique. **~ call** *n* coup *m* de téléphone. **~ number** *n* numéro *m* de téléphone.

telephoto *adj* **~ lens** téléobjectif *m*.

telescope *n* télescope *m*. ● *vt/i* (se) télescoper.

teletext *n* télétexte *m*.

televise *vt* téléviser.

television *n* télévision *f*; **~ set** poste *m* de télévision, téléviseur *m*.

telex *n* télex *m*. ● *vt* envoyer par télex.

tell *vt* (*pt* **told**) dire (sb sth qch à qn); (*story*) raconter; (distinguish) distinguer; ~ **sb to do sth** dire à qn de faire qch; ~ **sth from sth** voir la différence entre qch et qch. ● *vi* (show) avoir un effet; (know) savoir. □ ~ **off** 🔲 gronder.

temp *n* intérimaire *mf*. ● *vi* faire de l'intérim.

temper *n* humeur *f*; (anger) colère *f*; **lose one's** ~ se mettre en colère.

temperament *n* tempérament *m*.
temperamental *adj* capricieux.

temperature *n* température *f*; **have a** ~ avoir de la fièvre *or* de la température.

temple *n* temple *m*; (of head) tempe *f*.

temporary *adj* temporaire, provisoire.

tempt *vt* tenter; ~ **sb to do** donner envie à qn de faire.

ten *a* & *n* dix (*m*).

tenacious *adj* tenace.

tenancy *n* location *f*. **tenant** *n* locataire *mf*.

tend *vt* s'occuper de. ● *vi* ~ **to** (be apt to) avoir tendance à; (look after) s'occuper de. **tendency** *n* tendance *f*.

tender *adj* tendre; (sore, painful) sensible. ● *vt* offrir, donner. ● *vi* faire une soumission. ● *n* (Comm) soumission *f*; **be legal** ~ (money) avoir cours.

tendon *n* tendon *m*.

tennis *n* tennis *m*. ● *adj* (*court, match*) de tennis; ~ **shoes** tennis *mpl*.

tenor *n* (meaning) sens *m* général; (Mus) ténor *m*.

tense *n* (Gram) temps *m*. ● *adj* tendu. ● *vt* (*muscles*) tendre, raidir. ● *vi* (*face*) se crisper.

tension *n* tension *f*.

tent *n* tente *f*.

tentative *adj* provisoire; (hesitant) timide.

tenth *a* & *n* dixième (*mf*).

tepid *adj* tiède.

term *n* (word, limit) terme *m*; (of imprisonment) temps *m*; (School) trimestre *m*; ~**s** conditions *fpl*; **on good/bad** ~**s** en bons/mauvais termes; **in the short/long** ~ à court/long terme; **come to** ~**s with sth** accepter qch; ~ **of office** (Pol) mandat *m*. ● *vt* appeler.

terminal *adj* (*point*) terminal; (*illness*) incurable. ● *n* (oil, computer) terminal *m*; (Rail) terminus *m*; (Electr) borne *f*; (**air**) ~ aérogare *f*.

terminate *vt* mettre fin à. ● *vi* prendre fin.

terminus *n* (*pl* **-ni**) (station) terminus *m*.

terrace *n* terrasse *f*; (houses) rangée *f* de maisons contiguës; **the** ~**s** (Sport) les gradins *mpl*.

terracotta *n* terre *f* cuite.

terrible *adj* affreux, atroce.

terrific *adj* (huge) énorme; (great 🔲) formidable.

terrify *vt* terrifier; **be terrified of** avoir très peur de.

territory *n* territoire *m*.

terror *n* terreur *f*.

terrorism *n* terrorisme *m*.
terrorist *n* terroriste *mf*.

test *n* épreuve *f*; (written exam) contrôle *m*; (of machine, product) essai *m*; (of sample) analyse *f*; **driving** ~ examen *m* du permis de conduire. ● *vt* évaluer; (School) contrôler; (*machine, product*) essayer; (*sample*) analyser; (*patience, strength*) mettre à l'épreuve. ● *vi* ~ **for** faire une recherche de.

testament *n* testament *m*; **Old/New** **T**~ Ancien/Nouveau Testament *m*.

testicle *n* testicule *m*.

testify *vt/i* témoigner (to de; that que).

testimony *n* témoignage *m*.

test tube *n* éprouvette *f*.

tetanus *n* tétanos *m*.

text *n* texte *m*. ~**book** *n* manuel *m*.

texture *n* (of paper) grain *m*; (of fabric) texture *f*.

Thames *n* **the** ~ la Tamise.

than *conj* que, qu'; (with numbers) de; **more/less** ~ **ten** plus/moins de dix.

thank *vt* remercier; ~ **you!**, ~**s!** merci! **thankful** *adj* reconnaissant (for de). **thanks** *npl* remerciements *mpl*; ~**s to** grâce à. **Thanksgiving**

(**Day**) n (US) jour m d'Action de
Grâces (*fête nationale*).

that pl **those**

● *determiner*

····▶ ce, cet, cette, ces; ~ **dog** ce chien;
~ **man** cet homme; ~ **woman** cette
femme; **those books** ces livres; **at** ~
moment à ce moment-là.

❗ To distinguish from **this** and
these, you need to add -*là*
after the noun: **I prefer that
car** *je préfère cette voiture-là.*

● *pronoun*

····▶ cela, ça, ce; **what's** ~?, **what are
those?** qu'est-ce que c'est (que ça)?;
who's ~? qui est-ce?; ~ **is my
brother** c'est or voilà mon frère;
those are my parents ce sont mes
parents.

····▶ (emphatic) celui-là, celle-là,ceux-là,
celles-là; **all the dresses are nice but I
like** ~/**those best** toutes les robes
sont jolies mais je préfère celle-là/
celles-là.

● *relative pronoun*

····▶ (for subject) qui; **the man** ~ **stole
the car** l'homme qui a volé la
voiture.

····▶ (for object) que; **the girl** ~ **I met** la
fille que j'ai rencontrée.

❗ With a preposition, use *lequel/
laquelle/lesquels/lesquelles*:
the chair ~ **I was sitting on**
*la chaise sur laquelle j'étais
assis.*

❗ With a preposition that
translates as à, use *auquel/à
laquelle/auxquels/auxquelles*:
the girls ~ **I was talking to**
les filles auxquelles je parlais.

❗ With a preposition that
translates as *de*, use *dont*: **the
people** ~ **I've talked about**
les personnes dont j'ai parlé.

● *conjunction* que; **she said** ~ **she
would do it** elle a dit qu'elle le
ferait.

thatched adj de chaume; ~ **cottage**
chaumière f.

thaw vt/i (faire) dégeler; (*snow*)
(faire) fondre. ● n dégel m.

the *determiner*

····▶ le, l', la, les; ~ **dog** le chien; ~
tree l'arbre; ~ **chair** la chaise; **to** ~
shops aux magasins.

❗ With a preposition that
translates as à: à + *le* = *au* and
à + *les* = *aux*.

theatre n théâtre m.
theft n vol m.
their adj leur, pl leurs.
theirs pron le or la leur, les leurs.
them pron les; (after preposition) eux,
elles; (to) ~ leur; **phone** ~!
téléphone-leur!; **I know** ~ je les
connais; **both of** ~ tous/toutes les
deux.
themselves pron eux-mêmes, elles-
mêmes; (reflexive) se; (after preposition)
eux, elles.
then adv alors; (next) ensuite, puis;
(therefore) alors, donc. ● adj d'alors;
from ~ **on** dès lors.
theology n théologie f.
theory n théorie f.
therapy n thérapie f.
there adv là; (with verb) y; (over there)
là-bas; **he goes** ~ il y va; **on** ~ là-
dessus; ~ **is**, ~ **are** il y a; (pointing)
voilà. ● interj; ~, ~! allons, allons!
therefore adv donc.
thermal adj thermique.
thermometer n thermomètre m.
Thermos® n thermos® m or f inv.
thermostat n thermostat m.
thesaurus n (pl **-ri**) dictionnaire m
de synonymes.
these ⇒THIS.
thesis n (pl **theses**) thèse f.
they pron ils, elles; (emphatic) eux,
elles; (people in general) on.
thick adj épais; (stupid) bête; **be 6 cm**
~ avoir 6 cm d'épaisseur.
thief n (pl **thieves**) voleur/-euse m/
f.
thigh n cuisse f.
thin adj (**thinner**, **thinnest**) mince;
(*person*) maigre, mince; (sparse)

clairsemé; (fine) fin. ● *vt/i* (*pt*
thinned) ~ (**down**) (*paint*) diluer;
(*soup*) allonger.

thing *n* chose *f*; ~**s** (belongings)
affaires *fpl*; **the best** ~ **is to** le mieux
est de; **the** (**right**) ~ ce qu'il faut (**for
sb** à qn).

think *vt/i* (*pt* **thought**) penser
(**about, of** à); (carefully) réfléchir
(**about, of** à); (believe) croire; **I** ~ **so** je
crois que oui; ~ **of doing** envisager
de faire. □ ~ **over** bien réfléchir à;
~ **up** inventer.

third *adj* troisième. ● *n* troisième *mf*;
(fraction) tiers *m*. **T~ World** *n* tiers-
monde *m*.

thirst *n* soif *f*.

thirsty *adj* **be** ~ avoir soif; **make** ~
donner soif à.

thirteen *a* & *n* treize (*m*).

thirty *a* & *n* trente (*m*).

....

this *pl* **these**

● *determiner*

····▸ ce/cet/cette/ces; ~ **dog** ce chien;
~ **man** cet homme; ~ **woman** cette
femme; **these books** ces livres.

> To distinguish from **that** and
> **those**, you need to add -*ci*
> after the noun: **I prefer this
> car** *je préfère cette voiture-ci.*

● *pronoun*

····▸ ce; **what's** ~?, **what are these?**
qu'est-ce que c'est?; **who is** ~? qui
est-ce?; ~ **is the kitchen** voici la
cuisine; ~ **is Sophie** je te *or* vous
présente Sophie; **these are your
things** ce sont tes affaires.

····▸ (emphatic) celui-ci/celle-ci/ceux-ci/
celles-ci; **all the dresses are nice but I
like** ~/**these best** toutes les robes
sont jolies mais je préfère celle-ci/
celles-ci.

....

thistle *n* chardon *m*.

thorn *n* épine *f*.

thorough *adj* (detailed) approfondi;
(meticulous) minutieux. **thoroughly**
adv (clean, study) à fond; (very) tout à
fait.

those ⇒THAT.

though *conj* bien que. ● *adv* quand
même.

thought ⇒THINK. ● *n* pensée *f*, idée
f. **thoughtful** *adj* pensif; (kind)
prévenant.

thousand *a* & *n* mille (*m inv*); ~**s
of** des milliers de. **thousandth** *a* &
n millième (*mf*).

thread *n* (yarn & fig) fil *m*; (of screw)
pas *m*. ● *vt* enfiler; ~ **one's way** se
faufiler.

threat *n* menace *f*. **threaten** *vt/i*
menacer (**with** de).

three *a* & *n* trois (*m*).

threw ⇒THROW.

thrill *n* frisson *m*; (pleasure) plaisir *m*.
● *vt* transporter (de joie); **be** ~**ed**
être ravi. ● *vi* frissonner (de joie).

thrive *vi* (*pt* **thrived** *or* **throve**; *pp*
thrived *or* **thriven**) prospérer; **he**
~**s on it** cela lui réussit.

throat *n* gorge *f*; **have a sore** ~
avoir mal à la gorge.

throb *vi* (*pt* **throbbed**) (*heart*)
battre; (*engine*) vibrer. ● *n* (pain)
élancement *m*; (of engine) vibration *f*.
throbbing *adj* (*pain*) lancinant.

throne *n* trône *m*.

through *prep* à travers; (during)
pendant; (by means or way of, out of)
par; (by reason of) grâce à, à cause de.
● *adv* à travers; (entirely) jusqu'au
bout. ● *adj* (*train*) direct; **be** ~
(finished) avoir fini; **come** *or* **go** ~
(cross, pierce) traverser; **I'm putting
you** ~ je vous passe votre
correspondant.

throughout *prep* ~ **the country**
dans tout le pays; ~ **the day** pendant
toute la journée. ● *adv* (place)
partout; (time) tout le temps.

throw *vt* (*pt* **threw**; *pp* **thrown**)
jeter, lancer; (baffle) déconcerter; ~ **a
party** faire une fête. ● *n* jet *m*; (of
dice) coup *m*. □ ~ **away** (get rid of) se débarrasser de; ~ **off**
(get rid of) se débarrasser de; ~ **out**
jeter; (*person*) expulser; (reject)
rejeter; ~ **up** (*arms*) lever; (vomit 🄻)
vomir.

thrust *vt* (*pt* **thrust**) pousser. ● *n*
poussée *f*.

thud *n* bruit *m* sourd.

thug *n* voyou *m*.

thumb n pouce m. ● vt (book) feuilleter; ~ **a lift** faire de l'auto-stop. ~**-index** n répertoire m à onglets.

thump vt/i cogner (sur); (heart) battre fort. ● n coup m.

thunder n tonnerre m. ● vi (weather, person) tonner. ~**storm** n orage m.

Thursday n jeudi m.

thus adv ainsi.

thwart vt contrecarrer.

thyme n thym m.

tick n (sound) tic-tac m; (mark) coche f; (moment 🄸) instant m; (insect) tique f. ● vi faire tic-tac. ● vt ~ (**off**) cocher. □ ~ **over** tourner au ralenti.

ticket n billet m; (for bus, cloakroom) ticket m; (label) étiquette f. ~**-collector** n contrôleur/-euse m/f. ~**-office** n guichet m.

tickle vt chatouiller; (amuse: fig) amuser. ● n chatouillement m.

tidal adj (river) à marées; ~ **wave** raz-de-marée m inv.

tide n marée f; (of events) cours m.

tidy adj (-**ier**, -**iest**) (room) bien rangé; (appearance, work) soigné; (methodical) ordonné; (amount 🄸) joli. ● vt/i ~ (**up**) faire du rangement; ~ **sth up** ranger qch; ~ **oneself up** s'arranger.

tie vt (pres p **tying**) attacher; (knot) faire; (scarf) nouer; (link) lier. ● vi (in football) faire match nul; (in race) être ex aequo. ● n (necktie) cravate f; (fastener) attache f; (link) lien m; (draw) match m nul. □ ~ **down** attacher; ~ **in with** être lié à; ~ **up** attacher; (money) immobiliser; (occupy) occuper.

tier n étage m, niveau m; (in stadium) gradin m.

tiger n tigre m.

tight adj (clothes, budget) serré; (grip) ferme; (rope) tendu; (security) strict; (angle) aigu. ● adv (hold, sleep) bien; (squeeze) fort.

tighten vt/i (se) tendre; (bolt) (se) resserrer; (control) renforcer.

tights npl collant m.

tile n (on wall, floor) carreau m; (on roof) tuile f. ● vt carreler; couvrir de tuiles.

till n caisse f (enregistreuse). ● vt (land) cultiver. ● prep & conj = UNTIL.

timber n bois m (de construction); (trees) arbres mpl.

time n temps m; (moment) moment m; (epoch) époque f; (by clock) heure f; (occasion) fois f; (rhythm) mesure f; ~**s** (multiplying) fois fpl; **any** ~ n'importe quand; **for the** ~ **being** pour le moment; **from** ~ **to** ~ de temps en temps; **have a good** ~ s'amuser; **in no** ~ en un rien de temps; **in** ~ à temps; (eventually) avec le temps; **a long** ~ longtemps; **on** ~ à l'heure; **what's the** ~? quelle heure est-il?; ~ **off** du temps libre. ● vt choisir le moment de; (measure) minuter; (Sport) chronométrer. ~**-limit** n délai m.

timer n minuterie f; (for cooker) minuteur m.

time: ~**-scale** n délais mpl. ~**table** n horaire m. ~ **zone** n fuseau m horaire.

timid adj timide; (fearful) peureux.

tin n étain m; (container) boîte f; ~(**plate**) fer-blanc m. ● vt (pt **tinned**) mettre en boîte. ~ **foil** n papier m d'aluminium.

tingle vi picoter. ● n picotement m.

tin-opener n ouvre-boîtes m inv.

tint n teinte f; (for hair) shampooing m colorant. ● vt teinter.

tiny adj (-**ier**, -**iest**) tout petit.

tip n (of stick, pen, shoe, ski) pointe f; (of nose, finger, wing) bout m; (gratuity) pourboire m; (advice) tuyau m; (for rubbish) décharge f. ● vt/i (pt **tipped**) (tilt) pencher; (overturn) (faire) basculer; (pour) verser; (empty) déverser; (give money) donner un pourboire à. □ ~ **off** prévenir.

tiptoe n on ~ sur la pointe des pieds.

tire vt/i (se) fatiguer; ~ **of** se lasser de. ● n (US) pneu m.

tired adj fatigué; **be** ~ **of** en avoir assez de.

tiring adj fatigant.

tissue n tissu m; (handkerchief) mouchoir m en papier; ~ (**paper**) papier m de soie.

tit n (bird) mésange f; **give** ~ **for tat** rendre coup pour coup.

title n titre m. ~ **deed** n titre m de propriété.

to

● *preposition*

····▸ à; ~ **Paris** à Paris; **give the book** ~ **Jane** donne le livre à Jane; ~ **the office** au bureau; ~ **the shops** aux magasins.

····▸ (with feminine countries) en; ~ **France** en France.

····▸ (to + personal pronoun) me/te/lui/ nous/vous/leur; **she gave it** ~ **them** elle le leur a donné; **I'll say it** ~ **her** je vais le lui dire.

> **!** à + le = au
>   à + les = aux.

● *in infinitive*

to is not normally translated (**to go** *aller*, **to sing** *chanter*)

····▸ (in order to) pour; **he's gone into town** ~ **buy a shirt** il est parti en ville pour acheter une chemise.

····▸ (after adjectives) à; de; **be easy/ difficult** ~ **read** être facile/difficile à lire; **it's easy/difficult to read her writing** c'est facile/difficile de lire son écriture.

⟹ For verbal expressions using the infinitive 'to' such as **tell sb to do sth**, **help sb to do sth** ⇒**tell**, **help**.

toad n crapaud m.

toast n pain m grillé, toast m; (drink) toast m. ● vt (bread) faire griller; (drink to) porter un toast à. **toaster** n grille-pain m inv.

tobacco n tabac m.

tobacconist n marchand/-e m/f de tabac; ~**'s** (**shop**) tabac m.

toboggan n toboggan m, luge f.

today n & adv aujourd'hui (m).

toddler n bébé m (*qui fait ses premiers pas*).

toe n orteil m; (of shoe) bout m; **on one's** ~**s** vigilant. ● vt ~ **the line** se conformer.

together adv ensemble; (at same time) à la fois; ~ **with** avec.

toilet n toilettes fpl.

toiletries npl articles mpl de toilette.

token n (symbol) témoignage m; (voucher) bon m; (coin) jeton m. ● adj symbolique.

told ⇒TELL.

tolerance n tolérance f.

tolerate vt tolérer.

toll n péage m; **death** ~ nombre m de morts; **take its** ~ faire des ravages. ● vi (bell) sonner.

tomato n (pl ~**es**) tomate f.

tomb n tombeau m.

tomorrow n & adv demain (m); ~ **morning/night** demain matin/soir; **the day after** ~ après-demain.

ton n tonne f (= 1016 kg); (**metric**) ~ tonne f (= 1000 kg); ~**s of** 🄸 des masses de.

tone n ton m; (of radio, telephone) tonalité f. ● vt ~ **down** atténuer. ● vi ~ (**in**) s'harmoniser (**with** avec).

tongs npl (for coal) pincettes fpl; (for sugar) pince f; (for hair) fer m.

tongue n langue f.

tonic n (Med) tonique m. ● adj (effect, accent) tonique; ~ (**water**) tonic m, Schweppes® m.

tonight n & adv (evening) ce soir; (night) cette nuit.

tonsil n amygdale f.

too adv trop; (also) aussi; ~ **many people** trop de gens; **I've got** ~ **much/many** j'en ai trop; **me** ~ moi aussi.

took ⇒TAKE.

tool n outil m. ~**-box** n boîte f à outils.

toot n coup m de klaxon®. ● vt/i ~ (**the horn**) klaxonner.

tooth n (pl **teeth**) dent f. ~**ache** n mal m de dents. ~**brush** n brosse f à dents. ~**paste** n dentifrice m. ~**pick** n cure-dents m inv.

top n (highest point) sommet m; (upper part) haut m; (upper surface) dessus m; (lid) couvercle m; (of bottle, tube) bouchon m; (of beer bottle) capsule f; (of list) tête f; **on** ~ **of** sur; (fig) en plus de. ● adj (shelf, floor) du haut; (step, floor) dernier; (in rank) premier; (best) meilleur; (distinguished) éminent; (maximum) maximum. ● vt (pt

topped) (exceed) dépasser; (list) venir en tête de; ∼ **up** remplir; ∼**ped with** (*dome*) surmonté de; (*cream*) recouvert de.

topic *n* sujet *m*.

topless *adj* aux seins nus.

torch *n* (electric) lampe *f* de poche; (flaming) torche *f*.

tore ⇒TEAR[1].

torment *vt* tourmenter; (annoy) agacer.

torn ⇒TEAR[1].

torrent *n* torrent *m*.

tortoise *n* tortue *f*. ∼**shell** *n* écaille *f*.

torture *n* torture *f*; (fig) supplice *m*. ● *vt* torturer.

Tory *n & a* tory (*mf*), conservateur/-trice (*m/f*).

toss *vt* lancer; (*salad*) tourner; (*pancake*) faire sauter. ● *vi* se retourner; ∼ **a coin**, ∼ **up** tirer à pile ou face (**for** pour).

tot *n* petit/-e enfant *m/f*; (drink) petit verre *m*.

total *n & a* total (*m*). ● *vt* (*pt* **totalled**) (add up) additionner; (amount to) se monter à.

touch *vt* toucher; (tamper with) toucher à. ● *vi* se toucher. ● *n* (sense) toucher *m*; (contact) contact *m*; (of artist, writer) touche *f*; **a** ∼ **of** (small amount) un petit peu de; **get in** ∼ **with** se mettre en contact avec; **out of** ∼ **with** déconnecté de. □ ∼ **down** (Aviat) atterrir; ∼ **up** retoucher. ∼**down** *n* atterrissage *m*; (Sport) essai *m*. ∼**line** *n* ligne *f* de touche. ∼**tone** *adj* (phone) à touches.

tough *adj* (negotiator) coriace; (*law*) sévère; (*time*) difficile; (robust) robuste.

tour *n* voyage *m*; (visit) visite *f*; (by team) tournée *f*; **on** ∼ en tournée. ● *vt* visiter.

tourist *n* touriste *mf*. ● *adj* touristique. ∼ **office** *n* syndicat *m* d'initiative.

tournament *n* tournoi *m*.

tout *vi* ∼ (**for**) racoler 🄸. ● *vt* (sell) revendre. ● *n* racoleur/-euse *m/f*; revendeur/-euse *m/f*.

tow *vt* remorquer. ● *n* remorque *f*; **on** ∼ en remorque.

toward(s) *prep* vers; (of attitude) envers.

towel *n* serviette *f*.

tower *n* tour *f*. ● *vi* ∼ **above** dominer.

town *n* ville *f*; **in** ∼ en ville. ∼ **council** *n* conseil *m* municipal. ∼ **hall** *n* mairie *f*.

tow: ∼**path** *n* chemin *m* de halage. ∼ **truck** *n* dépanneuse *f*.

toxic *adj* toxique.

toy *n* jouet *m*. ● *vi* ∼ **with** (object) jouer avec; (idea) caresser.

trace *n* trace *f*. ● *vt* (*person*) retrouver; (*cause*) déterminer; (*life*) retracer; (draw) tracer; (with tracing paper) décalquer.

track *n* (of person, car) traces *fpl*; (of missile) trajectoire *f*; (path) sentier *m*; (Sport) piste *f*; (Rail) voie *f*; (on disc) morceau *m*; **keep** ∼ **of** suivre. ● *vt* suivre la trace *or* la trajectoire de. □ ∼ **down** retrouver. ∼ **suit** *n* survêtement *m*.

tractor *n* tracteur *m*.

trade *n* commerce *m*; (job) métier *m*; (swap) échange *m*. ● *vi* faire du commerce; ∼ **on** exploiter. ● *vt* échanger. ● *adj* (route, deficit) commercial. ∼**in** *n* reprise *f*. ∼ **mark** *n* marque *f* (de fabrique); (registered) marque *f* déposée.

trader *n* commerçant/-e *m/f*; (on stockmarket) opérateur/-trice *m/f*.

trade union *n* syndicat *m*.

trading *n* commerce *m*; (on stockmarket) transactions *fpl* (boursières).

tradition *n* tradition *f*.

traffic *n* trafic *m*; (on road) circulation *f*. ● *vi* (*pt* **trafficked**) faire du trafic (in de). ∼ **jam** *n* embouteillage *m*. ∼**lights** *npl* feux *mpl* (de circulation). ∼ **warden** contractuel/-le *m/f*.

trail *vt/i* traîner; (*plant*) ramper; (track) suivre; ∼ **behind** traîner. ● *n* (of powder) traînée *f*; (track) piste *f*; (path) sentier *m*.

trailer *n* remorque *f*; (caravan) caravane *f*; (film) bande-annonce *f*.

train *n* (Rail) train *m*; (underground) rame *f*; (procession) file *f*; (of dress) traîne *f*. ● *vt* (instruct, develop) former;

(*sportsman*) entraîner; (*animal*) dresser; (*ear*) exercer; (*aim*) braquer. ● *vi* être formé, étudier; (Sport) s'entraîner. **trained** *adj* (skilled) qualifié; (*doctor*) diplômé. **trainee** *n* stagiaire *mf*. **trainer** *n* (Sport) entraîneur/-euse *m/f*. **trainers** *npl* (shoes) chaussures *fpl* de sport. **training** *n* formation *f*; (Sport) entraînement *m*.

tram *n* tram(way) *m*.

tramp *vi* marcher (d'un pas lourd). ● *vt* parcourir. ● *n* (vagrant) clochard/-e *m/f*; (sound) bruit *m*.

trample *vt/i* ~ (on) piétiner; (fig) fouler aux pieds.

tranquil *adj* tranquille. **tranquillizer** *n* tranquillisant *m*.

transact *vt* négocier. **transaction** *n* transaction *f*.

transcript *n* transcription *f*.

transfer[1] *vt* (*pt* **transferred**) transférer; (*power*) céder; (*employee*) muter. ● *vi* être transféré; (*employee*) être muté.

transfer[2] *n* transfert *m*; (of employee) mutation *f*; (image) décalcomanie *f*.

transform *vt* transformer.

transitive *adj* transitif.

translate *vt* traduire. **translation** *n* traduction *f*. **translator** *n* traducteur/-trice *m/f*.

transmit *vt* (*pt* **transmitted**) transmettre. **transmitter** *n* émetteur *m*.

transparency *n* transparence *f*; (Photo) diapositive *f*.

transplant *n* transplantation *f*; (Med) greffe *f*.

transport[1] *vt* transporter.

transport[2] *n* transport *m*.

trap *n* piège *m*. ● *vt* (*pt* **trapped**) (jam, pin down) coincer; (cut off) bloquer; (snare) prendre au piège.

trash *n* (refuse) ordures *fpl*; (nonsense) idioties *fpl*. ~**can** *n* (US) poubelle *f*.

trauma *n* traumatisme *m*. **traumatic** *adj* traumatisant *m*.

travel *vi* (*pt* **travelled**, US **traveled**) voyager; (*vehicle, bullet*) aller. ● *vt* parcourir. ● *n* voyages *mpl*. ~ **agency** *n* agence *f* de voyages.

traveller, (US) **traveler** *n* voyageur/-euse *m/f*; ~**'s cheque** chèque *m* de voyage.

trawler *n* chalutier *m*.

tray *n* plateau *m*; (on office desk) corbeille *f*.

treacle *n* mélasse *f*.

tread *vi* (*pt* **trod**; *pp* **trodden**) marcher (**on** sur). ● *vt* fouler. ● *n* (sound) pas *m*; (of tyre) chape *f*.

treasure *n* trésor *m*. ● *vt* (*gift, memory*) chérir; (*friendship, possession*) tenir beaucoup à.

treasury *n* trésorerie *f*; **the T**~ le ministère des Finances.

treat *vt* traiter; ~ **sb to sth** offrir qch à qn. ● *n* (pleasure) plaisir *m*; (food) gâterie *f*. **treatment** *n* traitement *m*.

treaty *n* traité *m*.

treble *adj* triple; ~ **clef** clé *f* de sol. ● *vt/i* tripler. ● *n* (voice) soprano *m*.

tree *n* arbre *m*.

trek *n* randonnée *f*. ● *vi* (*pt* **trekked**) ~ **across/through** traverser péniblement; **go** ~**king** faire de la randonnée.

tremble *vi* trembler.

tremendous *adj* énorme; (excellent) formidable.

tremor *n* tremblement *m*; (**earth**) ~ secousse *f*.

trench *n* tranchée *f*.

trend *n* tendance *f*; (fashion) mode *f*. **trendy** *adj* 🅸 branché 🅸.

trespass *vi* s'introduire illégalement (**on** dans). **trespasser** *n* intrus/-e *m/f*.

trial *n* (Jur) procès *m*; (test) essai *m*; (ordeal) épreuve *f*; **go on** ~ passer en jugement; **by** ~ **and error** par expérience.

triangle *n* triangle *m*.

tribe *n* tribu *f*.

tribunal *n* tribunal *m*.

tributary *n* affluent *m*.

tribute *n* tribut *m*; **pay** ~ **to** rendre hommage à.

trick *n* tour *m*; (dishonest) combine *f*; (knack) astuce *f*; **do the** ~ 🅸 faire l'affaire. ● *vt* tromper. **trickery** *n* ruse *f*.

trickle vi dégouliner; ~ **in/out** arriver or partir en petit nombre. ● n filet m; (fig) petit nombre m.

tricky adj (task) difficile; (question) épineux; (person) malin.

trifle n bagatelle f; (cake) diplomate m; **a** ~ (small amount) un peu. ● vi ~ **with** jouer avec.

trigger n (of gun) gâchette f; (of machine) manette f. ● vt ~ **(off)** (initiate) déclencher.

trim adj (**trimmer**, **trimmest**) soigné; (figure) svelte. ● vt (pt **trimmed**) (hair, grass) couper; (budget) réduire; (decorate) décorer. ● n (cut) coupe f d'entretien; (decoration) garniture f; **in** ~ en forme.

trinket n babiole f.

trip vt/i (pt **tripped**) (faire) trébucher. ● n (journey) voyage m; (outing) excursion f.

triple adj triple. ● vt/i tripler. **triplets** npl triplés/-es m/fpl.

tripod n trépied m.

trite adj banal.

triumph n triomphe m. ● vi triompher (**over** de).

trivial adj insignifiant.

trod, trodden ⇒TREAD.

trolley n chariot m.

trombone n (Mus) trombone m.

troop n bande f; ~**s** (Mil) troupes fpl. ● vi ~ **in/out** entrer/sortir en bande.

trophy n trophée m.

tropic n tropique m; ~**s** tropiques mpl.

trot n trot m; **on the** ~ 🗈 coup sur coup. ● vi (pt **trotted**) trotter.

trouble n problèmes mpl; ennuis mpl; (pains, effort) peine f; **be in** ~ avoir des ennuis; **go to a lot of** ~ se donner du mal; **what's the** ~? quel est le problème? ● vt (bother) déranger; (worry) tracasser. ● vi ~ **(oneself) to do** se donner la peine de faire. ~**maker** n provocateur/-trice m/f. ~**shooter** n conciliateur/-trice m/f. (Tech) expert m.

troublesome adj ennuyeux.

trousers npl pantalon m; **short** ~ short m.

trout n inv truite f.

trowel n (garden) déplantoir m; (for mortar) truelle f.

truant n (School) élève mf qui fait l'école buissonnière; **play** ~ sécher les cours.

truce n trève f.

truck n (lorry) camion m; (cart) chariot m; (Rail) wagon m de marchandises. ~**-driver** n routier m.

true adj vrai; (accurate) exact; (faithful) fidèle.

truffle n truffe f.

truly adv vraiment; (faithfully) fidèlement; (truthfully) sincèrement.

trumpet n trompette f.

trunk n (of tree, body) tronc m; (of elephant) trompe f; (box) malle f; (Auto, US) coffre m; ~**s** (for swimming) slip m de bain.

trust n confiance f; (association) trust m; **in** ~ en dépôt. ● vt avoir confiance en; ~ **sb with** confier à qn. ● vi ~ **in** or **to** s'en remettre à. **trustee** n administrateur/-trice m/f. **trustworthy** adj digne de confiance.

truth n (pl -s) vérité f. **truthful** adj (account) véridique; (person) qui dit la vérité.

try vt/i (pt **tried**) essayer; (be a strain on) éprouver; (Jur) juger; ~ **on** or **out** essayer; ~ **to do** essayer de faire. ● n (attempt) essai m; (rugby) essai m.

T-shirt n tee-shirt m.

tub n (for flowers) bac m; (of ice cream) pot m; (bath) baignoire f.

tube n tube m; **the** ~ 🗈 le métro.

tuberculosis n tuberculose f.

tuck n pli m. ● vt (put away, place) ranger; (hide) cacher. ● vi ~ **in** or **into** 🗈 attaquer; ~ **in** (shirt) rentrer; (blanket, person) border.

Tuesday n mardi m.

tug vt (pt **tugged**) tirer. ● vi ~ **at/on** tirer sur. ● n (boat) remorqueur m.

tuition n cours mpl; (fee) frais mpl pédagogiques.

tulip n tulipe f.

tumble vi (fall) dégringoler. ● n chute f. ~**-drier** n sèche-linge m inv.

tumbler n verre m droit.

tummy n 🗈 ventre m.

tumour n tumeur f.

tuna n inv thon m.

tune n air m; **be in ~/out of ~**
(instrument) être/ne pas être en accord;
(singer) chanter juste/faux. ● vt
(engine) régler; (Mus) accorder. ● vi
~ in (to) (radio, TV) écouter. □ **~ up**
s'accorder.

Tunisia n Tunisie f.

tunnel n tunnel m; (in mine) galerie f.
● vi (pt **tunnelled**) creuser un
tunnel (**into** dans).

turf n (pl **turf** or **turves**) gazon m;
the ~ (racing) le turf. ● vt **~ out**
🄣 jeter dehors.

Turk n Turc m, Turque f. **Turkey** n
Turquie f.

turkey n dinde f.

Turkish adj turc. ● n (Ling) turc m.

turn vt/i tourner; (person) se tourner;
(to other side) retourner; (change) (se)
transformer (**into** en); (become)
devenir; (deflect) détourner; (milk)
tourner. ● n tour m; (in road)
tournant m; (of mind, events) tournure
f; **do a good ~** rendre service; **in ~**
à tour de rôle; **take ~s** se relayer.
□ **~ against** se retourner contre; **~
away** vi se détourner; vt (avert)
détourner; (refuse) refuser; (send back)
renvoyer; **~ back** vi (return)
retourner; (vehicle) faire demi-tour;
vt (fold) rabattre; **~ down** refuser;
(fold) rabattre; (reduce) baisser; **~ off**
(light) éteindre; (engine) arrêter;
(tap) fermer; (of driver) tourner; **~ on**
(light) allumer; (engine) allumer;
(tap) ouvrir; **~ out** vt (light)
éteindre; (empty) vider; (produce)
produire; vi **it ~s out that** il se
trouve que; **~ out well/badly** bien/
mal se terminer; **~ over** (se)
retourner; **~ round** (person) se
retourner; **~ up** vi arriver; (be found)
se retrouver; vt (find) déterrer; (collar)
remonter.

turning n rue f; (bend) virage m.

turnip n navet m.

turn: **~-out** n assistance f. **~over** n
(pie) chausson m; (money) chiffre m
d'affaires. **~table** n (for record)
platine f.

turquoise adj turquoise inv.

turtle n tortue f (de mer). **~-neck** n
col m montant.

tutor n (private) professeur m
particulier; (Univ) (GB) chargé/-e m/f
de travaux dirigés.

tutorial n (Univ) classe f de travaux
dirigés.

tuxedo n (US) smoking m.

TV n télé f.

tweezers npl pince f (à épiler).

twelfth a & n douzième (mf).

twelve a & n douze (m); **~ (o'clock)**
midi m or minuit m.

twentieth a & n vingtième (mf).

twenty a & n vingt (m).

twice adv deux fois.

twig n brindille f.

twilight n crépuscule m. ● adj
crépusculaire.

twin n & a jumeau/-elle (m/f). ● vt
(pt **twinned**) jumeler.

twinge n (of pain) élancement m; (of
conscience, doubt) accès m.

twinkle vi (star) scintiller; (eye)
pétiller. ● n scintillement m;
pétillement m.

twinning n jumelage m.

twist vt tordre; (weave together)
entortiller; (roll) enrouler; (distort)
déformer. ● vi (rope) s'entortiller;
(road) zigzaguer. ● n torsion f; (in
rope) tortillon m; (in road) tournant m;
(in play, story) coup m de théâtre.

twitch vi (person) trembloter;
(mouth) trembler; (string) vibrer. ● n
(tic) tic m; (jerk) secousse f.

two a & n deux (m); **in ~s** par deux;
break in ~ casser en deux.

tycoon n magnat m.

type n type m, genre m; (print)
caractères mpl. ● vt/i (write) taper (à
la machine). **~face** n police f (de
caractères). **~writer** n machine f à
écrire.

typical adj typique.

typist n dactylo mf.

tyrant n tyran m.

tyre n pneu m.

Uu

udder *n* pis *m*, mamelle *f*.

UFO *n* OVNI *m inv*.

UHT *abbr* (**ultra heat treated**) ~ milk lait *m* longue conservation.

ugly *adj* (**-ier, -iest**) laid.

UK *abbr* ⇒UNITED KINGDOM.

Ukraine *n* Ukraine *f*.

ulcer *n* ulcère *m*.

ulterior *adj* ultérieur; ~ **motive** arrière-pensée *f*.

ultimate *adj* dernier, ultime; (definitive) définitif; (basic) fondamental.

ultrasound *n* ultrason *m*.

umbilical cord *n* cordon *m* ombilical.

umbrella *n* parapluie *m*.

umpire *n* arbitre *m*. ● *vt* arbitrer.

umpteenth *adj* 🆄 énième.

UN *abbr* (**United Nations**) ONU *f*.

unable *adj* incapable; (through circumstances) dans l'impossibilité (**to do** de faire).

unacceptable *adj* (suggestion) inacceptable; (behaviour) inadmissible.

unanimous *adj* unanime. **unanimously** *adv* à l'unanimité.

unattended *adj* sans surveillance.

unattractive *adj* (idea) peu attrayant; (person) peu attirant.

unauthorized *adj* non autorisé.

unavoidable *adj* inévitable.

unbearable *adj* insupportable.

unbelievable *adj* incroyable.

unbiased *adj* impartial.

unblock *vt* déboucher.

unborn *adj* (child) à naître; (generation) à venir.

uncalled-for *adj* injustifié, déplacé.

uncanny *adj* (**-ier, -iest**) étrange, troublant.

uncivilized *adj* barbare.

uncle *n* oncle *m*.

uncomfortable *adj* (chair) inconfortable; (feeling) pénible; **feel** *or* **be** ~ (person) être mal à l'aise.

uncommon *adj* rare.

unconscious *adj* sans connaissance, inanimé; (not aware) inconscient (**of** de). ● *n* inconscient *m*.

unconventional *adj* peu conventionnel.

uncouth *adj* grossier.

uncover *vt* découvrir.

undecided *adj* indécis.

under *prep* sous; (less than) moins de; (according to) selon. ● *adv* au-dessous; ~ **it/there** là-dessous. ~ **age** *adj* mineur. ~**cover** *adj* secret. ~**cut** *vt* (*pt* **-cut**; *pres p* **-cutting**) (Comm) vendre moins cher que. ~**dog** *n* (Pol) opprimé/-e *m/f*; (socially) déshérité/-e *m/f*. ~**done** *adj* pas assez cuit. ~**estimate** *vt* sous-estimer. ~**fed** *adj* sous-alimenté. ~**go** *vt* (*pt* **-went**; *pp* **-gone**) subir. ~**graduate** *n* étudiant/-e *m/f* (qui prépare la licence).

underground *adj* souterrain; (secret) clandestin. ● *adv* sous terre. ● *n* (rail) métro *m*.

under: ~**line** *vt* souligner. ~**mine** *vt* saper.

underneath *prep* sous. ● *adv* (en) dessous.

under: ~**pants** *npl* slip *m*. ~**rate** *vt* sous-estimer.

understand *vt/i* (*pt* **-stood**) comprendre.

understanding *adj* compréhensif. ● *n* compréhension *f*; (agreement) entente *f*.

undertake *vt* (*pt* **-took**; *pp* **-taken**) entreprendre. ~**taker** *n* entrepreneur *m* de pompes funèbres. ~**taking** *n* (task) entreprise *f*; (promise) promesse *f*.

underwater *adj* sous-marin. ● *adv* sous l'eau.

under: ~**wear** *n* sous-vêtements *mpl*. ~**world** *n* (of crime) milieu *m*, pègre *f*.

undo *vt* (*pt* **-did**; *pp* **-done**) défaire, détacher; (wrong) réparer; (Comput) annuler.

undress *vt/i* (se) déshabiller; **get ~ed** se déshabiller.

undue *adj* excessif.

unearth *vt* déterrer.

uneasy *adj* (ill at ease) mal à l'aise; (worried) inquiet; (situation) difficile.

uneducated *adj* (person) inculte; (speech) populaire.

unemployed *adj* en chômage. ● *npl* **the ~** les chômeurs *mpl*.

unemployment *n* chômage *m*; **~ benefit** allocations *fpl* de chômage.

uneven *adj* inégal.

unexpected *adj* inattendu, imprévu. **unexpectedly** *adv* (arrive) à l'improviste; (small, fast) étonnamment.

unfair *adj* injuste.

unfaithful *adj* infidèle.

unfit *adj* (Med) pas en forme; (ill) malade; (unsuitable) impropre (**for** à); **~ to** (unable) pas en état de.

unfold *vt* déplier; (expose) exposer. ● *vi* se dérouler.

unforeseen *adj* imprévu.

unforgettable *adj* inoubliable.

unfortunate *adj* malheureux; (event) fâcheux.

ungrateful *adj* ingrat.

unhappy *adj* (-ier, -iest) (person) malheureux; (face) triste; (not pleased) mécontent (**with** de).

unharmed *adj* indemne, sain et sauf.

unhealthy *adj* (-ier, -iest) (climate) malsain; (person) en mauvaise santé.

unheard-of *adj* inouï.

unhurt *adj* indemne.

uniform *n* uniforme *m*. ● *adj* uniforme.

unify *vt* unifier.

unintentional *adj* involontaire.

uninterested *adj* indifférent (**in** à).

union *n* union *f*; (trade union) syndicat *m*; **U~ Jack** drapeau *m* du Royaume-Uni.

unique *adj* unique.

unit *n* unité *f*; (of furniture) élément *m*; **~ trust** ≈ SICAV *f*.

unite *vt/i* (s')unir.

United Kingdom *n* Royaume-Uni *m*.

United Nations *npl* Nations *fpl* Unies.

United States (of America) *npl* États-Unis *mpl* (d'Amérique).

unity *n* unité *f*.

universal *adj* universel.

universe *n* univers *m*.

university *n* université *f*. ● *adj* universitaire; (student, teacher) d'université.

unkind *adj* pas gentil, méchant.

unknown *adj* inconnu. ● *n* **the ~** l'inconnu *m*.

unleaded *adj* sans plomb.

unless *conj* à moins que.

unlike *adj* différent. ● *prep* contrairement à; (different from) différent de.

unlikely *adj* improbable.

unload *vt* décharger.

unlock *vt* ouvrir.

unlucky *adj* (-ier, -iest) malheureux; (number) qui porte malheur.

unmarried *adj* célibataire.

unnatural *adj* pas naturel, anormal.

unnecessary *adj* inutile.

unnoticed *adj* inaperçu.

unofficial *adj* officieux.

unpack *vt* (suitcase) défaire; (contents) déballer. ● *vi* défaire sa valise.

unpleasant *adj* désagréable (**to** avec).

unplug *vt* débrancher.

unpopular *adj* impopulaire; **~ with** mal vu de.

unprofessional *adj* peu professionnel.

unqualified *adj* non diplômé; (success) total; **be ~ to** ne pas être qualifié pour.

unravel *vt* (pt **unravelled**) démêler.

unreasonable *adj* irréaliste.

unrelated *adj* sans rapport (**to** avec).

unreliable *adj* peu sérieux; (machine) peu fiable.

unrest *n* troubles *mpl*.

unroll *vt* dérouler.

unruly *adj* indiscipliné.

unsafe *adj* (dangerous) dangereux; (*person*) en danger.

unscheduled *adj* pas prévu.

unscrupulous *adj* sans scrupules, malhonnête.

unsettled *adj* instable.

unsightly *adj* laid.

unskilled *adj* (worker) non qualifié.

unsound *adj* (*roof*) en mauvais état; (*investment*) douteux.

unsteady *adj* (step) chancelant; (*ladder*) instable; (*hand*) mal assuré.

unsuccessful *adj* (*result, candidate*) malheureux; (*attempt*) infructueux; **be ~** ne pas réussir (**in doing** à faire).

unsuitable *adj* inapproprié; **be ~** ne pas convenir.

unsure *adj* incertain.

untidy *adj* (**-ier, -iest**) (*person*) désordonné; (*room*) en désordre; (*work*) mal soigné.

untie *vt* (*knot, parcel*) défaire; (*person*) détacher.

until *prep* jusqu'à; **not ~** pas avant. ● *conj* jusqu'à ce que; **not ~** pas avant que.

untrue *adj* faux.

unused *adj* (new) neuf; (not in use) inutilisé.

unusual *adj* exceptionnel; (strange) insolite, étrange.

unwanted *adj* (useless) superflu; (*child*) non désiré.

unwelcome *adj* fâcheux; (*guest*) importun.

unwell *adj* souffrant.

unwilling *adj* peu disposé (**to** à); (*accomplice*) malgré soi.

unwind *vt/i* (*pt* **unwound**) (se) dérouler; (relax Ⅰ) se détendre.

unwise *adj* imprudent.

unwrap *vt* déballer.

up *adv* en haut, en l'air; (*sun, curtain*) levé; (out of bed) levé, debout; (finished) fini; **be ~** (*level, price*) avoir monté. ● *prep* (a hill) en haut de; (a tree) dans; (a ladder) sur; **come** *or* **go ~** monter; **~ in the bedroom** là-haut dans la chambre; **~ there** là-haut; **~ to** jusqu'à; (*task*) à la hauteur de; **it is ~ to you** ça dépend de vous (**to** de);

be ~ to sth (able) être capable de qch; (plot) préparer qch; **be ~ to** (in book) en être à; **be ~ against** faire face à; **~ to date** moderne; (*news*) récent. ● *n* **~s and downs** les hauts et les bas *mpl*.

up-and-coming *adj* prometteur.

upbringing *n* éducation *f*.

update *vt* mettre à jour.

upgrade *vt* améliorer; (*person*) promouvoir.

upheaval *n* bouleversement *m*.

uphill *adj* qui monte; (fig) difficile. ● *adv* **go ~** monter.

upholstery *n* rembourrage *m*; (in vehicle) garniture *f*.

upkeep *n* entretien *m*.

up-market *adj* haut-de-gamme.

upon *prep* sur.

upper *adj* supérieur; **have the ~ hand** avoir le dessus. ● *n* (of shoe) empeigne *f*. **~ class** *n* aristocratie *f*. **~most** *adj* (highest) le plus haut.

upright *adj* droit. ● *n* (post) montant *m*.

uprising *n* soulèvement *m*.

uproar *n* tumulte *m*.

uproot *vt* déraciner.

upset[1] *vt* (*pt* **upset**; *pres p* **upsetting**) (overturn) renverser; (*plan, stomach*) déranger; (*person*) contrarier, affliger. ● *adj* peiné.

upset[2] *n* dérangement *m*; (distress) chagrin *m*.

upside-down *adv* (lit) à l'envers; (fig) sens dessus dessous.

upstairs *adv* en haut. ● *adj* (*flat*) du haut.

uptight *adj* Ⅰ tendu, coincé Ⅰ.

up-to-date *adj* à la mode; (*records*) à jour.

upward *a* & *adv*, **upwards** *adv* vers le haut.

urban *adj* urbain.

urge *vt* conseiller vivement (**to do** faire); **~ on** encourager. ● *n* forte envie *f*.

urgency *n* urgence *f*; (of request, tone) insistance *f*. **urgent** *adj* urgent; (*request*) pressant.

urinal *n* urinoir *m*.

urine *n* urine *f*.

us *pron* nous; **(to)** ~ nous; **both of** ~ tous/toutes les deux.

US *abbr* ⇨UNITED STATES.

USA *abbr* ⇨UNITED STATES OF AMERICA.

use¹ *vt* se servir de, utiliser; (*consume*) consommer; ~ **up** épuiser.

use² *n* usage *m*, emploi *m*; **in** ~ en usage; **it is no** ~ **doing** ça ne sert à rien de faire; **make** ~ **of** se servir de; **of** ~ utile.

used¹ *adj* (*car*) d'occasion.

used² *v aux* **he** ~ **to smoke** il fumait (autrefois). ● *adj* ~ **to** habitué à.

useful *adj* utile.

useless *adj* inutile; (*person*) incompétent.

user *n* (of road, service) usager *m*; (of product) utilisateur/-trice *m/f*. ~**-friendly** *adj* facile d'emploi; (Comput) convivial.

usual *adj* habituel, normal; **as** ~ comme d'habitude. **usually** *adv* d'habitude.

utility *n* utilité *f*; (**public**) ~ service *m* public.

utmost *adj* (furthest, most intense) extrême; **the** ~ **care** le plus grand soin. ● *n* **do one's** ~ faire tout son possible.

utter *adj* complet, absolu. ● *vt* prononcer.

U-turn *n* demi-tour *m*; (fig) volte-face *f inv*.

Vv

vacancy *n* (post) poste *m* vacant; (room) chambre *f* disponible.

vacant *adj* (post) vacant; (seat) libre; (look) vague.

vacate *vt* quitter.

vacation *n* vacances *fpl*.

vaccinate *vt* vacciner.

vacuum *n* vide *m*. ~ **cleaner** *n* aspirateur *m*. ~**-packed** *adj* emballé sous vide.

vagina *n* vagin *m*.

vagrant *n* vagabond/-e *m/f*.

vague *adj* vague; (*outline*) flou; **be** ~ **about** ne pas préciser.

vain *adj* (conceited) vaniteux; (useless) vain; **in** ~ en vain.

valentine *n* ~ **(card)** carte *f* de la Saint-Valentin.

valid *adj* (argument, ticket) valable; (passport) valide.

valley *n* vallée *f*.

valuable *adj* (object) de valeur; (help) précieux. **valuables** *npl* objets *mpl* de valeur.

valuation *n* (of painting) expertise *f*; (of house) évaluation *f*.

value *n* valeur *f*; ~ **added tax** taxe *f* à la valeur ajoutée, TVA *f*. ● *vt* (appraise) évaluer; (cherish) attacher de la valeur à.

valve *n* (Tech) soupape *f*; (of tyre) valve *f*; (Med) valvule *f*.

van *n* camionnette *f*.

vandal *n* vandale *mf*.

vanguard *n* **in the** ~ **of** à l'avant-garde *f* de.

vanilla *n* vanille *f*.

vanish *vi* disparaître.

vapour *n* vapeur *f*.

variable *adj* variable.

varicose *adj* ~ **veins** varices *fpl*.

varied *adj* varié.

variety *n* variété *f*; (entertainment) variétés *fpl*.

various *adj* divers.

varnish *n* vernis *m*. ● *vt* vernir.

vary *vt/i* varier.

vase *n* vase *m*.

vast *adj* (space) vaste; (in quantity) énorme.

vat *n* cuve *f*.

VAT *abbr* (**value added tax**) TVA *f*.

vault *n* (roof) voûte *f*; (in bank) chambre *f* forte; (tomb) caveau *m*; (jump) saut *m*. ● *vt/i* sauter.

VCR *abbr* ⇨VIDEO CASSETTE RECORDER.

VDU *abbr* ⇨VISUAL DISPLAY UNIT.

veal *n* veau *m*.

vegan *a & n* végétalien/-ne (*m/f*).

vegetable *n* légume *m*. ● *adj* végétal.

vegetarian *a* & *n* végétarien/-ne (*m/f*).

vehicle *n* véhicule *m*.

veil *n* voile *m*.

vein *n* (in body, rock) veine *f*; (on leaf) nervure *f*.

velvet *n* velours *m*.

vending-machine *n* distributeur *m* automatique.

veneer *n* (on wood) placage *m*; (fig) vernis *m*.

venereal *adj* vénérien.

venetian *adj* ~ **blind** jalousie *f*.

vengeance *n* vengeance *f*; **with a** ~ de plus belle.

venison *n* venaison *f*.

venom *n* venin *m*.

vent *n* bouche *f*, conduit *m*; (in coat) fente *f*. ● *vt* (*anger*) décharger (**on** sur).

ventilate *vt* ventiler. **ventilator** *n* ventilateur *m*.

venture *n* entreprise *f*. ● *vt/i* (se) risquer.

venue *n* lieu *m*.

verb *n* verbe *m*.

verbal *adj* verbal.

verbatim *a* & *adv* mot pour mot.

verdict *n* verdict *m*.

verge *n* bord *m*; **on the** ~ **of doing** sur le point de faire. ● *vi* ~ **on** friser, frôler.

verify *vt* vérifier.

vermin *n* vermine *f*.

versatile *adj* (*person*) aux talents variés; (*mind*) souple.

verse *n* strophe *f*; (of Bible) verset *m*; (poetry) vers *mpl*.

version *n* version *f*.

versus *prep* contre.

vertebra *n* (*pl* -**brae**) vertèbre *f*.

vertical *adj* vertical.

vertigo *n* vertige *m*.

very *adv* très. ● *adj* (actual) même; **the** ~ **day** le jour même; **at the** ~ **end** tout à la fin; **the** ~ **first** le tout premier; ~ **much** beaucoup.

vessel *n* vaisseau *m*.

vest *n* maillot *m* de corps; (waistcoat: US) gilet *m*.

vet *n* vétérinaire *mf*. ● *vt* (*pt* **vetted**) (*candidate*) examiner (de près).

veteran *n* vétéran *m*; (**war**) ~ ancien combattant *m*.

veterinary *adj* vétérinaire; ~ **surgeon** vétérinaire *mf*.

veto *n* (*pl* ~**es**) veto *m*; (right) droit *m* de veto. ● *vt* mettre son veto à.

via *prep* via, par.

vibrate *vt/i* (faire) vibrer.

vicar *n* pasteur *m*.

vice *n* (depravity) vice *m*; (Tech) étau *m*.

vicinity *n* environs *mpl*; **in the** ~ **of** à proximité de.

vicious *adj* (spiteful) méchant; (violent) brutal; ~ **circle** cercle *m* vicieux.

victim *n* victime *f*.

victor *n* vainqueur *m*. **victory** *n* victoire *f*.

video *adj* (*game, camera*) vidéo *inv*. ● *n* (recorder) magnétoscope *m*; (film) vidéo *f*; ~ (**cassette**) cassette *f* vidéo. ● *vt* enregistrer.

videotape *n* bande *f* vidéo. ● *vt* (*programme*) enregistrer; (*wedding*) filmer avec une caméra vidéo.

view *n* vue *f*; **in my** ~ à mon avis; **in** ~ **of** compte tenu de; **on** ~ exposé; **with a** ~ **to** dans le but de. ● *vt* (watch) regarder; (consider) considérer (**as** comme); (*house*) visiter. **viewer** *n* (TV) téléspectateur/-trice *m/f*.

view: ~**finder** *n* viseur *m*. ~**point** *n* point *m* de vue.

vigilant *adj* vigilant.

vigour, (US) **vigor** *n* vigueur *f*.

vile *adj* (base) vil; (bad) abominable.

villa *n* pavillon *m*; (for holiday) villa *f*.

village *n* village *m*.

villain *n* scélérat *m*, bandit *m*; (in story) méchant *m*.

vindictive *adj* vindicatif.

vine *n* vigne *f*.

vinegar *n* vinaigre *m*.

vineyard *n* vignoble *m*.

vintage *n* (year) année *f*, millésime *m*. ● *adj* (*wine*) de grand cru; (*car*) d'époque.

viola *n* (Mus) alto *m*.

violate *vt* violer.

violence n violence f. **violent** adj violent.

violet n (Bot) violette f; (colour) violet m.

violin n violon m.

VIP abbr (**very important person**) personnalité f, VIP m.

virgin n (woman) vierge f.

Virgo n Vierge f.

virtual adj quasi-total; (Comput) virtuel. **virtually** adv pratiquement.

virtue n vertu f; (advantage) mérite m; by ~ of en raison de.

virus n virus m.

visa n visa m.

visibility n visibilité f. **visible** adj visible.

vision n vision f.

visit vt (pt **visited**) (person) rendre visite à; (place) visiter. ● vi être en visite. ● n (tour, call) visite f; (stay) séjour m. **visitor** n visiteur/-euse m/f; (guest) invité/-e m/f.

visual adj visuel. ~ **display unit** n visuel m, console f de visualisation.

visualize vt se représenter; (foresee) envisager.

vital adj vital.

vitamin n vitamine f.

vivacious adj plein de vivacité.

vivid adj (colour, imagination) vif; (description, dream) frappant.

vivisection n vivisection f.

vocabulary n vocabulaire m.

vocal adj vocal; (person) qui s'exprime franchement. ~ **cords** npl cordes fpl vocales.

vocation n vocation f. **vocational** adj professionnel.

voice n voix f. ● vt (express) formuler. ~ **mail** n messagerie f vocale.

void adj vide (of de); (not valid) nul. ● n vide m.

volatile adj (person) versatile; (situation) explosif.

volcano n (pl ~**es**) volcan m.

volley n (of blows, in tennis) volée f; (of gunfire) salve f.

volt n (Electr) volt m. **voltage** n tension f.

volume n volume m.

voluntary adj volontaire; (unpaid) bénévole.

volunteer n volontaire mf. ● vi s'offrir (**to do** pour faire); (Mil) s'engager comme volontaire. ● vt offrir.

vomit vt/i (pt **vomited**) vomir. ● n vomi m.

vote n vote m; (right) droit m de vote. ● vt/i voter; ~ **sb in** élire qn. **voter** n électeur/-trice m/f. **voting** n vote m (**of** de); (poll) scrutin m.

vouch vi ~ **for** se porter garant de.

voucher n bon m.

vowel n voyelle f.

voyage n voyage m (en mer).

vulgar adj vulgaire.

vulnerable adj vulnérable.

wad n (pad) tampon m; (bundle) liasse f.

wade vi ~ **through** (mud) patauger dans; (book: fig) avancer péniblement dans.

wafer n (biscuit) gaufrette f.

waffle n (talk 🇬🇧) verbiage m; (cake) gaufre f. ● vi 🇬🇧 divaguer.

wag vt/i (pt **wagged**) (tail) remuer.

wage vt (campaign) mener; ~ **war** faire la guerre. ● n (weekly, daily) salaire m; ~**s** salaire m. ~**-earner** n salarié/-e m/f.

wagon n (horse-drawn) chariot m; (Rail) wagon m (de marchandises).

wail vi gémir. ● n gémissement m.

waist n taille f. ~**coat** n gilet m.

wait vt/i attendre; **I can't** ~ **to start** j'ai hâte de commencer; **let's** ~ **and see** attendons voir; ~ **for** attendre; ~ **on** servir. ● n attente f.

waiter n garçon m, serveur m.

waiting-list n liste f d'attente.

waiting-room n salle f d'attente.

waitress n serveuse f.

waive vt renoncer à.

wake *vt/i* (*pt* **woke**; *pp* **woken**) ~
(**up**) (se) réveiller. ● *n* (track) sillage
m; **in the ~ of** (after) à la suite de. ~
up call *n* réveil *m* téléphoné.

Wales *n* pays *m* de Galles.

walk *vi* marcher; (not ride) aller à
pied; (stroll) se promener. ● *vt* (*streets*)
parcourir; (distance) faire à pied;
(*dog*) promener. ● *n* promenade *f*,
tour *m*; (gait) démarche *f*; (pace)
marche *f*, pas *m*; (path) allée *f*; **have a
~** faire une promenade. □ **~ out** (go
away) partir; (worker) faire grève; ~
out on abandonner.

walkie-talkie *n* talkie-walkie *m*.

walking *n* marche *f* (à pied). ● *adj*
(*corpse, dictionary*: fig) ambulant.

walkman® *n* walkman® *m*,
baladeur *m*.

walk: **~-out** *n* grève *f* surprise.
~-over *n* victoire *f* facile.

wall *n* mur *m*; (of tunnel, stomach) paroi
f. ● *adj* mural. **walled** *adj* (*city*)
fortifié.

wallet *n* portefeuille *m*.

wallpaper *n* papier *m* peint. ● *vt*
tapisser.

walnut *n* (nut) noix *f*; (tree) noyer *m*.

waltz *n* valse *f*. ● *vi* valser.

wander *vi* errer; (stroll) flâner;
(digress) s'écarter du sujet; (in mind)
divaguer.

wane *vi* décroître.

want *vt* vouloir (**to do** faire); (need)
avoir besoin de (**doing** d'être fait);
(ask for) demander; **I ~ you to do it** je
veux que vous le fassiez. ● *vi* ~ **for**
manquer de. ● *n* (need, poverty) besoin
m; (desire) désir *m*; (lack) manque *m*;
for ~ of faute de. **wanted** *adj*
(*criminal*) recherché par la police.

war *n* guerre *f*; **at ~** en guerre; **on
the ~path** sur le sentier de la
guerre.

ward *n* (in hospital) salle *f*; (minor: Jur)
pupille *mf*; (Pol) division *f* électorale.
● *vt* ~ **off** (*danger*) prévenir.

warden *n* directeur/-trice *m/f*; (of
park) gardien/-ne *m/f*; (**traffic**) ~
contractuel/-le *m/f*.

wardrobe *n* (furniture) armoire *f*;
(clothes) garde-robe *f*.

warehouse *n* entrepôt *m*.

wares *npl* marchandises *fpl*.

warfare *n* guerre *f*.

warm *adj* chaud; (hearty) chaleureux;
be *or* **feel ~** avoir chaud; **it is ~** il
fait chaud. ● *vt/i* ~ (**up**) (se)
réchauffer; (*food*) chauffer; (liven up)
(s')animer; (exercise) s'échauffer.

warmth *n* chaleur *f*.

warn *vt* avertir, prévenir; ~ **sb off
sth** (advise against) mettre qn en garde
contre qch; (forbid) interdire qch à
qn.

warning *n* avertissement *m*; (notice)
avis *m*; **without ~** sans prévenir. ~
light *n* voyant *m*. ~ **triangle** *n*
triangle *m* de sécurité.

warp *vt/i* (*wood*) (se) voiler; (pervert)
pervertir; (*judgment*) fausser.

warrant *n* (for arrest) mandat *m*
(d'arrêt); (Comm) autorisation *f*. ● *vt*
justifier.

warranty *n* garantie *f*.

wart *n* verrue *f*.

wartime *n* **in ~** en temps de guerre.

wary *adj* (**-ier, -iest**) prudent.

was ⇒BE.

wash *vt/i* (se) laver; (flow over)
baigner; ~ **one's hands of** se laver
les mains de. ● *n* lavage *m*; (clothes)
lessive *f*; **have a ~** se laver. □ ~ **up**
faire la vaisselle; (US) se laver.
~-basin *n* lavabo *m*.

washer *n* rondelle *f*.

washing *n* lessive *f*. **~-machine** *n*
machine *f* à laver. **~-powder** *n*
lessive *f*.

washing-up *n* vaisselle *f*. ~ **liquid**
n liquide *m* vaisselle.

wash: **~-out** *n* 🅵 fiasco *m*. **~-room**
n (US) toilettes *fpl*.

wasp *n* guêpe *f*.

wastage *n* gaspillage *m*.

waste *vt* gaspiller; (*time*) perdre.
● *vi* ~ **away** dépérir. ● *adj* superflu;
~ **products** *or* **matter** déchets *mpl*.
● *n* gaspillage *m*; (of time) perte *f*;
(rubbish) déchets *mpl*; **lay ~** dévaster.
wasteful *adj* peu économique;
(*person*) gaspilleur.

waste: ~ **land** *n* (desolate) terre *f*
désolée; (unused) terre *f* inculte; (in
town) terrain *m* vague. ~ **paper** *n*
vieux papiers *mpl*. **~-paper
basket** *n* corbeille *f* (à papier).

watch vt/i (television) regarder; (observe) observer; (guard, spy on) surveiller; (be careful about) faire attention à. ● n (for telling time) montre f; (Naut) quart m; **be on the ~** guetter; **keep ~ on** surveiller. □ **~ out** (take care) faire attention (**for** à); **~ out for** (keep watch) guetter.

water n eau f; **by ~** en bateau. ● vt arroser. ● vi (eyes) larmoyer; **my/his mouth ~s** l'eau me/lui vient à la bouche. □ **~ down** couper (d'eau); (tone down) édulcorer. **~colour** n (painting) aquarelle f. **~cress** n cresson m (de fontaine). **~fall** n chute f d'eau, cascade f. **~ heater** n chauffe-eau m. **watering-can** n arrosoir m. **~lily** n nénuphar m. **~melon** n pastèque f. **~proof** adj (material) imperméable. **~shed** n (in affairs) tournant m décisif. **~skiing** n ski m nautique. **~tight** adj étanche. **~way** n voie f navigable.

watery adj (colour) délavé; (eyes) humide; (soup) trop liquide.

wave n vague f; (in hair) ondulation f; (radio) onde f; (sign) signe m. ● vt agiter. ● vi faire signe (de la main); (move in wind) flotter.

waver vi vaciller.

wavy adj (line) onduleux; (hair) ondulé.

wax n cire f; (for skis) fart m. ● vt cirer; farter; (car) lustrer.

way n (road, path) chemin m (**to** de); (distance) distance f; (direction) direction f; (manner) façon f; (means) moyen m; **~s** (habits) habitudes fpl; **be in the ~** bloquer le passage; (hindrance: fig) gêner (qn); **be on one's** or **the ~** être sur son or le chemin; **by the ~** à propos; **by the ~side** au bord de la route; **by ~ of** comme; (via) par; **go out of one's ~** se donner du mal; **in a ~** dans un sens; **make one's ~ somewhere** se rendre quelque part; **push one's ~ through** se frayer un passage; **that ~** par là; **this ~** par ici; **~ in** entrée f; **~ out** sortie f. ● adv 🔲 loin.

we pron nous.

weak adj faible; (delicate) fragile.

weakness n faiblesse f; (fault) point m faible; **a ~ for** (liking) un faible pour.

wealth n richesse f; (riches, resources) richesses fpl; (quantity) profusion f.

wealthy adj (-ier, -iest) riche. ● n **the ~** les riches mpl.

wean vt (baby) sevrer.

weapon n arme f.

wear vt (pt **wore**; pp **worn**) porter; (put on) mettre; (expression) avoir. ● vi (last) durer; **~ (out)** (s')user. ● n (use) usage m; (damage) usure f. □ **~ down** user; **~ off** (colour, pain) passer; **~ out** (exhaust) épuiser.

weary adj (-ier, -iest) fatigué, las. ● vi **~ of** se lasser de.

weather n temps m; **under the ~** patraque. ● adj météorologique. ● vt (survive) réchapper de or à. **~ forecast** n météo f.

weave vt/i (pt **wove**; pp **woven**) tisser; (basket) tresser; (move) se faufiler. ● n (style) tissage m.

web n (of spider) toile f; (on foot) palmure f.

Web n (Comput) Web m. **~master** n administrateur m de site Internet. **~ site** n site m Internet.

wedding n mariage m. **~-ring** n alliance f.

wedge n (of wood) coin m; (under wheel) cale f. ● vt caler; (push) enfoncer; (crowd) coincer.

Wednesday n mercredi m.

weed n mauvaise herbe f. ● vt/i désherber; **~ out** extirper.

week n semaine f; **a ~ today/ tomorrow** aujourd'hui/demain en huit. **~day** n jour m de semaine. **~end** n week-end m, fin f de semaine.

weekly adv toutes les semaines. ● a & n (periodical) hebdomadaire (m).

weep vt/i (pt **wept**) pleurer (**for sb** qn).

weigh vt/i peser; **~ anchor** lever l'ancre. □ **~ down** lester (avec un poids); (bend) faire plier; (fig) accabler; **~ up** (examine 🔲) calculer.

weight n poids m; **lose/put on ~** perdre/prendre du poids. **~-lifting** n haltérophilie f. **~ training** n musculation f en salle.

weird *adj* mystérieux; (strange) bizarre.

welcome *adj* agréable; (timely) opportun; **be ~** être le *or* la bienvenu(e), être les bienvenu(e)s; **you're ~!** il n'y a pas de quoi!; **~ to do** libre de faire. ● *interj* soyez le *or* la bienvenu(e), soyez les bienvenu (e)s. ● *n* accueil *m*. ● *vt* accueillir; (as greeting) souhaiter la bienvenue à; (fig) se réjouir de.

weld *vt* souder. ● *n* soudure *f*.

welfare *n* bien-être *m*; (aid) aide *f* sociale. **W~ State** *n* État-providence *m*.

well[1] *n* puits *m*.

well[2] *adv* (**better**, **best**) bien; **do ~** (succeed) réussir; **~ done!** bravo! ● *adj* bien *inv*; **as ~** aussi; **be ~** (healthy) aller bien. ● *interj* eh bien; (surprise) tiens.

well: **~-behaved** *adj* sage. **~-being** *n* bien-être *m inv*.

wellington *n* (boot) botte *f* de caoutchouc.

well: **~-known** *adj* (bien) connu. **~-meaning** *adj* bien intentionné. **~ off** aisé, riche. **~-read** *adj* instruit. **~-to-do** *adj* riche. **~-wisher** *n* admirateur/-trice *m/f*.

Welsh *adj* gallois. ● *n* (Ling) gallois *m*.

went ⇒GO.

wept ⇒WEEP.

were ⇒BE.

west *n* ouest *m*; **the W~** (Pol) l'Occident *m*. ● *adj* d'ouest. ● *adv* vers l'ouest.

western *adj* de l'ouest; (Pol) occidental. ● *n* (film) western *m*. **westerner** *n* occidental/-e *m/f*.

West Indies *n* Antilles *fpl*.

westward *adj* (side) ouest *inv*; (journey) vers l'ouest.

wet *adj* (**wetter**, **wettest**) mouillé; (damp, rainy) humide; (paint) frais; **get ~** se mouiller. ● *vt* (*pt* **wetted**) mouiller. ● *n* **the ~** l'humidité *f*; (rain) la pluie *f*. **~ suit** *n* combinaison *f* de plongée.

whale *n* baleine *f*.

wharf *n* quai *m*.

what

● *pronoun*

····▸ (in questions as object pronoun) qu'est-ce que?; **~ are we going to do?** qu'est-ce que nous allons faire?

····▸ (in questions as subject pronoun) qu'est-ce qui?; **~ happened?** qu'est-ce qui s'est passé?

····▸ (introducing clause as object) ce que; **I don't know ~ he wants** je ne sais pas ce qu'il veut.

····▸ (introducing clause as subject) ce qui; **tell me ~ happened** raconte-moi ce qui s'est passé.

····▸ (with prepositions) quoi; **~ are you thinking about?** à quoi penses-tu?

● *determiner*

····▸ quel/quelle/quels/quelles; **~ train did you catch?** quel train as-tu pris?; **~ time is it?** quelle heure est-il?

whatever *adj* **~ book** quel que soit le livre. ● *pron* (no matter what) quoi que, quoi qu'; (anything that) tout ce qui; (object) tout ce que *or* qu'; **~ happens** quoi qu'il arrive; **~ happened?** qu'est-ce qui est arrivé?; **~ the problems** quels que soient les problèmes; **~ you want** tout ce que vous voulez; **nothing ~** rien du tout.

whatsoever *a* & *pron* = WHATEVER.

wheat *n* blé *m*, froment *m*.

wheel *n* roue *f*; **at the ~** (of vehicle) au volant; (helm) au gouvernail. ● *vt* pousser. ● *vi* tourner; **~ and deal** faire des combines. **~barrow** *n* brouette *f*. **~chair** *n* fauteuil *m* roulant.

when *adv* & *pron* quand. ● *conj* quand, lorsque; **the day/moment ~** le jour/moment où.

whenever *conj* & *adv* (at whatever time) quand; (every time that) chaque fois que.

where *adv*, *conj* & *pron* où; (whereas) alors que; (the place that) là où.

whereabouts *adv* (à peu près) où. ● *n* **sb's ~** l'endroit où se trouve qn.

whereas *conj* alors que.

wherever *conj* & *adv* où que; (everywhere) partout où; (anywhere) (là) où; (emphatic where) où donc.

whether *conj* si; **not know** ~ ne pas savoir si; ~ **I go or not** que j'aille ou non.

---

which

● *pronoun*

····▶ (in questions) lequel/laquelle/ lesquels/lesquelles; **there are three peaches,** ~ **do you want?** il y a trois pêches, laquelle veux-tu?

····▶ (in questions with superlative adjective) quel/quelle/quels/quelles; ~ **(apple) is the biggest?** quelle est la plus grosse?

····▶ (in relative clauses as subject) qui; **the book** ~ **is on the table** le livre qui est sur la table.

····▶ (in relative clauses as object) que; **the book** ~ **Tina is reading** le livre que lit Tina.

● *determiner*

····▶ quel/quelle/quels/quelles; ~ **car did you choose?** quelle voiture as-tu choisie?

---

whichever *adj* ~ **book** quel que soit le livre que *or* qui; **take** ~ **book you wish** prenez le livre que vous voulez. ● *pron* celui/celle/ceux/celles qui *or* que.

while *n* moment *m*. ● *conj* (when) pendant que; (although) bien que; (as long as) tant que. ● *vt* ~ **away** (*time*) passer.

whilst *conj* = WHILE.

whim *n* caprice *m*.

whine *vi* gémir, se plaindre. ● *n* gémissement *m*.

whip *n* fouet *m*. ● *vt* (*pt* **whipped**) fouetter; (Culin) fouetter, battre; (seize) enlever brusquement. ● *vi* (move) aller en vitesse. □ ~ **up** exciter; (cause) provoquer; (*meal* ⊞) préparer.

whirl *vt/i* (faire) tourbillonner. ● *n* tourbillon *m*. ~**pool** *n* tourbillon *m*. ~**wind** *n* tourbillon *m* (de vent).

whisk *vt* (snatch) enlever *or* emmener brusquement; (Culin) fouetter. ● *n* (Culin) fouet *m*.

whiskers *npl* (of animal) moustaches *fpl*; (of man) favoris *mpl*.

whisper *vt/i* chuchoter. ● *n* chuchotement *m*; (rumour: fig) rumeur *f*, bruit *m*.

whistle *n* sifflement *m*; (instrument) sifflet *m*. ● *vt/i* siffler; ~ **at** *or* **for** siffler.

white *adj* blanc. ● *n* blanc *m*; (person) blanc/-che *m/f*. ~ **coffee** *n* café *m* au lait. ~**-collar worker** *n* employé/-e *m/f* de bureau. ~ **elephant** *n* projet *m* coûteux et peu rentable. ~ **lie** *n* pieux mensonge *m*. W~ **Paper** *n* livre *m* blanc.

whitewash *n* blanc *m* de chaux. ● *vt* blanchir à la chaux; (*person*: fig) blanchir.

Whitsun *n* la Pentecôte.

whiz *vi* (*pt* **whizzed**) (through air) fendre l'air; (hiss) siffler; (rush) aller à toute vitesse. ~**-kid** *n* jeune prodige *m*.

who *pron* qui.

whoever *pron* (no matter who) qui que ce soit qui *or* que; (the one who) quiconque; **tell** ~ **you want** dites-le à qui vous voulez.

whole *adj* entier; (intact) intact; **the** ~ **house** toute la maison. ● *n* totalité *f*; (unit) tout *m*; **on the** ~ dans l'ensemble. ~**foods** *npl* aliments *mpl* naturels et diététiques. ~**-hearted** *adj* sans réserve. ~**meal** *adj* complet.

wholesale *adj* (*firm*) de gros; (fig) systématique. ● *adv* (in large quantities) en gros; (fig) en masse.

wholesome *adj* sain.

wholly *adv* entièrement.

whom *pron* (that) que, qu'; (after prepositions & in questions) qui; **of** ~ dont; **with** ~ avec qui.

whooping cough *n* coqueluche *f*.

whose *pron* & *a* à qui, de qui; ~ **hat is this?,** ~ **is this hat?** à qui est ce chapeau?; ~ **son are you?** de qui êtes-vous le fils?; **the man** ~ **hat I see** l'homme dont je vois le chapeau.

why *adv* pourquoi; **the reason** ~ la raison pour laquelle.

wicked *adj* méchant, mauvais, vilain.

wide *adj* large; (*ocean*) vaste. ● *adv* (*fall*) loin du but; **open** ~ ouvrir tout grand; ~ **open** grand ouvert;

~ **awake** éveillé. **widely** *adv*
(*spread, space*) largement; (*travel*)
beaucoup; (*generally*) généralement;
(*extremely*) extrêmement.

widespread *adj* très répandu.

widow *n* veuve *f.* **widowed** *adj*
(*man*) veuf; (*woman*) veuve.
widower *n* veuf *m.*

width *n* largeur *f.*

wield *vt* (*axe*) manier; (*power*: fig)
exercer.

wife *n* (*pl* **wives**) femme *f*, épouse *f.*

wig *n* perruque *f.*

wiggle *vt/i* remuer; (*hips*) tortiller;
(*worm*) se tortiller.

wild *adj* sauvage; (*sea, enthusiasm*)
déchaîné; (*mad*) fou; (*angry*) furieux.
● *adv* (*grow*) à l'état sauvage; **run ~**
(*free*) courir en liberté.

wildlife *n* faune *f.*

---

will¹

> *present* **will**; *present negative*
> **won't, will not**; *past* **would**

● *auxiliary verb*

····▶ (in future tense) **he'll come** il
viendra; **it ~ be sunny tomorrow** il
va faire du soleil demain.

····▶ (inviting and requesting) **~ you have
some coffee?** est-ce que vous voulez
du café?

····▶ (making assumptions) **they won't
know what's happened** ils ne doivent
pas savoir ce qui s'est passé.

····▶ (in short questions and answers) **you'll
come again, won't you?** tu
reviendras, n'est-ce pas?; '**they won't
forget**'—'**yes they ~**' 'ils n'oublieront
pas'—'si'.

····▶ (capacity) **the lift ~ hold 12**
l'ascenseur peut transporter 12
personnes.

····▶ (ability) **the car won't start** la
voiture ne veut pas démarrer.

● *transitive verb*

····▶ ~ **sb's death** souhaiter
ardemment la mort de qn.

---

will² *n* volonté *f*; (*document*) testament
m; **at ~** quand *or* comme on veut.

willing *adj* (*help, offer*) spontané;
(*helper*) bien disposé; ~ **to** disposé à.
willingly *adv* (with pleasure)
volontiers; (not forced)
volontairement. **willingness** *n*
empressement *m* (**to do** à faire).

willow *n* saule *m.*

will-power *n* volonté *f.*

win *vt/i* (*pt* **won**; *pres p* **winning**)
gagner; (*victory, prize*) remporter;
(*fame, fortune*) acquérir, trouver; ~
round convaincre. ● *n* victoire *f.*

winch *n* treuil *m.* ● *vt* hisser au
treuil.

wind¹ *n* vent *m*; (*breath*) souffle *m*; **get
~ of** avoir vent de; **in the ~** dans
l'air. ● *vt* essouffler.

wind² *vt/i* (*pt* **wound**) (s')enrouler;
(*of path, river*) serpenter; ~ (**up**) (*clock*)
remonter; ~ **up** (*end*) (se) terminer;
~ **up in hospital** finir à l'hôpital.

windmill *n* moulin *m* à vent.

window *n* fenêtre *f*; (*glass pane*) vitre
f; (in vehicle, train) vitre *f*; (in shop)
vitrine *f*; (*counter*) guichet *m*; (Comput)
fenêtre *f.* ~**-box** *n* jardinière *f.*
~**-cleaner** *n* laveur *m* de carreaux.
~**-dresser** *n* étalagiste *mf.*
~**-ledge** *n* rebord *m* de (la) fenêtre.
~**-shopping** *n* lèche-vitrines *m.*
~**-sill** *n* (inside) appui *m* de (la)
fenêtre; (outside) rebord *m* de (la)
fenêtre.

windscreen *n* pare-brise *m inv.* ~
wiper *n* essuie-glace *m.*

windshield *n* (US) = WINDSCREEN.

windsurfing *n* planche *f* à voile.

windy *adj* (**-ier, -iest**) venteux; **it is
~** il y a du vent.

wine *n* vin *m.* ~**-cellar** *n* cave *f* (à
vin). ~**glass** *n* verre *m* à vin.
~**grower** *n* viticulteur *m.* ~ **list** *n*
carte *f* des vins. ~**-tasting** *n*
dégustation *f* de vins.

wing *n* aile *f*; ~**s** (Theat) coulisses *fpl*;
under one's ~ sous son aile. ~
mirror *n* rétroviseur *m* extérieur.

wink *vi* faire un clin d'œil; (*light,
star*) clignoter. ● *n* clin *m* d'œil;
clignotement *m.*

winner *n* (of game) gagnant/-e *m/f*; (of
fight) vainqueur *m.*

winning ⇒WIN. ● *adj* (*number,
horse*) gagnant; (*team*) victorieux;

(*smile*) engageant. **winnings** *npl* gains *mpl*.

winter *n* hiver *m*.

wipe *vt* essuyer. ● *vi* ~ **up** essuyer la vaisselle. ● *n* coup *m* de torchon *or* d'éponge. □ ~ **out** (destroy) anéantir; (remove) effacer.

wire *n* fil *m*; (US) télégramme *m*.

wiring *n* (Electr) installation *f* électrique.

wisdom *n* sagesse *f*.

wise *adj* prudent, sage; (*look*) averti.

wish *n* (specific) souhait *m*, vœu *m*; (general) désir *m*; best ~**es** (in letter) amitiés *fpl*; (on greeting card) meilleurs vœux *mpl*. ● *vt* souhaiter, vouloir, désirer (**to do** faire); (bid) souhaiter. ● *vi* ~ **for** souhaiter; **I** ~ **he'd leave** je voudrais bien qu'il parte.

wishful *adj* it's ~ **thinking** c'est prendre ses désirs pour des réalités.

wistful *adj* mélancolique.

wit *n* intelligence *f*; (humour) esprit *m*; (person) homme *m* d'esprit, femme *f* d'esprit.

witch *n* sorcière *f*.

with *prep* avec; (having) à; (because of) de; (at house of) chez; **the man** ~ **the beard** l'homme à la barbe; **fill** ~ remplir de; **pleased/shaking** ~ content/frémissant de.

withdraw *vt/i* (*pt* **withdrew**; *pp* **withdrawn**) (se) retirer. **withdrawal** *n* retrait *m*.

wither *vt/i* (se) flétrir.

withhold *vt* (*pt* **withheld**) refuser (de donner); (retain) retenir; (conceal) cacher (**from** à).

within *prep* & *adv* à l'intérieur (de); (in distances) à moins de; ~ **a month** (before) avant un mois; ~ **sight** en vue.

without *prep* sans; ~ **my knowing** sans que je sache.

withstand *vt* (*pt* **withstood**) résister à.

witness *n* témoin *m*; (evidence) témoignage *m*; **bear** ~ **to** témoigner de. ● *vt* être le témoin de, voir. ~ **box**, ~ **stand** *n* barre *f* des témoins.

witty *adj* (**-ier**, **-iest**) spirituel.

wives ⇨WIFE.

wizard *n* magicien *m*; (genius: fig) génie *m*.

woke, **woken** ⇨WAKE.

wolf *n* (*pl* **wolves**) loup *m*. ● *vt* (*food*) engloutir.

woman *n* (*pl* **women**) femme *f*; ~ **doctor** femme *f* médecin; ~ **driver** femme *f* au volant.

women ⇨WOMAN.

won ⇨WIN.

wonder *n* émerveillement *m*; (thing) merveille *f*; **it is no** ~ ce *or* il n'est pas étonnant (**that** que). ● *vt* se demander (**if** si). ● *vi* s'étonner (**at** de); (reflect) songer (**about** à).

wonderful *adj* merveilleux.

won't = WILL NOT.

wood *n* bois *m*.

wooden *adj* en *or* de bois; (stiff: fig) raide, comme du bois.

wood: ~**wind** *n* (Mus) bois *mpl*. ~**work** *n* (craft, objects) menuiserie *f*.

wool *n* laine *f*. **woollen** *adj* de laine. **woollens** *npl* lainages *mpl*.

woolly *adj* laineux; (vague) nébuleux. ● *n* (garment 🎟) lainage *m*.

word *n* mot *m*; (spoken) parole *f*, mot *m*; (promise) parole *f*; (news) nouvelles *fpl*; **by** ~ **of mouth** de vive voix; **give/keep one's** ~ donner/tenir sa parole; **have a** ~ **with** parler à; **in other** ~**s** autrement dit. ● *vt* rédiger. **wording** *n* termes *mpl*.

word processing *n* traitement *m* de texte. **word processor** *n* machine *f* à traitement de texte.

wore ⇨WEAR.

work *n* travail *m*; (product, book) œuvre *f*, ouvrage *m*; (building work) travaux *mpl*; ~**s** (Tech) mécanisme *m*; (factory) usine *f*. ● *vi* (*person*) travailler; (*drug*) agir; (Tech) fonctionner, marcher. ● *vt* (Tech) faire fonctionner, faire marcher; (*land, mine*) exploiter; (shape, hammer) travailler; ~ **sb** (make work) faire travailler qn. □ ~ **out** *vt* (solve) résoudre; (calculate) calculer; (elaborate) élaborer; *vi* (succeed) marcher; (Sport) s'entraîner; ~ **up** *vt* développer; *vi* (to climax) monter vers; ~**ed up** (*person*) énervé.

workaholic *n* 🎟 bourreau *m* de travail.

worker n travailleur/-euse m/f;
(manual) ouvrier/-ière m/f.

work-force n main-d'œuvre f.

working adj (day, lunch) de travail;
~s mécanisme m; **in ~ order** en état
de marche.

working class n classe f ouvrière.
● adj ouvrier.

workman n (pl **-men**) ouvrier m.

work: ~ **out** n séance f de mise en
forme. ~**shop** n atelier m.
~**-station** n poste m de travail.

world n monde m; **best in the ~**
meilleur au monde. ● adj (power)
mondial; (record) du monde.

world-wide adj universel.

World Wide Web, **WWW** n World
Wide Web m, réseau m des réseaux.

worm n ver m. ● vt ~ **one's way into**
s'insinuer dans.

worn ⇒WEAR. ● adj usé. ~**-out** adj
(thing) complètement usé; (person)
épuisé.

worried adj inquiet.

worry vt/i (s')inquiéter. ● n souci m.

worse adj pire, plus mauvais; **be ~
off** perdre. ● adv plus mal. ● n pire
m. **worsen** vt/i empirer.

worship n (adoration) culte m. ● vt
(pt **worshipped**) adorer. ● vi faire
ses dévotions.

worst adj pire, plus mauvais; ● adv
(the) ~ (sing) le plus mal. ● n the ~
(one) (person, object) le or la pire; **the
~ (thing)** le pire.

worth adj **be ~ valoir; it is ~
waiting** ça vaut la peine d'attendre; **it
is ~ (one's) while** ça (en) vaut la
peine. ● n valeur f; **ten pence ~ of**
(pour) dix pence de. **worthless** adj
qui ne vaut rien. **worthwhile** adj
qui (en) vaut la peine.

worthy adj (-ier, -iest) digne (of
de); (laudable) louable.

would v aux **he ~ do/you ~ sing**
(conditional tense) il ferait/tu
chanterais; **he ~ have done** il aurait
fait; **I ~ come every day** (used to) je
venais chaque jour; **I ~ like some
tea** je voudrais du thé; ~ **you come
here?** voulez-vous venir ici?; **he
wouldn't come** il a refusé de venir.
~**-be** adj soi-disant.

wound[1] n blessure f. ● vt blesser;
the ~ed les blessés mpl.

wound[2] ⇒WIND[2].

wove, **woven** ⇒WEAVE.

wrap vt (pt **wrapped**) ~ (**up**)
envelopper. ● vi ~ **up** (dress warmly)
se couvrir; ~**ped up in** (engrossed)
absorbé dans.

wrapping n emballage m.

wreak vt ~ **havoc** faire des ravages.

wreath n (of flowers, leaves) couronne
f.

wreck n (sinking) naufrage m; (ship,
remains, person) épave f; (vehicle)
voiture f accidentée or délabrée. ● vt
détruire; (ship) provoquer le
naufrage de. **wreckage** n (pieces)
débris mpl; (wrecked building)
décombres mpl.

wrestle vi lutter, se débattre (with
contre).

wrestling n lutte f; (all-in) ~ catch
m.

wriggle vt/i (se) tortiller.

wring vt (pt **wrung**) (twist) tordre;
(clothes) essorer; ~ **out of** (obtain from)
arracher à.

wrinkle n (crease) pli m; (on skin) ride
f. ● vt/i (se) rider.

wrist n poignet m.

write vt/i (pt **wrote**; pp **written**)
écrire. □ ~ **back** répondre; ~
down noter; ~ **off** (debt) passer aux
profits et pertes; (vehicle) considérer
bon pour la casse; ~ **up** (from notes)
rédiger.

write-off n perte f totale.

writer n auteur m, écrivain m; ~ **of**
auteur de.

write-up n compte-rendu m.

writing n écriture f; ~(**s**) (works)
écrits mpl; **in ~** par écrit. ~**-paper**
n papier m à lettres.

written ⇒WRITE.

wrong adj (incorrect, mistaken) faux,
mauvais; (unfair) injuste; (amiss) qui
ne va pas; (clock) pas à l'heure; **be ~**
(person) avoir tort (to de); (be
mistaken) se tromper; **go ~** (err) se
tromper; (turn out badly) mal tourner;
it is ~ to (morally) c'est mal de; **what's
~?** qu'est-ce qui ne va pas?; **what is
~ with you?** qu'est-ce que vous avez?
● adv mal. ● n injustice f; (evil) mal

m; **be in the ~** avoir tort. ● *vt* faire
(du) tort à. **wrongful** *adj* injustifié,
injuste. **wrongfully** *adv* à tort.
wrongly *adv* mal; (*blame*) à tort.
wrote ⇨WRITE.
wrought iron *n* fer *m* forgé.
wrung ⇨WRING.

Xmas *n* Noël *m*.
X-ray *n* rayon *m* X; (*photograph*) radio
(graphie) *f*. ● *vt* radiographier.

yank *vt* tirer brusquement. ● *n* coup
m brusque.
yard *n* (*measure*) yard *m* (= *0.9144
metre*); (*of house*) cour *f*; (*garden: US*)
jardin *m*; (*for storage*) chantier *m*,
dépôt *m*. **~stick** *n* mesure *f*.
yawn *vi* bâiller. ● *n* bâillement *m*.
year *n* an *m*, année *f*; **school/tax ~**
année scolaire/fiscale; **be ten ~s old**
avoir dix ans.
yearly *adj* annuel. ● *adv*
annuellement.
yearn *vi* avoir bien *or* très envie
(**for, to** de).
yeast *n* levure *f*.
yell *vt/i* hurler. ● *n* hurlement *m*.
yellow *adj* jaune; (*cowardly* 🅵)
froussard. ● *n* jaune *m*.
yes *adv* oui; (*as answer to negative
question*) si. ● *n* oui *m inv*.
yesterday *n* & *adv* hier (*m*).
yet *adv* encore; (*already*) déjà. ● *conj*
pourtant, néanmoins.
yew *n* if *m*.

yield *vt* (*produce*) produire, rendre;
(*profit*) rapporter; (*surrender*) céder.
● *n* rendement *m*.
yoga *n* yoga *m*.
yoghurt *n* yaourt *m*.
yolk *n* jaune *m* (d'œuf).
you *pron* (*familiar form*) tu, *pl* vous;
(*polite form*) vous; (*object*) te, t', *pl* vous;
(*polite*) vous; (*after prep.*) toi, *pl* vous;
(*polite*) vous; (*indefinite*) on; (*object*)
vous; (**to**) **~** te, t', *pl* vous; (*polite*)
vous; **I gave ~ a pen** je vous ai
donné un stylo; **I know ~** je te
connais *or* je vous connais.
young *adj* jeune. ● *n* (*people*) jeunes
mpl; (*of animals*) petits *mpl*.
your *adj* (*familiar form*) ton, ta, *pl* tes;
(*polite form, & familiar form pl.*) votre, *pl*
vos.
yours *pron* (*familiar form*) le tien, la
tienne, les tien(ne)s; (*polite form, &
familiar form pl.*) le *or* la vôtre, les
vôtres; **~ faithfully/sincerely** je vous
prie d'agréer mes salutations les
meilleures.
yourself *pron* (*familiar form*) toi-même;
(*polite form*) vous-même; (*reflexive & after
prepositions*) te, t'; vous; **proud of ~**
fier de toi. **yourselves** *pron* vous-
mêmes; (*reflexive*) vous.
youth *n* jeunesse *f*; (*young man*) jeune
m. **~ hostel** *n* auberge *f* de
jeunesse.
Yugoslav *adj* yougoslave. ● *n*
Yougoslave *mf*.
Yugoslavia *n* Yougoslavie *f*.

zap *vt* 🅵 (*kill*) descendre; (*Comput*)
enlever.
zeal *n* zèle *m*.
zebra *n* zèbre *m*. **~ crossing** *n*
passage *m* pour piétons.
zero *n* zéro *m*.
zest *n* (*gusto*) entrain *m*; (*spice: fig*)
piment *m*; (*of orange or lemon peel*)
zeste *m*.

zip *n* (vigour) allant *m*; ∼(-fastener) fermeture *f* éclair®. ● *vt* (*pt* **zipped**) fermer avec une fermeture éclair®; (Comput) compresser. **Zip code** (US) *n* code *m* postal.

zodiac *n* zodiaque *m*.

zone *n* zone *f*.

zoo *n* zoo *m*.

zoom *vi* (rush) se précipiter. □ ∼ **off** *or* **past** filer (comme une flèche). ∼ **lens** *n* zoom *m*.

zucchini *n inv* (US) courgette *f*.

What are the equivalent tenses in English

Present indicative
je chante = *I sing, I'm singing*

Future indicative
je chanterai = *I will sing*

Imperfect indicative
je chantais = *I was singing*

Perfect indicative
j'ai chanté
= *I sang, I have sung*

Pluperfect indicative
j'avais chanté = *I had sung*

Present subjunctive
bien que je chante
= *although I sing*

Present conditional
si je pouvais, je chanterais
= *if I could, I would sing*

Past participle
chanté/chantée = *sung*

How to conjugate a reflexive verb

**Present indicative and other
simple tenses**
je me lave
tu te laves
il se lave
elle se lave
nous nous lavons
vous vous lavez
ils se lavent
elles se lavent

in the negative form
je ne me lave pas
tu ne te laves pas
il ne se lave pas
elle ne se lave pas
nous ne nous lavons pas
vous ne vous lavez pas
ils ne se lavent pas
elles ne se lavent pas

**Perfect indicative and other com-
pound tenses**
*(always with auxiliary **être**)*
je me suis lavé
tu t'es lavé
il s'est lavé
elle s'est lavée
nous nous sommes lavés
vous vous êtes lavés
ils se sont lavés
elles se sont lavées

in the negative form
je ne me suis pas lavé
tu ne t'es pas lavé
il ne s'est pas lavé
elle ne s'est pas lavée
nous ne nous sommes pas lavés
vous ne vous êtes pas lavés
ils ne se sont pas lavés
elles ne se sont pas lavées

French verbs

1 chanter

Present indicative

je	chante
tu	chantes
il	chante
nous	chantons
vous	chantez
ils	chantent

Present subjunctive

(que)	je	chante
(que)	tu	chantes
(qu')	il	chante
(que)	nous	chantions
(que)	vous	chantiez
(qu')	ils	chantent

Future indicative

je	chanterai
tu	chanteras
il	chantera
nous	chanterons
vous	chanterez
ils	chanteront

Present conditional

je	chanterais
tu	chanterais
il	chanterait
nous	chanterions
vous	chanteriez
ils	chanteraient

Imperfect indicative

je	chantais
tu	chantais
il	chantait
nous	chantions
vous	chantiez
ils	chantaient

Past participle

chanté/chantée

Pluperfect indicative

j'	avais	chanté
tu	avais	chanté
il	avait	chanté
elle	avait	chanté
nous	avions	chanté
vous	aviez	chanté
ils	avaient	chanté
elles	avaient	chanté

Perfect indicative

j'	ai	chanté
tu	as	chanté
il	a	chanté
elle	a	chanté
nous	avons	chanté
vous	avez	chanté
ils	ont	chanté
elles	ont	chanté

2 finir

Present indicative

je	finis
tu	finis
il	finit
nous	finissons
vous	finissez
ils	finissent

Present subjunctive

(que)	je	finisse
(que)	tu	finisses
(qu')	il	finisse
(que)	nous	finissions
(que)	vous	finissiez
(qu')	ils	finissent

Future indicative

je	finirai
tu	finiras
il	finira
nous	finirons
vous	finirez
ils	finiront

Present conditional

je	finirais
tu	finirais
il	finirait
nous	finirions
vous	finiriez
ils	finiraient

Imperfect indicative

je	finissais
tu	finissais
il	finissait
nous	finissions
vous	finissiez
ils	finissaient

Past participle

fini/finie

Pluperfect indicative

j'	avais	fini
tu	avais	fini
il	avait	fini
elle	avait	fini
nous	avions	fini
vous	aviez	fini
ils	avaient	fini
elles	avaient	fini

Perfect indicative

j'	ai	fini
tu	as	fini
il	a	fini
elle	a	fini
nous	avons	fini
vous	avez	fini
ils	ont	fini
elles	ont	fini

3 attendre

Present indicative

j'	attends
tu	attends
il	attend
nous	attendons
vous	attendez
ils	attendent

Present subjunctive

(que)	j'	attende
(que)	tu	attendes
(qu')	il	attende
(que)	nous	attendions
(que)	vous	attendiez
(qu')	ils	attendent

Future indicative

j'	attendrai
tu	attendras
il	attendra
nous	attendrons
vous	attendrez
ils	attendront

Present conditional

j'	attendrais
tu	attendrais
il	attendrait
nous	attendrions
vous	attendriez
ils	attendraient

Imperfect indicative

j'	attendais
tu	attendais
il	attendait
nous	attendions
vous	attendiez
ils	attendaient

Past participle

attendu/attendue

Pluperfect indicative

j'	avais	attendu
tu	avais	attendu
il	avait	attendu
elle	avait	attendu
nous	avions	attendu
vous	aviez	attendu
ils	avaient	attendu
elles	avaient	attendu

Perfect indicative

j'	ai	attendu
tu	as	attendu
il	a	attendu
elle	a	attendu
nous	avons	attendu
vous	avez	attendu
ils	ont	attendu
elles	ont	attendu

4 être

Present indicative

je	suis
tu	es
il	est
nous	sommes
vous	êtes
ils	sont

Present subjunctive

(que)	je	sois
(que)	tu	sois
(qu')	il	soit
(que)	nous	soyons
(que)	vous	soyez
(qu')	ils	soient

Future indicative

je	serai
tu	seras
il	sera
nous	serons
vous	serez
ils	seront

Present conditional

je	serais
tu	serais
il	serait
nous	serions
vous	seriez
ils	seraient

Imperfect indicative

j'	étais
tu	étais
il	était
nous	étions
vous	étiez
ils	étaient

Past participle

été (*invariable*)

Perfect indicative

j'	ai	été
tu	as	été
il	a	été
elle	a	été
nous	avons	été
vous	avez	été
ils	ont	été
elles	ont	été

Pluperfect indicative

j'	avais	été
tu	avais	été
il	avait	été
elle	avait	été
nous	avions	été
vous	aviez	été
ils	avaient	été
elles	avaient	été

5 avoir

Present indicative

j'	ai
tu	as
il	a
nous	avons
vous	avez
ils	ont

Present subjunctive

(que)	j'	aie
(que)	tu	aies
(qu')	il	ait
(que)	nous	ayons
(que)	vous	ayez
(qu')	ils	aient

Future indicative

j'	aurai
tu	auras
il	aura
nous	aurons
vous	aurez
ils	auront

Present conditional

j'	aurais
tu	aurais
il	aurait
nous	aurions
vous	auriez
ils	auraient

Imperfect indicative

j'	avais
tu	avais
il	avait
nous	avions
vous	aviez
ils	avaient

Past participle

eu/eue

Pluperfect indicative

j'	avais	eu
tu	avais	eu
il	avait	eu
elle	avait	eu
nous	avions	eu
vous	aviez	eu
ils	avaient	eu
elles	avaient	eu

Perfect indicative

j'	ai	eu
tu	as	eu
il	a	eu
elle	a	eu
nous	avons	eu
vous	avez	eu
ils	ont	eu
elles	ont	eu

[6] acheter
1 j'achète 2 j'achèterai
3 j'achetais 4 que j'achète
5 acheté

[7] acquérir
1 j'acquiers, nous acquérons,
ils acquièrent 2 j'acquerrai
3 j'acquérais 4 que
j'acquière 5 acquis

[8] aller
1 je vais, tu vas, il va, nous
allons, vous allez, ils vont
2 j'irai 3 j'allais 4 que
j'aille, que nous allions,
qu'ils aillent 5 allé

[9] asseoir
1 j'assois, tu assois, il assoit,
nous assoyons, vous assoyez,
ils assoient 2 j'assoirai
3 j'assoyais 4 que j'assoie,
que nous assoyions, qu'ils
assoient 5 assis

[10] avancer
1 nous avançons 3 j'avançais

[11] battre
1 je bats, il bat, nous battons
2 je battrai 3 je battais
4 que je batte 5 battu

[12] boire
1 je bois, il boit, nous
buvons, ils boivent 2 je
boirai 3 je buvais 4 que je
boive 5 bu

[13] bouillir
1 je bous, il bout, nous
bouillons, ils bouillent
2 je bouillirai 3 je bouillais
4 que je bouille 5 bouilli

[14] céder
1 je cède, nous cédons,
ils cèdent 2 je céderai 3 je
cédais 4 que je cède 5 cédé

[15] créer
1 je crée, nous créons 2 je
créerai 3 je créais 4 que je
crée 5 créé

[16] conclure
1 je conclus, il conclut, nous
concluons, ils concluent
2 je conclurai 3 je concluais
4 que je conclue 5 conclu
(*but* inclus)

[17] conduire
1 je conduis, nous
conduisons 2 je conduirai
3 je conduisais 4 que je
conduise 5 conduit (*but* lui,
nui)

[18] connaître
1 je connais, il connaît, nous
connaissons 2 je connaîtrai
3 je connaissais 4 que je
connaisse 5 connu

[19] coudre
1 je couds, il coud, nous
cousons, ils cousent 2 je
coudrai 3 je cousais 4 que
je couse 5 cousu

[20] courir
1 je cours, il court, nous
courons, ils courent 2 je
courrai 3 je courais 4 que
je coure 5 couru

[21] couvrir
1 je couvre 2 je couvrirai

---

1 Present Indicative 2 Future Indicative 3 Imperfect Indicative 4 Present Subjunctive 5 Past Participle

3 je couvrais 4 que je couvre
5 couvert

[22] craindre
1 je crains, il craint, nous
craignons, ils craignent
2 je craindrai 3 je craignais
4 que je craigne 5 craint

[23] croire
1 je crois, il croit, nous
croyons, ils croient 2 je
croirai 3 je croyais, nous
croyions 4 que je croie, que
nous croyions 5 cru

[24] croître
1 je croîs, il croît, nous
croissons 2 je croîtrai 3 je
croissais 4 que je croisse
5 crû/crue (*but* accru, décru)

[25] cueillir
1 je cueille 2 je cueillerai
3 je cueillais 4 que je cueille
5 cueilli

[26] devoir
1 je dois, il doit, nous devons,
ils doivent 2 je devrai 3 je
devais 4 que je doive, que
nous devions 5 dû/due

[27] dire
1 je dis, il dit, nous disons,
vous dites, ils disent 2 je
dirai 3 je disais 4 que je
dise 5 dit

[28] dissoudre
1 je dissous, il dissout, nous
dissolvons, ils dissolvent
2 je dissoudrai 3 je dissolvais
4 que je dissolve 5 dissous/
dissoute

[29] distraire
1 je distrais, il distrait, nous
distrayons 2 je distrairai
3 je distrayais 4 que je
distraie 5 distrait

[30] écrire
1 j'écris, il écrit, nous
écrivons 2 j'écrirai
3 j'écrivais 4 que j'écrive
5 écrit

[31] employer
1 j'emploie, nous employons,
ils emploient 2 j'emploierai
3 j'employais, nous
employions 4 que j'emploie,
que nous employions
5 employé

[32] envoyer
1 j'envoie, nous envoyons,
ils envoient 2 j'enverrai
3 j'envoyais, nous envoyions
4 que j'envoie, que nous
envoyions 5 envoyé

[33] faire
1 je fais, nous faisons (*say*
/fəzɔ̃/), vous faites, ils font
2 je ferai 3 je faisais (*say*
/fəzɛ/) 4 que je fasse, que
nous fassions 5 fait

[34] falloir (*impersonal*)
1 il faut 2 il faudra 3 il
fallait 4 qu'il faille 5 fallu

[35] fuir
1 je fuis, nous fuyons
2 je fuirai 3 je fuyais, nous
fuyions 4 que je fuie, que
nous fuyions 5 fui

---

1 Present Indicative 2 Future Indicative 3 Imperfect Indicative 4 Present Subjunctive 5 Past Participle

[36] haïr
1 je hais, il hait, nous haïssons, ils haïssent 2 je haïrai 3 je haïssais 4 que je haïsse 5 haï

[37] interdire
1 j'interdis, vous interdisez 2 j'interdirai 3 j'interdisais 4 que j'interdise 5 interdit

[38] jeter
1 je jette, nous jetons, ils jettent 2 je jetterai 3 je jetais 4 que je jette 5 jeté

[39] lire
1 je lis, il lit, nous lisons 2 je lirai 3 je lisais 4 que je lise 5 lu

[40] manger
1 je mange, nous mangeons 2 je mangerai 3 je mangeais 4 que je mange, que nous mangions 5 mangé

[41] maudire
1 je maudis, il maudit, nous maudissons 2 je maudirai 3 je maudissais 4 que je maudisse 5 maudit

[42] mettre
1 je mets, tu mets, nous mettons 2 je mettrai 3 je mettais 4 que je mette 5 mis

[43] mourir
1 je meurs, il meurt, nous mourons 2 je mourrai 3 je mourais 4 que je meure 5 mort

[44] naître
1 je nais, il naît, nous naissons 2 je naîtrai 3 je naissais 4 que je naisse 5 né

[45] oublier
1 j'oublie, nous oublions, ils oublient 2 j'oublierai 3 j'oubliais, nous oubliions, vous oubliiez 4 que nous oubliions, que vous oubliiez 5 oublié

[46] partir
1 je pars, nous partons 2 je partirai 3 je partais 4 que je parte 5 parti

[47] plaire
1 je plais, il plaît (*but* il tait), nous plaisons 2 je plairai 3 je plaisais 4 que je plaise 5 plu

[48] pleuvoir (*impersonal*)
1 il pleut 2 il pleuvra 3 il pleuvait 4 qu'il pleuve 5 plu

[49] pouvoir
1 je peux, il peut, nous pouvons, ils peuvent 2 je pourrai 3 je pouvais 4 que je puisse, que nous puissions 5 pu

[50] prendre
1 je prends, il prend, nous prenons 2 je prendrai 3 je prenais 4 que je prenne 5 pris

[51] prévoir
1 je prévois, il prévoit, nous prévoyons, ils prévoient 2 je prévoirai 3 je prévoyais,

1 Present Indicative 2 Future Indicative 3 Imperfect Indicative 4 Present Subjunctive 5 Past Participle

nous prévoyions **4** que je prévoie, que nous prévoyions **5** prévu

[52] recevoir
1 je reçois, il reçoit, nous recevons, ils reçoivent **2** je recevrai **3** je recevais **4** que je reçoive, que nous recevions **5** reçu

[53] résoudre
1 je résous, il résout, nous résolvons, ils résolvent **2** je résoudrai **3** je résolvais **4** que je résolve **5** résolu

[54] rire
1 je ris, nous rions, ils rient **2** je rirai **3** je riais, nous riions **4** que je rie, que nous riions **5** ri

[55] savoir
1 je sais, il sait, nous savons, ils savent **2** je saurai **3** je savais **4** que je sache, que nous sachions **5** su

[56] suffire
1 il suffit, ils suffisent **2** il suffira **3** il suffisait **4** qu'il suffise **5** suffi (*but* frit)

[57] suivre
1 je suis, il suit, nous suivons **2** je suivrai **3** je suivais **4** que je suive **5** suivi

[58] tenir
1 je tiens, il tient, nous

tenons, ils tiennent **2** je tiendrai **3** je tenais **4** que je tienne, que nous tenions **5** tenu

[59] vaincre
1 je vaincs, il vainc, nous vainquons, ils vainquent **2** je vaincrai **3** je vainquais **4** que je vainque **5** vaincu

[60] valoir
1 je vaux, il vaut, nous valons **2** je vaudrai **3** je valais **4** que je vaille, que nous valions **5** valu

[61] vêtir
1 je vêts, il vêt, nous vêtons **2** je vêtirai **3** je vêtais **4** que je vête **5** vêtu

[62] vivre
1 je vis, il vit, nous vivons, ils vivent **2** je vivrai **3** je vivais **4** que je vive **5** vécu

[63] voir
1 je vois, nous voyons, ils voient **2** je verrai **3** je voyais, nous voyions **4** que je voie, que nous voyions **5** vu

[64] vouloir
1 je veux, il veut, nous voulons, ils veulent **2** je voudrai **3** je voulais **4** que je veuille, que nous voulions **5** voulu

---

1 Present Indicative **2** Future Indicative **3** Imperfect Indicative **4** Present Subjunctive **5** Past Participle

French
Grammar

WILLIAM ROWLINSON

| Introduction

This French Grammar is more thorough and more practical than other paperback grammars. It is also more up to date. In the next 300 pages you will find:

■ All the basic grammar of French presented clearly, comprehensively, and succinctly.

■ Explanations that use everyday language, and a glossary of absolutely all the grammatical terms we have used.

■ Up-to-date explanations of modern French usage not found in other grammars of this size.

■ Short, simple, easy-to-follow French examples for points of basic grammar, and longer examples from modern French sources where they are needed to explain usage.

■ A clear layout.

This grammar is *really* comprehensive. It will explain problems met by beginners, it will be a reliable learning aid for GCSE and A level, and it will remain a first resource for quick reference and revision for French specialists who have reached university and polytechnic level. As well as covering all the grammar used in modern French, it has sections on translation problems and pronunciation traps, verb tables with the conjugation of more than a hundred irregular verbs, an alphabetical list of French prepositions and their use, sections on word order and punctuation, a glossary of grammatical terms and an easy-to-use index.

Contents

Verbs

TENSE FORMATION

The tenses of French verbs are either *simple*, in which case the verb is a single word, or *compound*, in which case it is normally formed from a part of the verb **avoir**, *to have*, followed by the past participle:

> simple tense: **je porte**, *I wear*
> compound tense: **j'ai porté**, *I have worn*

Regular verbs, what they are

Most French verbs are regular—that is they follow an entirely predictable pattern. The pattern they follow is determined by the way their infinitive ends. They divide into three groups (known as conjugations), each with its own infinitive ending:

> port**er**, *to wear*, first conjugation
> fin**ir**, *to finish*, second conjugation
> vend**re**, *to sell*, third conjugation

Most French verbs belong to the first conjugation, whose infinitives all end in **-er**. All invented new verbs are automatically first conjugation verbs. Verbs in the second conjugation all have an infinitive ending **-ir**, and those in the very small third conjugation all have an infinitive ending **-re**.

Irregular verbs, what they are

Some French verbs are irregular, following no pattern. In the simple tenses there is no way of predicting their stems (the part of the verb to which endings are added) or, quite frequently, the endings that are added to them. In the compound tenses, however, it is only the past participle which is irregular. So, for example, with **vouloir** (irregular), *to want*:

present (simple tense)	*perfect (compound tense)*
je veux	**j'ai voulu**
tu veux	**tu as voulu**
il veut	**il a voulu**
nous voulons	**nous avons voulu**
vous voulez	**vous avez voulu**
ils veulent	**ils ont voulu**

▶ There is a table of all the common irregular verbs with their conjugation on page 242.

Simple-tense formation, regular verbs

To form each simple tense a fixed set of endings is added to the verb's stem. The stem is the infinitive minus its **-er**, **-ir** or **-re** ending. Each conjugation has a different set of verb endings.

> **porter** → **port-** → **je porte**, *I wear*
> **finir** → **fin-** → **je finis**, *I finish*
> **vendre** → **vend-** → **je vends**, *I sell*

The ending of the verb corresponds to the subject of the verb:

> **je finis**, *I finish*
> **il finit**, *he finishes*

▶ The complete tense-formation of regular verbs is given on pp. 4–12, with the verb endings printed in bold.

Compound-tense formation, all verbs

To form a compound tense you need to know a verb's past participle. The past participle of a regular verb is formed by removing the **-er**, **-ir**, or **-re** of the infinitive. To this stem is added **-é** (first conjugation), **-i** (second conjugation), or **-u** (third conjugation):

infinitive		*past participle*
porter	→	port**é**
finir	→	fin**i**
vendre	→	vend**u**

The tenses of **avoir** used to form the compound tenses are:

> perfect tense:
> > present of **avoir**: j'**ai** porté
>
> pluperfect tense:
> > imperfect of **avoir**: j'**avais** porté
>
> future perfect tense:
> > future of **avoir**: j'**aurai** porté
>
> conditional perfect tense:
> > conditional of **avoir**: j'**aurais** porté
>
> past anterior tense:
> > past historic of **avoir**: j'**eus** porté
>
> perfect subjunctive:
> > present subjunctive of **avoir**: j'**aie** porté
>
> pluperfect subjunctive:
> > imperfect subjunctive of **avoir**: j'**eusse** porté

▶ Some very common French verbs form their compound tenses with **être** instead of **avoir**. See p. 12.

▶ In all the compound tenses the past participle may sometimes agree with its subject or its direct object, in gender and in number. See p. 14.

CONJUGATION OF -er VERBS

(First-conjugation verbs)

In all tenses **elle** (*she*), **on** (*one*) and singular nouns are followed by the **il** form of the verb; **elles** (*they*, feminine) and plural nouns are followed by the **ils** form of the verb.

infinitive	port**er**, *to wear*
present participle	port**ant**, *wearing*
past participle	port**é**, *worn*
imperative	port**e**, *wear...!*
	port**ons**, *let's wear...*
	port**ez**, *wear...!*

Simple tenses

present tense,	je port**e**	nous port**ons**
I wear, I am wearing	tu port**es**	vous port**ez**
	il port**e**	ils port**ent**
imperfect tense,	je port**ais**	nous port**ions**
I wore, I was wearing,	tu port**ais**	vous port**iez**
I used to wear	il port**ait**	ils port**aient**
past historic tense,	je port**ai**	nous port**âmes**
I wore	tu port**as**	vous port**âtes**
	il port**a**	ils port**èrent**
future tense,	je port**erai**	nous port**erons**
I shall wear, I shall	tu port**eras**	vous port**erez**
be wearing	il port**era**	ils port**eront**
conditional tense,	je port**erais**	nous port**erions**
I should wear	tu port**erais**	vous port**eriez**
	il port**erait**	ils port**eraient**
present subjunctive,	je port**e**	nous port**ions**
I wear, I may wear	tu port**es**	vous port**iez**
	il port**e**	ils port**ent**
imperfect subjunctive*,	je port**asse**	nous port**assions**
I wore, I might wear	tu port**asses**	vous port**assiez**
	il port**ât**	ils port**assent**

* archaic or literary

Compound tenses

perfect tense, *I wore, I have worn,* *I have been wearing*	j'**ai** porté tu **as** porté il **a** porté	nous **avons** porté vous **avez** porté ils **ont** porté
pluperfect tense, *I had worn, I had* *been wearing*	j'**avais** porté tu **avais** porté il **avait** porté	nous **avions** porté vous **aviez** porte ils **avaient** porté
future perfect tense, *I shall have worn, I* *shall have been* *wearing*	j'**aurai** porté tu **auras** porté il **aura** porté	nous **aurons** porté vous **aurez** porté ils **auront** porté
conditional perfect tense, *I should* *have worn*	j'**aurais** porté tu **aurais** porté il **aurait** porté	nous **aurions** porté vous **auriez** porté ils **auraient** porté
past anterior tense*, *I had worn*	j'**eus** porté tu **eus** porté il **eut** porté	nous **eûmes** porté vous **eûtes** porté ils **eurent** porté
perfect subjunctive, *I wore, I may* *have worn*	j'**aie** porté tu **aies** porté il **ait** porté	nous **ayons** porté vous **ayez** porté ils **aient** porté
pluperfect subjunctive*, *I* *had worn*	j'**eusse** porté tu **eusses** porté il **eût** porté	nous **eussions** porté vous **eussiez** porté ils **eussent** porté

Imperative of -er verbs

The **tu** form of the imperative of **-er** verbs (also verbs like **ouvrir**, see p. 29) has no **-s** except when followed by **y** or **en**:

> **donne-le-moi!**, *give it to me!*
> **donnes-en à ta sœur aussi!**, *give your sister some as well!*
> **vas-y!**, *go on!*

* archaic or literary

Spelling changes in some -er verbs

▶ Tenses with changes are given in detail in the verb tables on p. 239.

■ Verbs ending -e[CONSONANT]er change the e of the stem to è when a silent e follows:

mener → je mène

They also make this change in the future and conditional, where the e that follows is soft rather than silent:

je mènerai; je mènerais

■ verbs ending -eter and -eler, however, usually produce the open sound in the e by doubling the consonant:

jeter → je jette
rappeler → je rappelle

■ some verbs ending -eter and -eler follow the pattern of **mener**, changing the e to è:

acheter → j'achète
geler → je gèle

Most verbs that do this are, however, quite uncommon. The only ones you are at all likely to encounter are:

acheter, *buy*	**geler**, *freeze*
ciseler, *engrave*	**haleter**, *pant*
congeler, *(deep) freeze*	**modeler**, *model*
crocheter, *hook (up)*	**peler**, *peel*
déceler, *disclose*	**racheter**, *buy back,*
dégeler, *thaw*	*buy again*
démanteler, dismantle	

■ Verbs ending -é[CONSONANT]er change the é to è before a silent e in the same way, *except in the future and conditional tenses:*

espérer → j'espère, but
j'espérerai; j'espérerais

■ Verbs ending -cer and -ger change the c to ç and the g to ge before a and o. This keeps the c and the g soft:

commencer → nous commençons
manger → nous mangeons

■ Verbs ending -oyer and -uyer change the y to i before a silent e:

envoyer → j'envoie
appuyer → j'appuie

With verbs ending -ayer this change is optional:

payer → je paie or je paye

CONJUGATION OF -ir VERBS

(Second-conjugation verbs)

In all tenses **elle** (*she*), **on** (*one*), and singular nouns are followed by the **il** form of the verb; **elles** (*they*, feminine) and plural nouns are followed by the **ils** form of the verb.

infinitive	fin**ir**, *to finish*
present participle	fin**issant**, *finishing*
past participle	fin**i**, *finished*
imperative	fin**is**, *finish ...!*
	fin**issons**, *let's finish ...*
	fin**issez**, *finish ...!*

Simple tenses

present tense,	je fin**is**	nous fin**issons**
I finish, I am	tu fin**is**	vous fin**issez**
finishing	il fin**it**	ils fin**issent**

imperfect tense, *I finished, I was* *finishing, I used to* *finish*	je fin**issais** tu fin**issais** il fin**issait**	nous fin**issions** vous fin**issiez** ils fin**issaient**
past historic tense, *I finished*	je fin**is** tu fin**is** il fin**it**	nous fin**îmes** vous fin**îtes** ils fin**irent**
future tense, *I shall finish,* *I shall be finishing*	je fin**irai** tu fin**iras** il fin**ira**	nous fin**irons** vous fin**irez** ils fin**iront**
conditional tense, *I should finish*	je fin**irais** tu fin**irais** il fin**irait**	nous fin**irions** vous fin**iriez** ils fin**iraient**
present subjunctive, *I finish, I may* *finish*	je fin**isse** tu fin**isses** il fin**isse**	nous fin**issions** vous fin**issiez** ils fin**issent**
imperfect subjunctive*, *I finished, I might* *finish*	je fin**isse** tu fin**isses** il fin**ît**	nous fin**issions** vous fin**issiez** ils fin**issent**

Compound tenses

perfect tense, *I finished, I have* *finished*	j'**ai** fini tu **as** fini il **a** fini	nous **avons** fini vous **avez** fini ils **ont** fini
pluperfect tense, *I had finished*	j'**avais** fini tu **avais** fini il **avait** fini	nous **avions** fini vous **aviez** fini ils **avaient** fini
future perfect tense, *I shall have* *finished*	j'**aurai** fini tu **auras** fini il **aura** fini	nous **aurons** fini vous **aurez** fini ils **auront** fini
conditional perfect tense, *I should* *have finished*	j'**aurais** fini tu **aurais** fini il **aurait** fini	nous **aurions** fini vous **auriez** fini ils **auraient** fini

* archaic or literary

past anterior tense*, *I had finished*	j'**eus** fini tu **eus** fini il **eut** fini	nous **eûmes** fini vous **eûtes** fini ils **eurent** fini
perfect subjunctive, *I finished, I may have finished*	j'**ale** fini tu **ales** fini il **alt** fini	nous **ayons** fini vous **ayez** fini ils **alent** fini
pluperfect subjunctive*, *I had finished*	j'**eusse** fini tu **eusses** fini il **eût** fini	nous **eussions** fini vous **eussiez** fini ils **eussent** fini

CONJUGATION OF -re VERBS

(Third-conjugation verbs)

In all tenses **elle** (*she*), **on** (*one*), and singular nouns are followed by the **il** form of the verb; **elles** (*they*, feminine) and plural nouns are followed by the **ils** form of the verb.

infinitive	vend**re**, *to sell*
present participle	vend**ant**, *selling*
past participle	vend**u**, *sold*
imperative	vend**s**, *sell ...!* vend**ons**, *let's sell ...* vend**ez**, *sell ...!*

Simple tenses

present tense, *I sell, I am selling*	je vend**s** tu vend**s** il vend	nous vend**ons** vous vend**ez** ils vend**ent**
imperfect tense, *I sold, I was selling, I used to sell*	je vend**ais** tu vend**ais** il vend**ait**	nous vend**ions** vous vend**iez** ils vend**aient**

* archaic or literary

past historic tense,	je vend**is**	nous vend**îmes**
I sold	tu vend**is**	vous vend**îtes**
	il vend**it**	ils vend**irent**

future tense,	je vend**rai**	nous vend**rons**
I shall sell, I shall	tu vend**ras**	vous vend**rez**
be selling	il vend**ra**	ils vend**ront**

conditional tense,	je vend**rais**	nous vend**rions**
I should sell	tu vend**rais**	vous vend**riez**
	il vend**rait**	ils vend**raient**

present subjunctive,	je vend**e**	nous vend**ions**
I sell, I may sell	tu vend**es**	vous vend**iez**
	il vend**e**	ils vend**ent**

imperfect	je vend**isse**	nous vend**issions**
subjunctive*,	tu vend**isses**	vous vend**issiez**
I sold, I might sell	il vend**ît**	ils vend**issent**

Compound tenses

perfect tense,	j'**ai** vendu	nous **avons** vendu
I sold, I have sold,	tu **as** vendu	vous **avez** vendu
I have been selling	il **a** vendu	ils **ont** vendu

pluperfect tense,	j'**avais** vendu	nous **avions** vendu
I had sold, I had	tu **avais** vendu	vous **aviez** vendu
been selling	il **avait** vendu	ils **avaient** vendu

future perfect tense,	j'**aurai** vendu	nous **aurons** vendu
I shall have sold	tu **auras** vendu	vous **aurez** vendu
	il **aura** vendu	ils **auront** vendu

conditional perfect	j'**aurais** vendu	nous **aurions** vendu
tense, *I should*	tu **aurais** vendu	vous **auriez** vendu
have sold	il **aurait** vendu	ils **auraient** vendu

past anterior tense*,	j'**eus** vendu	nous **eûmes** vendu
I had sold	tu **eus** vendu	vous **eûtes** vendu
	il **eut** vendu	ils **eurent** vendu

* archaic or literary

perfect subjunctive, *I sold, I may have sold*	j'**aie** vendu tu **aies** vendu il **ait** vendu	nous **ayons** vendu vous **ayez** vendu ils **aient** vendu
pluperfect subjunctive*, *I had sold*	j'**eusse** vendu tu **eusses** vendu il **eût** vendu	nous **eussions** vendu vous **eussiez** vendu ils **eussent** vendu

COMPOUND TENSES

▶ For the formation of the compound tenses see p. 3.

Compound tenses formed with être

Although most verbs form their compound tenses with **avoir** as the auxiliary, two groups form these tenses with **être**: reflexive verbs and a small number of common verbs expressing motion or change of state.

■ Reflexive verbs

> **je me suis levé de bonne heure**, *I got up early*
> **tu t'étais couché tard?**, *you'd gone to bed late?*

▶ See p. 30 for the formation of reflexive verbs and p. 15 for their agreement.

■ 'Motion' verbs

This is a group of thirteen common (and a few more quite uncommon) verbs mainly expressing some kind of motion or change of state, and all intransitive (used without a direct object):

arriver, *arrive*	il est arrivé
partir, *set off*	il est parti
entrer, *enter*	il est entré
sortir, *go out*	il est sorti
aller, *go*	il est allé
venir, *come*	il est venu

* archaic or literary

monter, *go up*	**il est monté**
descendre, *go down*	**il est descendu**
mourir, *die*	**il est mort**
naître, *be born*	**il est né**
rester, *stay*	**il est resté**
tomber, *fall*	**il est tombé**
retourner, *return*	**il est retourné**

Accourir and **passer** used intransitively may take either **être** or **avoir**:

> **elle est accourue/elle a accouru**, *she ran up*

Except **convenir à** (*suit*), all compound verbs based on the above verbs also take **être** when used intransitively.

> **je suis parvenu à le faire**, *I managed to do it*
> **il est devenu soldat**, *he became a soldier*

but **cela ne lui a pas convenu**, *it didn't suit him*

▶ See p. 15 for the past-participle agreement with this group of verbs.

■ 'Motion' verbs used transitively

Some of the above verbs can also be used with a direct object (transitively). These verbs are:

> **descendre**, *to take down, to get down, to go down*
> **monter**, *to take up, to put up, to bring up, to go up*
> **entrer** (or more usually its compound, **rentrer**), *to put in, to let in, to bring in*
> **retourner**, *to turn (over)*
> **sortir**, *to take out, to bring out*

When they are used this way they take **avoir**, not **être**:

> **il a sorti un billet de cent francs de son portefeuille**, *he took a hundred-franc note from his wallet*
> **j'ai descendu l'escalier**, *I came down the stairs*

■ Verbs of motion and change of state other than those listed above always take **avoir**, whether used transitively or intransitively.

>**tu as beaucoup changé**, *you've changed a lot*

Past-participle agreement in compound tenses

■ Verbs conjugated with **avoir**

In most cases the past participle of a verb conjugated with **avoir** does not change at all. However, if an **avoir** verb has a direct object, and this precedes the verb, the past participle agrees with that object in gender and number, adding **-e** for feminine singular, **-s** for masculine plural and **-es** for feminine plural.

>**tes papiers, je les ai trouvés**, *those papers of yours, I found them*
>   – agreement, because direct object **les** precedes the verb
>**voilà les papiers que tu as cherchés toute la matinée**, *there are the papers you've been looking for all morning*
>   – agreement, because direct object **que**, referring to **les papiers**, precedes
>**quelle date as-tu choisie?**, *what date did you choose?*
>   – agreement, because direct object **quelle date** precedes

Notice that there is no agreement with an indirect object, or with **en**, or with a direct object that does not precede the verb:

>**j'ai trouvé les papiers**, *I've found the papers*
>   – no agreement, direct object **les papiers** follows

c'est à Sylvie que j'ai envoyé cet argent, *it's Sylvie I sent that money to*
- no agreement with **que**: it is the indirect object, standing for **à Sylvie**. The direct object **cet argent** follows.

les gâteaux? J'en ai mangé deux, *the cakes? I've eaten two of them*
- no agreement with **en**: it is not a true direct object

■ Verbs conjugated with **être**

□ Intransitive verbs of motion and change of state

The past participles of the thirteen 'motion' verbs and their compounds conjugated with **être** (see p. 12) agree with the subject in gender and number, adding **-e** for feminine singular, **-s** for masculine plural, **-es** for feminine plural:

elle est arrivée hier, *she arrived yesterday*
elles étaient parties bien avant midi, *they'd set off long before twelve o'clock*
ils seront déjà sortis, *they'll already have gone out*

□ Reflexive verbs

The past participles of reflexive verbs agree in gender and number with the preceding direct object, which in most cases will correspond to the subject:

elle s'est levée tard, *she got up late*
ils se sont dépêchés, *they hurried*

In some cases, however, the reflexive is an indirect object, and then there is no agreement:

elle s'est dit, « pourquoi pas? », *she said to herself, why not?*
ils se sont écrit toutes les semaines, *they wrote to each other every week*

>> **elle s'est cassé la cheville**, *she broke her ankle*
>> – **la cheville**, the ankle, is the direct object, **se** is
>> an indirect object indicating whose ankle she
>> broke

but notice:

>> **quelle cheville s'est-il cassée?,** *which ankle has
>> he broken?*
>> – the agreement is with **quelle cheville**, which is
>> the direct object, precedes, and is feminine.

■ Past participle used as an adjective

The past participle may also be used simply as an
adjective, in which case, like any other adjective, it agrees
with its noun:

>> **elles sont épuisées mais contentes**, *they are
>> exhausted but happy*

▶ See p. 38 for all the uses of the past participle.

USE OF TENSES

The present tense

French has only one form of the present tense,
corresponding to both the present simple and the present
continuous in English. So **je mange** translates both *I eat*
and *I am eating*. There is no possible translation of *I am
eating* using the present participle in French. If the
continuing nature of the action needs to be stressed, **être
en train de** is used:

>> **mais je suis en train de déjeuner!**, *but I'm still
>> eating my lunch!*

General uses of the present tense

■ As in English, the present is used not just to indicate
what is going on at the moment:

> **je mange un œuf,** *I'm eating an egg*

but also what habitually occurs:

> **je mange toujours un œuf au petit déjeuner,**
> *I always have an egg for breakfast*

■ It can also be used, again as in English, to indicate a future:

> **tu veux un œuf?,** *are you having (going to have) an egg?*

■ The present tense is used much more frequently than in English to narrate a past series of events, not just in spoken French but in written French also:

> **1945. A Hiroshima, la bombe explose. Toute discussion est terminée ...** *1945. In Hiroshima, the bomb exploded. All discussion was over*

This is called the historic present, and it is used to give more immediacy to past events. But see also p. 22.

Special uses of the present tense

■ Present tense with **depuis** (*for*), **depuis que** (*since*), **voilà ... que** (*since/for*) and **il y a ... que** (*since/for*)

□ **Depuis, depuis que**

With the preposition **depuis** and after the conjunction **depuis que** a French present tense is used where in English we should expect a perfect:

> **je suis ici depuis deux jours,** *I've been here (for) two days*
> **je le vois beaucoup plus souvent depuis que sa femme est partie,** *I've seen him a lot more often since his wife's gone*

With **depuis** plus a negative, however, the tense is the same as in English:

> **je ne l'ai pas vu depuis deux jours**, *I haven't seen him for two days*

And where the action is already completed the tense with **depuis** is also a past tense, as in English:

> **je l'ai terminé depuis deux heures**, *I finished it two hours ago*

▶ See also **depuis** + imperfect, p. 21.

☐ **Voilà ... que, il y a ... que**

All that has been said above about **depuis** also holds good for the constructions **voilà ... que** and **il y a ... que** (*since/for*):

> **voilà (il y a) deux jours que je suis ici**, *I've been here for two days*
>
> **voilà (il y a) deux jours que je ne l'ai pas vu**, *I haven't seen him for two days (it's two days since I've seen him)*

■ Present tense with **venir de**

With **venir de** (*to have just* done something) we find a present tense of **venir** corresponding to a perfect in English:

> **je viens de déjeuner**, *I've just had lunch*

The literal sense of the French is 'I'm coming from having lunch' (present) rather than the English 'I have just had lunch' (perfect). This French construction ('I'm coming from') is a quite logical equivalent to **je vais déjeuner**, *I'm going to have lunch* (see p. 24).

▶ See also **venir de** + imperfect, p. 21.

The perfect tense

The perfect has two main uses in French; as a 'true' perfect and as a past narrative tense.

■ The 'true' perfect (= *I have done*)

As in English, the true perfect is used to speak of something that happened in the past and has some bearing on what is being talked about in the present:

> **j'ai mangé tous tes chocolats**, *I've eaten all your chocolates* (now there's going to be trouble!)
>
> **je suis déjà tombé trois fois**, *I've fallen over three times already* (and he's asking me to go on the ice again!)

It also corresponds to the English perfect continuous:

> **j'ai regardé la télévision tout l'après-midi**, *I've been watching television all afternoon*

Don't be tempted to use an imperfect for this—**je regardais la télévision** means *I was watching television* (when all at once something happened).

■ The past-action perfect (= *I did*)

In French, the perfect is also used for an action in past narrative, especially in speech, where English uses a simple past tense:

> **je me suis levé à sept heures, j'ai allumé la radio et je suis entré dans la salle de bains**, *I got up at seven o'clock, switched on the radio and went into the bathroom*

However, for repeated past actions, where the English simple past, *I went*, really means *I used to go* or *I would go*, French uses the imperfect:

> **on allait chaque année à Torremolinos. C'était affreux!**, *we went (= used to go) to Torremolinos every year. It was (= used to be) dreadful!*

▶ See general uses of the imperfect, below.

The imperfect tense

General uses of the imperfect

■ To indicate a repeated action:

> **il venait me chercher tous les matins à huit heures**, *he came and picked me up (used to come and pick me up; would come and pick me up) every morning at eight*

■ To indicate a continuing action (which is often then interrupted by a single action, for which the perfect or past historic is used):

> **j'épluchais des pommes de terre quand elle sonna à la porte**, *I was peeling potatoes when she rang the doorbell*

■ To indicate a continuing state of affairs:

> **j'ai regardé par la fenêtre. Il pleuvait**, *I looked out of the window. It was raining*

Imperfect or not? Choosing the right French past tense

In general, an English 'was ... ing' indicates an imperfect, and so does 'would ...', unless this has an 'if' involved or implied (*I wouldn't do that ... if I were you*), in which case the tense is the conditional—see p. 26. However, if a simple past tense is to be translated into French, you must consider whether this is one single action (past historic or perfect) or a repeated action (imperfect).

Special uses of the imperfect

■ Imperfect for a single action

More and more frequently the imperfect is used by modern writers at all levels (literature, magazines, newspapers) as a single-action tense to give greater immediacy to an event. Here the newspaper *Le Figaro* is recounting individual events—in the imperfect:

> **Côté cinéma, Bernard Borderie décidait de saisir la balle au bond. Il choisissait pour interpréter le rôle la toute jeune Michèle Mercier.** *For the film, Bernard Borderie decided to grab his opportunity. He chose a really young actress to play the part, Michèle Mercier.*

Clearly 'deciding' and 'choosing' were single, not continous or repeated, actions. The feeling behind these imperfect tenses seems to be: 'there he was, deciding, choosing ...' Though this use of the imperfect should be recognized, it is not recommended that it be imitated.

■ Imperfect with **depuis** (*for*), **depuis que** (*since*), **voilà ... que** (*since/for*) and **il y avait ... que** (*since/for*)

Where English uses a pluperfect continuous (*I had been doing*) with these expressions, French uses an imperfect:

> **j'y étais depuis deux jours**, *I had been there (for) two days*
>
> **je le voyais beaucoup plus souvent depuis que sa femme était partie**, *I had been seeing him a lot more since his wife had gone*
>
> **il y avait deux jours que j'étais là**, *I had been there for two days*

All the other rules that apply to these expressions used with the present (see pp. 17, 18) also apply when they are used with the imperfect.

■ Imperfect with **venir de** (*to have just*)

Where English uses a simple past of *have just* ..., French uses an imperfect of **venir de**:

> **je venais de déjeuner**, *I had just had lunch*

▶ Compare **venir de** + present, p. 18.

■ Imperfect in **si** sentences

After **si** meaning *if*, the simple past in English always corresponds to an imperfect in French:

> **si j'avais ton numéro, je te téléphonerais**, *if I had your number I'd phone you*

Perfect or past historic are not possible after **si** meaning *if*; nor is the conditional, which you might be tempted to use because the main verb in such sentences is usually in the conditional.

However, as in English, the conditional can be used after **si** where it really means *whether*:

> **je ne savais pas s'il rappellerait**, *I didn't know if (whether) he would phone back*

▶ See also p. 26 for the conditional in **si** sentences.

The past historic tense

The past historic is mainly, though not exclusively, a written past narrative tense. In spoken French the perfect is usually used instead to recount past actions. However, the past historic can readily be heard in some French dialects and may also be used in standard spoken French where what is being narrated is clearly a self-contained story or a historical event.

Cases where the past historic is not used

■ The past historic is an alternative to the perfect as a narrative tense—it can never be substituted for the imperfect, or for the 'true' perfect (see p. 19).

■ In letter-writing and other personal writing the perfect, not the past historic, is normally used to narrate single actions in the past.

■ The present tense (known in this case as the historic present) may quite often be found with a past meaning, substituting for the past historic. The change to the

present from the past historic (or vice versa, from the
historic present to the past historic) is felt to lend more
immediacy to a narrative at the point at which it occurs.
The following example (here, historic present to past
historic at the important moment) is taken from the
magazine *Marie France*:

> Ensemble le soir, ils **font** la tournée des bistrots
> de la Butte, ce qui ne **va** pas sans dispute ni
> même sans coups … A l'époque Picasso **est** un
> petit gars noiraud et rablé; immenses yeux noirs,
> larges épaules et des hanches fines … Le coup de
> foudre **se produisit** sous une pluie battante: la
> jeune femme courait pour se mettre à l'abri,
> Picasso lui **barra** le passage en lui tendant un
> petit chat; elle **rit** et **accepta** sans plus de façon.
>
> *In the evenings they made the rounds of the
> Butte pubs together, not without rows, even blows.
> At the time Picasso was a swarthy, broad, stocky
> lad, with huge black eyes, big shoulders and
> narrow hips. Then, in a downpour of rain, came
> love at first sight: the girl was running for shelter,
> Picasso stood in her way offering her a kitten. She
> laughed, and accepted without more ado.*

The change to the past historic comes at **le coup de
foudre se produisit**.

● Future for past historic

The use of the future tense instead of the past historic
for past narrative is a not uncommon journalistic device.
See p. 25.

The future tense

Future tense and aller + infinitive

As well as the actual future tense (**je porterai** — *I shall
wear*), there is a future formed with **aller**, just as in

English futurity may be expressed by 'I am going to':

> **je vais partir**, *I'm going to leave*

This is sometimes called the 'immediate future', but the ordinary future tense can also be used for immediate happenings, and **aller** + infinitive can be used for things well into the distant future:

> **le défilé aura lieu cet après-midi**, *the processior will take place this afternoon*
>
> **on va retourner à Torremolinos l'année prochaine**. *we're going to go to Torremolinos again next year*

In fact, **aller** + infinitive is used to stress present intention:

> **je vais lui téléphoner demain matin**, *I'm going to (I intend to) phone him tomorrow morning*

or the relationship of the future event to something that is happening in the present:

> **si tu ne fais pas attention, tu vas te couper le doigt**, *if you don't look out you'll cut our finger (a direct consequence of not watching what you're doing!)*

This will often involve an event not too far into the future, but this is not necessarily the case (note the Torremolinos example above).

Special uses of the future tense

■ Future after **quand, lorsque, dès que, aussitôt que, tant que, pendant que**

Clauses beginning *when* (**quand, lorsque**), *as soon as* (**aussitôt que, dès que**), *as long as* (**tant que**) or *whilst* (**pendant que**) have a present tense in English with futurity implied. In French the tense must be future:

> **dès que le magasin ouvrira, nous serons à votre service**, *as soon as the shop opens we shall be at your service*

With these time conjunctions French follows the strict time-logic of the situation, so that in sentences such as the following a future perfect must be used:

> **je te dirai quand elle sera partie**, *I'll tell you when she's gone* (logically, *when she will have gone*)

Note that this strict time-logic does not extend to the conjunction **si**, *if*, which takes the same non-logical tense as English:

> **s'il est là quand je reviendrai**, *if he's there when I get back* (present tense, **est**, not the more logical future)

■ Future as a past narrative tense

The use of the future for past narrative is also becoming more common, especially in newspaper writing. The aim is to heighten the effect with a sense of 'what was destined to happen next was ...' This example comes from *Le Figaro*:

> Michèle **fera** tout pour échapper à cette cage dorée. Elle **finira** par quitter la France, **tentera** une nouvelle carrière aux États-Unis, **se lancera** dans la production, **se ruinera** avec une régularité métronomique pour «monter» des films qui n'**aboutiront** guère.
>
> *Michèle did everything possible to escape from this gilded cage. She ended up leaving France, tried a new career in the United States, launched herself into production, ruined herself over and over again putting on films that had little success.*

An effect similar to that of the French could be obtained in English using *was to* with each verb, but it would be considerably more clumsy than the French futures are.

The conditional tenses
(conditional and conditional perfect)

General uses of the conditional

■ The conditional can show future possibility (what might or might not happen if ...):

> **je ne ferais pas ça (si j'étais à ta place)**, *I shouldn't do that (if I were you)*

The 'if' clause may or may not be expressed.

■ The conditional can also show a 'future in the past'. In this use it indicates something that is to happen subsequently to some event narrated in a past tense (*would* is used for this in English):

> **elle m'a assuré qu'elle le ferait**, *she assured me she'd do it*

Conditional tenses used in si sentences

Conditional and conditional perfect tenses are very often found in sentences that include a clause beginning with **si**:

> **je serais content si elle venait**, *I'd be pleased if she came*
> **si elle était venue, j'aurais été tellement heureux**, *if she'd come I'd have been so happy*

The sequence is

> **si** + imperfect, + main clause conditional
> **si** + pluperfect, + main clause conditional perfect

▶ See also p. 22.

Special uses of the conditional tense

■ The conditional may express qualified possibility:

> **il serait peut-être temps de regarder votre avenir en face**, *it might perhaps be time to face your future*

■ The conditional may be used to avoid direct responsibility for the accuracy of a statement:

> **il y aurait quinze blessés**, *there are said to be (appear to be) fifteen injured*

■ The conditional may express a polite, hesitant request:

> **vous ne pourriez pas le revendre?**, *couldn't you perhaps sell it again?*

Literary tenses

One of the simple tenses, the imperfect subjunctive, and two of the compound tenses, the pluperfect subjunctive and the past anterior, are obsolescent or literary, to be recognized but not used.

The imperfect subjunctive

This is found in subjunctive clauses with a past meaning:

> **elle ne pensait pas qu'il le sût**, *she didn't think he knew it*

Everyday French would use a present subjunctive:

> **elle ne pensait pas qu'il le sache**

The pluperfect subjunctive

■ This is used where the verb has a pluperfect meaning:

> **il téléphona, bien qu'elle fût déjà partie**, *he telephoned, even though she had already left*

Here, everyday French would use a perfect subjunctive:

> **il téléphona, bien qu'elle soit déjà partie**

■ It is also used in literary French instead of the conditional perfect:

> **Rodrigue, qui l'eût cru? ... Chimène, qui l'eût dit? ...** *Rodrigue, who would have believed it?— Chimène, who would have said it?*
>
> (Corneille: *Le Cid*)

The past anterior

This is used with a pluperfect meaning after the conjunctions **quand, lorsque, dès que, aussitôt que**, but only when the verb in the main clause is in the past historic:

> **quand elle eut fini de parler, il se leva et sortit,** *when she had finished speaking, he got up and went out*

THE IMPERATIVE

The imperative is used to give orders or instructions or to express requests.

Formation of the imperative

The imperative has three forms, which are the same as the **tu, nous,** and **vous** parts of the present tense of the verb:

> **choisis,** *choose!*
> **choisissons,** *let's choose*
> **choisissez,** *choose!*

■ First conjugation (**-er**) verbs lose the final **-s** of the **tu** form of the imperative, unless followed by **y** or **en**:

> **donne-le-moi,** *give it to me*
> **donnes-en à ton amie,** *give some to your friend*
> **va dans ta chambre!,** *go to your room!*

So do irregular verbs whose **tu** form of the present ends in **-es**:

>**ouvre la porte**, *open the door*

▶ For form, order and position of pronoun objects with the imperative, see p. 106.

■ In the negative the **ne** and **pas** etc. go round the verb in the usual way:

>**ne choisissez pas encore**, *don't choose yet*

■ Third-person commands (*let him/her/it/them ...*) are expressed by using **que** plus the present subjunctive:

>**qu'il le trouve lui-même**, *let him find it himself!*

Alternatives to the imperative

An imperative need not be used to express a command. There are a number of other ways of doing it.

■ Politer than the imperative is **voulez-vous (veux-tu) ...**, *will you/would you ...*, or **auriez-vous l'amabilité de ...**, *would you be so kind as to ...*:

>**voulez-vous chercher mon sac?**, *would you look for my bag?*
>**auriez-vous l'amabilité de me passer ma valise?**, *would you be so kind as to pass me my case?*

■ The imperative of **vouloir** plus the infinitive is found as an alternative to the imperative in formal language and in the ending to formal letters:

>**veuillez signer ici**, *kindly sign here*
>**Veuillez agréer, chère madame, l'expression de mes sentiments les plus distingués**, *Yours sincerely*

■ In official notices and in recipes an infinitive, or **défense de ...**, or **... interdit** may be found instead of an imperative:

> **ne pas se pencher au dehors**, *do not lean out*
> **défense de fumer**, *no smoking*
> **entrée interdite**, *no entry*

■ The future tense may also express a command, as in English:

> **vous ferez exactement ce que je vous dirai**, *you'll do exactly what I say*

REFLEXIVE VERBS

Reflexive verbs are verbs whose direct or indirect object is the same as their subject (*he scratches himself; she allows herself a chocolate*). In French they consist of a simple verb preceded by a reflexive pronoun:

> **il arrête le train**, *he stops the train*—simple verb
> **le train s'arrête**, *the train stops (itself)*—reflexive verb

■ The reflexive pronouns

Apart from **se**, they are the same as the ordinary object pronouns:

> **me**, *(to) myself*
> **te**, *(to) yourself*
> **se**, *(to) himself, (to) herself, (to) itself, (to) oneself, (to) themselves*
> **nous**, *(to) ourselves*
> **vous**, *(to) yourself, (to) yourselves*

Me, te, and **se** become **m', t',** and **s'** before a vowel or **h** 'mute'. **Te** becomes **toi** when used with the imperative (see p. 107).

The reflexive pronoun corresponding to **on** is **se**:

> **on s'y habitue**, *you get used to it*

□ The reflexive pronouns are the same whether they are

direct or indirect objects, and stand before the verb in the same way as other object pronouns.

▶ For the order of object pronouns, including reflexives, see p. 106.

□ Reflexive pronouns in the plural—**nous, vous, se**—as well as meaning *(to) ourselves, (to) yourselves, (to) themselves,* can also mean *(to) one another* or *(to) each other.* This includes **se** when it refers to **on** with a plural meaning *(we, you, people,* etc.):

> **ils se détestent**, *they hate each other*
> **elles se téléphonent tous les soirs**, *they phone each other every evening*
> **on s'aime**, *we love one another*

If ambiguity might otherwise result, **l'un(e) l'autre / les un(e)s les autres** is added, where the reflexive is a direct object; or **l'un(e) à l'autre / les un(e)s aux autres**, where the reflexive is an indirect object:

> **nous nous sommes demandé, si ...**, *we wondered (asked ourselves) whether ...*
> **nous nous sommes demandé l'un à l'autre, si ...**, *we asked each other, whether ...*

■ Compound tenses of reflexive verbs are formed with **être**, not **avoir**.

In compound tenses the past participle of a reflexive verb agrees with a preceding direct object. Since direct object and subject are usually the same, this means that the past participle of a reflexive verb appears to agree with its subject. However, this is not always the case:

> **elle s'est lavée**, *she washed (herself)*
> **elle s'est lavé les cheveux**, *she washed her hair*

▶ See also p. 15.

■ A French reflexive verb may correspond to an English one:

    il se gratte, *he scratches himself*

but very often it does not:

    elle s'assoit, *she sits down*
    il se lave, *he washes*

■ Reflexive verbs are occasionally used in French where English uses a passive:

    je m'étonne: je croyais que c'était gratuit, *I'm
      surprised, I thought it was free*
    cela ne se vend pas ici, *it's not sold here*

▶ See p. 34 for this and other alternatives to the passive.

■ Reflexive verbs may sometimes have the sense of 'becoming':

    je m'ennuie, *I'm getting bored*
    elle s'impatientait, *she was becoming impatient*

THE PASSIVE

The passive forms of the tenses are those where the subject of the verb experiences the action rather than performs it (active: *he helped*; passive: *he was helped*).

Formation of the passive

The passive in English is formed with parts of the verb *to be* plus the past participle; in French it is formed in exactly the same way with parts of **être** plus the past participle:

    elle est détestée, *she is hated*
    il était protégé par sa femme, *he was protected by
      his wife*
    la ville avait été abandonnée par ses habitants,
      the town had been abandoned by its inhabitants

In the passive the past participle always agrees with the subject, in the same way that an adjective would.

■ In English the 'doer' of the action is indicated by *by* (as in this sentence you're reading). This is **par**, or sometimes **de**, in French. **Par** is more specific:

> **il a été tué par sa femme**, *he was killed by his wife*
>
> **elle est bien vue de tout le monde**, *she is well regarded by everyone*

However, where *by* refers to the instrument used, rather than the person doing the action, **de** is always used in French:

> **il a été tué d'un coup de revolver**, *he was killed by a revolver shot*

■ In English, the indirect object of an active verb may be made into the subject of the corresponding passive verb:

> *someone gave the book to me → I was given the book*
>
> *Paul gave the book to me → I was given the book by Paul*

This is impossible in French. *I was given the book* can be translated using **on**:

> **on m'a donné le livre** (literally, *someone has given me the book*)

However, in the second example, *I was given the book by Paul*, where the 'doer' of the action is stated, the sentence has to remain active in French:

> **Paul m'a donné le livre**

Or, if the English sentence stresses 'Paul':

> **c'est Paul qui m'a donné le livre**

Alternatives to the passive

The passive is frequently avoided in French, especially when the 'doer' of the action is not mentioned.

■ Most frequently **on** is used:

> **on l'avait abandonné**, *it had been abandoned*

■ Sometimes a reflexive verb may be used:

> **cela ne se fait pas!**, *that's not done!*
> **la porte s'ouvre**, *the door is (being) opened* (**la porte est ouverte** would mean *the door is— already—open*)

■ Or an active form may be preferred where English would use a passive:

> **ta lettre les a bouleversés**, *they've been shattered by your letter*

■ Occasionally, where the subject is a person, **se faire** is used:

> **il s'est fait renvoyer en Espagne**, *he's been sent (got himself sent) back to Spain*
> **nous nous sommes fait renvoyer**, *we've been sacked*

PARTICIPLES

The present participle

Formation of the present participle

The present participle (in English, the *-ing* part of the verb) is formed in French by substituting **-ant** for **-ons** in the **nous** form of the present tense of the verb:

> **choisir → nous choisissons → choisissant**

There are only three present participles which are exceptions to this rule:

> **être: étant**
> **avoir: ayant**
> **savoir: sachant** (but **savant** where the present
>   participle is used as an adjective: **un phoque**
>   **savant**, *a performing seal*)

Note also the two spellings of **fatiguant/fatigant**, the
second used adjectivally:

> **en fatiguant la salade**, *whilst dressing the salad*
> **une journée fatigante**, *an exhausting day*

Uses of the present participle

■ As an adjective

The present participle can be used as an adjective. When
it is so used, it behaves exactly as other adjectives. So it
agrees with its noun, and qualifying adverbs precede it:

> **l'année suivante**, *the following year*
> **une femme incroyablement charmante**, *an*
>   *incredibly charming woman*

■ As a verb

The present participle can also be used verbally in a
phrase with or without **en** (= *in, by, whilst*). When
the present participle is used verbally, pronoun objects stand
in front of it and adverbs after it, just as with any other
part of the verb:

> **en la rencontrant un jour dans la rue, il lui a**
>   **adressé la parole**, *(on) meeting her one day in*
>   *the street, he spoke to her*

Negatives go round it, as they go round other parts of
the verb:

> **ne sachant pas que vous étiez là, elle se tourna**
>   **vers moi**, *not knowing you were there, she*
>   *turned to me*

In this verbal use the present participle, since it is not an adjective, does not take adjective agreements.

☐ With or without **en**

When the present participle is used verbally without **en**, the two actions (that of the present participle and that of the main verb) follow one another. When the participle is used with **en** the actions go on simultaneously:

> **se retournant, elle répondit ...**, *turning round, she replied ...*
>
> **en tombant, elle a entraîné une lampe**, *in falling (as she fell), she brought down a lamp*
>
> **comment s'est-elle fait mal? — En tombant**, *how did she hurt herself? By falling (When she fell)*

En with a present participle usually corresponds to the English *on ... ing, by ... ing, in ... ing, whilst ... ing*.

☐ With **tout en**

The addition of **tout** to the above construction (**tout en ...**) draws attention to the fact that the two actions were going on together, often over a period of time. **Tout en** is usually translated as *whilst*:

> **tout en me parlant, il allumait sa pipe**, *whilst (all the time he was) speaking to me, he was lighting his pipe*

Tout en can also have the meaning of *whilst* (*on the one hand*):

> **tout en reconnaissant ce que vous avez fait, je dois vous dire que ...**, *whilst recognizing what you have done, I have to tell you that ...*

☐ With verbs of motion

English can make a verbal phrase by using a verb of motion plus a preposition (*swim away, fly off, run out*).

French has no equivalent construction and uses a variety
of strategies to deal with these concepts (**partir à la
nage, s'envoler**, etc.). One of these is to make the
preposition into a verb and then add a present participle
with **en**: **sortir en courant**, *run out*. This present-
participle construction is most frequently found with
courir.

▶ See also translation problems, p. 233.

■ As a noun

Present participles are occasionally used as nouns. They
add **-e** for feminine, **-(e)s** for plural forms: **l'occupant**,
occupier; **la passante**, *(woman) passer-by*; **des anciens
combattants**, *old soldiers*.

▶ The present participle can never be used in French
with an auxiliary verb, as it is in English. *I am sleeping*
has to be **je dors**. See p. 16.

The perfect participle

In English, the perfect participle is formed with the
present participle of *to have* plus the past participle of the
verb. In French the perfect participle is formed in an
exactly parallel way, using the present participle of **avoir**
plus the past participle of the verb:

> **ayant dit cela, elle s'assit**, *having said that, she
> sat down*

Verbs that form their compound tenses with **être** also
form their perfect participle with **être**:

> **étant arrivée de très bonne heure, elle acheta un
> journal**, *having arrived very early, she bought a
> newspaper*
> **s'étant déjà baigné, il revint sur la terrasse de la
> villa**, *having already had his dip, he came back on
> to the terrace of the villa*

As the above examples show, the use of the perfect participle in French exactly parallels its use in English.

The past participle

Formation of the past participle

Past participles of regular verbs are formed by removing the ending of the infinitive (**-er**, **-ir**, **-re**) and adding **-é**, **-i**, **-u**:

> **porter → porté**, *carried*
> **choisir → choisi**, *chosen*
> **vendre → vendu**, *sold*

▶ For the past participles of irregular verbs see the verb list, p. 242.

Uses of the past participle

■ The past participle is used to form all the compound tenses.

▶ See p. 3 (compound tense formation), p. 14 (past-participle agreement).

■ The past participle is used with **être** to form the passive.

▶ See p. 32.

■ The past participle may be used adjectivally; it then agrees with its noun, takes an adverb qualification, etc., just like any other adjective:

> **elle était complètement épuisée**, *she was completely exhausted*

■ The past participle may also occasionally be used as a noun:

> **le reçu**, *receipt*
> **les rescapés**, *survivors*

■ French sometimes uses a past participle where English

would use a present participle. Mostly this is to describe positions of the body. Common examples are:

accoudé, *leaning (on one's elbows)*	**couché**, *lying (e.g. in bed)*
agenouillé, *kneeling*	**étendu**, *lying (outstretched)*
appuyé, *leaning*	
assis, *sitting*	**(sus)pendu**, *hanging*

une seule lampe était suspendue au plafond, *just one lamp was hanging from the ceiling*

il était agenouillé devant l'autel, *he was kneeling before the altar*

THE SUBJUNCTIVE

The subjunctive, expressing doubt or unreality, barely exists any longer in English (*if I were you; if that be so; would that he were*). In French, though some of its tenses are literary or archaic, it is still in constant use in both the spoken and the written language.

The subjunctive is found in subordinate clauses beginning with **que** meaning *that*, though by no means all such clauses have a subjunctive. The subjunctive in French originally showed the speaker's attitude to an event in the light of his or her emotion (doubt, disbelief, pleasure, etc.). Nowadays it has become fixed as the form used after certain verbs or certain conjunctions, most of which still express some sort of emotion. In only a limited number of cases, however, noted below, is there still a choice between using or not using the subjunctive.

Formation of the subjunctive

The subjunctive has four tenses in French. Of these only the present subjunctive and, on the not very frequent occasions where a perfect meaning is necessary, the

perfect subjunctive are in modern everyday use. The
tenses are formed as follows:

■ Present subjunctive

The present subjunctive is formed from the **ils** form of
the present tense with endings as follows:

choisir → ils choisissent → choisiss-

je choisis**se**	nous choisiss**ions**
tu choisiss**es**	vous choisiss**iez**
il choisis**se**	ils choisiss**ent**

This normally produces, as with **choisir** above, **nous**
and **vous** forms identical with those of the imperfect
tense. In the few cases where this would not be so, **nous**
and **vous** forms of the imperfect tense are used for
present subjunctive **nous** and **vous**:

prendre → ils prennent → prenn-

je prenne	**nous prenions**
tu prennes	**vous preniez**
il prenne	ils prennent

The following verbs do not follow this pattern:

> **aller, avoir, être, faire, falloir, pouvoir, savoir,
> valoir, vouloir**

▶ For the subjunctive forms of these verbs, see the list
of irregular verbs, p. 242.

■ Perfect subjunctive

Use the present subjunctive of **avoir** or **être** with the
past participle of the verb:

j'aie choisi	**nous ayons** choisi
tu aies choisi	**vous ayez** choisi
il ait choisi	**ils aient** choisi
je sois arrivé(e)	**nous soyons** arrivé(e)s
tu sois arrivé(e)	**vous soyez** arrivé(e)(s)
il soit arrivé	**ils soient** arrivés

■ Imperfect subjunctive

The imperfect subjunctive is based on the past historic tense, as follows:

-er verbs (past historic: **je portai**):

je port**asse**	nous port**assions**
tu port**asses**	vous port**assiez**
il port**ât**	ils port**assent**

-ir and **-re** verbs (past historic: **je choisis, je vendis**):

je vend**isse**	nous vend**issions**
tu vend**isses**	vous vend**issiez**
il vend**ît**	ils vend**issent**

Irregular verbs that form their past historic with **-us** etc. form their imperfect subjunctive with **-usse**:

être:	je fu**sse**	nous fu**ssions**
	tu fu**sses**	vous fu**ssiez**
	il fû**t**	ils fu**ssent**

▶ See the irregular verb list, p. 242.

■ Pluperfect subjunctive

Formed from the imperfect subjunctive of **avoir** or **être** plus the past participle:

j'eusse choisi, etc.
je fusse parti, etc.

■ Future subjunctive

This tense does not exist. To express future meanings in subjunctive clauses, **devoir** must be used. See p. 67.

Uses of the subjunctive

■ The subjunctive is used after certain verbs; the ones listed are those most frequently met:

☐ Verbs of expectancy, wishing, wanting

> **vouloir que**, *wish; want*
> **souhaiter que**, *wish*
> **attendre que**, *wait until*
> **désirer que**, *want*
> **préférer que**, *prefer*
> **aimer mieux que**, *prefer*
> **il est préférable que**, *it is preferable*
> **il vaut mieux que**, *it is better*
> **il est important que**, *it is important*
>
> **il est important que tu le saches**, *it's important that you know*

With verbs of wishing, preferring, etc., English very often uses an infinitive dependent on an object—*they prefer us to go*. This is impossible in French and must always be translated by a dependent clause (= *they prefer that we should go*):

> **ils préfèrent que nous partions**, *they prefer us to go*
> **que voulez-vous qu'on fasse pour les jeunes chômeurs?**, *what do you want us to do for the young unemployed?*

Note that **espérer que**, *hope*, does not take the subjunctive.

☐ Verbs of necessity

> **il faut que**, *must*
> **il est nécessaire/urgent que**, *it is necessary/ urgent*
> **il faut que vous vous débrouilliez tout seul**, *you must sort it out on your own*

☐ Verbs of ordering, forbidding, allowing

> **ordonner que**, *order*
> **dire que**, *tell*

défendre que, *forbid*
permettre que, *allow*
s'opposer à ce que, *be opposed (to someone doing …)*

je ne permets pas que vous voyagiez seule, *I shall not allow you to travel alone*

With **dire que** there is a difference in meaning according to whether the subjunctive is used or not:

dites au messager qu'il part ce soir, *tell the courier he's leaving tonight* (piece of information)
dites au messager qu'il parte ce soir, *tell the courier to leave tonight* (command)

☐ Verbs of possibility

Il est possible que, *it is possible*
Il se peut que, *it is possible*
Il semble que, *it seems*
Il paraît que, *it seems*
Il est peu probable que, *it is improbable*
Il est impossible que, *it is impossible*

se peut-il qu'elle soit déjà là?, *is it possible that she's there already?*

Note that **il est probable que**, *it is probable*, and **il me semble/me paraît que**, *it seems to me*, do not generally take the subjunctive.

☐ Verbs of surprise and incomprehension

s'étonner que, *be surprised*
être surpris/étonné que, *be surprised*
quelle chance que, *what luck*
il me paraît curieux/surprenant/incroyable etc. **que**, *it seems odd/surprising/unbelievable*

je m'étonne qu'il y ait autant de chômeurs, *I'm surprised there are so many unemployed*

☐ Verbs of uncertainty

il n'est pas certain que, *it is not certain*
il n'est pas évident/vrai que, *it is not obvious/true*
je ne nie pas que, *I don't deny*
mettons/supposons que, *let us assume*

mettons que les réponses de ce sondage soient exactes, *let us assume that the replies to this poll are correct*

☐ Verbs of doubt and disbelief

douter que, *doubt*
il est douteux que,
   it is doubtful

penser que, *think*
croire que, *believe*
trouver, *think*
s'attendre à ce que, *expect*
être sûr/certain,
   be sure/certain

} in the negative or interrogative

je ne crois pas qu'elle t'ait dit des choses pareilles, *I don't believe she said things like that to you*

With the last five verbs above there is a difference in meaning according to whether the subjunctive is used or not:

je ne pense pas qu'il pleut, *I don't think it's raining* (I'm fairly sure it isn't)
je ne pense pas qu'il pleuve, *I don't <u>think</u> it's raining* (though it may be)

☐ Verbs of liking, pleasure, dislike, displeasure

aimer que, *like*
adorer que, *love*
ça me plaît que, *I'm glad*
être content/heureux/enchanté que, *be glad/ happy/delighted*
détester que, *hate*

j'aime que vous chantiez comme ça, *I like you to sing like that*

☐ Verbs of regret and concern

regretter que, *be sorry*

être désolé que, *be sorry*

c'est dommage que, *it's a pity*

avoir peur que ... (ne), *be afraid*

craindre que ... (ne), *be afraid*, (and the related conjunctions **de peur que ... (ne)**, **de crainte que ... (ne)**, *for fear that*)

être fâché que, *be annoyed that*

avoir honte que, *be ashamed that*

je suis désolé qu'elle ne puisse pas venir, *I'm sorry she can't come*

▶ The use of **ne** with **avoir peur que**, **craindre que**, and **de peur/crainte que** is formal or literary. See p. 162.

■ The subjunctive is used after certain conjunctions. The common ones are:

☐ **bien que/quoique**, *although*

bien que tout le monde se connaisse au village, personne ne lui parlait, *although everyone knew each other in the village, no-one would speak to him*

☐ **afin que/pour que**, *so that; for*

ils ont tout fait pour qu'il vienne le plus souvent possible, *they did everything so (that) he would come as often as possible*

☐ **à moins que ... (ne)**, *unless*

il y aura une catastrophe à moins que vous ne trouviez une solution rapidement, *there'll be a disaster unless you find a solution quickly*

▶ The use of **ne** (without **pas**, and with no negative

meaning) is still quite commonly found after **à moins que**, although even here it is tending to disappear except in formal or literary language. See p. 163.

☐ **que**, *whether*; **que ... que**, *whether ... whether*; **soit que ... soit que**, *whether ... whether* (literary)

> **les Français aiment le rock, qu'il soit hard ou qu'il ne le soit pas**, *the French like rock, whether it's hard or not*
>
> **qu'on parte ou non**, *whether we leave or not*

☐ **jusqu'à ce que/en attendant que**, *until*

> **restez là jusqu'à ce qu'elle vienne**, *wait there until she comes*

☐ **avant que ... (ne)**, *before*

> **ne bougez pas avant qu'elle parte**, *don't move before she goes*

The subjunctive is nowadays very commonly also used after **après que**, *after*, though not in careful or literary French.

▶ The use of **ne** after **avant que** is formal or literary. See p. 163.

☐ **pourvu que/à condition que**, *provided that*

> **oui, pourvu que vous le disiez au patron**, *yes, provided that you tell the boss*

☐ **si ... que**, *however*; **qui que**, *whoever*; **quoi que**, *whatever*

> **cet édifice, si imposant qu'il soit**, *this building, however impressive it may be*
>
> **qui qu'elle soit, quoi qu'elle dise, ne la crois pas**, *whoever she is, whatever she says, don't believe her*

▶ See also p. 233.

☐ **sans que,** *without*

> **faites-le, sans que nous en sachions rien,** *do it without us knowing anything about it*

☐ **de sorte que / de façon que / de manière que,** *so that* (= *with the inention that*)

> **on le fera, de sorte que vous puissiez voir toutes les possibilités,** *we'll do it, so that you can see all the possibilities*

Note that when these conjunctions express result, they are not followed by the subjunctive:

> **on l'a fait de sorte qu'ils ont pu voir toutes les possibilités,** *we did it in such a way that they could see all the possibilities*

■ The subjunctive is also used in the following cases:

☐ To relate back to a superlative, or to the adjectives **premier, dernier, seul, unique,** which convey a superlative idea

> **la Bretagne est la première province française qu'on ait dotée d'un programme d'action,** *Britanny is the first French province to have been provided with an action programme*

The subjunctive is not always found in these constructions.

☐ To express a 'required characteristic'

> **il cherchait quelque chose qui puisse le protéger,** *he was looking for something that could protect him*

With this construction the subjunctive is not used if the thing characterized is actually known to exist:

> **il cherchait la seule chose qui pouvait le protéger: son casque**, *he was looking for the only thing that could protect him, his helmet*

☐ To express a third person command

> **que le ciel soit loué!**, *heaven be praised!*

☐ In a second 'if' clause, where **que** is substituted for **si**

> **si tu veux nous accompagner, et que tu puisses être prêt avant huit heures, on t'emmènera**, *if you want to go with us, and you can be ready by eight o'clock, we'll take you*

The substitution of **que** for the second **si** is not obligatory; a second **si** would not be followed by the subjunctive.

☐ Instead of a conditional perfect in literary French. The tense used is the pluperfect subjunctive

> **il ne l'eût pas fait**, *he would not have done it*

Avoiding the subjunctive

Though the French use the subjunctive a great deal in everyday conversation, it is most frequently found after expressions of desire, necessity, and regret (**je veux que ..., il faut que ..., je suis désolé que ...**). Otherwise it tends to indicate high style, and expressions involving it are avoided wherever possible. So

> **il est possible qu'elle vienne aujourd'hui**, *it's possible that she'll come today*

becomes

> **peut-être qu'elle va venir aujourd'hui**, *perhaps she'll come today*

and

> **on le fera demain, à moins qu'elle ne vienne aujourd'hui**, *we'll do it tomorrow, unless she comes today*

becomes

> **on le fera demain, si elle ne vient pas aujourd'hui**, *we'll do it tomorrow, if she doesn't come today*

and

> **donne-le-lui avant qu'elle parte**, *give it to her before she goes*

becomes

> **donne-le-lui avant son départ**, *give it to her before her departure*

■ The subjunctive is also avoided where both verbs would have the same subject, by using the appropriate preposition and a dependent infinitive. English frequently does this too:

> **je suis désolé d'apprendre la mauvaise nouvelle de cette façon**, *I'm sorry to hear (that I should hear) the bad news in this way* (instead of '**je suis désolé que j'apprenne la mauvaise nouvelle de cette façon**')

▶ See p. 51 for the infinitive after verbs and pp. 51, 52 for the infinitive after adjectives.

■ In the same way, the subjunctive can be avoided with impersonal verbs by using a dependent infinitive:

> **il a fallu que je repense tout→il a fallu tout repenser**, *I had to rethink everything*

If there is any ambiguity about what the subject of the infinitive is, then a subjunctive clause must be used. The use of an indirect object with the main verb (**il m'a fallu tout repenser**) is literary.

THE INFINITIVE

The infinitive, what it is

Infinitives of French regular verbs end in **-er**, **-ir**, or **-re**, corresponding to the English *to ...* form of the verb:

> **porter**, *to wear*
> **choisir**, *to choose*
> **vendre**, *to sell*

The infinitive is the 'name' of the verb: it is really a sort of noun, and as such can be the subject or object of a verb, or stand after a preposition:

> **fumer, c'est dangereux**, *smoking is dangerous*
> **défense de fumer**, *no smoking*

Notice, in the examples above, that English usually uses the *-ing* form of the verb rather than the infinitive as the verbal noun.

Some infinitives have become true nouns and take an article. They are always masculine:

> **à prendre après manger**, *to be taken after meals* (**manger**, *to eat*)
> **un homme de savoir**, *a man of learning* (**savoir**, *to know*)

■ Pronoun objects stand in front of the infinitive:

> **pour le regarder**, *in order to look at it*

■ Both parts of a negative stand in front of the infinitive and its object pronouns:

un film à ne pas manquer, *a film not to be missed*
pour ne plus le regarder, *in order not to look at it
any more*

The infinitive after a verb

Infinitives usually follow another verb, and in English
they are joined to it by *to*. In French they are joined to it
by **à, de,** or nothing at all. Which of these is used
depends on the head verb, not on the infinitive, and it
doesn't vary—it is always, for instance, **se mettre
à** + infinitive (*begin to*), **essayer de** + infinitive (*try to*),
vouloir + infinitive (*want to*).

▶ For the correct preposition to use with any verb (**à,
de,** or nothing) see the alphabetical list on pp. 59–64.

■ It is normally impossible in French for an infinitive to
depend on the object of another verb as it can in English:

> *I want Fred to listen to me*—Fred is the object of
> *want*, but Fred is also the subject of *listen*.

A subordinate clause has to be used for this in French
(see p. 42):

> **je veux que Fred m'écoute**, *I want Fred to listen to
> me*

However, with a verb of perceiving (seeing, hearing,
feeling, etc.) a construction similar to the English one is
possible:

> **je l'ai regardé travailler**, *I watched him work*

▶ See also p. 232.

The infinitive after adjectives, nouns, and adverbs

Infinitives may also follow adjectives, nouns, and
adverbial expressions of quantity (**beaucoup, trop,** etc.).

A preposition is used before the infinitive and in most cases this is **de**:

> **je suis étonné de te voir**, *I'm surprised to see you*
> **je n'ai pas le temps de te parler**, *I haven't the time to speak to you*

Sometimes, however, the infinitive has a passive sense (*to be done* rather than *to do*), and in this case **à** is used:

> **j'ai beaucoup à faire**, *I've a lot to do* (= *to be done*)
> **j'ai deux pièces à tapisser**, *I've two rooms to paper* (= *to be papered*)
> **c'est une pièce très difficile à tapisser**, *it's a very difficult room to paper* (= *to be papered*).
> Compare: **il est très difficile de tapisser cette pièce**, *it's very difficult to paper this room*

There are one or two exceptions to this. In spite of the following infinitive having an active sense, **à** is always used with:

> **disposé à**, *willing to*
> **lent à**, *slow to*
> **prêt à**, *ready to*
> **prompt à**, *prompt in*
>
> **vous êtes prêts à partir?**, *you're ready to go?*

and with **unique, seul, dernier** and the ordinal numbers:

> **il était le seul à venir**, *he was the only one to come*

The infinitive after prepositions

▶ For infinitives following **à** and **de**:
after verbs, see pp. 55 and 56;
after adjectives, nouns and adverbs, see p. 51.

Infinitives may also follow the prepositions **après**, **par**, **sans**, and **pour**, and many compound prepositions formed with **de** (**au lieu de**, **avant de**, etc.):

> **sans bouger**, *without moving*
> **pour sortir**, *in order to go out*
> **je commence par citer Molière**, *I shall begin by quoting Molière*

■ In English, the part of the verb which follows a preposition is in almost all cases the present participle (*without looking*, *after eating*). In French it is always an infinitive, except after **en** where the present participle is used: **en revenant**, *on coming back*. See p. 35.

■ Always after **après**, and sometimes, according to meaning, after other prepositions, a perfect infinitive is used:

> **après l'avoir mangé**, *after eating (having eaten) it*
> **il est en prison pour avoir volé une voiture**, *he's in prison for having stolen a car*

▶ For the perfect infinitive, see below.

Other uses of the infinitive

■ In literary French the infinitive may be found, preceded by **de**, instead of a past historic:

> **et Yves de répondre «Mais non»**, *and Yves replied 'Of course not'*

■ The infinitive may also be used as an imperative. See p. 29.

The perfect infinitive

The perfect infinitive is formed with the infinitive of **avoir** or **être** plus the past participle of the verb:

> **avoir porté**, *to have worn*
> **être parti**, *to have gone*
> **s'être dépêché**, *to have hurried*

Past participles make the same agreements as in the compound tenses of the verb.

As well as being used after **après** and other prepositions (see p. 53), the perfect infinitive is used after a number of verbs where logic demands it. Common ones are:

> **se souvenir de/se rappeler**, *remember*
> **remercier de**, *thank for*
> **regretter de/être désolé de**, *be sorry for*
> **pardonner (à quelqu'un) de**, *forgive (somebody) for*

Beware: the tense of the equivalent English verb may not be the logical one!

> **je me souviens de l'avoir dit**, *I remember saying (having said) it*
> **je vous remercie d'avoir téléphoné**, *thank you for phoning (having phoned)*
> **elle est désolée de nous avoir dérangés**, *she's sorry to have (for having) disturbed us*
> **pardonne-moi de t'avoir retardé**, *forgive me for holding you up (having held you up)*

PREPOSITIONS AFTER VERBS

Prepositions with infinitives

In English a verb is linked to a following infinitive either by *to* (*I hope to go*) or by nothing at all (*I must go*). The constructions are invariable, we always use *hope + to*, *must* + *nothing*, whatever the infinitive that follows. The same is true of French, except that in French there are three possibilities, **de**, **à**, and nothing.

■ Verb + **de** + infinitive:

> **il essaye de le faire**, *he tries to do it*

This is by far the largest group and if a verb does not belong to one of the two other groups below, it should be assumed to take **de**.

■ Verb + nothing + infinitive

This is a relatively small group of rather common verbs. It includes:

☐ Verbs of expectancy (wanting, hoping)

> **j'espère vous revoir**, *I hope to see you again*

☐ Verbs of perception (seeing, hearing, feeling)

> **l'entends-tu venir?**, *can you hear him coming?*

☐ Verbs of liking and dislike

> **je déteste nager dans l'eau froide**, *I hate swimming in cold water*

☐ The modal verbs (**vouloir**, **pouvoir**, etc. See p. 64)

> **je ne sais pas nager**, *I can't swim*

☐ Intransitive verbs of motion (**aller**, **monter**, **sortir**, etc.)

> **va chercher ton père**, *go and look for your father* (note that the *and* used in English with these verbs is not used in French)

Pour may also be used with these verbs to stress the purpose of the action:

> **Il est entré dans le garage pour chercher une pelle**, *he went into the garage (in order) to look for a spade*

The most frequently met verbs taking an infinitive without a preposition are:

adorer, *adore*	**envoyer**, *send*	**prétendre**, *claim*
aimer (mieux), *prefer*	**espérer**, *hope*	**se rappeler**, *remember*
aller, *go*	**faillir**, *almost (do)*	**regarder**, *look at*
compter, *expect*	**faire**, *have (done)*	**rentrer**, *come in*
croire, *think*		**sembler**, *seem*
descendre, *come down*	**falloir**, *must*	**(se) sentir**, *feel*
désirer, *want*	**laisser**, *let*	**sortir**, *go out*
détester, *hate*	**monter**, *go up*	**souhaiter**, *wish*
devoir, *have to*	**oser**, *dare*	**valoir mieux**, *be better*
écouter, *listen to*	**paraître**, *seem*	
entendre, *hear*	**partir**, *go off*	**venir**, *come*
entrer, *come in*	**pouvoir**, *can*	**voir**, *see*
	préférer, *prefer*	**vouloir**, *want*

▶ For a fuller treatment of **faire** and **laisser** + infinitive see p. 71.

■ Verb + **à** + infinitive

This is also a small group of verbs. They are less heavily used, but still common. The **à** indicates aim or direction. The most frequently met verbs in this group are:

aider à, *help*	**chercher à**, *try*	**demander à**, *ask*
s'amuser à, *enjoy oneself*	**commencer à**, *begin*	**encourager à**, *encourage*
apprendre à, *learn*	**consentir à**, *consent*	**enseigner à**, *teach*
s'apprêter à, *get ready*	**consister à**, *consist (in)*	**forcer à**, *force*
arriver à, *manage*	**continuer à**, *continue*	**s'habituer à**, *get used*
s'attendre à, *expect*	**se décider à**, *decide; make up one's mind*	**hésiter à**, *hesitate*
avoir à, *have*		**s'intéresser à**, *be interested*
		inviter à, *invite*

se mettre à, start	**perdre du temps à**, waste time	**renoncer à**, *give up*
obliger à, *force*	**persister à**, persist	**rester à**, *be left*
parvenir à, *manage*		**réussir à**, *manage*
passer du temps à, spend time	**pousser à**, *urge*	**servir à**, *be used*
penser à, *think*	**(se) préparer à**, prepare	**songer à**, *think*
		tarder à, *be late*
		tenir à, *be keen*

▶ See p. 59 for an alphabetical list of infinitive and noun constructions after verbs.

Prepositions with nouns and pronouns

Most French verbs have the same preposition before a following noun as their English equivalents. There are three main groups where this is not the case.

■ Verbs with a direct object where we should expect a preposition:

> **attendez-moi**, *wait for me!*

The most frequently met verbs of this kind are:

approuver, *approve of*	**habiter**, *live at*
attendre, *wait for*	**mettre**, *put on*
chercher, *look for*	**payer**, *pay for*
demander, *ask for*	**regarder**, *look at*
écouter, *listen to*	**reprocher**, *blame for*
essayer, *try on*	

■ Verbs taking **de** where we should expect nothing:

> **elle joue du violon**, *she plays the violin*

The most frequently met verbs in this group are:

s'apercevoir de, *notice*	**discuter de**, *discuss*
s'approcher de, approach	**douter de**, *doubt*
avoir besoin de, *need*	**se douter de**, suspect
changer de, *change*	**s'emparer de**, *grab*

jouer de, *play*
(*an instrument*)
jouir de, *enjoy*
manquer de, *lack*

se méfier de, *mistrust*
se servir de, *use*
se souvenir de, *remember*
se tromper de, *mistake*

■ Verbs taking **à** where we should expect nothing:

elle joue au tennis, *she plays tennis*

The most frequently encountered verbs of this kind are:

assister à, *attend*
convenir à, *suit*
se fier à, *trust*
jouer à, *play* (*a game*)
nuire à, *harm*
(dés)obéir à, (*dis*)*obey*
pardonner à, *forgive*
(dé)plaire à, (*dis*)*please*

renoncer à, *renounce*
répondre à, *answer*
résister à, *resist*
ressembler à, *resemble*
succéder à, *succeed*
(*someone*)
survivre à, *outlive*
téléphoner à, *telephone*

Also in this group are a number of verbs that take **à** with the noun at the same time as an infinitive with **de**:

j'ai dit à Jean-Pierre de ne pas sortir, *I told Jean-Pierre not to go out*

These verbs are:

commander à ... de, *order*
conseiller à ... de, *advise*
défendre à ... de, *forbid*
demander à ... de, *ask*
dire à ... de, *tell*

ordonner à ... de, *order*
permettre à ... de, *allow*
promettre à ... de, *promise*
proposer à ... de, *suggest*

■ Verbs taking **à** or **de** where English has an entirely different preposition:

je l'ai acheté au fermier, *I bought it from the farmer*

These verbs are:

acheter à, *buy from*
arracher à, *snatch from*
blâmer de, *blame for*
boire à, *drink from*
cacher à, *hide from*
croire à, *believe in*
demander à, *ask for ... from*
dépendre de, *depend on*
doter de, *equip with*
emprunter à, *borrow from*
enlever à, *take away from*
féliciter de, *congratulate on*
s'intéresser à, *be interested in*

louer de, *praise for*
manquer à, *be missed by*
penser à, *think about*
prendre à, *take from*
punir de, *punish for*
récompenser de, *reward for*
réfléchir à, *think about*
remercier de, *thank for*
rêver à, *dream about*
rire de, *laugh at*
servir à, *be used for*
songer à, *think about*
témoigner de, *bear witness to*
toucher à, *meddle with*
vivre de, *live on*
voler à, *steal from*

Alphabetical list of verb constructions with prepositions

The list includes both verbs + preposition + infinitive, and verbs + preposition + noun. Only 'problem' verbs are included. If a verb is not included, assume that:

■ with a noun it will take the same construction as in English

■ before an infinitive it will take **de**

60 | Verbs

Abbreviations used:

> qn—**quelqu'un**
> qch—**quelque chose**
> sb—somebody
> sth—something
> INF—infinitive

acheter à qn	*buy from sb*
adorer + INF	*adore to*
aider à + INF	*help to*
aimer + INF	*like to*
aimer mieux + INF	*prefer to*
aller + INF	*go and; be going to*
s'amuser à + INF	*have fun … ing*
s'apercevoir de qch	*notice sth*
apprendre qch à qn	*teach sb sth*
apprendre à qn à + INF	*teach sb to*
apprendre à + INF	*learn to*
s'apprêter à + INF	*prepare to*
s'approcher de qn	*approach sb*
arracher à qn	*snatch from sb*
arriver à + INF	*manage to*
assister à qch	*attend/witness sth*
attendre qn	*wait for sb*
s'attendre à + INF	*expect to*
avoir qch à + INF	*have sth to*
avoir besoin de + INF	*need to*
blâmer de qch	*blame for sth*
boire à qch	*drink from/to sth*
cacher à qn	*hide from sb*
changer de qch	*change sth*
chercher qch	*look for sth*
chercher à + INF	*try to*
commander à qn de + INF	*order sb to*
commencer à (sometimes **de**) + INF	*begin to*

compter + INF	*intend to*
conseiller à qn de + INF	*advise sb to*
consentir à + INF	*agree to*
consentir à qch	*agree to sth*
consister en/dans qch	*consist of sth*
consister à + INF	*consist in*
continuer à (sometimes **de**) + INF	*continue to*
convenir à qn	*suit sb*
croire qn	*believe sb*
croire à/en qn/qch	*believe in sb/sth; trust in sb/sth*
se décider à + INF	*decide to; make up your mind to*
défendre à qn de + INF	*forbid sb to*
demander qn/qch	*ask for sb/sth*
demander qch à qn	*ask sb for sth*
demander à + INF	*ask to*
demander à qn de + INF	*ask sb to*
dépendre de qn/qch	*depend on sb/sth*
déplaire à qn	*displease sb*
descendre + INF	*go down and*
désirer + INF	*want to*
désobéir à qn	*disobey sb*
détester + INF	*hate to; detest ... ing*
devoir + INF	*have to*
dire à qn de + INF	*tell sb to*
discuter de qch	*discuss sth*
doter de qch	*equip with sth*
douter de qch	*doubt sth*
se douter de qch	*suspect sth*
écouter qn/qch	*listen to sb/sth*
écouter qn + INF	*listen to sb ... ing*
s'emparer de qch	*grab sth*
emprunter à qn	*borrow from sb*
encourager à + INF	*encourage to*

enlever à qn	*take away from sb*
enseigner qch à qn	*teach sb sth*
entendre qn + INF	*hear sb ... ing*
entrer + INF	*go/come in and*
envoyer qn + INF	*send sb to*
espérer + INF	*hope to*
essayer qch	*try sth on*
se fâcher de qch	*be annoyed about sth*
se fâcher contre qn	*be annoyed with sb*
se fier à qn	*trust sb*
faillir + INF	*almost do sth*
falloir + INF (il faut, etc.)	*must*
féliciter qn de qch	*congratulate sb on sth*
se fier à qn	*trust sb*
forcer à + INF	*force to*
habiter + PLACE	*live at/in*
habituer qn à + INF	*get sb used to ... ing*
s'habituer à + INF	*get used to ... ing*
hésiter à + INF	*hesitate to*
s'intéresser à qn/qch	*be interested in sb/sth*
s'intéresser à + INF	*be interested in ... ing*
inviter qn à + INF	*invite sb to*
jouer à qch	*play (a game)*
jouer de qch	*play (an instrument)*
jouir de qch	*enjoy sth*
laisser + INF	*let*
louer de qch	*praise for sth*
manquer de qch	*lack sth*
manquer à qn	*be missed by sb*
se marier avec qn	*marry sb*
se méfier de qn	*mistrust sb*
mettre qch	*put sth on*
se mettre à + INF	*begin to*
monter + INF	*go up (stairs) and*
nuire à qch	*harm sth*
obéir à qn	*obey sb*
obliger qn à + INF	*force sb to*

ordonner à qn de + INF	*order sb to*
oser + INF	*dare to*
paraître + INF	*appear to*
pardonner qch à qn	*forgive sb for sth*
partir + INF	*go off and; go off to*
parvenir à + INF	*manage to*
passer du temps à + INF	*spend time ... ing*
payer qch	*pay for sth*
penser à qn/qch	*think about sb/sth*
penser à + INF	*think of ... ing*
perdre du temps à + INF	*waste time ... ing*
permettre à qn de + INF	*allow sb to*
persister à + INF	*persist in ... ing*
plaire à qn	*please sb*
pousser à + INF	*urge to*
pouvoir + INF	*be able to*
préférer + INF	*prefer to*
prendre à qn	*take from sb*
préparer qn à + INF	*prepare sb to*
se préparer à	*get ready to*
prétendre + INF	*claim to*
promettre à qn de + INF	*promise sb to*
proposer à qn de + INF	*suggest to sb that they should*
punir de qch	*punish for sth*
se rappeler + PERFECT INF	*remember ... ing*
(*sometimes de* + PERF INF)	
récompenser de qch	*reward for sth*
réfléchir à qch	*think about sth*
regarder qn/qch	*look at sb/sth*
regarder qn + INF	*watch sb ... ing*
remercier de qch	*thank for sth*
renoncer à qch	*give sth up*
renoncer à + INF	*give up ... ing*
rentrer + INF	*come (back) in to*
répondre à qn/qch	*answer sb/sth*
reprocher qch à qn	*blame sb for sth*

résister à qch	*resist sth*
ressembler à qn/qch	*be like sb/sth*
rester à + INF	*remain to*
réussir à + INF	*manage to*
rêver à qn/qch	*dream about sb/sth*
rire de qn/qch	*laugh at sb/sth*
sembler + INF	*seem to*
sentir qch + INF	*feel sth ... ing*
se sentir + INF	*feel oneself ... ing*
servir à qch	*be used for sth*
servir à + INF	*be used to*
se servir de qch	*use sth*
songer à qn/qch	*think about sb/sth*
songer à + INF	*think about ... ing*
sortir + INF	*go out and*
souhaiter + INF	*want to*
se souvenir de qn/qch	*remember sb/sth*
succéder à qn	*succeed sb*
survivre à qn	*outlive sb*
tarder à + INF	*delay ... ing*
téléphoner à qn	*telephone sb*
témoigner de qch	*bear witness to sth*
tenir à + INF	*be keen to*
toucher à qch	*meddle with sth*
se tromper de qch	*mistake sth; be wrong about sth*
valoir mieux + INF	*be better to*
venir + INF	*come and; come to*
vivre de qch	*live on sth*
voir qn + INF	*see sb ... ing*
voler à qn	*steal from sb*
vouloir + INF	*want to*

MODAL VERBS

The modal verbs (auxiliary verbs of 'mood' like *can*, *must*, *will*, in English) always have a dependent infinitive:

je veux parler, *I want to speak*

Even if this infinitive is occasionally not expressed, it is always implied: **je veux bien!**, for instance, is really **je veux bien faire ce que tu as proposé!**

In French the five modal verbs are:

devoir, *must*
falloir (il faut), *have to*
pouvoir, *be allowed to*
savoir, *can*
vouloir, *will*

The meanings given above are in fact not really adequate. These verbs have a number of different meanings and shades of meaning in different uses of their various tenses. These are explained below.

Devoir

In its basic meaning **devoir** implies obligation, inner conviction, moral necessity (compare **falloir**, below). Its English equivalent is *have to* or *must*:

je dois rentrer, *I must (have to) go home*

■ Present

As well as *have to*, **devoir** in the present tense also has the sense of *should, is supposed to, is probably ... ing*:

il doit être là, *he should be there (by now)*

It can also mean *am to*:

je dois aller à Paris demain, *I'm to go to Paris tomorrow*

■ Imperfect

As well as *used to have to*, the imperfect of **devoir** can also mean *was to, was due to*:

> **on devait faire la vaisselle tous les matins avant
> sept heures**, *we used to have to wash up every
> morning before seven o'clock*
> **dans trois jours la guerre devait éclater**, *in three
> days war was to break out*

■ Perfect

The basic meaning of the perfect is *had to* (or *has had to*);
the perfect also means *must have*:

> **j'ai dû prendre le train**, *I had to (I've had to) take
> the train*
> **il a dû partir plus tôt**, *he must have left earlier*

■ Pluperfect

The pluperfect meaning is *had had to*, or *must have* (*must
have* is the same as the perfect—English has no separate
pluperfect form of *must*):

> **comme la voiture était en panne, j'avais dû
> prendre le train**, *as the car was off the road, I'd
> had to take the train*
> **elle nous répondit qu'il avait dû partir plus tôt**, *she
> replied that he must have left earlier*

■ Conditional

The conditional means *would have to*, and also *ought to* or
should:

> **s'il devenait président, on devrait quitter le pays**, *if
> he became president we should have to leave
> the country*
> **cela devrait faire votre affaire**, *that ought to
> (should) do the job for you*

■ Conditional perfect

The conditional perfect means *would have had to*, and
also *ought to have* or *should have*:

s'il était devenu président, on aurait dû quitter le pays, *if he had become president we should have had to leave the country*

il aurait dû répondre, *he ought to have (should have) replied*

■ Present subjunctive

Verbs have no future subjunctive. The present subjunctive of **devoir** is used where it is necessary to give other verbs in the subjunctive a future meaning:

je suis désolé qu'elle doive te suivre par avion, *I'm sorry she's going to fly out after you (**qu'elle te suive** could mean she's already set out)*

■ Note that **devoir** can be used impersonally, in all tenses, as an extension of **il y a**:

il doit y avoir trois cents personnes, *there must be three hundred people*

■ Used without a dependent infinitive, **devoir** means *to owe*. In this sense it is not a modal verb:

je vous dois mille francs, *I owe you a thousand francs*

Falloir

The basic meaning of **falloir** is *must* or *have to*, implying external necessity or constraint. Compare **devoir**, above.

tu dois rentrer déjà? — Mais oui, il faut absolument que je rentre: sinon, ma mère ne me permettra pas de sortir demain, *you must go home already? — Yes, I've really got to or my mother won't let me come out tomorrow*

■ **Falloir** is always an impersonal verb, used only in the **il** form (**il faut, il fallait**, etc.). The person need not be expressed at all if it is obvious who is involved:

> **Pierre, il faut téléphoner à ta grand–mère**, *you must phone your grandmother, Pierre*

The real subject can be expressed by a dative:

> **il me faut partir**, *I have to go*

but this is rather formal, and spoken French prefers a subjunctive clause if it is necessary to say who is involved:

> **il faut que je parte**, *I've got to go*

Pouvoir

Pouvoir means basically *can* or *be allowed to*. Parts of the English verb *can* are missing and *be able to* or *be allowed to* has sometimes to be substituted when translating.

> **peut-on sortir par ici?**, *can we (are we allowed to) go out this way?*
> **l'eau est bonne, on pourra nager**, *the water's fine, we'll be able to go swimming*

As well as *be allowed to* and *can*, **pouvoir** can also mean *may*, either as the politer form of *can*, or expressing possibility:

> **puis-je parler à votre patron?**, *may I speak to your boss?*
> **il peut toujours venir**, *he may still come*

Note too the reflexive form, **se pouvoir**:

> **cela se peut**, *that's possible*

■ Perfect

Means *was able to* or *could* (in a past sense), or *may have*:

> **je n'ai pas pu ouvrir la boîte**, *I couldn't open the tin*

> **elle a pu se tromper de train**, *she may have got the wrong train*

■ Conditional

Means *would be able to* or *could* (in a conditional sense), and also *might*:

> **si tu payais, je pourrais t'accompagner**, *if you paid I could (would be able to) come with you*
> **je crois qu'il pourrait neiger**, *I think it might snow*

■ Conditional perfect

Means *would have been able to* or *could have*, also *might have*:

> **si tu avais payé, j'aurais pu t'accompagner**, *if you'd paid, I could have (would have been able to) come with you*
> **elle aurait pu se présenter avant le début du spectacle**, *she might have turned up before the play started*

■ **Pouvoir** can be used impersonally as an extension of **il y a**:

> **il pourrait y en avoir mille**, *there might be a thousand of them*

■ With verbs of perception (**entendre, voir, sentir**) English uses *can* or *could* where French prefers the simple verb:

> **je le voyais atterrir**, *I could see it landing*

Savoir

Savoir means *can* in the sense of *know how to*. Compare **pouvoir** above.

> **l'eau est bonne, on peut nager — Mais moi, je ne sais pas nager**, *the water's fine, we can go swimming—But I can't swim*

■ Conditional

In careful or formal language, the negative conditional of **savoir** is used as a politer form of *I can't*. In this use the **pas** is always omitted:

> **je ne saurais faire cela**, *I don't really think I can do that*

With the full negative **je ne saurais pas** means *would not know how to*, *couldn't* (in a moral sense):

> **je ne saurais pas faire quelque chose comme ça**, *I couldn't do anything like that*

■ **Savoir** is most frequently found used without a dependent infinitive, meaning *to know*. In this use it is not a modal verb:

> **je sais qu'elle est là**, *I know she's there*

Vouloir

The basic meaning of **vouloir** is *to wish* or *want*:

> **je veux vous dire quelque chose**, *I want to tell you something*

It also means *will*, *be willing to*. **Bien** is used where English stresses *will*:

> **oui, je veux bien le faire**, *yes, I will do it*
> **la moto ne veut pas démarrer**, *the bike won't start*

It can also mean *attempt to* or *intend to*:

> **j'ai voulu l'embrasser**, *I tried to kiss her*
> **qu'est-ce qu'il veut faire?**, *what does he mean to do?*

■ Conditional, conditional perfect

As well as *should wish*, *should want* (conditional), and *should have wished*, *should have wanted* (conditional perfect), these tenses also have the meanings *should like* and *should have liked*:

> **je voudrais être à sa place**, *I'd like to be in her place*
>
> **j'aurais voulu la revoir**, *I'd have liked to see her again*

With this meaning **je voudrais** is a standard way of asking politely for things:

> **je voudrais deux cents grammes de pâté s'il vous plaît**, *I'd like two hundred grams of pâté, please*

■ Vouloir may also be used as a polite form of the imperative.

▶ See p. 29.

FAIRE + INFINITIVE AND SIMILAR CONSTRUCTIONS

Faire + infinitive

Faire + infinitive means *to have something done, to get something done, to get someone to do something*:

> **j'ai fait téléphoner à ses parents**, *I've got someone to phone his parents*
>
> **elle a fait enlever ce qui restait du repas**, *she had what was left of the meal taken away*

■ Position of objects with **faire** + infinitive

□ Noun objects of either verb follow both verbs

> **tu as fait jouer Pierre?**, *you got Pierre to play?*
>
> **tu as fait repeindre la porte?**, *you've had the door painted?*

☐ Pronoun objects of either verb come before both verbs

> **tu l'as fait jouer?**, *you got him to play?*
> **tu l'as fait repeindre?**, *you've had it painted?*

☐ If both verbs need an object, the object of **faire** is indirect (**à ...**), since in French a double direct object is impossible.

> **la nouvelle a fait perdre son sang-froid à mon**
> **père**, *the news made my father lose his temper*

■ **Faire** + reflexive verbs

If the dependent verb is reflexive it loses its object pronoun:

> **je les ai fait asseoir** (not **s'asseoir**), *I got them to*
> *sit down*
> **elle les a fait taire**, *she shut them up*

So if you find a reflexive pronoun in this construction it must belong to **faire** (*have oneself ..., get oneself ...*):

> **elle s'est fait virer du lycée**, *she got herself thrown*
> *out of school*

■ Agreement of past participle of **faire**

In the **faire** + infinitive construction the past participle **fait** is invariable: it never agrees with a preceding direct object. See the last two examples above (**je les ai fait ..., elle s'est fait ...**).

Laisser, voir, entendre, sentir + infinitive

■ **Laisser** + infinitive means *to let something be done* or *to let someone do something*:

> **tu l'as déjà laissé revenir?**, *you've let him come*
> *back already?*

j'ai dû le laisser passer, *I had to let him go through*

■ **Voir/entendre/sentir** + infinitive mean *to see/hear/ feel something happen*:

on l'a vu partir, *we saw him go*
je me sens guérir, *I can feel myself getting better*

■ All points made above with regard to **faire** concerning objects and past participle agreement may also apply to this group of verbs, though they are quite often ignored:

tu lui as laissé repeindre ta porte?, or very often
tu l'as laissé repeindre ta porte?, *you've let him paint your door?*

English equivalents of faire, etc. + infinitive

Some infinitive constructions of the verbs considered above are the equivalent of a simple verb or a verb plus preposition in English. The most common are:

entendre dire que, *hear that*
entendre parler de, *hear about*
faire entrer, *let in; show in*
faire sortir, *let out; show out*
faire venir, *send for*
faire voir, *show*
laisser tomber, *drop*

Similar constructions with other verbs used with an infinitive are:

aller chercher, *go for*
envoyer chercher, *send for*
venir chercher, *come for*
vouloir dire, *mean*

IMPERSONAL VERBS

Impersonal verbs are verbs whose subject is **il** or **ce/cela** meaning *it* or *there*.

Impersonal verbs with il

These are of two kinds: those that are always constructed with **il**, and those where **il** is simply a temporary subject so that the real subject can be held back until later in the sentence.

■ Real subject **il**

In this group are:

☐ Weather verbs, e.g.

il pleut, *it's raining*
il neige, *it's snowing*
il gèle, *it's freezing*
il tonne, *it's thundering*
il y a du brouillard, *it's foggy*
il fait du vent, *it's windy*
il fait beau, *it's fine*
il fait mauvais, *the weather's bad*
il fait chaud/froid, *it's hot/cold*

☐ **Être** used with time of day

il est cinq heures, *it's five o'clock*
il est midi et demi, *it's half past twelve*
il est tard, *it's late*

☐ **Il y a**, *there is, there are*

il y a trente mille personnes dans le stade, *there are thirty thousand people in the stadium*

Il y a is always singular.

▶ **Il y a** can also be used with **devoir** and **pouvoir**: **il peut y avoir ...**, *there may be ...* See pp. 67 and 69.

☐ A large number of other impersonal expressions, of which some of the commonest are:

> **Il s'agit de**, *it's a question of; it's about*
> **Il m'est arrivé de**, *I happened to*
> **Il faut (que)**, *you (we, they, etc.) must/need*
> **Il paraît que**, *it appears that*
> **Il semble que**, *it seems that*
> **Il suffit de**, *you only have to*
> **Il vaut mieux**, *it's better to*

Notice also

> **Il était une fois**, *once upon a time*

■ **Il** to hold back the real subject

Any verb can be used in this way; it remains singular, agreeing with **il**, even if the real subject is plural:

> **Il pousse beaucoup de fleurs au Sahara**, *there are lots of flowers (that grow) in the Sahara*
> **Il reste encore dix minutes**, *there are ten minutes still left*
> **Il me manque dix francs**, *I need ten francs* (literally: *there is lacking to me ten francs*)

☐ The real subject may be a noun, as in the examples above; or it may be a clause

> **Il me brûlait les lèvres de demander à quoi ça servait**, *I was dying to ask what that was for*

☐ The real subject may be an infinitive clause, following an adjective plus **de**. The pattern is: **il est** + adjective + **de** + infinitive clause

> **Il est difficile de concevoir quelque chose de plus imposant**, *it is difficult to conceive of anything more impressive*

In spoken French **c'est** is often used instead of **il est** in this construction.

□ The real subject may be a clause introduced by **que**, following an adjective. The pattern is: **il est** + adjective + **que** + clause

> **il est évident qu'elle mange trop**, *it's obvious that she eats too much*

Here too, **c'est** is often used instead of **il est** in spoken French.

Impersonal verbs with ce or cela/ça as subject

Ce (*it*) is used as the subject of **être**, and **cela/ça** (*it, that*) as the subject of any verb (including **être**), to stand for a previously expressed clause:

> **il est facile de mentir — Ah oui, c'est facile**, *it's easy to tell lies—Oh yes, it's easy* (**c'** refers back to **de mentir**)
>
> **si elle ment, c'est qu'elle ne veut pas vous parler de Jean-Claude**, *if she's lying, it's because she doesn't want to talk to you about Jean-Claude* (**c'** refers back to **si elle ment**)
>
> **tout ce que j'ai dit me paraît évident — Oui, cela prouve que tu es fou!**, *everything I've said seems obvious to me—Yes, that proves you're crazy!* (**cela** refers back to **tout ce que j'ai dit me paraît évident**)

C'est + adjective is also used extremely often in spoken French instead of **il est** + adjective:

> **c'est** (for: **il est**) **facile de mentir — Ah oui, c'est facile**

Articles

The definite article *77*
The indefinite and partitive articles *80*

Articles are words like *a* and *the*. Nouns are rarely used
without an article in French. If the noun has no article in
English, it is most likely to have a definite article in
French. There are, however, quite a number of
exceptions to this—see below.

THE DEFINITE ARTICLE

The definite article (*the* in English) has four forms, **le**,
la, or **l'** with singular nouns, **les** with plural nouns. **Le** is
used before a masculine singular noun, **la** before a
feminine singular noun, **l'** before a singular noun of
either gender beginning with a vowel or **h** 'mute'*. **Les** is
used before a plural noun of either gender:

> **le garçon**, *the boy*; **la fille**, *the girl*; **le haricot**, *the
> bean*
>
> **l'homme**, *the man*; **l'arbre**, *the tree*
>
> **les garçons**, *the boys*; **les filles**, *the girls*; **les
> haricots**, *the beans*;
>
> **les hommes**, *the men*; **les arbres**, *the trees*

Le and **les** compound with **à** and **de** to produce **au**,
aux (*to the*) and **du**, **des** (*of the*), thus:

---

* In older French some **h**'s were pronounced and some
were not, which accounts for **le haricot** and **l'homme**.
There is no pronunciation difference in modern French
(no **h**'s are pronounced), and there are no rules to
decide whether an **h** is 'mute' or not.

$$\begin{aligned}
\text{à} + \text{le} &= \text{au} & \text{de} + \text{le} &= \text{du} \\
\text{à} + \text{les} &= \text{aux} & \text{de} + \text{les} &= \text{des}
\end{aligned}$$

A la and **à l'**, **de la** and **de l'** do not change.

The same changes are found in the compound words **auquel, auxquels, auxquelles** (*to whom; to which*) and **duquel, desquels, desquelles** (*of whom; of which*).

Using the definite article

The definite article is used in French in a number of places where we should omit it in English.

■ When generalizing:

> **aimez-vous les animaux?**, *do you like animals?*
> (i.e. animals in general)

■ With abstract nouns:

> **c'est comme ça, la vie**, *life's like that*
> **l'amour de la patrie**, *love of country*

But not with abstract nouns after **avec** and **sans**:

> **avec difficulté**, *with difficulty*
> **sans occupation**, *unemployed*

■ With parts of the body, especially when used as the object of a verb:

> **levez le bras**, *raise your arm*

A reflexive indirect object pronoun is added in this construction when the action is done to, rather than with, the part of the body mentioned:

> **elle s'est lavé le visage**, *she has washed her face*

■ With names preceded by adjective or titles:

> **le vieux Corneille**, *old Corneille*
> **le président Mitterrand**, *President Mitterrand*

■ With names of countries, areas, mountains, lakes:

> **l'Angleterre**, *England*; **la Corse**, *Corsica* (but **en Angleterre**, **d'Angleterre**, *in/from England*; **en Corse**, **de Corse**, *in/from Corsica*); **le Mont-Blanc**, *Mont Blanc*; **le lac Trasimène**, *Lake Trasimeno*

■ With names of languages:

> **j'apprends le français**, *I'm learning French*
> **tu parles bien le français**, *you speak French well*

The article is omitted, however, after **parler** where the name of the language follows without any other qualification:

> **il parle français**, *he speaks French*

■ With days, mealtimes, seasons, religious festivals:

> **je déteste le lundi**, *I hate Monday(s)*
> **tu prends le petit déjeuner?**, *do you want breakfast?*
> **c'est l'hiver qui revient**, *winter's back*
> **le vendredi saint**, *Good Friday*
> **la Toussaint**, *All Saints' Day* (but the article is omitted with **Pâques**, *Easter*, and **Noël**, *Christmas*)

■ With school subjects and games:

> **aimes-tu les maths?**, *do you like maths?*
> **ici, on joue au rugby**, *here they play rugby*
> **il déteste les sports**, *he hates games*

Definite article for indefinite article

The definite article is used in a number of places where we should use the indefinite article (*a, an*).

■ When expressing quantity after price:

douze francs le kilo, *twelve francs a kilo*
cent francs la bouteille, *a hundred francs a bottle*

■ When expressing speed:

cent vingt kilomètres à l'heure, *120 km an hour*
(note the addition of **à** in French)

■ French also uses a definite article in a number of set expressions where in English we should use an indefinite article or no article at all:

il s'est couché le dernier/le premier, *he went to bed last/first*
l'un d'eux, *one of them*
au lit, *in bed*
au régime, *on a diet*
à la maison, *at home*
à l'école, *at school*
à l'église, *in church*

Omission of the definite article

The definite article is omitted in French in forming an attributive noun (a noun used as an adjective):

du pâté de campagne, *country pâté*
un tronc d'arbre, *a tree trunk*
les fromages de France, *French cheeses*

Compare these with:

un goût de la campagne, *a taste of the countryside*
le tronc de l'arbre, *the trunk of the tree*
le nord de la France, *the north of France*

THE INDEFINITE AND PARTITIVE ARTICLES

It is convenient to consider these two forms of article together, since there is much similarity in their use in French.

The indefinite article, what it is

The indefinite article (*a*, *an*, *some/any* in English) has
three forms: **un** with masculine singular nouns, **une** with
feminine singular nouns, **des** with plural nouns:

> **un garçon**, *a boy*; **une fille**, *a girl*; **un haricot**, *a
> bean*
> **un homme**, *a man*; **un arbre**, *a tree*
> **des garçons**, *some boys*; **des arbres**, *some trees*

The partitive article, what it is

The partitive article (*some* in English, or *any* in questions
and after negatives) has three forms, **du**, **de la**, and **de
l'**. They are used before singular 'uncountable' nouns,
i.e. nouns like *milk*, *sugar*, etc. that cannot normally be
used in the plural. **Du** is used before a masculine noun,
de la before a feminine noun, **de l'** before a noun of
either gender beginning with a vowel or **h** 'mute':

> **du chocolat**, *some chocolate*
> **de la confiture**, *some jam*
> **de l'argent**, *some money*

The partitive is sometimes said to have a plural form,
des. Strictly speaking, however, **des** is the plural of the
indefinite article: the singular of **des vins** is **un vin**, not
du vin.

Du/de la/des or le/la/les?

English sometimes does not use any article at all before
nouns:

> **vous prenez du lait?**, *do you take milk?*
> **je déteste le lait**, *I hate milk*

This raises the problem of whether to use **du/de la/des** or **le/la/les** where English has a noun with no article. **Du/de la/des** particularizes, **le/la/les** generalizes: **du/de la/des** means 'some', **le/la/les** implies 'all'. So:

> **vous avez du jus d'orange?**, *do you have orange juice?* (i.e., some orange juice)
>
> **j'aime le jus d'orange**, *I like orange juice* (i.e., orange juice in general, all orange juice)
>
> **il y a des mouches dans ma soupe**, *there are flies in my soup* (some flies, not all the flies that exist)
>
> **je n'aime pas les mouches**, *I don't like flies* (all flies, any flies at all, not just some flies)

De for des, etc.

■ After a negative the indefinite article (**un/une/des**) and the partitive article (**du/de la/de l'**) become **de** (**d'** before a vowel or **h** 'mute'). English may use *any* for this:

> **j'ai du temps**, *I have time*
>
> **je n'ai pas de temps à perdre**, *I've no time (I haven't any time) to lose*
>
> **il n'y a pas de pellicule dans l'appareil-photo**, *there isn't any film in the camera*
>
> **je n'ai pas d'appareil-photo**, *I don't have (haven't got) a camera*

Ne ... que is not regarded as negative as far as this rule is concerned:

> **je n'ai qu'un très vieil appareil**, *I've only a very old camera*

A negative *is* followed by an indefinite or partitive article if what is negated is the identity of the noun:

ce n'est pas un train, c'est un tramway, *it isn't a train, it's a tram*

■ The plural indefinite article **des** becomes **de** (**d'** before a vowel or **h** 'mute') when the noun following is preceded by an adjective:

j'ai eu d'incroyables difficultés, *I've had unbelievable difficulties*

This rule is often ignored where the meaning of the phrase centres on the noun rather than the adjective:

des jolies filles, *pretty girls*

It is always ignored where the adjective + noun pair forms a set expression:

des petits pois, *peas*
des petits pains, *bread rolls*

Before the adjective **autres**, however, you must keep to **d'**:

d'autres voyageurs ont dit ..., *other travellers have said ...*

■ After the preposition **de** (*of*) the partitive article **du/ de la/de l'** and the plural indefinite article **des** are always omitted:

j'ai besoin d'argent, *I need (some) money*
c'était un grand cratère plein d'eau, *it was a great crater full of (some) water*

This means that expressions of quantity, which all incorporate the preposition **de** (*of*), omit **du/de la/de l'/ des**:

un verre de vin, *a glass of wine*
beaucoup de vin, *a lot of wine*

But note that the definite article, meaning *the*, is NOT omitted in such cases:

> **j'ai acheté une bouteille du vin qu'il nous a fait goûter**, *I bought a bottle of the wine he let us taste*

Nor is the indefinite article in the singular omitted:

> **il lui restait quelques bouteilles d'un vin très ancien**, *he still had a few bottles of a very old wine*

The expressions of quantity **encore** (*more*) and **bien** (*many*) are intensifying adverbs not incorporating the preposition **de** and are followed by **du/de la/des**:

> **encore du pain, s'il vous plaît!**, *more bread please!*
> **bien des gens disent cela**, *many people say that*

Omission of the indefinite article

The indefinite article is omitted in French in the following cases where, in the singular, it would be used in English.

■ In apposition (i.e., where a second noun is placed directly after a first one in order to explain it):

> **M. Duval, ancien combattant de la guerre de quatorze-dix-huit**, *M. Duval, a veteran of the 14–18 war*

Definite articles, however, are not dropped in apposition:

> **M. Duval, l'ancien combattant dont nous parlons**, *M. Duval, the veteran we're speaking about*

■ After **il est/elle est/**NOUN **est**, followed by the name of a profession:

> **il est menuisier**, *he's a joiner*
> **son fils est avocat**, *his son's a lawyer*

But not after **c'est**:

> **c'est un menuisier**, *he's a joiner*

■ After **quel!**:

> **quel imbécile!**, *what a fool!*

■ After **sans**:

> **les voyageurs sans billet**, *passengers without a ticket*

The partitive article is also omitted in this case, as in English:

> **une journée sans vin est une journée sans soleil**, *a day without wine is a day without sunshine*

■ In lists, both the indefinite article and the partitive article may be omitted, as in English:

> **on y voyait des moutons**, *sheep could be seen there*

but:

> **on y voyait moutons, vaches, porcs, poules, tous mélangés**, *sheep, cattle, pigs, chickens could be seen there, all higgledy piggledy*

> **on nous offrait du mouton**, *we were offered lamb*

but:

> **on nous offrait mouton, porc, veau, bœuf ... toutes sortes de viandes**, *we were offered lamb, pork, veal, beef—all kinds of meat*

This use is rather literary.

Nouns

GENDER OF NOUNS

English has three genders: masculine, feminine, and neuter (*he, she, it*). French has only two: masculine and feminine. Most nouns denoting male people are masculine, most denoting female people are feminine. Names of inanimate objects may be either masculine or feminine. Unlike English nouns, French nouns make their gender obvious by means of the article in front of them and the adjectives that go with them.

The rules for gender in French are very far from watertight and there are many exceptions to all of them. As an overall rule of thumb for an unknown noun: if it ends in **-e** it is more likely to be feminine, if not it is more likely to be masculine.

Masculine groups

■ Workers, traders, names of males, and many names of animals are masculine:

> **le constructeur**, *builder*; **le boulanger**, *baker*; **le lion**, *lion*; **le fils**, *son*

Many but not all of these also have feminine forms: see p. 93. **Une autruche** (*ostrich*), **la baleine** (*whale*), **la girafe** (*giraffe*), **la panthère** (*panther*), **la souris** (*mouse*), **la fourmi** (*ant*) are always feminine.

■ Days, months, seasons, weights, measures, numerals, fractions, points of the compass, languages are masculine:

> **le vendredi**, *Friday*; **(le) janvier**, *January*; **le printemps**, *spring*; **le kilo**, *kilo*; **le kilomètre**, *kilometre*; **le douze**, *twelve*; **le quart**, *quarter*; **le sud**, *south*; **le français**, *French*

Exceptions: **la livre**, *pound*; **la tonne**, *(metric) ton*; **la moitié**, *half*

■ Trees, shrubs, metals are masculine:

> **le hêtre**, *beech*; **le laurier**, *laurel*; **le fer**, *iron*

Exceptions: **la bruyère**, *heather*; **la ronce**, *bramble*; **une aubépine**, *hawthorn*

■ Countries, rivers, vegetables and fruit not ending –e are masculine:

> **le Japon**, *Japan*; **le Nil**, *Nile*; **le chou**, *cabbage*; **le citron**, *lemon*

■ Most nouns of English origin are masculine:

> **le baby-foot**, *pin-table football*; **le hit-parade**, *hit parade*

Exception: **une interview**, *interview*

■ Words not originally nouns, when used as nouns, are masculine:

> **un joli rose**, *a pretty pink*
> **un oui suivi d'un non**, *a yes followed by a no*
> **on peut apporter son manger**, *you may bring your own food*

Exception: adjectives and participles used as nouns have the gender that their ending shows. So: **le passant, la passante**, *passer-by*; **une allée**, *path*; **la nouvelle**, *piece of news*; **la sortie**, *way out*

■ Nouns with the following endings are masculine:

-acle and **-icle**:

le spectacle, *show*; un article, *article*

-age:

le garage

Exceptions: la cage, *cage*; une image, *picture*;
la nage, *swimming*; la page, *page*; la plage,
beach; la rage, *rage, rabies*

-ail:

le travail, *work*

-asme and **-isme**:

le sarcasme, *sarcasm*; le communisme,
communism

-c:

le lac, *lake*

-é:

le péché, *sin*

-eau:

le bateau, *boat*

Exceptions: une eau, *water*; la peau, *skin*

-ège:

le collège, *secondary school*

-ème:

le poème, *poem*

Exception: la crème, *cream*

-er and **-ier**:

le clocher, *steeple*; le papier, *paper*

Exceptions: la mer, *sea*; la cuiller, *spoon* (also
spelled, and always pronounced, cuillère)

-ment:

le sentiment, *sentiment*

Exception: la jument, *mare*

-oir:

le couloir, *corridor*

-ou:

le trou, *hole*

■ Concrete nouns ending **-eur** are masculine:

> **le moteur**, *engine*

Abstract nouns ending **-eur** are feminine: **la grandeur**, *greatness*

■ Common traps! The following nouns ending **-e** look extremely feminine—they are all masculine:

> **le crime**, *crime*; **le disque**, *record*; **le groupe**, *group*; **le manque**, *lack*; **le mélange**, *mixture*; **le reste**, *remainder*; **le risque**, *risk*; **le silence**, *silence*; **le vice**, *vice*

Feminine groups

■ Feminine forms of traders, workers, animals; names of females:

> **la boulangère**, *baker*; **une électricienne**, *electrician*; **la lionne**, *lioness*; **la fille**, *girl*

Many feminine forms, for historical reasons, do not exist; many others (like **l'électricienne** above) are being newly coined; some (e.g. **la mairesse**, *mayoress*, i.e., *mayor's wife*) can still only refer to the wife of the male. In the animals group, no feminine forms exist of **un éléphant**, *elephant*, **un hippopotame**, *hippopotamus*, **le vautour**, *vulture*.

▶ See also p. 93 for the formation of feminine nouns.

■ Countries, rivers, vegetables and fruit ending **-e** are feminine:

> **la Hollande**, *Holland*; **la Tamise**, *Thames*; **la poire**, *pear*; **la carotte**, *carrot*; **la marguerite**, *daisy*

Exceptions: **le Mexique**, *Mexico*; **le Danube**; **le Rhône**; **le légume**, *vegetable*

■ Shops and trades, arts and sciences, religious festivals are feminine:

> **la boucherie**, *butcher's*; **la menuiserie**, *joinery*; **la sculpture**, *sculpture*; **la chimie**, *chemistry*; **la Pentecôte**, *Whitsun*; **la Toussaint**, *All Saints' Day*

Exception: **un joyeux Noël**, *happy Christmas* (but, in some parts of France, **à la Noël**, short for **à la fête** (*festival*) **de Noël**)

■ Nouns with the following endings are feminine:

-ace:
> **la grâce**, *grace*
> Exception: **un espace**, *space*

-ade:
> **la baignade**, *bathing*
> Exceptions: **le grade**, *grade*; **le stade**, *stadium*

-ance (and the similarly pronounced endings **-anse, -ence, ense**):
> **la dépendance**, *dependence*; **la danse**, *dance*; **la conscience**, *conscience*; **la défense**, *defence*
> Exception: **le silence**, *silence*

-che:
> **la tâche**, *task*
> Exceptions: **le manche**, *handle*; **le reproche**, *reproach*; **le caniche**, *poodle*

-ée:
> **la matinée**, *morning*
> Exceptions: **le musée**, *museum*; **le lycée**, *sixth-form college*

-elle:
> **la querelle**, *quarrel*

-ère:
> **la lumière**, *light*
> Exceptions: **le frère**, *brother*; **le père**, *father*; **le cimetière**, *cemetery*; **le mystère**, *mystery*; **le caractère**, *character*; **le cratère**, *crater*

-esse:

> **la faiblesse**, *weakness*

-ie:

> **la pluie**, *rain*
> Exceptions: **le génie**, *genius*; **un incendie**, *fire*;
> **le parapluie**, *umbrella*

-ine and -une:

> **la piscine**, *swimming pool*; **la fortune**, *fortune*

-ion:

> **la concentration**, *concentration*
> Exceptions: **le camion**, *lorry*; **un espion**, *spy*

-ison (and **-aison**):

> **la prison**, *prison*; **la maison**, *house*
> Exceptions: **le bison**, *bison*; **le vison**, *mink*

-oire:

> **la foire**, *fair*
> Exceptions: **le laboratoire**, *laboratory*; **le**
> **pourboire**, *tip*; **un observatoire**,
> *observatory*; **l'ivoire**, *ivory*

-onne:

> **la couronne**, *crown*

-te (and **-tte**, **-ette**):

> **la date**, *date*; **la patte**, *paw*; **la buvette**, *bar*
> Exception: **le squelette**, *skeleton*

-té and -tié:

> **la beauté**, *beauty*; **la pitié**, *pity*
> Exceptions: **le côté**, *side*; **le comté**, *county*; **le**
> **traité**, *treaty*; **le pâté**, (*meat, fish*) *pâté*

-ure:

> **la nature**, *nature*
> Exceptions: **le murmure**, *murmur*; **le mercure**,
> *mercury*

Very many of the above are abstract nouns: most abstract nouns, whatever their endings, are in fact feminine.

■ Abstract nouns ending **-eur** are feminine:

> **la chaleur**, *heat*

Exceptions: **le bonheur**, *happiness*; **le malheur**, *unhappiness*; **un honneur**, *honour*; **le déshonneur**, *dishonour*; **le labeur**, *labour*

Concrete nouns ending **-eur** are masculine: **le carburateur**, *carburettor*

■ Common traps! The following nouns ending in a consonant look extremely masculine—they are all feminine:

la chair, *flesh*; **la clef**, *key*; **la croix**, *cross*; **la façon**, *way, manner*; **la faim**, *hunger*; **la soif**, *thirst*; **la souris**, *mouse*; **la vis**, *screw*

Nouns with different meanings according to gender

masculine	*feminine*
l'aide, *assistant* (*male*)	**l'aide**, *assistance*; *assistant* (*female*)
le crêpe, *crêpe*	**la crêpe**, *pancake*
le critique, *critic*	**la critique**, *criticism*
le faux, *forgery*	**la faux**, *scythe*
le livre, *book*	**la livre**, *pound*
le manche, *handle*	**la manche**, *sleeve* (**la Manche**, *English Channel*)
le manœuvre, *labourer*	**la manœuvre**, *manœuvre*
le mémoire, *memorandum*	**la mémoire**, *memory*
le mode, *method; way*	**la mode**, *fashion; manner*
le mort, *dead man*	**la mort**, *death*
le moule, *mould*	**la moule**, *mussel*
un office, *office; religious service*	**une office**, *pantry*

le page, *page(boy)*	**la page**, *page (of a book)*
le pendule, *pendulum*	**la pendule**, *clock*
le physique, *physique*	**la physique**, *physics*
le poêle, *stove*	**la poêle**, *frying pan*
le poste, *set (e.g. TV); (military) post; (fire, police) station*	**la poste**, *post (= mail); post office*
le somme, *nap*	**la somme**, *sum*
le tour, *trick; tour*	**la tour**, *tower*
le vapeur, *steamer (boat)*	**la vapeur**, *steam*
le vase, *vase*	**la vase**, *mud; silt*
le voile, *veil*	**la voile**, *sail*

Gender of compound nouns

There are many exceptions, but

■ Compounds of two nouns or a noun plus adjective take the gender of the (first) noun:

le chou-fleur, *cauliflower*

■ Compounds where the first element is part of a verb are masculine:

le tire-bouchon, *corkscrew*

■ When in doubt about the gender of a compound noun, choose masculine.

FEMININE OF NOUNS

Professions, positions, nationalities, names of relationships, domestic animals (and a few wild ones) mostly have both masculine and feminine forms according to sex:

le vendeur, *salesman*	**la vendeuse**, *saleswoman*
le Français, *Frenchman*	**la Française**, *Frenchwoman*
le cousin, (*male*) *cousin*	**la cousine**, (*female*) *cousin*
le chien, *dog*	**la chienne**, *bitch*

With professions and positions the feminine form quite often still means *wife of the* ..., though this is not the case with the newer professions:

> **la mairesse**, *mayoress; wife of the mayor*
> **l'informaticienne**, (*female*) *computer programmer*

With animals, where two forms exist, the masculine form is used as the general term; the feminine form is only used where a specific distinction of sex is being made. Exception: **la chèvre** (general term for *goat*; masculine is **le bouc**, *billy-goat*)

■ The regular feminine endings are:

masculine noun	*feminine form*
-e	no change
le Russe, *Russian*	**la Russe**
-er	**-ère**
un ouvrier, *worker*	**une ouvrière**
-eur	**-euse**
le dormeur, *sleeper*	**la dormeuse**
-f	**-ve**
le veuf, *widower*	**la veuve**
-en, -on, -et	**-enne, -onne, -ette**
le chien, *dog*	**la chienne**
le Breton, *Breton*	**la Bretonne**
le cadet, *junior*	**la cadette**
-teur	**-teuse**: where the noun is based on the present participle of a verb

<table>
<tbody>
<tr><td></td><td>-trice: in all other cases</td></tr>
<tr><td>le menteur, lier</td><td>la menteuse (p.p. mentant)</td></tr>
<tr><td>le directeur, director</td><td>la directrice (p.p. dirigeant)</td></tr>
<tr><td>-x</td><td>-se</td></tr>
<tr><td>un époux, spouse,
husband</td><td>une épouse</td></tr>
</tbody>
</table>

With other endings the feminine, where it exists, is formed by adding **–e**:

un ami, *friend*	**une amie**
un Anglais, *Englishman*	**une Anglaise**

■ Nouns with an irregular feminine form:

masculine	*feminine*
un abbé, *abbot*	**une abbesse**
un ambassadeur, *ambassador*	**une ambassadrice**
un âne, *donkey*	**une ânesse**
le canard, *drake*	**la canne**, *duck*
le chat, *cat*	**la chatte**
le comte, *count*	**la comtesse**
le compagnon, *companion*	**la compagne**
le copain, *pal*	**la copine**
le dieu, *god*	**la déesse**
le dindon, *turkey*	**la dinde**
le duc, *duke*	**la duchesse**
un empereur, *emperor*	**une impératrice**
le fils, *son*	**la fille**, *daughter*
le Grec, *Greek*	**la Grecque**
le héros, *hero*	**l'héroïne**
l'hôte, *host*	**l'hôtesse**
un inspecteur, *inspector*	**une inspectrice**
le jumeau, *twin*	**la jumelle**

le loup, *wolf*	la louve
le maître, *master*	la maîtresse
le mulet, *mule*	la mule
le nègre (pejorative), *negro*	la négresse
le neveu, *nephew*	la nièce
le paysan, *peasant*	la paysanne
le pécheur, *sinner*	la pécheresse
le prêtre, *priest*	la prêtresse
le prince, *prince*	la princesse
le Suisse, *Swiss*	la Suissesse
le tigre, *tiger*	la tigresse
le traître, *traitor*	la traîtresse
le Turc, *Turk*	la Turque

■ Nouns with an entirely different feminine form.

As in English, the feminine form may be expressed by an entirely different word. Among the commonest of these are:

masculine	*feminine*
le cerf, *stag*	la biche, *hind*
le cheval, *horse*	la jument, *mare*
le coq, *cock*	la poule, *hen*
l'étalon, *stallion*	la jument, *mare*
le frère, *brother*	la sœur, *sister*
le garçon, *boy*	la fille, *girl*
l'homme, *man*	la femme, *woman*
le mari, *husband*	la femme, *wife*
l'oncle, *uncle*	la tante, *aunt*
le parrain, *godfather*	la marraine, *godmother*
le père, *father*	la mère, *mother*
le porc, *pig*	la truie, *sow*
le roi, *king*	la reine, *queen*
le serviteur, *servant*	la servante, *servant*
le taureau, *bull*	la vache, *cow*

■ Nouns unchanged in the feminine form:

un/une enfant, *child*

plus masculine nouns ending **-e**.

■ Nouns with only one gender, whatever the sex of the person they refer to:

un ange, *angel*

un amateur, *lover, amateur*

un assassin, *killer*

un auteur, *author*

le cadre, *executive*

la connaissance, *aquaintance*

le député, *MP*

le docteur, *doctor*

la dupe, *dupe*

un écrivain, *writer*

le facteur, *postman*

le guide, *guide*

un imposteur, *imposter*

un ingénieur, *engineer*

le juge, *judge*

le maire, *mayor*

le médecin, *doctor*

le ministre, *minister*

le peintre, *painter*

la personne, *person*

le poète, *poet*

le possesseur, *owner*

le professeur, *(secondary) teacher* (but, slang **le/la prof**)

la recrue, *recruit*

la sentinelle, *sentry*

le spectateur, *spectator*

le soldat, *soldier*

le témoin, *witness*

la vedette, *star*

la victime, *victim*

With professions, a specifically female form can be produced where needed by using **une femme** and adding the name of the profession attributively:

une femme auteur, *woman author, authoress*

Feminine forms of some of the above are now appearing in French (e.g., **une ministre**). They are not yet fully accepted and are at present best avoided.

For names of animals with only one gender (which is most animals), specifically male and female forms can be produced by using the adjectives **mâle, femelle**:

une souris mâle, *a male mouse*

un hamster femelle, *a female hamster*

PLURAL OF NOUNS
Plural formation

French nouns add **-s** to form their plural, except:

■ Nouns ending **-s**, **-x**, **-z** remain unchanged:

le tas, *heap*	**les tas**
la croix, *cross*	**les croix**
le nez, *nose*	**les nez**

■ Nouns ending **-au**, **-eau**, **-eu** add **-x**:

le tuyau, *drainpipe*	**les tuyaux**
le gâteau, *cake*	**les gâteaux**
le neveu, *nephew*	**les neveux**

Exceptions: **le bleu** (*bruise*) → **les bleus**; **le pneu** (*tyre*) → **les pneus**

■ Nouns ending **-al** change their ending to **-aux**:

le journal, *newspaper*	**les journaux**

Exceptions: **le bal** (*dance*) → **les bals**; **le festival** (*festival*) → **les festivals**

■ Four nouns ending **-ail** change it to **-aux** instead of adding **-s**:

le corail, *coral*	**les coraux**
l'émail, *enamel*	**les émaux**
le travail, *work*	**les travaux**
le vitrail, *stained-glass window*	**les vitraux**

■ Seven nouns ending **-ou** add **-x** instead of **-s**:

le bijou, *jewel*	**les bijoux**
le caillou, *pebble*	**les cailloux**
le chou, *cabbage*	**les choux**
le genou, *knee*	**les genoux**
le hibou, *owl*	**les hiboux**
le joujou, *toy*	**les joujoux**
le pou, *louse*	**les poux**

■ Letter names remain unchanged in the plural:

> **cela s'écrit avec deux p**, *you write it with two p's*

■ Family names usually remain unchanged in the plural; famous historical names add an -s:

> **les Robinson**, *the Robinsons*
> **les Bourbons**, *the Bourbons*

■ Irregular plurals:

l'aïeul, *ancestor*	**les aïeux**
le bonhomme, *fellow*	**les bonshommes**
le ciel, *sky*	**les cieux**
l'œil, *eye*	**les yeux**
madame, *Mrs*	**mesdames**
mademoiselle, *Miss*	**mesdemoiselles**
monsieur, *Mr*	**messieurs**

■ The following nouns have an extra meaning in the plural:

le ciseau, *chisel*	**les ciseaux**, *chisels; scissors*
la lunette, *telescope*	**les lunettes**, *telescopes; spectacles*
la vacance, *vacancy*	**les vacances**, *vacancies; holidays*
la gage, *pledge*	**les gages**, *pledges; wages*
l'affaire, *affair*	**les affaires**, *affairs; business*

Plural of compound nouns

There are many exceptions, but the following rules may help.

■ Compound nouns written as a single word, the plural is **-s**:

le pourboire, *tip*   **les pourboires**

■ Compound nouns formed of an adjective plus a noun or two nouns, both add **-s**:

la belle-mère, *mother-in-law*   **les belles-mères**
le chou-fleur, *cauliflower*   **les choux-fleurs**

■ Compound nouns formed of a noun plus a prepositional phrase, only the noun adds **-s**:

un arc-en-ciel, *rainbow*   **des arcs-en-ciel**

■ Compound nouns formed of a noun preceded by a preposition, the plural is the same as the singular:

le hors-d'œuvre, *starter*   **les hors-d'œuvre**

■ Compound nouns formed of a verb plus its object noun, the noun adds **-s**:

le tire-bouchon, *corkscrew*   **les tire-bouchons**
un essuie-glace, *windscreen-*   **des essuie-glaces**
wiper

But many compounds of this kind do not change in the plural:

le coupe-circuit, *circuit-*   **les coupe-circuit**
breaker

■ Compound nouns formed without a noun component, the plural is the same as the singular:

le passe-partout, *master key*   **les passe-partout**

Singular for plural

■ Plural (or usually plural) in English, but singular in French are:

le bétail, *cattle*; **la famille**, *family*; **la police**, *police*

The verb that follows them must be singular:

la famille est à table, *the family are sitting down to a meal*

■ Singular in English, but plural in French are:

les funérailles, *funeral*; **les nouvelles**, *news*; and (usually) **les fiancailles**, *engagement*; **les progrès**, *progress*

The verb that follows them must be plural:

les funérailles sont lundi prochain, *the funeral is next Monday*

Pronouns

SUBJECT PRONOUNS

The subject pronouns are

singular	*plural*
je, *I*	**nous**, *we*
tu, *you*	**vous**, *you*
il, *he, it*; **elle**, *she, it*	**ils**, **elles**, *they*

Je becomes **j'** before a word beginning with a vowel or **h** 'mute'.

■ **Il** is used for a person or a thing when referring to a masculine noun, **elle** when referring to a feminine noun.

■ **Ils** (*they*) is used to refer to more than one masculine (people or things) or a mixture of masculines and feminines, **elles** (*they*) to refer to more than one feminine.

■ **Vous** can be either plural:

> **toi et ta famille, vous êtes déjà allés en Corse?**, *have you and your family already been to Corsica?*

or a formal or polite form of the singular:

> **pourriez-vous ouvrir la fenêtre, monsieur?**, *will you please open the window (sir)?*

The polite **vous** is always used to strangers; **tu** is normally used to a close friend or colleague, a relation, a fellow-student. **Tu** is always used to address a child or an animal. Said to a stranger it may be purposely impolite. The same applies of course to all related forms (**ton**, **le tien**, etc.; **votre**, **le vôtre**, etc.).

■ The subject pronoun **on** takes the same form of the verb as **il**. It means *one* in the sense of 'people in general', and often corresponds to an indefinite *we* or *they* in English:

> **on part à trois heures trente-six**, *we leave at 3.36*
> **on écrit des choses vraiment incroyables**, *they write some really unbelievable things*

In spoken French **on** is almost always used instead of **nous**:

> **où on va ce soir?**, *where are we going tonight?*

On may be seen as feminine or plural when agreements are made, but it does not have to be:

> **ton père et moi, on était si fatigué(s)**, *we were so tired, your father and I*

▶ **On** is frequently used in French instead of the passive. See pp. 33, 34.

■ **Ce** (*this, that, it, those*) is used as an impersonal subject pronoun, but only with the verb **être**. In the plural **ce** is used with a plural form of **être** (**ce sont, c'étaient**, etc.):

> **c'est une Citroën**, *it's a Citroën*
> **ce sont des mouettes**, *those are seagulls*

With verbs other than **être** (and sometimes with **être** too), **cela** or the less formal **ça** is used:

> **ça (cela) ne se voit pas**, *that's* (*it's*) *not obvious*

▶ See also pp. 75, 76, and 225 for the use of **c'est** or **il est** + adjective and p. 84 and p. 224 for **c'est** or **il est** + noun.

▶ The stressed or disjunctive pronouns, **moi, toi**, etc. may also be used as subject pronouns in some circumstances. See p. 110.

OBJECT PRONOUNS

Forms of the object pronouns

■ The direct object pronouns are:

singular	plural
me, *me*	**nous**, *us*
te, *you*	**vous**, *you*
le, *him, it*; **la**, *her, it*	**les**, *them*

■ The indirect object pronouns are:

singular	plural
me, *to me*	**nous**, *to us*
te, *to you*	**vous**, *to you*
lui, *to him, to her, to it*	**leur**, *to them*

English often omits the *to* of the indirect object: *give it* (*to*) *me*. If you are not clear whether an English object without a *to* is indirect or not, simply insert the *to* and see if the sentence still makes sense.

■ The reflexive object pronouns are the same whether direct or indirect. They are:

singular	plural
me, (*to*) *myself*	**nous**, (*to*) *ourselves*
te, (*to*) *yourself*	**vous**, (*to*) *yourself/*
	yourselves
se, (*to*) *him-/her-/itself*	**se**, (*to*) *themselves*

▶ For the use of the reflexive pronouns see p. 30.

■ **Me, te, le, la, se** become **m', t', l', l', s'** before a vowel or **h** 'mute'.

Me and **te** become **moi** and **toi** in the positive imperative (**m'** and **t'** before a vowel). See p. 28 (formation of the imperative) and p. 106 (pronouns with the imperative).

■ **Y** (*to it, there*) and **en** (*of it, some*) are also treated as object pronouns. See p. 107.

Position of object pronouns

Object pronouns stand immediately before the verb (this includes infinitives, present participles, **voici** and **voilà**):

je t'explique le problème, *I'll explain the problem to you*

je vais t'expliquer le problème, *I'm going to explain the problem to you*

en t'expliquant le problème, *by explaining the problem to you*

le voilà, le problème, *that's it, that's the problem*

In the compound tenses they stand immediately before the auxiliary verb (**avoir** or **être**):

l'as-tu trouvé?, *have you found it?*

je l'ai trouvé dans l'armoire, *I found it in the cupboard*

Since they stand immediately before the verb, object pronouns follow the **ne** of a negative:

je ne l'ai pas trouvé, *I haven't found it*

▶ For the position of object pronouns with the imperative, see below.

Order of object pronouns

Where two object pronouns appear together they stand in this order:

me, m'				
te, t'	**le, l'**			
se, s'	**la, l'**	**lui**	**y**	**en**
nous	**les**	**leur**		
vous				

je te l'apporte, *I'll bring it to you*
elle le lui a emprunté, *she's borrowed it from him*
il n'y en a pas, *there isn't any*

Pronouns from the first and third columns cannot appear together. In the rare cases where this would happen the dative object is expressed by **à** + a disjunctive pronoun:

je vais vous conduire à eux, *I'm going to take you to them* (not **'vous leur'**)

Order of pronouns with the imperative

■ With the negative imperative the order of pronouns is as above:

ne me l'explique pas!, *don't explain it to me!*

■ With the positive imperative, object pronouns follow the verb, are hyphenated to it and to each other, and stand in the following order:

	moi, m'		
	toi, t'		
le	lui		
la	nous	y	en
les	vous		
	leur		

So:

> **donne-les-lui**, *give them to him*
>
> **donnez-la-leur**, *give it to them*

Me and **te** become **moi** and **toi** in the positive imperative; before **en** they become **m'** and **t'** and are not followed by a hyphen:

> **donne-les-moi**, *give them to me*
>
> **donne-m'en**, *give me some*

The pronouns y and en

■ **Y** stands for **à**, **sur** or **dans** + a thing or things. In this sense it usually means *to, at, in it/them*:

> **je m'y oppose formellement**, *I'm absolutely opposed to it*
>
> **il ne s'y intéresse pas du tout**, *he's not in the least interested in it*

It can also mean *there*, in which case it is really an adverb, though it still behaves as an object pronoun as far as its position in the sentence is concerned:

> **on y sera à l'ombre**, *we'll be in the shade there*

■ **En** stands for **de** + a thing or things. In this sense it usually means *of, with, from it/them*:

> **nous en parlerons demain**, *we'll speak of it tomorrow*

> **trois voyageurs en sont descendus**, *three passengers got out of it*

It often means *of it*, *of them* with an expression of quantity:

> **j'en ai beaucoup**, *I've got a lot of it*
> **il y en a trois**, *there are three of them*

With expressions of quantity English frequently drops *of it/them*. This is impossible in French—the **en** must always be there:

> **il faudra en remplacer un**, *you'll have to replace one (of them)*

With expressions of quantity, **en** can also stand for **de** + persons:

> **combien de frères as-tu? — J'en ai trois**, *how many brothers have you?—I've got three*

En can also mean *some* or *any*:

> **tu en as? Alors, donne-m'en**, *have you got any? Well, give me some*

Object pronouns to complete the sense

We have an example above (**il faudra en remplacer un**) of **en** used to complete the sense in French where in English *of it/them* is often omitted. This also occurs with the pronouns **le** (= *it*) and **y**:

> **je te l'ai dit**, *I told you (so)*
> **vous êtes la fille de cet homme? — Non, je le lui ai déjà dit**, *you are this man's daughter?—No, I've already told him (it)*
> **oui, j'y vais**, *all right, I'm going (there)*
> **elle sera déjà partie, je le sais**, *she'll have gone, I know (it)*

However, with **savoir** this **le** is very often dropped in a simple response to a statement:

> **elle est là — Oui, je (le) sais**, *she's there—Yes, I know*

DISJUNCTIVE PRONOUNS

The disjunctive, or stressed, pronouns are those that stand separated from ('disjoined from') verbs. There are no separate forms for these pronouns in English, ordinary subject or object pronouns being used. In French the disjunctive pronouns are:

moi, *me*	**nous**, *us*
toi, *you*	**vous**, *you*
lui, *him*	**eux**, *them* (masculine)
elle, *her*	**elles**, *them* (feminine)

The disjunctive corresponding to **on** is **soi**. It means *oneself*, *yourself*, and is only used after a preposition or **que** (see below). **Soi** in fact is the disjunctive that corresponds to all the indefinite pronouns (**chacun, tout le monde, personne**, etc.). See p. 127.

Disjunctives usually only refer to people, not to things. For the corresponding usage with things, see p. 112.

Use of the disjunctive pronouns

■ Disjunctives may stand completely alone in response to a question or statement:

> **qui l'a pris? — Moi!**, *who's taken it?—Me!*
> **tu l'as pris! — Moi?**, *you've taken it!—(What) me?*

■ They are used after prepositions:

> **comme nous**, *like us*
> **la plupart d'entre elles**, *most of them*
> **c'est à moi**, *it's mine* (*it belongs to me*)
> **chacun pour soi**, *each one for himself*

■ The preposition **à** plus a disjunctive pronoun is used with certain verbs instead of an indirect object, to refer to people. These verbs are:

> **penser/songer à**, *think about*
> **avoir affaire à**, *have business with; deal with*
> **prendre garde à**, *beware of*
>
> **je pense à toi**, *I'm thinking of you*

A disjunctive after **à** is also used with **venir** and **aller** where movement in space is indicated:

> **elle est venue à moi**, *she came to me*

but not otherwise:

> **ce kilt ne te va pas du tout**, *that kilt really doesn't suit you*

■ Disjunctive pronouns are used to specify the individual parts of a plural subject. A subject pronoun may or may not appear as well:

> **eux et moi, on se voit souvent**, *they and I see each other a lot*
> **les enfants et lui se taquinent toujours**, *he and the children always tease each other*
> **qui l'a fait, lui ou son copain?**, *who did it, he or his pal?*

■ They are used to give a subject or object pronoun more emphasis:

> **moi, je ne suis pas d'accord**, *I don't agree*
> **lui, je ne l'aime pas du tout**, *I don't like **him** at all*

■ They are used after **c'est**, **c'était**, etc. In this sense the disjunctives may refer to things as well as people:

> **c'est toi?** *it's you?*
> **c'est eux/elles!**, *it's them!*

In careful speech or writing **ce sont eux/elles** is used.

■ They are used after **que** in comparatives and after **ne ... que**, *only*, and **ne ... ni ... ni**, *neither ... nor*:

> **elle est plus jolie que moi**, *she's prettier than me*
> **on parle toujours des choses qui n'intéressent que soi**, *we always talk about things that only interest ourselves*

■ They are used before a relative pronoun:

> **lui, qui ne sait absolument rien, a été promu capitaine**, *he, who knows absolutely nothing, has been promoted captain*
> **elle m'aime, moi qui n'ai pas un sou**, *she loves me, I who haven't a penny*

This usage is rather literary.

■ They are used instead of subject pronouns with **aussi** and **seul**:

> **lui seul est resté dans la chambre**, *he alone remained in the room*
> **eux aussi l'ont essayé**, *they tried it too*

■ They combine with **-même** to produce emphatic forms:

> **moi-même**, *myself*
> **toi-même**, *yourself*
>
> **nous-mêmes**, *ourselves*
> **vous-même(s)**, *yourself*; *yourselves*
>
> **lui-même**, *himself*
> **elle-même**, *herself*
> **soi-même**, *oneself* etc.
>
> **eux-mêmes**, *themselves*
> **elles-mêmes**, *themselves*

> **tu l'as vraiment fait toi-même?**, *you really did it*
> *(all by) yourself?*

Substitutes for the disjunctive pronouns

The disjunctive pronouns are not normally used to refer
to things. For a preposition + *it/them* an adverb is
substituted:

> **sur lui → dessus**, *on it*
> **dans lui → dedans**, *in it*
> **derrière lui → derrière**, *behind it*
> **après lui → après**, *after it*
> **à côté de lui → à côté**, *beside it*
>   etc.

> **qu'est-ce qu'il y a dessus? Et dedans?**, *what's on*
> *it? And in it?*

Alternatively a demonstrative pronoun may be used:

> **je n'ai jamais eu une moto comme celle-là**, *I've*
> *never had a bike like it*

RELATIVE PRONOUNS

Relative pronouns introduce a clause within the sentence
and usually relate it back to a noun in the main clause. In
English they are *who*, *whom*, *whose*, *which*, *that*, *what*. In
French they are:

> **qui**, *who, which, that*
> **que**, *whom, which, that*
>
> **ce qui, ce que**, *what*
>
> **lequel**, *which*
>
> **de qui** or **dont**, *of whom, whose*

> **duquel** or **dont**, *of which, whose*
> **à qui**, *to whom*
> **auquel**, *to which*

and the less common

> **ce dont**, *that of which*
> **ce à quoi**, *that to which*

Que and **ce que** become **qu'** and **ce qu'** before a vowel. **Qui** and **ce qui** never change.

Relatives are sometimes omitted in English. In French this is not possible and it is important to recognize that a sentence like 'the man you want to see is here' has a hidden relative (*who* or *that*):

> **le client que tu voulais voir est là**, *the customer (that/who) you wanted to see is here*

Qui and que

■ **Qui** is the subject of the clause it introduces, **que** is the direct object:

> **la femme qui parle**, *the woman who is speaking*
> **la femme que tu connais**, *the woman (that) you know*

So **que** will be followed by a subject noun or pronoun (**tu** above), and **qui** will be followed by a verb, possibly preceded by **ne** and/or an object pronoun.

■ **Que** may not be the object of the verb it introduces but of an infinitive depending on that verb. This is similar to English:

> **la femme que tu espères épouser**, *the woman that you hope to marry* (you hope to marry her, you don't 'hope' her, so **que** is actually the object of **épouser**, not of **espères**)

■ After **que** a noun subject and the verb are often inverted if nothing else follows in that clause:

> **voilà la liste que réclame l'inspecteur**, *here's the list the inspector is asking for*

This does not happen with pronoun subjects, or if something else follows in the clause:

> **voilà la liste que vous demandez**, *here's the list you're asking for*
>
> **voilà la liste que l'inspecteur a demandée hier**, *here's the list the inspector asked for yesterday*

■ Beware! As well as being a relative, meaning *who*, *which*, *that*, **que** may also be a conjunction meaning *that* (this too may be omitted in English):

> **j'espère que tu te portes bien**, *I hope (that) you are well*

and it may also be part of a comparison, meaning *than*:

> **il est plus grand que toi**, *he's bigger than you*

Que = *what*, **qui** = *who*, and **lequel** = *which* may also introduce questions; here the question mark makes their meaning clear:

> **que dis-tu?**, *what are you saying?*

► See p. 118.

■ In order to avoid ambiguity **lequel** may sometimes be used instead of **qui/que**. This is because **lequel** shows gender and number:

> **j'ai écrit au père de sa femme, lequel est très riche**, *I've written to his wife's father, who is very rich*

► For the declension of **lequel** see p. 116.

Relative pronouns after prepositions

■ After prepositions **qui** is used for people (English *whom* or *that*). So *with/without/under whom* is **avec/sans/sous qui**:

> **la femme avec qui je parle**, *the woman to whom I'm speaking (that I'm speaking to)*

Notice that in English (as in the bracketed version above) we try to avoid the old-fashioned and formal word *whom*. So we often use *that* as the relative and push the preposition to the end of the clause. This is impossible in French: the preposition must come immediately before the relative.

□ After the prepositions **parmi**, *among*, and **entre**, *between*, **lesquels/lesquelles** is used instead of **qui** for people

> **les mineurs parmi lesquels tu vis**, *the miners among whom you live*

▶ For the declension of **lequel** see p. 116.

□ **De** + **qui** usually becomes **dont**, *whose, of whom*.

The word order after **dont** (or **de qui** or **duquel**) is always subject, verb, rest of clause. This is not the case in English, where the object is placed immediately after the word *whose*:

> **voilà l'homme dont (de qui) tu as volé la voiture**, *there's the man whose car you stole*

English also drops the definite article (*whose car*) which French does not (**dont … la voiture**).

Dont is used as the relative (for both people and things) with verbs that have an object preceded by **de**:

> **l'homme dont tu as besoin**, *the man you need* (= *of whom you have need*)

■ After prepositions **lequel** is used for things. So *with/ without/under which* is **avec/sans/sous lequel**. **Lequel** declines as follows:

	singular	*plural*
masculine	**lequel**	**lesquels**
feminine	**laquelle**	**lesquelles**

Lequel agrees in gender and number with the noun it refers back to.

□ **Lequel** combines with the prepositions **à** and **de** to produce the forms **auquel, auxquels, à laquelle, auxquelles** and **duquel, desquels, de laquelle, desquelles**

> **les autorités auxquelles j'écris**, *the authorities I'm writing to*
> **le pays duquel je parle**, *the country I'm speaking about*

However, the simpler word **dont**, *of which, whose*, is often substituted for **duquel** etc.

> **le pays dont je parle**, *the country I'm speaking of*
> **la voiture dont il a volé la radio**, *the car whose radio he stole*

Similarly, **où**, *where*, is often used instead of **auquel, dans lequel, sur lequel**, etc. where the meaning allows it:

> **la maison où (dans laquelle) il a passé sa vie**, *the house where (in which) he spent his life*

► See p. 115 for the word order after **dont** and **duquel**.

■ In English *whose* can be used after a preposition: *the nurse, without whose efforts I shouldn't be here*. **Dont** cannot be used in this way in French: **de qui/duquel** must be used instead:

> **cette infirmière, sans les soins de qui je ne serais plus ici, ne travaille plus dans cet hôpital,** *that nurse, without whose efforts I should no longer be here, doesn't work in this hospital any more*

This construction is often clumsy in French, however, and is usually avoided:

> **sans les soins de cette infirmière, je ne serais plus ici; mais elle ne travaille plus dans cet hôpital,** *without that nurse's efforts I should no longer be here today; but she doesn't work in this hospital any more*

Ce qui, ce que, ce dont, ce à quoi

■ *What* as a relative is **ce qui** or **ce que, ce qui** being the subject form and **ce que** the object form, as with **qui** and **que**. These relative pronouns introduce noun clauses:

> **je ne comprends pas ce que tu dis,** *I don't understand what you're saying*

If the main verb following a noun clause introduced by **ce qui/ce que** is **être**, a comma and **ce** are introduced, like this:

> **ce qui est difficile, c'est de jouer de la cornemuse,** *what's difficult is playing the bagpipes*

This construction is extremely common.

■ **Ce qui** and **ce que** are used instead of **qui** and **que** as relatives after **tout,** *all, everything*:

> **tout ce que tu dis est incompréhensible,** *everything (that) you say is incomprehensible*

■ **Ce qui** and **ce que** can also mean *which*, where this refers to an idea rather than a specific thing:

> **il va jouer de la cornemuse, ce qui est très difficile**, *he's going to play the bagpipes, which is very difficult* (*which* refers not to bagpipes but to playing them)

After prepositions the form of the relative meaning *which*, and referring back to an idea, is **quoi**:

> **je lui ait tout expliqué, sans quoi il aurait été vraiment fâché**, *I've explained everything to him, without which he would have been really angry* (*which* refers to my having explained things to him)

■ When the verb used in the relative clause takes **à** or **de** before its object, *what* as a relative is **ce à quoi** (**à** verbs) or **ce dont** (**de** verbs):

> **ce à quoi je pense, c'est d'aller jouer à la pétanque**, *what I'm thinking of is going to play pétanque* (the verb is **penser à**)
> **je peux t'envoyer ce dont tu as besoin**, *I can send you what you need* (*what you have need of*) (the verb is **avoir besoin de**)

De quoi is sometimes used instead of **ce dont**:

> **je ne comprends pas de quoi tu parles**, *I don't understand what you're talking about*

INTERROGATIVE PRONOUNS

The interrogative pronouns in English are *who?*, *what?*, and *which?* In English they have the same forms in both direct and indirect questions:

> *who did it?*—direct question
> *I want to know who did it*—indirect question

In French they have somewhat different forms in direct and in indirect questions.

Interrogative pronouns in direct questions

Referring to people

■ As the subject of the sentence the interrogative pronoun referring to people is **qui est-ce qui** or just **qui**. Both mean *who*:

> **qui est-ce qui arrive?**, *who's coming?*
> **qui vous a dit ça?**, *who told you that?*

The interrogative pronoun **qui** is always masculine singular—even if you know that the people who turned up were feminine and plural, you still ask **qui est arrivé?**

■ As the object of the sentence the interrogative pronoun referring to people is **qui est-ce que** or just **qui**. Both mean *who* (in older or formal English, *whom*). The **que** changes to **qu'** before a vowel:

> **qui est-ce qu'on a élu?**, *who did they elect?*
> **qui as-tu envoyé?**, *who did you send?*

■ After a preposition the interrogative pronoun referring to people is **qui est-ce que** or just **qui**. Both mean *who(m)*. The **que** changes to **qu'** before a vowel:

> **pour qui avez-vous fait cela?**, *who did you do it for? (for whom did you do it?)*
> **de qui est-ce que tu parles?**, *who are you talking about? (about whom are you talking?)*

Notice that in English the preposition may (and usually does) go to the end of its clause. This is impossible in French—it must always stand before the interrogative pronoun.

■ The longer forms of the interrogatives are common in speech.

Referring to things

■ As the subject of the sentence the interrogative pronoun referring to things is **qu'est-ce qui**, *what*:

> **qu'est-ce qui arrive?**, *what's happening?*

Notice that there is no alternative form here.

■ As the object of the sentence the interrogative pronoun referring to things is **qu'est-ce que** or just **que**. Both mean *what*. In both, **que** changes to **qu'** before a vowel:

> **qu'est-ce qu'on a trouvé?**, *what did they find?*
> **qu'as-tu fait de mon pullover blanc?**, *what have you done with my white pullover?*

Notice also the form **qu'est-ce que c'est qu'un ...?** (sometimes shortened to **qu'est-ce qu'un ...?**) meaning *what's a ...?*

> **qu'est-ce c'est qu'un ornithorynque?**, *what's a duck-billed platypus?*

■ After a preposition the interrogative pronoun referring to things is **quoi**, *what*:

> **avec quoi as-tu fait cela?**, *what did you do that with? (with what did you do that?)*

■ The longer forms of the interrogatives are common in speech.

Interrogative pronouns in indirect questions

Referring to people

■ The interrogative pronoun in indirect questions referring to people is always **qui**, *who(m)*, whether it is used as subject, object or after a preposition:

> **je ne sais pas qui sera président**, *I've no idea who will be president*

je me demande qui vous allez choisir, *I wonder
who you'll choose*
dis-moi à qui tu penses, *tell me who you're
thinking of*

Referring to things

■ As the subject of an indirect question, the
interrogative pronoun referring to things is **ce qui**, *what*:

je ne sais pas ce qui se passe ici, *I don't know
what's happening here*

■ As the object of an indirect question, the interrogative
pronoun referring to things is **ce que**, *what*:

explique-moi ce que tu penses, *explain to me what
you're thinking*

■ After prepositions, the interrogative pronoun in an
indirect question referring to things is **quoi**, *what*:

demande-lui de quoi elle a besoin, *ask her what
she needs*

The interrogative pronoun lequel

■ **Lequel** means *which* as an interrogative pronoun. It
refers to both people and things and is used in both
direct and indirect questions. It agrees with the noun it
refers to in gender and number:

	singular	*plural*
masculine	**lequel**	**lesquels**
feminine	**laquelle**	**lesquelles**

Notice that both parts of the word change.

lequel des deux préfères-tu?, *which of the two do
you prefer?*
il a répondu à trois questions — lesquelles?, *he's
answered three questions—which (ones)?*

je ne sais pas lequel des deux je préfère, *I don't know which of the two I prefer*

■ With the prepositions **à** and **de**, **lequel** forms the following compounds:

	singular	*plural*
masculine	**auquel, duquel**	**auxquels, desquels**
feminine	**à laquelle, de laquelle**	**auxquelles, desquelles**

auquel des trois donnez-vous votre voix?, *which of the three do you give your vote to?*

The interrogative adjective quel

■ The interrogative adjective corresponding to all the above pronouns is **quel**, *which, what*. **Quel** agrees with its noun in gender and number:

	singular	*plural*
masculine	**quel**	**quels**
feminine	**quelle**	**quelles**

avec quelle main l'as-tu fait?, *which hand did you do it with?*

quels gens fréquente-t-il?, *what (kind of) people does he go around with?*

je me demande à quel quai il va arriver, *I wonder which (what) platform it will arrive at*

■ With the verb **être**, **quel** may be divided from its noun by the verb:

quels sont ces gens?, *what (kind of) people are these? (who are these people?)*

▶ For questions introduced by other question-words see p. 212. For the formation of direct and indirect questions see pp. 211 and 213.

POSSESSIVE PRONOUNS

■ The forms of the possessive pronouns (*mine, yours,* etc. in English) are:

masc. sing.	fem. sing.	masc. plural	fem. plural	
le mien	la mienne	les miens	les miennes	*mine*
le tien	la tienne	les tiens	les tiennes	*yours*
le sien	la sienne	les siens	les siennes	*his, hers, its*
le nôtre	la nôtre	les nôtres		*ours*
le vôtre	la vôtre	les vôtres		*yours*
le leur	la leur	les leurs		*theirs*

> **ma mère et la vôtre sont parties ensemble**, *my mother and yours left together*

With **à**, **le/les** becomes **au/aux**; with **de**, **le/les** becomes **du/des**:

> **cet élève est un des miens**, *this pupil is one of mine*

■ The possessive pronouns do not agree with the *owner* of the object, but with the object itself. So **le sien** means either *his* or *hers*, referring to a masculine object, and **la sienne** means either *his* or *hers* referring to a feminine object:

> **mon argent, je l'ai toujours, mais Marie a dépensé tout le sien**, *I've still got my money, but Marie's spent all hers*

■ The possessive pronoun corresponding to **on** and other indefinite pronouns is **le sien**:

> **on s'occupe des siens**, *you look after your own (people)*

■ *It's mine, it's yours*, etc. may also be translated into French by **c'est à moi, c'est à toi**, etc. This use of à + disjunctive pronoun is only possible after **être**, where it is extremely common.

There is a slight difference in meaning between **c'est à moi** and **c'est le mien**. **C'est le mien** distinguishes between objects possessed: 'that one is mine, maybe some other is yours'; **c'est à moi** emphasizes the ownership of the object 'that's mine (so give it me!)'.

DEMONSTRATIVE PRONOUNS

The demonstrative pronouns—English *this (one), that (one), those*—point things out. In French they are **celui**, *this one here; that one there*, specifying, or **ceci / cela**, *this one / that one*, not specifying.

■ The forms of **celui** are:

	masculine	*feminine*	
singular	**celui**	**celle**	*this, that, the one*
plural	**ceux**	**celles**	*these, those*

They agree in gender and number with the noun they refer to.

■ **Celui** does not stand alone. It may be followed by a preposition, by **qui / que** or by **-ci / -là**.

Celui + preposition

The preposition most frequently found after **celui** is **de**. **Celui de** means *that of* and is the equivalent of the English **'s**:

> **celui de Nicole est cassé**, *Nicole's is broken*
> **la voiture? C'est celle de mon ami**, *the car? It's my friend's*

■ Other prepositions are also found after **celui**:

> **quel tapis? — Celui en laine,** which carpet?—The
> woollen one (the one in wool)

Celui à is frequently encountered when shopping:

> **quels abricots? — Ceux à neuf francs,** which
> apricots?—The ones at nine francs

Celui qui, celui que

Celui qui and **celui que** mean *the one who, the one that*
or in the plural *those who, those that*. The **qui** and **que**
are relative pronouns (see p. 112), so **celui qui** is the
subject of its clause and is followed by a verb, **celui que**
is the object and is followed by a pronoun or noun subject,
and then the verb:

> **celle qui habitait à côté de Jean-Luc a déménagé,**
> *that woman who lived next to Jean-Luc has moved*
> **lesquels? Ceux que tu trouves difficiles?,** *which?*
> *Those you find difficult?*

■ The relatives **à qui** and **dont** are also found after
celui when the verb that follows takes **à** or **de**:

> **celui à qui je pense,** *the one I'm thinking of*
> **(penser à)**
> **celle dont tu parles,** *the one you're talking about*
> **(parler de)**

Celui-ci, celui-là

Celui-ci means *this one*, **celui-là** means *that one* when
you are making a specific contrast:

> **celui-ci est bleu, celui-là est plutôt vert,** *this one's*
> *blue, that one's more green*

Because **là** is often used to mean *here* as well as *there* in modern French, **celui-là** is losing its ability to point to something at a distance when it is not contrasted, as in the example above, with **celui-ci**. To indicate something at a distance, therefore, **celui là-bas**, *that one over there*, is now often used instead of **celui-là**.

■ **Celui-ci** can also mean *the latter*, **celui-là** *the former*:

> **tu connais Luc et son frère? Alors, celui-ci a demandé de tes nouvelles hier soir**, *you know Luc and his brother? Well, the latter asked (his brother asked) about you last night*

Notice that *the former/the latter* are only used in formal English, whereas **celui-là/celui-ci** can be used with this meaning in French at all levels.

Cela, ça, ceci

Sometimes called neuter demonstratives, **cela** (and its more colloquial form **ça**) means *that* or *this* or *it*, **ceci** means *this*. **Cela/ça** is used much more frequently than **ceci**.

■ **Cela/ça** and **ceci** may refer to ideas, **cela** to one already mentioned, **ceci** to one about to be produced:

> **j'ai entendu tout ce que tu as dit, mais cela est très difficile à comprendre**, *I've heard all you've been saying, but that's (it's) very difficult to understand*
> **ça se comprend!** *that's obvious!*
> **écoutez ceci**, *listen to this*

or they may refer to objects, so far unnamed in the case of **ceci**:

> **je t'ai apporté ceci, c'est un petit cadeau**, *I've brought you this, it's a little present*

already known in the case of **cela/ça**:

> **ça te plaît?**, *do you like it?*

■ Whereas **celui-là** distinguishes between a number of objects, **cela/ça** simply points. Compare:

> **cela m'appartient**, *that's mine* (pointing to a single object)
> **celui-là m'appartient**, *that one's mine* (pointing to one among a number of similar objects)

Ce

The pronoun **ce** is a weaker form of **cela/ceci**, used only with **être**, and meaning *it* or *that*:

> **qui est-ce? — C'est moi**, *who's that?—It's me*

Ce becomes **c'** before **e**, **ç** before **a**:

> **ç'a été le plus grand problème**, *that's been the greatest problem*

■ The pronoun **ce** when used as the subject of **être** can also be plural:

> **ce sont des baleines**, *those are whales*

▶ See pp. 224 and 225 for **c'est** versus **il est**.

INDEFINITE PRONOUNS

Indefinite pronouns (*somebody*, *something*, *anybody*, etc. in English) all take the third person (**il** form) of the verb in French, as in English. The forms of object pronouns, reflexives, possessives corresponding to indefinite pronouns are also the third person forms (**le, la, lui; se; son, sa, ses; le sien** and their plurals); the corresponding form of the disjunctive is **soi**:

> **chacun doit s'asseoir à sa propre place**,
> *everybody must sit down in his or her own place*

Some indefinites only function as pronouns, some can also be adjectives—see below. See also indefinite adjectives, p. 148.

Used only as pronouns

■ **Chacun** (fem. **chacune**), *each one, everybody*:

chacun doit prendre une feuille de papier,
  everybody must take a sheet of paper

■ **Je ne sais quoi**, *something or other*

This phrase is used as if it were a simple pronoun. It may take an adjective, preceded by **de**:

elle a dit je ne sais quoi de complètement stupide,
  she said something or other completely stupid

■ **N'importe qui**, *anyone* (*at all*):

n'importe qui te dira ça, *anyone* (*at all*) *will tell you that*
ne le dis pas à n'importe qui, *don't tell just anyone*

■ **On**, *one, you, we, they, someone, people in general*:

on nous regarde, *somebody's looking at us*
qu'est-ce qu'on va faire?, *what are we going to do?*

▶ See also pp. 103, 109, and (**on** as a substitute for the passive) 34.

■ **Personne**, *nobody, not anybody*:

qui est là? — Personne, *who's there—Nobody*
je n'y vois personne, *I can't see anyone there*

Personne must have a **ne** with an associated verb, as in the second example above. See p. 159.

Any adjective with **personne** follows it, is masculine, and is preceded by **de**:

> **il n'y a personne de compétent**, *there is no one qualified*

■ **Quelque chose**, *something, anything*:

> **tu as vu quelque chose?**, *did you see anything?*
> **oui, il y a quelque chose qui bouge**, *yes, there's something moving*

Any adjective with **quelque chose** follows it, is masculine, and is preceded by **de**:

> **ça doit être quelque chose d'horrible!**, *it must be something horrible!*

The other **chose** compounds behave similarly:

> **autre chose**, *something else*
> **peu de chose**, *little*
> **pas grand-chose**, *not much*

■ **Quelqu'un**, *someone, anybody*:

> **il y a quelqu'un dans la grange**, *there's someone in the barn*
> **est-ce que tu entends quelqu'un?**, *can you hear anybody?*

Quelqu'un has masculine and feminine plural forms (**quelques-uns, quelques-unes**) but no feminine singular form (the masculine must be used even if you are aware that 'someone' is a woman):

> **il vit avec quelqu'un depuis trois ans**, *he's been living with somebody for three years*

The plural form, **quelques-un(e)s**, must have an **en** with its associated verb when it is used as the direct object:

> **ces dames-là? oui, j'en connais quelques-unes**, *those ladies? yes, I know some of them*

Any adjective with **quelqu'un** follows it and is preceded by **de**:

> **je cherche quelqu'un de beau**, *I'm looking for someone handsome*

■ **Quiconque**, *whoever; anybody*:

> **quiconque dit cela, ment!**, *whoever says that is lying!*
> **il joue mieux que quiconque**, *he plays better than anybody*

Qui que ce soit (qui/que) may be used, in rather less formal style, for **quiconque**. See p. 234.

■ **Rien**, *nothing, not anything*:

> **tu entends quelque chose? — Non, rien**, *can you hear anything?—No, nothing*
> **je n'entends absolument rien**, *I can hear absolutely nothing*

Rien must have a **ne** with an associated verb, as in the second example above. See p. 159.

Any adjective with **rien** follows it, is masculine, and is preceded by **de**:

> **ce n'est rien de spécial**, *it's nothing special*

■ **L'un** (fem. **l'une**), *(the) one*:

> **j'ai rencontré l'un d'eux en ville**, *I met one of them in town*
> **l'une chante, l'autre pas**, *one sings, the other doesn't*

As in the second example above, **l'un** is often followed later in the sentence by **l'autre**, *another, the other*. The plural is **les un(e)s ... les autres ...**

L'un(e) l'autre (plural **les un(e)s les autres**) is used to mean *one another, each other*:

> **ils se détestent l'un l'autre**, *they hate one another*

Used as both pronouns and adjectives

▶ For these indefinites used as adjectives, see p. 148.

■ **Aucun** (fem. **aucune**), *none, not any*:

> **tu as entendu ses disques? — Non, aucun**, *you've heard his records?—No, none of them*
>
> **il n'en a aucun**, *he hasn't any*

Aucun must have **en** before the verb when it is used as the direct object; it must also have a **ne** with an associated verb, as in the second example above. See p. 159.

Pas un (fem. **pas une**) and **nul** (fem. **nulle**) are found as alternatives to **aucun**, with the same meaning.

■ **Certains** (fem. **certaines**), *some (people)*:

> **certains ont dit qu'il a subtilisé l'argent**, *some people said he pinched the money*
>
> **certaines d'entre elles ont très bien parlé**, *some of them spoke very well*

Certain(e)s must have **en** before the verb when used as the direct object:

> **j'en connais certains**, *I know some of them*

■ **Plusieurs**, *several (people)*:

> **plusieurs sont venus sans savoir pourquoi**, *several came without knowing why*

Plusieurs must have **en** before the verb when used as the direct object:

> **il en a tué plusieurs**, *he killed several (of them)*

Any adjective with **plusieurs** follows it and is preceded by **de**:

> **il y en a plusieurs de verts**, *there are several green ones*

■ **Tous** (fem. **toutes**), *everybody, all*:

>**je vous connais tous**, *I know you all*
>**elles sont toutes là**, *they are all there*
>**tous sont venus à la réunion**, *all of them came to the meeting*

Tous usually follows the verb, as in the first two examples above, whether it refers to the subject or the object. It stands before the verb when it alone is the subject, as in the third example above.

■ **Tout**, *everything, all*:

>**tout est arrangé**, *all is arranged*
>**j'ai tout fait**, *I've done everything*

Adjectives

In French, adjectives are singular or plural and masculine or feminine according to the noun they refer to. To the basic masculine form **-e** is added to make the adjective feminine, **-s** to make it masculine plural, **-es** to make it feminine plural:

	singular	*plural*
masculine	**un stylo noir**, *a black pen*	**des stylos noirs**
feminine	**une boîte noire**, *a black box*	**des boîtes noires**

An adjective referring to two singular nouns is plural; if they are of different genders the adjective is masculine plural:

> **un complet et une cravate noirs**, *a black suit and tie*

Adjectives usually follow their noun; but see p. 138, position of adjectives.

FEMININE OF ADJECTIVES

Adjectives whose masculine form ends in **-e** remain unchanged in the feminine:

> **un stylo rouge**, *a red pen*
> **une boîte rouge**, *a red box*

otherwise all adjectives add **-e** to form their feminine.

■ Additional changes are made by adjectives with the following endings. Many of these changes are identical to those made by nouns to form their feminines—see p. 93.

masculine adjective	*feminine adjective*
-c	**-que**
public, *public*	**publique**
except:	
blanc, *white*	**blanche**
franc, *frank*	**franche**
grec, *Greek*	**grecque**
sec, *dry*	**sèche**
-er	**-ère**
dernier, *last*	**dernière**
-eur	**-euse**
trompeur, *deceptive*	**trompeuse**
except:	
inférieur, *lower*	**inférieure**
supérieur, *higher*	**supérieure**
intérieur, *inner*	**intérieure**
extérieur, *outer*	**extérieure**
majeur, *major*	**majeure**
mineur, *minor*	**mineure**
meilleur, *better*	**meilleure**
and see **-teur** below	

-f	**-ve**
informatif, *informative*	informative
except:	
bref, *brief*	brève
-gu	**-guë** (the tréma, ¨, indicates that the **e** is pronounced separately from the **u**)
aigu, *sharp*	aiguë
-teur	**-teuse**: where the adjective is based on the present participle of a verb
menteur, *lying*	menteuse (mentir, p.p. mentant)
	-trice: in all other cases
conservateur, *conservative*	conservatrice (conserver, p.p. conservant).
-x	**-se**
heureux, *happy*	heureuse
except:	
doux, *gentle*	douce
faux, *false*	fausse
roux, *red-haired*	rousse
vieux, *old*	vieille

■ Adjectives with the following endings double the consonant of their ending before adding **-e**:

masculine	*feminine*
-el	**-elle**
officiel, *official*	officielle
-en	**-enne**
ancien, *former*	ancienne
-et	**-ette**
net, *clear*	nette
except:	
complet, *complete*	complète
concret, *concrete*	concrète

discret, *discreet*	**discrète**
inquiet, *worried*	**inquiète**
secret, *secret*	**secrète**
-eil	**-eille**
pareil, *similar*	**pareille**
-on	**-onne**
bon, *good*	**bonne**

■ The following adjectives have a special form used before a masculine singular noun beginning with a vowel or 'mute' **h**, and their feminine form is derived from this:

masculine	*masc. before vowel*	*feminine*
beau, *fine*	**bel**	**belle**
fou, *mad*	**fol**	**folle**
mou, *soft*	**mol**	**molle**
nouveau, *new*	**nouvel**	**nouvelle**
vieux, *old*	**vieil**	**vieille**

■ Other adjectives with irregular feminine forms:

masculine	*feminine*
bas, *low*	**basse**
bénin, *benign*	**bénigne**
épais, *thick*	**épaisse**
favori, *favourite*	**favorite**
frais, *fresh*	**fraîche**
gras, *greasy*	**grasse**
gros, *big*	**grosse**
gentil, *nice*	**gentille**
jumeau, *twin*	**jumelle**
las, *tired*	**lasse**
long, *long*	**longue**
malin, *cunning*	**maligne**
nul, *no*	**nulle**
paysan, *peasant*	**paysanne**
sot, *foolish*	**sotte**

■ The following adjectives are usually invariable — they make no agreement at all with either a feminine or a plural noun:

> **châtain**, *chestnut*
> **impromptu**, *impromptu*
> **k(h)aki**, *khaki*
> **marron**, *brown*
> **snob**, *snobbish*

and all compound colour-adjectives:

> **une voiture bleu clair**, *a light blue car*
> **une boîte vert foncé**, *a dark green box*

The following adjectives make plural but no feminine agreements:

> **chic** (m. and f. plural **chics**), *chic*
> **maximum** (m. and f. plural, **maximums**), *maximum*
> **minimum** (m. and f. plural **minimums**), *minimum*

PLURAL OF ADJECTIVES

■ All feminine and most masculine adjectives form their plural by adding **-s** to their singular form. This also applies where the feminine singular is irregular:

	singular	*plural*
masculine	**bon**, *good*	**bons**
feminine	**bonne**	**bonnes**

■ Adjectives ending as follows have irregular masculine plurals. Their feminine plurals are formed regularly by adding **-s** to the feminine singular.

masculine singular	*masculine plural*
-s, -x	no change
gris, *grey*	**gris**
faux, *false*	**faux**

-eau	-eaux
beau, *fine*	**beaux**
-al	**-aux**
brutal, *brutal*	**brutaux**
except:	
banal, *trite*	**banals**
fatal, *fatal*	**fatals**
final, *final*	**finals**
naval, *naval*	**navals**

▶ A number of adjectives are invariable, remaining unchanged in both their feminine and their plural forms. See p. 137.

POSITION OF ADJECTIVES

The usual position for an adjective in French is immediately after the noun:

> **une robe verte**, *a green dress*

Two or more adjectives after the noun are joined with **et**:

> **une robe verte et blanche**, *a green and white dress*

Adjectives are also found in front of the noun, however, and some adjectives are almost always found in this position:

> **une jolie robe verte et blanche**, *a pretty green and white dress*

Adjectives that commonly precede are:

> **beau**, *fine*
> **bon**, *good* (and **meilleur**, *better, best*)
> **court**, *short*

gentil, *nice*
grand, *big; tall*
gros, *big*
jeune, *young*
joli, *pretty*
long, *long*
mauvais, *bad* (and **pire**, *worse, worst*)
méchant, *nasty*
nouveau, *new*
petit, *little* (and **moindre**, *less, least*)
vaste, *vast*
vieux, *old*
vilain, *ugly*

If in doubt place these adjectives before the noun, and all others after.

■ Most adjectives can in fact be placed before or after their noun, with a small but distinct difference in meaning. Placing the adjective after the noun indicates an objective distinction, placing it before shows a subjective feeling. So:

> **le long de cette côte s'étire une interminable plage**, *along this coastline stretches an endless beach* (travel agent's language: 'endless' is gushing and imprecise—'that seems as though it might go on for ever'; **une plage interminable**, however, means that the beach is literally or apparently interminable (and therefore boring and tiresome)

This use of adjectives before the noun is very common in modern French writing at all levels to strengthen the emotional content. The effect is often lost in written English: in spoken English we usually get it by stressing the adjective in some way:

ces superbes peintures, *these superb paintings*
une fantastique reproduction, *a fantastic reproduction*
cette magnifique vallée, *this magnificent valley*
d'une rare qualité, *of a really rare quality*

The adjectives listed on p. 138 above are rarely used as distinguishers: this is why they usually go before the noun. Some adjectives, however, such as colour adjectives, are almost always used to make an objective distinction and so they normally follow the noun.

■ There are some adjectives whose position is completely fixed:

□ Numbers, both cardinal (*one*, *two*, *three*, etc.) and ordinal (*first*, *second*, *third*, etc.), always precede the noun.

les trois mousquetaires, *the three musketeers*
le quatrième mousquetaire, *the fourth musketeer*

But in the following cases where the number follows in English it also follows in French.

numéro deux, *number two*
page cinq, *page five*
Henri quatre, *Henri the Fourth*
acte trois, *act three*

□ Demonstrative, possessive, and interrogative adjectives always precede.

cet enfant-là, *that child*
son parapluie, *his umbrella*
quelle difficulté?, *what difficulty?*

□ Indefinite adjectives like **chaque**, *each*, **tel**, *such*, **autre**, *other*, always precede. See p. 148.

une telle personne, *such a person*
chaque enfant, *each child*

☐ Past participles used as adjectives always follow.

> **un verre cassé**, *a broken glass*

☐ Adjectives of nationality always follow.

> **la révolution française**, *the French revolution*

☐ Scientific and technical adjectives always follow.

> **l'acide chlorhydrique**, *hydrochloric acid*

☐ Adjectives with a qualifying phrase always follow.

> **un bon champignon**, *a good mushroom*
> **un champignon bon à manger**, *an edible mushroom*

■ A small number of adjectives have quite different meanings according to whether they precede or follow the noun. They are:

ancien, *former/ancient*

> **un ancien professeur**, *a former teacher*
> **des meubles anciens**, *very old furniture*

certain, *certain (= I'm not sure what)/definite, (absolutely) sure*

> **un certain jour de mai**, *a certain day (one day) in May*
> **une date certaine**, *a definite date*

cher, *dear (= emotionally important)/dear (= expensive)*

> **mon cher Charles**, *my dear Charles*
> **une lampe chère**, *an expensive lamp*

dernier, *last (of a sequence)/last (= just gone)*

> **le dernier chèque de mon chéquier**, *the last cheque in my chequebook*
> **dimanche dernier**, *last Sunday*

divers, *various/varying*

> **j'ai eu diverses difficultés,** *I've had various difficulties*
> **on m'a donné des réponses diverses,** *I've been given varying replies*

même, *same/very*

> **la même chose,** *the same thing*
> **l'homme même,** *the very man*

Même before the article or before a pronoun means *even:*

> **même cet homme-là,** *even that man*
> **même vous,** *even you*

pauvre, *poor (= to be pitied)/poor (= not rich)*

> **ce pauvre enfant!,** *that poor child!*
> **une famille pauvre,** *a poor family*

propre, *own/clean*

> **mes propres mains,** *my own hands*
> **les mains propres,** *clean hands*

seul, *only/alone*

> **la seule solution,** *the only solution*
> **le roi seul a le droit de décider,** *the king alone has the right to decide* (this use is the equivalent of 'only the king', and **seul le roi** is equally possible)

vrai, *real (= genuine)/true (= not fictitious)*

> **un vrai mystère,** *a real mystery*
> **une histoire vraie,** *a true story*

COMPARATIVE AND SUPERLATIVE OF ADJECTIVES

■ English has two ways to form the comparative and superlative of adjectives:

> *fine*: *finer* (comparative), *finest* (superlative)
> *difficult*: *more difficult* (comparative), *most difficult* (superlative)

French forms the comparative and superlative in one way only, with **plus** (comparative) and **le/la/les plus** (superlative):

> **beau, plus beau, le plus beau**, *fine, finer, finest*
>
> **la voile est un plus beau sport que le tennis**, *sailing is a finer sport than tennis*
> **c'est le plus beau sport du monde**, *it's the finest sport in the world*
>
> **difficile, plus difficile, le plus difficile**, *difficult, more difficult, most difficult*
>
> **c'est une activité encore plus difficile**, *it's an even more difficult activity*
> **c'est l'activité la plus difficile**, *it's the most difficult activity*

■ The comparative or superlative comes in the same position, before or after the noun, that the adjective itself would take, and agrees in the same way as an ordinary adjective does. Notice that where it comes after the noun, the superlative adjective has its own definite article, independently of any article that already stands with the noun:

> **cette activité la plus difficile de toutes**, *this most difficult of all activities*

A superlative adjective immediately after a possessive (**mon, ma, mes; ton, ta, tes,** etc.) drops its definite article:

> **sa plus jolie jupe,** *her prettiest skirt*

■ The following comparative and superlative adjectives are exceptional:

> **bon, meilleur, le meilleur,** *good, better, best*
>
> **mauvais, plus mauvais, le plus mauvais,** or **mauvais, pire, le pire** (**pire, le pire** are less common. They are mainly used in some set phrases: **le remède est pire que le mal,** *the cure is worse than the disease*)
>
> **petit, plus petit, le plus petit,** *small, (physically) smaller, smallest,* or
>
> **petit, moindre, le moindre,** *little, less* (= *of less importance*), *least*

■ Comparisons, as well as being expressed by **plus ... que,** *more ... than,* can also be expressed by:

> **moins ... que,** *less ... than*
>
> **ton journal est moins intéressant que le mien,** *your paper's less interesting than mine*
>
> **aussi ... que,** *as ... as*
>
> **elle est aussi riche que son père,** *she's as rich as her father*
>
> **pas aussi** (or **pas si**) .,. **que,** *not as ... as*
>
> **elle n'est pas (aus)si riche que son grand-père,** *she's not as rich as her grandfather*

■ *Than* after a comparative is **que:**

> **vous êtes plus jeune qui moi,** *you're younger than me*

As after a comparative is also **que**:

> **elle n'est pas si vieille que lui**, *she's not as old as him*

In after a superlative is **de**:

> **le plus grand bâtiment du monde**, *the biggest building in the world*

By with either a comparative or a superlative is **de**:

> **il est de beaucoup le plus beau**, *he's by far the most handsome*

■ **Le/la/les moins** can also be used, like **le/la/les plus**, as a superlative:

> **l'enfant le moins gâté**, *the least spoiled child*

■ Where **plus** and **moins** are used to compare nouns rather than adjectives they are followed by **de**:

> **tu as plus de force que moi**, *you have more strength than I*
> **la ville a moins d'habitants qu'auparavant**, *the town has fewer inhabitants than formerly*

To express equal quantity **autant de**, *as much as*, is used:

> **elle a autant d'argent que son petit ami**, *she has as much money as her boyfriend*

More than, *less than* plus a quantity is also **plus de**, **moins de**:

> **il a plus de soixante ans**, *he's more than sixty*

■ *More and more* is **de plus en plus**, *less and less* **de moins en moins**:

> **le temps devient de plus en plus orageux**, *the weather's getting more and more stormy*
> **j'ai de moins en moins d'argent**, *I've less and less money*

▶ For the use of the subjunctive in a clause following a superlative, see p. 47.

DEMONSTRATIVE, POSSESSIVE, AND INTERROGATIVE ADJECTIVES

Demonstrative adjectives (*this*, *that* in English) and possessive adjectives (*my*, *your*, *his*, *her*, etc. in English) stand in exactly the same relationship to nouns as do definite and indefinite articles. They are in fact sometimes known as demonstrative and possessive articles.

■ The demonstrative adjective in French is **ce** (masculine singular), **cet** (masculine singular before a vowel or 'mute' **h**), **cette** (feminine singular), **ces** (plural):

> **ce jeune homme**, *this young man*
> **cet homme**, *this man*
> **cette fille**, *this girl*
> **ces gens**, *these people*

Where it is necessary to differentiate between *this* and *that*, **-ci** and **-là** are added to the following noun:

> **ce jeune homme-ci**, *this young man*
> **ces gens-là**, *those people*

However, just as French tends to use **là**, *there*, much more than **ici**, *here*, so **ce ... -là** is used in modern French in many cases where English would use *this*, with **ce ... là-bas** used for the more distant object:

> **tu sais quel train tu prends? Celui-là? — Non, ce train là-bas**, *do you know which train you're getting? This one?—No, that train (there)*

■ The possessive adjectives are:

	with masc. sing. noun	with fem. sing. noun	with plur. noun	
	mon	**ma**	**mes**	*my*
	ton	**ta**	**tes**	*your*
	son	**sa**	**ses**	*his, her, its*
		notre	**nos**	*our*
		votre	**vos**	*your*
		leur	**leurs**	*their*

Mon, **ton**, and **son** are also used before a feminine singular noun beginning with a vowel or 'mute' **h**.

> **c'est ma cassette**, *it's my cassette*
> **c'est ton orange**, *it's your orange* (**orange** is feminine)
> **c'est son pullover**, *it's his/her pullover*

Notice that **son**, **sa**, **ses**, like the rest of the possessives, have the gender of the object possessed, not of the person owning it. So **son pullover** is *his* or *her pullover*, **sa cassette** *his* or *her cassette*. Where it is necessary to differentiate, **à lui/à elle** are added:

> **c'est sa cassette à lui**, *it's <u>his</u> cassette*

■ The interrogative adjective in French is **quel?**, *which, what?* It agrees in gender and number with the noun that follows:

	singular	plural
masculine	**quel**	**quels**
feminine	**quelle**	**quelles**

> **quelle robe vas-tu porter?**, *which dress are you going to wear?*

Quel can be used to introduce an indirect question:

> **je ne sais pas quelle robe porter**, *I don't know
> what dress to wear*
> **je me demande quelle robe Sophie va porter**, *I
> wonder what dress Sophie will wear*

■ **Quel ...!** may also be an exclamation, meaning in the
singular *what a ...!*, *what ...!*, in the plural *what ...!*

> **quel bel enfant!**, *what a lovely child!*
> **quelle chance!**, *what luck!*
> **quelles vacances formidables!**, *what terrific
> holidays!*

INDEFINITE ADJECTIVES

Indefinite adjectives, as a group, include in English such
words as *several, certain, such*. The indefinite adjectives in
French are:

> **aucun, nul**, *no, not any*
> **autre**, *other*
> **certain**, *certain*
> **chaque**, *each*
> **même**, *same*
> **plusieurs**, *several*
> **quelque**, *some, any*
> **tel**, *such*
> **tout** (singular) *all, the whole of*; (plural) *all; every*

Chaque has no plural form, **plusieurs** no singular
form. **Plusieurs** is unchanged in both masculine and
feminine; **tel** and **tout** decline as follows:

	singular	*plural*
masculine	**tel; tout**	**tels; tous**
feminine	**telle; toute**	**telles; toutes**

Aucun and **nul** take **ne** with their verb, like negative
adverbs: see p. 159.

■ **Chaque, plusieurs, quelque, aucun, nul,** and **certains** (plural) are used without preceding article:

> **chaque employé recevra la même somme,** *each worker will be paid the same amount*
>
> **plusieurs d'entre eux sont là,** *several of them are there*
>
> **j'y vois quelques problèmes,** *I can see some problems there*
>
> **c'est à cause de certaines difficultés,** *it's because of certain difficulties*

■ **Tout** has the article following, as with *all* in English (but unlike the English usage with *every*):

> **tout le temps,** *all the time*
>
> **tous les soirs,** *every evening*

In the singular **tout** may be used without article to mean *all, any*:

> **cela exclut tout progrès dans cette affaire,** *that excludes any progress in this matter*

■ **Autre** and **tel** stand after the article like other adjectives. Notice that this is not the case with *such* in English:

> **les autres hommes,** *the other men*
>
> **un autre homme,** *another man*
>
> **un tel homme,** *such a man*

Such may also be used in English adverbially to qualify another adjective: *she has such big eyes*. In French this must be the adverb form **tellement,** or **si,** both of which mean *such* or *so*:

> **ses yeux sont tellement grands,** *her eyes are so big*
>
> **elle a de si grands yeux,** *she has such big eyes*

■ **Même** has four meanings according to position:

☐ Before the article, *even*

> **même son secrétaire le dit**, *even his secretary says so*

☐ Before the noun, or after the verb, *same*

> **c'est exactement la même chose**, *it's exactly the same thing*
>
> **ces deux filles sont toujours les mêmes**, *those two girls are always the same*

☐ After the noun, *very*

> **ce sont les paroles mêmes du président**, *they are the president's very words*

☐ Attached to a pronoun with a hyphen, *self*

> **il l'a fait lui-même**, *he did it himself*

NOUNS USED ADJECTIVALLY (ATTRIBUTIVE NOUNS)

English frequently uses nouns as adjectives: *a coffee pot, a steel saucepan, a box girder, a cat flap*. These imply something like 'used for', 'made from', 'in the form of', 'used by'. In French the adjectival (or attributive) noun is placed after the main noun, and joined to it with a preposition which makes clear this relationship. The prepositions used are **de**, **à**, and **en**:

de

☐ *of, appropriate for, belonging to*

> **un match de tennis**, *a tennis match* (= *a match of tennis*)

> **la route de Manieu**, *the Manieu road* (= *the road appropriate for Manieu*)
> **les feuilles d'automne**, *autumn leaves* (= *the leaves of autumn*)
> **des poulets de batterie**, *battery hens* (= *belonging to a battery*)

☐ *for the purpose of*

> **une salle d'attente**, *a waiting room* (= *a room for the purpose of waiting*)
> **un effet de choc**, *a shock effect* (= *an effect for the purpose of shocking*)

à

☐ *to contain, intended for*

> **un pot à café**, *a coffee pot* (= *a pot to contain coffee*. Compare **un pot de café**, *a pot of coffee*)
> **une boîte aux lettres**, *a letter box* (= *a box intended for letters*)

Verbal nouns (the -*ing* form in English, the infinitive in French) use **à** with this meaning to transform themselves into adjectives:

> **une salle à manger**, *a dining room* (= *a room intended for eating*)
> **une machine à laver**, *a washing machine* (= *a machine intended for washing*)

☐ *using, employing*

> **une poutre à caisson**, *a box girder* (= *a girder using a box shape*)
> **un moulin à vent**, *a windmill* (= *a mill that uses wind*)

☐ *with, possessing*

> **un chien à pedigree**, *a pedigree dog* (= *a dog possessing pedigree*)

en

□ *made from*

>**une casserole en acier**, *a steel saucepan* (= *a saucepan made from steel*)
>
>**un bracelet en or**, *a gold bracelet* (= *a bracelet made from gold*)

De is sometimes used in this way, too:

>**une barre de fer**, *an iron bar*

□ *in the form of*

>**un escalier en spirale**, *a spiral staircase* (= *a staircase in the form of a spiral*)

■ Sometimes, especially with modern words, the adjectival noun simply follows the main one, without any preposition, though often with a hyphen:

>**une cocotte-minute**, *a pressure cooker* ('minute casserole')
>
>**une bande-annonce**, *a film trailer* ('advertisement reel')

Adverbs

FORMATION OF ADVERBS

Adverbs formed from adjectives

■ Most French adverbs are formed by adding **-ment** to the feminine form of the adjective:

> **égal**, *equal* → feminine: **égale**
> → adverb: **également**, *equally*

■ If the masculine form of the adjective ends in a vowel, **-ment** is added to this masculine form:

> **vrai**, *real* → **vraiment**, *really*
> **forcé**, *forced* → **forcément**, *'forcedly'*, *necessarily*

Nouveau, mou, and **fou**, however, base their adverbs on their differing feminine forms **nouvelle, molle**, and **folle**:

> **nouveau** → **nouvellement**, *newly*
> **mou** → **mollement**, *softly*
> **fou** → **follement**, *madly*

■ Adjectives ending **-ent** and **-ant** form adverbs ending **-emment** and **-amment** (both pronounced as if they were spelled **-amment**):

> récent → récemment, *recently*
> constant → constamment, *constantly*

Exceptions: **lent → lentement**, *slowly*; **présent → présentement**, *presently*

■ A number of adjectives that do not end in **é** follow the pattern of **forcément**:

> aveugle → aveuglément, *blindly*
> commun → communément, *communally*
> confus → confusément, *confusedly*
> énorme → énormément, *enormously*
> exprès → expressément, *explicitly*
> impuni, *unpunished* → impunément, *with impunity, scot-free*
> intense, *intense* → intensément, *intensively*
> précis → précisément, *precisely*
> profond → profondément, *deeply*

■ The following adverbs are completely irregular in the way they are formed from their adjectives:

> bon → bien, *well*
> bref → brièvement, *briefly*
> continu → continûment, *continuously*
> gai → gaiement, *gaily*
> gentil → gentiment, *kindly*
> mauvais → mal, *badly*
> meilleur → mieux, *better*
> moindre → moins, *less*
> petit → peu, *little*
> traître → traîtreusement, *treacherously*

Adverbs not formed from adjectives

There are also many adverbs in French which are not formed from adjectives, mostly short words like **ainsi, donc, dedans**:

ainsi c'est entendu?, *so it's agreed?*

Some of these relate to conjunctions:

ainsi, *thus*, conjunction → **ainsi**, *so*, adverb

some to prepositions:

dans, *in*, preposition → **dedans**, *inside*, adverb

some are independent:

donc, *then*, adverb

Adverb alternatives

■ Adjectives are used as adverbs in a number of fixed expressions:

bas, haut	**parler bas, parler haut**, *speak softly/loudly*
bon, mauvais	**sentir bon, sentir mauvais**, *smell good/bad*
cher	**coûter cher, payer cher**, *cost/pay a lot*
court	**s'arrêter court, couper court**, *stop/cut short*
dur	**travailler dur**, *work hard*
juste / faux	**chanter juste, chanter faux**, *sing in/out of tune*
net	**refuser net**, *refuse point blank*

■ Adverb phrases commonly substitute for the longer and more cumbersome adverbs, and must be used where the adjective has no corresponding adverb, such as **content**, *happy*, *content*:

il me regarda d'un air content, *he looked at me contentedly*

— Ah non, dit-il d'une voix triste, *'Oh no,' he said sadly*

elle répondit à voix basse, *she answered softly*

je l'ai fait avec soin, *I did it carefully*

le régiment s'est battu avec beaucoup de courage, *the regiment fought very courageously*

elle l'a fait sans hésitation, *she did it unhesitatingly*

POSITION OF ADVERBS

Adverbs describe or modify a verb:

> **elle joue bien**, *she plays well* (adverb: **bien**)

or an adjective:

> **cela est complètement différent**, *that's completely different* (adverb: **complètement**)

or another adverb:

> **oui, très probablement**, *yes, very probably* (modifying adverb: **très**)

■ With adjectives and adverbs the modifying adverb stands immediately in front of the word it modifies, as in English. See the last two examples above.

■ With verbs:

□ In simple tenses adverbs usually stand immediately after the verb.

> **je connais intimement toute cette famille**, *I know all that family intimately*

□ In compound tenses adverbs follow the past participle if they take the stress.

> **je l'ai vu finalement**, *I saw him, in the end*
> **je lui ai finalement parlé**, *I finally <u>spoke</u> to him*

In practice this means that adverbs of place and precise adverbs of time (**aujourd'hui, demain, hier**, etc.) almost always stand after the past participle:

> **elle l'a mis là, sur le plancher**, *she's put it there, on the floor*
> **on l'a fait hier**, *we did it yesterday*

and short adverbs of degree (**bien, beaucoup, trop**, etc.) or imprecise adverbs of time (**déjà, souvent, bientôt**, etc.) stand before the past participle:

> **tu l'as très bien expliqué**, *you explained it very well*
>
> **il est déjà arrivé**, *he's already arrived*

☐ With a dependent infinitive the above points about adverbs with the past participle also apply.

> **je vais le faire finalement**, *I'm finally going to do it*
>
> **je vais finalement lui parler**, *I'm finally going to speak to him*

■ Adverbs, especially those of time and place, may be placed at the head of their clause for emphasis, as they sometimes are in English:

> **partout on voyait des coquelicots**, *everywhere poppies could be seen*
>
> **jamais je n'aurais fait cela**, *I'd never have done that*

■ Interrogative adverbs stand at the head of their clause, of course:

> **quand reviendra-t-elle?**, *when will she come back?*

► For the word order after interrogative adverbs, see p. 212.

COMPARATIVE AND SUPERLATIVE OF ADVERBS

In English the comparative and superlative are:

> *easily* →comparative: *more easily*
> superlative: *most easily*

In French the comparative and superlative of adverbs are formed in a similar way to those of adjectives (for which see p. 143):

> **facilement**, *easily*
>
> *comparative* **plus facilement**, *more easily*
>
> *superlative* **le plus facilement**, *most easily*

> **c'est comme ça que tu le feras le plus facilement**,
> *that's the way you'll do it most easily*

■ The superlative adverb always starts **le** (never **la** or **les**):

> **c'est elle qui le fera le plus facilement**, *she's the one who will do it most easily*

■ As with adjectives

> **moins … que**, *less … than*
>
> **aussi … que**, *as … as*
>
> **si … que**, *as* (after a negative)

can be used to form comparatives in the same way as **plus … que**:

> **elle part en vacances moins souvent que toi**, *she goes on holiday less often than you*
>
> **il ne conduit pas si vite que toi**, *he doesn't drive as fast as you*

Le moins …, *the least …*, can also be used in a similar way to **le plus …**, *the most …*, to form a superlative:

> **celui qui le fait le moins bien**, *the one who does it least well*

■ The following adverbs have irregular comparatives and superlatives:

beaucoup, *much*	**plus, le plus**, *more, the most*
bien, *well*	**mieux, le mieux**, *better, the best*
peu, *little*	**moins, le moins**, *less, the least*

The comparative adverb **pis**, *worse*, corresponding to the comparative adjective **pire**, is now only used in a few set expressions:

> **tant pis pour lui!**, *so much the worse for him!*

NEGATIVE ADVERBS

The negative adverbs in French are

> **aucun**, *no, none*
> **guère**, *hardly*
> **jamais**, *never*
> **ni**, *neither; nor*
> **nul**, *no*
> **nulle part**, *nowhere*
> **nullement**, *in no way*
> **pas**, *not*
> **personne**, *nobody*
> **plus**, *no longer*
> **que**, *only*
> **rien**, *nothing*

Negating a verb

The normal position for all the negative adverbs is after the verb in simple tenses, and before the past participle in compound tenses. In addition, they all have **ne** before the verb and any accompanying object pronouns. **Ne** becomes **n'** before a vowel or 'mute' **h**:

> **je ne le lui donne jamais**, *I never give it to him*
> **je n'ai rien dit**, *I haven't said anything*

■ **Nulle part** and **personne** normally come after the past participle in compound tenses:

> **ils n'ont vu personne**, *they haven't seen anyone*
> **on ne le trouve nulle part**, *it is not found anywhere*

■ **Ni**

☐ With two objects: the **ni** is repeated in front of each object. Any pronoun object must be a disjunctive (see p. 111)

> **je n'ai rencontré ni lui ni sa femme,** *I met neither him nor his wife*

☐ With two subjects: the **ni** is repeated in front of each subject. Any pronoun subject must be a disjunctive (see p. 111). The verb is usually plural

> **ni lui ni sa femme n'étaient là,** *neither he nor his wife was (were) there*

☐ With two verbs: the **ne** is repeated

> **il ne fume ni ne boit,** *he neither smokes nor drinks*

Neither without *nor* is **non plus**:

> **moi non plus,** *me neither!*
> **je ne l'ai pas vu non plus,** *I haven't seen him either*

■ **Que**, *only*, qualifying an object stands in front of the object. A pronoun object must be a disjunctive (see p. 111):

> **je n'aime que lui,** *I love only him*
> **je n'ai vraiment regardé que l'acteur principal,** *I only really looked at the main actor*

Que can also be made to qualify a verb by using the verb as an infinitive in the construction **ne faire que**:

> **cet enfant ne fait que crier,** *that child only cries (does nothing but cry)*

Que can itself be negated with **pas**:

> **il n'y a pas que Pierre qui soit invité,** *it's not only Pierre who's been invited*

■ **Aucun** and **nul** are actually adjectives, agreeing with the noun they stand in front of. They are used only in the singular; **nul** has the feminine form **nulle**.

In all other respects **aucun** and **nul** are like the other negative adverbs.

■ **Personne, rien, ni … ni …, aucun …** and **nul …** can stand as the subject of the sentence. The **ne** still appears before the verb (but beware—there is no **pas**!):

> **personne ne l'a entendu,** *nobody's heard him*

See indefinite pronouns, pp. 127 ff.

Negating an infinitive

■ With an infinitive both the **ne** and the negative adverb stand in front of the infinitive and its pronoun objects:

> **je peux ne pas venir,** *I may possibly not come* (as opposed to **je ne peux pas venir,** *I can't come*)

except in the case of those negative adverbs which follow the past participle (**personne, nulle part, ni, que, aucun, nul**), which also follow the infinitive:

> **je suis désolé de ne voir personne,** *I'm very sorry not to see anyone*
>
> **j'espère ne trouver ni difficultés ni problèmes,** *I hope to find neither difficulties nor problems*

■ **Sans** + infinitive can stand with all the negative adverbs, without a **ne**:

> **sans rien voir,** *without seeing anything*

Double negative adverbs

Plus and **jamais** can qualify another negative adverb. They stand in front of it:

>**je ne vois plus personne**, *I don't see anybody any more*
>
>**je n'achète jamais rien**, *I never buy anything*

Negatives with other parts of the sentence

■ *Not* with parts of the sentence other than the verb is either **pas** or **non,** or the stronger **non pas**. **Ne** does not appear in this case:

>**je veux des pommes, et non pas des pommes de terre!**, *I want apples, not potatoes!*

■ Most of the negative adverbs can be used without **ne** where no verb is expressed:

>**qui a téléphoné? — Personne**, *who phoned?— Nobody*
>
>**qu'est-ce que tu entends? — Plus rien**, *what can you hear?—Nothing any more*

Omission of ne and pas

■ **Ne** is omitted extremely frequently in spoken French:

>**Jean-Luc? Connais pas!**, *Jean-Luc? Don't know him!*
>
>**elle vient ce soir? — Oh, je sais pas**, *is she coming tonight?—Oh, I don't know*

■ **Pas** is omitted in literary French with the verbs **pouvoir, savoir, oser** + infinitive

>**je ne savais comment répondre**, *I did not know how to reply*

Non-negative ne

A non-negative **ne** is used in careful speech in clauses dependent on a number of expressions, mostly involving the subjunctive. The commonest are:

■ Verbs of fearing: **avoir peur que, craindre que**

> **j'ai peur qu'elle ne soit déjà là**, *I'm afraid she may be there already*

■ Conjunctions: **avant que, à moins que, de peur que, de crainte que**

> **je l'ai fait de peur qu'elle ne le fasse elle-même**, *I did it for fear she (in case she) might do it herself*

■ Comparisons: **plus ... que, moins ... que**

> **il est moins habile que vous ne pensez**, *he is less clever than you think*

This **ne** has no negative meaning and is not used in everyday spoken French.

► See uses of the subjunctive, pp. 41 ff.

Prepositions

Prepositions—words like *in*, *on*, *over*—stand in front of a noun or pronoun to relate it to the rest of the sentence:

> **il chante toujours dans la salle de bain**, *he always sings in the bathroom* (preposition: **dans**, *in*)

■ Prepositions can also stand in front of a verb—*without looking*, *by singing*. In English this part of a verb is the *-ing* form. In French it is the infinitive:

> **sans regarder**, *without looking*

except with the preposition **en**, which is followed by a present participle:

> **en chantant**, *whilst singing*

■ The prepositions **à** and **de** combine with the definite article to form **au**, **aux** and **du**, **des**. See p. 77.

■ The prepositions **à**, **de**, and **en** are usually repeated if they refer to more than one noun or pronoun. This is often not the case in English:

> **j'ai parlé à lui et à ses voisins**, *I spoke to him and his neighbours*

ALPHABETICAL LIST OF FRENCH PREPOSITIONS AND THEIR USE

The use of prepositions differs considerably from language to language. Below we give an alphabetical list of those French prepositions that may give difficulty, with their main and subsidiary meanings and examples of their use. The principal meaning (or meanings) is given first, with other meanings following in alphabetical order.

In addition, on p. 185 there is an alphabetical list of English prepositions with their various French equivalents, for cross-reference to the French list.

à, *at*

at (place)

> **on se retrouve à la gare routiere**, *we'll meet at the bus station*
> **à la maison**, *at home*
> **à l'école**, *at school*
> **au travail**, *at work*

at (time)

> **à midi et à une heure**, *at noon and at one o'clock*
> **au crépuscule**, *at twilight*
> **à l'aube**, *at dawn*
> **à Noël**, *at Christmas*

at (numbers)

> **à cent kilomètres à l'heure,** (*at*) *100 km. an hour*
> **à très peu de distance**, *at a very little distance*
> **ceux à vingt francs**, *those at 20 francs*

belonging to (English uses the possessive pronoun):

> **c'est à lui** (= it belongs to him), *it's his*

▶ See p. 123.

by

> **tu le reconnaîtras à sa moustache**, *you'll recognize him by his moustache*
> **des dentelles faites à la main** (= by hand), *hand-made lace*
> **cela se vend au kilo**, *we sell that by the kilo*

for (English uses an attributive noun)

> **un réservoir à essence** (= a tank for petrol), *a petrol tank*
>
> **un verre à vin** (= a glass for wine), *a wineglass* (compare **un verre de vin**, *a glass of wine*)

from

> **il l'a pris à ton frère**, *he took it from your brother* (and similarly **arracher à**, *snatch from*, **acheter à**, *buy from*, **boire à**, *drink from*, **cacher à**, *hide from*, **emprunter à**, *borrow from*, **voler à**, *steal from*)

in (place)

> **à la campagne**, *in the country* (but **en ville**, *in town*)
>
> **à la main**, *in my* (*her, your, etc.*) *hand*
>
> **au lit**, *in bed*
>
> **au ciel**, *in the sky*
>
> **au soleil**, *in the sun*
>
> **à Marseille**, *in Marseilles*
>
> **aux États-Unis**, *in the United States*
>
> **au Mexique**, *in Mexico* (but **en** with feminine singular countries: **en France**)

in (time)

> **au petit matin**, *in the early morning* (but without an adjective '*in*' with parts of the day is just **le**: **le matin**, *in the morning*; **l'après-midi**, *in the afternoon*; **le soir**, *in the evening*)
>
> **au XXᵉ siècle**, *in the twentieth century*
>
> **au mois de mai**, *in* (*the month of*) *May* (but **en mai**, *in May*)
>
> **au printemps**, *in spring* (but **en** with the other seasons: **en été**, *in summer*)
>
> **à son tour**, *in* (*his*) *turn*

in (manner)

> **à voix basse**, *in a soft voice*
>
> **des champignons à la grecque**, *mushrooms cooked the Greek way*
>
> **des tripes à la mode de Caen**, *Caen-style tripe*

on

> **au menu**, *on the menu*
>
> **ces peintures au mur**, *those paintings on the wall*
>
> **marqué au front**, *marked on the forehead*
>
> **à bicyclette, à pied, à cheval**, *on a bicycle (by bicycle), on foot, on horseback*
>
> **à droite/gauche**, *on the right/left*
>
> **à la page dix-huit**, *on page 18*

to

> **je vais à la boulangerie**, *I'm going to the baker's*
>
> **elle va à Paris, aux États-Unis, au Portugal**, *she's going to Paris, the USA, Portugal (but **en** with feminine singular countries: **elle va en Italie**, she's going to Italy)*
>
> **j'ai parlé à ton professeur**, *I've spoken to your teacher*
>
> **du matin au soir**, *from morning to (till) night*

using (English usually has an attributive noun)

> **un moteur à essence** (= using petrol), *a petrol engine*
>
> **un moulin à vent** (= using wind), *a windmill*
>
> **une locomotive à vapeur** (= using steam), *a steam locomotive*

with (= *containing, having*—English may use an attributive noun)

> **une pâté aux truffes** (= a pâté with truffles), *truffle pâté*
>
> **un chien à pedigree** (= a dog with a pedigree), *a pedigree dog*

l'homme au parapluie, *the man with the umbrella*
la femme aux yeux verts, *the woman with green eyes*

▶ For uses of **à** with verbs see p. 56.

▶ For **à** used after adjectives, nouns, and adverbs see p. 51.

à part, *except*

▶ See **au dehors de**, below.

à travers, *through*

▶ See **par**, p. 180.

après, *after*

after (time)

après trois heures, *after three o'clock*
après la guerre, *after the war*

after (place)

la troisième maison après la mairie, *the third house after the town hall*
elle court après lui, *she's running after him*

according to (notice the **d'**)

d'après Le Figaro, *according to Le Figaro*

▶ For **après** + perfect infinitive (*after ...ing*), see p. 53.

au-dehors de, *outside*

outside

ce chien reste au-dehors de la maison, *that dog stays outside the house*

The shorter form **hors de** locates less precisely:

> **ceux qui habitent hors de la ville**, *those who live
> (somewhere) outside the town*

Hors de also means *out of*:

> **elle était hors d'haleine**, *she was out of breath*

and, in literary usage, **hors** means *except*:

> **nous y sommes tous allés hors lui**, *we all went
> except him*

Except is, however, now more usually **à part**:

> **personne à part sa mère**, *no one except her
> mother*

au-dessous de, *under(neath), below*

▶ See **sous**, p. 183.

au-dessus de, *over*

over, above (physically)

> **le ciel au-dessus de la montagne**, *the sky over
> (above) the mountains*

Over, above with motion is **par-dessus**:

> **sauter par-dessus un obstacle**, *to leap over an
> obstacle*

Where *over* implies *touching* it is **sur**:

> **une serviette sur le bras**, *with a towel over his
> arm*

above, over (= *more than*)

> **ne paie pas au-dessus de cent francs**, *don't pay
> above (more than) 100 francs*

auprès de, *beside*

beside (nearness)

> **elle se tenait auprès du lit**, *she was standing beside the bed*

beside (= *compared to*)

> **son frère jumeau n'est rien auprès de lui**, *his twin brother is nothing beside (compared to) him*

avant, *before*

before (time)

> **avant le commencement du jeu**, *before the beginning of the match*
> **avant de sortir**, *before going out* (note the **de** before an infinitive)

before (place in a sequence of places)

> **vous descendez avant Genève?**, *are you getting out before Geneva?*

The older, formal use of *before* to mean *in front of* is **devant**:

> **il s'agenouilla devant l'autel**, *he knelt before the altar*

avec, *with*

with (= *together with*)

> **tu viens avec nous?**, *are you coming with us?*

with (= *by means of*)

> **tu n'y arriveras pas avec un tire-bouchon**, *you won't manage it with a corkscrew*

chez, *at X's*

at (or to) the house or shop of (English usually uses a possessive)

> **on va chez l'épicier**, *we're going to the grocer's*
> **on se voit chez Chantal**, *see you at Chantal's*
> **faites comme chez vous**, *make yourself at home*

with (= *as far as X is concerned*)

> **c'est une habitude chez elle**, *with her it's a habit*

among

> **chez les Esquimaux on ne joue pas beaucoup au tennis**, *not much tennis is played among the Eskimos*

in (*the works of*)

> **on ne trouve pas ce mot chez Racine**, *that word isn't found in Racine*

contre, *against*

against (in both concrete and abstract senses)

> **l'échelle est contre le garage**, *the ladder is against the garage*
> **nous sommes tous contre la guerre**, *we are all against war*

for

> **tu veux échanger ça contre mon tourne-disques?**, *do you want to exchange that for my record player?*

dans, *in*

in, into (place)

>**on va dans le jardin**, *we're going into the garden*
>
>**il y a deux hommes dans sa vie**, *there are two men in her life*

in (time, = *at the end of*)

>**je serai de retour dans dix minutes**, *I'll be back in ten minutes* (= *ten minutes from now*)

In = *within the space of* is **en**:

>**je le ferai en dix minutes**, *I'll do it in* (*within the space of*) *ten minutes*

from

>**je l'ai pris dans le tiroir**, *I took it from the drawer*

▶ See also **à**, *from*, p. 166. The French have in mind the original position of the object, from which it is then taken, snatched, etc.

de, *of*

of (possession or relation—English often uses a possessive or an attributive noun)

>**la voiture de Pierre**, *Pierre's car* (*the car of Pierre*)
>
>**la première femme de mon oncle**, *my uncle's first wife* (*the first wife of my uncle*)
>
>**la porte du jardin**, *the garden gate* (*the gate of the garden*)
>
>**la route de Versailles**, *the Versailles road* (*the road of Versailles*)
>
>**une partie de plaisir**, *a pleasure party* (*a party of pleasure*)

les vacances de Noël, *the Christmas holidays* (*the holidays of Christmas*)

of (= *containing*)

un verre de vin, *a glass of wine*

of (appositional, = *that is*)

au mois de septembre, *in the month of September* (*the month that is September*)

la ville de Paris, *the city of Paris*

about (= *concerning*)

elle est folle de ses animaux, *she's mad about her animals*

by

elle est Française de naissance, *she's French by birth*

il arriva accompagné de sa femme, *he arrived accompanied by his wife*

il a été blessé d'une balle, *he has been hit by a bullet* (See p. 33 for the use of **de** with the passive)

from

d'où vient-il?, *where has he come from?*

il revient de Paris, *he's just come back from Paris*

de temps en temps, *from time to time*

elle est différente de sa sœur, *she's different from her sister*

in (manner)

d'une voix tremblante, *in a trembling voice* (but **à voix basse/haute**, *in a low/loud voice*)

d'une manière impolie, *in a rude manner*

d'une façon stupide, *in a stupid way*

Similarly,

d'un air fâché, *with an angry look*

in (after a superlative or superlative-type word—see p. 145)

> **le meilleur du monde**, *the best in the world*
> **le premier de sa classe**, *the first in its class*

made of (English usually uses an attributive noun)

> **un coussin de soie**, *a silk cushion (a cushion made of silk)*
> **un chapeau de paille**, *a straw hat (a hat made of straw)*

than (with a quantity following a comparison)

> **plus de cinq fois**, *more than five times*
> **les enfants de moins de treize ans**, *children below (of less than) thirteen years*

to

> **tu es libre de supposer n'importe quoi**, *you are free to assume anything at all*

with

> **il est couvert de boue**, *he's covered with mud*
> **elle pleure de joie**, *she is weeping with joy*
> **il nous questionna d'un air soupçonneux**, *he questioned us with a suspicious look*

De is also used, with no equivalent word in English, in the following cases.

■ After expressions of quantity (this includes **un million**, *million*, and **un milliard**, *billion*, but not other numbers):

> **beaucoup de monde**, *a lot of people*
> **trop de questions**, *too many questions*
> **un million de chiens**, *a million dogs*

▶ See p. 83.

■ After **quelque chose, rien, personne**, etc.:

> **quelque chose de beau**, *something beautiful*
> **rien de spécial**, *nothing special*

▶ See pp. 128 ff.

■ To join two nouns where the second is used adjectivally (the attributive noun):

> **la salle de bain**, *the bathroom*
> **la salle de séjour**, *the sitting room*

▶ For **de** with verbs see p. 55.
▶ For **de** used after adjectives, nouns, and adverbs see p. 51.

depuis, *since*

since (a place or a point in time)

> **tu n'as rien mangé depuis ton arrivée**, *you haven't eaten anything since your arrival* (*since you got here*)
> **c'est le premier péage depuis Lyon**, *it's the first toll point since Lyons*

for (a length of time)

> **elle regarde la télévision depuis une demi-heure**, *she's been watching television for half an hour*

▶ *For* with time may also be **pendant** or **pour**. See pp. 181, 182.
▶ For tenses with both the above meanings of **depuis** see pp. 17 and 21.

from (a place or a time), in **depuis ... jusqu'à**, *from ... to*

> **la côte méditerranéenne depuis Toulon jusqu'à Nice**, *the Mediterranean coast from Toulon to (as far as) Nice*

> on est ouvert depuis huit heures du matin jusqu'à
> huit heures du soir, *we are open from eight in
> the morning until eight at night*

De ... à is less emphatic:

> **du matin au soir**, *from morning to night*

from (a place, = *out from*)

> **le panorama depuis le sommet est extraordinaire**,
> *the panorama from the summit is remarkable*

dès, *as soon as*

as soon as; no later than (with future time)

> **je le ferai dès demain**, *I'll do it no later than
> tomorrow*
> **dès son arrivée**, *as soon as she gets here*
> **dès maintenant**, *from now on*

as far back as; ever since (a point in past time onwards)

> **dès cette époque elle donnait des signes de folie**,
> *even at that period (as far back as that period) she
> was showing signs of madness*

devant, *in front of*

▶ See **avant**, p. 170.

en, *in*

En expresses *in* in a more abstract or less specific way
than does **dans**. It is always used without an article:

> **en ville**, *in town*
> **en question**, *in question*

except in a very few set expressions beginning with a
vowel or 'mute' **h**:

en l'absence de, *in the absence of*
en l'air, *in the air*
en l'an ..., *in (the year)* ...
en l'honneur de, *in honour of*

in

en réponse à votre lettre, *in reply to your letter*
en forme de collier, *in the form of a necklace*
elle sortit en colère, *she went out angry (in anger)*
la cuisine était peinte en vert, *the kitchen was painted (in) green*
habillé en short, *dressed in shorts*

in (time: months, seasons, years)

en février, *in February*
en été, en automne et en hiver, *in summer, autumn, and winter* (but au printemps, *in spring*)
en 1999, *in 1999* (but en l'an 1999—note the article)

in, into (languages)

en français, *in French*
traduisez ça en anglais, *translate that into English*

in, to (with feminine singular names of countries and of continents)

on va en France, *we're going to France*
nous vivons en Europe, *we live in Europe*

▶ Otherwise *in* or *to* with countries is **au / aux**. See à, pp. 166, 167.

in (time within which)

je le ferai en deux minutes, *I'll do it (I'll have it done) in two minutes*

In (= *at the end of which time*) is **dans**:

> **je le ferai dans deux minutes**, *I'll do it (I'll start the job) in two minutes*

▶ See **dans**, p. 172.

as (= *in the shape of, as if it were*)

> **Monsieur Charles, en parfait gentleman, les accueillit très poliment**, *Charles, as the perfect gentleman, welcomed them very politely*
> **il me traite toujours en enfant**, *he always treats me as a child*
> **elle était déguisée en duchesse**, *she was dressed as a duchess*

by (with a form of transport, usually when one is 'in' the vehicle)

> **nous y allons en avion**, *we're going by plane*
> **ceux qui roulent en auto et en moto**, *those who travel by car and by motorbike* (also **à moto**)

▶ See also **à** (p. 167) and **par** (p. 180) with this meaning.

by, whilst, on (followed by the present participle)

> **je l'ai rencontrée en sortant du supermarché**, *I met her (whilst I was) coming out of the supermarket*

▶ See present participle, p. 35.

in the form of (English sometimes uses an attributive noun)

> **des chaussettes en accordéon**, *wrinkled socks (in the form of an accordion)*
> **un escalier en spirale**, *a spiral staircase (in the form of a spiral)*

made of (English often uses an attributive noun)

> **une table en acajou**, *a mahogany table*

De is also used with this meaning (see p. 174). **En** tends to draw more attention to the material of which the article is made than does **de**:

>**une montre en or**, *a gold watch*

on

>**j'ai un chat qui me suit en promenade**, *I've a cat that follows me on my walks*
>**on part en vacances**, *we're leaving on holiday*

entre, *between*

between (two people or things)

>**entre lui et moi**, *between him and me*
>**entre dix heures et minuit**, *between ten o'clock and midnight*

among(st) (more than two people or things)

>**ici vous êtes entre amis**, *here you are among friends*
>**les gens parlaient entre eux**, *people were talking among themselves*

Among(st) is, however, more frequently **parmi**:

>**parmi tous ceux qui étaient là, elle était la seule à bouger**, *amongst all those who were there she was the only one to move*

of (after **de** (**d'entre**) in expressions of quantity before pronouns)

>**quatre d'entre eux**, *four of them*
>**beaucoup d'entre vous**, *many of you*

envers, *towards* (figurative)

▶ See **vers**, p. 185.

hors (de), *except; out of*

▶ See **au-dehors de**, p. 168.

par, *by*

by

> **on commence par discuter, on finit par se**
> **quereller**, *you begin by discussing, you end by*
> *falling out*
> **par la D565**, *by the D565 road*
> **par ici/là**, (*by*) *this/that way*

by (with passive)

> **elle a été blessée par son mari**, *she was injured*
> *by her husband*

▶ See passive, p. 33.

by (with a few forms of transport, as an alternative to **en**)

> **par le train**, *by train*
> **par le métro**, *by underground*
> **par avion**, *by plane*

from (= *out of*, reason)

> **elle ne fait rien par conviction**, *she does nothing*
> *from (out of) conviction*

on, to

> **il était étendu par terre**, *he was lying on the*
> *ground*
> **elle est tombée par terre**, *she fell over; she fell to*
> *the ground* (from a standing position). Compare:
> **tomber à terre**, *fall to the ground* (from a height)

on, in (weather)

> **par un jour froid d'hiver**, *on a cold winter's day*
> **par un temps superbe**, *in splendid weather*

per, *a* (after numbers)

> **cinquante fois par semaine**, *fifty times a week*
> **deux par personne**, *two per person*

through

> **elle m'a vu par la fenêtre**, *she saw me through the window*
> **il a longtemps erré par les rues de Paris**, *for a long time he wandered through the streets of Paris*

Through where some difficulty is implied is **à travers**:

> **il se fraya un chemin à travers la foule**, *he battled his way through the crowd*

via

> **tu peux passer par Lyon ou par Dijon**, *you can go via Lyons or Dijon*

parmi, *among(st)*

▶ See **entre**, p. 179.

pendant, *during*

during

> **pendant ma visite**, *during my visit*

for (a completed period of time in the past)

> **ce mois-ci il a chômé pendant treize jours**, *this month he was out of work for thirteen days*

▶ See also **pour** (p. 182) and **depuis** (p. 175) meaning *for* with time.

pour, *for*

for (= *in favour of*)

> **tu votes pour les socialistes?**, *are you voting for the socialists?*
>
> **il faut peser le pour et le contre**, *you've got to weigh the pros and cons*

for (= *on behalf of*)

> **morts pour la France**, *they died for France*
>
> **elle y répondra pour toi**, *she'll reply to it for you*

for (intention)

> **ceci est pour toi**, *this is for you*
>
> **l'avion part pour Paris à trois heures cinq**, *the plane leaves for Paris at 3.05*

for (= *because of*)

> **on vous donne une contravention pour avoir laissé votre voiture devant le commissariat**, *you've been given a parking ticket for having left (for leaving) your car in front of the police station*

for (= *in exchange for*)

> **qu'est-ce que tu me donnes pour mon vélo?**, *what will you give me for my bike?*

for (plus intended length of time)

> **tu y vas pour trois mois?**, *you're going for three months?*

▶ See also **depuis** (p. 175) and **pendant** (p. 181) meaning *for* with time.

for (+ an amount)

> **tu en as là pour vingt minutes**, *you've enough work there for twenty minutes*

pour cent francs de sans-plomb, s'il vous plaît, *100 francs worth ('for 100 francs') of unleaded, please*

as for

pour ma part, je voudrais bien le faire, *as far as I'm concerned (as for me), I'd like to do it*

Quant à is also used in this sense:

quant à vous, *as for you*

per

dix pour cent, *ten per cent*

to (= in order to)

pour faire fonctionner la pompe, il faut d'abord sortir le robinet, *(in order) to operate the pump, the nozzle must first be withdrawn*

to (after **trop** *+ adjective,* too ...*,* **assez** *+ adjective,* ... enough, *and the verb* **suffire,** *to be enough)*

tu es trop jeune pour y entrer, *you're too young to go in*

vous êtes assez informé pour savoir que ..., *you're well enough informed to know that ...*

cela suffira pour vous donner une idée de ce que nous pensons, *that will be enough to give you an idea of our thoughts*

quant à, *as for*

▶ See **pour**, above.

sous, *under*

under

ton hamster est sous ma chaise, *your hamster is under my chair*

Au-dessous de, *under,* implies *completely under* (= *underneath*), or means *below* in figurative senses:

> **les chiffres sont au-dessous de ce qu'on attendait**, *the figures are below what we expected*

in

> **tu ne peux pas sortir sous la pluie**, *you can't go out in the rain*
>
> **nous nous reverrons sous peu**, *we'll see each other shortly (in a little while)*
>
> **ils vécurent sous le règne de Louis XIV**, *they lived in the reign of Louis XIV*

sur, *on*

on, on to

> **je l'ai laissé sur le fauteuil**, *I left it on the armchair*
>
> **monte sur l'échelle**, *climb up (on to) the ladder*
>
> **elle était sur le point de m'interrompre**, *she was about to interrupt me (on the point of interrupting me)*
>
> **assis sur le mur**, *sitting on the wall (on = hanging on is* **à**. *See p. 167)*
>
> **sur notre droite**, *on our right*
>
> **je n'ai pas d'argent sur moi**, *I haven't any money on me*

by

> **douze centimètres de haut sur dix centimètres de large**, *12 cm. high by 10 cm. wide*

over

> **son autorité sur vous est très restreinte**, *his authority over you is very limited*
>
> **le pont sur l'estuaire de la Seine**, *the bridge over the Seine estuary*

▶ See also **au-dessus de,** *over*, p. 169.

in

> **j'ai laissé la clé sur la porte**, *I've left the key in the door*

in, out of

> **une personne sur dix**, *one person in ten*
> **dix-neuf sur vingt**, *19 out of 20*

upon

> **sur quoi, elle claqua la porte**, *whereupon (upon which) she slammed the door*

vers, *towards*

towards (place or point in time)

> **il s'en va vers la plage**, *he goes off towards the beach*
> **vers la fin de l'après-midi**, *towards the end of the afternoon*

Towards (figurative) is **envers**:

> **il est très bien intentionné envers nous**, *he is very well intentioned towards us*

about (with time of day)

> **vers dix heures et demie**, *about half past ten*

CROSS-REFERENCE LIST OF ENGLISH PREPOSITIONS

Prepositions presenting problems of translation are listed. These prepositions are cross-referenced to the list of French prepositions starting on p. 164. It is dangerous to take a French meaning from this list without subsequently checking its usage in the French list.

about
 = *concerning*, **de**, 173
 + time of day, **vers**, 185

according to
 d'après, 168

after
 place, **après**, 168
 time, **après**, 168

against
 contre, 171

among(st)
 chez, 171
 entre, 179
 parmi, 179

as
 = *in the shape of, as if it were*, **en**, 178

as far back as
 dès, 176

as for
 pour, 183

as soon as
 dès, 176

at
 numbers, **à**, 165
 place, **à**, 165
 time, **à**, 165

at X's (house, shop)
 chez, 171

above
 au-dessus de, 169
 par-dessus, 169

under
  sous, 183
  au-dessous de, 184

underneath
  au-dessous de, 184

upon
  sur, 185

using
  à, 167

via
  par, 181

whilst
  + present participle, **en**, 178

with
  de, 174
  manner, **de**, 173
  = *as far as X is concerned*, **chez**, 171
  = *by means of*, **avec**, 170
  = *containing, having*, **à**, 167
  = *together with*, **avec**, 170

| Conjunctions

■ Conjunctions are joining-words. They may join nouns or pronouns:

> **lui et son chien**, *he and his dog* (conjunction: **et**)

or phrases:

> **en arrivant ou en partant**, *on arriving or leaving* (conjunction: **ou**)

or clauses:

> **elle chante, mais elle ne joue pas**, *she sings but she doesn't play* (conjunction: **mais**)

■ They may also introduce a subordinate clause:

> **je le ferai quand j'aurai de l'argent**, *I'll do it when I have money* (conjunction: **quand**)

Many of the conjunctions that introduce subordinate clauses in French are two-word phrases with **que** as the second word:

> **je lui ai téléphoné pendant qu'elle travaillait**, *I phoned her whilst she was working* (conjunction: **pendant que**)

Quite often the first word of the phrase is a preposition with the same English meaning as the conjunction:

> **avant**, *before*, preposition
> **avant que**, *before*, conjunction

> **sans**, *without*, preposition
> **sans que**, *without*, conjunction

It is important to distinguish these—the preposition

will stand before a noun or (sometimes) the infinitive of a verb:

> **sans effort,** *without effort*
>
> **sans me regarder,** *without looking at me*

The conjunction will introduce a subordinate clause:

> **je l'organiserai avant qu'on leur parle,** *I'll organize it before anyone speaks to them*

▶ Many subordinating conjunctions are followed by the subjunctive. See p. 45.

■ The following conjunctions may give problems:

☐ **aussi,** *so, therefore*

After **aussi,** verb and pronoun subject are inverted:

> **elle n'y montrait aucun intérêt, aussi est-il parti sans plus rien dire,** *she wasn't showing any interest, so he left without saying anything more*

Aussi can of course also be an adverb, meaning *also*.

☐ **ni,** *nor*

After **sans, ni** is used where in English we should use *or*:

> **sans père ni mère,** *without father or mother*

☐ **où,** *where*

After definite expressions of time **où** is used where in English we should use *when* or *that* or nothing at all:

> **l'instant où elle s'est retournée,** *the moment (when, that) she turned round*

See also **que** below.

☐ **que,** *that*

Que becomes **qu'** before a vowel in written French. In spoken French it frequently remains as **que**.

After indefinite expressions of time **que** is used where in English we use *when*

>> **un jour qu'il faisait beau**, *one day when it was fine*

See also **où** above.

Que is often used to avoid repeating a conjunction

>> **quand tu viendras à Dijon et que tu verras la maison, tu seras enchanté**, *when you come to Dijon and (when you) see the house you'll be delighted*

When **que** replaces the conjunction **si** in this way it is followed by the subjunctive. See p. 48.

Que in comparisons means *than*

>> **il est plus fort que moi**, *he's stronger than me*

▶ **Que** can also be a relative pronoun. See p. 112.

■ Paired conjunctions.

These conjunctions are used in much the same way as in English. The common ones are:

ni ... ni, *neither ... nor*
non seulement ... mais encore, *not only ... but also*
et ... et, *both ... and*
ou (bien) ... ou (bien), *either ... or (else)*
soit ... soit, *either ... or*

>> **je n'ai ni argent ni ma carte Visa**, *I've neither money nor my Visa card*
>> **non seulement lui mais encore toute sa famille sont venus déjeuner**, *not only he but all his family came to lunch*
>> **on lui a pris et son agenda et son sac à main**, *they took both her diary and her handbag*
>> **ou vous lui demandez pardon, ou je vous tue**, *either you apologize to her or I kill you*

> **on voyagera soit par le train soit par avion**, *they'll travel either by train or by plane*

The last three pairs are used mostly in written French, a simple **et, ou**, or **ou bien** being used in the spoken language.

▶ For the use of **ne** with **ni ... ni** see p. 160.

Numbers, Time, Quantities

CARDINAL NUMBERS

The cardinal numbers are

0	zéro	24	vingt-quatre
1	un(e)	25	vingt-cinq
2	deux	26	vingt-six
3	trois	27	vingt-sept
4	quatre	28	vingt-huit
5	cinq	29	vingt-neuf
6	six	30	trente
7	sept	31	trente et un(e)
8	huit	32	trente-deux
9	neuf	40	quarante
10	dix	41	quarante et un(e)
11	onze	50	cinquante
12	douze	51	cinquante et un(e)
13	treize	60	soixante
14	quatorze	61	soixante et un(e)
15	quinze	70	soixante-dix
16	seize	71	soixante et onze
17	dix-sept	72	soixante-douze
18	dix-huit	80	quatre vingts
19	dix-neuf	81	quatre-vingt-un(e)
20	vingt	82	quatre-vingt-deux
21	vingt et un(e)	90	quatre-vingt-dix
22	vingt-deux	91	quatre-vingt-onze
23	vingt-trois	92	quatre-vingt-douze

100	cent	2 000	deux mille
101	cent un(e)	1 000 000	un million
200	deux cents	1 000 200	un million deux
201	deux cent un(e)		cents
1 000	mille	2 000 000	deux millions
1 001	mille un(e)	1 000 000 000	un milliard
1 002	mille deux	2 000 000 000	deux milliards

Thousands and millions are written with spaces (formerly sometimes with full stops) rather than, as in English, with commas. The comma is used for a decimal point—see p. 215.

■ There is no -s on the plural of **vingt** and **cent** when these are followed by another number.

■ There is never an -s on the plural of **mille** meaning *thousands*. **Le mille**, meaning *mile*, takes a plural -s.

■ **Million** and **milliard** are nouns. With a noun immediately following, they take **de**:

> **un million de soldats**, *a million soldiers*

but

> **un million deux cent mille soldats**, *1,200,000 soldiers*

All other numbers are adjectives. They are invariable, except that those ending in **un** agree with a following feminine noun (changing to **une**).

■ There is no **un** before **cent**, **mille**, meaning *one hundred, one thousand*:

> **mille francs**, *one thousand francs*

There is no **et** after **cent** or **mille**:

> **cent douze**, *a hundred and twelve*
> **mille un**, *one thousand and one*

except in the book title, *Les mille et une nuits*, *A Thousand and One Nights*.

■ Figures are grouped in twos when you speak telephone numbers:

> 33 56 08 = **trente-trois cinquante-six zéro huit**
>
> 445 35 71 = **quatre cent quarante-cinq trente-cinq soixante et onze**

■ In Belgium, Switzerland, and Canada **septante**, **octante** or **huitante**, and **nonante** are used for 70, 80, and 90.

■ The numbers **six** and **dix** have each three different pronunciations. Before a consonant the **-x** is not pronounced; before a vowel or **h** 'mute' it is pronounced **z**; where **six** and **dix** stand after the noun (**chapitre six**) or alone (**le dix**) the **-x** is pronounced **s**.

The final consonants of **cinq**, **huit**, and (usually) **neuf** are not pronounced before another consonant, except in dates.

The **f** of **neuf** is pronounced **v** before the words **ans**, *years*, and **heures**, *o'clock*; before other words beginning with a vowel or **h** 'mute' it is pronounced **f**.

The **t** of **vingt** is usually pronounced in the numbers 21–29; it is not pronounced in dates: **le vin[gt] août**.

■ Before **huit** and **onze**, **le** does not become **l'**:

> **tu as le huit de trèfle?**, *do you have the eight of clubs?*
>
> **le onze juin**, *the eleventh of June*

This also applies to the ordinal forms:

> **le huitième**, *the eighth*
>
> **le onzième**, *the eleventh*

ORDINAL NUMBERS

Ordinal numbers (*first*, *second*, *third*, etc.) are formed by removing the final **-e** of the cardinal number (if it ends in **-e**) and adding **-ième**:

8, **huit** → 8th, **huitième**
12, **douze** → 12th, **douzième**
21, **vingt et un** → 21st, **vingt et unième**

Exceptions:

premier (fem: **première**), 1st
cinquième, 5th
neuvième, 9th

la première fois, *the first time* (but **la trente et unième fois**, *the thirty-first time*)
le cinquième article, *the fifth article*
le vingt-neuvième livre, *the twenty-ninth book*

■ **Second** (fem: **seconde**) is an alternative to **deuxième**, mainly used where there is no reference to a third or subsequent thing or person. Notice though:

je suis en seconde, *I'm in the fifth form* (French secondary schools count their classes in the opposite order to English schools)

■ Ordinals may be abbreviated thus 1er, 2e, 3e, etc., or 1°, 2°, 3°, etc. The latter is short for the Latin *primo, secundo, tertio*, etc.

■ When cardinal and ordinal numbers are used together the order is the reverse of that in English:

les cinq premiers mois, *the first five months*

■ French uses cardinal numbers where we use ordinal numbers for days of the month and numbers of kings:

le vingt mai, *the twentieth of May*
Henri quatre, *Henri the Fourth*

However, for *first* French uses **premier**:

le premier septembre, *the first of September*
Charles premier, *Charles the First*

French, like English, uses cardinals for act, scene,

volume, and chapter numbers, but in all these cases uses **premier** for *one*:

>**acte premier**, *act one*
>**acte deux**, *act two*
>**chapitre premier**, *chapter one*

APPROXIMATE NUMBERS

Approximate numbers are formed in French by adding **-aine** to the cardinal number (the final **-e**, if any, is first dropped). They can only be based on 8, 15, tens up to 60, and 100. The resultant number is a feminine noun and is followed by **de**:

>**une quinzaine de francs**, *about fifteen francs*
>**une vingtaine de personnes**, *about twenty (a score of) people*
>**une cinquantaine de cahiers**, *about fifty exercise books*

■ **Mille**, *thousand*, forms **un millier**:

>**un millier de bateaux**, *about a thousand boats*

■ These nouns can be used in the plural:

>**des centaines de voitures**, *hundreds of cars*

■ **Une douzaine**, *a dozen*, though precise, is formed in the same way as the approximate numbers:

>**une douzaine d'œufs**, *a dozen eggs*

Une quinzaine can also be used precisely to mean *a fortnight*, and **une huitaine** is sometimes found as an alternative to **une semaine**, *a week*.

FRACTIONS

Ordinal numbers are used to express fractions, as in English:

$^1/_5$ = **un cinquième**
$^3/_8$ = **trois huitièmes**

Exceptions:

un quart = $^1/_4$, **trois quarts** = $^3/_4$
un tiers = $^1/_3$, **deux tiers** = $^2/_3$
un demi = $^1/_2$

■ *Half* as a mathematical term is **le demi**:

les deux demis, *the two halves*

but in ordinary language, *half of* something is **la moitié de**:

la moitié du temps il ne fait rien, *half the time he does nothing*

Half as an adjective is **demi**. It is hyphenated to the noun and is invariable:

une demi-journée, *a half day*
une demi-heure, *a half hour* (but **un quart d'heure**, *quarter of an hour*)

La demie is *the half-hour*:

la demie sonne, *it's striking half past*

■ Decimals are expressed in French with a comma:

1·5 → **1,5** (**un virgule cinq**)

■ The main mathematical signs are:

+ **plus**	÷ **divisé par**
− **moins**	^{2} **au carré**
× **fois**	% **pour cent**

trois plus deux égalent cinq, *three plus two equals five*
dix au carré, *ten squared*
onze pour cent, *eleven per cent*

TIME AND DATE

Time of day

Quelle heure est-il?, *what time is it?*
Avez-vous l'heure, monsieur/madame? (politer!)

Il est:

> **une heure,** *one o'clock*
> **une heure cinq,** *five past one*
> **deux heures,** *two o'clock*
> **deux heures et** (or **un**) **quart,** *quarter past two*
> **trois heures et demie, trois heures trente,** *half
> past three*
> **quatre heures moins le** (or **moins un**) **quart,**
> *quarter to four*
> **cinq heures moins une (minute),** *a minute to five*
> **midi,** *noon*
> **midi et demi, midi trente,** *half past twelve*
> **minuit,** *midnight*
> **minuit et demi, minuit trente,** *half past twelve*

■ **Heure(s)** is used where English uses *o'clock*. **Et
demie** is used after hours, **et demi** after **midi, minuit.**
With quarters the article **le** is used after **moins** but not
after **et**.

■ The forms **trois heures trente**, etc. are adopted
from the twenty-four hour clock, used in timetables and
all official documents. This follows the pattern:

> **une heure dix, 01h10**
> **douze heures quarante-cinq, 12h45**
> **dix-neuf heures cinquante-cinq, 19h55**

■ French has no equivalents to *a.m.* and *p.m.* Where
necessary, **du matin,** *in the morning,* **de l'après-midi,**
in the afternoon, or **du soir,** *in the evening,* are added as
appropriate:

trois heures du matin, *3 a.m.*

■ *In the morning (afternoon, evening)* is simply **le matin (l'après-midi, le soir)**. *At night* is **la nuit**. *Every morning* (etc.) is **tous les matins**.

Prepositions etc. with times of day

à, *at, by*

> **alors, on se revoit à trois heures précises**, *right, we'll meet at three o'clock sharp*
> **on sera là à midi**, *we'll be there by twelve*

à partir de, *from*

> **je serai au bureau à partir de neuf heures et demie**, *I shall be in the office from 9.30*

au bout de, *after*

> **au bout d'un petit instant elle recommença**, *after a moment she began again*

de ... à, *from ... to*

> **le restaurant est ouvert de midi à deux heures et demie**, *the restaurant is open from 12 to 2.30*

environ, *about*

> **il est environ sept heures** (or **sept heures environ**), *it's about seven o'clock*

jusqu'à, *until*

> **jusqu'à quatre heures de l'après-midi**, *until 4 p.m.*

pas plus tard que, *no later than*

> **il faut y arriver pas plus tard que deux heures et demie**, *you must get there no later than half past two*

passé, *past*

> **il est huit heures passées**, *it's past eight o'clock*

vers, *about*

> **il est parti vers les cinq heures**, *he left about five*

Days, months, seasons

days of the week	*months of the year*
dimanche, *Sunday*	**janvier**, *January*
lundi, *Monday*	**février**, *February*
mardi, *Tuesday*	**mars**, *March*
mercredi, *Wednesday*	**avril**, *April*
jeudi, *Thursday*	**mai**, *May*
vendredi, *Friday*	**juin**, *June*
samedi, *Saturday*	**juillet**, *July*
	août, *August*
today, etc.	**septembre**, *September*
avant-hier, *the day before yesterday*	**octobre**, *October*
hier, *yesterday*	**novembre**, *November*
aujourd'hui, *today*	**décembre**, *December*
demain, *tomorrow*	
après-demain, *the day after tomorrow*	*seasons*
	le printemps, *spring*
la veille, *the day before*	**l'été**, *summer*
le lendemain, *the day after*	**l'automne**, *autumn*
	l'hiver, *winter*

Days, months, and seasons are all masculine and are spelt with a small letter.

Parts of the day

hier, *yesterday*
ce (cet), *this*
demain, *tomorrow*
dimanche, *Sunday* (etc.)
le lendemain, *the day after*, *in the …*
⎱
matin, *morning*
après-midi, *afternoon*
soir, *evening*

on vous verra dimanche soir, *we'll see you Sunday evening*

cela est arrivé ce matin, *that happened this morning*

on s'est brouillés le lendemain soir, *we quarrelled the following evening*

The evening before is **la veille au soir**.

Cette nuit means either *tonight* or *last night*, according to context:

tu dormiras bien cette nuit!, *you'll sleep well tonight!*

je n'ai pas dormi cette nuit, *I didn't sleep last night*

Prepositions with days, months, seasons, etc.

■ *In* with months is **en** or **au mois de**:

en avril, *in April*
au mois d'août, *in August*

■ *In* with seasons is **en**, except **le printemps**:

en hiver, *in winter*
au printemps, *in spring*

■ *In* with years is **en** or **en l'an**. **Mil** is used instead of **mille** in writing years:

en l'an mil neuf cent quarante-cinq, *in 1945*

In spoken French **dix-neuf** (etc.) is very often used for **mil neuf** (etc.):

en seize cent douze, *in 1612*

In the eighties (etc.) is **dans les années quatre-vingt** (note spelling here: no **-s**, hyphen).

■ *In* with centuries is **au**:

> **au vingtième siècle**, *in the twentieth century*

■ *On* with days in the plural is **le**:

> **il ne travaille que le mercredi**, *he only works on Wednesdays*

■ *On* with days in the singular is not translated:

> **elle arrive mercredi**, *she's coming on Wednesday*
> **elle arrive mercredi matin**, *she's coming on Wednesday morning*

The date

The date is expressed with **le,** plus a cardinal number (except for **premier,** *first*), plus the month. *On* before a date is not translated:

> **on sera à Paris le quatorze juillet**, *we are going to be in Paris on the fourteenth of July*
> **nous sommes le premier juin**, *today's the first of June*

When the day is expressed, the article before the date is usually dropped:

> **lundi, vingt mai** or **le lundi vingt mai**, *Monday the twentieth of May*

MEASUREMENT

Length, breadth, height

Quelle est $\begin{Bmatrix} \text{la longueur} \\ \text{la largeur} \\ \text{la hauteur} \end{Bmatrix}$ **de cette pièce?,**

How $\begin{Bmatrix} \text{long} \\ \text{wide} \\ \text{high} \end{Bmatrix}$ *is this room?*

— Elle a trois mètres dix de $\begin{cases} \textbf{long} \\ \textbf{large} \\ \textbf{haut} \end{cases}$, *It's*

3.10 metres $\begin{cases} \textit{long} \\ \textit{wide} \\ \textit{high} \end{cases}$

■ **Faire** can be used instead of **avoir**:

> **elle fait trois mètres de long**, *it's three metres long*

■ *By* in measurements is **sur**:

> **cette pièce fait trois mètres sur quatre**, *this room is three metres by four*

Other common ways of expressing dimension

■ **Long** (etc.) **de**:

> **cette poutre est longue de trois mètres**, *this beam is three metres long*
> **une poutre longue de trois mètres**, *a beam three metres long*

■ **De longueur** (etc.):

> **cette poutre a trois mètres de longueur**, *this beam is three metres long*
> **une poutre de trois mètres de longueur**, *a beam three metres long*

■ **D'une longueur** (etc.) **de**:

> **cette poutre est d'une longueur de trois mètres**, *this beam is three metres long*
> **une poutre d'une longueur de trois mètres**, *a beam three metres long*

The same constructions can be used with **profond/la profondeur**, *deep/depth*, and **épais/l'épaisseur**, *thick/*

thickness, except the **de long** construction, which cannot be used with **épais** and **profond**.

Personal measurements

Quelle taille faites-vous?, *What size are you?*

Combien mesurez-vous?, *What is your height?*

Quel est votre tour de $\begin{Bmatrix} \text{poitrine} \\ \text{taille} \\ \text{hanches} \end{Bmatrix}$ **?**, *What is your* $\begin{Bmatrix} \text{bust} \\ \text{waist} \\ \text{hip} \end{Bmatrix}$ *size?*

Quelle pointure chaussez-vous/faites-vous?, *What is your shoe size?*

Notice the three meanings of **la taille**: *size, height, waist*. Only the context makes clear which is meant.

Word Order

Word order in French is generally the same as in English, except that:

- Adjectives usually follow their nouns. See p. 138.

- Object pronouns precede the verb. See p. 105.

- Adverbs follow the verb. See p. 156.

- Negatives stand in two parts around the verb. See p. 159.

- The 'strong' position in the French sentence is at the end, so where there are, for instance, two or more adverb phrases, the more important one goes to the end. Thus the answer to **quand l'as-tu retrouvé?** (*when did you find it?*) might be:

> **je l'ai retrouvé dans la voiture hier soir**, *I found it last night in the car*

English usage varies, but the more important phrase tends to come first in English, straight after the verb, as in the above example.

- Word order in direct and indirect questions is treated on pp. 211 and 213.

SPECIAL CASES

■ After direct speech, subject and 'saying' verb are inverted:

> «Bonjour, dit-il, ça va?», *'Hello,' he said, 'How are you?'*
>
> «Vraiment?» répondit l'agent, *'Really?' the policeman replied*

Notice what happens in compound tenses:

> «Bonjour, a-t-il dit, ça va?», *'Hello,' he said, 'How are you?'*
>
> «Vraiment?» a répondu l'agent, *'Really?' the policeman replied*

Although the pronoun inversion is like the question form (**a-t-il dit?**) the noun inversion is not (**l'agent a-t-il répondu?**).

■ In a clause beginning **peut-être**, *perhaps*, **à peine**, *scarcely*, or **aussi**, *therefore*, verb and subject pronoun are inverted:

> **peut-être a-t-elle froid**, *perhaps she's cold*
>
> **à peine son père était-il arrivé que le repas commença**, *his father had scarcely got there when the meal began*
>
> **maintenant tu me dis la vérité, aussi suis-je content**, *now you're telling me the truth, so I'm happy*

This inversion is literary, however. In everyday French it is avoided: **peut-être** would be placed after the verb, or the sentence would begin with **peut-être que**:

> **elle a peut-être froid**
>
> **peut-être qu'elle a froid**

A **peine** would similarly be placed after the verb, and **donc** would be substituted for **aussi**:

> **son père était à peine arrivé que le repas commença**
>
> **maintenant tu me dis la vérité, donc je suis content**

■ In exclamations after **comme** and **que** French has normal word order where English does not:

> **comme il est beau!**, *how handsome he is!*
> **que tu es bête!**, *how silly you are!*

■ After **dont** French always has normal word order where English sometimes does not:

> **le médecin dont tu connais la fille**, *the doctor whose daughter you know*
> **le médecin dont la fille est malade**, *the doctor whose daughter is ill*

▶ See also p. 115.

WORD ORDER IN DIRECT QUESTIONS

Simple questions

Simple questions are formed:

■ By a statement with an interrogative (rising) intonation. This is the commonest way to form a question in speech:

> **c'est une Française?**, *is she French?*

■ By prefixing **est-ce que** to the statement. This is also common in both speech and writing:

> **est-ce que vous prenez du sucre?**, *do you take sugar?*

■ By inverting verb and subject pronoun and putting a hyphen between them:

> **prenez-vous du café?**, *will you have some coffee?*

An extra **-t** is inserted where the verb ends in **-e** or **-a**:

> **a-t-il déjà dîné?**, *has he already eaten?*

In modern French there is, for most verbs, no inverted form of the interrogative with the **je** form of the present tense. **Est-ce que** or a simple question intonation is used.

Inversion is, however, still used with the **je** form of the present tense of **pouvoir**, **devoir**, **être**, and, occasionally, **avoir**:

> **puis-je vous revoir?**, *may I see you again?* (NB never 'peux-je')
> **que dois-je dire?**, *what am I to say?*
> **suis-je encore de tes amis?**, *am I still one of your friends?*
> **ai-je tout corrigé?**, *have I marked everything?*

■ By stating the noun subject and then asking the question about it using a pronoun. This produces the sequence noun, verb, hyphen, pronoun:

> **votre chien est-il toujours malade?**, *is your dog still ill?*

This construction is literary and is hardly ever found in everyday French.

Questions following question words (interrogative adverbs)

Questions following words such as **pourquoi**, *why*, **quand**, *when*, **où**, *where*, etc. are formed:

■ With a statement pronounced with an interrogative (rising) intonation, following the question word:

> **où tu vas?**, *where are you going?*

This construction is frowned upon in the written language but is extremely common in spoken French.

■ With the question word followed by **est-ce que** and a statement:

> **où est-ce que tu vas?**, *where are you going?*

This is common in both written and spoken French.

■ With the question word followed by the verb, a hyphen and the subject pronoun:

> **comment as-tu fait cela?**, *how did you do that?*

■ With the question word followed by the verb and the subject noun:

> **quand part le train de Marseille?**, *when does the Marseilles train go?*

This form is not possible after **pourquoi** and often sounds clumsy in compound tenses. In these cases one of the other forms is used.

■ With the question word followed by the noun subject, the question then being asked about this using a pronoun:

> **pourquoi le train de Marseille part-il de cette voie?**, *why does the Marseilles train leave from this platform?*

This construction is literary and is hardly ever found in everyday French.

▶ For questions introduced by the interrogative pronouns **qui, que**, etc. (*who, what*), see p. 119.

WORD ORDER IN INDIRECT QUESTIONS

An indirect question is one that is reported in some way (direct question: *why is he there?*, indirect question:

I don't know why he's there). As in English the word
order is: question word followed by normal order:

> **je ne sais pas pourquoi il est là**, *I don't know why
> he's there*

If the subject of the indirect question is a noun and the
verb would otherwise end the sentence, verb and noun
are inverted:

> **je me demande si ta copine est là**, *I wonder if
> your friend is there*
> **je me demande où est ta copine**, *I wonder where
> your friend is*

In this way French avoids leaving a weak word like **est**
in the strong position at the end of the sentence.

Punctuation

French punctuation is largely similar to English, with the following exceptions:

COMMAS

■ Commas are not used in writing large numbers in French. Where we would put a comma, modern French leaves a gap:

> English: 44,000,000   French: 44 000 000

■ Commas are used in decimals where we would use a decimal point or a full stop:

> English: 3·25 or 3.25   French: 3,25

CAPITAL LETTERS

Capitals are used much less frequently in French than in English. French uses small letters for:

■ Country adjectives:

> **il a l'air italien**, *he looks Italian*
> **une assiette anglaise**, *a plate of cold meats*

■ Language nouns:

> **elle parle français**, *she speaks French*

but not nouns of nationality:

> **c'est une Française**, *she's French*

■ Personal and professional titles, ranks:

> **monsieur Dubois** (but **M. Dubois**)
> **le docteur Artin**
> **le général Leclerc**

■ Street, square, avenue, etc., in names:

> **tu descends place de la Concorde**, *you get out at*
> *the Place de la Concorde*
> **la mer Méditerranée**, *the Mediterranean Sea*
> **elle demeure boulevard Raspail**, *she lives in the*
> *Boulevard Raspail*
> **7, rue Victor-Hugo**

■ Points of the compass:

> **le sud**, *the south*; **le nord**, *the north* (but **le Nord**,
> name of the region)

■ Names of days, months:

> **dimanche prochain**, *next Sunday*
> **en janvier dernier**, *last January*

■ Cheeses and wines named after places:

> **le camembert**, *Camembert*
> **le beaujolais**, *Beaujolais*

■ Quite often after an exclamation mark where the sense
is not complete. There are two examples in the Daudet
extract on p. 218 (in the section on inverted commas).

COLON AND DASH

Colon

The colon is used more frequently than in English.
As well as being used as a long pause, intermediate

between a semi-colon and a full stop (as in English), the colon is used where an amplification or explanation is to follow next. English often uses a dash for this, French hardly ever:

> **La seule solution: refaire le toit**, *The only solution—repair the roof*

Dash

■ Used at the beginning and end of parentheses, as in English:

> **Le patron parlait — il aimait beaucoup parler — et en même temps il tapait sur la table**, *The boss was speaking—he was very fond of speaking—and at the same time he was tapping on the table*

■ Used to mark off items in a list:

> **il sera nécessaire de**
> **— remplacer les poutres**
> **— refaire le toit**
> **— réparer les rebords des fenêtres**
> **— reconstruire les placards**

> *It will be necessary to*
> *replace the beams,*
> *redo the roof,*
> *repair the window-sills,*
> *remake the cupboards*

■ Used to indicate a change of speaker in direct speech (see below, inverted commas).

SUSPENSION POINTS (...)

These may indicate that the sentence breaks off, as in English. In French, they may also indicate that what is to come next is comic, incongruous, or unexpected. English often uses a dash here:

> **45 milliards de francs par mois ... la moitié du budget de l'État!**, *45 billion francs a year—half the national budget!*

INVERTED COMMAS

These are printed « » or " ". Single inverted commas ' ', are almost never used in French.

Inverted commas are placed at the beginning and end of a section of dialogue. Within that dialogue change of speaker is indicated by a new paragraph beginning with a dash (—), but the inverted commas are not closed or reopened. Short phrases indicating who is speaking, together with any adverbial qualifications, (e.g., **répondit-il d'un air distrait**) are included within the dialogue without closing or reopening the inverted commas. Longer interpolations (of at least one complete sentence) do entail closing and reopening the inverted commas.

The following extract from Daudet's *Lettres de mon moulin* illustrates all these points:

> **«C'est fini ... Je n'en fais plus.**
> **— Qu'est-ce qu'il y a donc, père Gaucher? demanda le prieur, qui se doutait bien un peu de ce qu'il y avait.**
> **— Ce qu'il y a, monseigneur? ... Il y a que je bois, que je bois comme un misérable ...**
> **— Mais je vous avais dit de compter vos gouttes.**
> **— Ah, bien oui! compter mes gouttes! c'est par gobelets qu'il faudrait compter maintenant ... Que le feu de Dieu me brûle si je m'en mêle encore!»**

C'est le chapitre qui ne riait plus.
«Mais, malheureux, vous nous ruinez! criait
l'argentier en agitant son grand-livre.
— Préférez-vous que je me damne?»

'It's over. I'm not making any more.'

'What's the matter then, père Gaucher?' asked
the prior, who rather suspected what the matter
was.

'What's the matter, monseigneur? The matter is,
I'm drinking, drinking like a scoundrel.'

'But I told you to count your sips.'

'Oh yes, count my sips! It's cupfuls I'd have to
be counting now. May the fire of God consume me
if I have anything more to do with it!'

Now it was the chapter who were no longer
laughing.

'But, you wretched man, you're ruining us!'
cried the treasurer, waving his ledger.

'Would you rather I damned myself?'

Translation Problems

The following list is alphabetical. It includes items not covered in the body of the grammar, or treated in a number of different places and more conveniently brought together here. Translation problems not covered here should be tackled via the index, or, in the case of prepositions, the alphabetical lists on pp. 185 (English) and 164 (French).

-ING

The *-ing* form of the verb is basically the present participle, but it has other uses in English, few of which correspond to the French.

■ *-ing* as adjective (the *-ing* word stands in front of a noun):

the setting sun
the deciding factor

In this case the French word will also be an adjective. It may be a present participle used as an adjective, as in English:

le soleil couchant, *the setting sun* (**se coucher**, *set* →present participle **couchant**)

or it may be an ordinary adjective:

le facteur décisif, *the deciding factor*

▶ See present participle, p. 34.

■ *-ing* as a verb in a phrase:

he spoke, looking at me closely
getting off the bus, I saw Micheline

In this case the *-ing* word is translated by a present participle, usually preceded by **en**, *whilst*:

il parla, en me regardant de près, *he spoke, looking at me closely*
en descendant de l'autobus, j'ai vu Micheline, *getting off the bus, I saw Micheline*

This construction can only be used where both verbs have the same subject (*he* spoke and *he* looked at me, *I* got off and *I* saw her). Where the subjects are different, **qui** (or alternatively, after verbs of perception only, an infinitive) has to be used:

j'ai vu Micheline qui descendait de l'autobus, or
j'ai vu Micheline descendre de l'autobus, *I saw Micheline getting off the bus*

In this case the subjects are different (*I* saw, but *Micheline* got off).

▶ For more detail see p. 35.

■ *-ing* after a preposition:

> *without stopping*
> *before eating*

This is an infinitive:

> **sans parler**, *without speaking*
> **avant de manger**, *before eating*

With some prepositions, notably **après**, *after*, the sense may demand a perfect infinitive:

> **après avoir mangé**, *after eating*
> **après être sorti**, *after going out*

After the preposition **en**, *whilst*, *by*, *in*, a present participle is used:

> **en tournant**, *whilst turning*

▶ For more detail see pp. 52 (infinitives after prepositions) and 53 (perfect infinitive).

■ *-ing* in 'continuous' tenses: *I am running, I was running, I shall be running, I have been running*, etc.

French does not use a present participle for these: *I run* and *I am running* are the same in French: **je cours**, *I have been running* and *I have run* are the same, **j'ai couru**. Only in the case of the imperfect does a special 'continuous' tense exist: **je courais**, *I was running*.

If the continuous nature of an action needs to be emphasized (which is not usually the case), **être en train de** is used:

> **je serai en train de déjeuner**, *I shall be eating my lunch*

▶ For more details see p. 16.

Superficially similar to the above are sentences such as 'she was leaning on the fence', 'he was lying on the ground'. In this case, however, French views *lying*, *leaning*, etc. as adjectives and uses **être** plus a past participle:

> **elle était accoudée sur la clôture**, *she was leaning on the fence*
>
> **il était couché par terre**, *he was lying on the ground*

▶ For further details see p. 39.

■ *-ing* after a verb:

> *he begins typing*
> *she stops telephoning*
> *they love swimming*

This is an infinitive in French, preceded by the preposition appropriate to the main verb:

> **il commence à taper à la machine**, *he begins typing*
> **elle s'arrête de téléphoner**, *she stops telephoning*
> **ils adorent nager**, *they love swimming*

■ *-ing* after a verb with an object:

> *he stops her telephoning*
> *she heard him laughing*

This is also an infinitive in French, preceded by the preposition appropriate to the main verb:

> **il l'empêche de téléphoner**, *he stops her telephoning*
> **elle l'a entendu rire**, *she heard him laughing*

▶ For the prepositions that verbs take before an infinitive see p. 51.

■ *-ing* as subject of the sentence (the verbal noun):

> *walking tires me*
> *telephoning is easier*

This is an infinitive in French:

> **me promener me fatigue**, *walking tires me*
> **téléphoner est plus simple**, *telephoning is easier*

However, French prefers to avoid this use of the infinitive at the beginning of the sentence, and usually makes the infinitive depend on the other verb:

> **ça me fatigue de me promener**, *it tires me to walk*
> **c'est plus simple de téléphoner**, *it's easier to telephone*

▶ See also the infinitive as verbal noun, p. 50.

■ *-ing* as a noun

English uses *-ing* nouns for many sorts of activity and sports. These are translated by other nouns in French:

> *fishing*, **la pêche**
> *swimming*, **la natation**
> *singing*, **le chant**
> *horse-riding*, **l'équitation**

IT IS

It is with nouns and adjectives

■ Where *it is* refers to a noun that has already been mentioned, it is translated by **il est** or **elle est** according to the gender of that noun:

> **la clé? Elle est sur la porte**, *the key? It's in the door*
> **ma nouvelle robe, ah oui, elle est bleue**, *my new dress, yes, it's blue*

■ Where *it is* introduces a noun or pronoun, it is translated by **c'est**, whatever the gender of the noun or pronoun. The plural (*those are*) is **ce sont**:

> **c'est une Citroën**, *it's a Citroën*
> **c'est moi!**, *it's me!*
> **ce sont des mouettes**, *those are seagulls*

C'est is similarly used to introduce adverbial expressions:

> **c'est à Noël qu'elle vient**, *it's at Christmas that she's coming*

■ Where *it is* refers back to something other than a noun (a noun clause, a previous sentence, etc.), **c'est** is used.

> **il parle italien? Oui, c'est possible**, *he speaks Italian? Yes, it's possible*

■ Where *it is* introduces an adjective followed by **que** or **de**, **il est** is used:

> **il est possible qu'il parle italien**, *it's possible that he speaks Italian*
> **il est difficile de traduire cela**, *it's difficult to translate that*

However, in the spoken language **c'est** is very often used in this case too:

> **c'est possible qu'il parle Italien**, *it's possible he speaks Italian*

■ In all cases except the last **cela est** may be used instead of **c'est**:

> **cela est possible**, *it's (that's) possible*

It is, with weather, time, etc.

■ *It* is **il** with:

□ Weather verbs, both simple verbs

> **il pleut**, *it's raining*
> **il neige**, *it's snowing*

and those constructed with **faire**

> **il fait du vent**, *it's windy*
> **il fait beau**, *it's fine*

☐ Time of day

> **il est cinq heures**, *it's five o'clock*
> **il est midi et demi**, *it's half past twelve*

☐ The time expressions: **tard**, *late*, **tôt**, *early*, **temps**, *time*

> **il est tard**, *it's late*
> **il est temps de partir**, *it's time to go*
> **il est temps que tu partes**, *it's time you went*

■ With other time expressions **c'est** is used:

> **c'est dimanche**, *it's Sunday*
> **c'est janvier**, *it's January*
> **c'est le printemps**, *it's spring*
> **c'est le 18 mai**, *it's the 18th of May*

■ **Pouvoir**, *can*, and **devoir**, *ought to*, *should*, may be introduced into these constructions:

> **ce doit être possible**, *it ought to be possible*
> **il peut neiger**, *it may snow*

▶ For further details see impersonal verbs, pp. 74 ff.

JUST (adverb)

■ *just = exactly*: **juste**; **justement**

> **tu as juste trois minutes**, *you have just three minutes*
> **c'est juste au-dessus de la porte**, *it's just above the door*
> **on a sonné juste au moment où je me mettais dans le bain**, *someone rang the bell just when I was getting into the bath*
> **c'est justement ce que je dis toujours**, *that's just what I always say*

■ *just = only*: **seul; seulement**

> **un seul**, *just one*
> **seulement deux, trois**, etc., *just two, three*, etc.
> **une seule fois**, *just once*

■ *just* in *have/had just*: **venir de** + infinitive

> **je viens de le faire**, *I've just done it*
> **on venait de l'ouvrir**, *they had just opened it*

▶ See pp. 18 and 21 for more details on tenses with **venir de**.

■ *just* in *just as* (= *equally*): **tout**

> **cela est tout aussi difficile**, *that's just as difficult*

■ *just* with a following verb: **ne faire que** + infinitive

> **elle n'a fait que pleurer**, *she just cried*

-SELF

■ *-self* as direct or indirect object: reflexive pronoun (**me, te, se**, etc.) before verb:

> **il s'est distingué**, *he distinguished himself*
> **je me disais la même chose**, *I was saying the same thing to myself*

▶ For further details see reflexive pronouns, p. 30.

■ *-self* as a strengthener of the subject: disjunctive pronoun + **-même** (**moi-même, toi-même**, etc.) placed after verb:

> **tu l'as fait toi-même?**, *you did it yourself?*

▶ For further details see disjunctive pronouns, p. 109 and disjunctives with **-même**, p. 111.

■ *-self* after preposition: disjunctive pronoun (**moi, toi,** etc.) with or without **-même**:

> **je ne parle que pour moi,** *I can only speak for myself*
>
> **il n'écrit que pour lui-même,** *he writes only for himself*

■ *oneself* is **soi(-même)**:

> **on ne peut pas le garder pour soi(-même),** *one can't keep it for oneself*

▶ For further details on the use of **soi** see p. 109.

SINCE

■ Preposition: **depuis**

> **je t'attends depuis deux heures et demie,** *I've been waiting for you since half past two*
>
> **je t'attendais depuis deux heures et demie,** *I had been waiting for you since half past two*

The tenses with **depuis** are different from the English ones in positive statements: *have been … ing* = French present, *had been … ing* = French imperfect. With a negative the tense is the same as in English:

> **je ne l'ai pas vue depuis la boum,** *I haven't seen her since the party*

▶ **Depuis** can also mean *for*. For more details on tenses with **depuis** see pp. 17 and 21.

■ Adverb: **depuis**

> **tu l'a vue depuis?,** *have you seen her since?*

The adverb **depuis** does not affect the tense of the verb.

■ Time conjunction: **depuis que**

> **elle travaille depuis que son mari est mort**, *she has been working (has worked) ever since her husband died*
>
> **elle allait à pied depuis que la voiture avait fini par tomber en panne**, *she had been walking (ever) since the car had finally broken down*
>
> **je ne dors plus depuis qu'il est de retour**, *I'm not sleeping any more since he's back*

Tenses with **depuis que,** conjunction, are the same as with **depuis,** preposition, above.

► For further information on **depuis que** see pp. 17 and 21.

■ Conjunction expressing reason: **puisque**

> **puisqu'il est si impoli je ne lui parle plus**, *since he's so rude I don't speak to him any more*

SOON AND *LATE*

Soon, early

■ *soon*: **bientôt**

> **on sera bientôt là**, *we'll soon be there*

■ *soon = early*: **tôt**

> **on est arrivé beaucoup trop tôt**, *we got there much too soon (early)*

■ *early = in good time*: **de bonne heure**

> **on est arrivé de bonne heure**, *we got there early*

■ *sooner = earlier*: **plus tôt**

> **nous sommes arrivés plus tôt qu'eux**, *we arrived sooner (earlier) than they did*

■ *sooner* = *in preference*; *rather*: **plutôt**

> **plutôt lui que moi**, *sooner him than me*

Late

■ *late*, time of day: **tard**

> **il est très tard, rentrons**, *it's very late, let's go home*

■ *late*, = *after the appropriate time*: **tard**

> **maintenant il est trop tard**, *now it's too late*

■ *late*, referring to people: **en retard**

> **nous sommes en retard**, *we're late*

■ *late*, adjective: **tardif**

> **à cette heure tardive**, *at this late hour*

■ *late*, adjective, = *dead*: **feu**

> **le tombeau de feu son père**, *his late father's grave*

Feu is invariable. Note its position.

TIME(S)

■ *time(s)* = *occasion(s)*: **la/les fois**

> **pour la première fois**, *for the first time*

■ *time* = *length, amount of time*: **le temps**

> **malheureusement je n'ai pas le temps**, *unfortunately I haven't got (the) time*

■ *time* = *point in time*: **le moment**

> **tu es arrivé au bon moment?**, *you got there at the right moment?*

On time is **à l'heure**; *in (the nick of) time* is **à temps**:

> **tu dois arriver à l'heure**, *you must get there on time*
> **tu es arrivé juste à temps**, *you got there just in time*

■ *time = time of day*: **l'heure**

> **vous avez l'heure?**, *do you have the (right) time?*

■ *time = period*: **l'époque**

> **à cette époque j'étais toujours au lycée**, *at that time I was still at college*

TO BE

To be is translated by verbs other than **être** in the following cases:

■ Location: **se trouver**

> **le garage se trouve derrière la maison**, *the garage is (located) behind the house*

■ Physical states: **avoir**

> **j'ai chaud/froid/faim/soif/sommeil/peur/honte**, *I'm hot/cold/hungry/thirsty/tired/frightened/ashamed*

Similarly: *to be right/wrong* is **avoir raison/tort**.

■ Health: **aller**

> **comment allez-vous?**, *how are you?*
> **maman va beaucoup mieux**, *mother's much better*

■ Weather: **faire**

> **il fait chaud/froid/beau/mauvais/du vent/du brouillard**, *it's hot/cold/fine/bad/windy/foggy*

■ Age: **avoir**

> **elle a vingt et un ans**, *she's twenty-one (years old)*

▶ *I am to/I was to* is translated by **devoir**. See p. 65.

VERB + OBJECT + INFINITIVE

Sentences such as *I want her to go, I like her to talk* cannot be translated directly into French, as, with the exception of a very few verbs (see below), this verb + object + infinitive construction does not exist in French. A clause has to be used instead:

> **je veux qu'elle parte**, *I want her to go* ('*I want that she should go*')
>
> **j'aime qu'il me gratte le dos**, *I like him to scratch my back* ('*I like that he scratches my back*')

Both **vouloir que** and **aimer que** in the above examples take the subjunctive.

A similar construction used in English with verbs of perception consists of verb + object + infinitive/present participle (*I hear him speak/speaking*). This construction, with verbs of perception (**voir, entendre, sentir**, etc.), can be translated directly into French. A dependent infinitive is used:

> **je l'entends parler**, *I hear him speak(ing)*

▶ For further details see p. 42 (subjunctive) and p. 51 (dependent infinitive)

VERB + PREPOSITION COMBINATIONS

Many English verbs consist of a simple verb plus a preposition (*cry out, run away, run back*). This verb-plus-preposition construction is impossible in French and such verbs, sometimes called phrasal verbs, have to be translated in one of the following ways.

■ By a simple verb:

> **crispée de douleur, elle commença à crier**,
> *contorted with pain, she began to cry out* (*cry out*: **crier**)

à la nuit tombante ils se sont enfuis, *at nightfall they ran away* (*run away*: **s'enfuir**)

■ By a verb based on the preposition, plus a dependent present participle (with **en**) or an adverb phrase:

ils sont retournés en courant, *they ran back* (*run back*: **retourner en courant**, '*go back running*')
ils sont partis à la hâte, *they hurried off* (*hurry off*: **partir à la hâte**, '*go off in a hurry*')

▶ For further details see p. 36.

■ Where the verb-phrase has an object, by a verb with a dependent infinitive:

laisse-le entrer!, *let him in*

Several of these are based on **faire**:

faire entrer, *show in*
faire sortir, *show out*
faire venir, *send for*

▶ See p. 73 for more details.

WHATEVER, WHOEVER

Whatever

■ Pronoun subject: **quoi que ce soit qui**; pronoun object: **quoi que** (both + subjunctive)

quoi que ce soit qui bouge, ne tirez pas!, *whatever moves, don't shoot*
quoi que ce soit qui ronge votre parquet, ce ne sont pas des souris, *whatever is eating your floorboards, it isn't mice*
quoi qu'il dise, je ne le crois pas, *whatever he says* (*may say*), *I don't believe him*

■ Adjective: **quel que soit**

> **quel que soit la somme qu'on vous offre**, *whatever money you are offered*
>
> **ne renoncez pas, quelles que soient les difficultés**, *don't give up, whatever the difficulties may be*

■ *Anything whatever* is **quoi que ce soit**, used as if it were a pronoun:

> **il ne se plaint pas de quoi que ce soit**, *he doesn't complain about anything whatever (anything at all)*

Whoever

■ **Qui que ce soit qui** (subject), **qui que ce soit que** (object) both + subjunctive:

> **qui que ce soit qui vous ait dit cela, c'est complètement faux**, *whoever told you that, it's completely untrue*
>
> **qui que ce soit qu'on propose comme candidat, je ne voterai pas**, *whoever they put up as candidate, I shall not vote*

Quiconque may be used (without the subjunctive), in rather more formal style, for **qui que ce soit qui/que**. See p. 130.

| Pronunciation Traps

To attempt to present the pronunciation of French as a whole in a grammar of this kind would be impossible and pointless. It is, however, useful to provide reference to those commonly used words whose pronunciation does not follow the usual patterns or with which learners consistently find pronunciation problems.

The following list gives such problem words alphabetically, with a very approximate imitated pronunciation followed by the exact pronunciation represented by the letters of the International Phonetic Alphabet. In general, related words show the same pronunciation changes (so **le sculpteur**, *sculptor*, is pronounced without a p, like **la sculpture**, listed below).

ail (m.), *garlic*	eye	aj
aile (f.), *wing*	el	ɛl
alcool (m.), *alcohol*	al-col (one o pronounced)	alkɔl
amener, *bring*	am-nay	amne
Amiens (the town)	am-ya	amjɛ̃
automne (m.), *autumn*	oh-tonn (m not pronounced)	otɔn
but, **automnal**, *autumnal*	oh-tom-nal (m often pronounced)	otɔmnal
bœuf (m.), *beef; ox*	berf	bœf
but plural **bœufs**, *cattle; oxen*	berh	bø
cent un, *101*; **cent onze** *111*	son-ern; son-onz (t not pronounced)	sɑ̃ œ̃; sɑ̃ ɔ̃:z
chef (m.), chief, *head*	shef	ʃɛf
but, **chef d'œuvre**, *masterpiece*	shed-er-vr (f not pronounced)	ʃɛdœ:vɾ

Christ (m.), *Christ*	creased (t pronounced)	krist
but **Jésus Christ**	jay-zoo-cree (t not pronounced)	ʒezy kri
condamner, *condemn*	con-da-nay (m not pronounced)	kɔ̃dane
cuiller (also spelled **cuillère**), (f.) *spoon*	kwee-yair (r pronounced)	kɥijɛːr
dix, *10* (standing alone) (before a consonant)	deese dee	dis di
(before a vowel)	deez	diz
dot, (f.) *dowry*	dot (t pronounced)	dɔt
emmener, *take away*	om-nay	ɑ̃mne
estomac (m.), *stomach*	esto-ma (c not pronounced)	ɛstɔma
eu, *had* (past participle of **avoir**)	ee (+ rounded lips)	y
fier, *proud*	fee-air (r pronounced)	fjɛːr
fils (m.), *son*	feese (s pronounced)	fis
but **fils** (m. pl.), *wires*	feel (s not pronounced)	fil
hais, hait, *hate(s)* (**je, tu** and **il** form of present, **haïr**)	eh (i not pronounced separately)	ɛ
hélas, *alas*	ay-lars (s pronounced)	elɑːs
jus (m.), *juice*	joo (s not pronounced)	ʒy
mademoiselle (f.), *miss*	mad-mwa-zel (first e not pronounced)	madmwazɛl
mille, *thousand*	meal (ll pronounced l)	mil

mœurs, (f. pl.), *manners*	merse (s usually pronounced)	mœrs
naïveté (f.), *naïvety*	na-eev-tay	naivte
neuf, *9*	nerf	nœf
but **neuf heures**	ner-vur	nœv œ:r
and **neuf ans**	ner-von (f pronounced v)	nœv ã
notre, *our*; **votre**, *your*	notr; votr	nɔtr̩; vɔtr̩
but, **nôtre**, *ours*; **vôtre**, *yours*	note-r, vote-r (o lengthened)	no:tr̩; vo:tr̩
œuf (m.), *egg*	erf	œf
but plural **œufs**, *eggs*	erh (fs not pronounced, vowel lengthened)	ø
oignon (m.), *onion*	on-yon	ɔɲɔ̃
os (m.), *bone*	os	ɔs
but plural **os**, *bones*	oh (s not pronounced, vowel lengthened)	o
poêle (m.), *stove*; (f.), *frying pan*	pwal	pwal
Reims, (*Rheims*, the town)	ranse	rɛ̃:s
rhum (m.), *rum* and **Rome**, *Rome*	rom	rɔm
sandwich (m.), *sandwich*	*sond-witch*	sãdwitʃ
sceptique, *sceptical*	sep-teek (c not pronounced)	sɛptik
sculpture (f.), *sculpture*	skill-tour (p not pronounced)	skylty:r
sens (m.), *sense*; *direction*	sonse (last s pronounced)	sã:s

six, *6* (standing alone)	cease	sis
(before a consonant)	sea	si
(before a vowel)	seas	siz
solennel, *solemn*	sol-a-nel	sɔlanɛl
	(first e pronounced a)	
tabac (m.),	ta-ba	taba
tobacco(nist's)	(c not pronounced)	
tiers (m.), *third*	tea-air	tjɛːr
	(s not pronounced)	
vieille (f.), *old*	vyay	vjɛːj
but **veille** (f.), *the day*	vay	vɛːj
before		
village (m.), *village*	vee-large	vilaːʒ
	(ll pronounced l)	
ville (f.), *town*	veel	vil
	(ll pronounced l)	
vingt, *20*	van	vɛ̃
but **vingt et un**, *21*	van-tay-ern	vɛ̃t e œ̃
vingt-deux, *22*, etc.	vant-der	vɛ̃t dø
	(t usually pronounced	
	from 21 on)	
wagon (m.), *carriage*	va-gon	vagɔ̃

Verb Tables

▶ See also pp. 7 and 8.

■ Verbs with infinitives ending -**e**[consonant]**er**:

☐ changing the -**e** to -**è** before a mute or unstressed **e**.
See p. 7 for a list of verbs in this group. Model: **acheter**,
to buy:

present		past participle
j'achète	nous achetons	acheté
tu achètes	vous achetez	
il achète	ils achètent	

future	past historic
j'achèterai	j'achetai

☐ doubling the consonant before a mute or unstressed
-**e**. Model: **jeter**, *to throw*:

present		past participle
je jette	nous jetons	jeté
tu jettes	vous jetez	
il jette	ils jettent	

future	past historic
je jetterai	je jetai

■ Verbs with infinitives ending **-é[consonant]er**:

The **é** changes to **è** before a mute **e**, but not in the future or conditional. Model: **préférer**, *to prefer*:

present		past participle
je préfère	**nous préférons**	**préféré**
tu préfères	**vous préférez**	
il préfère	**ils préfèrent**	

future	past historic
je préférerai	**je préférai**

■ Verbs with infinitives ending **-yer**:

The **y** changes to **i** before a mute or unstressed **e**. The change is optional with **-ayer** verbs. Model: **appuyer**, *to lean*:

present		past participle
j'appuie	**nous appuyons**	**appuyé**
tu appuies	**vous appuyez**	
il appuie	**ils appuient**	

future	past historic
j'appuierai	**j'appuyai**

■ Verbs with infinitives ending **-cer**:

The **c** changes to **ç** before **a** and **o**. Model: **commencer**, *to begin*:

present		past participle
je commence	**nous commençons**	**commencé**
tu commences	**vous commencez**	
il commence	**ils commencent**	

future		past historic
je commencerai		**je commençai**

present participle	imperfect	
commençant	**je commençais**	**nous commencions**
	tu commençais	**vous commenciez**
	il commençait	**ils commençaient**

■ Verbs with infinitives ending **-ger**:

The **g** changes to **ge** before **a** and **o**. Model: **manger**, *to eat*:

present		past participle
je mange	**nous mangeons**	**mangé**
tu manges	**vous mangez**	
il mange	**ils mangent**	

future		past historic
je mangerai		**je mangeai**

present participle	imperfect	
mangeant	**je mangeais**	**nous mangions**
	tu mangeais	**vous mangiez**
	il mangeait	**ils mangeaient**

IRREGULAR VERBS

Verbs, including common compound verbs, are in
alphabetical order. Verbs marked * are less common:
some parts of these verbs are very rarely met.

Verbs marked † form their compound tenses with **être**.

The parts given are the infinitive, the full present
tense, the past participle (from which all compound
tenses may be formed, see p. 3), the **je** form of the future
(from which the rest of the future and the conditional
may be formed), and the **je** form of the past historic
(from which the rest of the past historic may be formed).
The endings for these last three tenses are:

	future	_conditional_	_past historic_		
je	-ai	-ais	-ai	-is	-us
tu	-as	-ais	-as	-is	-us
il	-a	-ait	-a	-it	-ut
nous	-ons	-ions	-âmes	-îmes	-ûmes
vous	-ez	-iez	-âtes	-îtes	-ûtes
ils	-ont	-aient	-èrent	-irent	-urent

The conditional endings are added to the future stem
to form the conditional; the same endings are added to
the **nous** form of the present (without its **-ons**) to form
the imperfect.

For the formation of the present and imperfect
subjunctive see pp. 40 and 41.

infinitive; present	past participle	future	past historic
*acquérir *acquire*			
j'acquiers	acquis	j'acquerrai	j'acquis
tu acquiers			
il acquiert			
nous acquérons			
vous acquérez			
ils acquièrent			

accueillir, *welcome* → **cueillir**

admettre, *admit* → **mettre**

aller† *go*			
je vais	allé	j'irai	j'allai
tu vas			
il va			
nous allons			
vous allez			
ils vont			
pres. subjunctive: **j'aille, nous allions**			

apercevoir, *catch sight of* → **recevoir**

apparaître, *appear* → **connaître**

apprendre, *learn* → **prendre**

infinitive; present	past participle	future	past historic
s'asseoir† *sit down*			
je m'assieds	**assis**	**je m'assiérai**	**je m'assis**
tu t'assieds			
il s'assied			
nous nous asseyons			
vous vous asseyez			
ils s'asseyent			

more colloquial form of present: **je m'assois, tu t'assois, il s'assoit, nous nous assoyons, vous vous assoyez, ils s'assoient**

---

atteindre, *reach* → **peindre**

---

avoir *have*			
j'ai	**eu**	**j'aurai**	**j'eus**
tu as			
il a			
nous avons			
vous avez			
ils ont			

pres. subjunctive: **j'aie, nous ayons**, pres. participle: **ayant**, imperative: **aie, ayons, ayez**

---

*battre *beat*	regular except present: **je bats, tu bats, il bat, nous battons, vous battez, ils battent**

---

*se battre†, *fight* → **battre**

infinitive; present	past participle	future	past historic
boire *drink*			
je bois	**bu**	je boirai	je bus
tu bois			
il boit			
nous buvons			
vous buvez			
ils boivent			

*bouillir *boil*	regular except present: **je bous, tu bous, il bout, nous bouillons, vous bouillez, ils bouillent**

* combattre, *combat* → **battre**

commettre, *commit* → **mettre**

comprendre, *understand* → **prendre**

* concevoir, *conceive* → **recevoir**

infinitive; present	past participle	future	past historic
conduire *drive*			
je conduis	**conduit**	je conduirai	je conduisis
tu conduis			
il conduit			
nous conduisons			
vous conduisez			
ils conduisent			
connaître *know*			
je connais	**connu**	je connaîtrai	je connus
tu connais			
il connaît			
nous connaissons			
vous connaissez			
ils connaissent			

infinitive; present	past participle	future	past historic

construire, *construct* → **conduire**

* contraindre, *restrict* → **peindre**

* contredire, *contradict* → **dire** (present: **vous contredisez**)

* convaincre, *convince* → **vaincre**

* coudre
  sew

je couds	cousu	je coudrai	je cousis
tu couds			
il coud			
nous cousons			
vous cousez			
ils cousent			

courir
  run

je cours	couru	je courrai	je courus
tu cours			
il court			
nous courons			
vous courez			
ils courent			

couvrir
  cover

je couvre	couvert	je	je couvris
tu couvres		couvrirai	
il couvre			
nous couvrons			
vous couvrez			
ils couvrent			

craindre, *fear* → **peindre**

infinitive; present	past participle	future	past historic
croire *believe*			
je crois	cru	je croirai	je crus
tu crois			
il croit			
nous croyons			
vous croyez			
ils croient			
* croître *grow*			
je croîs	crû	je croîtrai	past hist.
tu croîs	(f.: **crue**)		not used
il croît			
nous croissons			
vous croissez			
ils croissent			
* cueillir *gather*			
je cueille	cueilli	je	je cueillis
tu cueilles		cueillerai	
il cueille			
nous cueillons			
vous cueillez			
ils cueillent			

* cuire, *cook* → **conduire**

décevoir, *deceive* → **recevoir**

découvrir, *discover* → **couvrir**

décrire, *describe* → **écrire**

* détruire, *destroy* → **conduire**

infinitive; present	past participle	future	past historic
devoir			
must; *owe*			
je dois	**dû**	**je devrai**	**je dus**
tu dois	(f.: **due,**		
il doit	m. pl.: **dus,**		
nous devons	f. pl.: **dues**)		
vous devez			
ils doivent			
dire			
say			
je dis	**dit**	**je dirai**	**je dis**
tu dis			
il dit			
nous disons			
vous dites			
ils disent			
dormir, *sleep* → **partir**			
écrire			
write			
j'écris	**écrit**	**j'écrirai**	**j'écrivis**
tu écris			
il écrit			
nous écrivons			
vous écrivez			
ils écrivent			

* **élire**, *elect* → **lire**

* **émouvoir**, *move*; *stir up* → **mouvoir** (past participle: **ému**)

* **s'enquérir**†, *enquire* → **acquérir**

infinitive; present	past participle	future	past historic
envoyer *send*			
j'envoie	**envoyé**	**j'enverrai**	**j'envoyai**
tu envoies			
il envoie			
nous envoyons			
vous envoyez			
ils envoient			

éteindre, *switch off*; *put out* → **peindre**

être *be*			
je suis	**été**	**je serai**	**je fus**
tu es			
il est			
nous sommes			
vous êtes			
ils sont			

pres. subjunctive: **je sois, nous soyons,**
pres. participle: **étant**, imperative: **sois, soyons, soyez**

* étreindre, *embrace* → **peindre**

faire *do; make*			
je fais			
tu fais	**fait**	**je ferai**	**je fis**
il fait			
nous faisons			
vous faites			
ils font			

pres. subjunctive: **je fasse, nous fassions**

infinitive; present	past participle	future	past historic
falloir *must*; *be* *necessary*			
il faut pres. subjunctive: **il faille**	**fallu**	**il faudra**	**il fallut**
* fuir *flee*			
je fuis **tu fuis** **il fuit** **nous fuyons** **vous fuyez** **ils fuient**	**fui**	**je fuirai**	**je fuis**
* haïr *hate*			
je hais **tu hais** **il hait** **nous haïssons** **vous haïssez** **ils haïssent**	**haï**	**je haïrai**	**je haïs**
(past. historic: **nous haïmes, vous haïtes**, imperfect subjunctive: **il haït**—but all three forms are virtually unused)			

* s'inscrire†, *have oneself registered* → **écrire**

interdire, *forbid* → **dire** (present: **vous interdisez**)

introduire, *introduce*; *put in* → **conduire**

joindre, *join* → **peindre**

infinitive; present	past participle	future	past historic
lire *read*			
je lis	lu	je lirai	je lus
tu lis			
il lit			
nous lisons			
vous lisez			
ils lisent			
*luire *shine*			
il luit	lui	il luira	past hist.
ils luisent	(no f.)		not used
mentir, *tell lies* → **partir**			
mettre *put*			
je mets	mis	je mettrai	je mis
tu mets			
il met			
nous mettons			
vous mettez			
ils mettent			
*moudre *grind*			
je mouds	moulu	je moudrai	je moulus
tu mouds			
il moud			
nous moulons			
vous moulez			
ils moulent			

infinitive; present	past participle	future	past historic
mourir† *die*			
je meurs	**mort**	**je mourrai**	**je mourus**
tu meurs			
il meurt			
nous mourons			
vous mourez			
ils meurent			
* mouvoir *drive;* *propel*			
je meus	**mû**	**je mouvrai**	**je mus**
tu meus	(f. **mue**)		(rare)
il meut			
nous mouvons			
vous mouvez			
ils meuvent			

* naître†, *be born* → **connaître** (past participle: **né**, past historic: **je naquis**)

* nuire, *harm* → **cuire** (past participle: **nui**)

offrir, *offer* → **couvrir**

ouvrir, *open* → **couvrir**

* paître, *graze* → **connaître** (no past participle or past historic)

paraître, *appear* → **connaître**

infinitive; present	past participle	future	past historic
partir†			
leave			
je pars	parti	je partirai	je partis
tu pars			
il part			
nous partons			
vous partez			
ils partent			
peindre			
paint			
je peins	peint	je peindrai	je peignis
tu peins			
il peint			
nous peignons			
vous peignez			
ils peignent			
* plaindre, *pity* → **peindre**			
* plaire			
please			
je plais	plu	je plairai	je plus
tu plais			
il plaît			
nous plaisons			
vous plaisez			
ils plaisent			
pleuvoir			
rain			
il pleut	plu	il pleuvra	il plut
pres. subjunctive: **il pleuve**			
poursuivre, *pursue* → **suivre**			

infinitive; present	past participle	future	past historic
pouvoir			
can; be able			
je peux			
(puis-je?)	pu	je pourrai	je pus
tu peux			
il peut			
nous pouvons			
vous pouvez			
ils peuvent			
pres. subjunctive: **je puisse, nous puissions**			

prendre			
take			
je prends	pris	je prendrai	je pris
tu prends			
il prend			
nous prenons			
vous prenez			
ils prennent			

produire, *produce* → **conduire**

*promouvoir, *promote:* only infinitive and past participle (**promu**) used

recevoir			
receive			
je reçois	reçu	je recevrai	je reçus
tu reçois			
il reçoit			
nous recevons			
vous recevez			
ils reçoivent			

reconnaître, *recognize* → **connaître**

infinitive; present	past participle	future	past historic
* réduire, *reduce* → **conduire**			
* se repentir†, *repent* → **partir**			
* résoudre *resolve*			
je résous	résolu	je	je résolus
tu résous		résoudrai	
il résout			
nous résolvons			
vous résolvez			
ils résolvent			
* restreindre, *restrain*; *limit* → **peindre**			
rire *laugh*			
je ris	ri	je rirai	je ris
tu ris			
il rit			
nous rions			
vous riez			
ils rient			
* rompre *break*			
je romps	rompu	je romprai	je rompis
tu romps			
il rompt			
nous rompons			
vous rompez			
ils rompent			

infinitive; present	past participle	future	past historic
savoir *know*			
je sais	su	je saurai	je sus
tu sais			
il sait			
nous savons			
vous savez			
ils savent			
pres. subjunctive: **je sache, nous sachions**			
pres. participle: **sachant**; used as adjective, **savant**			
imperative: **sache, sachons, sachez**			

*séduire, *seduce* → **conduire**

sentir, se sentir†, *feel* → **partir**

servir, *serve* → **partir**

sortir†, *go out* → **partir**

souffrir, *suffer* → **couvrir**

sourire, *smile* → **rire**

suffire, *be (quite) enough* → **lire**   (past participle: **suffi**, past historic: **je suffis**)

suivre *follow*			
je suis	suivi	je suivrai	je suivis
tu suis			
il suit			
nous suivons			
vous suivez			
ils suivent			

surprendre, *surprise* → **prendre**

*survivre, *survive* → **vivre**

infinitive; present	past participle	future	past historic

* se taire†, *be quiet* → **plaire** (present: **il se tait**)

tenir, *hold* → **venir**

traduire, *translate* → **conduire**

* vaincre
defeat

je vaincs	vaincu	je vaincrai	je vainquis
tu vaincs			
il vainc			
nous vainquons			
vous vainquez			
ils vainquent			

* valoir
be worth

je vaux	valu	je vaudrai	je valus
tu vaux			
il vaut			
nous valons			
vous valez			
ils valent			

pres. subjunctive: **je vaille, nous valions, ils vaillent**;
forms other than **il** extremely uncommon in all tenses

venir†
come

je viens	venu	je viendrai	je vins
tu viens			tu vins
il vient			il vint
nous venons			nous
vous venez			vînmes
ils viennent			vous vîntes
			ils vinrent

infinitive; present	past participle	future	past historic
* vêtir *dress*			
je vêts	vêtu	je vêtirai	je vêtis
tu vêts			
il vêt			
nous vêtons			
vous vêtez			
ils vêtent			
(present **nous vêtissons, vous vêtissez, ils vêtissent,** present part. **vêtissant,** and imperfect **je vêtissais** etc. are also found)			
vivre *live*			
je vis	vécu	je vivrai	je vécus
tu vis			
il vit			
nous vivons			
vous vivez			
ils vivent			
voir *see*			
je vois	vu	je verrai	je vis
tu vois			
il voit			
nous voyons			
vous voyez			
ils voient			

infinitive; present	past participle	future	past historic
vouloir *want*			
je veux	**voulu**	**je voudrai**	**je voulus**
tu veux			
il veut			
nous voulons			
vous voulez			
ils veulent			
pres. subjunctive: **je veuille, nous voulions**			
imperative: **veuille, veuillez** (= *would you kindly*)			

Glossary of Grammatical Terms

Abstract Noun The name of something that is not a concrete object or person. Words such as *difficulty*, *hope*, *discussion* are abstract nouns.

Active See Passive.

Adjective A word describing a noun. *A big, blue, untidy painting*—*big*, *blue*, *untidy* are adjectives describing the noun *painting*.

Adverb A word that describes or modifies (i) a verb: *he did it gracefully* (adverb: *gracefully*), or (ii) an adjective: *a disgracefully large helping* (adverb: *disgracefully*), or (iii) another adverb: *she skated extraordinarily gracefully* (adverbs: *extraordinarily*, *gracefully*).

Agreement In French, adjectives agree with nouns, verbs agree with subject nouns or pronouns, pronouns agree with nouns, etc. This is a way of showing that something refers to or goes with something else. Agreement is by number (showing whether something is singular or plural) and by gender (showing whether something is masculine or feminine). For instance: **des chaussettes bleues**, *blue socks*: **-e** is added to the adjective because **chaussette** is feminine, **-s** is added to **bleue** because **chaussettes** is plural.

Apposition Two nouns or noun phrases are used together, the second one explaining the first: *the station master, a big man with a moustache, came in.* 'A big man with a moustache' is in apposition to 'the station master'.

Articles The little words like *a* and *the* that stand in front of nouns. In English, *the* is the definite article (it defines a particular item in a category: *the hat you've got on*); *a* or *an* is the indefinite article (it doesn't specify which item in a category: *wear a hat, any hat*); *some* is the partitive article (it specifies a part but not the whole of a category: *I'd like some mustard*).

Attributive Noun A noun used as an adjective: *a petrol pump*: 'petrol' is an attributive noun, telling us what sort of pump.

Auxiliary Verb A verb used to help form a compound tense. In *I am walking, he has walked* the auxiliary verbs are *to be* (*am*) and *to have* (*has*).

Cardinal Numbers The numbers used in counting (*one, two, three, four*, etc.). Compare with Ordinal Numbers.

Clause A self-contained section of a sentence containing a verb: *He came in and was opening his mail when the lights went out*—'he came in', 'and (he) was opening his mail', 'when the lights went out' are clauses.

Comparative With adjectives and adverbs, the form produced by adding *-er* or prefixing *more*: *bigger, more difficult, more easily*.

Compound Noun Noun formed from two or more separate words, usually hyphenated in French: **le tire-bouchon**, *corkscrew*—both English and French words are compound nouns.

Compound Tense Tense of a verb formed by a part of that verb preceded by an auxiliary verb (*am, have, shall*, etc.): *am walking; have walked; shall walk*.

Compound Verb Verb formed by the addition of a prefix (*un-, over-, de-, dis-*, etc.) to another verb: simple verbs: *wind, take*; compound verbs: *unwind, overtake*.

Conditional Perfect Tense The tense used to express what might have happened (if something else had occurred) and formed in English with *should have* (*I* *should have walked, we should have walked*) or *would have* (*you would have walked, he would have walked, they would have walked*).

Conditional Tense The tense used to express what might happen (if something else occurred) and formed in English with *should* (*I should walk, we should walk*) or *would* (*you would walk, he would walk, they would walk*).

Conjugation The pattern which a type of verb follows. There is only one regular conjugation in English: *to walk*: present, *I walk, he walks*; past, *he walked*; perfect, *he has walked*, etc.

Conjunction A word like *and, but, when, because* that starts a clause and joins it to the rest of the sentence.

Consonant A letter representing a sound that can only be used in conjunction with a vowel. In French, the vowels are **a, e, i, o, u, y**. All the other letters of the alphabet are consonants.

Definite Article See Articles.

Demonstrative Adjective An adjective that is used to point out a particular thing: *I'll have that cake; this cake is terrible; give me those cakes*—*that, this, those* are demonstrative adjectives.

Demonstrative Article Alternative name for Demonstrative Adjective.

Demonstrative Pronoun A pronoun that is used to point out a particular thing: *I'll have that; this is terrible; give me those*—*that, this, those* are demonstrative pronouns.

Direct Object The noun or pronoun that experiences the action of the verb: *he hits me*, direct object: *me*. See also Indirect Object.

Disjunctive Pronoun Also called Stressed Pronoun. A pronoun that does not stand directly with a verb as its subject or object: *Who said that? Me!*—*me* is a disjunctive pronoun. Disjunctives in French have different forms from ordinary personal pronouns.

Ending See Stem.

Feminine See Gender.

First Conjugation Verb In French, a verb whose infinitive ends in **-er**.

First Person See Third Person.

Future Perfect Tense The tense used to express what, at some future time, will be a past occurrence. Formed in English with *shall have* (*I shall have walked, we shall have walked*) and *will have* (*you will have walked, he will have walked, they will have walked*).

Future Tense The tense used to express a future occurrence and formed in English with *shall* (*I shall walk, we shall walk*) or *will* (*you will walk, he will walk, they will walk*).

Gender In French, a noun or pronoun may be either masculine or feminine: this is known as the gender of the noun or pronoun. The gender may correspond to the sex of the thing named, or may not. In English gender only shows in pronouns (*he, she, it*, etc.) and corresponds to the sex of the thing named. See Agreement.

Historic Present Present tense used to relate past events, often in order to make the narrative more vivid: *So then I go into the kitchen and what do I see?*

Imperative The form of the verb that expresses a command. In English it is usually the same as the infinitive without *to*: infinitive, *to walk*, imperative, *walk!*

Imperfect Subjunctive One of the past tenses of the French subjunctive. See Subjunctive.

Imperfect Tense A French past tense formed by adding a set of endings (**-ais, -ais, -ait**, etc.) to the **nous** form of the present tense minus its **-ons**. Often corresponds to the English past continuous: **je marchais**, *I was walking*.

Impersonal Verb A verb whose subject is an imprecise *it* or *there*: *it is raining*; *there's no need for that*.

Indefinite Adjectives Adjectives such as *each*, *such*, *some*, *other*, *every*, *several*.

Indefinite Article See Articles.

Indefinite Pronouns Pronouns such as *somebody*, *anybody*, *something*, *anything*, *everybody*, *nobody*.

Indirect Object The noun or pronoun at which the direct object is aimed. In English it either has or can have *to* in front of it: *I passed it (to) him*, indirect object *(to) him*; *I gave her my address (I gave my address to her)*, indirect object *(to) her*. In these examples *it* and *my address* are direct objects. See Direct Object.

Indirect Question A question (without a question mark) in a subordinate clause. It is introduced by some such expression as *I wonder if, do you know where, I'll tell him when*. Direct question: *When is he coming?* Indirect question: *I don't know when he's coming*.

Infinitive The basic part of the verb from which other parts are derived. In English, it is normally preceded by *to*: *to walk*, *to run*.

Interrogative The question form of the verb.

Interrogative Adjective A question word (in English *which ...?* or *what ...?*) used adjectivally with a following noun: *which book do you mean?*

Interrogative Adverb An adverb that introduces a direct question, in English *why?*, *when?*, *how?*, etc. In indirect questions the same words function as conjunctions, joining the question to the main clause. *Why do you say that?*—direct question, *why* is an interrogative adverb; *I don't know why you say that*—indirect question, *why* is a conjunction.

Interrogative Pronoun A pronoun that asks a question, in English *who?* and *what?*

Intransitive Of verbs: having no direct object.

Irregular Verb In French, a verb that does not follow the pattern of one of the three regular conjugations.

Main Clause A clause within a sentence that could stand on its own and still make sense. For example: *He came in when he was ready. He came in* is a main clause (it makes sense standing on its own); *when he was ready* is a subordinate clause (it can't stand on its own and still make sense).

Masculine See Gender.

Modal Verbs (literally 'verbs of mood') These are the auxiliary verbs (other than *have* and *be*) that always appear with a dependent infinitive: *I can walk, I must walk, I will walk*—*can, must, will* are modal verbs.

Noun A word that names a person or thing. *Peter, box, glory, indecision* are nouns.

Noun Clause A clause that is the equivalent of a noun within the sentence: *I don't want to catch whatever you've got* (*whatever you've got* is a clause for which we might substitute a noun, e.g., *measles*).

Number With nouns, pronouns, etc.—the state of being either singular or plural. See Agreement.

Object See Direct Object and Indirect Object.

Ordinal (Number) A number such as *first, second, third, fourth*, normally used adjectivally about one thing in a series.

Partitive Article See Articles.

Passive The basic tenses of a verb are active. Passive tenses are the set of tenses that are used in order to make the person or thing experiencing the action of the verb (normally the object) into the subject of the verb. Active (basic tense): *I discover it*, passive: *it is discovered (by me)*; active: *he ate them*, passive: *they were eaten (by him)*.

Past Anterior Tense A French tense equivalent in time to the pluperfect, formed with the past historic of **avoir** or **être** + past participle: **j'eus marché**, *I had walked*.

Past Historic Tense A French past tense used in writing narrative instead of the perfect; often eqivalent to the English simple past tense: **je marchai**, *I walked*.

Past Participle The part of the verb used to form compound past tenses. In English, it usually ends in *-ed*; verb: *to walk*; past participle: *walked*; perfect tense: *I have walked*.

Perfect Continuous In English, the past tense formed using *was* + *-ing*, implying that something was continuing to occur: *I was walking*.

Perfect Infinitive The past form of the infinitive, formed in English from *to have* + past participle: *to have walked*.

Perfect Participle The part of the verb that in English is formed by *having* + past participle: *having walked away, he now came back*: *having walked* is a perfect participle.

Perfect Tense The past tense that, in English, is formed by using *have* + past participle: *I have walked*.

Personal Pronouns Subject and object pronouns referring to people or things (*he, him, she, her, it,* etc.).

Phrasal Verb In English, a verb made by combining a simple verb with a preposition: *run out, jump up, stand down*.

Phrase A self-contained section of a sentence that does not contain a full verb. *Being late as usual, he arrived at* *a quarter past eleven*: *at a quarter past eleven* is a phrase; present and past participles are not full verbs, so *being late as usual* is also a phrase. Compare Clause.

Pluperfect Continuous In English, the equivalent tense to the pluperfect using *had been* + *-ing*, implying that something had been going on (when something else happened), e.g.: *I had been walking for an hour, when* ...

Pluperfect Tense The past tense, that, in English, is formed by using *had* + past participle: *I had walked*.

Possessive Adjective An adjective that indicates possession; in English, *my*, *your*, *her*, etc.: *that is my book*.

Possessive Article Alternative name for Possessive Adjective.

Possessive Pronoun A pronoun that indicates possession; in English, *mine*, *yours*, *hers*, etc.: *that book is mine*.

Preposition A word like *in*, *over*, *near*, *across* that stands in front of a noun or pronoun relating it to the rest of the sentence.

Present Continuous See Present Tense.

Present Participle The part of the verb that in English ends in *-ing*: *to walk*: present participle, *walking*.

Present Tense The tense of the verb that refers to things now happening regularly (simple present: *I walk*), or happening at the moment (present continuous: *I am walking*).

Pronoun A word such as *he*, *she*, *which*, *mine* that stands instead of a noun (usually already mentioned).

Reflexive Verbs Verbs whose object is the same as their subject: *he likes himself*, *she can dress herself*. *Himself*, *herself* are reflexive pronouns.

Relative Pronoun A pronoun that introduces a subordinate clause and at the same time allows that clause to function as an adjective or noun. In English the relative pronouns are *who(m)*, *which*, *whose*, *that*, and *what*. *Tell me what you know!*: *what you know* is a noun clause and the direct object of *tell me*. It is introduced by the relative pronoun *what*. *That's the lad who stole my wallet*: *who stole my wallet* is an adjectival clause describing *lad*. It is introduced by the relative pronoun *who*.

Second Conjugation Verb In French, a verb whose infinitive ends in **-ir**.

Second Person See Third Person.

Simple Tense A one-word tense of a verb: *I walk, I run* (as opposed to a compound tense: *I am walking, I was running*).

Stem The part of a verb to which endings indicating tense, person, etc. are added. Verb: *to walk*: stem, *walk-*: *he walk-s, he walk-ed*, etc.

Stressed Pronouns See Disjunctive Pronouns.

Subject (of verb, clause, or sentence) The noun or pronoun that initiates the action of the verb: *George walked*, subject: *George*; *he hit George*, subject: *he*.

Subjunctive In French, a set of tenses that express doubt or unlikelihood. The subjunctive still exists in only a few expressions in English: *If I were you* [but I'm not], *I'd go now* (*I were* is subjunctive—the normal past tense is *I was*).

Subordinate Clause A clause in a sentence that depends, in order to make sense, on a main clause. See Main Clause.

Subordinating Conjunction The conjunction that introduces a subordinate clause.

Superlative With adjectives and adverbs, the form produced by adding *-est* or prefixing *most*: *biggest, most difficult, most easily*.

Tense The form of a verb that indicates when the action takes place (e.g., present tense: *I walk*; past tense: *I walked*).

Third Conjugation Verb In French, a verb whose infinitive ends in **-re**.

Third Person *He, she, it, they* (and their derivatives, like *him, his, her, their*), or any noun. The first person is *I* or *we* (and their derivatives), the second person is *you* (and its derivatives).

Transitive Of verbs: having a direct object.

Verb The word that tells you what the subject of the clause does: *he goes; she dislikes me; have you eaten it?, they know nothing—goes, dislikes, have eaten, know* are verbs.

Verbal Noun Part of the verb (in English, usually the present participle) used as a noun: *smoking is bad for you*: verbal noun, *smoking*.

Vowel A letter representing a sound that can be pronounced by itself without the addition of other sounds. In French the vowels are **a, e, i, o, u, y**.

| Index

English prepositions should be looked up in the alphabetical list on page 185.

French prepositions should be looked up in the alphabetical list on page 164.

Irregular verbs should be looked up in the alphabetical list on page 242.

The preposition a verb takes before an infinitive or noun will be found in the alphabetical list of verbs on page 59.

Words offering problems of pronunciation should be looked up in the alphabetical list on page 235.

Definitions of grammatical terms will be found in the glossary on page 260.